AP® BIOLOGY

First published 2021 by BIOZONE International Ltd

Third edition 2021
ISBN 978-1-98-856656-6

Printed by Integra Graphics Synergy

Acknowledgements

BIOZONE wishes to thank and acknowledge the team for their efforts and contributions to the production of this title.

Cover Photograph

Photo: Baranov / adobe.stock.com

The puma (*Puma concolor*) holds the Guinness world record for the mammal which has the highest number of different common names. In the English language alone, it has over 40, including cougar, panther and mountain lion. *https://www.guinnessworldrecords.com/world-records/78143-mammal-with-the-most-names*

BIOZONE Corporation

18801 E. Mainstreet, Suite 240,
Parker, CO, 80134-3445, UNITED STATES

855-246-4555
855-935-3555
sales@thebiozone.com

www.theBIOZONE.com

AP® BIOLOGY

About the Authors

Dr Tracey Greenwood *Senior Author*

Tracey has been writing resources for students since 1993 when she joined BIOZONE and enjoys the challenge of curriculum analysis and content development. Tracey has a PhD in biology, specializing in lake ecology and has taught both graduate and undergraduate biology, including implementing courses for medical intermediate students and remedial and foundation programs for nursing students. Since joining BIOZONE, Tracey has been a team leader in the design, development and production of targeted curricula for students and teachers in Australia, New Zealand, the UK and the US.

Kent Pryor *Author*

Kent has a BSc from Massey University majoring in zoology and ecology and taught secondary school biology and chemistry for 9 years before joining BIOZONE as an author in 2009.

Lissa Bainbridge-Smith *Author*

Lissa graduated with a Masters in Science (hons) from the University of Waikato. After graduation she worked in industry in a research and development capacity for eight years. Lissa joined BIOZONE in 2006 and is hands-on developing new curricula. Lissa has also taught science theory and practical skills to international and ESL students.

Contents

Using This Book vi
Using BIOZONE'S Resource Hub viii
Big Ideas and Enduring Understandings x
Science Practices and Skills xii

UNIT 1. Chemistry of Life

Learning Objectives 1
- ❑ 1 Water in Living Systems 2
- ❑ 2 The Biochemical Nature of the Cell 4
- ❑ 3 Nucleotides 6
- ❑ 4 Nucleic Acids 7
- ❑ 5 Amino Acids Make Up Proteins 9
- ❑ 6 Protein Structure is Hierarchical 11
- ❑ 7 Protein Shape is Related to Function 12
- ❑ 8 Comparing Fibrous and Globular Proteins 13
- ❑ 9 Carbohydrate Chemistry 15
- ❑ 10 Condensation and Hydrolysis of Sugars 16
- ❑ 11 Polysaccharides 17
- ❑ 12 Cellulose and Starch 19
- ❑ 13 Lipids 20
- ❑ 14 Phospholipids 22
- ❑ 15 Personal Progress Check 23

UNIT 2. Cell Structure and Function

Learning Objectives 27
- ❑ 16 Prokaryotic vs Eukaryotic Cells 28
- ❑ 17 Looking at Cells 29
- ❑ 18 Animal Cells 31
- ❑ 19 Plant Cells 33
- ❑ 20 Cell Structures and Organelles 35
- ❑ 21 A Closer Look at Chloroplasts and Mitochondria 37
- ❑ 22 Cell Sizes 39
- ❑ 23 Limitations to Cell Size 41
- ❑ 24 ● Surface Area and Cell Size 44
- ❑ 25 Efficient Exchanges with the Environment 46
- ❑ 26 The Structure of Membranes 48
- ❑ 27 Factors Affecting Membrane Permeability 50
- ❑ 28 The Role of the Cell Wall 52
- ❑ 29 Passive Transport 53
- ❑ 30 ● Diffusion and Osmosis in a Cell 55
- ❑ 31 Water Relations in Plants 56
- ❑ 32 Solute Potential and Cells 58
- ❑ 33 ● Osmosis in Potato Cells 59
- ❑ 34 Active Transport 60
- ❑ 35 Ion Pumps 61
- ❑ 36 Cytosis 62
- ❑ 37 Compartments in Cells 64
- ❑ 38 Origins of Cellular Compartments 66
- ❑ 39 Personal Progress Check 67

UNIT 3. Cellular Energetics

Learning Objectives 71
- ❑ 40 The Properties of Enzymes 72
- ❑ 41 How Enzymes Work 74
- ❑ 42 Denaturation 75
- ❑ 43 Factors Affecting Enzyme Activity 76
- ❑ 44 Enzyme Inhibitors 78
- ❑ 45 ● Investigating Enzyme Activity 80
- ❑ 46 Energy in Living Systems 82
- ❑ 47 Energy Transformations in Cells 85
- ❑ 48 Origin of Eukaryotic Photosynthesis 86
- ❑ 49 Photosynthesis 87
- ❑ 50 Pigments and Light Absorption 88
- ❑ 51 Light Dependent Reactions 89
- ❑ 52 Light Independent Reactions 91
- ❑ 53 ● Investigating Photosynthesis 92
- ❑ 54 Pathways for Obtaining Energy 93
- ❑ 55 Cellular Respiration Overview 94
- ❑ 56 The Biochemistry of Respiration 96
- ❑ 57 Chemiosmosis and the Proton Motive Force 98
- ❑ 58 ● Investigating Cellular Respiration 100
- ❑ 59 Anaerobic Pathways for ATP Production 103
- ❑ 60 Variation at the Molecular Level 104
- ❑ 61 Personal Progress Check 106

UNIT 4. Cell Communication and Cell Cycle

Learning Objectives 110
- ❑ 62 Types of Cell Signaling 111
- ❑ 63 Cell to Cell Communication 113
- ❑ 64 Communication Over Short and Long Distances 114
- ❑ 65 Signals and Signal Transduction 116
- ❑ 66 Types of Signal Transduction 118
- ❑ 67 Signal Transduction and Environment 120
- ❑ 68 Changes in Signal Transduction Pathways 122
- ❑ 69 Feedback 124
- ❑ 70 Cell Division 127
- ❑ 71 The Eukaryotic Cell Cycle 128
- ❑ 72 The Outcome of Mitosis 129
- ❑ 73 Mitosis and Cytokinesis 130
- ❑ 74 ● Modeling Mitosis 133
- ❑ 75 ● The Effect of Environment on Mitosis 134
- ❑ 76 Regulation of the Cell Cycle 135
- ❑ 77 Defective Gene Regulation in Cancer 137
- ❑ 78 ● Analyzing the Effects of Cell Cycle Errors 139
- ❑ 79 Personal Progress Check 140

CODES: **Activity** is marked: ❑ to be done ☑ when completed ● Support for practical investigation

Contents

UNIT 5. Heredity

	Learning Objectives	144
80	Meiosis	145
81	Modeling Meiosis	148
82	Mitosis vs Meiosis	150
83	What Do Shared Conserved Processes Tell Us?	151
84	Principles of Mendelian Genetics	152
85	Basic Genetic Crosses	154
86	Probability	156
87	Using Pedigrees to Analyze Inheritance Patterns	157
88	Recombination and Dihybrid Inheritance	159
89	Predicting the Outcomes of Genetic Crosses	160
90	Testing the Outcomes of Genetic Crosses	163
91	Non-Mendelian Inheritance	165
92	Codominance and Multiple Alleles	166
93	Incomplete Dominance	168
94	Lethal Alleles	169
95	Inheritance of Linked Genes	170
96 ●	Mapping Chromosomes Using Linked Genes	172
97	Detecting Linkage in Dihybrid inheritance	173
98	Sex Linkage	175
99	How Sex Determination Affects Inheritance	177
100	Multiple Genes	178
101	Non-nuclear Inheritance	180
102	Environmental Effects on Phenotype	181
103	Variation and Phenotypic Plasticity	184
104	The Chromosomal Basis of Inheritance	186
105	Chromosomal Inheritance and Human Disorders	187
106	Personal Progress Check	189

UNIT 6. Gene Expression and Regulation

	Learning Objectives	193
107	Genomes, Genes, and Alleles	194
108	Prokaryotic Chromosomes	195
109	Plasmid DNA	196
110	Eukaryotic Chromosomes	197
111	Creating a DNA Molecule	198
112	How Does DNA Replicate?	201
113	Enzyme Control of DNA Replication	203
114	What is Gene Expression?	204
115	What is the Genetic Code?	205
116	Transcription in Eukaryotes	207
117	mRNA Processing in Eukaryotes	208
118	Translation	209
119	Retroviruses: A Special Case in Information Flow	212
120	Structural and Regulatory Genes	213
121	Cell Differentiation and Gene Expression	214
122	Epigenetic Regulation of Gene Expression	215
123	Transcription Factors During Development	217
124	Gene Regulation in Prokaryotes	219
125	Eukaryotic Gene Structure and Regulation	221
126	Gene Expression and Phenotype	224
127	miRNA and Development	226
128	Mutations	227
129	Mutation and Phenotype	229
130	Changes to DNA	231
131	Changes to Chromosomes	233
132	Mutation, Variation, and Natural Selection	235
133	The Genetic Basis of Resistance in Bacteria	236
134	Recombining Genetic Material in Viruses	237
135	What is Genetic Engineering?	239
136	Gel Electrophoresis	241
137	Polymerase Chain Reaction	243
138	Bacterial Transformation and Gene Cloning	244
139 ●	Aseptic Technique and Streak Plating	246
140 ●	Testing for Transformation	248
141	DNA Analysis	249
142	Applications of Profiling	250
143 ●	DNA Profiling Lab	252
144	GM Techniques in Agriculture and Medicine	254
145	GM Techniques and Bioinformatics	256
146	Personal Progress Check	257

UNIT 7. Natural Selection

	Learning Objectives	261
147	A Pictorial History of Evolutionary Thought	262
148	Variation and Natural Selection	264
149	Adaptation and Fitness	266
150	Environment and Evolution	268
151	Natural Selection Acts on Phenotype	269
152	Selection Pressure in Populations	270
153	Phenotypic Variation and Fitness	271
154	Artificial Selection	273
155	Selection and Population Change	275
156	Artificial Selection in Crop Plants	276
157 ●	Selection in Fast Plants	278
158	Convergence: The Influence of Environment	280
159	Microevolutionary Processes in Gene Pools	283
160	Changes in a Gene Pool	285
161	Population Bottlenecks	286
162	Founder Effect	288
163	Genetic Drift	290
164	Calculating Allele Frequencies in Populations	291
165	Analysis of a Squirrel Gene Pool	293
166	The Evidence for Evolution	295

CODES: **Activity** is marked: ☐ to be done ☑ when completed ● Support for practical investigation

Contents

- 167 Fossils ... 296
- 168 Methods of Dating Fossils ... 298
- 169 Relative Dating and the Fossil Record ... 299
- 170 Chronometric Dating ... 301
- 171 Homologous Structures ... 303
- 172 Vestigial Structures ... 304
- 173 Homologous Proteins ... 305
- 174 What Can Highly Conserved Proteins Tell Us? ... 307
- 175 Genomic Comparisons and Relatedness ... 309
- 176 Gene Duplication and Evolution ... 311
- 177 Descent and Common Ancestry ... 312
- 178 The Origin of Eukaryotes ... 314
- 179 Continuing Evolution: Galápagos Finches ... 315
- 180 Master Genes and Evolutionary Change ... 317
- 181 Continuous Change in the Fossil Record ... 319
- 182 Modern Drivers in Evolution ... 321
- 183 The Emergence of New Diseases ... 323
- 184 What is a Phylogenetic Tree? ... 325
- 185 The Phylogeny of Animals ... 327
- 186 Constructing Phylogenies Using Cladistics ... 328
- 187 Why are Birds Dinosaurs? ... 330
- 188 Constructing a Cladogram ... 331
- 189 What is a Species? ... 332
- 190 Patterns of Evolution ... 333
- 191 Divergence is an Evolutionary Pattern ... 335
- 192 Adaptive Radiation in Mammals ... 337
- 193 Allopatric Speciation ... 339
- 194 Sympatric Speciation ... 342
- 195 Habitat Fragmentation: Speciation and Extinction ... 344
- 196 Prezygotic Isolating Mechanisms ... 345
- 197 Postzygotic Isolating Mechanisms ... 348
- 198 Extinction ... 349
- 199 Causes of Mass Extinctions ... 351
- 200 The Sixth Extinction ... 352
- 201 Diversity and Resilience ... 354
- 202 Investigating Molecular Diversity ... 356
- 203 The Origin of Life on Earth ... 358
- 204 Prebiotic Experiments ... 360
- 205 An RNA World ... 361
- 206 Landmarks in Earth's History ... 362
- 207 Personal Progress Check ... 364

UNIT 8. Ecology

- *Learning Objectives* ... 369
- 208 Responding to Changes in the Environment 370
- 209 Timing and Coordination in Plants ... 371
- 210 Tropisms and Growth Responses ... 373
- 211 Plant Hormones as Signal Molecules ... 374
- 212 Photoperiodism in Plants ... 376
- 213 ● Investigating Plant Transpiration ... 378
- 214 Kineses ... 381
- 215 Taxes ... 383
- 216 ● Choice Chamber Investigations ... 385
- 217 Stimuli and Behavior ... 387
- 218 Plant Responses to Threats ... 389
- 219 Communication ... 391
- 220 Courtship and Mating Behaviors ... 394
- 221 Territories and Breeding Behavior ... 396
- 222 Herds, Flocks, and Schools ... 398
- 223 The Adaptive Value of Cooperation ... 399
- 224 Honeybee Communication ... 401
- 225 Cooperation and Foraging Success ... 402
- 226 Cooperation and Improved Defense ... 404
- 227 Colony Behavior and Survival ... 405
- 228 Kin Selection ... 406
- 229 How Organisms Allocate Energy ... 407
- 230 Endothermy vs Ectothermy ... 409
- 231 Energy and Seasonal Breeding ... 412
- 232 Reproductive Allocation and Parental Care .. 413
- 233 Metabolism and Body Size ... 415
- 234 Energy in Ecosystems ... 417
- 235 The Flow of Energy in Ecosystems ... 420
- 236 Investigating Trophic Efficiencies ... 422
- 237 The Dynamics of Populations ... 425
- 238 Exponential Population Growth ... 427
- 239 The Effect of Density: Logistic Growth ... 428
- 240 Community Structure and Diversity ... 430
- 241 Species Interactions and Community Structure ... 433
- 242 Energy and Community Structure ... 438
- 243 Ecosystem Diversity and Resilience ... 440
- 244 The Role of Keystone Species ... 442
- 245 Adaptation and Environmental Change ... 444
- 246 Invasive Species and Community Change ... 446
- 247 Human Activity and Ecosystem Change ... 449
- 248 Natural Events and Ecosystem Change ... 452
- 249 Personal Progress Check ... 454

Science Practices for AP Biology

- *Learning Objectives* ... 458
- 250 Concept Explanation ... 459
- 251 Visual Representations ... 460
- 252 Questions and Methods ... 461
- 253 Representing and Describing Data ... 464
- 254 Statistical Tests and Data Analysis ... 467
- 255 Argumentation ... 471

Appendix 1: Summary of Mathematical Formulas ... 473
Appendix 2: Glossary ... 475
Image Credits ... 481
Index ... 482

CODES: **Activity** is marked: ☐ to be done ☑ when completed ● Support for practical investigation

Using This Book

This book is structured on the AP Biology Course and Exam Description (CED). It comprises 8 units, with an additional concluding chapter covering background and support for science practices (Chapter 9). The activities cover the course content and address the skills and knowledge requirements outlined in it. These are outlined in the Unit Introduction (below).

UNIT INTRODUCTIONS

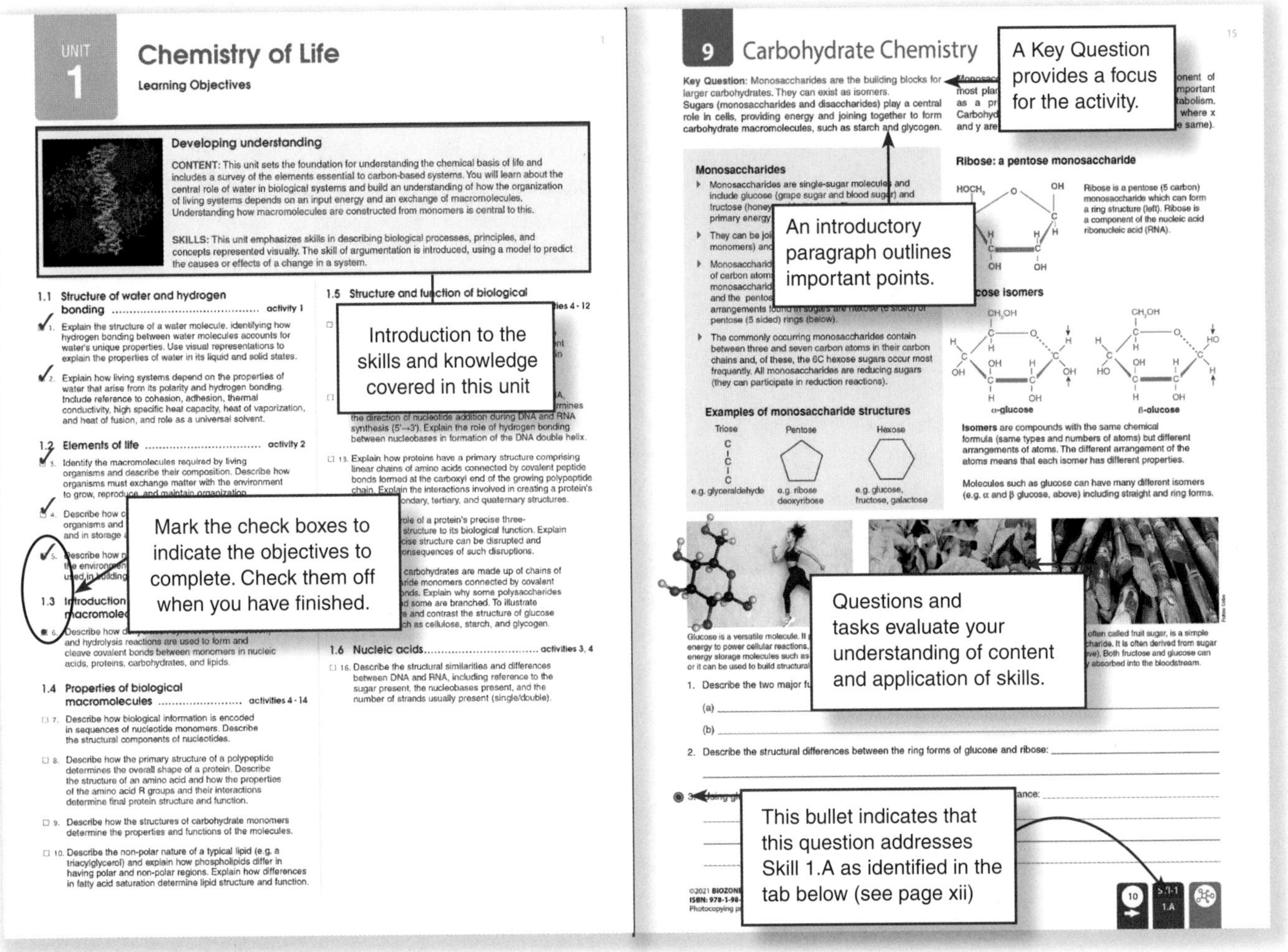

Introduction to the skills and knowledge covered in this unit

Mark the check boxes to indicate the objectives to complete. Check them off when you have finished.

A Key Question provides a focus for the activity.

An introductory paragraph outlines important points.

Questions and tasks evaluate your understanding of content and application of skills.

This bullet indicates that this question addresses Skill 1.A as identified in the tab below (see page xii)

The unit introductions begin with a synopsis of the skills and understanding you will develop in the unit. This is followed by a list of **learning objectives** aligned to the activities in the book. Tick off the objectives as you complete each activity and can answer the questions asked.

Activities make up most of the book. They present data and information as graphs, tables, diagrams, text, and labeled images. Questions and tasks allow you to test your understanding of content and competency in science practices. Skills addressed throughout the activity are identified with a colored bullet in the margin (see page xii).

SUPPORT FOR THE 13 INVESTIGATIONS

This book includes a number of activities providing support for specific aspects of each of the 13 investigations. These are integrated in context throughout and identified by a green bullet (●)in the contents pages (iii-v).

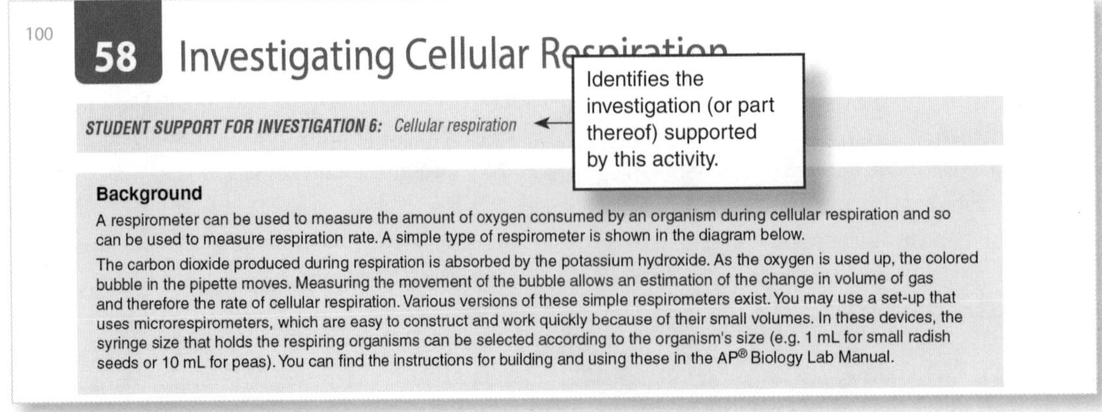

100

58 Investigating Cellular Respiration

STUDENT SUPPORT FOR INVESTIGATION 6: Cellular respiration

Identifies the investigation (or part thereof) supported by this activity.

Background

A respirometer can be used to measure the amount of oxygen consumed by an organism during cellular respiration and so can be used to measure respiration rate. A simple type of respirometer is shown in the diagram below.

The carbon dioxide produced during respiration is absorbed by the potassium hydroxide. As the oxygen is used up, the colored bubble in the pipette moves. Measuring the movement of the bubble allows an estimation of the change in volume of gas and therefore the rate of cellular respiration. Various versions of these simple respirometers exist. You may use a set-up that uses microrespirometers, which are easy to construct and work quickly because of their small volumes. In these devices, the syringe size that holds the respiring organisms can be selected according to the organism's size (e.g. 1 mL for small radish seeds or 10 mL for peas). You can find the instructions for building and using these in the AP® Biology Lab Manual.

FINDING YOUR WAY AROUND THIS BOOK

The activities in this book are furnished with a simple, easy-to-use tab system to help you identify the **big ideas** and the **science practices** and their associated **skills**. It will also help you to identify where the activity (or part of it) is supported with resources on **BIOZONE's Resource Hub**. Some of the tabs are at the bottom of the first page, while others are margin icons.

Tabs at the base of the page

Tabs at the bottom of the page help you to identify big ideas and skills, as well alerting you to connected activities and online resources.

The BIG IDEA/SKILL tab identifies the big idea to which the activity relates. The colored portion of the tab identifies the science practice (1-6) and the skill (A-F) addressed.

See pages x-xi for an explanation and map of big ideas and page xii for an explanation of the science practices and skills.

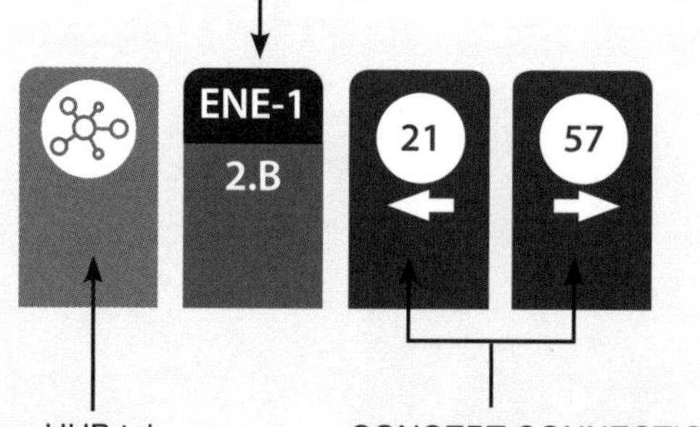

The gray HUB tab indicates that the activity has online support via the **Resource Hub** (see the next page for details)

CONCEPT CONNECTION tabs point you forward or back to activities with background you may wish to revisit, or activities covering related concepts.

Margin icons

Some icons in the margin help you understand the location of important material, identify where you should work in groups, or where an investigation involves use of a computer.

A group icon indicates you should work in pairs or groups for investigation or debate.

A computer icon next to an investigation indicates that it requires computer access.

Colored bullets in the margin indicate where a specific skill is addressed. The skill code is identified in the tab (left).

Concept explanation

Visual representations

Questions and methods

Representing and describing data

Statistical tests and data analysis

Argumentation

PERSONAL PROGRESS CHECKS

Each unit in this book finishes with a Personal Progress Check (PPC), which will help you in your preparation for the AP Biology exam. The Personal Progress Checks consist of ~20-40 multiple choice questions and two free response questions per unit. The question types are as outlined in the *AP Biology Course and Exam Description*. See pages x-xi for PPC details for each unit.

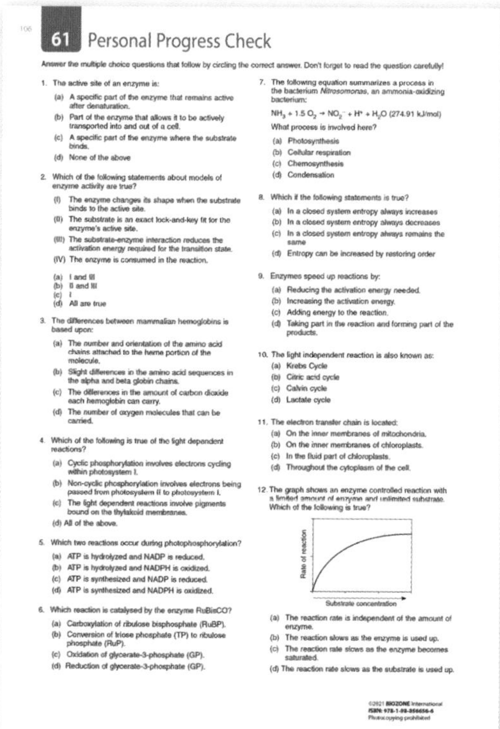

106

61 Personal Progress Check

Answer the multiple choice questions that follow by circling the correct answer. Don't forget to read the question carefully!

1. The active site of an enzyme is:
   (a) A specific part of the enzyme that remains active after denaturation.
   (b) Part of the enzyme that allows it to be actively transported into and out of a cell.
   (c) A specific part of the enzyme where the substrate binds.
   (d) None of the above

2. Which of the following statements about models of enzyme activity are true?
   (I) The enzyme changes its shape when the substrate binds to the active site.
   (II) The substrate is an exact lock-and-key fit for the enzyme's active site.
   (III) The substrate-enzyme interaction reduces the activation energy required for the transition state.
   (IV) The enzyme is consumed in the reaction.
   (a) I and III
   (b) II and III
   (c) I
   (d) All are true

3. The differences between mammalian hemoglobins is based upon:
   (a) The number and orientation of the amino acid chains attached to the heme portion of the molecule.
   (b) Slight differences in the amino acid sequences in the alpha and beta globin chains.
   (c) The differences in the amount of carbon dioxide each hemoglobin can carry.
   (d) The number of oxygen molecules that can be carried.

4. Which of the following is true of the light dependent reactions?
   (a) Cyclic phosphorylation involves electrons cycling within photosystem I.
   (b) Non-cyclic phosphorylation involves electrons being passed from photosystem II to photosystem I.
   (c) The light dependent reactions involve pigments bound on the thylakoid membranes.
   (d) All of the above.

5. Which two reactions occur during photophosphorylation?
   (a) ATP is hydrolyzed and NADP is reduced.
   (b) ATP is hydrolyzed and NADPH is oxidized.
   (c) ATP is synthesized and NADP is reduced.
   (d) ATP is synthesized and NADPH is oxidized.

6. Which reaction is catalysed by the enzyme RuBisCO?
   (a) Carboxylation of ribulose bisphosphate (RuBP).
   (b) Conversion of triose phosphate (TP) to ribulose phosphate (RuP).
   (c) Oxidation of glycerate-3-phosphate (GP).
   (d) Reduction of glycerate-3-phosphate (GP).

7. The following equation summarizes a process in the bacterium *Nitrosomonas*, an ammonia-oxidizing bacterium:
   $NH_3 + 1.5\ O_2 \rightarrow NO_2^- + H^+ + H_2O$ (274.91 kJ/mol)
   What process is involved here?
   (a) Photosynthesis
   (b) Cellular respiration
   (c) Chemosynthesis
   (d) Condensation

8. Which if the following statements is true?
   (a) In a closed system entropy always increases
   (b) In a closed system entropy always decreases
   (c) In a closed system entropy always remains the same
   (d) Entropy can be increased by restoring order

9. Enzymes speed up reactions by:
   (a) Reducing the activation energy needed.
   (b) Increasing the activation energy.
   (c) Adding energy to the reaction.
   (d) Taking part in the reaction and forming part of the products.

10. The light independent reaction is also known as:
    (a) Krebs Cycle
    (b) Citric acid cycle
    (c) Calvin cycle
    (d) Lactate cycle

11. The electron transfer chain is located:
    (a) On the inner membranes of mitochondria.
    (b) On the inner membranes of chloroplasts.
    (c) In the fluid part of chloroplasts.
    (d) Throughout the cytoplasm of the cell.

12. The graph shows an enzyme controlled reaction with a limited amount of enzyme and unlimited substrate. Which of the following is true?

    Rate of reaction
    Substrate concentration

    (a) The reaction rate is independent of the amount of enzyme.
    (b) The reaction slows as the enzyme is used up.
    (c) The reaction rate slows as the enzyme becomes saturated.
    (d) The reaction rate slows as the substrate is used up.

©2021 **BIOZONE** International
ISBN: 978-1-98-856656-6
Photocopying prohibited

109

Free Response Question: *Scientific investigation*

- The rate of photosynthesis can be investigated by measuring the substances involved in photosynthesis. These include measuring the uptake of carbon dioxide, the production of oxygen, or the change in biomass over time. Measuring the rate of oxygen production provides a good approximation of the photosynthetic rate and is relatively easy to carry out.

Aim

- To investigate the effect of light intensity on the rate of photosynthesis in an aquatic plant, *Cabomba aquatica*.

Method

- 0.8-1.0 grams of *Cabomba* stem were weighed on a balance. The stem was cut while submerged and inverted to ensure a free flow of oxygen bubbles.
- The stem was placed into a beaker filled with a solution containing 0.2 mol/L sodium hydrogen carbonate (to supply carbon dioxide). The solution was at approximately 20°C. A funnel was inverted over the *Cabomba* and a test tube filled with the sodium hydrogen carbonate solution was inverted on top to collect any gas produced.
- The beaker was placed at distances (20, 25, 30, 35, 40, 45, 50 cm) from a 60W light source and the light intensity measured with a lux meter at each interval.
- Before recording data at each new treatment, the *Cabomba* stem was left to acclimatize to the new light level for 5 minutes. Because the volumes of oxygen gas produced are very low, bubbles were counted for a period of three minutes at each distance.

1. **Describe** the biological basis for this investigation of photosynthesis: ____________________

2. (a) **Identify** the independent and dependent variables in this experiment: ____________________

   (b) **Identify** the part of the experimental procedure that made the assessment of light intensity quantitative: ____________________

3. **Predict** the how the rate of photosynthesis would change as the *Cabomba* is moved away from the light source.

4. **Justify** your prediction: ____________________

©2021 **BIOZONE** International
ISBN: 978-1-98-856656-6
Photocopying prohibited

Using BIOZONE's Resource Hub

- **BIOZONE's Resource Hub** provides links to online content supporting the activities in the book. From this page, you can also check for any errata or clarifications to the book since printing.
- Many of these external websites are narrowly focused animations and video clips directly relevant to that part of the activity identified by the hub icon. There is also material for data exploration, source material for activities, and some fact sheets, as well as 3D models and spreadsheet models. The hub provides great support for your studies.

www.BIOZONEhub.com

Then enter the code in the text field **APB1-6566**

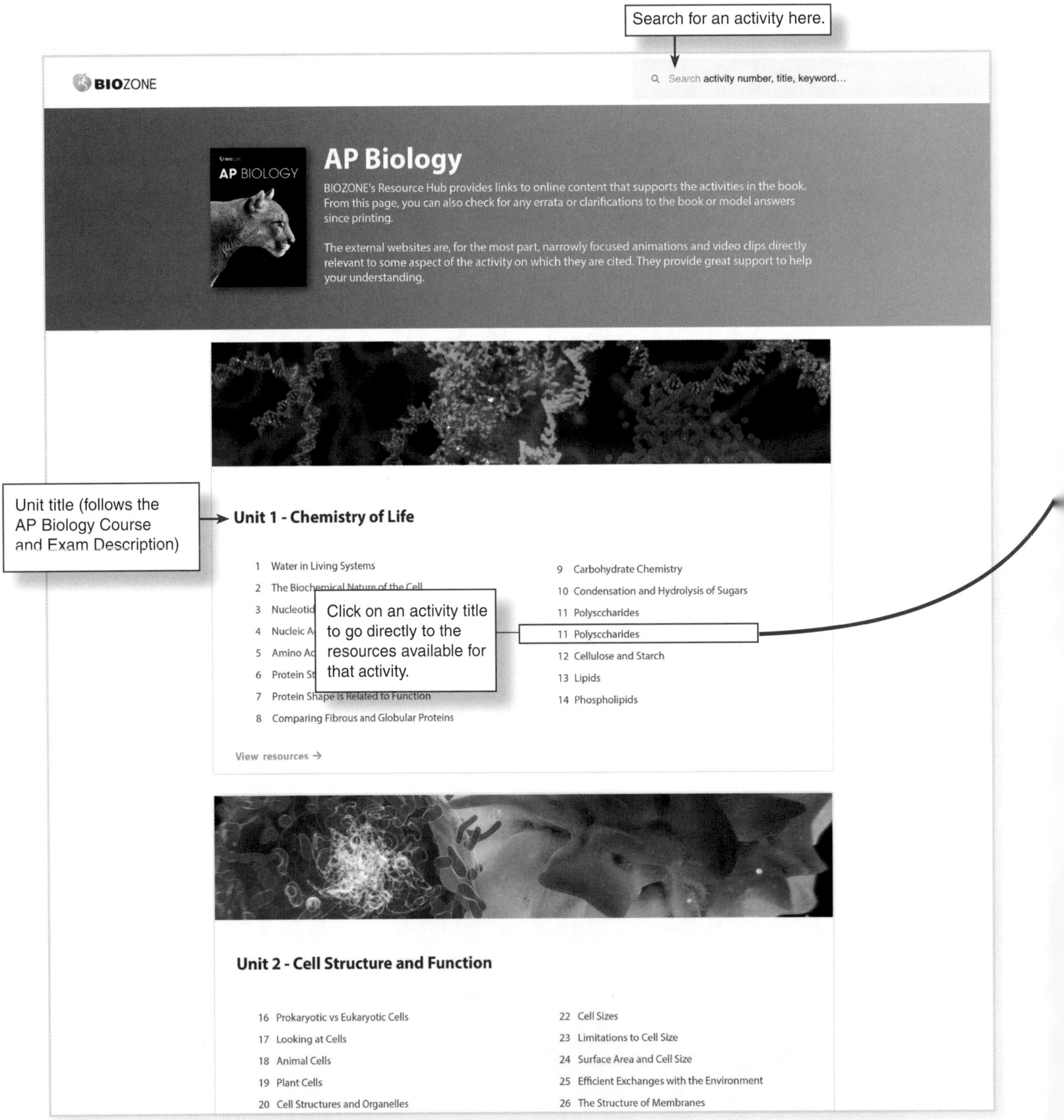

Search for an activity here.

BIOZONE

Search activity number, title, keyword...

AP Biology

BIOZONE's Resource Hub provides links to online content that supports the activities in the book. From this page, you can also check for any errata or clarifications to the book or model answers since printing.

The external websites are, for the most part, narrowly focused animations and video clips directly relevant to some aspect of the activity on which they are cited. They provide great support to help your understanding.

Unit title (follows the AP Biology Course and Exam Description)

Unit 1 - Chemistry of Life

1 Water in Living Systems
2 The Biochemical Nature of the Cell
3 Nucleotid
4 Nucleic A
5 Amino Ac
6 Protein St
7 Protein Shape is Related to Function
8 Comparing Fibrous and Globular Proteins
9 Carbohydrate Chemistry
10 Condensation and Hydrolysis of Sugars
11 Polysccharides
11 Polysccharides
12 Cellulose and Starch
13 Lipids
14 Phospholipids

Click on an activity title to go directly to the resources available for that activity.

View resources →

Unit 2 - Cell Structure and Function

16 Prokaryotic vs Eukaryotic Cells
17 Looking at Cells
18 Animal Cells
19 Plant Cells
20 Cell Structures and Organelles
22 Cell Sizes
23 Limitations to Cell Size
24 Surface Area and Cell Size
25 Efficient Exchanges with the Environment
26 The Structure of Membranes

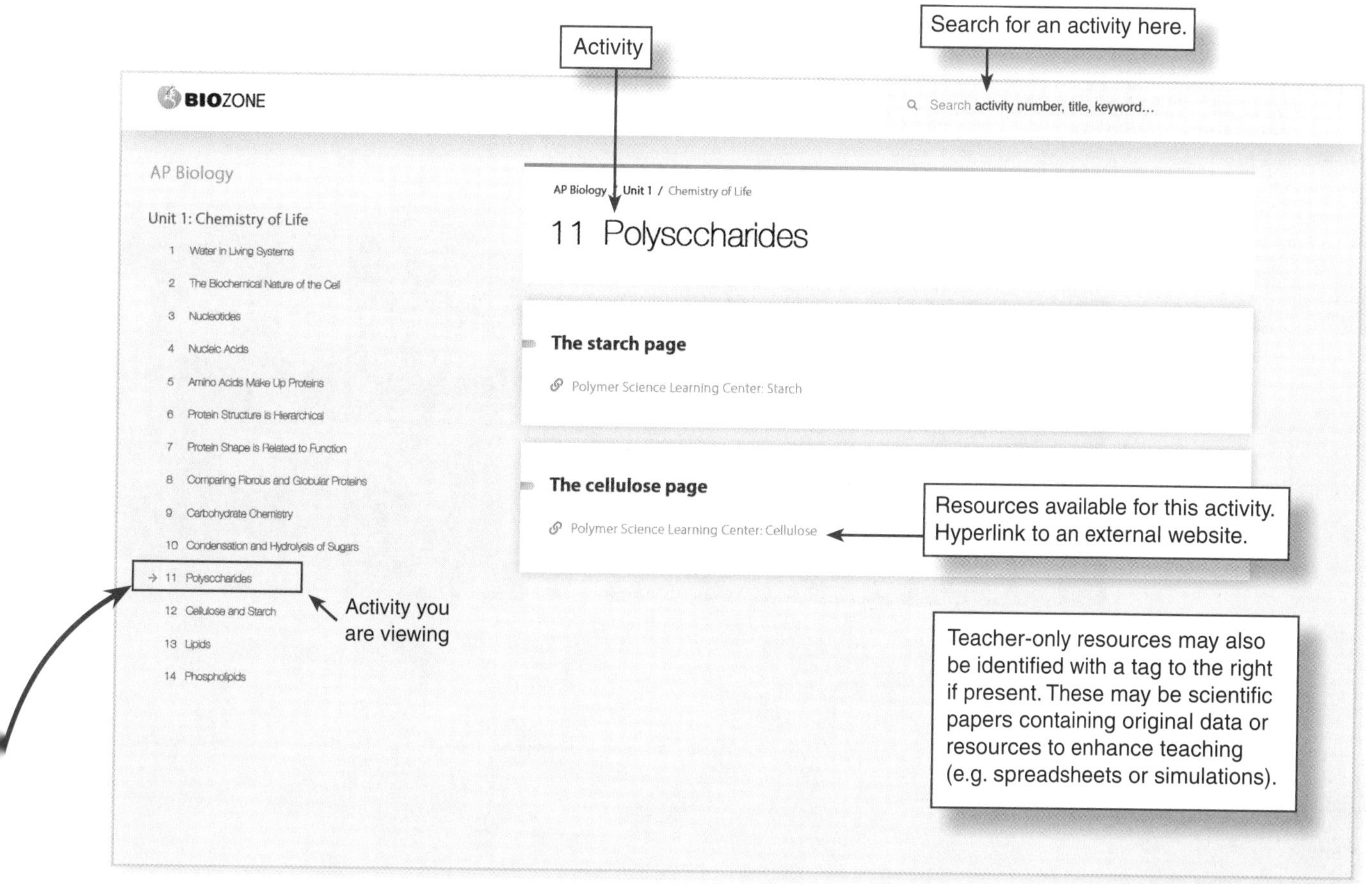

Activity

Search for an activity here.

BIOZONE

Search activity number, title, keyword...

AP Biology

Unit 1: Chemistry of Life

1 Water in Living Systems
2 The Biochemical Nature of the Cell
3 Nucleotides
4 Nucleic Acids
5 Amino Acids Make Up Proteins
6 Protein Structure is Hierarchical
7 Protein Shape is Related to Function
8 Comparing Fibrous and Globular Proteins
9 Carbohydrate Chemistry
10 Condensation and Hydrolysis of Sugars
→ 11 Polysccharides
12 Cellulose and Starch
13 Lipids
14 Phospholipids

Activity you are viewing

AP Biology / Unit 1 / Chemistry of Life

11 Polysccharides

The starch page

Polymer Science Learning Center: Starch

The cellulose page

Polymer Science Learning Center: Cellulose

Resources available for this activity. Hyperlink to an external website.

Teacher-only resources may also be identified with a tag to the right if present. These may be scientific papers containing original data or resources to enhance teaching (e.g. spreadsheets or simulations).

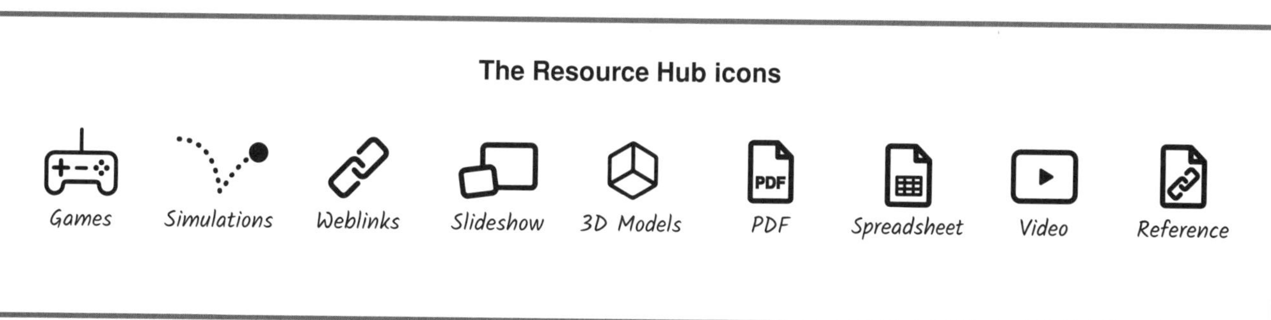

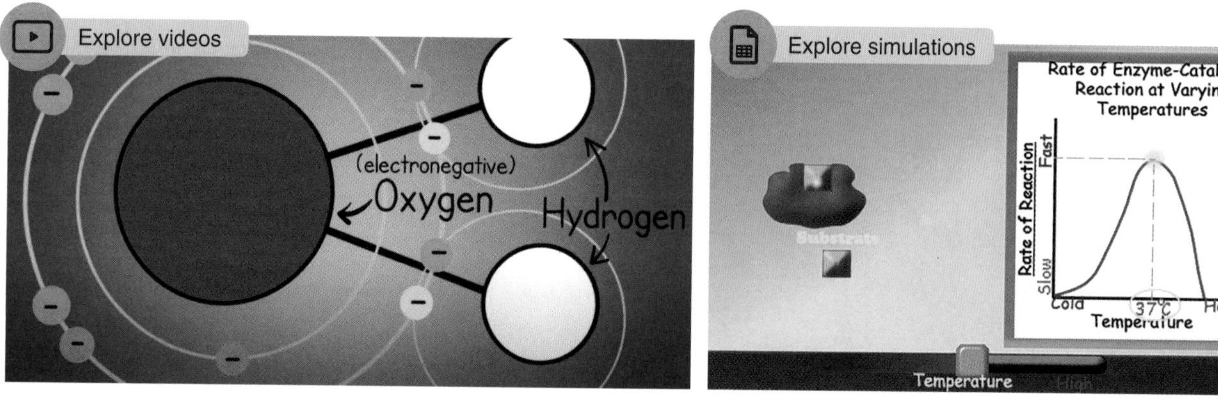

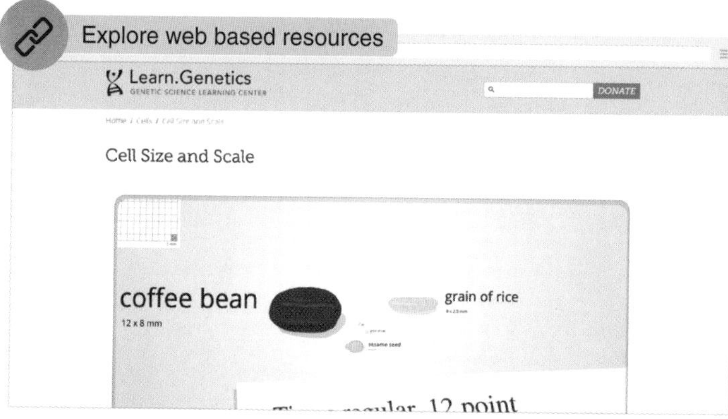

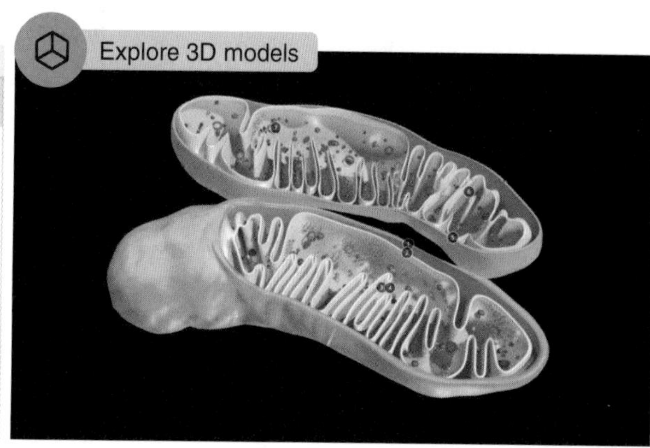

Big Ideas and Enduring Understandings

AP Biology is structured around four BIG IDEAS (below). These big ideas form threads that run throughout the entire course. The big ideas relate to several ENDURING UNDERSTANDINGS, which form the key concepts for learning and from which arise the learning objectives that form the basis of each unit introduction.

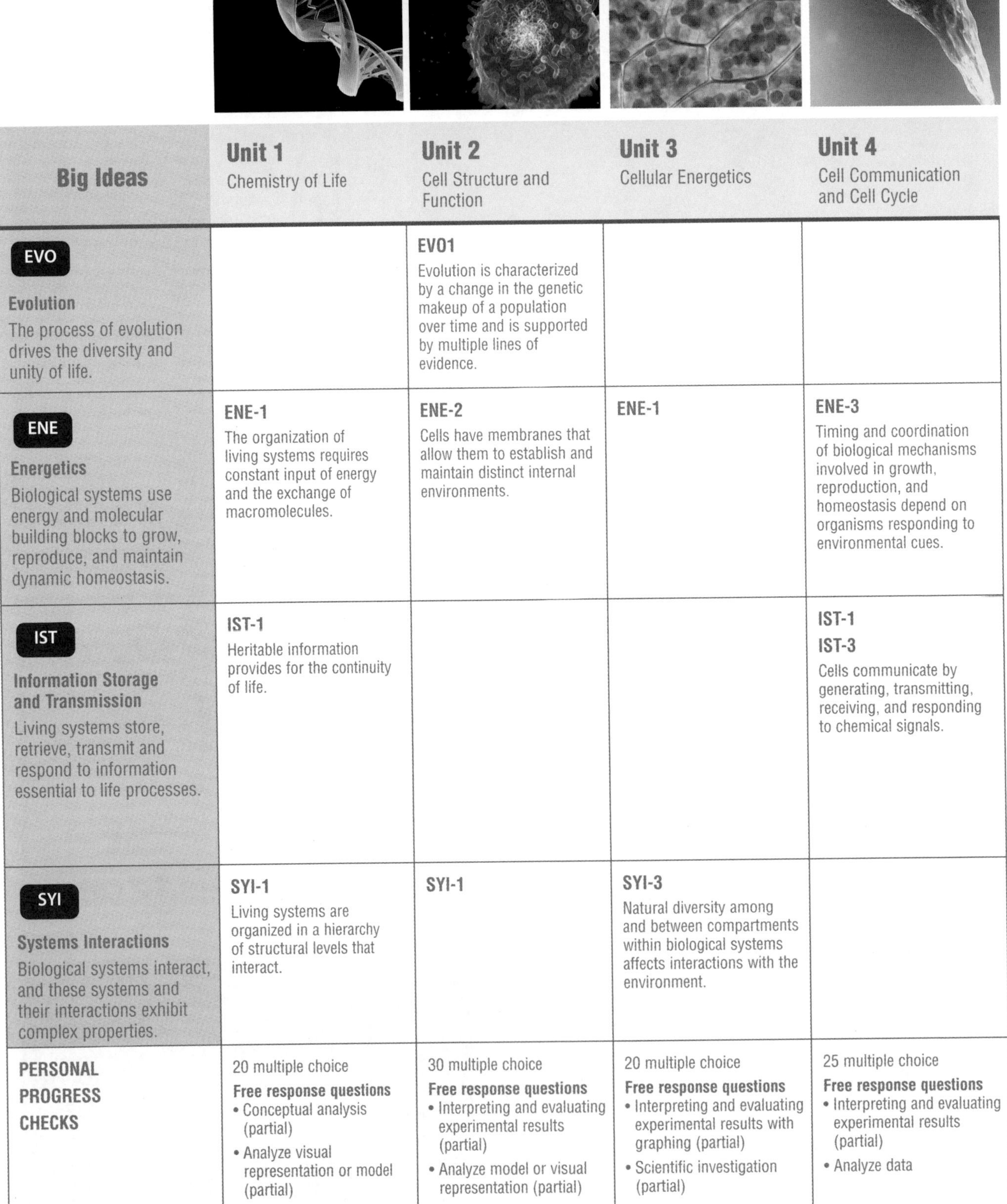

Big Ideas	**Unit 1** Chemistry of Life	**Unit 2** Cell Structure and Function	**Unit 3** Cellular Energetics	**Unit 4** Cell Communication and Cell Cycle
EVO **Evolution** The process of evolution drives the diversity and unity of life.		**EVO1** Evolution is characterized by a change in the genetic makeup of a population over time and is supported by multiple lines of evidence.		
ENE **Energetics** Biological systems use energy and molecular building blocks to grow, reproduce, and maintain dynamic homeostasis.	**ENE-1** The organization of living systems requires constant input of energy and the exchange of macromolecules.	**ENE-2** Cells have membranes that allow them to establish and maintain distinct internal environments.	**ENE-1**	**ENE-3** Timing and coordination of biological mechanisms involved in growth, reproduction, and homeostasis depend on organisms responding to environmental cues.
IST **Information Storage and Transmission** Living systems store, retrieve, transmit and respond to information essential to life processes.	**IST-1** Heritable information provides for the continuity of life.			**IST-1** **IST-3** Cells communicate by generating, transmitting, receiving, and responding to chemical signals.
SYI **Systems Interactions** Biological systems interact, and these systems and their interactions exhibit complex properties.	**SYI-1** Living systems are organized in a hierarchy of structural levels that interact.	**SYI-1**	**SYI-3** Natural diversity among and between compartments within biological systems affects interactions with the environment.	
PERSONAL PROGRESS CHECKS	20 multiple choice **Free response questions** • Conceptual analysis (partial) • Analyze visual representation or model (partial)	30 multiple choice **Free response questions** • Interpreting and evaluating experimental results (partial) • Analyze model or visual representation (partial)	20 multiple choice **Free response questions** • Interpreting and evaluating experimental results with graphing (partial) • Scientific investigation (partial)	25 multiple choice **Free response questions** • Interpreting and evaluating experimental results (partial) • Analyze data

As part of this learning structure, key science practices are integrated into the activities of this book. The science practices cover important skills students need to describe and analyze scientific ideas and data related to biology. These are described on page xii.

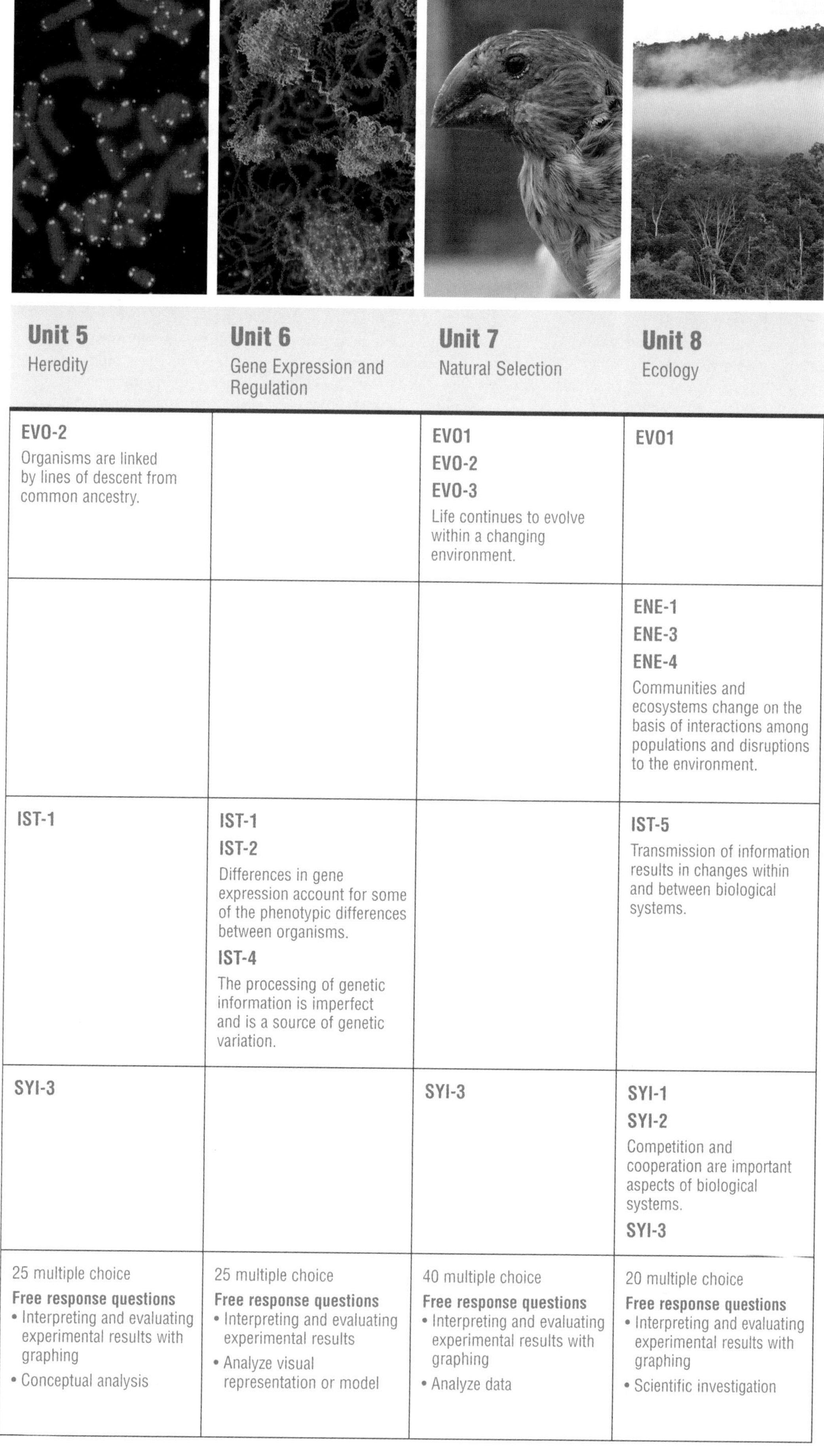

Unit 5 Heredity	**Unit 6** Gene Expression and Regulation	**Unit 7** Natural Selection	**Unit 8** Ecology
EVO-2 Organisms are linked by lines of descent from common ancestry.		**EVO1** **EVO-2** **EVO-3** Life continues to evolve within a changing environment.	**EVO1**
			ENE-1 **ENE-3** **ENE-4** Communities and ecosystems change on the basis of interactions among populations and disruptions to the environment.
IST-1	**IST-1** **IST-2** Differences in gene expression account for some of the phenotypic differences between organisms. **IST-4** The processing of genetic information is imperfect and is a source of genetic variation.		**IST-5** Transmission of information results in changes within and between biological systems.
SYI-3		**SYI-3**	**SYI-1** **SYI-2** Competition and cooperation are important aspects of biological systems. **SYI-3**
25 multiple choice **Free response questions** • Interpreting and evaluating experimental results with graphing • Conceptual analysis	25 multiple choice **Free response questions** • Interpreting and evaluating experimental results • Analyze visual representation or model	40 multiple choice **Free response questions** • Interpreting and evaluating experimental results with graphing • Analyze data	20 multiple choice **Free response questions** • Interpreting and evaluating experimental results with graphing • Scientific investigation

Science Practices and Skills

Science practices are things that scientists do in their everyday work, such as analyzing text and data, conducting experiments, and designing and evaluating solutions to problems. Competency in the skills associated with important practices in science are an integral part of the AP Biology course. The skills associated with each science practice (1-6) are identified in every activity and described below. As described on page vii, a margin bullet identifies exactly where on the page the skill is addressed. You will gain confidence and competence in these skills as you complete the activities. To help you, **refer at any time to the final chapter of this book**, which has an activity dedicated to each science practice.

Practice

1 Concept explanation
Explain biological concepts, processes, and models presented in written format.

SKILL 1.A	1.B	1.C
Describe biological concepts and/or processes.	Explain biological concepts and/or processes.	Explain biological concepts, processes, and/or models in applied contexts.

2 Visual representation
Analyze visual representations of biological concepts and processes.

SKILL 2.A	2.B	2.C	2.D
Describe characteristics of an biological concept, process, or model represented visually.	Explain relationships between different characteristics of biological concepts, processes, or models represented visually, in theoretical and applied contexts.	Explain how biological concepts and processes represented visually relate to larger biological principles, concepts, processes, or theories.	Represent relationships within biological models including mathematical models, diagrams, and flow charts.

3 Questions and methods
Determine scientific questions and methods.

SKILL 3.A	3.B	3.C	3.D	3.E
Identify or pose a testable question based on an observation, data, or a model	State the null and alternative hypotheses, or predict the results of an experiment,	Identify experimental procedures that are aligned to the question, including identifying variables and identifying and justifying controls.	Make observations, or collect data from representations of laboratory setups or results (not assessed).	Propose and new/next investigation based on an evaluation of the evidence from an experiment or an evaluation of the design/ methods.

4 Representing and describing data
Represent and describe data.

SKILL 4.A	4.B
Construct a graph,plot, or chart (*X,Y; Log Y; Bar; Histogram; Line; Dual Y; Box and Whisker; Pie*) with attention to orientation, labeling, units, scaling, plotting, type, and trend line.	Describe data from a table or graph including: a. Identifying specific data points b. Describing trends and/or patterns in the data c. Describing relationships between variables

5 Statistical tests and data analysis
Perform statistical tests and mathematical calculations to analyze and interpret data.

SKILL 5.A	5.B	5.C	5.D
Perform mathematical calculations, including mathematical equations in the curriculum, means, rates, ratios, and percentages.	Use confidence intervals and/or error bars (both determined using standard errors) to determine whether ample means are statistically significant.	Perform chi-square hypothesis testing.	Use data to evaluate a hypothesis (or prediction), including rejecting or failing to reject H_0 and supporting or refuting H_A

6 Argumentation
Develop and justify scientific arguments using evidence.

SKILL 6.A	6.B	6.C	6.D	6.E
Make a scientific claim.	Support a claim with evidence for biological principles, concepts, processes, and/ or data.	Provide reasoning to justify a claim by connecting evidence to biological theories.	Explain the relationship between experimental results and larger biological concepts, processes, or theories.	Predict the causes or effects of a change in, or disruption to, one or more components in a biological system based on: a. Biological concepts or processes b. A visual representation of a biological concept, process, or model c. Data

UNIT 1

Chemistry of Life

Learning Objectives

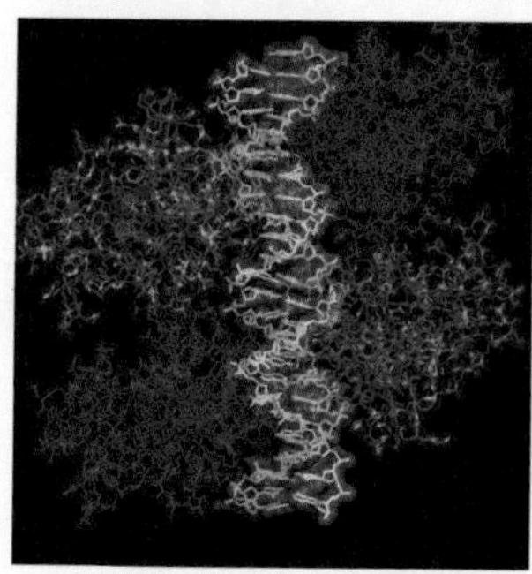

Developing understanding

CONTENT: This unit sets the foundation for understanding the chemical basis of life and includes a survey of the elements essential to carbon-based systems. You will learn about the central role of water in biological systems and build an understanding of how the organization of living systems depends on an input of energy and an exchange of macromolecules. Understanding how macromolecules are constructed from monomers is central to this.

SKILLS: This unit emphasizes skills in describing biological processes, principles, and concepts represented visually. The skill of argumentation is introduced, using a model to predict the causes or effects of a change in a system.

1.1 Structure of water and hydrogen bonding .... activity 1

☐ 1. Explain the structure of a water molecule, identifying how hydrogen bonding between water molecules accounts for water's unique properties. Use visual representations to explain the properties of water in its liquid and solid states.

☐ 2. Explain how living systems depend on the properties of water that arise from its polarity and hydrogen bonding. Include reference to cohesion, adhesion, thermal conductivity, high specific heat capacity, heat of vaporization, and heat of fusion, and role as a universal solvent.

1.2 Elements of life .... activity 2

☐ 3. Identify the macromolecules required by living organisms and describe their composition. Describe how organisms must exchange matter with the environment to grow, reproduce, and maintain organization.

☐ 4. Describe how carbon moves from the environment to organisms and how it is used to build biological molecules and in storage and cell formation in all organisms.

☐ 5. Describe how nitrogen and phosphorus move from the environment to organisms and how they are used in building new molecules in organisms.

1.3 Introduction to biological macromolecules .... activities 3-5, 10, 13

☐ 6. Describe how dehydration synthesis (condensation) and hydrolysis reactions are used to form and cleave covalent bonds between monomers in nucleic acids, proteins, carbohydrates, and lipids.

1.4 Properties of biological macromolecules .... activities 4-14

☐ 7. Describe how biological information is encoded in sequences of nucleotide monomers. Describe the structural components of nucleotides.

☐ 8. Describe how the primary structure of a polypeptide determines the overall shape of a protein. Describe the structure of an amino acid and how the properties of the amino acid R groups and their interactions determine final protein structure and function.

☐ 9. Describe how the structures of carbohydrate monomers determine the properties and functions of the molecules.

☐ 10. Describe the non-polar nature of a typical lipid (e.g. a triacylglycerol) and explain how phospholipids differ in having polar and non-polar regions. Explain how differences in fatty acid saturation determine lipid structure and function.

1.5 Structure and function of biological macromolecules .... activities 4-12

☐ 11. Explain how the nucleotides are organized into polymers called nucleic acids, including reference to the phosphodiester bonds that form between adjacent nucleotides. Interpret diagrams and models to explain the directionality of nucleic acids, defined by the 3' and a 5' carbons of the sugar in the nucleotide.

☐ 12. Explain the antiparallel, double helix structure of DNA, including how the directionality of the molecule determines the direction of nucleotide addition during DNA and RNA synthesis (5'→3'). Explain the role of hydrogen bonding between nucleobases in formation of the DNA double helix.

☐ 13. Explain how proteins have a primary structure comprising linear chains of amino acids connected by covalent peptide bonds formed at the carboxyl end of the growing polypeptide chain. Explain the interactions involved in creating a protein's primary, secondary, tertiary, and quaternary structures.

☐ 14. Explain the role of a protein's precise three-dimensional structure to its biological function. Explain how this precise structure can be disrupted and predict the consequences of such disruptions.

☐ 15. Explain how carbohydrates are made up of chains of monosaccharide monomers connected by covalent glycosidic bonds. Explain why some polysaccharides are linear and some are branched. To illustrate this, compare and contrast the structure of glucose polymers such as cellulose, starch, and glycogen.

1.6 Nucleic acids .... activities 3, 4

☐ 16. Describe the structural similarities and differences between DNA and RNA, including reference to the sugar present, the nucleobases present, and the number of strands usually present (single/double).

1 Water in Living Systems

Key Question: How does water's molecular structure account for its properties and for its central role in life's processes?

Water (H_2O) is the main component of living things, and typically makes up about 70% of any organism. Water is important in cell chemistry as it takes part in, and is a common product of, many reactions. Its cohesive, adhesive, thermal, and solvent properties come about because of its polarity and its ability to form hydrogen bonds with other polar molecules. Water's physical and chemical properties are essential for sustaining life. It is the universal solvent.

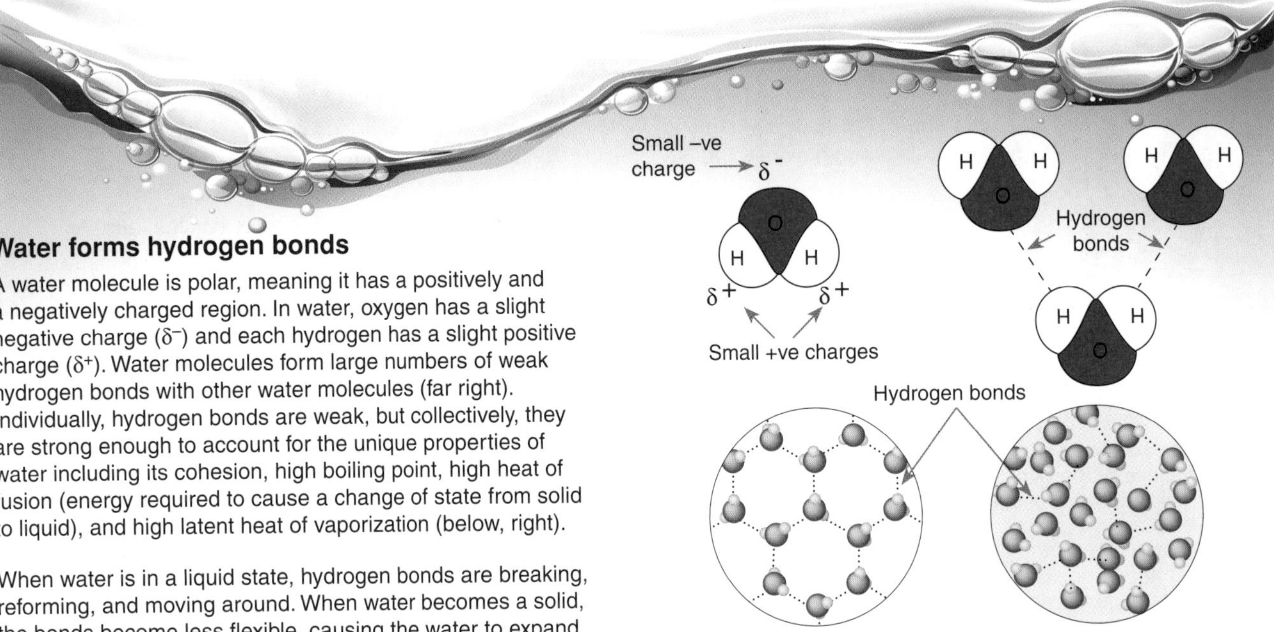

Water forms hydrogen bonds

A water molecule is polar, meaning it has a positively and a negatively charged region. In water, oxygen has a slight negative charge (δ^-) and each hydrogen has a slight positive charge (δ^+). Water molecules form large numbers of weak hydrogen bonds with other water molecules (far right). Individually, hydrogen bonds are weak, but collectively, they are strong enough to account for the unique properties of water including its cohesion, high boiling point, high heat of fusion (energy required to cause a change of state from solid to liquid), and high latent heat of vaporization (below, right).

When water is in a liquid state, hydrogen bonds are breaking, reforming, and moving around. When water becomes a solid, the bonds become less flexible, causing the water to expand. The expansion causes ice's density to decrease.

Intermolecular bonds between water and other polar molecules or ions are important for biological systems. Inorganic ions may have a positive or negative charge, e.g. positive sodium ion (Na^+) and negative chloride ion (Cl^-). The charged water molecules are attracted to charged ions and surrounds them. This formation of intermolecular bonds between water and the ions keeps ions dissolved in water. Polar molecules such as amino acids and carbohydrates also dissolve readily in water.

Ice: H-bonds are fixed in an interconnected framework.

Liquid water: H-bonds constantly break and reform.

Na⁺

Oxygen is attracted to the Na^+

Hydrogen is attracted to the Cl^-

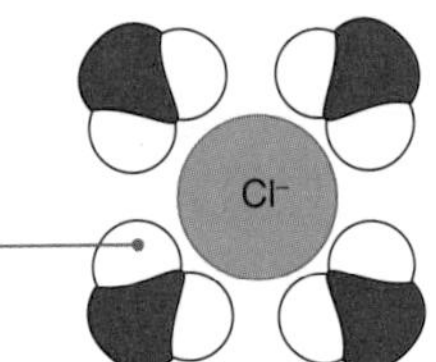

Water surrounding a positive ion (Na^+)

Water surrounding a negative ion (Cl^-)

Cohesive properties

Water molecules are cohesive, they stick together because hydrogen bonds form between water molecules. Cohesion allows water to form droplets and is responsible for the surface tension that many small organisms rely on.

Example: The cohesive and adhesive properties of water allow it to move as an unbroken column through the xylem of plants. This process is essential to water uptake from the soil.

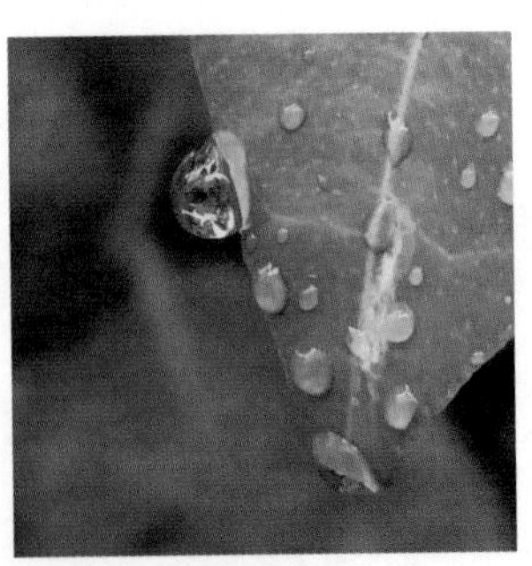

Adhesive properties

Water is attracted to other molecules because of its polar nature. Water will form thin films and "climb" up surfaces when the molecular forces between them (adhesive forces) are greater than the cohesive forces.

Example: Adhesion enables capillary action, i.e. the ability of a liquid to flow against gravity in a narrow space. This property is also shown by the meniscus of a liquid in a tube (above).

Solvent properties

Water's polarity allows it to dissociate ions in salts and bond to other polar substances (e.g. alcohols and acids), dissolving them. In contrast, non-polar substances such as fats and oils are not water soluble.

Example: Blood plasma in humans and other animals is largely water and transports many water-soluble substances, including ions, glucose, and amino acids, around the body.

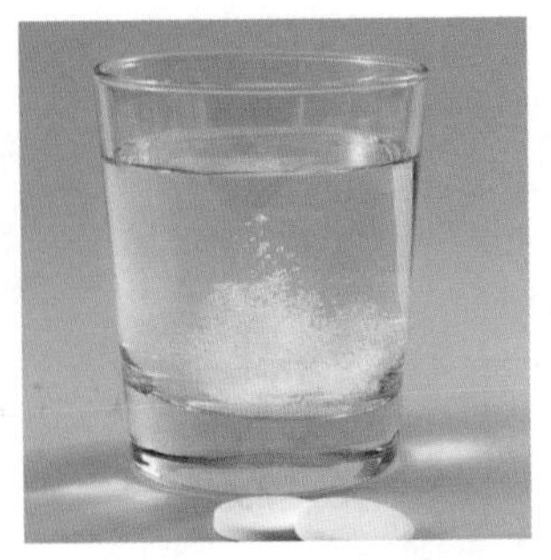

Thermal properties

Water has the highest specific heat capacity of all liquids, so it takes a lot of energy before it will change temperature. It also has high latent heat of vaporization, so it takes a lot of energy to transform it from the liquid to the gas phase.

Examples: High specific heat capacity means that large water bodies will maintain a relatively stable temperature. High heat of vaporization makes sweating a very effective cooling mechanism.

ISBN: 978-1-98-856656-6

The importance of water in biological systems

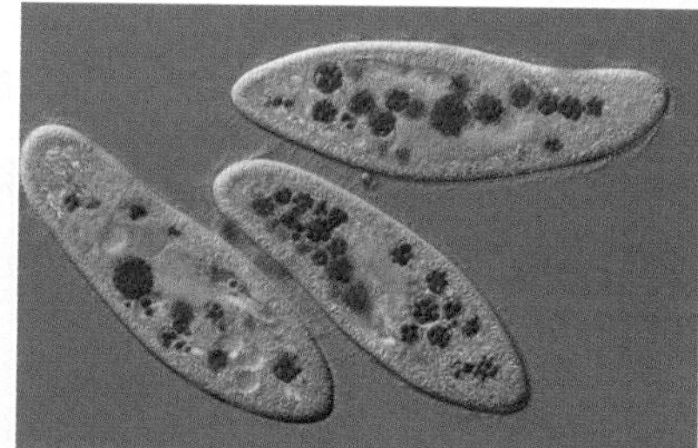

Water is liquid at room temperature. The liquid environment supports life and metabolic processes, which depend on dissolved reactants (solutes) coming into contact. Water can also act as an acid (donating H^+) or a base (receiving H^+) in chemical reactions.

Water provides an aquatic environment for organisms to live in. Water's cohesion is responsible for its high specific heat capacity (a function of its many hydrogen bonds). This means water bodies heat up and cool down only slowly, providing a relatively stable thermal environment.

Water's high latent heat of vaporization means that a change of state from liquid to gas absorbs a lot of energy. As the water in sweat evaporates from the skin's surface, heat from the body is transferred to the air, cooling the body. Panting in animals that do not sweat operates in the same way.

The lower density of ice relative to liquid water means that ice floats. This insulates the underlying water and maintains the aquatic habitat. A lot of energy is needed for water to change state, so water has a buffering effect on climate.

Water is known as the universal solvent, because many substances will dissolve in it. In natural waters, dissolved minerals, such as calcium, are available to aquatic organisms, e.g. shell building organisms such as the hard corals above.

Water is colorless, with a high transmission of visible light. Light penetrates aquatic environments, allowing photosynthesis to continue at depth. Coastal zones, where light penetration supports abundant algae are some of the most productive on Earth.

1. Explain how water's molecular structure accounts for each of the following:

(a) Water's cohesion and high heat capacity: weak hydrogen bonds

(b) Water's solvent properties: polarity allows to dissociate ions in salts + bond to other polar substances

(c) Water's high latent heat of vaporization: weak hydrogen bonds

2. (a) Use the diagram opposite to explain why water is less dense in its solid form (as ice) than in its liquid form:

bonds are stronger as well as closer / tightly packed together

(b) Explain the consequences of this to biological systems: Allows for icelands to be made, etcetera

3. Summarize the ways in which living systems depend on the properties of water arising from its molecular structure:

Water helps metabolic processes, sweating, maintaining organism's heat. Also provides many environment / ecosystems for several different species of orgdnisms.

ISBN: 978-1-98-856656-6

2 The Biochemical Nature of the Cell

Key Question: What atoms and molecules do organisms obtain from their environment and what do they do with them?

Water is the main component of cells and organisms, providing an aqueous environment in which metabolic reactions can occur. Apart from water, most other substances in cells are compounds of carbon, hydrogen, oxygen, and nitrogen. Life on Earth is carbon based. Carbon is able to form up to four valence bonds with other atoms simultaneously so it can combine with many other elements to form a large number of carbon-based (or organic) molecules. The organic molecules that make up living things can be grouped into four broad classes: carbohydrates, lipids, proteins, and nucleic acids. In addition, a small number of inorganic ions are also components of larger molecules.

The components of cells

Centrioles

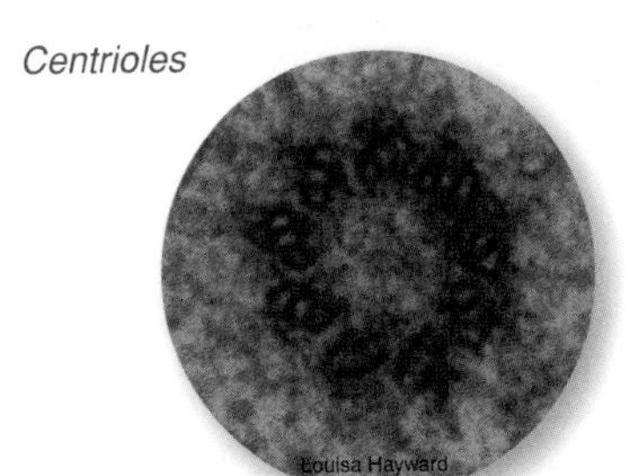

Chloroplasts in plant cells

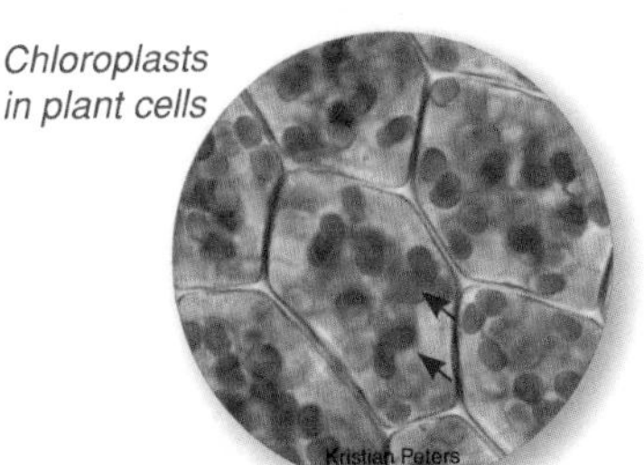

Plant epidermis

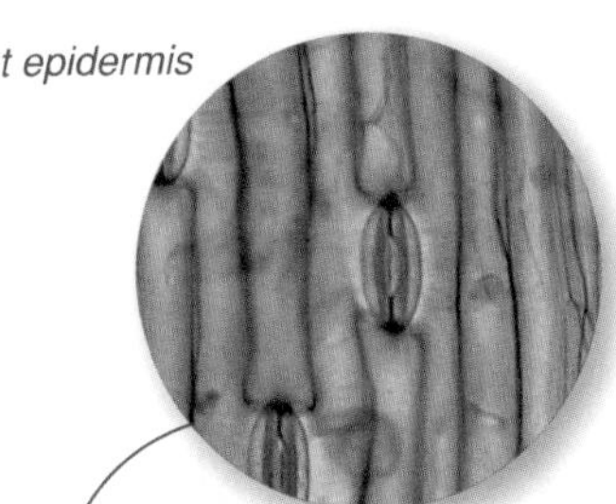

Proteins have an enormous number of structural and functional roles in plants and animals, e.g. as enzymes, structural materials (such as collagen), in transport, and movement (e.g. cytoskeleton and centrioles).
Components: **C, H, O, N, S, P**

Inorganic ions: Dissolved ions participate in metabolic reactions and are components of larger organic molecules, e.g. Mg^{2+} is a component of the green chlorophyll pigment in the chloroplasts of green plants.

Water is a major component of cells: many substances dissolve in it and metabolic reactions occur in it. In plant cells, fluid pressure against the cell wall provides turgor, which supports the cell.
Components: **H, O**

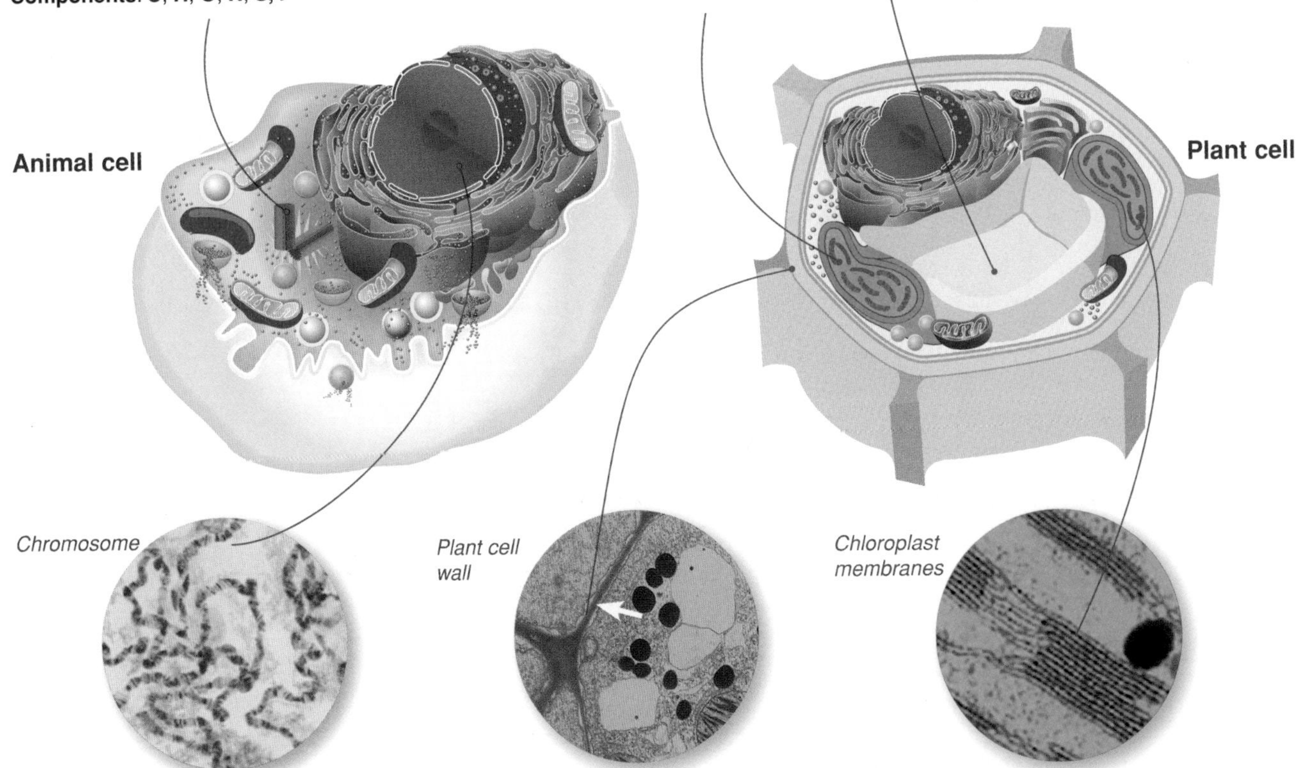

Chromosome

Plant cell wall

Chloroplast membranes

Nucleotides and nucleic acids
Nucleic acids encode information for the construction and functioning of an organism (DNA and RNA). ATP, a nucleotide derivative, is the energy carrier of the cell.
Components: **C, H, O, N, P**

Carbohydrates form the structural components of cells, e.g. cellulose cell walls (arrowed). They are important in providing usable energy as glucose, in energy storage and they are involved in cellular recognition.
Components: **C, H, O**

Simple lipids provide a concentrated source of energy. Phospholipids (a complex lipid) are a major component of cellular membranes, including the membranes of organelles such as chloroplasts and mitochondria.
Components: **C, H, O** (lipids)
C, H, O, P, N (phospholipids)

1. (a) List the four main macromolecule components of living organisms: carbohydrates, lipids, proteins, and nucleic acids

(b) List the elements that all these macromolecules share: made of carbon valence bonds

ISBN: 978-1-98-856656-6

The elements of life

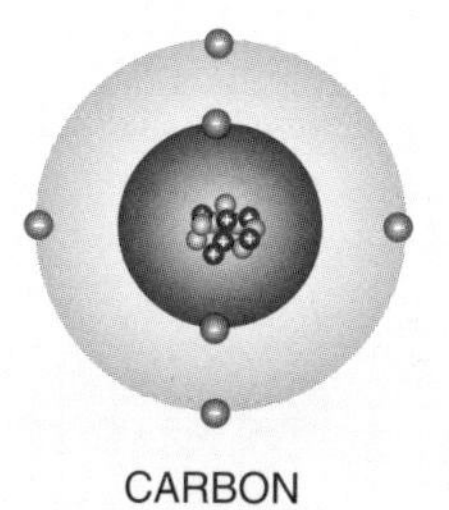

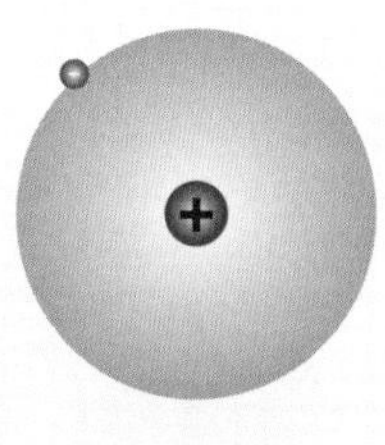

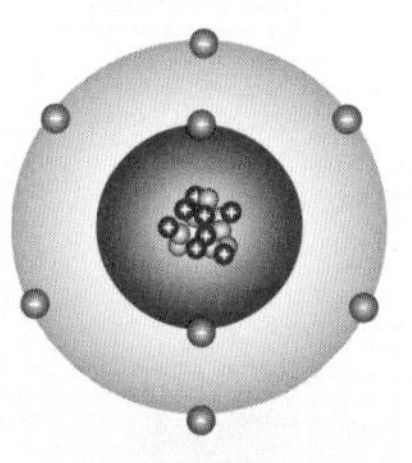

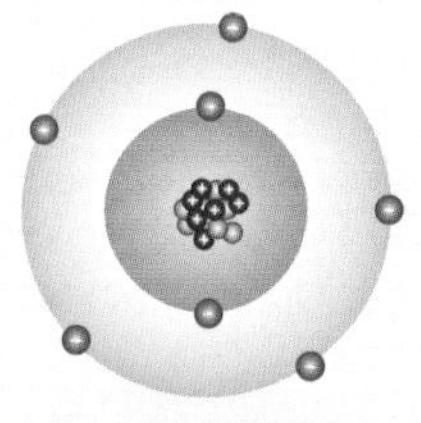

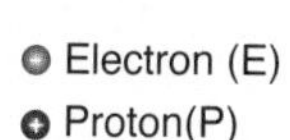

Carbon is very abundant. It has four valence (outer shell) electrons that are available to form up to four covalent (shared electron) bonds with other atoms. Complex biological molecules consist of carbon atoms bonded with other elements, especially oxygen and hydrogen, but also nitrogen, phosphorus, and sulfur. Carbon readily forms stable polymers that can participate in chemical reactions.

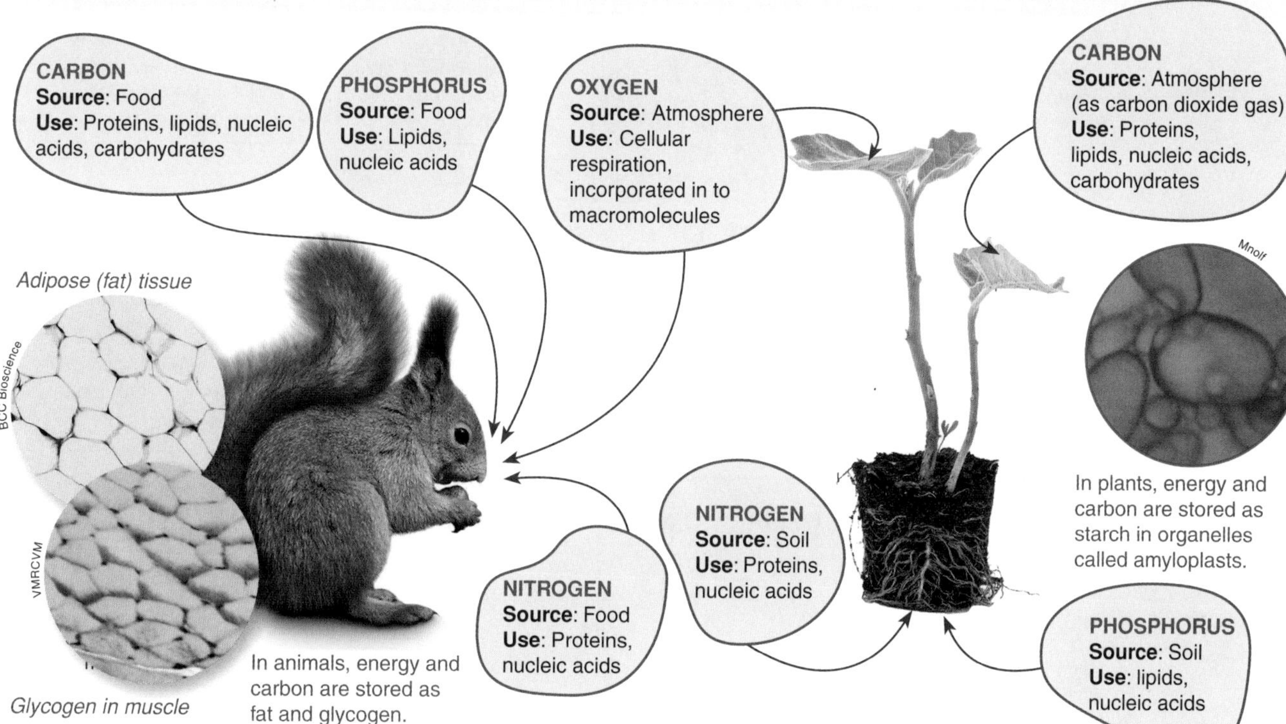

In animals, energy and carbon are stored as fat and glycogen.

In plants, energy and carbon are stored as starch in organelles called amyloplasts.

2. Summarize the role of each of the following cell components:

(a) Carbohydrates: provide usable energy as glucose

(b) Lipids: provide concentrated source of energy

(c) Proteins: numerous roles; structural materials in transport/movement

(d) Nucleic acids: encode information for construction/function of organism

(e) Inorganic ions: participate in metabolic reactions

(f) Water: substances dissolve in it + metabolic reactions occur in it.

3. Explain why carbon is so important for building the molecular components of an organism: It has 4 valence electrons that are available to form up to 4 covalent bonds w/ other atoms. Many molecules consist carbon atoms bonded w/ other elements.

4. State the main source of carbon, phosphorus, and nitrogen for animals: Food ~~soil~~

5. (a) State the main source of carbon for plants: atmosphere

(b) State the main source of phosphorus and nitrogen for plants: soil

ISBN: 978-1-98-856656-6

3 Nucleotides

Key Question: What are the components of a nucleotide monomer and how is it formed?

Nucleotides are the building blocks of nucleic acids (DNA and RNA), which are involved in the transmission of inherited information. Nucleotide derivatives, such as ATP, are involved in energy transfers in cells. A nucleotide has three components: a base, a sugar, and a phosphate group. Nucleotides may contain one of five bases. The combination of bases in the nucleotides making up DNA or RNA stores the information controlling the cell's activity.

Phosphate

Phosphate groups are represented by orange circles. With the pentose sugar they form the "backbone" of the DNA or RNA molecule.

$$HO-\overset{\displaystyle OH}{\underset{\displaystyle \|\atop O}{P}}-OH$$

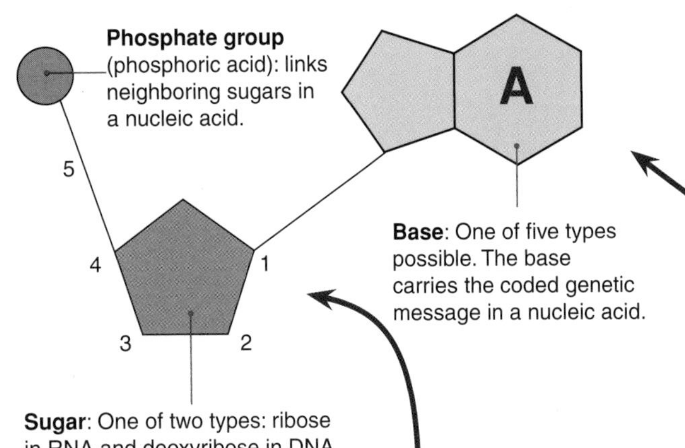

Phosphate group (phosphoric acid): links neighboring sugars in a nucleic acid.
A
5
4
1
3
2
Base: One of five types possible. The base carries the coded genetic message in a nucleic acid.
Sugar: One of two types: ribose in RNA and deoxyribose in DNA.

Pyrimidines

Thymine | Cytosine | Uracil

Pyrimidines are single ringed bases. DNA contains the pyrimidines cytosine (C) and thymine (T). RNA contains the pyrimidines cytosine and uracil (U).

Purines

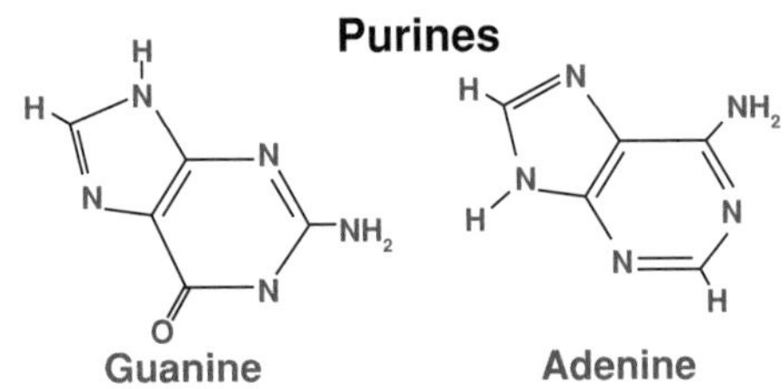

Guanine
Adenine

Purines are double ringed bases. Both DNA and RNA contain the purines adenine (A) and guanine (G).

Sugars

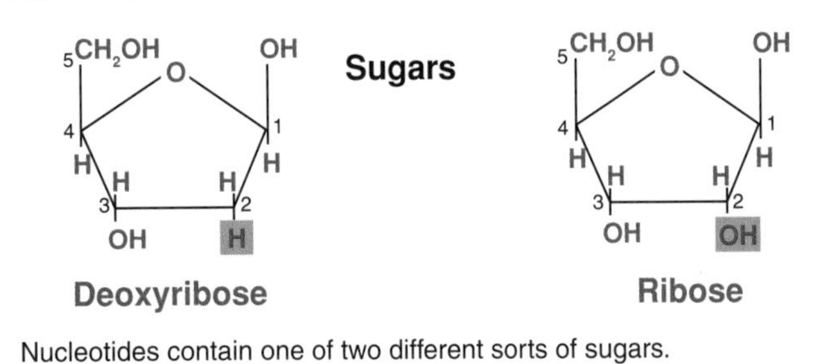

Deoxyribose
Ribose

Nucleotides contain one of two different sorts of sugars. **Deoxyribose** sugar is found in DNA. **Ribose** sugar is found in RNA.

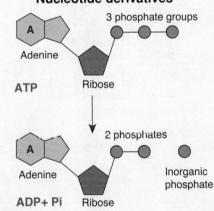

Nucleotide formation

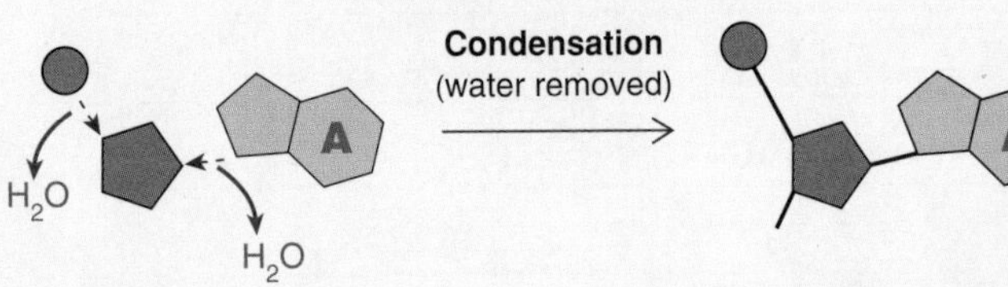

Condensation
(water removed)
A
A
H_2O
H_2O

In formation of a nucleotide, a phosphoric acid and a base are chemically bonded to a sugar molecule by **condensation** reactions in which water is given off. The reverse reaction is **hydrolysis**.

Nucleotide derivatives

3 phosphate groups | Adenine | Ribose | ATP

2 phosphates | Adenine | Ribose | Inorganic phosphate | ADP+ Pi

ATP is a nucleotide derivative that provides chemical energy for metabolism. It consists of an adenine linked to a ribose sugar and 3 phosphate groups. Energy is made available when a phosphate group is transferred to a target molecule. Other **nucleoside triphosphates** (NTPs) have similar roles.

1. Describe the basic structure of a nucleotide: base, sugar, phosphate group. Contain deoxyribose + ribose

2. Distinguish between purines and pyrimidines: purines - double ringed bases pyrimidines - single ringed bases.

3. Explain how a nucleotide is assembled from its component parts: phosphoric acid + base are chemically bonded to sugar molecule by condensation reactions.

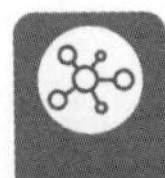
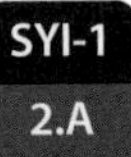

SYI-1
2.A

4

ISBN: 978-1-98-856656-6

4 Nucleic Acids

Key Question: How are nucleic acids formed and how do different nucleic acids differ in their structure and function?

DNA and RNA are nucleic acids involved in the transmission of inherited information. Nucleic acids have the capacity to store the information that controls cellular activity. The central nucleic acid is **DNA** (deoxyribonucleic acid). Ribonucleic acids (**RNA**) are involved in 'reading' and translating the information in DNA. All nucleic acids are made up of nucleotides linked together to form chains or strands. The strands vary in the sequence of the bases found on each nucleotide. It is this sequence that provides the coding for the amino acids that make up proteins, i.e. the 'genetic instructions' for the cell.

Nucleotides are joined by condensation polymerization

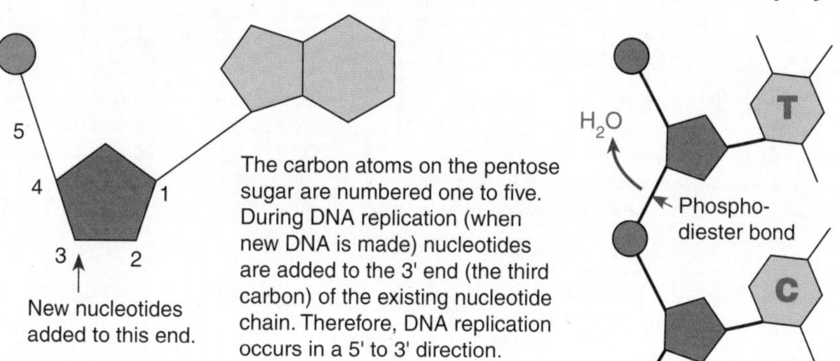

5
4
1
3
2
New nucleotides added to this end.
The carbon atoms on the pentose sugar are numbered one to five. During DNA replication (when new DNA is made) nucleotides are added to the 3' end (the third carbon) of the existing nucleotide chain. Therefore, DNA replication occurs in a 5' to 3' direction.
H_2O
T
Phospho-diester bond
C

In the formation of nucleic acids, nucleotides are joined together into polymers through a **condensation reaction** (dehydration synthesis) between the phosphate group of one nucleotide and the sugar of another. Water is released and a **phosphodiester bond** is formed, linking the 3' carbon atom of one sugar molecule and the 5' carbon atom of another. Because of the way they are formed, nucleic acids are called **condensation polymers**.

RNA molecule

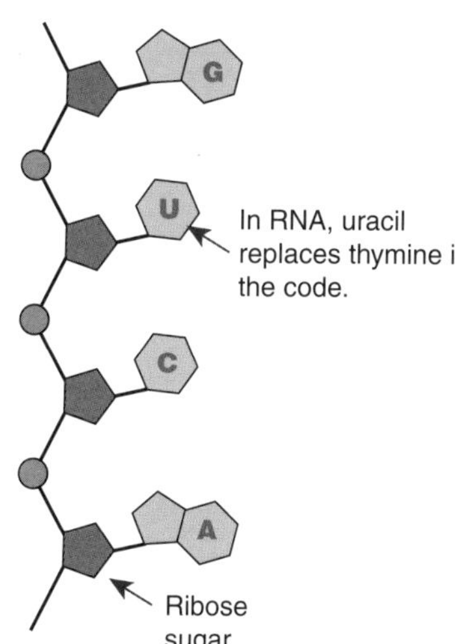

Ribonucleic acid (RNA) is made up of a single strand of nucleotides linked together. Although it is single stranded, it is often found folded back on itself, with complementary bases joined by hydrogen bonds.

DNA molecule

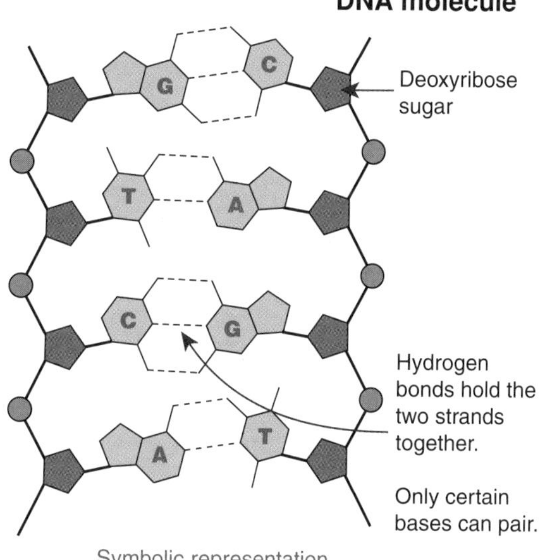

Symbolic representation

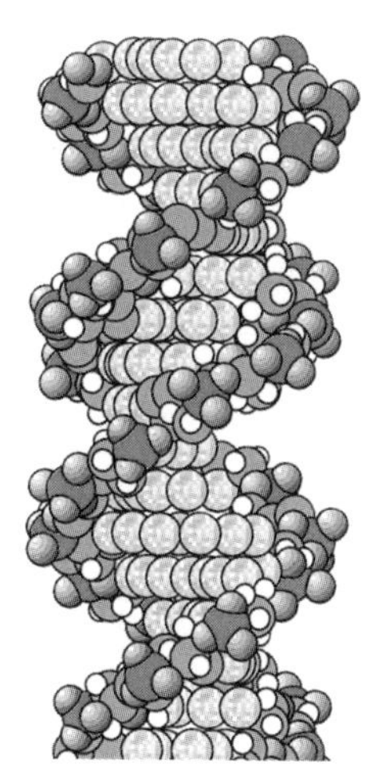

Space filling model

Deoxyribonucleic acid (DNA) is made up of a double strand of nucleotides linked together. It is shown unwound in the symbolic representation (above left). The DNA molecule takes on a double helix shape as shown in the space filling model above right.

Double-stranded DNA

The double-helix structure of DNA is like a ladder twisted into a corkscrew shape around its longitudinal axis. It is 'unwound' here to show the relationships between the bases.

- The DNA backbone is made up of alternating phosphate and sugar molecules, giving the DNA molecule an asymmetrical structure.
- The asymmetrical structure gives a DNA strand **direction**. Each strand runs in the opposite direction to the other.
- The ends of a DNA strand are labeled the 5' (five prime) and 3' (three prime) ends. The **5'** end has a terminal phosphate group (off carbon 5), the **3'** end has a terminal hydroxyl group (off carbon 3).
- The way the pairs of bases come together to form hydrogen bonds is determined by the number of bonds they can form and the configuration of the bases.

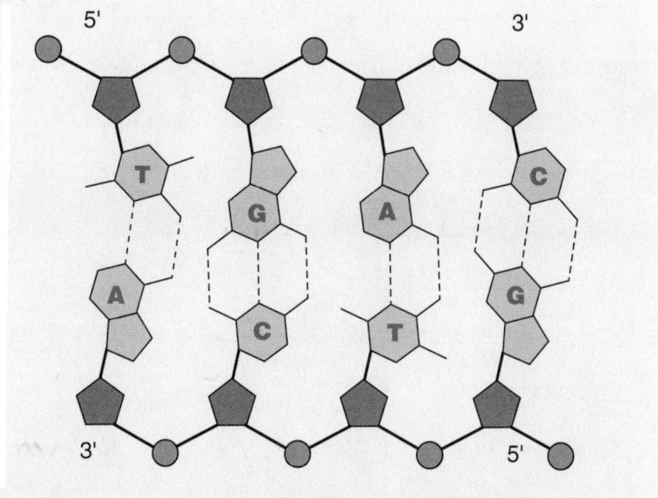

ISBN: 978-1-98-856656-6

RNAs are involved in decoding the genetic information in DNA, as messenger RNA (mRNA), transfer RNA (tRNA), and ribosomal RNA (rRNA). RNA is also involved in modifying mRNA after transcription and in regulating translation.

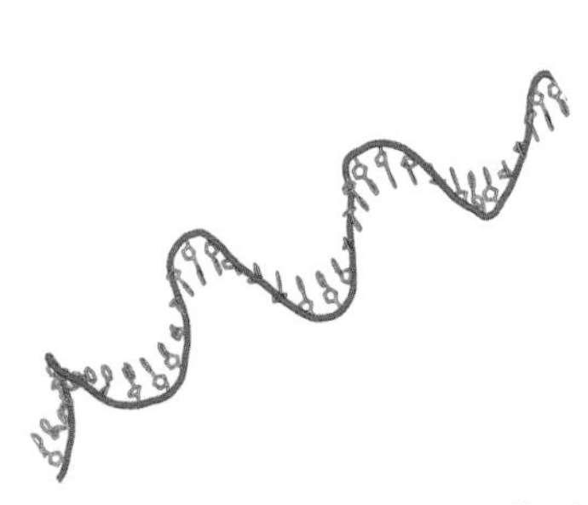

Messenger RNA (above) is transcribed (written) from DNA. It carries a copy of the genetic instructions from the DNA to ribosomes in the cytoplasm, where it is translated into a polypeptide chain.

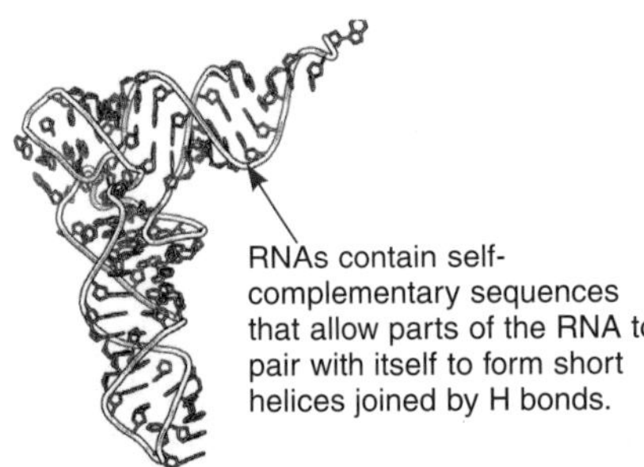

RNAs contain self-complementary sequences that allow parts of the RNA to pair with itself to form short helices joined by H bonds.

Transfer RNA (above) carries amino acids to the growing polypeptide chain. One end of the tRNA carries the genetic code in a three-nucleotide sequence called the **anticodon**. The amino acid links to the 3' end of the tRNA.

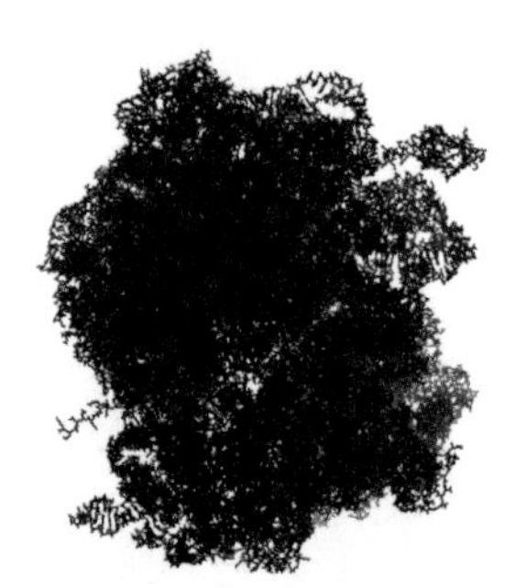

Ribosomal RNA (above) together with associated proteins make up ribosomes. Two separate ribosomal components (the large and small subunits) assemble amino acids into a polypeptide chain.

1. (a) Use the diagrams on the previous page to describe the base-pairing rule that applies in double-stranded DNA: Thymine + Cytosine are pyrimidines and guanine + adenine are purines. T pairs w/ A and C pairs w/ G.

   (b) How is the base-pairing rule for RNA different? uracil replaces thymine

   (c) What is the purpose of the hydrogen bonds in double-stranded DNA? Hydrogen bonds pair bases together and they are hard to take apart.

2. Describe how nucleic acids are formed: Nucleic acids are made of nucleotides linked together to form chains/strands. Nucleotides are joined together through a condensation reaction.

3. (a) If you wanted to use a radioactive or fluorescent tag to label only the RNA in a cell and not the DNA, what molecule(s) would you label?

   Molecules containing uracil bases

   (b) If you wanted to use a radioactive or fluorescent tag to label only the DNA in a cell and not the RNA, what molecule(s) would you label?

   Molecules containing adenine bases

4. (a) Why do the DNA strands have an asymmetrical structure? The asymmetrical structure gives a DNA strand direction. Each strand runs in the opposite direction to the other.

   (b) What are the differences between the 5' and 3' ends of a DNA strand? The 5' end has a terminal phosphate group, 3' end has a terminal hydroxyl group.

5. How can simple nucleotide units combine to store genetic information? DNA strands vary in the sequence of the bases found in each nucleotide. It is the sequence that provides the coding for the amino acids that make up proteins (genetic instructions for cells).

6. Summarize the differences between DNA and RNA molecules for each of the components identified below:

   (a) Sugar present i) DNA: ~~ribose~~ deoxyribose ii) RNA: ~~deoxyribo~~ ribose

   (b) Bases present i) DNA: 4, A-T, G-C ii) RNA: 4, A-U, G-C

   (c) Number of strands i) DNA: 2 ii) RNA: 1

ISBN: 978-1-98-856656-6

5 Amino Acids

Key Question: How do amino acid monomers come together and interact to form polypeptides?

Amino acids are the basic units from which proteins are made. Twenty amino acids commonly occur in proteins and they can be linked together in a linear sequence by condensation reactions to form polypeptides. Proteins are made up of one or more polypeptide molecules. These can be broken apart by hydrolysis into their constituent amino acids.

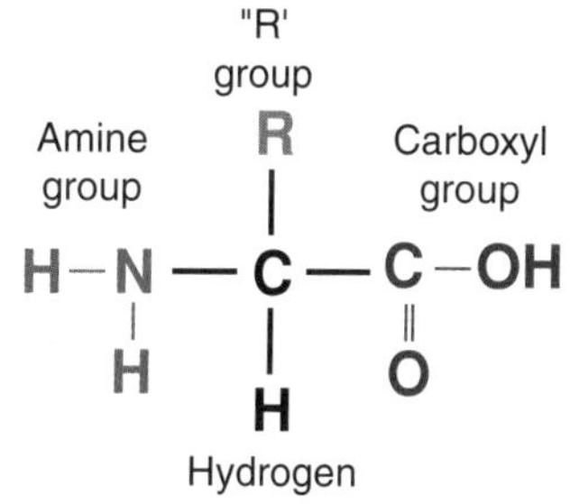

The structure and properties of amino acids

- Amino acids are the building blocks of proteins. They are linked by peptide bonds (below and next page) to form long chains called polypeptides, which are the basis of proteins. All amino acids have a common structure (left) with an amine group (blue), a carboxyl group (red), a hydrogen atom, and a functional or 'R' group (orange).
- Each type of amino acid has a different functional R group (side chain). Each functional R group has a different chemical property.
- Amino acids are represented by a single upper case letter or a three-letter abbreviation. For example, proline is known by the letter P or the three-letter symbol Pro.

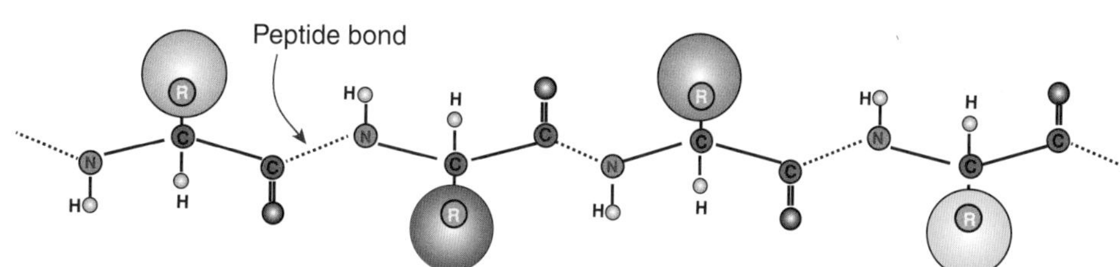

Different amino acids have different R groups

- The R group in the amino acid determines the chemical properties of the amino acid. Different amino acids have different R groups and therefore different chemical properties. Amino acids can be grouped according to these properties. Common groupings are nonpolar (hydrophobic), polar (hydrophilic), positively charged (basic), or negatively charged (acidic).
- The property of the R group determines how the amino acid will interacts with others and how the amino acid chain will fold up into a functional protein. For example, the hydrophobic R groups of soluble proteins will be folded into the protein's interior.

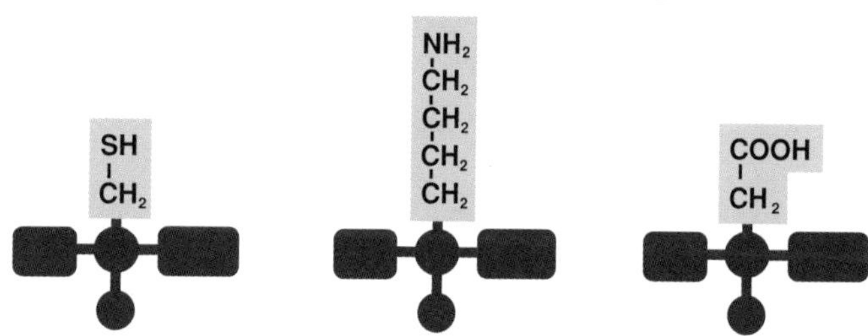

Cysteine
The 'R' group of cysteine forms **disulfide bridges** with other cysteines to create cross linkages in a polypeptide chain.

Lysine
The 'R' group of lysine gives the amino acid an **alkaline** property.

Aspartic acid
The 'R' group of aspartic acid gives the amino acid an **acidic** property.

1. What makes each of the amino acids in proteins unique and how does this uniqueness contribute to protein structure?

Different amino acids have different R groups, and this determines it's chemical properties + how it interacts w/ other amino acids

2. Do some research to assign each of the 20 amino acids found in proteins to one of the four groups below. Use a standard 3-letter code to identify each amino acid:

(a) Nonpolar (hydrophobic): ~~gly~~ ala, val, Ile, Leu, Met, phe, Tyr, Trp

(b) Polar (hydrophilic): Ser, thr, Asn, gln

(c) Positively charged (basic): Arg, His, Lys

(d) Negatively charged (acidic): Asp, Glu

3. (a) Which type(s) of amino acids would you find on the surface of a soluble protein? Which type(s) would you find in the interior? Explain:

you would find polar amino acids on the surface and nonpolar in the interior of the protein

(b) What distribution of amino acids would you expect to find in a protein embedded in a lipid bilayer?

you would find amino acids that are hydrophilic or polar.

ISBN: 978-1-98-856656-6

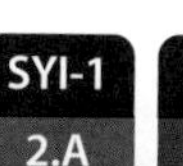

SYI-1 2.A

SYI-1 1.A

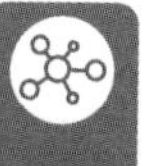

Polypeptides are made by condensation and broken down by hydrolysis

- Amino acids are linked by **peptide bonds** to form **polypeptide chains** of up to several thousand amino acids.
- Peptide bonds are covalent bonds formed between the carboxyl group of one amino acid and the amine group of another (right). Water is released when this bond is formed so the reaction is called a condensation reaction (or dehydration synthesis) because water is lost when building the molecule.
- The sequence of amino acids in a polypeptide is called the **primary structure** and is determined by the order of nucleotides in DNA and mRNA.

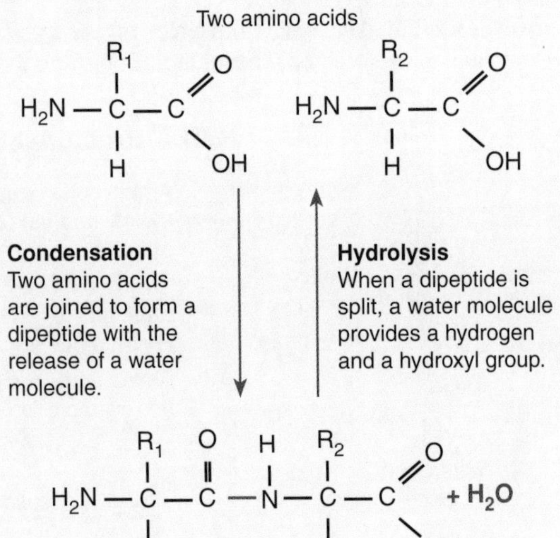

Polypeptide chain

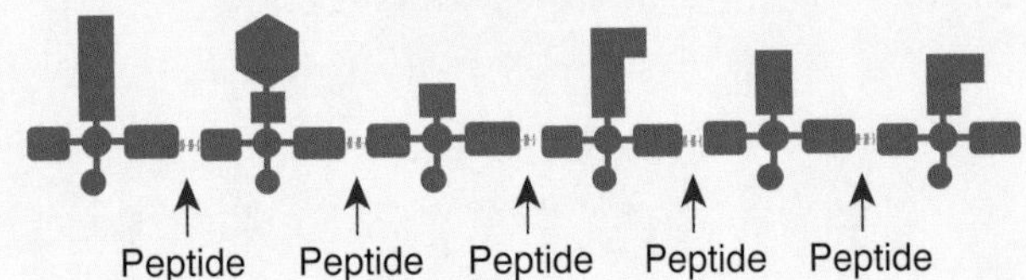

Links between amino acids

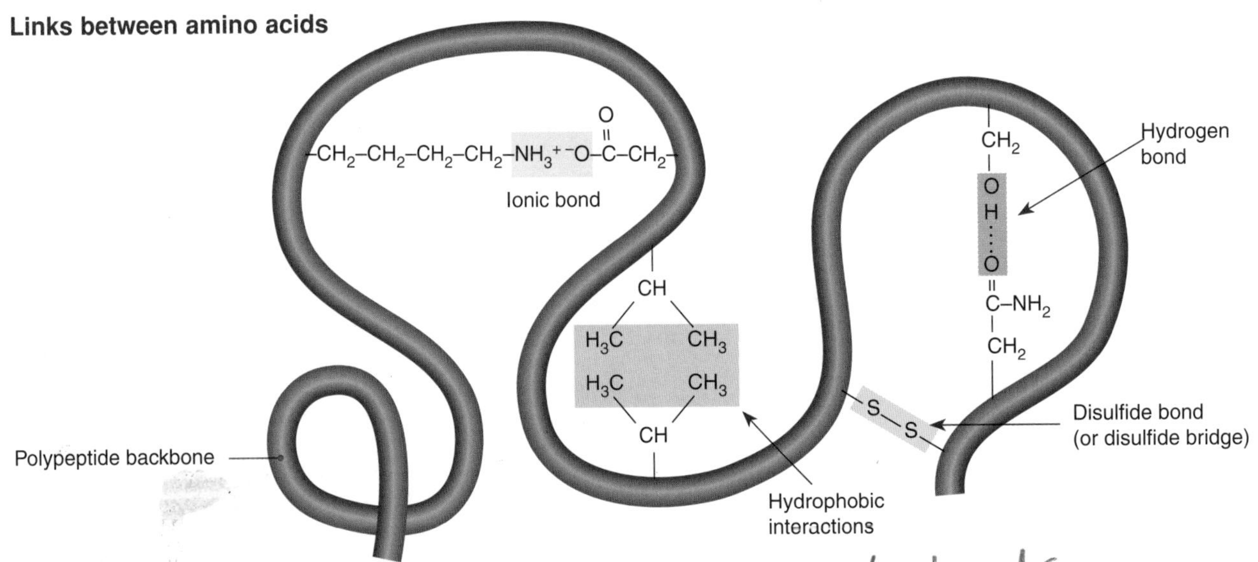

4. (a) What type of bond joins neighboring amino acids together? peptide bonds

   (b) How is this bond formed? through condensation (covalent bonds between carboxyl + amine groups of amino acids)

   (c) Where does this bond form? amine + carboxyl

   (d) How are di- and polypeptides broken down? hydrolysis

5. Use the diagram above to answer the following:

   (a) Name the different interactions that can shape the polypeptide: hydrophobic reactions, hydrogen bonds, disulfide bonds, ionic bonds

   (b) Which of the interactions would be the strongest? disulfide bond

6. In the diagram below identify following, *R group, amine group, peptide bond, carboxyl group*:

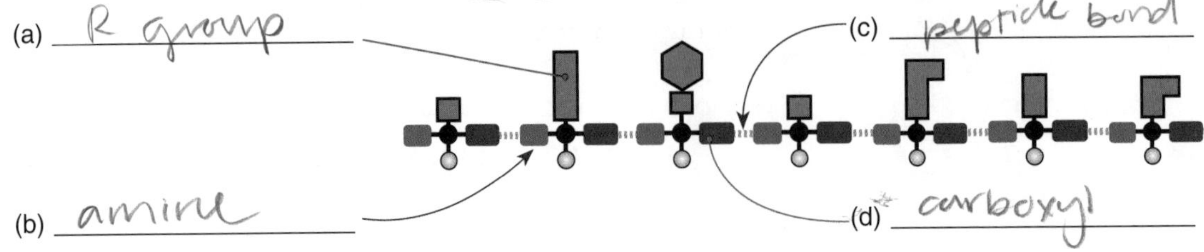

(a) R group

(b) amine

(c) peptide bond

(d) carboxyl

ISBN: 978-1-98-856656-6

6 Protein Structure is Hierarchical

Key Question: How do the sequence and types of amino acids in a protein determine its shape and function?

Proteins are large, complex macromolecules, built up from a linear sequence of amino acids. Proteins account for more than 50% of the dry weight of most cells and are important in virtually every cellular process. The various properties of the amino acids, which are conferred by the different R groups, determine how the polypeptide chain folds up. This three dimensional **tertiary structure** gives a protein its specific chemical properties and determine its functionality.

1. Describe the main features in the formation of each part of a protein's structure:

(a) Primary structure: Amino acids connected by peptide bonds.

(b) Secondary structure: maintained by hydrogen bonds between neighboring CO + NH groups. can be α-helix or β-pleated sheet. hydrogen bonds form between amino acid chains/chain

(c) Tertiary structure: has disulfide bridges, ionic bonds, and hydrophobic interactions. This structure is three dimensional. and more distant parts of the polypeptide chain interact

(d) Quaternary structure: This structure describes the arrangement + position of each of the subunits in a multiunit protein. Maintained by same interactions.

2. How are proteins built up into a functional structure?

Through different types of bonds that create bridges between amino acid sequences.

Primary (1°) structure (amino acid sequence)

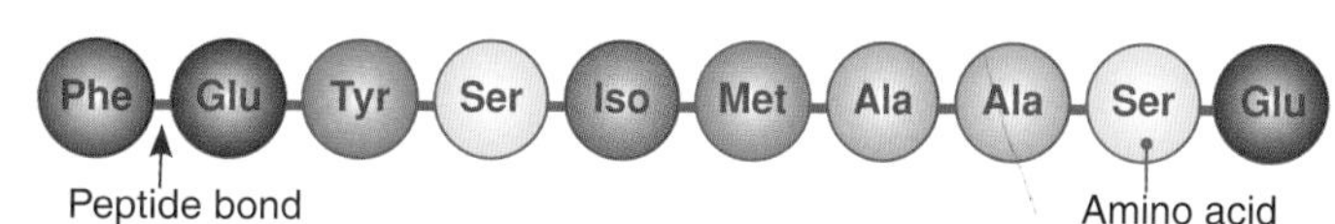

Hundreds of amino acids are linked by peptide bonds to form polypeptide chains. The attractive and repulsive charges on the amino acids determine the higher levels of organization in the protein and its biological function.

Secondary (2°) structure (α-helix or β-pleated sheet)

Secondary (2°) structure is maintained by hydrogen bonds between neighboring CO and NH groups. The hydrogen bonds are individually weak but collectively strong.

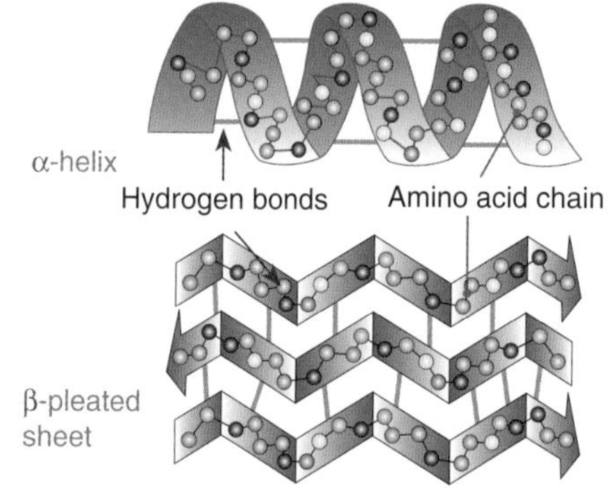

Polypeptide chains fold into a secondary (2°) structure based on H bonding. The coiled α-helix and β-pleated sheet are common 2° structures. Most globular proteins contain regions of both 2° configurations.

Tertiary (3°) structure (folding of the 2° structure)

Tertiary (3°) structure is maintained by more distant interactions such as **disulfide bridges** between cysteine amino acids, ionic bonds, and hydrophobic interactions.

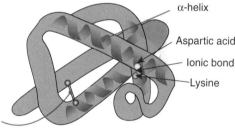

α-helix
Aspartic acid
Ionic bond
Lysine
Disulfide bond

A protein's 3° structure is the three-dimensional shape formed when the 2° structure folds up and more distant parts of the polypeptide chains interact.

Quaternary (4°) structure

Some complex proteins are only functional when as a group of polypeptide chains. Hemoglobin has a 4° structure made up of two alpha and two beta polypeptide chains, each enclosing a complex iron-containing prosthetic (or heme) group.

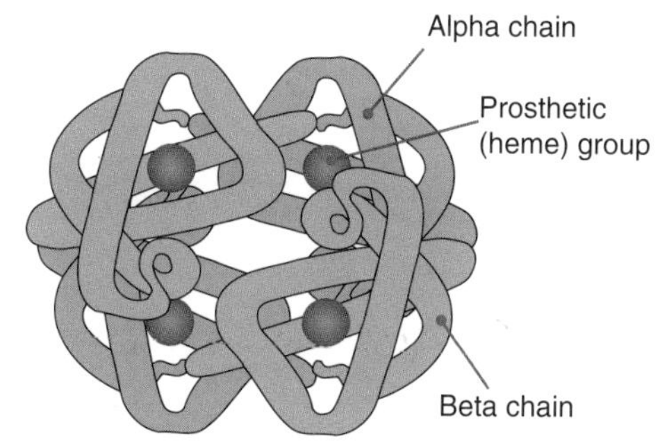

A protein's 4° structure describes the arrangement and position of each of the subunits in a multiunit protein. The shape is maintained by the same sorts of interactions as those involved in 3° structure.

ISBN: 978-1-98-856656-6

7 Protein Shape is Related to Function

Key Question: How does a protein's three dimensional shape reflect its role and enable it to function?

As we have seen, a protein may consist of one polypeptide chain, or several polypeptide chains linked together. Hydrogen bonds between amino acids cause the polypeptide chain to form its **secondary structure**, either an α-helix or a β-pleated sheet. The interaction between R groups causes a polypeptide to fold into its **tertiary structure**, a three dimensional shape held by ionic bonds and disulfide bridges (bonds formed between sulfur containing amino acids). If bonds are broken (through denaturation), the protein loses its tertiary structure, and its functionality.

The shape of a protein reflects its biological role

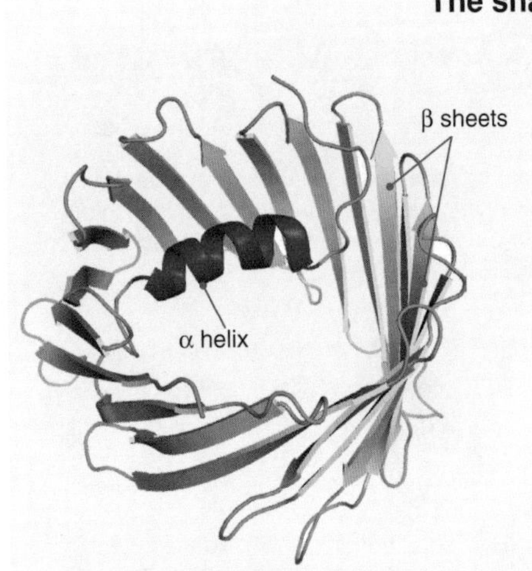

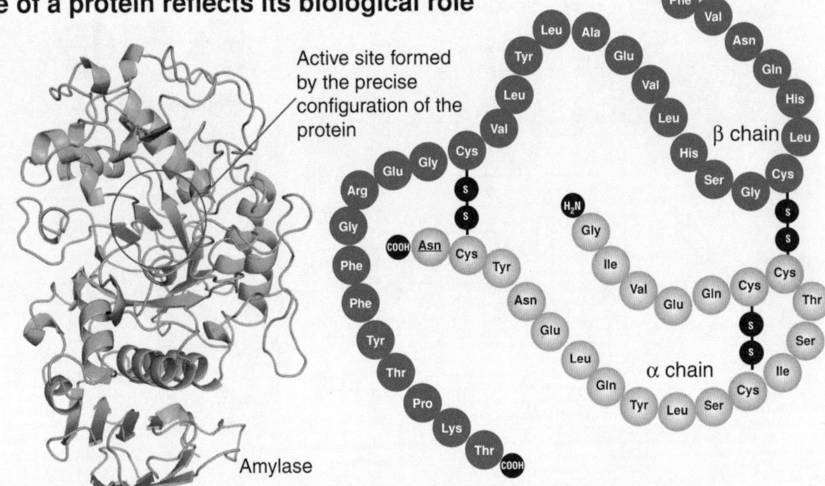

Channel proteins

Proteins that fold to form channels in the plasma membrane present non-polar R groups to the membrane and polar R groups to the inside of the channel. Hydrophilic molecules and ions are then able to pass through these channels into the interior of the cell. Ion channels are found in nearly all cells and many organelles.

Enzymes

Enzymes are globular proteins that catalyze reactions. They are specific to their substrates and their tertiary structure creates an **active site** where the substrate can bind and the reaction can occur. The specificity of the active site is determined by the interactions of amino acid R groups. Denaturation alters the active site and causes a loss of function.

Sub-unit proteins

Many proteins, e.g. insulin and hemoglobin, consist of two or more sub-units in a complex quaternary structure, often in association with a metal ion. Active insulin is formed by two polypeptide chains stabilized by disulfide bridges between neighboring cysteines. Insulin stimulates glucose uptake by cells.

Protein denaturation

When the chemical bonds holding a protein together become broken the protein can no longer hold its three dimensional shape. This process is called **denaturation**, and the protein usually loses its ability to carry out its biological function.

There are many causes of denaturation including exposure to heat or pH outside of the protein's optimum range. The main protein in egg white is albumin. It has a clear, thick fluid appearance in a raw egg (right). Heat (cooking) denatures the albumin protein and it becomes insoluble, clumping together to form a thick white substance (far right).

Raw (native) egg white

Cooked (denatured) egg white

1. Using the example of insulin, explain how interactions between R groups stabilize the protein's functional structure:

interactions between R groups helps a polypeptide to fold into its tertiary structure.

2. Why do channel proteins often fold with non-polar R groups to the channel's exterior and polar R groups to its interior?

Because hydrophylic molecules + ions are able to pass through channels into the interior of the cell. Ion channels are found in nearly all cells + many organelles.

3. Why does denaturation often result in the loss of protein functionality? Because a proteins structure and shape defines the way it functions. Denaturation breaks apart the protein's shape.

ISBN: 978-1-98-856656-6

8 Comparing Fibrous and Globular Proteins

Key Question: How do the structure and properties of globular and fibrous proteins reflect their contrasting roles?

Proteins can be classified according to structure or function. Globular and fibrous proteins form two of the main broad structural groups of proteins (the others being membrane proteins and disordered proteins such as casein). Globular proteins are spherical and somewhat soluble forming colloids in water (e.g. enzymes). Fibrous proteins have an elongated structure and are not water soluble. They provide stiffness and rigidity to the more fluid components of cells and tissues.

Globular proteins

The shape of globular proteins is a function of their tertiary structure. Some proteins (e.g. actin and tubulin) are globular and soluble as monomers, but polymerize to form long, stiff fibers.

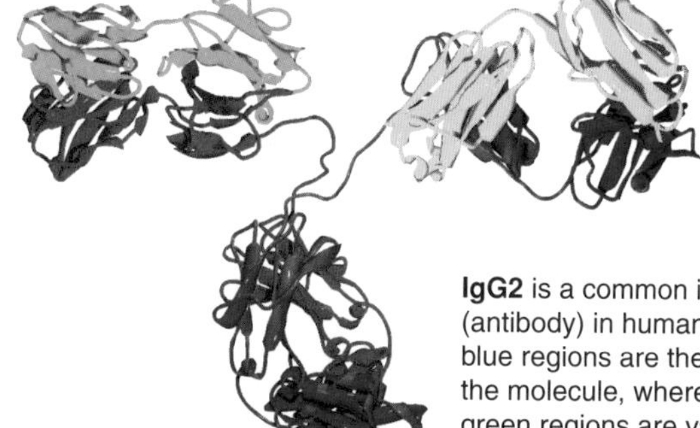

IgG2 is a common immunoglobulin (antibody) in human serum. The red and blue regions are the constant regions of the molecule, whereas the yellow and green regions are variable and determine antibody binding specificity.

Properties of globular proteins

- Easily water soluble
- Tertiary structure critical to function
- Polypeptide chains folded into a spherical shape

Functions of globular proteins

- Catalytic, *e.g. enzymes*
- Regulatory, *e.g. hormones (insulin)*
- Transport, *e.g. hemoglobin*
- Protective, *e.g. immunoglobulins (antibodies)*
- Structural (rarely), *e.g. actin and tubulin monomers (cytoskeletal elements)*

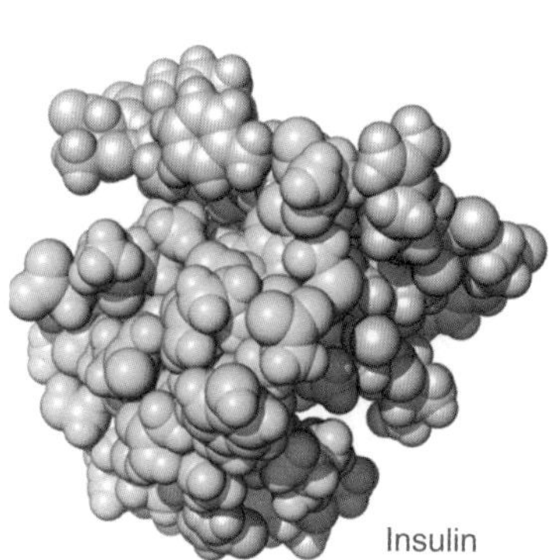

Insulin is a peptide hormone involved in the regulation of blood glucose. Insulin is composed of two peptide chains linked together by two disulfide bonds.

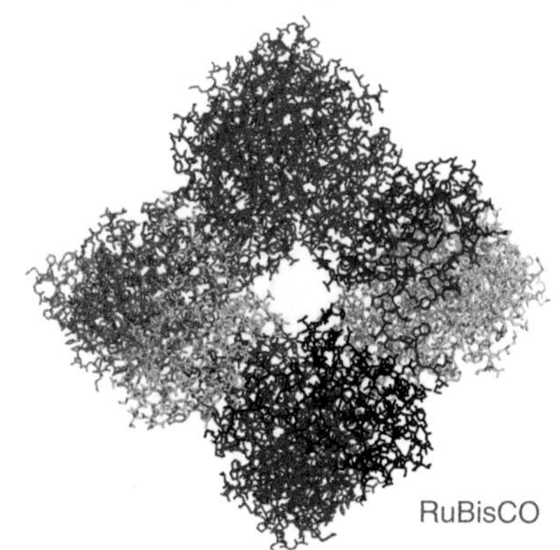

RuBisCo is a large multi-unit enzyme. It catalyzes the first step of carbon fixation in photosynthesis. It consists of 8 large and 8 small subunits and is the most abundant protein on Earth.

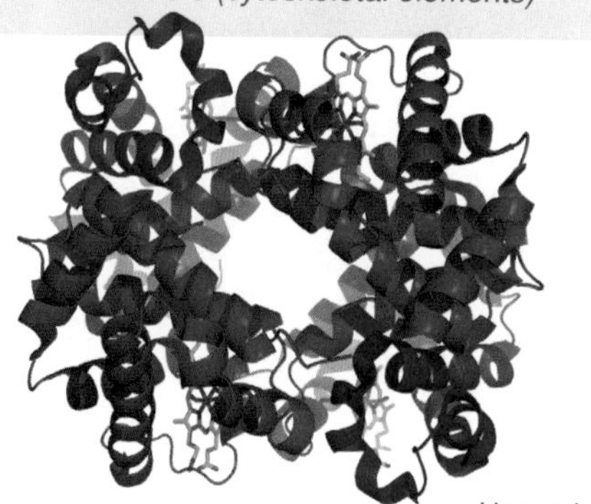

Zephyris CC 3.0

Hemoglobin is a multi-unit oxygen-transporting protein found in vertebrate red blood cells. One hemoglobin molecule consists of four polypeptide subunits (red and blue). Each subunit holds an oxygen-binding heme group (green).

1. How are globular proteins involved in the functioning of organisms? Use examples to help illustrate your answer: Globular proteins form one of the main broad structural groups of proteins. IgG2 is a common immunoglobulin (antibody) in human serum. The red/blue regions are the constant regions of the molecule, whereas the yellow/green regions are variable + determine antibody binding specificity.

2. (a) Explain how the shape and properties of a globular protein relate to its functional role: The shape of globular proteins is a function of their tertiary structure. Some proteins are globular + soluble as monomers, but polymerize to form long, stiff fibers

(b) How would its function be affected by a change in tertiary structure? changes in tertiary structure would change the entire function of the protein, since structure defines function

ISBN: 978-1-98-856656-6

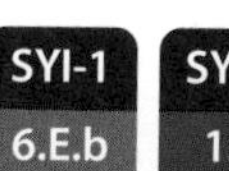

Fibrous proteins

Fibrous proteins are elongated and fibrous in nature or have a sheet like structure. These fibers and sheets are strong and water insoluble. Some, such as keratin, are even insoluble in organic solvents. They have important structural roles.

Properties of fibrous proteins	Functions of fibrous proteins
▶ Water insoluble ▶ Very tough physically; may be supple or stretchy ▶ Parallel polypeptide chains in long fibers or sheets	▶ Structural role in cells and organisms *e.g. collagen in connective tissues, skin, and blood vessel walls.* ▶ Contractile *e.g. myosin and actin polymers in muscles*

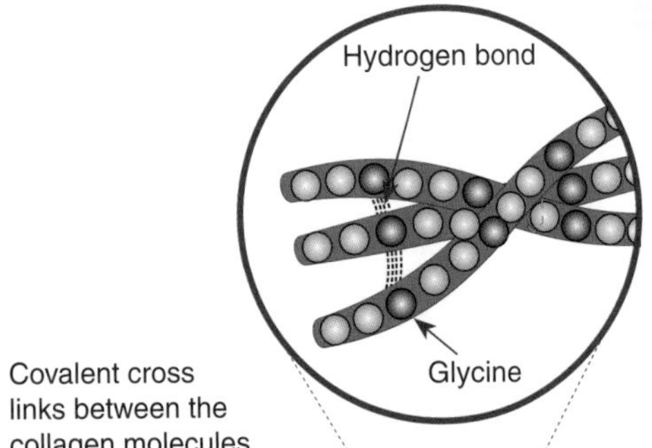

Collagen space filling model

Covalent cross links between the collagen molecules

Many collagen molecules form fibrils and the fibrils group together to form larger fibers.

A collagen molecule consists of three polypeptides wound together to form a helical 'rope'. Every third amino acid in each polypeptide is a glycine (Gly) where hydrogen bonding holds the three polypeptides together. Collagen molecules self assemble into **fibrils** held together by **covalent cross linkages**. Bundles of fibrils form fibers. Collagen is the main component of connective tissue, e.g. tendons and skin.

Mammalian hair and claws are α-keratin

The scales, beak, and feathers of birds are β keratin

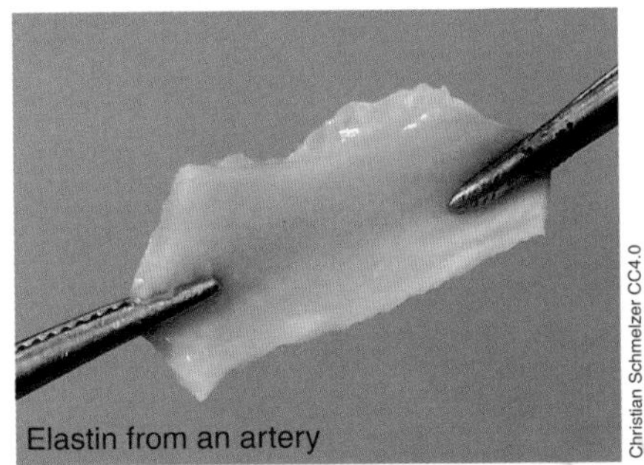

Elastin from an artery

Christian Schmelzer CC4.0

Keratins are found in hair, nails, claws, horn, hooves, wool, feathers, and the outer layers of skin. They fall into two classes: α keratins found in all vertebrates and the harder β keratins, found in reptiles and birds. The polypeptide chains are arranged in parallel sheets held together by hydrogen bonding. A distinguishing feature of keratins is the high sulfur content, with large numbers of disulfide bridges between cysteine residues. These form permanent, thermally stable covalent cross linkages and provide additional strength and rigidity.

Elastin is a connective tissue protein with elastic properties that enable tissues to resume their shape after stretching. Elastin has many hydrophobic amino acids, which form mobile hydrophobic regions flanked by covalent cross links between lysine residues.

3. How are fibrous proteins involved in the functioning of organisms? Use examples to help illustrate your answer:

Fibrous Proteins are found in things such as mammalian hair and claws, the scales, beak, and feathers of birds, and elastin from an artery. It is seen mainly in the surface of things.

4. Using an example, explain how the shape and properties of a fibrous protein relate to its functional role: A collagen molecule consists of three polypeptides wound together to form a helical 'rope'. Every 3rd amino acid in each polypeptide is a glycine where hydrogen bonding holds the 3 polypeptides together. Collagen is the main component of connective tissue.

5. What common feature contributes to the strength and stability of collagen, keratin, and elastin? Fibrous proteins are elongated + fibrouse in nature or have a sheet like structure. These fibers + sheets are strong and water insoluble.

ISBN: 978-1-98-856656-6

9 Carbohydrate Chemistry

Key Question: Monosaccharides are the building blocks for larger carbohydrates. They can exist as isomers.

Sugars (monosaccharides and disaccharides) play a central role in cells, providing energy and joining together to form carbohydrate macromolecules, such as starch and glycogen. Monosaccharide polymers form the major component of most plants (as cellulose). Monosaccharides are important as a primary energy source for cellular metabolism. Carbohydrates have the general formula $C_x(H_2O)_y$, where x and y are variable numbers (often but not always the same).

Monosaccharides

- Monosaccharides are single-sugar molecules and include glucose (grape sugar and blood sugar) and fructose (honey and fruit juices). They are used as a primary energy source for fuelling cell metabolism.
- They can be joined together to form disaccharides (two monomers) and polysaccharides (many monomers).
- Monosaccharides can be classified by the number of carbon atoms they contain. Some important monosaccharides are the hexoses (6 carbons) and the pentoses (5 carbons). The most common arrangements found in sugars are hexose (6 sided) or pentose (5 sided) rings (below).
- The commonly occurring monosaccharides contain between three and seven carbon atoms in their carbon chains and, of these, the 6C hexose sugars occur most frequently. All monosaccharides are reducing sugars (they can participate in reduction reactions).

Examples of monosaccharide structures

Triose

C
|
C
|
C

e.g. glyceraldehyde

Pentose

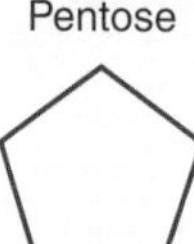

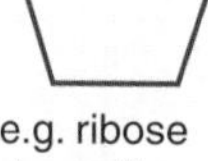

e.g. ribose deoxyribose

Hexose

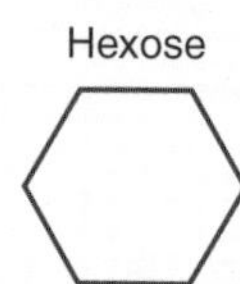

e.g. glucose, fructose, galactose

Ribose: a pentose monosaccharide

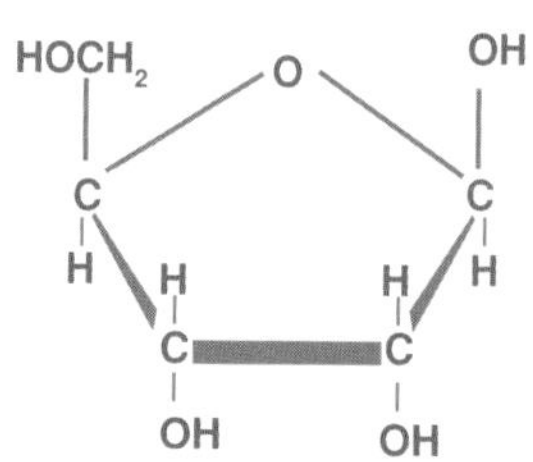

Ribose is a pentose (5 carbon) monosaccharide which can form a ring structure (left). Ribose is a component of the nucleic acid ribonucleic acid (RNA).

Glucose isomers

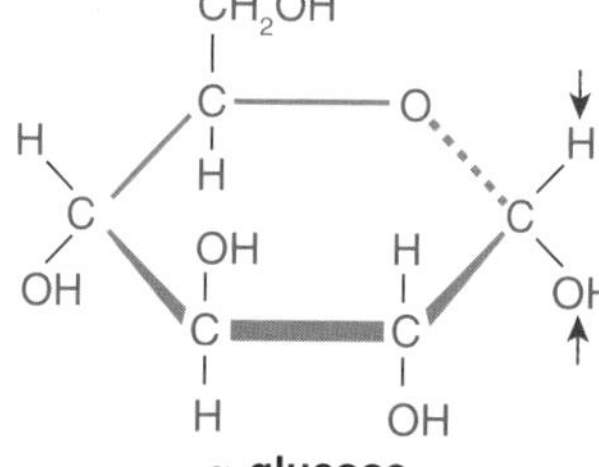

α-glucose

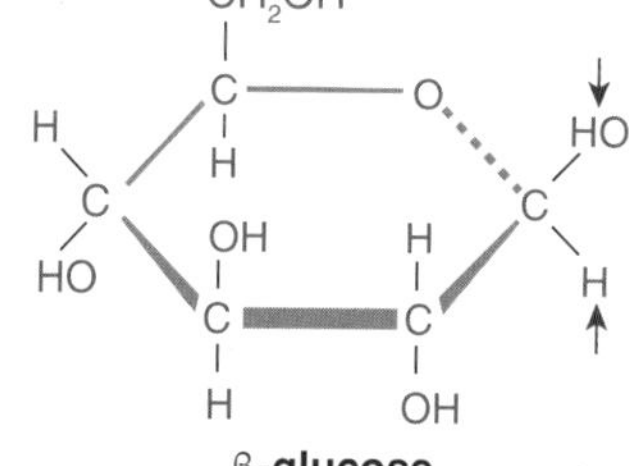

β-glucose

Isomers are compounds with the same chemical formula (same types and numbers of atoms) but different arrangements of atoms. The different arrangement of the atoms means that each isomer has different properties.

Molecules such as glucose can have many different isomers (e.g. α and β glucose, above) including straight and ring forms.

Glucose is a versatile molecule. It provides energy to power cellular reactions, can form energy storage molecules such as glycogen, or it can be used to build structural molecules.

Plants make their glucose via the process of photosynthesis. Animals and other heterotrophic organisms obtain their glucose by consuming plants or other organisms.

Rufino Uribe

Fructose, often called fruit sugar, is a simple monosaccharide. It is often derived from sugar cane (above). Both fructose and glucose can be directly absorbed into the bloodstream.

1. Describe the two major functions of monosaccharides:

(a) Form the major component of most plants (cellulose)

(b) Important as a primary energy source for metabolism.

2. Describe the structural differences between the ring forms of glucose and ribose: Ribose is a pentose monosaccharide, glucose is a hexose isomer.

3. Using glucose as an example, define the term isomer and state its importance: Isomers are compounds with the same chemical formula but different arrangements of atoms. The different arrangement of the atoms means that each isomer has different properties.

ISBN: 978-1-98-856656-6

10 Condensation and Hydrolysis of Sugars

Key Question: How do condensation and hydrolysis reactions form and break down disaccharides?

Monosaccharide monomers can be linked together by condensation reactions to produce disaccharides (and polysaccharides) by dehydration synthesis (building by loss of water). The reverse reaction, hydrolysis, breaks compound sugars down into their constituent monomers. Disaccharides are produced when two monosaccharides are joined together. Different disaccharides are formed by joining together different combinations of monosaccharides (below).

Condensation and hydrolysis reactions

Monosaccharides can combine to form compound sugars in what is called a condensation reaction. Compound sugars can be broken down by hydrolysis to simple monosaccharides.

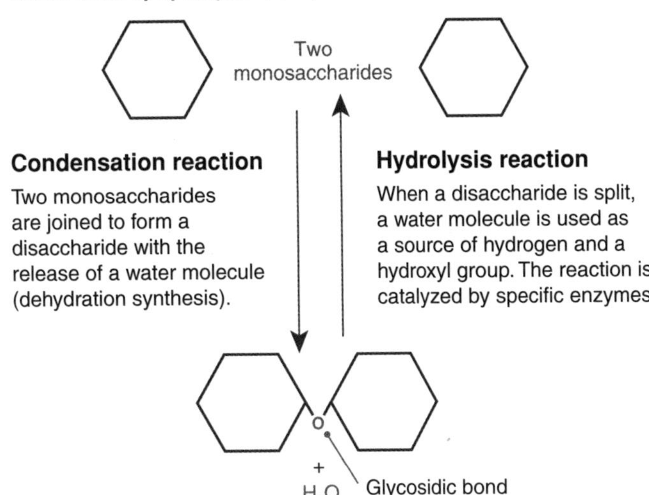

Two monosaccharides
Condensation reaction
Two monosaccharides are joined to form a disaccharide with the release of a water molecule (dehydration synthesis).
Hydrolysis reaction
When a disaccharide is split, a water molecule is used as a source of hydrogen and a hydroxyl group. The reaction is catalyzed by specific enzymes.
O
+
H_2O
Glycosidic bond

Disaccharide + water

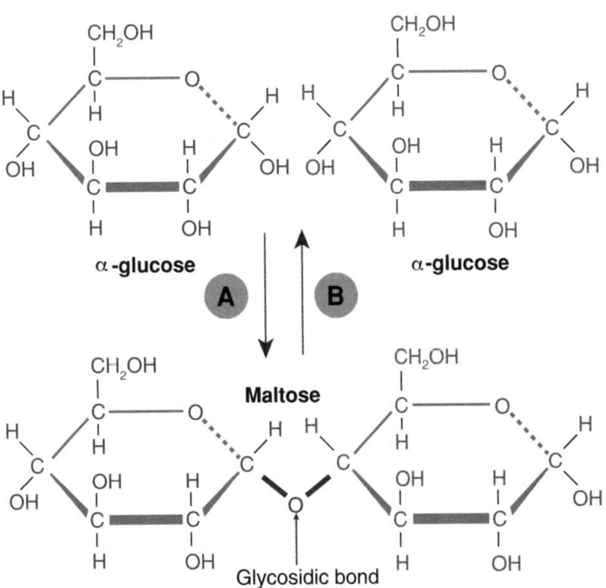

Disaccharide + water

Disaccharides

Disaccharides (below) are double-sugar molecules and are used as energy sources and as building blocks for larger molecules. They are important in human nutrition and are found in milk (lactose), table sugar (sucrose), and malt (maltose).

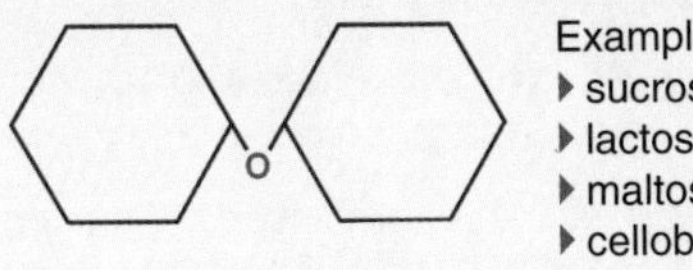

Examples
- sucrose
- lactose
- maltose
- cellobiose

The type of disaccharide formed depends on the monomers involved and whether they are in their α- or β- form. Only a few disaccharides (e.g. lactose) are classified as reducing sugars. Some common disaccharides are described below.

Lactose, a milk sugar, is made up of β-glucose + β-galactose. Milk contains 2-8% lactose by weight. It is the primary carbohydrate source for suckling mammalian young.

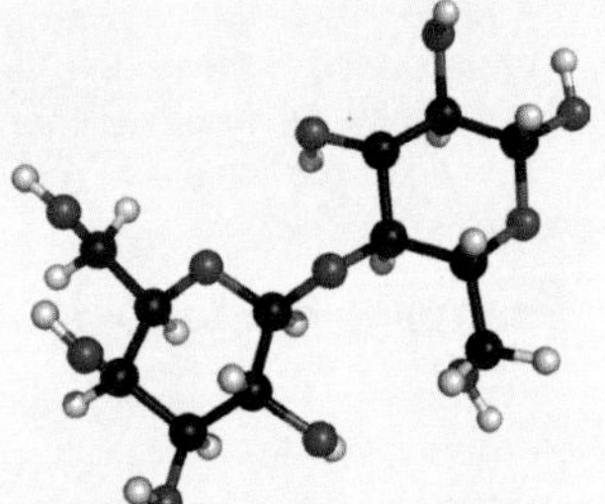

Maltose is composed of two α-glucose molecules. Germinating seeds contain maltose because the plant breaks down its starch stores to more easily mobilize glucose as an energy source for growth.

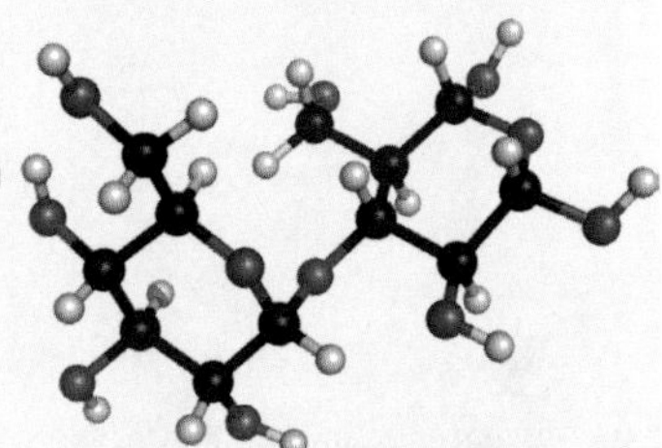

Sucrose (table sugar) is a simple sugar derived from plants such as sugar cane, sugar beet, or maple sap. It is composed of an α-glucose molecule and a β-fructose molecule.

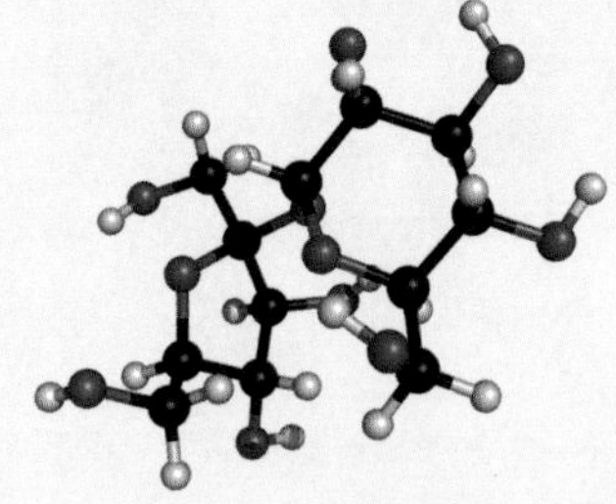

1. Explain briefly how disaccharide sugars are formed and broken down: Through a condensation reaction, 2 monosaccharides are joined to form a disaccharide w/ the release of a water molecule. Through hydrolysis, a disaccharide is split, + a water molecule is used as a source of hydrogen.

2. On the diagram above, name the reaction occurring at points **A** and **B** and name the product that is formed:
condensation - disaccharide + water
hydrolysis - two monosaccharides.

3. What determines the disaccharide made by condensation? monomers involved

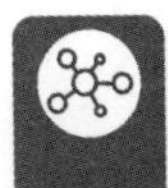
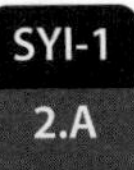

ISBN: 978-1-98-856656-6

11 Polysaccharides

Key Question: How are polysaccharides formed and what determines their functional properties?

Polysaccharides are macromolecules consisting of straight or branched chains of many monosaccharides. They can consist of one or more types of monosaccharides. The most common polysaccharides are cellulose, starch, and glycogen. These macromolecules contain only glucose, but their properties and their roles are very different. These differences are a function of the glucose isomer involved and the types of linkages joining the monomers. Different polysaccharides can thus be a source of readily available glucose or a structural material that resists digestion.

The structure of polysaccharides (also called complex carbohydrates) can be compared using molecular visualization software

Cellulose

Cellulose is a structural material found in the cell walls of plants. It is made up of unbranched chains of β-glucose molecules held together by β-1,4 glycosidic links. As many as 10,000 glucose molecules may be linked together to form a straight chain. Parallel chains become cross-linked with hydrogen bonds and form bundles of 60-70 molecules called **microfibrils**. Cellulose microfibrils are very strong and are a major structural component of plants, e.g. as the cell wall. Few organisms can break the β-linkages so cellulose is an ideal structural material.

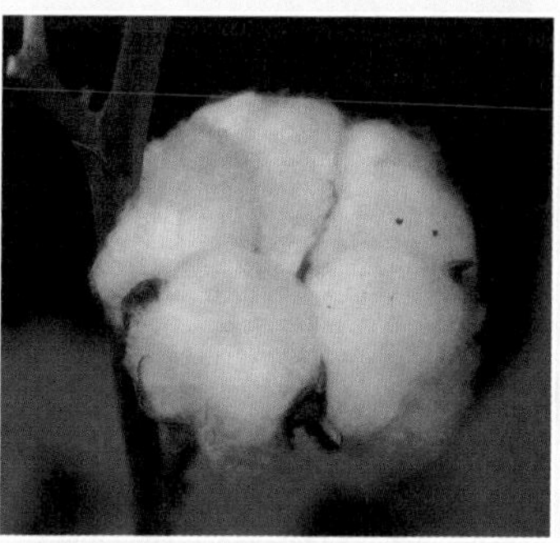
Cotton fibers contain more than 90% cellulose fiber.

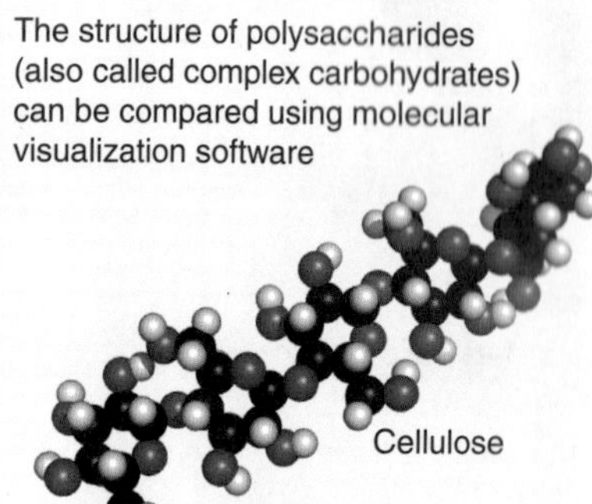

Starch

Starch is also a polymer of glucose, but it is made up of long chains of α-glucose molecules linked together. It contains a mixture of 25-30% **amylose** (unbranched chains linked by α-1,4 glycosidic bonds) and 70-75% **amylopectin** (branched chains with α-1, 6 glycosidic bonds every 24-30 glucose units). Starch is an energy storage molecule in plants and is found concentrated in insoluble starch granules within specialized plastids called amyloplasts in plant cells (see photo, right). Starch can be easily hydrolyzed by enzymes to soluble sugars when required.

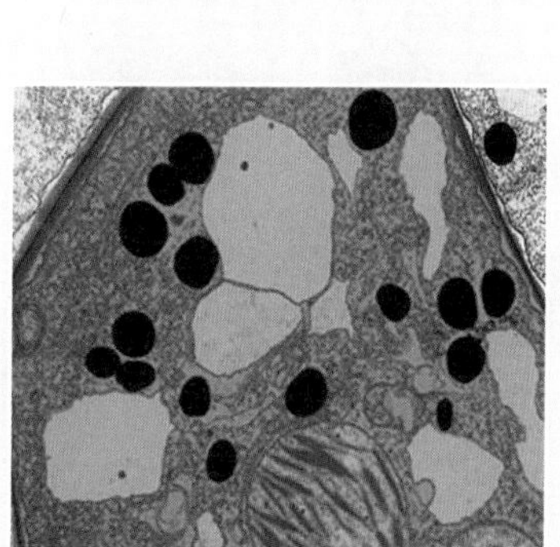
BF

Black starch granules in a plant cell (false color TEM).

Glycogen

Glycogen, like starch, is a branched polysaccharide. It is chemically similar to amylopectin, being composed of α-glucose molecules, but there are more α-1,6 glycosidic links mixed with α-1,4 links. This makes it more highly branched and more water-soluble than starch. Glycogen is a storage compound in animal tissues and is found mainly in liver and muscle cells (photo, right). It is readily hydrolyzed by enzymes to form glucose making it an ideal energy storage molecule for active animals.

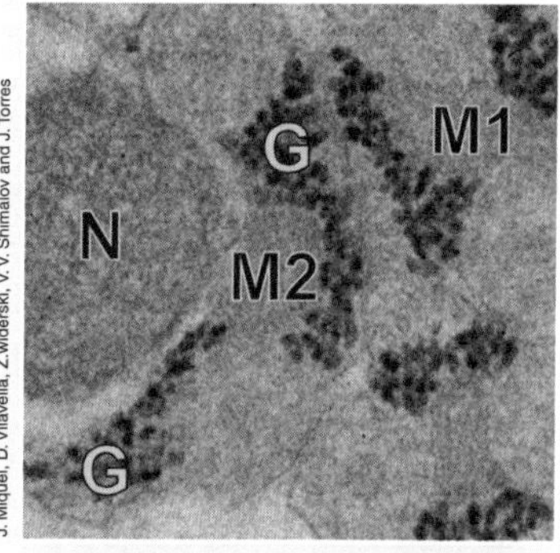

J. Miquel, D. Vilavella, Z. widerski, V. V. Shimalov and J. Torres

Glycogen (G) in the spermatozoa of a flatworm. M1, M2=mitochondria, N=nucleus.

Chitin

Chitin is a tough modified polysaccharide made up of chains of N-acetylglucosamine, a derivative of glucose. It is chemically similar to cellulose but each glucose has an amine group ($-NH_2-$) attached. The addition of the amine groups allows for stronger hydrogen bonding to occur than in cellulose. This makes chitin very strong. After cellulose, chitin is the second most abundant carbohydrate in nature. It is found in the cell walls of fungi and is the main component of the exoskeleton of insects (right) and other arthropods.

Chitinous insect exoskeleton.

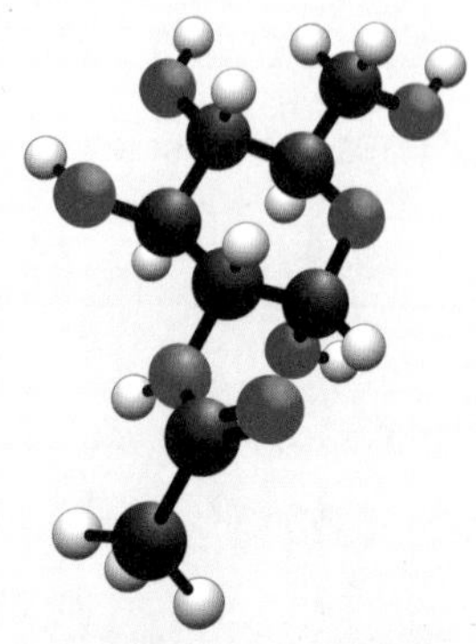
One N-acetylglucosamine (NAG) molecule, the monomeric unit of chitin. The nitrogen atom is green.

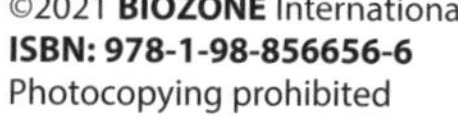

ISBN: 978-1-98-856656-6

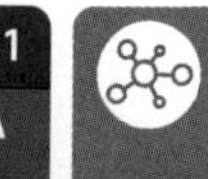

1. (a) What is a polysaccharide? a macromolecule consisting of straight or branched chains of many monosaccharides.

(b) What do all polysaccharides have in common? they consist monosaccharides.

2. Suggest why polysaccharides are such a good source of energy: These differences are a function of the glucose isomer involved + the types of linkages joining the monomers, which is why they are a good source of energy.

3. Contrast the properties of the polysaccharides starch, cellulose, and glycogen and relate these to their roles in the cell. Use the symbolic forms in the diagram right to help construct your explanation.

cellulose is made up of unbranched chains of β-glucose molecules held together by β-1,4 glycosidic links. They are formed as a straight chain. Starch contains long chains of a-glucose molecules linked together. It contains a mix of 25-30% amylose + 70-75% amylopectin. Glycogen is a branched polysaccharide. It is chemically similar to amylopectin, being composed of a-glucose molecules, but there are more a-1,6 glycosidic links mixed w/ a-1,4 links. Chitin is a tough modified polysaccharide made up of chains of N-acetylglucosamine, a derivative of glucose. Each glucose has an amine group ($-NH_2-$) attached.

Symbolic form of cellulose

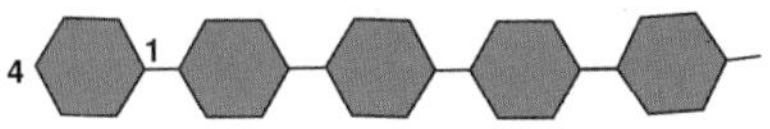

Symbolic form of amylopectin

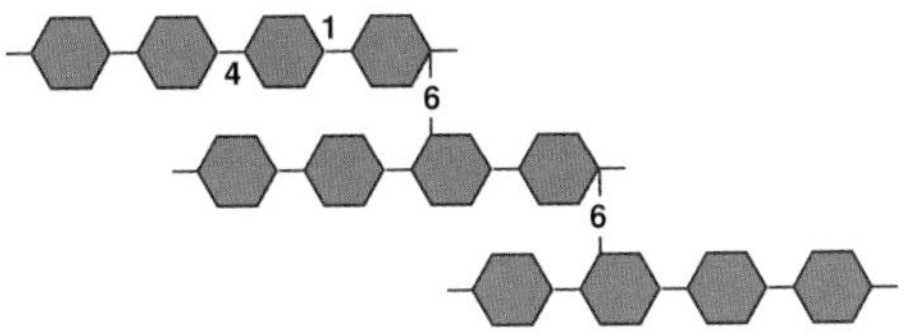

Symbolic form of glycogen

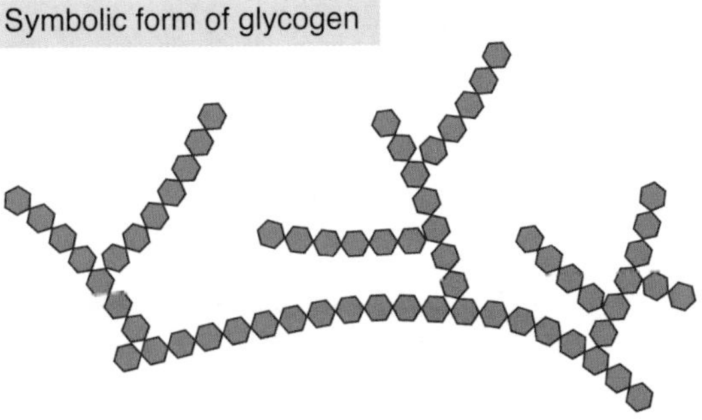

4. Amylopectin is very similar in structure to glycogen but is less soluble. Explain why: Because amylopectin is branched chains w/ a-1,6 glycosidic bonds every 24-30 glucose units. Glycogen is more highly branched.

5. (a) The symbolic structure of chitin is given below right. Which polysaccharide is it most similar to structurally?

cellulose

(b) Describe the major structural difference between chitin and the polysaccharide you named in (a):

chitin is fibrous and cellulose is an insoluble substance

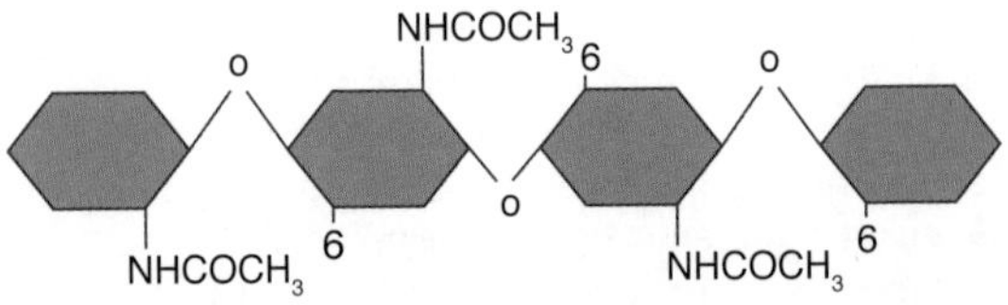

(c) Explain what functional advantage this structural difference provides to chitin: this is the major constituent in the exoskeleton of arthropods + the cell walls of fungi

Symbolic form of chitin

ISBN: 978-1-98-856656-6

12 Cellulose and Starch

Key Question: What structural and functional characteristics distinguish the plant polysaccharides, starch and cellulose?

Glucose monomers can be linked in condensation reactions to form large structural and energy storage polysaccharides. The glucose isomer involved and the type of glycosidic linkage determines the properties of the molecule. Starch is a storage carbohydrate made up of two α-glucose polymers. Cellulose is a structural β-glucose polymer.

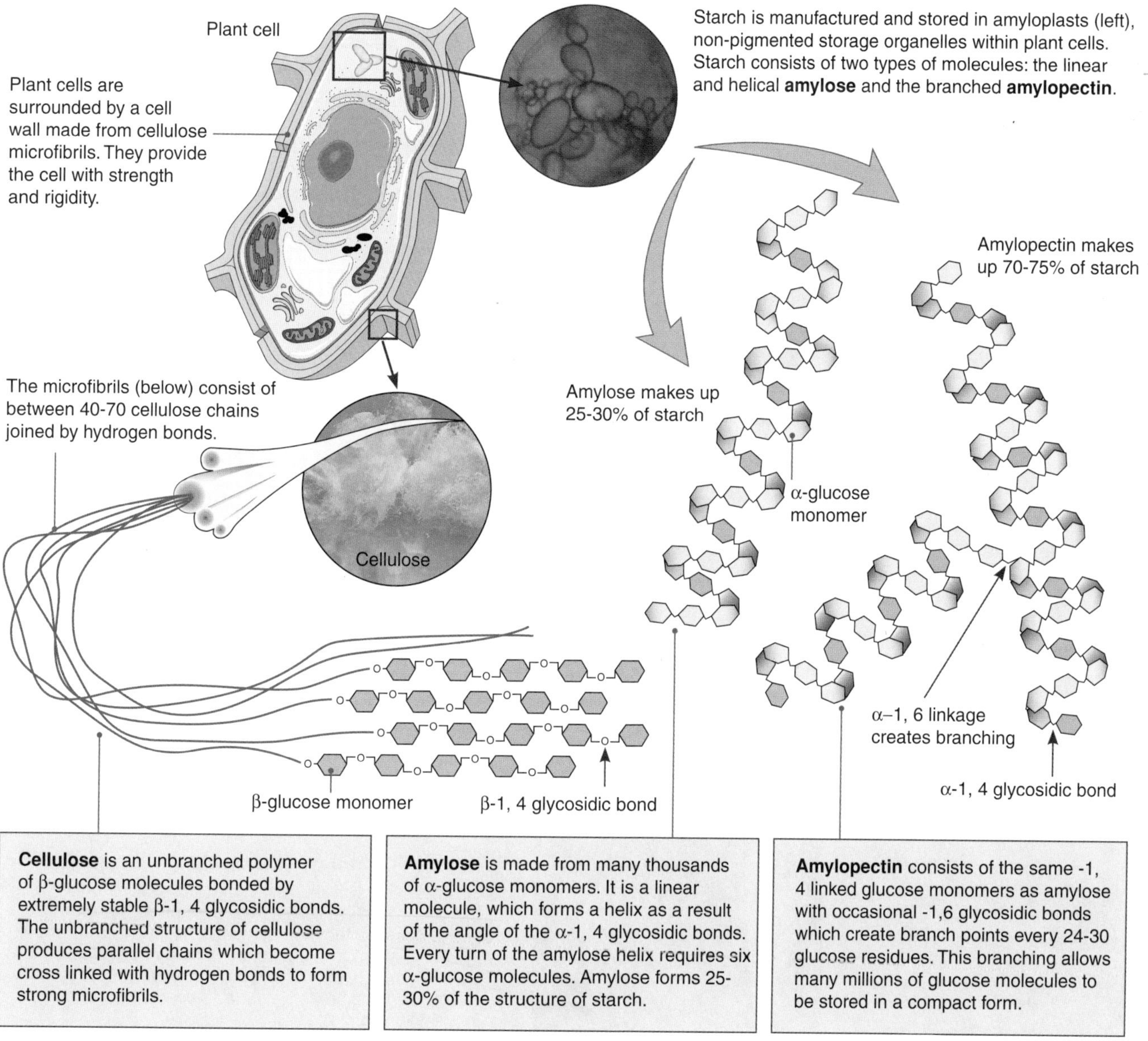

Plant cell

Plant cells are surrounded by a cell wall made from cellulose microfibrils. They provide the cell with strength and rigidity.

Starch is manufactured and stored in amyloplasts (left), non-pigmented storage organelles within plant cells. Starch consists of two types of molecules: the linear and helical **amylose** and the branched **amylopectin**.

The microfibrils (below) consist of between 40-70 cellulose chains joined by hydrogen bonds.

Cellulose

Amylose makes up 25-30% of starch

Amylopectin makes up 70-75% of starch

α-glucose monomer

α–1, 6 linkage creates branching

α-1, 4 glycosidic bond

β-glucose monomer

β-1, 4 glycosidic bond

Cellulose is an unbranched polymer of β-glucose molecules bonded by extremely stable β-1, 4 glycosidic bonds. The unbranched structure of cellulose produces parallel chains which become cross linked with hydrogen bonds to form strong microfibrils.

Amylose is made from many thousands of α-glucose monomers. It is a linear molecule, which forms a helix as a result of the angle of the α-1, 4 glycosidic bonds. Every turn of the amylose helix requires six α-glucose molecules. Amylose forms 25-30% of the structure of starch.

Amylopectin consists of the same -1, 4 linked glucose monomers as amylose with occasional -1,6 glycosidic bonds which create branch points every 24-30 glucose residues. This branching allows many millions of glucose molecules to be stored in a compact form.

1. (a) Where is starch stored in plants? amyloplasts

   (b) Where is cellulose found in plants? cell wall of plant cells.

2. Compare and contrast the structure of amylose and amylopectin: amylose is made from many thousands of a-glucose monomers, is linear, which forms a helix as a result of the angle of a-1,4 glycosidic bonds. Amylopectin consists of the sam -1,4 linked glucose monomers as amylose w/ occassional -1,6 glycosidic bonds

3. Account for the differences in structure between cellulose and starch: Cellulose is an unbranched polymer of B glucose molecules bonded by extremely stable B-1,4 glycosidic bonds. Starch is manufactered + stored in amyloplasts, it consists of 2 types of molecules: the linear + helical amylose + the branched amylopectin.

ISBN: 978-1-98-856656-6

13 Lipids

Key Question: What features characterize lipid molecules, how are they formed, and what are their biological roles?

Lipids are organic compounds that are mostly nonpolar (have no overall charge) and hydrophobic, so they do not dissolve in water. Simple lipids (fats and waxes) are distinct from complex lipids, such as phospholipids and fat-soluble cell components such as steroids. Fatty acids are a major component of neutral fats and phospholipids. Most fatty acids consist of an even number of carbon atoms, with hydrogen bound along the length of the chain.

Triglycerides (triacylglycerols)

H_2C-O
$HC-O$
H_2C-O

9 12 15

Glycerol Ester bond Fatty acids

Triglyceride: an example of a neutral fat

Neutral fats and oils are the most abundant lipids in living things. They make up the fats and oils found in plants and animals. Neutral fats and oils consist of a glycerol attached to one (mono-), two (di-) or three (tri-) fatty acids by **ester bonds**.

Esterification: A condensation reaction of an alcohol (e.g. glycerol) with an acid (e.g. fatty acid) to produce an ester and water. In the diagram right, the ester bonds are indicated by thick red lines.

Lipolysis: The breakdown of lipids. It involves hydrolysis of triglycerides into glycerol molecules and free fatty acids.

Triglycerides are formed by condensation

Triglycerides form when glycerol bonds with three fatty acids. Glycerol is an alcohol containing three carbons. Each of these carbons is bonded to a hydroxyl (-OH) group. When glycerol bonds with the fatty acid, an **ester bond** is formed and water is released. Three separate condensation (or dehydration synthesis) reactions are involved in producing a triglyceride.

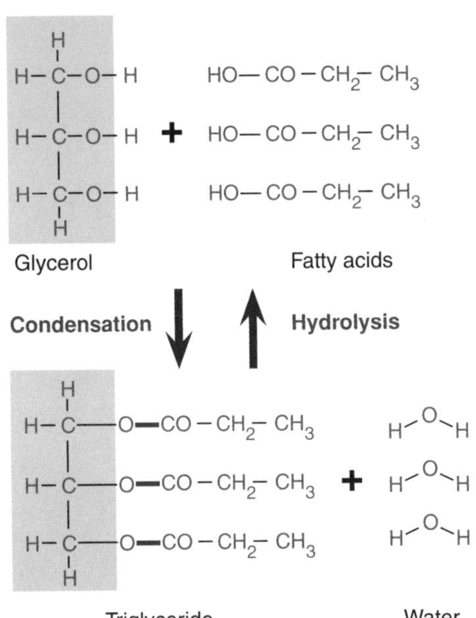

The biological roles of lipids

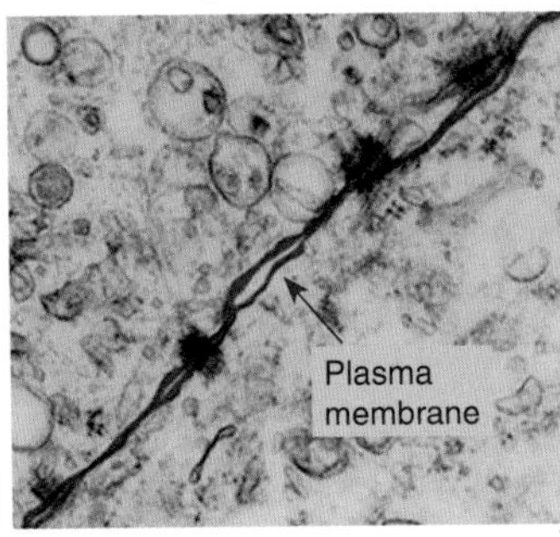

Phospholipids form the basic structure of cellular membranes in prokaryotes and eukaryotes.

Waxes and oils secreted on to surfaces provide waterproofing in plants and animals.

Oxidation of fat provides large amounts of energy and metabolic water. In some desert dwelling animals (e.g. kangaroo rat) this provides all the water they need.

As well as storing energy, fat stores provide insulation, reducing heat losses to the environment. Fat also absorbs shocks cushioning and protecting internal organs.

Why are lipids a good source of energy?

- Lipids have a high proportion of hydrogen present in the fatty acid chains. Being so reduced and anhydrous (without water), they are an economical way to store fuel reserves, and provide more than twice as much energy as the same quantity of carbohydrate. Fatty acids (mainly as triglycerides) are the most common form of stored fuel in animals and to a lesser extent in plants.
- Triglycerides are metabolized through a stepwise process called beta oxidation. Two-carbon units are removed in a stepwise fashion to produce $FADH_2$, NADH, and acetyl CoA. These enter usual respiratory pathways and are oxidized to carbon dioxide and water as with other fuels. Triglycerides have many 2-carbon units so they can provide large amounts of energy and water (below).

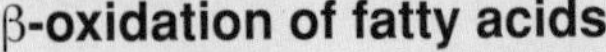

β-oxidation of fatty acids

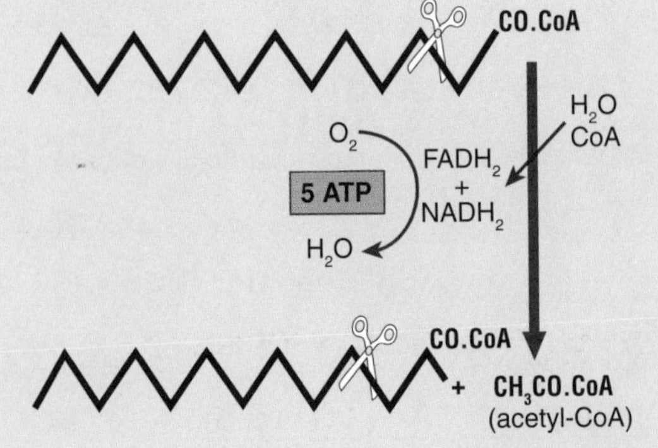

ISBN: 978-1-98-856656-6

Saturated and unsaturated fatty acids

Fatty acids are carboxylic acids (meaning they have a terminal -COOH) with long hydrocarbon chains. They are classed as either saturated or unsaturated. **Saturated fatty acids** contain the maximum number of hydrogen atoms. **Unsaturated fatty acids** contain some double-bonds between carbon atoms and are not fully saturated with hydrogens. A chain with only one double bond is called monounsaturated, whereas a chain with two or more double bonds is called polyunsaturated.

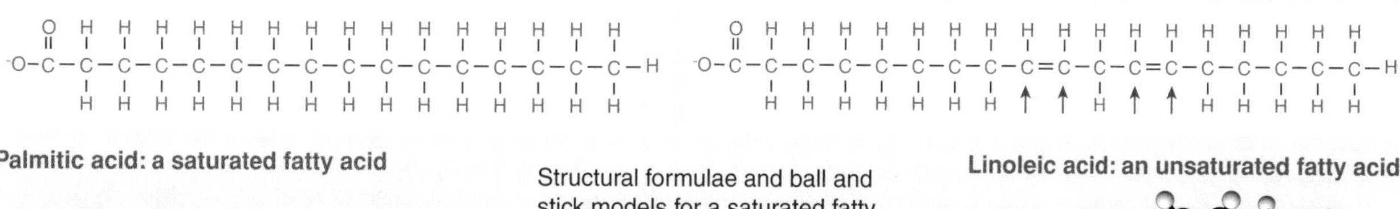

Palmitic acid: a saturated fatty acid

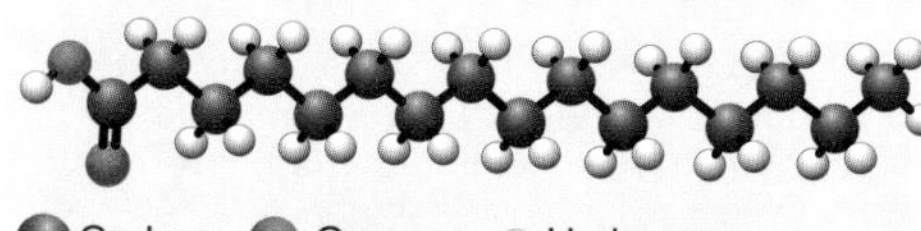

Carbon Oxygen Hydrogen

Butter

Structural formulae and ball and stick models for a saturated fatty acid, palmitic acid (left) and an unsaturated fatty acid, linoleic acid (right). The arrows indicate double bonded carbon atoms that are not fully saturated with hydrogens.

Lipids containing a high proportion of saturated fatty acids tend to be solids at room temperature (e.g. butter). Lipids with a high proportion of unsaturated fatty acids are oils and tend to be liquid at room temperature (e.g. olive oil). This is because the unsaturation causes kinks in the straight chains so that the fatty acid chains do not pack closely together.

Linoleic acid: an unsaturated fatty acid

Olive oil

1. Identify the main components (a-c) of the symbolic triglyceride right:

   (a) glycerol (b) ester bond (c) fatty acids

   a b c

2. Why do lipids have such a high energy content? they have a high proportion of hydrogen present in the fatty acid chains. They are an economical way to store fuel reserves w/o water.

3. (a) Distinguish between saturated and unsaturated fatty acids: saturated contain the max # of hydrogen atoms. Unsaturated contain some double bonds between carbon atoms + are not fully saturated w/ hydrogens.

   (b) Relate the properties of a neutral fat to the type of fatty acid present: Neutral fats and oils are the most abundant lipids in living things. They made of a glycerol attached to one, two, or three fatty acids by ester bonds.

4. (a) Describe what happens during the esterification (condensation) process to produce a triglyceride: when glycerol bonds w/ the fatty acid, an ester bond is formed + water is released.

   (b) Describe what happens when a triglyceride is hydrolyzed: it creates glycerol and fatty acids.

5. Discuss the biological role of lipids: Phospholipids form the basic structure of cellular membranes in prokaryotes + eukaryotes. Waxes + oils secreted on to surfaces provide waterproofing in plants + animals. Oxidation of fat provides large amounts of energy + metabolic water. Fat stores provide insulation, reducing heat losses in the environment.

ISBN: 978-1-98-856656-6

14 Phospholipids

Key Question: How are phospholipids formed, what are their characteristics, and what are their biological roles?

A phospholipid is structurally similar to a triglyceride except that a phosphate group and a nitrogen-containing compound replace one of the fatty acids attached to the glycerol. Phospholipids naturally form bilayers in aqueous solutions and are the main component of cellular membranes. The fatty acid tails can be saturated (straight chains) or unsaturated (kinked chains). The proportion of saturated versus unsaturated fatty acids affects the fluidity of the phospholipid bilayer.

Phospholipids

Phospholipids consist of a glycerol attached to two fatty acid chains and a phosphate (PO_4^{3-}) group. The phosphate end of the molecule is attracted to water (hydrophilic) while the fatty acid end is repelled (hydrophobic). The hydrophobic ends turn inwards to form a **phospholipid bilayer**.

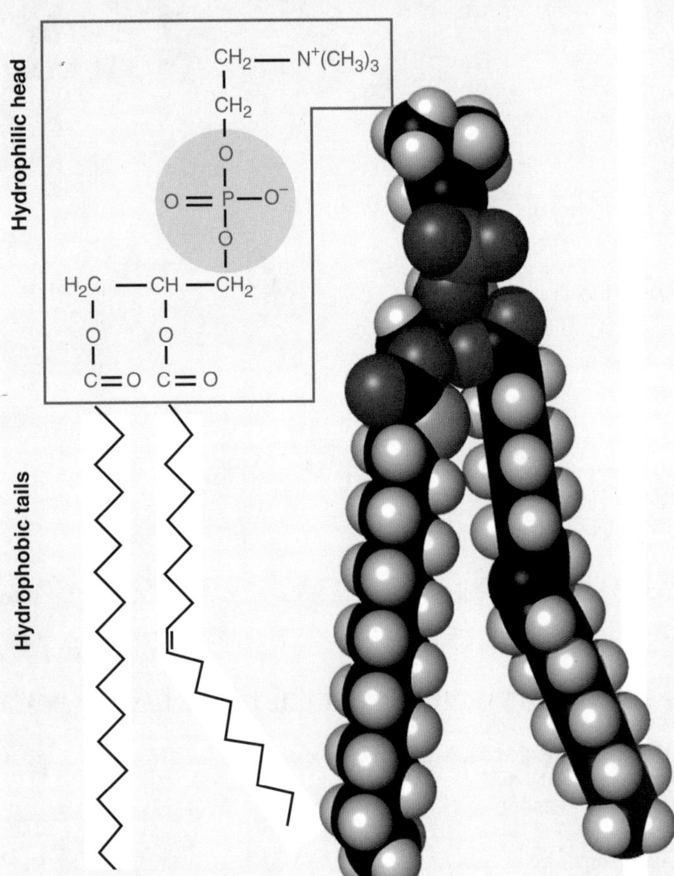

Phospholipids and membranes

The amphipathic (having hydrophobic and hydrophilic ends) nature of phospholipids means that when in water they spontaneously form bilayers. This bilayer structure forms the outer boundary of cells or organelles. Modifications to the different hydrophobic ends of the phospholipids cause the bilayer to change its behavior. The greater the number of double bonds in the hydrophobic tails, the greater the fluidity of the membrane.

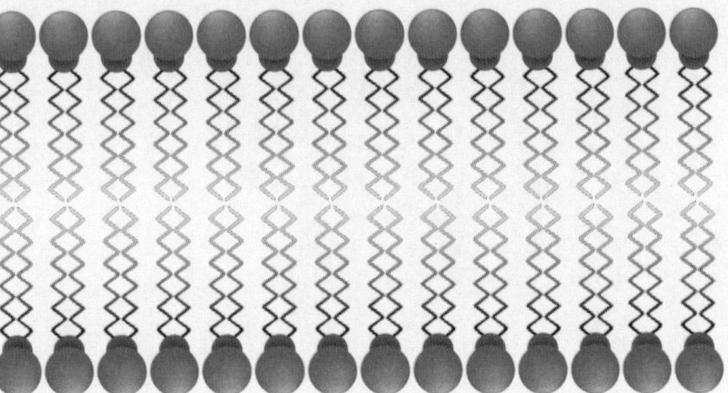

Membrane containing only phospholipids with saturated fatty acid tails.

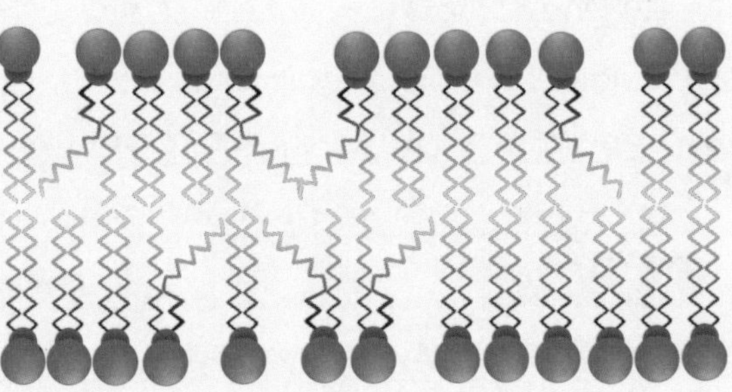

Membrane containing phospholipids with unsaturated fatty acid tails. The fact that the phospholipids do not stack neatly together produces a more fluid membrane.

1. (a) Relate the structure of phospholipids to their chemical properties and their functional role in cellular membranes: The amphipathic nature of phospholipids means that when in water they spontaneously form bilayers. This bilayer structure forms the outer boundary of cells or organelles.

(b) Suggest how the cell membrane structure of an Arctic fish might differ from that of tropical fish species: One cell membrane may have more fluidity than the other.

2. Explain why phospholipid bilayers containing many phospholipids with unsaturated tails are particularly fluid: The fact that the phospholipids do not stack neatly together produces a more fluid membrane

ISBN: 978-1-98-856656-6

15 Personal Progress Check

Answer the multiple choice questions that follow by circling the correct answer. Don't forget to read the question carefully!

1. The property of water that accounts for evaporative cooling is:
   (a) Its cohesion
   (b) Its high specific heat capacity
   (c) Its high latent heat of vaporization
   (d) Its solvent properties

2. Which type of bond involves sharing of electron pairs between atoms:
   (a) Hydrophobic bond
   (b) Ester bond
   (c) Ionic bond
   (d) Covalent bond

3. Water shows a number of emergent properties that are important to life on Earth. These properties are mostly the result of:
   (a) Water's ability to act as an acid or a base
   (b) Water's abundance on Earth
   (c) The hydrogen bonds linking water molecules together
   (d) Water's buffering effect on climate

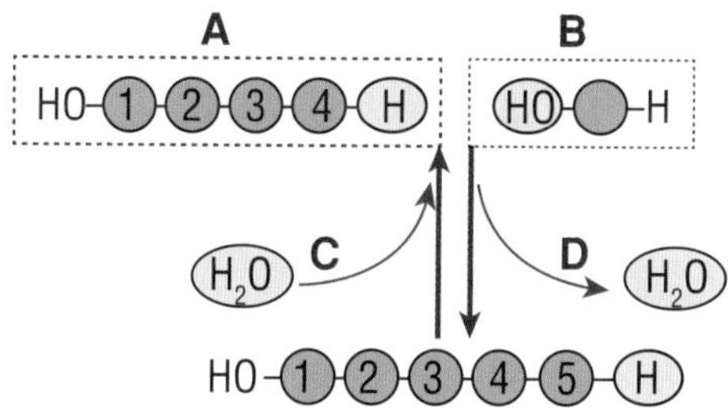

Questions 4-5 refer to the diagram above.

4. Which part of the diagram shows a condensation reaction?
   (a) A
   (b) B
   (c) C
   (d) D

5. Which part of the diagram shows a monomer?
   (a) A
   (b) B
   (c) C
   (d) D

6. Water is less dense as a solid because:
   (a) The hydrogen bonds expand between the water molecules to form a crystal.
   (b) The covalent bonds expand between the water molecules to form a crystal.
   (c) The covalent bonds contract between the water molecules to form a crystal.
   (d) The hydrogen bonds contract between the water molecules to form a crystal.

7. Which of the following is not a macromolecule:
   (a) Triglyceride
   (b) Nucleotide
   (c) Nucleic acid
   (d) Polysaccharide

8. Select all of the following statements about the fatty acids in lipids that are true:
   1. Saturated fatty acids are kinked because of their double bonds.
   2. Unsaturated fatty acids are kinked because of their double bonds.
   3. Saturated fats tend to be solids at room temperature and unsaturated fatty acids tend to be liquids at room temperature.
   4. Saturated fatty acids contain the maximum number of hydrogen atoms possible for the molecule.
   5. Saturated fatty acids pack together very loosely.

   (a) Statement 1
   (b) Statements 2, 3, and 4.
   (c) Statements 2 and 4.
   (d) Statement 5.

9. Which of the following elements is not found in carbohydrates:
   (a) Carbon
   (b) Nitrogen
   (c) Oxygen
   (d) Hydrogen

10. Which of the following elements is not found in nucleic acids:
    (a) Oxygen
    (b) Nitrogen
    (c) Sulfur
    (d) Phosphorus

11. Which of the following form the structure of biological membranes:
    (a) Neutral fats
    (b) Phospholipids
    (c) Fibrous proteins
    (d) Carbohydrates

12. Which statement best describes hydrolysis:
    (a) The reaction in which a polymer is broken down by adding water
    (b) The process of breaking down a water molecule
    (c) The reaction in which a polymer is formed while releasing water
    (d) The reaction in which a polymer is broken down while releasing water

ISBN: 978-1-98-856656-6

13. What determines the function of a protein?
 (a) The size of the protein
 (b) The protein's specific 3 dimensional structure
 (c) The tissue that produces the protein
 (d) The number of peptide bonds.

14. The monomeric unit of cellulose is:
 (a) β-glucose.
 (b) α-glucose.
 (c) amylose
 (d) N-acetylglucosamine

15. Neutral fats yield a lot of energy because:
 (a) They are very large macromolecules
 (b) They are very reduced and anhydrous
 (c) They are not easily oxidized
 (d) Neutral fats do not yield much energy.

16. Neutral fats are metabolized to provide energy via a stepwise process called:
 (a) Digestion
 (b) Hydrolysis
 (c) Beta oxidation
 (d) Lipolysis

17. The bond between glycerol and fatty acids in lipids is:
 (a) A peptide bond
 (b) A glycosidic bond
 (c) An ester bond
 (d) A disulfide bond

18. The bond between amino acids in a protein is:
 (a) A peptide bond
 (b) A glycosidic bond
 (c) An ester bond
 (d) A disulfide bond

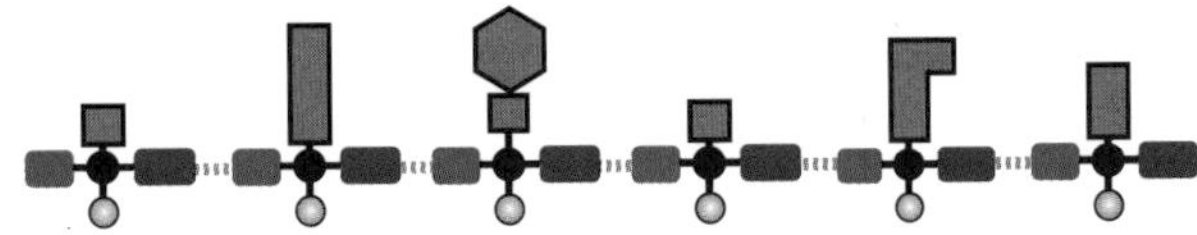

Questions 19-21 refer to the schematic above.

19. The schematic shown above represents:
 (a) A lipid
 (b) A phospholipid
 (c) A nucleic acid
 (d) A polypeptide

20. The R group in this molecule is represented by the color:
 (a) Black
 (b) Red
 (c) Orange
 (d) Blue

21. The R group in amino acids determine:
 (a) The properties of the amino acid
 (b) The interactions that will occur in a polypeptide's folded structure
 (c) Both (a) and (b)
 (d) Neither of (a) and (b)

22. Condensation reactions are involved in the formation of:
 (a) The formation of dipeptides
 (b) The formation of nucleic acids
 (c) The formation of disaccharides
 (d) All of the above

23. Globular proteins have an important role in:
 (a) Catalyzing biochemical reactions
 (b) Forming the structure of hair and skin
 (c) Connective tissue
 (d) None of the above

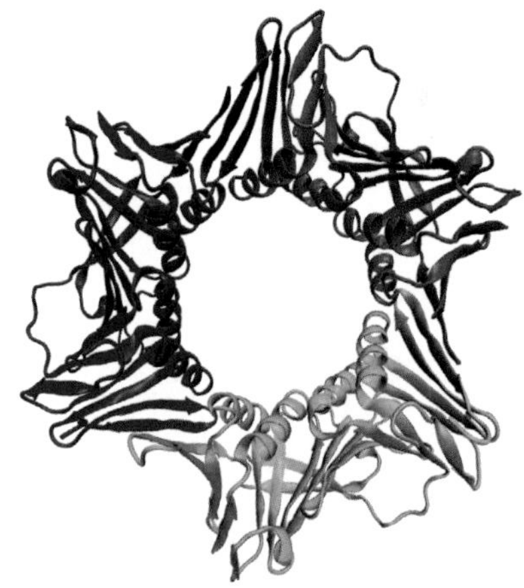

24. The image above depicts the quaternary structure of a protein in humans involved in DNA replication. We know this protein has quaternary structure because:
 (a) It has a lot of alpha helices
 (b) It has a lot of beta pleated sheets
 (c) It has three associated monomers
 (d) It is globular protein

25. Which of the following are typical features of fibrous proteins?
 (a) Soluble in water with a tertiary structure that is critical to function.
 (b) Insoluble in water and physically tough
 (c) Often have catalytic function
 (d) None of the features above apply to fibrous proteins.

26. Which of the features below is important in the structural and functional diversity of polysaccharides?
 (a) The R group
 (b) Tertiary structure
 (c) Isomerism
 (d) Directionality

ISBN: 978-1-98-856656-6

***Free Response Question:** Conceptual analysis*

Milk processing

- Heat treatment is an essential part of milk processing by inhibiting microbial growth and extending its shelf-life. However, heating raw milk can also cause irreversible changes in the structure of the milk proteins.
- Cow's milk contains 30-35 g/L protein of which 80-85% is casein. Casein is a simple protein with relatively little tertiary structure. It is relatively hydrophobic so is found in milk as a suspension of spherical particles called casein micelles. Casein is unchanged by heat treatment but low pH causes its coagulation, as is used in cheese making.
- The remainder of milk's protein is made up of whey proteins. The most abundant whey protein by far is β-lactoglobulin (β-lg).

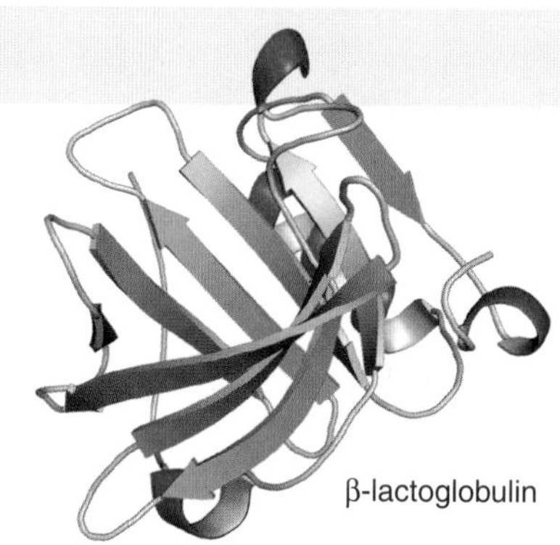

β-lg is a relatively small protein and makes up most of the volume of whey proteins in milk. It is acid stable but when exposed to heat it forms large aggregates by associating with the casein micelles. These aggregations compromise milk quality and digestibility in people with reduced digestive ability.

Researchers wanted to study the effect of different heat treatments on the extent of whey protein denaturation and combination with casein micelles. Raw milk was subjected to heat treatments at different temperatures (75-95°C) and for varying lengths of time (0-30 minutes). The proportion of whey proteins denatured or combining with casein micelles was determined.

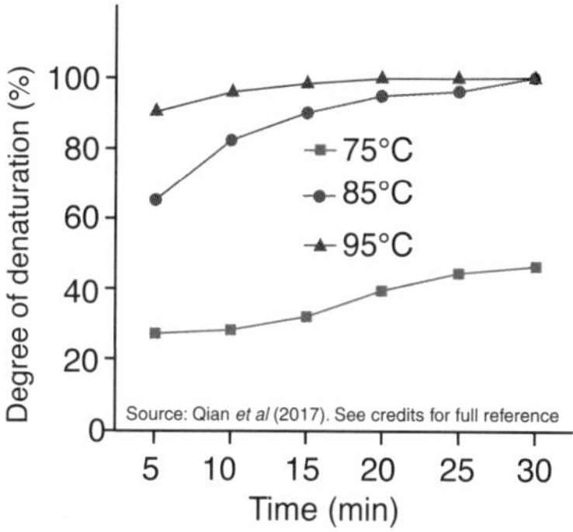

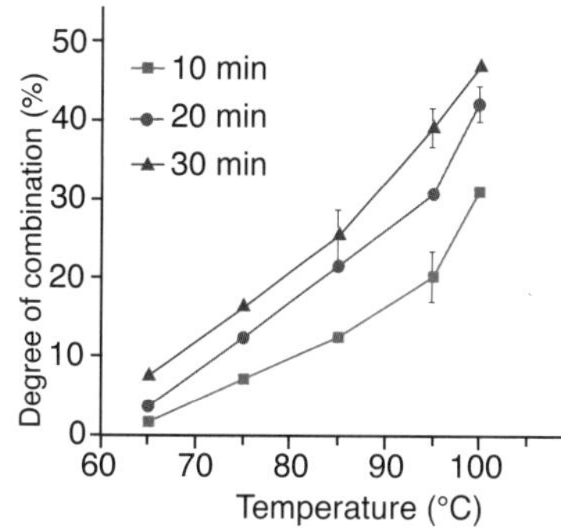

1. **Describe** what happens as a result of protein denaturation and identify likely causes: ______________________

2. **Explain** why protein denaturation causes a change in the properties or biological function of a protein:

3. Based on the data above, **predict** the effect of heating milk to 100°C for 45 minutes: ______________________

4. **Justify** your prediction based on the data presented: ______________________

ISBN: 978-1-98-856656-6

***Free Response Question:** Analyze a model or visual representation*

Nucleic acids

Scientists, artists, and students use different types of models to represent the structure of DNA. These images show different representations of DNA: **A**- **F**.

A: Space-filling model **B**: Schematic

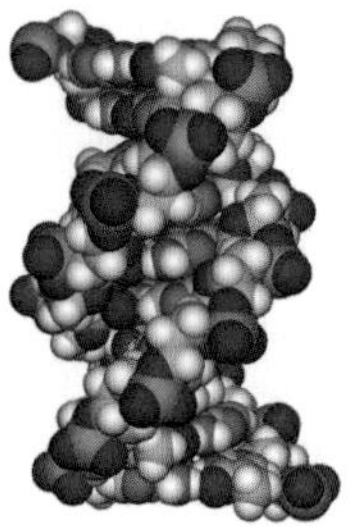

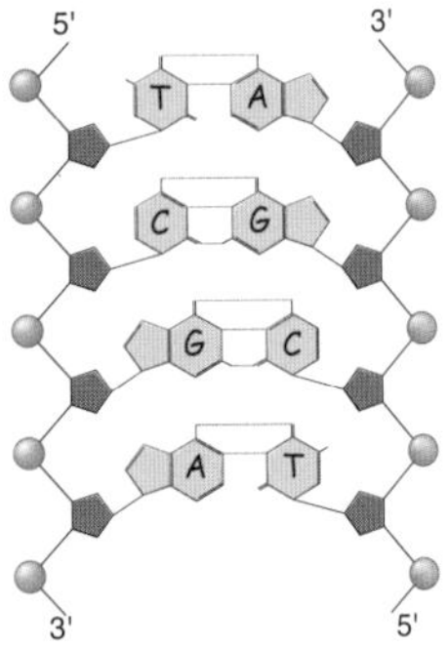

5' 3'

T A

C G

G C

A T

3' 5'

C: Stick model 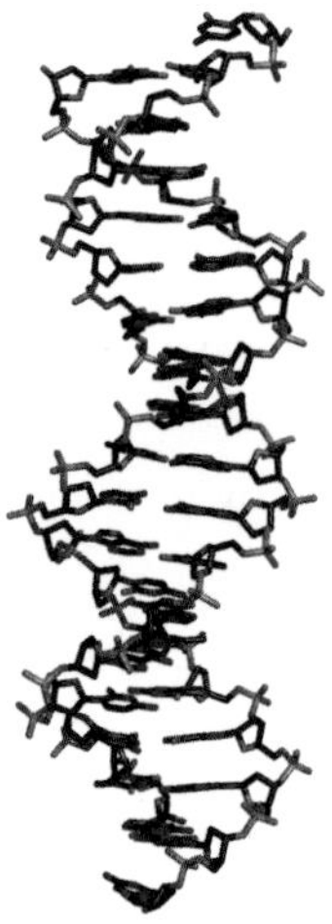 **D**: 3-D model 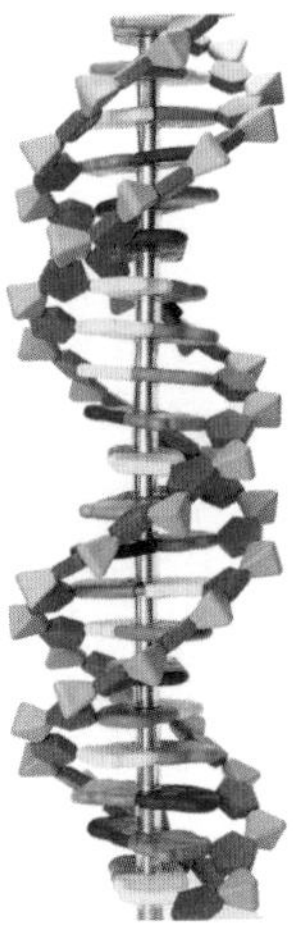 **E**: Cartoon 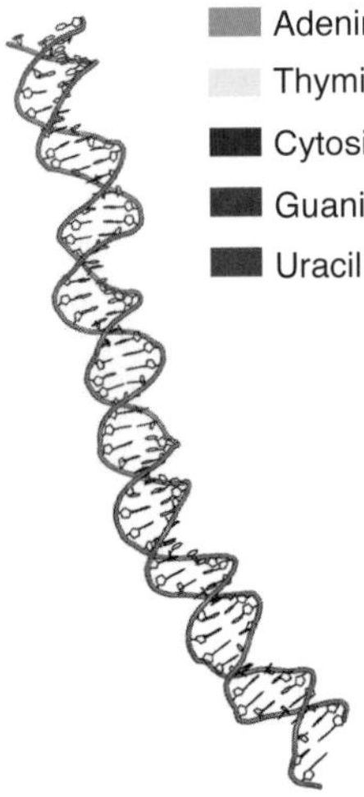 **F**: Schematic with key (left) and an RNA molecule to the right

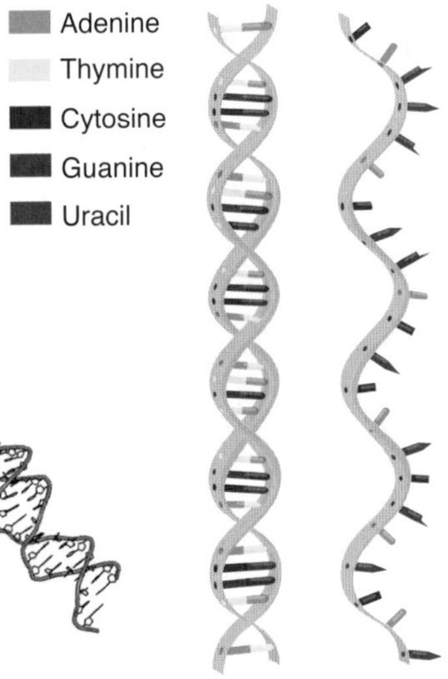

Adenine
Thymine
Cytosine
Guanine
Uracil

1. Examine the models above and **describe** the characteristics that they all share:

2. **Explain** the relationships between the different components represented in the models:

3. Use the models to **explain** how the components of a DNA molecule are organized to produce its functional structure:

4. Use the models to **explain** how DNA's structure accounts for its ability to act as an information molecule:

ISBN: 978-1-98-856656-6

UNIT 2

Cell Structure and Function

Learning Objectives

Developing understanding

CONTENT: This unit explores cells as the units of life. How do cells contribute to the organization of life and provide the environment in which organelles can function? Cells and cellular organelles have membranes that enable them to establish and maintain an internal environment and control exchanges with the external cellular environment. The maintenance of internal and external cellular environments is called homeostasis. An understanding of the principles of cellular homeostasis is important to understanding the material in the units that follow.

SKILLS: This unit emphasizes skills in explaining the relationships between structure and function of organelles and cellular components on the subcellular and cellular levels. You should become proficient in describing data, making calculations, and analyzing different types of data.

2.1 Cell structure: subcellular components .... activities 16 - 21

☐ 1. Describe the structure and/or function of subcellular components and organelles to include ribosomes, rough and smooth endoplasmic reticulum (ER), the Golgi complex, mitochondria, lysosomes, vacuoles, and chloroplasts.

2.2 Cell structure and function............ activities 16 - 21

☐ 2. Explain how subcellular components and organelles contribute to cell function with reference to ER, mitochondria, lysosomes, and vacuoles.

☐ 3. With reference to membrane infolding in prokaryotes, and chloroplasts and mitochondria in eukaryotes, describe the structural features of a cell that allow organisms to capture, store, and use energy.

2.3 Cell size .... activities 22 - 25

☐ 4. Explain the effect of surface area-to-volume ratios on the exchange of materials between cells or organisms and the environment. Describe the strategies and specializations of organisms that increase the efficiency of these exchanges.

2.4 Plasma membranes........................... activity 26

☐ 5. Describe the components of the plasma (cell) membrane, including phospholipids and proteins, and their roles in maintaining the internal environment of the cell. Describe the fluid mosaic model of membrane structure and explain how this model explains membrane behavior.

2.5 Membrane permeability .... activities 27 - 28

☐ 6. Explain how the selective permeability of cell membranes is a direct consequence of membrane structure. Which molecules pass freely across the membrane and which move across through channel and carrier proteins?

☐ 7. With respect to prokaryotes, plants, and fungi, describe the role of the cell wall in maintaining cell structure and function.

2.6 Membrane transport .... activities 29, 34 - 36

☐ 8. Describe the mechanisms that organisms use to maintain solute and water balance, including the distinction between passive and active transport.

☐ 9. Describe how organisms transport large molecules across the plasma membrane. Include reference to how selective permeability allows for the formation of concentration gradients across the membrane, and how endocytosis and exocytosis enable movement of materials into and out of the cell using energy.

2.7 Facilitated diffusion .... activity 29

☐ 10. Using examples, explain the role of membrane proteins in the facilitated diffusion of large polar molecules and ions across the plasma membrane. Contrast facilitated diffusion with active transport processes, which also involve membrane proteins, but require the expenditure of energy (e.g. the Na^+/K^+ ion pump, which maintains membrane potential).

2.8 Tonicity and osmoregulation......... activities 29 - 33

☐ 11. Explain how external environments can be hypotonic, hypertonic, or isotonic to the internal environment of the cell. Explain the components of water potential and use water potential to explain the movement of water into and out of cells by osmosis.

☐ 12. Using examples, explain the role of osmoregulation in the health and survival or organisms. Examples could include the contractile vacuoles of protists and the vacuoles of plants. Determine the solute potential (osmolarity) and water potential of plant cells (e.g. potato cells) through investigation and calculation ($\psi_S = -iCRT$).

2.9 Mechanisms of transport ...... activities 29, 34 - 36

☐ 13. Summarize the passive and active transport processes that enable ions and other molecules to move across membranes. Include reference to diffusion osmosis, facilitated diffusion, primary active transport (e.g. the Na^+/K^+ pump) and secondary active transport (e.g. the Na^+/glucose co-transporter), endocytosis, and exocytosis.

2.10 Compartmentalizaton........................ activity 37

☐ 14. Describe the membrane-bound structures of eukaryotic cells and explain their role in providing cellular compartments within which specific reaction sequences can occur. Explain how the process of compartmentalization improves the efficiency of cellular functions.

2.11 Origins of cell compartments .... activity 38

☐ 15. Describe similarities and/or differences in compartmentalization in prokaryotic and eukaryotic cells and comment of the significance of these similarities/differences. Outline the endosymbiotic theory for the origin of cellular organelles in eukaryotes and describe the evidence for it.

☐ 16. Describe the relationship between the functions of eukaryotic cellular organelles (specifically chloroplasts and mitochondria) and their free-living ancestral counterparts.

16 Prokaryotic vs Eukaryotic Cells

Key Question: What features distinguishes the two types of cellular life: prokaryotes and eukaryotes?

Cells are divided into two broad groups based on their size and organization. Prokaryotic cells (Bacteria and Archaea) are small, single cells with a simple internal structure. Eukaryotic cells are larger and more complex with specialized membranous compartments. All multicellular and some unicellular organisms are eukaryotic.

Prokaryotic cells

- Prokaryotic cells are small (~0.5-10 µm) single cells. They lack any membrane-bound organelles.
- They are relatively unstructured with little cellular organization. Their DNA, ribosomes, and enzymes are free floating within the cell's cytoplasm. The ribosomes (70S) are smaller than eukaryotic ribosomes.
- They have a single, circular chromosome of naked DNA (not associated with protein). They commonly have small, circular accessory chromosomes called plasmids.
- Photosynthetic bacteria have enzymes and light capturing membranes like those in eukaryotic chloroplasts.
- Prokaryotes have cell walls, but they are different in composition to the cell walls of eukaryotes.
- Examples of bacterial cells include the gut bacterium *Escherichia coli* and the cyanobacterium *Anabaena*.

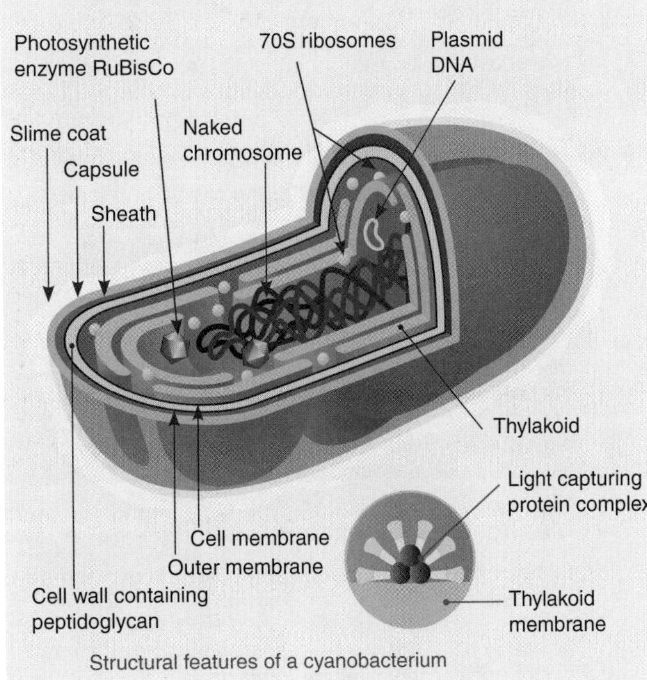

Structural features of a cyanobacterium

Eukaryotic cells

- Eukaryotic cells have a complex cell structure, with a high degree of organization including a membrane-bound nucleus and other membrane-bound organelles.
- Plant cells, animal cells, fungal cells, and protists are all eukaryotic cells.
- Eukaryotic cells are large (30-150 µm). They may exist as single cells (below) or as part of a multicellular organism.
- Their genetic material is found as multiple linear chromosomes consisting of DNA and associated proteins.
- Ribosomes (80S) are larger than in prokaryotes, except those in mitochondria and chloroplasts, which are 70S.

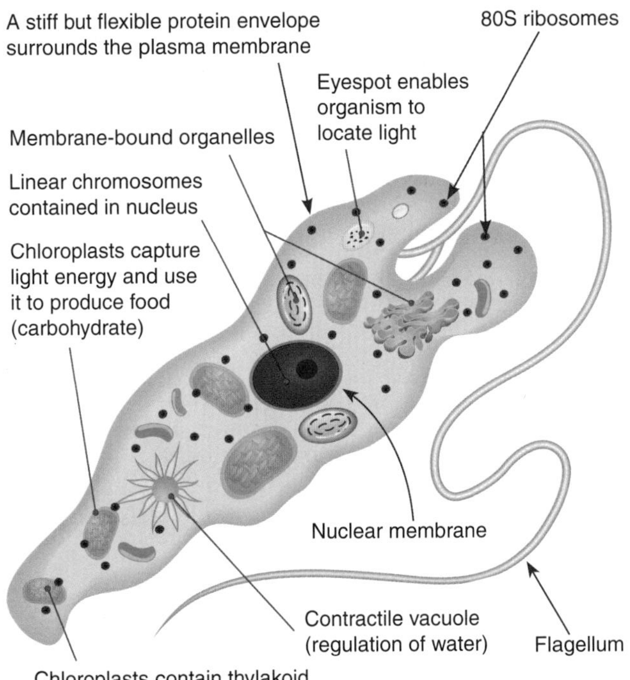

Euglena is a protist: a relatively simple single-celled photosynthetic eukaryote.

1. The cells of prokaryotes and eukaryotes are diverse. Identify the features that distinguish them:

prokaryotes - small, single cells w/ simple internal structure
eukaryotic cells - larger, complex, specialized membranous organelles

2. What is interesting about the ribosomes of prokaryotes and the ribosomes found in eukaryote chloroplasts?

they are free floating, and only differ in size

3. Cyanobacterial cells (above left) and *Euglena* (above right) are both photosynthetic organisms. Describe features of these organisms that enable them to capture and store energy:

Light capturing protein complex as well as chloroplasts that capture light energy + use it to produce food (carbohydrate)

ISBN: 978-1-98-856656-6

17 Looking at Cells

Key Question: What features of cells can be seen under different microscope views and magnifications?

The microscope is an important tool in biology for viewing cells and their features, which are far too small to be seen by the human eye. High power compound light microscopes use visible light and a combination of lenses to magnify objects up to several 100 times. Electron microscopes use beams of electrons and computer imaging to capture extremely fine detail of either surface or internal cellular features. They can magnify images up to 500,000 times. Scanning Tunnelling Microscopes (STMs) can magnify object ten times more than that. With a resolution of 0.1 nanometers, STMs operate at the edge of the quantum realm and are able to image some types of atoms.

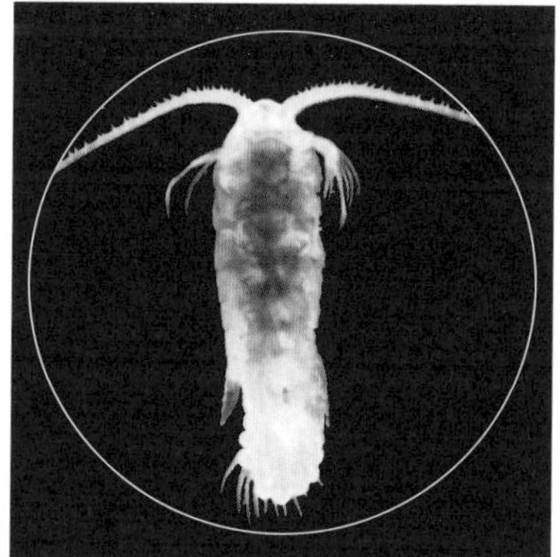

Dissecting microscopes are used for dissections, observing microbial cultures, and for identifying and sorting organisms, like this small crustacean.

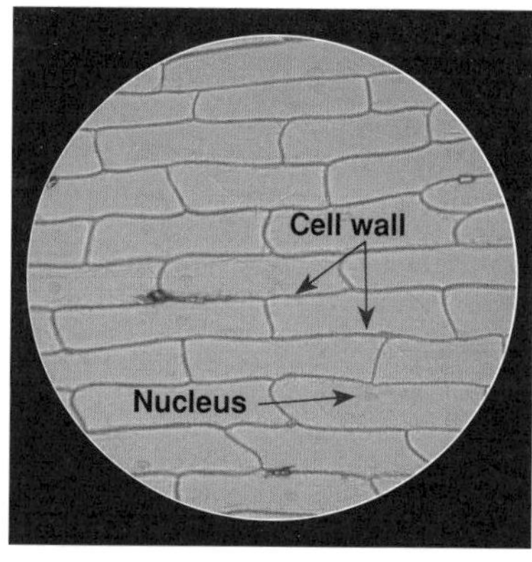

These onion epidermal cells are viewed with standard **bright field** lighting. Very little detail can be seen. The cell nuclei are barely visible.

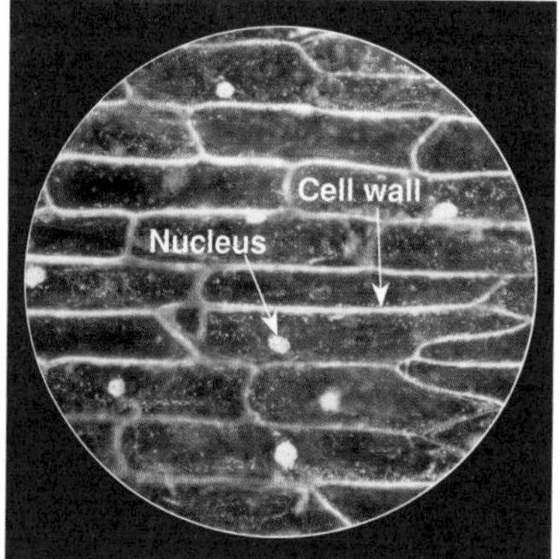

Dark field illumination is excellent for viewing specimens that are almost transparent. The nuclei of these onion epidermal cells are clearly visible.

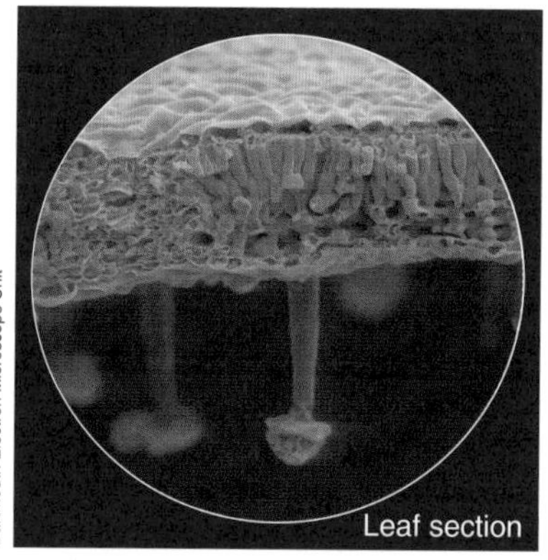

Scanning Electron Microscopes (SEMs) produce extremely high resolution images of the surface of cells and objects.

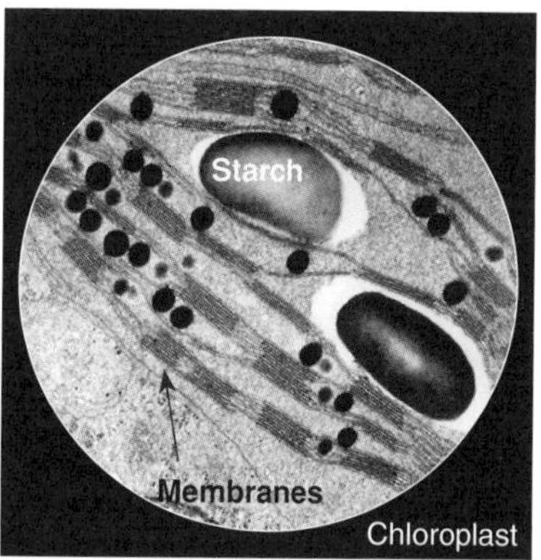

Transmission Electron Microscopes (TEMs) produce extremely high resolution images of the interior of cells and transparent objects.

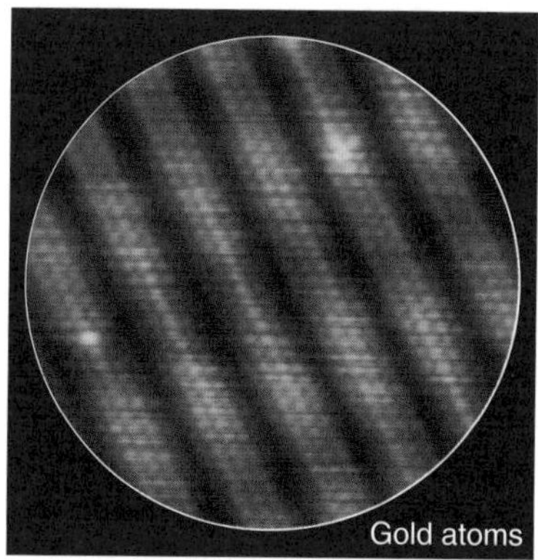

Scanning Tunnelling Microscopes (STMs) produce images based on current variation between an extremely fine needle and the object it moves over.

Staining

Some parts of the cell take up stains (chemical dyes) better than others. Stains can be used to highlight parts of the cell for better viewing with a microscope or they can improve contrast. A wide range of chemicals act as stains, including iodine and methylene blue.

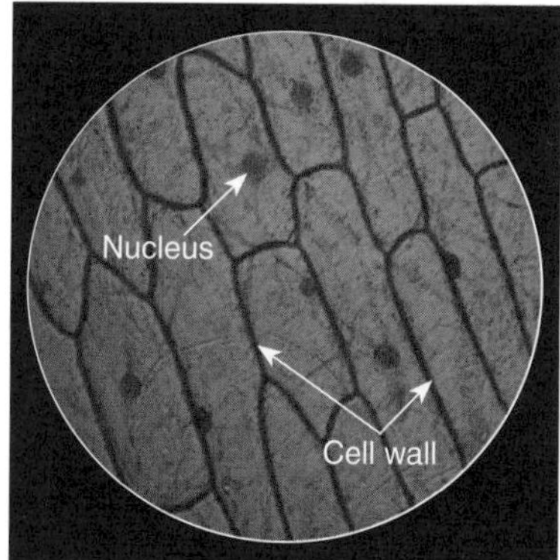

Iodine is used to increase the contrast in transparent tissues, such as this onion epidermis. Iodine stains are also used to show the presence of starch, binding starch to produce a blue-black color.

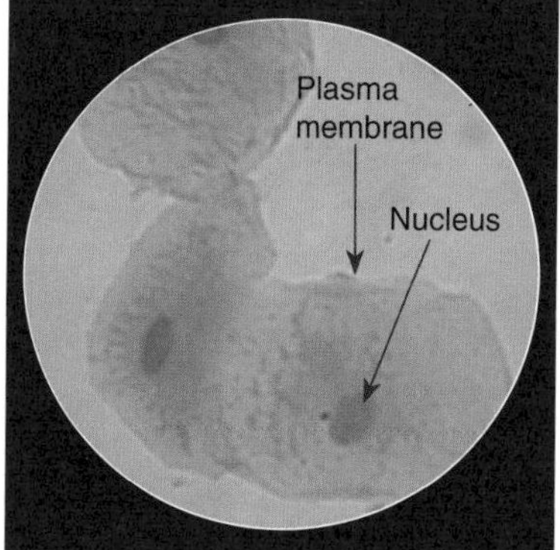

Methylene blue is a positively charged stain commonly used when viewing animal cells. It has a strong affinity for DNA (in the nucleus) and a weaker affinity for RNA (in the cytoplasm).

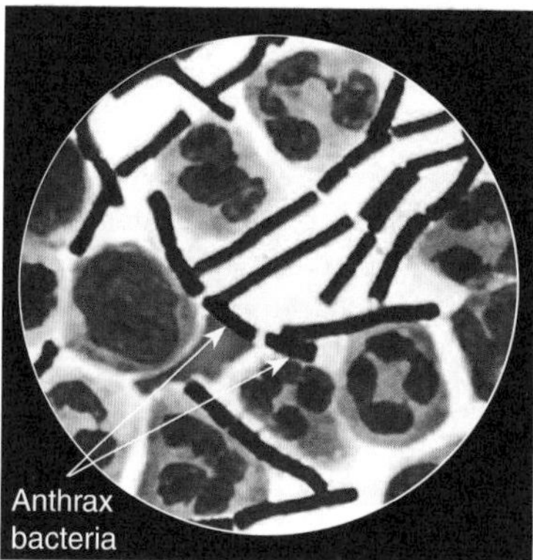

Some bacteria can be identified and viewed using Gram staining. Bacteria are classed as Gram positive and Gram negative depending on whether or not the stain is retained by the cell wall.

ISBN: 978-1-98-856656-6

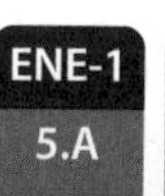

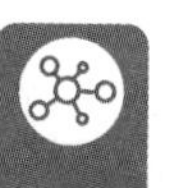

What is magnification?

Magnification refers to the number of times larger an object appears compared to its actual size.

$$\text{Magnification} = \frac{\text{measured size of the object}}{\text{actual size of the object}}$$

$$\text{Actual object size} = \frac{\text{size of the image}}{\text{magnification}}$$

What is resolution?

Resolution is the ability to distinguish between close together but separate objects. Resolution is a function of wavelength of light used to view the object. Examples of high and low resolution for separating two objects viewed under the same magnification are given below.

High resolution 

Low resolution 

1. Calculate the length or magnification of the object or organism:

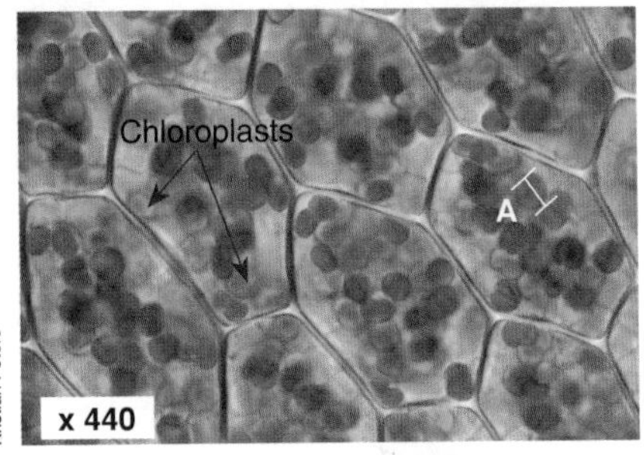

x 440

Kristian Peters

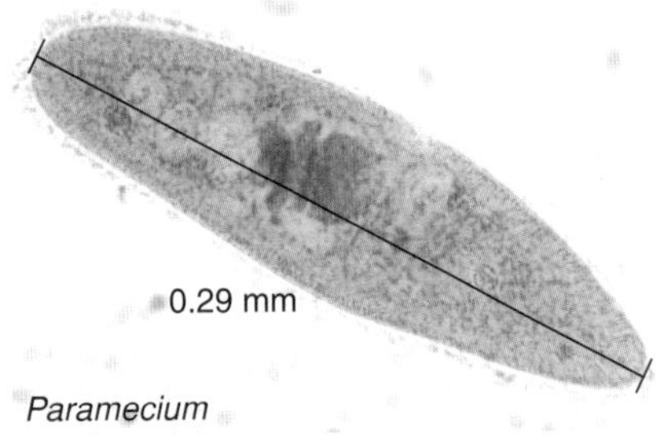

Paramecium

EII

Dust mites

(a) Length of A: 0.29

(b) Magnification: 0.5

(c) Magnification: 0.97

2. Identify which type of microscope (optical microscope, SEM, or TEM) was used to produce each of the images in the photos below (a to f):

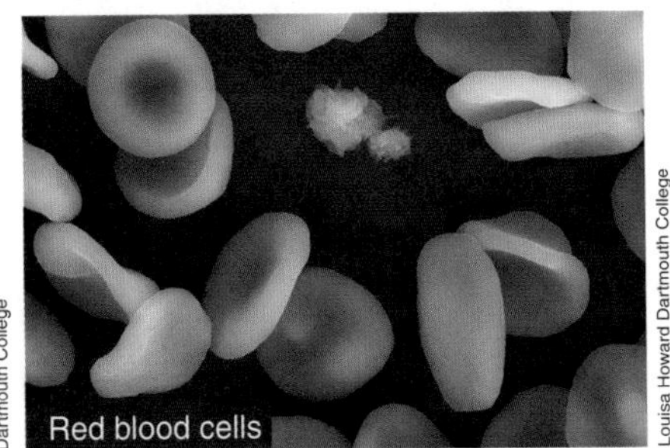
Red blood cells

Dartmouth College

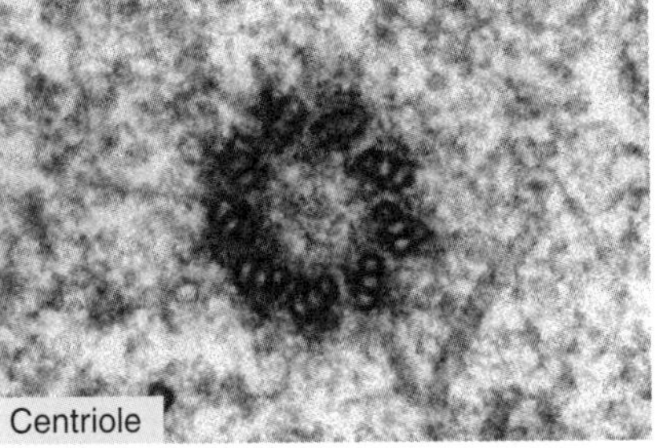
Centriole

Louisa Howard Dartmouth College

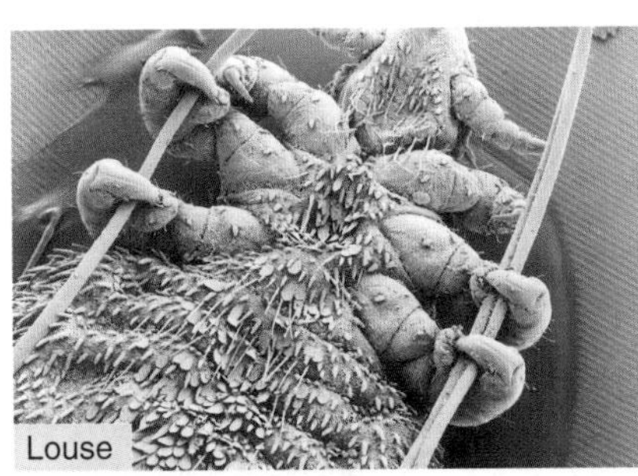
Louse

(a) TEMS

(b) STMS

(c) SEMS

Wool

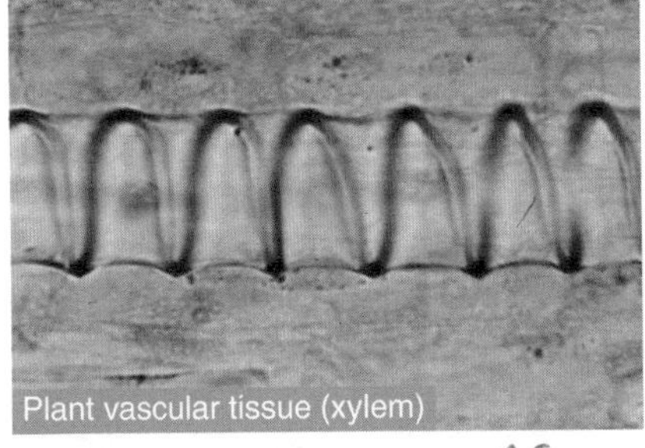
Plant vascular tissue (xylem)

BAN127

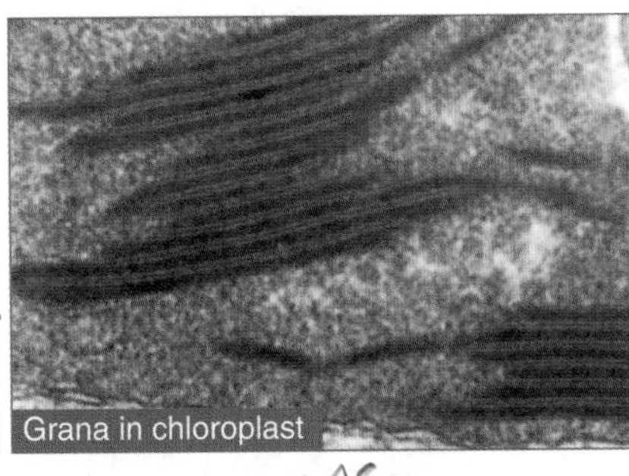
Grana in chloroplast

Dartmouth College

(d) SEMS

(e) ~~SE~~ TEMS

(f) STMS

3. Identify the labeled structures:

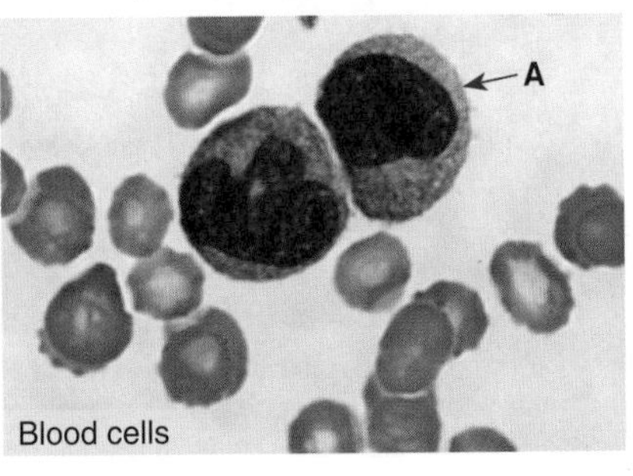

Blood cells

Dr Graham Beards

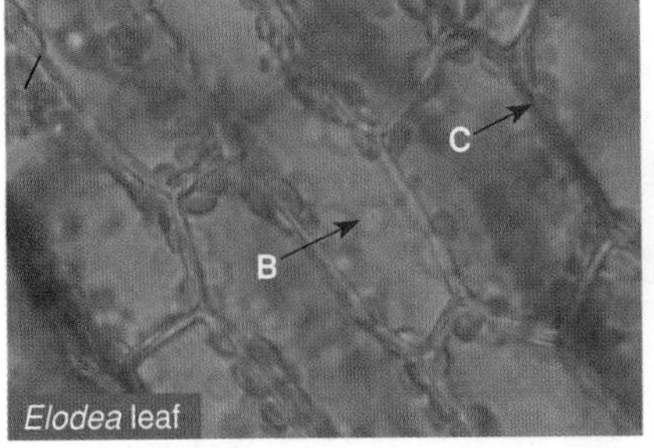

Elodea leaf

toony

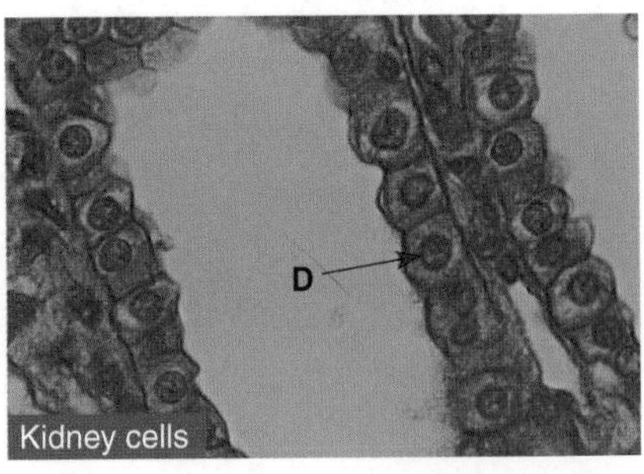

Kidney cells

(a) TBMS

(b) TBMS

(c) STMS

(d) ~~STMS~~ TEMS

ISBN: 978-1-98-856656-6

18 Animal Cells

Key Question: What features characterize animal cells?
Animal cells, unlike plant cells, do not have a regular shape. Plant cells are constrained by their rigid cell wall, but many animal cells (such as phagocytes) are able to alter their shape for various purposes (e.g. engulfing foreign material).

The diagram below shows the structure and organelles of a liver cell, a relatively unspecialized human cell. Note the differences between this cell and the generalized plant cell (next activity). The plant cells activity provides further information on the organelles identified but not described.

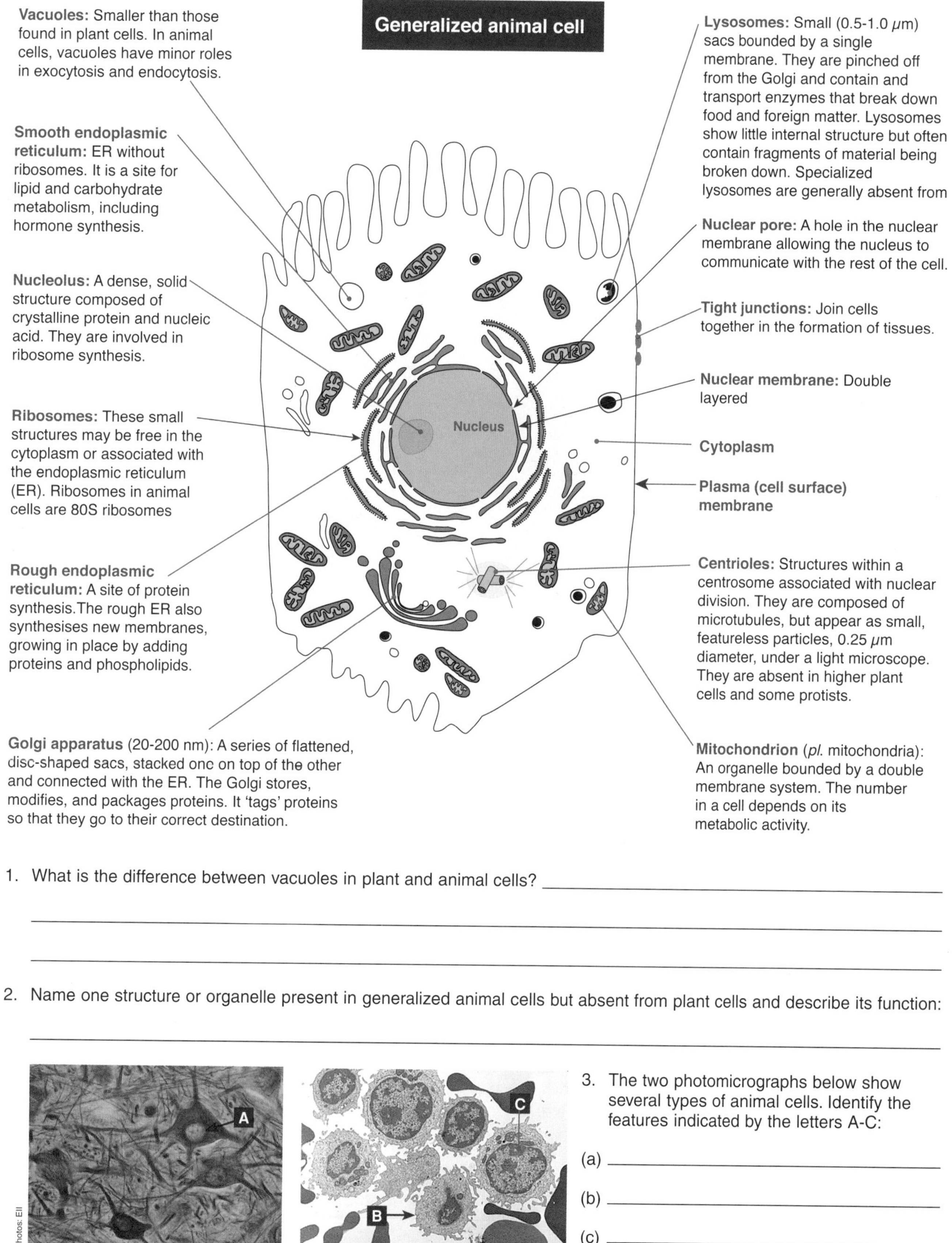

Generalized animal cell
Vacuoles: Smaller than those found in plant cells. In animal cells, vacuoles have minor roles in exocytosis and endocytosis.
Smooth endoplasmic reticulum: ER without ribosomes. It is a site for lipid and carbohydrate metabolism, including hormone synthesis.
Nucleolus: A dense, solid structure composed of crystalline protein and nucleic acid. They are involved in ribosome synthesis.
Ribosomes: These small structures may be free in the cytoplasm or associated with the endoplasmic reticulum (ER). Ribosomes in animal cells are 80S ribosomes
Rough endoplasmic reticulum: A site of protein synthesis.The rough ER also synthesises new membranes, growing in place by adding proteins and phospholipids.
Golgi apparatus (20-200 nm): A series of flattened, disc-shaped sacs, stacked one on top of the other and connected with the ER. The Golgi stores, modifies, and packages proteins. It 'tags' proteins so that they go to their correct destination.
Nucleus
Lysosomes: Small (0.5-1.0 μm) sacs bounded by a single membrane. They are pinched off from the Golgi and contain and transport enzymes that break down food and foreign matter. Lysosomes show little internal structure but often contain fragments of material being broken down. Specialized lysosomes are generally absent from
Nuclear pore: A hole in the nuclear membrane allowing the nucleus to communicate with the rest of the cell.
Tight junctions: Join cells together in the formation of tissues.
Nuclear membrane: Double layered
Cytoplasm
Plasma (cell surface) membrane
Centrioles: Structures within a centrosome associated with nuclear division. They are composed of microtubules, but appear as small, featureless particles, 0.25 μm diameter, under a light microscope. They are absent in higher plant cells and some protists.
Mitochondrion (*pl.* mitochondria): An organelle bounded by a double membrane system. The number in a cell depends on its metabolic activity.
A
C
B
Photos: Ell

1. What is the difference between vacuoles in plant and animal cells? ______________________

____

____

2. Name one structure or organelle present in generalized animal cells but absent from plant cells and describe its function:

____

Nerve cells in the spinal cord

White blood cells and red blood cells

3. The two photomicrographs below show several types of animal cells. Identify the features indicated by the letters A-C:

(a) ______________________

(b) ______________________

(c) ______________________

ISBN: 978-1-98-856656-6

4. Identify and label the structures in the TEM of the animal cell below using the following list of terms: *cytoplasm, plasma membrane, rough endoplasmic reticulum, mitochondrion, nucleus, centriole, Golgi apparatus, lysosome*

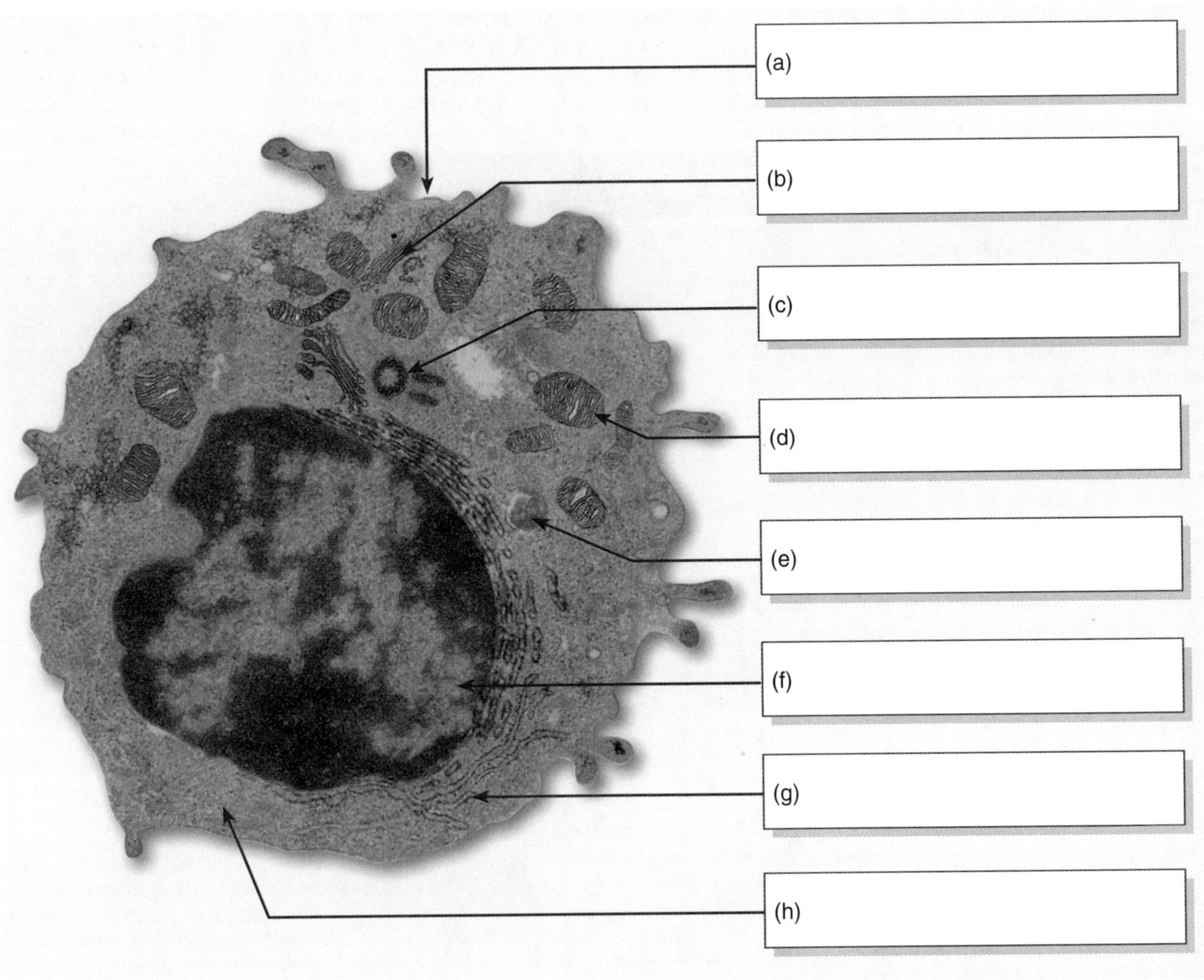

5. Which of the organelles in the TEM above are obviously shown in both transverse and longitudinal section?

6. Why do plants lack any of the mobile phagocytic cells typical of animal cells?

7. The animal cell pictured above is a lymphocyte. Describe the features that suggest to you that:

(a) It has a role in producing and secreting proteins:

(b) It is metabolically very active:

8. What features of the lymphocyte cell above identify it as eukaryotic?

9. If you were to see the cell above with no other references, how would you be able to identify it as an animal cell?

ISBN: 978-1-98-856656-6

19 Plant Cells

Key Question: What are the features of a plant cell that make it a eukaryote, and what features does it share with an animal cell? Which are unique?

Eukaryotic cells have a similar basic structure, although they may vary tremendously in size, shape, and function. Certain features are common to almost all eukaryotic cells, including their three main regions: a nucleus, surrounded by a watery cytoplasm, which is itself enclosed by the plasma membrane. Plant cells are enclosed in a cellulose cell wall, which gives them a regular, uniform appearance. The cell wall protects the cell, maintains its shape, and prevents excessive water uptake. It provides rigidity to plant structures but permits the free passage of materials into and out of the cell.

Generalized plant cell

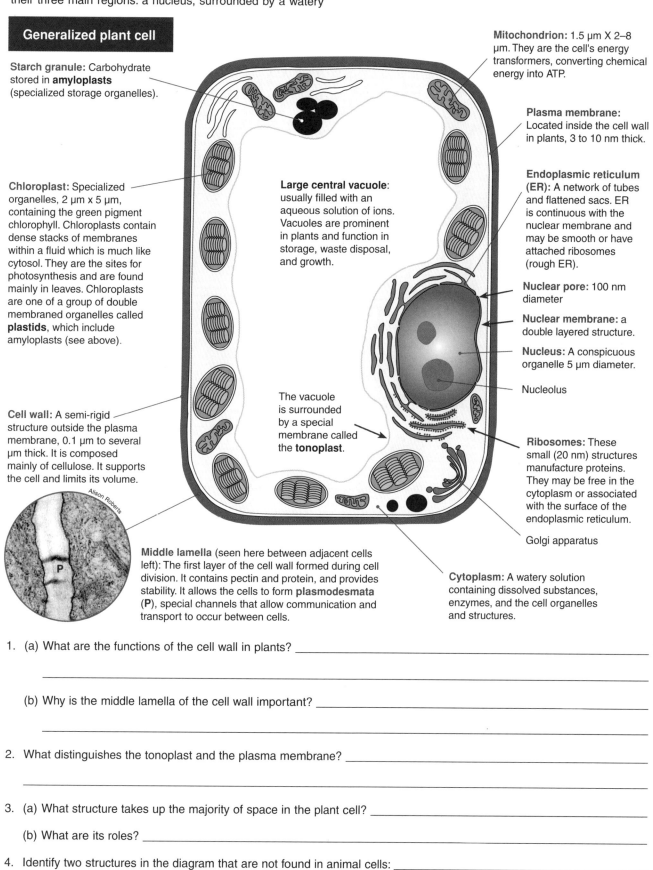

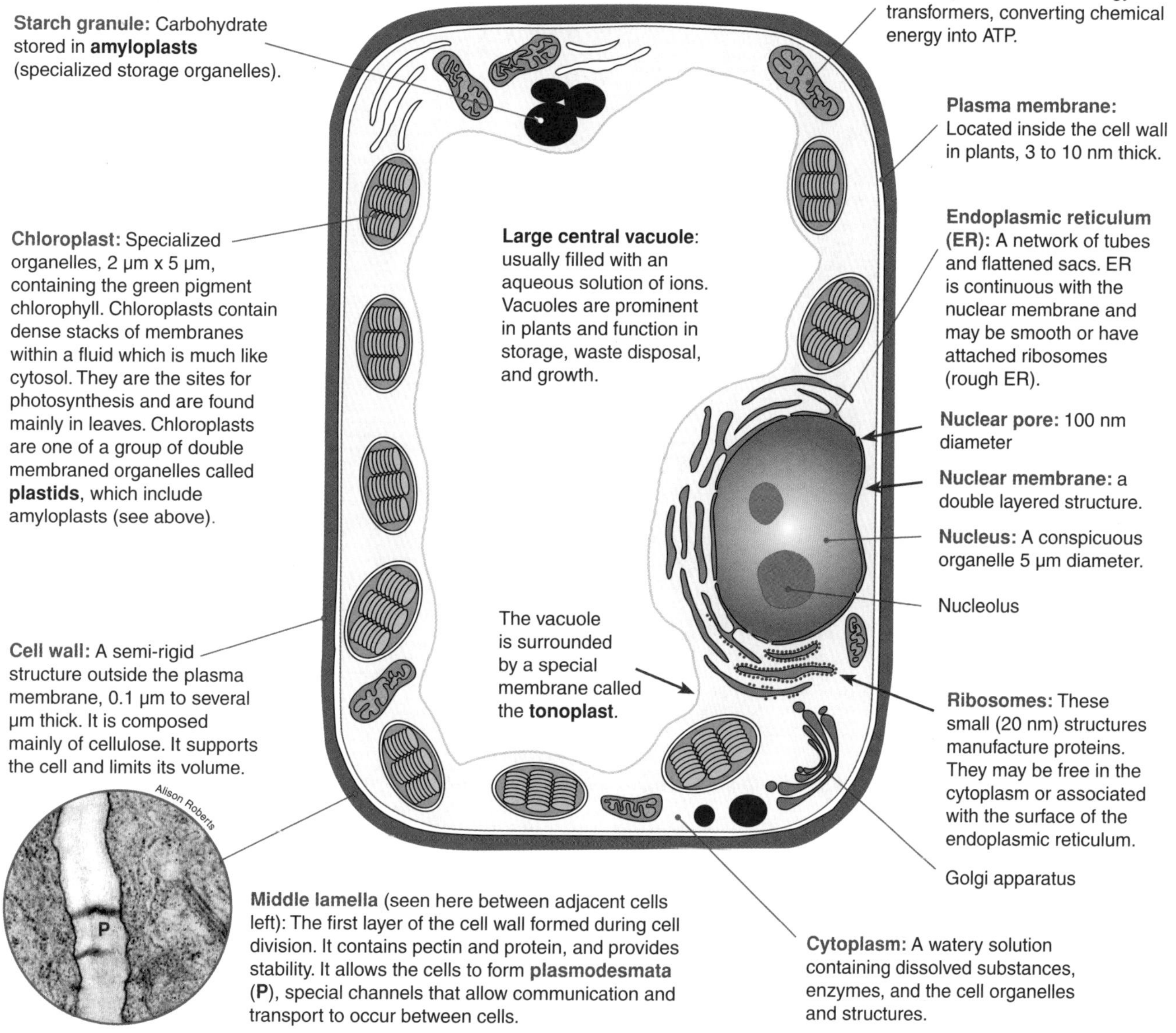

Starch granule: Carbohydrate stored in **amyloplasts** (specialized storage organelles).

Chloroplast: Specialized organelles, 2 µm x 5 µm, containing the green pigment chlorophyll. Chloroplasts contain dense stacks of membranes within a fluid which is much like cytosol. They are the sites for photosynthesis and are found mainly in leaves. Chloroplasts are one of a group of double membraned organelles called **plastids**, which include amyloplasts (see above).

Cell wall: A semi-rigid structure outside the plasma membrane, 0.1 µm to several µm thick. It is composed mainly of cellulose. It supports the cell and limits its volume.

Alison Roberts

P

Middle lamella (seen here between adjacent cells left): The first layer of the cell wall formed during cell division. It contains pectin and protein, and provides stability. It allows the cells to form **plasmodesmata** (**P**), special channels that allow communication and transport to occur between cells.

Large central vacuole: usually filled with an aqueous solution of ions. Vacuoles are prominent in plants and function in storage, waste disposal, and growth.

The vacuole is surrounded by a special membrane called the **tonoplast**.

Mitochondrion: 1.5 µm X 2–8 µm. They are the cell's energy transformers, converting chemical energy into ATP.

Plasma membrane: Located inside the cell wall in plants, 3 to 10 nm thick.

Endoplasmic reticulum (ER): A network of tubes and flattened sacs. ER is continuous with the nuclear membrane and may be smooth or have attached ribosomes (rough ER).

Nuclear pore: 100 nm diameter

Nuclear membrane: a double layered structure.

Nucleus: A conspicuous organelle 5 µm diameter.

Nucleolus

Ribosomes: These small (20 nm) structures manufacture proteins. They may be free in the cytoplasm or associated with the surface of the endoplasmic reticulum.

Golgi apparatus

Cytoplasm: A watery solution containing dissolved substances, enzymes, and the cell organelles and structures.

1. (a) What are the functions of the cell wall in plants? ______________________

____

(b) Why is the middle lamella of the cell wall important? ______________________

____

2. What distinguishes the tonoplast and the plasma membrane? ______________________

____

3. (a) What structure takes up the majority of space in the plant cell? ______________________

(b) What are its roles? ______________________

4. Identify two structures in the diagram that are not found in animal cells: ______________________

ISBN: 978-1-98-856656-6

5. Study the diagrams on the other pages in this chapter to familiarize yourself with the structures found in eukaryotic cells. Identify the 11 structures in the cell below using the following word list: *cytoplasm, smooth endoplasmic reticulum, mitochondrion, starch granule, chromosome, nucleus, vacuole, plasma membrane, cell wall, chloroplast, nuclear membrane*

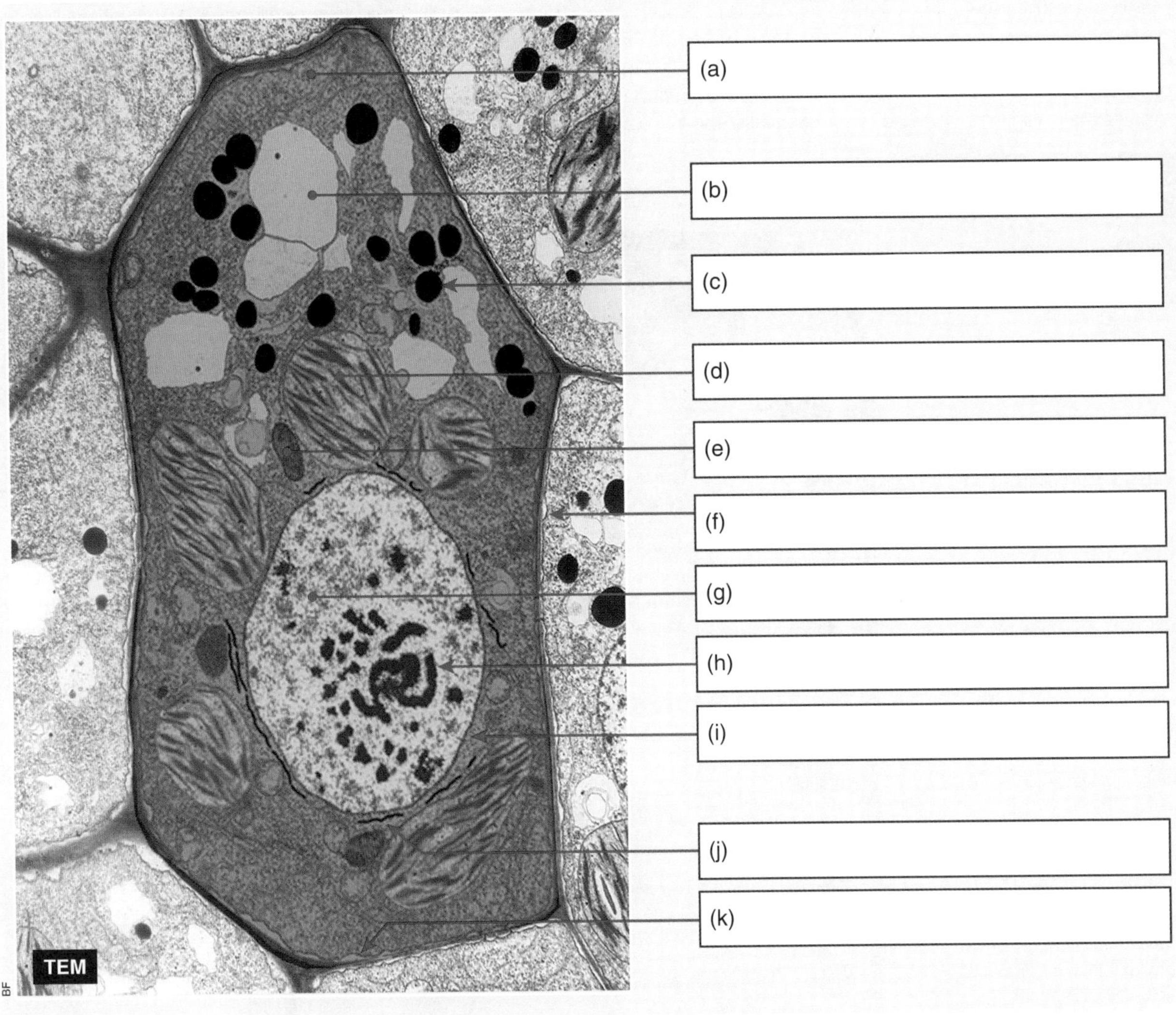

6. State how many cells, or parts of cells, are visible in the electron micrograph above: ______

7. Describe the features that identify this cell as a plant cell: ______

8. (a) Explain where cytoplasm is found in the cell: ______

(b) Describe what the cytoplasm is made up of: ______

9. Describe two structures, pictured in the cell above, that are associated with storage:

(a) ______

(b) ______

ISBN: 978-1-98-856656-6

20 Cell Structures and Organelles

Key Idea: Each type of organelle in a cell has a specific role. Not all cell types contain every type of organelle.

The diagram below provides spaces for you to summarize information about the organelles found in eukaryotic cells. The log scale of measurements (top of next page) illustrates the relative sizes of some cellular structures.

1. (a) Name this organelle:

   (b) Structure and location:

   (c) Function:

5. (a) Name this organelle:

   (b) Structure and location:

   (c) Function:

2. (a) Name this organelle:

   (b) Structure and location:

   (c) Function:

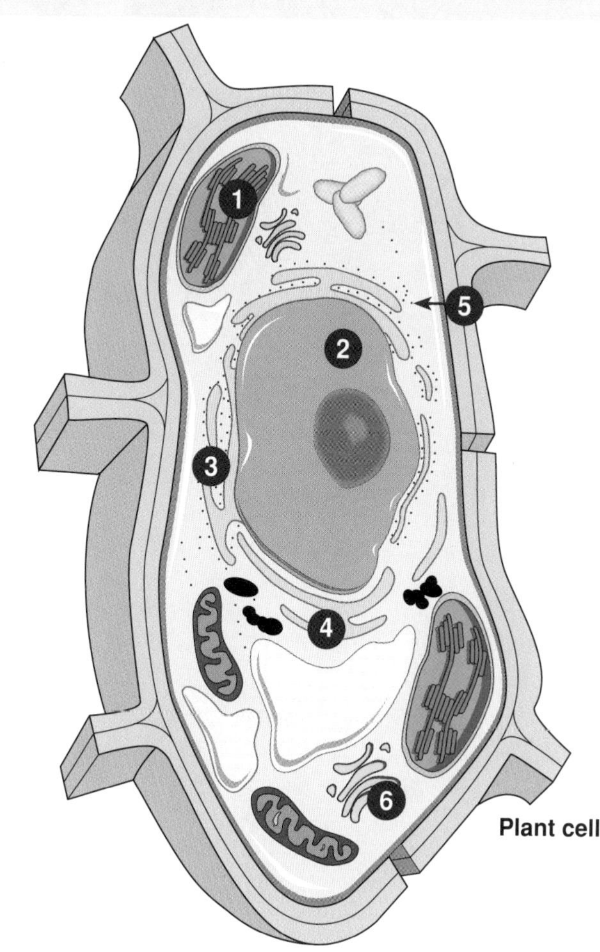

3. (a) Name this organelle:

   (b) Structure and location:

   (c) Function:

4. (a) Name this organelle:

   (b) Structure and location:

   (c) Function:

6. (a) Name this organelle:

   (b) Structure and location:

   (c) Function:

ISBN: 978-1-98-856656-6

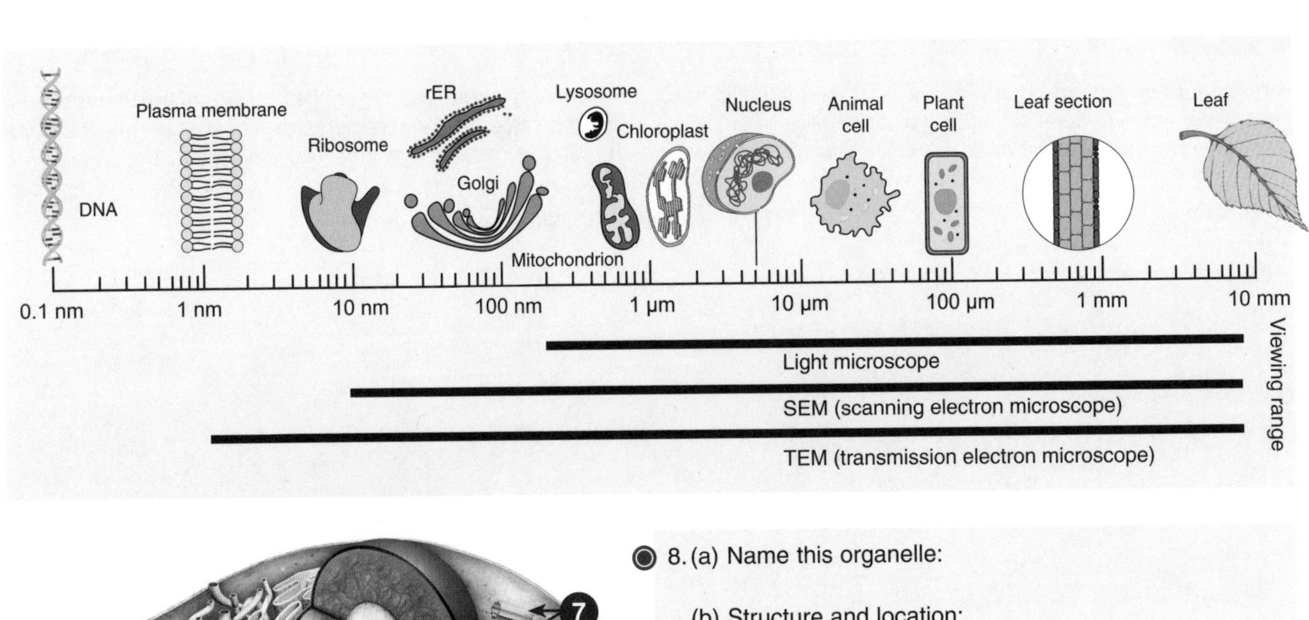

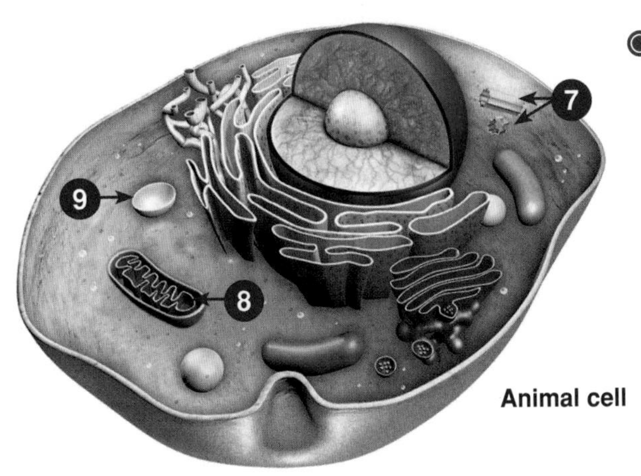

8. (a) Name this organelle:

(b) Structure and location:

(c) Function:

7. (a) Name this organelle:

(b) Structure and location:

(c) Function:

9. (a) Name this organelle:

(b) Structure and location:

(c) Function:

10. Use the scale at the top of the page and the information on previous activities to identify which of the organelles (1-9):

(a) Can be seen with a high power light microscope: ____________________

(b) Require a TEM to be seen: ____________________

11. (a) Which of the organelles (1-9) is/are not found in animal cells: ____________________

(b) Which of the organelles (1-9) is/are not found in plant cells: ____________________

(c) Which organelles (1-9) is/are found in plant and animal cells: ____________________

12. Identify one unlabeled structure in the plant cell on the previous page and describe its function: ____________________

____

____

____

ISBN: 978-1-98-856656-6

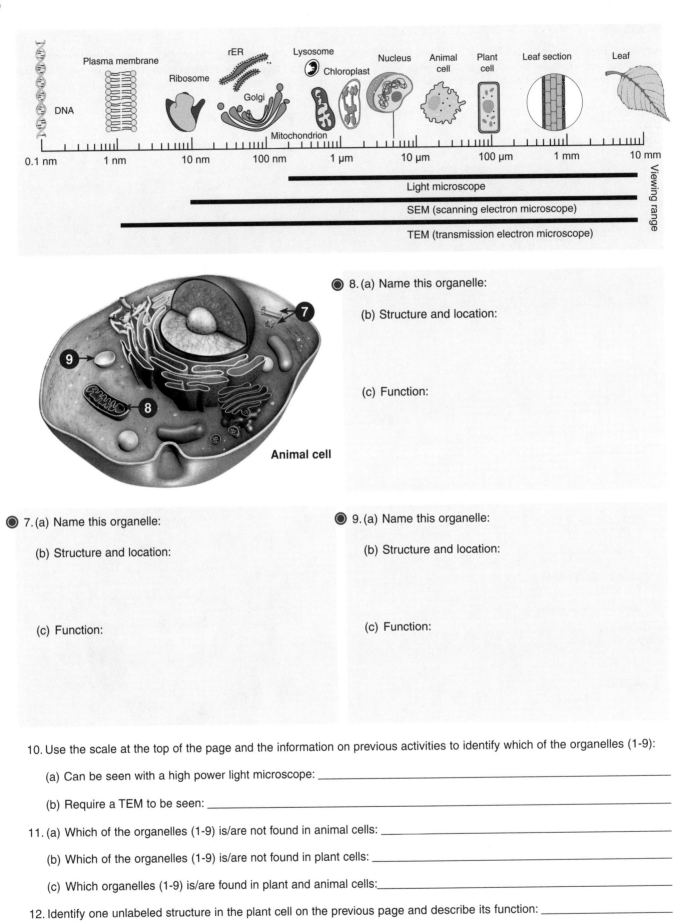

21 A Closer look at Chloroplasts and Mitochondria

Key Question: What are the important structural features of mitochondria and chloroplasts?

Chloroplasts and mitochondria are organelles involved in the production of energy storage molecules in cells. Both are membranous organelles in which specialized biochemical reactions occur. Chloroplasts are found only in plant cells and some protists, whereas mitochondria are found in all eukaryotic cells. Mitochondria contain proteins (including ATP synthase) involved in the production of ATP, the energy storage molecule of cells. The number of mitochondria in each cell is variable. Red blood cells have no mitochondria, whereas a heart cell can have up to 5000. Chloroplasts are the organelles responsible for photosynthesis. A mesophyll leaf cell contains between 50-100 chloroplasts. Chloroplasts have an internal structure characterized by a system of membranous structures with bound light-capturing pigments. These absorb light of specific wavelengths, capturing light energy, which is then used to fix carbon into carbohydrates.

The structure of a mitochondrion

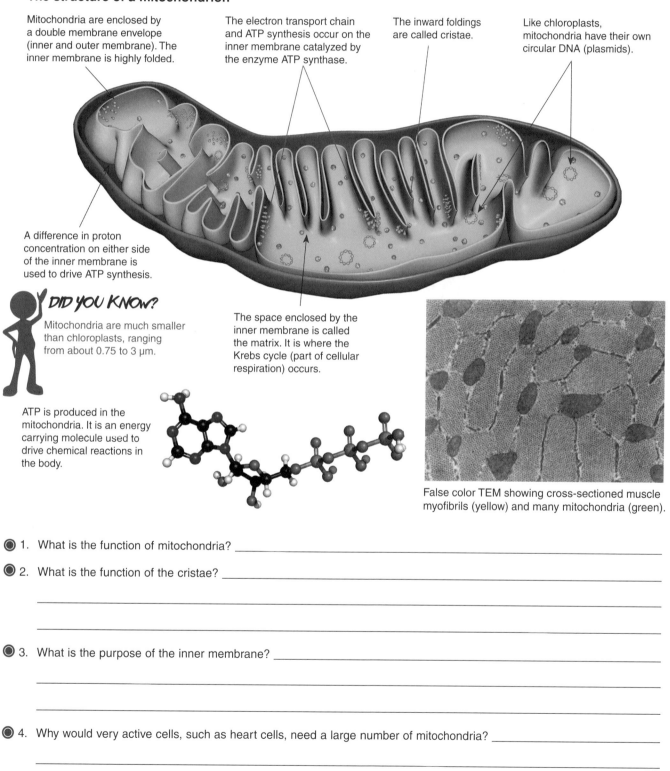

Mitochondria are enclosed by a double membrane envelope (inner and outer membrane). The inner membrane is highly folded.

The electron transport chain and ATP synthesis occur on the inner membrane catalyzed by the enzyme ATP synthase.

The inward foldings are called cristae.

Like chloroplasts, mitochondria have their own circular DNA (plasmids).

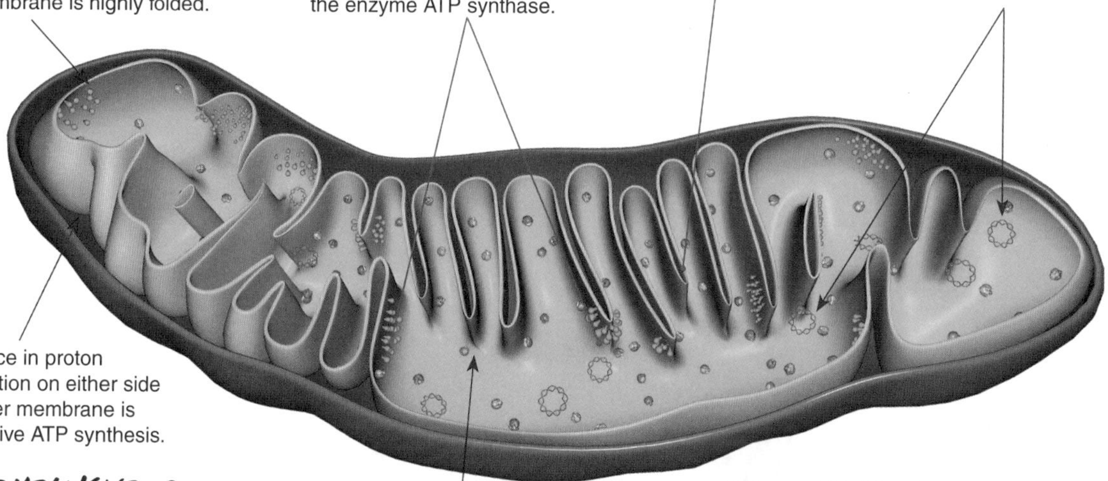

A difference in proton concentration on either side of the inner membrane is used to drive ATP synthesis.

The space enclosed by the inner membrane is called the matrix. It is where the Krebs cycle (part of cellular respiration) occurs.

DID YOU KNOW?

Mitochondria are much smaller than chloroplasts, ranging from about 0.75 to 3 μm.

ATP is produced in the mitochondria. It is an energy carrying molecule used to drive chemical reactions in the body.

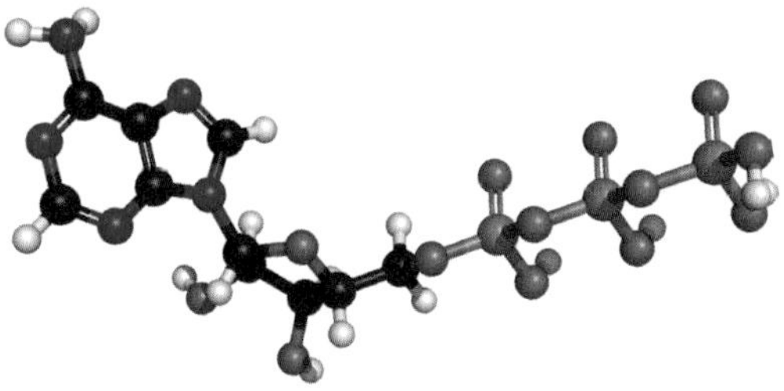

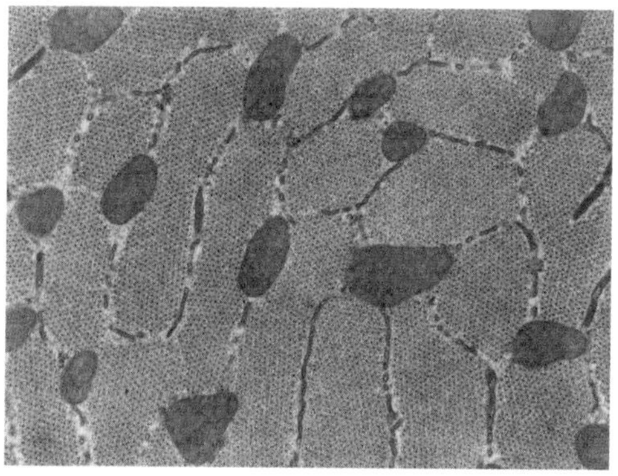

False color TEM showing cross-sectioned muscle myofibrils (yellow) and many mitochondria (green).

1. What is the function of mitochondria? ___

2. What is the function of the cristae? ___

3. What is the purpose of the inner membrane? ___

4. Why would very active cells, such as heart cells, need a large number of mitochondria? ___

ISBN: 978-1-98-856656-6

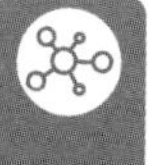

The structure of a chloroplast

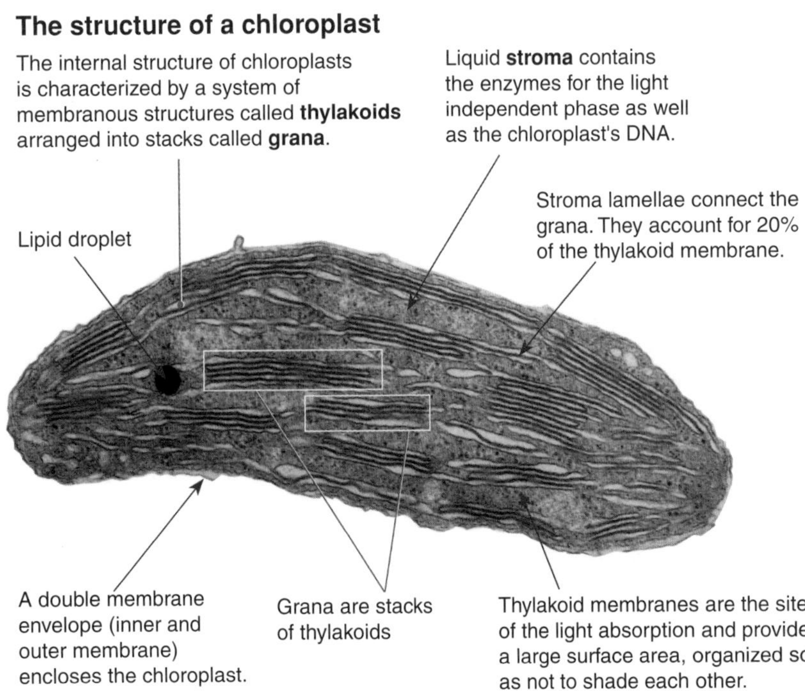

The internal structure of chloroplasts is characterized by a system of membranous structures called **thylakoids** arranged into stacks called **grana**.
Liquid **stroma** contains the enzymes for the light independent phase as well as the chloroplast's DNA.
Stroma lamellae connect the grana. They account for 20% of the thylakoid membrane.
Lipid droplet
A double membrane envelope (inner and outer membrane) encloses the chloroplast.
Grana are stacks of thylakoids
Thylakoid membranes are the site of the light absorption and provide a large surface area, organized so as not to shade each other.

False color TEM image of a single chloroplast

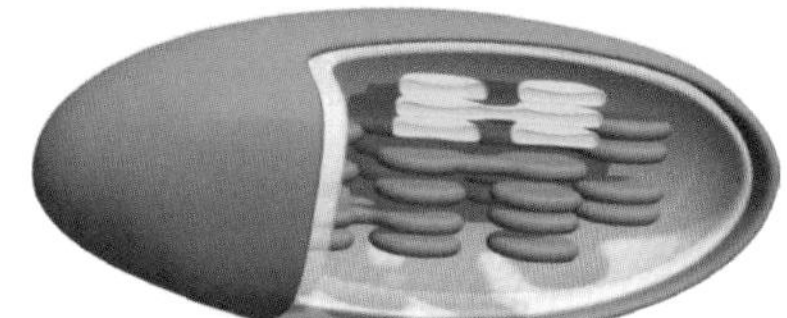

3D model of a chloroplast

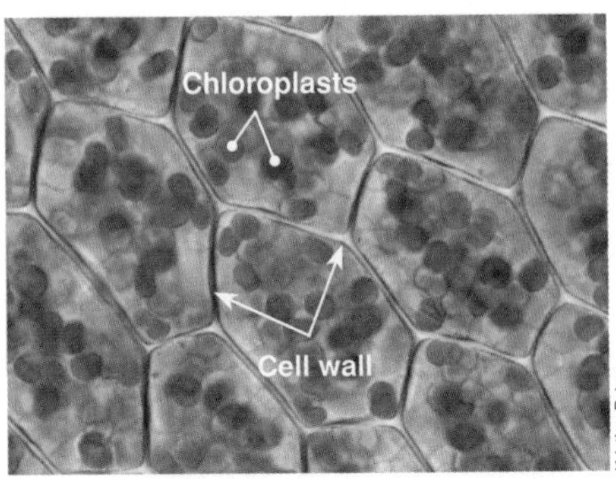

Chloroplasts visible in leaf cells. They appear green because they absorb blue and red light, reflecting green light. The chloroplasts are generally aligned so that their broad surface runs parallel to the cell wall to maximize the surface area available for light absorption.

5. Label the transmission electron microscope image of a chloroplast below:

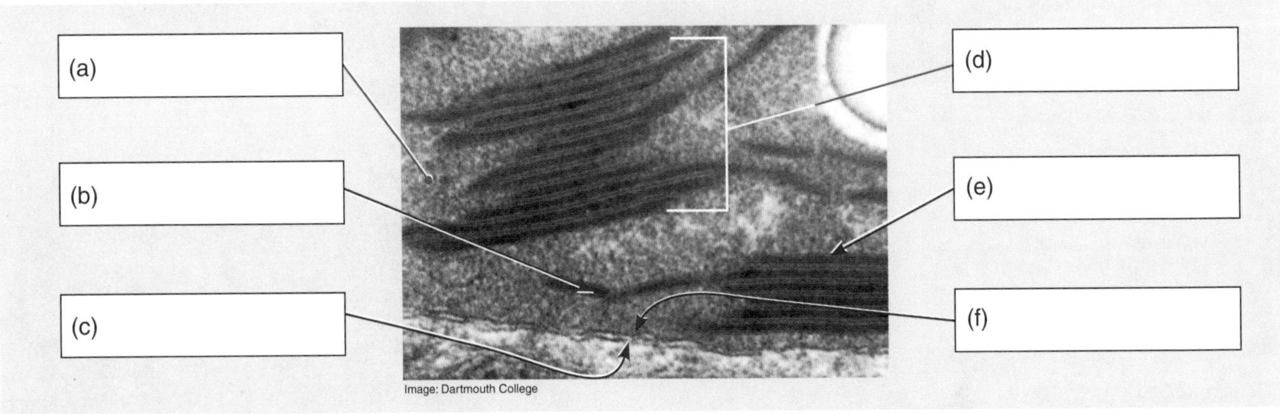

6. (a) Where is chlorophyll found in a chloroplast? ____________________

(b) Why is chlorophyll found there? ____________________

7. Explain how the internal structure of chloroplasts helps absorb the maximum amount of light: ____________________

8. Explain why plant leaves appear green: ____________________

9. Describe the difference in functions of the stroma and the thylakoid membranes: ____________________

ISBN: 978-1-98-856656-6

22 Cell Sizes

Key Question: How do different types of cells vary in size? Different types of cells have different sizes. Eukaryotic cells are much larger than prokaryotic cells, but even they vary widely in size. Cells also have different shapes. Many have no fixed shape, but others have shapes approximating spheres, e.g. *Streptococcus,* cylinders, e.g. *E. coli*, or rectangular prisms, e.g. plant cells. The volume of these cells can then be estimated using the appropriate formula for their shape.

Typical sizes of cells and viruses

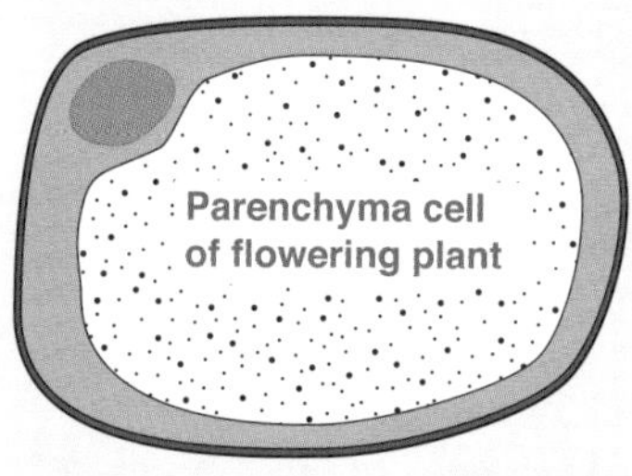

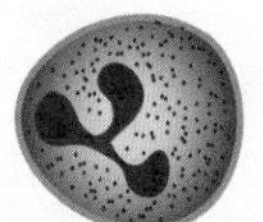

Human white blood cell

Eukaryotic cells
(e.g. plant and animal cells)
Size: 10-100 µm diameter.
Cellular organelles may be up to 10 µm.

Prokaryotic cells
Size: Typically 2-10 µm length, 0.2-2 µm diameter. Upper limit 30 µm long.

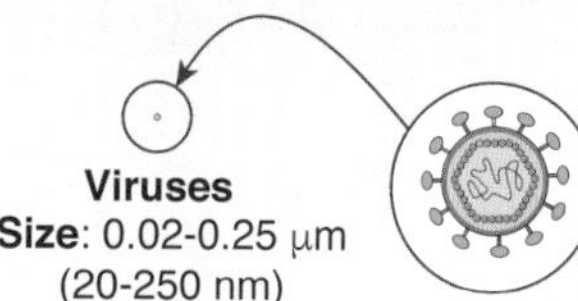

Viruses
Size: 0.02-0.25 µm (20-250 nm)

Unit of length (international system)		
Unit	**Meters**	**Equivalent**
1 meter (m)	1 m	= 1000 millimeters
1 millimeter (mm)	10^{-3} m	= 1000 micrometers
1 micrometer (µm)	10^{-6} m	= 1000 nanometers
1 nanometer (nm)	10^{-9} m	= 1000 picometers

Micrometers are sometimes referred to as microns. Smaller structures are usually measured in nanometers (nm) e.g. molecules (1 nm) and plasma membrane thickness (10 nm).

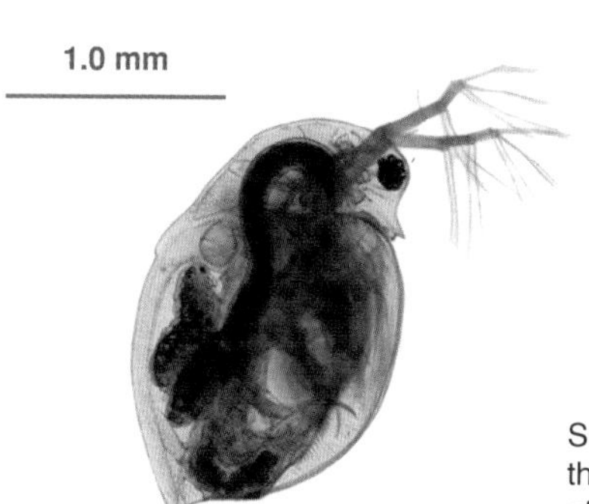

Daphnia is a small crustacean found as part of the zooplankton of lakes and ponds.

SEM of *Giardia*, a protozoan that infects the small intestines of many vertebrate groups.

Paramecium is a protozoan commonly found in ponds.

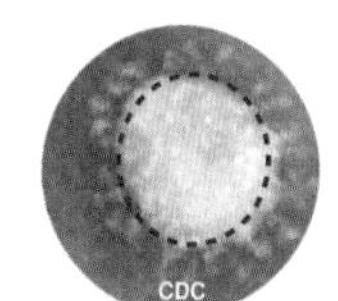

Coronavirus is the virus responsible for SARS.

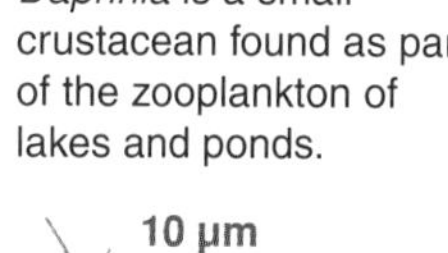

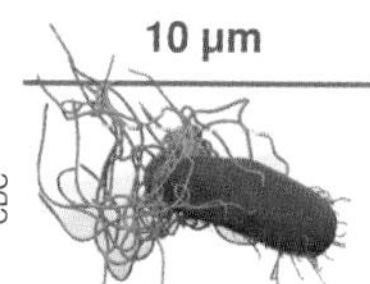

Salmonella is a bacterium found in many environments and causes food poisoning in humans.

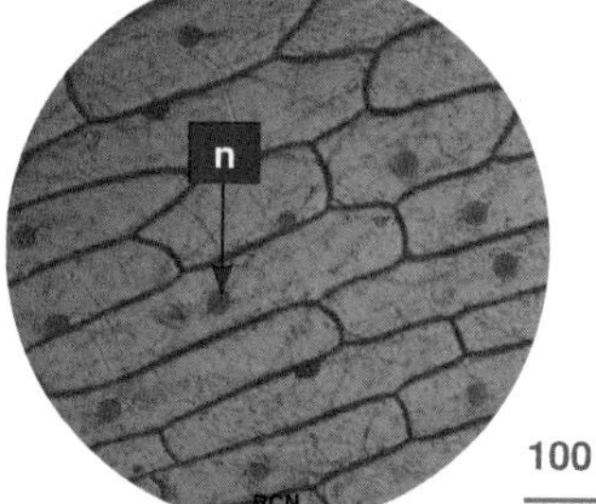

Onion epidermal cells: the nucleus (n) is just visible.

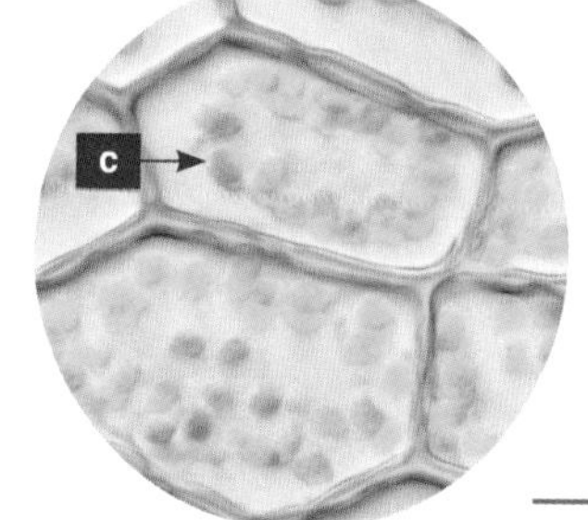

Mosses are low growing primitive plants. In these cells, the chloroplasts (c) can be seen, mostly around the cell edges.

1. Using the measurement scales provided on each of the photographs above, determine the longest dimension (length or diameter) of the cell/animal/organelle indicated in µm and mm. Do not include cilia or flagella. Attach your working:

(a) *Daphnia*: ________ µm ________ mm

(b) *Giardia*: ________ µm ________ mm

(c) Nucleus ________ µm ________ mm

(d) *Elodea* leaf cell: ________ µm ________ mm

(e) Chloroplast: ________ µm ________ mm

(f) *Paramecium*: ________ µm ________ mm

(g) *Salmonella*: ________ µm ________ mm

(h) *Coronavirus*: ________ µm ________ mm

2. Mark and label the examples above on the log scale below according to their size:

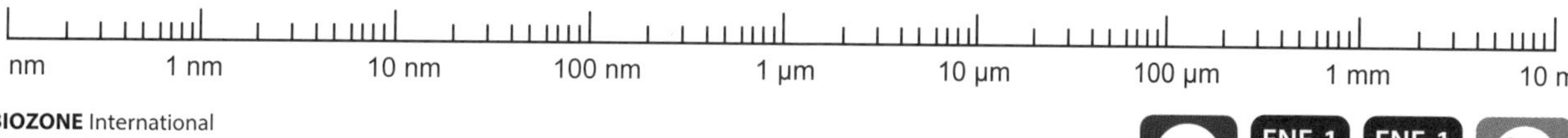

ISBN: 978-1-98-856656-6

Volume of simple three dimensional shapes

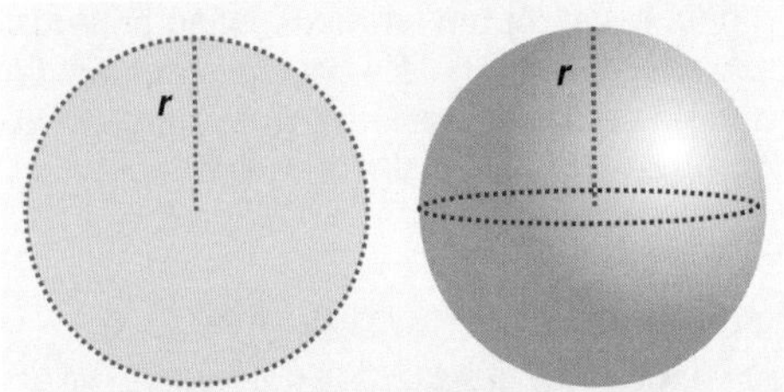

The **circumference** is the linear distance around the edge of a circle or sphere and is given by the formula $2\pi r$

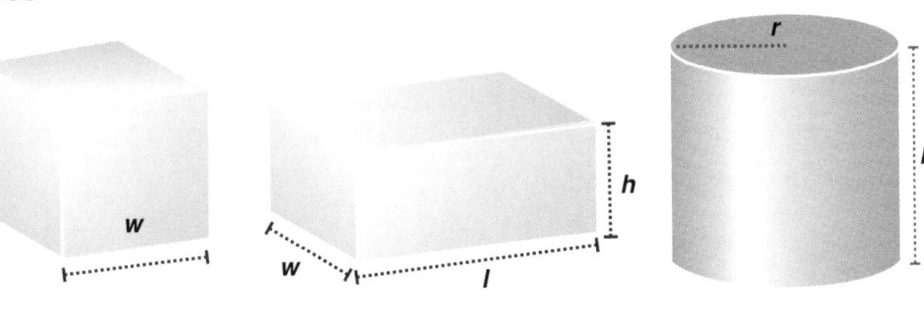

r = radius **l** = length **w** = width **h** = height π = 3.14

	Sphere	Cube	Rectangular prism	Cylinder
Biological example.	*Staphylococcus* bacterial cell	Kidney tubule cell	Intestinal epithelial cell	Axon of neuron
Surface area: The sum of all areas of all shapes covering an object's surface.	$4\pi r^2$	$6w^2$	$2(lh + lw + hw)$	$(2\pi r^2) + (2\pi rh)$
Volume: The amount that a 3-dimensional shape can hold.	$\frac{4}{3}\pi r^3$	w^3	lwh	$\pi r^2 h$

3. For a sphere with a radius of 2 cm, calculate the:

   (a) Circumference: ___

   (b) Surface area: ___

   (c) Volume: ___

4. For a rectangular prism with the dimensions l = 3 mm, w = 0.3 mm, and h = 2 mm calculate the:

   (a) Surface area: ___

   (b) Volume: ___

5. For a cylinder with a radius of 4.9 cm and height of 11 cm, calculate the:

   (a) Surface area: ___

   (b) Volume: ___

6. Find the radius of a cylinder with a volume of 27 cm^3 and a height of 3 cm: ___

7. A spherical bacterium with a radius of 0.2 μm divides in two. Each new cell has a radius that is 80% of the original cell.

   (a) Calculate the surface area of the 'parent' bacterial cell: ___

   (b) Calculate the volume of the 'parent' bacterial cell: ___

   (c) Calculate the surface area of each new cell: ___

   (d) Calculate the volume of each new cell: ___

   (e) Which cell has the greatest surface area to volume ratio? Show your working: ___

8. Many plant cells are rectangular prisms. Measure the moss cell with the chloroplast on the previous page. Assume cell width and height are equal (as above). Record these measurements and calculate the approximate cell volume in μm^3:

ISBN: 978-1-98-856656-6

23 Limitations to Cell Size

Key Question: What sets the limits to a cell's size and how does a cell overcome these limitations?

In order to function, a cell must obtain the raw materials it needs and dispose of the waste products of metabolism. These exchanges must occur across the plasma membrane. In a spherical cell, the cell volume increases faster than the corresponding surface area. As the cell becomes larger, it becomes more and more difficult for it to obtain all the materials it needs to sustain its metabolism. This constraint ultimately limits the size of the cell.

Diffusion

Diffusion is the movement of particles down a concentration gradient. Diffusion is a **passive process**, meaning it needs no input of energy to occur. During diffusion, molecules move randomly about, eventually becoming evenly dispersed.

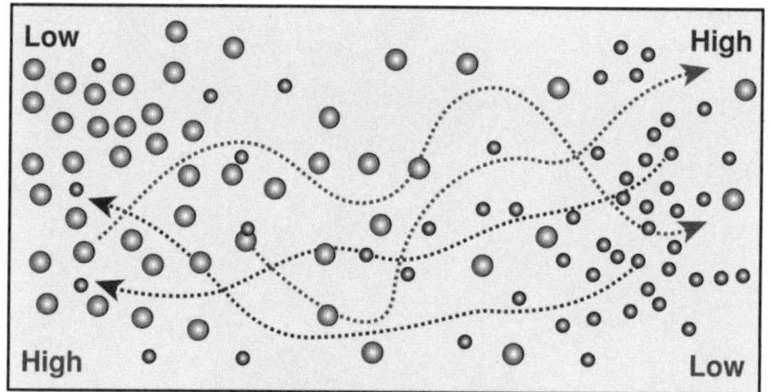

Concentration gradient

If molecules can move freely, they move from high to low concentration (down a concentration gradient) until evenly dispersed. Each molecule moves down its own concentration gradient independent of the concentration gradients of other molecules.

Factors affecting the rate of diffusion

Concentration gradient	The rate of diffusion is higher when there is a greater difference between the concentrations of two regions.
The distance moved	Diffusion over shorter distance occurs at a greater rate than over a larger distance.
The surface area involved	The larger the area across which diffusion occurs, the greater the rate of diffusion.
Barriers to diffusion	Thick barriers have a slower rate of diffusion than thin barriers.
Temperature	Particles at a high temperature diffuse at a greater rate than at a low temperature.
Solubility	Lipid-soluble or non-polar molecules pass across membranes more easily than polar materials, so their rates of diffusion are faster.
Solvent density	As the density of a solvent increases, the rate of diffusion decreases. Cellular dehydration adversely affects diffusion rates within cells.

The effect of increasing size

- The transport of substances across membranes allows cells to exchange matter with their environment. Simple diffusion and transport involving membrane proteins are both affected by cell size and shape because these things affect the amount of surface area available relative to the cell's volume. The larger a cell is the more materials (e.g. oxygen) it needs and the further molecules need to move to reach their destination within the cell.
- A cell's surface area is important in determining how many molecules it can obtain. Its volume is important in determining how quickly molecules can reach certain parts of the cell. Surface area to volume ratio is therefore crucial to cell function.
- The diagram below shows four hypothetical cells of different sizes. They range from a small 2 cm cube to a 5 cm cube (not to scale). How does this change in size affect the surface area and the volume of the cell?

(a) 2 cm cube

(b) 3 cm cube

(c) 4 cm cube

(d) 5 cm cube

1. Use the formulas provided in the previous activity to calculate the surface area (SA), volume (V), and the ratio of surface area to volume (SA:V) for each of the four cuboidal cells **(a)-(d)** above. Show your calculations.

   (a) SA: ____________ V: ____________ SA:V ____________

   (b) SA: ____________ V: ____________ SA:V ____________

   (c) SA: ____________ V: ____________ SA:V ____________

   (d) SA: ____________ V: ____________ SA:V ____________

2. (a) Calculate the SA:V ratios for a 2 μm spherical cell and a 5 μm spherical cell: ____________

   ____

   ____

   (b) What happens to the SA:V ratio of a spherical cell as its size increases? ____________

ISBN: 978-1-98-856656-6

Solving the problem of declining surface area to volume ratios

- The size and shape of a cell reflects its function and the need for essential molecules to move in and out. The greater the spherical diameter of a cell, the more material it contains and the further molecules have to move in order to reach the center. At the same time, its metabolic requirements for raw materials increase. Molecules diffusing into the cell are used up faster than they can be supplied and may not reach the cell's center, leaving it starved of essential molecules (e.g. oxygen).
- The problem of supply and demand can be solved by reducing the diameter of the cell along one axis or elongating it along another. An elongated sphere or cylinder (e.g. a rod shaped cell) has a greater surface area than a sphere of the same volume. In this way, a cell can grow larger while still gaining the materials it needs. The cells of multicellular organisms are often highly specialized to maximize SA: V. The three images below are all to scale.

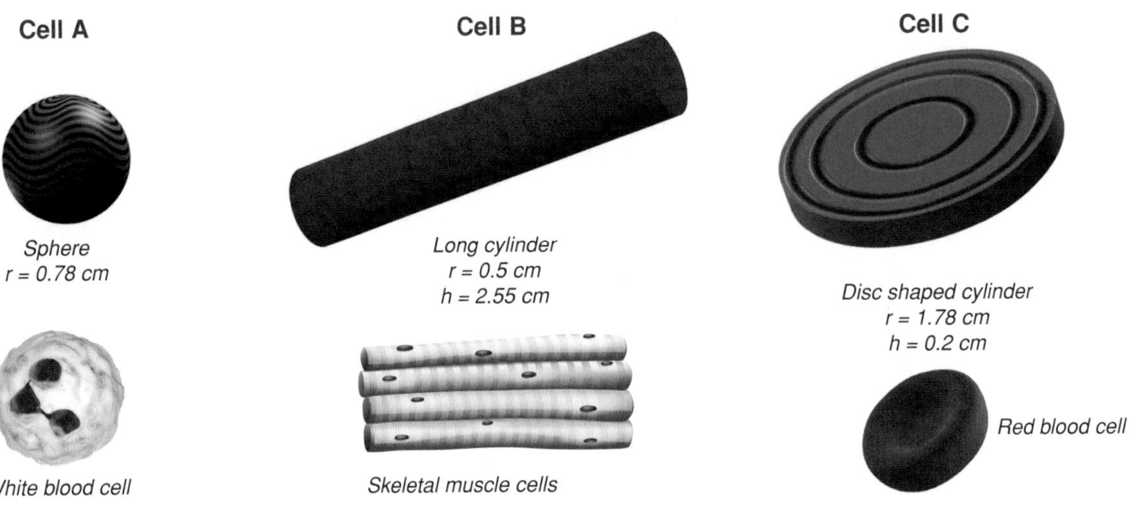

- Compartmentalizing within the cell also helps with issues of size. Specialized organelles can concentrate the reactants they require and so are able to carry out reactions more easily and with greater efficiency.

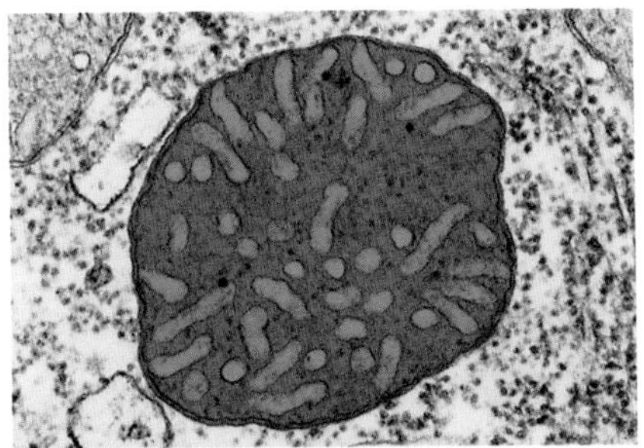

Aerobic cellular respiration occurs within mitochondria, which themselves have specific regions in which different phases occur. A large area of internal membrane is important.

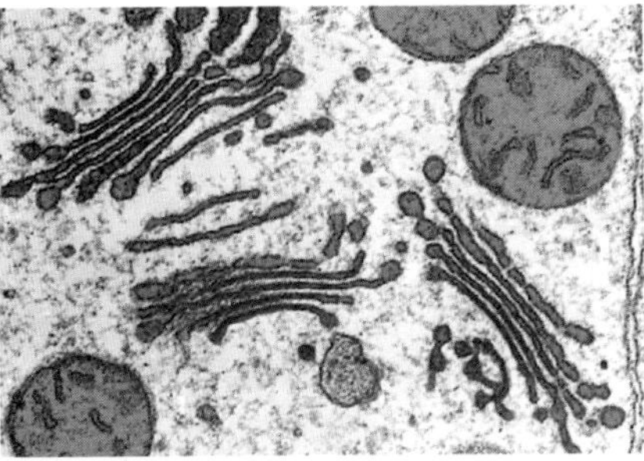

The membrane-bound compartments of the Golgi (green) are responsible for modifying and packaging proteins for secretion. These events are localized for greater efficiency.

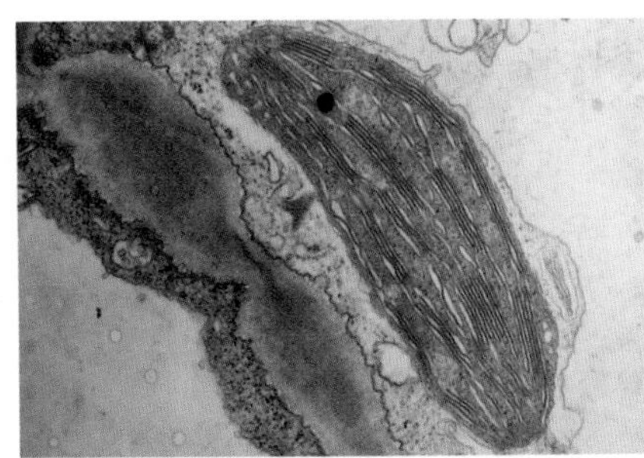

Chloroplasts in plant cells isolate the reactions of photosynthesis from the rest of the cell. Compartments within the chloroplast further isolate the different reaction phases.

3. Use the formulas for a sphere and a cylinder in Activity 22 to calculate the surface area of cell A, B, and C.

   (a) SA cell A: ______________________ (c) SA cell C: ______________________

   (b) SA cell B: ______________________

4. Use the formulas for a sphere and a cylinder in Activity 22 to calculate the volume of cell A, B, and C.

   (a) Volume cell A: ______________________ (c) Volume cell C: ______________________

   (b) Volume cell B: ______________________

5. Which of the cells above (A, B, C) has the greater surface area to volume ratio? Describe how changing the shape of a cell affects its surface area and its ability to obtain nutrients and dispose of wastes:

____

____

____

____

____

ISBN: 978-1-98-856656-6

- Small objects, such as cells, have a large surface area relative to their volume, so diffusion is an effective way to move materials in and out. As an object becomes larger, its surface area to volume ratio decreases and diffusion becomes a less effective way to transport materials to the inside.
- The effectiveness of diffusion is the controlling factor determining how big an individual cell can become. As organisms become larger, their SA:V decreases. This affects their ability to make efficient exchanges with the environment (e.g. for nutrients, gases, and heat). In large, multicellular organisms, specialized systems deliver materials to the cells that make up the body's tissues.

Single-celled organisms

Single-celled organisms (e.g. *Amoeba*), are small and have a large surface area relative to the cell's volume. The cell's requirements can be met by the diffusion or active transport of materials into and out of the cell (below).

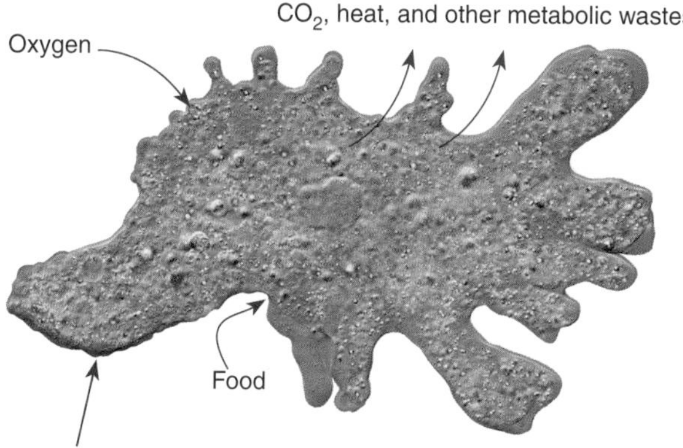

The plasma membrane, which surrounds every cell, regulates movements of substances into and out of the cell. For each square micrometer of membrane, only so much of a particular substance can cross per second.

Multicellular organisms

Multicellular organisms (e.g. plants and animals) generally have a small surface area compared to their volume. They require specialized body systems to transport the materials they need to and from the cells and tissues in their body.

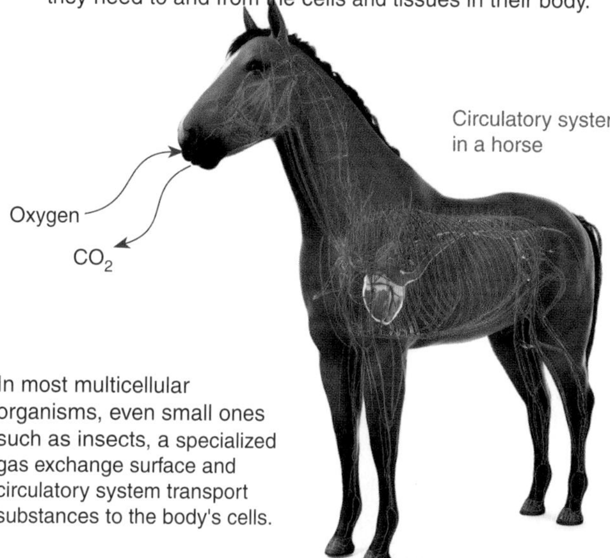

In most multicellular organisms, even small ones such as insects, a specialized gas exchange surface and circulatory system transport substances to the body's cells.

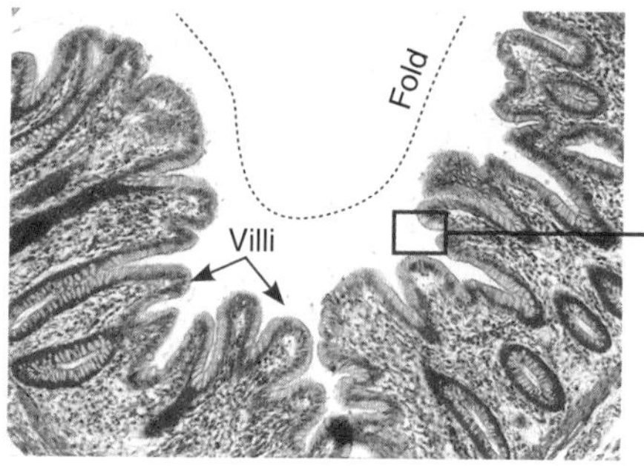

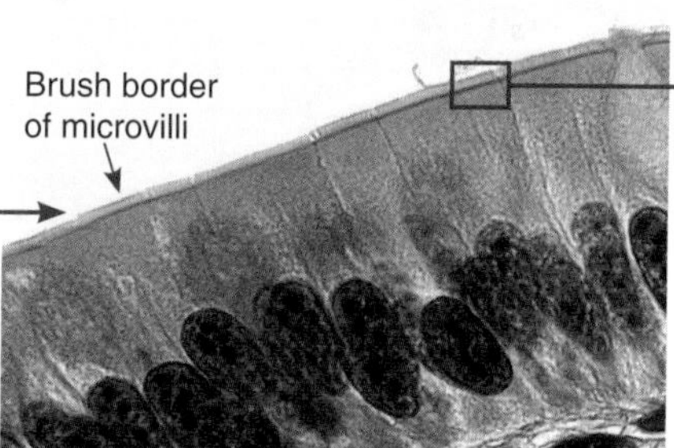

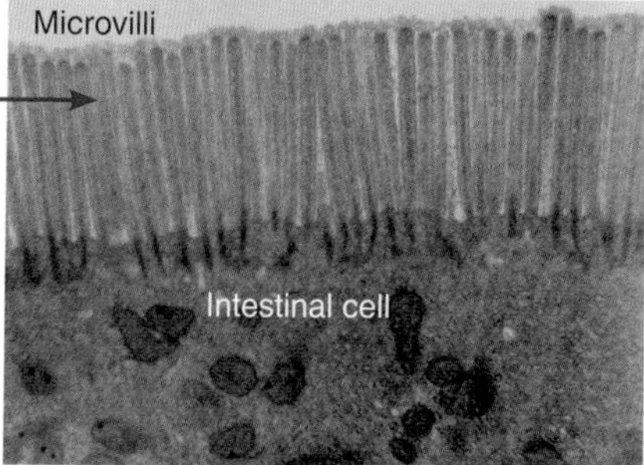

Animal tissues are also organized to increase surface area. Here, the **intestinal wall** has many folds and on those folds are projections or **villi** (image left). Epithelial cells line each villus, each with a brush border of microvilli (image center). The tiny microvilli are extensions of the cell's membrane (image right) and greatly increase the surface area for absorbing nutrients and binding digestive enzymes.

6. What is the purpose of compartmentalization in cells? ______________________

____

____

7. Describe two ways in which eukaryotic cells can efficiently obtain the raw materials they need for metabolism, even as they become larger:

(a) ______________________

(b) ______________________

8. Explain how multicellular organisms have overcome the limitations to size: ______________________

____

____

____

____

ISBN: 978-1-98-856656-6

24 Surface Area and Cell Size

STUDENT SUPPORT FOR INVESTIGATION 4, Procedure 1: *Surface area and cell size*

- As described in the previous activity, the efficiency of diffusion decreases as cell size increases. This can be demonstrated easily in a model system. In this activity you will investigate the effect of surface area: volume ratios on diffusion in model cells.

The aim

To investigate the effect of cell size on diffusion.

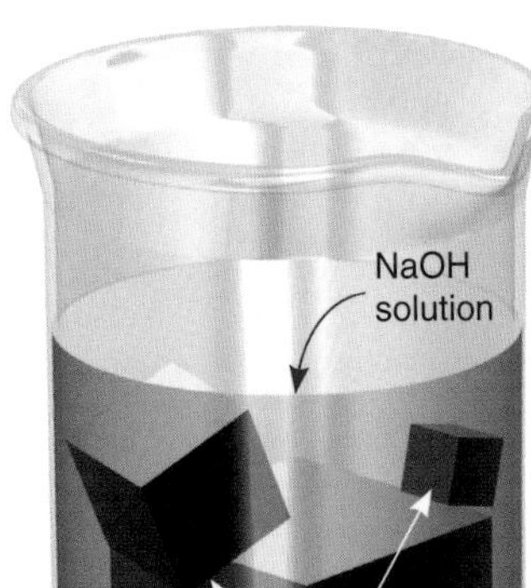

Agar blocks

Background

Oxygen, water, cellular waste, and many nutrients are transported into and out of cells by diffusion. However, at a certain surface area to volume ratio, diffusion becomes inefficient. This activity investigates the relationship between cell size and rate or efficiency of diffusion using agar block as model cells.

- Diffusion of molecules into a cell can be modeled using agar cubes infused with phenolphthalein indicator and soaked in sodium hydroxide (NaOH).
- Phenolphthalein is an acid/base indicator. It turns pink in the presence of a base. As the NaOH diffuses into the agar, the phenolphthalein changes to pink, indicating how far into the agar block the NaOH has diffused (right).
- By cutting an agar block into cubes of various sizes, it is possible to investigate the effect of cell size on diffusion.

Method

Students cut an agar block infused with phenolphthalein into three model cells of 1 cm^3, 2 cm^3, and 4 cm^3. The blocks were placed into a beaker of NaOH and left to soak for 5 minutes (right). The "cells" were then removed and blotted dry. They were cut in half and the region of color change was measured.

The diagram below shows the results.

1. Write a hypothesis for the investigation above: ____________________

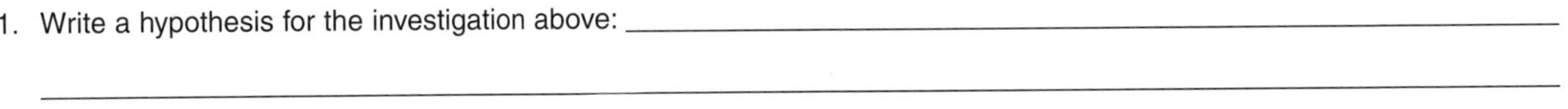

2. Use the diagrams of the cubes below to fill in Table 1. The cubes and color penetration are to scale:

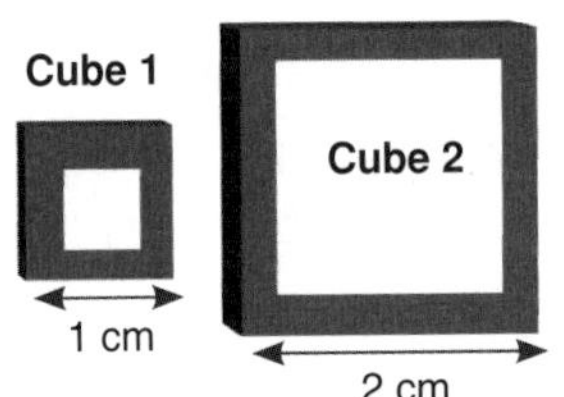

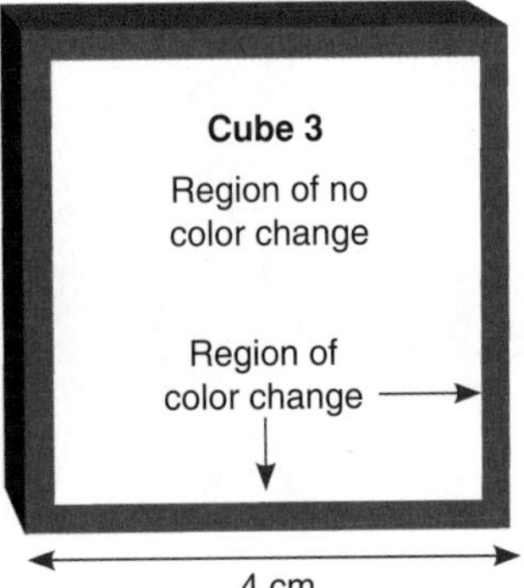

Table 1: Calculations for SA:V and diffusion in agar cubes

	A	B	C	D	E	F	G	H	I
		$= 6A^2$	$= A^3$	= B/C		= C – E	= F/C x 100		= H/5
Cube no.	Length of side of agar cube (cm)	Total surface area of cube (cm^2)	Total volume of the cube (cm^3)	Surface area to volume ratio	Volume not pink (cm^3)	Diffused volume (cm^3)	% diffused	Distance solution diffuses in 5 min (cm)	Rate of diffusion (cm/min)
1									
2									
3									

3. (a) Is there any difference in the rate of diffusion as the size of the agar cubes increases?

____

(b) What happens to the % diffusion as cube size increases? ____________________

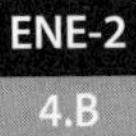
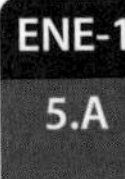

ISBN: 978-1-98-856656-6

4. Diffusion of substances into and out of a cell occurs across the plasma membrane. For a cuboid cell, explain how increasing cell size affects the ability of diffusion to provide the materials required by the cell:

5. (a) Plot the surface area: volume ratio vs the percentage diffusion from Table 1 on the grid below.

(b) What is the % diffusion of a 3 cm^3 cube?

6. A student made an agar cell that was 1 cm high by 2 cm wide by 4 cm long and placed it into a beaker of NaOH for five minutes. If the NaOH diffused into the agar at the same rate as the previous experiment, what would be the percentage diffusion of this cell? How does it compare to the 2 x 2 x 2 cm cell in the previous experiment?

7. (a) What might happen to the % diffusion (in 5 minutes) if the temperature of the NaOH was increased by 5°C?

(b) What might happen to the % diffusion (in 5 minutes) if the temperature of the NaOH was decreased by 5°C?

8. Write a conclusion for this experiment:

ISBN: 978-1-98-856656-6

25 Efficient Exchanges with the Environment

Key Question: How do organisms exchange nutrients with the environment or eliminate metabolic wastes?

The strategy an organism uses to obtain the materials it needs for survival and eliminate its metabolic wastes depends on the size of the organism and its lifestyle. Single celled organisms can meet their needs by diffusion alone, but multicellular organisms must have mechanisms to overcome the size of their body. These include regional specialization (e.g. organs) and transport networks to remove wastes and move nutrients around to where they are needed.

Efficiency starts in the cell

- You have already seen how specific reactions occur within particular organelles within the cells. Membrane-bound organelles increase metabolic efficiency for two reasons. Firstly, reaction pathways, such as cellular respiration, are restricted to a region where all the necessary metabolic components are located together. Secondly, because reactants and products must enter and leave reaction pathways by crossing a membrane, the rate of the reactions can be regulated more easily. The activity of the enzymes in the respiratory pathways within the mitochondrion is regulated by levels of ATP and NADH, and ATP production itself is regulated by ADP supply. The mitochondrion and its specialized internal structure enable precise regulation of substrates and end-products.

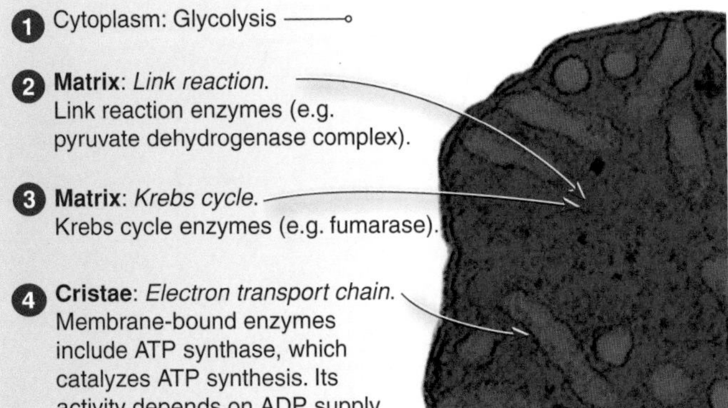
1 Cytoplasm: Glycolysis
2 Matrix: Link reaction. Link reaction enzymes (e.g. pyruvate dehydrogenase complex).
3 Matrix: Krebs cycle. Krebs cycle enzymes (e.g. fumarase).
4 Cristae: Electron transport chain. Membrane-bound enzymes include ATP synthase, which catalyzes ATP synthesis. Its activity depends on ADP supply.
Mitochondrion
WMU

Exchanges in simple organisms

- As we saw for the single celled *Amoeba* earlier, single celled organisms (e.g. *Euglena*, *Amoeba*, and *Paramecium*) can meet their gas exchange requirements by simple diffusion or active transport directly across the plasma membrane. Food is obtained by engulfing food particles to form membrane-bound food vacuoles (*Amoeba*) or by photosynthesis (*Euglena*).
- Some simple multicellular organisms, such as flatworms, can meet their needs for gas exchange by simple diffusion across the body surface. Food is digested by secretion of enzymes outside the body and the digested material is taken up into a simple, highly branched gut.
- In a similar way, insects have a network of tubes, which open to the outside and branch internally to allow gases to penetrate into the tissues. Such systems are only effective for relatively small organisms.

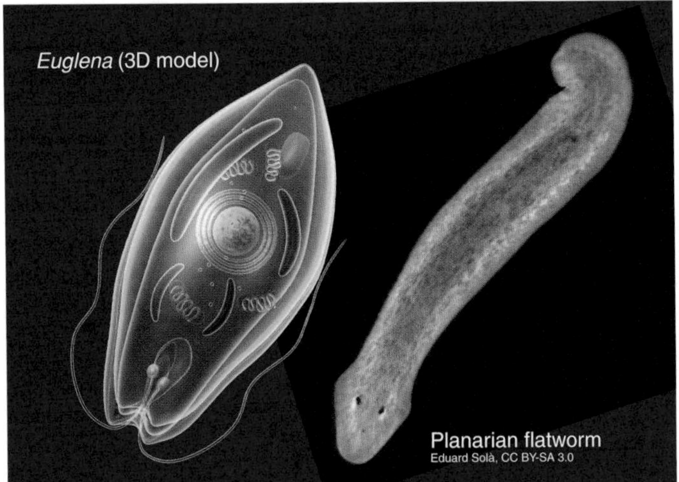
Euglena (3D model)

Planarian flatworm
Eduard Solà, CC BY-SA 3.0

Exchanges in vascular plants

- Plants must overcome two "supply and demand" difficulties. They must have a way to allow carbon dioxide into the leaf to provide the raw material for photosynthesis, but they must limit water loss. The stomata (leaf pores), guard cells (flanking the stomata), and the plant cell vacuole all play important roles in permitting exchanges with the environment.
- Guard cells are specialized cells that occur in pairs in the plant epidermis. They are unevenly thickened and control gas exchange through rapid changes in turgor. When they are swollen (turgid), the stomatal pore is open and water and gases can enter and leave the leaf. When the guard cells lose turgor, they collapse, closing the pore. This reduces water loss but also prevents gas exchange.
- Guard cells make these rapid turgor changes by regulating the movements of osmotically active solutes and so also the osmotic pressure of their vacuoles. The vacuoles either take up or lose water, and consequently enlarge or shrink, changing the turgor of the cell.
- Plants depend on their roots to absorb water and nutrients from the soil. The surface area available for these exchanges is greatly increased by the presence of root hairs, which are lateral extensions of single cells. The root hair cells lack a waterproof cuticle so nutrient and water uptakes can be maximized.

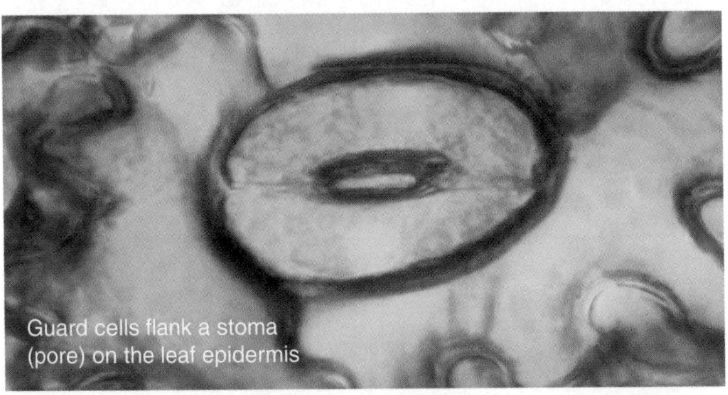
Guard cells flank a stoma (pore) on the leaf epidermis

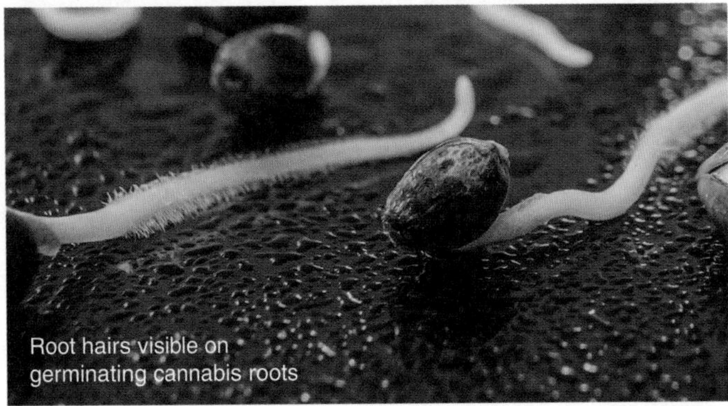
Root hairs visible on germinating cannabis roots

ISBN: 978-1-98-856656-6

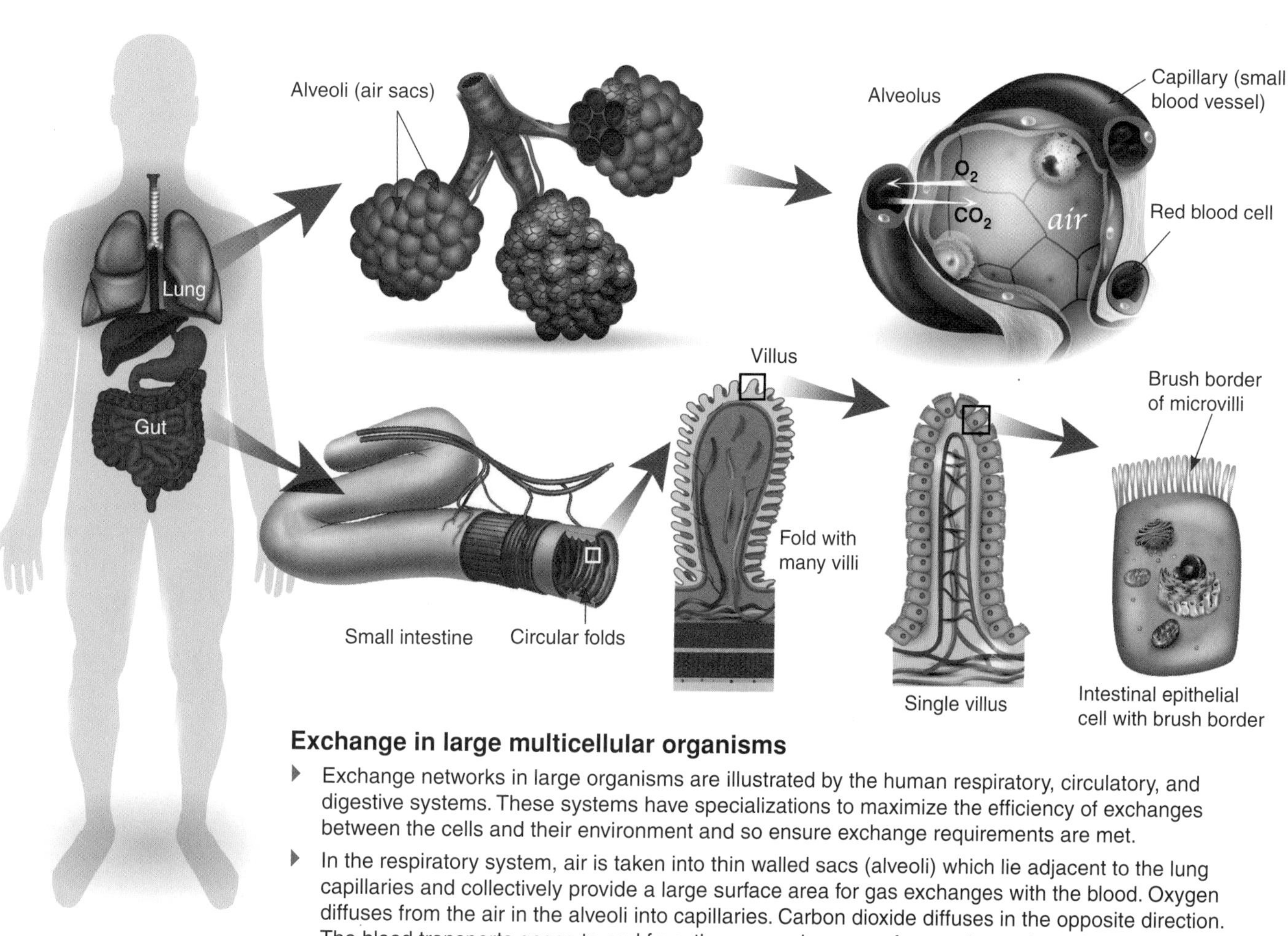

Exchange in large multicellular organisms

- Exchange networks in large organisms are illustrated by the human respiratory, circulatory, and digestive systems. These systems have specializations to maximize the efficiency of exchanges between the cells and their environment and so ensure exchange requirements are met.
- In the respiratory system, air is taken into thin walled sacs (alveoli) which lie adjacent to the lung capillaries and collectively provide a large surface area for gas exchanges with the blood. Oxygen diffuses from the air in the alveoli into capillaries. Carbon dioxide diffuses in the opposite direction. The blood transports gases to and from the gas exchange surface and, together with lung ventilation (breathing), this maintains the concentration gradients for diffusion.
- In the digestive system, surface area for nutrient exchange is increased by several levels of organization. 1) The gut is folded into circular folds. 2) These folds bear many projections called villi, which are lined with epithelial cells. 3) Each epithelial cell has a fringe of microvilli (see Activity 23).

1. Use examples from the opposite page to explain how cells and organisms use specialized exchange surfaces to obtain or release molecules from or into the surrounding environment:

2. Use the diagram above to explain how the organization of tissues in large, multicellular organisms increases the efficiency of exchanges with the environment through increased surface area:

ISBN: 978-1-98-856656-6

26 The Structure of Membranes

Key Question: What are cellular membranes made of and how do they regulate entry into and exit from the cell?

The plasma (or cell surface) membrane encloses the cell's contents and regulates many of the cell's activities. Importantly, it controls what enters and leaves the cell by the use of carrier and channel proteins.

Fluid mosaic model of membrane structure

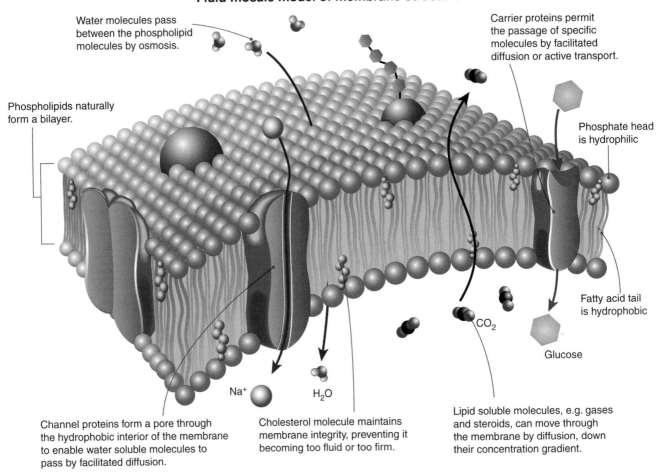

Water molecules pass between the phospholipid molecules by osmosis.

Carrier proteins permit the passage of specific molecules by facilitated diffusion or active transport.

Phospholipids naturally form a bilayer.

Phosphate head is hydrophilic

Fatty acid tail is hydrophobic

CO_2

Glucose

Na^+

H_2O

Channel proteins form a pore through the hydrophobic interior of the membrane to enable water soluble molecules to pass by facilitated diffusion.

Cholesterol molecule maintains membrane integrity, preventing it becoming too fluid or too firm.

Lipid soluble molecules, e.g. gases and steroids, can move through the membrane by diffusion, down their concentration gradient.

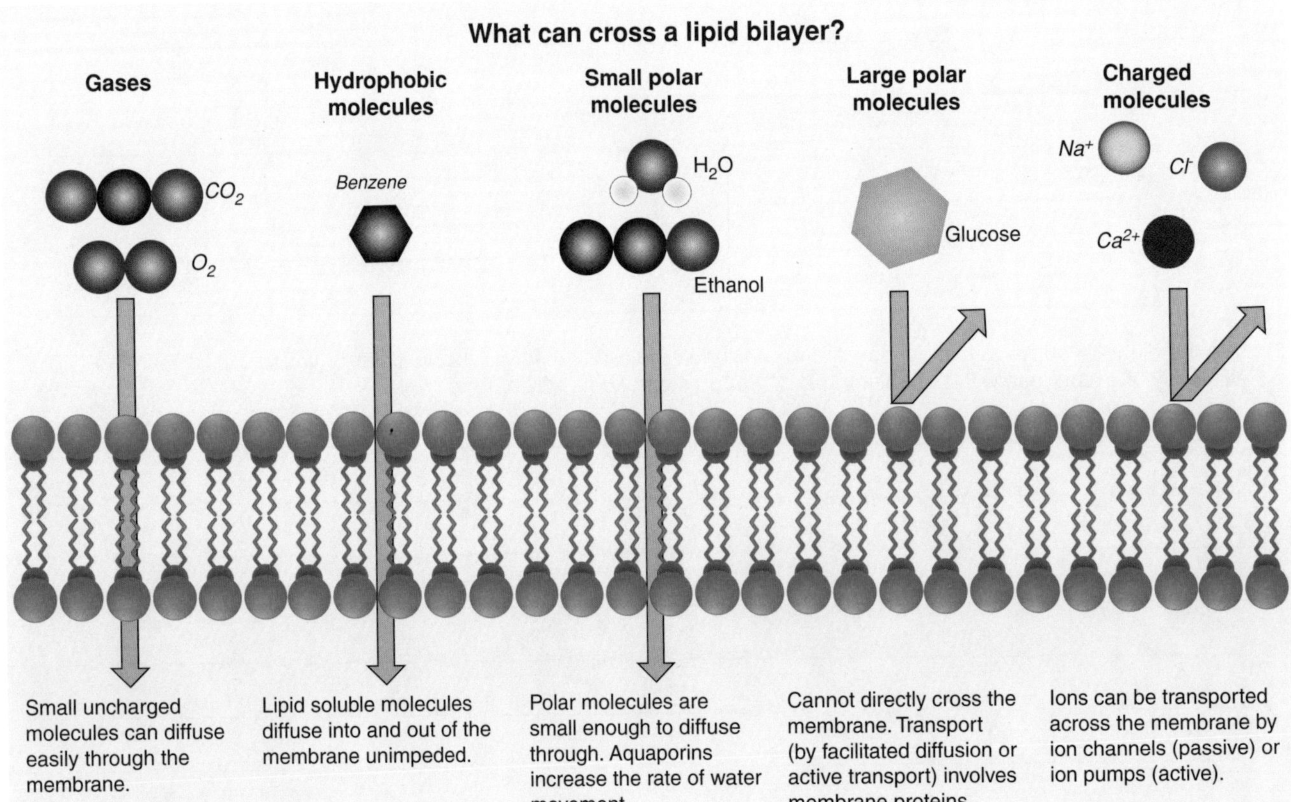

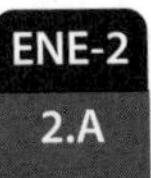

ISBN: 978-1-98-856656-6

What do proteins in the cell surface membrane really look like?

The structure of membrane proteins enables them to perform their particular function in transport, cell signalling, or cell recognition. The proteins are integral to the membrane, and often have parts of their structure projecting from both internal and external sides of the membrane. Note the two types of folding structure in membrane proteins: the alpha helix and the beta pleated sheet.

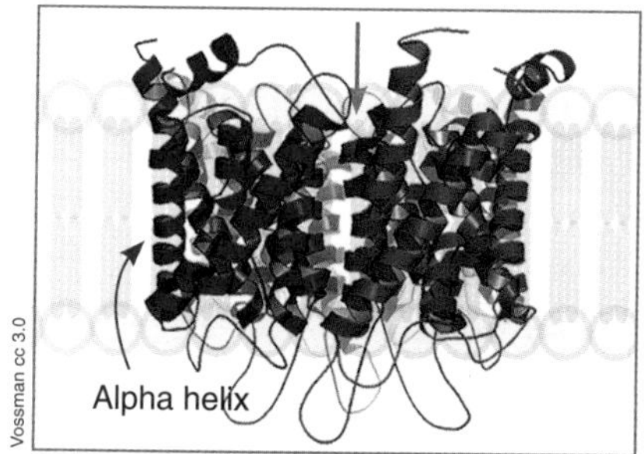

Aquaporins are a special type of channel protein that speed up the passage of water molecules across the membrane. Their tertiary structure creates a pore through the centre of the protein through which molecules can pass (arrow).

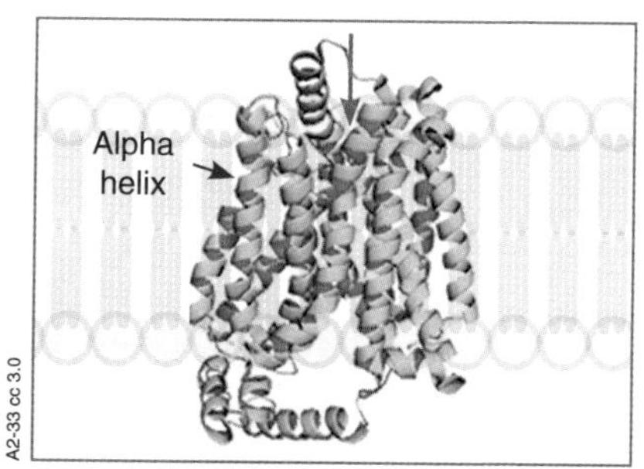

The GLUT1 glucose transporter is a carrier protein that facilitates the transport of glucose across the plasma membranes of mammalian cells. It increases the rate of glucose transport by 50,000X (high enough to supply the cell's energy needs).

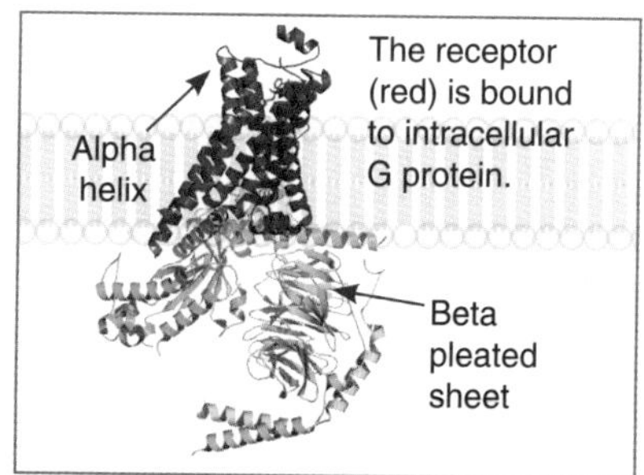

G-protein coupled receptors are proteins involved in signaling pathways. A signal molecule binds to the receptor protein outside the cell to trigger a reaction involving intracellular G protein. In this example, the receptor binds to adrenaline.

1. Describe the general structure and properties of the plasma membrane: Plasma membranes are made up of 2 layers of phospholipids joined together. This called a bilayer. Channel proteins form a pore through the hydrophobic interior of the membrane to enable water soluble molecules to pass by facilitated diffusion.

2. What is the purpose of carrier proteins in the membrane? Carrier proteins permit the passage of specific molecules by facilitated diffusion or active transport.

3. What is the purpose of channel proteins in the membrane? Channel proteins form a pore through the hydrophobic interior of the membrane to enable water soluble molecules to pass by facilitated diffusion.

4. Identify the molecule(s) that:

(a) Can diffuse through the plasma membrane on their own: gases, hydrophobic molecules, small polar molecules.

(b) Can diffuse through the membrane via channel proteins: large polar molecules

(c) Must be transported across the membrane by carrier proteins: charged molecules.

5. Describe the role of the following proteins in the plasma membrane:

(a) Aquaporins: speed up the passage of water molecules across the membrane.

(b) GLUT1 protein: a carrier protein that facilitates the transport of glucose across the plasma membranes of mammals.

(c) G protein: proteins involved in signaling pathways.

ISBN: 978-1-98-856656-6

27 Factors Affecting Membrane Permeability

Key Question: How do temperature and solvents affect the structure of cellular membranes and alter their permeability?

Membrane permeability can be disrupted if membranes are subjected to high temperatures or solvents. At temperatures above the optimum, the membrane proteins become denatured. Alcohols, e.g. ethanol, can also denature proteins. In both instances, the denatured proteins no longer function properly and the membrane loses its selective permeability and becomes leaky. What's more, the combination of alcohol and high temperature can also dissolve lipids.

The aim and hypothesis

To investigate the effect of ethanol concentration on membrane permeability. The students hypothesized that the amount of pigment leaking from the beetroot cubes would increase with increasing ethanol concentration.

Beetroot cubes

Background

Plant cells often contain a large central vacuole surrounded by a membrane called a **tonoplast**. In beetroot plants, the vacuole contains a water-soluble red pigment called betacyanin, which gives beetroot its color. If the tonoplast is damaged, the red pigment leaks out into the surrounding environment. The amount of leaked pigment relates to the amount of damage to the tonoplast.

Method for determining effect of ethanol concentration on membrane permeability

Raw beetroot was cut into uniform cubes using a cork borer with a 4 mm internal diameter. The cubes were trimmed to 20 mm lengths and placed in a beaker of distilled water for 30 minutes. The following ethanol concentrations were prepared using serial dilution: 0, 6.25, 12.5, 25, 50, and 100%.

Eighteen clean test tubes were divided into six groups of three and labeled with one of the six ethanol concentrations. Three cm^3 of the appropriate ethanol solution was placed into each test tube. A beetroot cube (dried by blotting) was added to each test tube. The test tubes were covered with parafilm (plastic paraffin film with a paper backing) and left at room temperature. After one hour the beetroot cubes were removed and the absorbance measured at 477 nm. Results are tabulated, below.

Absorbance of beetroot samples at varying ethanol concentrations

Ethanol concentration (%)	Absorbance at 477 nm			Mean
	Sample 1	Sample 2	Sample 3	
0	0.014	0.038	0.038	0.03
6.25	0.009	0.015	0.023	0.016
12.5	0.010	0.041	0.018	0.023
25	0.067	0.064	0.116	0.082
50	0.945	1.100	0.731	0.925
100	1.269	1.376	0.907	1.184

1. Why is it important to wash the beetroot cubes in distilled water prior to carrying out the experiment? It helps w/ cleaning the cubes on a balanced temperature level.

2. Complete the table above by calculating the mean absorbance for each ethanol concentration:

3. What is absorbance measuring and why is it increasing with increasing ethanol concentration? The absorbance measures how much water and oxygen was taken in by the cubes.

ISBN: 978-1-98-856656-6

4. What was the purpose of the 0% ethanol solution in the experiment described opposite? control group ~~of~~ because of its 0% ethanol concentration

5. (a) Why do you think the tubes were covered in parafilm? so that nothing can contaminate it

(b) How could the results have been affected if the test tubes were not covered with parafilm? there would be unaccounted variables.

6. (a) Plot a line graph of ethanol concentration against mean absorbance on the grid (right):

(b) Describe the effect of ethanol concentration on the membrane permeability of beetroot: ethanol makes the beetroot more permeable.

7. Some students wanted to find out how temperature affected membrane permeability. They prepared the beetroot cubes the same way as in the previous experiment.

(a) Write a hypothesis for their experiment: the higher the temperature the more permeable the membrane becomes.

(b) List an appropriate range of temperatures for the experiment: 0°C, 32°C, 80°C

(c) Write the method for the experiment: create 3 different tubes/cubes, put them in distilled water, each w/ different temperatures and record the results after conducting it 3 times.

(d) Make a prediction about the results based on your understanding of cellular processes: I think the high temperature will break down the membrane of the beetroot + it will turn pale.

ISBN: 978-1-98-856656-6

28 The Role of the Cell Wall

Key Question: How does the structure and function of cell walls vary among different organisms?

Cell walls are structural components of cells external to the plasma membrane. They are composed of complex carbohydrates: cellulose in plants, chitin in fungi and peptidoglycan in bacteria (although not Archaea). Cell walls provide support and protection for the cell, preventing over expansion when the pressure inside a cell rises. In bacteria, cell wall composition is important in distinguishing bacterial groups and may also contribute to virulence.

Capkuckokos CC 4.0

Xylem cell wall (plant)

Functions of the cell wall

- **Support**: Maintains mechanical strength and supports the cell.
- **Offsets osmotic influx**: Internal pressure from the cell's contents (turgor pressure) presses the plasma membrane against the cell wall. Turgor pressure limits cell volume and is important for supporting primary plant tissues.
- **Regulate growth**: The cell wall helps regulate the cell cycle.
- **Permeability**: The cell wall is freely permeable to water, ions, and other small molecules including small proteins, but molecules larger than 60,000 Da can't cross, so the cell wall represents a permeability barrier to some molecules. Larger molecules can move between cells via cellular connections through the cell wall called plasmodesmata.
- **Protection**: Because it excludes larger particles, the cell wall provides some protection against viruses and bacteria.
- **Storage**: The cell wall is a major store of complex carbohydrate.

Plant cell walls

Carbohydrates: cellulose, hemicellulose, pectin

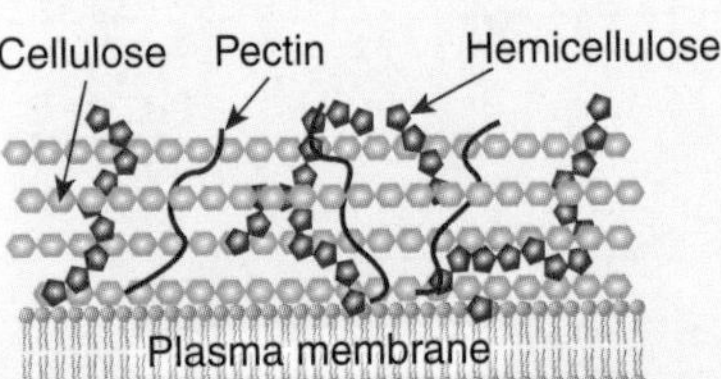

Bacterial cell walls

Carbohydrate: peptidoglycan

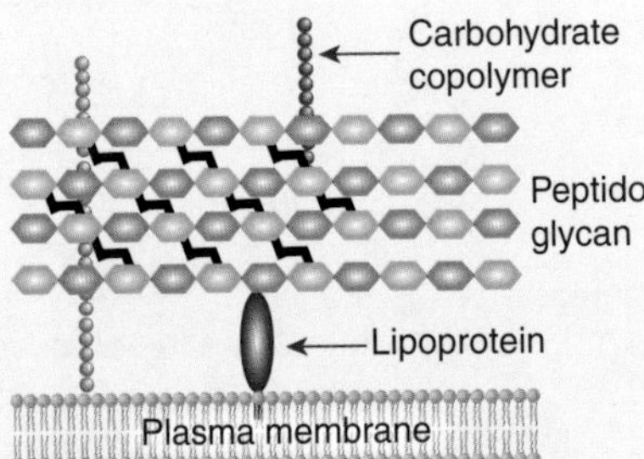

Fungal cell walls

Carbohydrates: chitin, glucan

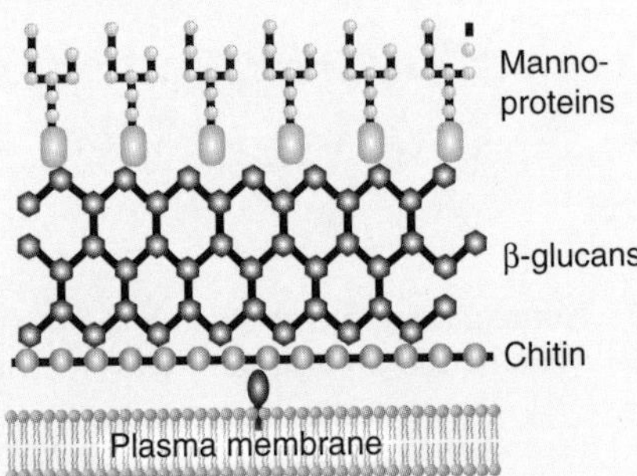

- **Plant cell walls** have three major elements: cellulose, hemicellulose, and pectin. Hemicellulose links the cellulose into a matrix, which is embedded with pectin, an acidic polysaccharide.
- **Bacterial cell walls** are divided into two major groups, Gram-positive or Gram-negative, based on the wall's retention of a crystal violet stain. Gram positive cell walls (above) contain more peptidoglycan than Gram negative walls, which have only a thin peptidoglycan layer sandwiched between an inner (plasma) and outer membrane. Bacterial cell walls provide structural support and determine shape. The composition of the wall also contributes to virulence and is a factor in antibiotic sensitivity.
- **Fungal cell walls** are a unique structure of chitin, β-glucans (β-D-glucose polysaccharides), and mannoproteins (proteins with mannose sugar attached). The wall provides cell rigidity and shape and helps the fungus adhere to nutrient-rich substrates.

1. Describe the roles of the cell wall in organisms: Maintains mechanical strength + supports the cell, offsets osmotic influx, regulate growth, permeability, protection, and storage.

2. (a) How are the cell walls of bacteria, plants, and fungi similar? Each one contains carbohydrates.

(b) What makes them different? plant cells have 3 elements, bacteria has 2, and fungal has a lot more

3. Predict the effect on a plant cell if the cell wall structure is compromised by disease: The cell will most likely self destruct in apoptosis.

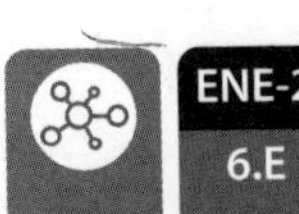
ENE-2 6.E 19

ISBN: 978-1-98-856656-6

29 Passive Transport

Key Question: How do cells facilitate and control diffusion of molecules into and out of the cell?

In biological systems, most diffusion occurs across membranes. Some molecules move freely (unassisted) across the membrane by simple diffusion. For other molecules, their diffusion is facilitated by specific carrier and channel proteins in the membrane. Diffusion is important in allowing cells to make exchanges with their extracellular environment (e.g. the blood and fluids that bathe them) and is crucial to the regulation of water content.

Diffusion across the membrane

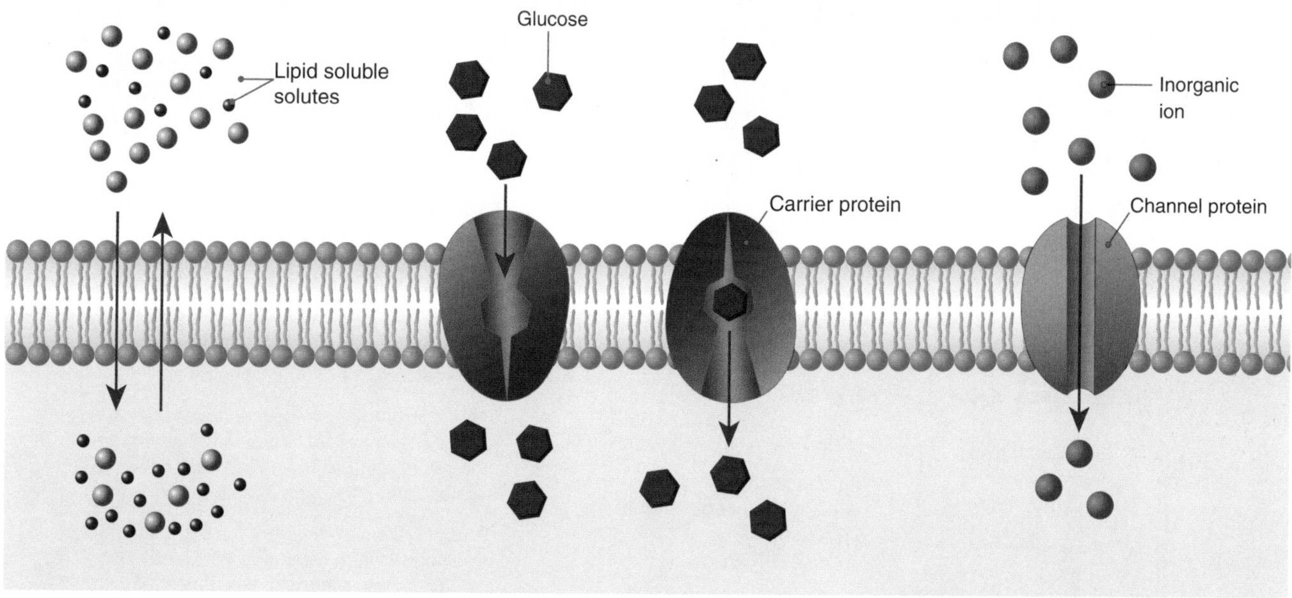

Simple diffusion
Molecules move directly through the plasma membrane without assistance. Example: O_2 diffuses into the blood and CO_2 diffuses out. Diffusion gradients are maintained because substances are constantly being imported, made, or used by the cell.

Facilitated diffusion involving carrier proteins
Carrier proteins in the membrane allow large lipid-insoluble molecules that cannot cross the membrane by simple diffusion to be transported into the cell. Example: The transport of glucose into red blood cells.

Facilitated diffusion involving channel proteins (hydrophilic pores)
Channel proteins (water-filled pores) in the plasma membrane allow inorganic ions to pass through. **Aquaporins** are special channel proteins for rapid diffusion of water. Example: K^+ ions exiting nerve cells to restore resting potential.

1. What do the three types of diffusion described above all have in common? They all involve the transport of different types of molecules.

2. How does facilitated diffusion differ from simple diffusion? Facilitated diffusion occurs through channel/carrier proteins and simple diffusion occurs w/o assistance

3. Why is carbon dioxide able to continually diffuse out of cells? Because it is a molecule that can cross the cell membrane through simple diffusion.

4. Why would a thin flat cell have a greater rate of diffusion to and from its centre than a thick spherical cell?
Because through a thin wall, molecules can pass through much faster compared to a thicker wall.

ISBN: 978-1-98-856656-6

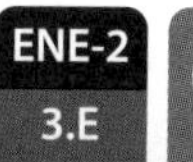

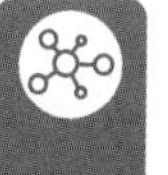

- **Osmosis** is the diffusion of water molecules from regions of lower solute concentration (higher free water concentration) to regions of higher solute concentration (lower free water concentration) across a partially permeable membrane. A partially permeable membrane allows some molecules, but not others, to pass through.
- Water molecules will diffuse across a partially permeable membrane until an equilibrium is reached and net movement is zero. The plasma membrane of a cell is an example of a partially permeable membrane. Osmosis is a passive process and does not require any energy input.

Demonstrating osmosis

Osmosis can be demonstrated using dialysis tubing in a simple experiment (described below). Dialysis tubing, like all cellular membranes, is a partially permeable membrane.

A sucrose solution (high solute concentration) is placed into dialysis tubing and the tubing is placed into a beaker of distilled water (low solute concentration). The difference in sucrose (solute) concentration between the two solutions creates an osmotic gradient. Water moves by osmosis into the sucrose solution and the volume of the solution inside the dialysis tubing increases.

The dialysis tubing acts as a partially permeable membrane, allowing water to pass freely, while keeping the sucrose inside.

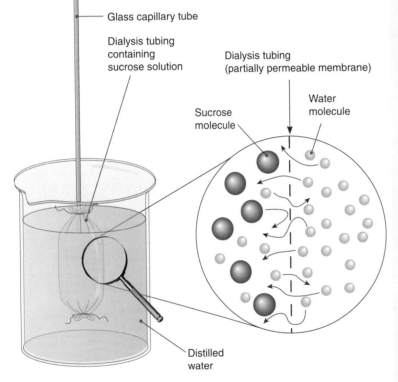

Glass capillary tube

Dialysis tubing containing sucrose solution

Dialysis tubing (partially permeable membrane)

Water molecule

Sucrose molecule

Distilled water

Osmotic potential

The presence of solutes (dissolved substances) in a solution increases the tendency of water to move into that solution. This tendency is called the osmotic potential or osmotic pressure. The more total dissolved solutes a solution contains, the greater its osmotic potential.

Osmolarity and tonicity

Osmolarity and tonicity are related but distinct terms and often confused. Both terms compare the solute concentrations of two solutions separated by a membrane, but terms ending in -osmotic (e.g. isosmotic) are not equivalent to terms ending in -tonic (e.g. isotonic). The difference relates to whether the solutes can cross the membrane (penetrating) or not (non-penetrating).

Osmolarity (osmotic concentration) takes into account the total concentration of penetrating and non-penetrating solutes. The greater the solute concentration, the higher the osmolarity.

Tonicity is the measure of the osmotic pressure gradient between two solutions. Unlike osmolarity, tonicity is only influenced by solutes that cannot cross the semipermeable membrane, because these are the only solutes influencing the osmotic pressure gradient and osmosis must occur for the two solutions to reach equilibrium. Solutions are usually categorized as isotonic, hypotonic, or hypertonic depending of whether they have the same, lower, or higher solute concentration relative to another solution across a membrane.

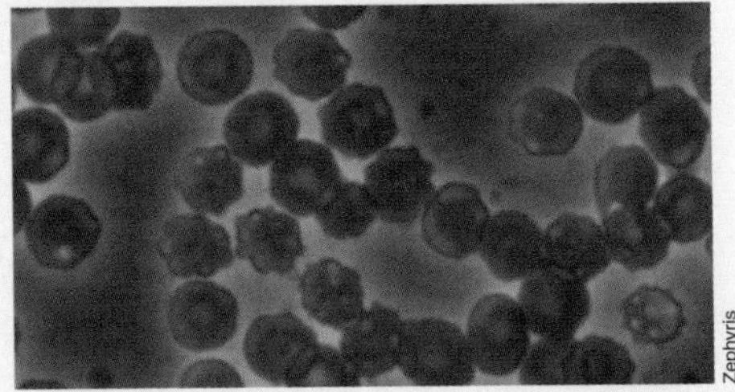

The red blood cells above were placed into a hypertonic solution. As a result, the cells have lost water and shrunk, losing their discoid shape.

5. What is osmosis? Osmosis is the diffusion of water molecules from regions of lower solute concentration to regions of higher solute concentration.

6. (a) In which direction (left or right) will be the net movement of water in the diagram above? low to high

   (b) Why did water move in this direction? Because there were more solutes inside the tubing and more concentration of water on the outside.

7. Propose a method for increasing the height the water travels in the capillary tube: you can fill the inside of the tube w/ greater amounts of solute.

ISBN: 978-1-98-856656-6

30 Diffusion and Osmosis in a Cell

STUDENT SUPPORT FOR INVESTIGATION 4, Procedure 2: *Diffusion and osmosis*

The pores of the dialysis tubing determine the size of the molecules that can pass through. The experiment described below demonstrates the difference between sucrose and glucose when placed into partially permeable membrane with pores large enough only for glucose and water (but not sucrose) to move through.

Aim

To demonstrate how the size difference between sucrose and glucose affects diffusion osmosis using a partially permeable membrane.

Hypothesis

Sucrose is larger than glucose and will remain inside the model cell and the cell will gain mass (water) by osmosis. The glucose cell will gain less mass as some glucose diffuses out of the cell, reducing osmotic gain.

Background

Dialysis tubing acts as a partially (or selectively) permeable membrane. It comes in many pore sizes and only allows molecules smaller than the size of the pore to pass through.

Glucose is a monosaccharide whereas sucrose is a disaccharide (consisting of a glucose and a fructose molecule joined together). Sucrose is effectively twice the size and mass of glucose.

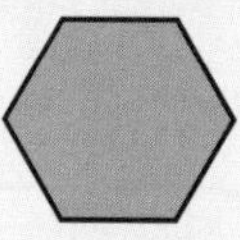
Glucose

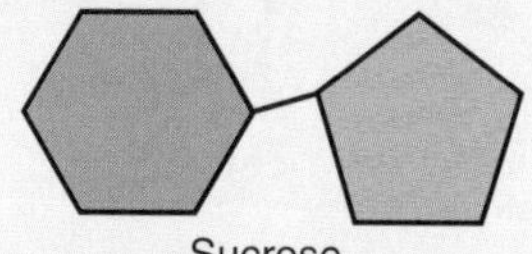
Sucrose

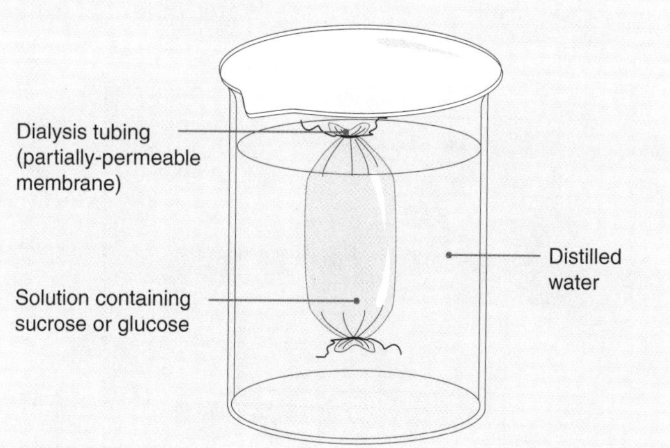

Method

Two model cells of dialysis tubing were filled with 5 cm^3 each of a 1 mol/L sucrose solution and a 1 mol/L glucose solution.

The dialysis tubing cells were tied off and weighed to 2 decimal places. They were then placed in separate beakers of distilled water for 10 minutes.

After 10 minutes the cells were removed from the distilled water and blotted dry with a paper towel. They were reweighed and their masses recorded.

The experiment was carried out three times.

Results

Sucrose				
Cell	Final mass (g)	Initial mass(g)	change (g)	% change
1	11.22	10.39		
2	11.23	10.33		
3	12.03	10.98		
Mean				

Glucose				
Cell	Final mass (g)	Initial mass(g)	change (g)	% change
1	11.00	10.35		
2	11.15	10.47		
3	11.28	10.55		
Mean				

1. Calculate the mean percentage change in mass for the sucrose and glucose cells in the table above:

2. Explain the result in terms of movement of the molecules, diffusion, and osmosis, given that sucrose has a relative mass of 342.3 g/mol, glucose a relative mass of 180.2 g/mol, and water a relative mass of 18 g/mol.

ISBN: 978-1-98-856656-6

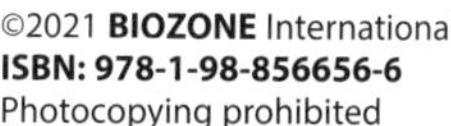

31 Water Relations in Plant Cells

Key Question: What is water potential and how can it be used to explain the tendency of water to move from one region to another by osmosis?

The **water potential** of a solution, denoted by the Greek letter psi (ψ) is the term given to the tendency for water molecules to enter or leave a solution by osmosis. The tendency for water to move into or out of a living cell can be calculated on the basis of the water potential of the cell sap relative to its surrounding environment. The use of water potential to express water relations of plant cells is used in preference to osmotic potential and osmotic pressure, although these terms are often used in medicine and animal physiology.

Water potential (ψ) and water movement

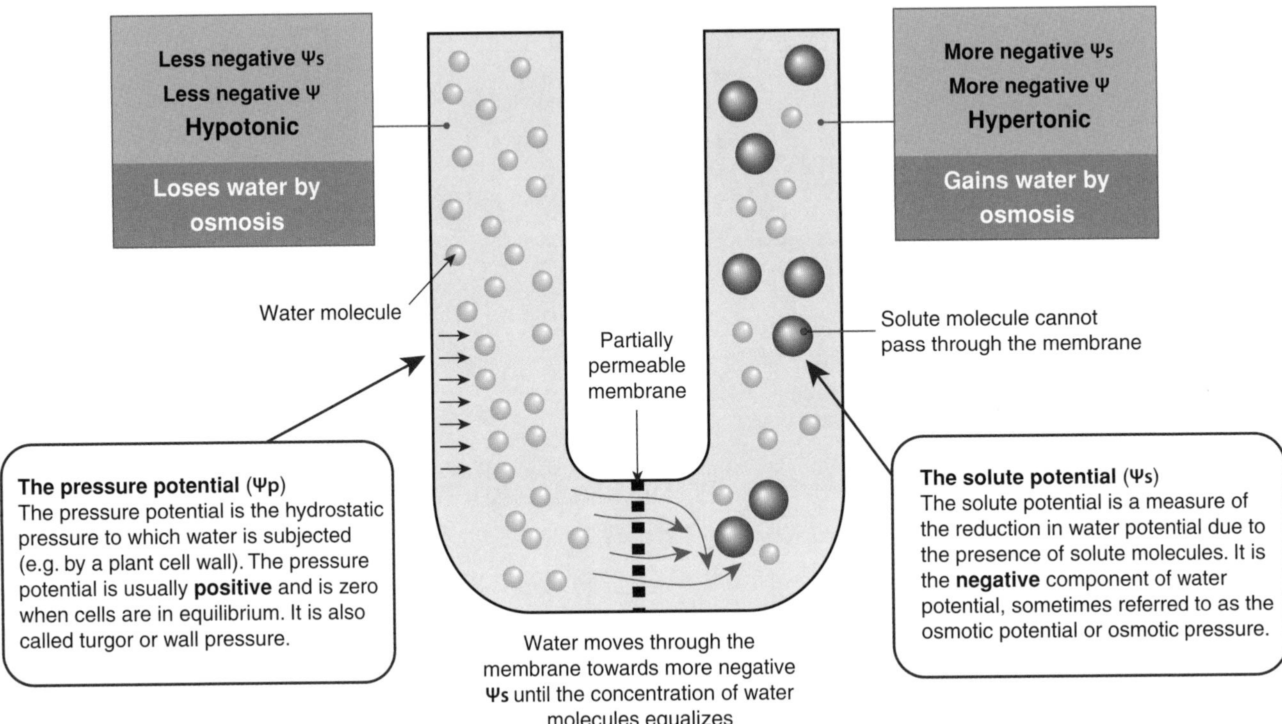
Less negative Ψs
Less negative Ψ
Hypotonic
Loses water by osmosis
More negative Ψs
More negative Ψ
Hypertonic
Gains water by osmosis
Water molecule
Partially permeable membrane
Solute molecule cannot pass through the membrane
The pressure potential (Ψp)
The pressure potential is the hydrostatic pressure to which water is subjected (e.g. by a plant cell wall). The pressure potential is usually positive and is zero when cells are in equilibrium. It is also called turgor or wall pressure.
The solute potential (Ψs)
The solute potential is a measure of the reduction in water potential due to the presence of solute molecules. It is the negative component of water potential, sometimes referred to as the osmotic potential or osmotic pressure.
Water moves through the membrane towards more negative Ψs until the concentration of water molecules equalizes

As water molecules move around, some collide with the plasma membrane and create pressure on the membrane called water potential (ψ).The greater the movement of water molecules, the higher their water potential. The presence of solutes (e.g. sucrose) lowers water potential because the solutes restrict the movement of water molecules. Pure water has the highest water potential (zero). Dissolving any solute in water lowers the water potential (makes it more negative).

Water always diffuses from regions of less negative to more negative water potential. Water potential is determined by two components: the **solute potential**, ψ_s (of the cell sap) and the **pressure potential**, ψ_p, expressed by:

$$\Psi_{cell} = \Psi_s + \Psi_p$$

The closer a value is to zero, the higher its water potential.

1. What is the water potential of pure water? 0

2. The diagrams below show three hypothetical situations where adjacent cells have different water potentials. For each pair (a)-(c) calculate ψ for each side and describe the net direction of water flow (A→B, B→A or no net movement):

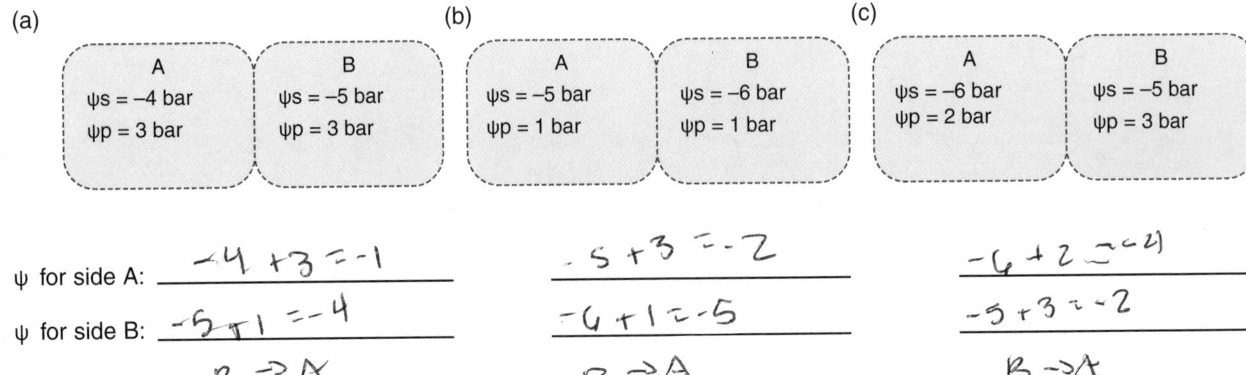
(a)
A
ψs = –4 bar
ψp = 3 bar
B
ψs = –5 bar
ψp = 3 bar
(b)
A
ψs = –5 bar
ψp = 1 bar
B
ψs = –6 bar
ψp = 1 bar
(c)
A
ψs = –6 bar
ψp = 2 bar
B
ψs = –5 bar
ψp = 3 bar
ψ for side A: -4 + 3 = -1 | -5 + 3 = -2 | -6 + 2 = -4
ψ for side B: -5 + 1 = -4 | -6 + 1 = -5 | -5 + 3 = -2
Direction: B → A | B → A | B → A

ISBN: 978-1-98-856656-6

- When the contents of a plant cell push against the cell wall they create **turgor** (tightness). Turgor provides support for the plant body. When cells lose water, there is a loss of turgor and the plant wilts. Complete loss of turgor from a cell is called **plasmolysis** and is irreversible.

- The diagram below shows the state of a cell when the external water potential is more negative than the cell's contents (left) and when it is less negative than the cell's contents (right). When the external water potential is the same as that of the cell, there is no net movement of water.

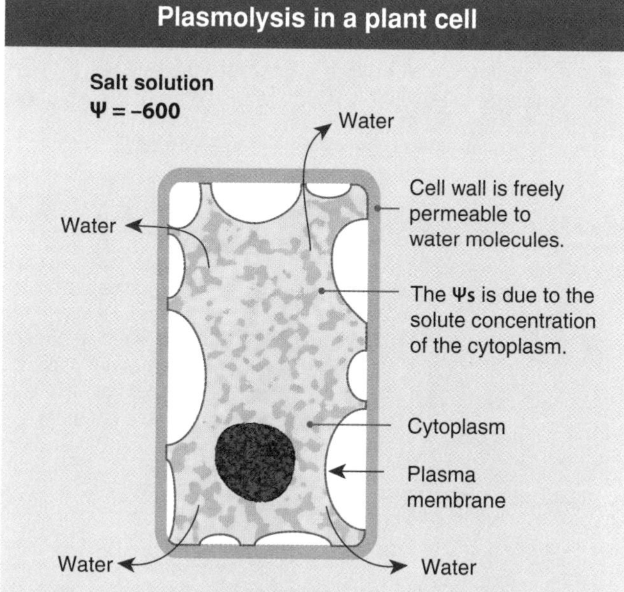

When external water potential is more negative than the water potential of the cell ($\Psi_{cell} = \Psi_s + \Psi_p$), water leaves the cell and, because the cell wall is rigid, the plasma membrane shrinks away from the cell wall. This process is termed **plasmolysis** and the cell becomes flaccid ($\Psi_p = 0$). Full plasmolysis is irreversible because the cell cannot recover by taking up water.

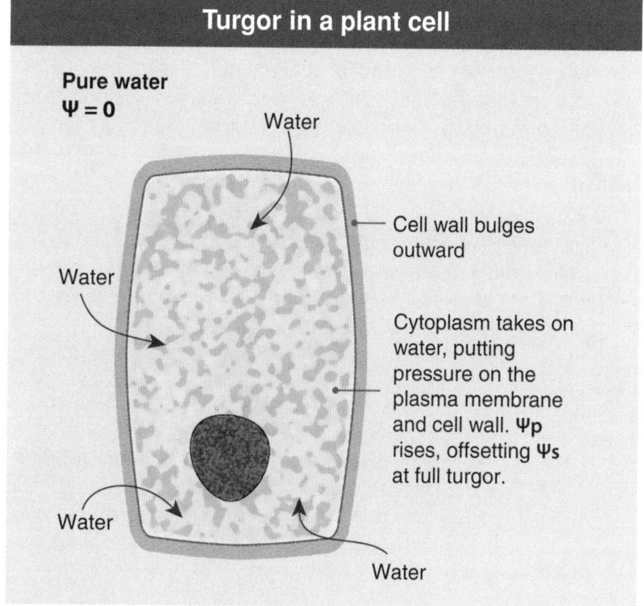

When the external water potential is less negative than the Ψ_{cell}, water enters the cell. A pressure potential is generated when sufficient water has been taken up to cause the cell contents to press against the cell wall. Ψ_p rises progressively until it offsets Ψ_s. Water uptake stops when the $\Psi_{cell} = 0$. The rigid cell wall prevents cell rupture. Cells in this state are **turgid**.

3. What is the effect of dissolved solutes on water potential? dissolved solutes reduce water potential

4. Why don't plant cells burst when water enters them? the cell wall bulges outward and the cytoplasm takes in the water to put pressure on the cell wall to bulge out

5. (a) Distinguish between plasmolysis and turgor: plasmolysis is when external water potential is more negative than the water potential of the cell water leaves the cell (plasma shrinks)

   (b) Describe the state of the plant in the photo on the right and explain your reasoning: The plant is drooping down and seems to have too much water.

6. (a) Explain the role of pressure potential in generating cell turgor in plants: Pressure potential generates turgor because pressure from water on the plasma membrane creates a bulge outward

   (b) Explain the purpose of cell turgor to plants: it creates a rigid cell wall to prevent cell rupture.

ISBN: 978-1-98-856656-6

32 Solute Potential and Cells

Key Question: How is solute potential calculated and how can it be used to determine a cell's water potential?

Recall the contributors to a cell's water potential and their relationship to the movement of water into and out of cells. The water potential of a plant cell can be calculated by measuring the gain or loss in mass when the cells are placed into solutions with a range of known concentrations. Cells placed into different concentrations will either gain or lose water depending on whether their internal water potential (ψ) is higher (less negative) or lower (more negative) than the solution's. Cells with a water potential equal to the surrounding solution will neither gain or lose water (mass). A solution in an open beaker has no pressure acting on it ($\psi_p = 0$). For cells in this system, the only important factor in determining a cell's water potential is the solute potential of the solution. If the cell neither gains nor loses water, then its water potential is equal to the solute potential of the solution:

$$\psi_{cell} = \psi_{beaker} = \psi_{p(beaker)} (=0) + \psi_{s(beaker)}$$

Solute potential

- Solute potential is the pressure needed to be applied to a solution to stop the inward flow of water across a partially permeable membrane due to solutes. It is always negative in a plant cell and zero in distilled water. It is measured in bars (1 bar = 1 atmosphere at sea level).
- Solute potential can be calculated using the formula:

$$\psi_s = -iCRT$$

i = ionization constant (this is the number of particles produced per unit when dissolved. For example the ionization constant for sucrose is 1, whereas for NaCl it is 2 (Na^+ and Cl^-).

C = molar concentration (mol/L)

R = pressure constant = 0.0831 liter bars/mole K

T = temperature (K) = 273 + °C of solution.

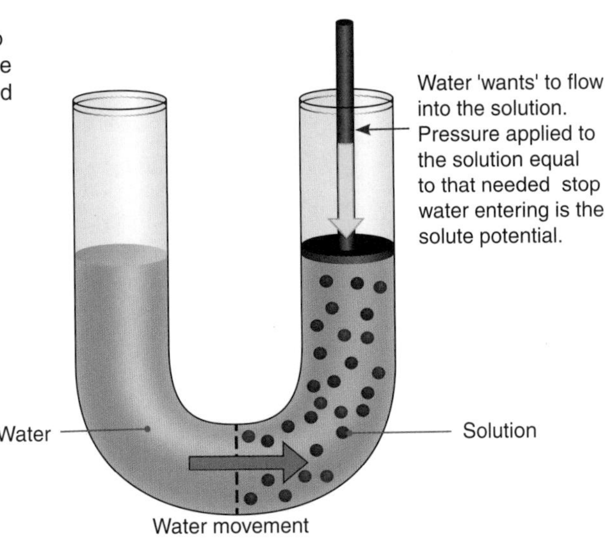

Water 'wants' to flow into the solution. Pressure applied to the solution equal to that needed stop water entering is the solute potential.
Water
Solution
Water movement

1. What is the ionization constant for the following substances?

(a) Glucose: 1 (b) KCl: 10.1 (c) $MgCl_2$: 30.4

2. A student made up three solutions of sucrose with the following concentrations: 1.00 mol/L, 0.50 mol/L, and 0.25 mol/L. Calculate the solute potentials for each solution at 22°C:

(a) 1.00 mol/L: -1 CRT = -1 (1) (0.0831) (295K) = -24.5

(b) 0.50 mol/L: -1 (0.5) (0.0831) (295K) = -12.3

(c) 0.25 mol/L: -1 (0.25) (0.0831) (295K) = 6.13

3. Plot a graph of the of solute potential vs sucrose concentration on the grid below:

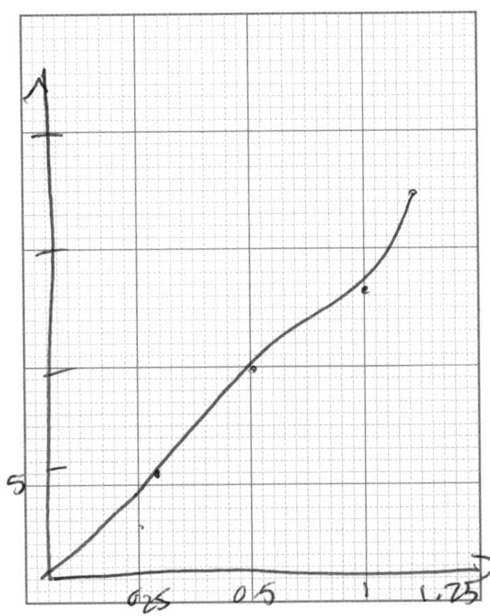

4. Use the plot to determine the solute potential of a 0.75 mol/L solution: ≈ 17 mol/L

ISBN: 978-1-98-856656-6

33 Osmosis in Potato Cells

STUDENT SUPPORT FOR INVESTIGATION 4, Procedure 3: *Observing osmosis in living cells*

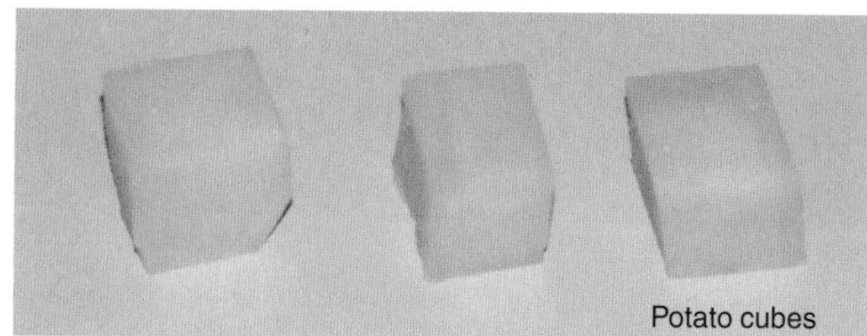
Potato cubes

KP

1. Complete the table (below right) by calculating the total mass of the potato cubes, the total change in mass, and the total % change in mass for all the sucrose concentrations.

2. Use the grid below to draw a line graph of the sucrose concentration vs total percentage change in mass:

3. (a) Use the graph to estimate the osmolarity of the potato at equilibrium (the point of no change in mass):

   (b) What is the pressure potential (ψp) of the solution in the beaker?

   (c) What is the solute potential (ψs) of the solution in the beaker at equilibrium?

   (d) Use the equation ψ = ψs + ψp to determine the water potential of the potato cells at equilibrium:

See the previous activity for background information.

Aim

To determine the water potential of potatoes by placing potato cubes in varying solutions of sucrose, $C_{12}H_{22}O_{11}$.

Method

Fifteen identical 1.5 cm^3 cubes of potato were cut and weighed in grams to two decimal places. Five solutions of sucrose were prepared in the following range (in mol/L): 0.00, 0.25, 0.50, 0.75, 1.00. Three potato cubes were placed in each solution, at 22°C, for two hours, stirring every 15 minutes. The cubes were then retrieved, patted dry on blotting paper and weighed again.

Results

	Potato sample	Initial mass (I) (g)	Final mass (F) (g)
[Sucrose] 0.00 mol/L	1	5.11	6.00
	2	5.15	6.07
	3	5.20	5.15
Total			
Change (C) (F-I) (g)			
% change (C/I x 100)			
[Sucrose] 0.25 mol/L	1	6.01	4.98
	2	6.07	5.95
	3	7.10	7.00
Total			
Change (C) (F-I) (g)			
% change (C/I x 100)			
[Sucrose] 0.50 mol/L	1	6.12	5.10
	2	7.03	6.01
	3	5.11	5.03
Total			
Change (C) (F-I) (g)			
% change (C/I x 100)			
[Sucrose] 0.75 mol/L	1	5.03	3.96
	2	7.10	4.90
	3	7.03	5.13
Total			
Change (C) (F-I) (g)			
% change (C/I x 100)			
[Sucrose] 1.00 mol/L	1	5.00	4.03
	2	5.04	3.95
	3	6.10	5.02
Total			
Change (C) (F-I) (g)			
% change (C/I x 100)			

ISBN: 978-1-98-856656-6

34 Active Transport

Key Question: How does active transport move molecules against their concentration gradient across a partially permeable membrane?

Active transport is the movement of molecules (or ions) from regions of low concentration to regions of high concentration across a cellular membrane by a transport protein. Active transport needs energy to proceed because molecules are being moved against their concentration gradient.

- The energy for active transport comes from ATP (adenosine triphosphate). Energy is released when ATP is hydrolysed (water is added) forming ADP (adenosine diphosphate) and inorganic phosphate (Pi).
- Transport (carrier) proteins in the membrane are used to actively transport molecules from one side of the membrane to the other (below).
- Active transport can be used to move molecules into and out of a cell.
- Active transport can be either primary or secondary. **Primary active transport** directly uses ATP for the energy to transport molecules. In **secondary active transport**, energy is stored in a concentration gradient. The transport of one molecule is coupled to the movement of another down its concentration gradient, ATP is not directly involved in the transport process.

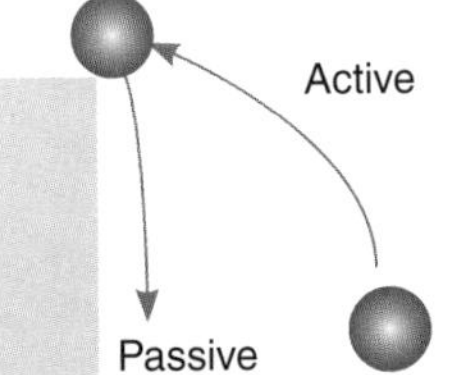

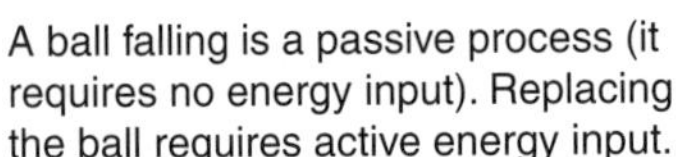
A ball falling is a passive process (it requires no energy input). Replacing the ball requires active energy input.

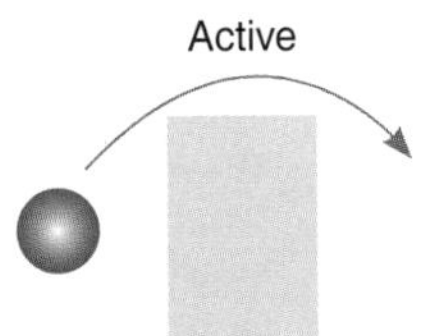

It requires energy to actively move an object across a physical barrier.

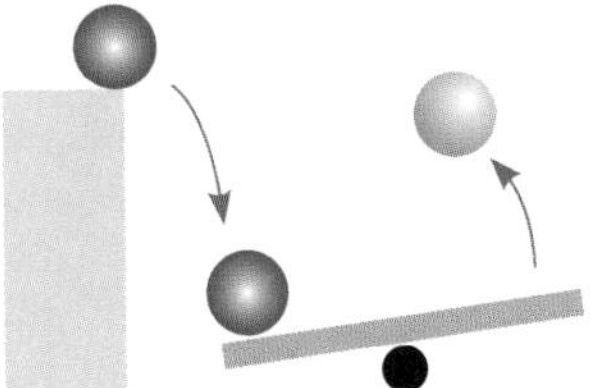
Sometimes the energy of a passively moving object can be used to actively move another. For example, a falling ball can be used to catapult another (left).

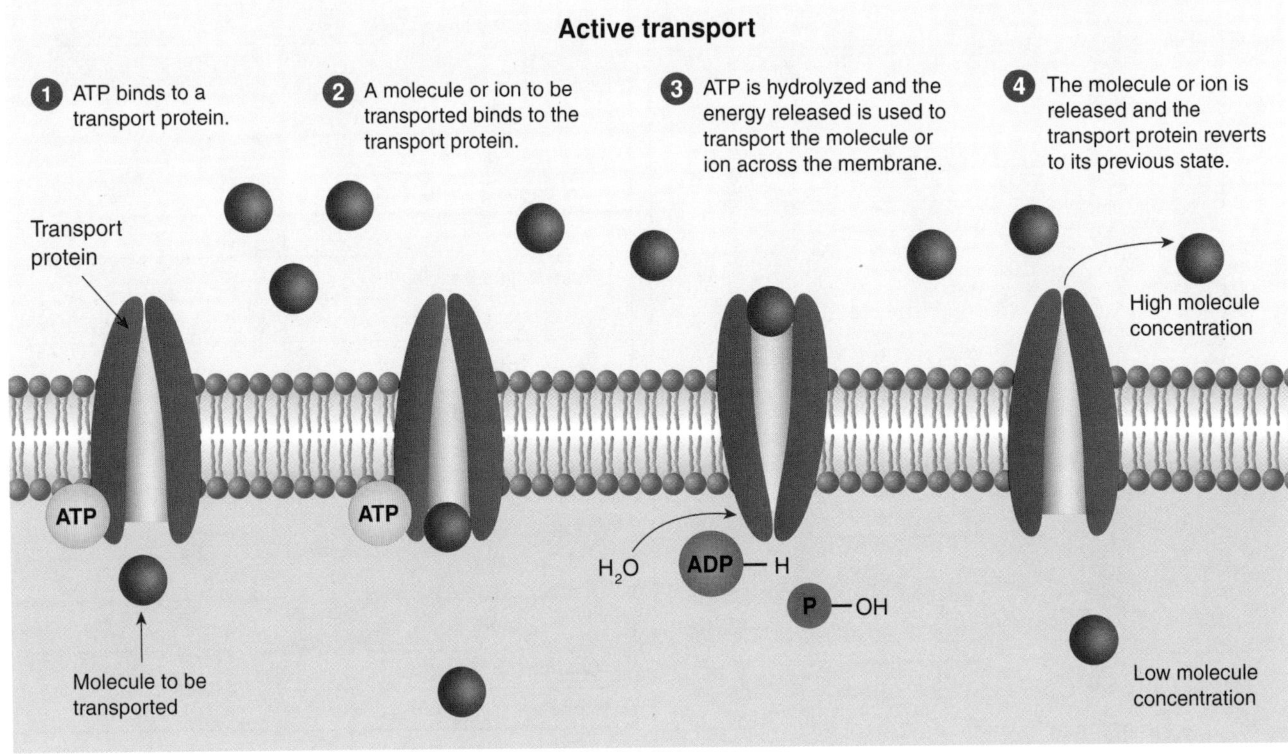

Active transport
1 ATP binds to a transport protein.
2 A molecule or ion to be transported binds to the transport protein.
3 ATP is hydrolyzed and the energy released is used to transport the molecule or ion across the membrane.
4 The molecule or ion is released and the transport protein reverts to its previous state.
Transport protein
ATP
ATP
Molecule to be transported
H2O
ADP — H
P — OH
High molecule concentration
Low molecule concentration

1. (a) What is the essential feature of active transport? ______

   (b) How is active transport used in the cell? ______

2. Where does the energy for active transport come from? ______

3. Explain the difference between primary active transport and secondary active transport: ______

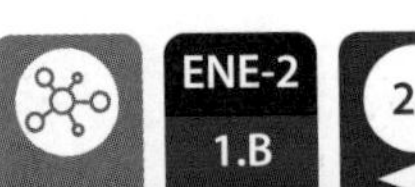

ISBN: 978-1-98-856656-6

35 Ion Pumps

Key Question: What are ion pumps and how do they move molecules and ions against their concentration gradients?

Molecules or ions are often needed in concentrations that diffusion alone cannot supply, or they cannot diffuse through the plasma membrane. In this case, ion pumps are used to transport them across the membrane. Ions are charged, so their movements can create a potential difference (voltage) across membranes. The combination of concentration gradient and voltage that affects an ion's movement is called an **electrochemical gradient**. The electrochemical gradient created by ion pumps is often coupled to the transport of other molecules such as glucose across the membrane.

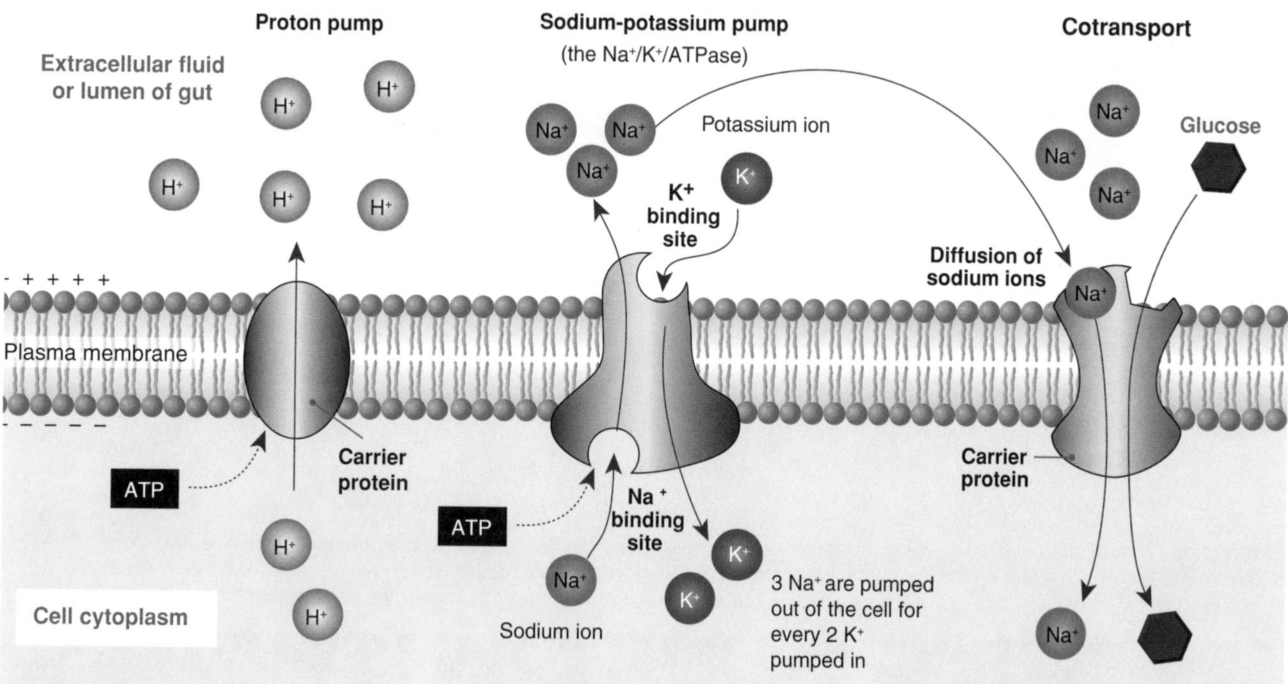

Proton pumps

Proton pumps create a potential difference across a membrane by using energy (ATP or electrons) to move H^+ from one side of the membrane to the other. This difference can be coupled to the transport of other molecules. In cell respiration and the light reactions of photosynthesis, the energy for moving the H^+ comes from electrons, and the flow of H^+ back across the membrane drives ATP synthesis via the membrane-bound enzyme ATP synthase.

Sodium-potassium pump

The sodium-potassium pump is a transmembrane protein that uses energy from ATP to exchange Na^+ for K^+ across the membrane. The unequal balance of Na^+ and K^+ across the membrane creates large electrochemical gradients that can be used to drive transport of other substances (e.g. cotransport of glucose). The Na^+/K^+ pump also helps to maintain ion balance and so helps regulate the cell's water balance.

Cotransport (coupled transport)

A gradient in sodium ions drives the active transport of **glucose** in intestinal epithelial cells. The specific transport protein couples the return of Na^+ down its electrochemical gradient to the transport of glucose into the intestinal epithelial cell. Glucose diffuses from the epithelial cells and is transported away in the blood. A low intracellular concentration of Na^+ (and therefore the concentration gradient) is maintained by a sodium-potassium pump.

1. Why is ATP required for membrane pump systems to operate? __________

2. (a) Explain what is meant by cotransport: __________

   (b) How is cotransport used to move glucose into the intestinal epithelial cells? __________

   (c) What happens to the glucose that is transported into the intestinal epithelial cells? __________

3. Describe two consequences of the extracellular accumulation of sodium ions: __________

ISBN: 978-1-98-856656-6

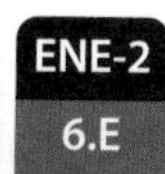

36 Cytosis

Key Question: How does the folding of the plasma membrane enable the cell to bring in or export material?

Cytosis is an active process involving the plasma membrane. In exocytosis, vesicles merge with the plasma membrane to export material from the cell. Endocytosis is a general term for engulfing of material by infolding of the plasma membrane.

Exocytosis

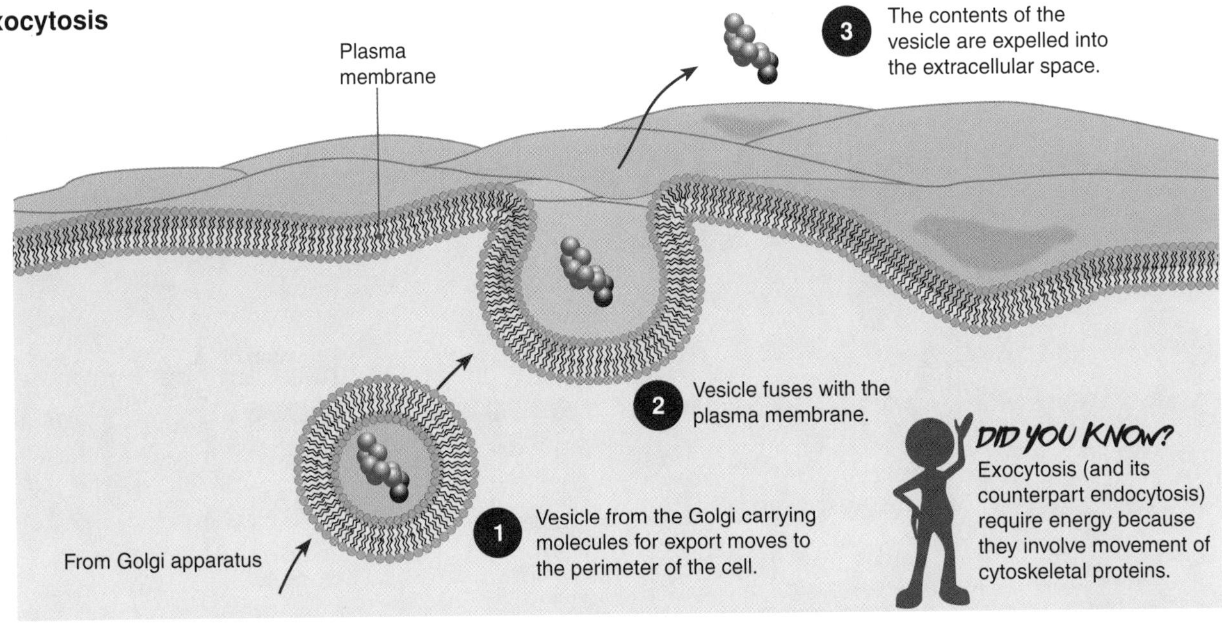

Plasma membrane
3 The contents of the vesicle are expelled into the extracellular space.
2 Vesicle fuses with the plasma membrane.
1 Vesicle from the Golgi carrying molecules for export moves to the perimeter of the cell.
From Golgi apparatus
DID YOU KNOW?
Exocytosis (and its counterpart endocytosis) require energy because they involve movement of cytoskeletal proteins.

Exocytosis (above) is an active transport process in which a secretory vesicle fuses with the plasma membrane and expels its contents into the extracellular space. In multicellular organisms, various types of cells (e.g. endocrine cells and nerve cells) are specialized to manufacture products, such as proteins, and then export them from the cell to elsewhere in the body or outside it.

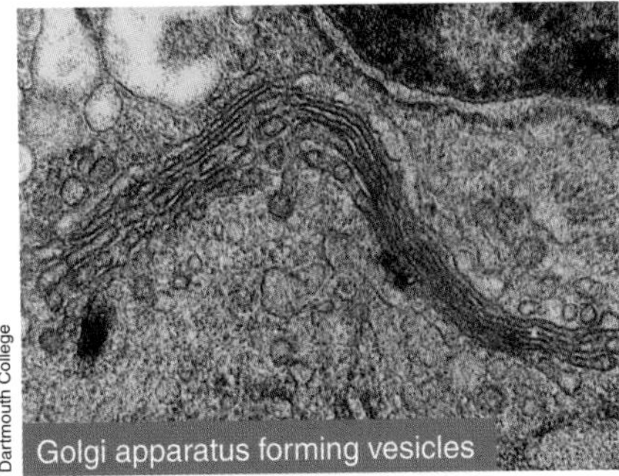

The transport of Golgi vesicles to the edge of the cell and their expulsion from the cell occurs through the activity of the cytoskeleton. This requires energy (ATP).

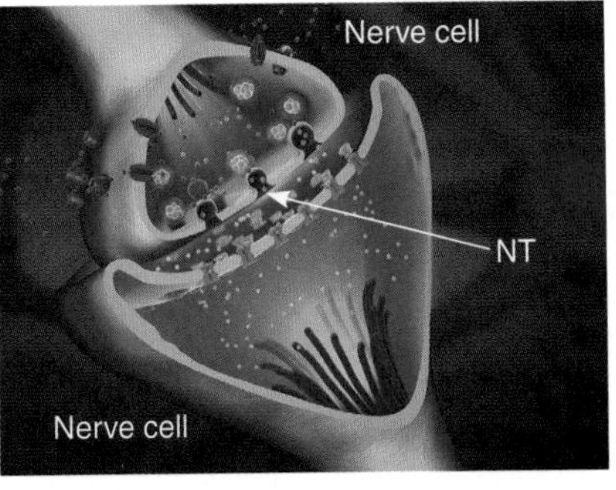

Exocytosis is important in the transport of neurotransmitters (NT) into the junction (synapse) between nerve cells to transmit nervous signals, as shown in this illustration.

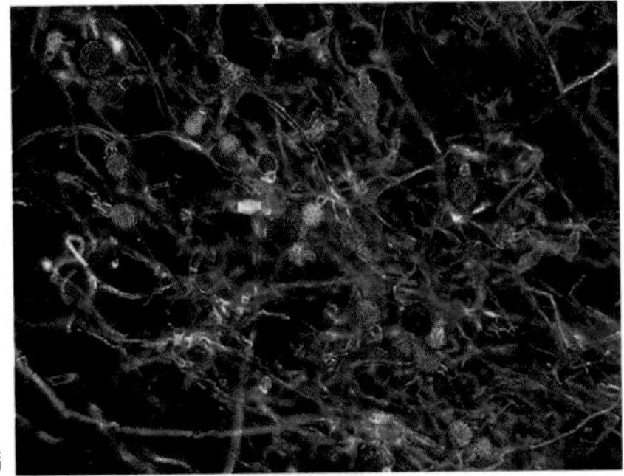

Fungi and bacteria use exocytosis to secrete digestive enzymes, which break down substances extracellularly so that nutrients can be absorbed (by endocytosis).

1. (a) What is the purpose of exocytosis? ______________________

____

(b) How does it occur? ______________________

____

____

2. Describe two examples of the role of exocytosis in cells:

(a) ______________________

____

____

(b) ______________________

____

____

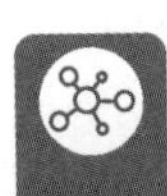
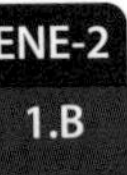

ISBN: 978-1-98-856656-6

Endocytosis

Endocytosis is a type of active transport in which the plasma membrane folds around a substance to transport it across the plasma membrane into the cell. The ability of cells to do this is a function of the fluid nature of the plasma membrane.

Material (solids or fluids) that are to be brought into the cell are engulfed by an infolding of the plasma membrane.

Plasma membrane

Vesicle buds inwards from the plasma membrane

The vesicle carries molecules into the cell. The contents may then be digested by enzymes delivered to the vacuole by lysosomes.

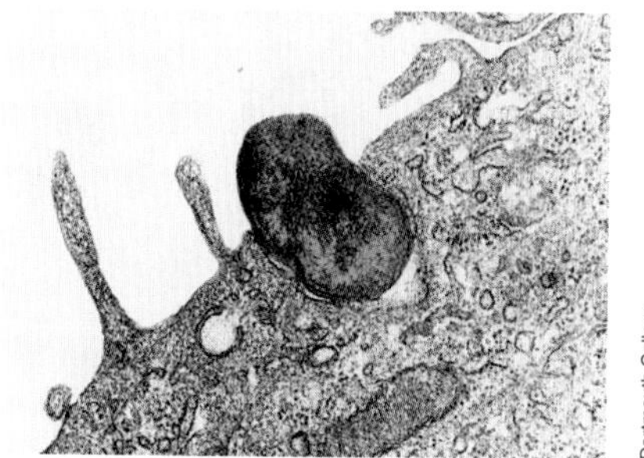

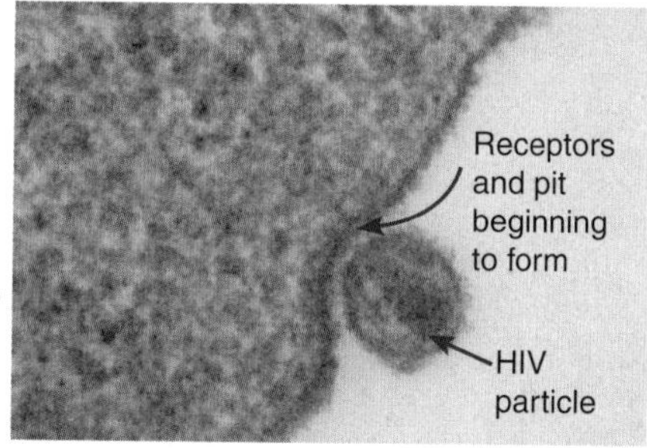

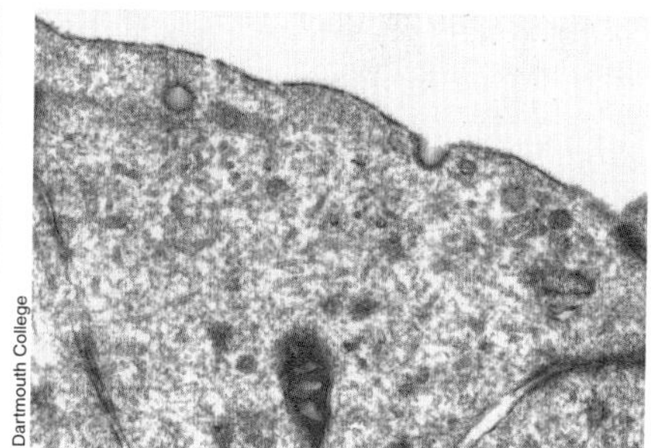

Phagocytosis (or 'cell-eating') involves the cell engulfing solid material to form large phagosomes or vacuoles (e.g. food vacuoles). It may be non-specific or receptor-mediated. Examples: Feeding in *Amoeba*, phagocytosis of foreign material and cell debris by neutrophils and macrophages.

Receptor mediated endocytosis is triggered when certain metabolites, hormones, or viral particles bind to specific receptor proteins on the membrane so that the material can be engulfed. Examples: The uptake of lipoproteins by mammalian cells and endocytosis of viruses (above).

Pinocytosis (or 'cell-drinking') involves the non-specific uptake of liquids or fine suspensions into the cell to form small pinocytic vesicles. Pinocytosis is used primarily for absorbing extracellular fluid. Examples: Uptake in many protozoa, some cells of the liver, and some plant cells.

3. What is the purpose of endocytosis? ____

____

4. Is endocytosis active or passive transport? ____

5. Describe the following types of endocytosis:

(a) Phagocytosis: ____

____

(b) Receptor mediated endocytosis: ____

____

(c) Pinocytosis: ____

____

6. Explain how the plasma membrane can form a vesicle: ____

____

ISBN: 978-1-98-856656-6

37 Compartments in Cells

Key Question: How are eukaryotic cells compartmentalized and what is the purpose of these compartments?

The cell can be compared to an office or business with specific departments where tasks are carried out. An office may have an executive, who produces instructions for the rest of the office. It may have a design department, sales, accounts, or IT departments. All these smaller groups work together to produce a product and keep the business going. Materials are brought into the business and used, and products and wastes are exported. In a similar way, a cell compartmentalizes certain operations. This increases the cell's overall efficiency because specific areas are focused on specific tasks. Cells create compartments (organelles) using membranes. Like the plasma membrane, the membranes of organelles control entry and exit of materials to and from their compartments. Membranes also allow attachment of proteins for specific tasks and help create chemical gradients to power the biochemical reactions necessary to sustain life.

Compartments and processes in an animal cell

Containment of damaging oxidative reactions

peroxisomes

Isolate damaging oxidation reactions, such as beta oxidation. Peroxisomes are derived from the ER.

Protein synthesis

nucleus, rough endoplasmic reticulum, free ribosomes

Genetic information in the nucleus is translated into proteins by attached or free ribosomes.

Transport in and out of the cell

plasma membrane

Diffusion and active transport mechanisms move substances across the plasma membrane.

Cellular respiration

cytoplasm, mitochondria

Glucose is broken down, supplying the cell with energy to carry out the many other reactions involved in metabolism.

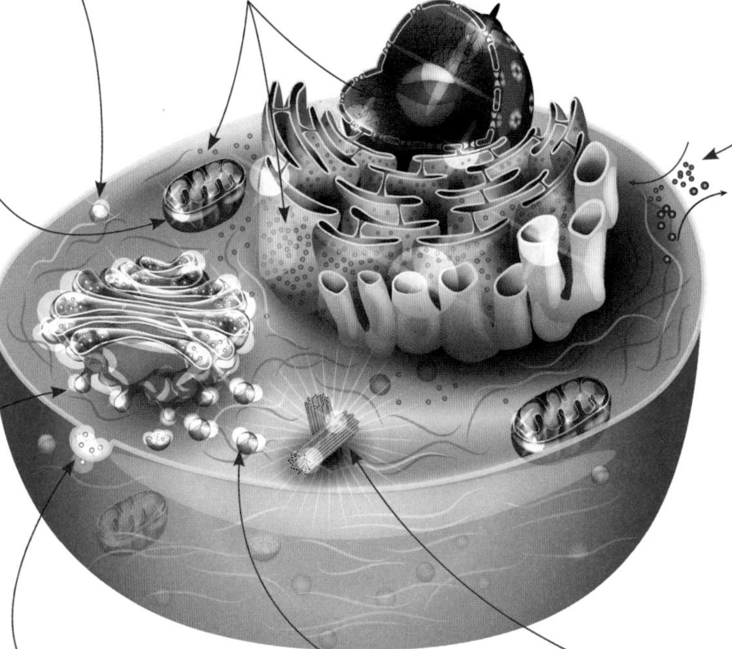

Secretion

Golgi apparatus, plasma membrane

The Golgi produces secretory vesicles (small membrane-bound sacs) that are used to modify and move substances around and export them from the cell (e.g. hormones, digestive enzymes).

Cytosis

plasma membrane, vacuoles

Material can be engulfed to bring it into the cell (endocytosis) or the plasma membrane can fuse with secretory vesicles to expel substances from the cell (exocytosis). In animal cells, cytosis may involve vacuoles.

Breakdown

lysosomes

Contain hydrolytic enzymes to destroy unwanted cell organelles and foreign material. Lysosomes are derived from the Golgi.

Cell division

nucleus, centrioles

Centrioles are microtubular structures involved in key stages of cell division. They are part of a larger organelle called the centrosome. The centrosomes of higher plant cells lack centrioles.

Plant cells carry out photosynthesis

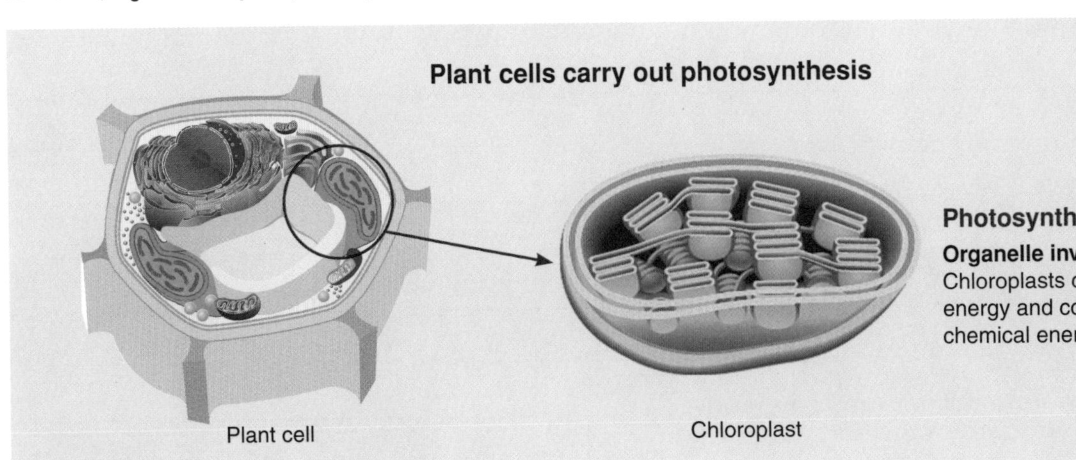

Photosynthesis (plant cell)

Organelle involved: *chloroplast.*

Chloroplasts capture light energy and convert it into useful chemical energy (as sugars).

ISBN: 978-1-98-856656-6

Membranes allow compartmentalization of reactions and processes

Membranes play an important role in separating regions within the cell (and within organelles) where particular reactions occur. Specific enzymes are therefore often located in particular organelles. The reaction rate is controlled by controlling the rate at which substrates enter the organelle and therefore the availability of the raw materials required for the reactions.

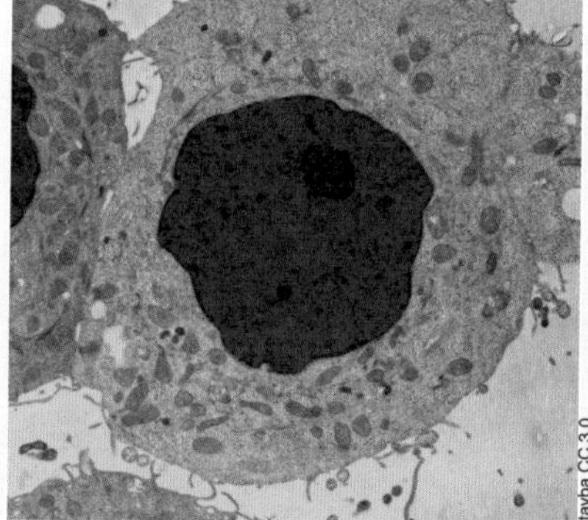

The nucleus is surrounded by a double-membrane structure called the nuclear envelope, which forms a separate compartment containing the cell's genetic material (DNA).

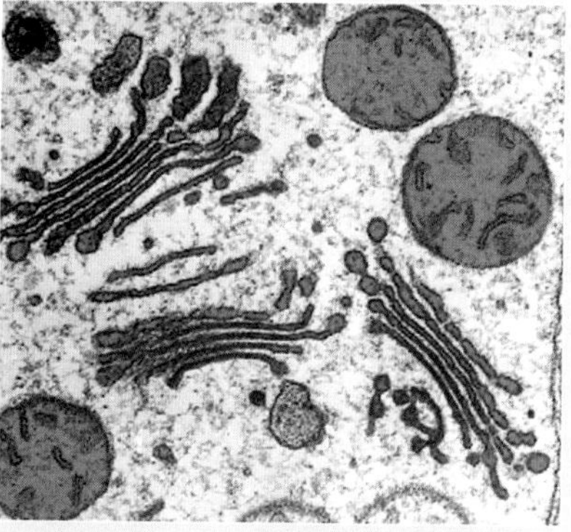

The Golgi apparatus (green) is a specialized membrane-bound organelle that compartmentalizes the modification, packing, and secretion of substances such as proteins and hormones.

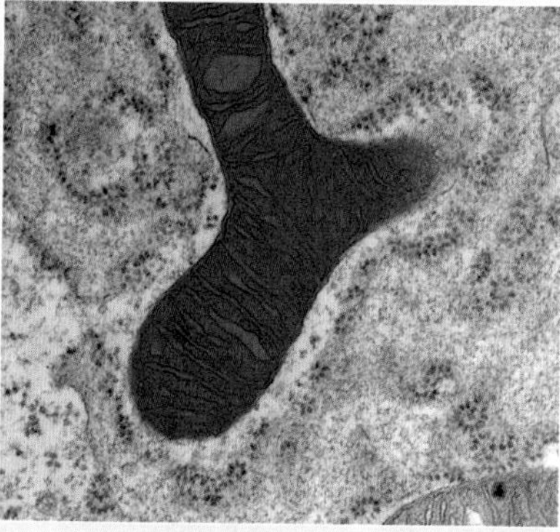

The inner membrane of a mitochondrion provides attachments for enzymes involved in cellular respiration. It allows ion gradients to be produced that can be used in the production of ATP.

1. For each of the processes listed below, identify the organelles or structures associated with that process (there may be more than one associated with a process):

   (a) Secretion: ____________________

   (b) Respiration: ____________________

   (c) Endocytosis: ____________________

   (d) Protein synthesis: ____________________

   (e) Photosynthesis: ____________________

   (f) Cell division: ____________________

   (g) Autolysis: ____________________

   (h) Transport in/out of cell: ____________________

2. Identify two examples of intracellular membranes and describe their functions:

   (a) ____________________

   (b) ____________________

3. Explain how compartmentalization within the cell is achieved and how it contributes to functional efficiency:

4. Explain how compartmentalization has enabled the evolution of larger cells: ____________________

ISBN: 978-1-98-856656-6

38 Origins of Cellular Compartments

Key Question: What was the origin of cellular compartments and what is the evidence for these origins?

It is thought that eukaryotic cells evolved from pre-eukaryotic (bacterial) cells that ingested other free-floating bacteria. They formed a symbiotic relationship with the cells they engulfed (a hypothesized process called **endosymbiosis**). The two organelles that evolved in eukaryotic cells as a result of bacterial endosymbiosis were **mitochondria**, for aerobic respiration, and **chloroplasts**, for photosynthesis in aerobic conditions. Primitive eukaryotes probably acquired mitochondria by engulfing purple bacteria. Similarly, chloroplasts may have been acquired by engulfing photosynthetic cyanobacteria. Other organelles may have formed from infolding of the plasma membrane.

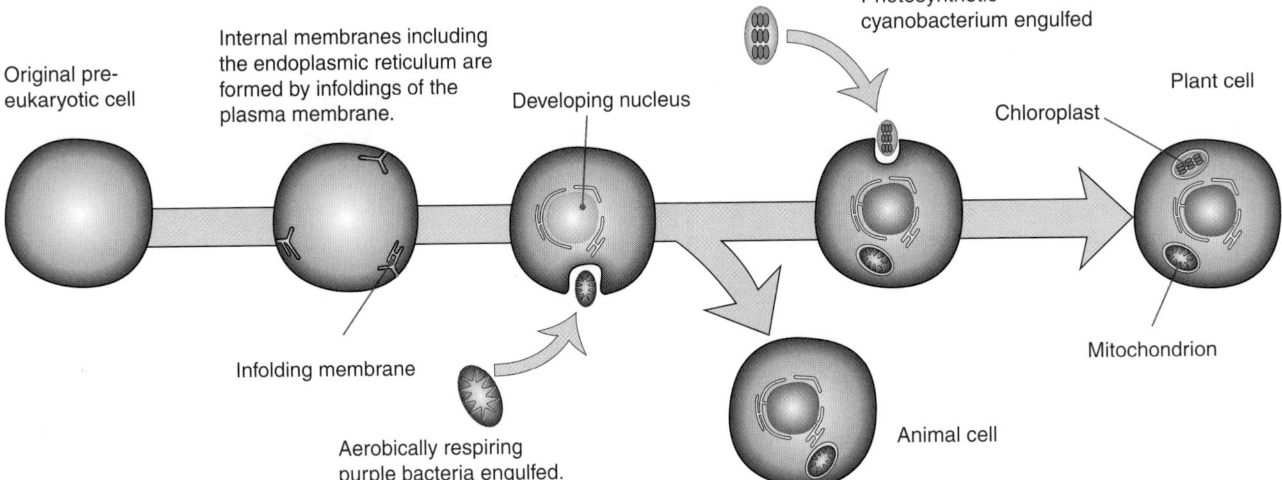

Evidence for the bacterial origins for organelles

Evidence for the bacterial origin of chloroplasts and mitochondria by endosymbiosis includes:

- Mitochondria and, in particular, chloroplasts, have a similar morphology to bacteria.
- Mitochondria and chloroplasts divide by binary fission, splitting in half to form new organelles, just like bacteria. Thus new mitochondria and chloroplasts arise from preexisting ones; they are not manufactured by the cell.
- Both mitochondria and chloroplasts have a chemically distinct inner membrane. The outer membrane is similar to the plasma membrane (as if a vesicle formed around the engulfed cell) but the inner membrane is similar to the bacterial membrane.
- Bacterial DNA is a single circular molecule. Mitochondria and chloroplasts also have their own single circular DNA. Like bacterial DNA, this DNA has no intervening non-protein-coding regions or associated proteins. Also the DNA mutates at a different rate to the nuclear DNA.
- Mitochondria and chloroplasts contain ribosomes that are more similar in size to bacterial ribosomes than ribosomes in the cytoplasm.
- Antibiotics that inhibit protein synthesis in bacteria also inhibit protein synthesis in mitochondria and chloroplasts.
- Analysis of chloroplast DNA has shown that they are related to cyanobacteria.

Examples of engulfment

Paramecium bursaria

Paramecium bursaria (below) is a single celled protozoan. It engulfs cells of *Zoochlorella*, a photosynthetic green alga. It houses the algae and carries them to lighted areas in a pond where they can photosynthesize. In return, it uses the food made by the algae.

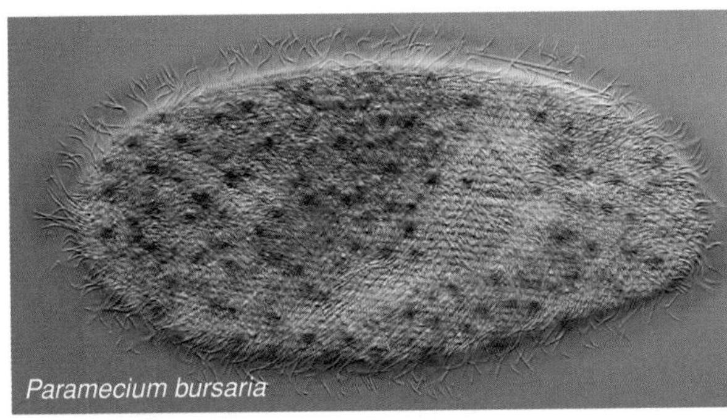
Paramecium bursaria

Amoeba proteus

From 1972, microbiologist Kwang Jeon studied the infection of *Amoeba proteus* by *Legionella*-like bacteria. He found that most infected amoebae died. The few that survived and their descendants functioned well with the bacteria still thriving inside. When antibiotics were used to kill the bacteria inside the amoebae, the amoebae also died, having become dependent on a bacterial protein. A symbiosis has evolved.

1. Which endosymbiosis occurred first in the evolution of eukaryotic cells? Explain your reasoning: ______________________

____

____

2. How would symbiosis benefit both the engulfed bacterium and the eukaryotic cell? ______________________

____

____

ISBN: 978-1-98-856656-6

39 Personal Progress Check

Answer the multiple choice questions that follow by circling the correct answer. Don't forget to read the question carefully!

1. The primary barrier to the passage of ions and polar molecules through the plasma membrane is the:
   (a) Boundary layer of carbohydrates
   (b) Hydrophobic nature of the proteins in the plasma membrane
   (c) Hydrophobic nature of the lipid bilayer
   (d) The thickness of the plasma membrane

2. The cell component not found in a prokaryotic cell is:
   (a) Plasma membrane
   (b) Chromosome
   (c) Ribosomes
   (d) Nucleus

3. Which of the following relationships between cell structures and their respective functions is correct?
   (a) Cell wall: support, protection
   (b) Chloroplasts: chief sites of cellular respiration
   (c) Chromosomes: cytoskeleton of the nucleus
   (d) Ribosomes: secretion

4. Which of the following is an important cause of size limits for certain types of cells?
   (a) The evolution of larger cells after the evolution of smaller cells.
   (b) The difference in plasma membranes between prokaryotes and eukaryotes.
   (c) The evolution of eukaryotes after the evolution of prokaryotes.
   (d) The need for sufficient surface area to allow adequate exchanges with the environment.

5. What kind of cell would you not expect to contain a larger than average number of mitochondria?
   (a) A cell with a regularly contracting function
   (b) A cell with a primarily transport function
   (c) A cell detoxifying various waste molecules
   (d) A highly active motile cell

6. Which organelle is primarily involved in the synthesis of oils, phospholipids, and steroids?
   (a) Ribosome
   (b) Lysosome
   (c) Smooth endoplasmic reticulum
   (d) Mitochondrion

7. Which structure is the site of the synthesis of proteins to be exported from the cell?
   (a) Rough ER
   (b) Lysosomes
   (c) Plasmodesmata
   (d) Golgi vesicles

8. Which of the following contains hydrolytic enzymes?
   (a) Lysosome
   (b) Mitochondrion
   (c) Golgi apparatus
   (d) Peroxisome

9. Which one of the organelles below is the main producer of ATP in a cell?
   (a) Lysosome
   (b) Vacuole
   (c) Mitochondrion
   (d) Golgi apparatus

10. In which of the following organelles would you expect to find DNA?
    (a) Mitochondria
    (b) The nucleus
    (c) Chloroplasts
    (d) All of the above

11. Grana, thylakoids, and stroma are all components found in:
    (a) Vacuoles
    (b) Chloroplasts
    (c) Mitochondria
    (d) Nuclei

12. The cell component not found in an animal cell is:
    (a) Plasma membrane
    (b) Mitochondria
    (c) Chloroplast
    (d) Nucleus

13. Which of the following relationships between cell structures and their respective functions is incorrect?
    (a) Plasma membrane: control of material's entry to and exit from a cell
    (b) Mitochondria: main site of cellular respiration
    (c) Golgi apparatus: main site of ribosome production
    (d) Nucleus: stores nuclear DNA

14. Protein synthesis is carried out in:
    (a) The nucleus, rough endoplasmic reticulum and free ribosomes
    (b) The Golgi apparatus and plasma membrane
    (c) The nucleus and centrioles
    (d) The plasma membrane and vacuoles

15. Cristae, matrix, and ATP synthase are all components found in:
    (a) Vacuoles
    (b) Chloroplasts
    (c) Mitochondria
    (d) Nuclei

ISBN: 978-1-98-856656-6

16. Cell walls containing chitin are unique to:
    (a) Fungi
    (b) Plants
    (c) Gram positive bacteria
    (d) Gram negative bacteria

17. A cell wall is found:
    (a) Only in plant cells
    (b) External to the plasma membrane
    (c) Internal to the plasma membrane
    (d) None of the above

18. Ions diffuse across membranes down their
    (a) Chemical gradients
    (b) Concentration gradients
    (c) Electrical gradients
    (d) Electrochemical gradients

19. Which of the following types of transport requires ATP?
    (a) Diffusion
    (b) Facilitated transport
    (c) Active transport
    (d) All of the above

20. A cell placed in distilled water would:
    (a) Shrivel up because the water is hypotonic relative to the cell's contents.
    (b) Burst because the water is hypotonic compared to the cell's contents.
    (c) Shrivel up because the water is hypertonic compared to the cell's contents.
    (d) The cell would not change because the cell and water are isotonic.

21. The selective permeability of the plasma membrane is the result of:
    (a) Receptor proteins
    (b) Channel proteins
    (c) Phospholipids
    (d) All of the above

22. Which of the following are common to eukaryotic and prokaryotic cells?
    (a) Mitochondria
    (b) Ribosomes
    (c) Nuclear envelope
    (d) Chloroplasts

23. Which of the following statements about diffusion is correct?
    (a) Diffusion is very rapid over long distances.
    (b) Diffusion requires energy expenditure by the cell.
    (c) Diffusion is a passive process in which molecules move from a region of higher concentration to a region of lower concentration.
    (d) Diffusion is an active process in which molecules move from a region of lower concentration to a region of higher concentration

24. Which structure is not part of the endomembrane system of a eukaryotic cell?
    (a) Nuclear envelope
    (b) Chloroplast
    (c) Golgi apparatus
    (d) ER

25. Water passes quickly through cell membranes because:
    (a) It moves through aquaporins in the membrane.
    (b) It moves through hydrophobic channels.
    (c) Water movement is tied to ATP hydrolysis.
    (d) It is a small, polar, charged molecule.

26. Which structure is common to plant and animal cells?
    (a) Chloroplast
    (b) Cellulose cell wall
    (c) Central vacuole
    (d) Mitochondrion

27. The endosymbiont theory proposes that mitochondria descended from endosymbiotic bacteria that lived inside other cells. Which of the following statements would best support that theory?
    (a) Both bacteria and mitochondria possess similar ribosomes and genetic material.
    (b) Both bacteria and mitochondria possess similar nuclei.
    (c) Neither bacteria nor mitochondria have nuclear membranes.
    (d) Microtubules are present in both bacteria and mitochondria.

28. Which of the statements about water is incorrect?
    (a) Water is a polar molecule
    (b) Water is a solvent for hydrophilic molecules
    (c) Water is a solvent for hydrophobic molecules
    (d) Water is produced in condensation reactions

29. A person at one end of a room opens two perfume bottles A and B at the same time. The person at the other end of the room smells perfume A first. Four statements were made relating to the diffusion of perfumes A and B:

1. Perfume A has lighter molecules than perfume B so they diffused more quickly
2. Perfume A was more concentrated so its particles diffused faster
3. Perfume B was colder than perfume a so its molecules moved more slowly that perfumes A's
4. Perfume A's molecules were larger than B's so took up more of the room's space.

Which could be correct?
(a) 1 and 2
(b) 1 and 3
(c) 2 and 3
(d) 3 and 4

ISBN: 978-1-98-856656-6

Free Response Question: *Interpreting and evaluating experimental results*

- An experiment was carried out in which red blood cells were placed in NaCl solutions of differing concentrations and a urea solution isosmotic with the blood plasma. NaCl cannot freely cross the plasma membrane, but urea can. The cells and solutions were mixed gently and after 10 minutes the samples were centrifuged to separate the cells from the solution.
- The packed cell volume (hematocrit) was then measured. The hematocrit indicates how many intact cells remain to contribute to packed cell volume. The amount of hemolysis (bursting of blood cells) was measured using reference tubes. After centrifugation, fully hemolyzed blood is uniformly red because all the hemoglobin has been released from the cells into solution.
- Treatments and results tabulated right.

	Sample	Percentage hematocrit	Percentage hemolysis
A	Blood + 0.462 mol/L NaCl (hypertonic)	6	2.1
B	Blood + 0.154 mol/L NaCl (isotonic)	10	2.1
C	Blood + 0.077 mol/L NaCl (hypotonic)	12	66.7
D	Blood + distilled water	0	100
E	Blood + isosmotic urea (total solute concentration equal to blood cells)	0	100
F	Non-hemolyzed blood (control)	9	1.1

Source: Goodhead and MacMillan (2017) See credits for full citation.

1. (a) **Describe** what is meant by tonicity: ______

   (b) **Explain** what causes cells to increase or decrease in volume: ______

2. (a) **Identify** the independent variable: ______

   (b) **Identify** the dependent variable: ______

   (c) Explain why non-hemolyzed blood acted as the control: ______

3. **Analyze** the hematocrit results for each of the solutions:

   A: ______

   B: ______

   C: ______

   D: ______

   E: ______

4. **Predict** the result if red blood cells were placed in an isosmotic solution of sucrose. **Justify your prediction**: ______

ISBN: 978-1-98-856656-6

Free Response Question: *Analyze a model or visual representation*

Using pulse and chase to track protein secretion

- The export of proteins from the cell can be tracked using what is called a **pulse-chase experiment**. George Palade and his colleagues (1967) used this technique to track the movement of synthesized proteins in cultured pancreatic cells, which secrete digestive enzymes.
- The experiment begins when a brief (3 minute) pulse of radiolabeled amino acid is added to the cells.
- This pulse is followed by a chase when the modified amino acid is washed out and replaced with a non-labeled version of the same amino acid.
- The researchers based their experiment on following a small population of radiolabeled proteins over time. Their summarized results are plotted, right.

Data: Jamieson and Palade (1967). See credits for full citation.

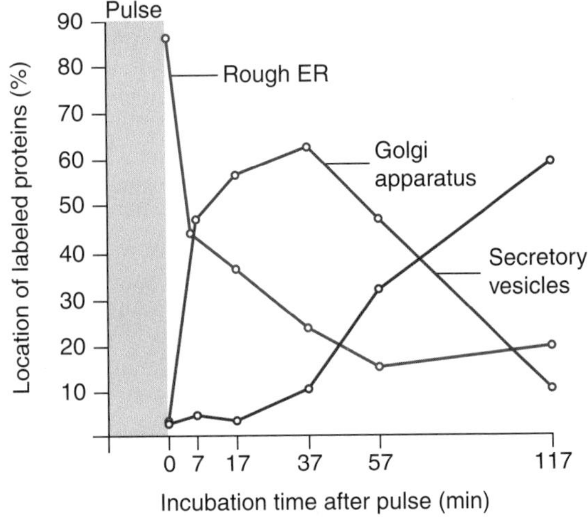

1. Identify the organelles involved in the synthesis and export of proteins from the cell and **describe** their role:

2. **Explain** the relationships between these different organelles as indicated by the results of Palade's "pulse and chase" experiment presented in the graph above:

3. In the drawing of the cell right, **represent the data above** by marking the drawing with colored dots and numbers to indicate the radiolabeled proteins and their location at time 0, time +37 minutes, and time +117 minutes after the pulse.

4. **Explain** how the findings of Palade's experiment contributed to our understanding of processes in secretory cells:

ISBN: 978-1-98-856656-6

UNIT 3 Cellular Energetics

Learning Objectives

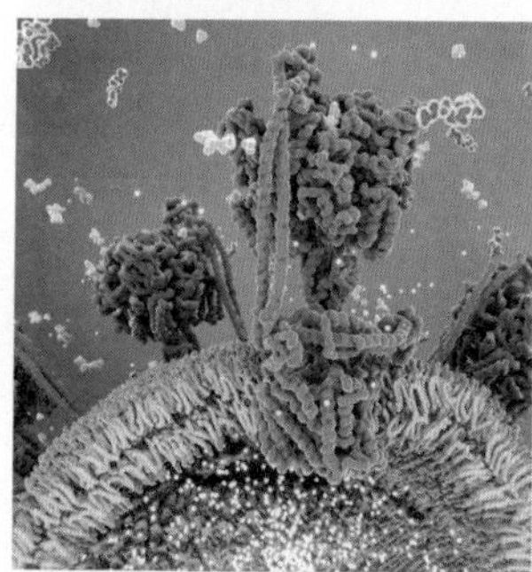

Developing understanding

CONTENT: In this unit, you will build on your knowledge of cell structure and function by focusing on cellular energetics. You will develop an understanding of why cells need a constant energy input, and explore the concepts of energy capture and use. You will learn about enzymes and the role of the environment in enzyme activity. You will develop a deeper understanding of photosynthesis and cellular respiration, which you can apply later in the course.

SKILLS: This unit focuses on explaining biological concepts and processes, analyzing experimental procedures, presenting and describing data, and constructing arguments from evidence. Other skills include interpreting visual representations and data analysis.

3.1 Enzyme structure .... activity 40

☐ 1. Describe the structure and role of enzymes, including reference to the active site and what determines its properties. Describe how the charge and shape of the substrate must be compatible with the enzyme's active site in order for an enzyme-mediated chemical reaction to occur. Understand that the precise configuration of the active site determines the specificity of the enzyme to its substrate.

☐ 2. Describe the induced fit model for enzyme function, with reference to the enzyme-substrate complex, enzyme-product complex, and product formation.

3.2 Enzyme catalysis .... activity 41

☐ 3. Explain how enzymes catalyze reactions by lowering the activation energy and identify this on a plot of the progress of the reaction against the free energy. Understand the role of enzymes in regulating the biochemical reactions in living things (collectively called metabolism).

☐ 4. Distinguish between anabolic and catabolic reactions and recognize these in visual representations. Categorize cellular respiration and photosynthesis using these terms.

3.3 Environmental impacts on enzyme function .... activities 42 - 46

☐ 5. Explain how changes to an enzyme's structure affect its activity by affecting rate or by denaturation (loss of function). Describe situations in which enzyme denaturation can be reversible, allowing an enzyme to regain its activity.

☐ 6. Explain how environmental pH can alter the efficiency of enzyme activity by disrupting the stability of the bonds that maintain the active site. Analyze data on the effect of pH on the activity of an enzyme, e.g. turnip peroxidase.

☐ 7. Analyze data to describe the effect of changes in enzyme concentration and substrate concentration on enzyme activity. How do the relative concentrations of substrates and products affect the efficiency of an enzymatic reactions?

☐ 8. Explain how temperature affects enzyme reaction rates. Why is high temperature denaturation generally irreversible?

☐ 9. Explain how enzyme inhibitors alter enzyme reaction rates, distinguishing between competitive and non-competitive inhibitors and between reversible and non-reversible inhibition. Describe the role of non-competitive inhibitors in feedback inhibition of metabolic pathways.

3.4 Cellular energy .... activities 46, 47

☐ 10. Describe the role of energy in living organisms, including the role of energy inputs in maintaining order in systems that otherwise move towards maximum entropy.

☐ 11. Describe the sequential nature of energy related pathways in biological systems, which enables a more controlled and efficient transfer of energy. Use examples to describe how the product of a reaction in a metabolic pathway is generally the reactant for a subsequent step in the pathway.

3.5 Photosynthesis .... activities 48 - 53

☐ 12. Describe the photosynthetic processes that allow organisms to capture and store energy. Describe how eukaryotic photosynthesis evolved from prokaryotic photosynthetic pathways and describe the evidence for this and for the role of photosynthesis in producing an oxygenated atmosphere.

☐ 13. Recall the structure of chloroplasts, and explain the role of pigments in light capture. Which wavelengths of light are most effective in driving photosynthesis and why?

☐ 14. Describe the inputs and outputs of the light dependent stage of photosynthesis. Outline the events in the light dependent reactions of photosynthesis, including absorption of light, transfer of excited electrons between carriers in the thylakoid membranes, generation of ATP and NADPH, and the photolysis of water.

☐ 15. Describe the inputs and outputs of the light independent stage of photosynthesis (the Calvin cycle), including the role of the enzyme RuBisCo. Outline the events in the Calvin cycle, including the fixation of carbon and the production of triose phosphate using reduced NADPH and ATP.

3.6 Cellular respiration .... activities 47, 54 - 59

☐ 16. Describe the role of cellular respiration and fermentation as energy yielding pathways characteristic of all forms of life.

☐ 17. Describe the main inputs, outputs, and location of glycolysis, the Krebs cycle, and the electron transport chain, including ATP yield. Explain the main steps in cellular respiration to include glycolysis, Krebs cycle, and electron transport chain (ETC). Understand that glycolysis is an almost universal pathway in cells and can yield ATP in anaerobic conditions.

☐ 18. Describe how electron transfer and the generation of a proton gradient are used to generate ATP by chemiosmosis in photosynthesis and respiration. Recall how the conversion of ATP to ADP releases energy to power metabolism.

☐ 19. Explain how fermentation allows glycolysis to proceed without oxygen, with reference to alcoholic fermentation in yeast and lactic acid fermentation in mammalian muscle.

3.7 Fitness .... activity 60

☐ 20. Use examples, e.g. hemoglobin diversity, to explain the connection between molecular variation in cells and the ability of organisms to survive and reproduce.

40 The Properties of Enzymes

Key Question: What are enzymes and what do they do?

Enzymes catalyze chemical reactions in living organisms. **Enzymes** are **biological catalysts** because they speed up biochemical reactions, but the enzyme itself remains unchanged. It is not used up in the reaction and carries out the same reaction many times. Most enzymes are globular proteins, with a specific shape that is determined by the protein's tertiary structure. Each enzyme catalyzes only one type of chemical reaction, so enzymes usually only act on one specific chemical or **substrate** (reactant). In some instances an enzyme will act on a small group of similar substrates. This specificity is a result of the precise configuration of the catalytic region or **active site**, where the substrate binds and the chemical reaction occurs to form the product.

The active site

An enzyme acts on a specific chemical called the **substrate**. The substrate binds to a specific part of the enzyme called the **active site**.

The properties of the active site are specific to an enzyme and are a function of its tertiary structure. The active site accounts for an enzyme's specificity for its substrate (the substrate has a shape and charge to interact correctly with the active site).

Extremes of temperature or pH can alter the enzyme's active site and lead to loss of function. This process is called **denaturation**.

Amylase breaks starch (a glucose polymer) into smaller 2-3 glucose units.

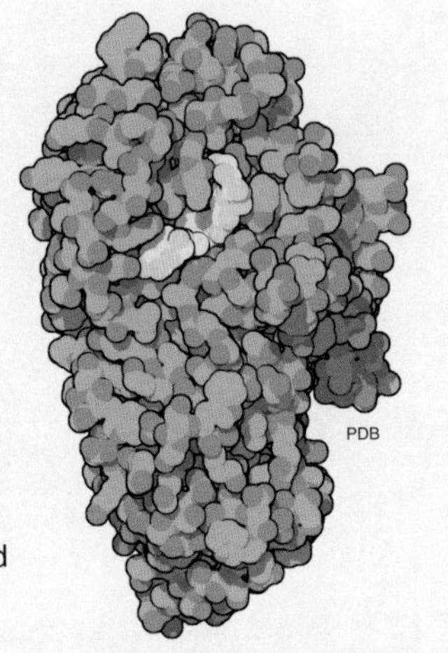

Amylase (blue) with bound glucose (yellow) in the active site

Intracellular and extracellular enzymes

Enzymes can be defined based on where they are produced relative to where they are active.

An **Intracellular enzyme** performs its functions within the cell that produces it. Most enzymes are intracellular enzymes, e.g. respiratory enzymes.

Example: Catalase (a type of peroxidase).

Many metabolic processes produce hydrogen peroxide, which is harmful to cells. Catalase converts hydrogen peroxide into water and oxygen gas (below) to prevent damage to cells and tissues.

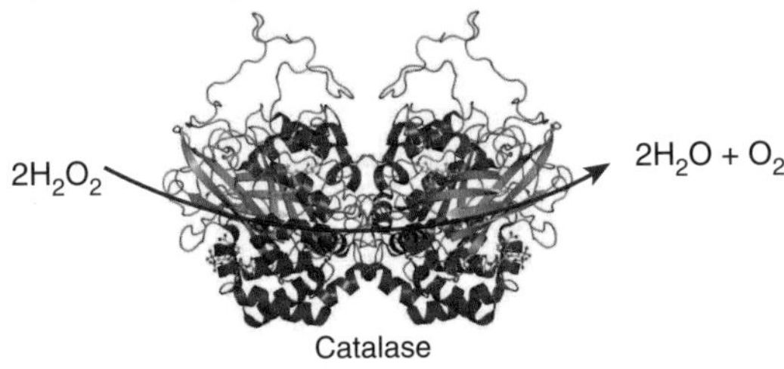

Catalase

Substrates collide with an enzyme's active site

For a reaction to occur reactants must collide with sufficient speed and with the correct orientation. Enzymes enhance reaction rates by providing a site for reactants to come together in such a way that a reaction will occur. They do this by orientating the reactants so that the reactive regions are brought together. They may also destabilize the bonds within the reactants making it easier for a reaction to occur.

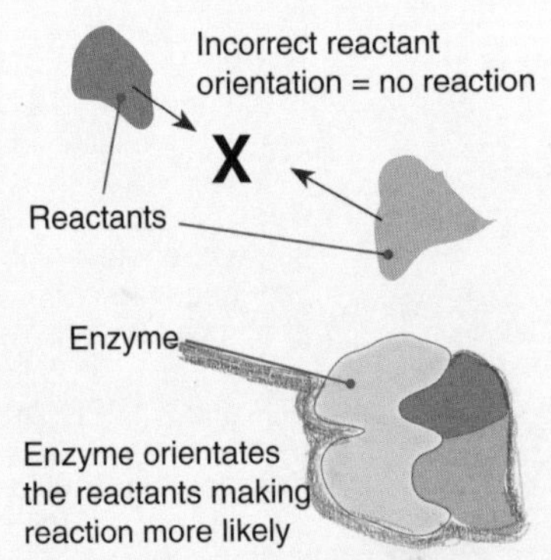

An **extracellular enzyme** is an enzyme that functions outside the cell from which it originates (i.e. it is produced in one location but active in another).

Examples: Trypsin and α-amylase.

Trypsin is a protein-digesting enzyme and hydrolyses the peptide bond immediately after a basic residue (e.g. arginine). It is produced in an inactive form (called trypsinogen) and secreted into the small intestine by the pancreas. It is activated in the intestine by the enzyme enteropeptidase to form trypsin. Active trypsin can convert more trypsinogen to trypsin.

Alpha amylase is a digestive enzyme produced in the salivary glands and pancreas in humans. It acts in the mouth and small intestine respectively to hydrolyse starch by cleaving the α-1,4 glycosidic bond. The end-products are sugars (maltose, dextrin).

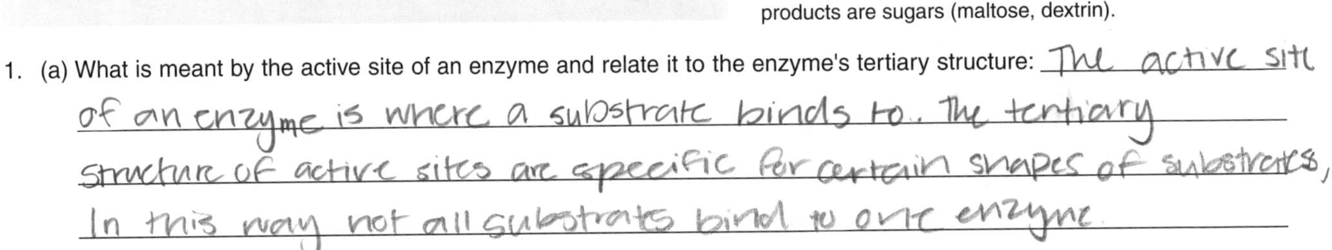

1. (a) What is meant by the active site of an enzyme and relate it to the enzyme's tertiary structure: The active site of an enzyme is where a substrate binds to. The tertiary structure of active sites are specific for certain shapes of substrates, In this way not all substrates bind to one enzyme.

   (b) Explain why enzymes are specific to one substrate (or group of closely related substrates): this is because each enzyme catalyzes only one type of chemical reaction.

2. Explain how substrate molecules come into contact with an enzyme's active site: the substrate must collide w/sufficient speed/correct orientation. They bind + cause a chemical reaction which produces the products.

3. (a) Suggest why digestion (the breakdown of large macromolecules) is largely performed by extracellular enzymes: so newly broken down nutrients can be absorbed by nearby cells.

   (b) Explain why an extracellular enzyme would be secreted in an inactive form: so it doesn't activate in the cell

ISBN: 978-1-98-856656-6

The induced fit model of enzyme action

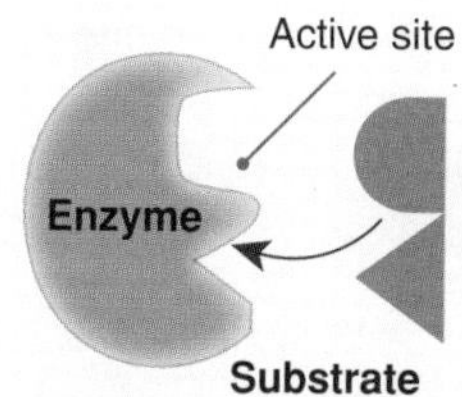

1 A substrate molecule is drawn into the enzyme's active site by its particular properties (resulting from its amino acid side chains). The active site is like a cleft into which the substrate molecule(s) fit.

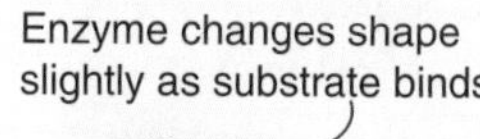

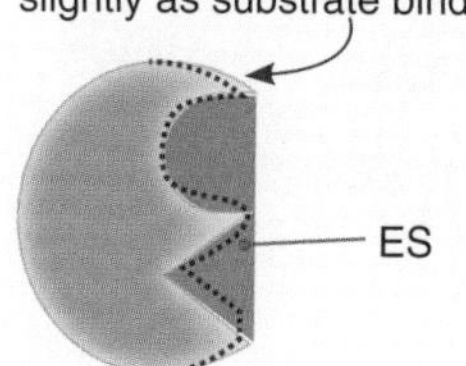

2 The enzyme changes shape as the substrate binds, forming an enzyme-substrate (ES) complex. Chemical and electrostatic interactions are important in forming the ES complex. The shape change makes a change in the substrate more likely. In this way, the enzyme's interaction with its substrate is an induced fit.

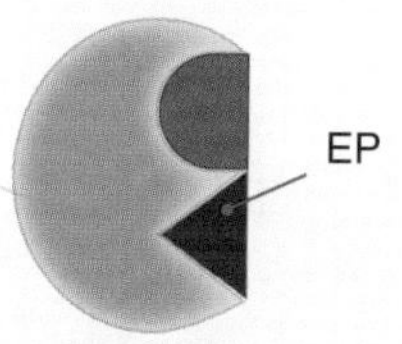

3 The ES interaction results in an intermediate enzyme-product (EP) complex. The substrate becomes bound to the enzyme by weak chemical bonds, straining bonds in the substrate and allowing the reaction to proceed more readily.

End products released

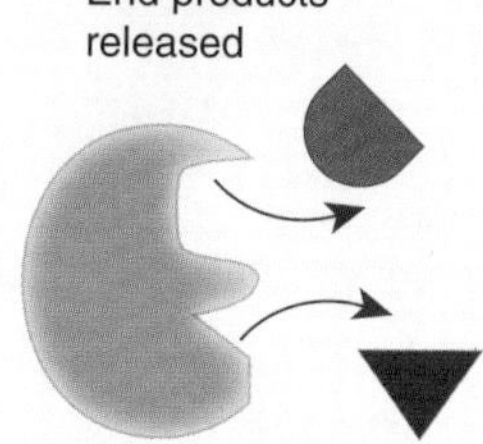

4 The end products are released and the enzyme returns to its previous shape.

Once the substrate enters the active site, the shape of the active site changes to form an active complex. The formation of an ES complex strains substrate bonds and lowers the energy required to reach the transition state, which allows the reaction to proceed. The **induced-fit model** is supported by X-ray crystallography, chemical analysis, and studies of enzyme inhibitors, which show that enzymes are flexible and change shape when interacting with the substrate.

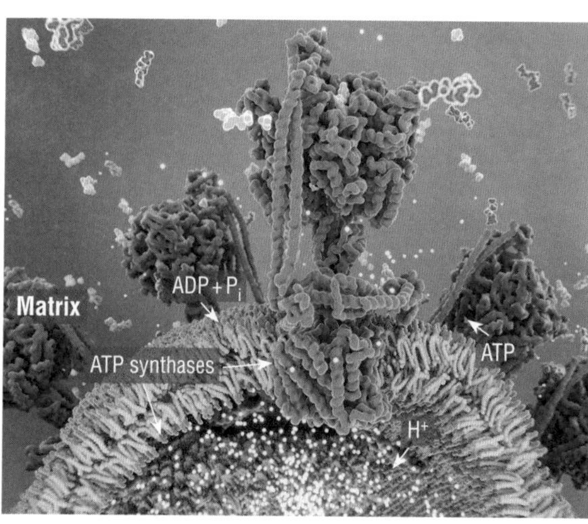

ATP synthase is a transmembrane enzyme that catalyzes the synthesis of ATP from ADP and inorganic phosphate, driven by a proton gradient generated by electron transfer. The image shows ATP synthase in the membrane of a mitochondrion, but it is also found in the membranes of chloroplasts, where ATP is generated in the light dependent reactions of photosynthesis. ATP synthase is classified as a type of ligase because the catalysis involves the formation of P-O (phosphodiester) bond. It has three active sites.

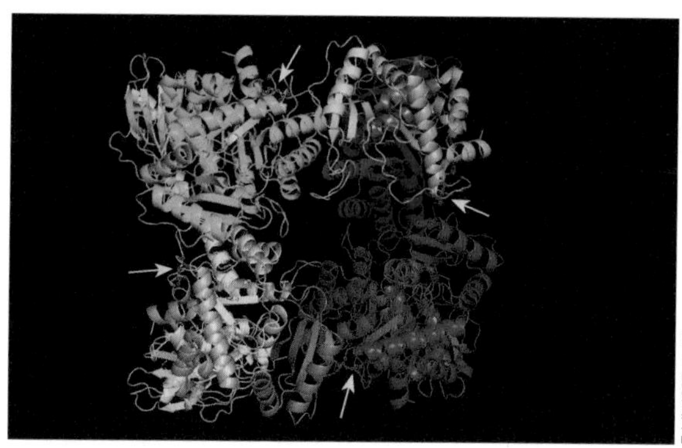

RuBisCo is an enzyme involved in the first main step of carbon fixation in plants and other photosynthetic organisms. It catalyzes the attachment of CO_2 to a 5-C sugar derivative called RuBP. The active sites are indicated by arrows.

4. Explain how an enzyme interacts with its substrate in an 'induced' fit model: A substrate molecule is drawn into the enzyme's active site by its particular properties. The active site is like a cleft into which the substrate moecule fits. The enzyme changes shape as the substrate binds, forming an enzyme-substrate complex. The shape change makes a change in the substrate more likely. In this way, the enzymes interaction w/ its substrate is an induced fit.

5. In the 1960s, it was proposed that ATP synthesis depended on a shape change in ATP synthase generated by rotation of membrane-bound subunit. This rotation has now been demonstrated experimentally. Explain how this provided evidence for the induced fit model of enzyme function:

Enzymes are flexible and change shape when interacting with the substrate, this allows for the chemical reactions to occur after the binding of enzymes and substrates.

ISBN: 978-1-98-856656-6

41 How Enzymes Work

Key Question: How do enzymes act as biological catalysts?

Chemical reactions in cells are accompanied by energy changes. The amount of energy released or taken up is directly related to the tendency of a reaction to run to completion (for all the reactants to form products). Any reaction needs to raise the energy of the substrate to an unstable **transition state** before the reaction will proceed (below). The amount of energy needed to do this is the **activation energy** (E_a). Enzymes lower the E_a by destabilizing bonds in the substrate so that it is more reactive.

Enzymes lower the activation energy for biochemical reactions

- The presence of an enzyme simply makes it easier for a reaction to take place. All catalysts speed up reactions by influencing the stability of bonds in the reactants. They may also provide an alternative reaction pathway, thus lowering the activation energy (E_a) needed for a reaction to take place (below). These reactions are accompanied by energy changes.
- When the reactants have lower energy than the product, the reaction requires energy input and is endergonic. When the reactants have higher energy than the product, energy is released in product formation and the reaction is exergonic.

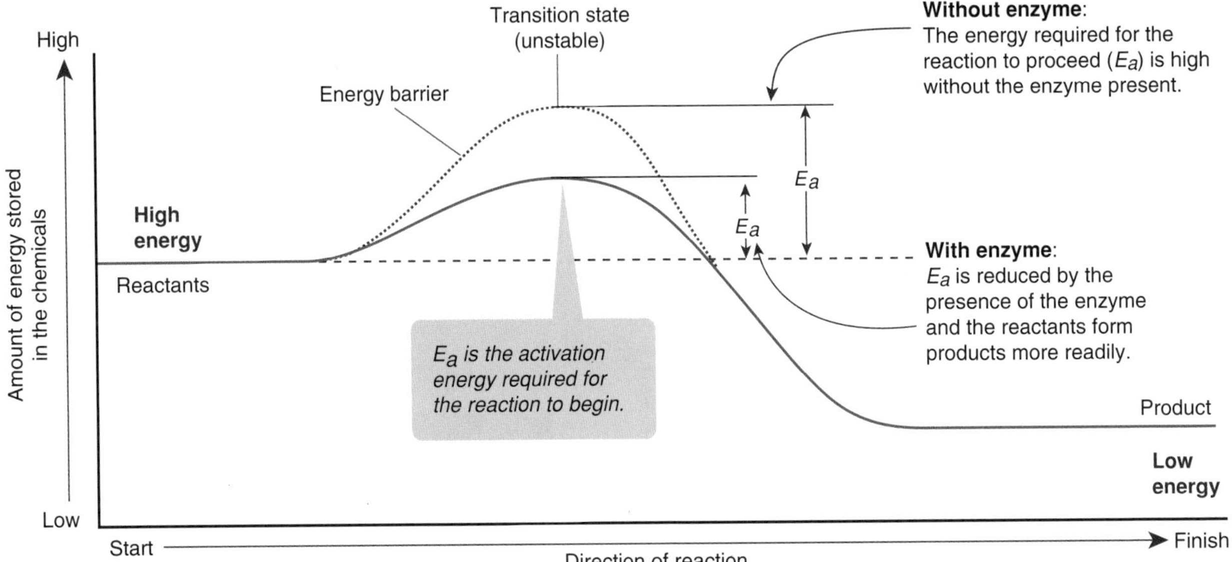

Enzymes can catalyze the break down of molecules

The properties of an enzyme's active site can draw in a single substrate molecule. Chemical bonds are broken, cleaving the substrate molecule to form two separate molecules. Reactions that break down complex molecules into simpler ones are called **catabolic reactions** and involve a net release of energy (they are **exergonic**). Examples: *cellular respiration, digestion.*

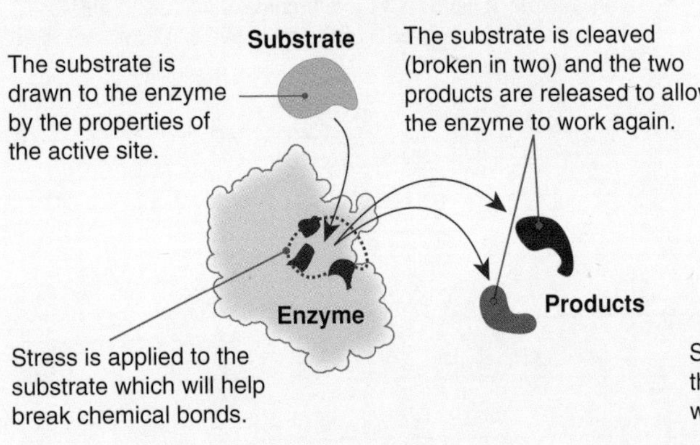

Substrate
The substrate is drawn to the enzyme by the properties of the active site.
The substrate is cleaved (broken in two) and the two products are released to allow the enzyme to work again.
Enzyme
Products
Stress is applied to the substrate which will help break chemical bonds.

Enzymes can catalyze the building of molecules

The properties of an enzyme's active site can draw in two substrate molecules. The two substrate molecules form bonds and become a single molecule. Reactions that build more complex molecules and structures from simpler ones are called **anabolic reactions** and involve a net use of energy (they are **endergonic**). Examples: *photosynthesis, protein synthesis.*

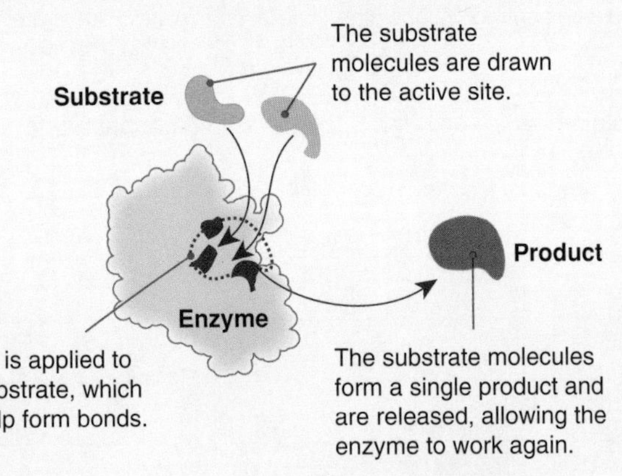

The substrate molecules are drawn to the active site.
Substrate
Product
Enzyme
Stress is applied to the substrate, which will help form bonds.
The substrate molecules form a single product and are released, allowing the enzyme to work again.

1. Explain how enzymes lower the activation energy for a reaction: They make it easier for a reaction to take place. They speed up the reaction, thus lowering the activation energy needed for the reaction to occur.

2. Anabolic reactions are responsible for the bulking up of muscle seen in bodybuilders: true or false? true

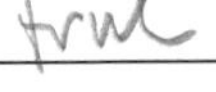

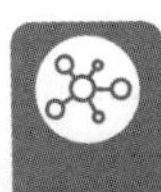
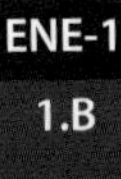

ISBN: 978-1-98-856656-6

42 Denaturation

Key Question: How do changes to an enzyme's three dimensional structure affect its function?

When an enzyme (or any protein) loses its specific tertiary structure, it also loses its ability to carry out its functional role. The change in shape with associated loss of function is called **denaturation** and it can occur when environmental factors (e.g. extremes of pH or temperature) disrupt the chemical bonds between amino acids. In enzymes, the physical and chemical nature of the active site are also altered. Recall that the active site will only interact with a specific substrate. When the shape of the active site is altered, the substrate can no longer bind and the enzyme loses its catalytic function. Denaturation can be reversible, depending on the enzyme and the nature of the denaturing agent.

Hydrophobic interactions and chemical bonds between amino acids hold a protein in its three dimensional functional shape. Bonds (red lines on the diagram, right) include hydrogen bonds, ionic bonds, and disulfide bonds.

All enzymes have optimal conditions, i.e. the environmental conditions in which they work best. Outside of the optimal conditions, enzyme activity slows down, and will stop completely if the enzyme is denatured (stabilizing bonds are broken). Denaturation can be caused by extremes of temperature or pH.

As temperature increases, the enzyme molecule gains kinetic energy. Above a certain temperature, the energy is so great that stabilizing hydrogen bonds and hydrophobic interactions are shaken apart and the enzyme unfolds.

pH is a measure of the number of hydrogen ions in solution.

$$pH = -\log[H^+]$$

Changes in the concentrations of H^+ ions (pH) will affect those bonds which contain a charge, i.e. hydrogen and ionic bonds. These bonds help maintain the tertiary structure and the active site so they are very vulnerable to changes in hydrogen ion concentration. The reaction does not proceed because the substrate does not enter the active site or does not align properly.

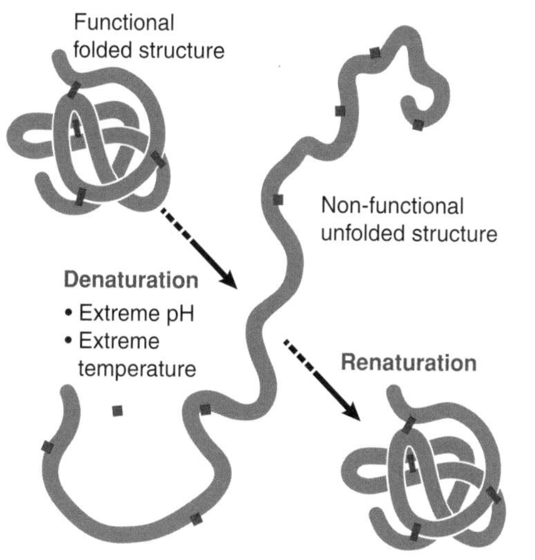

Sometimes enzymes can regain their original shape and activity. This is called renaturation (refolding back to the original shape). Renaturation is more likely to occur if a moderate pH change caused denaturation and the environment has returned to a suitable pH. Temperature induced denaturation is usually irreversible.

1. Pepsin is a protein digesting enzyme in the stomach. It is most active between pH 1.5-2.5 (the pH of the stomach). Pepsin is inactive at pH 6.5 or above, but does not become fully denatured until pH 8.0.

   (a) When the stomach empties, the partially digested food and enzyme mixture is released into the small intestine. The pH of the small intestine ranges between 6.0-7.4. Would pepsin be active in the small intestine? Explain your answer:

   Partially, but most likely no. The pepsin is inactive at 6.5 or above.

   (b) Predict what would happen to pepsin activity under the following conditions. Explain your answer:

   (i) A pepsin solution at pH 7.0 was adjusted to pH 1.5: enzyme mixture would become active.

   (ii) A pepsin solution at pH 8.5 was adjusted to pH 1.5: enzyme can become active, depending if the denaturing can be reversible

2. The graph (right) shows enzyme reaction rate versus temperature for hypothetical enzyme X.

   (a) In terms of enzyme activity, what is happening at point A? the product was made after the reaction

   (b) Enzyme X catalyzes a reaction in a critical metabolic pathway. Predict what would happen if the temperature remained high (close to point A):

   the temperature would affect the enzyme activity through denaturization

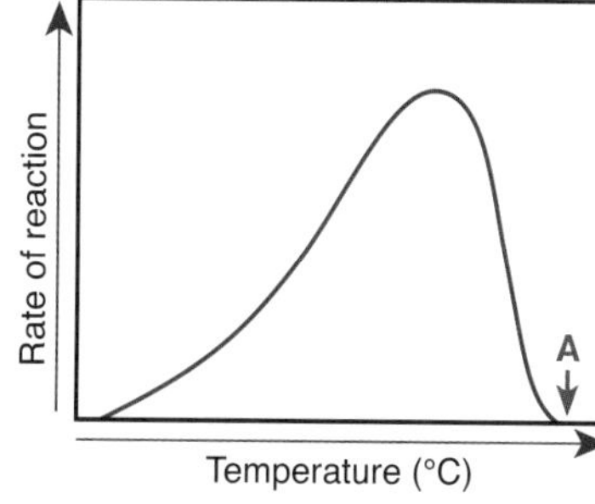

ISBN: 978-1-98-856656-6

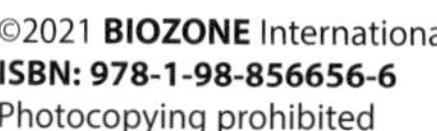

43 Factors Affecting Enzyme Activity

Key Question: What factors influence enzyme activity rates? Enzymes have an optimum set of conditions (e.g. of pH and temperature) where their activity is highest. As you explored in the previous activity, outside of the optimum, enzyme activity falls off and will stop altogether if the enzyme is denatured.

Most enzymes work best at moderate temperatures, but some enzymes have very high optimal temperatures (e.g. bacteria found in hot springs). Within their normal operating conditions, enzyme reaction rates are influenced by enzyme and substrate concentration in a predictable way.

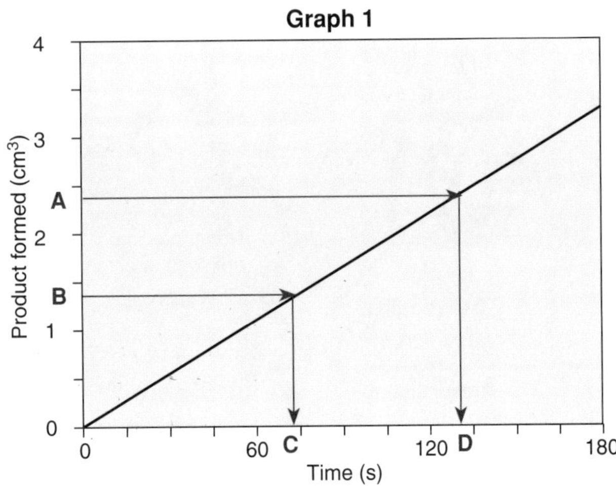

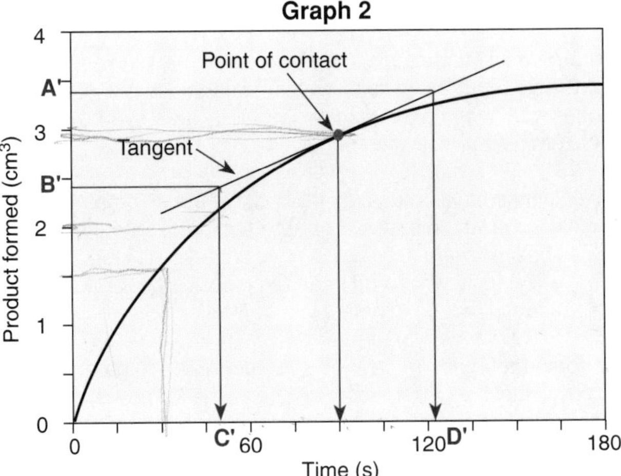

The rate of a reaction can be calculated from the amount of product produced during a given time period. For a reaction in which the rate does not vary (graph 1) the reaction rate calculated at any one point in time will be the same. For example: B/C = A/D = A-B/D-C = ($\Delta p/\Delta t$) (the change in product divided by the change in time).

In a reaction in which the rate varies (graph 2) a reaction rate can be calculated for any instantaneous moment in time by using a tangent. The tangent must touch the curve at only one point. The gradient of the tangent can then be used to calculate the rate of reaction at that point in time (A'-B'/D'-C').

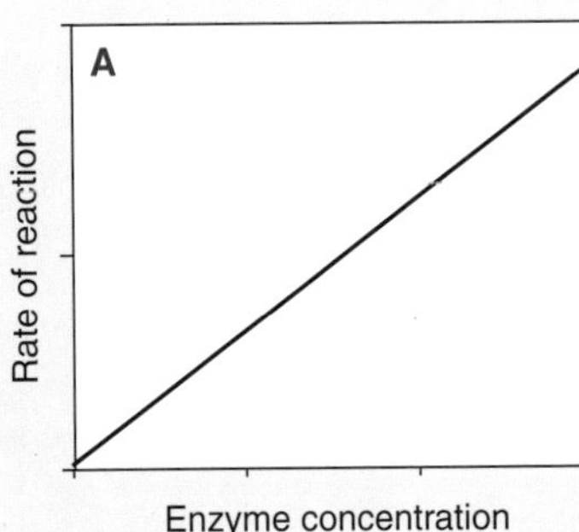

Given an unlimited amount of substrate, the rate of reaction will continue to increase as enzyme concentration increases. More enzyme means more reactions between substrates can be catalyzed in any given time (graph A).

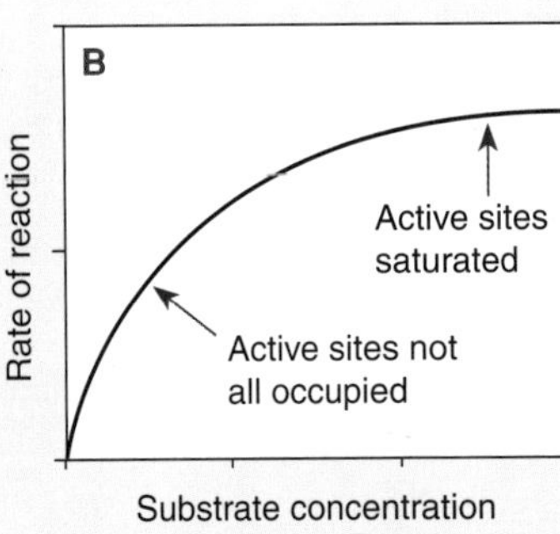

If there is unlimited substrate but the enzyme is limited, the reaction rate will increase until the enzyme is saturated, at which point the rate will remain static (graph B).

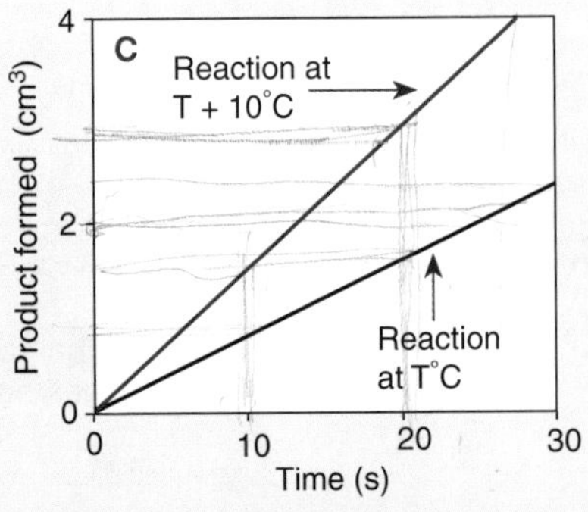

The effect of temperature on a reaction rate is expressed as the temperature coefficient, usually given as the Q_{10}. Q_{10} expresses the increase in the rate of reaction for every rise of 10°C. **Q10 = rate of reaction at (T + 10°C)/ rate of reaction at T**, where T is the temperature in °C (graph C).

1. Calculate the reaction rate in graph 1: 0.5 cm³/s

2. (a) For graph 2, calculate:

   (a) The reaction rate at 90 seconds: 0.03 cm³/s

   (b) The reaction rate at 30 seconds: 0.5 cm³/s

3. (a) What must be happening to the reaction mix in graph 1 to produce the straight line (constant reaction rate)?

   unlimited amount of substrate and increasing enzyme concentra

   (b) Explain why the reaction rate in graph 2 changes over time: there is limited enzyme

4. Explain why a reaction rate might drop off as the enzyme-catalyzed reaction proceeds over time: the enzyme becomes saturated, at which point the rate remains static

ISBN: 978-1-98-856656-6

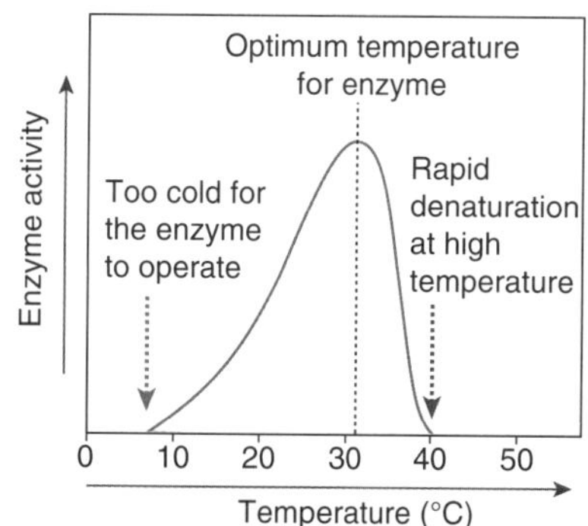

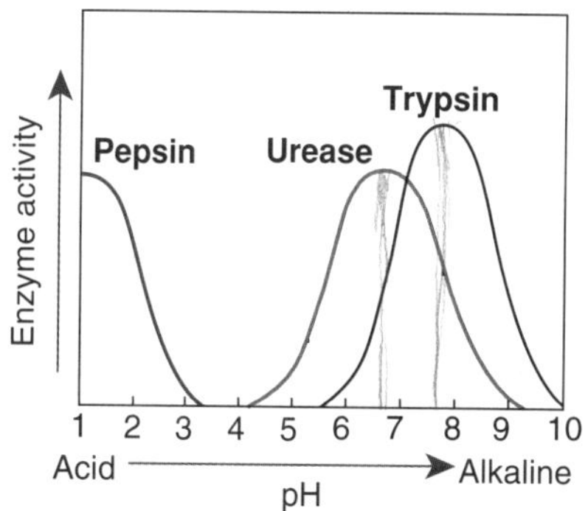

Higher temperatures increase the speed with which molecules in a solution move. This increases the frequency of collisions between a substrate and the active site, increasing reaction rate. However, few enzymes can tolerate temperatures higher than 50–60°C, and enzymes become denatured. The temperature at which an enzyme works at its maximum rate is the **optimum temperature**.

Enzymes performing the same function in species in different environments are very slightly different in order to maintain optimum performance. For example, the enzyme acetylcholinesterase has an optimum temperature of -2°C in the nervous system of an Antarctic icefish but an optimum temperature of 25°C in grey mullet found in the Mediterranean.

Like all proteins, enzymes are denatured by extremes of pH (very acid or alkaline). Within these extremes, most enzymes have a specific pH range for optimum activity. For example, digestive enzymes are specific to the region of the gut where they act: pepsin in the acid of the stomach and trypsin in the alkaline small intestine. Urease catalyzes the hydrolysis of urea at a near neutral pH.

5. (a) Describe the change in reaction rate when the enzyme concentration is increased and the substrate is not limiting:

More enzyme means more reactions between substrates can be catalyzed in any given time.

(b) Suggest how a cell may vary the amount of enzyme present:

6. Describe the change in reaction rate when the substrate concentration is increased (with a fixed amount of enzyme):

the reaction rate will increase until the enzyme is saturated

7. (a) Describe what is meant by an optimum temperature for enzyme activity: there is a certain temperature in which enzymes are most active

(b) Predict the effect on enzyme activity if an enzyme with a temperature optimum of 37°C was added to its substrate and incubated at 25°C. What would happen if the temperature was slowly increased to the optimum? Explain:

The reaction rate would be slow at first, than become faster due to the increase in temperature.

(c) For graph C on the previous page, calculate the Q_{10} for the reaction: 0.15/.08 = 1.875 = Q_{10}

8. (a) State the optimum pH for each of the enzymes:

Pepsin: 1 pH Trypsin: 7.8 pH Urease: 6.8 pH

(b) Explain how the pH optima of each of these enzymes is suited to its working environment: enzymes performing the same function in species in different environments are very slightly different in order to maintain optimum performance

ISBN: 978-1-98-856656-6

44 Enzyme Inhibitors

Key Question: What are the different types of enzyme inhibition and how is enzyme activity affected?

Enzyme activity can be stopped, temporarily or permanently, by chemicals called enzyme inhibitors. **Irreversible inhibitors** bind tightly to the enzyme and are not easily displaced. **Reversible inhibitors** can be displaced from the enzyme and have a role as enzyme regulators in metabolic pathways.

Competitive inhibitors compete directly with the substrate for the active site and their effect can be overcome by increasing the concentration of available substrate. A **non-competitive inhibitor** does not occupy the active site, but distorts it so that the substrate and enzyme can no longer interact. Both competitive and non-competitive inhibition may be irreversible, in which case the inhibitors act as poisons.

Competitive inhibition

Competitive inhibitors compete with the normal substrate for the enzyme's active site.

Competitive inhibitors compete directly with the substrate for the active site, and their effect can be overcome by increasing the substrate concentration.

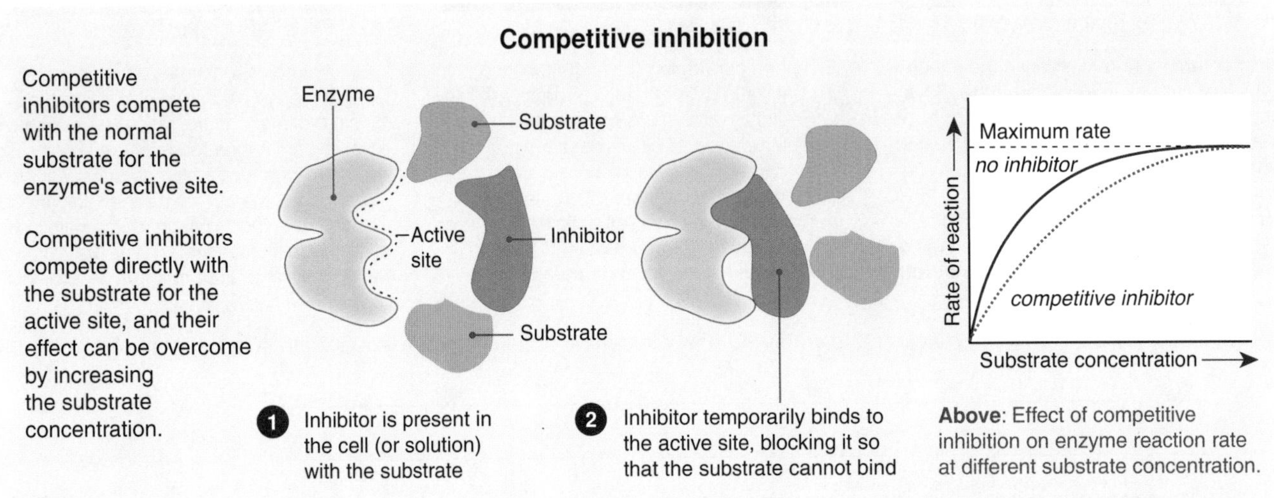

1. Inhibitor is present in the cell (or solution) with the substrate
2. Inhibitor temporarily binds to the active site, blocking it so that the substrate cannot bind

Above: Effect of competitive inhibition on enzyme reaction rate at different substrate concentration.

Non-competitive inhibition

Non-competitive inhibitors bind with the enzyme at a site other than the active site.

They inactivate the enzyme by altering its shape so that the substrate and enzyme can no longer interact.

Non-competitive inhibition cannot be overcome by increasing the substrate concentration.

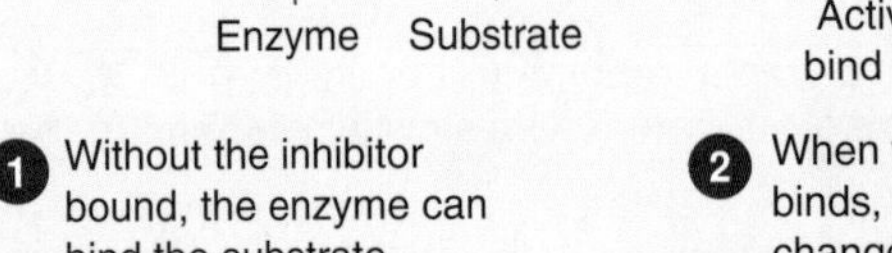

1. Without the inhibitor bound, the enzyme can bind the substrate
2. When the inhibitor binds, the enzyme changes shape.

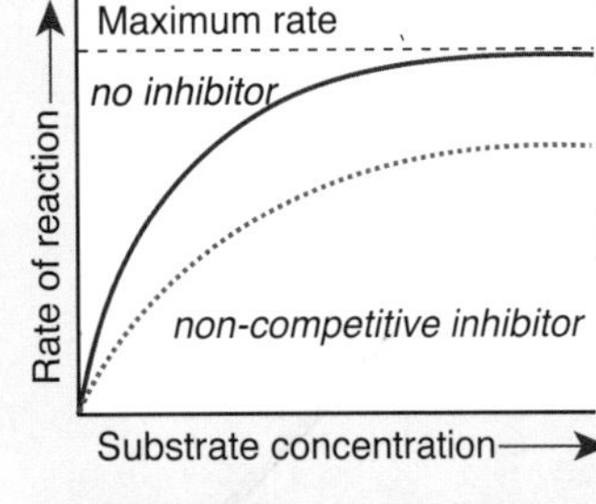

Above: Effect of non-competitive inhibition on enzyme reaction rate at different substrate concentration.

Allosteric enzyme regulation

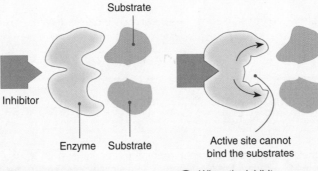

Allosteric site: The place on an enzyme where a molecule that is not a substrate may bind. The allosteric binding site is never the active site.

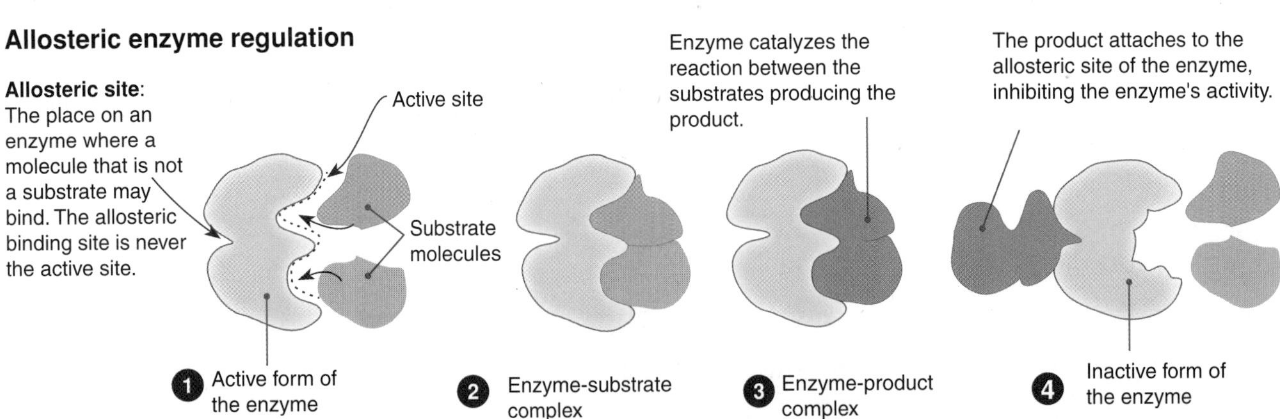

Active site
Substrate molecules
Enzyme catalyzes the reaction between the substrates producing the product.
The product attaches to the allosteric site of the enzyme, inhibiting the enzyme's activity.

1. Active form of the enzyme
2. Enzyme-substrate complex
3. Enzyme-product complex
4. Inactive form of the enzyme

Allosteric regulation is a form of non-competitive regulation where the regulatory molecule (*an activator or inhibitor*) binds to an enzyme somewhere other than the active site. Most non-competitive inhibition is a form of allosteric regulation. Allosteric regulation controls the enzymes in many metabolic pathways, and enzyme activity can be regulated by the products produced in the pathway. The action is usually by **feedback inhibition** (negative feedback). When the concentration of the end product is high, the end product will bind to the allosteric site of the first enzyme in the pathway, inhibiting the enzyme and shutting down the pathway. When the concentration of the end product is reduced, the allosteric site is vacated and the pathway is activated again.

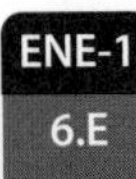

ISBN: 978-1-98-856656-6

Poisons are irreversible inhibitors

Some enzyme inhibitors are poisons because the binding of enzyme and inhibitor is irreversible. Irreversible inhibitors form strong covalent bonds with an enzyme. These inhibitors may act at, near, or remotely from the active site and modify the enzyme's structure to such an extent that it ceases to work. For example, the poison cyanide is an irreversible enzyme inhibitor that combines with the copper and iron in the active site of cytochrome *c* oxidase and blocks cellular respiration.

Since many enzymes contain sulfhydryl (-SH), alcohol, or acidic groups as part of their active sites, any chemical that can react with them may act as an irreversible inhibitor. Heavy metals, Ag^+, Hg^{2+}, or Pb^{2+}, have strong affinities for -SH groups and destroy catalytic activity. Most heavy metals are non-competitive inhibitors.

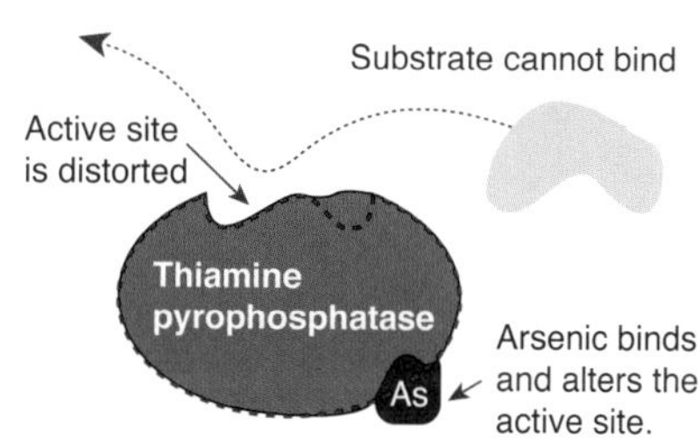

Arsenic and phosphorus share some structural similarities so arsenic will often substitute for phosphorus in biological systems. It therefore targets a wide variety of enzyme reactions. Arsenic can act as either a competitive or a non-competitive inhibitor (as above) depending on the enzyme.

Drugs

Many drugs work by irreversible inhibition of a pathogen's enzymes. Penicillin (below) and related antibiotics inhibit transpeptidase, a bacterial enzyme that forms some of the linkages in the bacterial cell wall. Susceptible bacteria cannot complete cell wall synthesis and cannot divide. Human cells are unaffected by the drug.

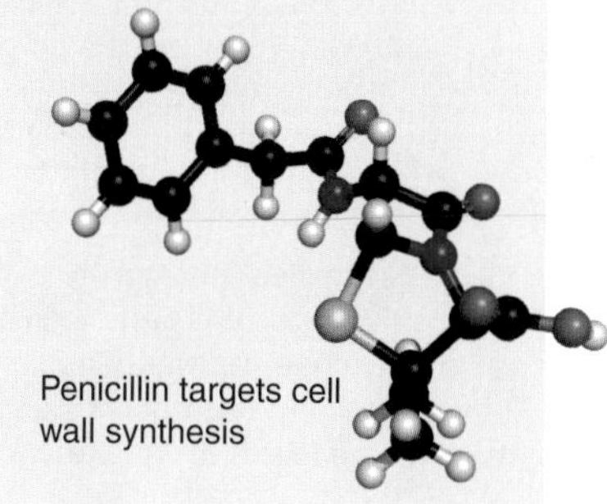

Penicillin targets cell wall synthesis

1. Distinguish between competitive and non-competitive inhibition: competitive inhibitors compete directly w/ the substrate for the active site + their effect can be overcome by increasing the concentration of available substrate. A non competitive does not occupy the active site, but distorts it so that the substrate + enzyme can no longer interact.

2. Predict the effect of competitive inhibition on the rate of an enzyme controlled reaction at:

   (a) Low substrate concentration: high reaction rate

   (b) High substrate concentration: low reaction rate → static rate

   (c) Suggest how you could distinguish between competitive and non-competitive inhibition in an isolated system: In competitive inhibition, the inhibitor binds to the active site where in noncompetitive it does not

3. Describe how an allosteric regulator can regulate enzyme activity: It controls the enzymes in many metabolic pathways, and enzyme activity can be regulated by the products produced in the pathway.

4. Explain why heavy metals, such as lead and arsenic, are poisonous: they have strong affinities for -SH groups + destroy catalytic activity. They can stop enzyme activity since they are non-competitive inhibitors.

5. (a) In the context of enzymes, explain how penicillin is exploited to control human diseases: It inhibits transpeptidase, a bacterial enzyme that forms some of the linkages in the bacterial cell wall. Humans aren't affect, yet bacteria cannot complete cell wall synthesis + cannot divide.

   (b) Explain why the drug is poisonous to the target organism, but not to humans: * read answer above*

ISBN: 978-1-98-856656-6

45 Investigating Enzyme Activity

STUDENT SUPPORT FOR INVESTIGATION 13, Procedure 2: *Investigating the effect of pH on peroxidase activity*

- Use the information provided and your own understanding of enzymes to investigate the effect of pH on enzyme activity.

Background

Hydrogen peroxide (H_2O_2) is a toxic by-product of respiration and must be broken down in order to avoid cellular damage. **Peroxidase** acts in the presence of naturally occurring organic reducing agents (electron donors) to catalyze the breakdown of H_2O_2 into water and oxidized organic substrates.

$$2H_2O_2 + 2AH_2 \xrightarrow{\text{Peroxidase}} 4H_2O + A_2$$

Like all enzymes, the activity of peroxidase is highest within specific ranges of pH and temperature, and activity drops off or is halted altogether when the conditions fall outside of the optimal range. The conversion of H_2O_2 is also influenced by other factors such as the levels of substrate and enzyme.

The effect of peroxidase on H_2O_2 breakdown can be studied using a common reducing agent called guaiacol. Oxidation of guaiacol (as in the equation above) forms tetraguaiacol, which is a dark orange color. The rate of the reaction can be followed by measuring the intensity of the orange color as a function of time.

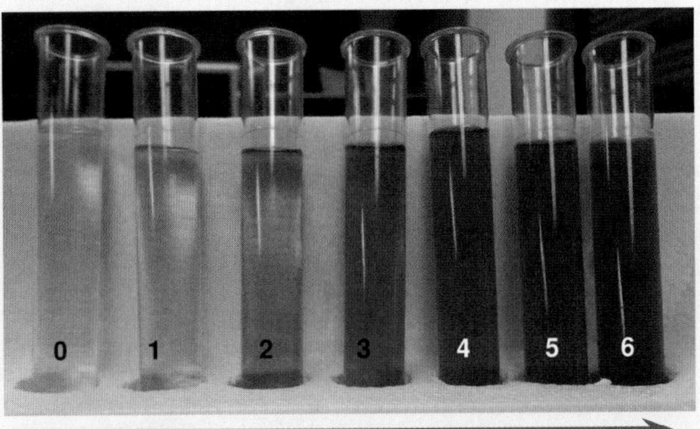

Increasing levels of oxygen production over time (minutes)

A time-color palette is shown above. You can use it as a reference against which to compare your own results from the investigation below. The palette was produced by adding a set amount of peroxidase to a solution containing hydrogen peroxide and water. The color change was recorded at set time points (0-6 minutes).

Determining the effect of pH on peroxidase activity

Students examined the effect of pH on peroxidase activity using the following procedure:

- **Substrate tubes** were prepared by adding 7 mL of distilled water, 0.3 mL of 0.1% H_2O_2 solution, and 0.2 mL of prepared guaiacol solution into 6 clean test tubes. The tubes were covered with parafilm and mixed.
- **Enzyme tubes** were prepared by adding 6.0 mL of prepared buffered pH solution (pH 3, 5, 6, 7, 8, 10) and 1.5 mL of prepared turnip peroxidase solution into 6 clean test tubes. The tubes were covered with parafilm and mixed.
- The substrate and enzyme tubes were combined, covered in parafilm, mixed and placed back into a test tube rack at room temperature. Timing began immediately. Students took photos with their phones to record the color change (relative to the reference color palette) every minute from time 0-6 minutes. Results are provided in Table 1.

Table 1. Effect of pH on peroxidase activity

	Color reference number					
	0 min	1 min	2 min	3 min	4 min	5 min
pH 3	0	2	2	3	3	3
pH 5	0	2	4	5	6	6
pH 6	0	3	3	3	3	3
pH 7	0	3	4	4	4	4
pH 8	0	3	3	3	3	3
pH 10	0	0	0	0	0	0

1. Graph the students' results on the grid (right).

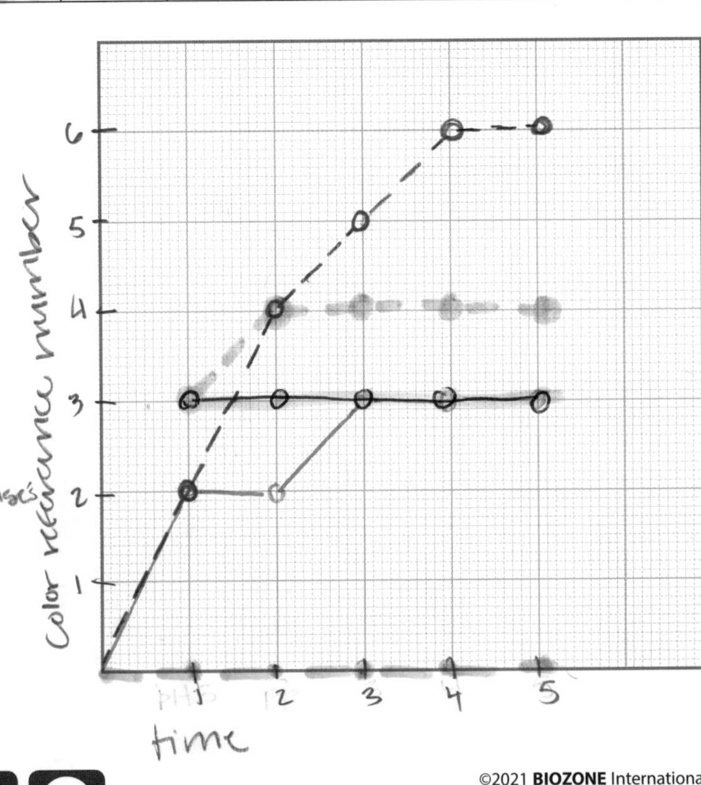

2. (a) Describe the effect of pH on peroxidase activity:

pH 5 is the most optimal pH for peroxidase activity. If pH is too low, the peroxidase's reaction rate is slow. If pH is too high, the enzyme eventually becomes denaturized and doesn't function (ex) pH 10).

ISBN: 978-1-98-856656-6

(b) No color change was recorded at pH 10. Explain why and relate this finding to the enzyme's structure and the way it interacts with its substrate:

The high pH denaturizes the enzyme resulting in no way for the enzyme to interact with it's substrate (because it's unfolded).

3. The color palette (opposite) shows the relative amounts of tetraguaiacol formed when oxygen binds to guaiacol. How can this be used to determine enzyme activity?

The darker (or greater) the color change describes the enzyme activity measured in the trials.

4. In the pH experiment, the students measured the rate of enzyme activity by comparing their results against a color palette. How could they have measured the results quantitatively?

They could watch/measure the color change

5. How might the results be affected if the students did not begin timing immediately after mixing the enzyme and substrate tubes together?

The time related to color reference would not be accurate, due to enzyme activity occurring in the unrecorded time.

6. Why is peroxidase written above the arrow in the equation for enzymatic breakdown of H_2O_2? Because it is being added to the reaction to create the end product.

7. Using the information provided, design an experiment to test the effect of concentration of turnip peroxidase on oxygen production. In the space below, summarize your method as step by step instructions. Design and justify your control. Explain how you will record and display the data and any limitations or sources of potential error with your design:

Step #1 - Gather materials + make sure to label the test tubes (one substrate + enzyme) #2 - prepare substrate tube #3 - prepare the enzyme tube. #4 - combine the contents into one tube. Cover w/ film + invert twice to mix. Take photo of immediate reaction. Start timing. #5 - Observe the color change for the next five minutes. Record color every minute. #6 - Use the color chart to help measure amount of color change. #7 - Repeat steps 2-6 once w/ .5% turnip peroxidase, another w/ 2% turnip peroxidase.

ISBN: 978-1-98-856656-6

46 Energy in Living Systems

Key Question: What is the role of ATP in living organisms?

All organisms require energy to be able to perform the metabolic processes required for them to function and reproduce. Energy input must exceed energy loss in order to power cellular processes. This energy is obtained by **cellular respiration**, a set of metabolic reactions that convert biochemical energy from 'food' into the nucleotide **ATP** (adenosine triphosphate). ATP is considered to be a universal energy carrier, transferring chemical energy within the cell for use in metabolic processes such as biosynthesis, cell division, cell signaling, thermoregulation, cell mobility, and active transport of substances across membranes.

Adenosine triphosphate (ATP)

- The ATP molecule consists of three components; a purine base (adenine), a pentose sugar (**ribose**), and **three phosphate groups** which attach to the 5' carbon of the pentose sugar. Adenine + ribose form adenosine (the "A" in ATP). The structure of ATP is shown right.
- The bonds between the phosphate groups contain electrons in a high energy state which store a large amount of energy. The energy is released during ATP hydrolysis. Typically, hydrolysis is coupled to another cellular reaction to which the energy is transferred. The end products of the reaction are adenosine diphosphate (ADP) and an inorganic phosphate (Pi).
- Note that energy is released during the formation of bonds during the hydrolysis reaction, not the breaking of bonds between the phosphates (which requires energy input).

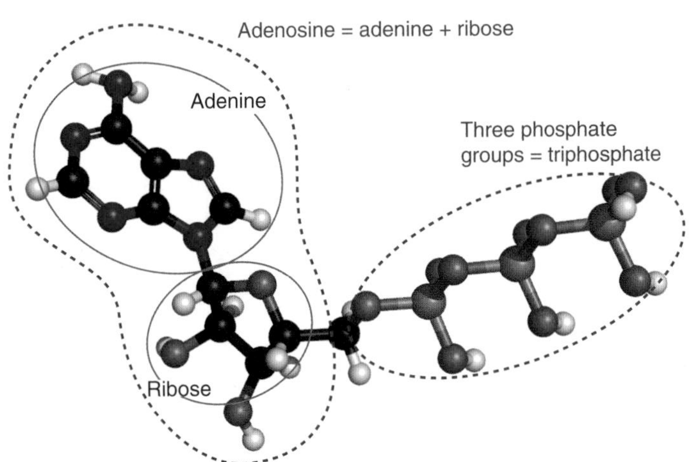

ATP powers metabolism

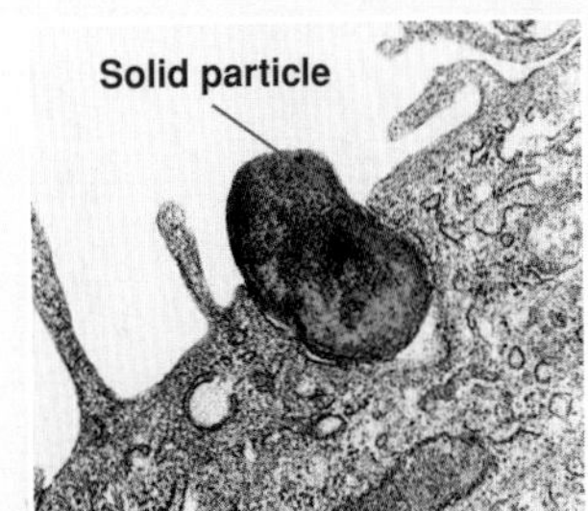

The energy released from the removal of a phosphate group of ATP is used for active transport of molecules and substances across the plasma membrane e.g. **phagocytosis** (above) and other active transport processes.

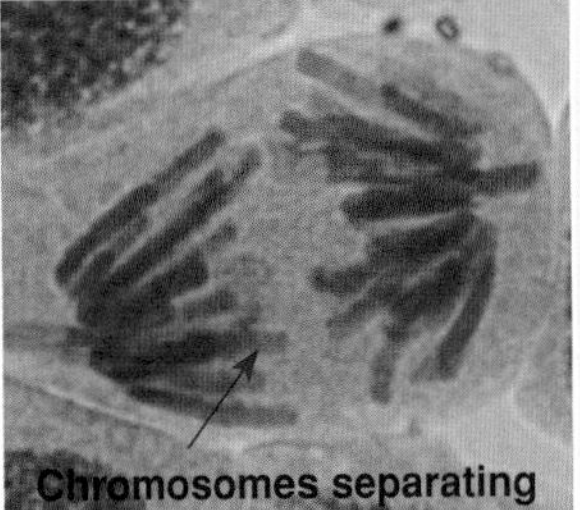

Mitosis, as seen in this stained onion cell, requires ATP to proceed. Formation of the mitotic spindle and chromosome separation both involve activity of cytoskeletal proteins and require the energy provided by ATP hydrolysis to occur.

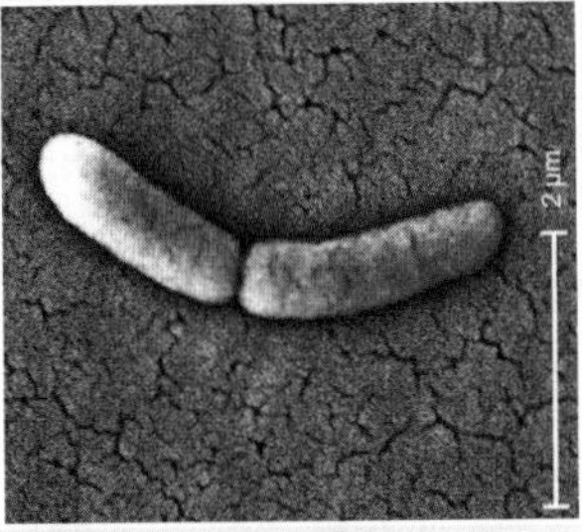

ATP is required when bacteria divide by binary fission (above). For example, ATP is required in DNA replication, for polymerization of organizing proteins, and to synthesize components of the peptidoglycan cell wall.

Not all of the energy released in the oxidation of glucose is captured in ATP. The rest is lost as heat. This heat energy can be used to maintain body temperature. Thermoregulatory mechanisms such as shivering and sweating also use ATP.

1. What process produces ATP in a cell? cellular respiration

2. Identify the three distinct elements of the space filing model of ATP, labeled (a)-(c) below right:

(a) adenine (b) ribose (c) triphosphate

3. Which two of the elements you labeled in question 2 make up adenosine? adenine + ribose

4. Explain why thermoregulation requires the expenditure of energy:

some energy in the oxidation of glucose is lost as heat. Thermoregulatory mechanisms such as shivering + sweating also use ATP.

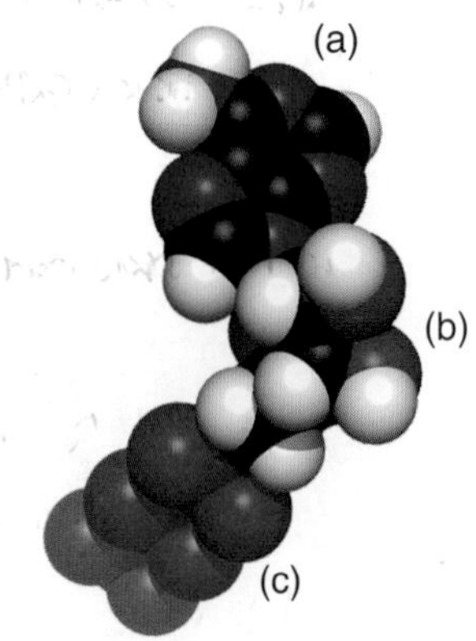

5. How does ATP act as a supplier of energy to power metabolic reactions? ATP is used for several metabolic reactions such as phagocytosis and mitosis

ISBN: 978-1-98-856656-6

- Thermodynamics lays out the fundamental laws of energy that govern the universe. The first law of thermodynamics states that the energy in an isolated system is constant (energy is neither created or destroyed). The second law of thermodynamics states that as energy is transferred or transformed, less is available to be used for work and it degenerates into a more disordered state (**entropy**). Entropy increases over time. To maintain order within a system, there must be an input of energy.
- Living organisms follow these laws by using energy in the form of light, inorganic substances, or food to drive the chemical reactions that maintain order in their bodies. Without the input of energy, order in a living system is quickly lost and organisms die. The disorder in their constituent parts then continues to increase until it reaches an equilibrium with the environment.

Entropy

Entropy is a measure of the disorder in a system, or the amount of energy not available to do work, and increases with time. The greater the entropy, the greater the disorder in the system.

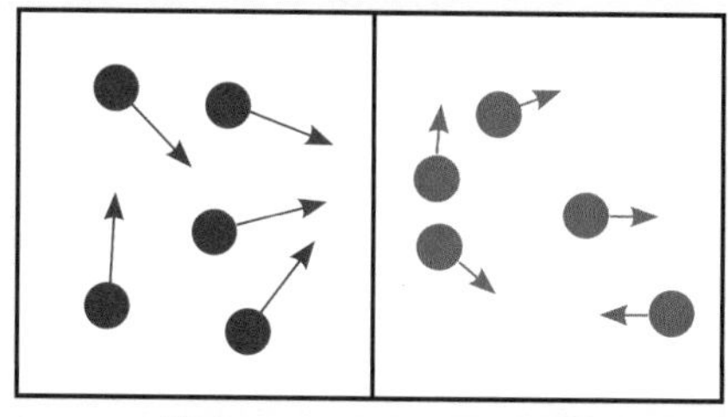

The system shown above has order. Hot, fast-moving molecules (high energy, long arrows) are separated from cold, slow moving molecules (low energy, short arrows).

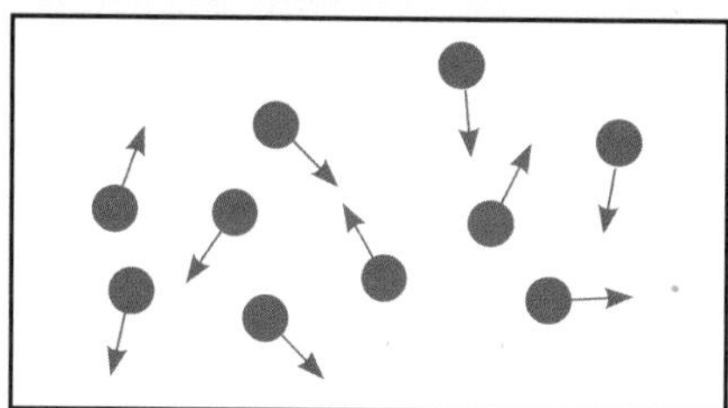

If the separation in the system is removed, the high energy molecules move into the area of low energy molecules. Collisions of the high energy molecules with the low energy molecules decrease the energy of the high energy molecules and increase the energy of the low energy molecules. Energy is also lost as heat. Eventually all molecules will have the same energy (equilibrium is reached). Entropy in the system has increased to its maximum level.

Order and the cell

Cells maintain order by using energy, either directly or indirectly. ATP can be used to directly drive a chemical reaction or it can used to produce a gradient, which is then used to move molecules into or out of the cell.

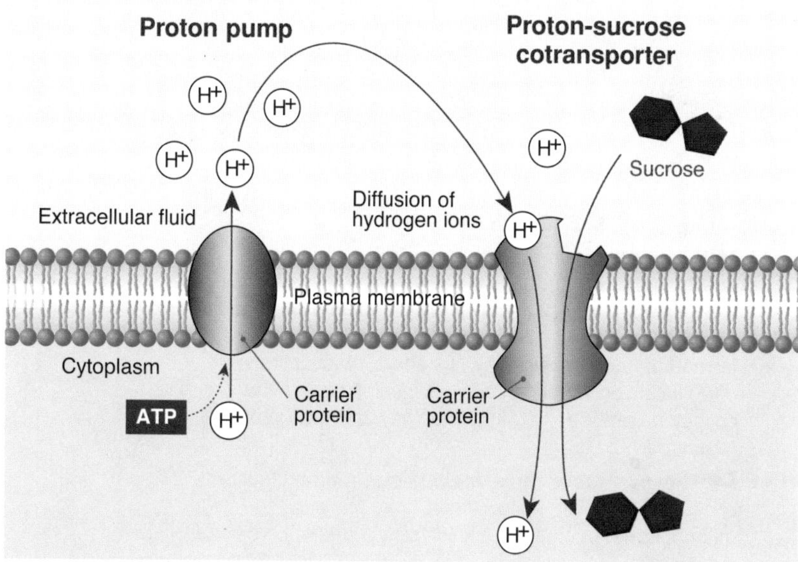

The proton-sucrose co-transporter shown above is common in the plasma membranes of plant cells. Energy in ATP is used to pump protons out of the cell, decreasing entropy with respect to the protons and producing a gradient. Sucrose is coupled to the flow of protons back down the gradient (increasing entropy with respect to the protons). Thus as the entropy with respect to the protons increases, the entropy with respect to the sucrose decreases.

The arrow of time

Entropy provides an answer as to why time moves forward (not backwards) and why we age. The universe is (we assume) an isolated system and its entropy can never decrease. Thus time is a result of the entropy of the universe moving towards its maximum. Aging can be viewed as an increase in the body's entropy. Death is effectively the highest and therefore most thermodynamically favored level of entropy. So favorable, in fact, that no amount of energy input can prevent it.

6. (a) Define entropy: a measure of the disorder in a system

   (b) Why has the entropy in the hot-cold system in the blue panel increased in the second image? Because in the 2nd pic, the separation is removed and there is more disorder, thus increasing the entropy.

7. (a) Explain how living organisms maintain order in their cells: cells maintain order by using energy, either directly or indirectly.

   (b) How does the proton-sucrose co-transporter decrease entropy with respect to the sucrose inside and outside a cell? entropy decreases by increasing the sucrose concentration within the cell, which is done by the increase of entropy of H+ and ATP.

ISBN: 978-1-98-856656-6

Metabolic pathways are sequential

- Metabolic pathways consist of a series of sequential steps. The product of one step in the pathway is generally the reactant (substrate) for the following step. The failure of one step therefore blocks all subsequent steps.
- You have already seen how feedback inhibition operates through the activity of allosteric inhibitors. Metabolic pathways are commonly regulated by feedback inhibition in this way, as illustrated by the end-product inhibition of the pathway that converts the amino acid threonine (one of 9 essential amino acids) to isoleucine.

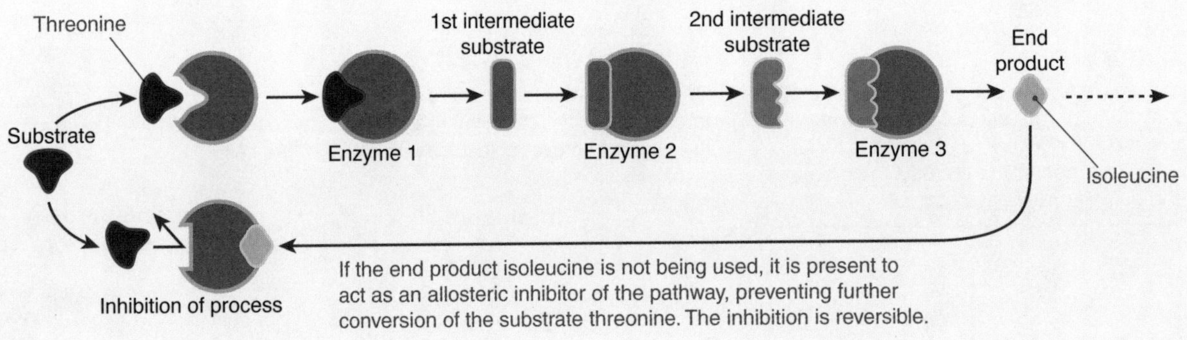

If the end product isoleucine is not being used, it is present to act as an allosteric inhibitor of the pathway, preventing further conversion of the substrate threonine. The inhibition is reversible.

Achieving efficiency by inhibition

- Metabolic pathways are tightly controlled to prevent energy being wasted. As shown above, if a product is not needed, the pathway for its production will shut down to conserve energy. This energy conservation is termed metabolic efficiency. Metabolic reactions are often localized within specific organelles so that the collected components of the pathway are more easily regulated.
- For instance, Krebs cycle, and the electron transport chain (oxidative phosphorylation) take place in the mitochondria. In contrast, glycolysis occurs in the cell's cytoplasm.
- Like simpler pathways, these complex pathways are regulated by feedback inhibition. For example, Krebs cycle is regulated mainly by the concentration of ATP and NADH. The key control points are the allosteric dehydrogenase enzymes in the cycle. Through feedback inhibition, the rate of the cycle is precisely regulated to meet the ATP needs of the organism.

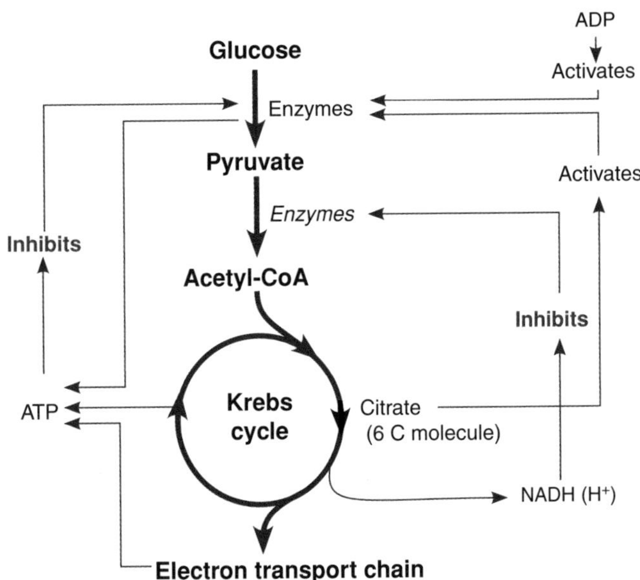

8. What does metabolic efficiency mean? When a product is not needed, the pathway for its production will shut down to conserve energy. This energy conservation is called metabolic efficiency.

9. Study the schematics above and use them to provide evidence to justify the claim that metabolic efficiencies are achieved by feedback inhibition:

Metabolic reactions are often localized within specific organelles so that the collected components of the pathway are more easily regulated. Feedback inhibition operates through the activity of allosteric inhibitors. Metabolic pathways are commonly regulated by feedback inhibition this way, as illustrated by the end product inhibition of the pathway that converts the amino acid threonine to isoleucine

ISBN: 978-1-98-856656-6

47 Energy Transformations in Cells

Key Question: How is energy from sunlight captured, stored and used to power the production of ATP?

The energy from sunlight is captured and stored as glucose, which powers the production of ATP in the process of cellular respiration. Hydrolysis of ATP provides the energy for the chemical reactions in living systems. Energy flow in the cell of a photoautotroph (a plant) is shown below. Note that ATP has a central role in acting as an energy carrier to power metabolic reactions. Heterotrophic cells (animals, fungi, and some bacteria) have a similar flow except the glucose is supplied by ingestion or absorption of food molecules rather than by photosynthesis. The energy not immediately stored in chemical bonds is lost as heat. Note that ATP provides the energy for most metabolism, including photosynthesis.

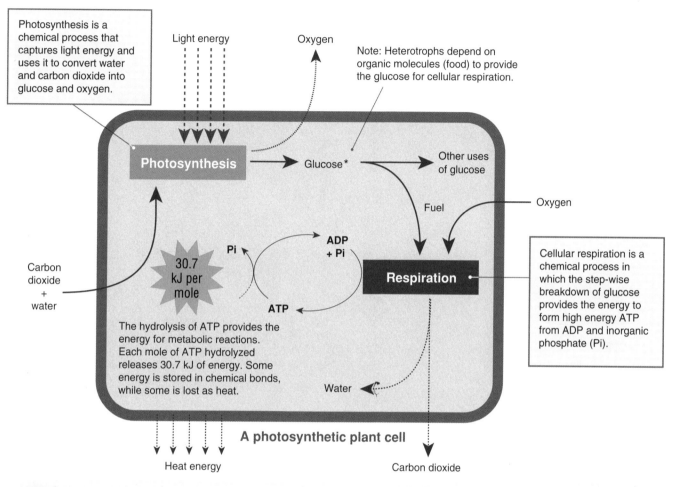

Photosynthesis is a chemical process that captures light energy and uses it to convert water and carbon dioxide into glucose and oxygen.

Light energy

Oxygen

Note: Heterotrophs depend on organic molecules (food) to provide the glucose for cellular respiration.

Photosynthesis

Glucose*

Other uses of glucose

Fuel

Oxygen

Pi

ADP + Pi

30.7 kJ per mole

Carbon dioxide + water

Respiration

Cellular respiration is a chemical process in which the step-wise breakdown of glucose provides the energy to form high energy ATP from ADP and inorganic phosphate (Pi).

ATP

The hydrolysis of ATP provides the energy for metabolic reactions. Each mole of ATP hydrolyzed releases 30.7 kJ of energy. Some energy is stored in chemical bonds, while some is lost as heat.

Water

A photosynthetic plant cell

Heat energy

Carbon dioxide

DID YOU KNOW?

It takes energy to break bonds, so how does the hydrolysis of ATP provide energy for metabolic reactions?
The hydrolysis of ATP is linked to the formation of a reactive intermediate, which can be used to do work. The reactions that make the energy in ATP available occur virtually simultaneously, so the reaction is simplified to omit the intermediates:

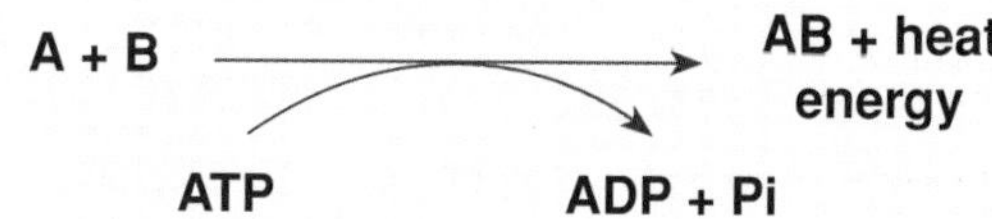

1. The diagram above depicts energy flow in an autotroph. But some autotrophs can derive their energy to fix carbon from inorganic compounds, such as hydrogen sulfide, rather than sunlight. For example, at deep sea hydrothermal vents, bacteria oxidize hydrogen sulfide to produce sugar, sulfur, and water: $CO_2 + 4H_2S + O_2 \rightarrow CH_2O + 4S + 3H_2O$:

   (a) Suggest why different pathway for fixing carbon dioxide evolved in deep sea vents: To provide CO^2 for plants without light in deep sea.

   (b) How are the end products of this pathway different to that shown above? The products are completely different ~~[illegible]~~ $(CH_2O + 4S + 3H_2O)$

2. In what way are the processes pictured above (photosynthesis and cellular respiration) connected? The products for each reaction are the reactants for the other reaction (recycled)

ISBN: 978-1-98-856656-6

48 Origin of Eukaryotic Photosynthesis

Key Question: How did oxygenic photosynthesis arise and what effect did it have on the Earth's atmosphere?

Photosynthesis is the process by which phototrophic organisms convert sunlight energy into chemical energy. Ancient prokaryotic organisms first evolved the ability to carry out anoxygenic photosynthesis, a bacterial photosynthesis that occurs under anaerobic conditions and produces no oxygen. Oxygenic photosynthesis, which releases oxygen, arose in a cyanobacterial ancestor around 2.7 billion years ago (bya). Over time, the abundance of photosynthesizing cyanobacteria resulted in an accumulation of oxygen the Earth's atmosphere and oceans, shifting them from being weakly reducing to oxidizing. This part of Earth's history, about 2.5 bya, is known as the **Great Oxygenation Event** (GOE). It resulted in a rapid increase in mineral diversity and led to the evolution of multicellular eukaryotes, including eukaryotic photoautotrophs such as red and green algae and land plants.

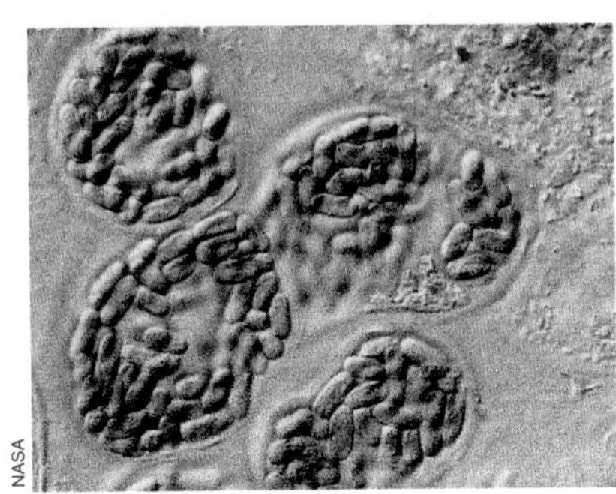

Chloroplasts are the photosynthetic organelles in eukaryotes. Cyanobacteria (above) are considered to be the ancestors of chloroplasts. The evidence for this comes from similarities in the ribosomes and membrane organization, as well as from genetic studies. Chloroplasts were acquired by eukaryotic cells independently of mitochondria, from a different bacterial lineage, but by the similar process of endosymbiosis.

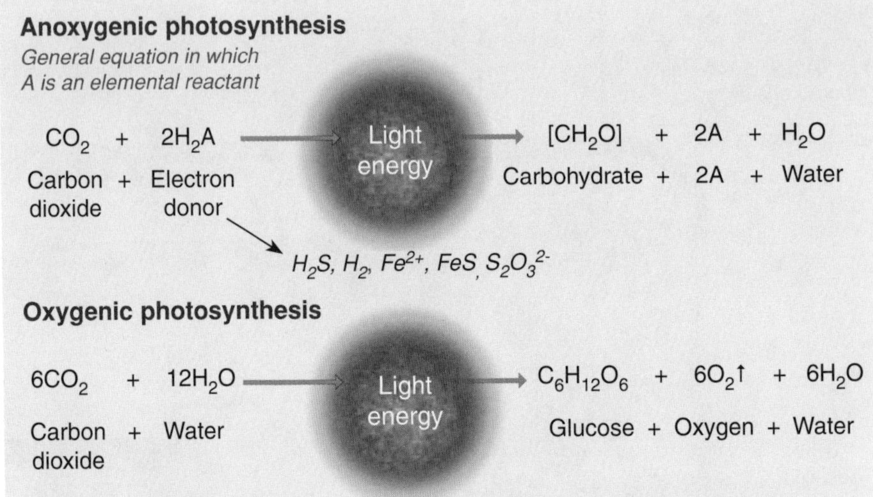

Many phototrophic bacteria carry out anoxygenic photosynthesis. They use strong electron donors other than water (above) and no oxygen is generated. Cyanobacteria and photosynthetic eukaryotes carry out oxygenic photosynthesis. These organisms use water as the electron donor, producing oxygen as a by-product. Prokaryotic synthetic pathways were the foundation of eukaryotic photosynthesis.

1. Describe the main difference between anoxygenic photosynthesis and oxygenic photosynthesis: Anoxygenic photosynthesis is a bacterial photosynthesis that occurs under anaerobic conditions + produces no oxygen. Oxygenic photosynthesis releases oxygen.

2. What evidence is there that cyanobacteria are the ancestors of chloroplasts? The evidence for this comes from similarities in the ribosomes + membrane organization, as well as from genetic studies.

3. Study the graph (right).

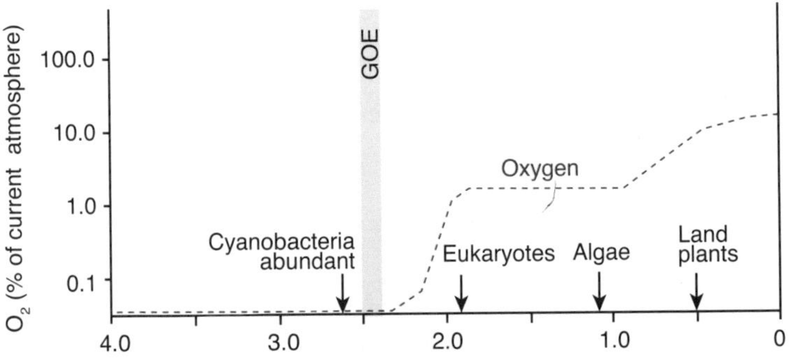

(a) What evidence is there that cyanobacteria were responsible for the GOE?

GOE rose when cyanobacteria were abundant.

(b) Suggest why atmospheric oxygen levels continued to increase up until present day:

The need for oxygen by newly made organisms like eukaryotes.

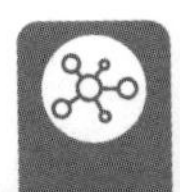
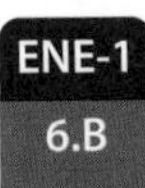

ISBN: 978-1-98-856656-6

49 Photosynthesis

Key Question: What are the net inputs and outputs of oxygenic photosynthesis?

Oxygenic photosynthesis is of fundamental importance to living things because it transforms sunlight energy into chemical energy stored in molecules, releases free oxygen gas, and absorbs carbon dioxide (a waste product of cellular metabolism). Photosynthesis (and from here on this means oxygenic photosynthesis within the chloroplasts of green plants) has two sets of reactions. In the **light dependent phase**, in the thylakoid membranes of chloroplasts, light energy is converted to chemical energy (ATP and NADPH). In the **light independent phase**, in the stroma of chloroplasts, the ATP and NADPH are used to synthesize carbohydrate. In photosynthesis, water is split and electrons are transferred together with hydrogen ions from water to CO_2, reducing it to triose phosphates (these are then converted to sugars).

Light dependent phase (LDP):

In the first phase of photosynthesis, chlorophyll captures light energy, which is used to split water, producing O_2 gas (waste). Electrons and H^+ ions are transferred to the molecule NADPH. ATP is also produced. The light dependent phase occurs in the thylakoid membranes of the grana.

Light independent phase (LIP):

The second phase of photosynthesis occurs in the stroma and uses the NADPH and the ATP to drive a series of enzyme-controlled reactions (the **Calvin cycle**) that fix carbon dioxide to produce triose phosphate. This phase does not need light to proceed.

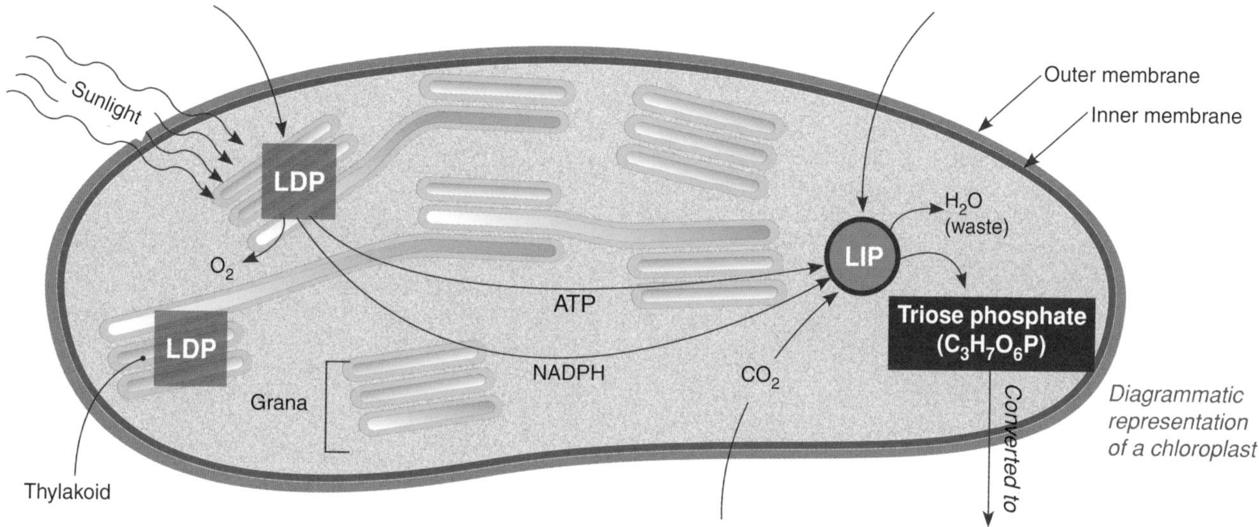

Diagrammatic representation of a chloroplast

CO_2 from the air provides raw materials for glucose production.

Monosaccharides (e.g. **glucose**) and other carbohydrates, lipids, and amino acids.

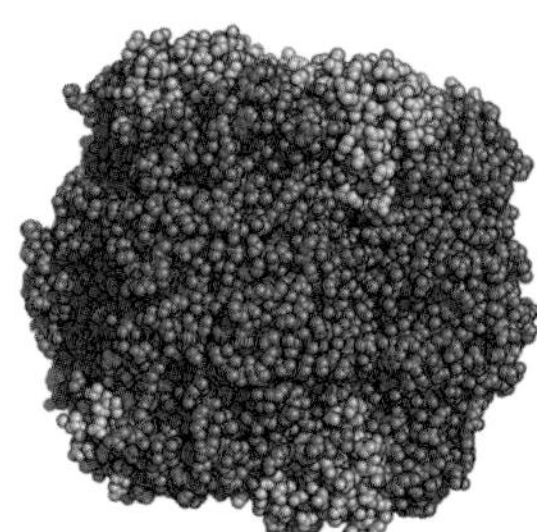

RuBisCo (left) is the central enzyme in the LIP of photosynthesis (carbon fixation) catalyzing the first step in the Calvin cycle. However it is remarkably inefficient, processing just three reactions a second. To compensate, RuBisCo makes up almost half the protein content of chloroplasts.

The general equation for photosynthesis

$$6CO_2 + 6H_2O \xrightarrow[\text{Chlorophyll}]{\text{Light}} C_6H_{12}O_6 + 6O_2$$

1. Identify the two phases of photosynthesis and their location in the cell:

(a) light dependent phase - chlorophyll

(b) light independent phase (calvin cycle) - stroma

2. (a) What is the role of the enzyme RuBisCo? catalyzes 1st step of calvin cycle.

(b) RuBisCo is the most abundant protein on Earth. Suggest a reason for this: Because it is remarkably inefficient, so there needs to be an abundance of it to work.

3. State the origin and fate of the following molecules involved in photosynthesis:

(a) Carbon dioxide: provides raw materials for glucose production.

(b) Oxygen: Produced as waste in LDP

(c) Hydrogen: split from water in LDP

ISBN: 978-1-98-856656-6

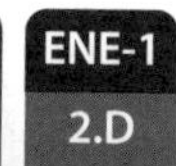
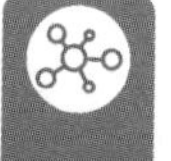

50 Pigments and Light Absorption

Key Question: How do chlorophyll pigments absorb light and capture light energy for photosynthesis?

The ability of phototrophic organisms to capture light energy is a function of the membrane-bound pigments they possess. **Pigments** are substances that absorb visible light, and different pigments absorb light of different wavelengths. The amount of light absorbed vs the wavelength of light is called the **absorption spectrum** of that pigment. The absorption spectrum of different photosynthetic pigments provides clues to their role in photosynthesis, since light can only perform work if it is absorbed. An **action spectrum** profiles the effectiveness of different wavelengths of light in fueling photosynthesis. It is obtained by plotting wavelength against a measure of photosynthetic rate (e.g. O_2 production).

The electromagnetic spectrum

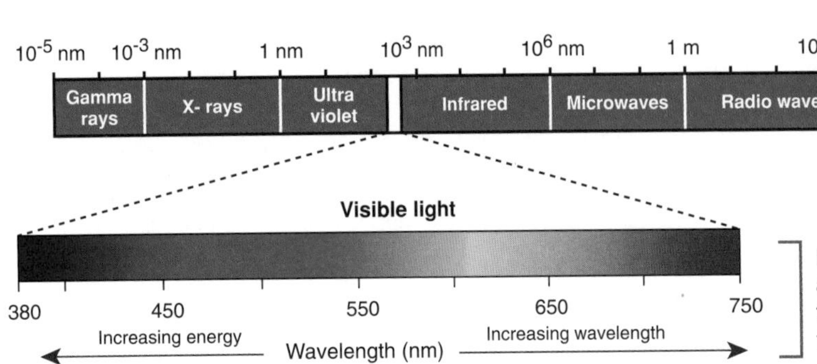

Light is a form of energy known as electromagnetic radiation (EMR). The segment of the electromagnetic spectrum most important to life is the narrow band between about 380 nm and 750 nm. This radiation is known as visible light because it is detected as colors by the human eye. It is visible light that drives photosynthesis.

EMR travels in waves, where wavelength provides a guide to the energy of the photons. The greater the wavelength of EMR, the lower the energy of the photons in that radiation.

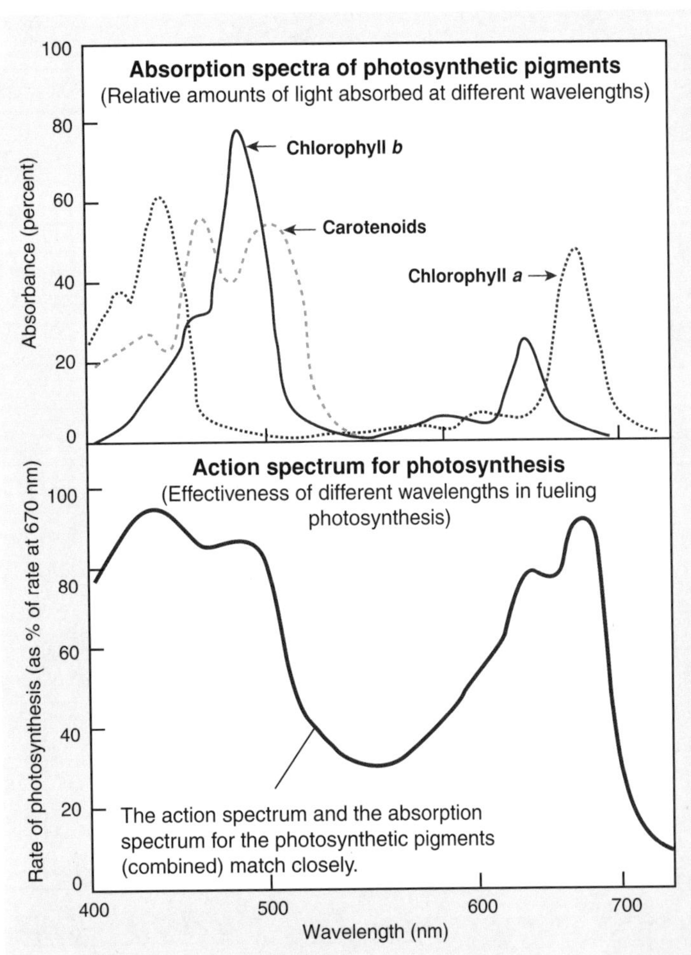

The photosynthetic pigments of plants

The photosynthetic pigments of plants fall into two categories: **chlorophylls** (which absorb red and blue-violet light) and **carotenoids** (which absorb strongly in the blue-violet and appear orange, yellow, or red). The pigments are located on the chloroplast membranes (the thylakoids) and are associated with membrane transport systems.

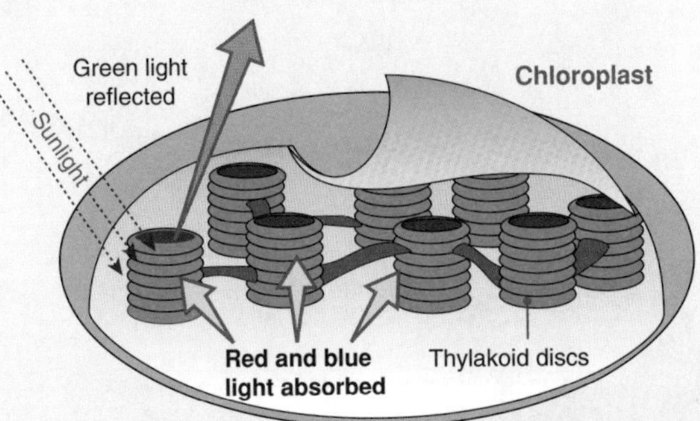

The pigments of chloroplasts in higher plants (above) absorb blue and red light, and the leaves therefore appear green (which is reflected). Each photosynthetic pigment has its own characteristic absorption spectrum (top left). Only chlorophyll *a* participates directly in the light reactions of photosynthesis, but the accessory pigments (chlorophyll *b* and carotenoids) can absorb wavelengths that chlorophyll *a* cannot and pass the energy (photons) to chlorophyll *a*, broadening the spectrum that can drive photosynthesis.

Left: Graphs comparing absorption spectra of photosynthetic pigments compared with the action spectrum for photosynthesis.

1. What is meant by the absorption spectrum of a pigment? provides clues to their role in photosynthesis since light can only perform work if it is absorbed.

2. Use the graphs above to explain why the action spectrum for photosynthesis doesn't exactly match the absorption spectrum of chlorophyll *a*:

The pigments of chloroplasts in higher plants absorb blue + red light and the leaves appear green.

ISBN: 978-1-98-856656-6

51 Light Dependent Reactions

Key Question: How is light energy used to drive the reduction of NADP+ and the production of ATP.

Photosynthesis is a redox process where water is split, and electrons and hydrogen ions are transferred from water to CO_2, reducing it to sugar. The electrons increase in potential energy as they move from water to sugar. The energy to do this is provided by light. Photosynthesis has two phases. In the **light dependent reactions**, light energy is converted to chemical energy (ATP and NADPH). In the **light independent reactions**, the chemical energy is used to synthesize carbohydrate. The light dependent reactions most commonly involve **non-cyclic phosphorylation**, which produces ATP and NADPH in roughly equal quantities. The electrons lost are replaced from water. In **cyclic phosphorylation**, the electrons lost from photosystem II are replaced by those from photosystem I. ATP is generated, but not NADPH.

Non-cyclic phosphorylation

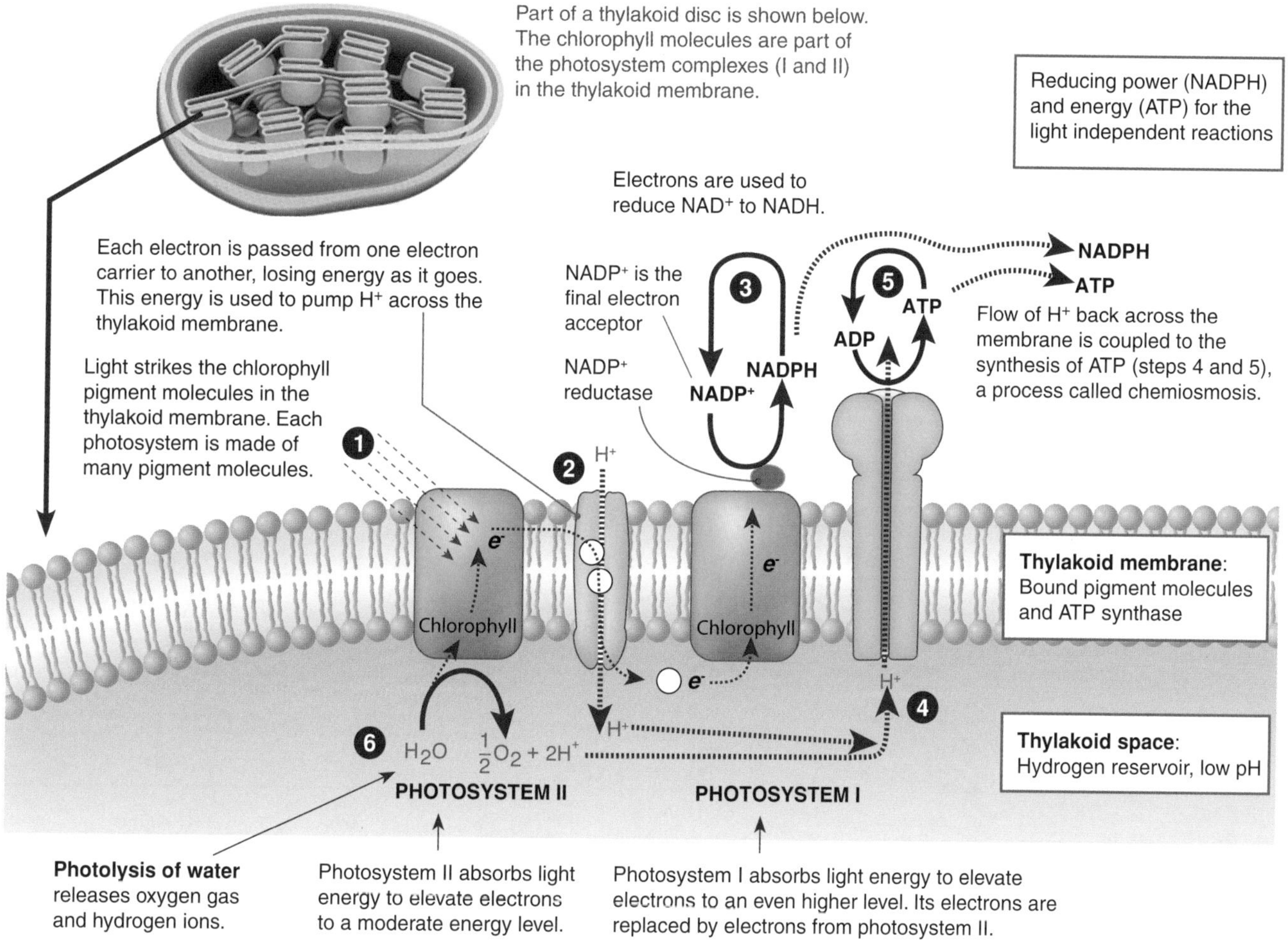

Part of a thylakoid disc is shown below. The chlorophyll molecules are part of the photosystem complexes (I and II) in the thylakoid membrane.

Reducing power (NADPH) and energy (ATP) for the light independent reactions

Electrons are used to reduce NAD+ to NADH.

Each electron is passed from one electron carrier to another, losing energy as it goes. This energy is used to pump H+ across the thylakoid membrane.

Light strikes the chlorophyll pigment molecules in the thylakoid membrane. Each photosystem is made of many pigment molecules.

NADP+ is the final electron acceptor

NADP+ reductase

1, 2, 3, 4, 5, 6

NADP+ NADPH ADP ATP H+ e- Chlorophyll

NADPH

ATP

Flow of H+ back across the membrane is coupled to the synthesis of ATP (steps 4 and 5), a process called chemiosmosis.

Thylakoid membrane: Bound pigment molecules and ATP synthase

Thylakoid space: Hydrogen reservoir, low pH

H_2O → $\frac{1}{2}O_2 + 2H^+$

PHOTOSYSTEM II **PHOTOSYSTEM I**

Photolysis of water releases oxygen gas and hydrogen ions.

Photosystem II absorbs light energy to elevate electrons to a moderate energy level.

Photosystem I absorbs light energy to elevate electrons to an even higher level. Its electrons are replaced by electrons from photosystem II.

Cyclic phosphorylation

Cyclic phosphorylation involves only photosystem I and no NADPH is generated. Electrons from photosystem I are shunted back to the electron carriers in the membrane so this pathway produces ATP only. The Calvin cycle uses more ATP than NADPH, so cyclic phosphorylation makes up the difference. It is activated when NADPH levels build up, and remains active until enough ATP is made to meet demand.

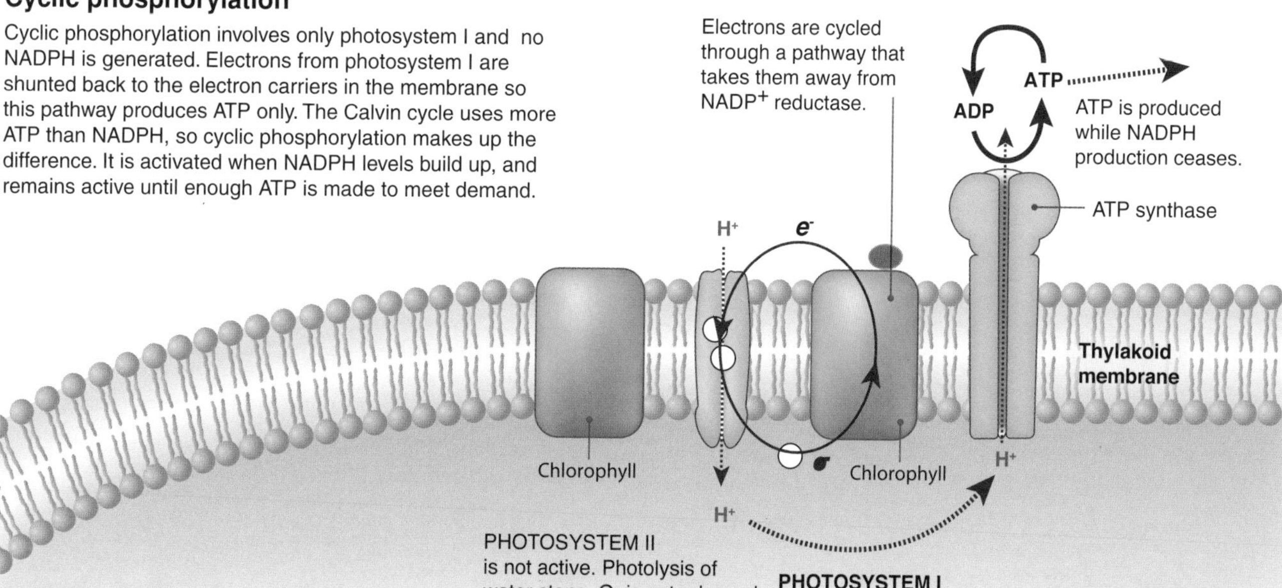

Electrons are cycled through a pathway that takes them away from NADP+ reductase.
ATP
ADP
ATP is produced while NADPH production ceases.
ATP synthase
H+
e-
Thylakoid membrane
Chlorophyll
Chlorophyll
H+
H+
PHOTOSYSTEM II is not active. Photolysis of water stops. O2 is not released.
PHOTOSYSTEM I

ISBN: 978-1-98-856656-6

1. Describe the role of the carrier molecule NADP in photosynthesis: NADP+ is the final electron acceptor.

2. Explain the role of chlorophyll molecules in photosynthesis: The chlorophyll molecules are part of the photosystem complexes (I and II) in the thylakoid membrane.

3. (a) Where do the light dependent reactions occur? thylakoid

(b) Summarize the events of the light dependent reactions: light energy is converted to chemical energy. The chemical energy is used to synthesize carbohydrate. Non-cyclic phosphorylation produces ATP in roughly equal quantities.

4. Explain how ATP generation is linked to the light dependent reactions of photosynthesis: In the light dependent reactions, the chemical energy is used to synthesize carbohydrate. The light dependent reactions most ~~importantly~~ commonly involve non-cyclic phosphorylation, which produces ATP and NADPH in roughly equal quantities. In cyclic phosphorylation the electrons lost from photosystem II are replaced by I and ATP is generated.

5. (a) Explain what you understand by the term non-cyclic phosphorylation: The light dependent reactions most commonly involve non-cyclic phosphorylation which produces ATP + NADPH in roughly equal quantities

(b) Suggest why this process is also known as non-cyclic photophosphorylation: The products are non cycled back as the reactants of the pathway

6. (a) Describe how cyclic photophosphorylation differs from non-cyclic photophosphorylation: ~~Non~~ only involves photosystem I and no NADPH is generated. Electrons from photosystem I are shunted back to the electron carriers in the membrane so this pathway produces ATP only.

(b) Both cyclic and non-cyclic pathways operate to varying degrees during photosynthesis. Since the non-cyclic pathway produces both ATP and NAPH, explain the purpose of the cyclic pathway of electron flow:

It is activated when NADPH builds up, and remains active until enough ATP is made to meet demand.

7. Bacteria that carry out anoxygenic photosynthesis lack a functional equivalent to photosystem II and use only cyclic phosphorylation. Explain how this accounts for their inability to generate oxygen from photosynthesis:

Bacteria ~~does~~ are prokaryotes and do not use oxygen to form energy.

ISBN: 978-1-98-856656-6

52 Light Independent Reactions

Key Question: What are the features of the Calvin cycle?

In the **light independent reactions** (commonly also called the **Calvin cycle**) hydrogen (H^+) is added to CO_2 and a 5C intermediate to make carbohydrate. The H^+ and ATP are supplied by the light dependent reactions. The Calvin cycle uses more ATP than NADPH, but the cell uses cyclic phosphorylation (which does not produce NADPH) when it runs low on ATP to make up the difference.

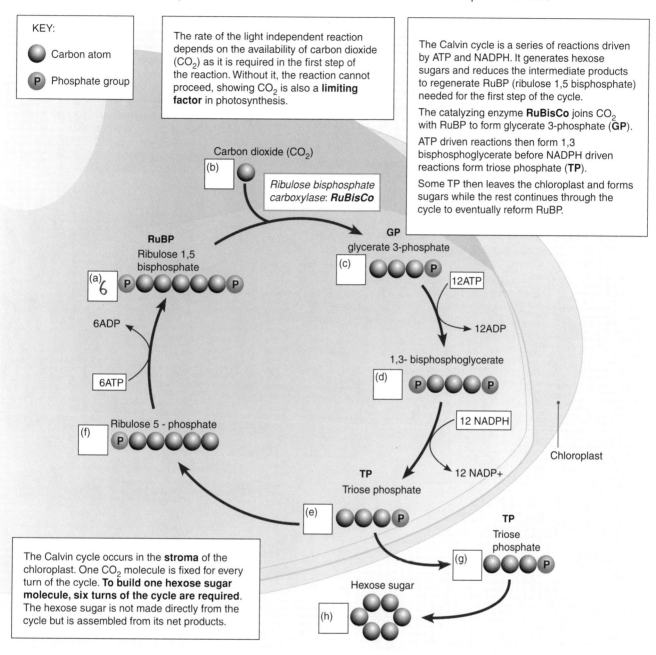

KEY:
- Carbon atom
- P Phosphate group

The rate of the light independent reaction depends on the availability of carbon dioxide (CO_2) as it is required in the first step of the reaction. Without it, the reaction cannot proceed, showing CO_2 is also a **limiting factor** in photosynthesis.

The Calvin cycle is a series of reactions driven by ATP and NADPH. It generates hexose sugars and reduces the intermediate products to regenerate RuBP (ribulose 1,5 bisphosphate) needed for the first step of the cycle.

The catalyzing enzyme **RuBisCo** joins CO_2 with RuBP to form glycerate 3-phosphate (**GP**).

ATP driven reactions then form 1,3 bisphosphoglycerate before NADPH driven reactions form triose phosphate (**TP**).

Some TP then leaves the chloroplast and forms sugars while the rest continues through the cycle to eventually reform RuBP.

Carbon dioxide (CO_2) (b)

Ribulose bisphosphate carboxylase: ***RuBisCo***

RuBP Ribulose 1,5 bisphosphate (a) 6

GP glycerate 3-phosphate (c)

12ATP → 12ADP

1,3- bisphosphoglycerate (d)

12 NADPH → 12 NADP+

TP Triose phosphate (e)

Ribulose 5 - phosphate (f)

6ATP → 6ADP

TP Triose phosphate (g)

Hexose sugar (h)

Chloroplast

The Calvin cycle occurs in the **stroma** of the chloroplast. One CO_2 molecule is fixed for every turn of the cycle. **To build one hexose sugar molecule, six turns of the cycle are required.** The hexose sugar is not made directly from the cycle but is assembled from its net products.

1. In the boxes on the diagram above, write the number of molecules formed at each step during the formation of **one hexose sugar molecule**. The first one has been done for you:

2. Explain the importance of RuBisCo in the Calvin cycle: The catalyzing enzyme RuBisCo joins CO_2 w/ RuBP to form glycerate 3-phosphate

3. Identify the actual end product on the Calvin cycle: hexose sugar

4. Write the equation for the production of one hexose sugar molecule from carbon dioxide: CO_2 + 12ATP + 12 NADPH = hexose sugar

5. Explain why the Calvin cycle is likely to cease in the dark for most plants, even though it is independent of light: It needs some form of energy to be able to function

ISBN: 978-1-98-856656-6

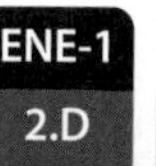

ENE-1 2.A
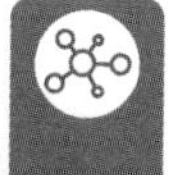

53 Investigating Photosynthesis

***STUDENT SUPPORT FOR INVESTIGATION 5:** Investigating the effect of wavelength on photosynthetic rate*

Aim

To investigate the effect of wavelength of light (light color) on the rate of photosynthesis in a green plant.

Method

- A student selected several green leaves of the same type. They used a hole punch to cut out 50 discs of a uniform size (avoiding major leaf veins). The discs were placed into a large syringe containing a 0.2% solution of sodium bicarbonate ($NaHCO_3$). The student then placed a finger tightly over the tip of the syringe and slowly pulled back on the plunger, repeating until all the discs sunk. The syringe was kept in the dark until needed. Any discs still floating were not used.
- Four 150 mL glass beakers were labeled red, blue, green, or white. 100 mL of 0.2% $NaHCO_3$ solution and 5 mL of detergent was added to each beaker. Next, 10 drops of the appropriate food coloring was added to the appropriate beaker. No food coloring was added to the white beaker.
- Ten leaf discs were placed into a beaker, and the beaker was placed 15 cm from a 100 watt light bulb. A timer was immediately started and the time taken for all 10 leaf discs to float was recorded. The student repeated the procedure with the remaining colored solutions.

Background

Leaf disc assays are commonly used to investigate photosynthesis in the classroom because they are simple to perform and do not require any specialized equipment. The bicarbonate solution under pressure removes any oxygen in the leaf by replacing the air in the leaf air spaces and it also serves as a source of CO_2 during the experiment. As photosynthesis occurs, O_2 is produced and the leaf disks become buoyant and eventually float. The rate of flotation is an indirect measure of the rate of photosynthesis. The detergent is added to break down the water-repellent barrier on the leaf surface, allowing the sodium bicarbonate to enter the leaf more easily.

Results

The results from the experiment are shown below.

Light color	Time taken for 10 discs to float (*s*)
Blue	162
Red	558
Green	998
White	694

1. Generate a brief hypothesis for this experiment: The beakers with red and blue solution will be most effective in photosynthesis due to the colors' light absorbancy.

2. Why do the leaf discs float? As photosynthesis occurs, O_2 is produced, and the leaf disks become buoyant and eventually float.

3. (a) Graph the results on the grid provided (right):

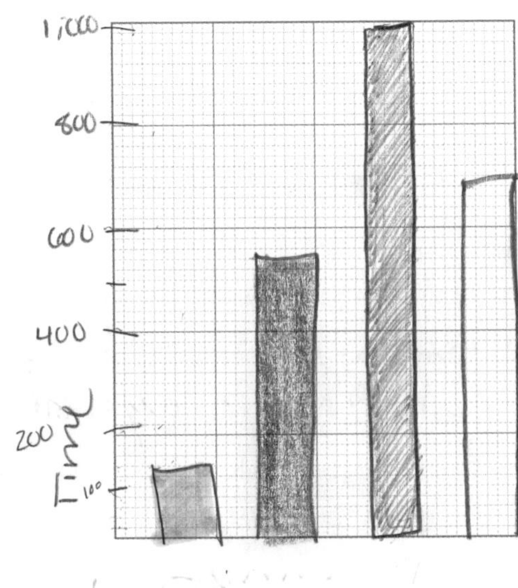

(b) Describe how photosynthesis was affected by light color: Each color solution have different light absorbencies, so the solutions that were more light absorbent would have photosynthesis occurring faster.

4. Did the results support your hypothesis? Explain: Yes because the blue + red solutions had the leaf disks float the fastest.

ISBN: 978-1-98-856656-6

54 Pathways for Obtaining Energy

Key Question: What are the different metabolic pathways organisms use to generate ATP and what are the ATP yields?

In most energy-yielding pathways the initial source of chemical energy is glucose, a 6C sugar. The first step, **glycolysis**, is an anaerobic process that converts glucose to pyruvate. It is an almost universal pathway. Different energy yielding pathways diverge after this step. Some are **aerobic** (require oxygen) while others are **anaerobic** (do not require oxygen). Cellular respiration can be aerobic or anaerobic. Anaerobic bacteria in oxygen-free environments use only anaerobic respiration. Plants, animals, and some prokaryotes respire aerobically. Some will also generate ATP anaerobically using fermentation pathways, which do not require oxygen, but the only ATP generated comes from glycolysis.

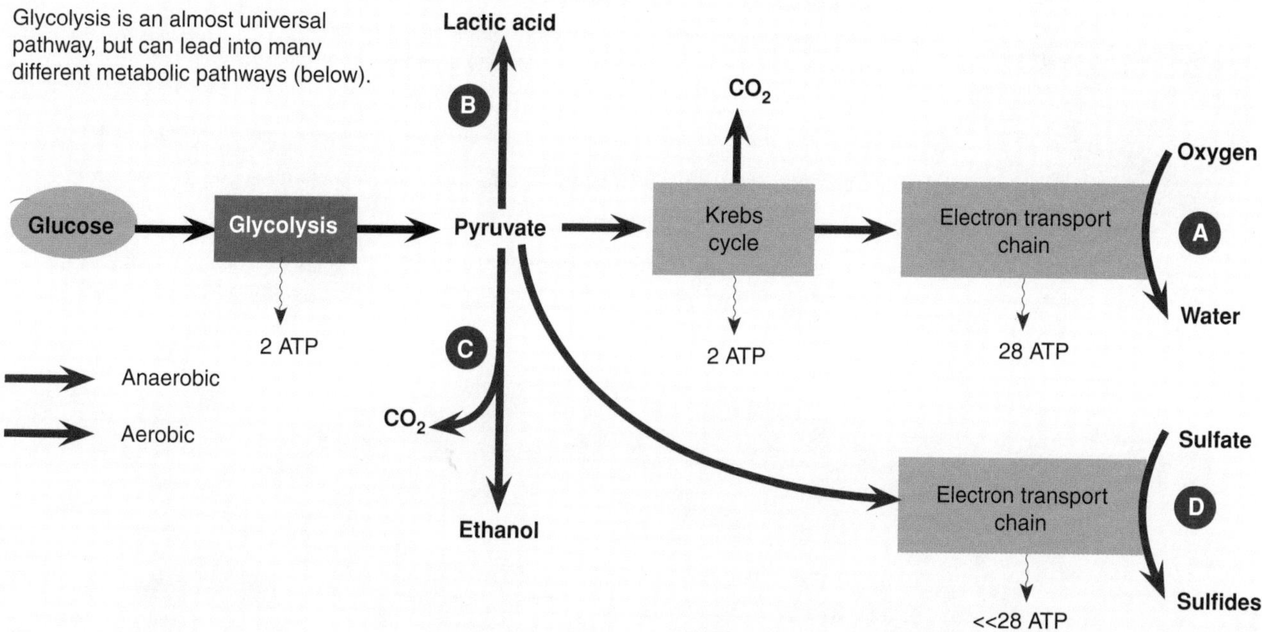

A Aerobic respiration

Aerobic respiration produces the energy (as ATP) needed for metabolism using oxygen as a final electron acceptor. The rate of aerobic respiration is limited by the amount of oxygen available. In animals and plants, the oxygen supply is sufficient to maintain aerobic metabolism most of the time. Aerobic respiration produces a high yield of ATP per molecule of glucose because the electron transport chain couples multiple redox reactions to ATP synthesis by oxidative phosphorylation.

ATP yield: high (30-32 ATP)

B Lactic acid fermentation

Lactic acid fermentation occurs in some bacteria and in animal cells, particularly muscle cells. During maximum physical activity when oxygen is limited, or if pyruvate is building up faster than it can be metabolized, anaerobic metabolism provides an alternative pathway for continued ATP generation. In mammalian muscle, metabolism of pyruvate produces lactate, which provides fuel for working muscle and produces a low yield of ATP.

ATP yield: low (2 ATP)

C Alcoholic fermentation

The process of brewing utilizes the anaerobic metabolism of Brewer's yeasts, which preferentially use anaerobic metabolism in the presence of excess sugars. This process, called **alcoholic fermentation**, produces ethanol and CO_2 from a derivative of pyruvate. It is carried out in vats that prevent entry of O_2. Brewer's yeast is a facultative anaerobe meaning it can also use aerobic pathways, depending on availability of oxygen and concentration of glucose.

ATP yield: low (2 ATP)

D Anaerobic respiration

Many bacteria and Archaea (ancient prokaryotes) are anaerobic, using molecules other than oxygen (e.g. nitrate or sulfate) as the terminal electron acceptor of their electron transport chain. These electron acceptors are not as efficient as oxygen as terminal electron acceptors. They have a lower reduction potential than oxygen so less energy is released per oxidized molecule, so the ATP yield from anaerobic respiration is generally low relative to aerobic metabolism.

ATP yield: << aerobic respiration

1. What is the difference between aerobic respiration and the other ATP production pathways shown above?
Aerobic respiration requires oxygen as the other ATP production pathways do not require it.

2. What process is common to all the pathways above? glycolysis

3. Why does anaerobic respiration produce less ATP than aerobic respiration? Because the only ATP generated in anaerobic respiration is from glycolysis.

ISBN: 978-1-98-856656-6

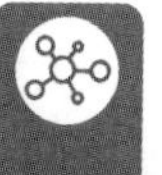

55 Cellular Respiration Overview

Key Question: What are the recognizable stages in cellular respiration that produce ATP for a eukaryotic cell?

Aerobic respiration releases the energy in glucose via a series of connected reactions. In eukaryotes, the first stage (glycolysis) occurs in the cytoplasm, and subsequent stages occur within the mitochondrion. In prokaryotes, all stages except the last occur in the cytoplasm. The final stage, electron transport, is associated with proteins attached to the plasma membrane. However, in both prokaryotes and eukaryotes, the processes are essentially identical.

An overview of cellular respiration

- **Cellular respiration** involves three metabolic stages, plus a link reaction, summarized below.

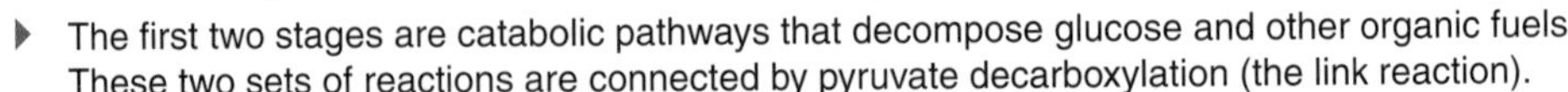

- The first two stages are catabolic pathways that decompose glucose and other organic fuels. These two sets of reactions are connected by pyruvate decarboxylation (the link reaction).
- In the third stage, the electron transport chain accepts electrons from the first two stages and passes these from one electron acceptor to another. The energy released at each stepwise transfer is used to make ATP. The final electron acceptor in this process is molecular oxygen.

1. **Glycolysis**. In the cytoplasm, glucose is broken down into two molecules of pyruvate.

L. **The link reaction**. In the mitochondrial matrix, pyruvate is split and added to coenzyme A.

2. **Krebs cycle**. In the mitochondrial matrix, a derivative of pyruvate is decomposed to CO_2.

3. **Electron transport and oxidative phosphorylation**. This occurs in the inner membranes of the mitochondrion and accounts for almost 90% of the ATP generated by respiration.

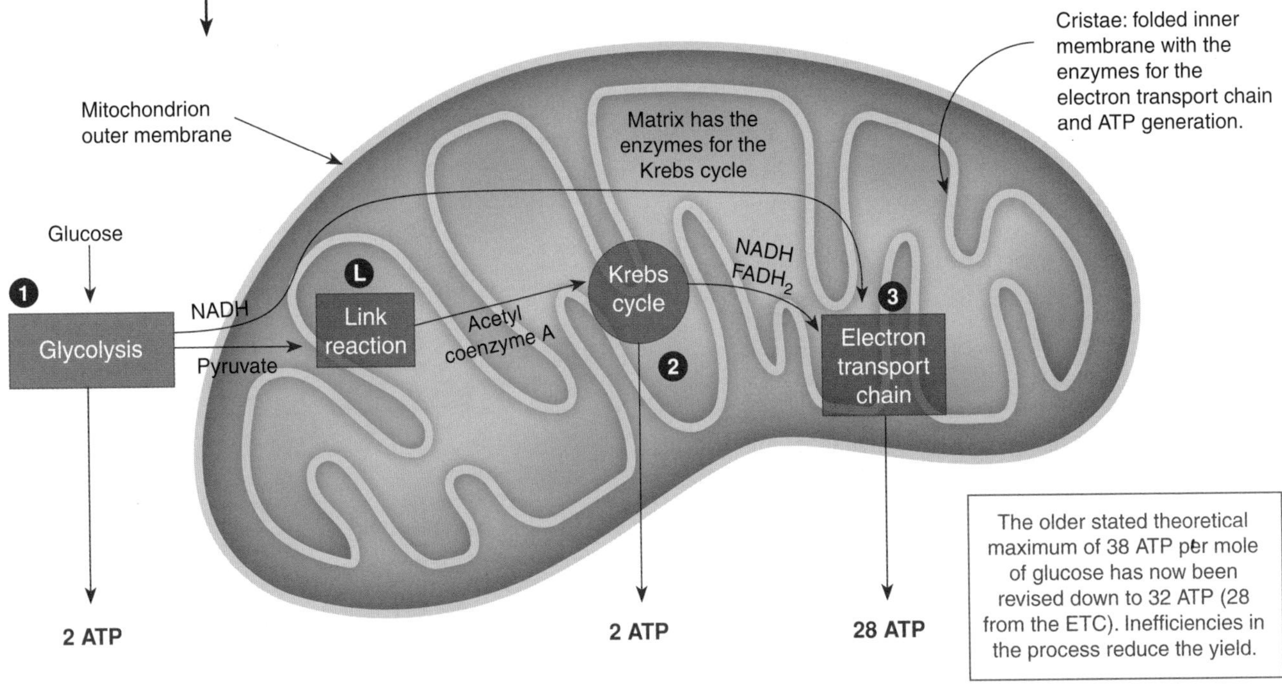

The older stated theoretical maximum of 38 ATP per mole of glucose has now been revised down to 32 ATP (28 from the ETC). Inefficiencies in the process reduce the yield.

The general equation for cellular respiration

$$C_6H_{12}O_6 + 6O_2 \longrightarrow 6CO_2 + 6H_2O + \text{energy}$$

1. Describe precisely in which part of a eukaryotic cell the following take place:

   (a) Glycolysis: cytoplasm - glucose broken down 2 molecules of pyruvate

   (b) The link reaction: mitochondrial matrix - pyruvate split, added to coenzyme A

   (c) Krebs cycle reactions: mitochondrial matrix - a derivative of pyruvate, decomposed to C

   (d) Electron transport chain: Inner membrane of mitochondrion - accounts for 90% of AT

2. Write a word equation for the general equation for cellular respiration: glycolysis → link reaction → Krebs cycle → electron transport chain

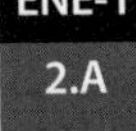

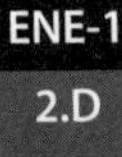

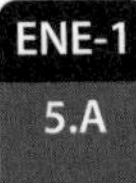

ISBN: 978-1-98-856656-6

How does cellular respiration provide energy?

- Glucose contains 16 kJ of energy per gram (2870 kJ/mol). The simplest way of releasing the energy in glucose is to burn it in oxygen (combustion).
- In this case, glucose + oxygen → carbon dioxide + water. The reaction is not controlled and occurs in one step.
- Living cells control the reaction of glucose and oxygen to release the energy stored in the glucose in steps that allow the energy to be captured. The reaction pathway is not a simple reaction of oxygen and glucose (as in combustion), and includes many dozens of steps, but it can be simplified to the same equation. Therefore the process releases the same energy overall.

Energy loss from glucose via combustion

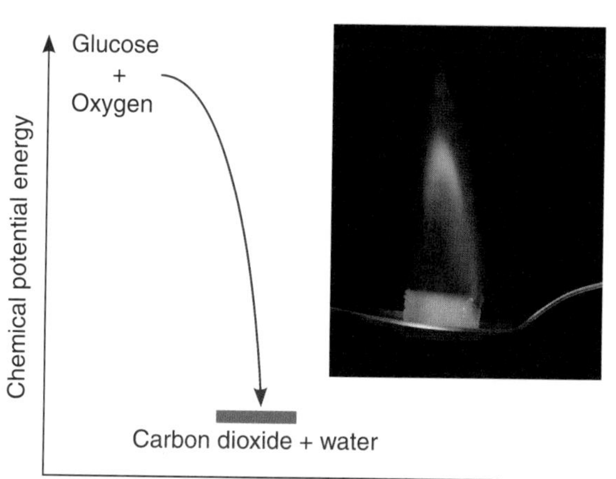

ATP production and energy transfer from glucose via cellular respiration

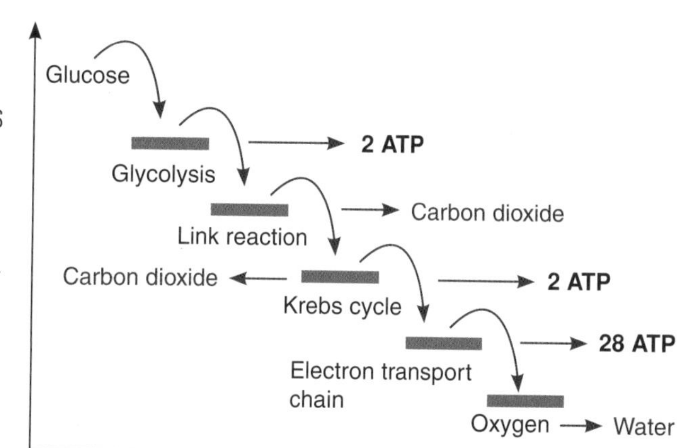

- In a direct combustion of glucose to water and carbon dioxide the same amount of energy is released, but all of it as heat and light (above left). Energy released during the conversion of glucose to water and carbon dioxide can be captured by coupling it to reactions that produce ATP in successive steps (above right).

3. What is the total number of ATP produced from one glucose molecule? 28 ATP

4. Describe three functions of glycolysis in the process of cellular respiration: glycolysis converts glucose to pyruvate, produces NADH for the ETC, and it produces 2 ATP.

5. Describe two functions of the Krebs cycle in the process of cellular respiration: The Krebs cycle produces 2 ATP as well as NADH, $FADH_2$ for the electron transport chain (ETC)

6. One mole of glucose contains 2870 kJ of energy. The hydrolysis of one mole of ATP releases 30.7 kJ of energy. Calculate the percentage of energy that is transformed to useful energy in the body. Show your working.

2870 kJ − 30.7 kJ = 2,839.3 / 2870 = 98.9% of energy is transformed to useful energy

7. Not all the energy in a glucose molecule is captured by the cell. What happens to the energy that is not captured?

It's released as heat

8. In what way is cellular respiration like the combustion of glucose? In what way is it different? It both uses glucose and oxygen to produce carbon dioxide and water. The difference is that respiration produces energy in the form of ATP where in combustion energy is lost. There are many more steps occurring in cellular respiration as well whereas combustion only has one.

ISBN: 978-1-98-856656-6

56 The Biochemistry of Respiration

Key Question: What are the specific steps in aerobic respiration and how is ATP produced?

The oxidation of glucose is a catabolic, energy yielding pathway. The breakdown of glucose and other organic fuels (such as fats and proteins) to simpler molecules releases energy for ATP synthesis. Glycolysis and the Krebs cycle supply electrons to the electron transport chain, which drives oxidative phosphorylation. Glycolysis nets two ATP. The conversion of pyruvate (the end product of glycolysis) to acetyl CoA links glycolysis to the Krebs cycle. One "turn" of the cycle releases carbon dioxide, forms one ATP, and passes electrons to three NAD^+ and one FAD. Most of the ATP generated in cellular respiration is produced by oxidative phosphorylation when NADH + H^+ and $FADH_2$ donate electrons to the series of electron carriers in the electron transport chain. At the end of the chain, electrons are passed to molecular oxygen, reducing it to water. Electron transport is coupled to ATP synthesis.

Steps in cellular respiration

Glycolysis

Glycolysis is the beginning of cellular respiration. Glycolysis initially uses two ATP but produces four ATP. It therefore produces a net of two pyruvate molecules, each of which can then enter the Krebs cycle. NADH is produced for use in the electron transport chain. **The numbers shown are for one glucose molecule.**

Link reaction

The link reaction removes CO_2 from pyruvate and adds coenzyme A, producing the 2C molecule acetyl coenzyme A, which enters the Krebs cycle. NADH is also produced and flows to the electron transport chain.

Krebs cycle

In the Krebs cycle, acetyl coenzyme A is attached to the 4C molecule oxaloacetate and coenzyme A is released. Oxaloacetate is eventually remade in a cyclic series of reactions that produce more NADH and $FADH_2$ for the electron transport chain. Two ATP are also made by substrate level phosphorylation.

Electron transport chain

Electrons carried by NADH and $FADH_2$ are passed to a series of electron carrier enzymes embedded in the inner membrane of the mitochondria. The energy from the electrons is used to pump H^+ ions across the inner membrane from the matrix into the intermembrane space. These are allowed to flow back to the matrix via the enzyme ATP synthase which uses their energy to produce ATP. The electrons are coupled to H^+ and oxygen at the end of the electron transport chain to form water.

Substrate level phosphorylation

An enzyme transfers a phosphate group directly from a substrate (such as glucose) to ADP to form ATP. Net ATP yield from substrate level phosphorylation shown in black below.

Oxidative phosphorylation

Glucose is oxidized in a series of reduction and oxidation reactions that provide the energy to form ATP. This is achieved by the flow of reducing power (as NADH and $FADH_2$) to the electron transport chain (ETC). Net ATP yield from this process shown in red below.

Glycolysis
Glucose
Pyruvate
2ATP
2NADH → ETC → 5ATP
$2CO_2$
Acetyl coenzyme A
2NADH → ETC → 5ATP
Krebs cycle
2ATP
$4CO_2$
6NADH → ETC → 15ATP
$2FADH_2$ → ETC → 3ATP
Electron transport chain (ETC)
H^+ H^+ H^+ H^+
NADH
NAD^+
e^-
$FADH_2$ FAD
H_2O
$H^+ + ½O_2$
H^+
Total
28ATP

1. (a) What is substrate level phosphorylation? an enzyme transfers a phosphate group directly from a substrate to ADP to form ATP

(b) How many ATP are produced this way during cellular respiration (per molecule of glucose)? 2ATP

2. (a) What is oxidative phosphorylation? glucose is oxidized in a series of reduction and oxidation reactions that provide the energy to form ATP

(b) How many ATP are produced this way during cellular respiration (per molecule of glucose)? 5ATP

ISBN: 978-1-98-856656-6

Mitochondria (*sing.* mitochondrion) are organelles found in most eukaryotic cells. They vary in diameter from 0.75 - 3.0 µm, and can be quite long in comparison to their diameter.

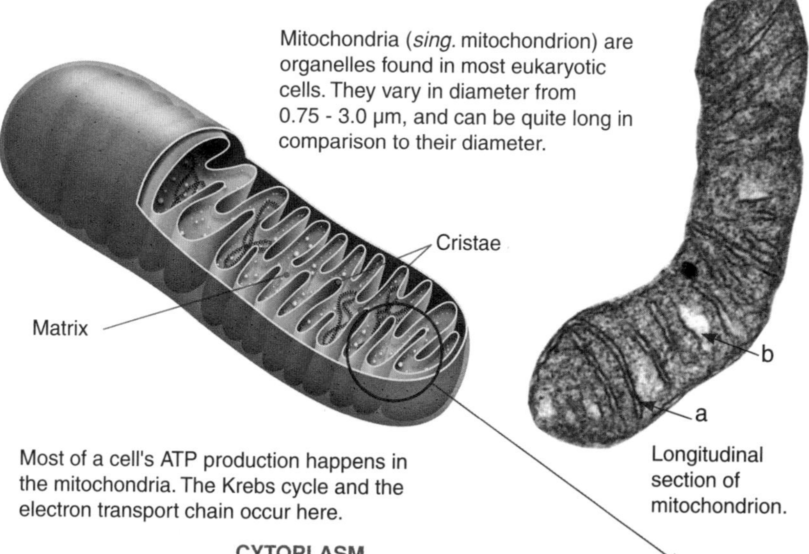

Longitudinal section of mitochondrion.

Most of a cell's ATP production happens in the mitochondria. The Krebs cycle and the electron transport chain occur here.

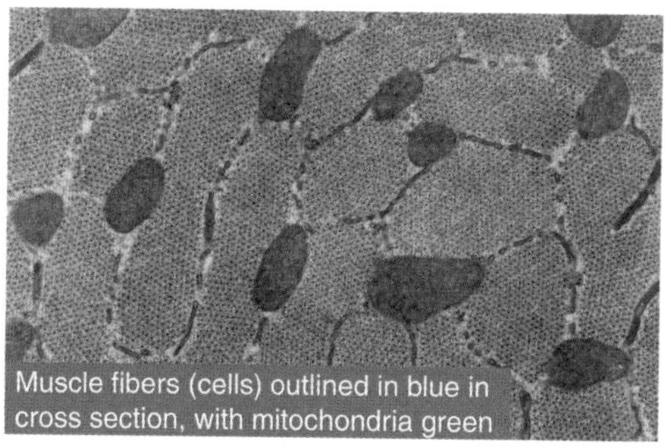

Muscle fibers (cells) outlined in blue in cross section, with mitochondria green

Cells that require a lot of ATP for cellular processes have a lot of mitochondria. Sperm cells contain a large number of mitochondria near the base of the tail. In skeletal muscle fibers (above) mitochondria (green) can occupy up to 20% of the cytoplasmic space. In liver cells, the figure is about 25% and in heart muscle cells, it can be as high as 40%.

CYTOPLASM | MITOCHONDRION

Outer membrane
Inner membrane forming cristae
Electron transport chain
ATP synthase
H+ H+ H+ H+
½O_2 + $2H^+$ → H_2O
6 NADH + H^+ + 2 $FADH_2$
2 NADH + H^+
Glucose → 2 pyruvate
2 ATP
Glycolysis
2 NADH + H^+
2 Acetyl-CoA
$2CO_2$
Link reaction
Krebs cycle → $4CO_2$
2 ATP
28 ATP
Mitochondrial matrix is the space within the membranes.

3. In the longitudinal section of a mitochondrion (above), identify the regions (a) cristae (b) matrix

4. Explain the purpose of the link reaction: removes CO_2 from pyruvate + adds coenzyme A, producing the 2C molecule acetyl coenzyme A, which enters the Krebs cycle. NADH is also produced + flows to the ETC

5. How many ATP molecules **per molecule of glucose** are generated during the following stages of respiration?

(a) Glycolysis: 4 (b) Krebs cycle: 2 (c) Electron transport chain: 28 (d) Total: 32

6. Explain what happens to the carbon atoms lost during respiration. When are they lost? In the Krebs cycle, acetyl coenzyme A is attached to the 4C molecule oxaloacetate + is released.

7. Describe how ATP is produced in the electron transport chain: electrons carried by NADH + $FADH_2$ are passed to a series of electron carrier enzymes embedded in the inner membrane of the mitochondria. The energy from the electrons is used to pump H^+ ions across the inner membrane from the matrix into the intermembrane space. ATP synthase uses energy to produce ATP.

8. What is the purpose of NADH and $FADH_2$ in cellular respiration? This is achieved by the flow of reducing power to ETC → (as NADH + $FADH_2$)

ISBN: 978-1-98-856656-6

57 Chemiosmosis and the Proton Motive Force

Key Question: What is chemiosmosis and how is it related to ATP synthesis?

Chemiosmosis occurs in the membranes of mitochondria, the chloroplasts of plants, and across the plasma membrane of bacteria. Chemiosmosis involves the establishment of a proton (hydrogen) gradient across a membrane. The concentration gradient is used to drive ATP synthesis. Chemiosmosis has two key components: an **electron transport chain** sets up a proton gradient as electrons pass along it to a final electron acceptor, and an enzyme called **ATP synthase** uses the proton gradient to catalyze ATP synthesis. In cellular respiration, electron carriers on the inner membrane of the mitochondrion oxidize NADH + H^+ and $FADH_2$. The energy released from this process is used to move protons against their concentration gradient, from the mitochondrial matrix into the space between the two membranes. The return of protons to the matrix via ATP synthase is coupled to ATP synthesis. Similarly, in the chloroplasts of green plants, ATP is produced when protons pass from the thylakoid lumen to the chloroplast stroma via ATP synthase.

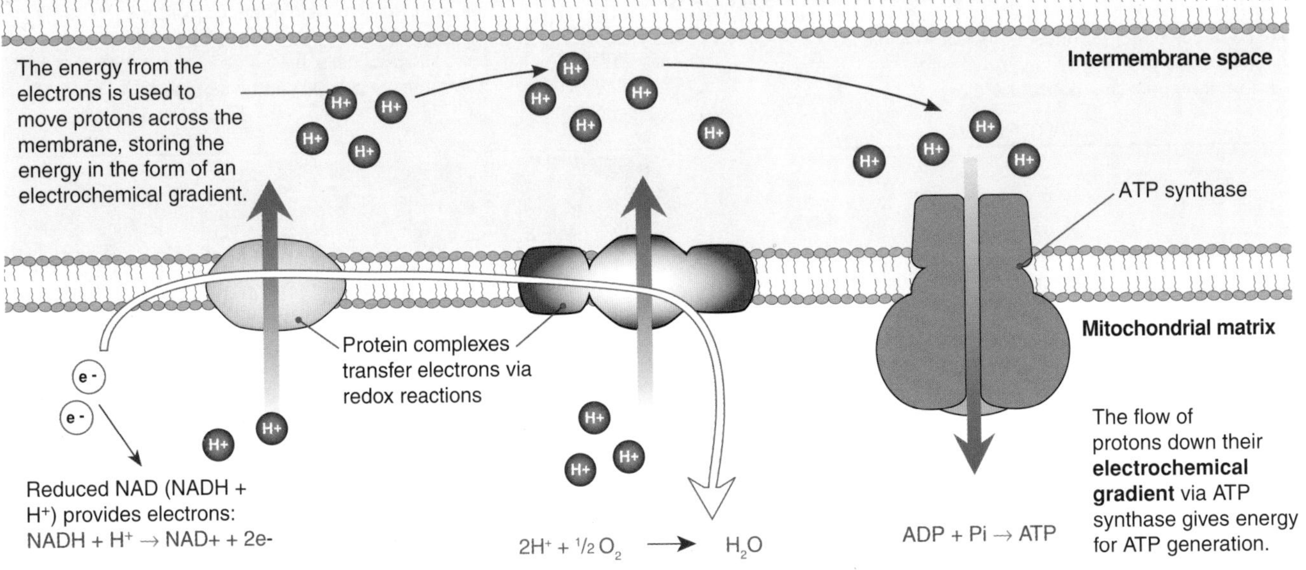

The energy from the electrons is used to move protons across the membrane, storing the energy in the form of an electrochemical gradient.
Intermembrane space
ATP synthase
Mitochondrial matrix
Protein complexes transfer electrons via redox reactions
Reduced NAD (NADH + H+) provides electrons: NADH + H+ → NAD+ + 2e-
2H+ + 1/2 O2 → H2O
ADP + Pi → ATP
The flow of protons down their electrochemical gradient via ATP synthase gives energy for ATP generation.

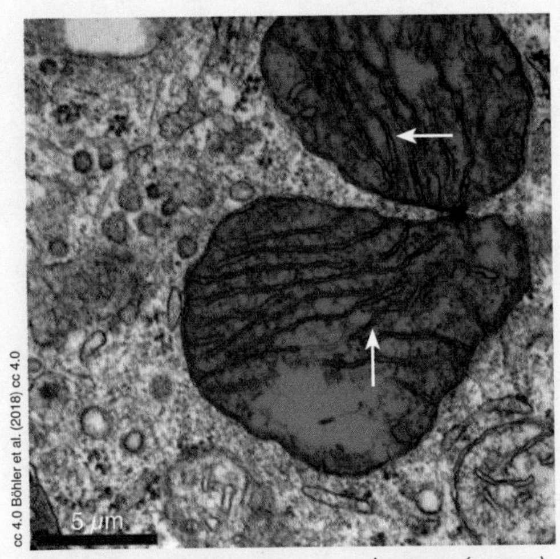

5 µm
cc 4.0 Böhler et al. (2018) cc 4.0

The intermembrane spaces can be seen (arrows) in this transverse section of mitochondria.

The evidence for chemiosmosis

The British biochemist Peter Mitchell proposed the chemiosmotic hypothesis in 1961. He proposed that, because living cells have membrane potential, electrochemical gradients could be used to do work, i.e. provide the energy for ATP synthesis. Scientists at the time were skeptical, but the evidence for chemiosmosis was extensive and came from studies of isolated mitochondria and chloroplasts. Evidence included:

- The outer membranes of mitochondria were removed leaving the inner membranes intact. Adding protons to the treated mitochondria increased ATP synthesis.
- When isolated chloroplasts were illuminated, the medium in which they were suspended became alkaline.
- Isolated chloroplasts were kept in the dark and transferred first to a low pH medium (to acidify the thylakoid interior) and then to an alkaline medium (low protons). They then spontaneously synthesized ATP (no light was needed).

1. Summarize the process of chemiosmosis in a mitochondrion: 2 key components: An ETC sets up a proton gradient as electrons pass along it to a final electron acceptor, and an enzyme called ATP synthase uses the proton gradient to catalyze ATP synthesis. Cellular respiration, electron carriers on the inner membrane of the mitochondrion oxidize NADH + H+ and FADH2. Energy is released from this process to move protons against their concentration gradient, from the mitochondrial matrix into the space between the 2 membranes.

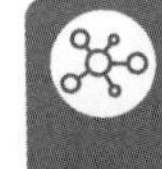
ENE-1 2.B

ENE-1 6.B

21 56

ISBN: 978-1-98-856656-6

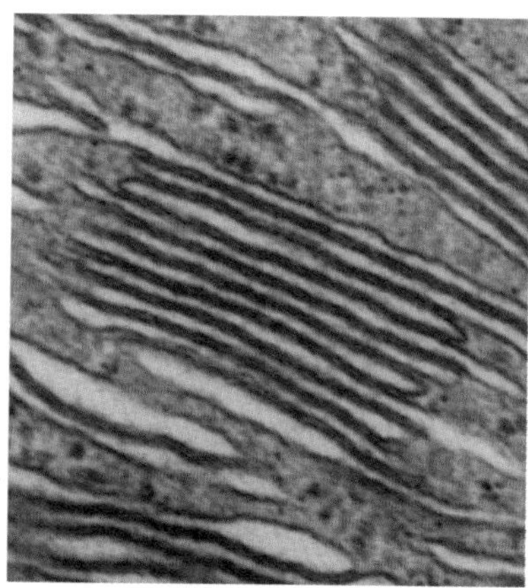

Chemiosmosis in plants

The light reactions that occur in the chloroplasts of plants exploit the same chemiosmotic process as mitochondria. In this case, electrons are excited by the energy of photons and flow down the ETC causing protons to move across the thylakoid membrane into the stroma.

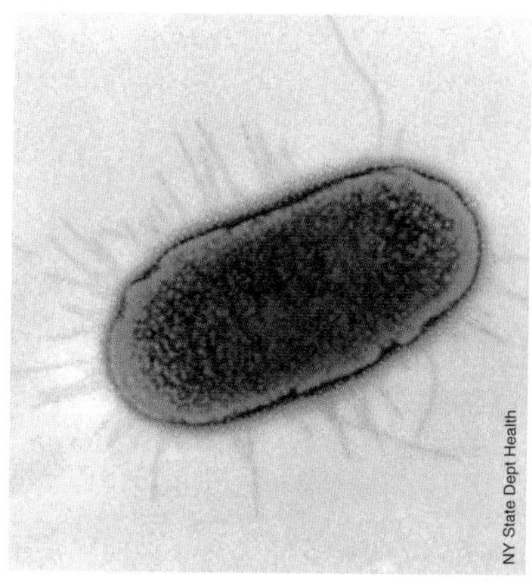

Chemiosmosis in prokaryotes

Prokaryotes also use chemiosmosis to produce ATP. Their electron transport chains are located in the plasma membrane and as electrons move down the ETC, H^+ are pumped out of the cell. H^+ flow back into the cell through the ATP synthase complex generating ATP.

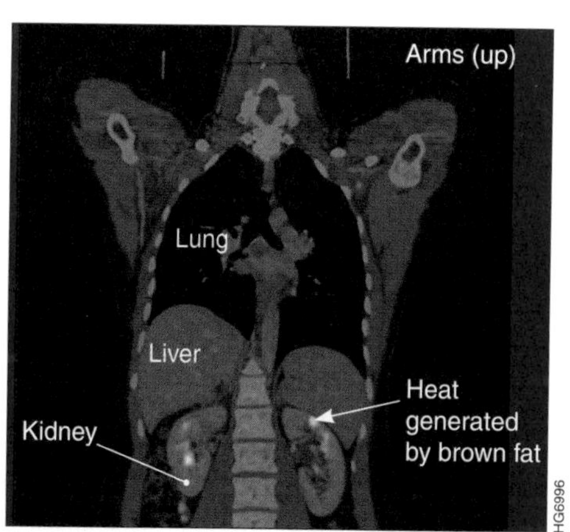

Uncoupling H^+ flow and ATP generation

In some cells, such as the brown fat cells of mammals, 'uncoupling' proteins in the inner mitochondrial membrane act as channels, allowing protons to pass directly to the matrix without traveling through ATP synthase. This route for H^+ flow allows the energy of the gradient to be dissipated, generating body heat (bright spots).

2. Why did the addition of protons to the treated mitochondria increase ATP synthesis? The return of protons to the matrix via ATP synthase is coupled to ATP synthesis. ATP is produced when protons pass from the thylakoid lumen to the chloroplast stroma via ATP synthase.

3. Why did the suspension of isolated chloroplasts become alkaline when illuminated? Isolated chloroplasts were kept in the dark + transferred first to a low pH medium + then to an alkaline medium

4 (a) What was the purpose of transferring the chloroplasts first to an acid then to an alkaline medium? The thylakoid interior needed to be acidified then an alkaline medium created a gradient as protons were able to flow.

(b) Why did ATP synthesis occur spontaneously in these treated chloroplasts? When these chloroplasts are then transferred to a slightly alkaline medium, that is, one w/ a lower concentration of protons and given a supply of ADP + inorganic phosphate.

5. Compare and contrast how and where chemiosmosis occurs in animals, plants, and prokaryotes: The light reactions that occur in chloroplasts of plants exploit the same chemiosmotic process as mitochondria. Prokaryotes also use chemiosmosis to produce ATP. Their electron transport chains are located in the plasma membrane and as electrons move down the ETC, H^+ are pumped out of the cell. H^+ flow back into the cell through the ATP synthase complex generating ATP.

6. (a) In mammals, what happens to energy stored in the proton gradient if it is not used to generate ATP? It would be released as heat.

(b) Suggest how this apparently wasteful process might benefit a hibernating mammal: In a cold environment, it cold help maintain the body heat of the animal where it is hibernating

ISBN: 978-1-98-856656-6

58 Investigating Cellular Respiration

STUDENT SUPPORT FOR INVESTIGATION 6: *Cellular respiration*

Background

A respirometer can be used to measure the amount of oxygen consumed by an organism during cellular respiration and so can be used to measure respiration rate. A simple type of respirometer is shown in the diagram below.

The carbon dioxide produced during respiration is absorbed by the potassium hydroxide. As the oxygen is used up, the colored bubble in the pipette moves. Measuring the movement of the bubble allows an estimation of the change in volume of gas and therefore the rate of cellular respiration. Various versions of these simple respirometers exist. You may use a set-up that uses microrespirometers, which are easy to construct and work quickly because of their small volumes. In these devices, the syringe size that holds the respiring organisms can be selected according to the organism's size (e.g. 1 mL for small radish seeds or 10 mL for peas). You can find the instructions for building and using these in the AP® Biology Lab Manual.

Aim

To investigate the rate of respiration in germinating pea seeds.

Method

- Students labeled three vials 1, 2, and 3. They placed cotton wool soaked in 15% KOH in the bottom of all three vials. They then placed dry non-absorbent gauze on top.
- The students placed 25 newly germinating pea seeds into vial 2, and the same number of non-germinating (dormant) seeds into vial 3 (making up the volume with glass beads). Vial number 1 had only glass beads added, and was made up to the same volume as in the other two vials. The students determined the volumes using a water displacement method.
- Once the vials had been prepared, they capped each vial with a stopper fitted with a 1 mL pipette, tip pointing outward. A weight (two metal washers) was added to each vial.
- A drop of food coloring was inserted into the tip of each pipette to seal off the system.
- All three respirometers were placed in a 25°C water bath supported so that the pipette tips stayed out of the water (see diagram right). They were left for 10 minutes to equilibrate.
- After the 10 minutes of equilibration, the position of the food coloring bubble was recorded and a timer was started.
- The movement of the colored bubble was recorded at 5 minute intervals for 25 minutes.
- The recorded movement of the colored bubble in tube 1 (glass beads) accounted for any pressure fluctuations. The changes recorded in tube 1 were subtracted from the changes in each of tube 2 and 3 to obtain the corrected volume changes caused by the use of oxygen.

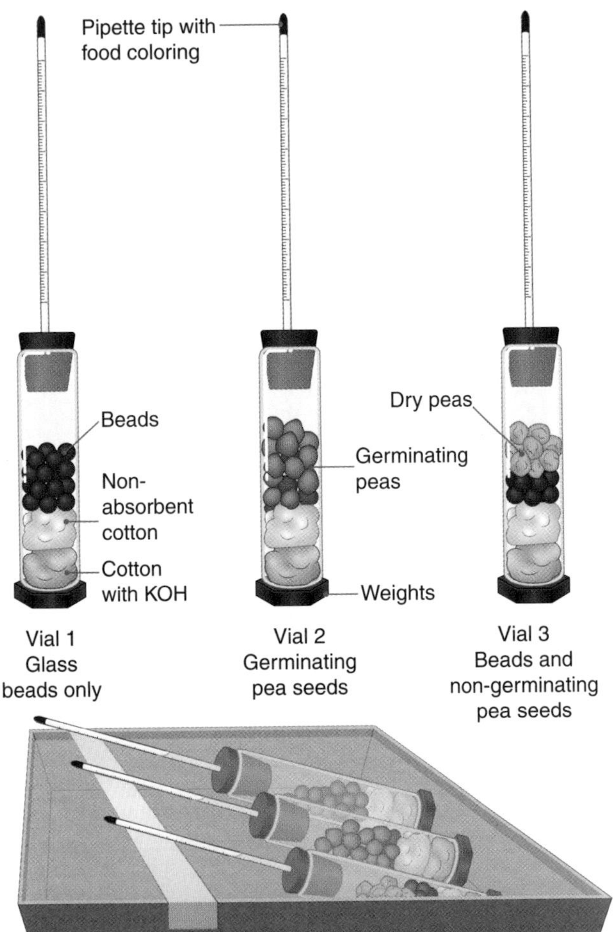

Vials in 25°C water bath

1. Explain the purpose of the following in the experiment:

   (a) KOH: ______________________________

   (b) Equilibration period: ______________________________

   (c) The test tube with the ungerminated seeds: ______________________________

   (d) The test tube with the glass beads: ______________________________

ISBN: 978-1-98-856656-6

Results

	Tube 1: Beads alone		Tube 2: Geminating peas				Tube 3: Dry peas and beads			
Time X	Reading at time X (mL)	Difference (correction)	Reading at time X	Difference	Corrected volume (mL)	Respiration rate (mL/min)	Reading at time X	Difference	Corrected volume (mL)	Respiration rate (mL/min)
0	0.74	—	0.66	—	—	—	0.81	—	—	—
5	0.73	0.01	0.57	0.09			0.80	0.01		
10	0.73	0.01	0.50	0.16			0.79	0.02		
15	0.73	0.01	0.42	0.24			0.79	0.02		
20	0.73	0.01	0.36	0.30			0.78	0.03		
25	0.73	0.01	0.31	0.35			0.77	0.04		

2. (a) Calculate the corrected distance the bubble moved in tubes 2 (germinating seeds) and 3 (non germinating seeds) by subtracting the distance moved in tube 1 (glass beads) from each value (pale green column above). Record these values in the appropriate columns in the table above.

(b) Use the corrected distance the bubble moved to calculate the rate of respiration for germinating and non-germinating (dormant) peas. Record these values in the appropriate columns in the table above.

(c) Plot the rate of respiration for tubes 2 and 3 on the grid (below). Include an appropriate title and axis labels.

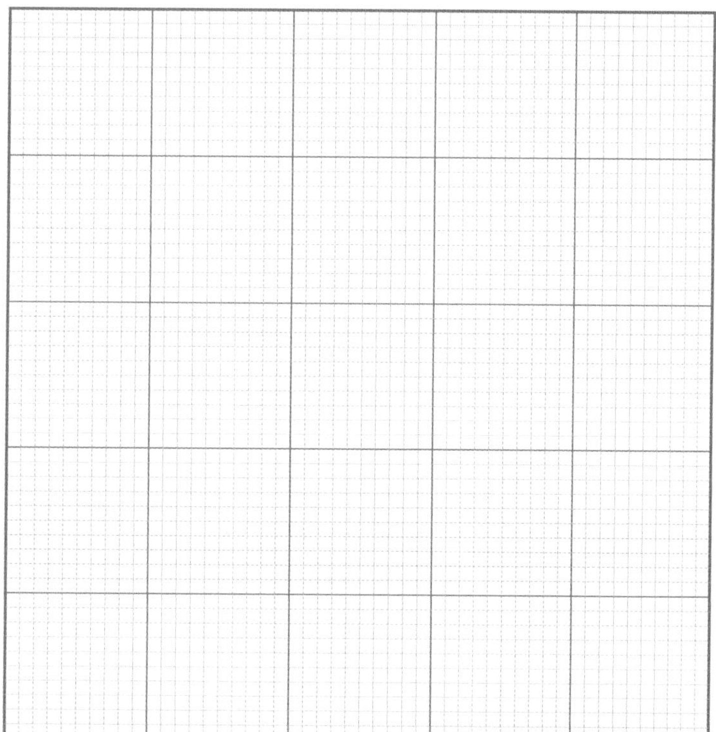

(d) What does your plot show? ______

ISBN: 978-1-98-856656-6

3. Why does the bubble in the capillary tube move?

4. Where are the sources of error in measuring respiration rate with respirometers? How could you minimize them?

5. What conclusion can you make about cellular respiration in germinated and ungerminated (dormant) seeds?

6. How would you have to modify the experiment if you were measuring respiration in a plant instead of seeds?

7. Design an experimental protocol to test the respiration of seeds at 25°C and 10°C:

8. A student repeated the respirometer experiment using maggots instead of seeds. Their results are tabulated below:

Time (minutes)	Distance bubble moved (mm)	Rate (mm/min)
0	0	
5	25	
10	65	
15	95	
20	130	
25	160	

(a) Calculate the rates and record them in the table above:

(b) Graph the rates on the grid above right.

(c) Describe the results:

ISBN: 978-1-98-856656-6

59 Anaerobic Pathways for ATP Production

Key Question: What pathways do eukaryotes use to generate ATP in the absence of oxygen?

Aerobic respiration occurs in the presence of oxygen. When oxygen is absent or limited, eukaryotic organisms can often generate ATP from substrate phosphorylation alone using only the glycolytic pathway and a molecule other than oxygen as the terminal electron acceptor. In alcoholic fermentation in yeasts, the electron acceptor is ethanal. In lactic acid fermentation, which occurs in mammalian muscle even when oxygen is present, the electron acceptor is pyruvate itself.

Alcoholic fermentation

In alcoholic fermentation, the H^+ acceptor is ethanal which is reduced to ethanol with the release of carbon dioxide (CO_2). Yeasts respire aerobically when oxygen is available but can use alcoholic fermentation when it is not. At ethanol levels above 12-15%, the ethanol produced by alcoholic fermentation is toxic and this limits their ability to use this pathway indefinitely. The root cells of plants also use fermentation as a pathway when oxygen is unavailable but the ethanol must be converted back to respiratory intermediates and respired aerobically.

Lactic acid fermentation

Skeletal muscles produce ATP in the absence of oxygen using lactic acid fermentation. In this pathway, pyruvate is reduced to lactic acid, which dissociates to form lactate and H^+. The conversion of pyruvate to lactate is reversible and this pathway operates alongside the aerobic system all the time to enable greater intensity and duration of activity. Lactate can be metabolized in the muscle itself or it can enter the circulation and be taken up by the liver to replenish carbohydrate stores. This 'lactate shuttle' is an important mechanism for balancing the distribution of substrates and waste products.

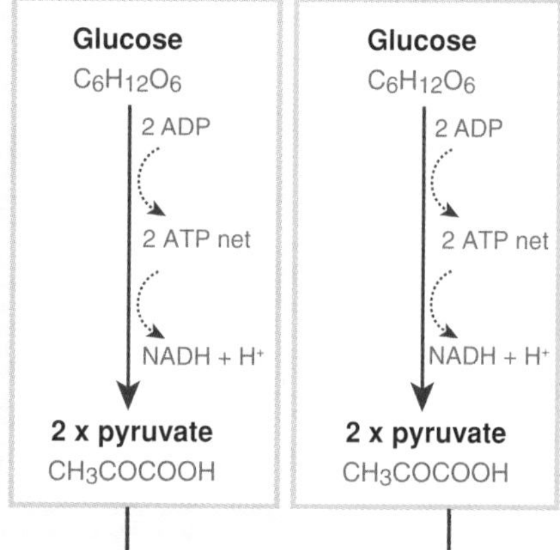

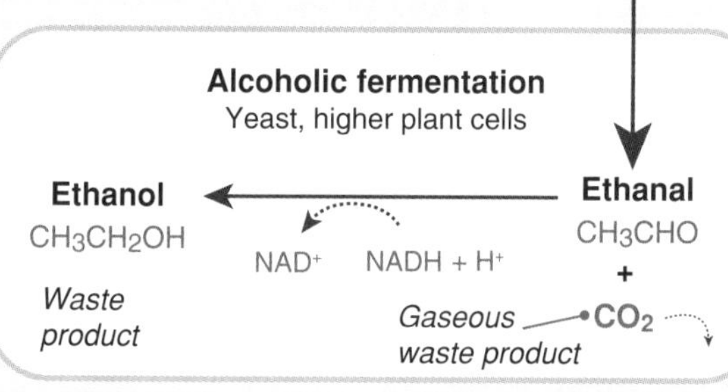

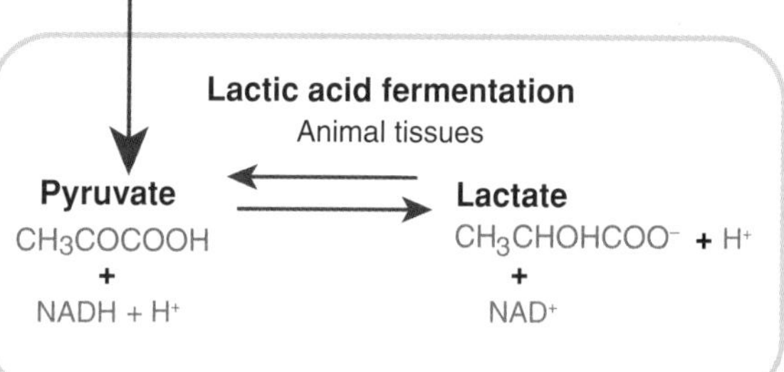

The alcohol and CO_2 produced from alcoholic fermentation form the basis of the brewing and baking industries. In baking, the dough is left to ferment and the yeast metabolizes sugars to produce ethanol and CO_2. The CO_2 causes the dough to rise.

Yeasts are used to produce almost all alcoholic beverages (e.g. wine and beers). The yeast used in the process breaks down the sugars into ethanol (alcohol) and CO_2. The alcohol produced is a metabolic by-product of fermentation by the yeast.

The lactate shuttle in vertebrate skeletal muscle works alongside the aerobic system to enable maximal muscle activity. Lactate moves from its site of production to regions within and outside the muscle (e.g. liver) where it can be respired aerobically.

1. Describe the key difference between aerobic respiration and fermentation: aerobic respiration uses oxygen while fermentation does not

2. (a) Refer to pages 94-97 and determine the efficiency of fermentation compared to aerobic respiration: 19 %

   (b) Why is the efficiency of these anaerobic pathways so low? they generate ATP from substrate phosphorylation alone

3. Why can't alcoholic fermentation go on indefinitely? Because the toxic waste in it will kill it.

ISBN: 978-1-98-856656-6

60 Variation at the Molecular Level

Key Question: How does molecular diversity in the cell allow organisms to survive different environments?

Variation in related molecules allows those molecules to function in slightly different ways or in slightly different environments. This can happen both within the same organism (e.g. hemoglobin and myoglobin) or between different organisms (e.g. different hemoglobin molecules in different organisms). These differences allow organisms to survive and reproduce in a variety of environments and so contribute to evolutionary fitness.

Variation in hemoglobin

- Hemoglobin (Hb) is a respiratory pigment (a pigmented protein) capable of combining reversibly with oxygen, hence increasing the amount of oxygen that can be carried by the blood. All vertebrates use hemoglobin to transport blood through the body.

Taxon	Oxygen capacity (cm^3 O_2 per 100 cm^3 blood)	Pigment
Fishes	2 - 4	Hemoglobin
Reptiles	7 - 12	Hemoglobin
Birds	20 - 25	Hemoglobin
Mammals	15 - 30	Hemoglobin

- The oxygen carrying capacity of hemoglobin is not the same for all vertebrates. Variations in its structure change both its capacity to carry oxygen and its ability to take up and release oxygen. In general, the oxygen carrying capacity of blood in vertebrates increases from fish, to reptiles, to birds and mammals, and is correlated with metabolic rate. Fish blood frequently possesses several hemoglobins. This allows them to move between different environments while maintaining the oxygen carrying capacity of their blood.
- The hemoglobin of small mammals releases oxygen more readily than larger mammals because it has a lower affinity for oxygen. This is related to the higher per mass metabolic rate of small mammals. They consume oxygen at a higher rate than larger mammals and so require a faster delivery of oxygen.

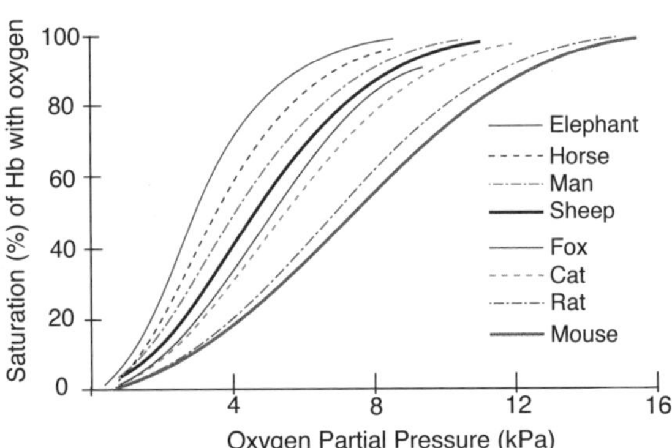

- Adaptations of hemoglobin have enabled some mammals to live in places with low oxygen content. Llamas and their relatives live at high altitudes with low oxygen pressure. Moles (below) live underground where carbon dioxide levels can be high and oxygen levels low. The hemoglobin in some moles has lost the ability to bind the molecule DPG (which inhibits oxygen binding in deoxygenated tissues). This increases the amount of oxygen and carbon dioxide that can be transported in the blood.

1. The oxygen carrying capacity of hemoglobin varies between mammals. What is the cause of this difference in carrying capacity?

The more oxygen available, the more hemoglobin can transport molecules.

2. (a) Describe the relationship between hemoglobin's affinity for oxygen and body size in mammals:

Temperature, hydrogen ions and CO_2 are different based on body size.

(b) Give a likely reason for this relationship:

This influences hemoglobin's affinity for oxygen.

3. Llamas are able to live at very high altitudes. What would their hemoglobin need to be able to do in order for this to happen?

Their hemoglobin is able to carry max amount of oxygen allowing llamas to live at high altitudes.

4. Explain how moles are able to live a low oxygen underground environment:

Moles also have the ability to live in low oxygen environments be their hemoglobin can carry max amount of oxygen.

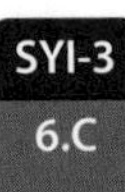 SYI-3 2.A
 SYI-3 6.C
8 ←
 202 →

ISBN: 978-1-98-856656-6

Variation in oxygen carrying molecules

- Adult hemoglobin is different to fetal hemoglobin. The two different hemoglobins (Hb) are needed because of the different environments they function in. Fetal Hb needs to be able to obtain oxygen from the mother's blood (via the placenta). It therefore has a higher affinity for oxygen than adult Hb and carries 20-30% more than maternal Hb.
- Hemoglobin, as a tetramer with quaternary structure, exhibits a behavior called cooperative binding. This means that the more oxygen is bound to Hb, the easier it is for more oxygen to bind (its dissociation curve is sigmoidal).
- Myoglobin (Mb) in skeletal muscle has a very high affinity for oxygen and will take up oxygen from Hb in the blood. Its high affinity also means it is less inclined to release the oxygen. It therefore acts to store oxygen rather than transport it.
- Myoglobin is related to Hb and carries the same heme group for binding oxygen. However, it is a monomer with one oxygen binding site. This means it cannot show cooperative binding and its affinity for oxygen does not change as the oxygen concentration changes.

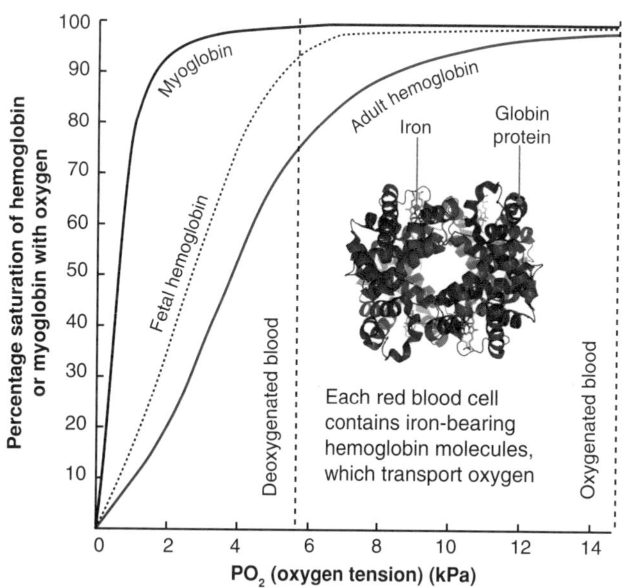

Above: Oxygen dissociation curves show differences in oxygen affinity of fetal and adult hemoglobins and myoglobin at different oxygen tensions.

Humans vs whales

- Whales such as the sperm whale are able to hold their breath for long periods of time while diving to depths of up to 1000 m. Whales are able to do this because their muscle cells hold up to 20 times more myoglobin than human muscle cells can.
- Importantly, the muscle cells of whales produce a much more stable type of myoglobin than human muscle cells (up to 60 times more stable). This means much more can be produced and stored.
- The difference occurs because of slight differences in the amino acid sequences of human and whale myoglobin.

5. Describe the relationship between hemoglobin saturation and the oxygen level in the blood: Oxygen levels in the blood, if shifted, can cause a decrease / increase in oxygen affinity of hemoglobin

6. (a) How is the behavior of fetal Hb different to adult Hb? It has a stronger oxygen affinity

   (b) Explain the significance of this difference: It increases the transport's speed when it trafers fetus within the uterus.

7. Why is the very high affinity of myoglobin for oxygen important? It is important bc it will be less inclined to release oxygen once it has been bound.

8. A scientist hypothesized that all deep diving mammals will be found to have high levels of myoglobin in their muscle cells. Justify the scientist's hypothesis, relating your answer to how diving mammals live:

   Diving mammals need to have/be able to keep oxygen in, especially with swimming in deep waters w/ less oxygen and more pressure.

ISBN: 978-1-98-856656-6

61 Personal Progress Check

Answer the multiple choice questions that follow by circling the correct answer. Don't forget to read the question carefully!

1. The active site of an enzyme is:
   (a) A specific part of the enzyme that remains active after denaturation.
   (b) Part of the enzyme that allows it to be actively transported into and out of a cell.
   (c) A specific part of the enzyme where the substrate binds.
   (d) None of the above

2. Which of the following statements about models of enzyme activity are true?
   (I) The enzyme changes its shape when the substrate binds to the active site.
   (II) The substrate is an exact lock-and-key fit for the enzyme's active site.
   (III) The substrate-enzyme interaction reduces the activation energy required for the transition state.
   (IV) The enzyme is consumed in the reaction.

   (a) I and III
   (b) II and III
   (c) I
   (d) All are true

3. The differences between mammalian hemoglobins is based upon:
   (a) The number and orientation of the amino acid chains attached to the heme portion of the molecule.
   (b) Slight differences in the amino acid sequences in the alpha and beta globin chains.
   (c) The differences in the amount of carbon dioxide each hemoglobin can carry.
   (d) The number of oxygen molecules that can be carried.

4. Which of the following is true of the light dependent reactions?
   (a) Cyclic phosphorylation involves electrons cycling within photosystem I.
   (b) Non-cyclic phosphorylation involves electrons being passed from photosystem II to photosystem I.
   (c) The light dependent reactions involve pigments bound on the thylakoid membranes.
   (d) All of the above.

5. Which two reactions occur during photophosphorylation?
   (a) ATP is hydrolyzed and NADP is reduced.
   (b) ATP is hydrolyzed and NADPH is oxidized.
   (c) ATP is synthesized and NADP is reduced.
   (d) ATP is synthesized and NADPH is oxidized.

6. Which reaction is catalyzed by the enzyme RuBisCO?
   (a) Carboxylation of ribulose bisphosphate (RuBP).
   (b) Conversion of triose phosphate (TP) to ribulose phosphate (RuP).
   (c) Oxidation of glycerate-3-phosphate (GP).
   (d) Reduction of glycerate-3-phosphate (GP).

7. The following equation summarizes a process in the bacterium *Nitrosomonas*, an ammonia-oxidizing bacterium:

   $NH_3 + 1.5\ O_2 \rightarrow NO_2^- + H^+ + H_2O$ (274.91 kJ/mol)

   What process is involved here?
   (a) Photosynthesis
   (b) Cellular respiration
   (c) Chemosynthesis
   (d) Condensation

8. Which if the following statements is true?
   (a) In a closed system entropy always increases
   (b) In a closed system entropy always decreases
   (c) In a closed system entropy always remains the same
   (d) Entropy can be increased by restoring order

9. Enzymes speed up reactions by:
   (a) Reducing the activation energy needed.
   (b) Increasing the activation energy.
   (c) Adding energy to the reaction.
   (d) Taking part in the reaction and forming part of the products.

10. The light independent reaction is also known as:
    (a) Krebs Cycle
    (b) Citric acid cycle
    (c) Calvin cycle
    (d) Lactate cycle

11. The electron transfer chain is located:
    (a) On the inner membranes of mitochondria.
    (b) On the inner membranes of chloroplasts.
    (c) In the fluid part of chloroplasts.
    (d) Throughout the cytoplasm of the cell.

12. The graph shows an enzyme controlled reaction with a limited amount of enzyme and unlimited substrate. Which of the following is true?

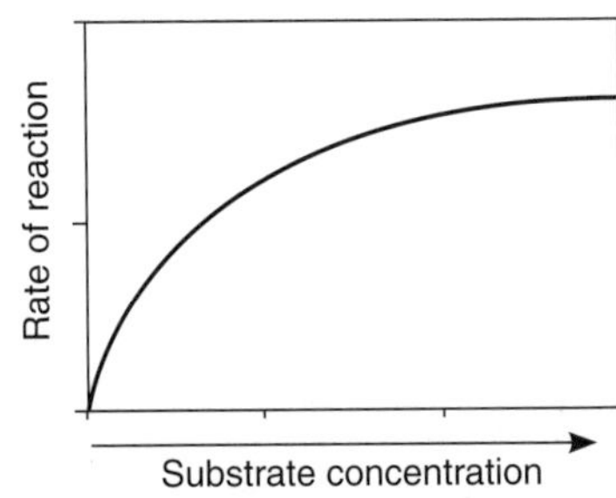

    (a) The reaction rate is independent of the amount of enzyme.
    (b) The reaction slows as the enzyme is used up.
    (c) The reaction rate slows as the enzyme becomes saturated.
    (d) The reaction rate slows as the substrate is used up.

ISBN: 978-1-98-856656-6

Question 13 and 14 relate the to the process of photosynthesis shown below:

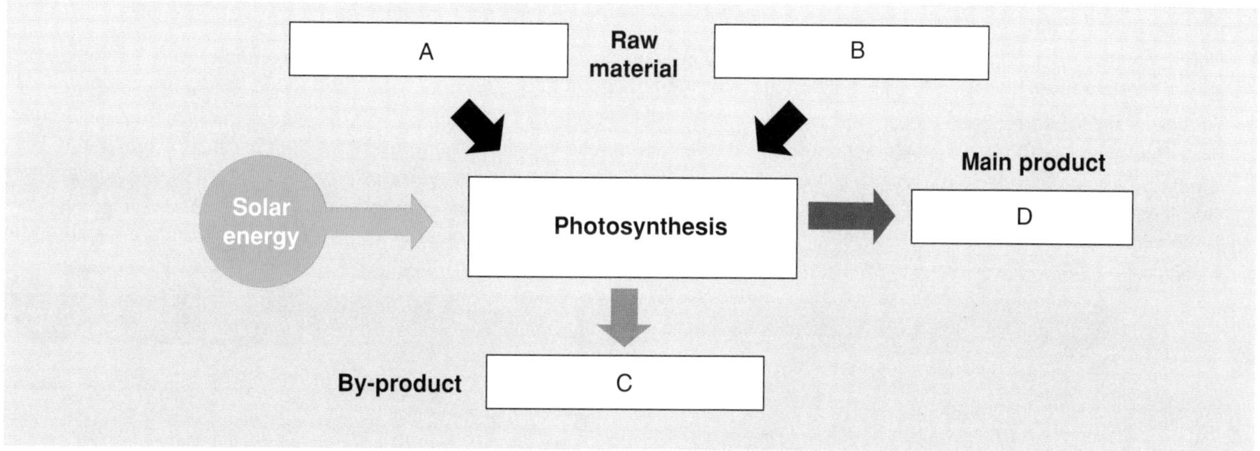

13. Raw materials A and B are:
    (a) Oxygen, carbon dioxide
    (b) Carbon dioxide, water
    (c) Water, oxygen
    (d) Water, glucose

14. Main product D and by-product C are
    (a) D: Oxygen C: Glucose
    (b) D: Carbon dioxide C: Oxygen
    (c) D: Glucose C: Oxygen
    (d) D: Water C: Glucose

15. Which of the following is produced in mammalian muscle cells operating anaerobically?
    (a) Citrate
    (b) Ethanal
    (c) Lactate
    (d) Oxalate

16. Which process does not produce ATP?
    (a) Electron transport chain
    (b) Krebs cycle
    (c) Light dependent reactions
    (d) Light independent reactions

Refer to the diagram below for questions 17-20

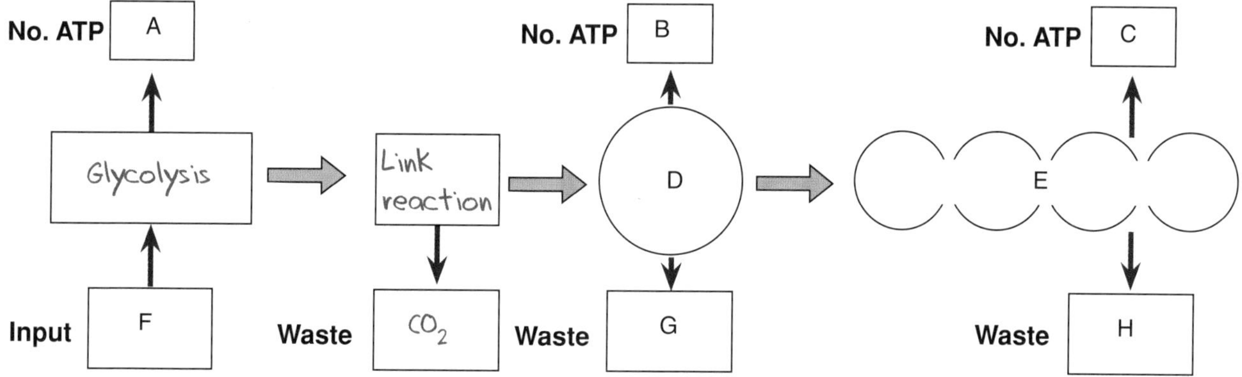

17. The total number of ATP molecules produced in steps A, B, and C is:
    (a) Approximately 20
    (b) Approximately 28
    (c) Approximately 32
    (d) Approximately 38

18. The waste products G and H are
    (a) G: Oxygen H: Carbon dioxide
    (b) G: Carbon dioxide H: Oxygen
    (c) G: Water H: Carbon dioxide
    (d) G: Carbon dioxide H: Water

19. Which process above also occurs in fermentation?
    (a) Glycolysis
    (b) Link reaction
    (c) Process D
    (d) Process E

20. Which of the molecules below transfer electrons to the Electron transport chain in aerobic respiration?
    (a) NADH and $FADH_2$
    (b) NADPH and $FADH_2$
    (c) $NADP^+$ and $FADH^+$
    (d) ATP and NADH

ISBN: 978-1-98-856656-6

***Free Response Question:** Interpreting and evaluating experimental results with graphing*

- During cellular respiration, glucose is oxidized through a stepwise process that results in the generation of ATP. The indicator triphenyl tetrazolium chloride (TTC) is a colorless hydrogen acceptor and intercepts the H^+ produced during respiration.
- TTC turns red when reduced (accepts H^+) so the rate of color change of TTC can be used to indicate the rate of respiration of cells in a test tube. To quantify the color change, samples are placed in a colorimeter and the light absorbance measured.
- Yeast respire aerobically when oxygen is present and glucose is limited. The effect of temperature on the respiration rate of yeast cells was investigated using the TTC indicator method. Four test tubes of a yeast suspension (10 g yeast in 1.5 g/L glucose) containing TTC were placed in water baths at each of 25°C and 40°C. Absorbances at 1.5, 3.0, and 4.5 hours are tabulated below.
- A yeast-glucose tube at 25°C included no TTC. This is a positive control used to validate the procedure (yeast will grow).

	Absorbance at 25°C or 40°C												
	25°C						40°C						Control
	Tube number				Mean	95%CI	Tube number				Mean	95%CI	Tube
Time (hr)	1	2	3	4			5	6	7	8			9
1.5	1.13	1.02	1.20	1.18	1.13	0.13	2.34	2.33	2.29	2.30	2.32	0.04	0.40
3.0	1.96	1.88	2.04	2.06	1.99	0.13	5.85	5.89	5.80	5.92	5.87	0.08	0.51
4.5	2.76	2.69	2.81	2.80	2.77	0.09	7.84	7.88	7.80	7.82	7.84	0.05	0.62

1. (a) **Describe** where the H^+ intercepted by TTC comes from:

(b) **Explain** why measuring the rate of TTC reduction provides a measure of respiration rate:

2. **Construct and label** an appropriate graph of the data tabulated above (mean ±95% CI) using the grid supplied right.

3. **Analyze** the data, explaining what the results indicate about the effect of temperature on the respiration rate of yeast:

4. **Predict** the likely result if the experiment was repeated at 32.5°C. **Justify** your prediction based on the data:

ISBN: 978-1-98-856656-6

Free Response Question: *Scientific investigation*

- The rate of photosynthesis can be investigated by measuring the substances involved in photosynthesis. These include measuring the uptake of carbon dioxide, the production of oxygen, or the change in biomass over time. Measuring the rate of oxygen production provides a good approximation of the photosynthetic rate and is relatively easy to carry out.

Aim

- To investigate the effect of light intensity on the rate of photosynthesis in an aquatic plant, *Cabomba aquatica*.

Cabomba aquatica, a common aquarium plant

Piotr Kuczynski CC 3.0

Method

- 0.8-1.0 grams of *Cabomba* stem were weighed on a balance. The stem was cut while submerged and inverted to ensure a free flow of oxygen bubbles.
- The stem was placed into a beaker filled with a solution containing 0.2 mol/L sodium hydrogen carbonate (to supply carbon dioxide). The solution was at approximately 20°C. A funnel was inverted over the *Cabomba* and a test tube filled with the sodium hydrogen carbonate solution was inverted on top to collect any gas produced.
- The beaker was placed at distances (20, 25, 30, 35, 40, 45, 50 cm) from a 60W light source and the light intensity measured with a lux meter at each interval.
- Before recording data at each new treatment, the *Cabomba* stem was left to acclimatize to the new light level for 5 minutes. Because the volumes of oxygen gas produced are very low, bubbles were counted for a period of three minutes at each distance.

1. **Describe** the biological basis for this investigation of photosynthesis: ______

2. (a) **Identify** the independent and dependent variables in this experiment: ______

   (b) **Identify** the part of the experimental procedure that made the assessment of light intensity quantitative:

3. **Predict** the how the rate of photosynthesis would change as the *Cabomba* is moved away from the light source:

4. **Justify** your prediction: ______

ISBN: 978-1-98-856656-6

UNIT 4

Cell Communication and Cell Cycle

Learning Objectives

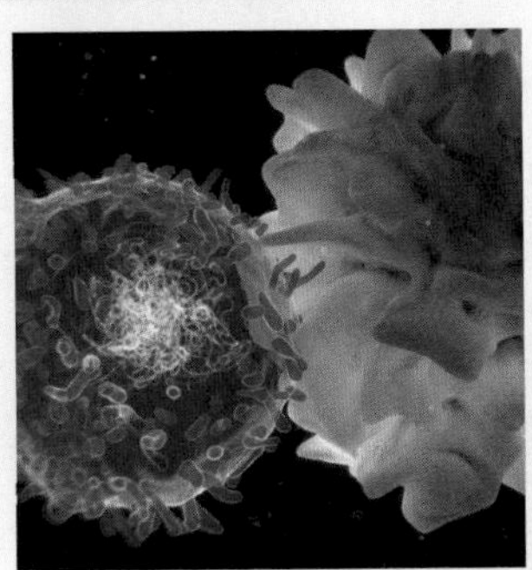

Developing understanding

CONTENT: In this unit, you will continue to learn about cells, focusing on how they use energy and transmit information to communicate and replicate. Signal transduction enables cells to communicate with each other. Cells can generate and receive signals, and coordinate their responses to the environment. These responses enable them to maintain homeostasis. They can also regulate their replication as part of the cell cycle that provides for the continuity of life.

SKILLS: This unit builds on your ability to describe and explain biological concepts and processes relating to the cell cycle. You will develop your skills in formulating questions and planning investigations, and continue to build skills in analysis and scientific communication.

4.1 Cell communication .... activities 62 - 64

☐ 1. Describe the different ways in which cells communicate over different distances using chemical signaling, including how they can produce and respond to their own signals.

☐ 2. Explain how cells communicate by direct cell-to-cell contact and describe examples, e.g. cell communication by plasmodesmata in plants and cell-to-cell contact between cells of the mammalian immune system.

☐ 3. Explain cell signaling by local regulators and how it is used, e.g. in the plant immune response and in nerve transmission.

☐ 4. Explain cell signaling over greater distances using hormones as chemical messengers and describe examples.

4.2 Introduction to signal transduction .... activities 65, 66

☐ 5. Describe how signal transduction pathways link signal reception with cellular responses. Giving examples, describe the components of a signal transduction pathway, including the role of ligands (signal molecules) and receptor proteins. Describe how signal cascades amplify signals and how signal amplification results in a cellular response.

☐ 6. Describe the events occurring after a ligand binds to a receptor protein, including shape change in the intracellular domain of the receptor and the role of second messengers such as cyclic AMP.

4.3 Signal transduction .... activity 67

☐ 7. Describe how changes in the environment trigger changes in cellular responses through signal transduction pathways. Describe the different types of cellular response elicited by different types of signal transduction pathways.

☐ 8. Use examples to provide evidence for how signal transduction pathways operate in different environments. Examples include the use of chemical messengers (autoinducers) in quorum sensing in bacteria, epinephrine stimulation of glycogen breakdown in mammalian liver or muscle cells, and regulation of gene expression by cytokines involved in blood cell differentiation (hematopoiesis).

4.4 Changes in signal transduction pathways... activity 68

☐ 9. Explain how changes in elements of a signal transduction pathway can alter the cellular response. Changes may include mutations (genetic errors) that alter the shape or behavior of a signal molecule or its receptor.

☐ 10. Use examples to explain how chemicals (drugs) can be used to activate or inhibit cell signaling pathways. When are these drugs used and what is the outcome?

4.5 Feedback .... activity 69

☐ 11. Describe how organisms use feedback mechanisms to maintain their internal environments and respond appropriately to changes in their environment.

☐ 12. Using examples, explain how negative (counterbalancing) feedback maintains homeostasis (steady state) and explain why it is so important in regulating physiological systems. Examples include regulation of blood glucose and body temperature (thermoregulation).

☐ 13. Using examples, explain how positive (reinforcing) feedback operates and describe its role in bringing about a system change in certain situations. Describe the effect of positive feedback on homeostasis and explain why it is less common in physiological systems than negative feedback. Examples include fruit ripening, blood clotting, lactation, childbirth, and fever in response to infection.

4.6 Cell cycle .... activities 70 - 75

☐ 14. Describe the role of cell division in the life cycle of organisms, distinguishing mitosis and meiosis.

☐ 15. Describe the sequence of events in the cell cycle: interphase (G_1, S, G_2) and M phase (mitosis and cytokinesis).

☐ 16. Recognize G_0 phase as the point where cells exit the cycle in response to chemical cues.

☐ 17. Explain how mitosis transmits the genetic information in chromosomes from one generation of cells to the next. Describe the sequential stages of mitosis: prophase (including early prophase and prometaphase), metaphase, anaphase, telophase). Create these stages in a model and identify them in light micrographs.

☐ 18. Use experimental data to evaluate the effect of environment, including the chemical environment, on mitosis.

4.7 Regulation of the cell cycle .... activities 76 - 78

☐ 19. Describe the role of internal checkpoints in regulating the progression of the cell cycle. Where do these checkpoints occur and what criteria must be met before the cell progresses to the next stage?

☐ 20. Recall G_0 phase and describe the characteristics of cells in this phase, and their potential fates.

☐ 21. Describe the interactions between cyclins and cyclin-dependent kinases (CdK) and explain their role in cell cycle progression. Recognize the trigger for mitosis as a CdK called M-phase promoting factor (MPF).

☐ 22. Describe the effects of disruptions to the cell cycle caused by failure of (mutations to) regulatory genes such as p53. Include reference to apoptosis and cancer.

62 Types of Cell Signaling

Key Question: How do cells use chemical messengers to communicate and to gather information about, and respond to, changes in their cellular environment.

In order to communicate and respond to changes in their environment, cells must be able to send, receive, and process signals. Most signals are chemicals (signal molecules or ligands). To alter cellular behavior, a ligand must be able to interact with the cell and initiate a cellular response. This interaction occurs via receptors, either on the cell's plasma membrane or inside the cell itself. Cells with the receptors to bind a particular ligand are the **target cells** for that specific ligand. If a cell does not have the 'right' receptor, it is unaffected by the signal. Signal molecules may act over varying distances, having localized or far reaching effects.

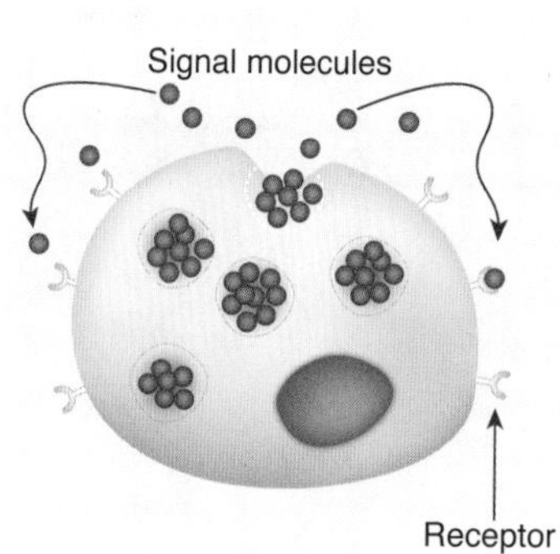

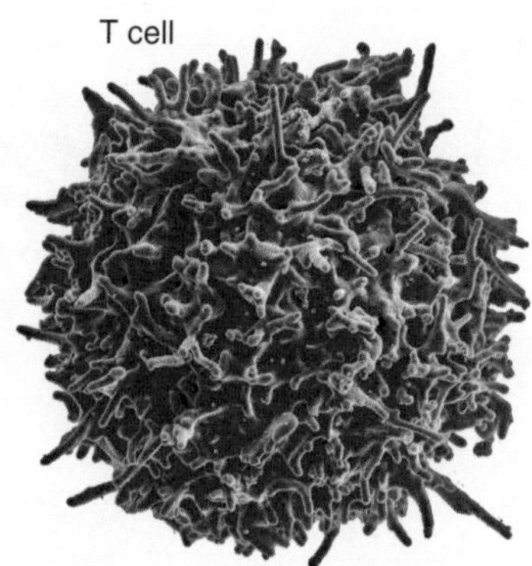

Autocrine signaling

Cells can produce and react to their own signals. This type of signaling is important during growth and development and in the functioning of the immune system.

Example: In vertebrates, the presence of a foreign antibody causes T-cells to produce a growth factor to stimulate their own production. The increased number of T-cells helps to fight the infection.

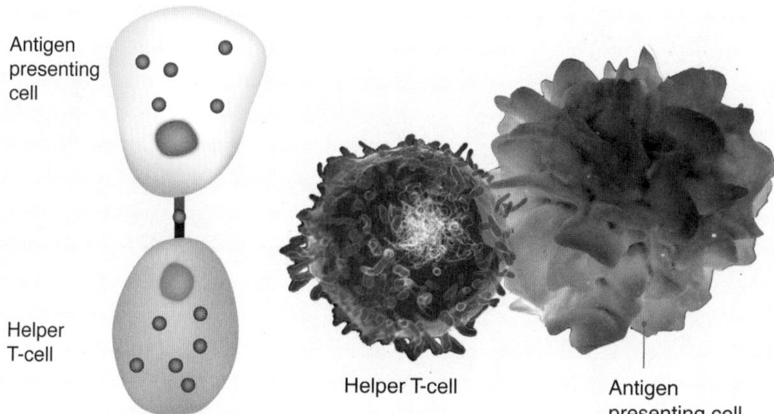

Cell-to-cell communication

Cell-to-cell communication involves cells interacting directly with one another. There are two forms: 1) communication via special channels between adjacent cells and 2) two cells bind to and communicate with each other because they have complementary proteins on their surfaces.

Example: Plasmodesmata are microscopic channels that run through the cell wall of adjacent plant cells. Signal molecules can pass through to the next cell.

Example: In the immune system, antigen presenting cells present antigens to helper T-cells for destruction.

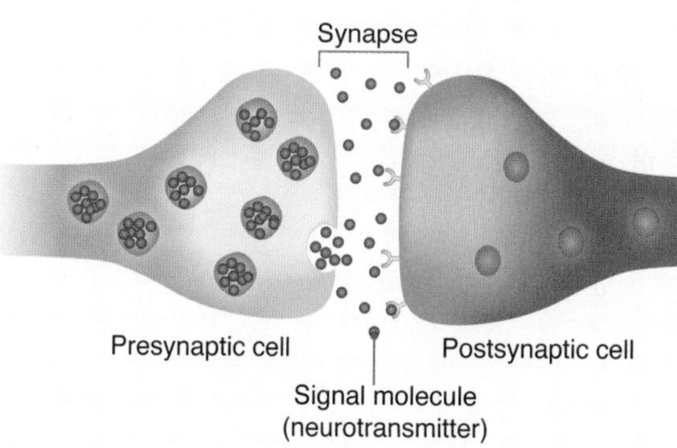

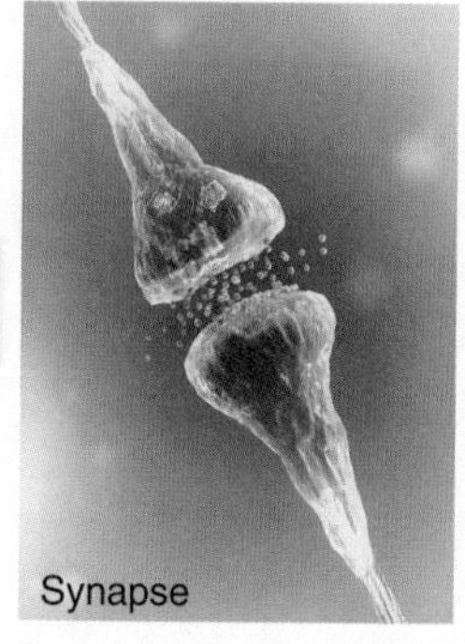

Signaling by local regulators

Some cell signaling occurs between cells that are close together. The signal molecule binds to receptors on a nearby cell causing a response. Both neurotransmitters (signaling molecules in the nervous system) and cytokines (small molecules produced by a range of different cells) are involved in this type of local regulation.

Example: Neurotransmitters released from a nerve cell travel across the synapse (gap) to another cell to cause a response.

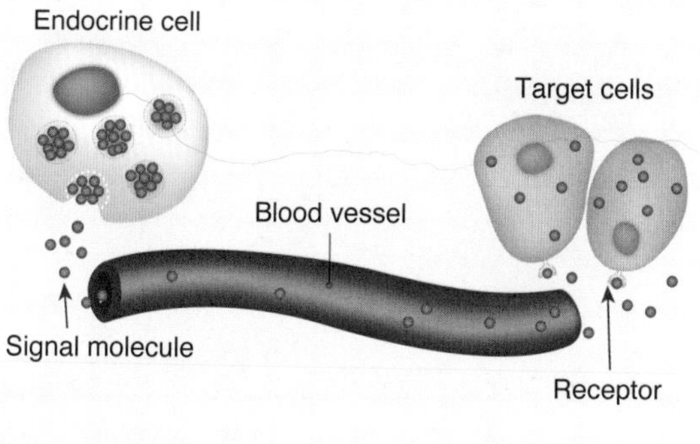

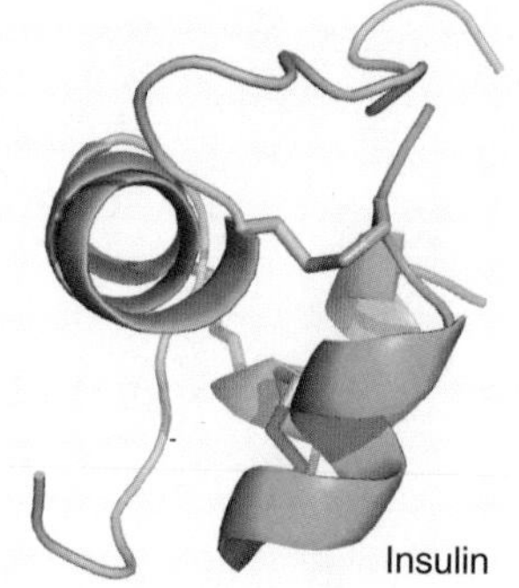

Endocrine signaling

A signal is carried in the bloodstream to target cells, often some distance away.

Endocrine signaling may involve hormones (released from the cells of endocrine glands) or cytokines as the signaling molecule although cytokines are also important in local regulation and circulate in more variable concentrations than hormones.

Example: Insulin from the pancreas stimulates the cellular uptake of glucose.

ISBN: 978-1-98-856656-6

What is a receptor?

Chemical signals must be received by a cell in order to exert their effect. Reception of signal molecules (ligands) is the job of proteins called receptors, which bind ligands and link them to a biochemical pathway to cause a cellular response. The specificity of receptors to their particular signal molecule increases the efficiency of cellular responses and saves energy. The binding sites of cell receptors are specific only to certain ligands. This stops them reacting to every signal the cell encounters. Receptors generally fall into two main categories:

Intracellular receptors

Intracellular (cytoplasmic) receptors are located within the cell's cytoplasm and bind ligands that can cross the cell membrane.

Extracellular receptors

Extracellular (transmembrane) receptors span the cell membrane with regions both inside and outside the cell. They bind ligands that cannot cross the cell membrane (right).

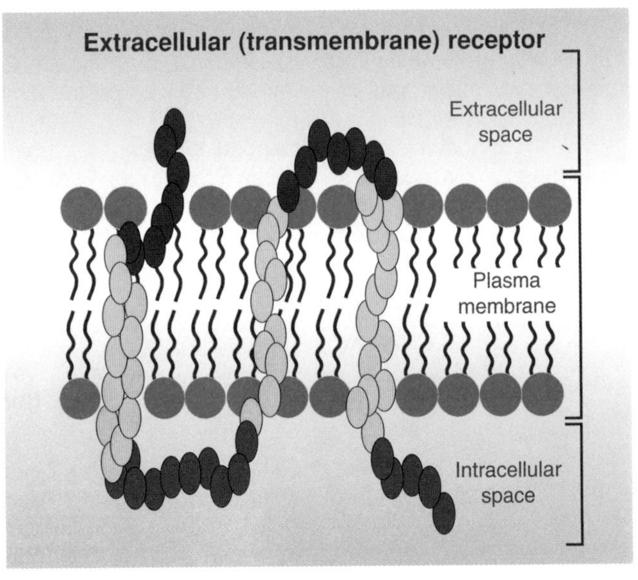

1. Describe the following types of cell signaling:

(a) Autocrine signaling: cells can produce + react to their own signals. This type of signaling is important during growth and development + in the functioning of the immune system

(b) Cell-to-cell communication: Involves cells interacting directly w/ one another. there are 2 forms: 1) communication via special channels between adjacent cells + 2) 2 cells bind to + communicate w/ each other because they have complementary proteins on the surface

(c) Local regulation: occurs between cells that are close together. The signal molecule binds to receptors on a nearby cell causing a response. Both neurotransmitters + cytokines are involved.

(d) Endocrine signaling: a signal is carried in the bloodstream to target cells. May involve hormones or cytokines as the signaling molecule although cytokines are also important in local regulation + circulate in more variable concentrations than hormones.

2. Explain the features shared by all types of communication by signaling: All types of of communication by signaling involve signal molecules (ligands) as well as receptors for these molecules.

3. Explain how cells are able to communicate over varying distances using different types of signaling: Cell to cell communication is where cells interact directly w/ one another. Endocrine signaling occurs over long distances as signals are carried through bloodstreams. Autocrine signals are produced by its own cell. And signaling by local regulators occurs locally.

4. Cytokines and hormones are both involved in endocrine signaling. Explain how they differ: cytokines are small proteins while hormones can be proteins, steroids, amino acid derivatives, fatty acid derivatives, etc

ISBN: 978-1-98-856656-6

63 Cell-to-Cell Communication

Key Question: How do plant and animal cells use cell signaling to interact directly?

Cell-to-cell signaling requires close contact between adjacent cells. It is also known as contact dependent signaling. There are several mechanisms by which cell-to-cell communication can occur. Plant and animal cells may have connecting microscopic channels running between adjacent cells allowing for communication to occur. In animal cells these are called **gap junctions** and in plant cells they are **plasmodesmata** (*sing.* plasmodesma). A second form of cell-to-cell communication occurs when a receptor of one cell interacts directly with the receptor of a second cell. This type of cell signaling is important in embryonic development and the immune response.

Cell-to-cell communication in animal cells

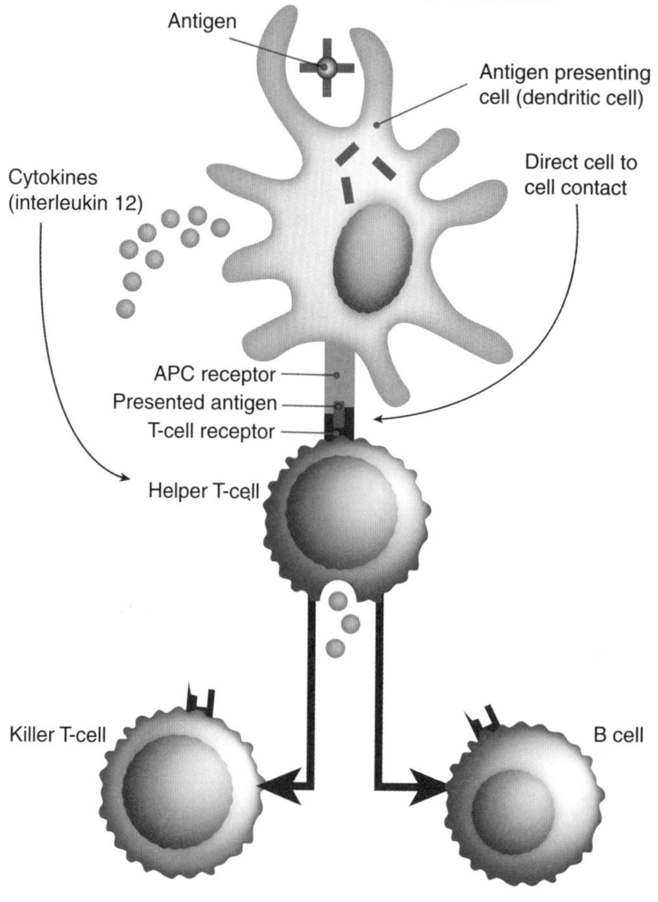

Helper T-cells are activated by direct cell-to-cell signaling with antigen presenting cells

In the immune system, T helper cells and antigen presenting cells (APCs) communicate directly through cell-to-cell contact. APCs, such as dendritic cells and macrophages, ingest antigens, process them, and present them on the cell surface where they are recognized by T helper cells. This presentation (along with cytokines released from the APC) stimulates the production of T killer cells and B cells and helps an organism to destroy foreign antigens.

Cell-to-cell communication in plant cells

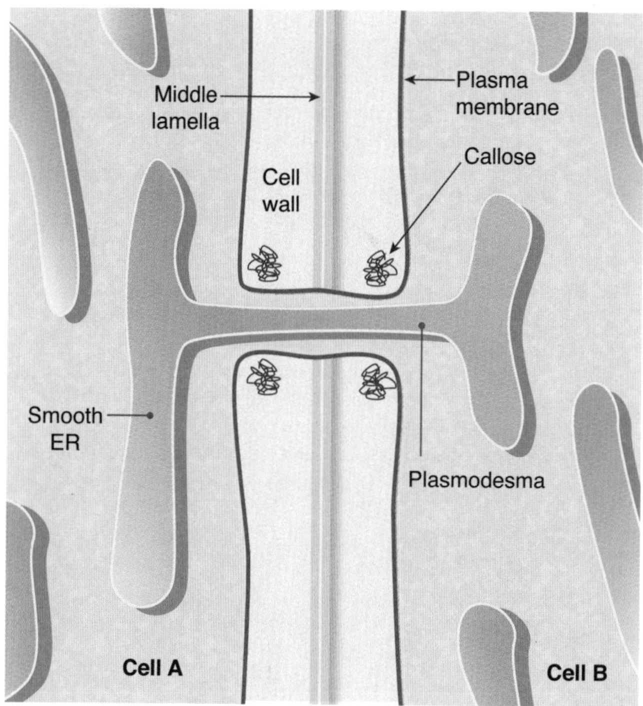

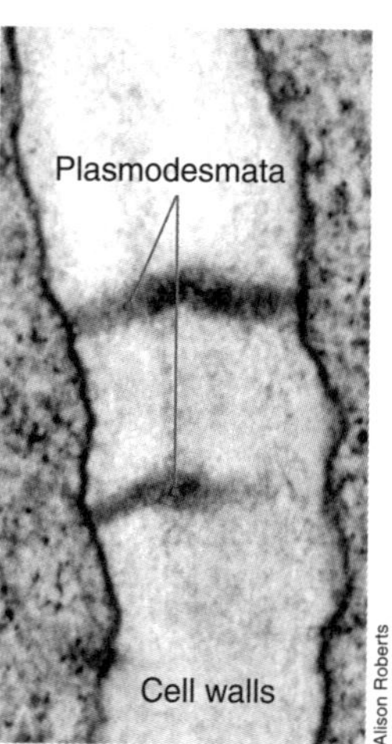

Plasmodesmata allow adjacent plant cells to communicate directly

Each cell has 10^3-10^5 cytoplasmic connections called plasmodesmata, laid down at the time of development. They are dynamic channels, regulating the passage of signaling and information molecules, such as transcription factors, between adjacent cells. Intercellular communication allows the plant to coordinate tissue or organ responses to environmental stress or as required for growth and development. The permeability of plasmodesmata is regulated by changes in the amount of a polysaccharide called callose at the opening of the plasmodesma.

1. Compare direct cell-to-cell communication between animal cells of the immune system and adjacent plant cells:

In animals, T helper cells + antigen presenting cells communicate directly through cell to cell contact. In plants, each cell has 10^3-10^5 cytoplasmic connections (plasmodesmata), laid down at development. They are dynamic channels, regulating the passage of signaling + information molecules between adjacent cells.

2. Explain how plants can regulate the level of cell signaling occurring through plasmodesmata: The permeability of plasmodesmata is regulated by changes in the amount of a polysaccharide called callose at the opening of the plasmodesma.

ISBN: 978-1-98-856656-6

64 Communication Over Short and Long Distances

Key Question: How do cells use signal molecules to communicate over short and long distances?

Cells in close proximity can communicate using **local regulators**, i.e. signal molecules that travel only a short distance from the secreting cell to the target cell before being inactivated. A number of cells in the immediate vicinity of the emitting cell may be stimulated, causing a specific cellular response, such as a nerve impulse. If distantly separated cells within an organism are to communicate, signal molecules (hormones) must be transported in a medium, usually blood. Target cells with receptors that can bind the hormone will be able to respond to these endocrine signals. Often these target cells are concentrated within a specific tissue, but they may be widespread throughout the body.

Local regulation between animal cells

- Local regulation across synapses occurs in the nervous system and takes place between a neuron (nerve cell) and another cell (e.g. another neuron or a muscle cell).
- In this 'synaptic signaling', an electrical impulse travels along a long conducting process of the neuron called an axon. It eventually reaches the synapse (the gap between the two cells) where it triggers the release of chemical signal molecules called neurotransmitters from the axon terminals.
- The neurotransmitter travels across the synapse to affect the target cell. The effect can increase a response (excitatory) or decrease a response (inhibitory) depending on the cell and neurotransmitter involved. Chemical changes in the cell bring about a range of specific cellular responses (e.g. opening ion channels, causing muscle contraction, and regulation of heart rate and blood pressure).

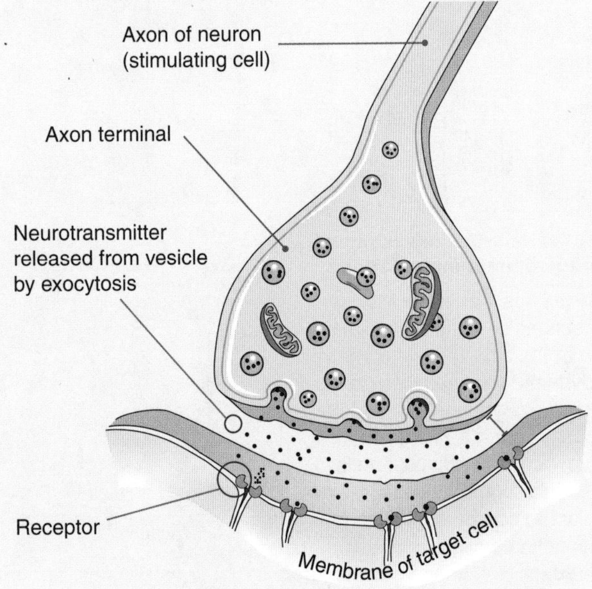

The neurotransmitter is broken down (inactivated) or reabsorbed after diffusing across the synapse. This prevents continued response by the target cell.

Local regulation between plant cells

In plants, local regulation occurs via a process called **transcellular transport**. Signaling molecules are transferred between cells over a short distance, but without the use of plasmodesmata. This involves transport across membranes and includes import and export mechanisms such as secretion, receptor-mediated endocytosis, and channel- and carrier-based transport (active transport or facilitated diffusion). Transcellular transport mechanisms are used by plants to launch an immune response to disease.

Example: Salicylic acid is produced in response to pathogens (disease-causing organisms). It results in activating genes involved in defense which may:

- Close stomata (to prevent more pathogens entering).
- Produce proteins with antimicrobial activity.
- Target and destroy non-plant nucleic acids.

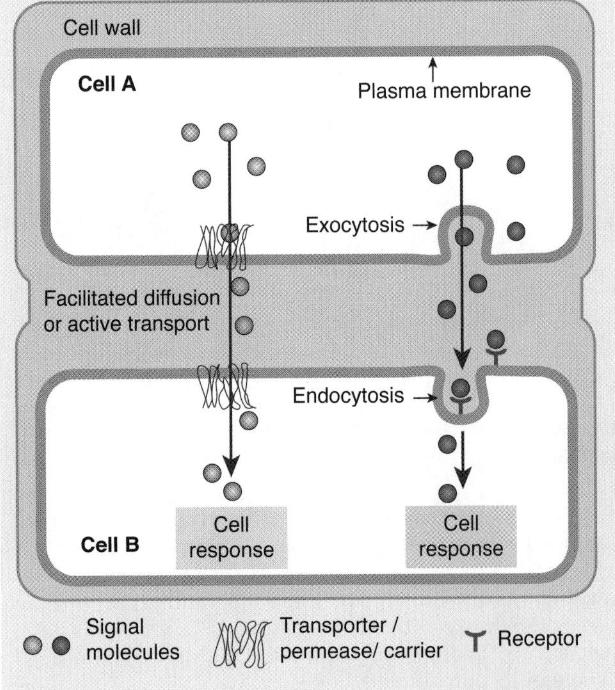

1. Explain how local regulation is used in cell to cell communication in plants and animals: In animal cells, local regulation across synapses occurs in the nervous system and takes place between a neuron + another cell. In plants, it occurs via transcellular transport.

2. In what way are the mechanisms of local regulation similar in plants and animals? The similarities between them are the proximity of the cells and the neurotransmitters.

ISBN: 978-1-98-856656-6

Endocrine signaling: communicating over distance

- You have seen earlier how hormones are chemical messengers in endocrine signaling pathways. Hormones are secreted from endocrine glands and distributed throughout the body in the blood. This allows hormones to reach the same targets at much the same time, even when those targets are at different places in the body.
- Endocrine control acts more slowly than signaling through local regulators (as in nerve pathways) because the distances involved are greater. The effects of hormones are often wide ranging affecting may different tissues. Their effects may be long-lasting, affecting development (e.g. the estrogens), or more immediate (e.g. insulin promoting cellular uptake of glucose).

ESTROGENS (e.g. estradiol, estrone)
Produced in the ovaries with widespread but specific effects on target tissues and organs.

Estrogens (e.g. estradiol) are lipid-soluble steroid hormones and pass through the plasma membrane to bind with nuclear receptors, exerting their effects at the genomic level. By altering gene expression, estrogens regulate specific aspects of female reproduction and development.

INSULIN
Produced by beta endocrine cells in the pancreas. Insulin signaling allows the body's cells to take up glucose and promotes glucose storage (as glycogen) in the liver. Its effect is to lower blood glucose level.

Endocrine cells of the pancreas are sensitive to blood glucose levels.
Beta cells
Muscle fiber
Insulin promotes uptake of glucose in tissues, e.g. muscle.
High levels of glucose in the blood stimulate beta cells to release insulin into the blood.
Glucose
Insulin
Glucose transporter
Insulin receptor

Insulin is linked to glucose transport
This highly simplified schematic shows how insulin binding activates glucose transporters allowing glucose to enter the cell.

3. (a) What type of signaling do the examples of insulin and estrogen above represent? endocrine

(b) Explain your answer: estrogen + insulin are secreted from endocrine glands and distributed throughout the body in blood, allowing them to reach targets in different areas of the body

4. Using the example of estrogens, explain how hormones are able to have such widespread and long-lasting effects:
Estrogens are lipid-soluble steroid hormones + pass through the plasma membrane to bind w/ nuclear receptors, exerting their effects at the genomic level. They also travel through endocrine signaling, so in the bloodstream to reach many parts of the body.

5. In simple terms, explain how insulin is able to promote uptake of glucose by cells: through endocrine signaling that promotes this.

ISBN: 978-1-98-856656-6

65 Signals and Signal Transduction

Key Question: How does signal transduction convert an external signal into a functional change within the cell.

Signal transduction is the process by which molecular signals are converted from one form to another so that they can be transmitted from outside the cell to inside and bring about a response. The transduction involves an external signal molecule binding to a receptor and triggering a series of biochemical reactions. The series of biochemical reactions is often called a cascade and usually involves phosphorylation of a number of molecules in a sequence. The type of cellular response varies and may include activation of a metabolic pathway, gene expression (to produce a specific protein), or membrane permeability (to allow entry of specific molecules). The process is outlined in simple form below.

An overview of signal transduction

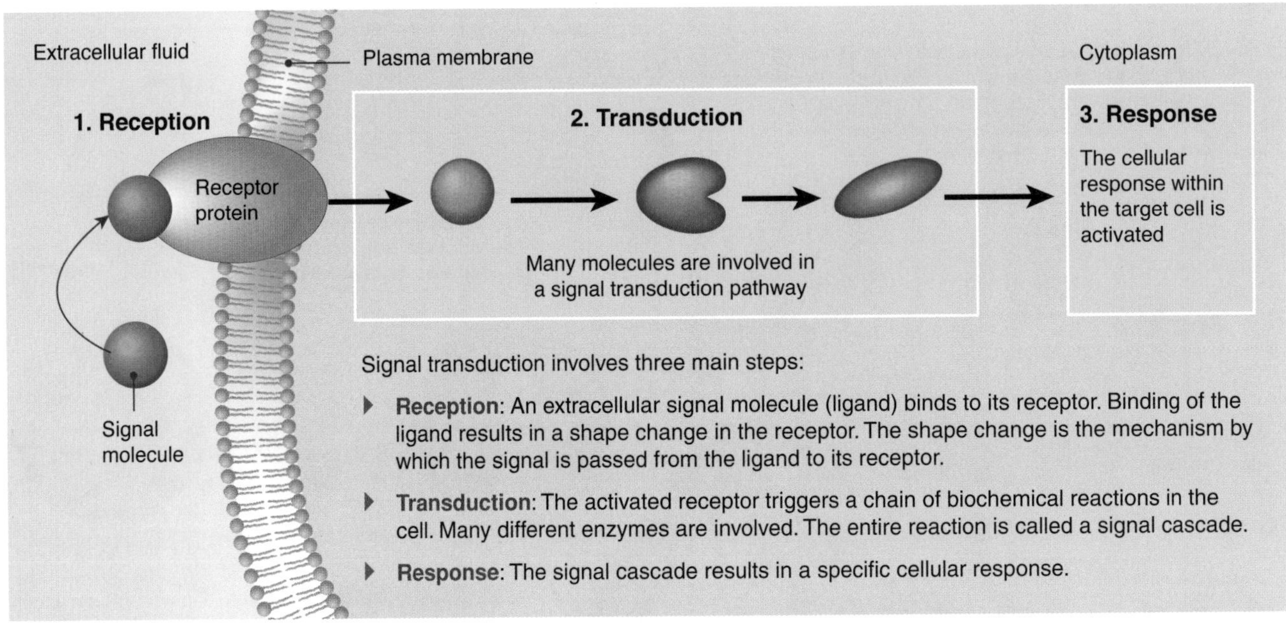

Signal transduction involves three main steps:

- **Reception:** An extracellular signal molecule (ligand) binds to its receptor. Binding of the ligand results in a shape change in the receptor. The shape change is the mechanism by which the signal is passed from the ligand to its receptor.
- **Transduction:** The activated receptor triggers a chain of biochemical reactions in the cell. Many different enzymes are involved. The entire reaction is called a signal cascade.
- **Response:** The signal cascade results in a specific cellular response.

1. Describe the three stages of signal transduction:

(a) reception-ligand binds to its receptor. This results in a shape change in the receptor. This is the mechanism by which the signal is passed from the ligand to its receptor.

(b) transduction-activated receptor triggers a chain of biochemical reaction in the cell. Many enzymes involved. Reaction is called a signal cascade.

(c) Response-the signal cascade results in a specific cellular response.

2. (a) Why doesn't every cell respond to a particular signal molecule? Because they may have different receptor proteins, not for that particular molecule.

(b) Why is this important? So that the cell isn't always responsive and overdoing its job.

3. The images below show a signaling pathway, but the steps are out of order. Assign each image a number (1-4) to indicate its correct position in the sequence:

(a) 1 (b) 3 (c) 4 (d) 2

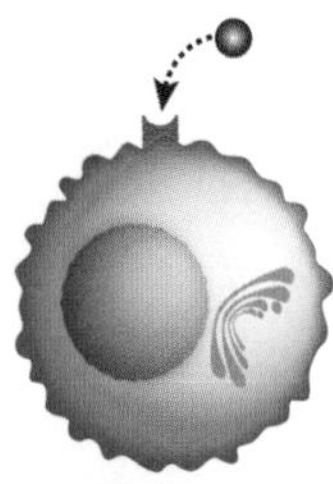
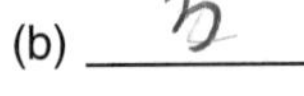

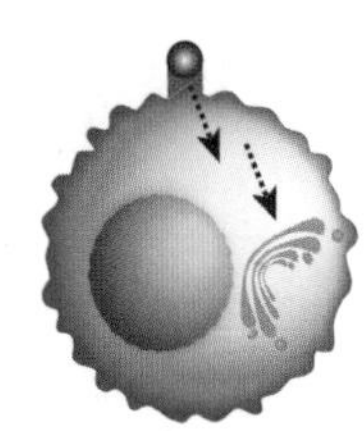
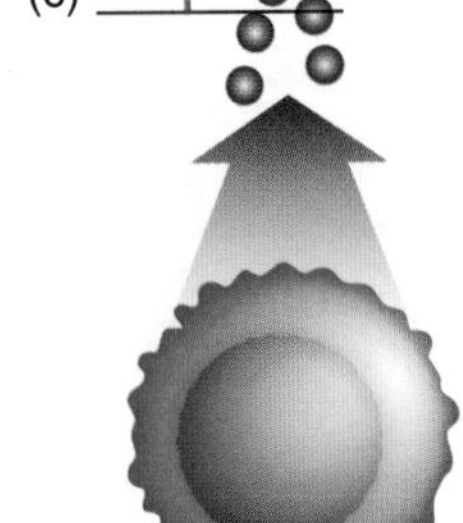

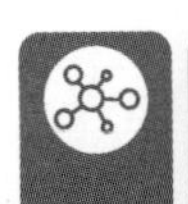
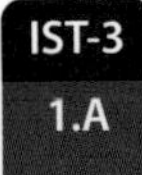

ISBN: 978-1-98-856656-6

How signal transduction generates a cellular response

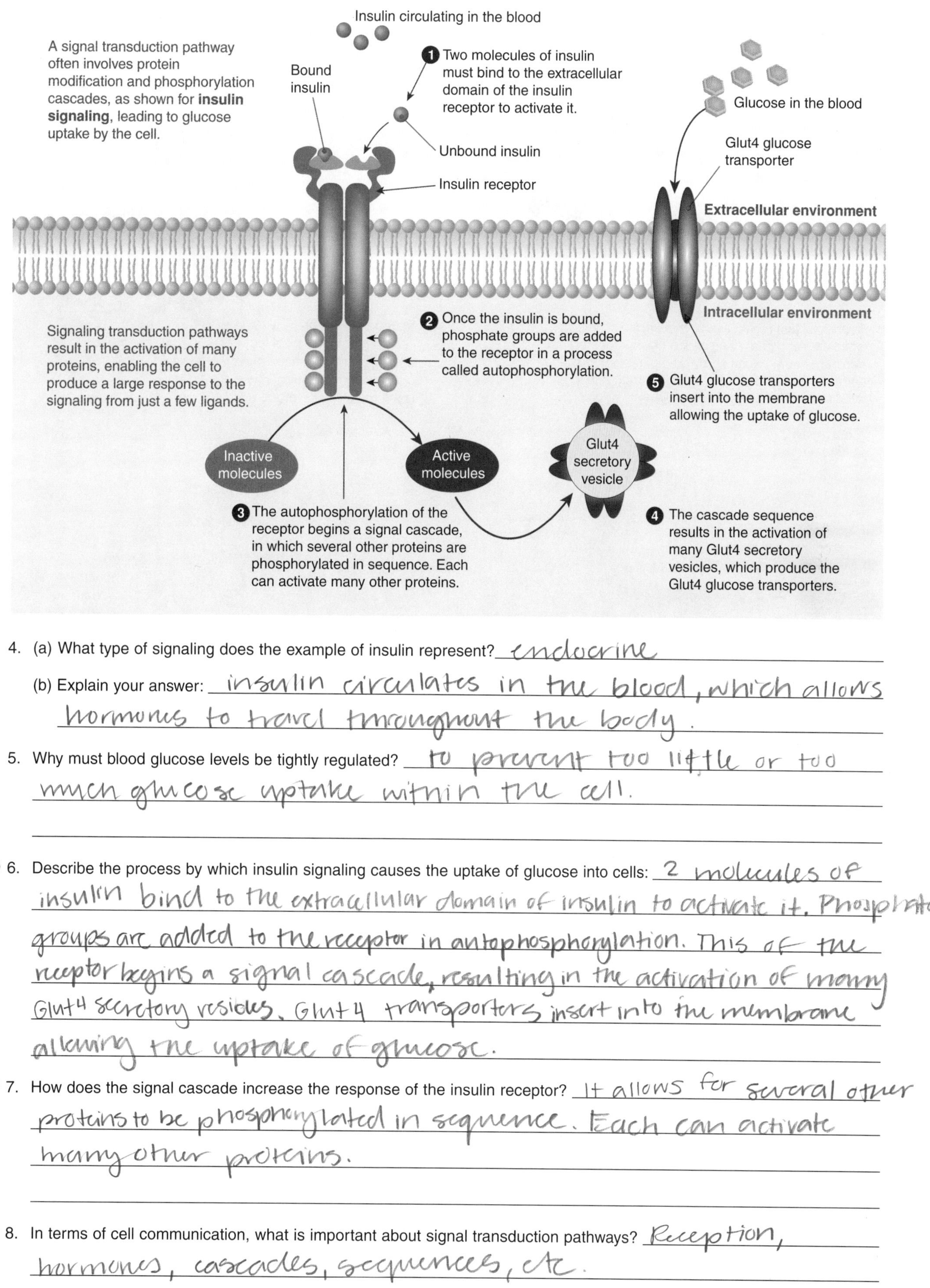

Insulin circulating in the blood
A signal transduction pathway often involves protein modification and phosphorylation cascades, as shown for insulin signaling, leading to glucose uptake by the cell.
Bound insulin
1 Two molecules of insulin must bind to the extracellular domain of the insulin receptor to activate it.
Unbound insulin
Insulin receptor
Glucose in the blood
Glut4 glucose transporter
Extracellular environment
Intracellular environment
Signaling transduction pathways result in the activation of many proteins, enabling the cell to produce a large response to the signaling from just a few ligands.
2 Once the insulin is bound, phosphate groups are added to the receptor in a process called autophosphorylation.
5 Glut4 glucose transporters insert into the membrane allowing the uptake of glucose.
Inactive molecules
Active molecules
Glut4 secretory vesicle
3 The autophosphorylation of the receptor begins a signal cascade, in which several other proteins are phosphorylated in sequence. Each can activate many other proteins.
4 The cascade sequence results in the activation of many Glut4 secretory vesicles, which produce the Glut4 glucose transporters.

4. (a) What type of signaling does the example of insulin represent? endocrine

(b) Explain your answer: insulin circulates in the blood, which allows hormones to travel throughout the body.

5. Why must blood glucose levels be tightly regulated? to prevent too little or too much glucose uptake within the cell.

6. Describe the process by which insulin signaling causes the uptake of glucose into cells: 2 molecules of insulin bind to the extracellular domain of insulin to activate it. Phosphate groups are added to the receptor in autophosphorylation. This of the receptor begins a signal cascade, resulting in the activation of many Glut4 secretory vesicles. Glut4 transporters insert into the membrane allowing the uptake of glucose.

7. How does the signal cascade increase the response of the insulin receptor? It allows for several other proteins to be phosphorylated in sequence. Each can activate many other proteins.

8. In terms of cell communication, what is important about signal transduction pathways? Reception, hormones, cascades, sequences, etc.

ISBN: 978-1-98-856656-6

66 Types of Signal Transduction

Key Question: How do the properties of signal molecules determine the nature of the signal transduction pathway?

Cell receptors fall into two broad classes.n**Extracellular receptors** bind hydrophilic signal molecules outside of the cell. The signal molecule does not have to pass across the plasma membrane to cause a cellular response. Most cell receptors are extracellular receptors. **Intracellular receptors** bind hydrophobic signal molecules that pass into the cell directly across the plasma membrane. Intracellular receptors may be located in the cytoplasm or on the nucleus.

Hydrophilic signal molecules are received by extracellular receptors

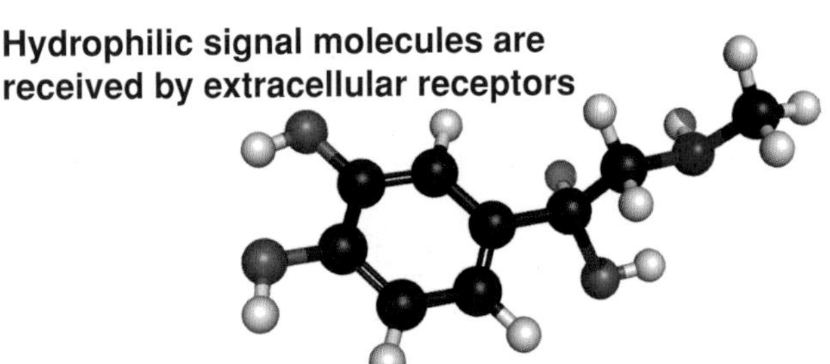

Hydrophilic signal molecules such as epinephrine are water soluble and cannot cross the plasma membrane. The epinephrine receptor is an example of a G-coupled receptor. Epinephrine accelerates heart rate and is involved in the fight or flight response.

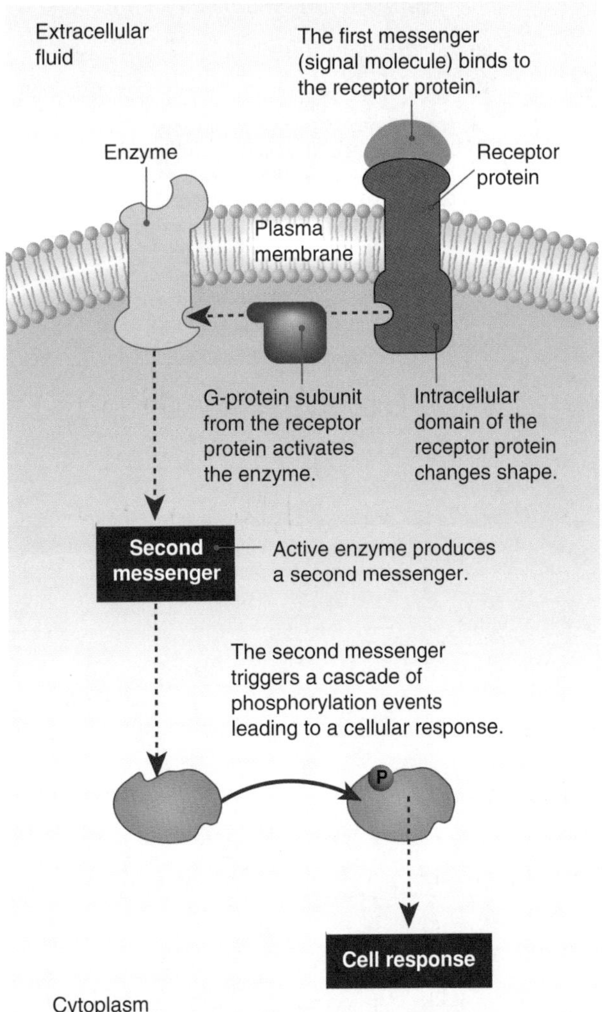

Hydrophilic signal molecules cannot cross the plasma membrane and must exert their effect by interacting with an extracellular receptor. Hydrophilic signals include water soluble hormones such as epinephrine and insulin. The signal molecule is the **first messenger**. When it binds, the extracellular receptor changes shape, triggering a sequence of biochemical reactions, including activation of a **second messenger**. As a consequence, the original signal is amplified, bringing about a cellular response. This pathway is given in more detail in the next activity.

Hydrophobic signal molecules are received by intracellular receptors

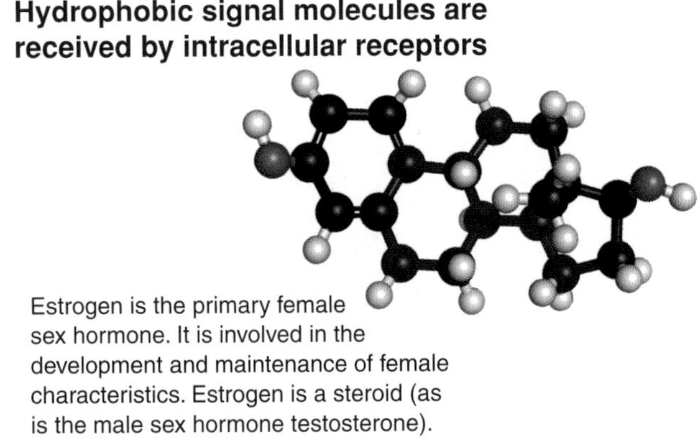

Estrogen is the primary female sex hormone. It is involved in the development and maintenance of female characteristics. Estrogen is a steroid (as is the male sex hormone testosterone).

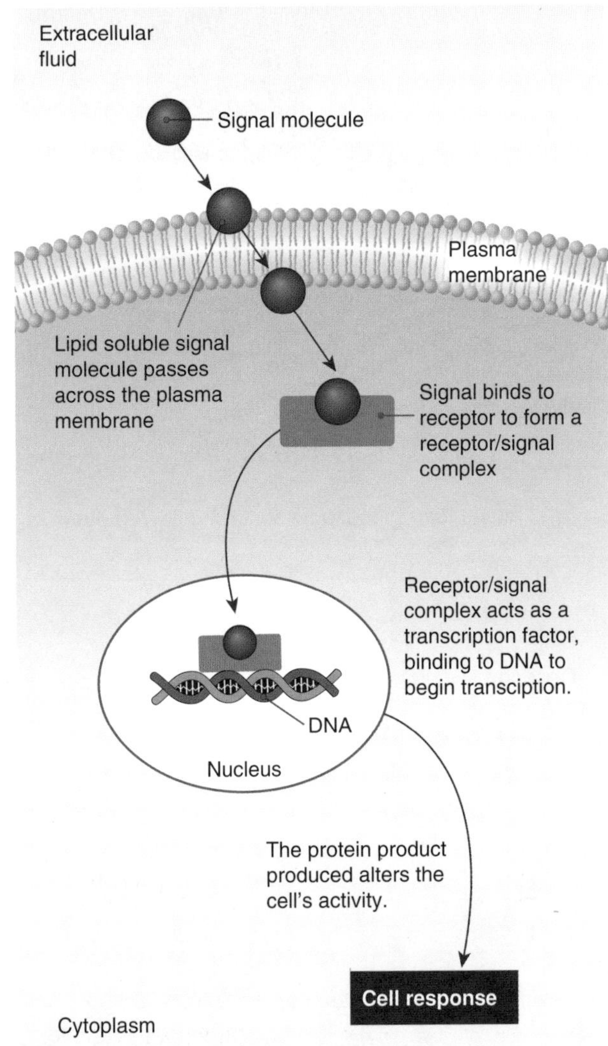

Hydrophobic hormones, such as steroids (e.g. estrogen), diffuse freely across the plasma membrane and into the cytoplasm of target cells. Once inside the cell, they bind to intracellular receptors in the cytoplasm to form a receptor-signal complex. The complex moves to the cell nucleus where it binds directly to the DNA and acts as a **transcription factor**, resulting in the transcription of a one or more specific genes. Concentrations of the different gene products (proteins) change as a result (a phenotypic change).

ISBN: 978-1-98-856656-6

1. Describe the differences between an intracellular receptor and an extracellular receptor: extracellular receptors bind hydrophilic signal molecules outside of the cell. Intracellular receptors bind hydrophobic signal molecules that pass into the cell directly across the plasma membrane

2. What must a signal molecule do in order to activate a receptor? It must bind to the receptor

3. In terms of their ability to cross the plasma membrane, describe the difference between a hydrophobic signal molecule and a hydrophilic signal molecule:
Hydrophilic signal molecules cannot cross the plasma membrane. Hydrophobic hormones diffuse freely across the plasma membrane.

4. (a) Describe the process of signal transduction via an extracellular receptor: hydrophilic signal molecules bind to these receptors, causing the receptors to change shape, triggering a sequence of biochemical reactions (including second messenger). Original signal is amplified, bringing about a cellular response.

   (b) Describe the differences between a first messenger and a second messenger: 1st messanger binds to the receptor protein. The second messenger triggers a cascade of phosphorylation events leading to a cellular response.

5. Describe the process of signal transduction via an intracellular receptor: Hydrophobic hormones cross the plasma membrane + bind to these receptors in the cytoplasm to form a receptor-signal complex, which moves to the cell nucleus where it binds directly to the DNA + acts as a transcription factor. Concentration of the different gene products change as a result.

6. The diagram on the right represents a cell signaling process.

   Plasma membrane
   A
   B
   Cellular response

   (a) Does this diagram represent an extracellular or intracellular signaling process? Explain your answer:
   extracellular, the signal molecules bind to the receptor outside the plasma membrane

   (b) What type of receptor is B? extracellular

   (c) What does A represent? hydrophilic signal molecule.

   (d) Would A be hydrophobic or hydrophilic? Explain your answer: Hydrophilic since they cannot cross the plasma membrane + must exert their effect by interacting w/ an extracellular receptor.

ISBN: 978-1-98-856656-6

67 Signal Transduction and Environment

Key Question: What is the role of the cellular environment in eliciting a cellular response.

Cellular environments are dynamic. To survive and grow, cells must be able to respond appropriately to changes in the environment. As we have seen, this involves responding to signals that indicate environmental change. In multicellular organisms, this might mean responding to changes in the level of a circulating hormone. For unicellular organisms, it may involve making appropriate responses to changes in cell density or chemicals in the wider environment. These dynamic responses are mediated through signal transduction pathways and may include changes in the activity of preexisting enzymes, changes in the rates of synthesis of new enzymes, or changes in membrane-transport processes.

Signaling via epinephrine

Cytokines are non-hormone signaling molecules

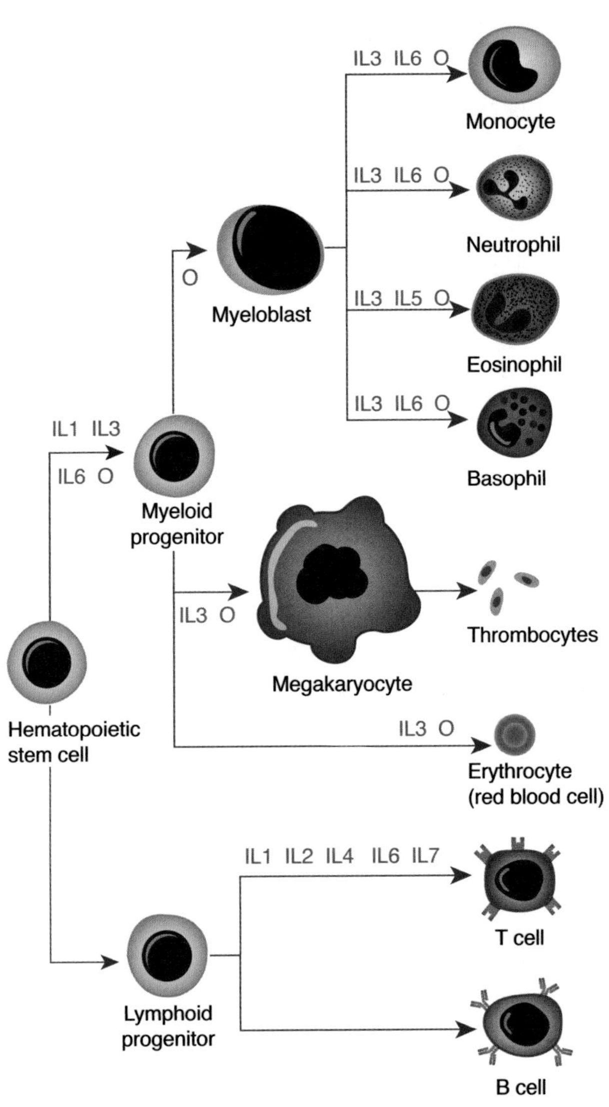

Signal transduction involving epinephrine

As you saw in the precious activity, second messengers relay a signal received by an extracellular receptor to a target within the cell to bring about a specific response such as enzyme activation. The process involves a signal cascade, which amplifies the original signal, so many molecules are activated. Common second messengers include cyclic AMP (cAMP) and Ca^{2+}.

Signal transduction pathways involving phosphorylation cascades work by activating a chain of protein kinases (enzymes that transfer phosphates). In the example shown above, epinephrine binds to receptors on a liver cell. The end result is the breakdown of stored glycogen into glucose monomers. Epinephrine is a hormone released as part of the fight-or-flight response. Rapid mobilization of glucose to provide energy is just one of its effects.

Signaling pathways control cell differentiation

Cytokines are a diverse group of small signaling proteins with roles in regulating immunity, inflammation, and the formation and differentiation of blood cells (hematopoiesis). They cannot cross the plasma membrane so also operate through extracellular (cell surface) receptors. Cytokines are involved in autocrine, paracrine and endocrine signaling.

Interleukins (IL) are common cytokines in hematopoiesis (above). The unique sequence in which different cytokines are expressed, along with other control processes such as DNA methylation, determine blood cell fate during differentiation. This diagram shows the involvement of multiple factors in cell differentiation. It is not intended that you memorize these.

ISBN: 978-1-98-856656-6

Quorum sensing and bioluminescence in bacteria

- **Quorum sensing** is a process of cell to cell communication between bacterial cells. It involves extracellular signaling molecules called **autoinducers**. Bacteria share information about cell density in their environment and then alter their cellular response through changes in gene expression.
- Quorum sensing allows the bacterial population to act together in a coordinated way. A critical number (quorum) is required for the action to be beneficial. Quorum sensing helps to ensure that energy and resources are not expended unnecessarily. It regulates many activities in bacteria, including symbiosis, virulence, motility, antibiotic production, and biofilm formation.

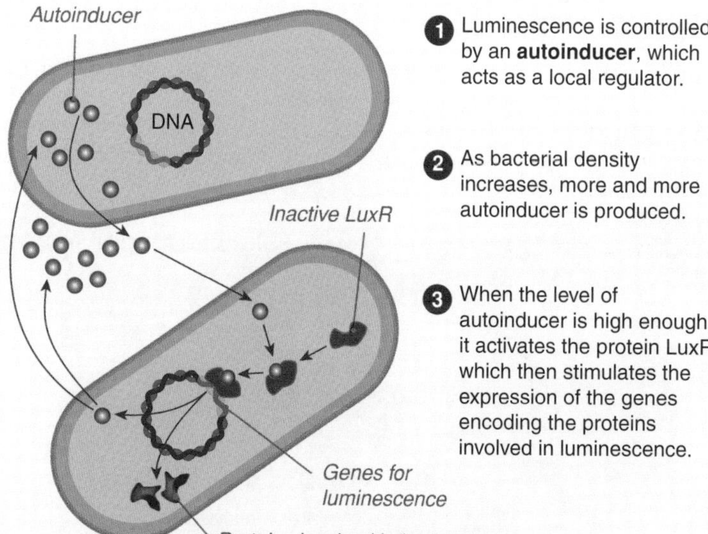

1. Luminescence is controlled by an **autoinducer**, which acts as a local regulator.

2. As bacterial density increases, more and more autoinducer is produced.

3. When the level of autoinducer is high enough, it activates the protein LuxR, which then stimulates the expression of the genes encoding the proteins involved in luminescence.

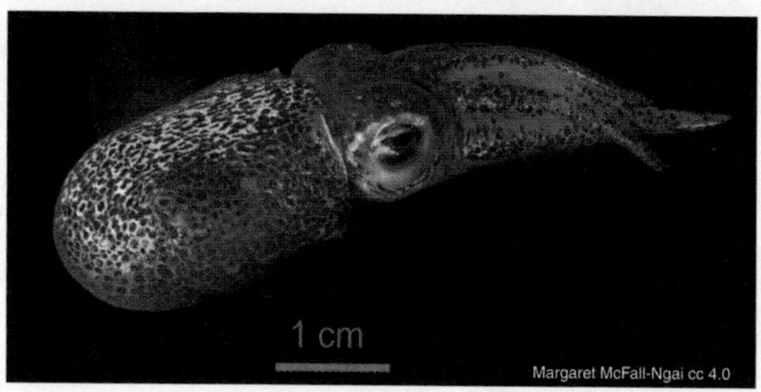

The Hawaiian bobtail squid (left) lives in a mutually beneficial symbiotic relationship with the bacterium *Aliivibrio fischeri*, which luminesces when the bacterial population reaches a certain density. Hatchling squid capture bacteria from the environment and house them at high densities in a light organ. The bacteria receive sugars and amino acids and the squid uses the luminescing bacterial to provide camouflage through counter-illumination (producing light on their bellies to match the light coming down from above).

Luminescent bacteria produce light as the result of a chemical reaction that converts chemical energy to light energy.

1. Explain the significance of signal amplification in signal transduction pathways: ______

2. Explain why each molecule in the cAMP signal cascade is phosphorylated: ______

3. How does the bobtail squid make use of the quorum sensing abilities of *Aliivibrio fischeri*? ______

4. Use the information presented above and opposite to justify the claim that signal transduction pathways influence how cells respond to their environment: ______

ISBN: 978-1-98-856656-6

68 Changes in Signal Transduction Pathways

Key Question: What are the consequences when cell signaling pathways fail to operate properly?

Almost as soon as biologists realized the importance of signal transduction pathways in the body, their importance in the development of disease became obvious. Failure of a pathway to operate properly would cause significant detrimental effects. Many therapeutic drugs focus on blocking the effects of overactive pathways or restoring signaling pathways when they fail. The negative effects of many toxins are caused by their actions on signal transduction pathways.

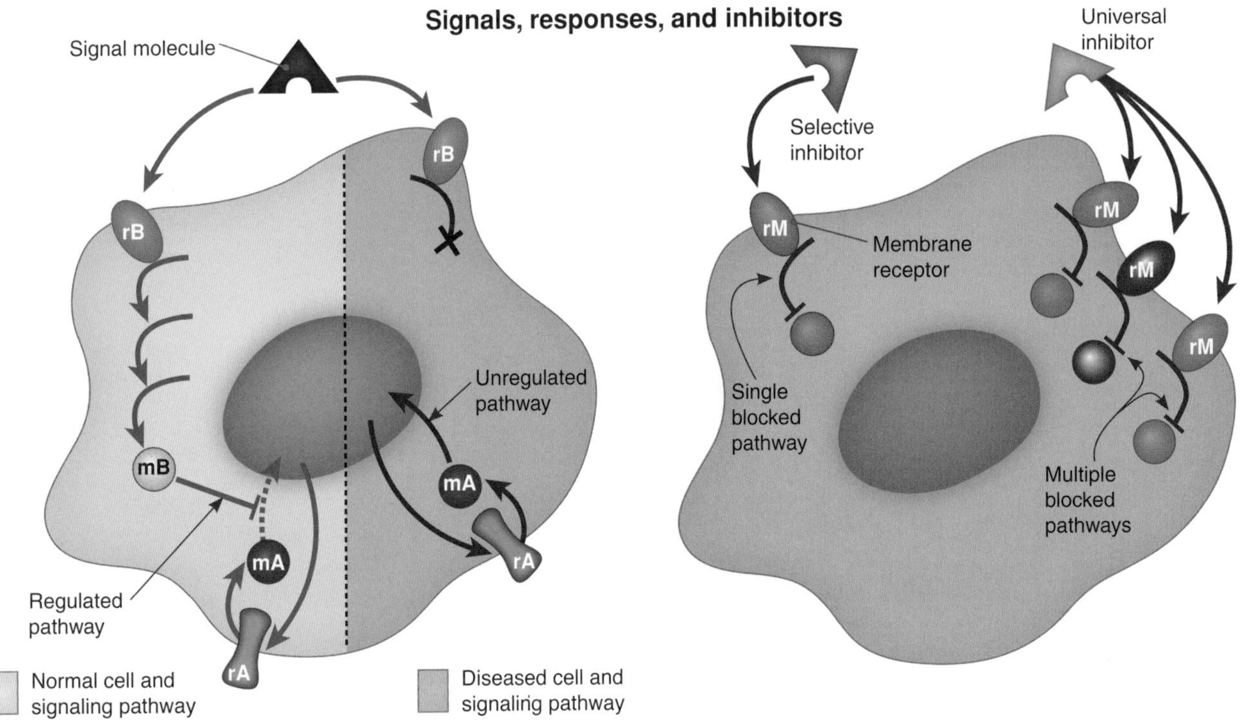

In order to correct a signal transduction pathway, it is important to understand its normal operation. The signaling pathways of diseased cells (e.g. tumor cells) are often overactive (e.g. over expressing receptors for growth factors). In the example above, receptor rA signals the production of more receptor rA via the messenger molecule mA. Receptor rB initiates a signal cascade activating molecule mB, which inactivates molecule mA and so regulates receptor rA's production. The diseased cell fails to make molecule mB and so cannot regulate receptor rA's production.

Selecting inhibitors as drugs also involves the question of how many membrane receptors (**rM**) are affected by a particular drug. **Universal signal transduction inhibitors** (top right) affect diseased cells by blocking many signal pathways, but also affect healthy cells, and so can cause damage outside the target area. **Selective signal transduction inhibitors** (top left) target a single overactive pathway, thus causing no damage outside the target area. However the specificity of these drugs may mean many different types are required to treat a disease effectively.

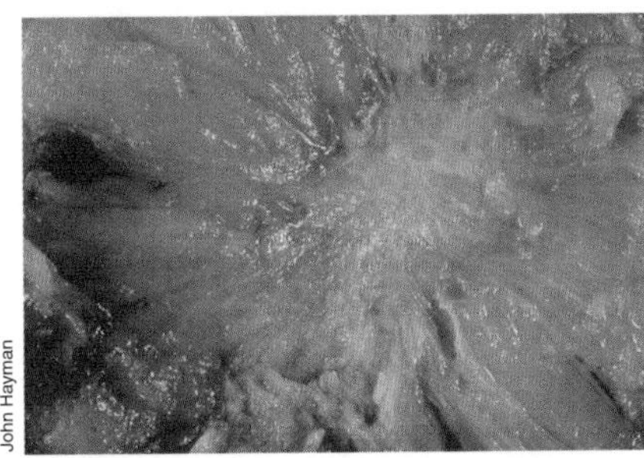

Breast cancer (like all cancers) is the result of cells dividing out of control. In breast cancer, the HER2 receptor protein has been identified as a major cause.

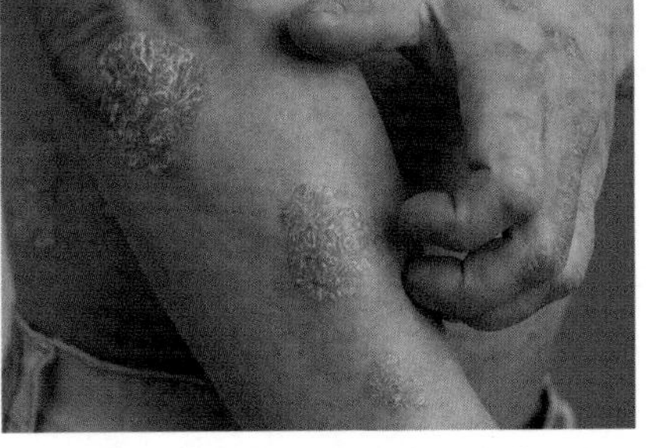

Psoriasis results from the hyper-proliferation of keratinocytes (epidermal cells) which is driven by EGFR (epidermal growth factor receptor) causing scaly patches or plaques on the skin.

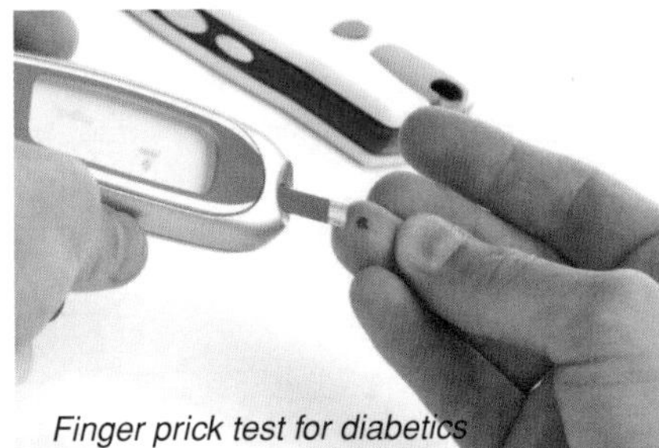

Finger prick test for diabetics

Type 2 (adult onset) diabetes is caused by the failure of cells to respond to signaling by the hormone insulin, which results in the failure of cells to take up glucose.

1. Predict the consequences to the cellular response in the unregulated pathway of the diseased cell (above, left):

ISBN: 978-1-98-856656-6

Pesticides and signals

Many pesticides work by affecting signaling in nerve cells. They may block uptake of signaling molecules or they may facilitate higher rates of uptake than normal.

Cholinesterase inhibitors work by blocking the enzyme responsible for breaking down acetylcholine after it has transmitted a message across a synapse. As a result, the receiving neuron continues to fire, causing over-stimulation and death.

Neonicotinoid insecticides (NNIs) mimic the action of acetylcholine in synapses. This again causes the over-stimulation of the nerve cells and results in death. Recent evidence links use of NNIs to persistent negative effects on reproduction in bees.

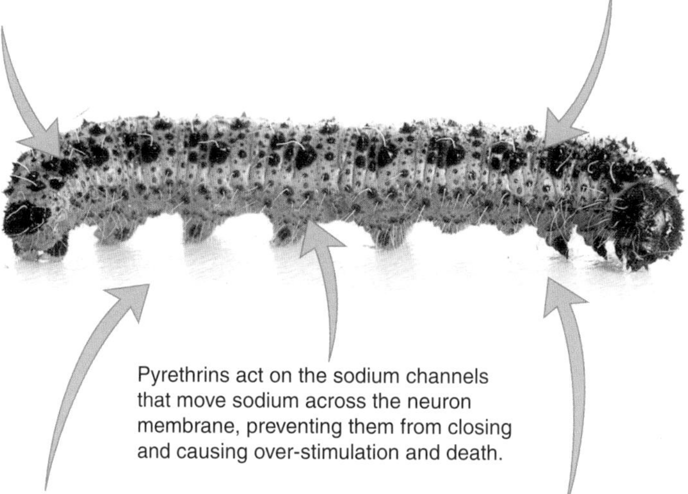

Pyrethrins act on the sodium channels that move sodium across the neuron membrane, preventing them from closing and causing over-stimulation and death.

Organochlorines inhibit the GABA receptor, which itself has an inhibitory function in nerve cells. The result is over-stimulation of the nervous system and death.

Chitin is a major part of an insect's exoskeleton. Pesticides block the chitin synthesis pathway, preventing the insect from growing a new exoskeleton and molting (so it can't grow), eventually killing the insect.

Action of antihistamine

Hayfever and similar allergic reactions occur when mast cells produce the chemical histamine as part of an immune response to foreign particles such as pollen. Histamine triggers the inflammatory response and results in swelling, red eyes, and a runny nose.

Antihistamines block the histamine receptor of cells and so block the signal for the inflammatory response.

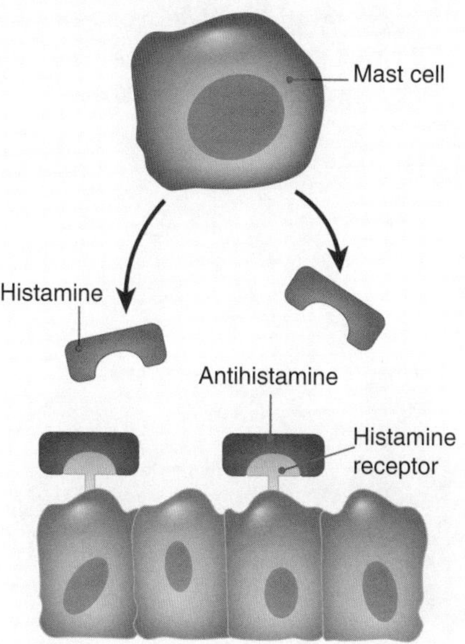

2. (a) Explain the link between signal transduction and disease: ______

(b) Explain why understanding the link is important: ______

3. (a) Describe the action of drugs that inhibit the activity of membrane receptors: ______

(b) Predict a likely biological consequences if the wrong type of inhibitor was used to treat a signaling disorder: ______

4. Acetylcholine and GABA are neurotransmitters in a wide range of animals, including humans. Predict the toxicity to humans of organochlorines and cholinesterase inhibitors relative to pesticides based on inhibition of chitin synthesis: ______

5. Explain how antihistamines prevent hayfever: ______

ISBN: 978-1-98-856656-6

69 Feedback

Key Question: How do feedback mechanisms operate to stabilize dynamic systems or to bring about a specific result? Most organisms are able to regulate the internal conditions of their bodies in order to maintain a steady state when the environment around them is changing. To do this, they must detect environmental change through sensory systems and coordinate appropriate responses through nervous or hormonal mechanisms. Two types of feedback operate in biological systems. Counterbalancing or **negative feedback** stabilizes systems against fluctuations outside a set range. Reinforcing or **positive feedback** amplifies a response, usually to achieve a specific outcome. Positive feedback is unstable, so it is rarer in biological systems than the negative feedback that controls most physiological processes.

Negative feedback keeps body temperature at ~37°C

- Negative (or counterbalancing) feedback is a control system that maintains the body's internal environment at a relatively steady state. Negative refers to the sign used in mathematical models of feedback.
- Negative feedback has a stabilizing effect by discouraging variations from a set point. When variations are detected by the body's receptors, negative feedback returns internal conditions back to a steady state (below).

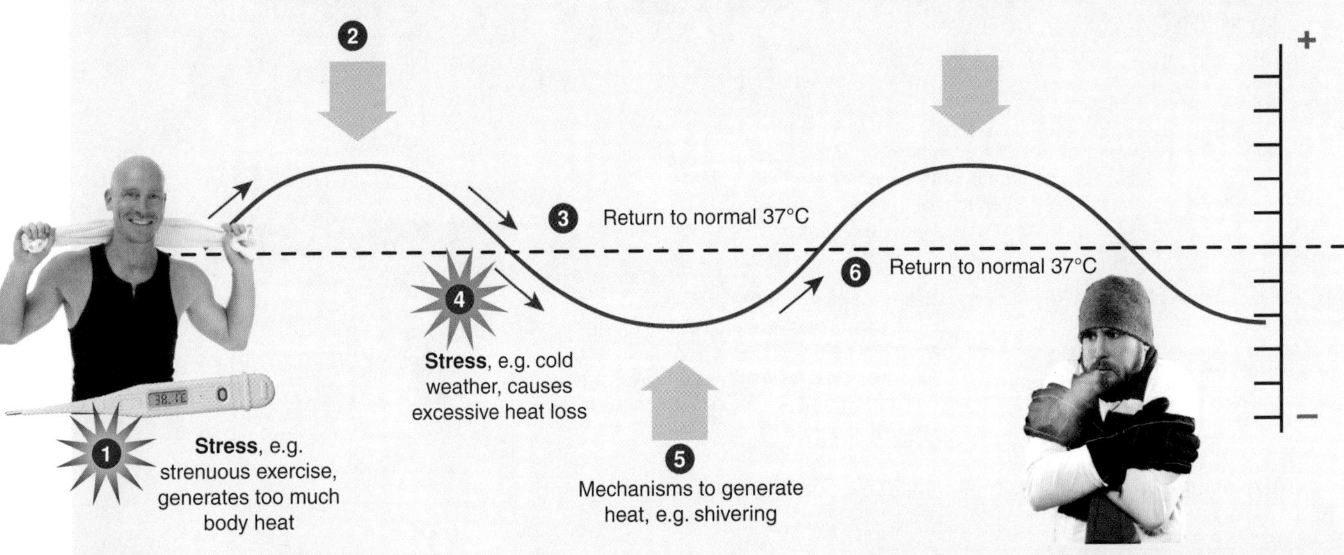

We know when we are too cold but we are unaware of most of the negative feedback operating in our bodies. Yet it keeps our body systems stable.

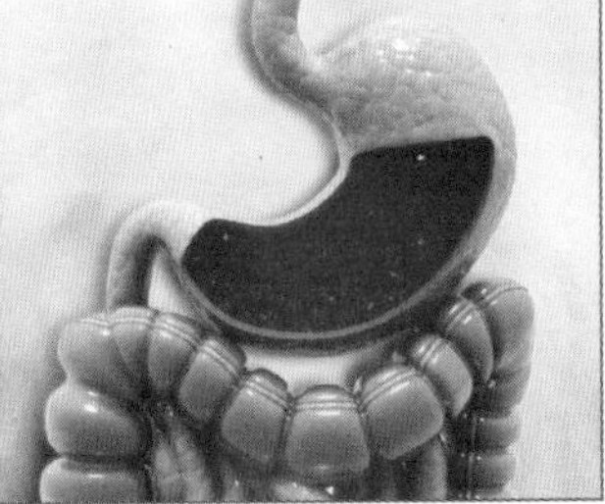

Food in the stomach activates stretch receptors, stimulating gastric secretion and motility. As the stomach empties, the stimulus for gastric activity declines.

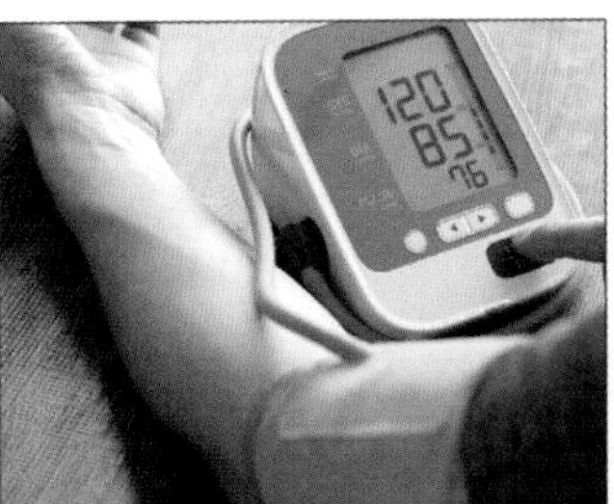

Negative feedback controls almost all the body's functioning processes including heart rate, blood glucose, blood pressure, and pituitary secretions.

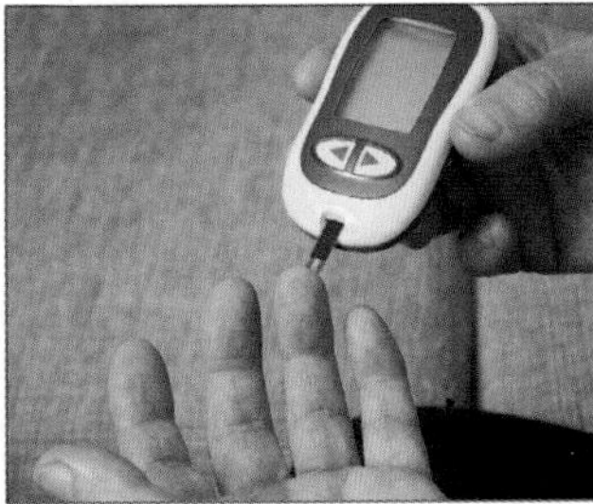

Maintaining stable blood glucose levels is an important homeostatic function regulated by negative feedback involving two antagonistic (opposing) hormones.

1. How does the behavior of a negative feedback system maintain homeostasis? ______________________

____

____

____

2. Why do you think it is important that the regulation of the body's critical functions depends on negative feedback?

____

____

____

ISBN: 978-1-98-856656-6

Understanding negative feedback: regulation of blood glucose

- Blood glucose levels are controlled by negative feedback involving two hormones, insulin and glucagon. These hormones are produced by the islet cells of the pancreas, and act in opposition to control blood glucose levels.
- As you saw earlier in this chapter, insulin lowers blood glucose by promoting the cellular uptake of glucose and the conversion of glucose into the storage molecule glycogen in the liver.
- Glucagon opposes insulin's action. It increases blood glucose by stimulating the breakdown of stored glycogen and the synthesis of glucose from amino acids. Negative feedback stops hormone secretion when normal blood glucose is restored. Blood glucose homeostasis allows energy to be available to cells as required. The liver has a central role in these carbohydrate conversions.

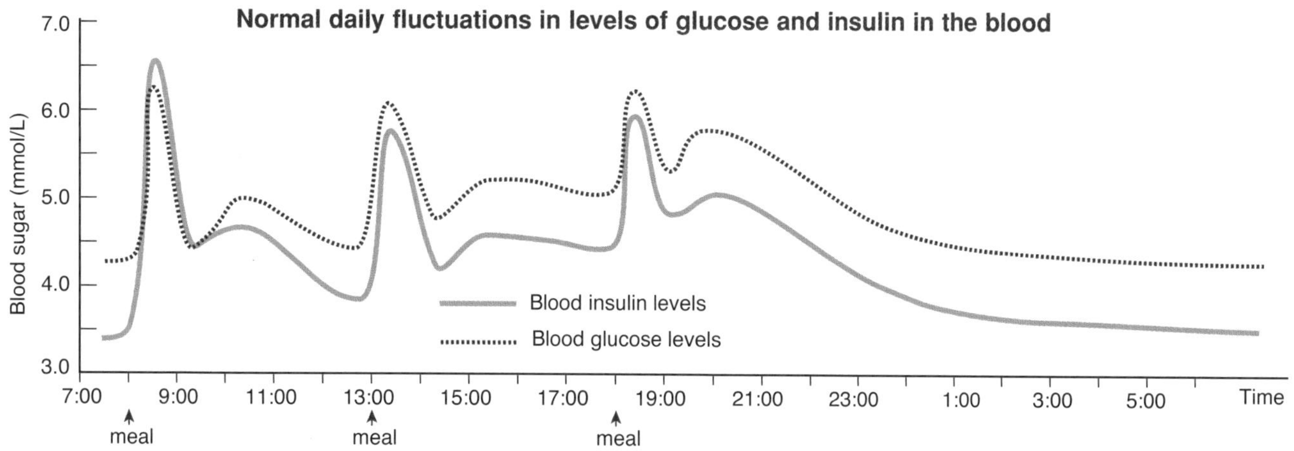

Negative feedback in blood glucose regulation

Blood glucose (**BG**) can be tested using a finger prick test. The glucose in the blood reacts with an enzyme electrode, generating an electric charge proportional to the glucose concentration. This is displayed as a digital readout.

5.2 mmol/L

beta cells

Stimulates β cells to secrete insulin

Uptake of glucose by cells. Glucose converted to glycogen or fat in the liver.

Rise in BG

Normal blood glucose (BG) level 3.9-5.6 mmol /L

Decreases blood glucose.

alpha cells

Stimulates α cells to secrete glucagon

Fall in BG

Breakdown of glycogen to glucose in the liver.

Release of glucose into the blood.

3. (a) Identify the stimulus for the release of insulin: ______

(b) Identify the stimulus for the release of glucagon: ______

(c) How does glucagon increase blood glucose level? ______

(d) How does insulin decrease blood glucose level? ______

4. Using the information above, predict the consequences of a lack of insulin (as occurs in type 1 diabetes): ______

ISBN: 978-1-98-856656-6

Positive feedback

- Positive feedback mechanisms amplify (increase) a response in order to achieve a particular result. Examples of positive feedback include fruit ripening, fever, blood clotting, childbirth (labor) and lactation (production of milk) in mammals.
- A positive feedback mechanism stops when the end result is achieved (e.g. the baby is born, a pathogen is destroyed by a fever, or ripe fruit falls off a tree). Positive feedback is less common than negative feedback in biological systems because the escalation in response is unstable. Unresolved positive feedback responses (e.g. high fevers) can be fatal.

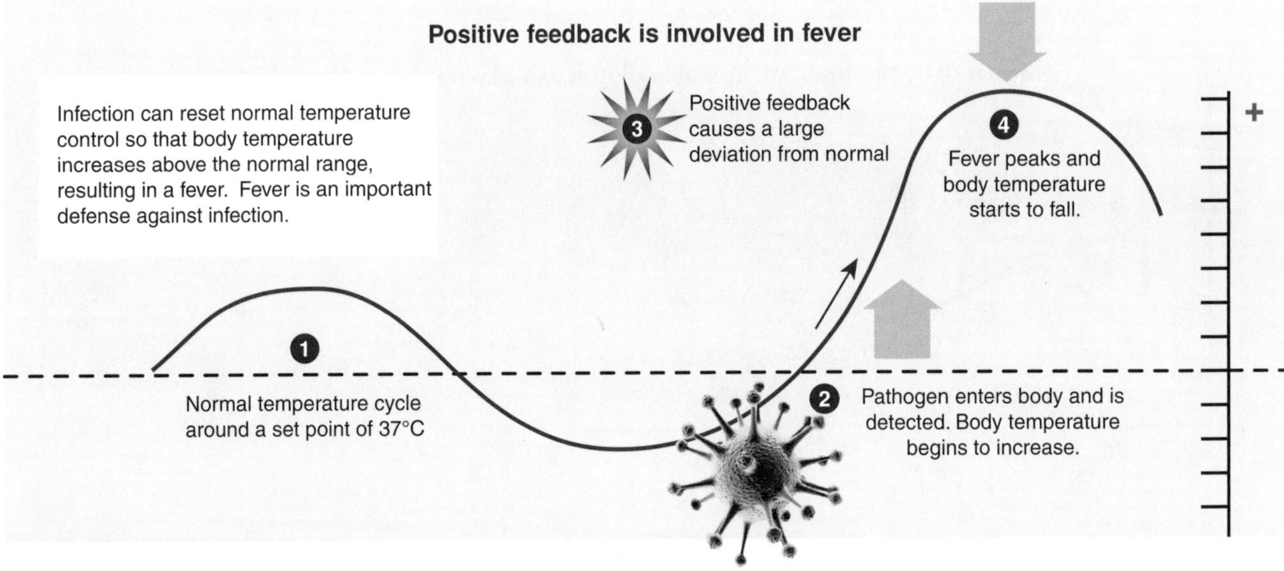
Positive feedback is involved in fever
Infection can reset normal temperature control so that body temperature increases above the normal range, resulting in a fever. Fever is an important defense against infection.
3 Positive feedback causes a large deviation from normal
4 Fever peaks and body temperature starts to fall.
+
1 Normal temperature cycle around a set point of 37°C
2 Pathogen enters body and is detected. Body temperature begins to increase.

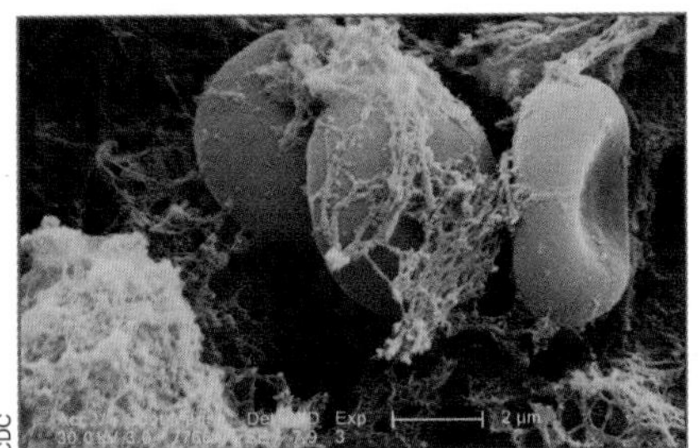
CDC

Positive feedback is involved in blood clotting. A wound releases chemicals to activate platelets in the blood. Activated platelets release chemicals to activate more platelets, so a blood clot is formed.

Ragesoss

Ethylene is a gaseous plant hormone involved in fruit ripening. It accelerates ripening in nearby fruits, so these also ripen, releasing more ethylene. Too much ethylene causes over-ripening.

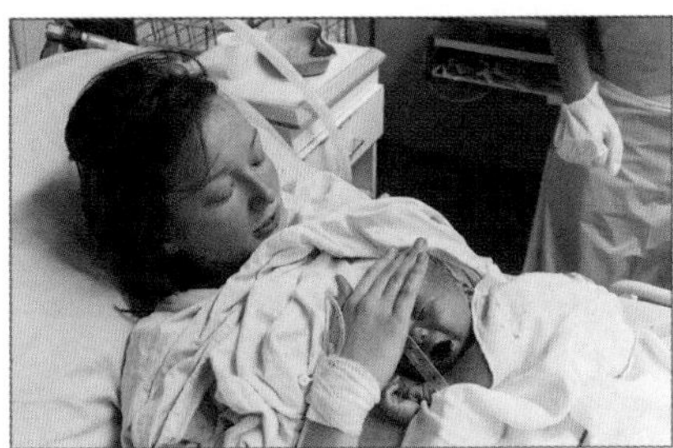

Childbirth involves positive feedback. Pressure of the baby's head causes release of a hormone that increases contractions even more. The feedback loop ends when the baby is born.

5. (a) Why is positive feedback much less common than negative feedback in body systems? ____________________

(b) How can positive feedback lead to a runaway response in the body? ____________________

(c) Why can positive feedback be dangerous if it continues on for too long? ____________________

(d) How is a positive feedback loop normally stopped? ____________________

(e) Predict what could happen if a person's temperature continued increasing during a fever (did not peak and fall): ____________________

ISBN: 978-1-98-856656-6

70 Cell Division

Key Question: What roles do the two types of cell division, mitosis and meiosis, play in the life cycles of organisms?

New cells are formed when existing cells divide. In eukaryotes, cell division begins with the replication of a cell's DNA followed by division of the nucleus. There are two forms of cell division. **Mitosis** produces two identical daughter cells from each parent cell. Mitosis is responsible for growth and repair processes in multicellular organisms, and asexual reproduction in some eukaryotes, e.g. yeasts. **Meiosis** is a special type of cell division concerned with producing haploid cells for sexual reproduction. It occurs in the sex organs of plants and animals. Meiosis is covered in the next unit.

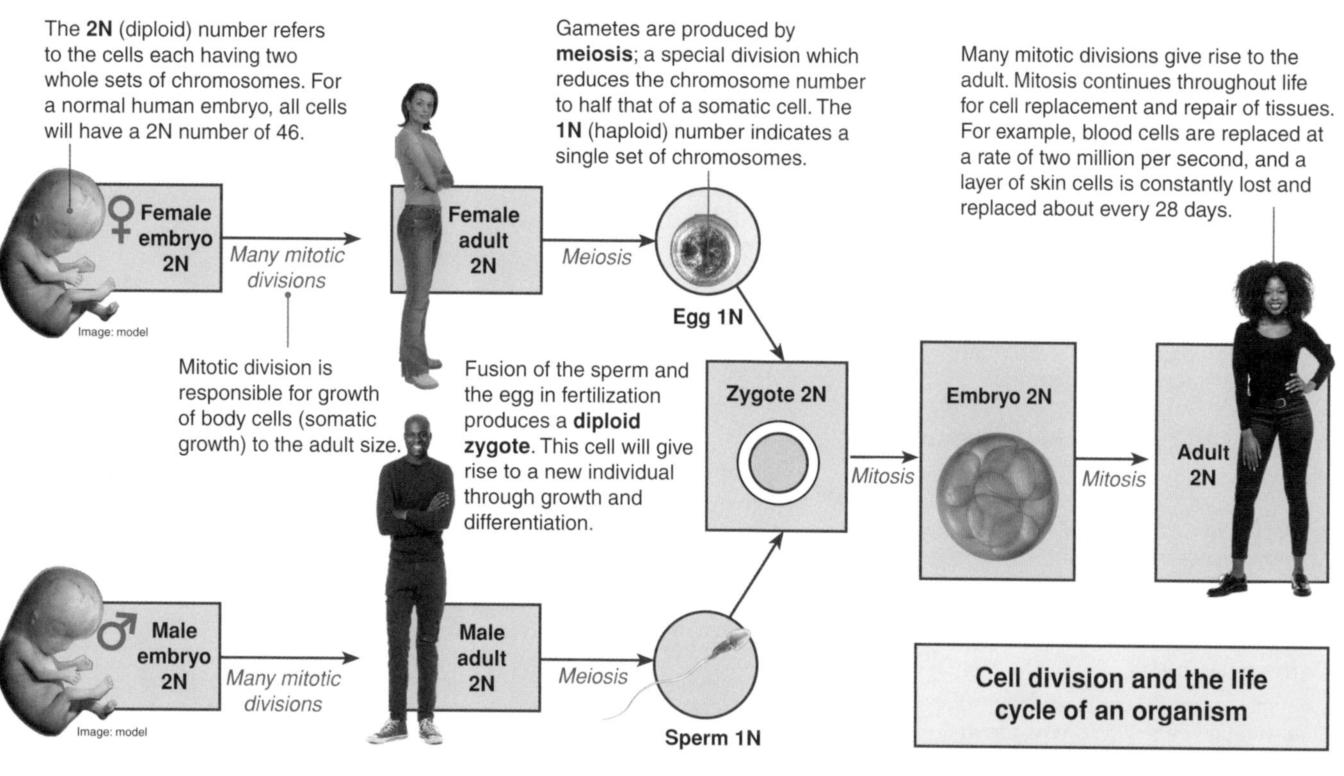

The **2N** (diploid) number refers to the cells each having two whole sets of chromosomes. For a normal human embryo, all cells will have a 2N number of 46.
Gametes are produced by **meiosis**; a special division which reduces the chromosome number to half that of a somatic cell. The **1N** (haploid) number indicates a single set of chromosomes.
Many mitotic divisions give rise to the adult. Mitosis continues throughout life for cell replacement and repair of tissues. For example, blood cells are replaced at a rate of two million per second, and a layer of skin cells is constantly lost and replaced about every 28 days.
♀ Female embryo 2N
Many mitotic divisions
Female adult 2N
Meiosis
Egg 1N
Image: model
Mitotic division is responsible for growth of body cells (somatic growth) to the adult size.
Fusion of the sperm and the egg in fertilization produces a **diploid zygote**. This cell will give rise to a new individual through growth and differentiation.
Zygote 2N
Mitosis
Embryo 2N
Mitosis
Adult 2N
♂ Male embryo 2N
Many mitotic divisions
Male adult 2N
Meiosis
Sperm 1N
Image: model
Cell division and the life cycle of an organism

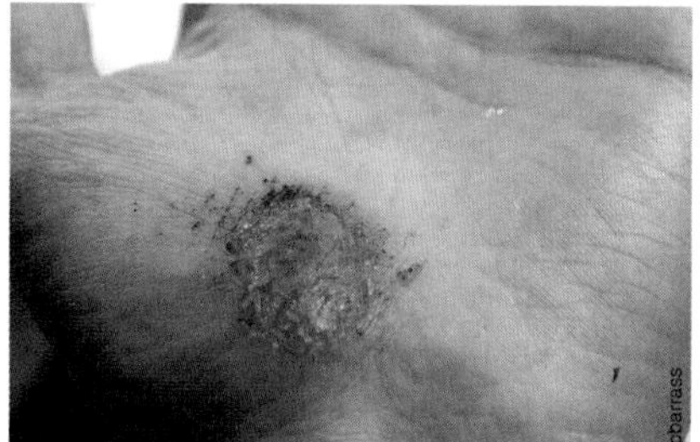

Mitosis for repair: Mitosis is vital in the repair and replacement of damaged cells. When you break a bone, or graze your skin, identical new cells are generated to repair the damage. Some organisms, such as sea stars, can generate new limbs if they are broken off.

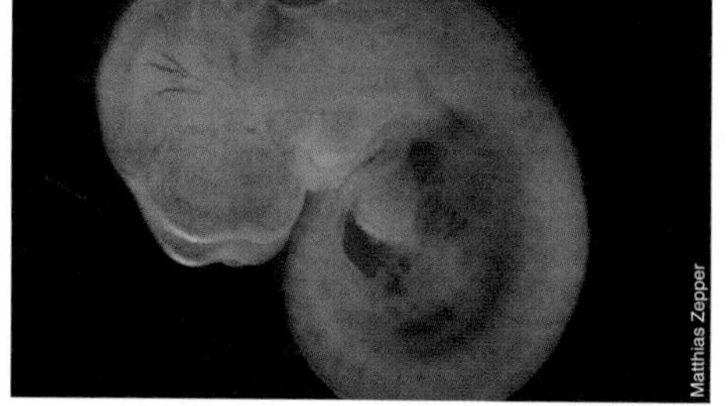

Mitosis for growth: Multicellular organisms develop from a single fertilized cell (zygote). Organisms, such as this 12 day old mouse embryo, grow by increasing their cell number. Cell growth is highly regulated and once the mouse reaches its adult size, growth stops.

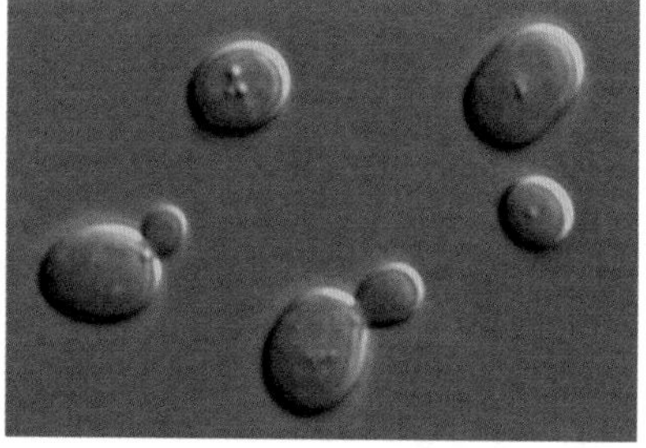

Mitosis for reproduction: Some eukaryotes, such as these yeast cells, reproduce asexually by mitotic division at a specific site. The daughter cell buds off from the parent cell, eventually separating from it. It is genetically identical to the parent.

1. (a) Where does mitosis take place in animals? ______

   (b) What are the roles of mitosis? ______

2. (a) Where does meiosis take place in animals? ______

   (b) What is the purpose of meiosis? ______

3. Why do gametes produced by meiosis have a haploid chromosome number? ______

ISBN: 978-1-98-856656-6

71 The Eukaryotic Cell Cycle

Key Question: What are the major phases of the cell cycle and what characterizes each phase?

The life cycle of a eukaryotic cell is called the cell cycle. It can be divided broadly into **interphase**, which is the time between cell divisions, and M phase, during which the cell divides. Aspects of the cell cycle can vary enormously between cells of the same organism. For example, intestinal cells divide around twice a day, while cells in the liver divide once a year, and those in muscle tissue do not divide at all. If any of these tissues is damaged, however, cell division increases rapidly until the damage is repaired. This variety of length in the cell cycle can be explained by the existence of regulatory mechanisms that are able to slow down or speed up the cell cycle in response to changing conditions.

Interphase

Cells spend most of their time in interphase. Interphase is divided into three stages:

- The first gap phase (G_1).
- The S-phase (S).
- The second gap phase (G_2).

During interphase the cell increases in size, carries out its normal activities, and replicates its DNA in preparation for cell division. Interphase is not a stage in mitosis.

Mitosis and cytokinesis (M-phase)

Mitosis and cytokinesis occur during M-phase. During mitosis, the cell nucleus (containing the replicated DNA) divides in two equal parts. Cytokinesis occurs at the end of M-phase. During cytokinesis the cell cytoplasm divides, and two new daughter cells are produced.

Exiting the cycle

Cells may exit the cycle in response to chemical cues and enter a resting phase, called G_0.

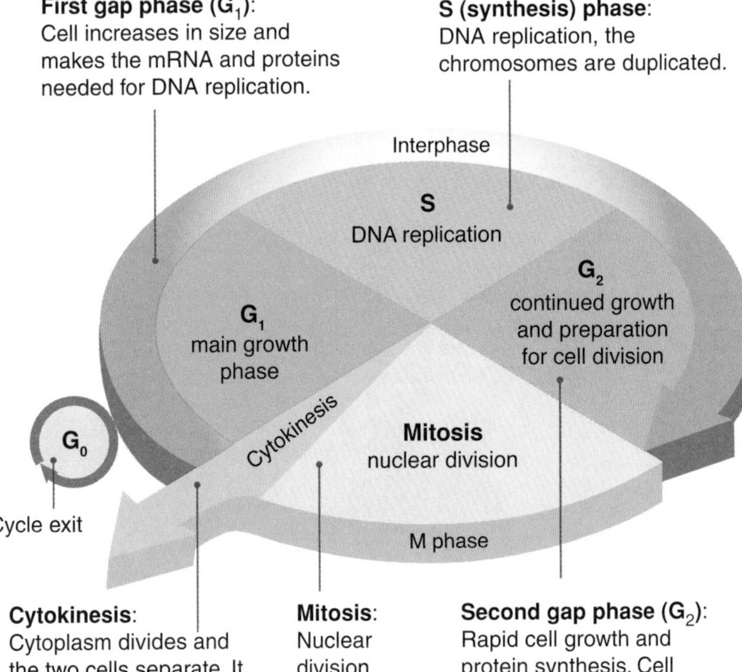
First gap phase (G_1):
Cell increases in size and makes the mRNA and proteins needed for DNA replication.
S (synthesis) phase:
DNA replication, the chromosomes are duplicated.
Interphase
S
DNA replication
G_2
continued growth and preparation for cell division
G_1
main growth phase
Cytokinesis
Mitosis
nuclear division
G_0
Cycle exit
M phase
Cytokinesis:
Cytoplasm divides and the two cells separate. It is distinct from mitosis.
Mitosis:
Nuclear division
Second gap phase (G_2):
Rapid cell growth and protein synthesis. Cell prepares for mitosis.

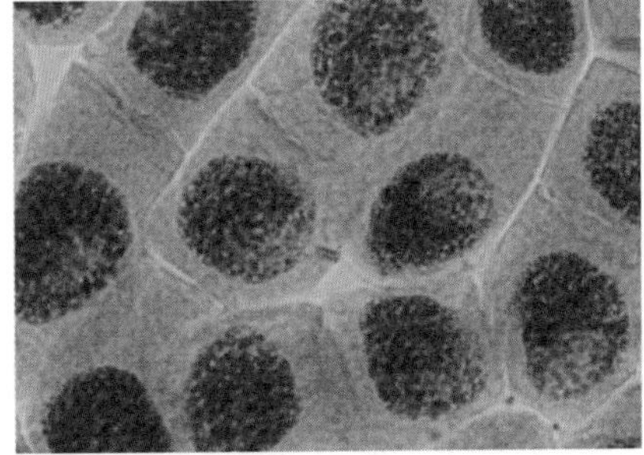

During the first stages of interphase, the cell grows and acquires the materials needed to undergo mitosis. It also prepares the nuclear material for separation by replicating it.

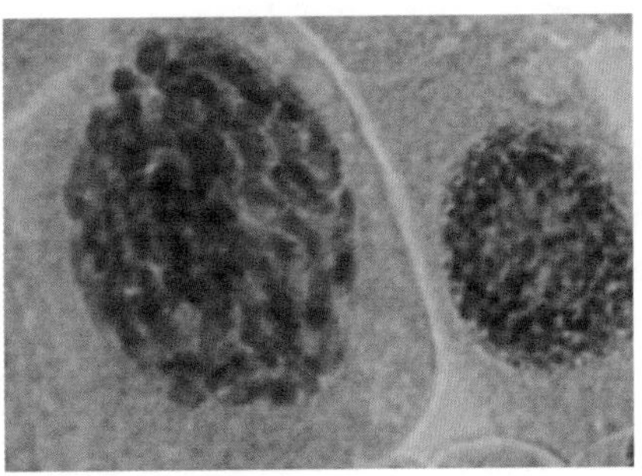

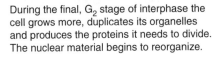

During the final, G_2 stage of interphase the cell grows more, duplicates its organelles and produces the proteins it needs to divide. The nuclear material begins to reorganize.

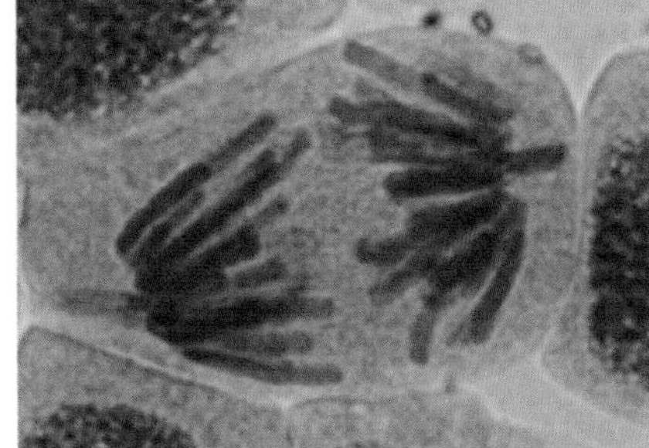

During mitosis the condensed chromosomes are separated. Mitosis is a highly organized process and the cell must pass checkpoints before it proceeds to the next phase.

1. Summarize the events occurring during the following phases of the cell cycle:

(a) Interphase: ______

(b) Mitosis: ______

(c) Cytokinesis: ______

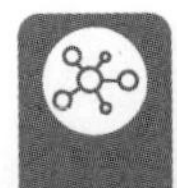

IST-1
1.A

73

76

111

ISBN: 978-1-98-856656-6

72 The Outcome of Mitosis

Key Question: What are the genetic and cellular outcomes of mitosis and where do we find dividing cells?

Mitosis is part of the cell cycle in which an existing parent cell divides into two new daughter cells. During interphase, which precedes mitosis, the cell's DNA is duplicated. In mitosis, the genetic material is apportioned equally to the two daughter cells. Each daughter cell is genetically identical to the parent cell and there is no change in chromosome number.

Mitosis is a stage in the cell cycle

- M-phase (**mitosis** and cytokinesis) is the part of the cell cycle in which the parent cell divides to produce two genetically identical daughter cells (right).
- Mitosis results in the separation of the nuclear material and division of the cell. It does not result in a change of chromosome number.
- Mitosis is one of the shortest stages of the cell cycle. When a cell is not undergoing mitosis, it is said to be in interphase. At any one time, only a small proportion of the cells in an organism will be undergoing mitosis. The majority of the cells will be in interphase.
- In animals, mitosis takes place in the somatic (body) cells. Somatic cells are any cell of the body except sperm and egg cells.
- In plants, mitosis takes place in the meristems. The meristems are regions of growth (where new cells are produced), such as the tips of roots and shoots.

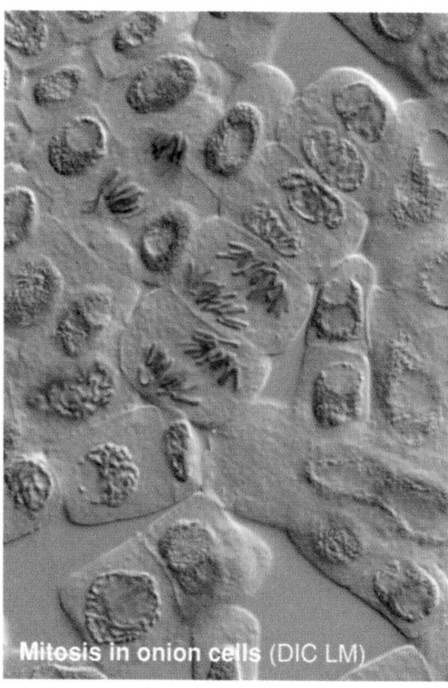

Mitosis in onion cells (DIC LM)

The **mitotic index** (number of cells in mitosis ÷ total number of cells) gives a measure of cell proliferation. The mitotic index is high in areas of rapid growth.

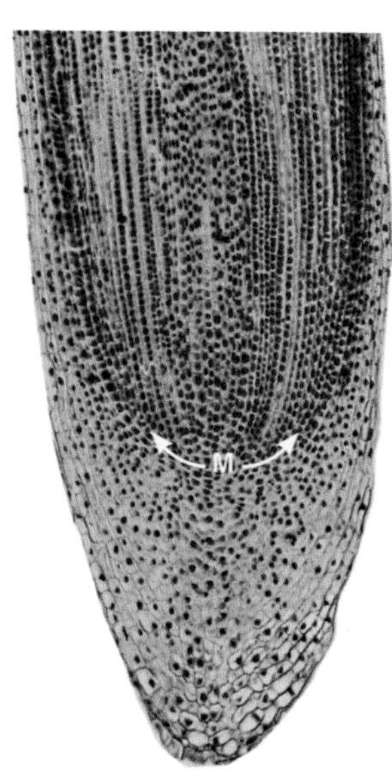

The growing tip (meristem, M) is the site of mitosis in this onion root. The root cap below the meristem protects the dividing cells.

Mitosis produces identical daughter cells

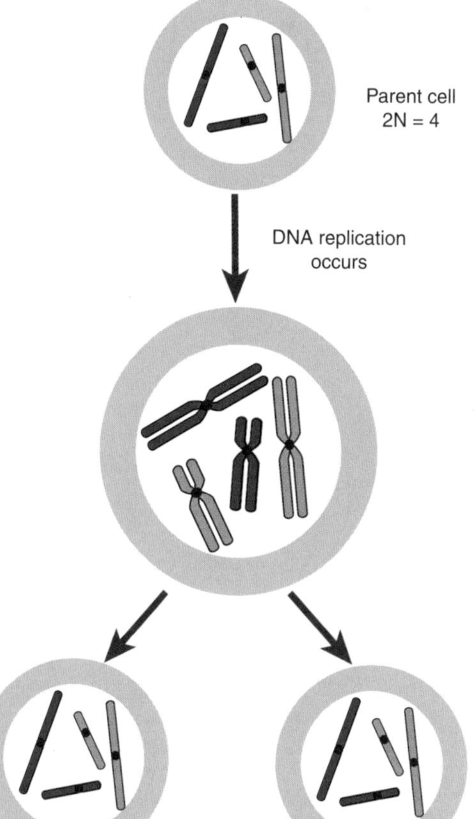

Hypothetical cell where the diploid chromosome number is 4 (2N=4). The cell divides forming two identical daughter cells. The chromosome number remains the same as the parent cell.

1. Contrast the location of mitosis in plants and animals: In animals, mitosis takes place in somatic cells, in plants it takes place in the meristems.

2. When a slide of plant meristematic tissue is examined, only a small proportion of the cells are dividing. Explain why: these cells continue to divide until a time when they lose the ability to.

3. A cell with 10 chromosomes undergoes mitosis.

   (a) How many daughter cells are created? 2

   (b) How many chromosomes does each daughter cell have? 10

   (c) Is the genetic material of the daughter cells the same as the parent cell? yes

4. What feature of mitosis is central to its role in repairing and replacing damaged tissues in an adult organism? It can create the same identical cells to replace the damaged ones.

ISBN: 978-1-98-856656-6

73 Mitosis and Cytokinesis

Key Question: What are the key features of mitosis and cytokinesis and how is mitotic activity quantified?

Mitosis refers to the division of the nuclear material and it is followed immediately by division of the cell. Although mitosis is part of a continuous cell cycle, it is divided into stages to help distinguish the processes occurring during its progression. Mitosis is one of the shortest stages of the cell cycle. Cytokinesis (the division of the newly formed cells) is part of M-phase but it is distinct from nuclear division. During cytokinesis the cell divides into two.

The cell cycle and stages of mitosis in an animal cell

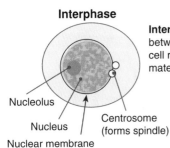

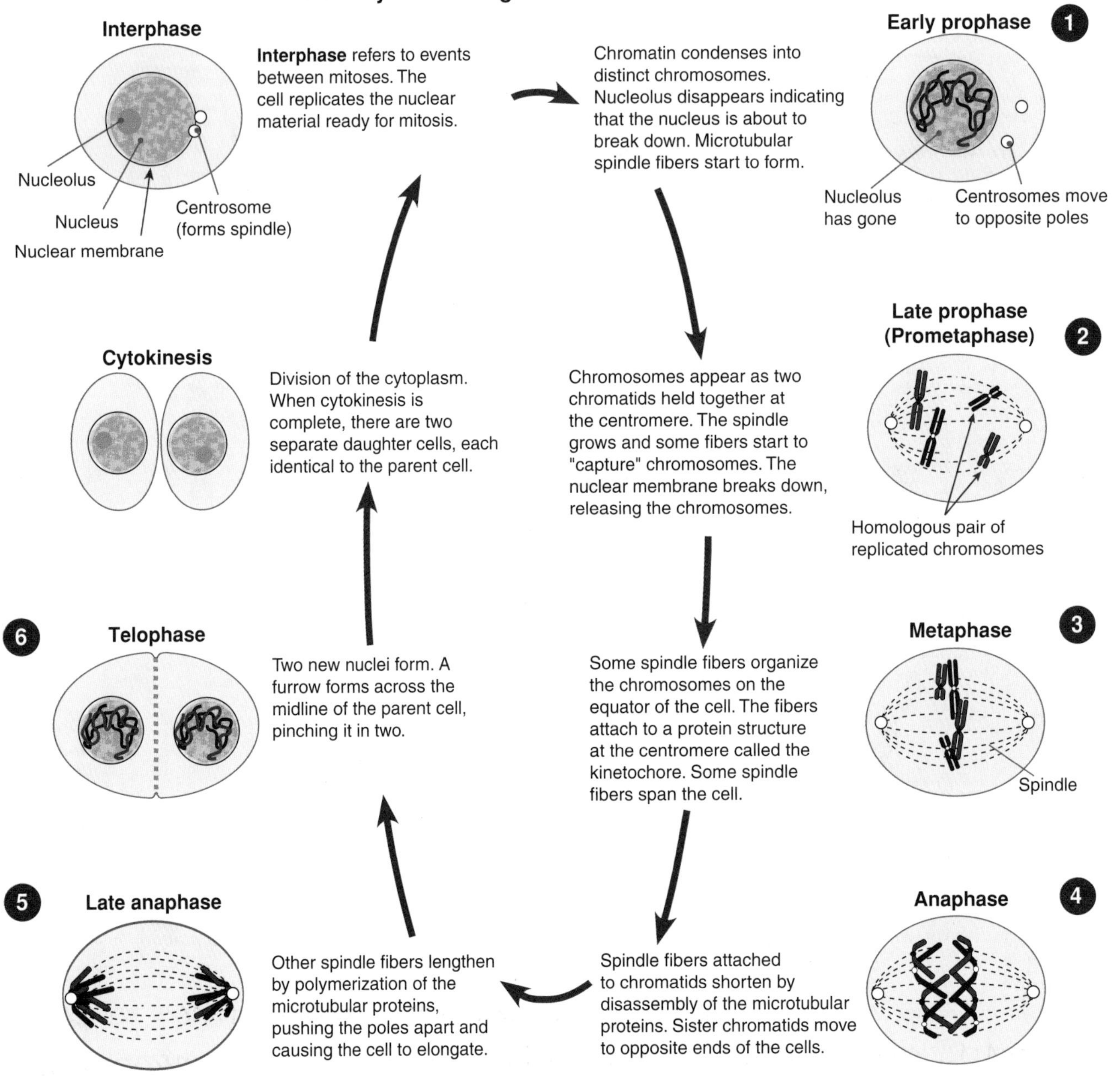

Interphase

Nucleolus

Nucleus

Nuclear membrane

Centrosome (forms spindle)

Interphase refers to events between mitoses. The cell replicates the nuclear material ready for mitosis.

Early prophase 1

Chromatin condenses into distinct chromosomes. Nucleolus disappears indicating that the nucleus is about to break down. Microtubular spindle fibers start to form.

Nucleolus has gone

Centrosomes move to opposite poles

Late prophase (Prometaphase) 2

Chromosomes appear as two chromatids held together at the centromere. The spindle grows and some fibers start to "capture" chromosomes. The nuclear membrane breaks down, releasing the chromosomes.

Homologous pair of replicated chromosomes

Metaphase 3

Some spindle fibers organize the chromosomes on the equator of the cell. The fibers attach to a protein structure at the centromere called the kinetochore. Some spindle fibers span the cell.

Spindle

Anaphase 4

Spindle fibers attached to chromatids shorten by disassembly of the microtubular proteins. Sister chromatids move to opposite ends of the cells.

5 **Late anaphase**

Other spindle fibers lengthen by polymerization of the microtubular proteins, pushing the poles apart and causing the cell to elongate.

6 **Telophase**

Two new nuclei form. A furrow forms across the midline of the parent cell, pinching it in two.

Cytokinesis

Division of the cytoplasm. When cytokinesis is complete, there are two separate daughter cells, each identical to the parent cell.

1. What must occur before mitosis takes place? interphase

2. (a) What is the purpose of the spindle fibers? to pull apart chromatids to opposite sides of the cell, allowing the cell to split.

(b) Where do the spindle fibers originate? from the centromeres.

3. Suggest why mitosis and cytokinesis are energetically demanding processes: The cells have to duplicate everything and split to make two identical daughter cells, the process must be very precise.

ISBN: 978-1-98-856656-6

Cytokinesis (division of the cytoplasm)

Animal cells: Cytokinesis (below left) begins shortly after the sister chromatids have separated in anaphase of mitosis. A ring of microtubules assembles in the middle of the cell, next to the plasma membrane, constricting it to form a cleavage furrow. In an energy-using process, the cleavage furrow moves inwards, forming a region where the two cells will separate.

Plant cells (below right): Cytokinesis involves construction of a cell plate (a precursor of the new cell wall) in the middle of the cell. The cell wall materials are delivered by vesicles derived from the Golgi. The vesicles join together to become the plasma membranes of the new cell surfaces.

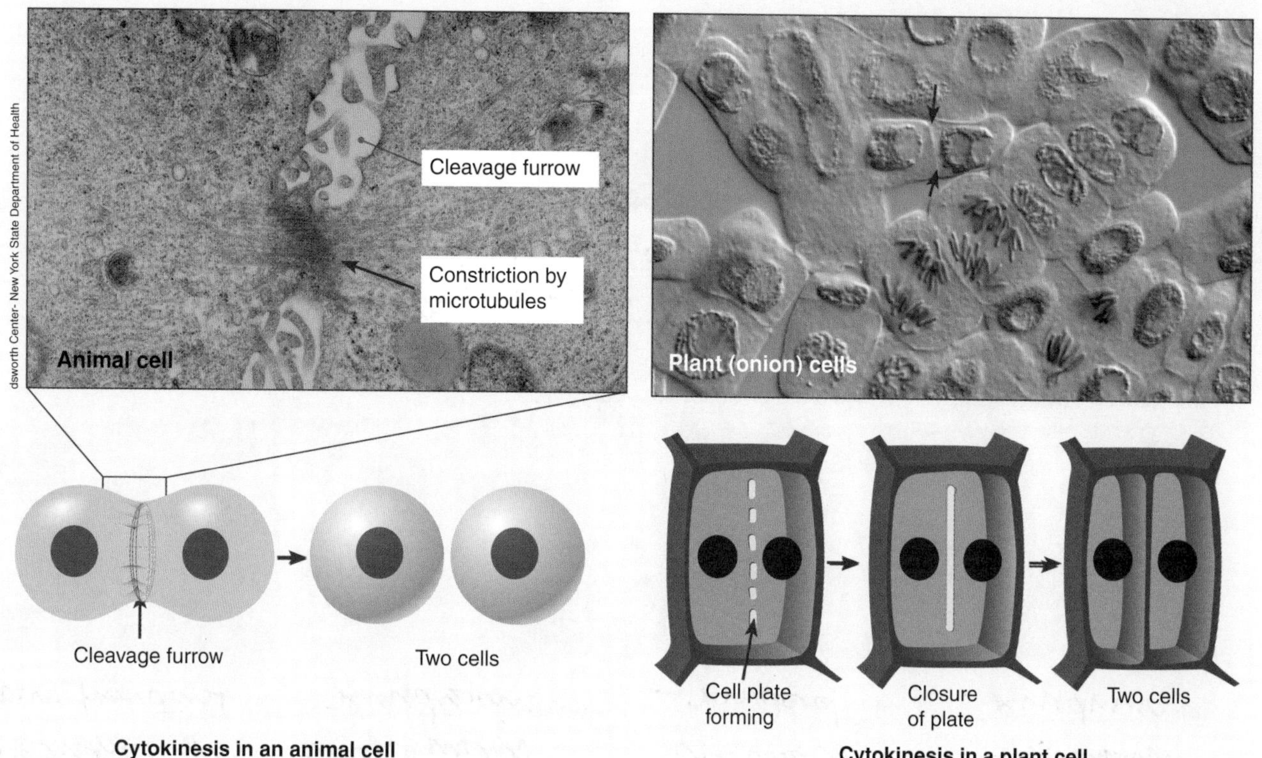

Cytokinesis in an animal cell

Cytokinesis in a plant cell

4. Summarize what happens in each of the following phases of mitosis:

(a) Prophase: chromatin condenses, spindle fibers start to form, nucleolus starts to disappear, chromosomes start to form

(b) Metaphase: spindle fibers organize the chromosomes on the equator of the cell. Fibers attach to centromeres.

(c) Anaphase: spindle fibers attatched to chromatids, separating them, and lengthening the cell (elongation)

(d) Telophase: two nuclei form. A furrow forms across the midline of the parent cell, pinching it in two.

5. (a) What is the purpose of cytokinesis? Cytokenesis completes mitosis by splitting the prior parent cell to two identical daughter cells.

(b) Describe the differences between cytokinesis in an animal cell and a plant cell: In an animal cell, a ring of microtubules assemble in the middle of the cell, and forms a cleavage furrow. The cleavage furrow separates the cell. In plant cells, a cell plate is constructed in the middle of the cell. The cell wall materials are delivered by vesicles from the Golgi. They join together to become the plasma membranes of the new cell surfaces.

ISBN: 978-1-98-856656-6

The mitotic index

The mitotic index measures the ratio of cells in mitosis to the number of cells counted. It is a measure of cell proliferation and can be used to diagnose cancer (because cancerous cells divide very quickly). In areas of high cell growth the mitotic index is high such as in plant apical meristems or the growing tips of plant roots. The mitotic index can be calculated using the formula below:

$$\text{Mitotic index} = \frac{\text{Number of cells in mitosis}}{\text{Total number of cells}}$$

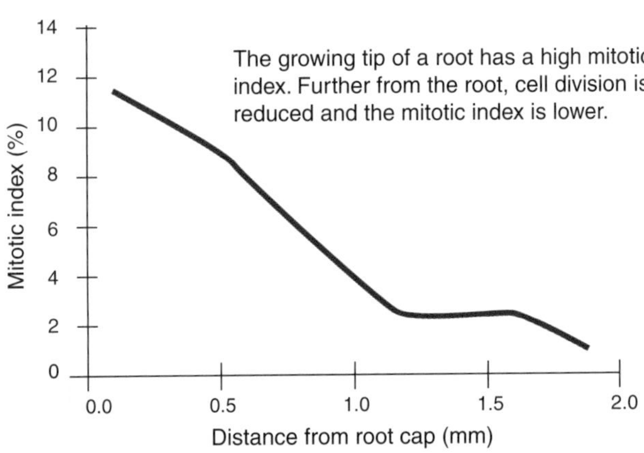

6. Describe what happens to the proportion of cells in mitosis with distance from the root cap (tip):

Further from the root (due to the tip w/ high mitotic index) cell division is reduced + the mitotic index is lower.

7. Use the information at the start of this activity to identify the stage of mitosis shown in each of the photographs below. Underneath your identification, briefly state the reason for your choice.

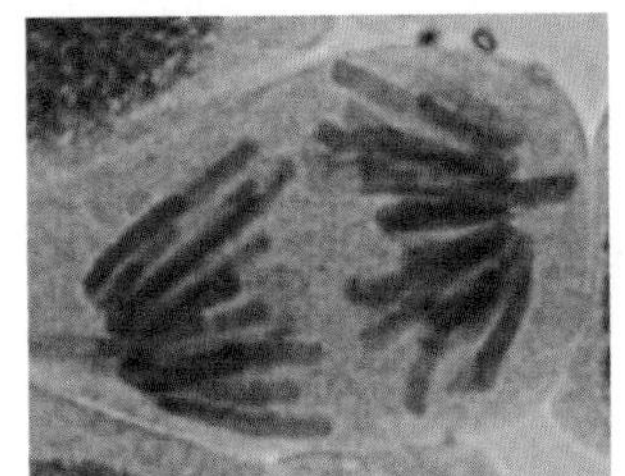
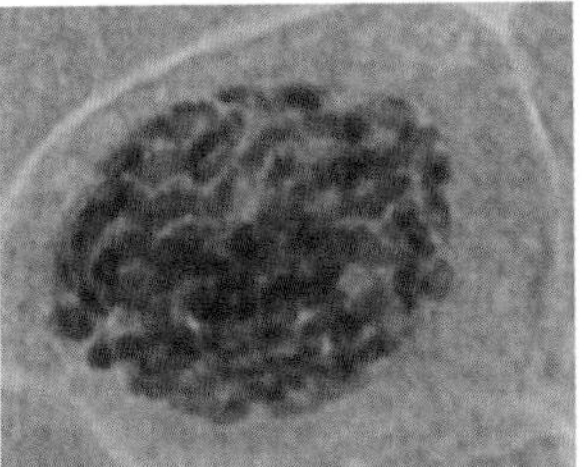
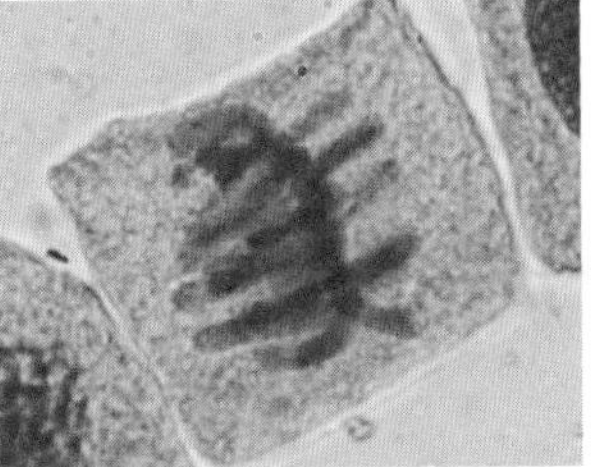
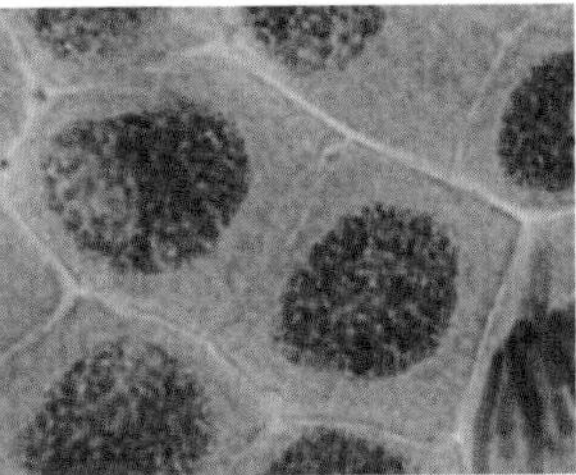

(a) anaphase - chromatids separating

(b) prophase - chromatin condensing

(c) metaphase chromatids in middle

(d) telophase/cytokenesis cells separating

8. (a) The light micrograph (right) shows a section of cells in an onion root tip. These cells have a cell cycle of approximately 24 hours. The cells can be seen to be in various stages of the cell cycle. By counting the number of cells in the various stages it is possible to calculate how long the cell spends in each stage of the cycle. Count and record the number of cells in the image that are in mitosis and those that are in interphase. Cells in cytokinesis can be recorded as in interphase. Estimate the amount of time a cell spends in each phase.

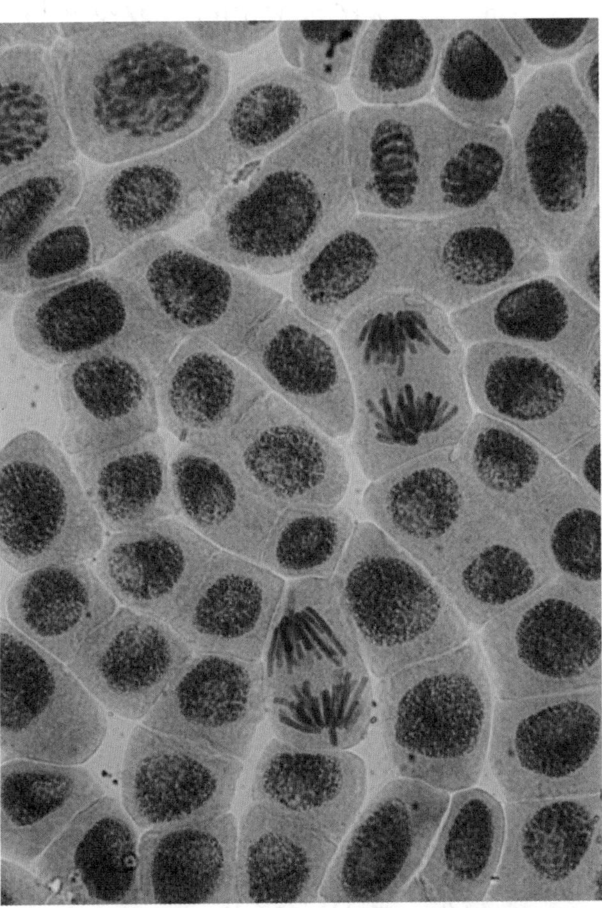

Stage	No. of cells	% of total cells	Estimated time in stage
Interphase	48	90.6	21 hrs 44 min
Mitosis	5	9.4	2 hrs 16 min
Total	53	100	24 hrs

$\frac{9.4}{100} = \frac{x}{24}$

(b) Use your counts from 8(a) to calculate the mitotic index for this section of cells.

0.094

9. What would you expect to happen to the mitotic index of a population of cells that loses the ability to divide as they mature?

declines

ISBN: 978-1-98-856656-6

74 Modeling Mitosis

***STUDENT SUPPORT FOR INVESTIGATION 7, Part 1:** Modeling mitosis*

Modeling clay or chenille stems and yarn can be used to model stages of mitosis in an animal cell. For simplicity, it is easiest to start with 4 chromosomes (2N = 4). Typical images are shown below. How could you improve on this in your own model?

1. Image 1 represents the stage just before mitosis begins. The red circular structures are the centrosomes.

   (a) Name the stage shown in the image: interphase

   (b) Why are there two copies of the centrosomes? to separate chromatids on each end

   (c) What has happened to the chromosomes in this image? condensing

Image 1

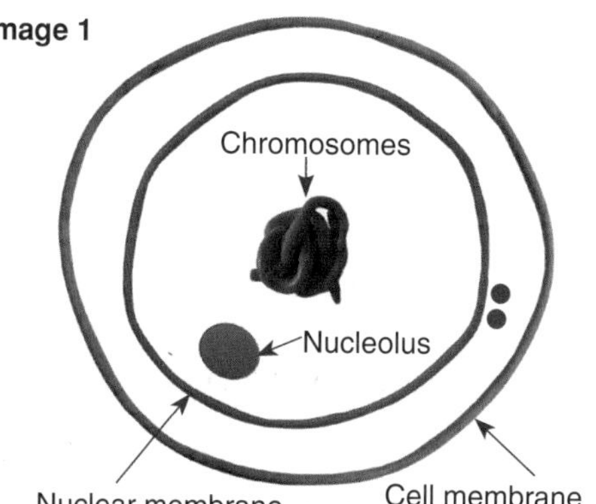

2. Study the image sequence 2-6 below. Identify the stage of mitosis shown in each and briefly describe what is occurring:

Image 2

Image 3

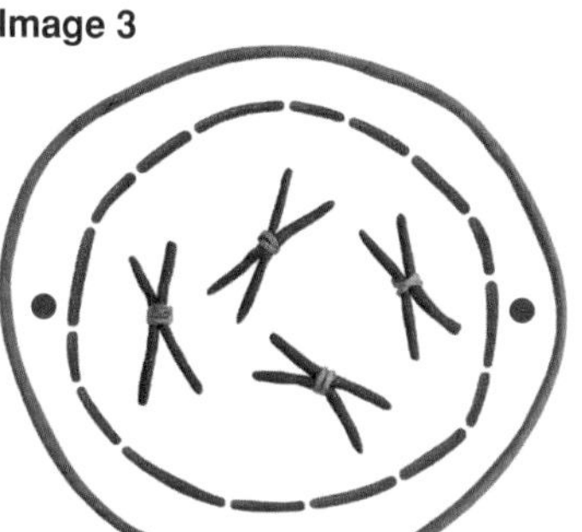

Image 4

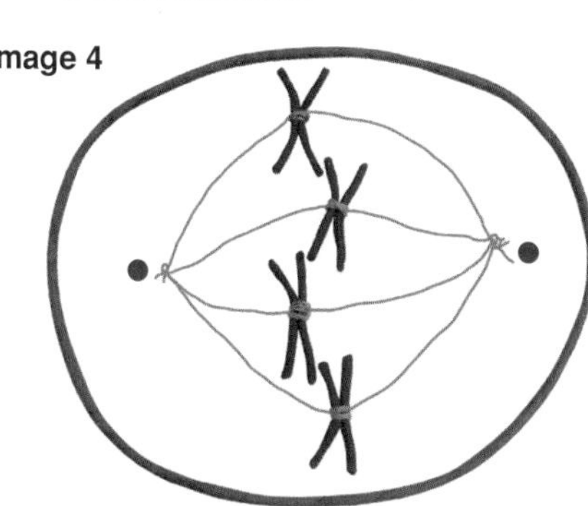

Image 5

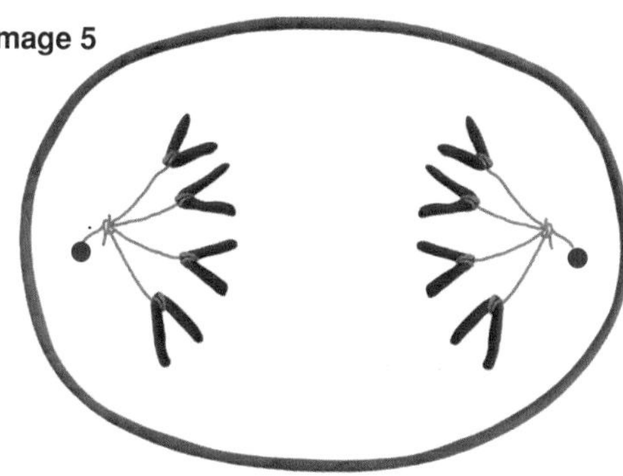

Image 6

   (a) Image 2: prophase - chromatid created, spindle fibers go on each side of cell

   (b) Image 3: prometaphase - nucleolus starts to disappear, centromeres of chromatin created.

   (c) Image 4: metaphase - chromatin lined up in the middle, spindle fibers attatch to centromeres

   (d) Image 5: anaphase - the chromatids are pulled apart by spindle fibers to opposite sides of the cell.

   (e) Image 6: telophase - cell pinches in the middle, nucleolus forms around 2 new sets of chromosomes.

3. Describe what happens next. What is the name of the stage? The cell splits during cytokinesis.

ISBN: 978-1-98-856656-6

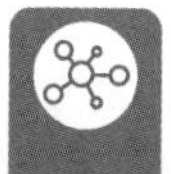

75 The Effect of Environment on Mitosis

STUDENT SUPPORT FOR INVESTIGATION 7, Part 2: *Effects of environment on mitosis*

Some environmental factors, such as presence of the carbohydrate-binding proteins **lectins**, have been shown to increase the rate of mitosis in blood cells. Students wanted to determine if PHA-M (a lectin) would increase the level of mitosis in the root tip cells of onion plants. They exposed the roots of some onion plants to a 50 mg/L solution of PHA-M and others to a control solution (water). After an exposure period of 2 days, they prepared and stained the samples so they could count the number of cells in mitosis and interphase.

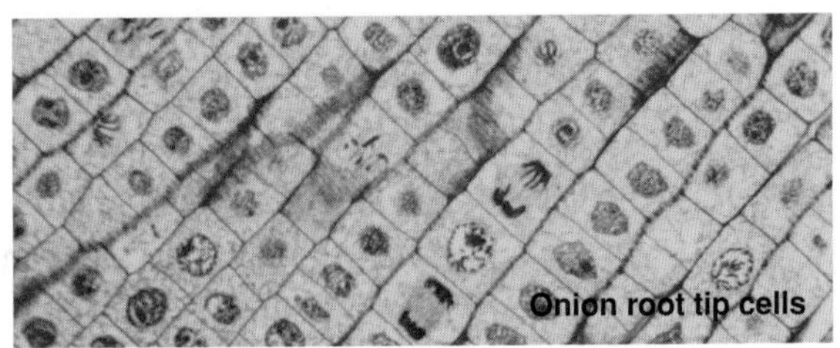
Onion root tip cells

1. Generate a null hypothesis and an alternative hypothesis for this experiment:

(a) Null hypothesis (H_0): PHA-M has no effect on the level of mitosis in the root tip cells of onion plants.

(b) Hypothesis (H_A): ~~[illegible]~~ Lectins cannot increase the rate of mitosis in blood cells.

Procedure

- The combined class data is given in Table 1. The percentage of cells in interphase or mitosis for the control and treated samples are presented in Table 2.
- A chi-squared test (χ^2) was used to determine if the null hypothesis should be accepted or rejected at P=0.05 (see Table 3). Expected values (E) were calculated by applying the control percentages in Table 2 (blue column) to the treated total (i.e. 0.81 x 1712 = 1386). At the end of the calculation, a chi-squared value ($\Sigma(O-E)^2 / E$) is generated.
- The χ^2 value is compared to a critical value of χ^2 for the appropriate degrees of freedom (number of groups – 1). For this test it is 1 (2–1=1). For this data set, **the critical value is 3.84** (at 5% probability and 1 degree of freedom). If χ^2 is < 3.84, the result in not significant and H_0 cannot be rejected. If χ^2 is ≥ 3.84, H_0 can be rejected in favor of H_A.

Table 1: Class data

	Number of cells		
	Interphase	**Mitosis**	**Total**
Control	1292	302	1598
Treated	1406	306	1712

1.48 16.85 5.68 47.37

Table 2: Percentage of cells in interphase or mitosis

	% of cells	
	Control	**Treated**
Interphase cells	81	82
Mitotic cells	19	18

1.20 0.36 = 0.65 1.69 1.2 2.89 .36 3.15

Table 3: Calculation of chi-squared value

	Observed (O)	Expected (E)	(O - E)	$(O - E)^2$	$(O - E)^2 / E$
Interphase cells	1406	1386	20	400	0.289
Mitosis cells	306	325	-19	361	1.11
				$\Sigma(O-E)^2 / E$	1.399

2. Calculate the chi-squared value by completing Table 3. χ^2 = 1.399

3. (a) Should the null hypothesis be accepted or rejected? ~~rejected~~ accepted

(b) Is the result you would have expected? Explain: the result was lower than the chi square value, ~~meaning~~ meaning the result wasn't significant so we have to accept the null hypothesis.

4. Suggest further investigations to verify the results presented here. Use more paper and attach it here if you wish: Factors could have interferred w/ the experiment – resulting in insignifacant results.

ISBN: 978-1-98-856656-6

76 Regulation of the Cell Cycle

Key Question: What is the role of regulatory checkpoints in the cell cycle and how are cyclins involved?

Cell cycle checkpoints provide a way for cells to make sure that necessary processes at one stage have been completed successfully before the cell transitions to the next stage. There are three checkpoints in the cell cycle. At each checkpoint, a set of conditions determines whether or not the cell will continue into the next phase. Cancer can result when the pathways regulating the checkpoints fail. Non-dividing cells enter a resting phase (G_0), where they may remain for a few days or up to several years. Under specific conditions, they may re-enter the cell cycle.

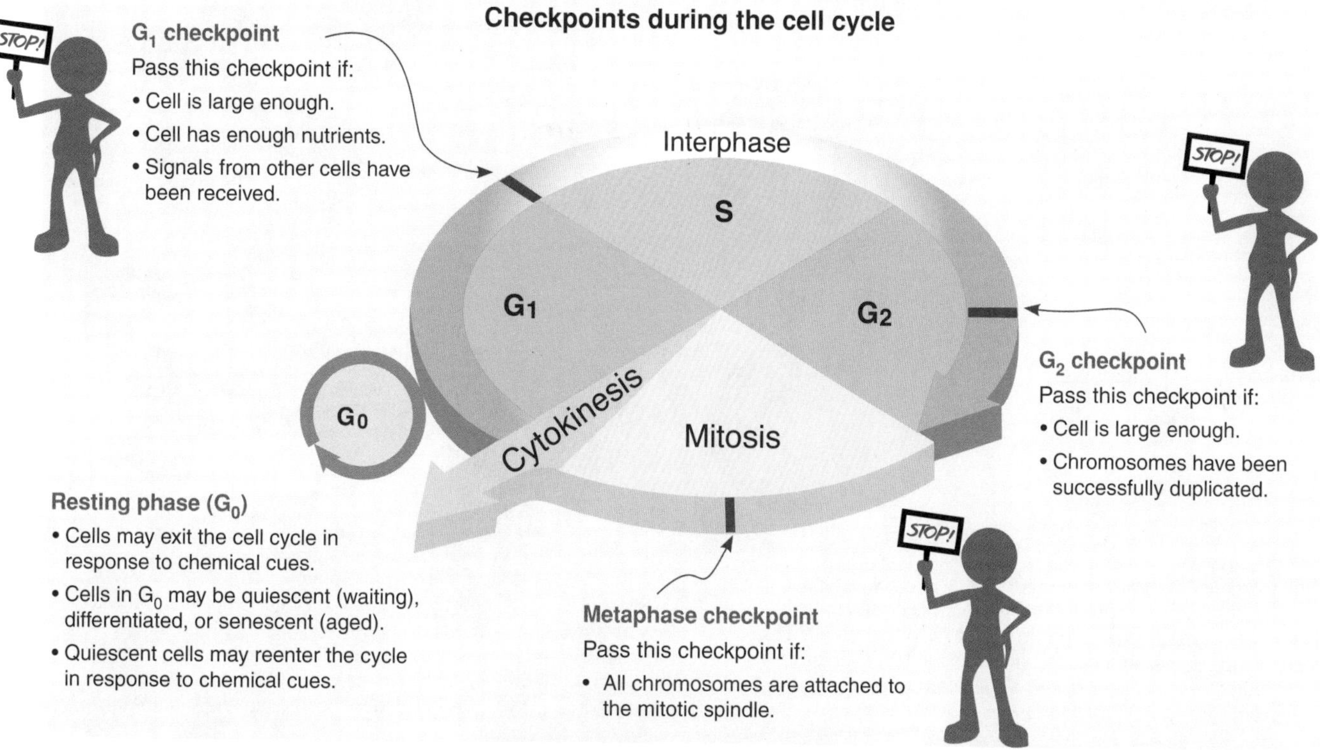
Checkpoints during the cell cycle
STOP!
G_1 checkpoint
Pass this checkpoint if:
• Cell is large enough.
• Cell has enough nutrients.
• Signals from other cells have been received.
Interphase
S
G1
G2
Go
Cytokinesis
Mitosis
STOP!
G_2 checkpoint
Pass this checkpoint if:
• Cell is large enough.
• Chromosomes have been successfully duplicated.
Resting phase (G_0)
• Cells may exit the cell cycle in response to chemical cues.
• Cells in G_0 may be quiescent (waiting), differentiated, or senescent (aged).
• Quiescent cells may reenter the cycle in response to chemical cues.
STOP!
Metaphase checkpoint
Pass this checkpoint if:
• All chromosomes are attached to the mitotic spindle.

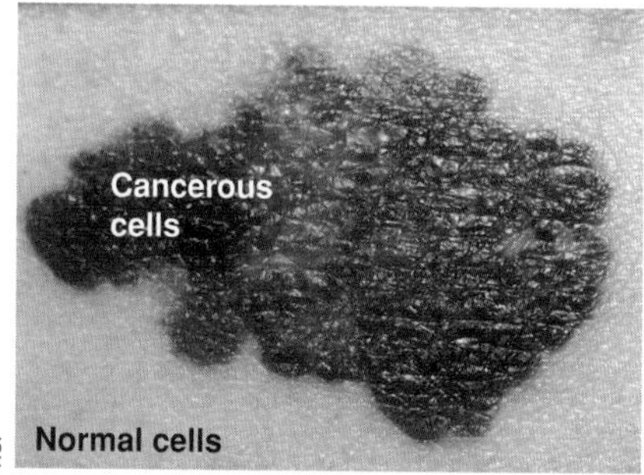
Cancerous cells
Normal cells
NCI

Skin cancer (melanoma). The cancer cells grow more rapidly than the normal skin cells because normal cell regulation checkpoints are ignored. This is why the cancerous cells sit higher than the normal cells and can rapidly spread (a process called metastasis).

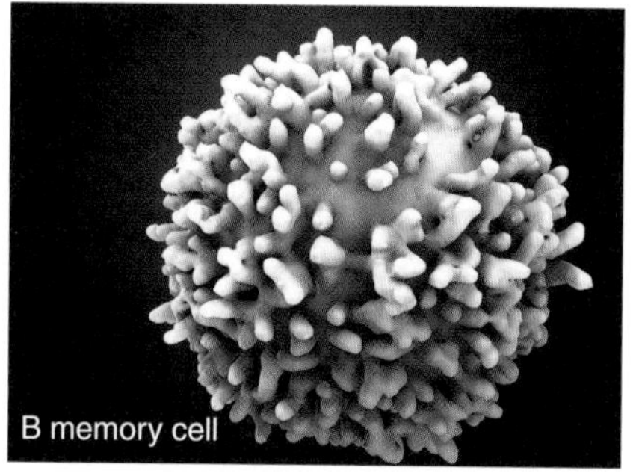
B memory cell

Most lymphocytes in human blood are in the resting G_0 phase and remain there unless they are stimulated by specific antigens to re-enter the cell cycle via G_1. G_0 phase cells are not completely dormant, continuing to carry out essential cell functions in reduced form.

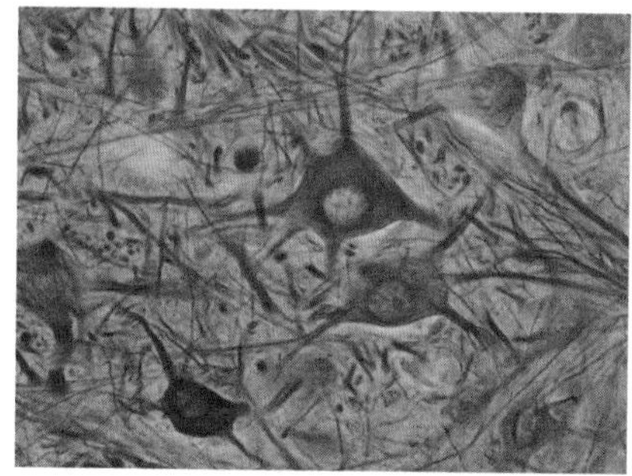
EII

Many fully differentiated (specialized) cells, e.g. neurons (above), exit the cell cycle permanently and stay in G_0. These cells continue their functional role in the body, but do not proliferate. Senescent cells have accumulated mutations, lose function, and die.

1. Explain the importance of cell cycle checkpoints: ____________________

2. In terms of the cell cycle and the resting phase (G_0), distinguish between the behavior of fully differentiated cells, such as neurons, and cells that are quiescent, such as B memory cells:

____

ISBN: 978-1-98-856656-6

The trigger for mitosis

Experiments with the eggs of the African clawed frog (*Xenopus laevis*) provided evidence that a substance found in an M-phase cell could induce a G_2 cell to enter M phase. The substance was called **M-phase promoting factor** (**MPF**).

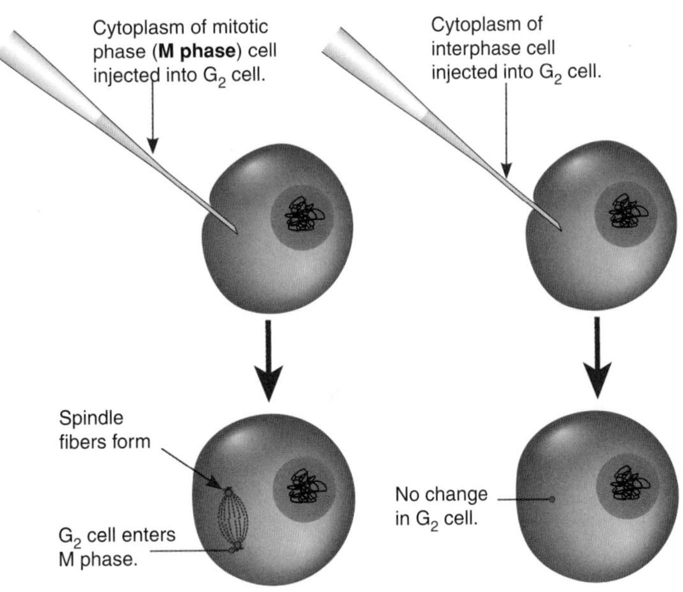
Cytoplasm of mitotic phase (**M phase**) cell injected into G_2 cell.
Cytoplasm of interphase cell injected into G_2 cell.
Spindle fibers form
G_2 cell enters M phase.
No change in G_2 cell.

Other studies have shown that MPF is made up of two subunits. The first subunit is a **protein kinase**, which activates proteins by transferring a phosphate group from ATP to the protein. The second subunit, called a **cyclin**, activates the first subunit. The first subunit is known as a **cyclin-dependent kinase** or **CdK**).CdK is constantly present in the cell, whereas cyclin is not.

Checkpoints and the role of cyclins

The cell cycle is driven by cyclin-CdK complexes. CdK without cyclin is inactive. Once cyclin is bound, it forms an active enzyme complex that can target the proteins involved in that phase of the cell cycle.

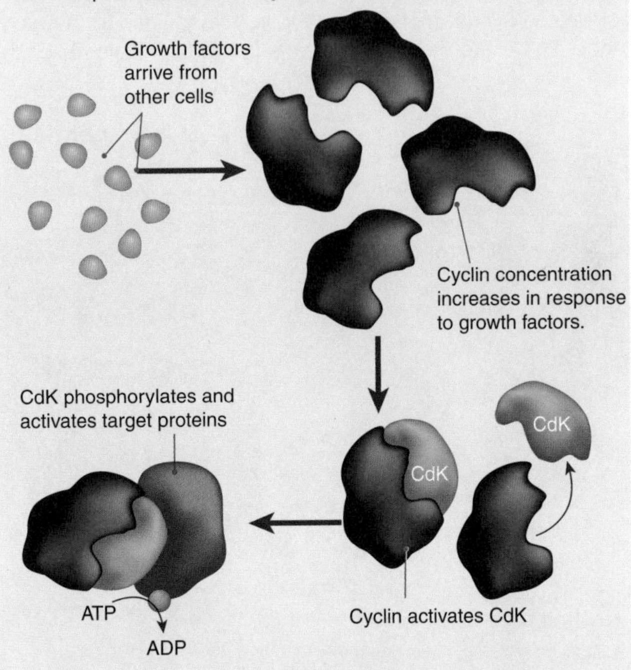
Growth factors arrive from other cells
Cyclin concentration increases in response to growth factors.
CdK phosphorylates and activates target proteins
CdK
CdK
ATP
ADP
Cyclin activates CdK

The cyclin-CdK complexes have periodic spikes of activity associated with orderly progression of the cell cycle. Cyclins are synthesized in response to growth factors from other cells and different cyclins are associated with each phase of the cell cycle. For example, M cyclins send CdKs to M phase protein targets, e.g. to cause break down of the nuclear membrane.

3. Explain why the cytoplasm from a M-phase cell could induce a G_2 cell to enter M phase: ______

4. (a) Which checkpoint ensures that replicated chromosomes will separate correctly? ______

   (b) Why is this important? ______

5. Suggest why signals (growth factors) from other cells play a part in regulating the cell cycle: ______

6. Cyclin D is synthesized during G_1 and is important in the G_1 checkpoint and the G_1/S transition. Predict a likely consequence of errors resulting in an over-production of cyclin D: ______

ISBN: 978-1-98-856656-6

77 Defective Gene Regulation in Cancer

Key Question: What happens when cell checkpoints fail? Cells that become damaged beyond repair normally undergo a controlled process of programmed cell death called apoptosis. However, cancerous cells evade this control and become immortal, continuing to divide without any checks on their proliferation even though they are faulty. Agents capable of causing cancer are called **carcinogens**. Most carcinogens are also mutagens (they damage DNA). Any one of a number of cancer-causing factors (including defective genes) may interact to disrupt the cell cycle and result in cancer.

Cancer: cells out of control

Cancerous transformation results from changes in the genes controlling normal cell growth and division. The resulting cells become immortal and no longer carry out their functional role.

Proto-oncogenes and tumor-suppressor genes

- Two types of gene are normally involved in controlling the cell cycle: **proto-oncogenes**, which start cell division and are essential for normal cell development, and **tumor-suppressor genes**, which switch off cell division.
- In their normal form, these types of gene work together, enabling the body to repair defective cells and replace dead ones. Mutations in these genes can disrupt this regulation.
- Proto-oncogenes, through mutation, can give rise to oncogenes, which cause uncontrolled cell division. Mutations to tumor-suppressor genes initiate most human cancers. The best studied tumor-suppressor gene is **p53**, which encodes a protein that halts the cell cycle so that DNA can be repaired before division. P53 acts at the G_1-S checkpoint and initiates DNA repair or apoptosis.

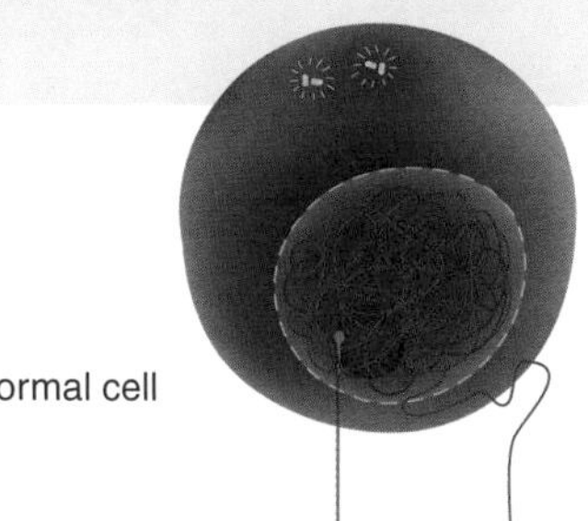

Normal cell

If the damage is too serious to repair, the p53 gene activates other genes to cause the cell to enter apoptosis (programmed cell death).

Tumor-suppressor genes
When damage occurs, the tumor suppressor gene p53 commands other genes to bring cell division to a halt. If repairs are made, then the p53 gene allows the cell cycle to continue.

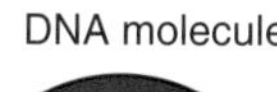

DNA molecule

Damaged DNA

Proto-oncogenes
Genes that turn on cell division. The mutated form or oncogene leads to unregulated cell division. A mutation to one or two controlling genes might cause a benign (non-malignant) tumor. A large number of mutations can cause loss of control, causing a cell to become cancerous (left).

Cancerous cell showing the membrane protrusions that are important in cancer cell adhesion and migration.

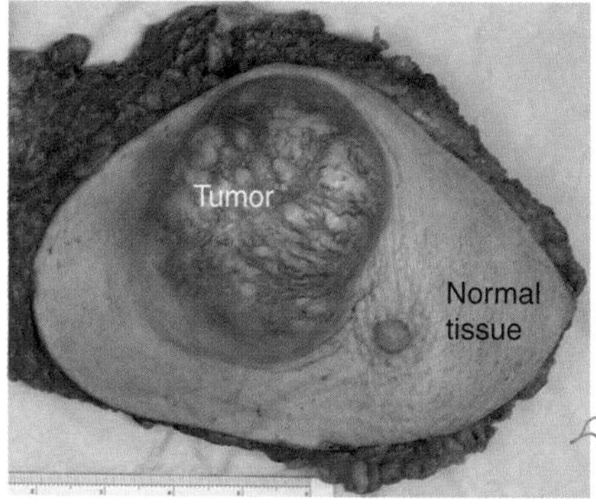

Emmanuelm cc3.0

The product of the gene BRCA1 is involved in repairing damaged DNA and BRCA1 deficiency is associated with abnormalities in cell cycle checkpoints. Mutations to this gene and another gene called BRCA2 are found in about 10% of all breast cancers and 15% of ovarian cancers.

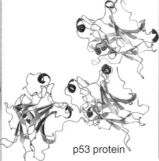

p53 protein

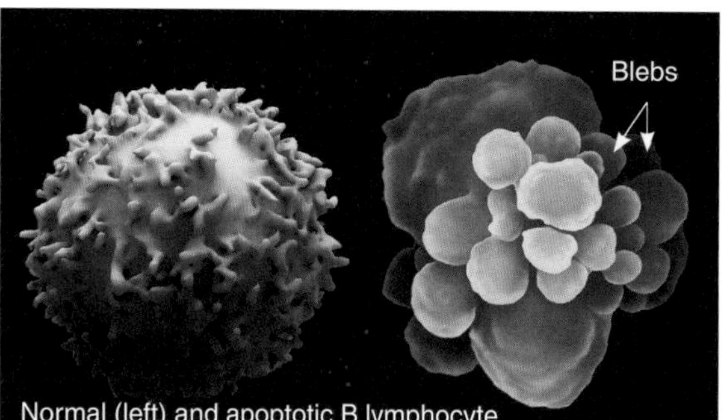

Normal (left) and apoptotic B lymphocyte

Felix Hicks

One of the most important proteins in regulating the cell cycle is the protein produced by the gene p53. The p53 tumor-suppressor protein helps regulate the cell cycle, apoptosis, and genomic stability. Mutations to the p53 gene are found in about 50% of cancers. Apoptosis is a controlled process that involves cell shrinkage, blebbing (above), and DNA fragmentation. Apoptosis removes damaged or abnormal cells before they can multiply. When apoptosis malfunctions it can cause disease, including cancer. When cell cycle checkpoints fail, the normal rate of apoptosis falls. This allows a damaged cell to divide without regulation.

ISBN: 978-1-98-856656-6

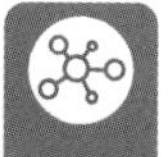

Reduction in rates of apoptosis can cause cancer

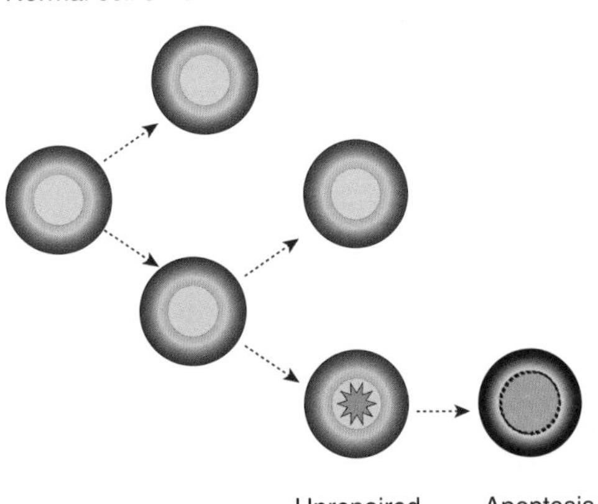

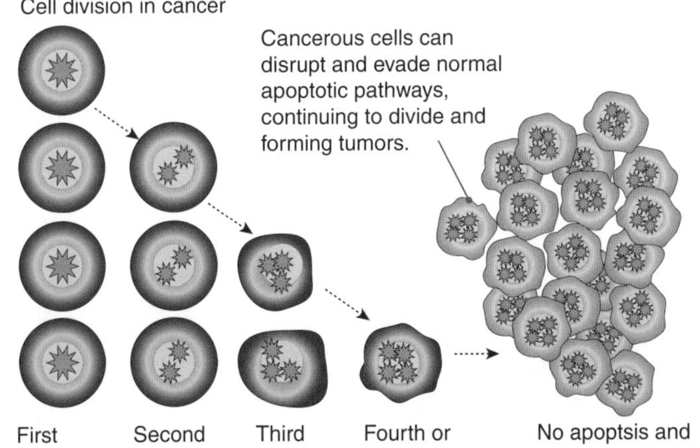

Tumor suppressor genes, e.g. the p53 gene, normally halt cell division of DNA damaged cells until the damage is repaired. If the damage cannot be repaired, apoptosis, a process of controlled cell death, is triggered.

Cancerous cells may inhibit the expression of the p53 gene. Around 50% of all human tumors contain p53 gene mutations. Factors known to disrupt normal cell cycle controls include defective genes, some viruses, and a number of chemical and environmental factors.

Viruses can inhibit apoptosis

Some viruses, such as human papillomavirus (HPV), invade human cells and inhibit apoptosis. HPV is a known carcinogen. Nearly all cases of cervical cancer can be attributed to HPV infection. HPV integrates its DNA into the host's DNA promoting genomic instability and producing a protein that binds to and inactivates the p53 protein. Inactivation of p53 promotes unregulated cell division, cell growth, and cell survival.

HeLa is an immortal cell line widely used in scientific research. The line is derived from the cervical cancer cells of Henrietta Lacks (HeLa cells) after being taken from her and cultured without her consent just before her death from cervical cancer. The cell line was the first to be cultured successfully and is robust and very aggressive.

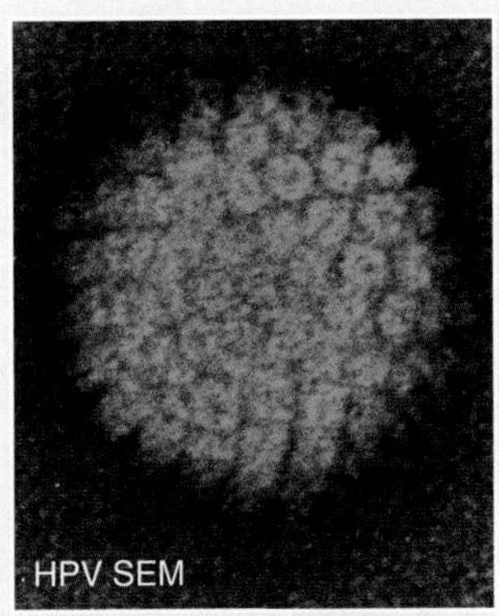

False color SEM of human papillomavirus, a causative agent in cervical cancer.

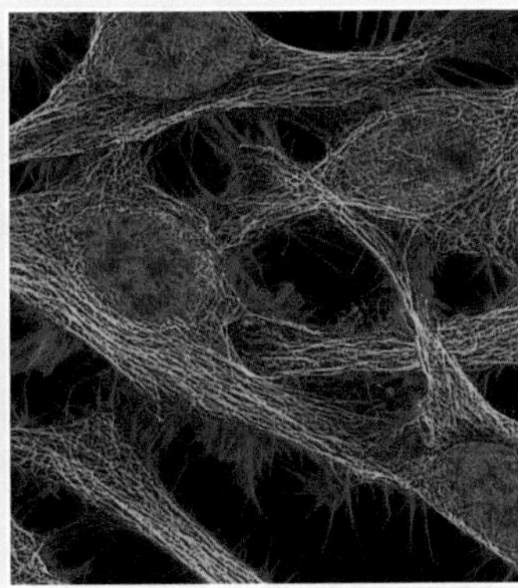

Stained HeLa cells showing nuclei (blue), actin filaments (red), and microtubules (cyan).

1. How do cancerous cells differ from normal cells? ______________________

2. Describe the involvement of regulatory genes in control of the cell cycle: ______________________

3. (a) Explain how the normal controls over the cell cycle can be lost: ______________________

(b) How can these failures result in cancer? ______________________

ISBN: 978-1-98-856656-6

78 Analyzing the Effects of Cell Cycle Errors

***STUDENT SUPPORT FOR INVESTIGATION 7, Part 3:** Loss of cell cycle control in cancer*

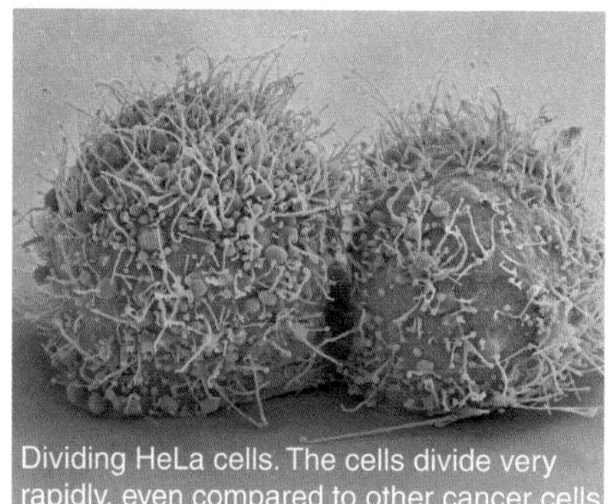

Dividing HeLa cells. The cells divide very rapidly, even compared to other cancer cells

As described opposite, the HeLa cells cultured from Henrietta Lacks' are remarkably robust in culture. While Lacks' original genome has the normal 46 chromosomes, most HeLa cells have 70-90 chromosomes, a consequence of integration of the HPV genome into the genome of cervical cells.

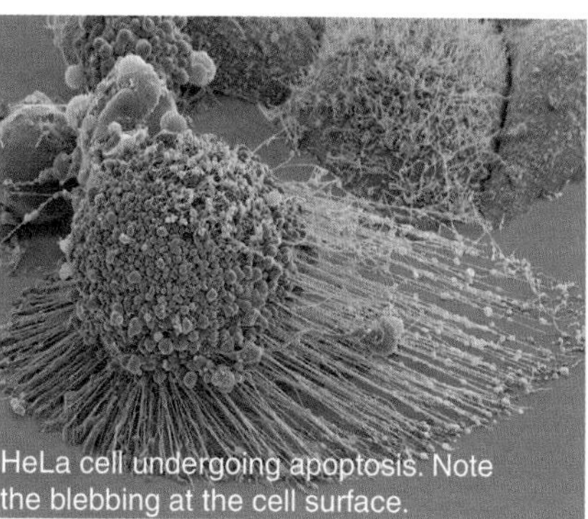

HeLa cell undergoing apoptosis. Note the blebbing at the cell surface.

The genomes of HeLa cells, like many tumors, carry many errors including with over 20 translocation mutations, some involving multiple chromosomal rearrangements. Looking for treatments that induce apoptosis in HeLa cells is one of the ways the HeLa cell lines are used in medical research.

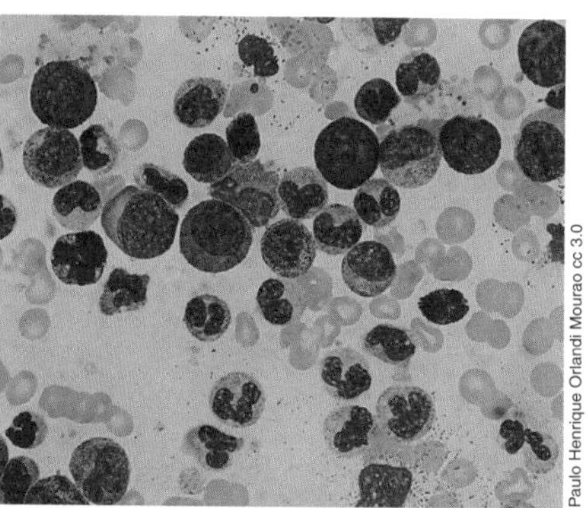

Blood smear from a patient with chronic myelogenous leukemia, a disease in which the granulocytic white blood cells (neutrophils, eosinophils, and basophils) proliferate out of control. The disease is associated with a recognizable karyotype with chromosomal abnormalities (karyogram B below).

Karyogram* A: Normal individual (male and female sex chromosomes are both shown)

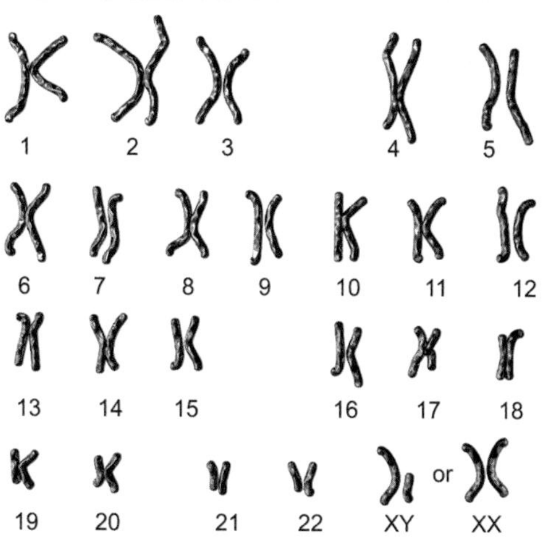

Karyogram B: Individual with chronic myelogenous leukemia (male and female sex chromosomes are both shown)

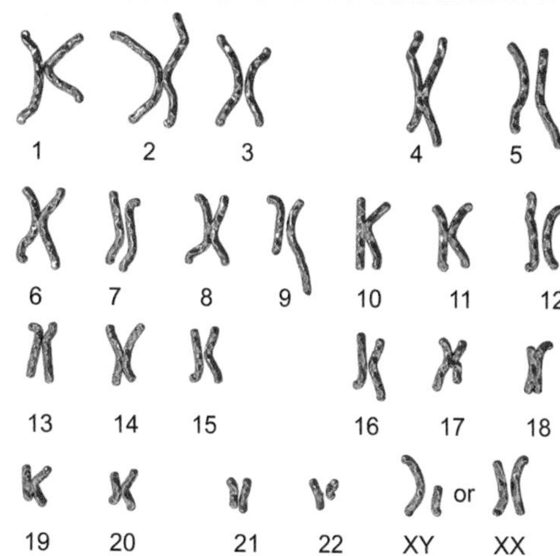

*A karyotype is the number and appearance of chromosomes in an organism. A karyogram is a standardized image of the karyotype.

1. Study the two karyograms above and answer the following questions:

   (a) How does karyogram B differ from karyogram A? ______________________

   (b) Suggest what has happened in the karyogram depicting chronic myelogenous leukemia: ______________________

   (c) The result of the changes in karyogram B is an abnormal gene (BCR_ABL1). It promotes cell division and blocks apoptosis. Predict the effect of this on the spread of cancerous cells:

   ____

2. (a) What feature would help you distinguish a HeLa cell karyotype from a normal karyotype? ______________________

   (b) How would this characteristic arise? ______________________

3. Find out more about the story of Henrietta Lacks' cell line. As a group, discuss the ethical issues surrounding the origin of the cell line and its continued use. Would this happen today? If you wish, present your group's arguments to the class.

ISBN: 978-1-98-856656-6

79 Personal Progress Check

Answer the multiple choice questions that follow by circling the correct answer. Don't forget to read the question carefully!

1. In local regulation, the signaling molecule affects only:
   (a) Target cells distant from the secreting cell
   (b) Target cells close to the secreting cell
   (c) Both (a) and (b)
   (d) None of the above

2. Cytokines can act as:
   (a) Local regulators
   (b) Endocrine regulators
   (c) Both (a) and (b)
   (d) None of the above

3. Synaptic transmission involves signaling molecules called?
   (a) G proteins
   (b) Neurotransmitters
   (c) Second messengers
   (d) Cylic AMP

4. When a ____________ reaches its ____________, the response of the cell depends on it having the correct specialized ____________?
   (a) Signaling molecule, receptor, G protein.
   (b) Signaling molecule, target cell, G protein.
   (c) Signaling molecule, target cell, receptor.
   (d) Signaling molecule, receptor, kinase.

5. Which of the following is true about a hydrophilic signaling molecule?
   (a) It is a steroid.
   (b) Its receptor is located in the cytoplasm of the target cell.
   (c) It might trigger a signal cascade that causes an effect in a cell.
   (d) It can enter the cell, so it directly affects some specific cell process.

6. What is the name of the hormone that alters glucose uptake, and where would its receptors be located?
   (a) Epinephrine; liver
   (b) Insulin; different cell types that use glucose for fuel
   (c) Insulin; beta cells of pancreas
   (d) Epinephrine, beta cells of pancreas

7. Hydrophobic signal molecules are ____________ and include ____________ like ____________.
   (a) Lipid soluble; steroid hormones; estrogen
   (b) Lipid insoluble; protein hormones; insulin
   (c) Lipid soluble; amino acid derivatives; epinephrine
   (d) Lipid insoluble; steroid hormones; estrogen

8. Signal transduction pathways may be regulated by:
   (a) Second messengers
   (b) Transcription factors
   (c) Protein methylation
   (d) All of the above

9. Which of the following involve(s) cell to cell communication?
   (a) Activation of helper T cells by antigen presenting cells
   (b) Transfer of signal molecules via plasmodesmata
   (c) Both (a) and (b)
   (d) None of the above

10. Signal transduction may involve:
    (a) Phosphorylation cascades
    (b) Activation of transcription factors
    (c) Second messengers
    (d) All of the above

11. Cyclic AMP is a common ____________ in cell signaling pathways:
    (a) Hormone
    (b) Cytokine
    (c) Second messenger
    (d) Kinase

12. Quorum sensing is a type of cell to cell communication common in:
    (a) Invertebrates
    (b) Bacteria
    (c) Plants
    (d) Mammals

13. Errors in signaling pathways are implicated in:
    (a) Cancers
    (b) Psoriasis
    (c) Type 2 diabetes
    (d) All of the above

14. Negative feedback regulation is involved in:
    (a) Thermoregulation
    (b) Physiological regulation requiring maintenance of steady state
    (c) Blood glucose regulation
    (d) All of the above

15. Positive feedback is involved in:
    (a) Fruit ripening
    (b) Childbirth
    (c) Blood clotting
    (d) All of the above

ISBN: 978-1-98-856656-6

Question 16 refers to the plot below, which shows fluctuations in serum insulin and blood glucose after sucrose-rich or starch-rich meals.

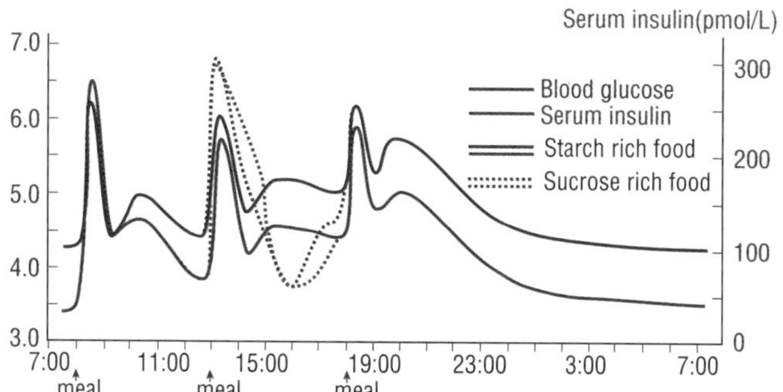

16. The plot shows that:
    (a) Blood glucose levels rises after a meal and serum insulin levels rise immediately after.
    (b) Blood glucose fluctuates less when sucrose-rich food is eaten rather than starch rich food.
    (c) Fluctuations in serum insulin appear unrelated to fluctuations in blood glucose.
    (d) None of the above is true.

17. Which statement about daughter cells following mitosis and cytokinesis is correct:
    (a) They are genetically different from each other and from the parent cell.
    (b) They are genetically identical to each other and to the parent cell.
    (c) They are genetically identical to each other but different to the parent cell.
    (d) Only one of the daughter cells is identical to the parent cell.

18. If the DNA content of a non-dividing cell is X, what would be its content at the start of interphase, during telophase, and after cytokinesis respectively:
    (a) 2X, X, X
    (b) X, 2X, X
    (c) X, X, 2X
    (d) 2X, 2X, X

19. Progression through the cell cycle is regulated by oscillations of which type of molecule?
    (a) Cyclins
    (b) Cyclin-dependent kinases
    (c) p53 and other tumor suppressor proteins
    (d) Phosphorylases

20. Which is the primary growth phase of a cell?
    (a) G_1
    (b) G_2
    (c) M
    (d) G_0

21. Which checkpoint controls the progression of the cell to its DNA replication phase in the cell cycle?
    (a) G_1
    (b) G_2
    (c) M
    (d) S

Questions 22-23 refers to the image below.

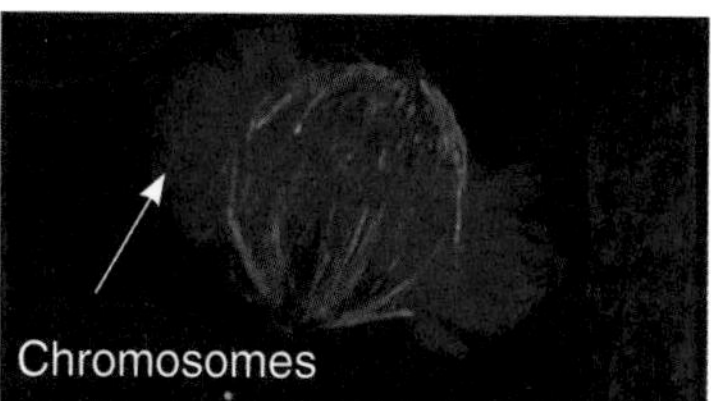

22. The phase of mitosis pictured is.
    (a) Prophase
    (b) Telophase
    (c) Metaphase
    (d) Anaphase

23. The green fluorescent structures are:
    (a) Centromeres
    (b) Spindle fibers
    (c) Kinetochores
    (d) An artifact of slide preparation

24. Cdk is a protein at the center of cell cycle regulation. It:
    (a) Binds to different cyclins
    (b) Is only active in mitosis
    (c) Must be phosphorylated to be active
    (d) Controls growth

25. Cells that no longer divide (such as certain specialized cells in the brain) stay in which phase of the cell cycle?
    (a) S phase
    (b) G_0 phase
    (c) G_1 phase
    (d) Interphase

26. Errors in which of the following genes are involved in cancer?
    (a) BRCA1
    (b) p53
    (c) (a) and (b)
    (d) None of the above

27. The phase of mitosis that is associated with the formation of the nuclear envelope, is:
    (a) Prophase
    (b) Metaphase
    (c) Anaphase
    (d) Telophase

28. The phase of mitosis that is associated with the breakdown of the nuclear envelope, is:
    (a) Prophase
    (b) Prometaphase
    (c) Metaphase
    (d) Anaphase

29. The phase of mitosis that is associated with the separation of chromatids to opposite poles, is:
    (a) Prometaphase
    (b) Metaphase
    (c) Anaphase
    (d) Telophase

ISBN: 978-1-98-856656-6

Free Response Question: Interpreting and evaluating experimental results

- To study the morphology of chromosomes, cells can be arrested during mitosis at prometaphase. In beans (*Phaseolus vulgaris*) and other plants, this can be achieved by subjecting root tips to a period of low temperature. Low temperature blocks the continuation of mitosis by preventing the chromosomes aligning on the metaphase plate.
- This experiment reports the effect of low temperature (4°C) treatment on the frequency of mitotic stages in bean root tips. Recovery of mitosis at 23°C was also recorded.
- Small lots (10 seeds per lot) of germinating seeds were placed in a low temperature incubator at 4°C. After time 0.5, 1.0, 1.5, 2.0, 3.0, and 6 hours at 4°C, root tip lots were excised and fixed, then sectioned, stained, and mounted.
- The recovery treatment involved placing small lots of the germinating seeds at 4°C for 3 hours and then placing them in another incubator at 23°C. Recovery of mitosis once at the higher temperature was recorded at 0.5, 1.0, 1.5, 3.0, and 6.0 hours by taking root tip samples as above.
- The results at the 3 hour interval (when mitotic percentages became relatively static) are plotted right for cells in prophase, prometaphase, and metaphase-anaphase-telophase collectively.

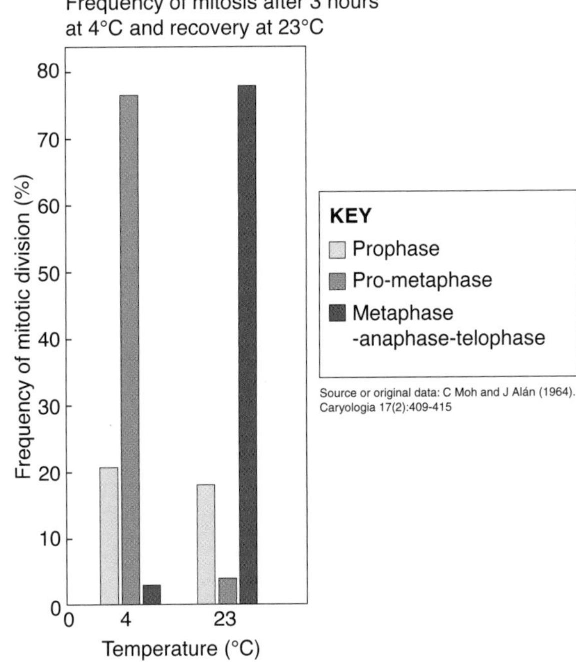

Source or original data: C Moh and J Alán (1964). Caryologia 17(2):409-415

1. (a) **Describe** the main events occurring in prometaphase and metaphase of mitosis:

   (b) **Explain** why mitosis is arrested when chromosomes cannot align on the metaphase plate:

2. (a) **Identify** the independent variable:

   (b) **Identify** the dependent variable:

3. (a) **Describe** the effect of low temperature on the progression of mitosis in bean root tips:

   (b) **Describe** the effect of returning the root tips to room temperature after 3 hours at 4°C:

4. **Predict** the effect of returning the recovering 23°C seeds to 4°C after only 1.5 hours. **Justify** your prediction:

ISBN: 978-1-98-856656-6

Free Response Question: Analyze data

- Much cancer research is directed at finding ways to identify cell cycle errors and target stages in the cell cycle that can slow or stop the unregulated division of cancer cells.
- Taxol is one of a number of anticancer drugs that target cytoskeletal proteins. It stabilizes spindle microtubules, preventing their disassembly. Chromosomes cannot achieve a metaphase spindle configuration, and this blocks the progression of mitosis.
- Stathmin is a protein that regulates the cell cycle. One of its normal roles is promote depolymerization (instability) of spindle microtubules. Its activity is regulated by cell-cycle-specific phosphorylation. In normal cells, stathmin activity is switched off by phosphorylation as the cell enters M phase. Phosphatases remove these phosphates in late mitosis so the cell can exit M-phase. Aggressive forms of breast cancer are resistant to Taxol chemotherapy alone. In these cancers, the stathmin gene is overexpressed.

HYPOTHESIS

- The researchers hypothesized that because stathmin decreases the stability of microtubules, switching off its production would enhance the ability of Taxol to stabilize microtubules and cause mitosis to be arrested more effectively in cancerous cells.

INVESTIGATION AND RESULTS

- Researchers investigated tumor volume over time in mice with aggressive cancers under three treatments: No treatment (control), Taxol treatment, and Taxol treatment with the stathmin gene expression suppressed.
- The results of the different treatments on tumor volume are plotted right. Error bars represent ± *sd* of the mean.

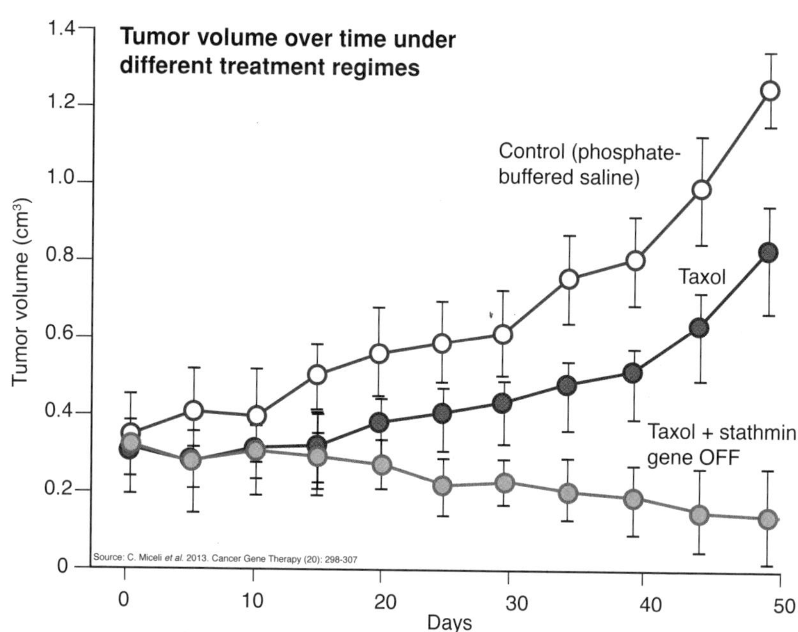

1. **Describe** the results plotted in the figure above right: ______

2. **Explain** the results plotted in the figure above right: ______

3. Use the data presented to **evaluate** the hypothesis and prediction of the researchers: ______

4. **Explain** what the results tell you about the regulation of the cell cycle and treatments for cancer: ______

ISBN: 978-1-98-856656-6

UNIT 5

Heredity

Learning Objectives

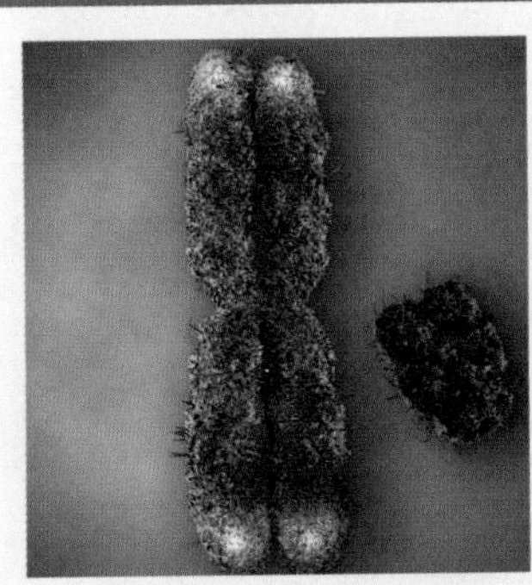

Developing understanding

CONTENT: In this unit, you will focus on heredity and the biological concepts and processes involved in ensuring the continuity of life. You will explore how meiosis ensures genetic diversity and gain a deeper understanding of Mendelian inheritance through problem solving. You will also learn to recognize patterns of inheritance that do not follow Mendelian rules. This unit also explores chromosomal inheritance, non-disjunction, and the role of environment on inheritance.

SKILLS: This unit builds on your ability to describe and explain biological concepts and processes relating to inheritance. You will develop your skills in hypothesis testing using chi-squared, and continue to build skills in the calculation of genotypic and phenotypic ratios.

5.1 Meiosis .... activities 80 - 82

- ☐ 1. Describe the basic characteristics of meiosis as a process, including its outcome and its two sequential steps.
- ☐ 2. Summarize the roles of mitosis and meiosis in the life cycle of sexually reproducing organisms, recognizing the role of mitosis in growth and repair and meiosis in producing haploid gametes prior to fertilization. Compare and contrast the processes in terms of the way the chromosomes segregate, the number of cells produced, and the genetic content of the daughter cells.

5.2 Meiosis and genetic diversity ...... activities 80 - 82

- ☐ 3. Explain how the process of meiosis generates genetic diversity by outlining the significance of the following events:
  - Crossing over between homologous chromosomes in prophase I resulting in recombination of alleles.
  - Independent assortment of homologous chromosomes in metaphase I.
  - The non-dividing centromere in metaphase I.
- ☐ 4. Explain how sexual reproduction in eukaryotes, including the events in meiosis and random union of gametes in fertilization, increases genetic variation in the offspring.

5.3 Mendelian genetics............... activities 83 - 87, 89

- ☐ 5. Explain how shared, conserved features and processes support a common ancestry for all organisms. These include nucleic acids, ribosomes, the genetic code, ATP, and core metabolic pathways such as glycolysis.
- ☐ 6. Explain the inheritance of genes and traits as described by Mendelian laws. Explain the laws of segregation and independent assortment and how Mendel arrived at these through his study of pea plant inheritance. Recognize that Mendelian laws apply to genes on separate chromosomes.
- ☐ 7. Recall how fertilization involves the fusion of haploid gametes, restoring the diploid number and creating new allele combinations in the zygote. Explain how the rules of probability can be applied to analyze the passage of single gene traits from parents to offspring.
- ☐ 8. Given parental genotypes and phenotypes or pedigrees, predict offspring genotypes and phenotypes for different patterns of inheritance, including monohybrid, dihybrid, linked and sex-linked genes.

5.4 Non-Mendelian genetics .... activities 88 - 101

- ☐ 9. Explain what is meant by genetic linkage (linked genes) and explain its biological consequences. Describe the dihybrid inheritance of linked genes. Explain how the probability that linked genes will segregate as a unit can be used to calculate the map distance between them.
- ☐ 10. Explain how you can recognize patterns of inheritance that do not follow Mendelian rules. Use the chi-squared test to test the outcome of genetic crosses against predicted outcomes and to provide evidence for genotype and linkage.
- ☐ 11. Use Punnett squares to predict the frequencies of genotypes and phenotypes in crosses involving incomplete dominance and codominance (including in multiple allele systems). Describe the features of these inheritance patterns.
- ☐ 12. Explain how the presence of lethal alleles can be detected from phenotypic ratios in the offspring of genetic crosses.
- ☐ 13. Describe different systems for sex determination in animals. For mammals and flies, with an XX/XY system, X linked recessive traits are always expressed in males.
- ☐ 14. Explain what is meant by a sex-linked trait. What are the characteristics of inheritance of X-linked dominant traits? Of X-linked recessive traits? Predict patterns of X-linked inheritance in pedigrees.
- ☐ 15. Explain inheritance involving multiple genes (polygeny) and explain how it contributes to continuous variation in a population. Describe the contribution of environment to the continuous variation observed for phenotypes determined by the inheritance of multiple genes.
- ☐ 16. Describe how traits that are the result of non-nuclear inheritance, i.e. inheritance through chloroplast or mitochondrial DNA, are inherited through the maternal line. Explain why such traits do not follow simple Mendelian rules.

5.5 Environmental effects on phenotype .... activities 102, 103

- ☐ 17. Describe how genotype, environmental factors, and epigenetic factors contribute to produce the phenotype of an organism. Recall the basis of quantitative and qualitative traits in organisms and explain why quantitative traits are often heavily influenced by the environment.
- ☐ 18. Using different examples, explain how the same genotype can result in multiple phenotypes under different conditions. Provide evidence for how this phenotypic plasticity contributes to fitness by allowing organisms to respond to changes in their environment.

5.6 Chromosomal inheritance......... activities 104, 105

- ☐ 19. Describe how chromosomal inheritance generates genetic variation in sexual reproduction through segregation, independent assortment of chromosomes, and fertilization. Explain how the chromosomal basis of inheritance explains the patterns of genetic transmission from parent to offspring
- ☐ 20. Explain how genetic disorders in humans can be attributed to the inheritance of a single mutated allele or to chromosomal changes arising from non-disjunction.

80 Meiosis

Key Question: How does meiosis produce haploid sex cells for the purpose of sexual reproduction?

Meiosis involves a single chromosomal duplication followed by two successive nuclear divisions, and results in a halving of the diploid chromosome number. Meiosis occurs in the sex organs of animals and the sporangia of plants. If genetic mistakes (**mutations**) occur here, they will be passed to the offspring (inherited). The first division in meiosis is a reduction division (the chromosome number is halved). The second meiotic division is similar to mitosis in that chromatids are pulled apart and the chromosome number remains the same. Meiosis creates genetic variation in the sex cells through two important processes: crossing over and independent assortment. These are described on the next page.

KEY EVENTS

Interphase
- DNA is copied and the cell prepares to divide.

REMEMBER! Homologous chromosomes (or homologs) are chromosome pairs with the same gene sequence. One comes from the mother (called maternal) and one comes from the father (called paternal).

MEIOSIS I (separation of homologous chromosomes)

Prophase I
- Chromosomes condense
- Homologs pair up
- Recombination of alleles occurs as homologous chromosomes exchange DNA in crossing over.

Metaphase I
- Random alignment of homologous chromosomes at the equator.
- Chromatids still held at centromere.

Anaphase I
- The pairs of chromosomes separate and move to opposing poles.

Telophase I
- Nuclear membranes reform, the cell divides and two cells are formed, each with N = 2 chromosomes.
- The spindle fibers disassemble.

MEIOSIS II (separation of chromatids)

Prophase II
- There are now two cells.
- DNA does not replicate again.
- Recombination of alleles occur

Metaphase II
- Individual chromosomes line up along the equator of the cell.

Anaphase II
- The chromatids split at the centromere and are moved by the spindle fibers to opposite poles of the cell.

Telophase II
- Nuclear membranes reform.
- There are 4 new haploid daughter cells.

2N = 4

Maternal chromosome

Paternal chromosome

When a cell is not dividing (interphase) the chromosomes are not visible, but the DNA is being replicated. The cell shown is **2N**, where N is the number of copies of chromosomes in the nucleus. N = one copy of each chromosome (haploid). 2N = two copies of each chromosome (diploid).

Meiosis starts here

Spindle apparatus begins to form.

In **prophase I**, replicated chromosomes appear as two **sister chromatids** held together at the **centromere** (a specialized DNA sequence that holds the sister chromatids together). Homologous chromosomes pair up (synapsis). **Crossing over** may occur at this time making sister chromatids differ from one another.

In **metaphase I**, homologous pairs line up in the middle of the cell (equator) independently of each other. This results in paternal and maternal chromosomes **assorting independently** into the gametes.

In **anaphase I**, homologs separate, pulled apart by the disassembly of the spindle fibers that are attached to the kinetochores (protein discs) on the centromeres. Other spindle fibers grow longer to push the cell poles apart and elongate the cell.

N = 2

In **telophase I**, two intermediate cells form.

In **prophase II**, the spindle apparatus reforms. Chromosomes migrate towards the metaphase plate at the equator of the cell.

In **metaphase II**, the chromosomes line up on the metaphase plate.

In **anaphase II**, the centromere divides and sister chromatids (now individual chromosomes) are separated, moving to opposite poles of the cell.

Telophase II produces four haploid gametes. Each one is N = 2.

N N N N

ISBN: 978-1-98-856656-6

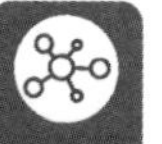

Crossing over and recombination

- Chromosomes replicate during interphase, before meiosis begins, to produce replicated chromosomes with sister chromatids held together at the **centromere** (below). The centromere is a specialized DNA sequence that links a pair of sister chromatids.
- When the replicated chromosomes are paired during the first stage of meiosis, non-sister chromatids may become entangled and segments may be exchanged in a process called **crossing over**. Crossing over results in the **recombination** of alleles (gene variants) producing greater variation in the offspring than would otherwise occur.

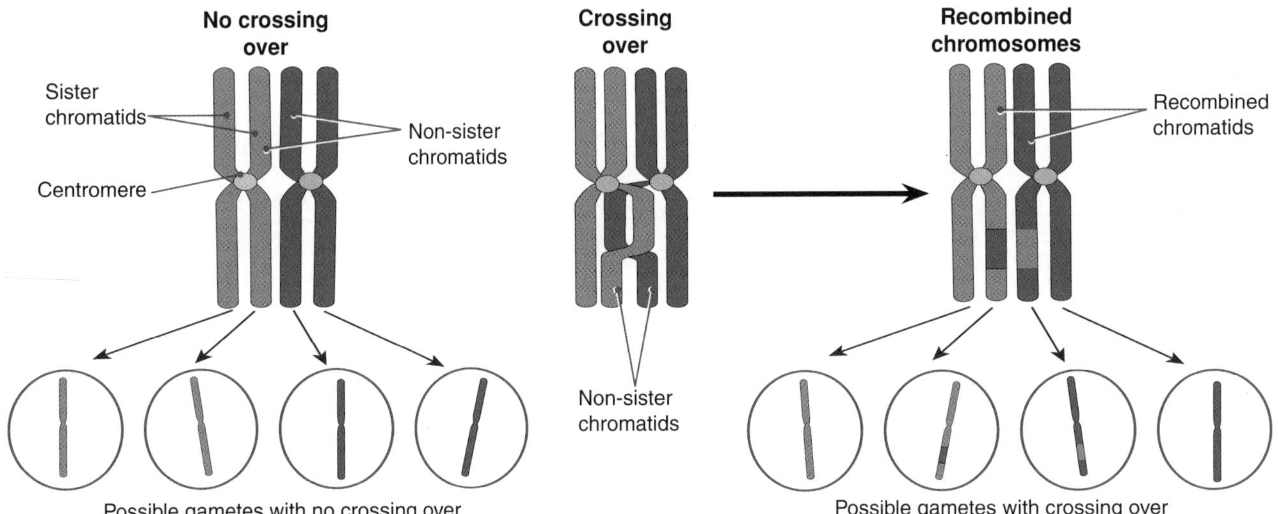

Independent assortment

- Independent assortment describes the random alignment and distribution of chromosomes during meiosis. Independent assortment is an important mechanism for producing variation in gametes.
- During the first stage of meiosis, replicated homologous chromosomes pair up along the middle of the cell. The way the chromosomes pair up is random. For the homologous chromosomes right, there are two possible ways in which they can line up resulting in four different combinations in the gametes. The intermediate steps of meiosis have been left out for simplicity.

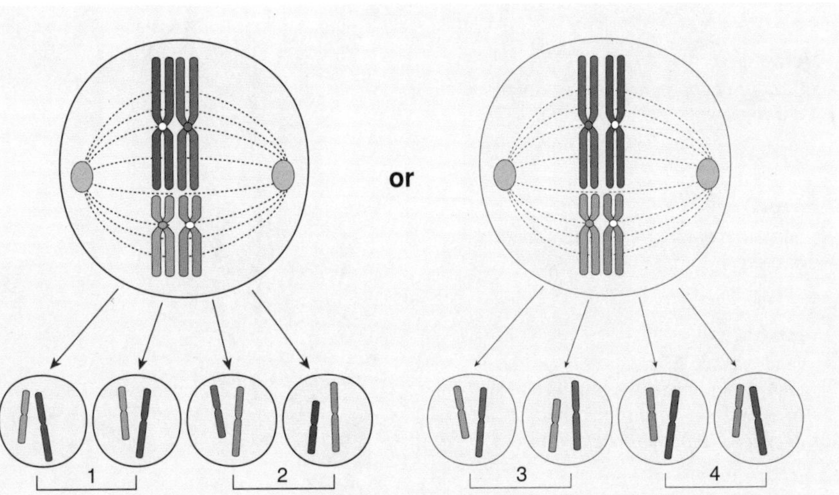

1. Describe the behavior of the chromosomes in the first and then the second division in meiosis: In the first division, chromosomes are replicated then recombined, in the 2nd division, chromosomes cross over + split, resulting in various genetic infos.

2. Explain how independent assortment increases the variation in gametes: It describes random alignment + distribution of chromosomes during meiosis

3. (a) What is crossing over? Crossing over is where non-sister chromatids may become entangled + segments may be exchanged

   (b) Explain how crossing over increases the variation in the gametes (and hence the offspring): It results in the recombination of alleles, producing greater variation in the offspring than would otherwise occur.

ISBN: 978-1-98-856656-6

The diagram below shows a pair of homologous chromosomes about to undergo crossing over during meiosis I. There are known crossover points along the length of the chromatids (same on all four chromatids shown in the diagram). In the prepared spaces below, draw the gene sequences after crossing over has occurred on three unrelated and separate occasions (it would be useful to use different colored pens to represent the genes from the two different chromosomes).

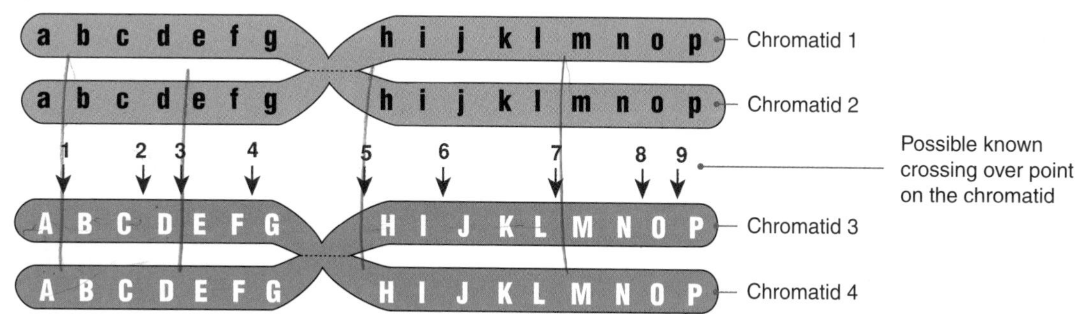

4. At which stage of meiosis does crossing over occur? prophase I

5. Crossing over occurs at a single point between the chromosomes above.

   (a) Draw the gene sequences for the four chromatids (on the right), after crossing over has occurred at crossover point **2**.

   (b) Which genes have been exchanged with those on its homolog (neighbor chromosome)?

   -ABC, abc

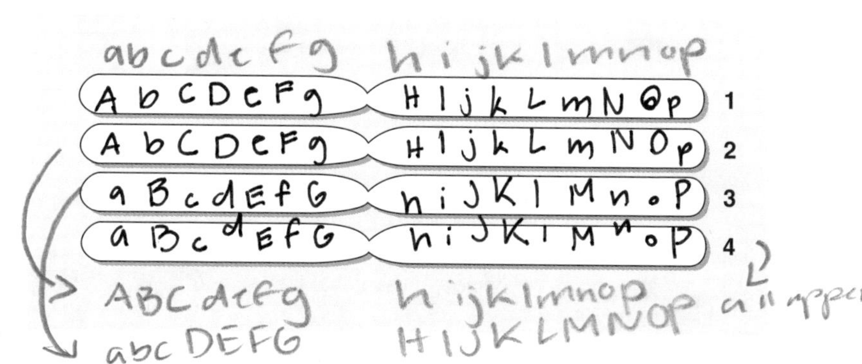

6. Crossing over occurs at two points between the chromosomes above.

   (a) Draw the gene sequences for the four chromatids (on the right), after crossing over has occurred between crossover points **6** and **7**.

   (b) Which genes have been exchanged with those on its homolog (neighbor chromosome)?

   -JkL, jkl

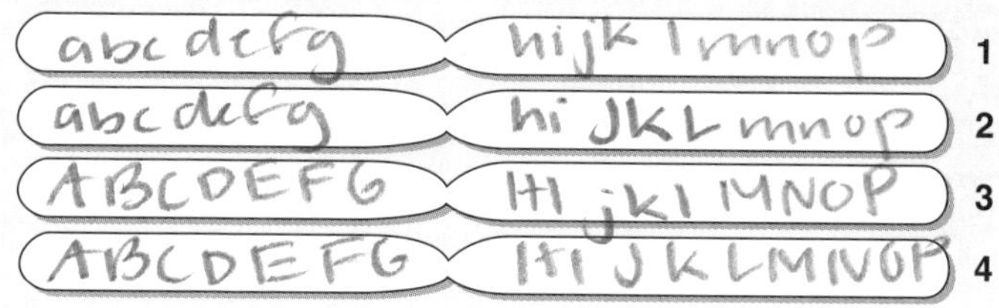

7. Crossing over occurs at four points between the chromosomes above.

   (a) Draw the gene sequences for the four chromatids (on the right), after crossing over has occurred between crossover points **1** and **3**, and **5** and **7**.

   (b) Which genes have been exchanged with those on its homolog (neighbor chromosome)?

   -bcd, hijkl

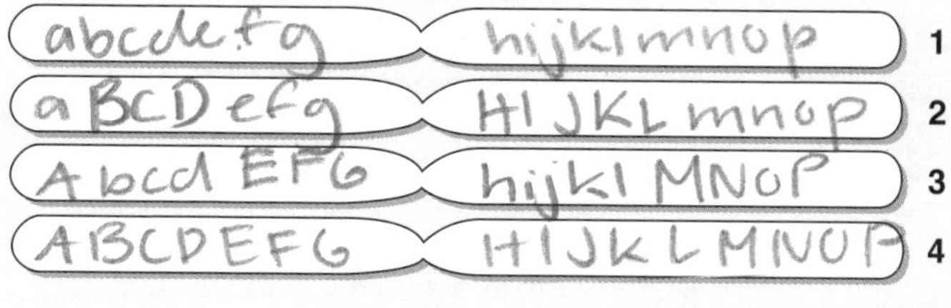

8. What would be the genetic consequences if there was no crossing over between chromatids during meiosis?

   then there would be no genetic variation and identical daughter cells w/ the same genetic information would be produced.

ISBN: 978-1-98-856656-6

81 Modeling Meiosis

STUDENT SUPPORT FOR INVESTIGATION 7, Part 4: *Modeling Meiosis*

This is a practical activity that simulates the production of gametes (sperm and eggs) by meiosis and shows how crossing over increases genetic variability. This is demonstrated by studying the inheritance of two of your own alleles by a "child" produced at the end of the activity. Completing this activity will help you to visualize and understand meiosis. It will take 25-45 minutes.

Background

Each of your somatic cells contains 46 chromosomes as 22 homologous pairs, plus the sex chromosomes. For simplicity, the number of chromosomes used here has been reduced to four (two homologous pairs). To study the effect of crossing over on genetic variability, you will look at the inheritance of two of your own traits: **handedness** and the ability to **tongue roll**.

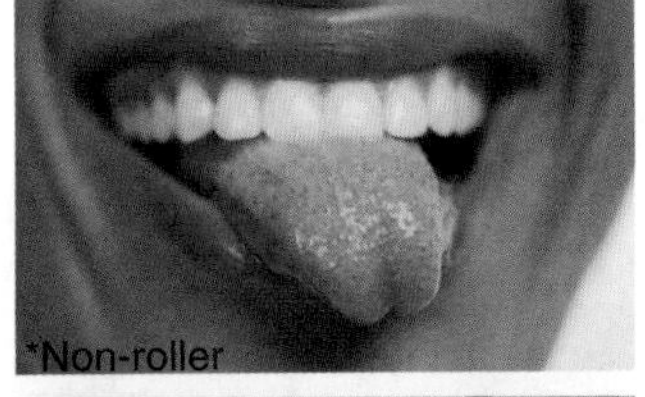
*Non-roller

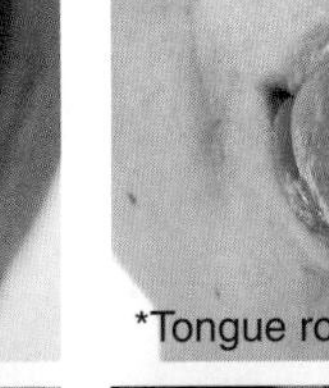
*Tongue roller

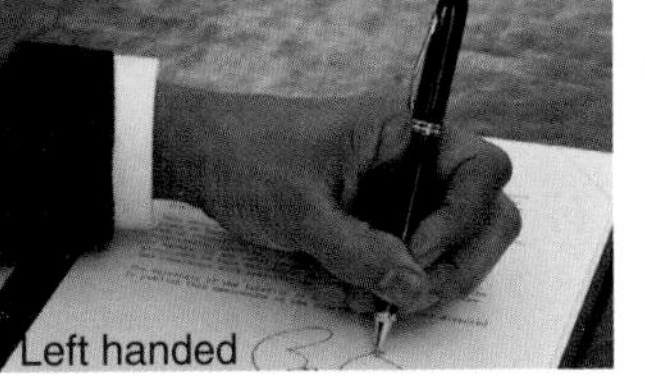
Left handed

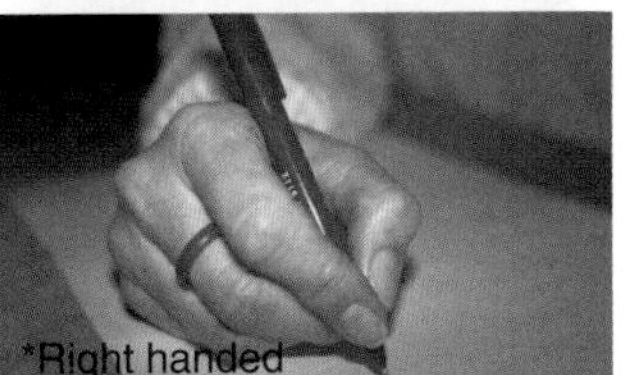
*Right handed

*Before beginning, bear in mind that most common phenotypic traits often identified as following simple Mendelian rules are not controlled by a single gene. Modifier genes and environment are important. This applies to tongue-rolling, handedness, cleft chin and many others. They are used here for simplicity but in genetics, things are often not as simple as they might appear!

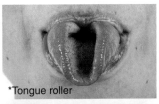

Chromosome #	Phenotype	Genotype
10	Tongue roller	TT, Tt
10	Non-tongue roller	tt
2	Right handed	RR, Rr
2	Left handed	rr

Record your phenotype and genotype for each trait in the table below. If you have a dominant trait, you will not know if you are heterozygous or homozygous for that trait, so you can choose either genotype.

Trait	Phenotype	Genotype
Handedness	Tt	TT
Tongue rolling	TT	TT

BEFORE YOU START THE SIMULATION: Partner up with a classmate. Your gametes will combine with theirs (fertilization) at the end of the activity to produce a "child". Decide who will be the female, and who will be the male. You will need to work with this person again at step 8.

1. Collect four craft sticks. These represent four chromosomes. Use colored sticks or color two blue or mark them with a P. These are the paternal chromosomes. The plain (or yellow) sticks are the maternal chromosomes. Write your initials on each of the four sticks. Label each chromosome with its chromosome number.

   Label four sticky dots with the alleles for each of your phenotypic traits and stick them on to the appropriate chromosomes. For example, if you are left handed and heterozygous for tongue rolling, your chromosomes will look like something like this (below).

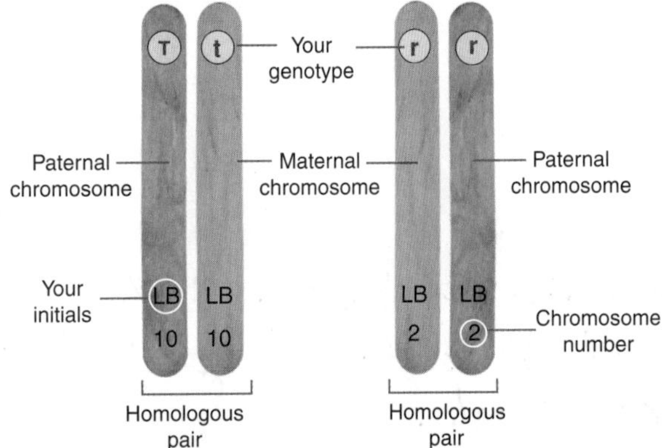

2. Randomly drop the chromosomes onto a table. This represents a cell in the testes or ovaries. **Duplicate** your chromosomes (to simulate DNA replication) by adding four more identical sticks to the table (below). This is **interphase**.

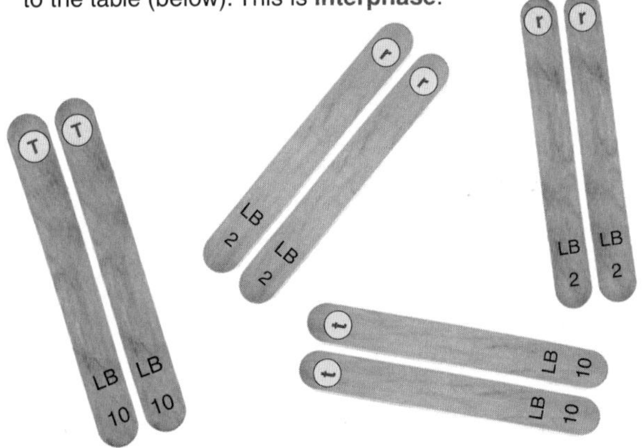

3. Simulate **prophase I** by lining up each duplicated chromosome with its homolog (below). For each chromosome number, you will have four sticks touching side-by-side (A). At this stage crossing over occurs. Simulate this by swapping sticky dots between adjoining homologs (B).

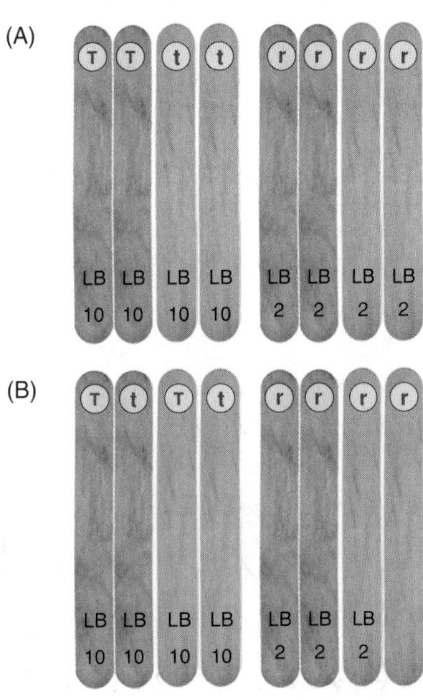

ISBN: 978-1-98-856656-6

4. Randomly align the homologous chromosome pairs to simulate alignment on the metaphase plate (as occurs in metaphase I).

5. Simulate anaphase I by separating chromosome pairs. For each group of four sticks, two are pulled to each pole.

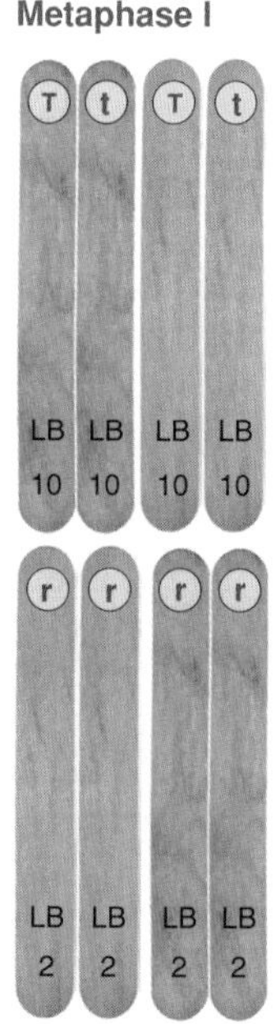

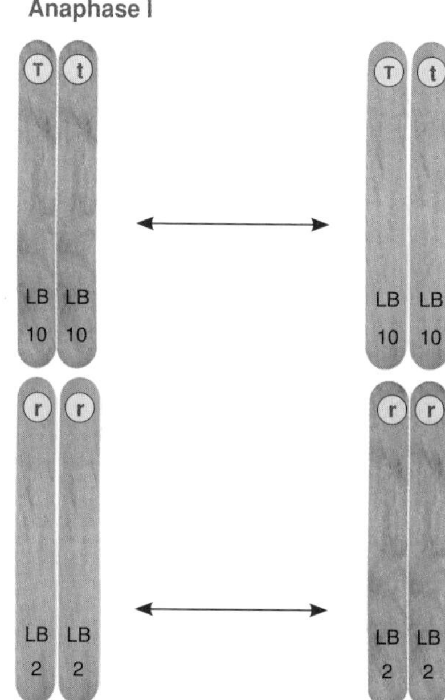

6. **Telophase I**: Two intermediate cells are formed. If you have been random in the previous step, each intermediate cell will contain a mixture of maternal and paternal chromosomes. This is the end of meiosis I.
7. Now that meiosis I is completed, your cells need to undergo **meiosis II**. Carry out prophase II, metaphase II, anaphase II, and telophase II. Remember, there is no crossing over in meiosis II. At the end of the process, each intermediate cell will have produced two haploid gametes (below).

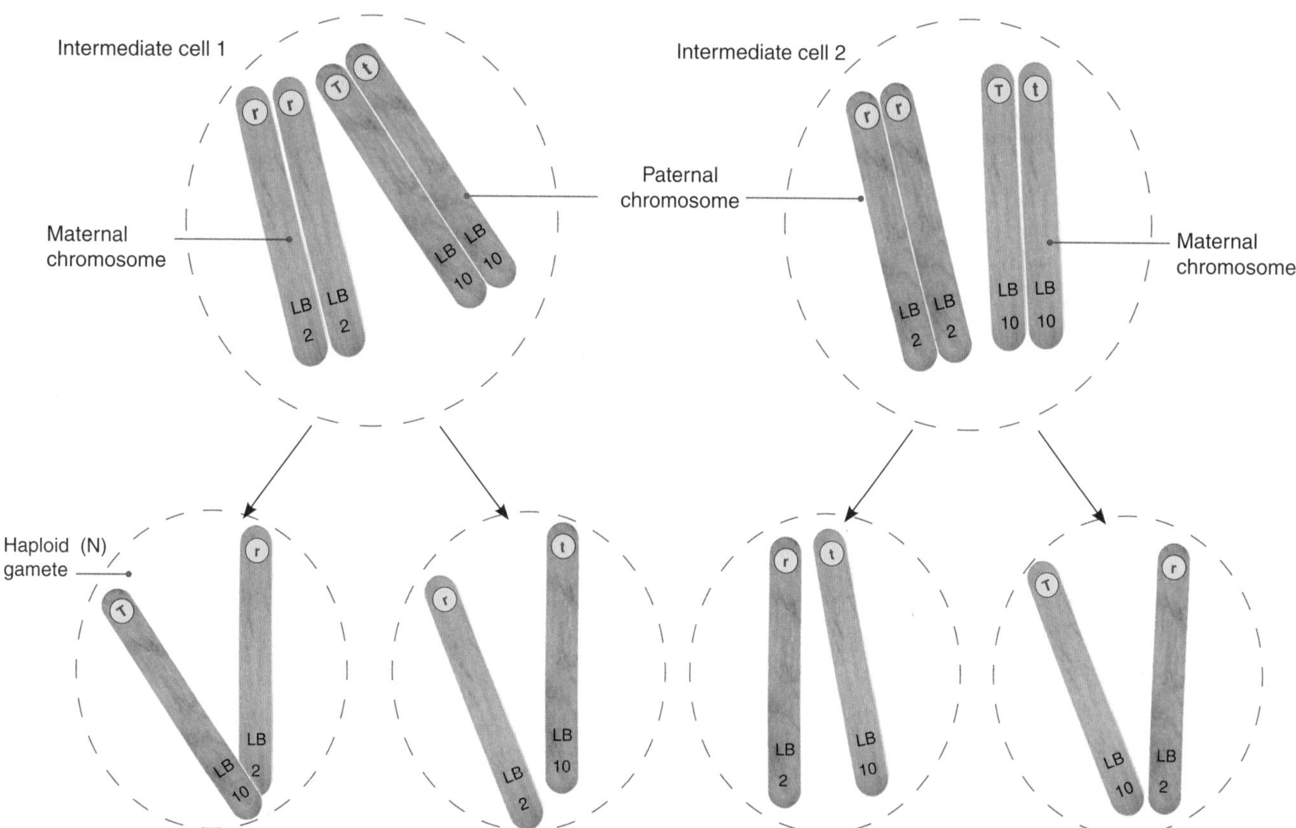

8. Pair up with the partner you chose at the beginning of the exercise to carry out fertilization. Randomly select one sperm and one egg cell. The unsuccessful gametes can be removed from the table. Combine the chromosomes of the successful gametes. You have created a child! Fill in the following chart to describe the child's genotype and phenotype for tongue rolling and handedness. How did meiosis generate variation in the offspring?

Trait	Phenotype	Genotype
Handedness	Tt	TT
Tongue rolling	TT	TT

ISBN: 978-1-98-856656-6

82 Mitosis vs Meiosis

Key Question: How do the processes and outcomes of mitosis and meiosis differ?

Cell division is fundamental to all life, as cells arise only by the division of existing cells. All types of cell division begin with replication of the cell's DNA. In eukaryotes, this is followed by division of the nucleus. Recall from Unit 4 that the two forms of cell division, **mitosis** and **meiosis**, have quite different purposes and outcomes. Mitosis produces two identical daughter cells from each parent cell and is responsible for growth and repair processes in multicellular organisms. Meiosis involves a **reduction division** in which haploid gametes are produced for the purposes of sexual reproduction. Fusion of haploid gametes in fertilization restores the diploid cell number in the zygote.

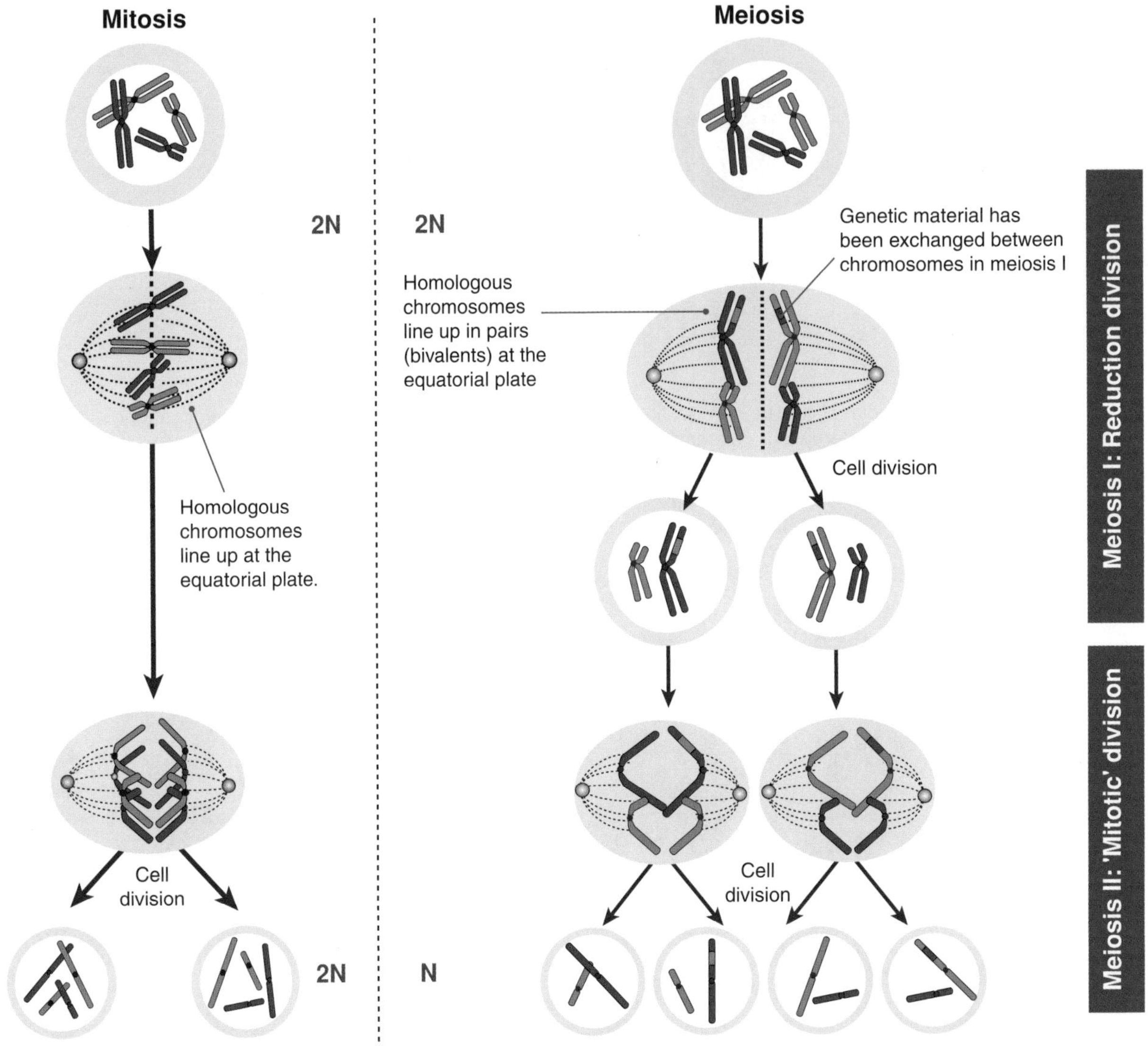

Mitosis

2N

Homologous chromosomes line up at the equatorial plate.

Cell division

2N

Meiosis

2N

Homologous chromosomes line up in pairs (bivalents) at the equatorial plate

Genetic material has been exchanged between chromosomes in meiosis I

Cell division

Cell division

N

Meiosis I: Reduction division

Meiosis II: 'Mitotic' division

1. Explain how mitosis conserves chromosome number while meiosis reduces the number from diploid to haploid:

2. Describe a fundamental difference between the first and second divisions of meiosis:

3. Explain how the differences between mitosis and meiosis account for their different roles in organisms:

ISBN: 978-1-98-856656-6

83 What Do Shared Conserved Processes Tell Us?

Key Question: How do we know that all life is descended from a common ancestor?

Powerful evidence for the common ancestry of all life comes from the universal nature of nucleic acids and the genetic code, and from the similarities in the molecular machinery of all cells, including ribosomes and ATP synthases.

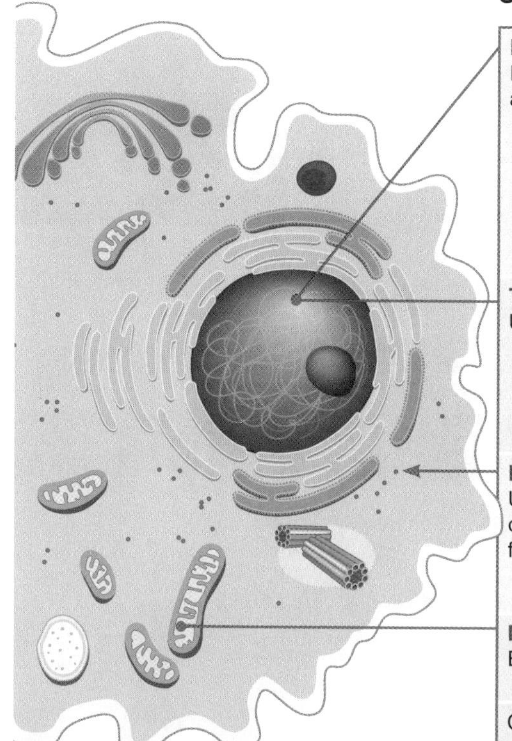

Shared core processes and features

DNA and RNA Information storage and retrieval	All life as we know it uses DNA and to store genetic information and RNA as a way of transferring that information to cell machinery for processing into proteins.
	All DNA is made up of the same four nucleotides (A, T, C, G). All RNA is made up of the same four nucleotides (A,U, C, G).
	DNA can be transferred between life forms (e.g. from eukaryotes to prokaryotes) and the cellular machinery to store and use DNA in the cells of all life forms is the same.
The genetic code Universality of rules	The genetic code is shared by all living systems
	Virtually all life translates RNA to proteins using the same three letter code on the RNA (codons).
	The start and stop codons for ribosomes reading the RNA are the same for all cells.
Ribosomes Universality of occurrence and function	Ribosomes are found in every living system on Earth. They synthesize all the proteins in all living systems.
	Although prokaryotic and eukaryotic ribosomes are slightly different, they share important core structures (i.e. the same DNA codes for these core structures).
Metabolic pathways Energy transfers	ATP is the universal energy transfer molecule. Essentially the same structure and activity of ATP synthase enzymes are present in all domain. Glycolysis is a universal pathway.
Cell communication	Cell communication in all cells involves transduction stimulatory or inhibitory signals from other cells.

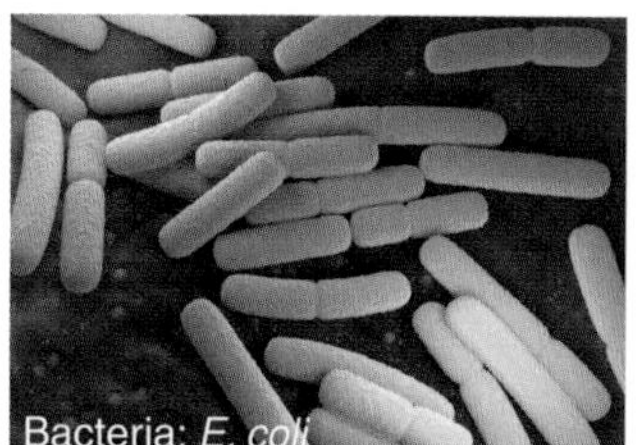
Bacteria: *E. coli*

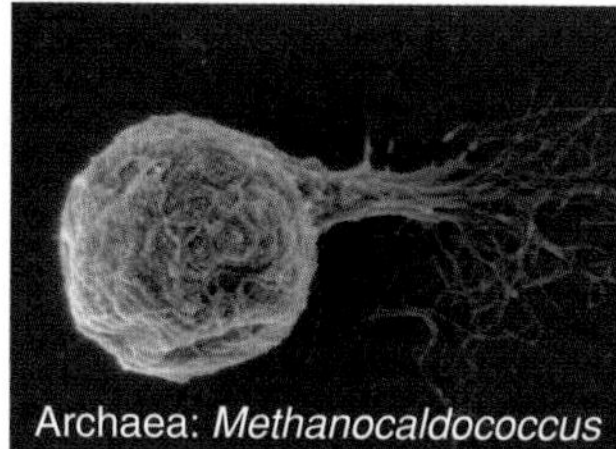
Archaea: *Methanocaldococcus*

Eukarya: *Paramecium bursaria*

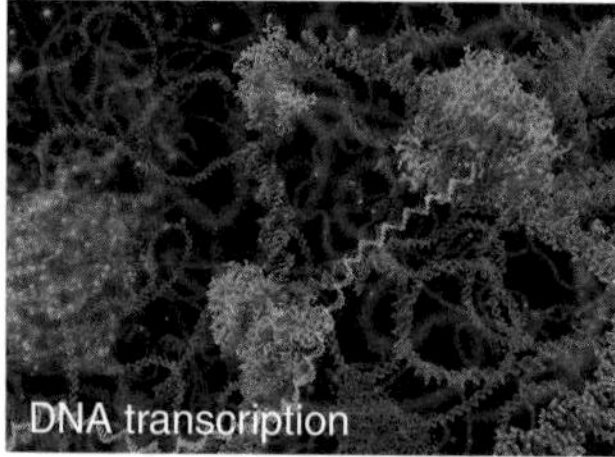
DNA transcription

Bacteria, Archaea, and all Eukaryota, including very simple protistans, share the same cellular machinery for information storage and retrieval. These shared conserved processes and structures provide a wealth of evidence to support a common ancestry for all organisms.

1. Describe how evidence from each of following supports a common ancestry for all living systems:

(a) DNA and RNA: ______________________________

____

____

(b) The genetic code: ______________________________

____

____

(c) Ribosomes: ______________________________

____

____

(d) Metabolic pathways: ______________________________

____

____

ISBN: 978-1-98-856656-6

84 Principles of Mendelian Genetics

Key Question: How do genes produce phenotypic traits that are inherited in predictable ratios, as shown by Mendel's pea experiments?

Gregor Mendel (1822-1884), right, was an Austrian monk who carried out the pioneering studies of inheritance. Mendel bred pea plants to study the inheritance patterns of a number of **traits** (specific characteristics). He showed that characters could be masked in one generation but could reappear in later generations and proposed that inheritance involved the transmission of discrete units of inheritance from one generation to the next. At the time the mechanism of inheritance was unknown, but further research has provided an accepted mechanism and we know these units of inheritance are **genes**. The entire genetic makeup of an organism is its **genotype**.

Mendel examined six traits and found that they were inherited in predictable ratios, depending on the **phenotypes** (the physical appearance) of the parents. Some of his results from crossing heterozygous plants are tabulated below. The numbers in the results column represent how many offspring had those traits.

1. Study the results for each of the six experiments below. Determine which of the two phenotypes is dominant, and which is the recessive. Place your answers in the spaces in the **dominance** column in the table below.

2. Calculate the ratio of dominant phenotypes to recessive phenotypes (to two decimal places). The first one has been done for you (5474 ÷ 1850 = 2.96). Place your answers in the spaces provided in the table below:

Trait	Possible phenotypes	Results	Dominance	Ratio
Seed shape	*Wrinkled* / *Round*	Wrinkled 1850 Round 5474 **TOTAL 7324**	Dominant: Round Recessive: Wrinkled	2.96 : 1
Seed color	*Green* / *Yellow*	Green 2001 Yellow 6022 **TOTAL 8023**	Dominant: Recessive	
Pod color	*Green* / *Yellow*	Green 428 Yellow 152 **TOTAL 580**	Dominant: Recessive	
Flower position	*Axial* / *Terminal*	Axial 651 Terminal 207 **TOTAL 858**	Dominant: Recessive	
Pod shape	*Constricted* / *Inflated*	Constricted 299 Inflated 882 **TOTAL 1181**	Dominant: Recessive	
Stem length	*Tall* / *Dwarf*	Tall 787 Dwarf 277 **TOTAL 1064**	Dominant: Recessive	

3. Mendel's experiments identified that two heterozygous parents should produce offspring in the ratio of three times as many dominant offspring to those showing the recessive phenotype.

(a) Which three of Mendel's experiments provided ratios closest to the theoretical 3:1 ratio?

____

(b) Suggest why these results deviated less from the theoretical ratio than the others: _______________

____

____

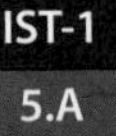
IST-1
5.A

85

ISBN: 978-1-98-856656-6

Mendel's laws of inheritance

Mendel's laws of inheritance were based on his observations and govern how genes are passed to the offspring.

Particulate inheritance

Characteristics of both parents are passed on to the next generation as discrete entities (genes).

This model explained many observations that could not be explained by the idea of blending inheritance, which was universally accepted prior to this theory. The trait for flower color (right) appears to take on the appearance of only one parent plant in the first generation, but reappears in later generations.

White X Purple **Parent plants**

X **Generation 1**

The offspring are inbred (self-pollinated)

Generation 2

Law of segregation

During gametic meiosis, the two members of any pair of alleles segregate unchanged and are passed into different gametes.

These gametes are eggs (ova) and sperm cells. The allele in the gamete will be passed on to the offspring.

NOTE: This diagram has been simplified, omitting the stage where the second chromatid is produced for each chromosome.

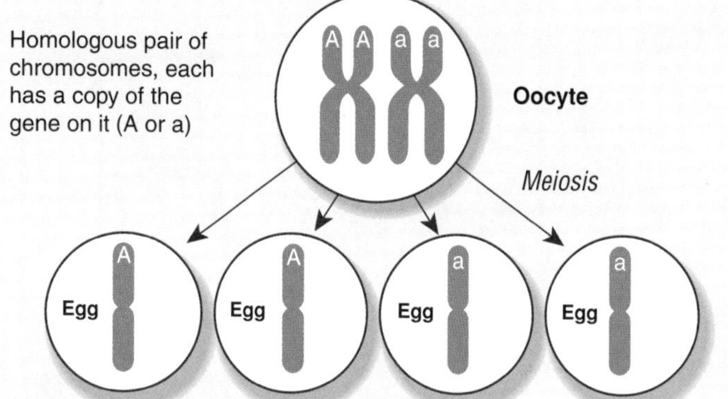

Law of independent assortment

Allele pairs separate independently during gamete formation, and traits are passed on to offspring independently of one another (this is only true for unlinked genes).

This diagram shows two genes (A and B), which code for different traits. Each of these genes is represented twice, one allele on each of two homologous chromosomes.

The genes A and B are located on different chromosomes and, because of this, they will be inherited independently of each other, i.e. the gametes may contain any combination of the parental alleles.

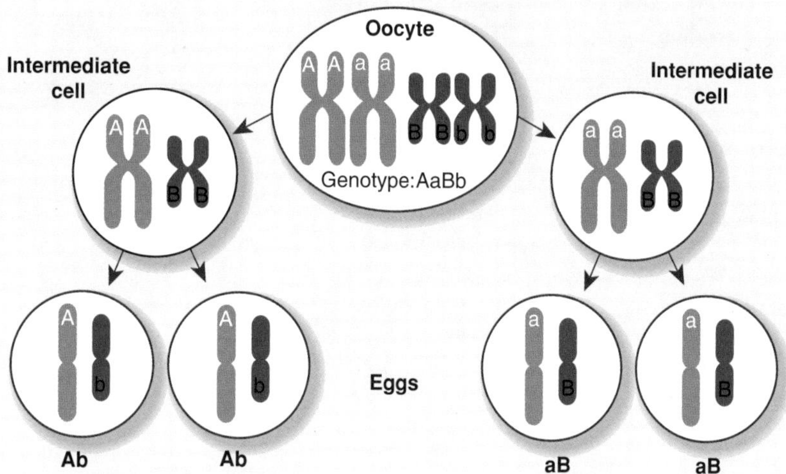

4. State the **property of genetic inheritance** that allows parent pea plants of different flower color to give rise to flowers of a single color in the first generation, with both parental flower colors reappearing in the following generation:

____

____

5. The oocyte is the egg producing cell in the ovary of an animal. In the diagram illustrating the **law of segregation** above:

   (a) State the genotype for the oocyte (adult organism): ____________________

   (b) State the genotype of each of the **four** gametes: ____________________

   (c) State how many different kinds of gamete can be produced by this oocyte: ____________________

6. The diagram illustrating the **law of independent assortment** (above) shows only one possible result of the random sorting of the chromosomes to produce: Ab and aB in the gametes.

   (a) Give other possible combinations of genes in gametes from the same oocyte: ____________________

   (b) How many different gene combinations are possible for the oocyte? ____________________

ISBN: 978-1-98-856656-6

85 Basic Genetic Crosses

Key Question: How can Punnett squares be used to show the outcome of genetic crosses?

Examine the diagrams below depicting monohybrid (one gene) and dihybrid (two gene) inheritance. The F_1 generation describes the offspring of a cross between **true-breeding** (homozygous) parents. A **back cross** is a cross between an offspring and one of its parents. If the back cross is to a homozygous recessive, it can be used as a **test cross**.

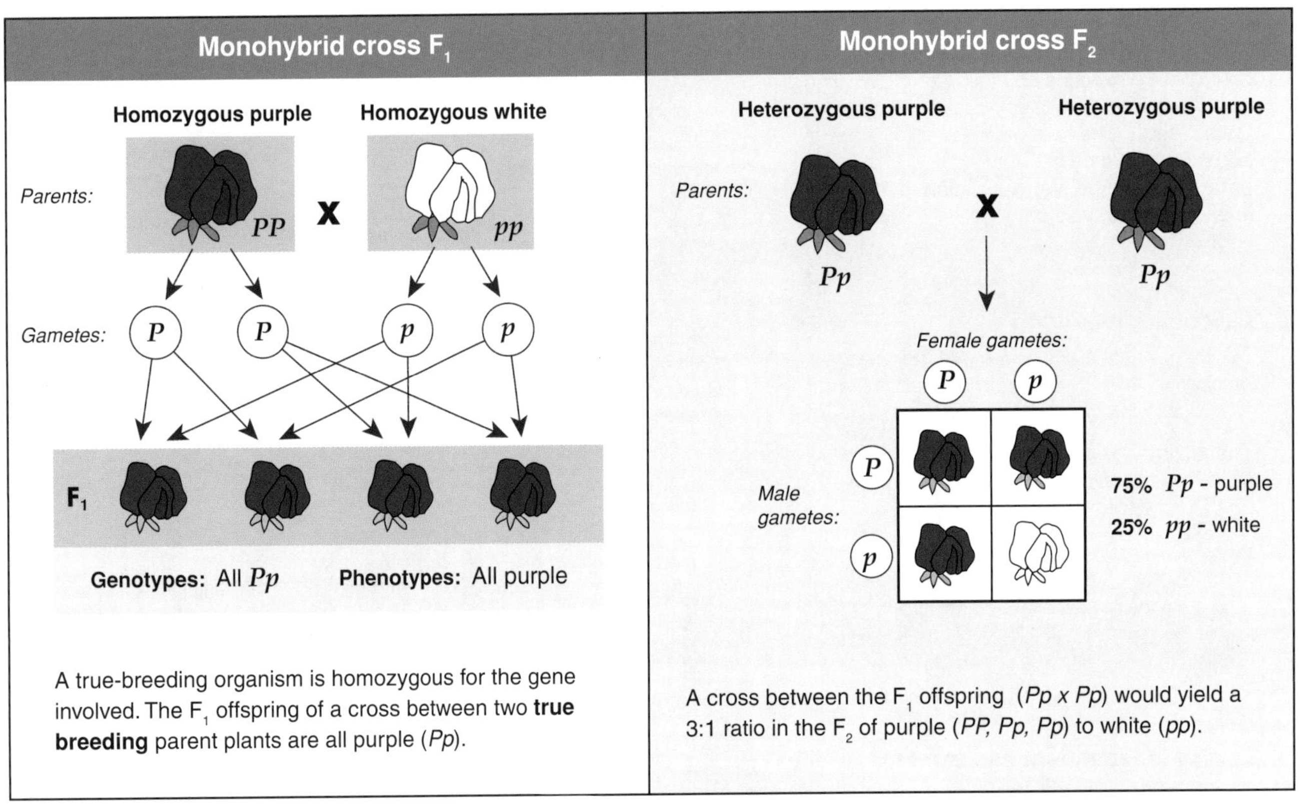

A true-breeding organism is homozygous for the gene involved. The F_1 offspring of a cross between two **true breeding** parent plants are all purple (*Pp*).

A cross between the F_1 offspring (*Pp x Pp*) would yield a 3:1 ratio in the F_2 of purple (*PP, Pp, Pp*) to white (*pp*).

Dihybrid cross

A dihybrid cross studies the inheritance patterns of two genes. In pea seeds, yellow color (*Y*) is dominant to green (*y*) and round shape (*R*) is dominant to wrinkled (r). Each **true breeding** parental plant has matching alleles for each of these characters (*YYRR* or *yyrr*). F_1 offspring will all have the same genotype and phenotype (yellow-round: *YyRr*).

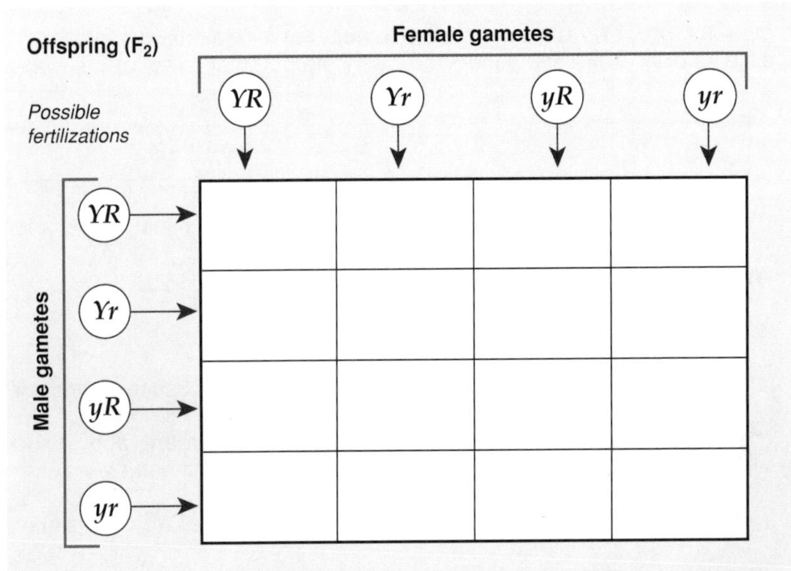

1. Fill in the Punnett square (below right) to show the genotypes of the F_2 generation.

2. In the boxes below, use fractions to indicate the numbers of each phenotype produced from this cross.

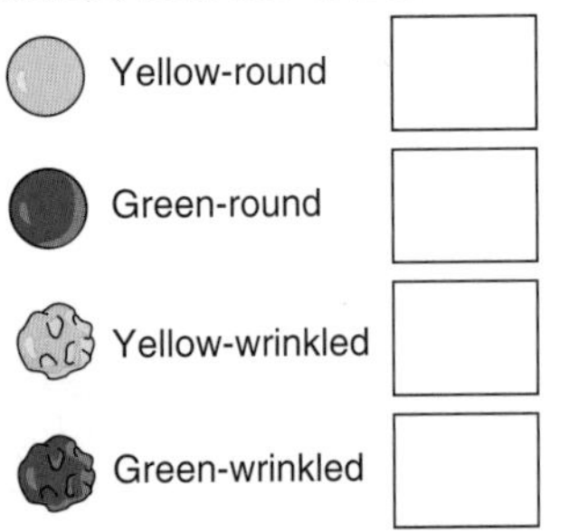

3. Express these numbers as a ratio:

____

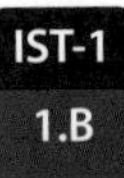

ISBN: 978-1-98-856656-6

The test cross

- It is not always possible to determine an organism's genotype by its appearance because gene expression is complicated by patterns of dominance and by gene interactions. The **test cross** is a special type of back cross used to determine the genotype of an organism with the dominant phenotype for a particular trait.
- The principle is simple. The individual with the unknown genotype is bred with a homozygous recessive individual for the trait(s) of interest. The homozygous recessive can produce only one type of allele, so the phenotypes of the offspring will reveal the genotype of the unknown parent (below). The test cross can be used to determine the genotype of single or multiple genes.

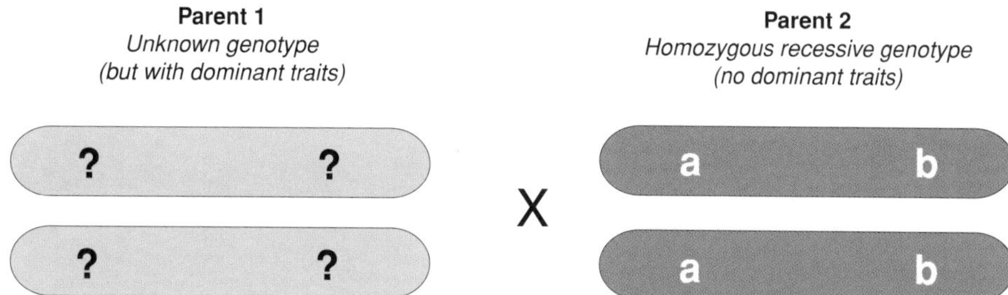

- The common fruit fly (*Drosophila melanogaster*) is often used to illustrate basic principles of inheritance because it has several easily identified phenotypes, which act as genetic markers. Once such phenotype is body color. Wild type (normal) *Drosophila* have yellow-brown bodies. The allele for yellow-brown body color (E) is dominant. The allele for an ebony colored body (e) is recessive. The test crosses below show the possible outcomes for an individual with homozygous and heterozygous alleles for ebony body color.

A. A homozygous recessive female (ee) with an ebony body is crossed with a homozyogous dominant male (EE).

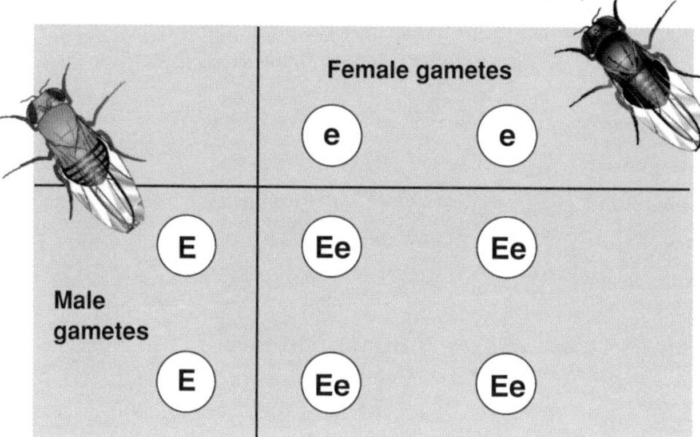

Cross A:

(a) Genotype frequency: 100% Ee

(b) Phenotype frequency: 100% yellow-brown

B. A homozygous recessive female (ee) with an ebony body is crossed with a heterozygous male (Ee).

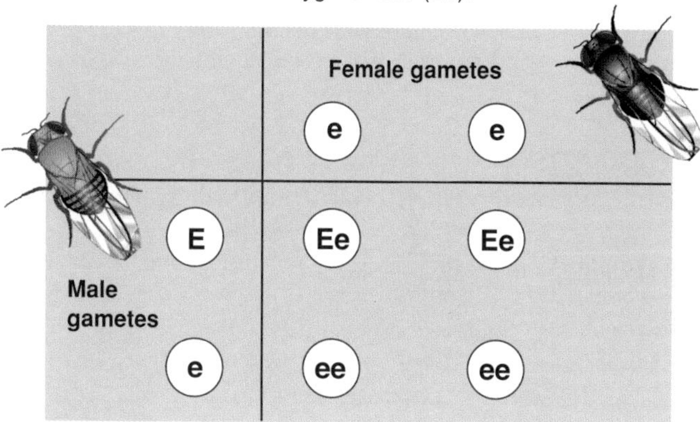

Cross B:

(a) Genotype frequency: 50% Ee, 50% ee

(b) Phenotype frequency: 50% yellow-brown, 50% ebony

- In crosses involving Drosophila, the wild-type alleles are dominant but are given an upper case symbol of the mutant phenotype. This is because there are many alternative mutant phenotypes to the wild type, e.g. vestigial wings and curled wings are both mutant phenotypes, whereas the wild type is straight wing. This can happen in other crosses too, e.g. guinea pigs, if a letter is already used for another character.

4. In *Drosophila*, the allele for brown eyes (b) is recessive, while the red eye allele (B) is dominant. Explain (using text or diagrams) how you would carry out a test cross to determine the genotype of a male with red eyes:

5. Of the test cross offspring, 50% have red eyes and 50% have brown eyes.

   What is the genotype of the male *Drosophila*? ______

ISBN: 978-1-98-856656-6

86 Probability

Key Question: What mathematical rules can be used to predict genetic crosses?

Most events cannot be predicted with absolute certainty, but we can determine how likely it is that an event will happen. This calculated likelihood is called **probability** and it ranges from 0 to 1. The sum of all probabilities equals 1. In biology, probability is used to calculate the statistical significance of a difference between means or the probability of an event occurring, e.g. getting certain genotypic or phenotypic ratios in the offspring of a genetic cross.

- Tossing a coin and predicting whether it will land heads (H) up or tails (T) up is a good example to illustrate probability.
- There are two possible outcomes; the coin will either land heads up or tails up, and only one outcome can occur at a time. Therefore the probability of a coin landing heads up is 1/2. The likelihood of a coin landing tails up is also 1/2.
- Remember probability is just an indication of how likely something will happen. Even though we predict that heads and tails will come up 50 times each if we toss a coin 100 times, it might not be exactly that.

Probability of an event happening = $\frac{\textbf{Number of ways it can happen}}{\textbf{Total number of outcomes}}$

The rules for calculating probability

- Probability rules are used when we want to predict the likelihood of two events occurring together or when we want to determine the chances of one outcome over another. The rules are useful when we want to determine the probably of certain outcomes in genetic crosses, especially when large numbers of alleles are involved. The probability rule used depends on the situation.

PRODUCT RULE for independent events

For independent events, A & B, the probability (P) of them both occurring (A&B) = P(A) X P(B)

Example: If you roll two dice at the same time, what is the probability of rolling two sixes?

Solution: The probability of getting six on two dice at once is 1/6 x 1/6 = 1/36.

SUM RULE for mutually exclusive events

For mutually exclusive events, A & B, the probability (P) that one will occur (A or B) = P(A) + P(B)

Example: A single die is rolled. What are the chances of rolling a 2 **or** a 6?

Solution: P(A or B) = P(A) + P(B). 1/6 + 1/6 = 2/6 (1/3). There is a 1/3 chance that a 2 or 6 will be rolled.

1. In a cross Aa x Aa, use the sum rule to determine the probability of the offspring having a dominant phenotype:

2. Use the product rule to determine the probability of a first and second child born to the same parents both being boys:

3. In a cross of rabbits both heterozygous for genes for coat color and length (BbLl x BbLl), determine the probability of the offspring being BbLl. HINT: Calculate probabilities for Bb and Ll separately and then use the product rule. Test your calculation using the Punnett square (right).

4. In a cross of two individuals with various alleles of four unlinked genes: AaBbCCdd x AabbCcDd, explain how you would calculate the probability of getting offspring with the dominant phenotype for all four traits:

5. Predict the probability of getting offspring with the dominant phenotype for all four traits if the heterozygous Bb in Q4 above was changed to bb:

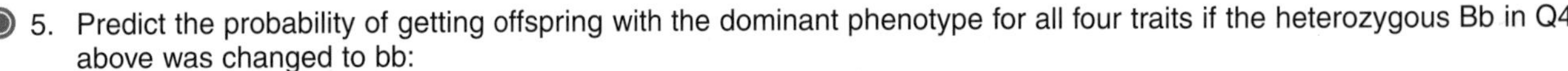

ISBN: 978-1-98-856656-6

87 Using Pedigrees to Analyze Inheritance Patterns

Key Question: What are pedigree charts and how are they be used to study the inheritance of genetic disorders?

One way in which to analyze the family history of an observable trait is to use a pedigree chart, which follows certain rules and uses particular symbols to indicate the sex and genotype of individuals across generations.

Pedigree charts

A pedigree chart is a diagram that shows the occurrence of a particular gene or trait from one generation to the next. In humans, pedigree charts are often used to analyze the inheritance of heritable conditions. In domestic animals, pedigree charts are often used to trace the inheritance of traits in selective breeding programs.

Pedigree charts use symbols to indicate an individual's particular traits. The key (right) explains the meaning of the symbols. Particular individuals are identified by their generation number and their order in that generational row. For example, **II-6** is the sixth person in the second generation. The arrow indicates the person through whom the pedigree was discovered (i.e. reported the condition).

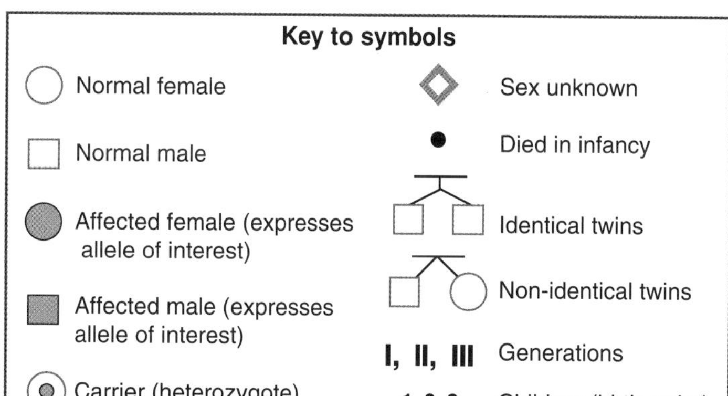

The chart on the right represents three generations: grandparents (I-1 and I-2) with three sons and one daughter. Two of the sons (II-3 and II-4) are identical twins, but did not have any children. The other son (II-1) had a daughter and another child (sex unknown). The daughter (II-5) had two sons and two daughters (plus a child that died in infancy). Pedigrees can also indicate if a trait shows autosomal or sex linked inheritance. In autosomal patterns, both males and females are generally equally affected (more or less).

For the particular trait being studied, the grandfather was expressing the phenotype (showing the trait) and the grandmother was a carrier. One of their sons and one of their daughters also show the trait, together with one of their granddaughters (arrow).

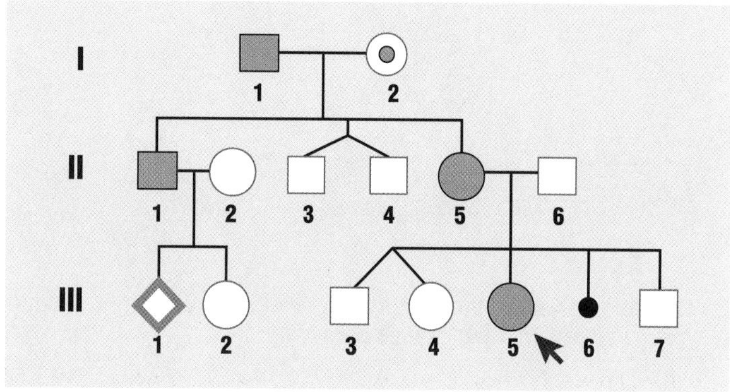

1. (a) Brown eyes are the result of a dominant eye-color allele and blue eyes are recessive. A brown-eyed man (A) whose mother had blue eyes and whose father had brown eyes marries a blue-eyed woman (B) whose parents are both brown-eyed. They have a daughter who is blue-eyed. Draw a pedigree showing all four grandparents, the two parents, and the daughter. Indicate each individual's possible genotype. Use filled shapes to indicate the recessive trait.

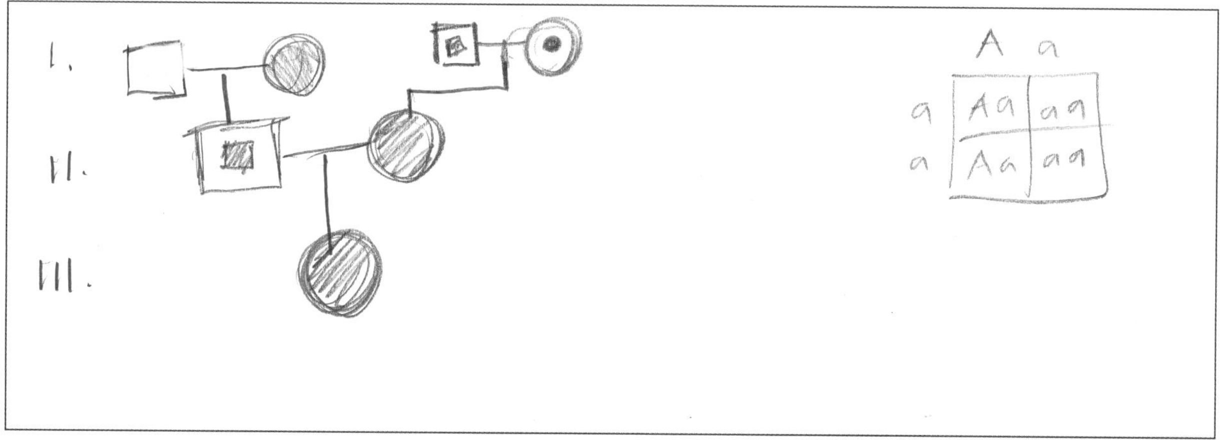

(b) Identify the individuals that are definitely heterozygous (carriers): mom's parents, dad

(c) Identify the individual that could be heterozygous (a carrier): dad's dad

(d) What is the probability of couple A and B having a blue-eyed boy as their next child? 50%

(e) Explain your reasoning: the dad is heterozygous and the mom is homozygous recessive. If you put their alleles in a punnett square, they have a 50/50 of having a blue or brown eyed child.

ISBN: 978-1-98-856656-6

The pedigree of lactose intolerance

Lactose intolerance is the inability to digest the milk sugar lactose. It occurs because some people do not produce lactase, the enzyme needed to break down lactose. The pedigree chart below was one of the original studies to determine the inheritance pattern of lactose intolerance.

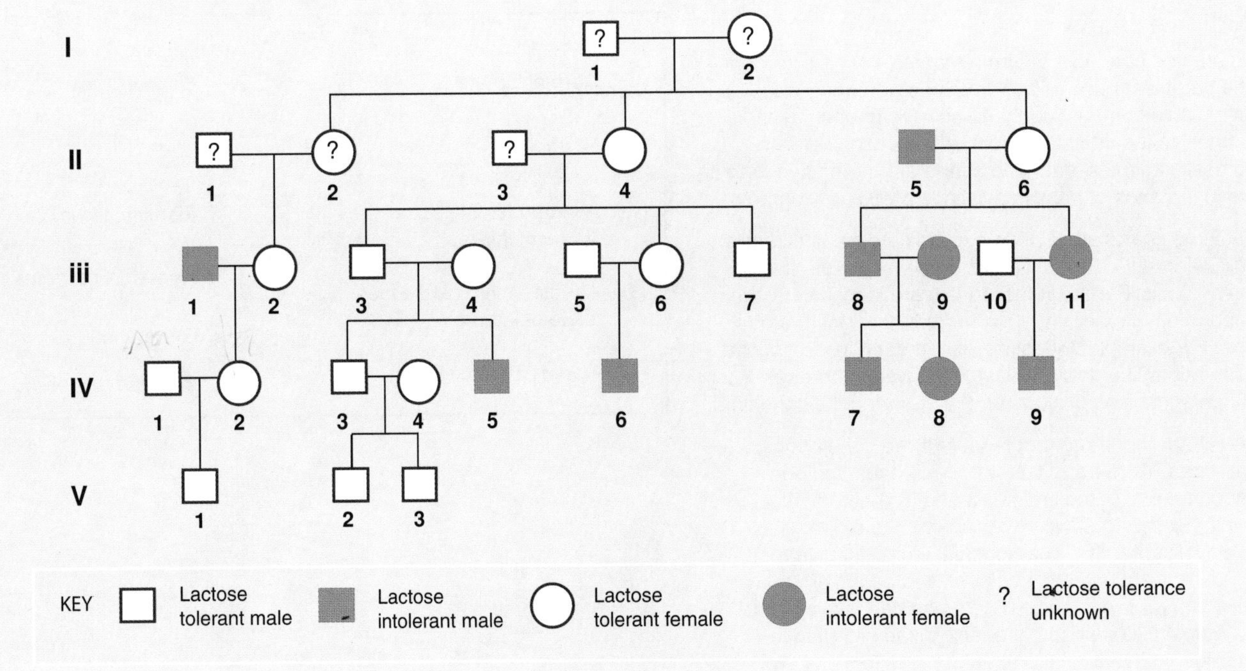

2. Use an analysis of the pedigree above to make a claim about the inheritance pattern of lactose intolerance. Support your claim with at least two pieces of evidence:

Lactose intolerance is a recessively inherited trait. According to the pedigree chart, it shows that even if the parents both are not lactose intolerant, they can be carriers and pass it onto the children. The offspring can also become carriers or fully dominant homozygous from two heterozygous parents.

3. (a) Use the Punnett square below to show the cross between III-10 and III-11 in the pedigree chart above. Use the capital letter L for the dominant allele and the letter l for the recessive allele.

(b) Explain how you can be certain about III-10's genotype:

If it was homozygous dominant, its offspring would not express the recessive trait.

Female alleles \ Male alleles	L	l
l	Ll	ll
l	Ll	ll

4. What is the probability that V-1 is heterozygous for lactose intolerance (Ll)? Show your working or justification:

There is a 50% chance that V1 can be heterozygous because his grandfather was lactose intolerant meaning his mom is most likely heterozygous. If his dad is also heterozygous, in a punnet square it shows 50% chance as well.

5. How do we know that the original parents (row I) could not both have been homozygous dominant? Explain: II-6 would be (AA) meaning none of their children would express lactose intolerance, but they did.

ISBN: 978-1-98-856656-6

88 Recombination and Dihybrid Inheritance

Key Question: How is it that genes on the same chromosomes can sometimes behave as if they are inherited independently of each other?

As you saw earlier, alleles on non-sister chromatids can be exchanged during crossing over in prophase I of meiosis. In the diagram below, alleles B and Pr can remain linked on the same chromatid, or the alleles Pr and pr could be exchanged.

Then all possible combinations of gametes (BPr, Bpr, bPr,and bpr) from parent 1 are possible. Offspring formed from these gametes are called **recombinants** and show combinations of characteristics not seen in the parents. However these recombinants are not produced in the numbers that would be expected had the alleles been on separate chromosomes (independent assortment).

Overview of recombination

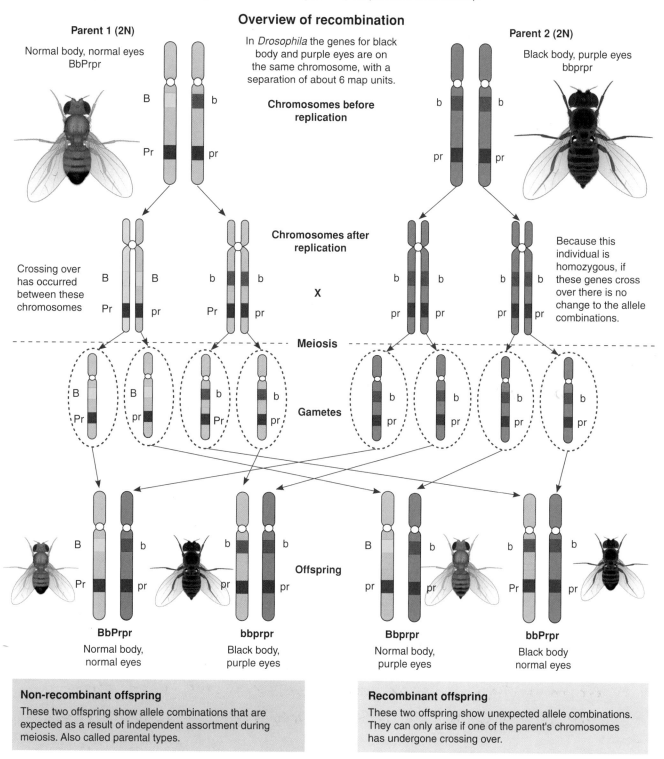

In *Drosophila* the genes for black body and purple eyes are on the same chromosome, with a separation of about 6 map units.

Parent 1 (2N)
Normal body, normal eyes
BbPrpr

Parent 2 (2N)
Black body, purple eyes
bbprpr

Chromosomes before replication

B, Pr | b, pr — b, pr | b, pr

Chromosomes after replication

Crossing over has occurred between these chromosomes

B Pr | B pr | b Pr | b pr — X — b pr | b pr | b pr | b pr

Because this individual is homozygous, if these genes cross over there is no change to the allele combinations.

Meiosis

Gametes

B Pr | B pr | b Pr | b pr | b pr | b pr | b pr | b pr

Offspring

BbPrpr
Normal body, normal eyes

bbprpr
Black body, purple eyes

Bbprpr
Normal body, purple eyes

bbPrpr
Black body normal eyes

Non-recombinant offspring
These two offspring show allele combinations that are expected as a result of independent assortment during meiosis. Also called parental types.

Recombinant offspring
These two offspring show unexpected allele combinations. They can only arise if one of the parent's chromosomes has undergone crossing over.

1. Describe the effect of recombination on the inheritance of genes: creates genetic variation. and unexpected allele combinations.

2. What would be the effect on the number of different kinds of gametes produced if no recombination occurred?
There would be identical gametes and no difference

ISBN: 978-1-98-856656-6

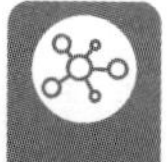

89 Predicting Outcomes of Genetic Crosses

Key Question: Can you use what you have learned so far to solve these problems?

The following problems mostly involve Mendelian crosses and probability. Some involve recombination. The alleles involved are associated with phenotypic traits controlled by a single gene or pairs of genes. The problems are to give you practice solving simple Mendelian inheritance problems and using probability to predict the outcomes of genetic crosses.

1. A dominant gene (**W**) produces wire-hair in dogs. Its recessive allele (**w**) produces smooth hair. Heterozygous wire-hair dogs were crossed and their F_1 progeny then test-crossed. Determine the expected genotypic and phenotypic ratios among the **test cross** progeny:

2. In sheep, black wool is due to a recessive allele (**b**) and white wool to its dominant allele (**B**). A white ram is crossed to a white ewe. Both animals carry the black allele (b). They produce a white ram lamb, which is then back crossed to the female parent. Determine the probability of the **back cross** offspring being black:

   There is a 25% chance for the back cross offspring being black because the female parent is heterozygous (Bb) and the offspring can be either (Bb) or (BB). If it's heterozygous there's a 25% chance

3. A homozygous recessive allele, **aa**, is responsible for albinism. Humans can exhibit this phenotype. In each of the following cases, determine the possible genotypes of the mother and father, and their children:

   (a) Both parents have normal phenotypes; some of their children are albino and others are unaffected:

   Aa, aa, AA

   (b) Both parents are albino and have only albino children: aa

   (c) The woman is unaffected, the man is albino, and they have one albino child and three unaffected children:

   Aa, aa

4. (a) Two plants with the genotypes Aa and aa were crossed. What is the probability that a seed resulting from the cross will have an aa genotype?

   50% chance

   (b) If 300 seeds were collected from the cross in (a), how many of them would be expected to have the genotype aa?

   150

   (c) How many would be expected to have the dominant phenotype? 150

   (d) The collected seeds were planted and all germinated. 163 of the seedlings showed the recessive phenotype. Explain why this is possible:

   probability is never exact, which is why it is by chance. It is just a prediction of outcomes.

5. A plant grower accidently mixed up seeds of a plant that produces orange or yellow flowers depending on if they expressed the dominant or recessive phenotype. The seeds were planted to find out which was which. When the plants flowered, 22 had yellow flowers and 60 had orange flowers. Which phenotype is dominant and why?

   Orange, dominant phenotypes usually are more expressed or have a higher chance of being shown in phenotypes in both heterozygous + homozygous alleles

ISBN: 978-1-98-856656-6

6. In cats, the following alleles are present for coat characteristics: black (B), brown (b), short (L), long (l), tabby (T), blotched tabby (tb). Use the information to complete the dihybrid crosses below:

(a) A black short haired (BBLl) male is crossed with a black long haired (Bbll) female. Determine the genotypic and phenotypic ratios of the offspring:

Genotype ratio: 1:2:2

Phenotype ratio: 1:1

(b) A tabby, short haired male (TtbLl) is crossed with a blotched tabby, short haired (tbtbLl) female. Determine the offspring ratios:

Genotype ratio: 2:2:2:2:4:4 = 1:1:1:1:2:2

Phenotype ratio: 3:3:1:1

6-short tabby 2=long tabby

7. A plant with orange-striped flowers was cultivated from seeds. The plant was self-pollinated and the F_1 progeny appeared in the following ratios: 89 orange with stripes, 29 yellow with stripes, 32 orange without stripes, 9 yellow without stripes.

(a) Determine the genotype of the original plant with orange striped flowers: Aa Bb

(b) A seed was chosen at random from the F_1 progeny of the selfed plant with orange striped flowers. The seed was grown and crossed with a plant grown from a randomly chosen seed from the plant with yellow non-striped flowers. What is the probability that a yellow striped flower will be produced?

8. In rabbits, spotted coat **S** is dominant to solid color **s,** while for coat color, black **B** is dominant to brown **b**. A brown spotted rabbit is mated with a solid black one and all the offspring are black spotted (the genes are not linked).

(a) State the genotypes: bbSS, BBss

Parent 1: bbSS Parent 2: BBss Offspring: BbSs

(b) Use the Punnett square to show the outcome of a cross between the F_1:

(c) Using ratios, state the phenotypes of the F_2 generation:

solid black - III solid brown - I

spotted black - ~~IIII~~ IIII spotted brown - III

1:3:3:8

9. In a cross of AaBb and AABb, what is the probability of both the dominant phenotypes appearing in any offspring?

50% for Bb, 100% for Aa, 75% for both

ISBN: 978-1-98-856656-6

10. Complete the recombination diagram right, adding the gametes in the ovals and offspring genotypes and phenotypes in the rectangles:

11. Explain how recombination increases the amount of genetic variation in offspring:

Recombination through crossing over results a unique combination of genes in each zygote.

12. Explain why it is not possible to have a recombination frequency of greater than 50% (half recombinant progeny):

random assortment of genes generates 50% recombination

13. A second pair of *Drosophila* are mated. The female is Cucu YY (straight wing, gray body), while the male is Cucu yy (straight wing, yellow body). Assuming recombination, perform the cross and list the offspring genotypes and phenotypes:

Cucu yy - straight wing, gray body
Cucu Yy - straight wing gray body
cucu yy - curled wing, yellow body
Cucu yy straight wing, yellow body
cucu Yy - curled wing, gray body

An example of recombination

In the female parent, crossing over occurs between the linked genes for wing shape and body color

	Wild type female	Mutant male
Parent	**Wild type female**	**Mutant male**
Phenotype	Straight wing Gray body	Curled wing Ebony body
Genotype	Cucu Ebeb	cucu ebeb
Linkage	*Cu* *Eb* / *cu* *eb*	*cu* *eb* / *cu* *eb*

Meiosis

Gametes from female fly (N)
Crossing over has occurred, giving four types of gametes

Gametes from male fly (N)
Only one type of gamete is produced in this case

Non-recombinant offspring **Recombinant offspring**

The sex of the offspring is irrelevant in this case

14. A hypothetical plant has the following alleles. A tall plant is dominant (T) and a short plant is recessive (t). Purple flowers are dominant (P) and white flowers are recessive (p). Two tall, purple flowered plants are crossed. One has genotype TtPP and the other has genotype TtPp.

(a) What is the probability of producing tall plants with purple flowers? ______

(b) What is the probability of producing dwarf plants with white flowers? ______

(c) What is the probability of producing tall plants with white flowers? ______

(d) What is the probability of producing both tall plants with purple flowers and dwarf plants with purple flowers? Explain:

15. Brown eyes (B) are dominant to blue eyes (b). A man with blue eyes marries a woman with brown eyes. The woman does not know her genotype. If they have a child what is the probability it will have brown eyes?

16. A dog breeder crosses two dogs of genotype BbCc where B = black coat, b = yellow coat, C = straight coat, and c = curly coat. Assuming the genes assort independently, predict the proportion of BbCc puppies in the offspring:

ISBN: 978-1-98-856656-6

90 Testing the Outcomes of Genetic Crosses

Key Question: How can the chi-squared test for goodness of fit be used to determine if the outcome of a genetic cross is significantly different from the expected?

When using the chi-squared test, the null hypothesis predicts the ratio of offspring of different phenotypes according to the expected Mendelian ratio for the cross, assuming independent assortment of alleles (no linkage). Significant departures from the predicted Mendelian ratio indicate linkage of the alleles in question. Raw counts should be used and a large sample size is required for the test to be valid.

Using χ^2 in Mendelian genetics

- In genetic crosses, certain ratios of offspring can be predicted based on the known genotypes of the parents The chi-squared test is a statistical test to determine how well observed offspring numbers match (or fit) expected numbers. Raw counts should be used and a large sample size is required for the test to be valid.
- In a chi-squared test, the null hypothesis predicts the ratio of offspring of different phenotypes is the same as the expected Mendelian ratio for the cross, assuming independent assortment of alleles (no linkage, i.e. the genes involved are on different chromosomes).
- Significant departures from the predicted Mendelian ratio indicate linkage (the genes are on the same chromosome) of the alleles in question.
- In a *Drosophila* genetics experiment, two individuals were crossed (the details of the cross are not relevant here). The predicted Mendelian ratios for the offspring of this cross were 1:1:1:1 for each of the four following phenotypes: gray body-long wing, gray body-vestigial wing, ebony body-long wing, ebony body-vestigial wing.
- The observed results of the cross were not exactly as predicted. The following numbers for each phenotype were observed in the offspring of the cross:

Gray body, vestigial wing **88**

Gray body, long wing **98**

Ebony body, long wing **102**

Ebony body, vestigial wing **112**

Table 1: Critical values of χ^2 at different levels of probability. By convention, the critical probability for rejecting the null hypothesis (H_0) is 5%. If the test statistic is less than the tabulated critical value for $P = 0.05$ we cannot reject H_0 and the result is not significant. If the statistic is greater than the tabulated value for $P = 0.05$ we reject (H_0) in favor of the alternative hypothesis.

Degrees of freedom	Level of probability (P)					
	0.50	0.20	0.10	0.05	0.02	0.01
1	0.455	1.64	2.71	3.84	5.41	6.64
2	1.386	3.22	4.61	5.99	7.82	9.21
3	2.366	4.64	6.25	7.82	9.84	11.35
4	3.357	5.99	7.78	9.49	11.67	13.28
5	4.351	7.29	9.24	11.07	13.39	15.09
	← Do not reject H_0				Reject H_0 →	

Steps in performing a χ^2 test for goodness of fit

1 Enter the observed value (O).

Enter the values of the offspring into the table (below) in the appropriate category (column 1).

2 Calculate the expected value (E).

In this case the expected ratio is 1:1:1:1. Therefore the number of offspring in each category should be the same (i.e. total offspring/ no. categories). 400 / 4 = 100 (column 2).

3 Calculate O–E and $(O-E)^2$

The difference between the observed and expected values is calculated as a measure of the deviation from a predicted result. Since some deviations are negative, they are all squared to give positive values (columns 3 and 4).

4 Calculate χ^2

For each category, calculate $(O - E)^2 / E$. Then sum these values to produce the χ^2 value (column 5).

$$\chi^2 = \sum \frac{(O - E)^2}{E}$$

5 Calculate degrees of freedom

The probability that any particular χ^2 value could be exceeded by chance depends on the number of degrees of freedom. This is simply one less than the total number of categories (this is the number that could vary independently without affecting the last value) In this case 4 – 1 = 3.

6 Use χ^2 table

On the χ^2 table with 3 degrees of freedom, the calculated χ^2 value corresponds to a probability between 0.2 and 0.5. By chance alone a χ^2 value of **2.96** will happen 20% to 50% of the time. The probability of 0.0 to 0.5 is higher than 0.05 (i.e 5% of the time) and therefore the null hypothesis cannot be rejected. We have no reason to believe the observed values differ significantly from the expected values.

	1	2	3	4	5
Category	O	E	O–E	$(O-E)^2$	$(O-E)^2/E$
GB, LW	98	100	-2	4	0.04
GB, VW	88	100	-12	144	1.44
EB, LW	102	100	2	4	0.04
EB, VW	112	100	12	144	1.44
				χ^2 →	2.96

ISBN: 978-1-98-856656-6

The following problems examine the use of the chi-squared (χ^2) test in genetics.

1. In a tomato plant experiment, two heterozygous individuals were crossed (the details of the cross are not relevant here). The predicted Mendelian ratios for the offspring of this cross were **9:3:3:1** for each of the **four following phenotypes**: purple stem-jagged leaf edge, purple stem-smooth leaf edge, green stem-jagged leaf edge, green stem-smooth leaf edge.

   The observed results of the cross were not exactly as predicted.
   The numbers of offspring with each phenotype are provided below:

Observed results of the tomato plant cross

Purple stem-jagged leaf edge	**12**	Green stem-jagged leaf edge	**8**
Purple stem-smooth leaf edge	**9**	Green stem-smooth leaf edge	**0**

   (a) State your null hypothesis for this investigation (Ho): ______________________

   (b) State the alternative hypothesis (HA): ______________________

2. Use the chi-squared (χ^2) test to determine if the differences between the observed and expected phenotypic ratios are significant. Use the table of critical values of χ^2 at different P values on the previous page.

   (a) Enter the observed values (number of individuals) and complete the table to calculate the χ^2 value:

Category	O	E	O — E	(O — E)^2	$\frac{(O-E)^2}{E}$
Purple stem, jagged leaf					
Purple stem, smooth leaf					
Green stem, jagged leaf					
Green stem, smooth leaf					
	Σ				Σ

   (b) Calculate χ^2 value using the equation:

$$\chi^2 = \sum \frac{(O-E)^2}{E} \qquad \chi^2 = \_\_\_\_\_\_$$

   (c) Calculate the degrees of freedom: __________

   (d) Using the χ^2 table, state the *P* value corresponding to your calculated χ^2 value:

   ____

   (e) State your decision: *(circle one)*
   reject Ho / do not reject Ho

3. Students carried out a pea plant experiment, where two heterozygous individuals were crossed. The predicted Mendelian ratios for the offspring were **9:3:3:1** for each of the **four following phenotypes**: round-yellow seed, round-green seed, wrinkled-yellow seed, wrinkled-green seed.

   The observed results were as follows:

Round-yellow seed	**441**	Wrinkled-yellow seed	**143**
Round-green seed	**159**	Wrinkled-green seed	**57**

   Use a separate piece of paper to complete the following:

   (a) State the null and alternative hypotheses (Ho and HA).

   (b) Calculate the χ^2 value.

   (c) Calculate the degrees of freedom and state the *P* value corresponding to your calculated χ^2 value.

   (d) State whether or not you reject your null hypothesis: reject Ho / do not reject Ho (circle one)

4. Comment on the whether the χ^2 values obtained above are similar. Suggest a reason for any difference:

____

____

____

____

ISBN: 978-1-98-856656-6

91 Non-Mendelian Inheritance

Key Question: What are the characteristics of the most common non-Mendelian inheritance patterns?

Not all genetic crosses follow Mendel's laws. In fact Mendel was fortunate in that the traits he studied in pea plants were associated with genes that were all on different chromosomes and had simple single gene dominant-recessive relationships. Not all genes behave this way, in fact most do not. This activity summarizes different kinds of non-Mendelian inheritance.

Inheritance pattern and description	Examples
Linked genes Linked genes are genes carried on the same chromosome. As a result they do not assort independently.	The genes for the β and δ **hemoglobin proteins** are linked on chromosome 11. They are inherited together. HbA has 2α and 2β chains. HbA2 has 2α and 2δ chains. Dihybrid crosses of linked genes do not follow the expected Mendelian 9:3:3:1 ratio. Emw (left) and Zephyris (right) cc 3.0
Codominance Both alleles are fully expressed in the phenotype. Neither allele is dominant or recessive.	ABO blood group system in humans, roan coat phenotype in cattle and horses, and flower petal color in **camellias**. A monohybrid cross between heterozygotes produces three distinct phenotypes.
Incomplete dominance The effect of one allele does not mask the effect of the other, producing a blend of the two parental phenotypes.	Flower color in **roses**, snapdragons, and four o'clocks. A monohybrid cross between homozygous dominant and recessive genotypes produces an phenotype that is intermediate between the parental phenotypes.
Multiple alleles Genes with more than two alleles in the population (a heterozygote will still possess only two alleles).	The ABO blood group system in humans has alleles A, B, and O. A person could be any combination of two of the alleles. The HLA genes coding for the MHC antigens on cell surfaces (image, right) also have multiple alleles.
Lethal alleles Lethal alleles may be lethal in the homozygote or the heterozygote, and may be dominant or recessive.	**Yellow mice**, Manx gene in cats, Huntington disease in humans. In cases where the lethal condition occurs before birth, the Mendelian ratio is affected as homozygous genotypes are not born.
Sex-linked genes Genes located on sex (X or Y) chromosomes. Many X linked genes do not have a matching gene on the Y chromosome.	**Color-blindness** in humans, hemophilia, orange coat color in cats. Males tend to be more commonly affected because they have only one X chromosome, so the effect of a recessive allele is not masked. X-linked conditions are much more common than those that are Y-linked.
Multiple genes One phenotypic trait is determined by more than one gene (polygeny).	**Skin color**, eye color, height, and hair color are all polygenic traits. Because of the way these genes interact and the influence of environmental factors, polygenic traits often do not show expected Mendelian phenotypic ratios.
Pleiotropy One gene influences two or more seemingly unrelated phenotypic traits.	Phenylketonuria, an inherited disorder affecting levels of the amino acid **phenylalanine**. A defect to one gene affects multiple systems.
Non-nuclear inheritance Some DNA is inherited via mitochondria and (in plants) via the chloroplasts and not via the nuclear DNA.	All your **mitochondria** (and so your mitochondrial DNA) is inherited from your mother at fertilization via mitochondria in her egg cell. In plants, chloroplast DNA is inherited from the female parent via egg cells.

1. Why did Mendel's result not show any of the non-Mendelian inheritance patterns described above? ____________________

2. Why would crosses involving linked genes not produce offspring phenotypes in the ratios expected by Mendelian rules?

3. Explain why a cross between heterozygotes involving codominant alleles produces three distinct phenotypes:

ISBN: 978-1-98-856656-6

92 Codominance

Key Question: How does the equal and independent expression of alleles affect inheritance patterns?

Codominance is an inheritance pattern in which both alleles in a heterozygote contribute to the phenotype and both alleles are independently and equally expressed. Examples include the human blood group AB and roan coat color in horses and cattle. Red coat color is equally dominant with white. Animals with both alleles have coats that are roan (both red and white hairs are present). There are various roan phenotypes depending on the base color (red roan, blue roan etc).

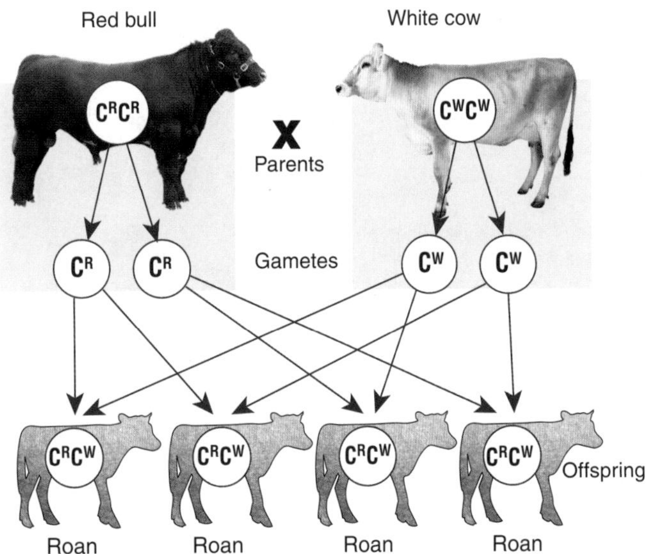

A roan shorthorn heifer

In the shorthorn cattle breed, coat color is inherited. White shorthorn parents always produce calves with white coats. Red parents always produce red calves. However, when a red parent mates with a white one, the calves have a coat color that is different from either parent; a mixture of red and white hairs, called roan. Use the example (left) to help you to solve the problems below.

1. Explain how codominance of alleles can result in offspring with a phenotype that is different from either parent:

____

2. A white bull is mated with a roan cow (right):

   (a) Fill in the spaces to show the genotypes and phenotypes for parents and calves:

   (b) What is the phenotype ratio for this cross?

   ____

   (c) How could a cattle farmer control the breeding so that the herd ultimately consisted of only red cattle:

   ____

   ____

   ____

   ____

   ____

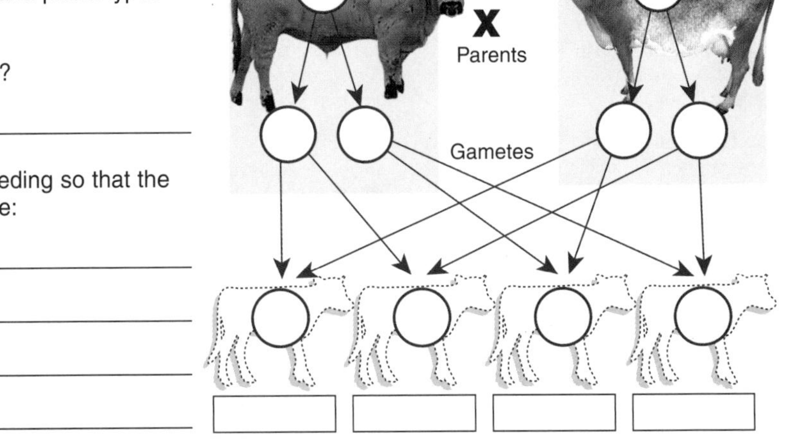

3. A farmer has only roan cattle on his farm. He suspects that one of the neighbors' bulls may have jumped the fence to mate with his cows earlier in the year because half the calves born were red and half were roan. One neighbor has a red bull, the other has a roan.

   (a) Fill in the spaces (right) to show the genotype and phenotype for parents and calves.

   (b) Which bull (red or roan) serviced the cows? ____________

4. Describe the classical phenotypic ratio for a codominant gene resulting from the cross of two heterozygous parents (e.g. a cross between two roan cattle):

____

____

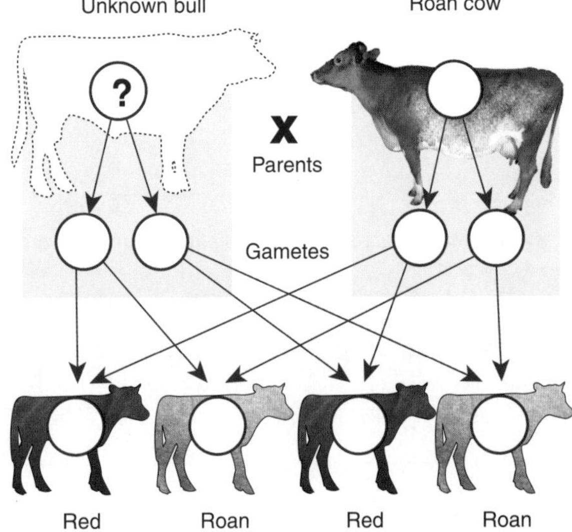

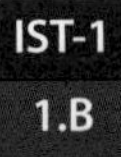

ISBN: 978-1-98-856656-6

- The human ABO blood group system also shows codominance. The four common blood groups of the human 'ABO blood group system' are determined by three alleles: A, B, and O. The ABO antigens consist of sugars attached to the surface of red blood cells. The alleles code for enzymes (proteins) that join these sugars together.
- The allele O is recessive. It produces a non-functioning enzyme that cannot make any changes to the basic sugar molecule.
- The other two alleles (A, B) are codominant and are expressed equally. They each produce a different functional enzyme that adds a different, specific sugar to the basic sugar molecule.
- The blood group A and B antigens are able to react with antibodies present in the blood of other people so blood must always be matched for transfusion.

Recessive allele: ***O*** produces a non-functioning protein
Dominant allele: ***A*** produces an enzyme that forms **A antigen**
Dominant allele: ***B*** produces an enzyme that forms **B antigen**

If a person has the ***AO*** allele combination then their blood group will be group **A**. The presence of the recessive allele has no effect on the blood group in the presence of a dominant allele. Another possible allele combination that can create the same blood group is ***AA***.

5. Use the information above to complete the table for the possible genotypes for blood group B and group AB.

6. Below are four crosses possible between couples of various blood groups. The first example has been completed for you. Complete the genotype and phenotype for the other three crosses below:

Blood group (phenotype)	Possible genotypes	Percentage frequency in North America		
		White	Black	Native American
O	OO	45	49	79
A	AA AO	40	27	16
B		11	20	4
AB		4	4	1

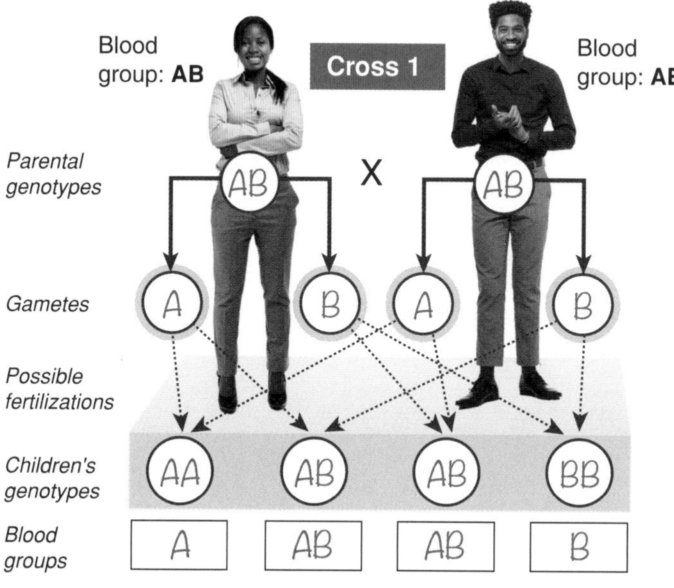

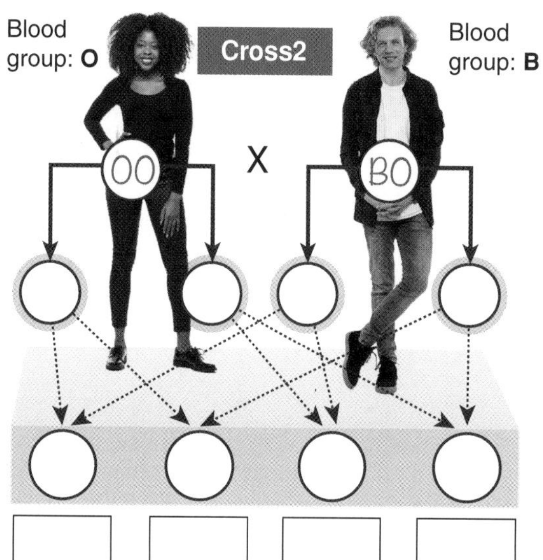

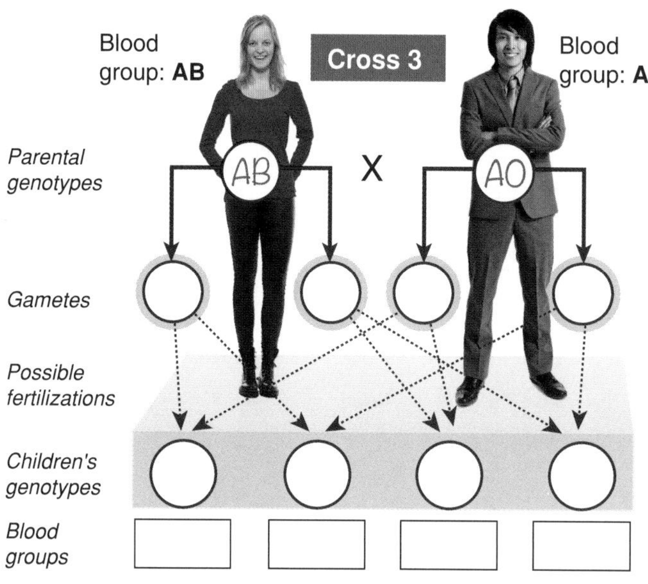

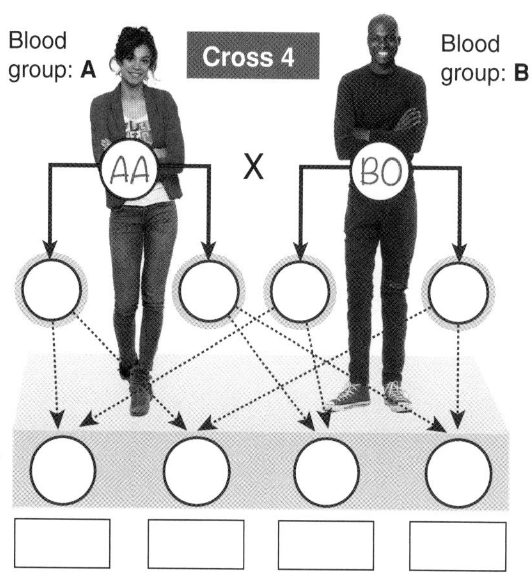

ISBN: 978-1-98-856656-6

93 Incomplete Dominance

Key Question: What is incomplete dominance and how does it affect Mendelian inheritance?

In incomplete dominance the heterozygous offspring are intermediate in phenotype between the contrasting homozygous parental phenotypes. In crosses involving incomplete dominance, the phenotype and genotype ratios are identical. The phenotype of heterozygous offspring results from the partial influence of both alleles. Examples of incomplete dominance includes flower color in snapdragons (*Antirrhinum*) and four o'clocks (*Mirabilis*) (below).

Red flower C^RC^R **X** *Parents* White flower C^WC^W

Gametes C^R C^R C^W C^W

Offspring C^RC^W Pink, C^RC^W Pink, C^RC^W Pink, C^RC^W Pink

Pure breeding snapdragons produce red or white flowers (left). When red and white-flowered parent plants are crossed a pink-flowered offspring is produced. If the offspring (F_1 generation) are then crossed together, all three phenotypes (red, pink, and white) are produced in the F_2 generation.

Four o'clocks (above) are also known to have flower colors controlled by alleles that show incomplete dominance. Pure breeding four o'clocks produce crimson, yellow or white flowers. Crimson flowers (above) crossed with yellow flowers produced reddish-orange flowers, while crimson flowers crossed with white flowers produce magenta (reddish-pink) flowers.

1. Explain how incomplete dominance of alleles differs from complete dominance: ______________________

____

____

____

2. A plant breeder wanted to produce snapdragons for sale that were only pink or white (i.e. no red). Determine the phenotypes of the two parents necessary to produce these desired offspring. Use the Punnett square (right) to help you:

____

____

____

Gametes from male

Gametes from female

3. Another plant breeder crossed two four o'clocks, known to have its flower color controlled by alleles that show incomplete dominance. Pollen from a magenta flowered plant was placed on the stigma of a crimson flowered plant.

(a) Fill in the spaces on the diagram on the right to show the genotype and phenotype for parents and offspring.

(b) State the phenotype ratio:

____

____

____

____

Magenta flower **X** Crimson flower

Gametes

Possible fertilizations

Offspring

Phenotypes

IST-1 1.B

ISBN: 978-1-98-856656-6

94 Lethal Alleles

Key Question: Why do phenotypic outcomes involving lethal alleles not follow expected Mendelian ratios?

Lethal alleles are usually a result of mutations in essential genes. They may result in death of an organism because an essential protein is not produced. Some lethal alleles are lethal in both homozygous dominant and heterozygous conditions. Others are lethal only in the homozygous condition (either dominant or recessive). Furthermore, lethal alleles may take effect at different stages in development, e.g. symptoms of Huntington disease usually appear after 30 years of age.

When Lucien Cuenot investigated inheritance of coat color in yellow mice in 1905, he reported a peculiar pattern.

When he mated two yellow mice, about 2/3 of their offspring were yellow, and 1/3 were non-yellow (a 2:1 ratio). This was a departure from the expected Mendelian ratio of 3:1.

A test cross of the yellow offspring showed that all the yellow mice were heterozygous. No homozygous dominant yellow mice were produced because they had two copies of a lethal allele (Y). The Y allele is a mutation of the wild type agouti gene (A).

Yellow mouse A^YA | Yellow mouse A^YA

Gametes: A^Y, A, A^Y, A

Possible fertilizations

Dead ¼ A^YA^Y | Yellow, Yellow ½ A^YA | Non-yellow ¼ AA

Cats possess a gene for producing a tail. The tailless **Manx** phenotype in cats is produced by an allele that is lethal in the homozygous state. The Manx allele $\mathbf{M^L}$ severely interferes with normal spinal development. In heterozygotes ($\mathbf{M^LM}$), this results in the absence of a tail. In $\mathbf{M^LM^L}$ homozygotes, the double dose of the gene produces an extremely abnormal embryo, which does not survive.

1. In Manx cats, the allele for taillessness ($\mathbf{M^L}$) is incompletely dominant over the recessive allele for normal tail (M). Tailless Manx cats are heterozygous ($\mathbf{M^LM}$) and carry a recessive allele for normal tail. Normal tailed cats are MM. A cross between two Manx (tailless) cats, produces two Manx to every one normal tailed cat (not a regular 3 to 1 ratio).

   (a) Complete the Punnett square for the cross:

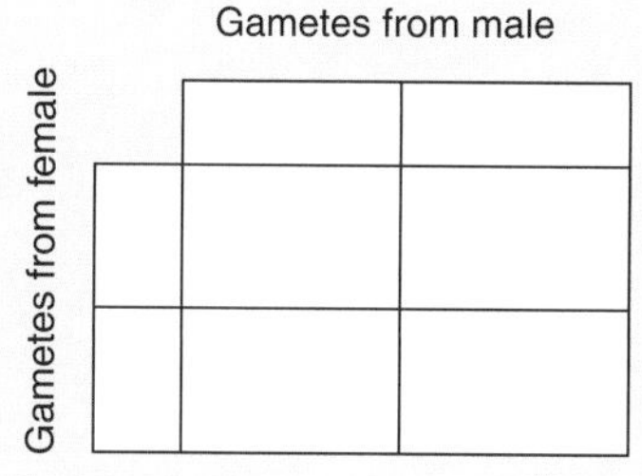

   (b) State the phenotype ratio of Manx to normal cats and explain why it is not the expected 3:1 ratio:

2. Huntington disease (HD) is caused by an autosomal dominant mutation in either of the alleles of the gene Huntingtin. Explain why HD persists in the human population when it is caused by a lethal, dominant allele:

ISBN: 978-1-98-856656-6

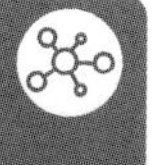

95 Inheritance of Linked Genes

Key Question: What is the effect of linkage on the amount of variation we see in the offspring of genetic crosses?

Genes are **linked** when they are on the same chromosome. Linked genes tend to be inherited together but the further apart they are, the more likely it is that crossing over will occur between them in prophase I. This also means that the extent of crossing over (the frequency of recombination) can be used to work out how close together the genes are. In genetic crosses, linkage is indicated when a greater proportion of the offspring from a cross are of the parental type (than would be expected if the alleles were on separate chromosomes and assorting independently).

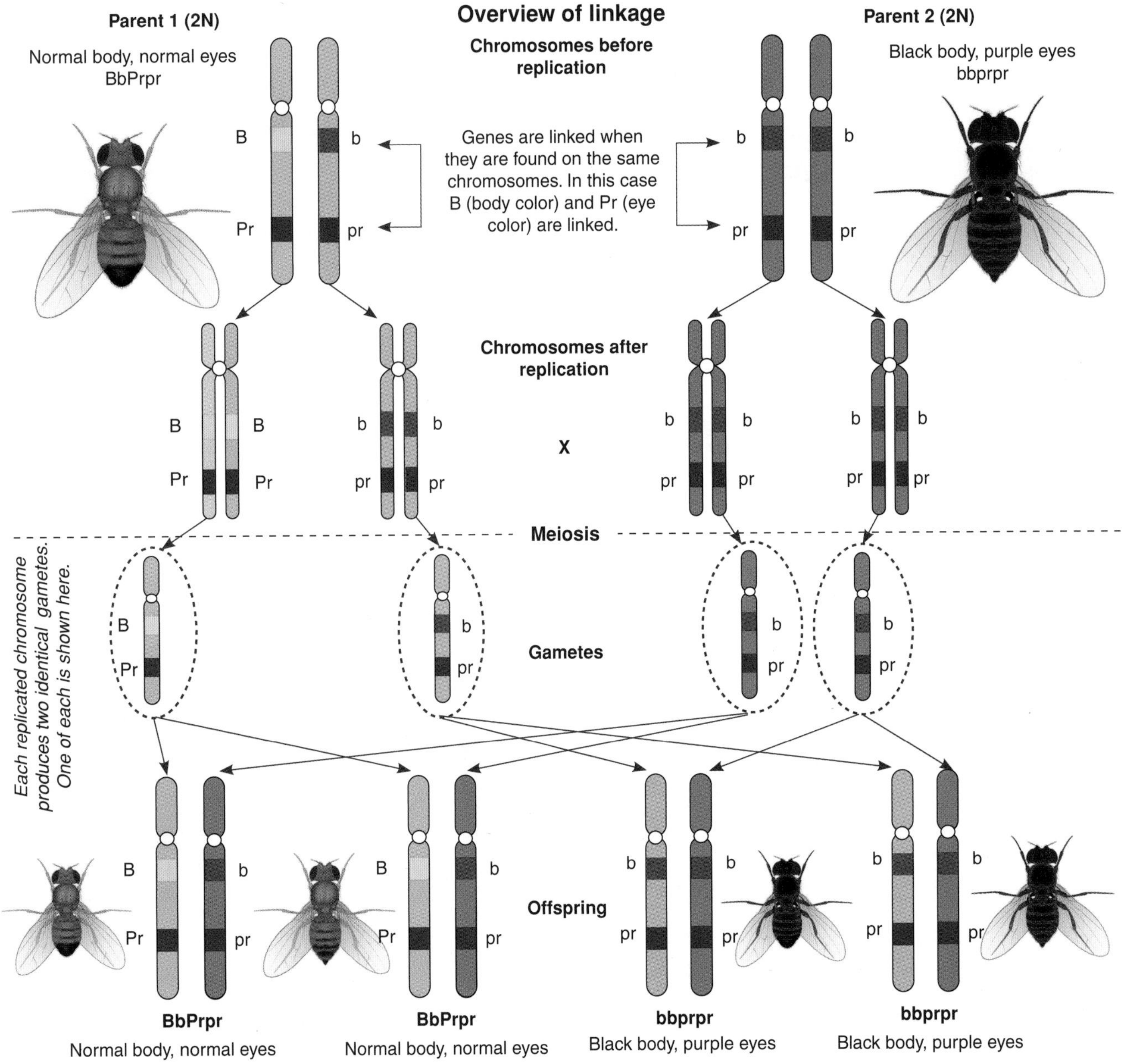

Overview of linkage

Parent 1 (2N)

Normal body, normal eyes
BbPrpr

Parent 2 (2N)

Black body, purple eyes
bbprpr

Chromosomes before replication

B, Pr | b, pr

b, pr | b, pr

Genes are linked when they are found on the same chromosomes. In this case B (body color) and Pr (eye color) are linked.

Chromosomes after replication

B B, Pr Pr | b b, pr pr **X** b b, pr pr | b b, pr pr

Meiosis

Each replicated chromosome produces two identical gametes. One of each is shown here.

Gametes

B, Pr | b, pr | b, pr | b, pr

Offspring

B, Pr / b, pr	B, Pr / b, pr	b, pr / b, pr	b, pr / b, pr
BbPrpr	**BbPrpr**	**bbprpr**	**bbprpr**
Normal body, normal eyes	Normal body, normal eyes	Black body, purple eyes	Black body, purple eyes

Possible offspring

Only two kinds of genotype combinations are possible. They are they same as the parent genotype.

1. What is the effect of linkage on the inheritance of genes? ______________________________

____

____

2. Explain how linkage decreases the amount of genetic variation in the offspring: ______________________________

____

____

____

ISBN: 978-1-98-856656-6

An example of linked genes in *Drosophila*

The genes for wing shape and body color are linked (they are on the same chromosome)

Parent	Wild type female	Mutant male
Phenotype	Straight wing Gray body	Curled wing Ebony body
Genotype	Cucu Ebeb	cucu ebeb

Linkage

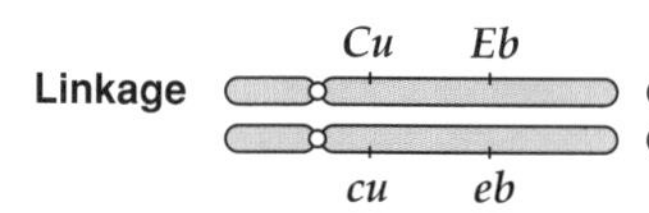

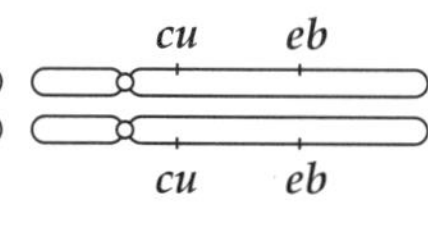

Meiosis

Gametes from female fly (N) Gametes from male fly (N)

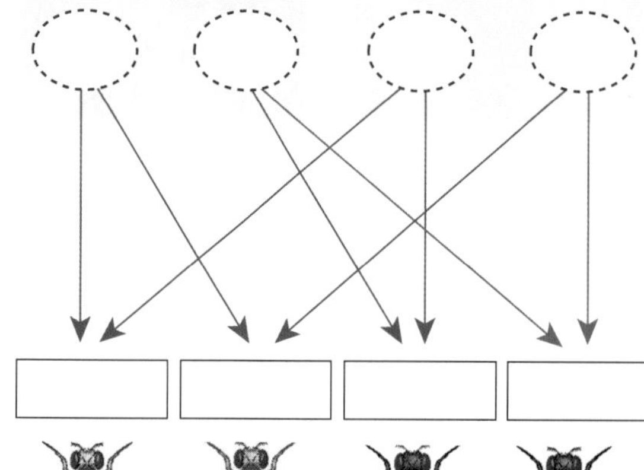

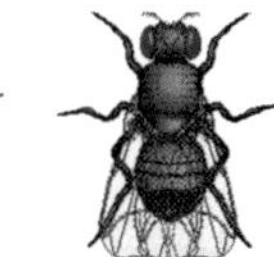

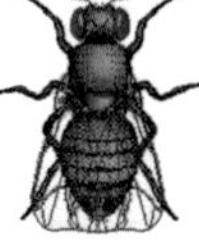

Drosophila and linked genes

In the example shown left, wild type alleles are dominant and are given an upper case symbol of the mutant phenotype (Cu or Eb). This notation used for *Drosophila* departs from the convention of using the dominant gene to provide the symbol. This is necessary because there are many mutant alternative phenotypes to the wild type (e.g. curled and vestigial wings). A lower case symbol of the wild type (e.g. ss for straight wing) would not indicate the mutant phenotype involved.

Drosophila melanogaster is known as a **model organism**. Model organisms are used to study particular biological phenomena, such as mutation. *Drosophila melanogaster* is particularly useful because it produces such a wide range of heritable mutations. Its short reproduction cycle, high offspring production, and low maintenance in culture make it ideal for studying in the lab.

Drosophila showing variations in eye and body color. The wild type is marked with a **w** in the photo above. The body is a gray-yellow (denoted gray) and the eyes are red.

3. Complete the linkage diagram above by adding the gametes in the ovals and offspring genotypes in the rectangles.

4. (a) List the possible genotypes in the offspring (above, left) if genes Cu and Eb had been on **separate chromosomes**:

   (b) If the female *Drosophila* had been homozygous for the dominant wild type alleles (CuCu EbEb), state:

   The genotype(s) of the F_1: The phenotype(s) of the F_1:

5. A second pair of *Drosophila* are mated. The female genotype is Vgvg EbEb (straight wings, gray body), while the male genotype is vgvg ebeb (vestigial wings, ebony body). Assuming the genes are linked, carry out the cross and list the genotypes and phenotypes of the offspring. Note vg = vestigial (no) wings:

   The genotype(s) of the F_1: The phenotype(s) of the F_1:

6. Explain why *Drosophila* is often used as a model organism in the study of genetics:

ISBN: 978-1-98-856656-6

96 Mapping Chromosomes Using Linked Genes

***STUDENT SUPPORT FOR INVESTIGATION 7, Part 5:** Meiosis and crossing over*

Identifying offspring genotype frequencies

- Recall that linked genes do not assort independently. As a result, the offspring will have the parental phenotype. Also recall that linked genes can be exchanged between non-sister chromatids during crossing over at a frequency determined by their distance apart. If this happens, genetic crosses will produce recombinant offspring, which will have a phenotype different from either parent. The further apart the linked genes are on the chromosome, the more likely it is that they will cross over.
- These three ideas can then be used to work out the relative distances of genes from each other. Genes close to each other will cross over less often and fewer recombinants will be produced than if the genes are more distant from each other.
- The method below shows how to work out the distance between two genes in **map units** or centimorgans (cM). The cM was named after Thomas Hunt Morgan who discovered genes as the unit of heredity and worked on gene linkage using *Drosophila*.

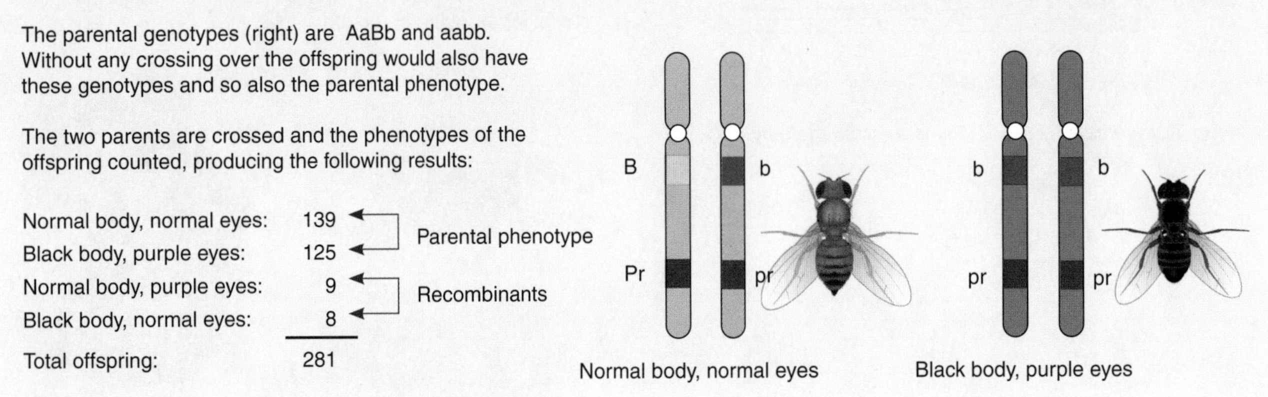

The parental genotypes (right) are AaBb and aabb. Without any crossing over the offspring would also have these genotypes and so also the parental phenotype.
The two parents are crossed and the phenotypes of the offspring counted, producing the following results:
Normal body, normal eyes: 139
Black body, purple eyes: 125
Normal body, purple eyes: 9
Black body, normal eyes: 8
Total offspring: 281
Parental phenotype
Recombinants
B
b
Pr
pr
Normal body, normal eyes
b
b
pr
pr
Black body, purple eyes

The crossover value is calculated from the number of recombinants and the total number of offspring.

The crossover value is then used to produce the map unit or centimorgan.

Each percent of crossover is equivalent to one centimorgan. So a crossover value of 30% is equal to 30 centimorgans

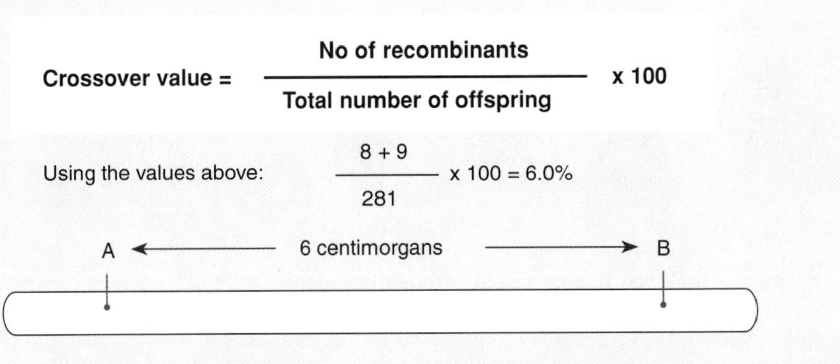

Crossover value = No of recombinants / Total number of offspring x 100
Using the values above: 8 + 9 / 281 x 100 = 6.0%
A
6 centimorgans
B

The known map distances between pairs of genes can be used to build up a map of the genes on a chromosome. For example if the genes A, B, and C had the crossover values of A-B 22%, B-C 12%, and A-C 10% then the chromosome map is:

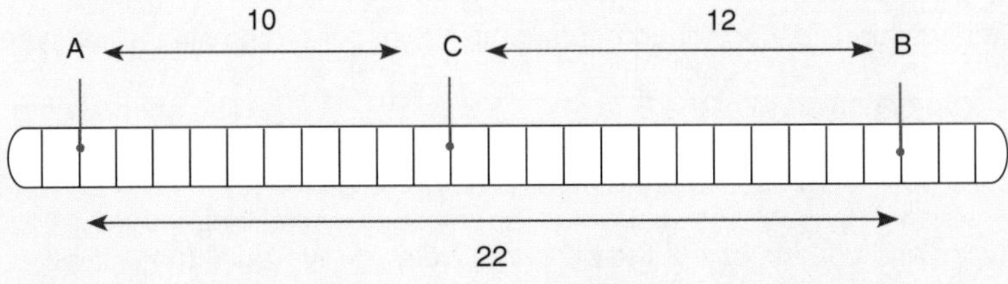

1. *Drosophila* males with the phenotype gray body, normal wings (BbVgvg) were crossed with females with the phenotype black body, vestigial wings (bbvgvg). The genes for these phenotypes are known to be *Drosophila*'s chromosome 2. The resulting offspring have the phenotypes: gray body, normal wings (964), black body, vestigial wings (945), gray body, vestigial wings (207), and black body, normal wings (184).

   (a) Identify the recombinant phenotypes: ______

   (b) What is the total number of recombinants? ______

   (c) What is the total number of offspring? ______

   (d) Calculate the distance between the two genes in centimorgans: ______

   (e) Would you say these genes are relatively close to each other or far away? ______

ISBN: 978-1-98-856656-6

97 Detecting Linkage in Dihybrid Crosses

Key Question: How can we detect linkage between genes? Shortly after the rediscovery of Mendel's work early in the 20th century, it became apparent that his ratios of 9:3:3:1 for heterozygous dihybrid crosses did not always hold true. Experiments on sweet peas by William Bateson and Reginald Punnett, and on *Drosophila* by Thomas Hunt Morgan, showed that there appeared to be some kind of coupling between many of the genes they studied. This coupling, which we now know to be linkage, did not follow any genetic relationship known at the time.

Pedigree for nail-patella syndrome

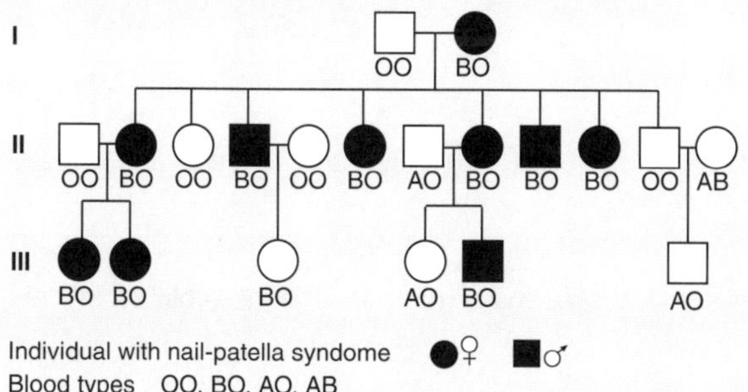

Linked genes can be detected by pedigree analysis. The diagram above shows the pedigree for the inheritance of nail-patella syndrome, which results in small, poorly developed nails and kneecaps in affected people. The nail-patella syndrome gene is linked to the ABO blood group locus.

Sweet pea cross

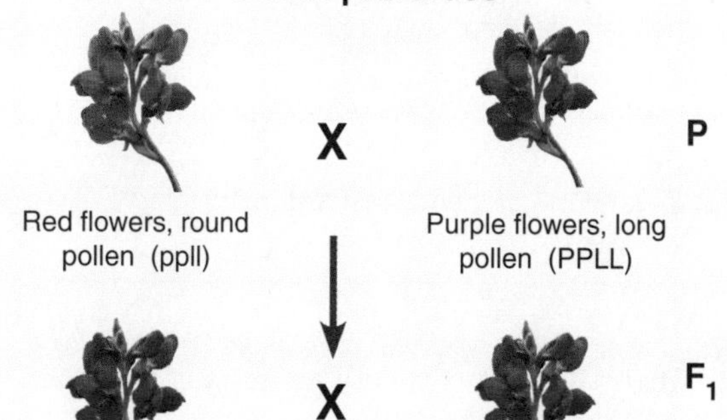

Bateson and Punnett studied sweet peas in which purple flowers (P) are dominant to red (p), and long pollen grains (L) are dominant to round (l). If these genes were unlinked, the outcome of an cross between two heterozygous sweet peas should have been a 9:3:3:1 phenotypic ratio.

Table 1: Sweet pea cross results

	Observed	Expected
Purple long (P_L_)	284	
Purple round (P_ll)	21	
Red long (ppL_)	21	
Red round (ppll)	55	
Total	381	381

1. Fill in the missing numbers in the **expected** column of **Table 1**, remembering that a 9:3:3:1 ratio is expected:

2. (a) Fill in the missing numbers in the **expected** column of **Table 2**, remembering that a 1:1:1:1 ratio is expected:

   (b) Add the gamete type (parental/recombinant) to the gamete type column in Table 2:

   (c) What type of cross did Morgan perform here?

3. (a) Use the pedigree chart above to determine if nail-patella syndrome is dominant or recessive, giving reasons for your choice:

   (b) What evidence is there that nail-patella syndrome is linked to the ABO blood group locus?

   (c) Suggest a likely reason why individual III-3 is not affected despite carrying the B allele:

Drosophila cross

Morgan performed experiments to investigate linked genes in *Drosophila*. He crossed a heterozygous red-eyed normal-winged (Prpr Vgvg) fly with a homozygous purple-eyed vestigial-winged (prpr vgvg) fly. The table (below) shows the outcome of the cross.

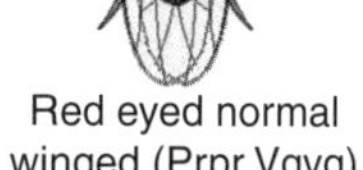
X

Red eyed normal winged (Prpr Vgvg)

Purple eyed vestigial winged (prpr vgvg)

Table 2: *Drosophila* cross results

Genotype	Observed	Expected	Gamete type
Prpr Vgvg	1339		Parental
prpr Vgvg	152		
Prpr vgvg	154		
prpr vgvg	1195		
Total	2840	2840	

ISBN: 978-1-98-856656-6

95 IST-1 5.C IST-1 5.A

4. A group of students bred two corn plants together. The first corn plant was known to have grown from a kernel that was colorless (c) and did not have a waxy endosperm (w). The second corn plant was grown from a seed that was colored (C) but with a waxy endosperm (W). When the corn plant (offspring) matured, the students removed a corn ear and counted the different phenotypes in the corn kernels.

The students noticed the observed results of the cross are presented (right). From the results the students argued:

(1) The plant with the dominant phenotype must have been heterozygous for both traits.

(2) The genes for kernel color and endosperm waxiness must be linked (on the same chromosome).

Observed results of corn kernels

Colored, waxy	**201**	Colorless, waxy	**86**
Colored, not waxy	**85**	Colorless, not waxy	**210**

(a) Defend the students' first argument: ______________________________

____

(b) Use a chi-squared test to provide evidence for or against the students' second argument. Use the table of critical values for χ^2 at different *P* values on page 163.

(i) State your null hypothesis for this investigation (H_0): ______________________________

____

(ii) State the alternative hypothesis (H_A): ______________________________

____

(iii) Enter the observed and expected values (number of individuals) and complete the table to calculate the χ^2 value.

Category	O	E	O – E	$(O – E)^2$	$(O – E)^2/E$
Colored - waxy					
Colored - not waxy					
Colorless - waxy					
Colorless - not waxy					
					Σ

(d) Calculate the χ^2 value using the equation: $\chi^2 = \sum \frac{(O - E)^2}{E}$

(e) Calculate the degrees of freedom: ______________________________

(f) Using the χ^2 table, state the P value corresponding to your calculated χ^2 value: ______________________________

(g) State your decision: reject H_0 / do not reject H_0 : ______________________________

5. Use the data for the sweet pea F_1 cross (previous page) to determine if the genes for flower color and pollen shape are in fact linked or unlinked.

(a) State the null hypothesis for the test: ______________________________

____

Category	O	E	O – E	$(O – E)^2$	$(O – E)^2/E$
Purple-long					
Purple-round					
Red-long					
Red-round					
					Σ

(b) Calculate chi-squared value as above:

(c) State your decision: reject H_0 / do not reject H_0 : ______________________________

ISBN: 978-1-98-856656-6

98 Sex Linkage

Key Question: How do X-linked sex linked genes affect the expression of phenotypic traits in males?

Sex linkage occurs when a gene is located on a sex chromosome (usually the X). The result of this is that the character encoded by the gene is commonly seen only in the sex with two differing sex chromosomes. In humans, recessive sex linked genes cause a number of heritable disorders in males, e.g. hemophilia. Women who have a recessive allele are **carriers**. X-linked inheritance is also common in the genes determining some coat colors in cats.

X-linkage in cats

One of the gene loci controlling coat color in cats is sex-linked. The two alleles, red and non-red (or black), are found only on the X-chromosome. When sex linkage affects the X-chromosome, it is often called X-linkage.

Allele types	Genotypes		Phenotypes
X_o = Black	X_oX_o, X_oY	=	Black coated female, male
X_O = Red	X_OX_O, X_OY	=	Orange coated female, male
	X_OX_o	=	Tortoiseshell (black and orange in fur) in female cats only

1. An owner of a cat is thinking of mating her black female cat with an orange male cat. Before she does this, she would like to know what possible coat colors could result from such a cross. Use the symbols above to fill in the diagram on the right. Summarize the possible genotypes and phenotypes of the kittens in the tables below.

	Genotypes	Phenotypes
Male kittens		

	Genotypes	Phenotypes
Female kittens		

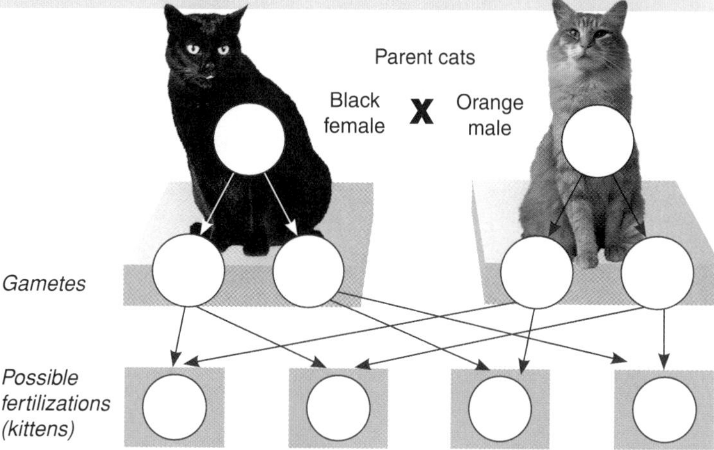

2. A female tortoiseshell cat mated with an unknown male cat in the neighborhood and has given birth to a litter of six kittens. The owner of this female cat wants to know what the appearance and the genotype of the father was of these kittens.

   Use the symbols above to fill in the diagram on the right.

   Describe the father cat's:

   (a) Genotype: ______________________

   (b) Phenotype: ______________________

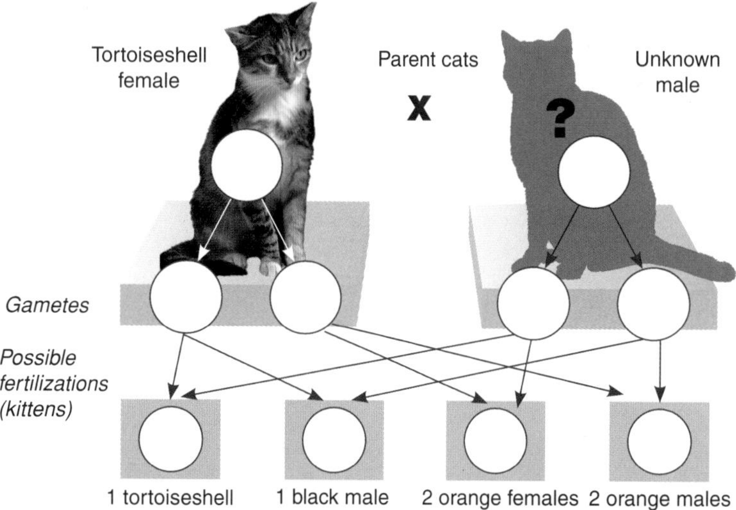

3. The owner of another cat, a black female, also wants to know which cat fathered her two tortoiseshell female and two black male kittens.

   Use the symbols above to fill in the diagram on the right.

   Describe the father cat's:

   (a) Genotype: ______________________

   (b) Phenotype: ______________________

   (c) Was it the same male cat that fathered both this litter and the one above?

   ____

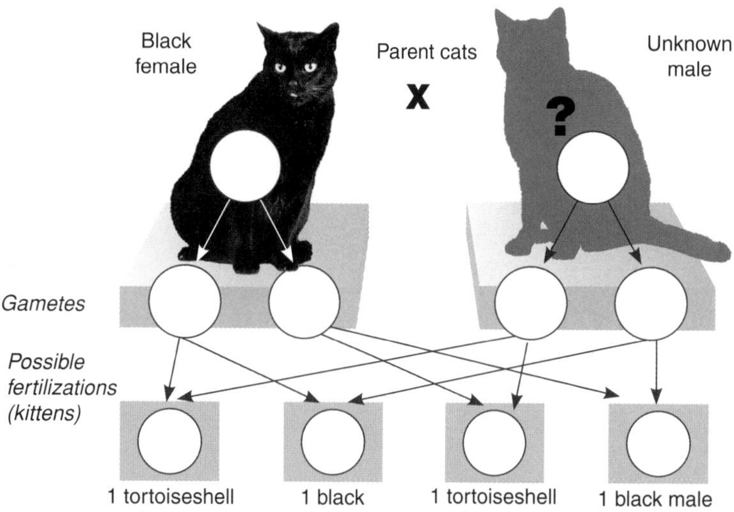

ISBN: 978-1-98-856656-6

Inheritance of sex-linked recessive traits in humans

Inheritance of **hemophilia** is sex linked. Hemophilia impairs the body's blood clotting, so that hemophiliacs suffer uncontrolled bleeding. Males with the recessive (hemophilia) allele, are affected. Females can be carriers. The allele types, genotypes, and phenotypes are as follows:

Allele types	Genotypes		Phenotypes
X^h = hemophilia	XX, XY	=	Affected female
X = normal	X^hY	=	Affected male
	XX^h	=	Carrier female
	X^hX^h	=	Affected female
	XX, XY	=	Unaffected female, male

4. Using the information for sex-linked hemophilia above:

   (a) Enter the parent phenotypes and complete the Punnett square for a cross between an unaffected male and a carrier female.

Female parent

Male parent

   (b) What is the probability of child being hemophiliac?

   ____

5. **X-linked recessive traits** can be identified in a pedigree because if a female shows a trait, so too must all her sons as well as her father.

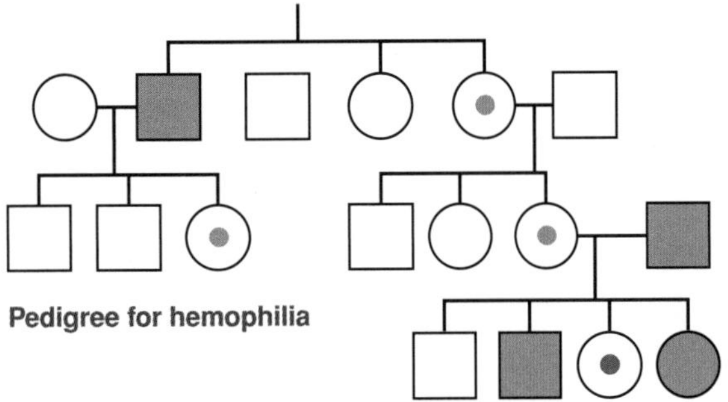

Pedigree for hemophilia

In the pedigree above, can an unaffected mother have affected sons? Explain:

____

____

6. Explain why males much more likely to inherit X-linked recessive disorders than females:

____

____

____

____

____

____

Inheritance of sex-linked dominant traits in humans

A rare form of **rickets** in humans is determined by a dominant allele of a gene on the X chromosome (there is no copy on the Y chromosome). This condition is not successfully treated with vitamin D therapy. The allele types, genotypes, and phenotypes are as follows:

Allele types	Genotypes		Phenotypes
X^R = Rickets	X^RX^R, X^RX	=	Affected female
X = Normal	X^RY	=	Affected male
	XX, XY	=	Unaffected female, male

7. Using the information for sex-linked rickets above:

   (a) Enter the parent phenotypes and complete the Punnett square for a cross between an affected male and an unaffected female.

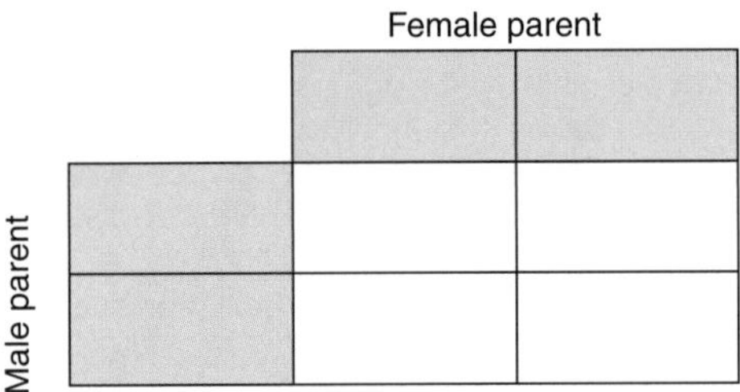

   (b) Determine the probability of having an affected girl:

   ____

8. **X-linked dominant traits** can be identified in a pedigree because if a male shows the trait, so must all his daughters as well as his mother.

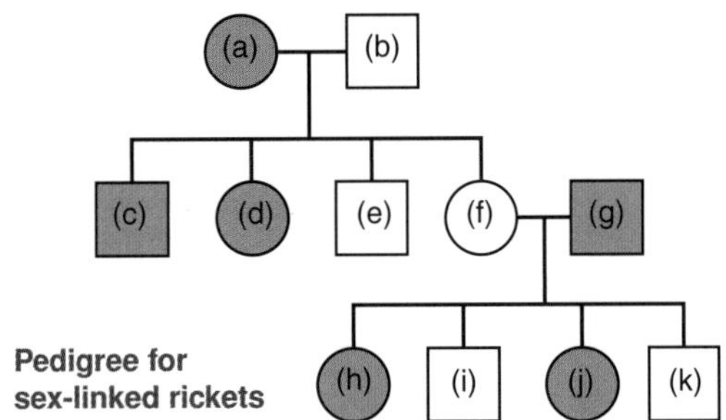

Pedigree for sex-linked rickets

Identify the genotypes in the pedigree above:

(a) __________ (e) __________ (i) __________

(b) __________ (f) __________ (j) __________

(c) __________ (g) __________ (k) __________

d) __________ (h) __________

9. In the pedigree above, can an unaffected mother have affected sons (or an affected father)? Explain:

____

____

____

____

____

ISBN: 978-1-98-856656-6

99 How Sex Determination Affects Inheritance

Key Question: How is sex determined in different species?

The determination of the sex of an organism is controlled in most cases by the sex chromosomes provided by each parent. These have evolved to regulate the ratios of males and females produced and preserve the genetic differences between the sexes. In humans, males are the heterogametic sex because each somatic cell has one X and one Y chromosome. The determination of sex is based on the presence or absence of the Y chromosome. Without the Y, an individual will develop into a female. In mammals, the male is always the heterogametic sex, but this is not necessarily the case in other animal taxa. In birds and butterflies, the female is the heterogametic sex, and in some insects the male is simply X whereas the female is XX.

The XY type

Female: XX Male XY

Examples: Mammals (including humans), fruit flies (*Drosophila*), some dioecious (separate male and female) plants such as kiwifruit.

The female is homogametic and has two similar sex chromosomes (XX) and the male is the heterogametic sex with two unlike chromosomes (XY). The primary sexual characteristics (possessing ovaries, uterus, breasts etc.) are initiated by special genes on the X chromosomes. Females must have a double dose (2X chromosomes). Maleness is determined by the presence of the Y chromosome.

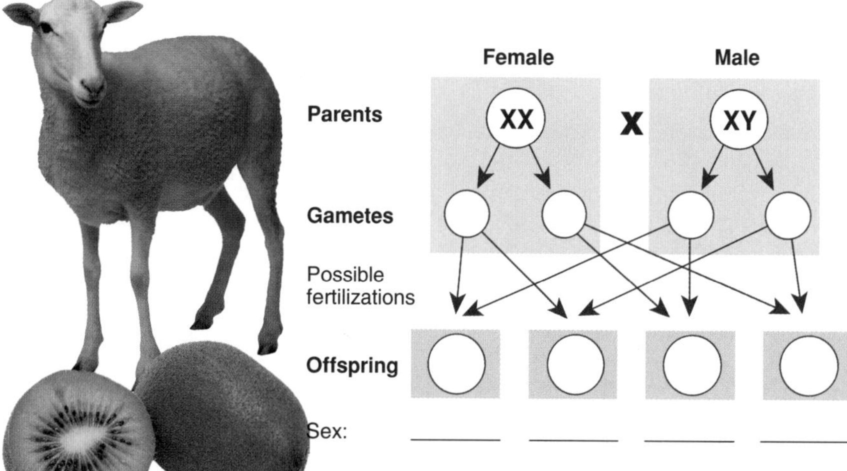

The XO type

Female: XX Male XO

Examples: Grasshoppers and relatives, aphids, honeybees, many true bugs.

In some insect orders, the female has two sex chromosomes while the male only has one (a system called haplodiploidy). In sperm produced by males, there is a 50% chance that it will have a sex chromosome and create a female offspring when it fertilizes an egg.

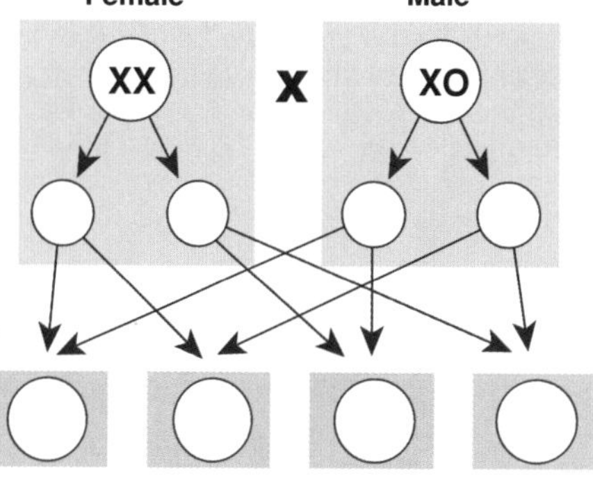

The WZ type

Female: WZ Male ZZ

Examples: Birds, lepidopterans (butterflies and moths), some fish.

The male is the homogametic sex with two chromosomes of the same type, while the female has two differing kinds of sex chromosome. Unlike the two other sex determination mechanisms described above, it is the female that determines the sex of the offspring.

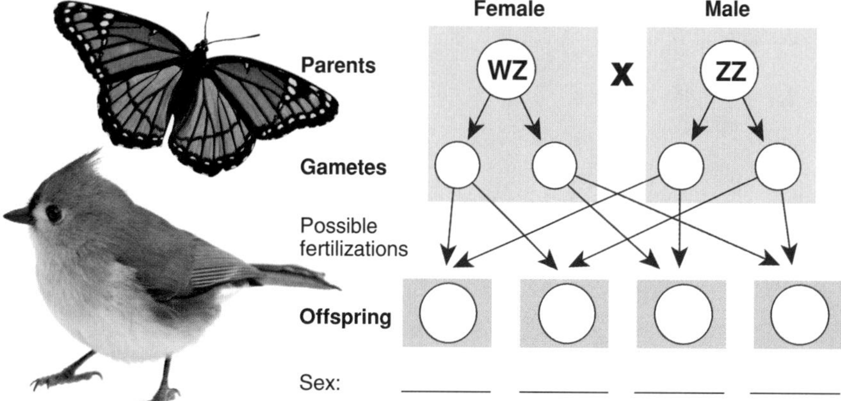

1. Complete the diagrams above, to show the resulting gametes, genotype and sex of the offspring:

2. Explain what determines the sex of the offspring at the moment of conception in humans: ____________________

3. Distinguish between the different modes of sex determination in animals: ____________________

ISBN: 978-1-98-856656-6

100 Multiple Genes

Key Question: How do multiple genes affect phenotypes?

Many phenotypes are controlled by more than one gene, a situation known as polygeny or polygenic inheritance. As there are many genes and therefore many alleles controlling the phenotype, there are a large range of possible phenotypes. Combined with environmental effects, this produces **continuous variation** within the population. Two examples in humans are skin color and height.

Polygenic traits

Polygenic traits are usually identified by

- Traits are usually quantified by measuring rather than counting.
- Two or more genes contribute to the phenotype.
- Phenotypic expression is over a wide range (often in a bell shaped curve).
- Polygenic phenotypes include skin color, height, eye color, and weight.

It is estimated that skin color is controlled by at least eight genes (probably more). There are various ways to compare skin color. One is shown right, in which there are seven shades ranging from very pale to very dark. Most individuals are somewhat intermediate in skin color.

Very pale	Light	Medium light	Medium	Medium dark	Dark	Black
0	1	2	3	4	5	6

The table below shows the results of an F_1 cross involving three genes for skin color, A, B, and C, each with two alleles (AaBbCc x AaBbCc). This is sufficient to give the seven shades of skin color shown above. The shaded boxes indicate their effect on skin color when combined. No dominant allele results in a lack of dark pigment (aabbcc). Full pigmentation (black) requires six dominant alleles (AABBCC). Note that for three genes with two alleles each there are $2^3 \times 2^3 = 8 \times 8 = 64$ possible genotypes. How many would there be if eight genes were included in the table?

Gametes	ABC	ABc	AbC	Abc	aBC	aBc	abC	abc
ABC	AABB CC	AABB Cc	AABb CC	AABb Cc	AaBB CC	AaBB Cc	AaBb CC	AaBb Cc
ABc	AABB Cc	AABB cc	AABb Cc	AABb cc	AaBB Cc	AaBB cc	AaBb Cc	AaBb cc
AbC	AABb CC	AABb Cc	AAbb CC	AAbb Cc	AaBb CC	AaBb Cc	Aabb Cc	Aabb Cc
Abc	AABb Cc	AABb cc	AAbb Cc	AAbb cc	AaBb Cc	AaBb cc	Aabb Cc	Aabb cc
aBC	AaBB CC	AaBB Cc	AaBb CC	AaBb Cc	aaBB CC	aaBB Cc	aaBb CC	aaBb Cc
aBc	AaBB Cc	AaBB cc	AaBb Cc	AaBb cc	aaBB Cc	aaBB cc	aaBb Cc	aaBb cc
abC	AaBb CC	AaBb Cc	Aabb CC	Aabb Cc	aaBb CC	aaBb Cc	aabb CC	aabb Cc
abc	AaBb Cc	AaBb cc	Aabb Cc	Aabb cc	aaBb Cc	aaBb cc	aabb Cc	aabb cc

A dark knight to rescue the fair maiden?

Read a fairy tale and inevitably the princess is fair-complexioned and light of hair. The knight sent to save her is darker or tanned, with wild black or dark hair. Really? It's just a fairy tale, isn't it?... Well, not entirely.

Research shows that, in any human population, women on average have a lighter skin color than men. In European populations, women have skin 15.2% lighter than men while, in African populations, women have skin 11.1% lighter than men. The same research shows men are generally attracted to women with lighter skin, whereas women are attracted to men with darker skin.

Why? Although preference is undoubtedly linked to cultural values, there is an evolutionary advantage for women to have lighter skin. It enables them to absorb more UV light, which helps manufacture the vitamin D needed to absorb calcium from the diet. High calcium levels are needed for pelvic development, the development of the fetal skeleton, and to produce milk to feed the growing infant.

So, is there something in those old fairy tales after all?

1. (a) What is polygeny? ______

   (b) How does polygeny contribute to continuous variation? ______

2. Identify two continuous phenotypic characteristics in humans and explain why the they are continuous: ______

3. Study the cross between the A, B, and C genes above. Write down the frequencies of the seven phenotypes (0-6): ______

ISBN: 978-1-98-856656-6

4. Explain the differences between continuous and discontinuous variation, giving examples to illustrate your answer:

5. From a sample of no less than 30 adults (or similar aged teenagers), collect data (by request or measurement) for one continuous variable (e.g. height, foot length, or hand span). Record and tabulate your results in the space below, and then plot a frequency histogram of the data on the grid below:

Raw data

Tally chart (frequency table)

Variable: ....

Frequency

(a) Calculate the following for your data and attach your working:

Mean: ______ **Mode**: ______ **Median**: ______

Standard deviation: ______

(b) Describe the pattern of distribution shown by the graph, giving a reason for your answer:

(c) What is the genetic basis of this distribution?

(d) What is the importance of a large sample size when gathering data relating to a continuous variable?

ISBN: 978-1-98-856656-6

101 Non-Nuclear Inheritance

Key Question: How is the DNA in mitochondria (mtDNA) and chloroplasts (cpDNA) transmitted?

Mitochondrial and chloroplast DNA replicates independently of the main genome and contains genes essential for that organelle's function, e.g. mitochondrial DNA contains genes for producing some of the proteins associated with the electron transport chain. Mitochondria and chloroplasts are passed on via the maternal line. Because mitochondria and chloroplasts are distributed randomly in gametes, the traits determined by their genes do not follow simple Mendelian rules.

Mitochondrial DNA

In most multicellular organisms, the mtDNA and cpDNA are inherited via the maternal line. Mitochondria in the cytoplasm are randomly divided between dividing primary oocytes so that the final egg cell has a random selection of mitochondria from the original cell. Mitochondria are numerous in sperm cells, providing the energy to power the tail. However, they do not enter the egg cell, or are destroyed by enzymes within it. Human mtDNA encodes 13 proteins associated with oxidative phosphorylation.

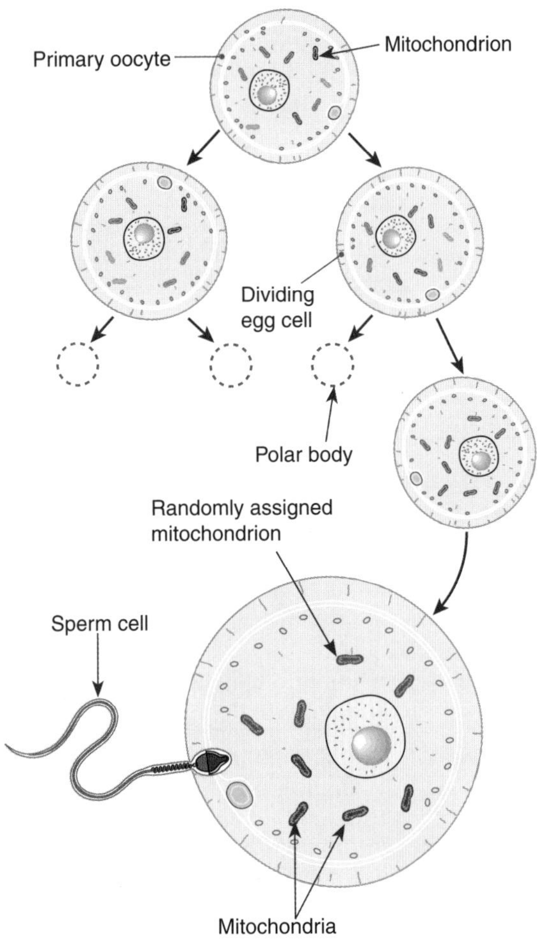

Chloroplast DNA

In 1909, Carl Correns, a German geneticist, noticed that the branches of the four o'clock (*Mirabilis jalapa*) developed leaves that could be green, white, or variegated (green and white). After performing a series of crosses, Correns noticed that seeds from branches with solid green leaves grew into plants with solid green leaves, even if the pollen was from a branch with white or variegated leaves (below).

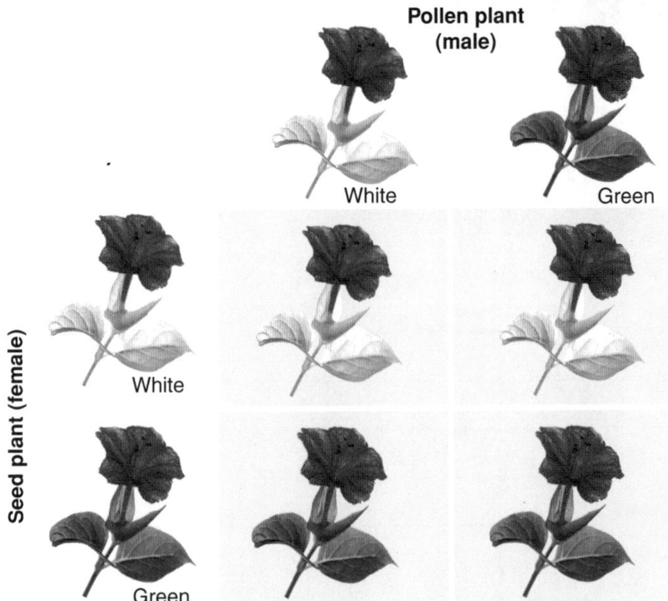

- Seeds from branches with variegated leaves produced plants with all three leaf types. Again, where the pollen came from did not matter. In addition, the appearance of these three types was never in any predictable Mendelian ratio.
- Correns concluded that the trait was being passed via the maternal line. We now know a defect in the cpDNA of the four o'clock causes the white color and these, like mitochondria, are passed randomly to the offspring.

1. (a) Explain why mtDNA and cpDNA are only passed along the maternal line: ______

   (b) Explain why the inheritance patterns of mtDNA and cpDNA do not follow predictable Mendelian rules?

2. mtDNA and cpDNA are inherited via the maternal line. Each type of DNA tends to mutate at a predicable rate. Explain how this information can be used to trace lineage:

ISBN: 978-1-98-856656-6

102 Environmental Effects on Phenotype

Key Question: How does the external or internal environment affect the development of an organism?

The development of an organism is influenced by its genome and a combination of environmental factors. The effects might be very obvious, such as differences in growth as a result of differences in nutrition (in animals) or soil chemistry (in plants), or they can be more subtle, such as differences in susceptibility to disease as a result of epigenetic tagging.

- **Cancers** are caused by a complex interaction of the environment, genes, and epigenetic factors. The relatively new field of epigenetics (meaning "on top of genetics") is highlighting the role of gene-environment interactions in gene expression. **Epigenetics** alters the way the genes are read and expressed **but not the genes themselves**.
- Epigenetic processes include DNA methylation (in which methyl groups are added to cysteine bases in DNA) and histone modification. There is increasing evidence that lifestyle, including diets high in sugars, high alcohol consumption, obesity, and lack of exercise, cause epigenetic changes to the DNA encoding microRNAs, which have roles in gene regulation.
- One example is the microRNA miR-182, which has a role in regulating the *BRCA1* gene. *BRCA1* is a tumor suppressor gene and produces a protein that helps repair DNA. Epigenetic modifications increase the activity of miR-182 which in turn decreases *BRCA1* activity, which can lead to breast cancer.

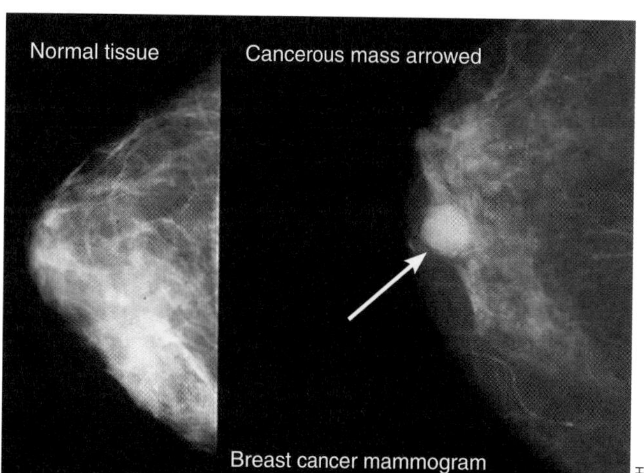

Breast cancer mammogram

Snowshoe hares are well known for their change of coat color as the seasons change. During fall, the hares molt, replacing their brown coat with white. In spring, the brown coat replaces white. The change in coat color is triggered by changes in day length and regulated by hormonal changes. Little is known about the genes involved in the color change but a 2014 study showed at least 568 genes were differentially expressed between the white coat stage and the brown coat stage, while another 186 were involved in the molt from white to brown.

The transition from white to brown and back helps with camouflaging the hare and so reducing predation. Because the change is based on the photoperiod and not temperature some scientists have expressed concerns over the effect of global warming and a mismatch of the environment and the timing of the color change.

Winter morph

Summer morph

Saccharomyces cerevisiae has two mating types, a and α (both haploid). The presence of pheromones (signaling molecules between organisms) from either type can induce the other to express genes that code for proteins that inhibit the cell cycle. The two cells fuse to form a diploid cell. This grows and, under starvation, begins meiosis, producing four haploid spores. Under the right conditions these germinate and undergo mitotic growth.

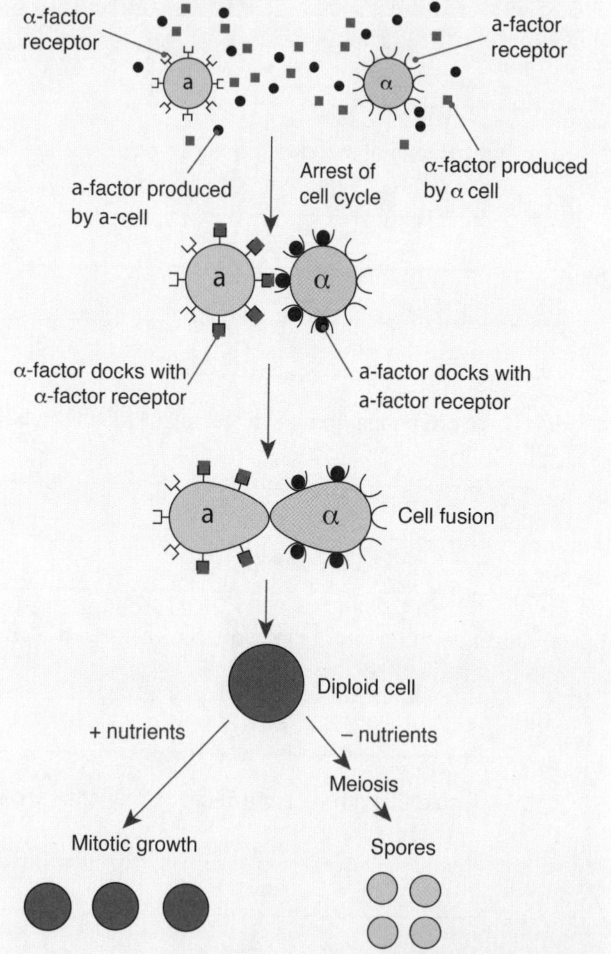

ISBN: 978-1-98-856656-6

Plants respond to herbivores in a variety of ways including increasing trichome (leaf hair) density with increasing herbivory and increasing the concentration of distasteful chemicals in their leaves. Observations of *Acacia* trees in Kenya noted those that were regularly browsed had significantly longer thorns than unbrowsed trees. What's more, trees that were regularly pruned also produced longer thorns. Together with this, leaves were longer at the tops of the trees (above 5 m) than lower down where they were shorter than the thorns, presumably to avoid browse damage by giraffes and other herbivores.

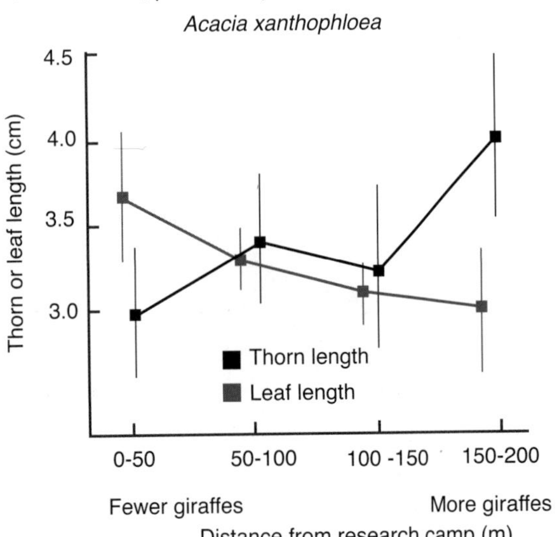

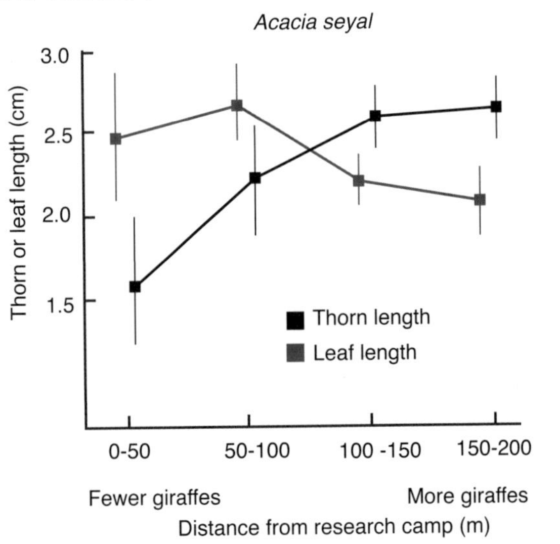

A. Milewski *et. al.* (1990). See credits for full citation

1. What is epigenetics and what role does it play in determining phenotype?

2. Using an example, explain how lifestyle factors and epigenetic changes can lead to cancers:

3. Explain the cause of a snowshoe hare's color change and its survival advantages:

4. How do pheromones from an 'a' yeast cell affect the behavior of an 'α' yeast cell?

5. (a) Describe the effect of herbivore browsing on the phenotype of *Acacia* trees:

   (b) Why would this growth pattern occur only after browsing damage?

ISBN: 978-1-98-856656-6

How do chemicals affect hydrangea flowers?

- Changes in the chemical environment influence flower color in hydrangeas (right). They have blue flowers when they are grown in acidic soil (pH <7.0) and pink flowers when grown in neutral to basic soils (≥ 7.0).
- The color change is a result of the mobility and availability of aluminum ions (Al^{3+}) at different pH.
- At low pH Al^{3+} is highly mobile. It binds with other ions and is taken up into the plant, reacting with the usually red/pink pigment in the flowers to form a blue color.
- In soil pH at or above 7.0, the aluminum ions combine with hydroxide ions to form insoluble and immobile aluminum hydroxide ($Al(OH)_3$). The plant doesn't take up the aluminum and remains red/pink.
- Other conditions (e.g. high phosphorus levels) can also affect aluminum mobility and availability.

Soil pH <7.0: blue flowers

Soil pH > 7.0: pink flowers

The environment can determine sex

- The sex of turtles, crocodiles, and the American alligator is determined by the incubation temperature during embryonic development. In some species, high incubation temperatures produce males and low temperatures produce females. In other species, the opposite is true.
- In turtles, males are produced at lower incubation temperatures than females. In one of the best studied species, the European pond turtle (right), eggs incubated above 30°C produce all-female broods, while temperatures below 25°C produce all-male broods. At the threshold of 28.5°C, the sex ratio is even. At higher temperatures, the temperature dependent enzyme aromatase converts the male hormone testosterone to estrogen to produce females, but it is unclear whether the temperature sensitivity resides in the gene or the protein.

European pond turtle, *Emys orbicularis* hatching. Reptiles incubate their eggs by burying them in the substrate, e.g. sand or soil.

6. Explain why soil pH affects the color of hydrangea flowers:

7. Temperature regulated sex determination may provide an advantage by preventing inbreeding. How might this work?

8. How might climate change affect the survival of many reptile species? Explain:

9. The graph on the right shows the effect of altitude on tree growth in both crowded and uncrowded areas. Explain the effect shown on the graph:

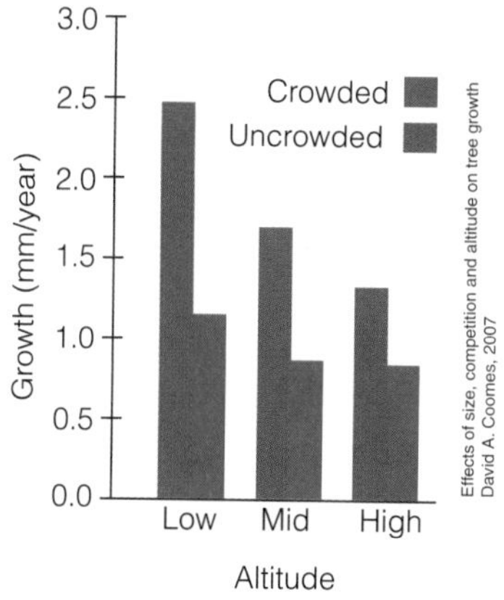

Growth (mm/year)
3.0
2.5
2.0
1.5
1.0
0.5
0.0
Crowded
Uncrowded
Low
Mid
High
Altitude
Effects of size, competition and altitude on tree growth David A. Coomes, 2007

ISBN: 978-1-98-856656-6

103 Variation and Phenotypic Plasticity

Key Question: How much phenotypic variation is the result of environment and how can we detect its influence?

As we saw in the previous activity, the phenotype encoded by genes is a product not only of the genes themselves, but of their internal and external environment and the variations in the way those genes are controlled (epigenetics). You will learn more about this in Unit 6. An organism's phenotype is not necessarily fixed. For many phenotypic traits, especially those controlled by multiple genes, organisms may show varying degrees of flexibility in their observable phenotype, called **phenotypic plasticity**. Plasticity can apply at both the individual level (e.g. aerial and submerged leaves in aquatic plants) and species level (e.g. winged and wingless morphs in aphids and different morphs in peppered moths).

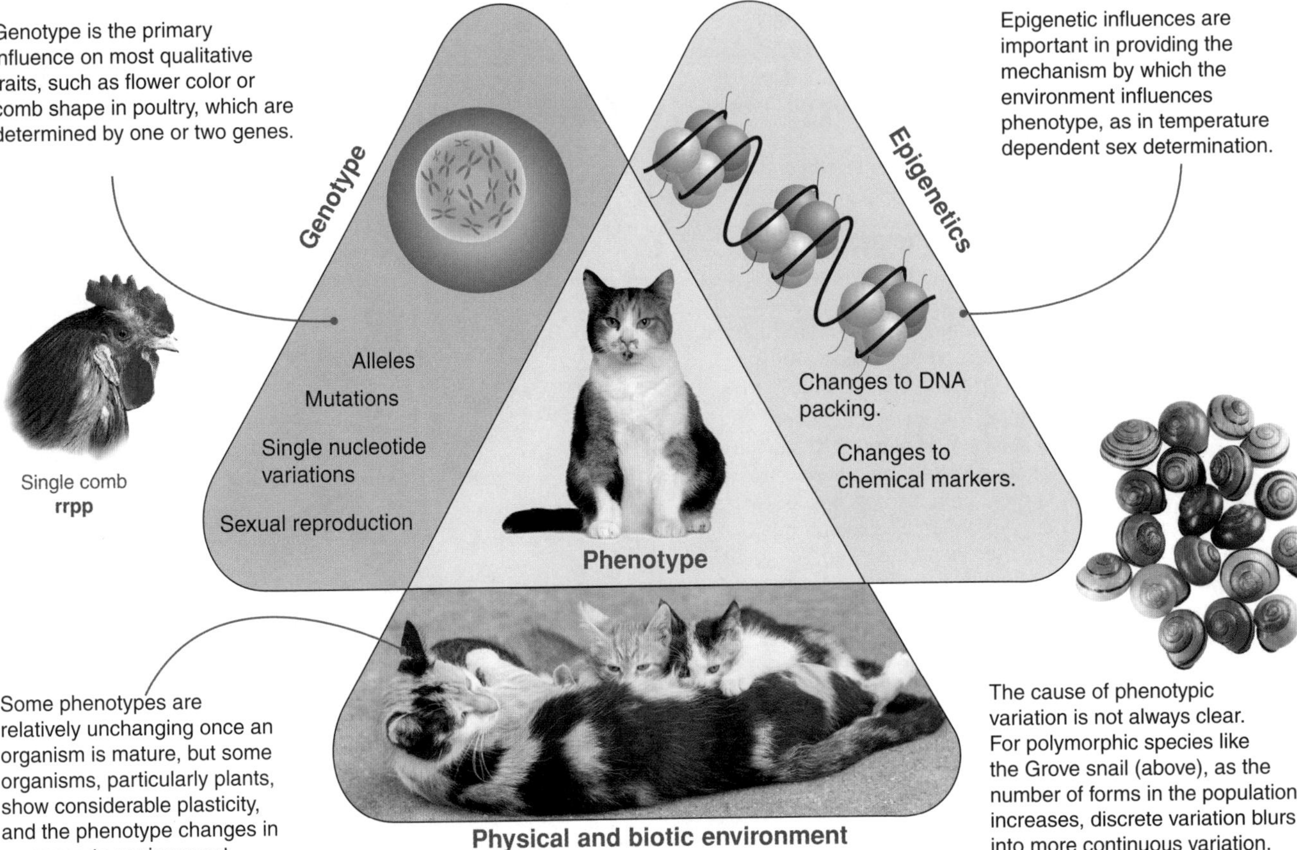

Genotype is the primary influence on most qualitative traits, such as flower color or comb shape in poultry, which are determined by one or two genes.
Epigenetic influences are important in providing the mechanism by which the environment influences phenotype, as in temperature dependent sex determination.
Genotype
Epigenetics
Alleles
Mutations
Single nucleotide variations
Sexual reproduction
Changes to DNA packing.
Changes to chemical markers.
Phenotype
Single comb
rrpp
Physical and biotic environment
Some phenotypes are relatively unchanging once an organism is mature, but some organisms, particularly plants, show considerable plasticity, and the phenotype changes in response to environment.
The cause of phenotypic variation is not always clear. For polymorphic species like the Grove snail (above), as the number of forms in the population increases, discrete variation blurs into more continuous variation.

What does variation look like?

- As you have seen earlier in this chapter, phenotypic variation is often either **continuous**, with a large number of phenotypic variants or **discontinuous**, with only a limited number of phenotypic variants in the population.
- Phenotypic characteristics showing discontinuous variation are determined by only one or two genes, e.g. flower color. These traits are qualitative and tend to be less influenced by environment. Temperature dependent sex determination is an exception.
- Phenotypic characteristics showing continuous variation are determined by multiple genes. These quantitative traits are commonly heavily influenced by environment and are the most likely to show phenotypic plasticity.
- **Phenotypic plasticity** refers to changes in an organism's phenotype in response to a unique environment. Plasticity occurs within genetically constrained extremes.

Flower color in snapdragons is a **qualitative trait** determined by two alleles (red and white) Heterozygotes exhibit an intermediate pink phenotype.

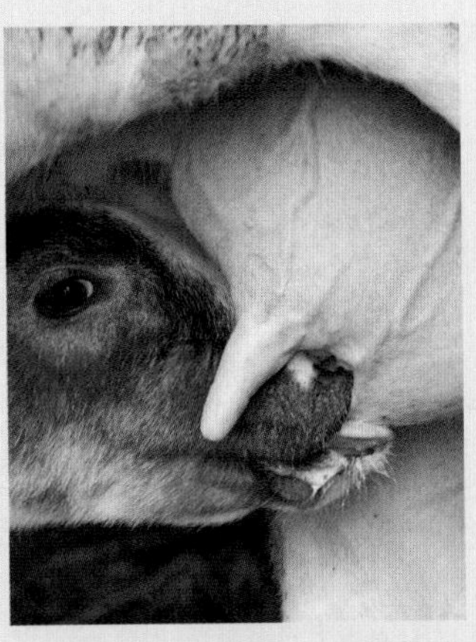
Milk production in mammals is a **quantitative trait** and heavily influenced by environment, although in some livestock there is a strong genetic component.

1. Identify each of the following phenotypic traits as continuous (quantitative) or discontinuous (qualitative):

(a) Wool production in sheep: ______________________

(b) Hand span in humans: ______________________

(c) Blood groups in humans: ______________________

(d) Albinism in mammals: ______________________

(e) Body weight in mice: ______________________

(f) Flower color in snapdragons: ______________________

ISBN: 978-1-98-856656-6

The importance of phenotypic plasticity

- The amount of change in a phenotype due to environmental influences is called its phenotypic plasticity. Plants often have high phenotypic plasticity because they are unable to move and so must adjust to environmental changes throughout their lives. Phenotypic plasticity contributes to fitness by allowing organisms to exploit changes in their environment.
- **Polyphenism** is a particular case of phenotypic plasticity in which multiple, discrete phenotypes can arise from a single genotype as a result of differing environmental conditions. Some polyphenisms are seasonal, while others are the result of environmental factors such as predation or resource limitation.
- Examples include the caste system in ants and bees, seasonal coat color changes in arctic foxes, seasonal changes in wing patterns in peacock pansy butterflies, and changes in body color in response to food resources in peppered moth larvae.

Color polyphenism in peppered moth larvae depends on the color or their food source branches. It is unrelated to the genetic polymorphism for melanic phenotypes in adult moths and is direct, because background color induces a similar phenotype in the larva.

Seasonal polyphenism is common in butterflies such as the peacock pansy butterflies. It may be related to seasonal changes in predators.

Seasonal polyphenism is also seen in birds and mammals, such as the arctic fox, which becomes white in winter as snow camouflage.

1. Buckeye butterflies change color as the breeding season progresses. The graph below left shows this as a change in reflectance of the wings.

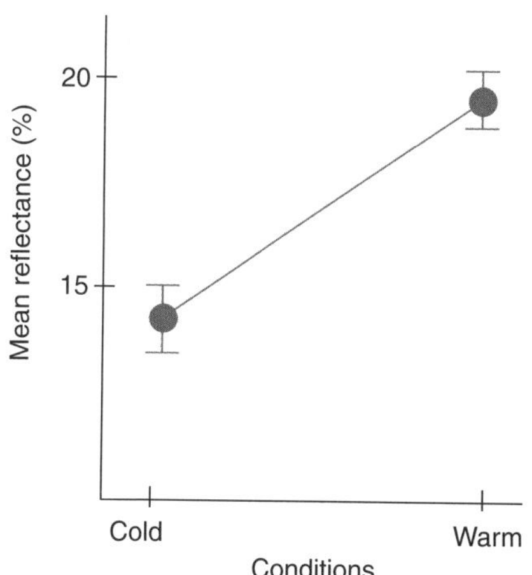

Fall buckeye (low reflectance)

Early summer buckeye (high reflectance)

(a) How does temperature affect the coloration of the buckeye butterfly? ______________________

(b) Using other examples, explain how phenotypic plasticity helps survival of polyphenic species: ______________________

ISBN: 978-1-98-856656-6

104 The Chromosomal Basis of Inheritance

Key Question: What is the chromosomal basis of inheritance? Gregor Mendel's laws of segregation and independent assortment were not immediately accepted. Observations of meiosis by Walter Sutton and the outcomes of crosses in *Drosophila* by Thomas Hunt Morgan helped them link inheritance to chromosomes and so to Mendel's work.

Building the chromosomal theory of inheritance

- Although **Gregor Mendel's** work on pea plants is today recognized as a seminal work on genetics, it was generally unrecognized for more than 30 years after its publication in 1865.
- It was not until 1902 that **Walter Sutton** linked his work on the chromosomes of grasshoppers to Mendel's, resulting in what is now known as the chromosomal basis of inheritance.
- In his observations, Sutton noticed that the assortment of chromosomes during meiosis was entirely random. There was never a specific side of the cell that a chromosome was found on and each chromosome acted independently of the others. He also noted that the chromosomes always maintained their individuality.
- In the closing statement of his 1902 paper Sutton wrote *"I may finally call attention to the probability that the association of paternal and maternal chromosomes in pairs and their subsequent separation... ...may constitute the physical basis of the Mendelian law of heredity".*
- This chromosome theory was later demonstrated by **Thomas Hunt Morgan** and **Lilian Vaughan Morgan**. It was known that fruit flies have two sex chromosomes. Males have an XY configuration, females have an XX configuration. A male fly was noticed to have white eyes instead of the normal red eyes. Breeding experiments showed that the gene for eye color was on the X chromosome and the white eye allele was recessive.
- The chromosome theory predicted that the white eye genotype should only appear in females if they had two recessive alleles. However a cross between a heterozygous female and a normal male produced a white eyed female. This appeared to go against the chromosome theory.
- Morgan showed that the white eyed female was XXY and this must have happened due to the X chromosome not separating (non-disjunction) during the second phase of meiosis. This helped confirm the chromosome theory of inheritance (right).

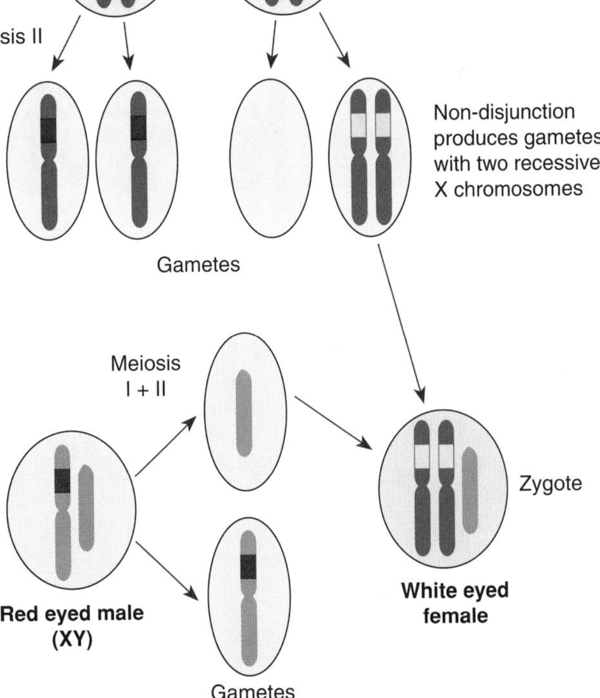

Non-disjunction in fruit fly, *Drosophila*

A heterozygous red eyed female when mated to a red eyed male should not be able to produce a white eyed female offspring. The only explanation for the production of a white eyed female is via the non-disjunction of X chromosomes.

1. Given that the gene for eye color is sex linked what is the expected phenotypic outcome for the cross above? Explain:

2. Explain why a heterozygous female fly should not be able to produce white eyed female offspring when mated to a red eyed male:

3. Explain how the non-disjunction event helped confirm the chromosomal basis of inheritance:

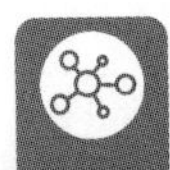
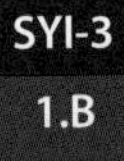
SYI-3 1.B

105

131

ISBN: 978-1-98-856656-6

105 Chromosomal Inheritance and Human Disorders

Key Question: How are some human disorders related to chromosomal inheritance?

There are more than 6000 human diseases attributed to mutations in single genes, although most are uncommon. Human disorders may also result from chromosomal abnormalities, resulting from non-disjunction during meiosis.

Huntington disease (HD)

Incidence: An uncommon disease affecting 3-7 per 100,000 people of European descent. Less common in other ethnicities (e.g. Chinese, Japanese, African).

Gene type: Autosomal dominant mutation of the HTT gene caused by a trinucleotide repeat expansion on the short arm of chromosome 4. In the mutation (mHTT), the number of CAG repeats increases from the normal 6-30 to 36-125. The severity of the disease increases with the number of repeats. The repeats result in an abnormally long version of the huntingtin protein.

Symptoms: The long huntingtin protein is cut into small toxic fragments. These build up in nerve cells and eventually kill them. The disease becomes apparent in mid-adulthood, with jerky, involuntary movements and loss of memory, reasoning, and personality.

Inheritance: Autosomal dominance pattern. Affected people may be homozygous or heterozygous for the mutant allele.

Gene location: Chromosome 4

American singer-songwriter and folk musician Woody Guthrie died from complications of HD

Sickle cell disease

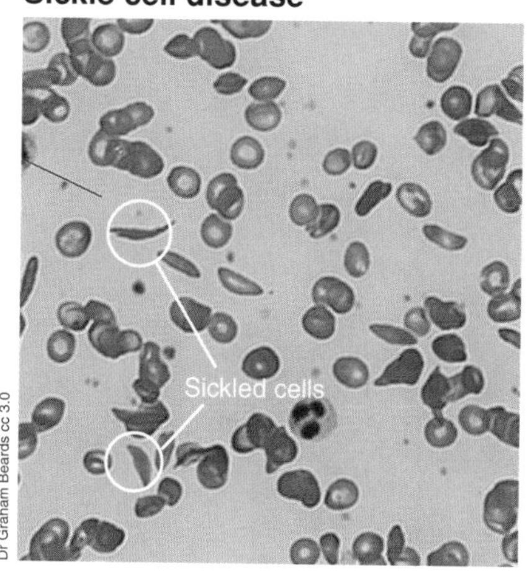

Incidence: Occurs most commonly in people of African descent. West Africans: 1% (10-45% are carriers). West Indians: 0.5%.

Gene type: Autosomal mutation involving substitution of a single nucleotide in the HBB gene. The gene codes for the beta chain of hemoglobin and the substitution causes a change in a single amino acid. The alleles (normal and mutant) are codominant. The mutated hemoglobin behaves differently when deprived of oxygen, causing distortion of the red blood cells, anemia, and circulatory problems.

Symptoms: Sickling of the red blood cells, which are removed from circulation, anemia, pain, damage to tissues and organs.

Inheritance: Autosomal codominance pattern. People who are homozygous for the mutant allele have sickle cell disease. Heterozygotes (carriers) are only mildly affected and show greater resistance to malaria than people without the mutation.

Gene location: Chromosome 11

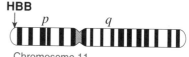

In a person heterozygous for the sickle cell allele, only some of the red blood cells are deformed.

HBB
p q
Chromosome 11

1. For each of genetic disorder below, indicate the following:

   (a) Sickle cell anemia: Gene name: ____________ Chromosome: ______________ Mutation type: ______________

   (b) Huntington disease: Gene name: ____________ Chromosome: ______________ Mutation type: ______________

2. Explain why mHTT, which is dominant and lethal, does not disappear from the population: ______________

3. What is the cause of Huntington disease? ______________

4. Explain why the sickle cell mutation has been maintained in populations, despite being lethal: ______________

5. What is the cause of sickle cell disease? ______________

ISBN: 978-1-98-856656-6

91

Chromosomes and non-disjunction

- In meiosis, chromosomes are usually distributed to daughter cells without error. Occasionally, homologous chromosomes fail to separate properly in meiosis I, or sister chromatids fail to separate in meiosis II. In these cases, one gamete receives two of the same type of chromosome and the other gamete receives no copy.
- This error is known as **non-disjunction** and it results in abnormal numbers of chromosomes in the gametes. The union of an aberrant and a normal gamete at fertilization produces offspring with an abnormal chromosome number (known as **aneuploidy**).

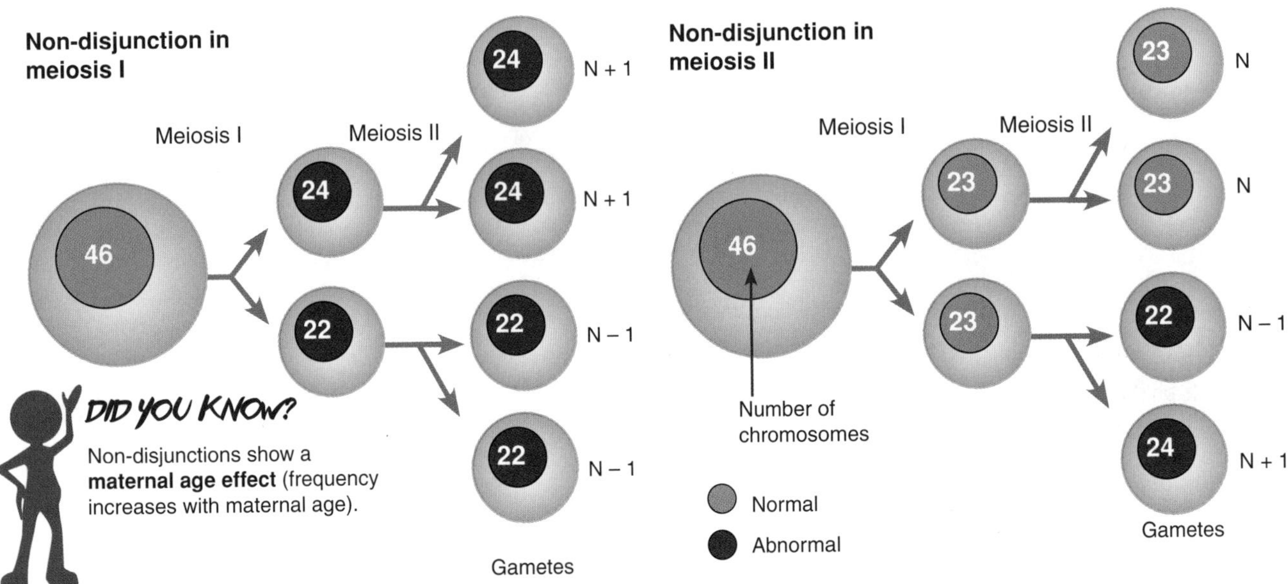

DID YOU KNOW?

Non-disjunctions show a **maternal age effect** (frequency increases with maternal age).

Down Syndrome (Trisomy 21)

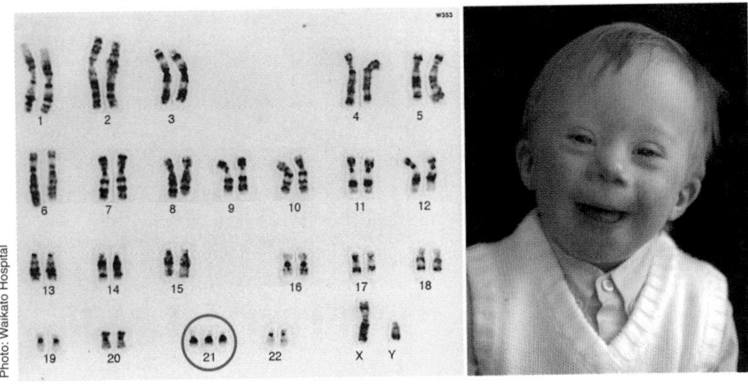

Incidence: Down syndrome is the most common of the human aneuploidies. The incidence rate in humans is about 1 in 800 births for women aged 30 to 31 years, with a **maternal age effect**.

Inheritance: Nearly all cases (approximately 95%) result from **non-disjunction** of chromosome 21 during **meiosis**. When this happens, a gamete (most commonly the oocyte) ends up with 24 rather than 23 chromosomes, and fertilization produces a trisomic offspring.

Far left: A karyogram for an individual with trisomy 21. The chromosomes are circled.

6. Describe the consequences of non-disjunction during meiosis: ______

7. Explain why non-disjunction in meiosis I results in a higher proportion of faulty gametes than non-disjunction in meiosis II: ______

8. What is the maternal age effect and what are its consequences? ______

9. Predict the outcome of non-disjunction occurring to all chromosomes during meiosis I: ______

ISBN: 978-1-98-856656-6

106 Personal Progress Check

Answer the multiple choice questions that follow by circling the correct answer. Don't forget to read the question carefully!

1. Alternate forms of the same gene are known as:
   (a) Gametes
   (b) Homozygotes
   (c) Genotypes
   (d) Alleles

2. The information within a Punnett square is used to predict:
   (a) The phenotypes of the offspring
   (b) The phenotypes of the parents
   (c) The genotypes of the offspring
   (d) The genotypes of the parents

3. The law of independent assortment:
   (a) Describes how alleles of different genes sort independently of one another during meiosis
   (b) Holds true only for unlinked genes
   (c) Was first described by Gregor Mendel
   (d) All of the above

The information relates to question 4 - 6: The ABO blood group system describes how humans have three different allele kinds (A, B, and O) for blood antigens.

4. When the A and B alleles are present both A and B antigens are expressed on the surface of the blood cell. This is:
   (a) Codominance
   (b) Incomplete dominance
   (c) A dominant inheritance pattern
   (d) A recessive inheritance pattern

5. The number of genotypes that could form in the ABO blood group system is:
   (a) 3
   (b) 4
   (c) 6
   (d) 8

6. How many phenotypes of would be seen in the ABO blood group system:
   (a) 3
   (b) 4
   (c) 5
   (d) 6

7. In humans, a gene involved in a sex-linked trait is located on:
   (a) The X chromosome
   (b) The Y chromosome
   (c) Any autosome
   (d) Either the X or Y chromosome

8. In *Drosophila*, normal wings are dominant to vestigial wings. If a heterozygous normal winged male is mated to a vestigial winged female, the phenotype of the offspring will:
   (a) All have normal wings
   (b) Al have vestigial wings
   (c) All will have wings smaller than normal but larger than vestigial
   (d) A mix of normal and vestigial wings.

9. Two flowers heterozygous for a single gene are crossed. The probability any of the F_1 generation will be homozygous recessive is:
   (a) 0.25
   (b) 0.5
   (c) 0.75
   (d) 1

10. Recombination occurs when:
    (a) Unlinked genes cross over during meiosis
    (b) Linked genes cross over during mitosis
    (c) The full 2N chromosome number is restored during fertilization
    (d) Genes on non-sister chromatids cross over during meiosis

11. For a color blind female, which of the following is not true?
    (a) Her father is also color blind
    (b) Both parents must be color blind
    (c) If she has a son, he will be color blind
    (d) Her mother had at least one allele for color-blindness

12. If a male is color blind, from whom did he receive the recessive allele?
    (a) Mother
    (b) Father
    (c) Either mother or father
    (d) Not enough information

13. Human females are much less likely to be color blind than males because:
    (a) Female eyes are more sensitive than male eyes
    (b) Females need two recessive alleles two become color blind, rather than one in males
    (c) Females only ever have the dominant allele
    (d) None of the above

14. Which are the following are evidence of the universal common ancestry of life?
    (a) DNA, ribosomes, the genetic code, ATP
    (b) ATP, mitochondria, chloroplasts, DNA
    (c) DNA, ATP, mitochondria, ribosomes
    (d) The genetic code, DNA, RNA, chloroplasts

ISBN: 978-1-98-856656-6

15. A test cross:

(a) Crosses two unknown genotypes to find out what the F_1 will be.
(b) Crosses two known genotypes to find out the F_1 genotypes.
(c) Crosses an unknown genotype with a recessive genotype, using the F_1 to find out the parental unknown.
(d) Crosses an unknown genotype with a heterozygous genotype, using the F_1 to find out the parental unknown.

16. Study the chromosome map below:

Which pair of genes would display the highest recombination frequency?

(a) 1 - 2
(b) 2 - 3
(c) 1 - 4
(d) 2 - 4

17. The crossover frequencies of four genes A, B, C, and D, where used to map their positions. The crossover frequencies were:

A-C 17%
A-B 25%
D-C 8%
C-B 8%

The chromosome map is:

(a) 

(b) 

(c) 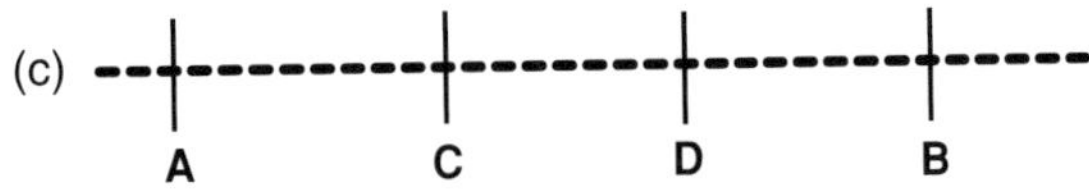

(d) 

18. A cross between homozygous purple-flowered and homozygous white-flowered pea plants results in offspring with purple flowers. This demonstrates

(a) The blending model of genetics
(b) True-breeding
(c) Dominance
(d) A dihybrid cross

19. In a hypothetical gene, the alleles F and G are codominant. For the cross below:

	F	G
F	FF	FG
G	FG	GG

How many phenotypes will there be?

(a) 2
(b) 3
(c) 4
(d) 5

20. A color-blind man plans to have a child with a woman who is a carrier for color-blindness. The probability that will be both male and color blind is:

(a) 0.25
(b) 0.33
(c) 0.5
(d) 0.75

21. Black fur in mice (B) is dominant to brown fur (b). Short tails (T) are dominant to long tails (t). What fraction of the offspring of the cross BbTt x BBtt will have black fur and long tails?

(a) 1/16
(b) 3/16
(c) 1/2
(d) 9/16

22. For the cross AaBbCc x AaBbCc what is the probability of producing a AABBCc genotype?

(a) 0.25
(b) 0.0625
(c) 0.0312
(d) 0.0156

23. Study the pedigree chart below. The inheritance pattern is:

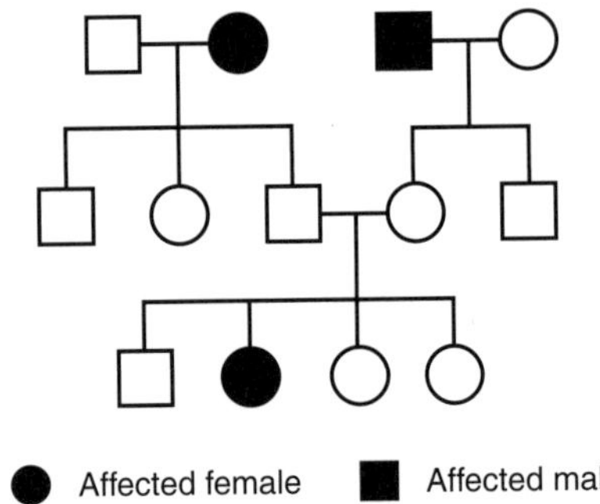

(a) Dominant
(b) Recessive
(c) Codominant
(d) Incomplete dominance

ISBN: 978-1-98-856656-6

Free Response Question: *Interpreting and evaluating experimental results with graphing*

- Browsing by large mammals can alter plant phenotype by providing selection pressure for browsing defenses such as thorns or hairs. Browsing can also constrain the growth and reproduction of woody plants, leading to reductions in plant height and a decrease in the number and length of shoots.
- Researchers studied the effects of reindeer browsing on the growth and reproduction of willow (a favored browse species) in an experimental setup in which willows were exposed to browsing or protected with fencing. The experiment involved 20 randomized plots of similar habitat each with four willow plants. The plants in each plot were cut back to the base to stimulate growth (rejuvenated) and in each plot half the plants were fenced against deer and half were left open. The experiment was run over 5 years.

1. **Describe** the likely effect of browsers on the growth of rejuvenated willows over 5 years when browsed versus protected from browsing. **Explain** your reasoning based on biological concepts involved:

RESULTS

TABLE 1: Mean height of willow in browsed and fenced plots. SE = standard error of the mean.

Year	Mean height of willows (cm)					
	Open	SE	95% CI	Fenced	SE	95% CI
1997	0	0.5	1.01	0	0.5	1.01
1998	13	3.0	6.07	21.0	2.8	5.66
1999	23	3.0	6.07	42.0	3.5	7.08
2000	30	3.8	7.69	51.0	3.0	6.07
2001	32	3.2	6.47	59.0	4.0	8.09
2002	29.0	4.0	8.09	62.0	2.5	5.06

Adapted from data in M. Den Herder, R. Virtanen, & H. Roininen (2004). See credits for full citation

2. Use table 1 to **plot a labeled graph** of change in mean height of willow over time in fenced and open areas (±95% CI):

3. (a) **Describe** the results:

(b) Was there a significant difference between fenced and open areas between the start of the experiment and the end?

4. **Predict** the consequences to willow mean height if the fences were removed. **Justify** your prediction:

ISBN: 978-1-98-856656-6

Free Response Question: Conceptual analysis

Temperature changes to sex determination and inheritance in flatfish

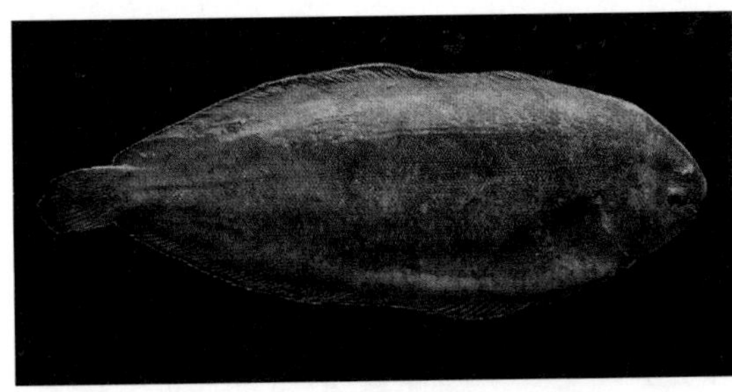

- The tongue sole (right) is a tropical to sub-tropical flat fish whose sex is determined mainly by the inheritance of sex chromosomes (genetic sex determination) but also affected by environmental temperature (environmental sex determination).
- In the normal temperature rearing conditions (22°C), the sex of tongue sole is determined by the ZW/ZZ sex determination system. ZZ fish develop into males and ZW fish develop into females.
- However, which fish are raised at high temperatures (28°C), the Z chromosome is modified (Z*). and genetic females can develop into fertile phenotypic males and can pass the Z* chromosome to their offspring even when those offspring are raised at lower temperature (in other words, the sex reversal could be inherited).
- At least one Z or Z* chromosome is required for survival of the fish.
- A cross between a ZW female and a Z*Z male is shown in the Punnett square (right).

Male gametes	Female gametes: Z	Female gametes: W
Z*	Z*Z	Z*W
Z	ZZ	ZW

Primary source of information: Jiang and Hengde (2017). See credits for full citation.

1. (a) Which sex determines the sex of the offspring in tongue sole: ______

   (b) **Describe** the effect of temperature on the genetic expression of sex in tongue sole: ______

   (c) Determine the percentage of phenotypic males among the F_1 offspring in the cross shown in the Punnett square above if the offspring are raised at 22°C. Do the ratios differ from the expected? **Explain**:

2. A researcher crossed two offspring from the cross above and observed a 2:1 ratio of males to females in the offspring. Based on the information provided, identify the genotype of the male parent in the cross. **Explain** your reasoning. You can use the working space provided:

3. **Predict** the consequences to this fish species of an increase in sea temperatures to 28°C during the breeding season:

4. **Justify** your prediction: ______

ISBN: 978-1-98-856656-6

UNIT 6

Gene Expression and Regulation

Learning Objectives

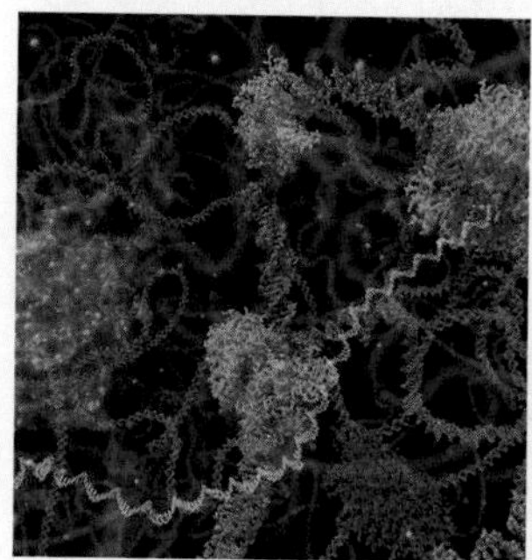

Developing understanding

CONTENT: In this unit, you will build on your knowledge of nucleic acids, looking in more detail at the differences between DNA and RNA. This unit explores the relationship between genotype and phenotype, linking this to gene expression. Understanding protein synthesis is essential to answering questions about gene expression and its regulation. The importance of these processes to survival lays the foundation for exploring natural selection in Unit 7.

SKILLS: This unit focuses on describing, analyzing, and creating models and representations to explain or illustrate biological processes. The are multiple opportunities to develop your skills in argumentation and problem solving using real work contexts.

6.1 DNA and RNA structure .... activities 107 - 111

☐ 1. Recall the structure and role of DNA and RNA as information molecules. Explain how the structure of these nucleic acids enables them to store information that can be passed from generation to generation.

☐ 2. Understand what is meant by a genome and compare genome size in different organisms. Describe the structure and role of plasmids and compare and contrast the structure of prokaryotic and eukaryotic chromosomes.

☐ 3. Create a model of DNA to demonstrate an understanding of the base pairing rule and its role in enabling the transmission of hereditary information.

6.2 Replication .... activities 112 - 113

☐ 4. Describe the semi-conservative process of DNA replication, including the roles of key enzymes (helicase, topoisomerase, DNA polymerase, and ligase) and the significance of the direction (5'→ 3') of synthesis.

6.3 Transcription and RNA processing .... activities 114 - 117

☐ 5. Provide an overview of the flow of genetic information in cells (the central dogma).

☐ 6. Describe how the sequence of RNA bases and the structure of the RNA molecule determine RNA function, distinguishing between mRNA, tRNA, and rRNA.

☐ 7. Describe transcription as the first stage in protein synthesis, identifying the significance of the sequence of bases in mRNA codons, the role of RNA polymerase, and the direction of synthesis. Contrast the location of transcription in prokaryotes and eukaryotes.

☐ 8. Describe modifications to the primary transcript in eukaryotic cells to include addition of caps and tails, removal of introns, and exon splicing. Explain the roles of these modifications.

6.4 Translation .... activities 115, 118 - 119

☐ 9. Explain how translation of mRNA by ribosomes produces the proteins that link genotype to phenotype. Identify the location of translation in prokaryotes and eukaryotes and explain why translation in prokaryotes can occur while genes are still being transcribed.

☐ 10. Describe important features of the genetic code and explain the significance of its degeneracy and universality.

☐ 11. Describe the sequence of steps in translation to include initiation, elongation, and termination. Describe important features of each stage including the role of the ribosomes, start and stop codons, and tRNA molecules.

☐ 12. Explain how retroviruses provide an exception to the central dogma through an alternate flow of information made possible by reverse transcriptase. Explain how retroviruses use this method of information storage and retrieval to propagate new viral progeny.

6.5 Regulation of gene expression... activities 120 - 125

☐ 13. Describe the role of gene regulation in determining phenotype, including the importance of the genes expressed but also the order and timing of expression and the role of transcription factors in this.

☐ 14. Describe how epigenetic changes affect gene expression through reversible modifications of DNA or histone proteins. Describe evidence for the heritability of epigenetic tags (although most are reset in the gametes).

☐ 15. Explain how prokaryotic genes are clustered as operons consisting of structural genes under the control of a single promoter. Using an example, describe the role of regulatory genes in controlling the activity of prokaryotic operons.

☐ 16. Explain how transcription factors (encoded by regulatory genes) regulate gene expression in eukaryotes.

6.6 Gene expression and cell specialization..................... activities 121, 123 - 127

☐ 17. Explain the link between the regulation of gene expression and phenotypic differences in cells and organisms. Include reference to the roles of differential gene expression and small RNA molecules in determining cellular outcomes.

6.7 Mutations................................ activities 128 - 134

☐ 18. Describe types of mutation and their effects of phenotype to include positive, negative, and neutral mutations.

☐ 19. Recognize mutation as the source of all new alleles. Use examples to explain how changes in genotype (through mutation) can result in phenotypic changes. Include reference to gene and chromosome mutations (including aneuploidy in humans and polyploidy in plants).

☐ 20. Explain how changes to the DNA sequence contribute to variation that can be subject to natural selection. Include reference to the horizontal acquisition of genetic information in bacteria and recombination in viruses. Recognize that reproductive processes that increase genetic variation are evolutionarily conserved and shared by various organisms.

6.8 Biotechnology .... activities 135 - 145

☐ 21. Use examples to explain the use of genetic engineering techniques in analyzing and manipulating DNA. Include reference to gel electrophoresis, PCR, bacterial transformation, and DNA sequencing.

107 Genomes, Genes, and Alleles

Key Question: What is a genome and how does genome size relate to genes and alleles and to organism complexity?

The **genome** refers to all the genetic material in one haploid set of chromosomes. The genome contains all of the information the organism needs to function and reproduce. Every cell in an individual has a complete copy of the genome. Within the genome are sections of DNA, called **genes**, which code for proteins. Collectively, genes determine what an organism looks like (its traits). Eukaryotes have two copies of each gene (one inherited from each parent), so it is possible for one individual to have two different versions of a gene. These different versions are called **alleles**.

The location and size of the genome varies between organisms

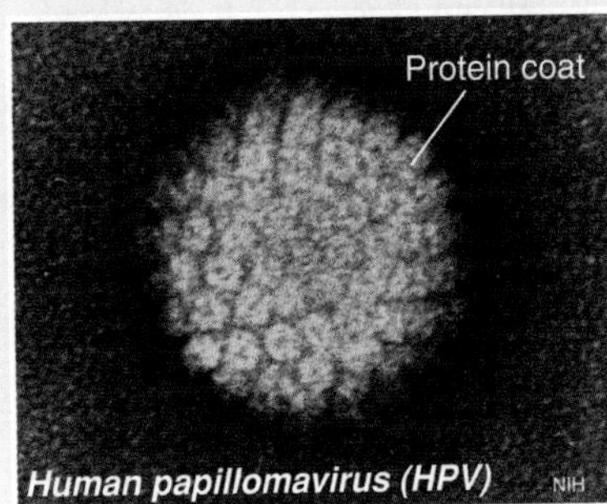

Human papillomavirus (HPV)

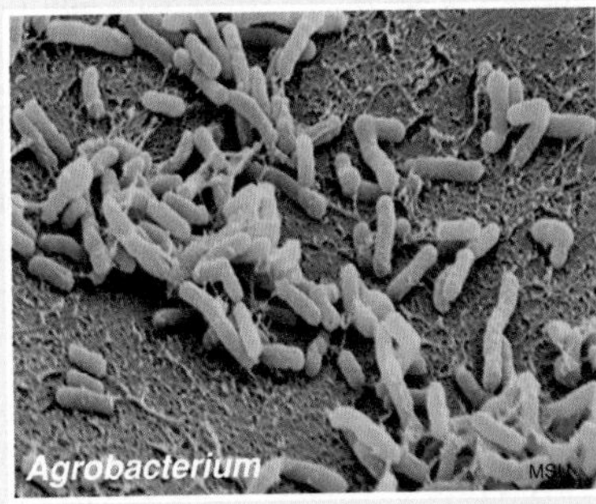
Agrobacterium

Human: a eukaryote

Genome size: Small → Large

Number of genes: Few → Many

The viral genome is contained within the virus's outer protein coat. Viral genomes are typically small and highly variable. They can consist of single stranded or double stranded DNA or RNA and contain only a small number of genes.

The HPV genome consists of a double stranded circular DNA molecule ~8000 bp long.

In bacteria (prokaryotes) most of the DNA is located within a single circular chromosome, which makes them haploid (i.e. one allele) for most genes. Many bacteria also have small accessory chromosomes called plasmids, which carry genes for special functions such as antibiotic resistance and substrate metabolism.

The *Agrobacterium* genome is 5.7 Mb long and consists of a linear chromosome and two plasmids, one of which enables it to infect plants.

In eukaryotes, most of the DNA is located inside the cell's nucleus. A small amount resides in the mitochondria and chloroplasts (in plants). The DNA is arranged into linear chromosomes and most eukaryotes are diploid, with two sets of chromosomes, one from each parent.

The human genome is ~3000 Mb long in 23 chromosomes. The diploid number is 46 chromosomes.

Measuring genomes

Genome size is often expressed as the number of base pairs. The unit most often used to show the size of a genome is the megabase (Mb). Note: 1 megabase = 1 million base pairs. The image right is of the ϕX174 bacteriophage, a virus that infects bacterial cells. Its entire genome is only 5375 base pairs long (0.005375 Mb) and it contains only nine genes, coding for nine different proteins. At least 2000 times this amount of DNA would be found in a single bacterial cell. Half a million times the quantity of DNA would be found in the genome of a single human cell.

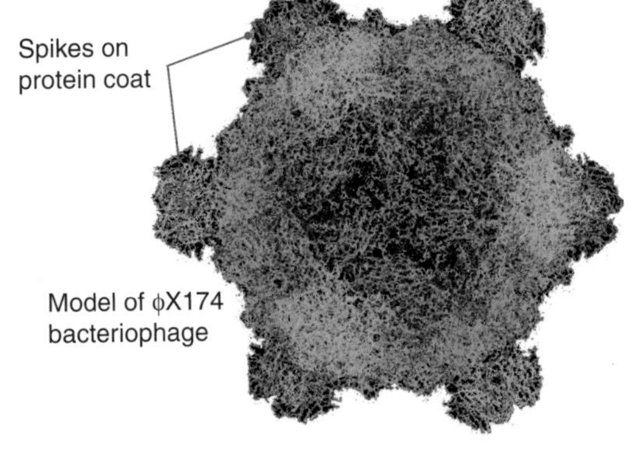

Model of ϕX174 bacteriophage

1. Define the following terms:

   (a) Genome: ______

   (b) Gene: ______

   (c) Allele: ______

2. Describe the general trend for genome size and gene number for viruses, bacteria, and eukaryotic organisms:

   ______

3. Explain why an individual eukaryote can have different versions of a gene (allele) but viruses and bacteria do not:

   ______

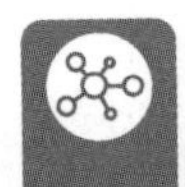

ISBN: 978-1-98-856656-6

108 Prokaryotic Chromosomes

Key Question: How is prokaryote DNA packaged within the cell and how does this account for their genomic makeup?

DNA is a universal carrier of genetic information but it is packaged differently in prokaryotic and eukaryotic cells. Unlike eukaryotic chromosomes, the prokaryotic chromosome is not enclosed in a nuclear membrane and is not associated with protein. It is a single circular (rather than linear) molecule of double stranded DNA, attached to the plasma membrane and located in a nucleoid region, which is in direct contact with the cytoplasm. As well as the bacterial chromosome, bacteria often contain small circular, double-stranded DNA molecules called plasmids. Plasmids are independent of the main bacterial chromosome and usually contain 5-100 genes that are not crucial to cell survival under normal conditions.

The prokaryotic genome

- In contrast to eukaryotes, prokaryotic DNA consists almost entirely of protein coding genes and their regulatory sequences. It was the study of prokaryotic genomes that gave rise to the **one gene-one protein hypothesis**, which still holds true for bacteria.
- The chromosomal DNA is located in a **nucleoid region**. It is not enclosed in a membrane. The nucleoid may take up as much as 20% of the cell's volume in actively growing cells.
- Most bacteria have a single, circular chromosome. This makes them haploid for most genes, unless copies are located on **plasmids** (small circular auxiliary DNA strands). Plasmids are generally circular but can also exist as linear or supercoiled structures.

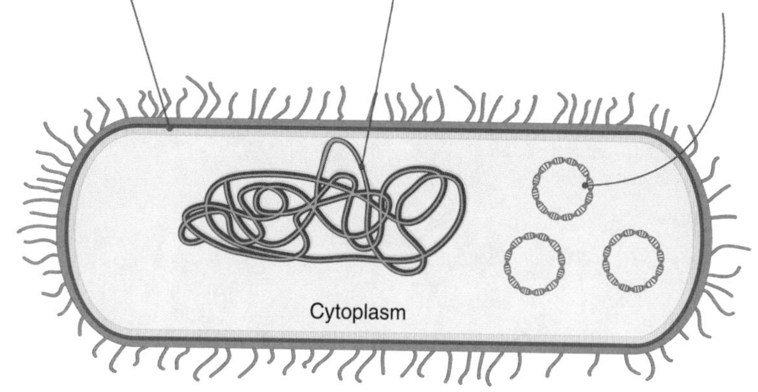
Proteins associated with the plasma membrane carry out DNA replication and segregate the chromosomes to the daughter cells in cell division.
Single circular chromosome is attached to the plasma membrane and not associated with proteins.
Plasmids occur in the cytoplasm. Plasmids replicate independently of the main chromosome.
Cytoplasm

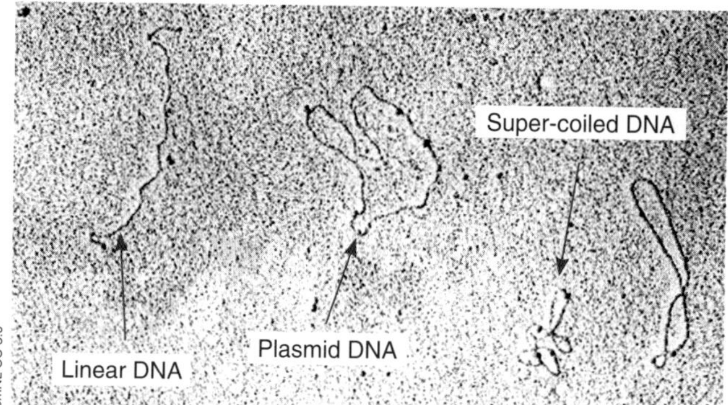
Super-coiled DNA
Linear DNA
Plasmid DNA
emNL CC 3.0

Plasmids vary in size from 1000 base pairs (bp) to hundreds of thousands of base pairs. In bacteria, they play an important role in providing extra genetic material that confers properties such as antibiotic resistance. Plasmids can be transferred between bacterial cells by a process of plasmid transfer called **conjugation** (right)

Horizontal gene transfer via conjugation

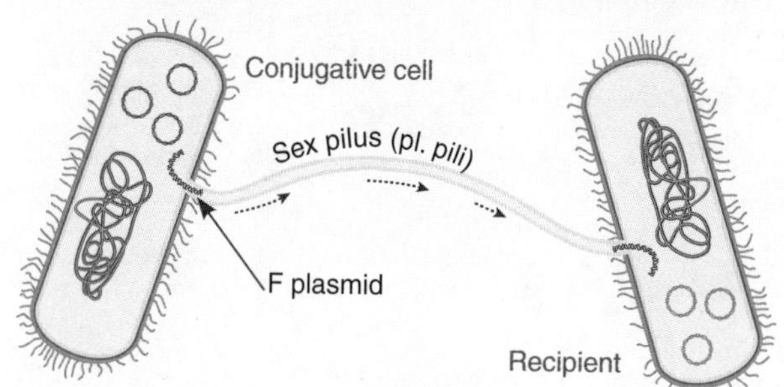
Conjugative cell
Sex pilus (pl. pili)
F plasmid
Recipient

Conjugation: Special conjugative (F) plasmids contain transfer genes, which enable conjugation and the transfer of genetic information between bacterial cells. The transfer occurs via a **sex pilus**, which briefly connects the donor and the recipient. Conjugation provides another route for acquiring genes to vertical transfer via binary fission.

1. State three important ways in which prokaryotic chromosomes differ from eukaryotic chromosomes:

   (a) ______________________________

   (b) ______________________________

   (c) ______________________________

2. Explain the consequences to protein synthesis of the prokaryotic chromosome being free in the cytoplasm: ______________

   ____

   ____

3. Most of the bacterial genome comprises protein coding genes and their regulatory sequences. What is the consequence of this to the relative sizes of bacterial and eukaryotic genomes:

   ____

   ____

ISBN: 978-1-98-856656-6

109

108

IST-1
1.C

109 Plasmid DNA

Key Question: What are the special characteristics of plasmids and what role do they have in prokaryotes?

Prokaryotes store most of their genetic information in one large chromosome but a small proportion can commonly be found as independently replicating, circular, extra-chromosomal pieces of DNA known as **plasmids**. Plasmids may carry important genes, such as those for the production of toxins that eliminate prokaryote competitors. Plasmids are less common in eukaryotes but some species, such as the yeast *Saccharomyces,* do have them. The genetic material from viruses may form plasmid-like structures called episomes once they have infected a cell.

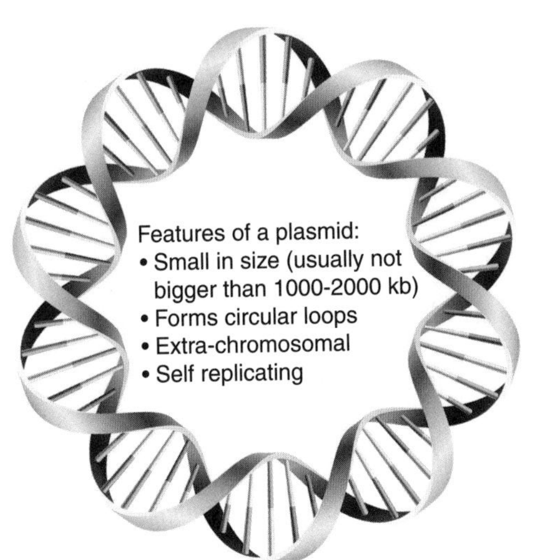

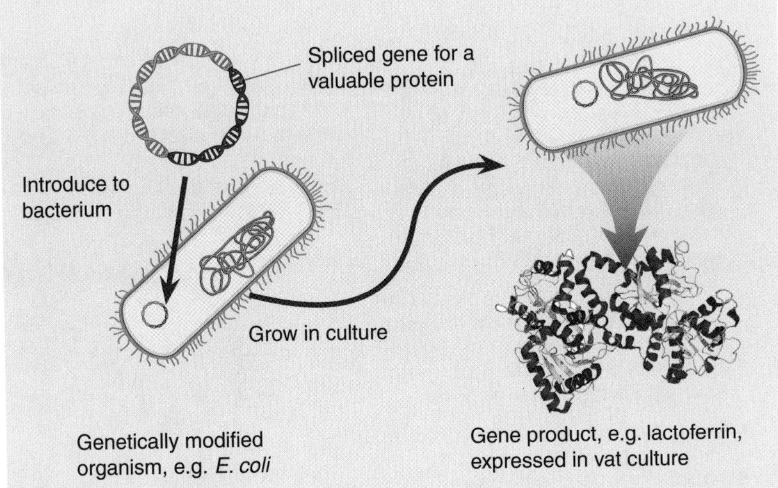

The properties of plasmids enable them to be used as tools to introduce genetic material into organisms. A gene is spliced into a plasmid and the plasmid inserted into a recipient organism (e.g. a bacterium). The recipient will then produce the gene product as part of its normal metabolism. This technique has enabled the industrial-scale production of valuable gene products, such as human proteins, from bacteria.

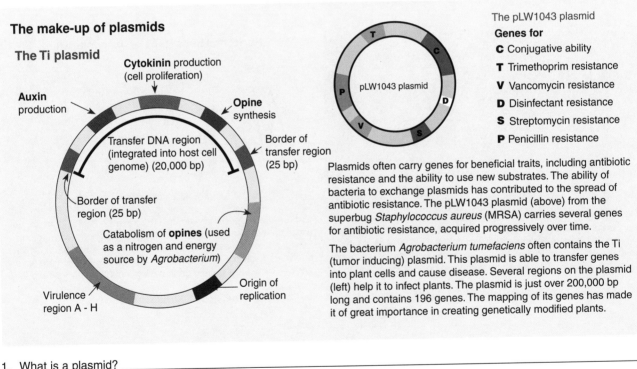

The make-up of plasmids

The Ti plasmid

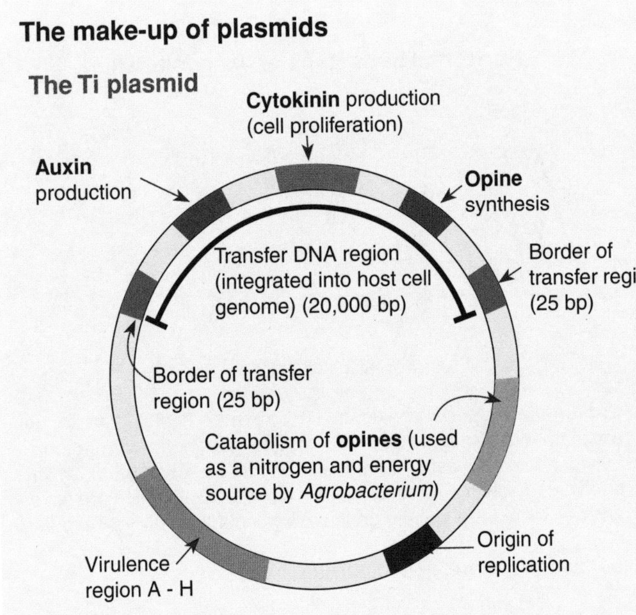

The pLW1043 plasmid

pLW1043 plasmid
T C D S V P

Genes for

C Conjugative ability
T Trimethoprim resistance
V Vancomycin resistance
D Disinfectant resistance
S Streptomycin resistance
P Penicillin resistance

Plasmids often carry genes for beneficial traits, including antibiotic resistance and the ability to use new substrates. The ability of bacteria to exchange plasmids has contributed to the spread of antibiotic resistance. The pLW1043 plasmid (above) from the superbug *Staphylococcus aureus* (MRSA) carries several genes for antibiotic resistance, acquired progressively over time.

The bacterium *Agrobacterium tumefaciens* often contains the Ti (tumor inducing) plasmid. This plasmid is able to transfer genes into plant cells and cause disease. Several regions on the plasmid (left) help it to infect plants. The plasmid is just over 200,000 bp long and contains 196 genes. The mapping of its genes has made it of great importance in creating genetically modified plants.

1. What is a plasmid? ________________

2. Explain how a plasmid can convey a survival advantage to bacteria under certain conditions: ________________

____

____

3. (a) Why are plasmids (such as the Ti plasmid) useful to genetic engineers? ________________

____

(b) Into which region of the Ti plasmid would you insert a gene in order for it to be transferred into a host plant cell?

____

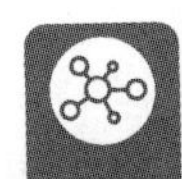

ISBN: 978-1-98-856656-6

110 Eukaryotic Chromosomes

Key Question: How is DNA packaged into the cell's nucleus?

The DNA in eukaryotes is packaged as discrete linear chromosomes. The number of chromosomes varies from species to species. The extent of DNA packaging changes during the life cycle of the cell, but classic chromosome structures (below) appear during metaphase of mitosis.

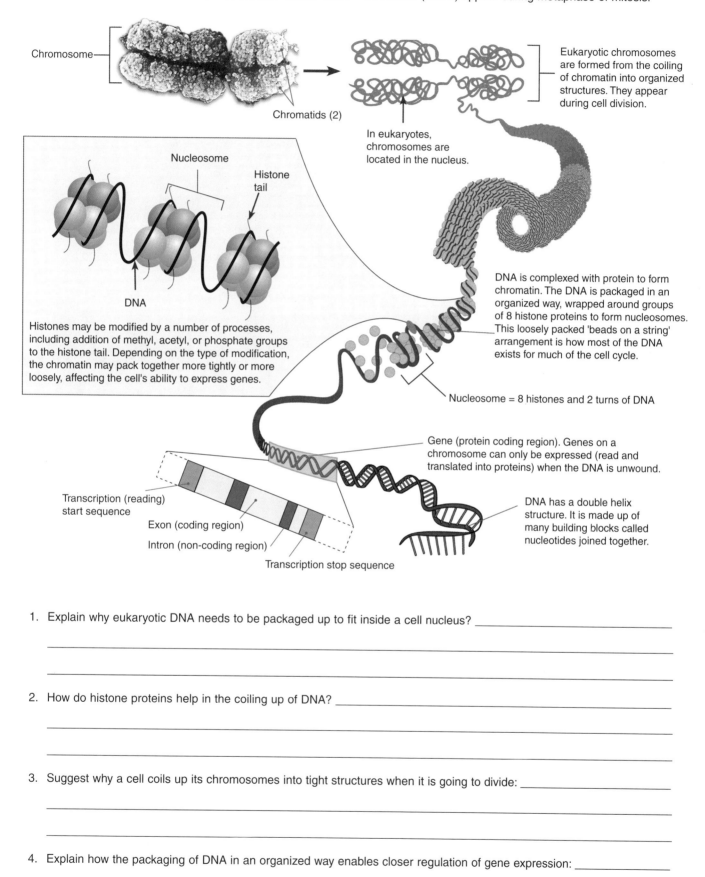

Chromosome

Chromatids (2)

Eukaryotic chromosomes are formed from the coiling of chromatin into organized structures. They appear during cell division.

In eukaryotes, chromosomes are located in the nucleus.

Nucleosome

Histone tail

DNA

Histones may be modified by a number of processes, including addition of methyl, acetyl, or phosphate groups to the histone tail. Depending on the type of modification, the chromatin may pack together more tightly or more loosely, affecting the cell's ability to express genes.

DNA is complexed with protein to form chromatin. The DNA is packaged in an organized way, wrapped around groups of 8 histone proteins to form nucleosomes. This loosely packed 'beads on a string' arrangement is how most of the DNA exists for much of the cell cycle.

Nucleosome = 8 histones and 2 turns of DNA

Gene (protein coding region). Genes on a chromosome can only be expressed (read and translated into proteins) when the DNA is unwound.

Transcription (reading) start sequence

Exon (coding region)

Intron (non-coding region)

Transcription stop sequence

DNA has a double helix structure. It is made up of many building blocks called nucleotides joined together.

1. Explain why eukaryotic DNA needs to be packaged up to fit inside a cell nucleus? ____________

2. How do histone proteins help in the coiling up of DNA? ____________

3. Suggest why a cell coils up its chromosomes into tight structures when it is going to divide: ____________

4. Explain how the packaging of DNA in an organized way enables closer regulation of gene expression: ____________

ISBN: 978-1-98-856656-6

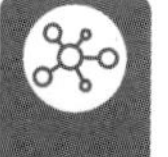

111 Creating a DNA Model

Key Question: What are the base pairing rules for DNA. How can they be modeled?

Recall that DNA is made up of structures called nucleotides. Two primary factors control the way in which these nucleotide building blocks are linked together: the available space within the DNA double helix and the hydrogen-bonding capability of the bases. These factors cause the nucleotides to join together in a predictable way, referred to as the **base pairing rule**. It is derived from Chargaff's rules which state that % A = %T and %C = %G for both strands of the DNA.

DNA base pairing rule			
Adenine	is always attracted to	**Thymine**	A ⟷ T
Thymine	is always attracted to	**Adenine**	T ⟷ A
Cytosine	is always attracted to	**Guanine**	C ⟷ G
Guanine	is always attracted to	**Cytosine**	G ⟷ C

1. (a) Cut out the opposite page. Cut out the gray template strand. Dark black lines should be cut. The dashed gray lines represent the hydrogen bonds. Fold on the red dotted lines so that the gray surfaces are facing (a valley fold). Do not cut around the hydrogen bonds on each base. These are just to show you where you will join your bases.
   (b) Cut out the complementary strand. The first base (G) is already in position as a guide. Again fold on the red line so that the blue surfaces are facing each other.

2. Fill in the table below to help you place the remaining bases in the correct order on the complementary strand:

Template strand	Complementary strand
Cytosine (C)	Guanine (G)
Guanine (G)	(a)
Thymine (T)	(b)
Adenine (A)	(c)
Thymine (T)	(d)
Adenine (A)	(e)
Thymine (T)	(f)
Thymine (T)	(g)
Cytosine (C)	(h)
Guanine (G)	(i)

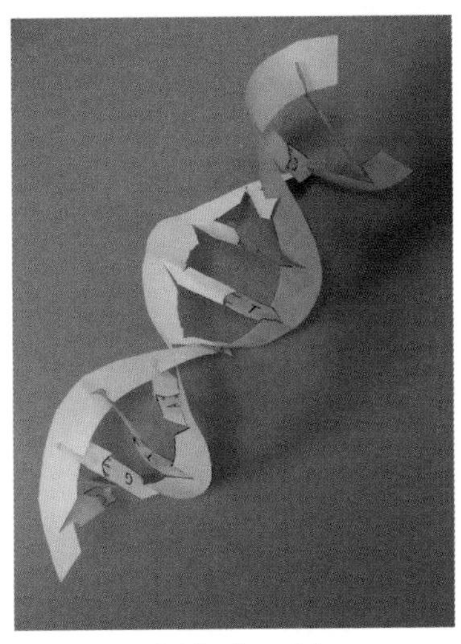
A finished model

3. Cut out the bases and slot them into the slots on the complementary strand using the order in the table above. Use tape to fix them in position. Make sure the blue surfaces are facing and the base is in the same orientation as the guide (G).

4. Line up the first base pairs (C and G) and stick them together with tape. Note that the bases are facing in opposite directions.

5. Continue sticking base pairs together, working your way around the helix, to complete the DNA molecule.

6. What does anti-parallel mean? ______________________________

____

7. Explain how the concept of base pairing allowed you to easily model a DNA molecule using the template provided:

____

____

____

____

____

ISBN: 978-1-98-856656-6

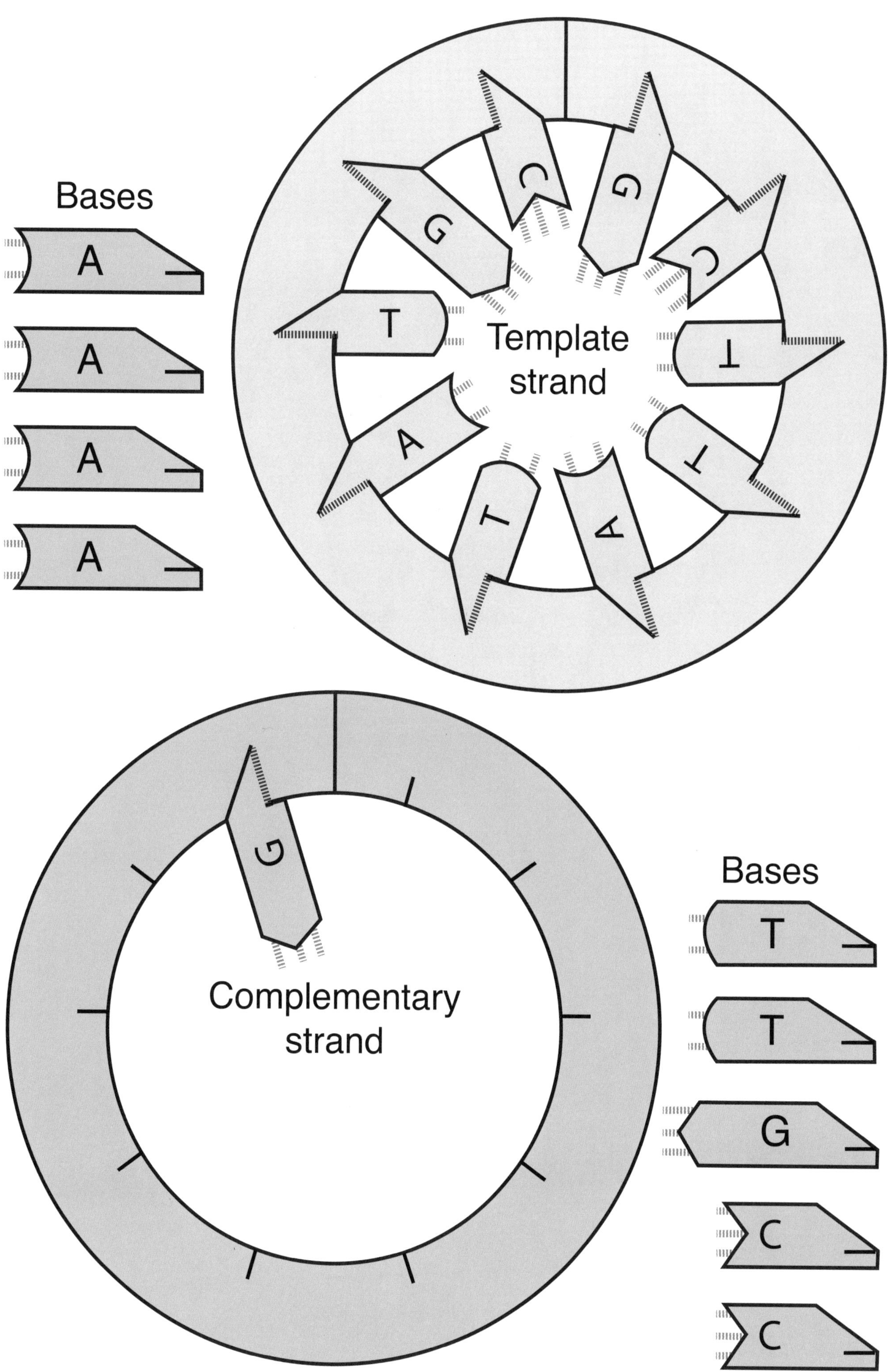

ISBN: 978-1-98-856656-6

The page has been deliberately left blank

ISBN: 978-1-98-856656-6

112 How Does DNA Replicate?

Key Question: How does DNA carry out semi-conservative replication and what is the outcome of this process?

Before a cell can divide, it must double its DNA. It does this by a process called **DNA replication**. This process ensures that each resulting cell receives a complete set of genetic instructions from the parent cell. After the DNA has replicated, each chromosome is made up of two chromatids, joined at the centromere. The two chromatids will become separated during cell division to form separate chromosomes. During DNA replication, nucleotides are added at the replication fork. Enzymes are responsible for all of the key events. DNA replication is semi-conservative, meaning each new DNA molecule is made of one strand from the parent DNA and one strand from the daughter DNA.

Step 1
Unwinding the DNA molecule

A normal chromosome consists of an unreplicated DNA molecule. Before cell division, this long molecule of double stranded DNA must be replicated.

For this to happen, it is first untwisted and separated (unzipped) at high speed at its replication fork by an enzyme called **helicase**. Another enzyme relieves the strain that this generates by cutting, winding and rejoining the DNA strands.

Step 2
Making new DNA strands

The formation of new DNA is carried out mostly by an enzyme complex called **DNA polymerase**.

DNA polymerase catalyses the condensation reaction that joins adjacent nucleotides. The strand is synthesized in a 5' to 3' direction, with the polymerase moving 3' to 5' along the strand it is reading. Thus the nucleotides are assembled in a continuous fashion on one strand but in short fragments on the other strand. These fragments are later joined by an enzyme to form one continuous length.

Step 3
Rewinding the DNA molecule

Each of the two new double-helix DNA molecules has one strand of the original DNA (green and white) and one strand that is newly synthesized (blue). The two DNA molecules rewind into their double-helix shape again.

DNA replication is **semi-conservative**, with each new double helix containing one old (parent) strand and one newly synthesized (daughter) strand. The new chromosome has twice as much DNA as a non-replicated chromosome. The two chromatids will become separated in the cell division process to form two separate chromosomes.

3' 5'

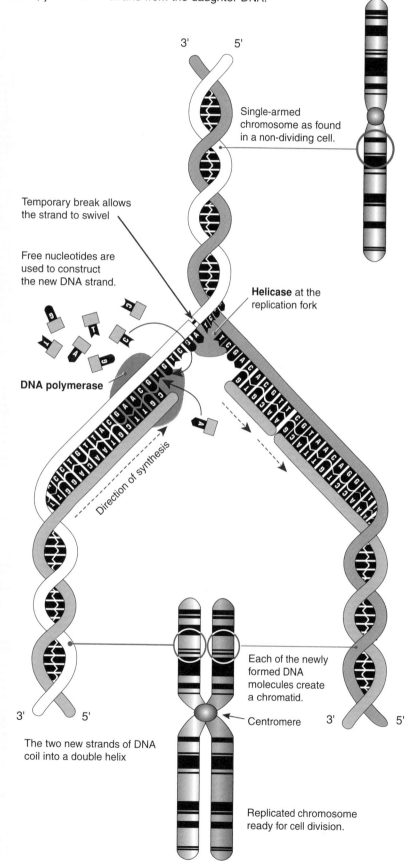

Single-armed chromosome as found in a non-dividing cell.

Temporary break allows the strand to swivel

Free nucleotides are used to construct the new DNA strand.

Helicase at the replication fork

DNA polymerase

Direction of synthesis

Each of the newly formed DNA molecules create a chromatid.

Centromere

3' 5' 3' 5'

The two new strands of DNA coil into a double helix

Replicated chromosome ready for cell division.

ISBN: 978-1-98-856656-6

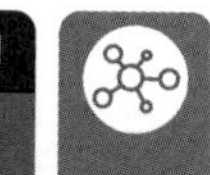

1. What is the purpose of DNA replication?

2. Summarize the three main steps involved in DNA replication:

(a)

(b)

(c

3. For a cell with 22 chromosomes, state how many chromatids would exist following DNA replication:

4. What percentage of DNA in each daughter cell is new and what percentage is original?

5. What does it mean when we say DNA replication is semi-conservative?

6. How are the new strands of DNA lengthened during replication:

7. What rule ensures that the two new DNA strands are identical to the original strand?

8. Use the diagram to explain why one strand of DNA needs to be copied in fragments that are joined together later:

9. Match the statements in the table below to form complete sentences, then put the sentences in order to make a coherent paragraph about DNA replication and its role:

The enzymes also proofread the DNA during replication...	...is required before mitosis or meiosis can occur.
DNA replication is the process by which the DNA molecule...	...by enzymes.
Replication is tightly controlled...	...to correct any mistakes.
After replication, the chromosome...	...and half new DNA.
DNA replication...	...during mitosis.
The chromatids separate...	...is copied to produce two identical DNA strands.
A chromatid contains half original ...	...is made up of two chromatids.

Write the complete paragraph here:

ISBN: 978-1-98-856656-6

113 Enzyme Control of DNA Replication

Key Question: How is the process of DNA replication controlled?

DNA replication involves many enzyme-controlled steps. They are shown below as separate, but many of the enzymes are clustered together as enzyme complexes. As the DNA is replicated, enzymes 'proof-read' it and correct mistakes. The polymerase enzyme can only work in one direction, so that one new strand is constructed as a continuous length (the leading strand) while the other new strand (the lagging strand) is made in short segments to be later joined together.

DNA replication occurs at a rate of ~1000 nucleotides per second in *E. coli* and ~50 nucleotides per second in humans.

Nucleotides are present as deoxynucleoside triphosphates (dNTPs), e.g. dATP. When hydrolyzed, these provide the energy for incorporating the nucleotide into the strand (INSET).

DS DNA
5' 3'
Overall direction of replication

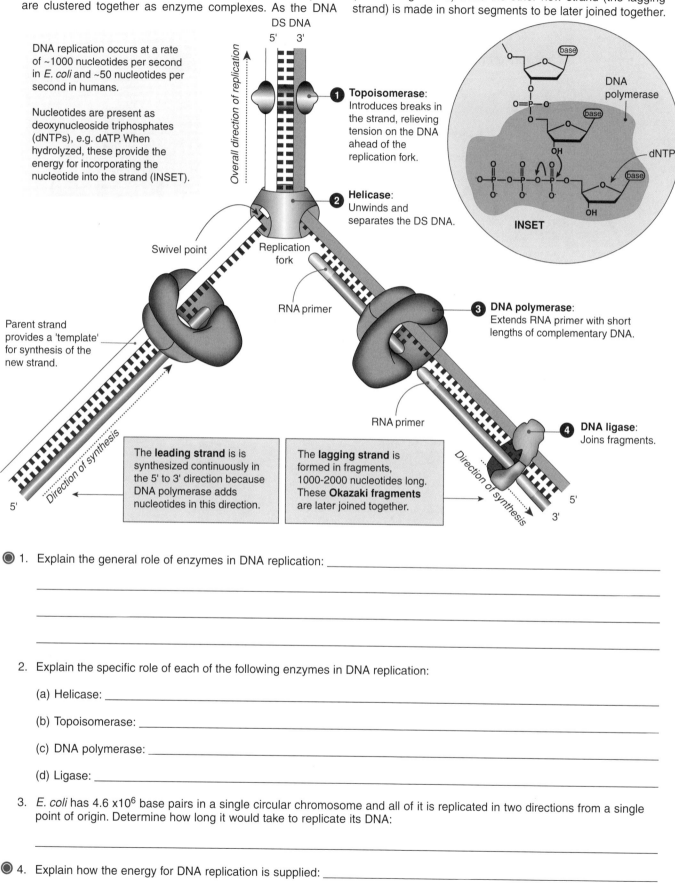

1 Topoisomerase: Introduces breaks in the strand, relieving tension on the DNA ahead of the replication fork.

2 Helicase: Unwinds and separates the DS DNA.

DNA polymerase
dNTP
base
OH
INSET

Swivel point
Replication fork
RNA primer

3 DNA polymerase: Extends RNA primer with short lengths of complementary DNA.

Parent strand provides a 'template' for synthesis of the new strand.

RNA primer

4 DNA ligase: Joins fragments.

3' 5'
Direction of synthesis

The **leading strand** is is synthesized continuously in the 5' to 3' direction because DNA polymerase adds nucleotides in this direction.

The **lagging strand** is formed in fragments, 1000-2000 nucleotides long. These **Okazaki fragments** are later joined together.

Direction of synthesis
5' 3'

1. Explain the general role of enzymes in DNA replication: ____________________

2. Explain the specific role of each of the following enzymes in DNA replication:

   (a) Helicase: ____________________

   (b) Topoisomerase: ____________________

   (c) DNA polymerase: ____________________

   (d) Ligase: ____________________

3. *E. coli* has 4.6 $\times 10^6$ base pairs in a single circular chromosome and all of it is replicated in two directions from a single point of origin. Determine how long it would take to replicate its DNA:

   ____

4. Explain how the energy for DNA replication is supplied: ____________________

ISBN: 978-1-98-856656-6

114 What is Gene Expression?

Key Question: How does the process of gene expression use the information in genes to produce proteins?

Gene expression is the process by which the information in genes is used to synthesize a protein or polypeptide. It involves **transcription** of the DNA into mRNA and **translation** of the mRNA into a polypeptide. Eukaryotic genes include non-protein coding regions called introns. Intronic DNA must be edited out before the mRNA can translated by the ribosomes. Transcription and editing occur in the nucleus. Translation of the mRNA by the ribosomes occurs in the cytoplasm. This flow of information from DNA to RNA to protein is known in biology as the **central dogma**.

A summary of eukaryotic gene expression

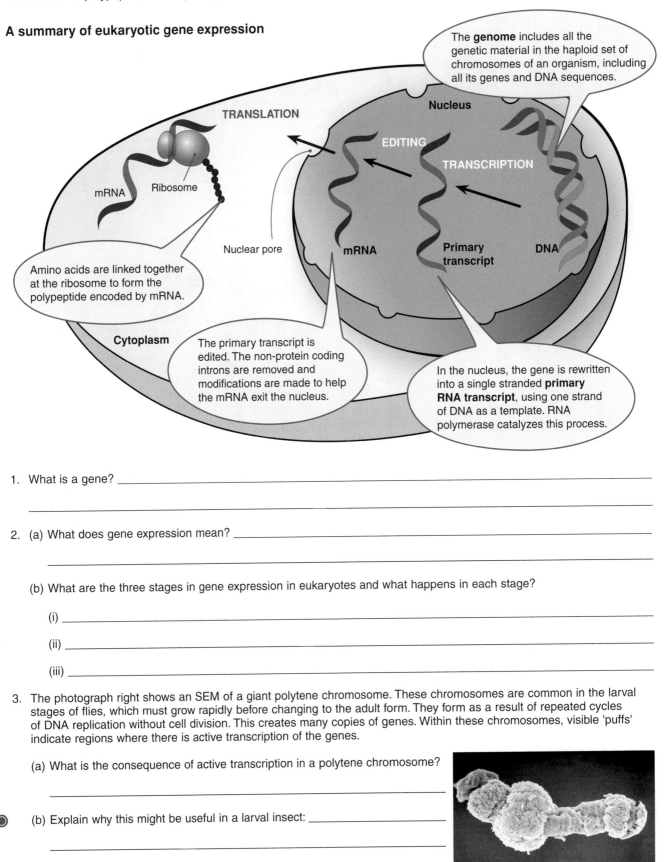

The **genome** includes all the genetic material in the haploid set of chromosomes of an organism, including all its genes and DNA sequences.

Nucleus

TRANSLATION

EDITING

TRANSCRIPTION

mRNA

Ribosome

Nuclear pore

mRNA

Primary transcript

DNA

Amino acids are linked together at the ribosome to form the polypeptide encoded by mRNA.

Cytoplasm

The primary transcript is edited. The non-protein coding introns are removed and modifications are made to help the mRNA exit the nucleus.

In the nucleus, the gene is rewritten into a single stranded **primary RNA transcript**, using one strand of DNA as a template. RNA polymerase catalyzes this process.

1. What is a gene? ______________________________

____

2. (a) What does gene expression mean? ______________________________

____

(b) What are the three stages in gene expression in eukaryotes and what happens in each stage?

(i) ______________________________

(ii) ______________________________

(iii) ______________________________

3. The photograph right shows an SEM of a giant polytene chromosome. These chromosomes are common in the larval stages of flies, which must grow rapidly before changing to the adult form. They form as a result of repeated cycles of DNA replication without cell division. This creates many copies of genes. Within these chromosomes, visible 'puffs' indicate regions where there is active transcription of the genes.

(a) What is the consequence of active transcription in a polytene chromosome?

____

(b) Explain why this might be useful in a larval insect: ______________________________

____

____

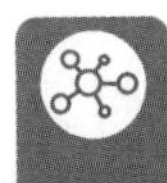

IST-1

2.B

ISBN: 978-1-98-856656-6

115 What is the Genetic Code?

Key Question: How does the three letter triplet code of DNA provide the information to assemble proteins?

The genetic information for the assembly of amino acids into polypeptides is stored as a series of three-base sequences on mRNA called **codons**. Each codon represents one of 20 amino acids used to make proteins. The code is effectively universal, being the same in all living things (with a few minor exceptions). The genetic code is summarized in a mRNA-amino acid table, which identifies the amino acid encoded by each mRNA codon. The code is degenerate, meaning there may be more than one codon for each amino acid. Most of this degeneracy is in the third nucleotide of a codon.

The mRNA - amino acid table

The table on the right is used to 'decode' the genetic code. It identifies the amino acid encoded by each mRNA codon. There are 64 different codons possible, 61 code for amino acids, and three are stop codons.

Amino acid names are written as three letter abbreviations, e.g. Ser = serine (or sometimes one-letter abbreviations, e.g. S = serine). To work out which amino acid a codon codes for, carry out the following steps:

- i Find the first letter of the codon in the row on the left hand side of the table. AUG is the start codon.
- ii Find the column that intersects that row from the top, second letter, row.
- iii Locate the third base in the codon by looking along the row on the right hand side that matches your codon. e.g. GAU codes for Asp (aspartic acid)

Read second letter here

First letter	Second letter: U	C	A	G	Third letter
U	UUU Phe	UCU Ser	UAU Tyr	UGU Cys	U
	UUC Phe	UCC Ser	UAC Tyr	UGC Cys	C
	UUA Leu	UCA Ser	UAA STOP	UGA STOP	A
	UUG Leu	UCG Ser	UAG STOP	UGG Trp	G
C	CUU Leu	CCU Pro	CAU His	CGU Arg	U
	CUC Leu	CCC Pro	CAC His	CGC Arg	C
	CUA Leu	CCA Pro	CAA Gln	CGA Arg	A
	CUG Leu	CCG Pro	CAG Gln	CGG Arg	G
A	AUU Ile	ACU Thr	AAU Asn	AGU Ser	U
	AUC Ile	ACC Thr	AAC Asn	AGC Ser	C
	AUA Ile	ACA Thr	AAA Lys	AGA Arg	A
	AUG Met	ACG Thr	AAG Lys	AGG Arg	G
G	GUU Val	GCU Ala	GAU Asp	GGU Gly	U
	GUC Val	GCC Ala	GAC Asp	GGC Gly	C
	GUA Val	GCA Ala	GAA Glu	GGA Gly	A
	GUG Val	GCG Ala	GAG Glu	GGG Gly	G

Read first letter here

Read third letter here

1. (a) Use the base-pairing rule for to create the complementary strand for the DNA template strand shown below.

Template strand

DNA TAC CCA ATG GAC TCC CAT TAT GCC CGT GAA ATC

Complementary strand (this is the DNA coding strand)

(b) For the same DNA template strand, determine the mRNA sequence and use the mRNA-amino acid table to determine the amino acid sequence. Note that in mRNA, uracil (U) replaces thymine (T) and pairs with adenine.

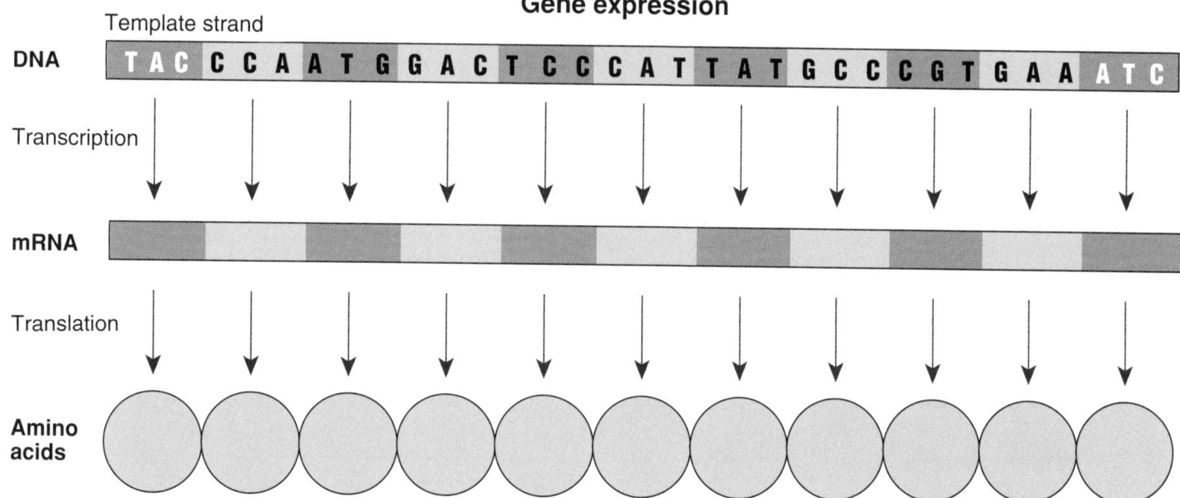

2. What do you notice about the sequence on the DNA coding strand and the mRNA strand? ______

______

ISBN: 978-1-98-856656-6

Redundancy and degeneracy

Redundancy and degeneracy are important concepts in understanding the **genetic code.**

- **Redundancy** occurs when the same function is performed by identical elements.
- **Degeneracy** refers to the ability of structurally different elements to perform the same function or yield the same output.

Degeneracy and redundancy are often confused or used synonymously but they are subtly different. Degeneracy is common in biological systems but true redundancy is less so (the main source of genetic redundancy being gene duplication). Examples of redundancy and degeneracy are illustrated below. In modern aircraft, redundant features add safety by making sure if one system fails others will ensure a safe flight. Degeneracy can be seen in proteins when different proteins have the same function.

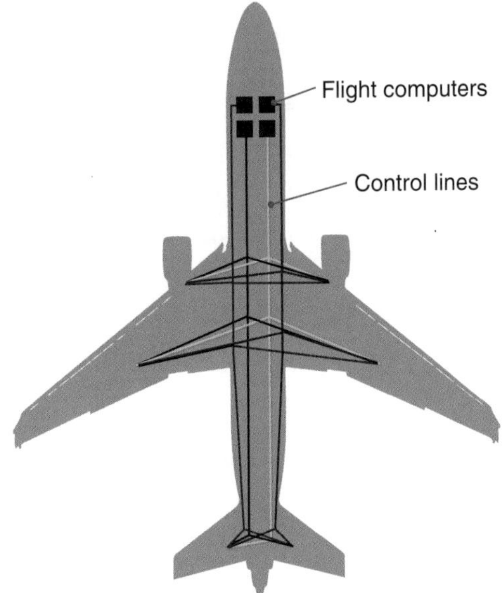

Modern aircraft (left) have multiple redundant features for safety. Often there are three or four flight computers linked independently to the flight surfaces and other input/output devices. If one computer or control line fails the others can continue to fly the plane normally.

Degeneracy is seen in the production of the enzymes salivary and pancreatic amylase. The enzymes are encoded by different genes (AMY1A and AMY2A) but are structurally and functionally equivalent (right). Salivary amylase breaks down carbohydrates in the mouth, whereas pancreatic amylase does so in the small intestine.

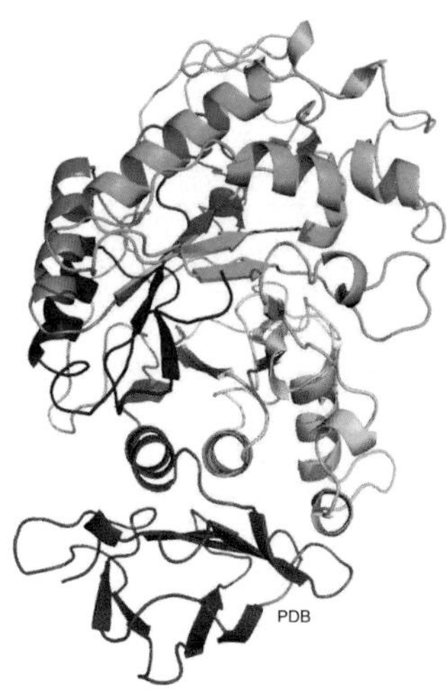

Salivary amylase (above) is structurally different to pancreatic amylase, but has the same function.

The genetic code shows **degeneracy**. This means that a number of 3 base combinations specify one amino acid. The codons for the same amino acid often differ by only a single letter (often the second or third). For example, proline is encoded by four different codons.

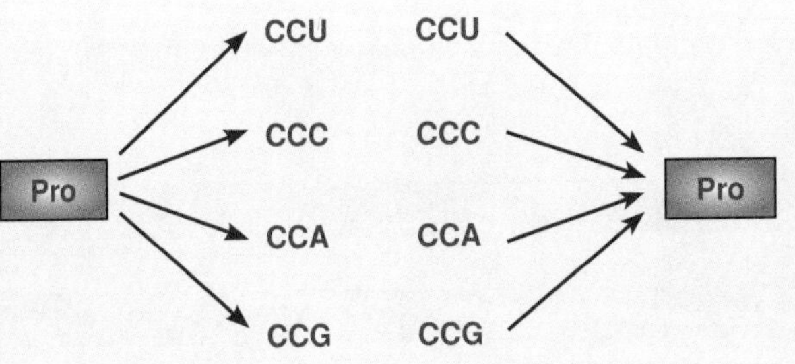

Although there is degeneracy in the genetic code, so that several codons code for the same amino acid (e.g. CCU, CCC, CCA, and CCG code for proline), there is no ambiguity (uncertainty). A particular codon in mRNA will always be encode the same amino acid or stop signal.

3. Explain how degeneracy adds "safety" to the coding of protein chains: ______________________________

____

____

____

4. The genetic code shows degeneracy but no ambiguity. What does this mean and why is it important? ______________________________

____

____

____

5. Identify the following:

   (a) The codons that encode valine (Val): ______________________________

   (b) The codons that encode aspartic acid (Asp): ______________________________

6. (a) Arginine (Arg) is encoded in how many ways? ______________________________

   (b) Glycine (Gly) is encoded in how many ways? ______________________________

   (c) Which amino acid(s) are encoded in only one way? ______________________________

ISBN: 978-1-98-856656-6

116 Transcription in Eukaryotes

Key Question: What is the purpose of transcription, where does it occur, and what are the key steps in the process?

Transcription is the first stage of gene expression. It takes place in the nucleus and is carried out by the enzyme RNA polymerase, which rewrites the DNA into a primary RNA transcript using a single template strand of DNA. The protein-coding portion of a gene is bounded by an upstream start (promoter) region and a downstream terminator region. These regions control transcription by telling RNA polymerase where to start and stop transcription. In eukaryotes, non protein-coding sections called **introns** must first be removed and the remaining **exons** spliced together to form the mature mRNA before the gene can be translated into a protein. This editing process also occurs in the nucleus.

Transcription is carried out by RNA polymerase (RNAP)

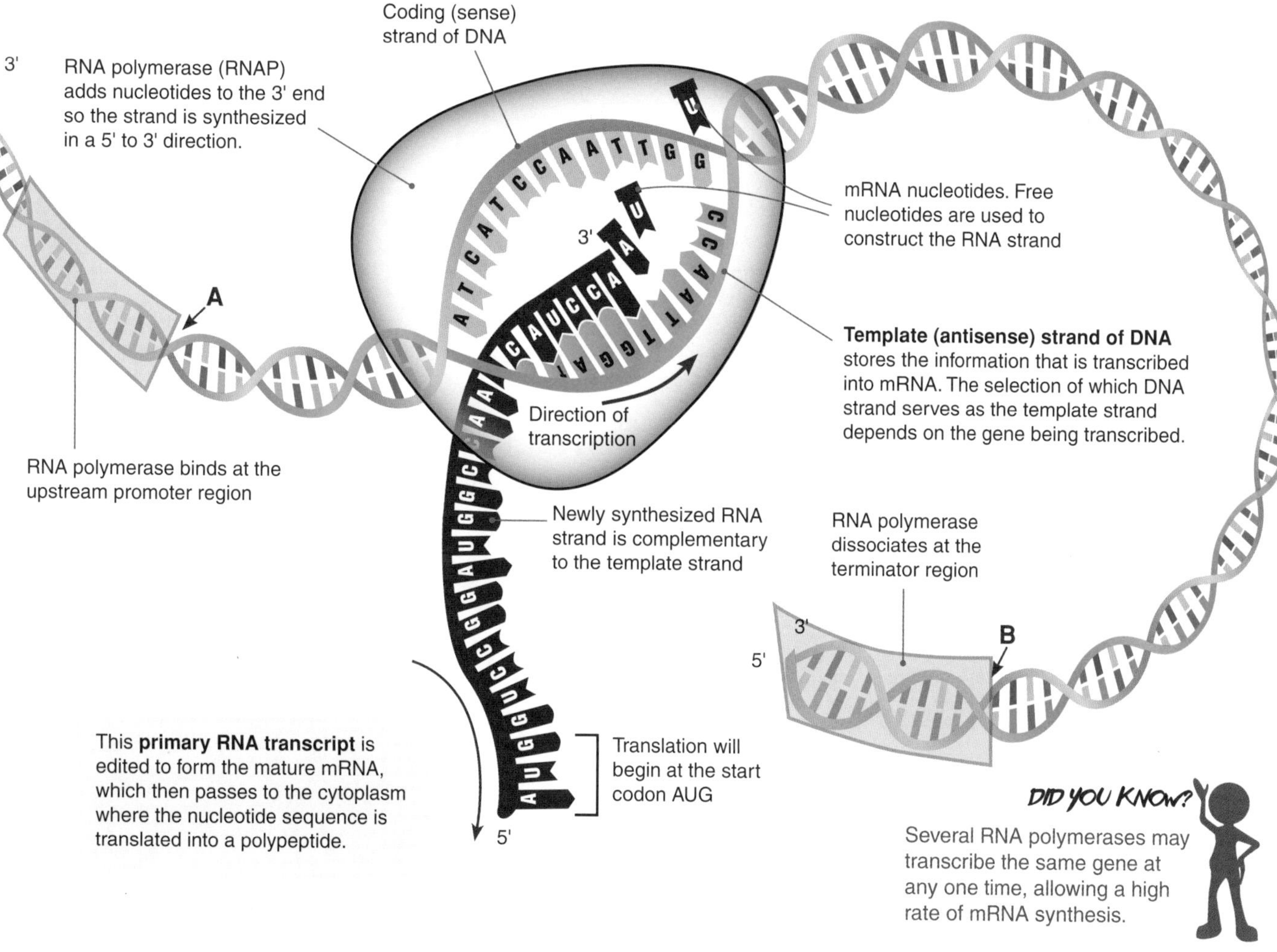

Coding (sense) strand of DNA
3'
RNA polymerase (RNAP) adds nucleotides to the 3' end so the strand is synthesized in a 5' to 3' direction.
mRNA nucleotides. Free nucleotides are used to construct the RNA strand
3'
A
Template (antisense) strand of DNA stores the information that is transcribed into mRNA. The selection of which DNA strand serves as the template strand depends on the gene being transcribed.
Direction of transcription
RNA polymerase binds at the upstream promoter region
Newly synthesized RNA strand is complementary to the template strand
RNA polymerase dissociates at the terminator region
3'
5'
B
This **primary RNA transcript** is edited to form the mature mRNA, which then passes to the cytoplasm where the nucleotide sequence is translated into a polypeptide.
Translation will begin at the start codon AUG
5'

DID YOU KNOW?

Several RNA polymerases may transcribe the same gene at any one time, allowing a high rate of mRNA synthesis.

1. (a) Name the enzyme responsible for transcribing the DNA: ______

   (b) What strand of DNA does this enzyme use? ______

   (c) Is the code on this strand the same as or complementary to the RNA being formed: ______

   (d) Which nucleotide base replaces thymine in mRNA? ______

   (e) Explain what is represented by points **A** and **B** on the diagram: ______

2. (a) In which direction is the RNA strand synthesized? ______

   (b) Explain why this is the case: ______

3. (a) Why is AUG called the start codon? ______

   (b) What would the three letter code be on the DNA coding strand? ______

ISBN: 978-1-98-856656-6

117 mRNA Processing in Eukaryotes

Key Question: How is the primary transcript modified after transcription and what do the modifications achieve?

Once a gene is transcribed, the primary transcript is modified to produce the mRNA strand that will be translated in the cytoplasm. Modifications to the 5' and 3' ends of the transcript enable the mRNA to exit the nucleus and remain stable long enough to be translated. Other post transcriptional modifications remove non-protein coding intronic DNA and splice exons in different combinations to produce different protein end products.

Primary RNA is modified by the addition of caps and tails

CAP A guanine nucleotide cap at the 5' end of the primary transcript stops degradation during transport from the nucleus and helps in the first phase of translation.

5' | 5' UTR | Coding sequence | 3' UTR | 3'

After transcription, the primary RNA transcript is modified by enzymes to create 'caps' and 'tails'. These modifications are part of the untranslated region (UTR) at each end of a gene. They stabilize the RNA, protect it from degradation, and help its transport through the nuclear pore. They are also important in translation although they are not translated themselves. The START and STOP points of translation are marked by darker green lines.

POLY-A TAIL Adenosine nucleotides are added to the primary transcript. These poly-A tails aid nuclear export, translation, and stability of the mRNA.

Modification after transcription

- As you have seen earlier, introns are removed from the primary mRNA transcript and the exons are spliced together. However, exons can be spliced together in different ways to create variations in the translated proteins. Exon splicing occurs in the nucleus, either during or immediately after transcription.
- In mammals, the most common method of alternative splicing involves exon skipping, in which not all exons are spliced into the final mRNA (below).

DID YOU KNOW?

Human DNA contains 25,000 genes, but produces up to 1 million different proteins. Modifications after transcription and translation allow several proteins to be produced from just one gene.

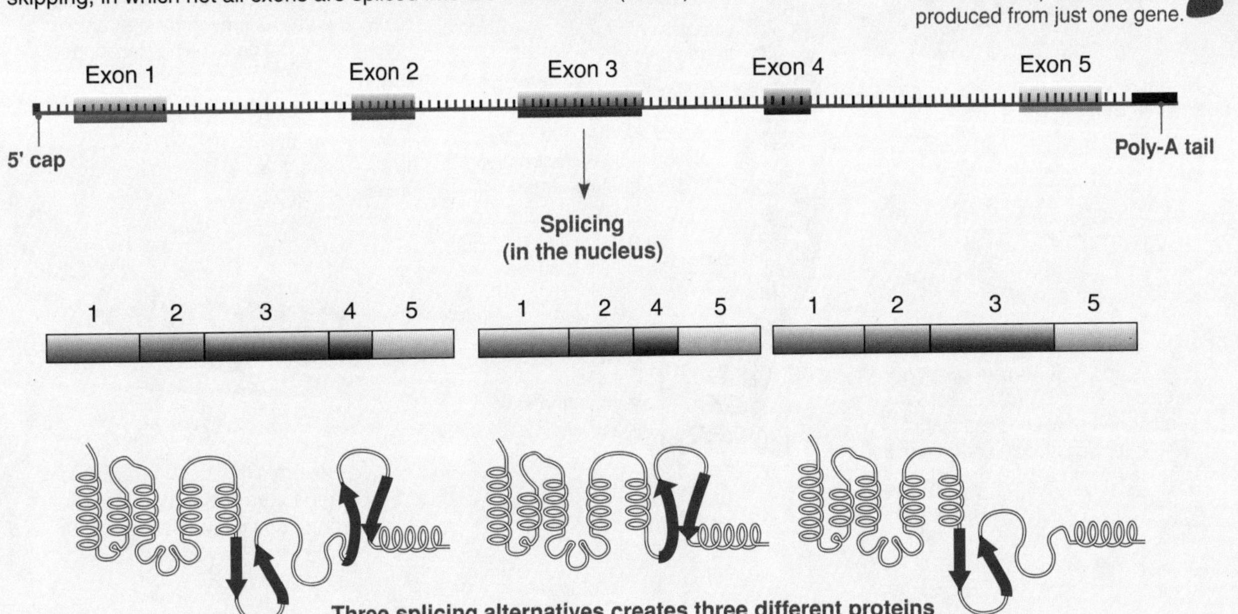

Three splicing alternatives creates three different proteins

1. Explain the purpose of the caps and tail on mRNA? ______________________________

2. (a) What happens to the intronic sequences in DNA after transcription? ______________________________

   (b) What is one possible fate for these introns? ______________________________

3. Explain how so many proteins can be produced from a much smaller number of genes: ______________________________

4. If a human produces 1 million proteins, but human DNA codes for only 25,000 genes, on average how many proteins are produced per gene?

IST-1
2.B

ISBN: 978-1-98-856656-6

118 Translation

Key Question: What is the purpose of translation, where does it occur, and what are the key steps in the process?

In eukaryotes, translation occurs in the cytoplasm either at free ribosomes or ribosomes on the rough endoplasmic reticulum. Ribosomes translate the code carried in the mRNA molecules, providing the catalytic environment for the linkage of amino acids delivered by transfer RNA (tRNA) molecules. Protein synthesis begins at the start codon and, as the ribosome wobbles along the mRNA strand, the polypeptide chain elongates. On reaching a stop codon, the ribosome subunits dissociate from the mRNA, releasing the polypeptide chain.

Ribosome structure

Ribosomes are made up of a complex of ribosomal RNA (rRNA) and ribosomal proteins. These small cellular structures direct the catalytic steps required for protein synthesis and have specific regions that accommodate transfer RNA (tRNA) molecules loaded with amino acids.

Ribosomes exist as two separate sub-units (below) until they are attracted to a binding site on the mRNA molecule, when they come together around the mRNA strand.

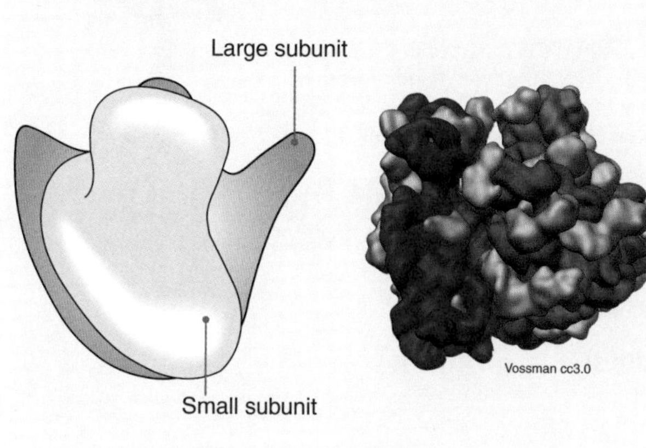

tRNA structure

tRNA molecules are RNA molecules, about 80 nucleotides long, which transfer amino acids to the ribosome as directed by the codons in the mRNA. Each tRNA has a 3-base anticodon, which is complementary to a mRNA codon. There is a different tRNA molecule for each possible codon and, because of the degeneracy of the genetic code, there may be up to six different tRNAs carrying the same amino acid.

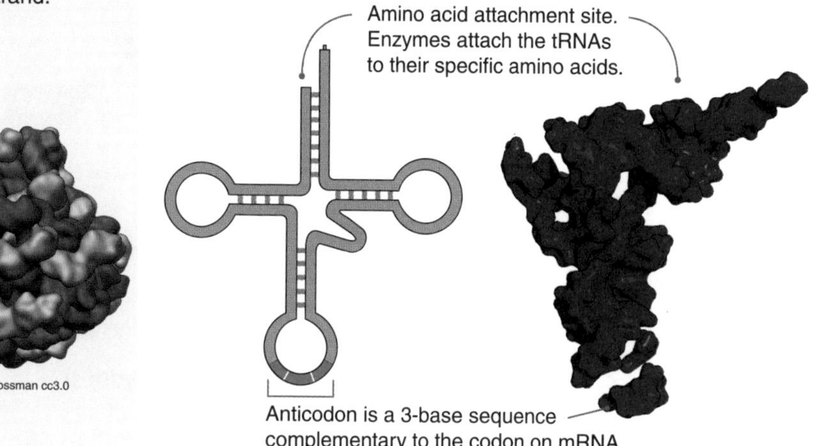

Amino acid attachment site. Enzymes attach the tRNAs to their specific amino acids.
Anticodon is a 3-base sequence complementary to the codon on mRNA.

1. Describe the structure of a ribosome: ______________________

____

2. What is the role of each of the following components in translation?

(a) Ribosome: ______________________

(b) tRNA: ______________________

(c) Amino acids: ______________________

(d) Start codon: ______________________

(e) Stop codon: ______________________

3. There are many different types of tRNA molecules, each with a different anticodon (HINT: see the mRNA table).

(a) How many different tRNA types are there, each with a unique anticodon? ______________________

(b) Explain your answer: ______________________

____

____

(c) Determine the mRNA codons and the amino acid sequence for the following tRNA anticodons:

tRNA anticodons: U A C U A G C C G C G A U U U

Codons on the mRNA: ______________________

Amino acids encoded: ______________________

ISBN: 978-1-98-856656-6

tRNA molecules deliver amino acids to ribosomes

tRNA molecules match amino acids with the appropriate codon on mRNA. As defined by the genetic code, the anticodon specifies which amino acid the tRNA carries. The tRNA delivers its amino acid to the ribosome, where enzymes join the amino acids to form a polypeptide chain. During translation the ribosome "wobbles" along the mRNA molecule joining amino acids together. Enzymes and energy are involved in charging the tRNA molecules (attaching them to their amino acid) and elongating the peptide chain.

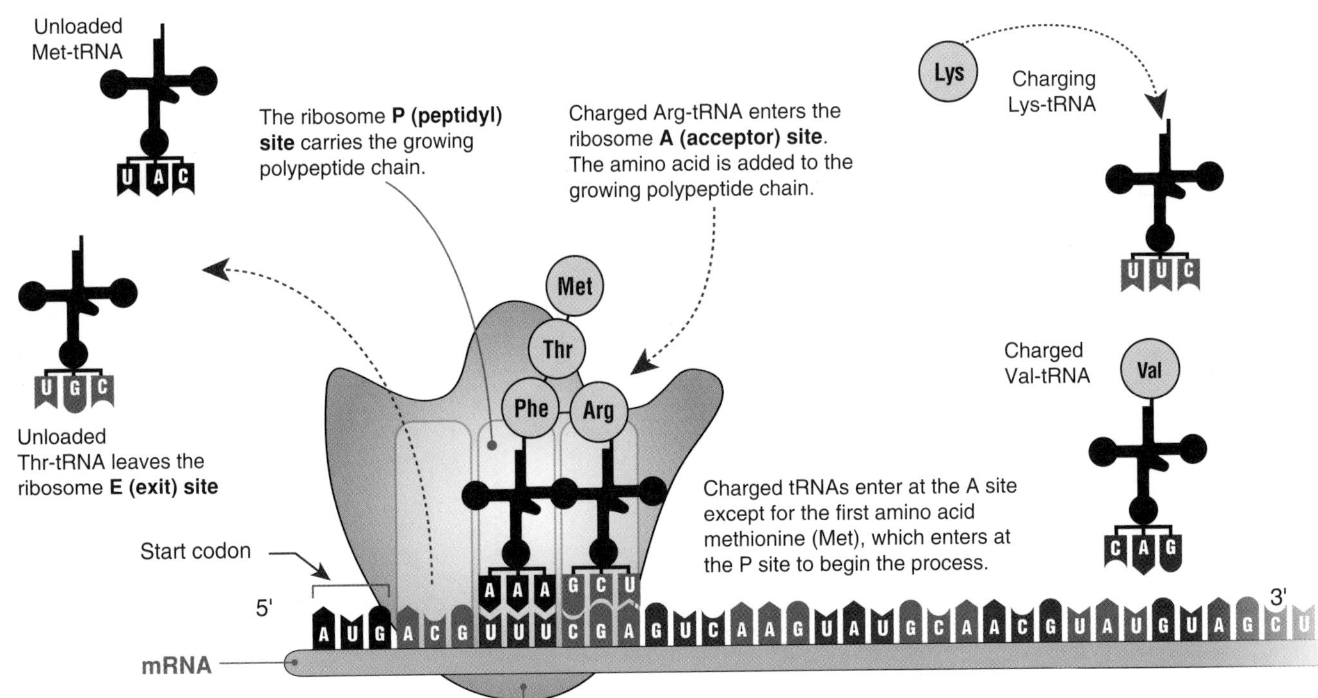

The polypeptide chain grows as more amino acids are added

Initiation

Protein synthesis begins when the ribosome reads the start codon (AUG).

Elongation

The polypeptide chain continues to grow as more amino acids are added.

Termination

Protein synthesis stops when a stop codon is reached (UGA, UAA, or UAC). The ribosome falls off the mRNA and the polypeptide is released.

START

STOP

5'

3'

Direction of protein synthesis

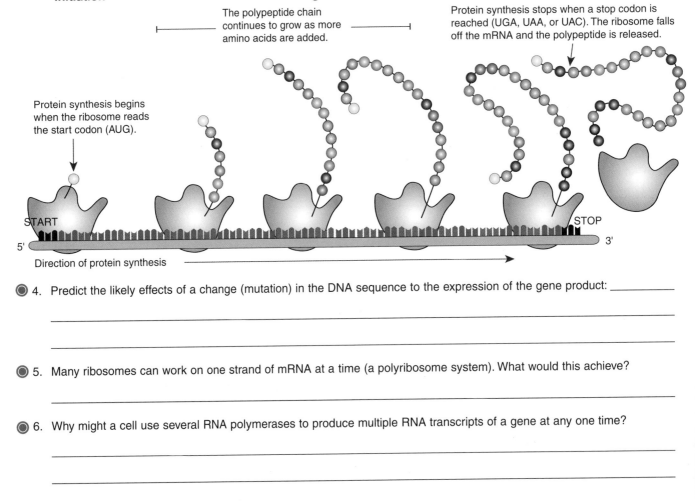

4. Predict the likely effects of a change (mutation) in the DNA sequence to the expression of the gene product: ______________

5. Many ribosomes can work on one strand of mRNA at a time (a polyribosome system). What would this achieve?

6. Why might a cell use several RNA polymerases to produce multiple RNA transcripts of a gene at any one time?

ISBN: 978-1-98-856656-6

Comparing gene expression in prokaryotes and eukaryotes

In both prokaryotes and eukaryotes, genes are transcribed by RNA polymerase and translated by ribosomes. However, there are some important differences. In eukaryotes, primary RNA must be edited and processed before passing from the nucleus to the cytoplasm. In prokaryotes, there is no nucleus and ribosomes can begin translating a gene while it is still being transcribed.

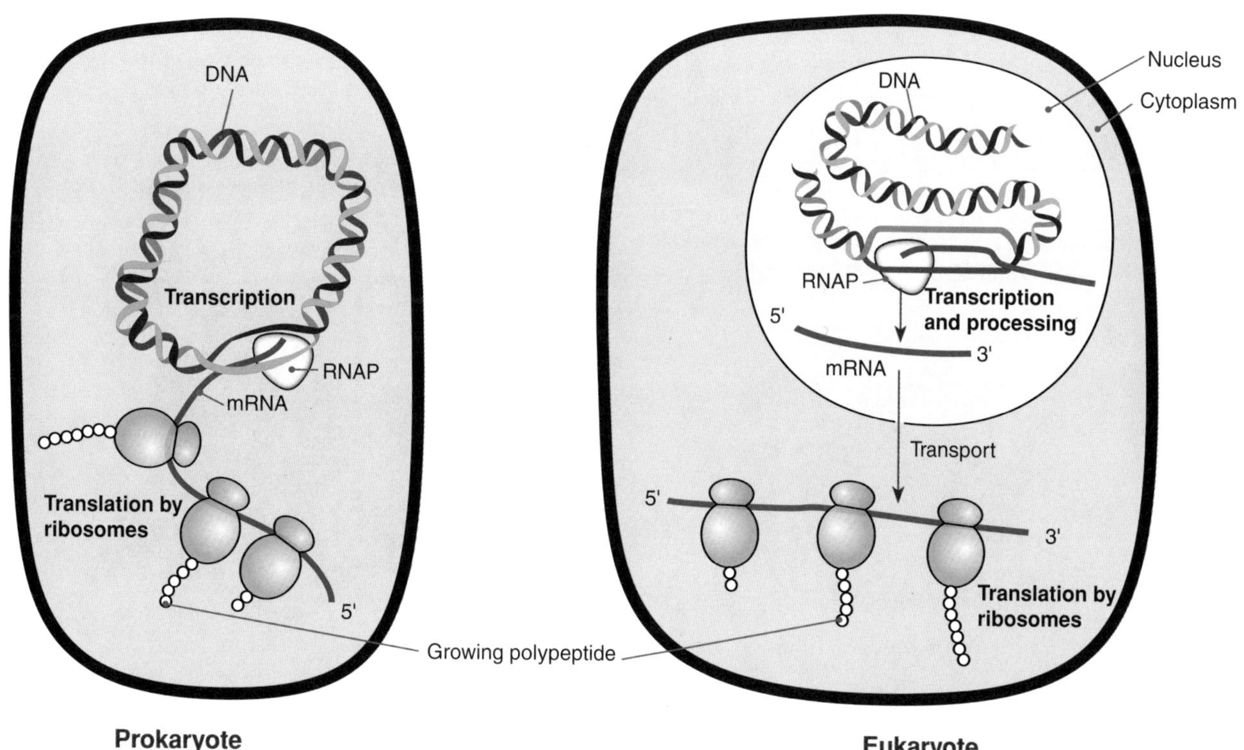

7. Draw a flowchart to represent the process of translation pictured opposite. A starting point has been provided:

8. Based on the diagram above, describe two differences between gene expression in prokaryotes and eukaryotes:

(a) ______________________________

(b) ______________________________

9. Based on the diagram above, how is gene expression in prokaryotes and eukaryotes similar? ______________________________

____

____

10. What benefit might there be to the way in which prokaryotes can begin translation while a gene is still being transcribed?

____

____

ISBN: 978-1-98-856656-6

119 Retroviruses: A Special Case in Information Flow

Key Question: How does the flow of genetic information in retroviruses differ from the central dogma?

As we have seen, living cells store their genetic information as double stranded DNA. This is transcribed to mRNA, then translated into proteins. In most viruses, this central dogma of DNA→RNA→protein is followed. However, one group of viruses store their genetic information as two single strands of RNA rather than DNA. In these **retroviruses**, RNA is first copied into DNA before it is integrated into the host cell's DNA. This is done using the enzyme reverse transcriptase. The discovery of this reverse flow of genetic information from RNA to DNA violated the central dogma.

A retrovirus such as HIV below, contains two positive single strand RNA molecules (+ssRNA) in association with two reverse transcriptase enzymes. When the virus enters the cell these +ssRNAs and the **reverse transcriptase** and **integrase enzymes** are released into the host cell's cytoplasm.

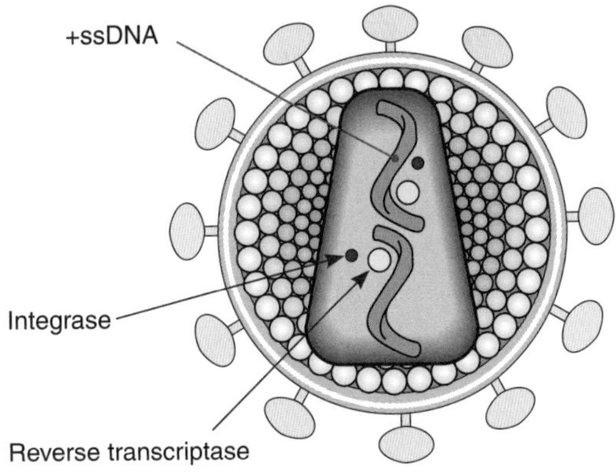

Life cycle of HIV, a retrovirus

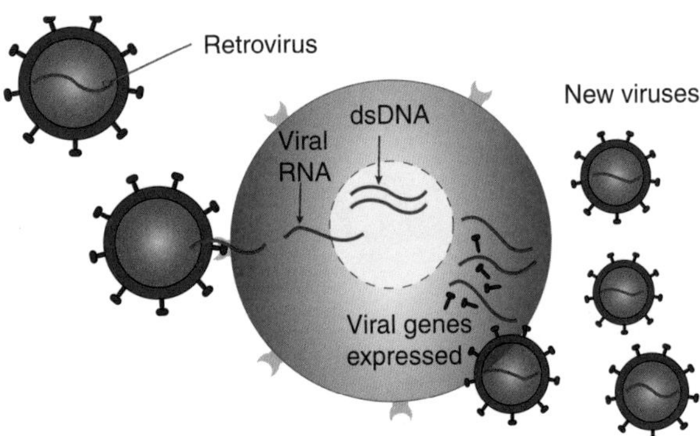

Once the RNA has been reverse transcribed into DNA, the DNA is integrated into the host's DNA by the enzyme **integrase**. The viral genes are expressed (transcribed and translated) and the cellular machinery of the host cell produces the components of the new viruses.

Reverse transcriptase is made of two subunits. A groove runs through the middle of the enzyme where the DNA is seated (shown in blue).

The reverse transcriptase copies the +ssRNA into single strand DNA (ssDNA) using the host cell's nucleotides. At the same time, the +ssRNA is broken down into single nucleotides which are released.

PDB

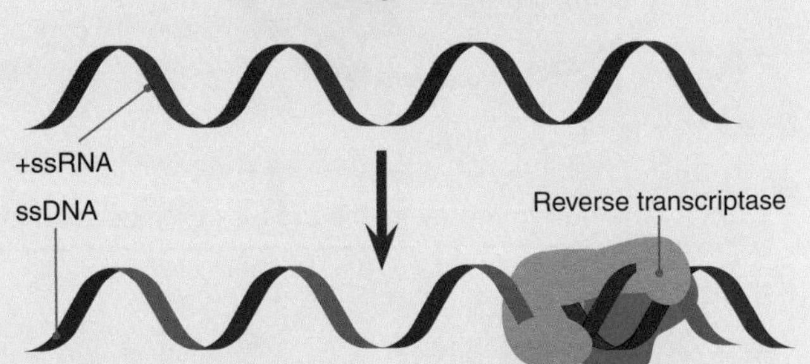

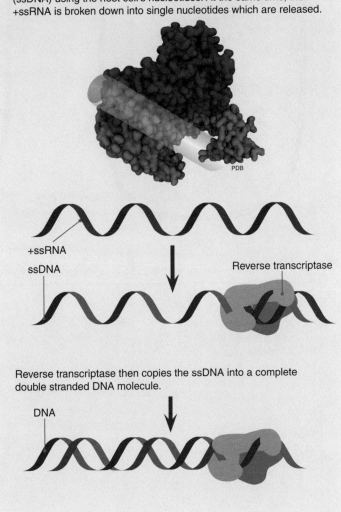

Reverse transcriptase then copies the ssDNA into a complete double stranded DNA molecule.

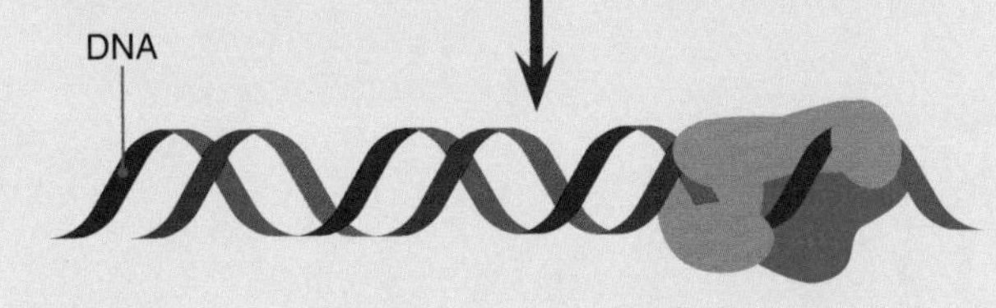

1. Describe the flow of genetic information to proteins in a living cell: ______

2. Describe the flow of genetic information to proteins in a retrovirus: ______

3. Use the diagrams to explain how reverse transcriptase produces DNA: ______

4. Describe the life cycle of a retrovirus: ______

ISBN: 978-1-98-856656-6

120 Structural and Regulatory Genes

Key Question: What are the functional differences between structural and regulatory genes?

Genes are sections of DNA that code for proteins (or other mRNA products). They are divided broadly into structural genes and regulatory genes. **Structural genes** code for any protein product other than a regulatory protein. The proteins encoded by structural genes are diverse and have roles in maintaining the structure or function of a cell. **Regulatory genes** code for proteins and other small molecules, such as microRNAs, that control the expression of structural genes. These regulatory genes may be some distance from the structural genes they control. Expressed structural genes are also bounded by **untranslated regions** called UTRs. UTRs contain regulatory sequences that directly control protein synthesis. These are arranged differently in prokaryotes and eukaryotes (below).

Prokaryotic gene structure

- In prokaryotes, several structural genes with related functions are grouped together between UTRs (below). These groupings of structural genes and their regulatory elements are called **operons**. The UTR upstream of the structural genes contains a regulatory sequence to initiate transcription of the structural genes. The downstream UTR stops transcription of the genes.
- In prokaryotes, the entire transcribed mRNA sequence for the structural genes is translated into proteins (there is no gene editing). Upstream of the operon, there is also a regulatory gene, which encodes a regulatory protein (not shown).

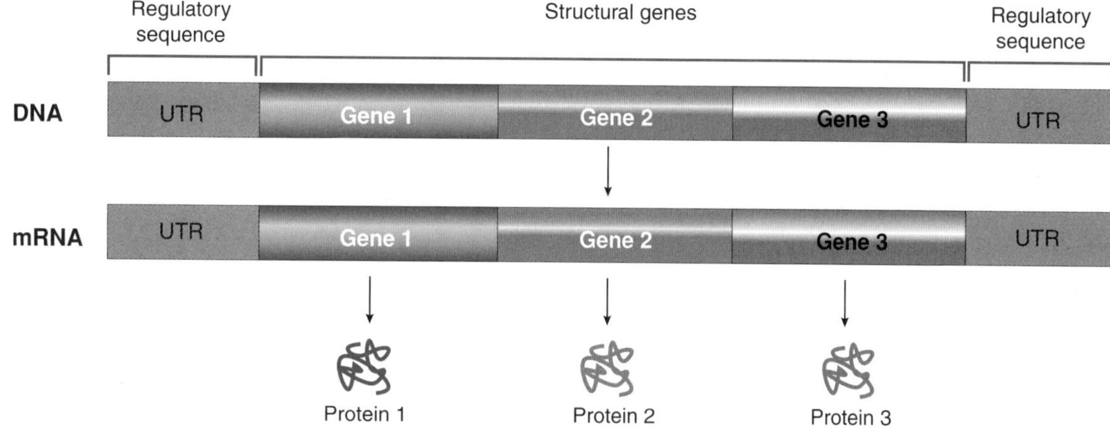

Eukaryotic gene structure

- In eukaryotes, structural genes are also under the control of regulatory sequences. However, only one structural gene is enclosed by UTRs and there is no 'bulk control' of a structural gene sequence as seen in prokaryotes (i.e. no operon).
- It is important to remember that before the primary RNA transcript is translated in eukaryotes, the non-protein coding introns are removed (only the protein-coding exons form the mature mRNA for translation).

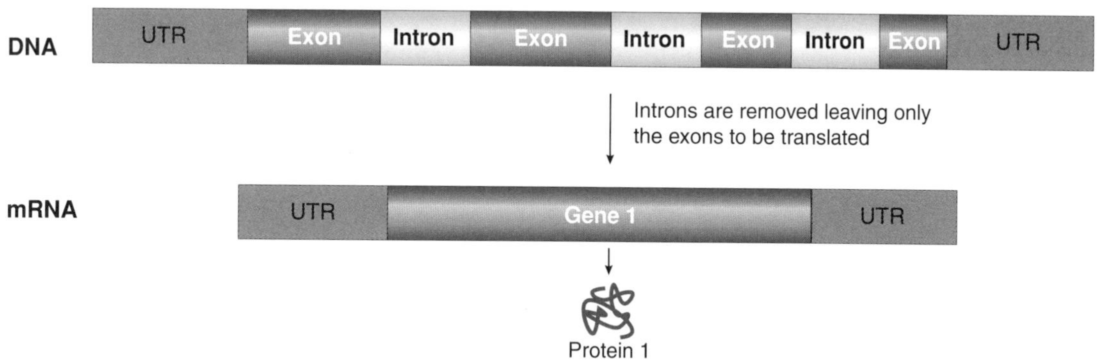

1. Describe the difference between a regulatory gene and a structural gene: ______________________________

____

____

2. Using the diagrams above, describe how gene expression in prokaryotes differs from gene expression in eukaryotes:

____

____

____

____

____

ISBN: 978-1-98-856656-6

121 Cellular Differentiation and Gene Expression

Key Question: What is cellular differentiation and how is it controlled to produce all the different cells in the body?

Multicellular organisms consist of many different types of cells, each specialized to carry out a particular function. A zygote and its first few divisions can differentiate to form any cell type in the body. During development, these cells divide and follow different developmental pathways, giving rise to specialized cells that make up the tissues and organs of the body. This process by which more specialized cells develop from more generalized ones is called **cellular differentiation**. It is achieved by switching on and off genes with regulatory proteins called **transcription factors**. Different transcription factors active at different times determine the fate of cells by regulating their developmental pathway.

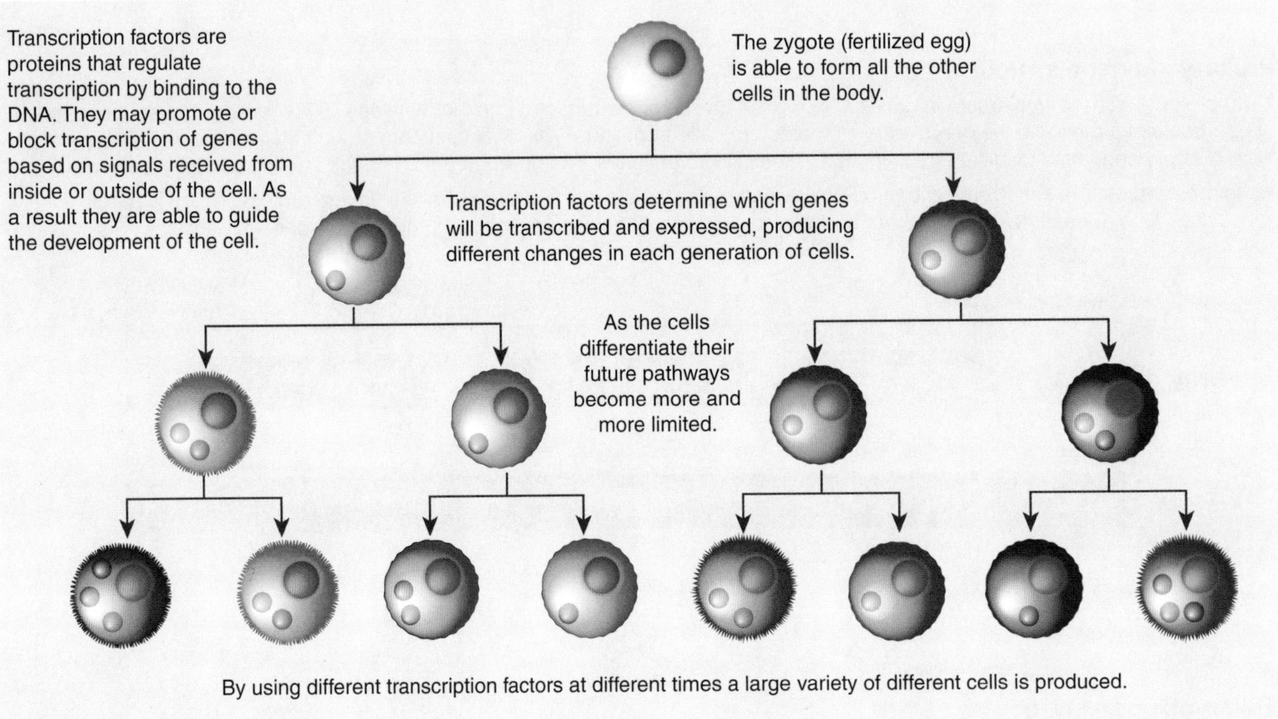

Transcription factors are proteins that regulate transcription by binding to the DNA. They may promote or block transcription of genes based on signals received from inside or outside of the cell. As a result they are able to guide the development of the cell.
The zygote (fertilized egg) is able to form all the other cells in the body.
Transcription factors determine which genes will be transcribed and expressed, producing different changes in each generation of cells.
As the cells differentiate their future pathways become more and more limited.
By using different transcription factors at different times a large variety of different cells is produced.

Signaling controls cell differentiation

The retina is the light sensitive tissue layer at the back of the eye. The retina is made up of several different cell types, all originating from retinal precursor cells. Many transcription factors control retinal cell fate during embryogenesis. Improper regulation of the signaling pathways can cause eyes to form in the wrong place or improper eye development.

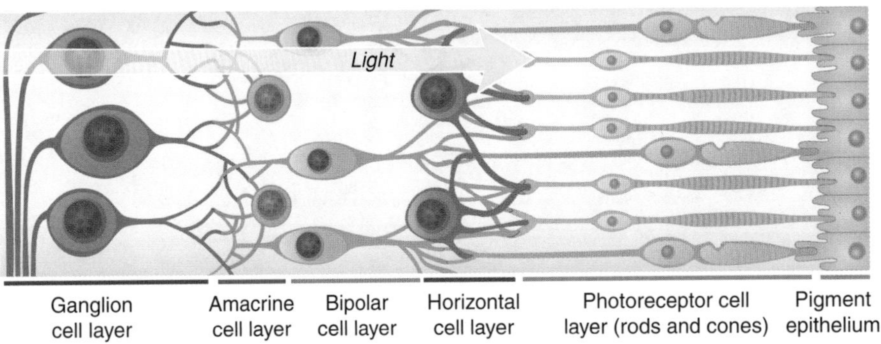

1. Multicellular organisms consist of many different cell types. Use the diagram above to explain how it is possible for these all to arise from a single fertilized egg (zygote):

2. What role do transcription factors play in cellular differentiation of the retina?

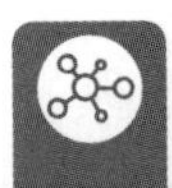

ISBN: 978-1-98-856656-6

122 Epigenetic Regulation of Gene Expression

Key Question: What is epigenetics, what does it involve, and how does it affect gene expression?

As you saw earlier, gene expression can be influenced in part by the environment. But how is the influence of environment moderated? Sometimes the environment directly influences a protein's function. Most often though, the regulation is epigenetic. **Epigenetic factors** are the chemical tags and markers external to the DNA. Epigenetic regulation is achieved by modifying the way the DNA is packaged and its availability to be transcribed. The DNA sequence is unchanged. Just as organisms have a genome, the collection of chemical tags an individual possess is called its **epigenome**.

The regulation of gene expression in eukaryotes is a complex process beginning before the DNA is even transcribed. The packaging of DNA regulates gene expression either by making the nucleosomes in the chromatin pack together tightly (**heterochromatin**) or more loosely (**euchromatin**). This affects whether or not RNA polymerase can attach to the DNA and transcribe it. Almost all of the chemical tags on DNA that make up the epigenome are reset in germ cells (eggs and sperm) and in the very earliest stages of development of an embryo.

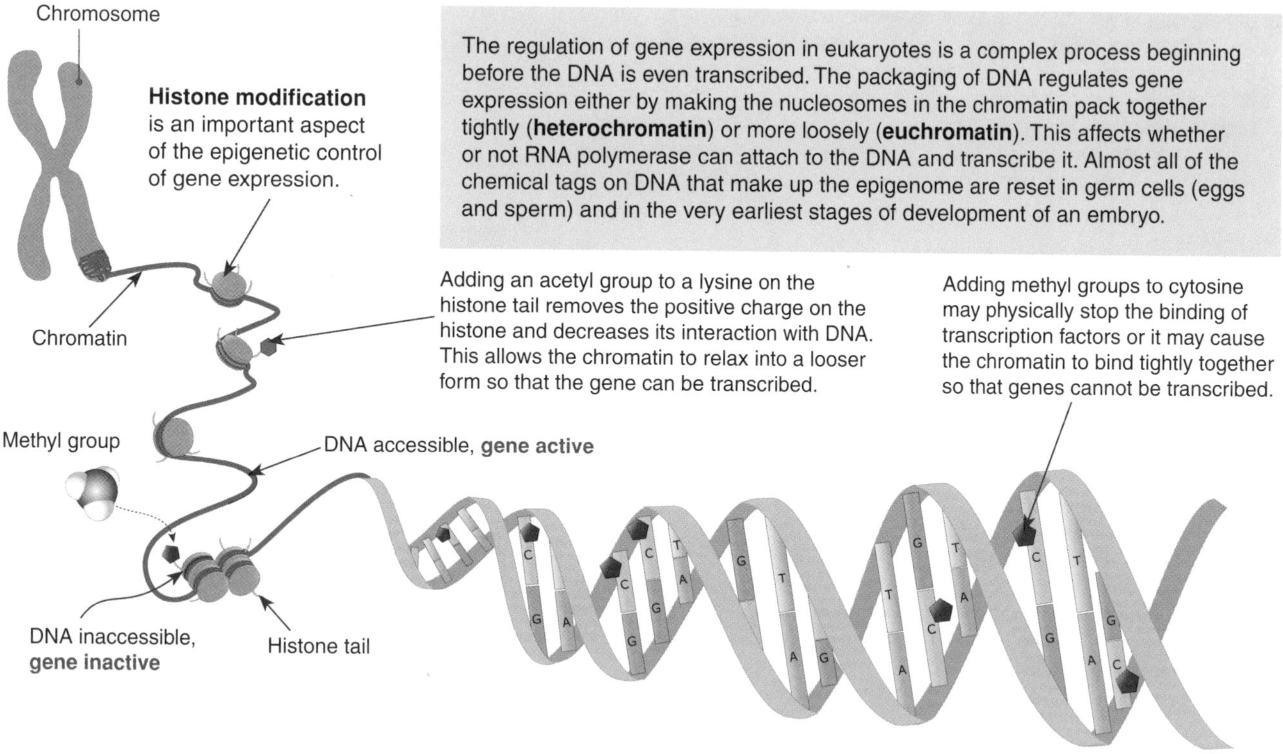

Chromosome
Histone modification is an important aspect of the epigenetic control of gene expression.
Chromatin
Methyl group
DNA accessible, **gene active**
DNA inaccessible, **gene inactive**
Histone tail
Adding an acetyl group to a lysine on the histone tail removes the positive charge on the histone and decreases its interaction with DNA. This allows the chromatin to relax into a looser form so that the gene can be transcribed.
Adding methyl groups to cytosine may physically stop the binding of transcription factors or it may cause the chromatin to bind tightly together so that genes cannot be transcribed.

1. What is epigenetics? ______________________________

____

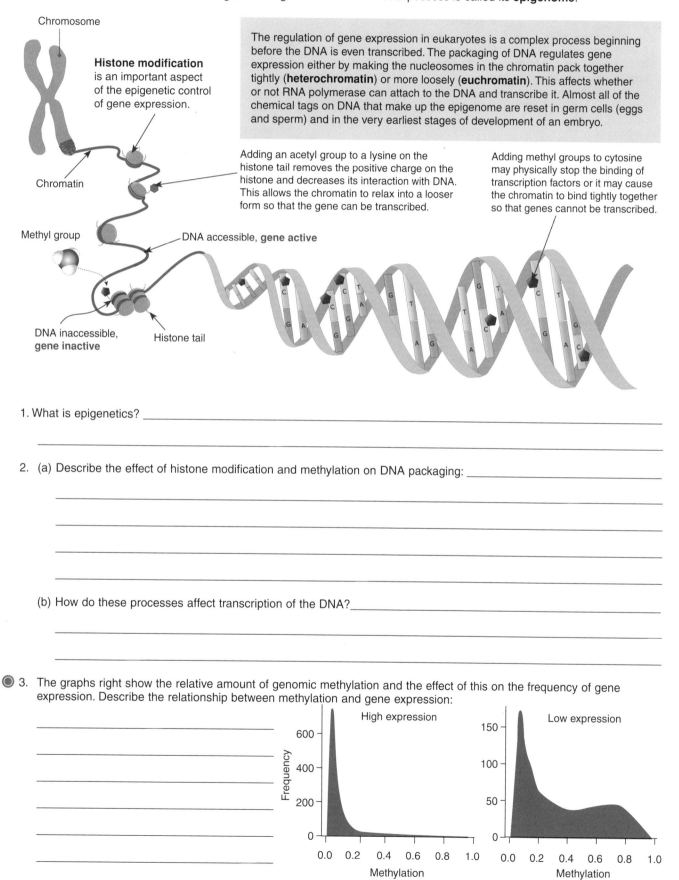

2. (a) Describe the effect of histone modification and methylation on DNA packaging: ______________________________

____

____

____

____

(b) How do these processes affect transcription of the DNA? ______________________________

____

____

3. The graphs right show the relative amount of genomic methylation and the effect of this on the frequency of gene expression. Describe the relationship between methylation and gene expression:

____

____

____

____

____

____

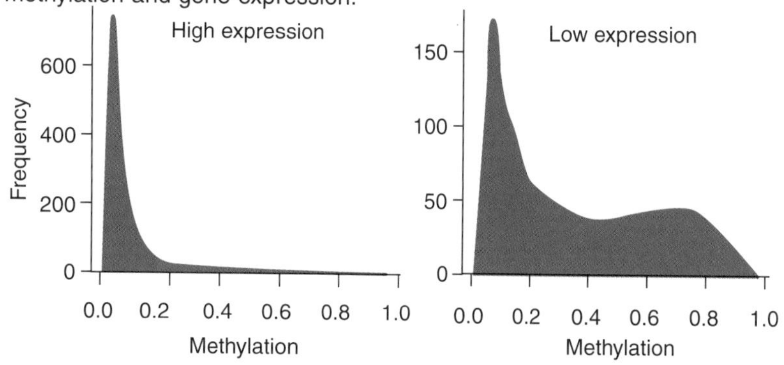

ISBN: 978-1-98-856656-6

Epigenetics and gene expression

Epigenetics affects development

- One of the biggest debates in the study of development is the idea of nature versus nurture. To what extent do genes or the environment affect development and phenotype?
- A 2004 study of the grooming of rat pups by their mothers helps provide some insight. In this study, the quality of care by a pup's mother affected how the pup behaved when it reached adulthood.
- Rat pups that were groomed more often by their mother were better at coping with stress than pups that received less grooming. What's more, it was shown that the effect was caused by changes in the expression of the glucocorticoid receptor, which plays a role in the response to stress.
- DNA analysis found differences in the way the DNA was chemically tagged. Rats that received a lot of grooming had DNA that allowed for greater transcription and so had higher expression of the glucocorticoid receptor. The opposite was true for rats who received little grooming.

Twins in space

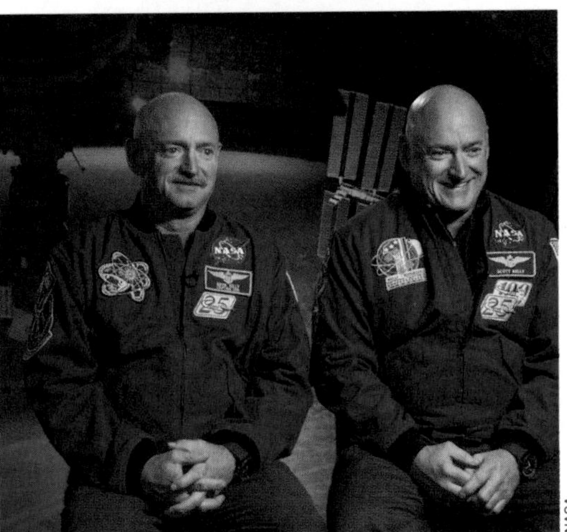

NASA

- Twin studies can provide a lot of information about how the environment affects gene expression. The studies are often done when identical twins have been separated at birth (usually because one or both of them are adopted out). Their similarities and differences can then be studied to assess how much the environment influenced their development.
- In 2015, NASA astronaut Scott Kelly blasted into space for a year long stay on the International Space Station. His identical twin brother Mark remained on Earth. This gave NASA a chance to study the real effects of space travel on the human body. Importantly, the gene expression of the men could be measured before and after Scott went to space.
- It was found that six months after Scott's return, 7% of his genes had not returned to their normal level of gene expression. Also, although there was no decrease in Scott's cognitive abilities, there was a decrease in his speed and accuracy until his readjustment to Earth gravity. The space environment had altered Scott Kelly's gene expression compared to his identical twin Mark Kelly.

4. (a) Describe how grooming by mother rats on their pups affected the pups in the long term: ______________________

   ____

   (b) How could this have been achieved by epigenetics? ______________________

   ____

   ____

5. How might twin studies help the study of gene-environment responses? ______________________

   ____

   ____

   ____

6. What evidence is there that epigenetics can have long term to permanent effects on gene expression?

   ____

   ____

   ____

   ____

7. When a zygote forms at fertilization most of the epigenetic tags are erased so that cells return to a genetic 'blank slate' ready for development to begin. However some epigenetic tags are retained and inherited. Why do you think it might be advantageous to inherit some epigenetic tags from a parent?

   ____

   ____

   ____

ISBN: 978-1-98-856656-6

123 Transcription Factors During Development

Key Question: How do signal molecules produced in the embryo affect embryonic development?

The differentiation of cells is controlled by cell signaling, either by producing a gradient of molecules through the embryo or by signaling a specific cell that then signals other cells in sequence. Cell signals regulate transcription factors that in turn control the differential gene expression that shapes embryos. This process, called **embryonic induction**, takes hours to days, while the time a cell can respond to an inducing signal is strictly limited.

Development in *Drosophila*

Morphogen concentration and cell fate

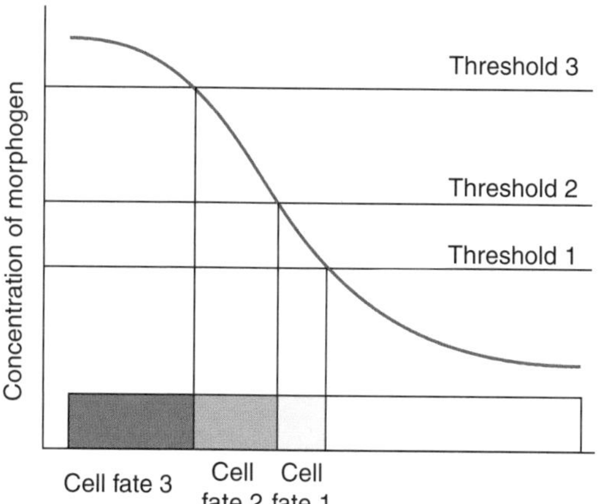

Morphogens are signal molecules that govern patterns of tissue development. Morphogens induce cells in different positions to adopt different fates by diffusing from an area of production through a field of cells. Bicoid protein (right) is an example of a morphogen.

The **bicoid gene** is important in *Drosophila* development. After fertilization, bicoid mRNA from the mother is passed to the egg where it is translated into bicoid protein. Bicoid protein forms a concentration gradient in the developing embryo, which determine where the anterior (front) and posterior (rear) develop.

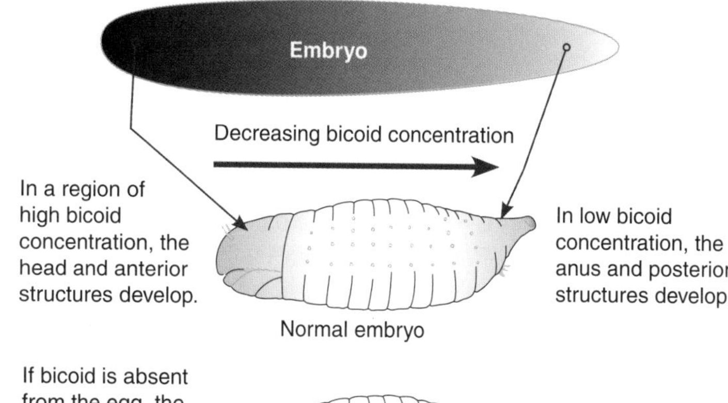

Embryo
Decreasing bicoid concentration
In a region of high bicoid concentration, the head and anterior structures develop.
In low bicoid concentration, the anus and posterior structures develop.
Normal embryo
If bicoid is absent from the egg, the embryo develops two posterior ends and no head. Development stops.
Bicoid mutant

Development in *Caenorhabditis elegans*

The nematode worm, *Caenorhabditis elegans*, is a model organism for developmental studies as its simple body plan and short life cycle makes it easy to study.

The development of *C. elegans* never varies. Exactly 1090 cells are generated to form an adult hermaphrodite. Of these 1090 cells exactly 131 cells undergo programmed cell death (apoptosis).

The death of these cells is controlled by the genes *ced-3* and *ced-4*, which are themselves regulated by gene *ced-9*. There are three waves of apoptosis. The first removes 113 cells, the second removes 18 more cells, and the third removes half of the developing egg cells (oocytes). This process is so tightly regulated that cell death events occur at the same time and same place in all *C. elegans* individuals.

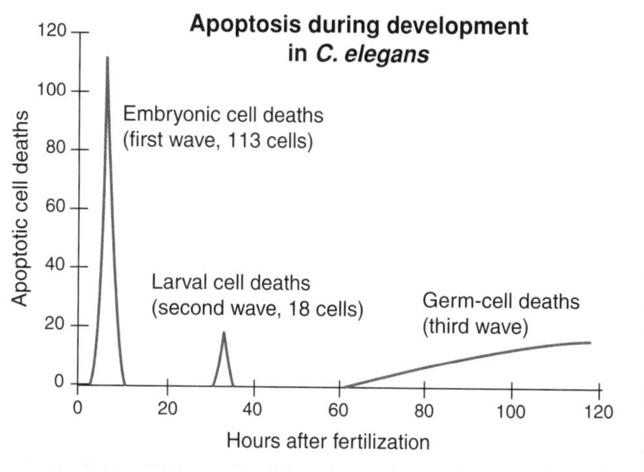

G Lettre and M Hengartner, Nature.com 2007

1. (a) What is a morphogen? ______________________________

   (b) Explain the purpose of the bicoid protein in *Drosophila*: ______________________________

2. Describe the pattern of apoptosis in the development of *C. elegans*: ______________________________

ISBN: 978-1-98-856656-6

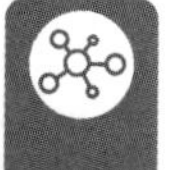

Cell signaling and transcription factors: Gibberellic acid activation of α-amylase

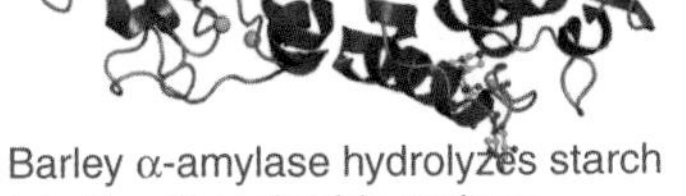
Barley α-amylase hydrolyzes starch into the disaccharide maltose.

- In plants, the hormone gibberellic acid (GA) is involved in seed germination. GA acts as a signal molecule which signals for the transcription factor Myb to be produced.
- Myb stimulates the production of the enzyme α-amylase. The α-amylase hydrolyzes (breaks down) starch into simple sugars, which the plant can use.

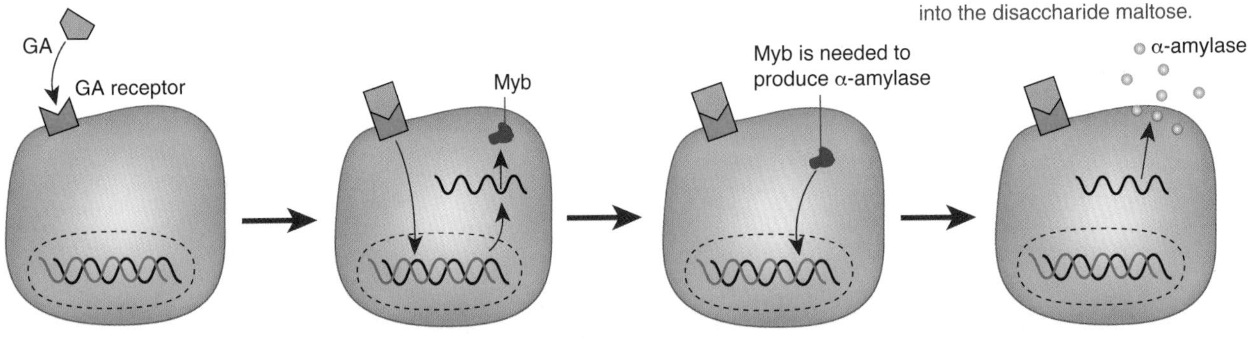

GA binds to a receptor on the plasma membrane.

GA receptor signals for the production of a transcription factor called Myb protein.

Myb protein binds to DNA and activates transcription of α-amylase enzyme.

α-amylase is produced and hydrolyzes the starch in the seeds into simple sugars.

3. Describe the role of GA in α-amylase production and in germination. Provide evidence for your claim:

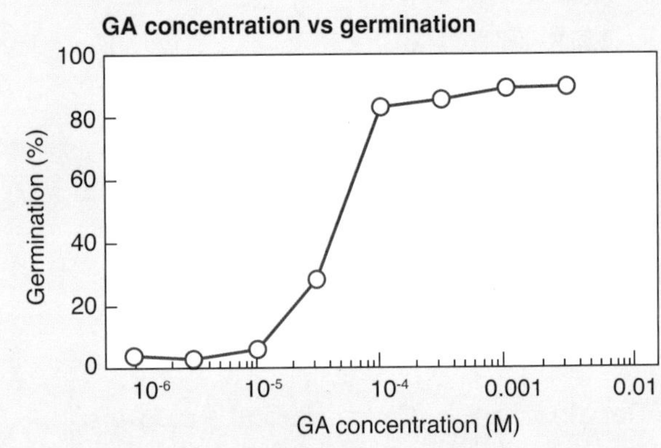

4. How does temperature affect α-amylase activity?

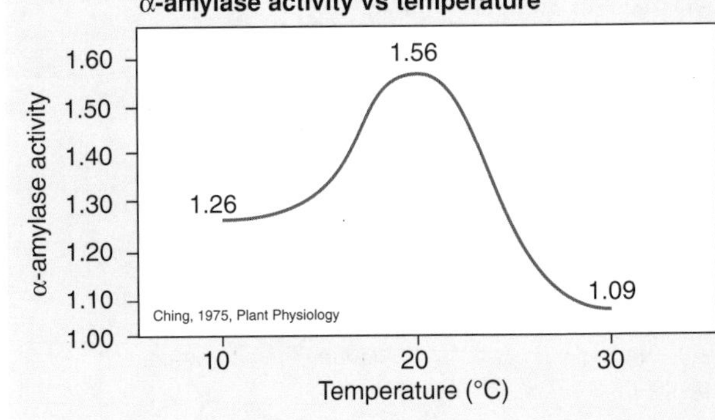

5. Study the graph relating to germination vs temperature:

(a) Which plant(s) have the best germination success?

(b) Would you choose corn if you were planting crops in environmental conditions below 20°C? Explain:

Percentage germination vs temperature in crops

Wheat strain A

Wheat strain B

Wheat strain C

Corn (*Zea mays*)

Germination (%): 0, 20, 40, 60, 80, 100

Temperature (°C): 0, 10, 20, 30, 40

Mendeny, 2007, World Journal Ag.

ISBN: 978-1-98-856656-6

124 Gene Regulation in Prokaryotes

Key Question: How are prokaryotic operons regulated?

Prokaryotic genes are organized as operons. An **operon** is a cluster of several structural genes under the control of the same regulatory genes and sequences. The ***lac* operon** is an operon required for the transport and metabolism of lactose in many bacteria including *Escherichia coli* (*E.coli*). It is a model for operon function in prokaryotes. The operon model applies only to prokaryotes because eukaryotic genes are not found as operons. Transcription of the structural genes in an operon is controlled by the promoter and the operator. The regulator gene can produce a repressor molecule that can bind to the operator and block the transcription of the structural genes. The presence or absence of a functional repressor molecule switches the structural genes on or off and controls the metabolic pathway. Two mechanisms operate in this model: gene induction and gene repression. In **gene induction** (below), genes are switched on when an inducer binds to the repressor and deactivates it. In **gene repression** (next page), genes are normally on but will be switched off when the end-product of the metabolic pathway is present in excess.

Prokaryotic genes occur as operons

A number of structural genes encoding the enzymes for a metabolic pathway are under the control of the same regulatory elements.

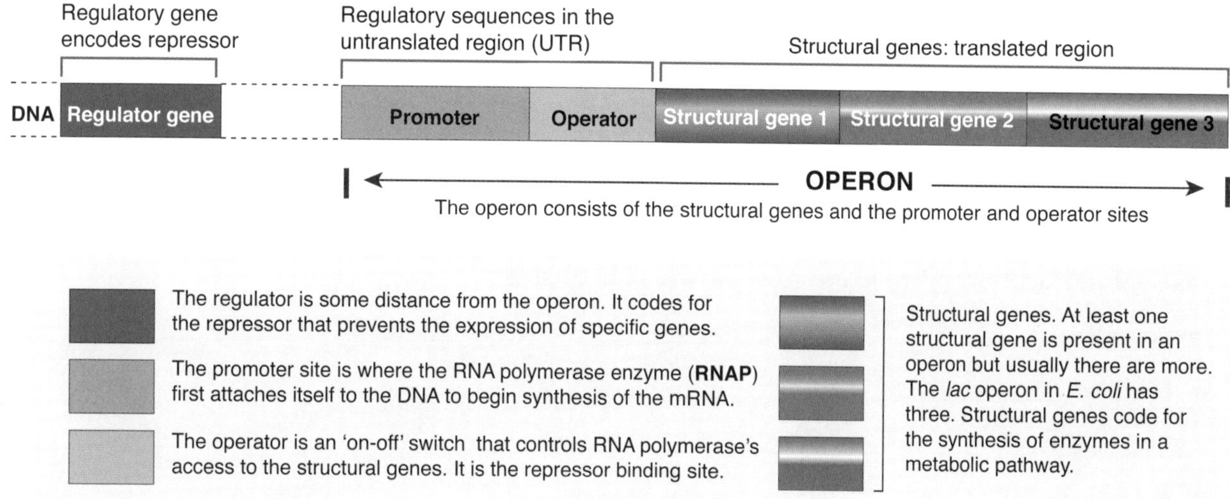

Regulatory gene encodes repressor
Regulatory sequences in the untranslated region (UTR)
Structural genes: translated region
DNA
Regulator gene
Promoter
Operator
Structural gene 1
Structural gene 2
Structural gene 3
OPERON
The operon consists of the structural genes and the promoter and operator sites
The regulator is some distance from the operon. It codes for the repressor that prevents the expression of specific genes.
The promoter site is where the RNA polymerase enzyme (RNAP) first attaches itself to the DNA to begin synthesis of the mRNA.
The operator is an 'on-off' switch that controls RNA polymerase's access to the structural genes. It is the repressor binding site.
Structural genes. At least one structural gene is present in an operon but usually there are more. The lac operon in E. coli has three. Structural genes code for the synthesis of enzymes in a metabolic pathway.

The *lac* operon: an inducible operon

Repressor is active and the genes are normally switched off

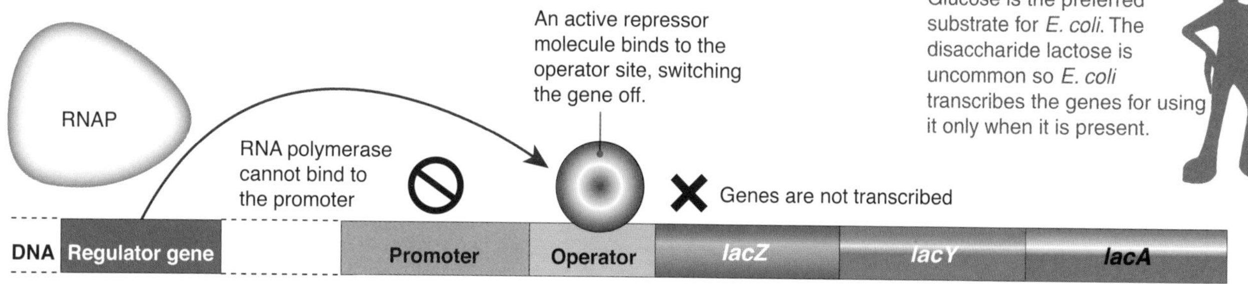

DID YOU KNOW?

Glucose is the preferred substrate for *E. coli*. The disaccharide lactose is uncommon so *E. coli* transcribes the genes for using it only when it is present.

Lactose switches the *lac* operon on

Presence of lactose results in inactivation of the repressor so the genes can be transcribed

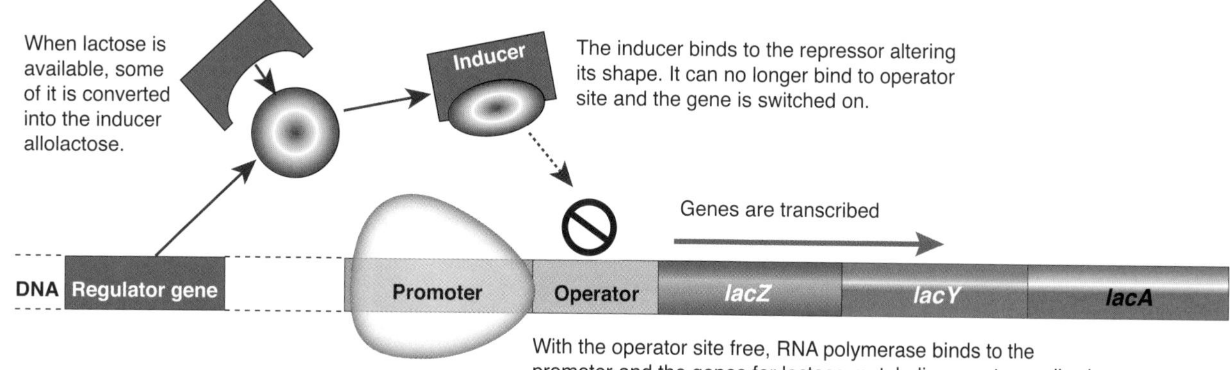

When lactose is available, some of it is converted into the inducer allolactose.

ISBN: 978-1-98-856656-6

The *trp* operon: a repressible operon

Transcription is normally on and must be switched off.

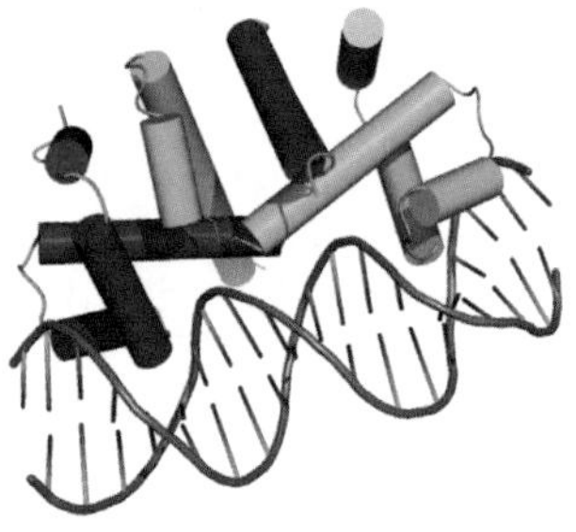

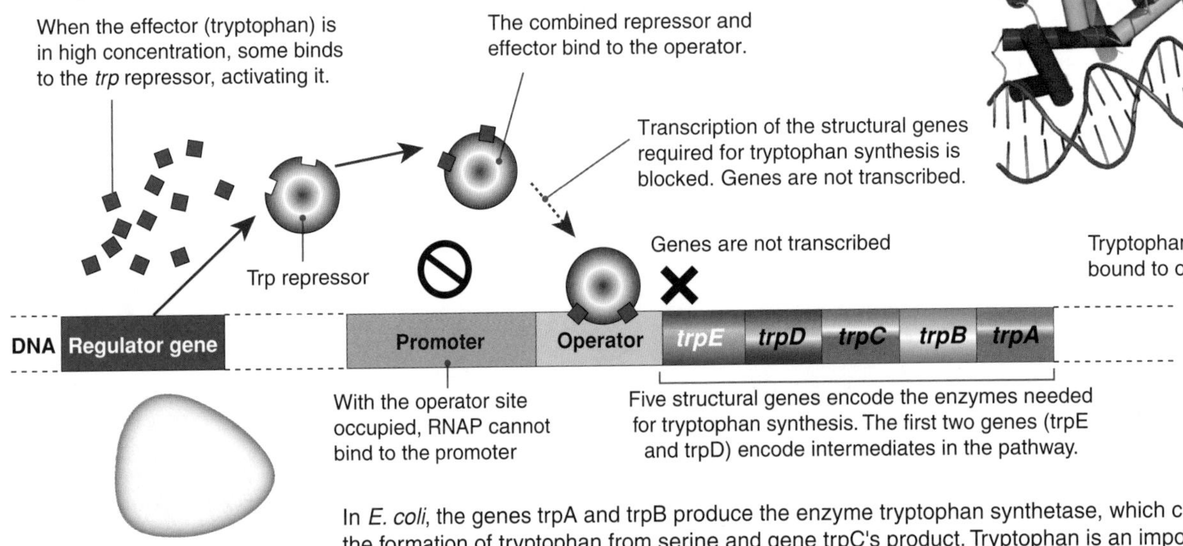

When the effector (tryptophan) is in high concentration, some binds to the *trp* repressor, activating it.

The combined repressor and effector bind to the operator.

Transcription of the structural genes required for tryptophan synthesis is blocked. Genes are not transcribed.

Trp repressor

Genes are not transcribed

Tryptophan repressor bound to operator.

DNA Regulator gene

Promoter

Operator

trpE *trpD* *trpC* *trpB* *trpA*

With the operator site occupied, RNAP cannot bind to the promoter

Five structural genes encode the enzymes needed for tryptophan synthesis. The first two genes (trpE and trpD) encode intermediates in the pathway.

In *E. coli*, the genes trpA and trpB produce the enzyme tryptophan synthetase, which catalyzes the formation of tryptophan from serine and gene trpC's product. Tryptophan is an important amino acid so the genes for producing it are normally switched on. When tryptophan is present in excess, some of it acts as an effector (or co-repressor), activating the repressor and preventing transcription of the structural genes.

1. Describe the role of each of the following components of an operon:

   (a) Promoter: ______________________________

   (b) Operator: ______________________________

   (c) Structural genes: ______________________________

2. Describe the role of the repressor molecule in operon function: ______________________________

   ____

3. Summarize the function of the *lac* operon by completing the following (write the correct answer in the space):

   (a) When lactose is absent, the repressor is (active / inactive) __________, RNA polymerase (can / cannot) __________, bind, and the structural genes (are / are not) __________ transcribed.

   (b) When lactose is present, the repressor is (active / inactive) __________, RNA polymerase (can / cannot) __________, bind, and the structural genes (are / are not) __________ transcribed.

4. (a) Explain why the *lac* operon is usually switched off in *E.coli*: ______________________________

   ____

   (b) Explain is the advantage in having an inducible enzyme system that is regulated by the presence of a substrate?

   ____

   ____

   ____

   (c) Suggest when it would not be an advantage to have an inducible system for metabolism of a substrate: __________

   ____

5. Using the diagrams, describe how the *lac* operon differs from the *trp* operon and explain reasons for the difference:

   ____

   ____

   ____

   ____

ISBN: 978-1-98-856656-6

125 Eukaryotic Gene Structure and Regulation

Key Question: How are eukaryotic genes organized and how does this organization affect regulation?

A eukaryotic gene includes more than just the region of **ex**onic (**ex**pressed) DNA that is translated into protein. It also contains introns, regulatory untranslated regions (UTRs), a promoter to which the RNA polymerase binds, and a terminator region, which signals the stop point of transcription. The control sequences ensure that transcription begins and ends at the correct points and that the necessary sequences are present to create a mature mRNA molecule capable of exiting the nucleus. The promoter region is the binding site for regulatory proteins called transcription factors and it contains several **highly conserved** regions (sequences that have remained unchanged throughout evolution). Transcription's dependence on sequence recognition and transcription factors provides close control over the expression of genes.

The structure of eukaryotic genes

A gene contains both translated and untranslated regions, including control sequences

Upstream control elements

TATA box

Transcription start (+1) 25-35 base pairs downstream of the TATA box.

Poly-A tail signal sequence within the 3' UTR

5' Enhancers | 5' UTR | Exon | Intron | Exon | Intron | Exon | 3' UTR | 3'

DNA coding strand

Promoter region
RNA polymerase recognizes and binds

Terminator sequence
signals STOP transcription

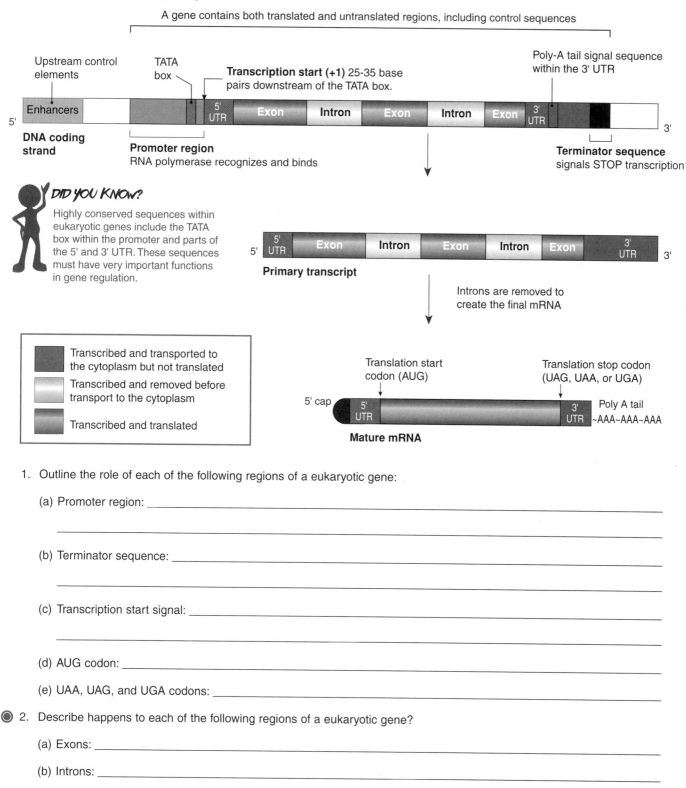

DID YOU KNOW?
Highly conserved sequences within eukaryotic genes include the TATA box within the promoter and parts of the 5' and 3' UTR. These sequences must have very important functions in gene regulation.

5' | 5' UTR | Exon | Intron | Exon | Intron | Exon | 3' UTR | 3'

Primary transcript

Introns are removed to create the final mRNA

Transcribed and transported to the cytoplasm but not translated

Transcribed and removed before transport to the cytoplasm

Transcribed and translated

Translation start codon (AUG)

Translation stop codon (UAG, UAA, or UGA)

5' cap | 5' UTR | | 3' UTR | Poly A tail ~AAA~AAA~AAA

Mature mRNA

1. Outline the role of each of the following regions of a eukaryotic gene:

   (a) Promoter region:

   (b) Terminator sequence:

   (c) Transcription start signal:

   (d) AUG codon:

   (e) UAA, UAG, and UGA codons:

2. Describe happens to each of the following regions of a eukaryotic gene?

   (a) Exons:

   (b) Introns:

   (c) 5' and 3' UTR:

ISBN: 978-1-98-856656-6

120

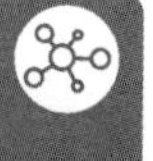

RNA polymerase can only transcribe genes in the presence of transcription factors

- In eukaryotes, RNA polymerase cannot initiate the transcription of structural genes alone. It requires the presence of **transcription factors**. Transcription factors are encoded by regulatory genes and have a role in creating an initiation complex for transcription.
- Transcription factors bind to distinct regions of the DNA, including the **promoter** and upstream **enhancers**. They will act as a guide to indicate to RNA polymerase where transcription should start.
- Once bound to the promoter sequence, the transcription factors capture RNA polymerase, which can then begin transcription.
- Transcription is activated when a hairpin loop in the DNA brings the transcription factors (activators) attached to the enhancer sequence in contact with the transcription factors bound to RNA polymerase at the promoter (bottom).

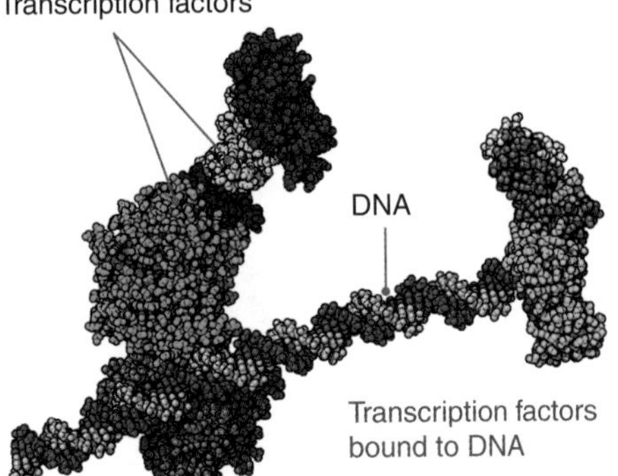

Assembly of the transcription initiation complex

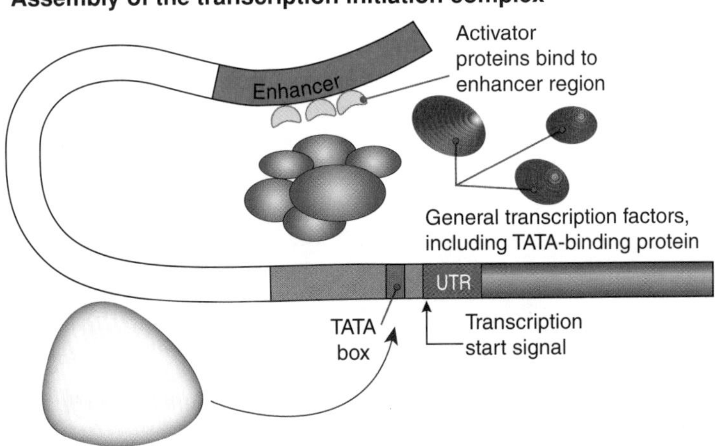

RNA polymerase binds and transcription begins

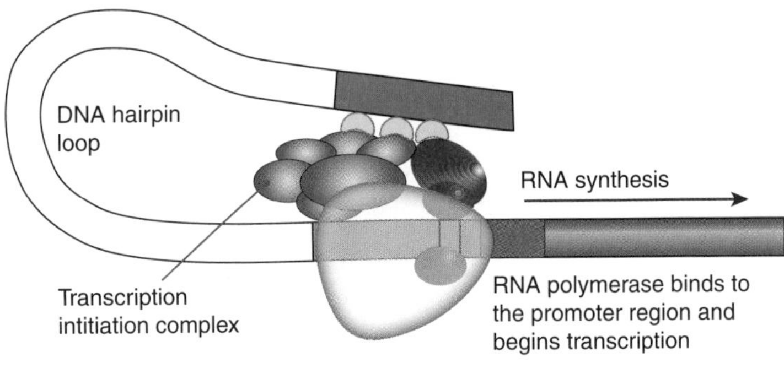

3. Why would a gene contain regions that are transcribed but not translated? ____________________

____

4. (a) What is a transcription factor? ____________________

____

____

(b) What sort of genes encode transcription factors? ____________________

(c) Use the diagram to describe how transcription factors are involved in the regulation of gene expression: ____________________

____

____

5. (a) What does it mean to say a DNA sequence is highly conserved? ____________________

____

____

(b) Some of the most highly conserved regions of genes include untranslated sequences. Why do you think this is?

____

____

____

____

ISBN: 978-1-98-856656-6

Eukaryotic gene repression

Like prokaryotes, eukaryotic gene transcription can also be inhibited by negative regulatory molecules (repressors). Eukaryotic repressors bind to DNA sequences called **silencers**. Repressors inhibit transcription in three main ways.

1. **Competition**: The silencer and the enhancer may overlap or be identical. The repressor and activator then compete for the same DNA binding site. When the repressor molecule is bound to the silencer, the activator molecules cannot bind.
2. **Inhibition**: The repressor binds directly to the activator and inhibits transcription by protein-protein interactions with the activator. The repressor may or may not bind to the silencer.
3. **Direct repression**: When bound to the silencer, the repressor may directly repress the transcription complex by protein-protein interactions.

Inhibition of galactose metabolism in yeast

- In yeast, a number of different genes are involved in the metabolism of galactose. When galactose is not present the genes need to be inhibited.
- The transcription activator GAL4 binds to the GAL4 site to help activate transcription of genes associated with galactose metabolism.
- When there is no galactose present, the repressor molecule GAL80 binds to the GAL4 protein and inhibits it (inhibition above).
- When galactose is present, a third protein, GAL3, binds to the galactose molecule. This causes GAL3 to be able to bind GAL80, removing it from GAL4.
- GAL4 is then able to help activate transcription of the genes associated with galactose metabolism.

Competition

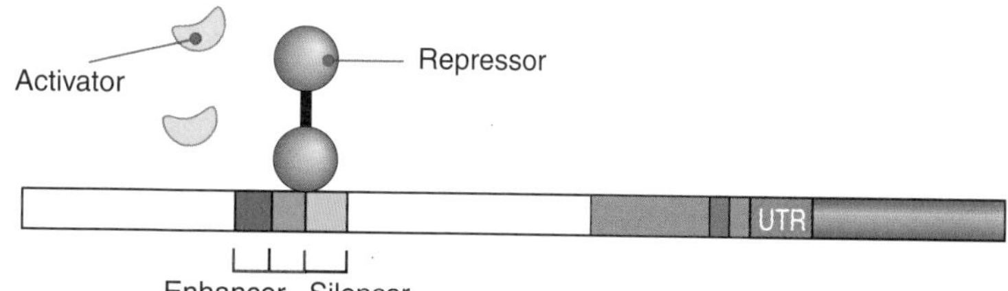

Inhibition

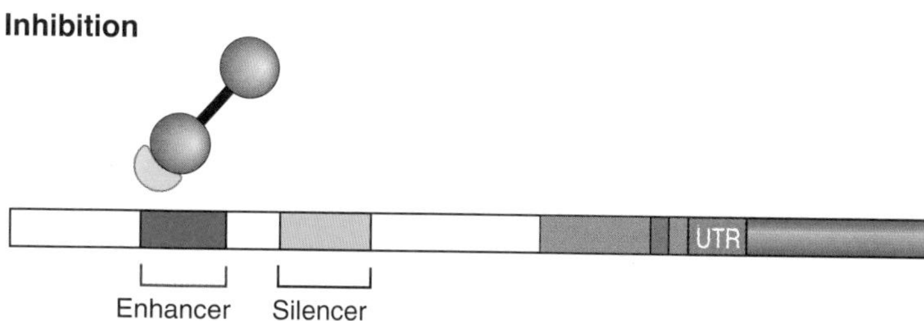

Direct repression

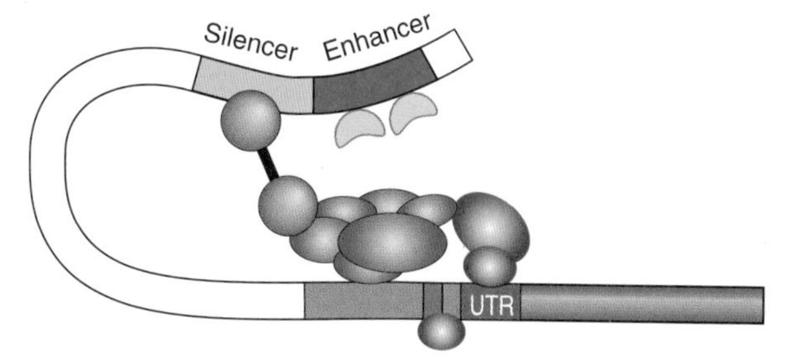

6. Use the diagram above to describe the ways negative regulatory molecules can regulate DNA transcription: ____________

7. Draw a diagram to show how galactose metabolism is regulated in yeast cells:

ISBN: 978-1-98-856656-6

126 Gene Expression and Phenotype

Key Question: How do differences in gene regulation result in different phenotypes?

The role of genes in determining different phenotypes can be investigated by transplanting genes from one type of cell into another. The zygote has the ability to differentiate into any of the body's cells, but as cells differentiate, they lose this ability and their fate becomes determined. This is because specific regulatory genes become inactivated at each division and are never reactivated. Experimental studies of development show how genes and their regulation affect phenotype.

Timing in gene expression

- As an embryo develops, populations of undifferentiated cells pass a point where they become committed to becoming a certain type of cell.
- During an organism's development, its various cells become committed to a particular fate, such as skin cells or muscle cells.
- It is possible to determine the timing of these commitments by transplanting genes from one cell line to another. This was first carried out by Harold Weintraub in 1986 on myoblasts (below).

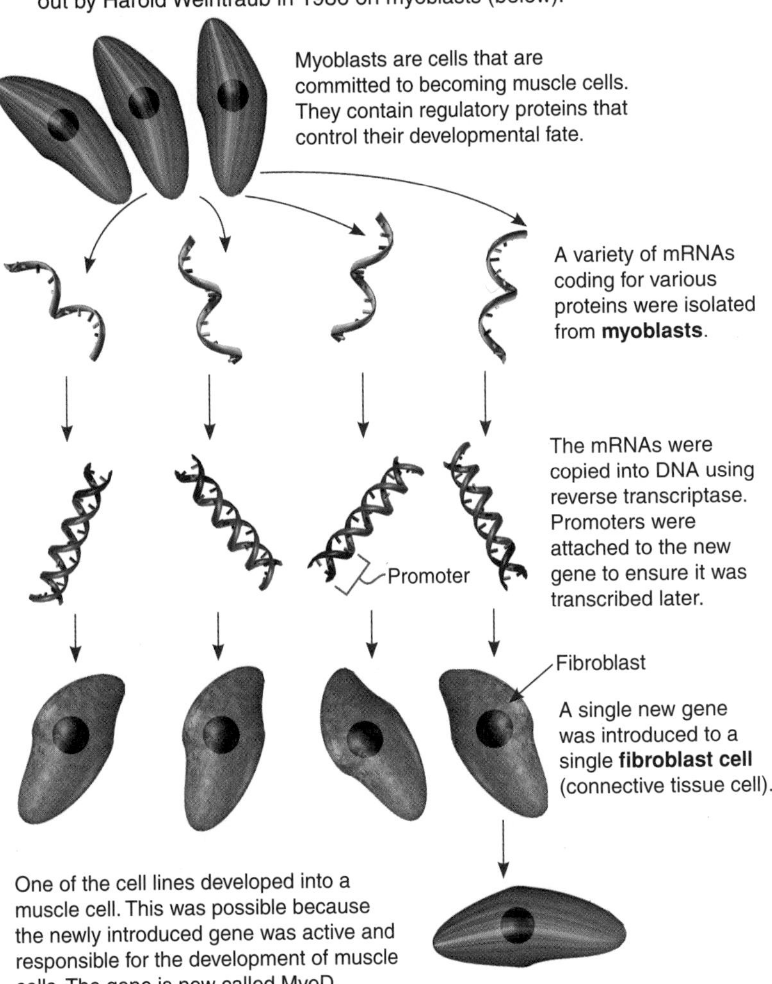

Myoblasts are cells that are committed to becoming muscle cells. They contain regulatory proteins that control their developmental fate.
A variety of mRNAs coding for various proteins were isolated from **myoblasts**.
The mRNAs were copied into DNA using reverse transcriptase. Promoters were attached to the new gene to ensure it was transcribed later.
Promoter
Fibroblast
A single new gene was introduced to a single **fibroblast cell** (connective tissue cell).

One of the cell lines developed into a muscle cell. This was possible because the newly introduced gene was active and responsible for the development of muscle cells. The gene is now called MyoD (myoblast determination). It was the first master regulatory gene discovered.

Transplanting eye genes into blind cavefish

The Mexican tetra (*Astyanax mexicanus*), or blind cavefish, is a freshwater fish that can develop two distinct forms. Cavefish living in areas with light have functioning eyes, whereas those living in caves (no light) do not. Both forms can interbreed.

The eyes of both forms begin development in the early embryo stage, but development stops soon after in the blind form. Researchers thought that a gene in the eye cells might be regulating the eye's development. To test this they took a lens from an eyed *Astyanax* and transplanted it into a blind embryo. The eye in the blind embryo then developed normally, showing the cells in the lens were producing the substances required for eye development. This also showed that the cells in the eye of blind cavefish embryos are able to develop into correctly functioning eyes if they are given the correct signals at the correct time.

When two different and geographically isolated populations of blind cavefish were bred together, the offspring developed functioning eyes. This was because eye development is controlled by numerous genes. Each isolated population of cavefish developed blindness through mutations to different genes. The hybrid offspring gained a working version of each gene, one from each parent, enabling normal eye development.

1. What does transferring the active MyoD gene into fibroblasts tell us about gene expression and phenotype?

2. What do the results of the cavefish gene transplantation experiment tell us about genes and normal development?

ISBN: 978-1-98-856656-6

- Genes play a critical role in regulating normal development. However, if a gene becomes mutated (its DNA sequence changes) the genetic message can be altered and a different gene product (protein) will be produced. If the protein is critical to development, the mutations can disrupt normal development.
- Gene regulation can be studied by investigating the effect of particular mutations on the development of an individual. A much studied group of developmental genes is the ***Hox* gene** cluster. *Hox* genes are genes involved in regulating the body plan of organisms by ensuring that the correct structures form in the correct places of the body. Each *Hox* gene encodes a transcription factor, so the order of *Hox* gene expression determines when particular transcription factors are present.

Eight *Hox* genes control development in *Drosophila*

Mutations to highly conserved *Hox* genes can drastically alter the body plan of affected individuals, giving rise to abnormal phenotypes. The fruit fly *Drosophila melanogaster* is a model organism for genetics and has been extensively studied to determine how gene expression can affect developmental processes. The general principles learned by studying *Drosophila* can be applied to understanding development in other organisms.

Drosophila have eight *Hox* genes to control body development. They are clustered into two complexes, the antennapedia complex (**ANT-C**), which consists of five genes, and the bithorax complex (**BX-C**), which consists of three genes (right).

- The **antennapedia (Antp) gene** directs the development of the second pair of legs and so is normally highly expressed in the second thoracic segment. The name antennapedia simply means antenna-foot.
- Expression of the Antp gene in other regions of the body can result in mutant strains of *Drosophila*. Antp expression in the head region (where it is usually not expressed at all) results in legs instead of antennae growing (photo, right). This type of mutation is called a **gain-of-function** mutation and is dominant (a leg will always form if this gene is expressed).
- Another mutant form of *Drosophila* is the recessive **loss-of-function** Antp mutant. In these individuals the Antp gene is not expressed in the second thoracic segment, and antennae form instead of legs.

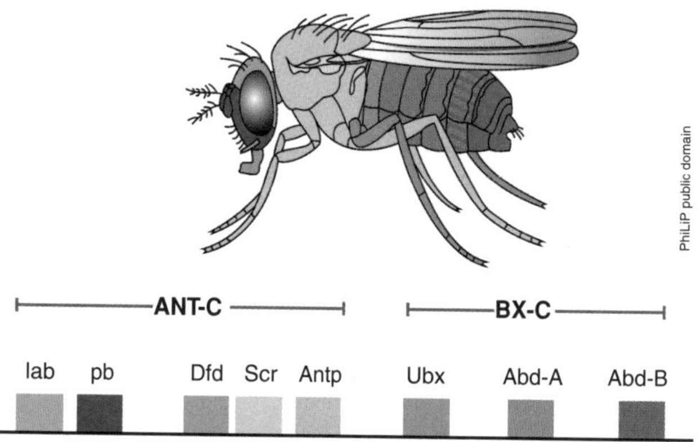

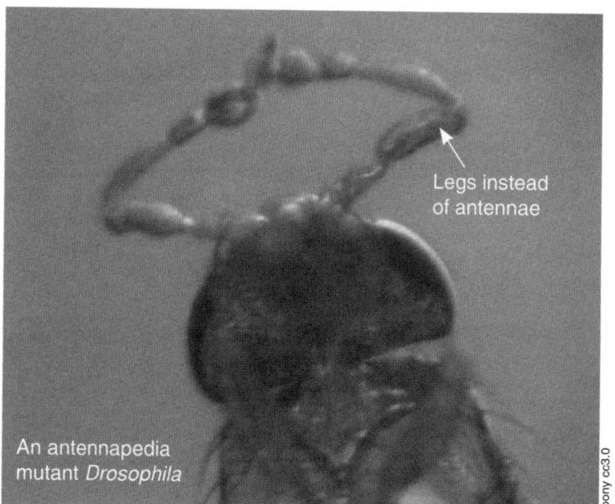

3. Describe the role of the Antp gene in *Drosophila* development: ____________________

4. (a) Where is the Antp gene usually expressed in a normal *Drosophila* individual? ____________________

   (b) Where is the Antp gene expressed in an antennapedia mutant *Drosophila*? ____________________

   (c) What is the effect of the mutation in the antennapedia mutant? ____________________

   (d) What happens if the Antp gene is not expressed in the second thoracic segment? ____________________

5. Why is the antennapedia mutation considered to be dominant? ____________________

6. In the third thoracic segment, Ubx directs the development of a pair of legs and a pair of halteres (very reduced wings used for balance). It operates largely by suppressing wing formation. Predict the effect in Ubx loss-of-function mutants:

7. Explain the evidence from the *Drosophila Hox* cluster that supports the role of transcription factors in development:

ISBN: 978-1-98-856656-6

127 miRNA and Development

Key Question: What are microRNAs and how do they affect gene expression?

MicroRNAs (**miRNA**) are small, highly conserved RNA molecules found in plants and animals and some DNA based viruses. They are around 22 nucleotide bases in length and are non-coding RNA in that they are not translated into protein. miRNAs play important roles in gene regulation through interactions with mRNA. This is achieved through three mechanisms: 1) cleavage of mRNA, 2) mRNA destabilization, and 3) reduction in the efficiency of mRNA translation so that less protein product is produced. Many studies of embryos have shown that miRNA activity is required for normal development in multicellular eukaryotes. The enzyme dicer is important in producing miRNAs.

Evidence for the role of miRNA in development

MicroRNAs originate in the nucleus. They are cut into functional miRNAs in the cytoplasm by the **dicer** enzyme. Making dicer nonfunctional prevents the functional miRNA being produced. Researchers can then study how dicer's absence and nonfunctional miRNAs affect developmental processes.

- Zebrafish embryos contain maternal dicer enzyme. When maternal dicer is removed, the embryos continue to develop normally for 24 hours. This indicates that miRNA activity is not important in regulating early development.
- After the initial normal development, the dicer mutant embryos showed many physical defects and died 5-8 days after fertilization. This indicates that miRNA is critical for controlling embryonic development at this stage.
- This information is also supported by expression studies which show that in zebrafish most miRNAs are not expressed early on, but are highly expressed in specific tissues at later stages of development. This also suggests that miRNAs are involved in cellular differentiation.

Zebrafish (*Danio rerio*)

Azul cc 0

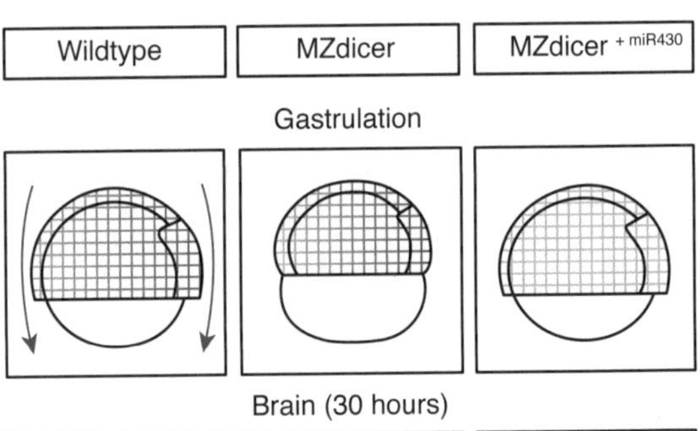

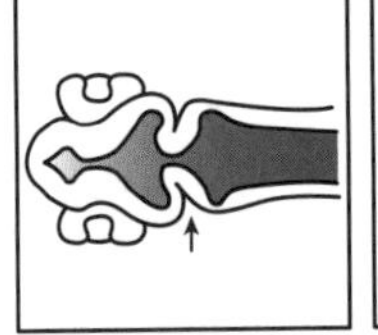

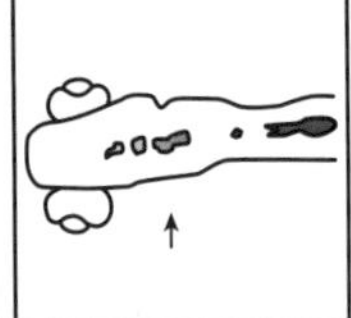

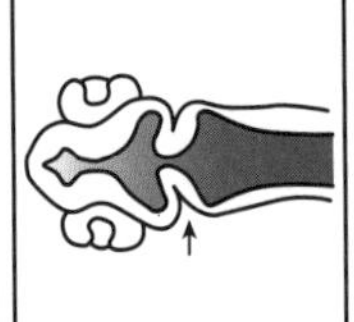

Adapted from Schier, A.F and Giraldex, A.J MicroRNA function and mechanism: Insights from zebra fish Cold Spring Harbor Symposia on Quantitative Biology, 2006

KEY:

- Wildtype: individuals with normal dicer activity
- MZdicer: individuals with all dicer activity removed
- MZdicer $^{+miR430}$: individuals with all dicer activity removed, but injected with miRNA430 at the onset of zygotic transcription (around the 500 cell stage).

The results above show gastrulation and brain development in the three study groups. Wildtype and MZdicer $^{+miR430}$ individuals developed normally. MZdicer individuals showed developmental defects and died on day 5.

The arrows on the images of the 30 hour brain indicate the midbrain-hindbrain boundary.

1. What evidence is there that miRNA is not important in early embryonic development (up to 24 hours)? ______

______

______

2. Why was it important to remove all dicer enzyme when studying the effect of miRNA on embryonic development?

______

______

3. (a) Compare the wildtype and MZdicer development results (above right): ______

______

______

______

(b) What effect did injecting miR430 have on the MZdicer $^{+miR430}$ individuals? ______

______

(c) What do these results reveal about the role of miRNA on developmental processes? ______

______

______

ISBN: 978-1-98-856656-6

128 Mutations

Key Question: What are mutations?

A **mutation** is a permanent change to the DNA sequence of an organism. Mutations are the ultimate source of new alleles. They can be small, such the change of a single nucleotide (e.g. A to G) or they may be large, such as the duplication of entire genes or sometimes entire genomes. Most mutations are harmful because they disrupt some important cellular process, often by causing a protein to fold incorrectly. Occasionally they may cause some beneficial change, such as making an enzyme more efficient. Although the DNA replication process is very accurate, it is estimated that, in humans, a mutation occurs once every 30 million base pairs copied during DNA replication prior to meiosis. This means that every person has about 200-300 new mutations that their parents did not have. In most cases, these mutations have little to no effect and are called silent mutations.

Some mutations are retained, others are eliminated

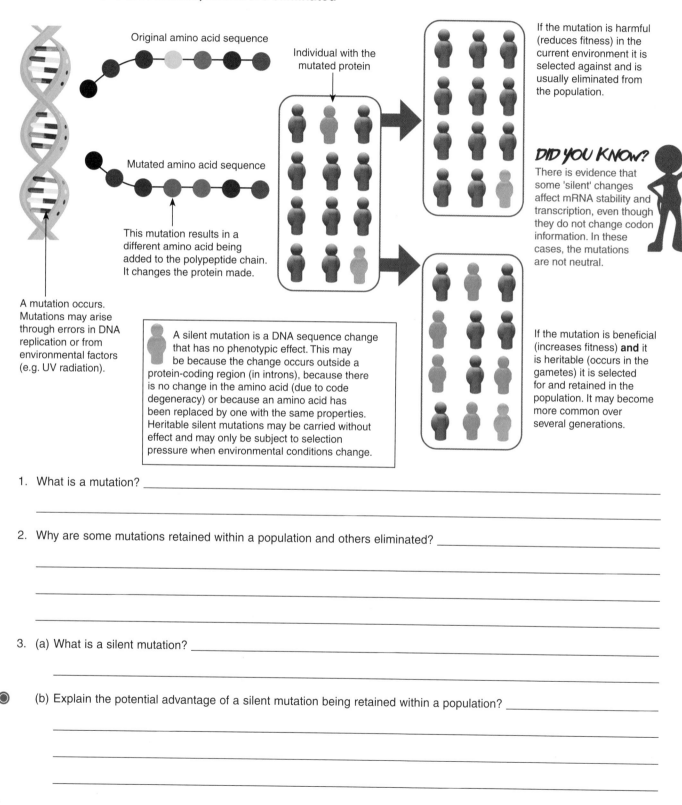

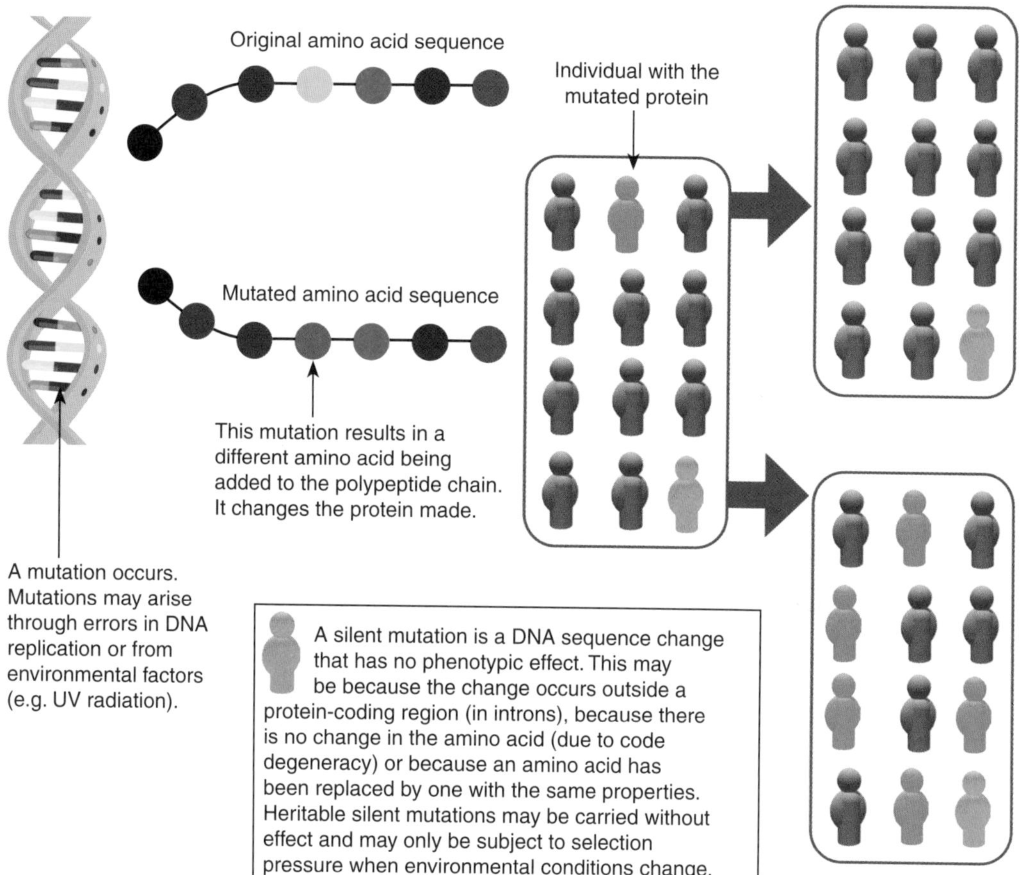

Original amino acid sequence

Mutated amino acid sequence

This mutation results in a different amino acid being added to the polypeptide chain. It changes the protein made.

A mutation occurs. Mutations may arise through errors in DNA replication or from environmental factors (e.g. UV radiation).

Individual with the mutated protein

If the mutation is harmful (reduces fitness) in the current environment it is selected against and is usually eliminated from the population.

If the mutation is beneficial (increases fitness) **and** it is heritable (occurs in the gametes) it is selected for and retained in the population. It may become more common over several generations.

A silent mutation is a DNA sequence change that has no phenotypic effect. This may be because the change occurs outside a protein-coding region (in introns), because there is no change in the amino acid (due to code degeneracy) or because an amino acid has been replaced by one with the same properties. Heritable silent mutations may be carried without effect and may only be subject to selection pressure when environmental conditions change.

DID YOU KNOW?

There is evidence that some 'silent' changes affect mRNA stability and transcription, even though they do not change codon information. In these cases, the mutations are not neutral.

1. What is a mutation? ______________________________

2. Why are some mutations retained within a population and others eliminated? ______________________________

3. (a) What is a silent mutation? ______________________________

(b) Explain the potential advantage of a silent mutation being retained within a population? ______________________________

ISBN: 978-1-98-856656-6

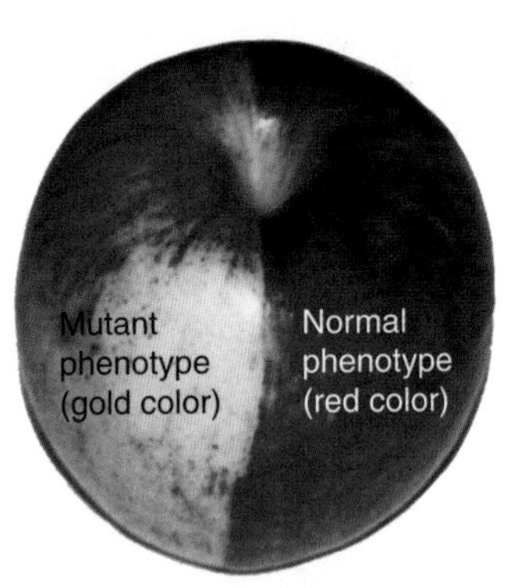

- Gametic cells are the reproductive (sex) cells of an organism (the egg and sperm). Mutations occurring in these cells are called **gametic mutations**.
- Somatic cells (body cells) are all the remaining cells. Mutations to these cells are called **somatic mutations**.
- Only gametic mutations will be inherited. Somatic mutations are not inherited but may affect an organism in its lifetime (e.g. a cancer).
- The red delicious apple (right) is a natural chimera (an organism with a mixture of two or more different genotypes). In the apple, a mutation occurred in the part of the flower that developed into the fleshy part of the apple. The seeds are unaffected by the mutation, so it is not inherited.

Somatic mutation		Gametic mutation
Sperm cell; Egg cell	**Parental gametes**	Gametic mutation to sperm
Somatic mutation affects a local group of cells	**Embryo**	All cells are carrying the mutation
Patch of affected area	**Organism**	Entire organism carries the mutation
None of the gametes carry the mutation	**Gametes of offspring**	Half of the gametes carry the mutation

4. Distinguish between somatic and gametic mutations: ____________________

____

____

____

____

5. Explain the consequences of these different mutation locations: ____________________

____

____

6. Chimeras can be produced artificially in both plants and animals. What kind of information could these organisms provide in studies of gene expression and gene regulation?

____

____

____

____

ISBN: 978-1-98-856656-6

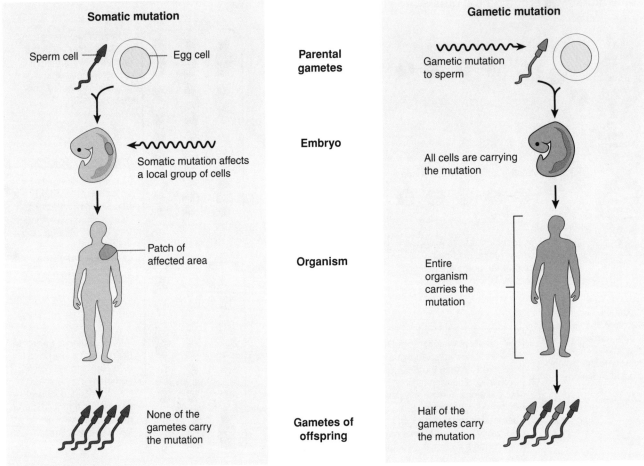

129 Mutation and Phenotype

Key Question: How do mutations affect fitness?

A mutation can have a positive or negative effect on an organism depending on the environment and the prevailing selection pressures. For example a mutation may increase the efficiency of an enzyme. This might give the organism an advantage in an environment where a resource is scarce, allowing it to process the resource more quickly. But it could be a disadvantage if the resource is plentiful and the enzyme is energetically costly to produce. The examples in this activity highlight these ideas. The advantage or disadvantage of a change in coat color in mice depends on the environment. The cystic fibrosis mutation is, in most cases, detrimental (indeed it is fatal), but in some extreme circumstances there is some evidence it can help survival.

Mice and coat color

- The MC1R gene is important in determining hair (coat) color in mammals. Mutations in the gene are in part responsible for the different coat colors in mammals. The genetic basis of coat color has been well studied in populations of oldfield mice (also called beach mice) in Florida, USA.
- Oldfield mice are found in two distinct habitats in Florida. In inland (mainland) areas, which are vegetated with dark, loamy soil, and in coastal sand dunes, which have little vegetation and brilliant white sand. Mice in these different habitats have distinct coat-colors. Mainland mice have a darker brown coat, whereas beach mice, such as the one pictured right, are very pale.
- Researchers hypothesized that these rodents rely on camouflage to avoid detection by predators. Two phenotypes for coat color are common; dark and light (or white). Their hypothesis was tested and supported in an experiment using clay models painted to resemble beach and mainland forms. Relative predation rates on dark and light models in mainland (top right) and beach (bottom right) habitats are shown in a column graph. Column color is matched to model color.
- Genetic studies have shown that the mice along the Gulf coast form one genetically distinct population, whereas the mainland mice and the mice along the Atlantic coast form a separate, less defined genetic group. The genetic data indicate that light colored fur must have evolved independently in the Gulf coast and Atlantic coast populations.
- Genetic analysis also shows that the genes responsible for the light fur are different in the two groups. The light color in the Gulf coast populations is the result of mutation in the MC1R gene and all the Gulf coast beach mice probably arose from a few founding individuals. The light color in the Atlantic coast beach mice has several different genetic causes. Lighter fur provides a survival advantage in beach habitats, so pale mice are more common there, regardless of the genetic mechanism by which the light color arises.

Alabama beach mouse

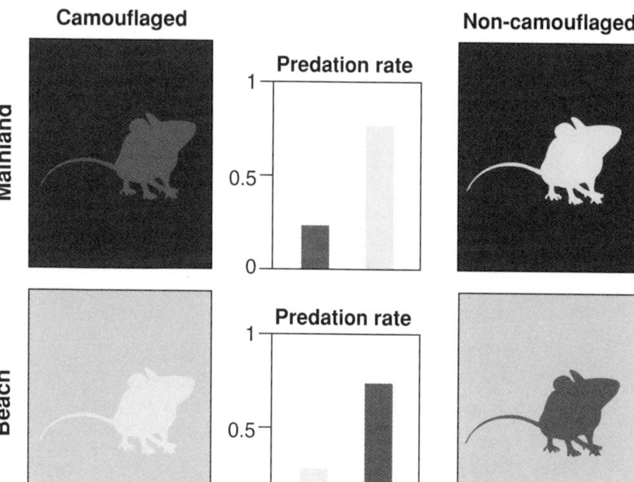

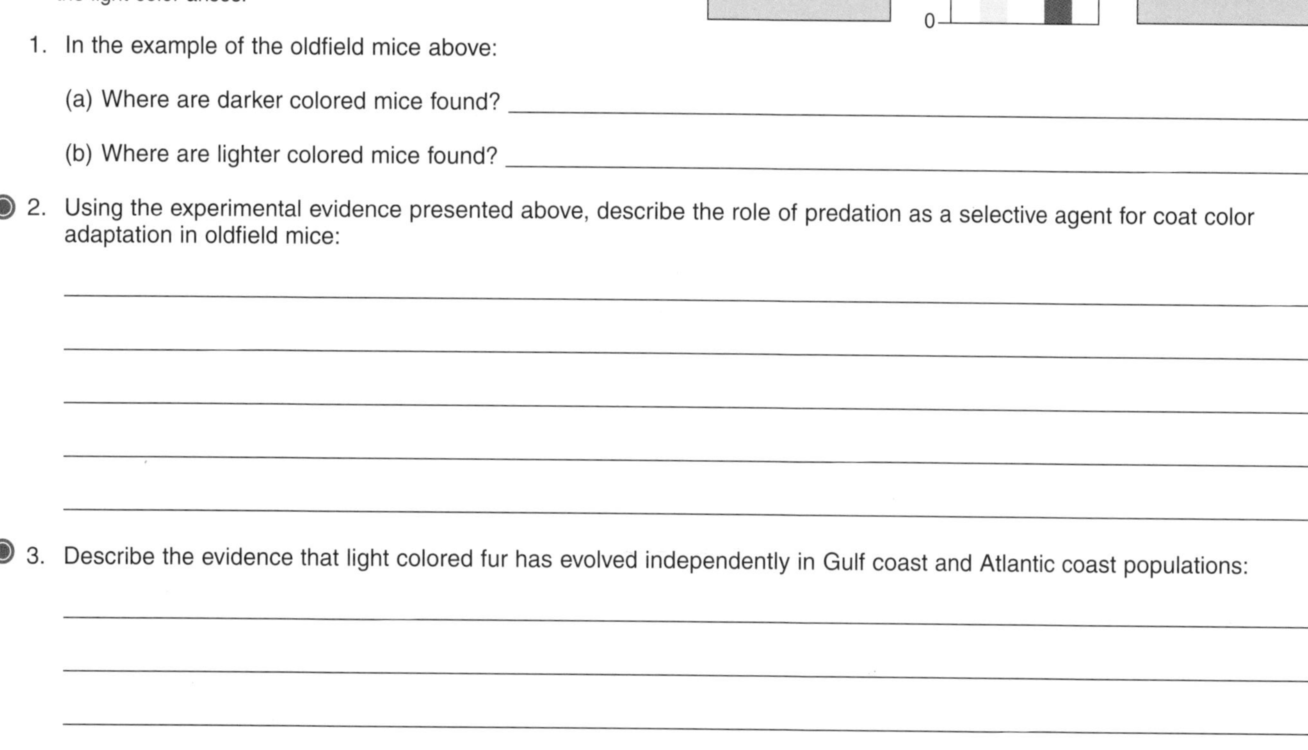

1. In the example of the oldfield mice above:

   (a) Where are darker colored mice found? ______

   (b) Where are lighter colored mice found? ______

2. Using the experimental evidence presented above, describe the role of predation as a selective agent for coat color adaptation in oldfield mice:

3. Describe the evidence that light colored fur has evolved independently in Gulf coast and Atlantic coast populations:

ISBN: 978-1-98-856656-6

Mutation and cystic fibrosis

- Cystic fibrosis (CF) is an inherited disorder caused by a mutation of the CFTR gene. It is one of the most common lethal autosomal recessive conditions affecting people of European descent (4% are carriers). The CFTR gene's protein product is a membrane-based protein that regulates chloride transport in cells.
- Over 500 mutations of the CFTR gene are known, causing disease symptoms of varying severity. The Δ(delta)F508 mutation accounts for more than 70% of all defective CFTR genes. This mutation leads to an abnormal CFTR, which cannot take its proper position in the membrane (below) nor perform its transport function.
- Studies of cystic fibrosis in mice shows that the heterozygous condition reduces the effects of a cholera infection by about 50%. There was also evidence of some resistance to typhoid and tuberculosis. Models show that historical cases of these diseases in humans might explain the prevalence of cystic fibrosis in people of European descent.

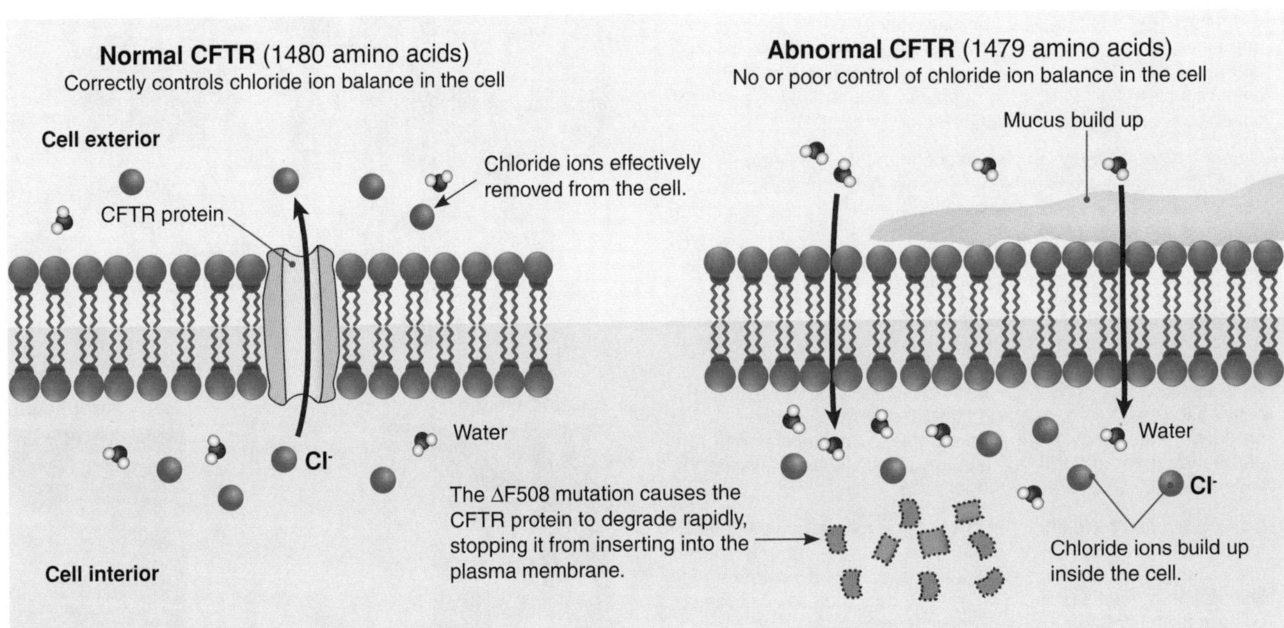

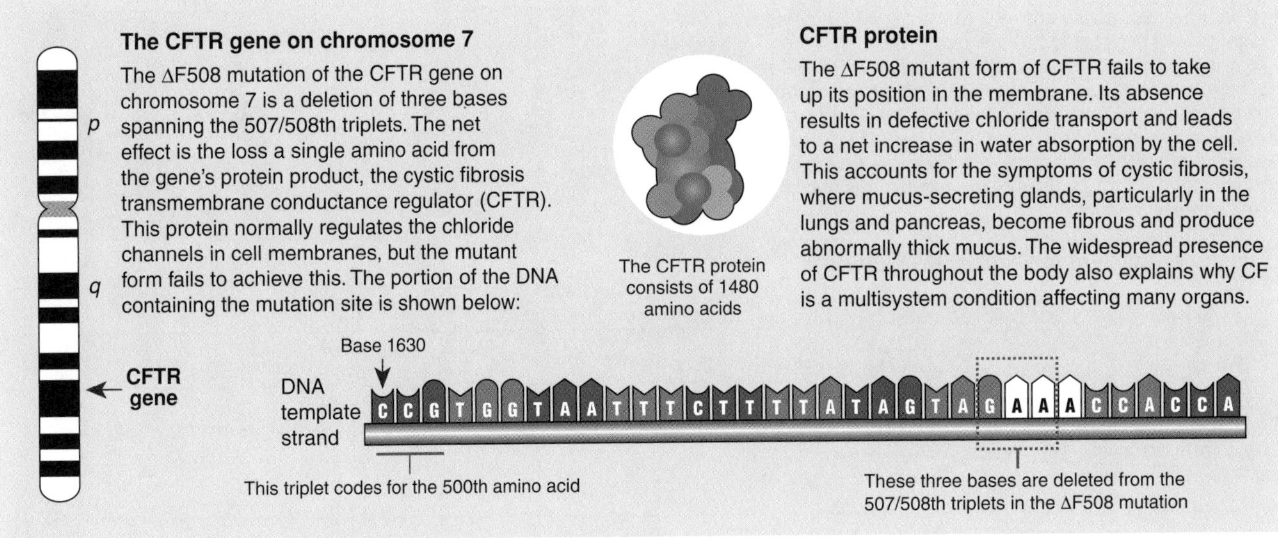

The CFTR gene on chromosome 7

The ΔF508 mutation of the CFTR gene on chromosome 7 is a deletion of three bases spanning the 507/508th triplets. The net effect is the loss a single amino acid from the gene's protein product, the cystic fibrosis transmembrane conductance regulator (CFTR). This protein normally regulates the chloride channels in cell membranes, but the mutant form fails to achieve this. The portion of the DNA containing the mutation site is shown below:

CFTR protein

The ΔF508 mutant form of CFTR fails to take up its position in the membrane. Its absence results in defective chloride transport and leads to a net increase in water absorption by the cell. This accounts for the symptoms of cystic fibrosis, where mucus-secreting glands, particularly in the lungs and pancreas, become fibrous and produce abnormally thick mucus. The widespread presence of CFTR throughout the body also explains why CF is a multisystem condition affecting many organs.

4. Explain why the abnormal CFTR fails to transport Cl^- correctly: ______

5. Explain why mucus secretions become thick and sticky in people with the ΔF508 mutation: ______

6. A cholera infection causes extreme dehydration by causing transmembrane proteins to let water and salt out of intestinal cells. How might the ΔF508 mutation help reduce this effect?

ISBN: 978-1-98-856656-6

130 Changes to DNA

Key Question: How do mutations change the DNA sequence?

Mutations can change the DNA sequence in many different ways. These include deletions, insertions, and substitutions of bases. These may involve just a single nucleotide, a few, or many. In some cases whole sections of genes or chromosomes may be deleted or duplicated. Mutations more commonly involve just one or a few nucleotides and occur during replication where the enzymes involved in replication occasionally inserts or leaves out a nucleotide. These mistakes are normally repaired by proof reading enzymes, but not always. More mutations become more common in the presence of certain chemicals or environmental conditions. Mutations accumulated during a lifetime become more obvious with age, such as many cancers.

Changes to DNA

- Mutations may occur during replication or when the DNA is repaired after being damaged (e.g. from exposure to UV radiation).
- These mutations often involve a single (point mutation) or just a few nucleotides and may be substitutions, insertion, or deletions. The type of mutation can have an important effect on the outcome of translation and the amino acid chain (below).

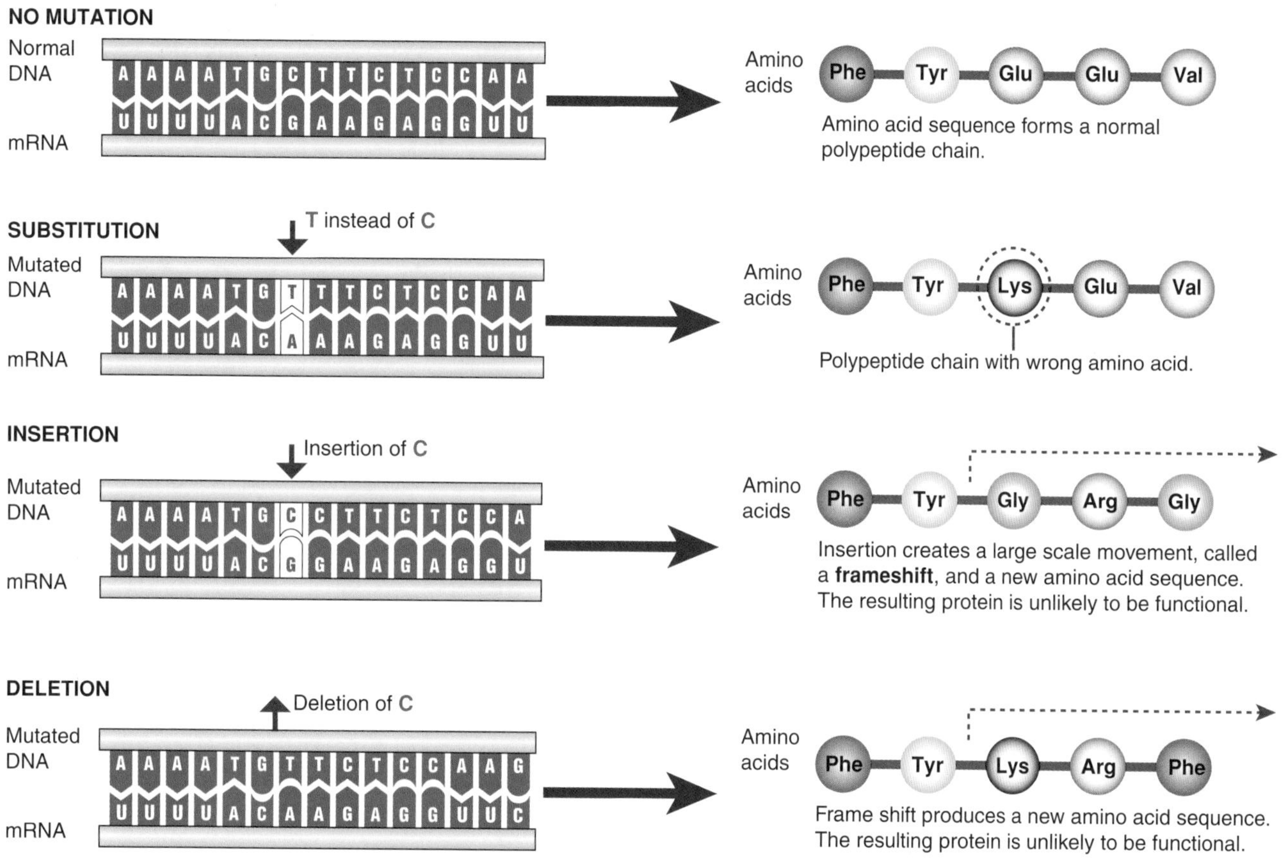

NO MUTATION

Normal DNA: A A A A T G C T T C T C C A A

mRNA: U U U U A C G A A G A G G U U

Amino acids: Phe – Tyr – Glu – Glu – Val

Amino acid sequence forms a normal polypeptide chain.

SUBSTITUTION

T instead of C

Mutated DNA: A A A A T G T T T C T C C A A

mRNA: U U U U A C A A A G A G G U U

Amino acids: Phe – Tyr – Lys – Glu – Val

Polypeptide chain with wrong amino acid.

INSERTION

Insertion of C

Mutated DNA: A A A A T G C C T T C T C C A

mRNA: U U U U A C G G A A G A G G U

Amino acids: Phe – Tyr – Gly – Arg – Gly

Insertion creates a large scale movement, called a **frameshift**, and a new amino acid sequence. The resulting protein is unlikely to be functional.

DELETION

Deletion of C

Mutated DNA: A A A A T G T T C T C C A A G

mRNA: U U U U A C A A G A G G U U C

Amino acids: Phe – Tyr – Lys – Arg – Phe

Frame shift produces a new amino acid sequence. The resulting protein is unlikely to be functional.

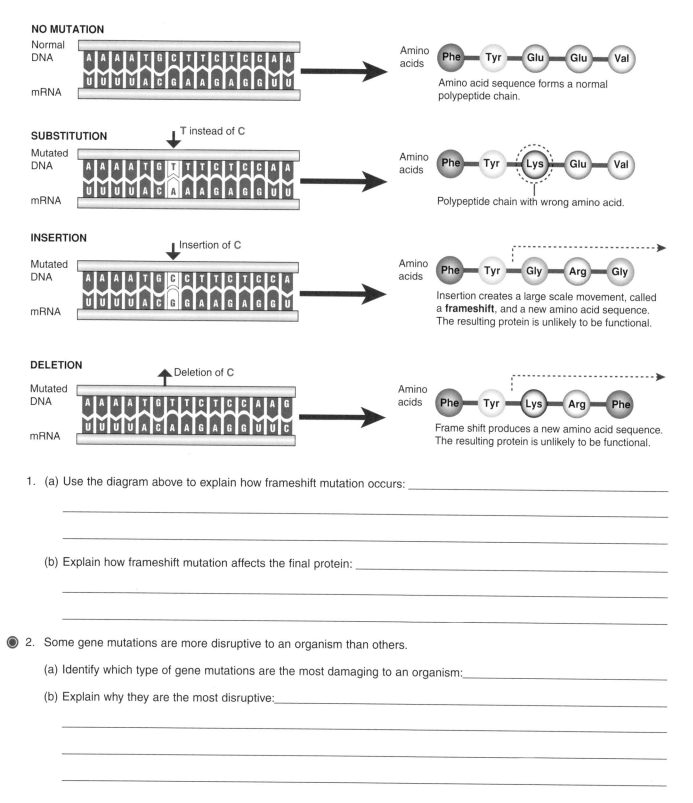

1. (a) Use the diagram above to explain how frameshift mutation occurs: ______

   (b) Explain how frameshift mutation affects the final protein: ______

2. Some gene mutations are more disruptive to an organism than others.

   (a) Identify which type of gene mutations are the most damaging to an organism: ______

   (b) Explain why they are the most disruptive: ______

ISBN: 978-1-98-856656-6

Environmental factors can cause mutations

- Mutations occur naturally via mistakes in DNA replication or meiosis but the rate of mutations can be increased by mutagens. Mutagens may be chemicals or physical factors in the environment that increase the risk of errors in DNA replication. The longer a person is exposed to these factors the greater their effect will be and the greater the risk of serious consequences occurring.
- In most cases the somatic cells will be affected and a possible outcome will be cancer (e.g. skin cancer). Most cancers are caused by environmental factors. In some cases the gametes or zygote will be affected and so the embryo will be affected.

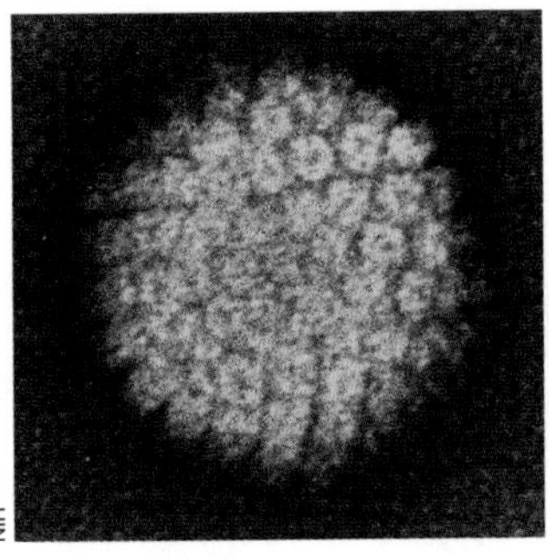

NIH

Viruses and microorganisms

Some viruses integrate into the human chromosome, upsetting genes and triggering cancers. Examples include hepatitis B virus (liver cancer) and HPV (above) which is implicated in cervical cancer. Those at higher risk of viral infections include intravenous drug users and those with unsafe sex practices.

Poisons and irritants

Many chemicals are mutagenic. Synthetic and natural examples include organic solvents such as benzene, asbestos, formaldehyde and tobacco tar. Those most at risk include workers in the chemicals industries. People involved in environmental clean-up of toxic spills are at high risk of exposure to mutagens.

Ionizing radiation

The most common exposure to ionizing radiation is from UV rays in sunlight. Too much exposure causes sunburn. Being sunburnt many times greatly raises the risk of skin cancer. People working with X-rays (from X-ray machines) and nuclear radiation are also at higher risk of cancers.

Lifestyle

One of the most important factors in increasing the risk of mutations is lifestyle. This includes diet, alcohol consumption, and whether we smoke. Smoking causes lung cancer, while heavy drinking causes liver damage and increases cancer risk. Heavy drinking at the time of conception and in early pregnancy severely affects fetal development.

3. In the following DNA sequence, replace the **G** of the **second codon** with an A to create a new mutant DNA, then determine the new mRNA sequence, and the amino acid sequence. Refer to the mRNA-amino acid table to identify the amino acids coded in each case.

   (a) Original DNA: CGT ATG AAA CTG GGG CTG TCA CCT AAT

   Mutated DNA: ______________________________

   mRNA: ______________________________

   Amino acids: ______________________________

   (b) Identify the amino acid coded by codon 2 (ATG) in the original DNA: ______________________________

   (c) Explain the effect of the mutation: ______________________________

4. Explain how mutagens cause mutations: ______________________________

5. Mutation breeding is a biotechnology technique in which plant seeds are exposed to mutagens and then grown.

   (a) What would be the purpose of this technique? ______________________________

   (b) Pollen is also treated with mutagens. What would the effect of this on the plant produced using this pollen?

ISBN: 978-1-98-856656-6

131 Changes to Chromosomes

Key Question: How do chromosome abnormalities arise and what are their phenotypic effects?

Chromosome abnormalities include missing or extra chromosomes, or chromosomes with irregular portions (e.g. duplications). These abnormalities usually occur during cell division in mitosis or meiosis where the homologous chromosomes or chromatids fail to separate correctly (nondisjunction). In many cases of nondisjunction the result will be one extra (2N+ 1) or one missing (2N-1) chromosome in the final cell (an aneuploid). Occasionally nondisjunction occurs to all of the chromosomes and the final cell may be 3N or more (a polyploid).

Aneuploidy in humans

- Aneuploidy is the condition where the chromosome number is not an exact multiple of the normal haploid set for the species (the number may be more, e.g. 2N+2, or less, e.g. 2N–1). It may occur with any chromosome (both autosomes and sex chromosomes) with specific phenotypic effects being associated with each different aneuploidy.
- The examples below show three aneuploidies, two autosomal aneuploids and one sex chromosome aneuploid.

Turner syndrome

The incidence rate of Turner syndrome is 1 in 5000 live female births. Typically Turner syndrome features include a characteristic residual web neck. Low levels of reproductive hormones result in poor development of secondary sexual characteristics (almost always infertile), puffy fingers with deep set, hyperconvex finger nails.

Edward syndrome

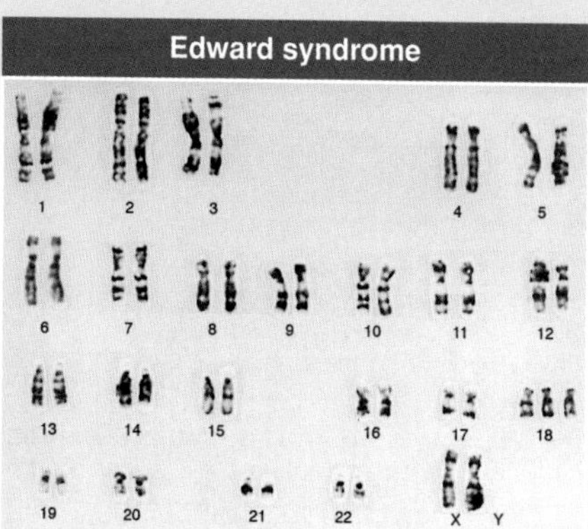

Edward syndrome has an incidence rate of 1 in 5000 live births (with a maternal age effect). Features include severely reduced intellectual ability, low set, malformed ears, congenital heart defects, small mouth and rocker-bottom feet. Survival beyond a year is less than 10%. About 95% of the affected fetuses are spontaneously aborted

Down syndrome

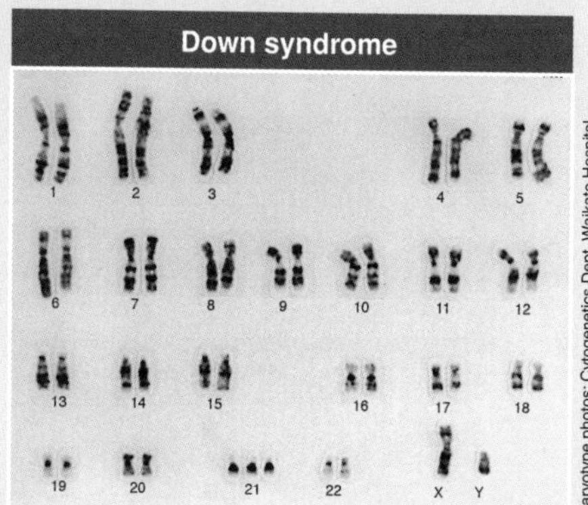

Karyotype photos: Cytogenetics Dept, Waikato Hospital

Down syndrome is the most common of the human aneuploidies. The most common form of this condition arises when meiosis fails to separate the pair of chromosome number 21s in the eggs that are forming in the woman's ovaries. Features include reduced intellectual ability, poor immune function, and reduced growth.

1. For each of the three human aneuploids above identify the chromosome or chromosome number where the extra or missing chromosome has occurred:

   (a) Turner Syndrome: ______________ (b) Edward syndrome: ______________ (c) Down syndrome: ______________

2. (a) Complete the cross of the sex chromosomes for humans below.

Faulty egg production

Faulty meiosis during egg cell production can result in egg cells with 0 to up to 4 X chromosomes (nondisjunction in meiosis I and II).

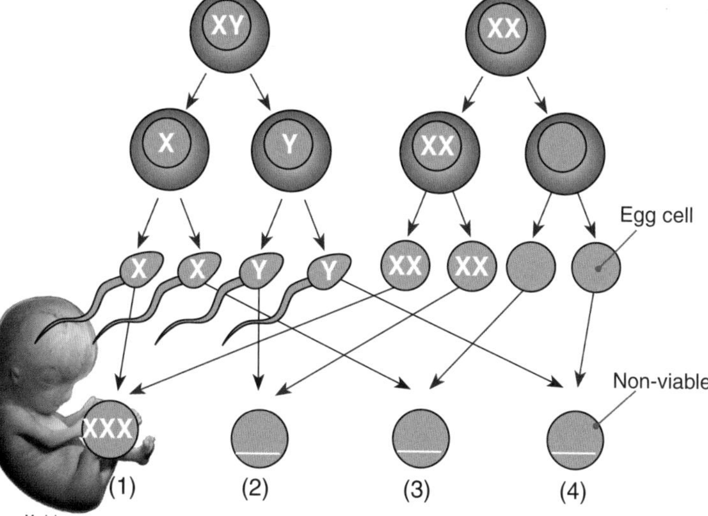

Faulty sperm production

Faulty meiosis during sperm cell production can result in an uneven distribution of X and Y chromosomes.

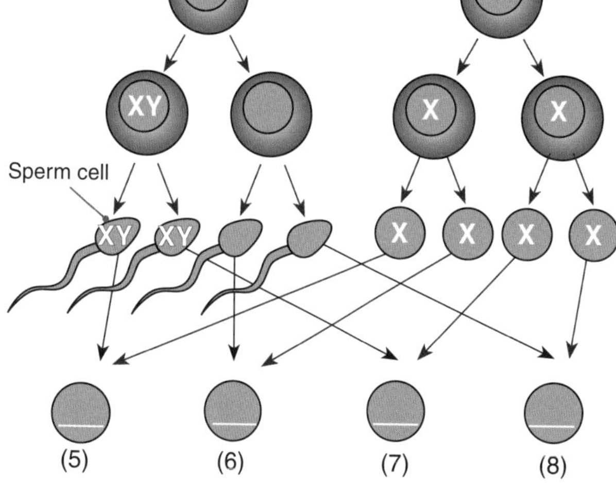

(b) Which of the aneuploids correspond to Turner syndrome? ______________________________

ISBN: 978-1-98-856656-6

Polyploidy

- **Polyploidy** is a condition in which a cell or organism contains three or more times the haploid number of chromosomes (**3N** or more). Polyploidy is rare in animals, but more common in plants. Natural polyploid species occur in animals particularly among hermaphrodites (those having both male and female sex organs), such as flatworms and earthworms.
- The high frequency of polyploidy in plants indicates that polyploidy provides an adaptive advantage. Often this advantage is the result of hybrid vigor, where the hybrid shows improvements over the parents (e.g. by being larger or growing more vigorously). The increase in heterozygosity (heterozygous for a large number of genes) reduces the frequency of (expressed) recessive mutations and also contributes to hybrid vigor.
- Polyploidy results in gene redundancy and provides opportunities to diversify gene function. Extra copies of the gene not required for its original function can be adapted for use in a different way. This can provide an evolutionary advantage. Many polyploids show novel variation or morphologies relative to their parental species.
- New plant varieties can be made by inducing non-disjunction with chemicals. The induction of polyploidy is a common technique to overcome hybrid sterility during plant breeding.

3. Explain why the presence of an extra chromosome has such a profound effect on phenotype: ______

4. Study the examples of polyploidy in plants below.

   (a) Show the **1N** number of chromosomes (haploid state of the **original** population before polyploidy).

   (b) For each plant, describe the condition of the polyploid (e.g. octaploid, tetraploid)

Plant name:	Common wheat	Kiwifruit	Fuji apple	Tobacco	Banana	Boysenberry	Strawberry
Polyploid number:	6N = 42	Naturally 6N	Naturally 3N	4N = 48	3N = 27	7N = 49	8N = 56
1N number:	1N = 7	NA	NA	______	______	______	______
Condition:	Hexaploid	______	______	______	______	______	______

5. Explain why polyploidy is much more common in plants than in animals: ______

6. Explain how nondisjunction results in polyploidy: ______

7. How might nondisjunction result in an instant new species? ______

ISBN: 978-1-98-856656-6

132 Mutations, Variation, and Natural Selection

Key Question: How can mutation enhance survival?

Many mutations have a negative effect on an organism because they interfere with important cellular processes. Many are silent and appear to have no effect on phenotype. A few mutations have a beneficial effect and convey some sort of advantage to the organism. Whether or not a mutation is beneficial often depends on the selection pressures placed on the organism by its environment. Mutations produce new alleles and so are the source of variation on which natural section acts. Bacteria are well known for their ability to become resistant to antibiotics. Resistance can arise through random mutations or can be acquired by transfer of genes in conjugation. Viruses also mutate rapidly; so rapidly that producing a vaccine can be very difficult for some. Organisms with short generation times are able to evolve very quickly in response to changing selection pressures. This is why pesticide resistance in insects and multiple drug resistance in bacteria have evolved so quickly.

Beneficial mutations

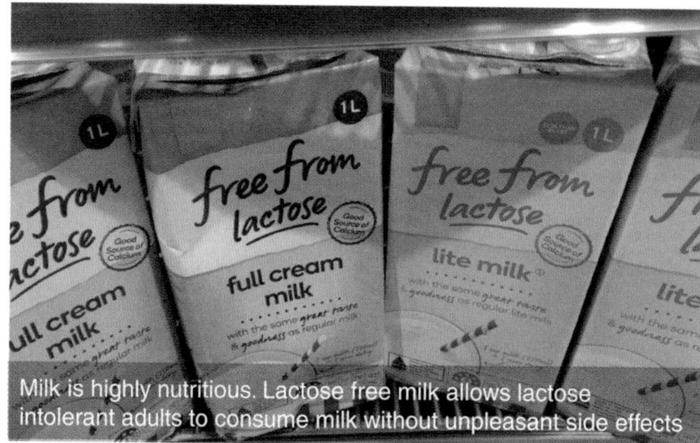

Milk is highly nutritious. Lactose free milk allows lactose intolerant adults to consume milk without unpleasant side effects

TG

- The ability to use various energy sources provides an important survival advantage. Normally mammals stop being able to drink milk (digest lactose) and mothers stop making milk (saving them energy) soon after the offspring's infancy.
- In humans of Northern European, East African, and Middle Eastern descent, lactase production persists and lactose tolerance persists into adulthood. This would be a disadvantage if no milk was available. However humans began farming livestock about 10,000 years ago (about the same time as the mutation for lactose tolerance became prominent). The lactase-persistence mutation involves a single nucleotide change to a regulatory sequence and has been an important and beneficial mutation in human history.

Harmful mutations

Albino

Non-albino

- There are many well-documented examples of mutations that cause harmful effects. Examples are the mutations giving rise to cystic fibrosis (CF) and sickle cell disease. The sickle cell mutation involves a change to only one base in the DNA sequence, whereas the CF mutation involves the loss of a single triplet (three nucleotides).
- Changes in the genes for coat color in mammals are well studied. A number of mutations can produce a lack of coat pigmentation and all are recessive. True albinos (such as the gray squirrel above left) also lack pigmentation in the eyes, which appear pink, distinguishing them from seasonal white morphs. Albinism makes the animal more vulnerable to predators and sensitive to high light.

1. (a) Explain why the mutation for lactase persistence would have first become apparent in cattle-raising populations?

(b) Explain the advantage of being able to digest lactose as an adult?

2. Explain why beneficial mutations do not necessarily spread through the entire human population:

3. Explain why some mutations are harmful only under certain conditions:

ISBN: 978-1-98-856656-6

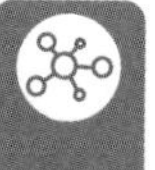

133 The Genetic Basis of Resistance in Bacteria

Key Question: How are bacteria able to quickly acquire new genetic material and become resistant antibiotics?

Bacteria are well known for their ability to become resistant to antibiotics. This can be achieved through a random mutation in a gene that gives the bacterium resistance. Mutations can then be passed on to the next generation during binary fission (vertical gene transfer). However, even though bacteria can produce enormous numbers in a very short time, acquiring resistance in this way is inefficient and does not allow the resistance to spread to other bacterial populations (including other strains). A more important way for acquiring resistance in bacteria is via horizontal gene transfer (HGT). This is the transfer of genes directly without involving cell division. In this way, bacteria can acquire genes for resistance from other strains of bacteria or from the environment, allowing the gene to spread more quickly through many bacterial populations.

1. Which of the methods described right show horizontal gene transfer (HGT)?

____

2. Explain how HGT contributes to the rapid spread of drug resistance in bacteria:

____

____

____

____

____

____

____

3. Explain how transposons contribute to genetic variation that can be subject to natural selection:

____

____

____

____

4. How do viruses contribute to the acquisition of new genetic information in bacteria?

____

____

____

____

____

5. Which of the methods by which bacteria acquire new genetic information would be useful in genetic engineering. Explain:

____

____

____

____

____

____

Methods by which bacteria acquire resistance

Spontaneous and induced resistance

Mutation caused by radiation, chemicals, or transcription error.

Mutated gene codes for antibiotic resistance

Conjugation

Plasmid is transferred via a sex pilus between the bacteria

This bacterium has plasmids that give resistance to antibiotics 1 and 2.

Plasmid giving resistance to antibiotic 2

Plasmid giving resistance to antibiotic 1

Transduction

A viral vector (bacteriophage), which has picked up an antibiotic resistance gene from one bacterium, transfers it to another.

The gene is integrated into the genome of the bacterial cell where it confers resistance.

Gene for antibiotic resistance

Transformation

Naked DNA containing a gene for antibiotic resistance is taken up by a bacterium....

... and integrated into its genome.

Transposition

DNA contains elements called transposons

Transposons are able to change positions in the DNA producing new sequences that may confer antibiotic resistance.

Transposon

Transposon

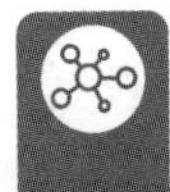

ISBN: 978-1-98-856656-6

134 Recombining Genetic Material in Viruses

Key Question: How does recombining material in viruses confer a survival advantage?

Although viruses are not alive, they still evolve in a similar way to living organisms. Viruses that are able to avoid a host's immune system, reproduce, and spread will survive and those that can't will become extinct over time. One example is smallpox. Before the invention of vaccines, this virus spread rapidly and caused numerous epidemics. After a smallpox vaccine was developed, the virus was unable to evolve defenses against it quickly enough and it declined to extinction in the natural population. Compare this to HIV, which evolves so quickly, no vaccine has yet been produced.

Influenzavirus

- Influenza (flu) is a disease of the upper respiratory tract caused by the viral genus *Influenzavirus*. Three *Influenzavirus* types (A, B, and C) affect humans.
- The most common and most virulent of these is *Influenzavirus* A (right). Influenza viruses undergo genetic changes continually, either by **antigenic drift**, which involves small incremental changes, or by **antigenic shift**, which involves two subtypes recombining to create a new subtype.
- These genetic changes result in changes to the proteins (antigens) presented on the viral surface. The changes prevent the human immune system from recognizing the virus easily, and allow the virus to reinfect people who may have had a previous strain of the flu in the past.
- *Influenzavirus* subtypes are classified by the N and H antigens (e.g. H1N1) which cover their surface. The genetic material in *Influenzavirus* is stored as eight RNA sequences. All eight RNA segments can be reassorted. Two of the RNA segments code for the H and N antigens.

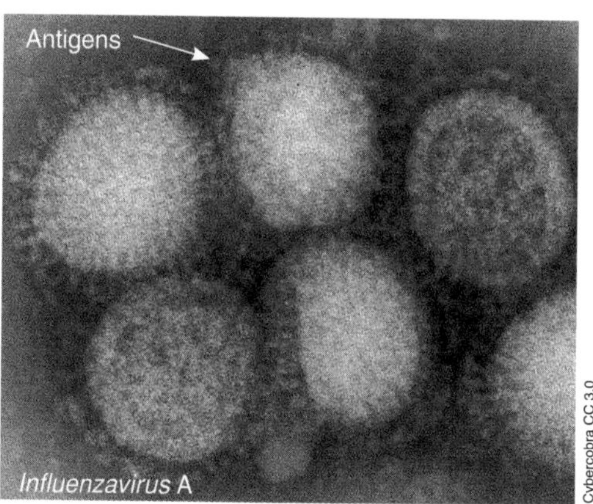

Cybercobra CC 3.0

Antigenic drifts are small incremental changes (caused by mutations) in the virus that happen continually over time. The changes affect the H and N surface antigens. Accumulated changes result in the immune system not recognizing the virus. As a result, the influenza vaccine, which prepares the immune system for infection, must be adjusted each year to include the most recently circulating influenza viruses.

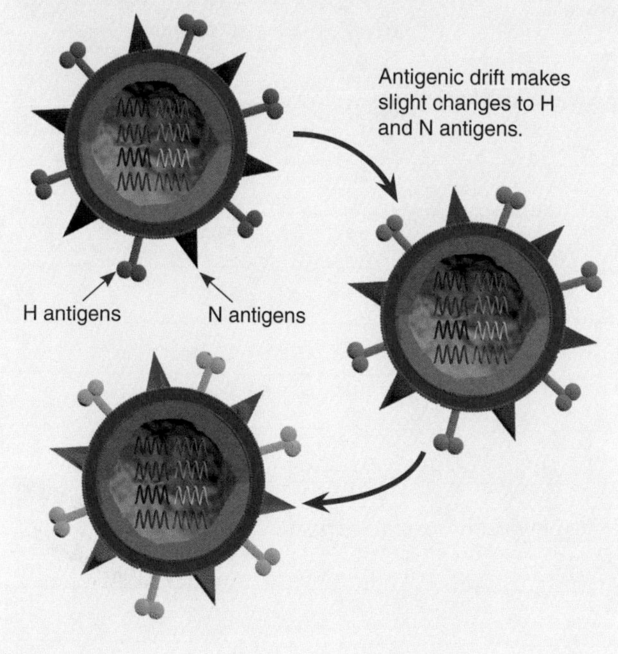

Antigenic drift makes slight changes to H and N antigens.
H antigens
N antigens

Antigenic shift occurs when two or more different viral strains (or different viruses) infect the same cell and recombine to form a new subtype. The changes are large and sudden, and most people lack immunity to the new subtype. New influenza viruses arising from antigenic shift have caused influenza pandemics that have killed millions people over the last century. *Influenzavirus* A is dangerous to human health because it is capable of antigenic shift.

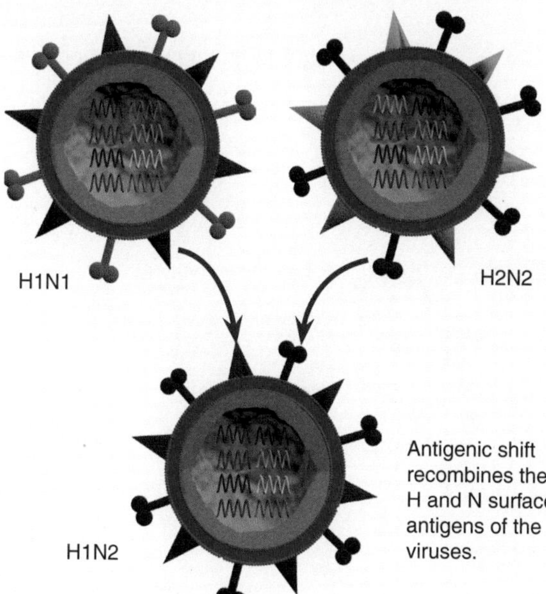

1. Explain how the difference between antigenic drift and antigenic shift accounts for the different responses in the host:

ISBN: 978-1-98-856656-6

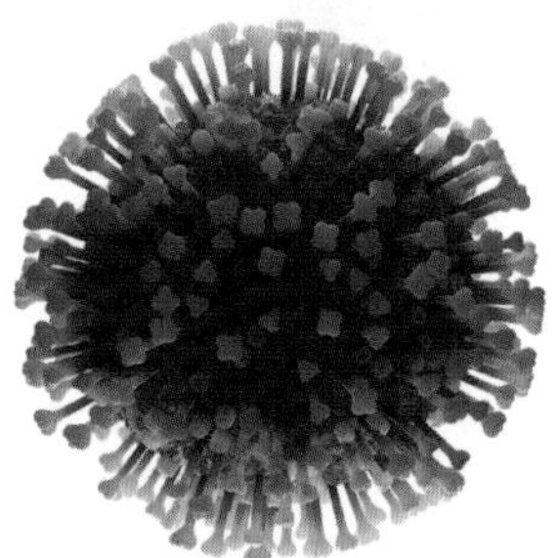
H1N1 *Influenzavirus* (model)

Antigenic shift and outbreaks

- Subtypes of *Influenzavirus* can reassort genetic material with each other to produce new subtypes, often never encountered by humans. For example, seasonal flu mutates so rapidly that vaccinations only last a year.
- Reassortment is a genetic recombination exclusive to segmented RNA viruses in which infection of a host cell with multiple viruses results in complete gene segments being reshuffled to generate novel viruses.
- **Example**: The novel H1N1 *Influenzavirus*, which caused the 2009 swine flu pandemic, evolved from several reassortments of genes from human, pig, and avian viruses over several decades (below).

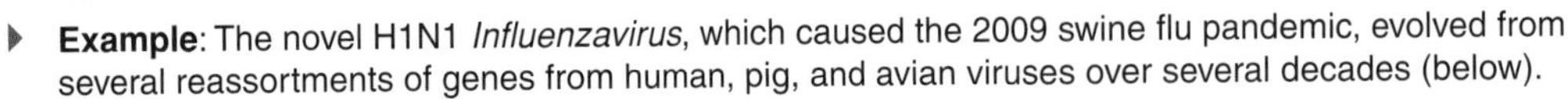

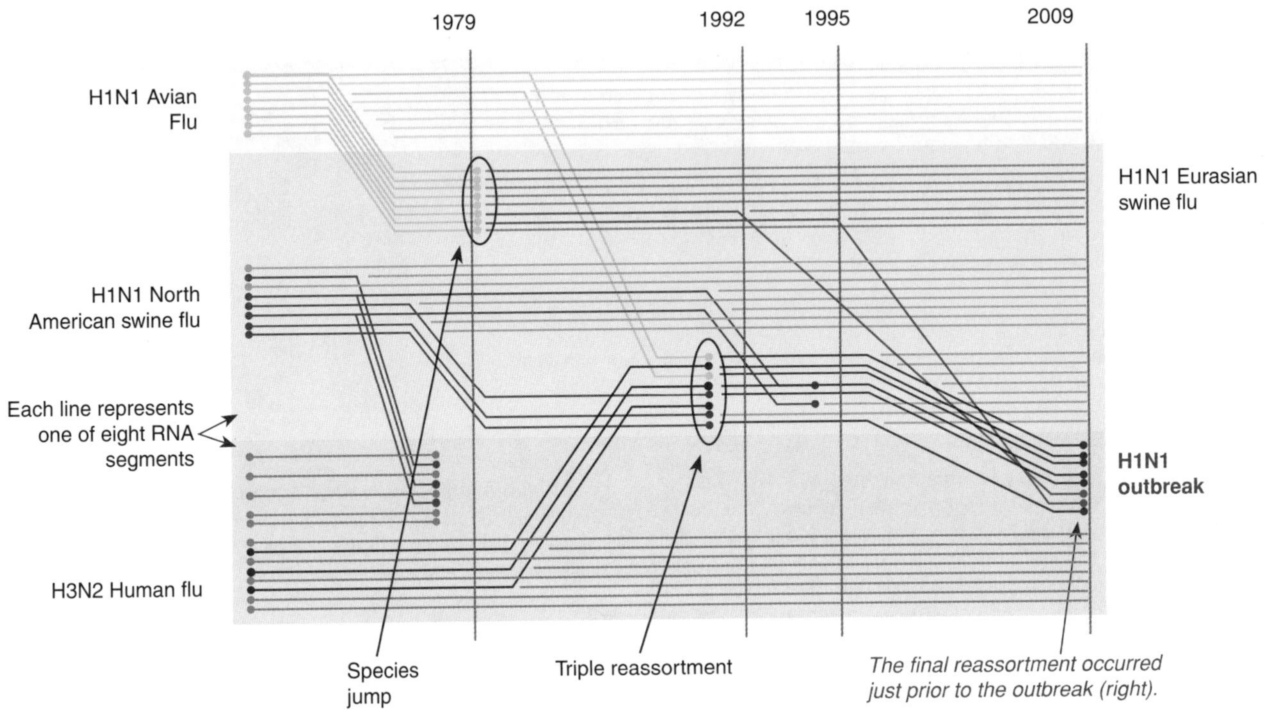

2. The *Influenzavirus* is able to mutate readily and alter the composition of H and N spikes on its surface.

   (a) Explain why the virus can mutate so rapidly: ____________________

   (b) Explain how this affects the ability of the virus to survive and spread: ____________________

3. Why does a person need to be infected by at least two different subtypes of *Influenzavirus* for antigenic shift to occur?

4. The H1N1 subtype of 2009 spread across the globe very quickly. Describe how this new subtype evolved: ____________________

ISBN: 978-1-98-856656-6

135 What is Genetic Engineering?

Key Question: What is genetic engineering (GE) and how can GE techniques be applied to areas of biotechnology?

DNA manipulation (also called genetic engineering) involves the direct manipulation of an organism's genome using many different technologies. These technologies can also be applied to a wide range of uses outside direct gene manipulation, including food technology, industry, agriculture, environmental cleanup, vaccine development, and production of pharmaceuticals. It is the application of genetic engineering technologies to these areas and more that has changed our understanding of the world, from producing genetically modified organisms, to improving forensics, to rewriting or confirming our understanding of evolutionary relationships between organisms.

Basic tools in genetic engineering

- Restriction endonucleases (restriction enzymes or REs) are an important tool in genetic engineering. REs cleave DNA into fragments at or near specific recognition sites. This means that DNA with a gene of interest and the DNA of a vector such as a plasmid can be cut with the same RE and the pieces can then be joined together using DNA ligase (right).
- Restriction digests are a common tool to create recombinant DNA and to prepare DNA for analysis, gene (molecular) cloning, or **bacterial transformation** (below).

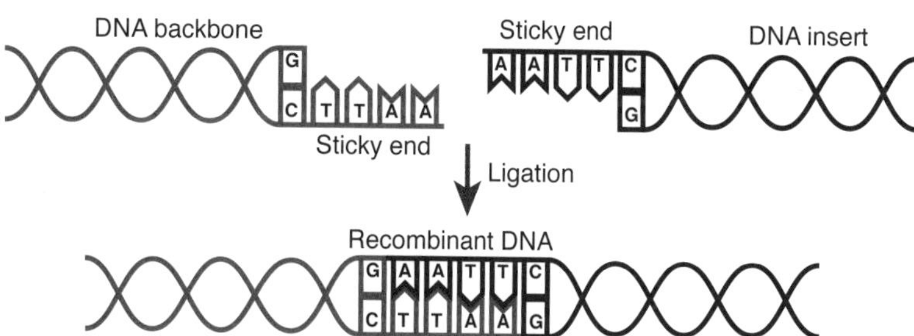

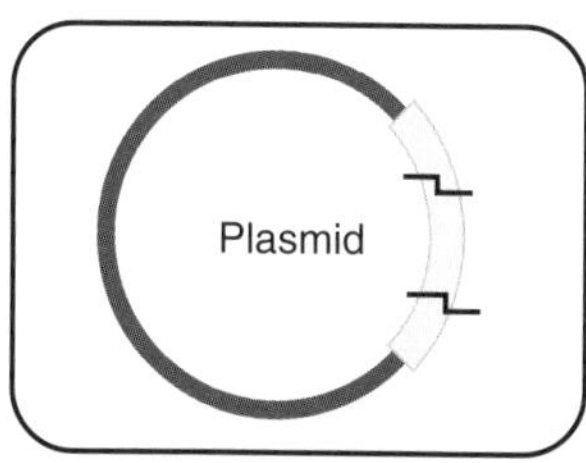

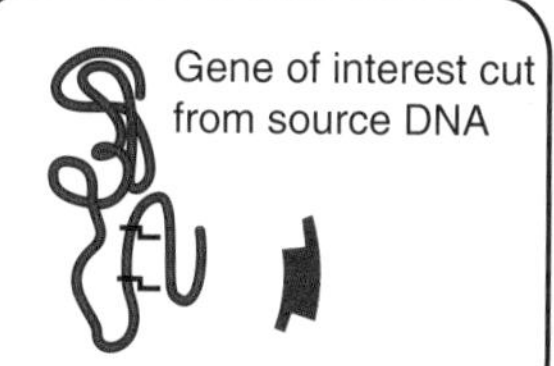

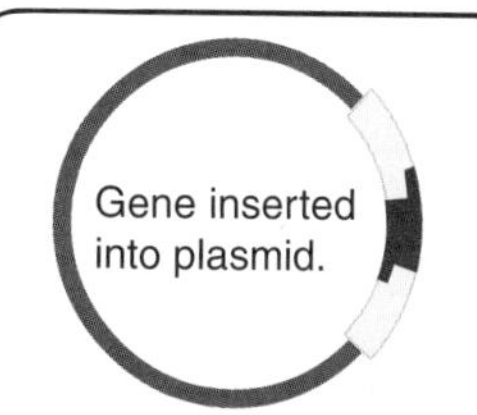

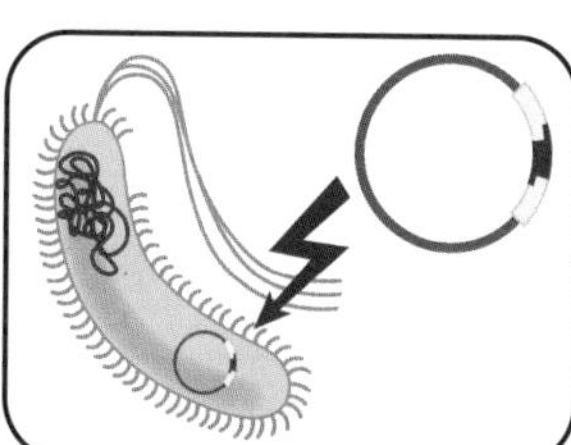

Restriction digestion of vector → Restriction digestion of gene of interest → Ligation → Transformation

CRISPR-Cas9 is a powerful gene editing tool

Single guide RNA (sgRNA) is a short synthetic RNA sequence designed to guide Cas9 to the site of interest (e.g. a faulty gene sequence). It contains a nucleotide section which is complementary to the DNA of interest.

Cas9 unwinds the DNA and cuts both strands at a specific point.

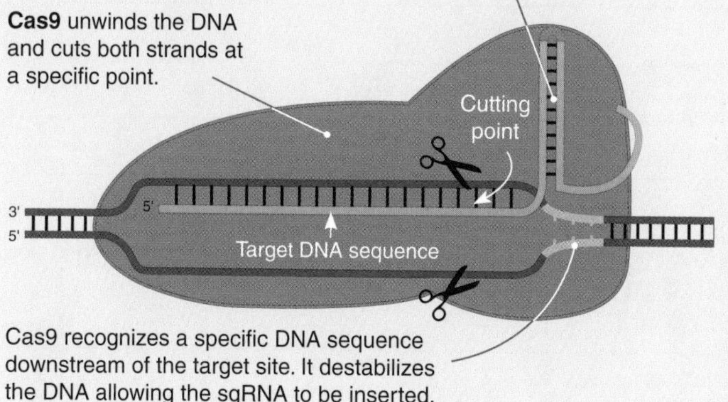

Cas9 recognizes a specific DNA sequence downstream of the target site. It destabilizes the DNA allowing the sgRNA to be inserted.

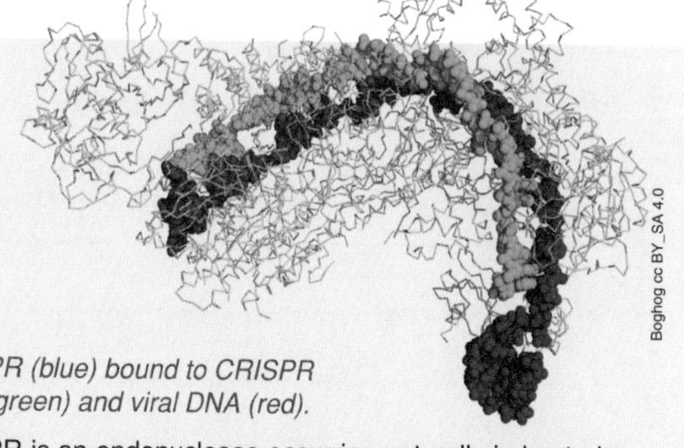

CRISPR (blue) bound to CRISPR RNA (green) and viral DNA (red).

- CRISPR is an endonuclease occurring naturally in bacteria, which use it to edit the DNA of invading viruses. It is able to find specific stretches of DNA and edit it at precise locations.
- CRISPR requires an **RNA guide**, which locates and binds to the target piece of DNA, and the **Cas9 enzyme**, which unwinds and cuts the DNA. If genes are edited in the gametes or the early embryo the edits will be passed to developing individual.
- The CRISPR-Cas9 system makes it possible to replace faulty sequences (knock-in) or to silence genes (gene knock-out).

1. What is DNA manipulation and what does it involve? ______________________________

____

____

____

____

ISBN: 978-1-98-856656-6

138

137
136

109

IST-1 2.B

Applying genetic engineering techniques

Phylogenetics
Technologies involved in GE, including gel electrophoresis, restriction digestion, and DNA probes, have been applied to genomic analysis, allowing the genomes of multiple organisms to be compared for their genetic relationships.

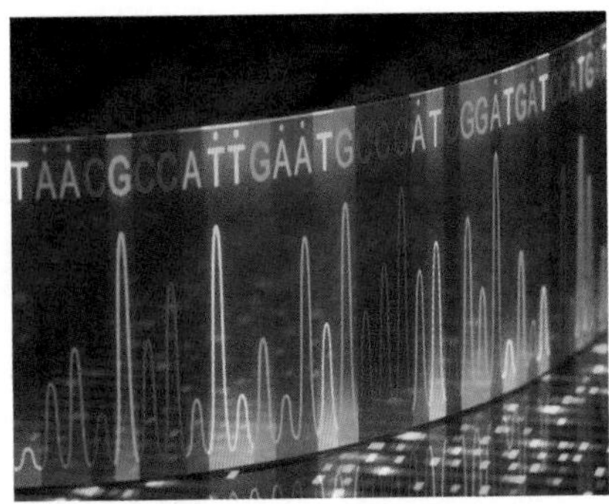

Analysis of the differences in DNA sequences have been able to establish genetic relationships between species.

Forensics
Restriction digestion coupled with gel electrophoresis have transformed forensics. Investigators can collect and analyze DNA from a crime scene. Many cold cases have been solved by analyzing stored DNA samples.

By analyzing short DNA segments unique to individuals forensic scientists can link an accused to a crime scene

Producing GMOs
Genetically modified organisms are produced with a vast range of abilities. Many proteins once obtained from animals are now produced by bacteria, and many crops plants produce their own pesticides or are herbicide resistant.

Adding, removing or silencing genes has produced organisms with a wide range of characteristics useful for humans.

2. Identify two genetic engineering tools and describe how they can be used: ______

3. Describe some broad applications of genetic engineering technologies: ______

4. One of the key concepts of DNA manipulation and genetic engineering is that DNA from a donor species can be transferred to a host species and that the transferred DNA will behave in the same way in the host species as in the donor species. Explain how this is possible and why this is so important for genetic engineering:

ISBN: 978-1-98-856656-6

136 Gel Electrophoresis

Key Question: What is gel electrophoresis, how does it work, and what kind of information does it provide?

Gel electrophoresis is a tool used to isolate DNA of interest for further study. It is also used for DNA profiling (comparing individuals based on their unique DNA banding profiles). DNA has an overall negative charge, so when an electrical current is run through a gel, the DNA moves towards the positive electrode. The rate at which the DNA molecules move through the gel depends primarily on their size and the strength of the electric field. The gel they move through is full of pores (holes). Smaller DNA molecules move through the pores more quickly than larger ones. At the end of the process, the DNA molecules can be stained and visualized as a series of bands. Each band contains DNA molecules of a particular size. The bands furthest from the start of the gel contain the smallest DNA fragments.

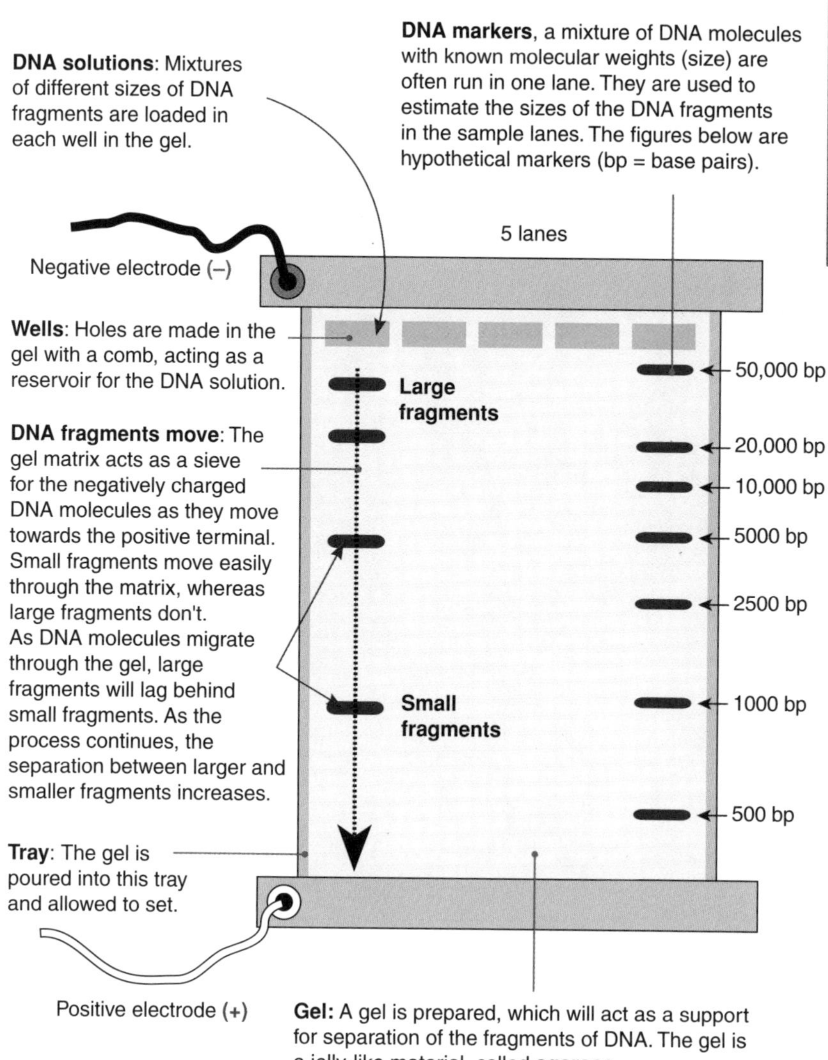

DNA solutions: Mixtures of different sizes of DNA fragments are loaded in each well in the gel.
DNA markers, a mixture of DNA molecules with known molecular weights (size) are often run in one lane. They are used to estimate the sizes of the DNA fragments in the sample lanes. The figures below are hypothetical markers (bp = base pairs).
5 lanes
Negative electrode (–)
Wells: Holes are made in the gel with a comb, acting as a reservoir for the DNA solution.
Large fragments
50,000 bp
20,000 bp
10,000 bp
5000 bp
2500 bp
1000 bp
500 bp
DNA fragments move: The gel matrix acts as a sieve for the negatively charged DNA molecules as they move towards the positive terminal. Small fragments move easily through the matrix, whereas large fragments don't.
As DNA molecules migrate through the gel, large fragments will lag behind small fragments. As the process continues, the separation between larger and smaller fragments increases.
Small fragments
Tray: The gel is poured into this tray and allowed to set.
Positive electrode (+)
Gel: A gel is prepared, which will act as a support for separation of the fragments of DNA. The gel is a jelly-like material, called agarose.

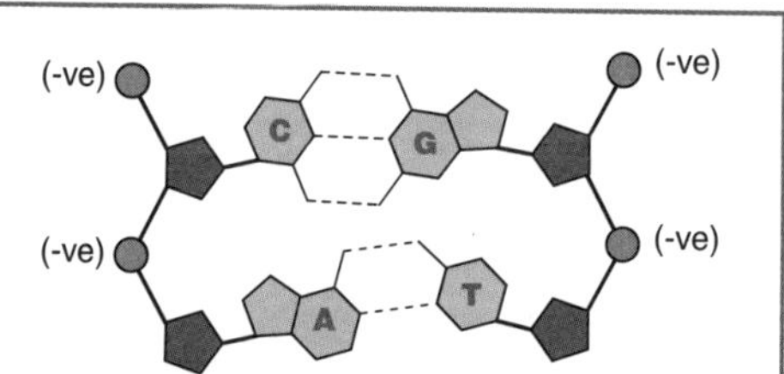

DNA is **negatively charged** because the phosphates (blue) that form part of the backbone of a DNA molecule have a negative charge.

Steps in the process of gel electrophoresis of DNA

1. The gel is placed in an electrophoresis chamber and the chamber is filled with buffer, covering the gel. This allows the electric current from electrodes at either end of the gel to flow through the gel.
2. DNA samples are mixed with a "loading dye" to make the DNA sample visible. The dye also contains glycerol or sucrose to make the DNA sample heavy so that it will sink to the bottom of the well.
3. The gel is covered, electrodes are attached to a power supply and turned on.
4. When the dye marker has moved through the gel, the current is turned off and the gel is removed from the tray.
5. DNA molecules are made visible by staining the gel with methylene blue or ethidium bromide which binds to DNA and will fluoresce in UV light.
6. The band or bands of interest are cut from the gel and dissolved in chemicals to release the DNA. This DNA can then be studied in more detail (e.g. its nucleotide sequence can be determined).

1. What is the purpose of gel electrophoresis? ____________________

2. Describe the two forces that control the speed at which fragments pass through the gel:

(a) ____________________

(b) ____________________

3. Why do the smallest fragments travel through the gel the fastest? ____________________

ISBN: 978-1-98-856656-6

142

IST-1
6.D

Once made, an electrophoresis gel must be interpreted. If a specific DNA base sequence was being investigated, then the band pattern can be used to determine the DNA sequence and the protein that it encoded. Alternatively, depending on how the original DNA was treated, the banding pattern may be used as a profile for a species or individual. Commonly, the gene for cytochrome oxidase I (COXI), a mitochondrial protein, is used to distinguish animal species. The genetic information from this gene is both large enough to measure differences between species and small enough to have the differences make sense (i.e. the differences occur in small regions and aren't hugely varied).

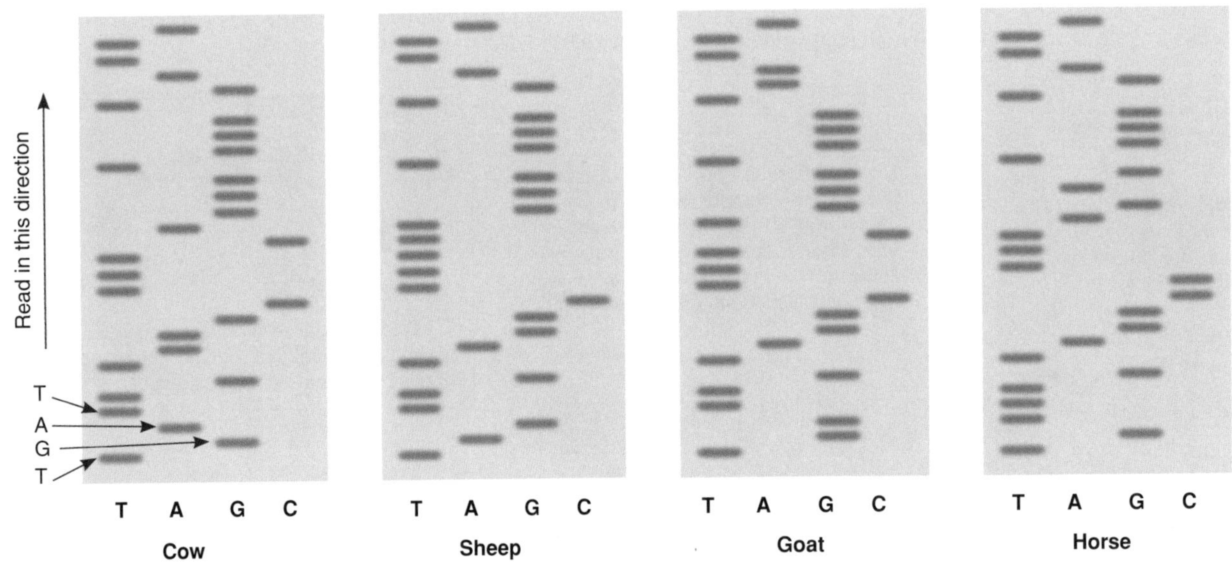

4. The photographs above show gel electrophoresis results for four species.

   (a) For each of the species determine the sequence of DNA:

   Cow DNA sequence: ______________________

   Sheep DNA sequence: ______________________

   Goat DNA sequence: ______________________

   Horse DNA sequence: ______________________

   Based on the number of differences in the DNA sequences:

   (b) Identify the two species that are most closely related: ______________________

   (c) Identify the two species that are the least closely related: ______________________

5. What makes COXI useful for comparing species by gel electrophoresis? ______________________

____

____

6. Determine the relatedness of each individual (A-E) using each banding pattern on the set of DNA profiles below. When you have done this, complete the phylogenetic tree by adding the letter of each individual.

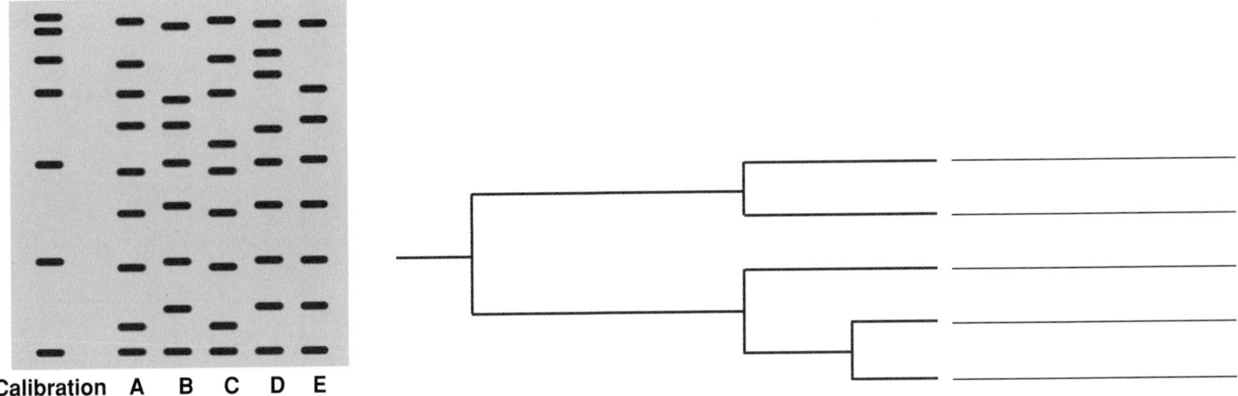

ISBN: 978-1-98-856656-6

137 Polymerase Chain Reaction

Key Question: What are the principles behind the polymerase chain reaction and why is it useful in biotechnology?

Often it is very hard to get enough DNA to analyze (e.g. DNA from a crime scene or from an extinct organism). Researchers need to increase the amount of DNA they have to work with, this is done using **polymerase chain reaction** (PCR). PCR can make billions of copies of a target DNA sequence of interest so that it can be analyzed. The technique is carried out *in vitro* (e.g. in tubes) rather than in a living organism. An overview of PCR given below.

A single cycle of PCR

DNA polymerase: A thermally stable form of the enzyme is used (e.g. ***Taq* *polymerase***). This is extracted from thermophilic (heat tolerant) bacteria.

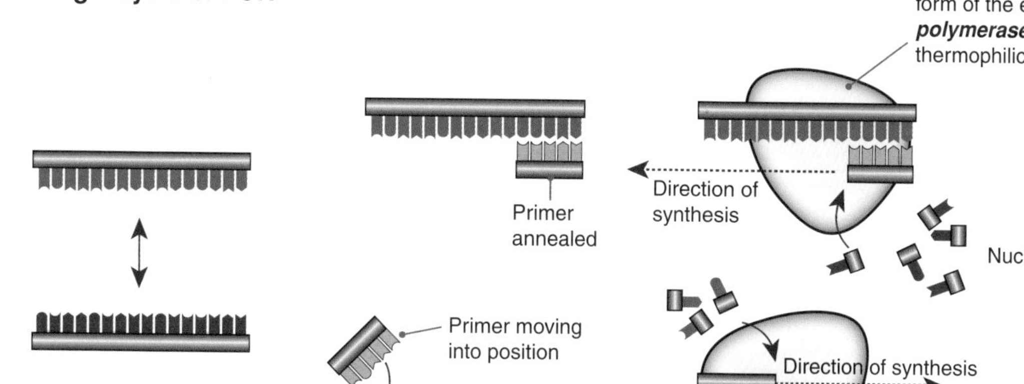

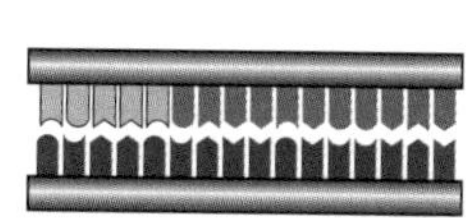

1. Denaturing
A DNA sample (called target DNA) is obtained. It is denatured (DNA strands are separated) by heating at 98°C for 5 minutes.

2. Annealing
The sample is cooled to 60°C. Primers are annealed (bonded) to each DNA strand. In PCR, the primers are short strands of DNA; they provide the starting sequence for DNA extension.

3. Extension/elongation
Free nucleotides and DNA polymerase are added. DNA polymerase binds to the primers and synthesises complementary strands of DNA, using the free nucleotides.

4. Completed strands
After one cycle, there are now two copies of the original DNA.

Repeat cycle of heating and cooling until enough copies of the target DNA have been produced

1. Describe the process of PCR: ______________________________

2. (a) Explain the purpose of PCR: ______________________________

(b) Give two examples where PCR is needed to amplify DNA: ______________________________

3. After only two cycles of replication, four copies of the double-stranded DNA exist. Calculate how much a DNA sample will have increased after:

(a) 10 cycles: ______________ (b) 25 cycles: ______________

4. Researchers take great care to avoid DNA contamination during PCR preparation. Explain why: ______________________________

ISBN: 978-1-98-856656-6

138 Bacterial Transformation and Gene Cloning

Key Question: How is the ability of bacteria to take up plasmids from the environment used in biotechnology?

We have already seen that recombinant DNA techniques can be used to insert a gene into a plasmid. The plasmid can then be used to transmit the gene to another organism (e.g. *E. coli* bacteria). Once inside *E. coli*, the gene is replicated along with the host DNA. This technique is called **gene cloning** (or molecular cloning) and produces multiple copies of the gene. The recombinant plasmid must be able to replicate inside its host, it must have one or more sites at which a restriction enzyme can cut, and it must have some kind of genetic marker that allows them to be identified. **Replica plating** is often used to identify organisms that have produced the gene of interest.

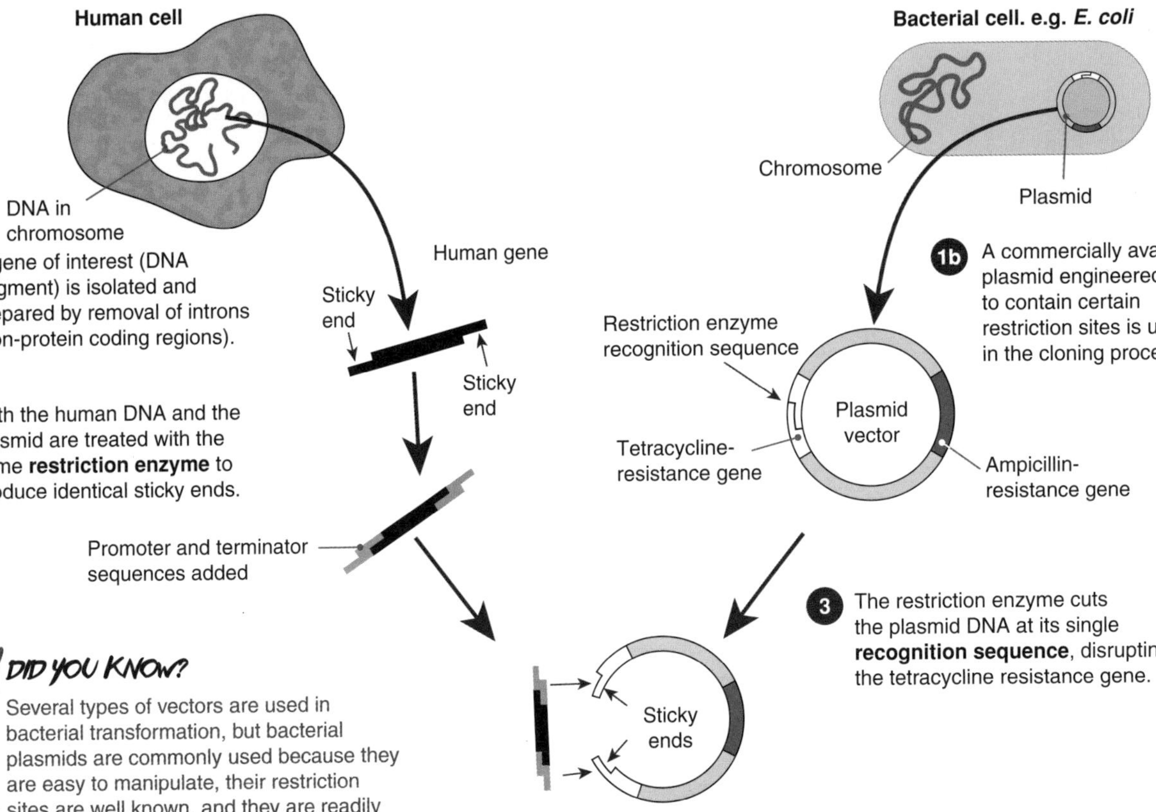

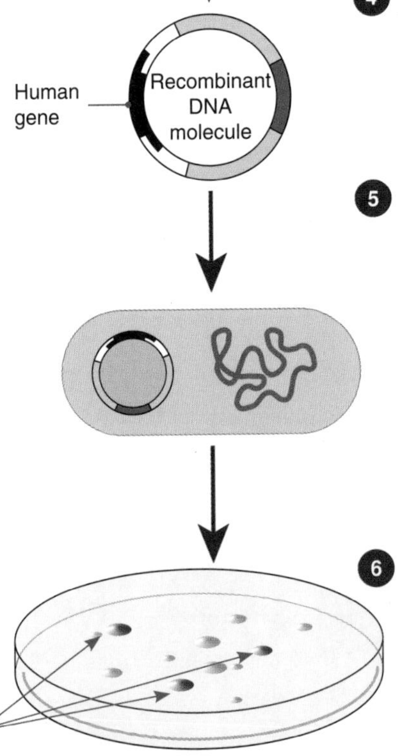

Human cell

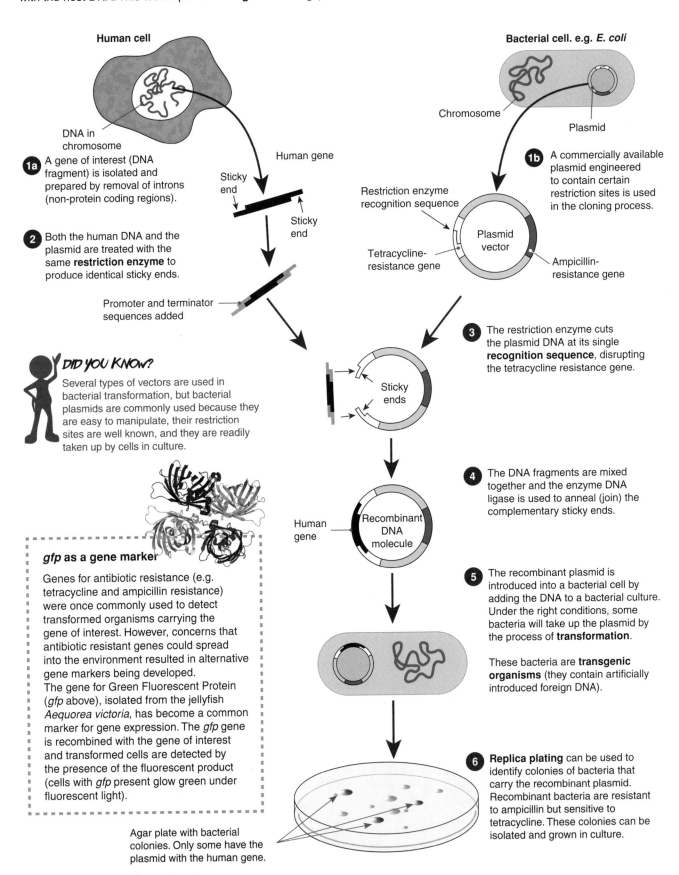

DNA in chromosome

1a A gene of interest (DNA fragment) is isolated and prepared by removal of introns (non-protein coding regions).

Human gene

Sticky end

Sticky end

2 Both the human DNA and the plasmid are treated with the same **restriction enzyme** to produce identical sticky ends.

Promoter and terminator sequences added

Bacterial cell. e.g. *E. coli*

Chromosome

Plasmid

1b A commercially available plasmid engineered to contain certain restriction sites is used in the cloning process.

Restriction enzyme recognition sequence

Plasmid vector

Tetracycline-resistance gene

Ampicillin-resistance gene

3 The restriction enzyme cuts the plasmid DNA at its single **recognition sequence**, disrupting the tetracycline resistance gene.

Sticky ends

DID YOU KNOW?

Several types of vectors are used in bacterial transformation, but bacterial plasmids are commonly used because they are easy to manipulate, their restriction sites are well known, and they are readily taken up by cells in culture.

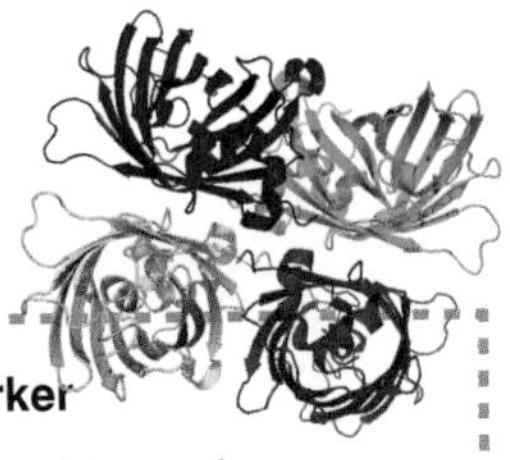

4 The DNA fragments are mixed together and the enzyme DNA ligase is used to anneal (join) the complementary sticky ends.

Human gene

Recombinant DNA molecule

5 The recombinant plasmid is introduced into a bacterial cell by adding the DNA to a bacterial culture. Under the right conditions, some bacteria will take up the plasmid by the process of **transformation**.

These bacteria are **transgenic organisms** (they contain artificially introduced foreign DNA).

6 **Replica plating** can be used to identify colonies of bacteria that carry the recombinant plasmid. Recombinant bacteria are resistant to ampicillin but sensitive to tetracycline. These colonies can be isolated and grown in culture.

Agar plate with bacterial colonies. Only some have the plasmid with the human gene.

gfp as a gene marker

Genes for antibiotic resistance (e.g. tetracycline and ampicillin resistance) were once commonly used to detect transformed organisms carrying the gene of interest. However, concerns that antibiotic resistant genes could spread into the environment resulted in alternative gene markers being developed.

The gene for Green Fluorescent Protein (*gfp* above), isolated from the jellyfish *Aequorea victoria*, has become a common marker for gene expression. The *gfp* gene is recombined with the gene of interest and transformed cells are detected by the presence of the fluorescent product (cells with *gfp* present glow green under fluorescent light).

ISBN: 978-1-98-856656-6

Replica plating identifies colonies with desirable qualities

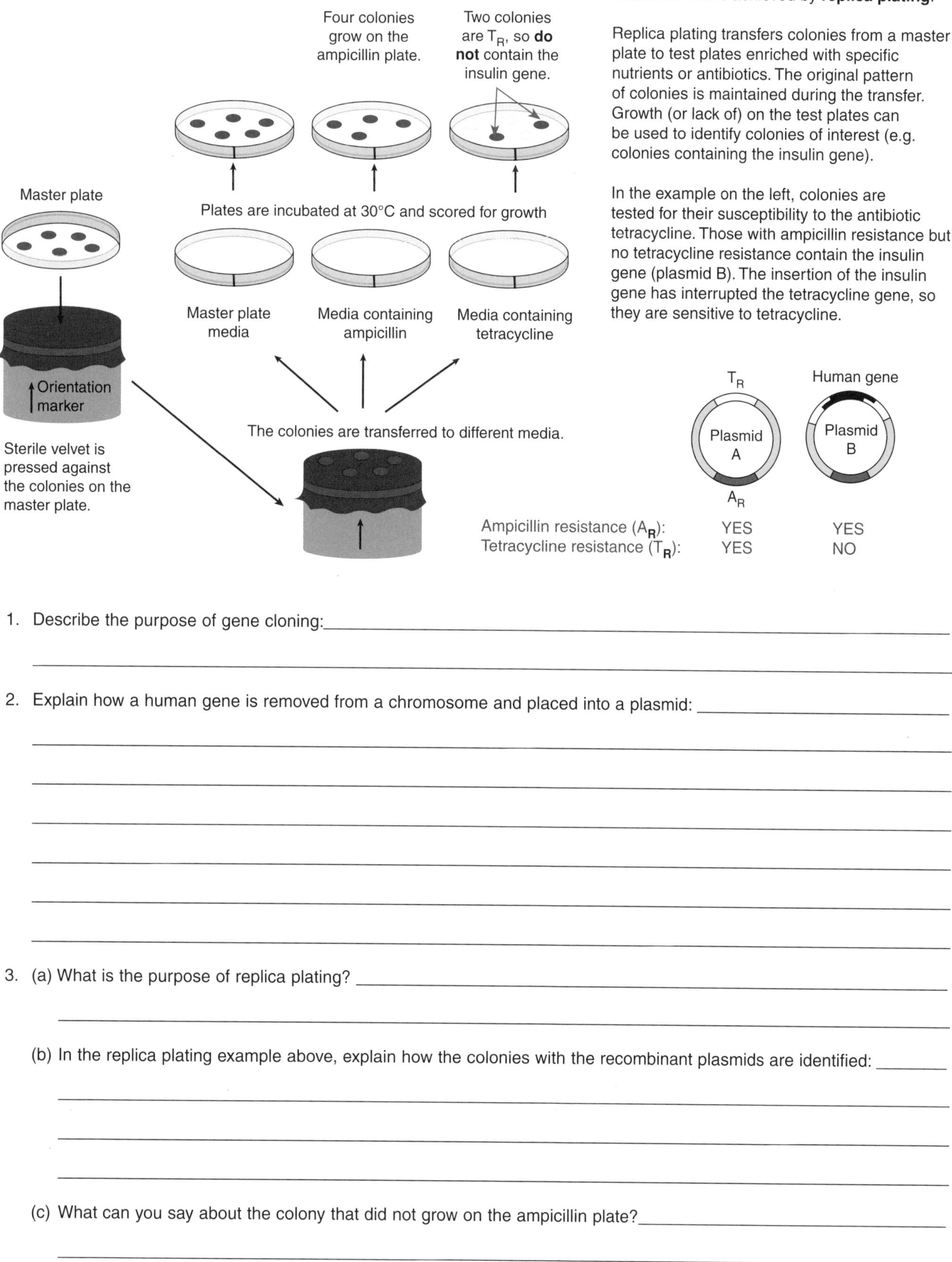

After gene cloning, it is important to be able to identify the colonies in which transformation has occurred. This is achieved by **replica plating**.

Replica plating transfers colonies from a master plate to test plates enriched with specific nutrients or antibiotics. The original pattern of colonies is maintained during the transfer. Growth (or lack of) on the test plates can be used to identify colonies of interest (e.g. colonies containing the insulin gene).

In the example on the left, colonies are tested for their susceptibility to the antibiotic tetracycline. Those with ampicillin resistance but no tetracycline resistance contain the insulin gene (plasmid B). The insertion of the insulin gene has interrupted the tetracycline gene, so they are sensitive to tetracycline.

1. Describe the purpose of gene cloning: ______________________

2. Explain how a human gene is removed from a chromosome and placed into a plasmid: ______________________

3. (a) What is the purpose of replica plating? ______________________

(b) In the replica plating example above, explain how the colonies with the recombinant plasmids are identified: ______________________

(c) What can you say about the colony that did not grow on the ampicillin plate? ______________________

4. Explain why the *gfp* marker is a more desirable gene marker than genes for antibiotic resistance: ______________________

ISBN: 978-1-98-856656-6

139 Aseptic Technique and Streak Plating

STUDENT SUPPORT FOR INVESTIGATION 8: *Bacterial transformation*

- The most common way of separating bacterial cells on an agar surface is the **streak plate method**. This method dilutes the sample by mechanical means. Contamination is minimized using a procedure called **aseptic technique**.
- After incubation, the area at the beginning of the streak pattern will show confluent growth (growth as a continuous sheet), while the area at the end of the streak will show individual colonies.
- Isolated colonies can be removed using aseptic techniques, and transferred to a sterile medium. After incubation, assuming aseptic techniques have been used, all organisms in the new culture will be descendants of the same organism (i.e. a pure culture). The organism can then be identified and studied (e.g. for sensitivity to particular antibiotics).

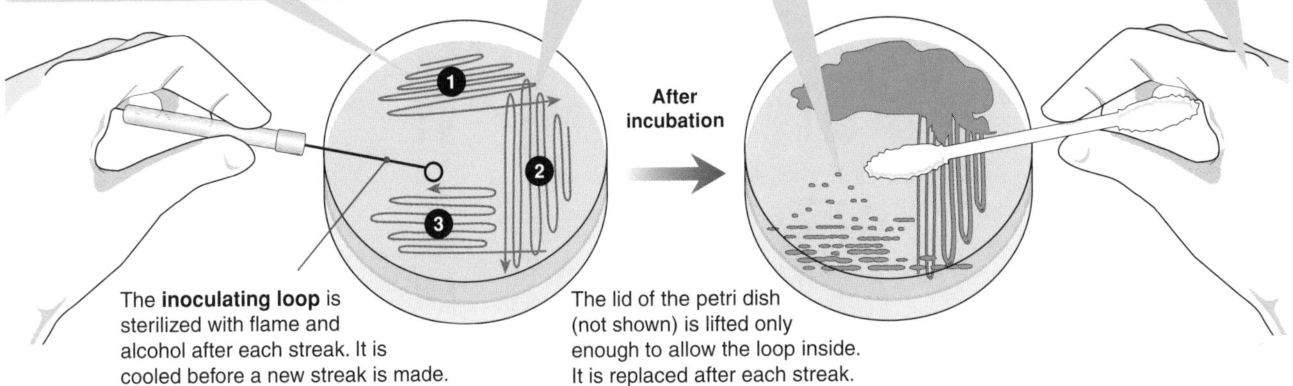

The streaking starts here. Streaks are made in the order indicated by the numbers on the plate. The first streak is made from the initial bacterial mixture.
In each streak, the loop picks up bacteria from the previous series, diluting the number of cells each time.
Individual colonies (arising from one cell) should be obtained here. These can be removed and then cultured separately.
Latex gloves ensure no contamination from either bacteria or fungi on the hands.
1
2
3
After incubation
The **inoculating loop** is sterilized with flame and alcohol after each streak. It is cooled before a new streak is made.
The lid of the petri dish (not shown) is lifted only enough to allow the loop inside. It is replaced after each streak.

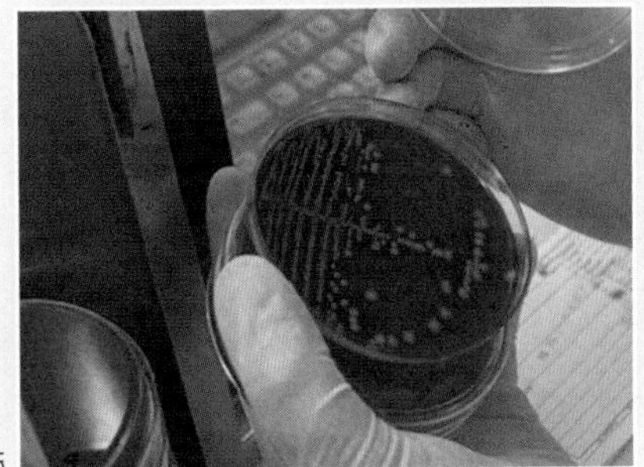

Colonies become visible when approximately 10 to 100 million bacterial cells are present. Note the well-isolated colonies in the photo above. A single colony may be removed for further investigation.

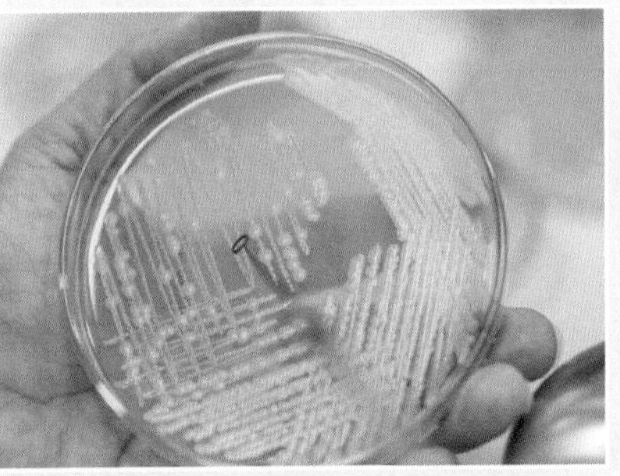

A swab containing a single strain of bacteria is used to inoculate additional nutrient plates to produce pure cultures of bacteria.

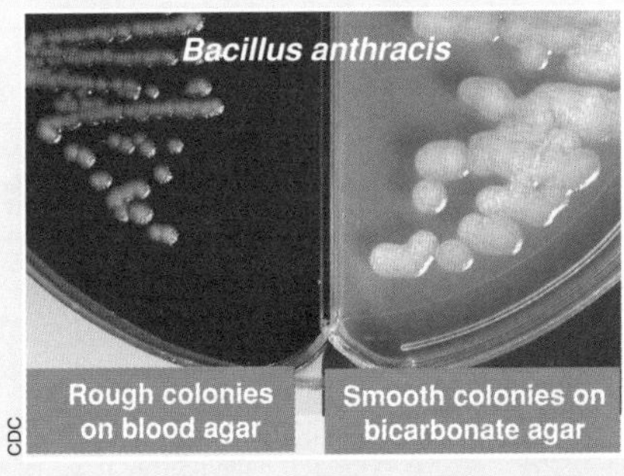

To test purity, a sample of a culture can be grown on a selective medium that promotes the growth of a single species. A selective medium may contain a nutrient specific to a particular species.

1. What is the purpose of streak plating? ______

2. Describe the process of streak plating: ______

3. Why is the lid only partially removed during streaking? ______

4. (a) How would you know if your streak plating had been effective? ______

   (b) What could you do to test that all your colonies were the same species? ______

ISBN: 978-1-98-856656-6

Aseptic technique

Aseptic technique is a fundamental skill in microbiology as it prevents unwanted microorganisms contaminating a laboratory culture. The technique involves the use of heat (a flame) and sometimes alcohol to sterilize the tools used to transfer a microbial inoculum to the growth medium.

Exposure of the culture media to the environment is limited to reduce the risk of contamination from the environment. For this reason, the lid of an agar plate or screw cap of a liquid broth are only partially opened for as little time as possible to inoculate the media. Aseptic technique also minimizes the risk of microbes being released into the environment. This is especially important when dealing with pathogenic (disease causing) microbes. The example provided (right) shows inoculation of an agar plate using aseptic technique.

Sources of contamination

Sources of contamination include:

- Airborne microbes
- Contamination from the researcher's body
- Dirty (unsterilized) equipment or bench top
- Contaminated culture media

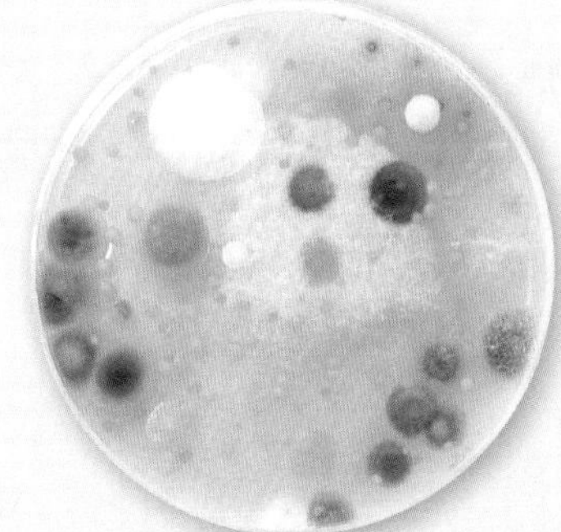

The environment contains many microbes that could potentially contaminate an inoculum if correct aseptic technique is not followed. The agar plate above was left exposed in a laboratory for one hour and then incubated. Many different types of microbes have grown on it.

1. Always wear gloves when working with microbes. Wipe the work surface down with a disinfectant such as ethanol.

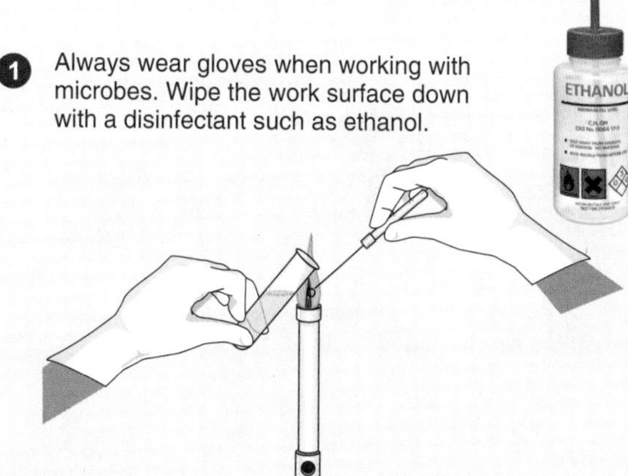

2. Hold the inoculating loop in the flame until it glows red hot. Remove the lid from the culture broth and pass the neck of the bottle through the flame.

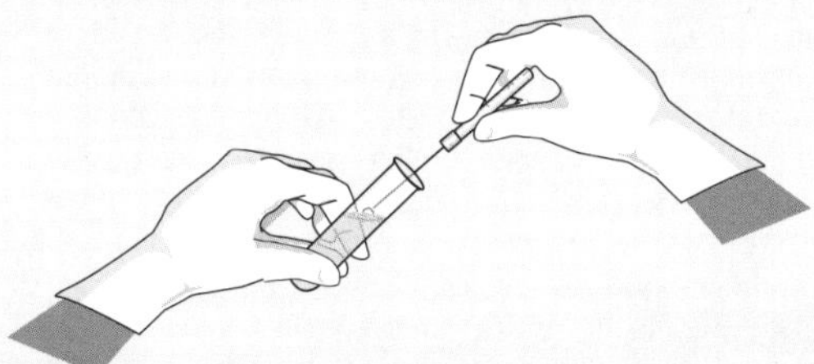

3. Dip the cool inoculating loop into the broth. Flame the neck of the bottle again and replace the lid.

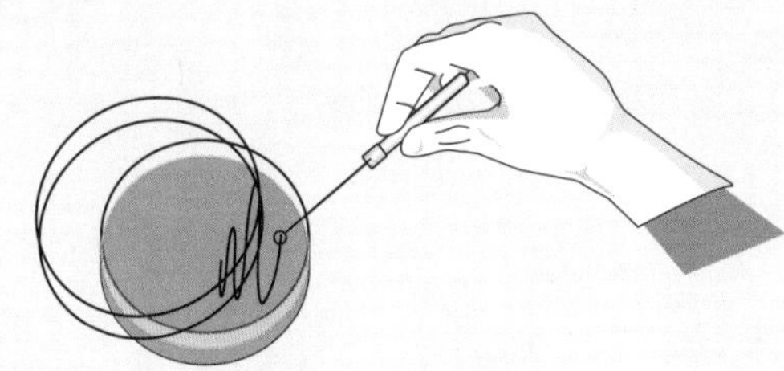

4. Raise the lid of the plate just enough to allow the loop to streak the plate. Streak the surface of the media.

5. Describe three sources of contamination and how contamination from them can be minimized:

(a) ____

____

(b) ____

____

(c) ____

____

6. Why is it important to use aseptic technique when growing microbial cultures? ______________________

____

____

7. What would happen if you did not cool the inoculation loop before you dipped it into the culture broth? ______________

____

____

ISBN: 978-1-98-856656-6

140 Testing for Transformation

STUDENT SUPPORT FOR INVESTIGATION 8: *Bacterial transformation*

Bacteria may obtain new genetic material via mutation, obtain it from other bacteria, or by taking up naked genetic material from the environment, a process call transformation. Transformation efficiency is a measure of the ability of bacteria to take up extracellular DNA. Bacteria that are able to do this are termed **competent**. Transformation is commonly used in genetic engineering to insert novel genes into bacteria in order to produce proteins on an industrial scale.

Aim

To investigate the efficiency of transformation in *E. coli* bacteria when mixed with a plasmid containing a variant of GFP (green fluorescent protein) gene and the ampicillin resistance gene.

Background

GFP is a common marker gene that is used to indicate bacterial colonies that have acquired a target plasmid. GFP glows under fluorescent light. The variant of this gene also causes the bacterial colonies to turn yellow-green in ordinary white light (*E. coli* colonies normally have a whitish appearance). GFP is normally a preferred alternative to using a gene for resistance to ampicillin (an antibiotic) as it reduces the risk of antibiotic resistance spreading in bacteria. In this example, both genes are being used as only transformed bacterial colonies are being counted and the ampicillin resistance makes this simpler because untransformed colonies can be eliminated by using ampicillin-containing agar plates. Colonies can be assumed to be derived from individual bacterial cells, so the number of colonies relates directly to the number of cells originally on the agar plate.

Method for transforming *E. coli*

250 μL of ice cold $CaCl_2$ was transferred to two microcentrifuge tubes using a sterile transfer pipette. One tube was labeled +plasmid, the other was labeled -plasmid. Both tubes were placed on ice. A starter colony was transferred to each tube from an agar plate of *E. coli* using a sterile inoculation loop. The tubes were inverted several times to ensure mixing, then returned to the ice.

10 μL of 0.005 μg/μL solution of plasmid was transferred by sterile pipette to the tube labeled +plasmid. Both tubes were then incubated on ice for 10 minutes. The tubes were then placed in a water bath at 42°C for 50 seconds to heat shock the bacteria, after which the tubes were returned to ice for two minutes.

Each tube then had 250 μL of nutrient broth added and were incubated at room temperature for ten minutes.

Two plates containing nutrient agar and two plates containing nutrient agar and ampicillin were prepared. 100 μL of -plasmid was transferred to one of each type of plate and streaked using a sterile inoculating loop. The same was done with the +plasmid.

The plates were then covered and placed in an incubator at 37°C for 24 hours. The number of colonies on the plate containing the +plasmid and ampicillin agar were counted and recorded.

Results

The four agar plates are shown below:

● Transformed *E.coli* ● Untransformed *E.coli*

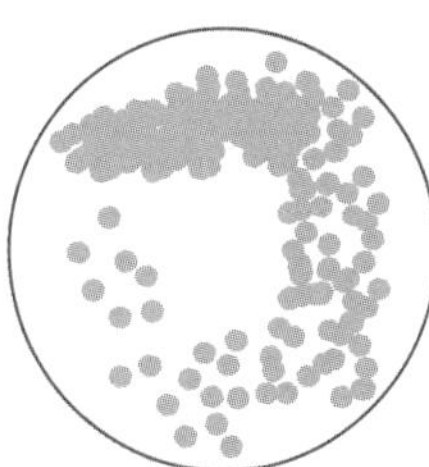

Plate 1:
No ampicillin -plasmid

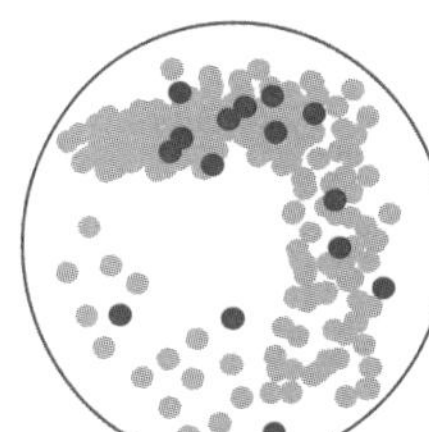

Plate 2:
No ampicillin +plasmid

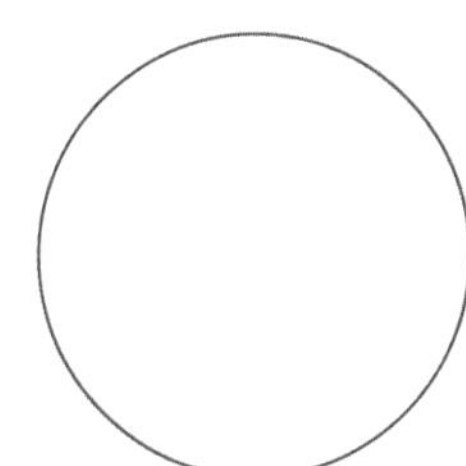

Plate 3:
Ampicillin -plasmid

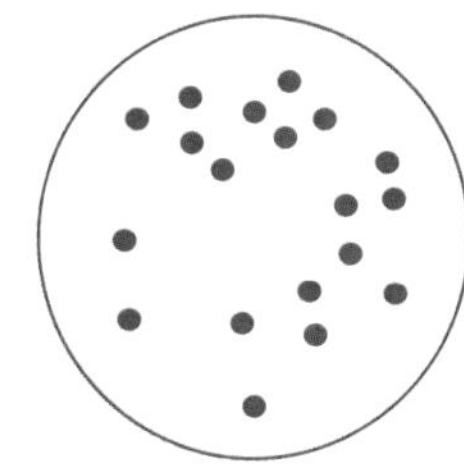

Plate 4:
Ampicillin +plasmid

1. (a) Determine the mass of plasmid pipetted into the microcentrifuge tubes.
Use the formula mass (μg) (of plasmid) = concentration (μg/μL) x volume (μL):

___

(b) Determine the fraction of this amount spread on the plate (volume spread on plate ÷ total volume in tube):

___

(c) Determine the mass of plasmid spread on the plate (answer 1. (a) x answer 1. (b)): ___

(d) Calculate the transformation efficiency (transformants per μg) using the number of colonies ÷ mass of DNA spread:

___

2. What is the purpose of the -plasmid tube? ___

3. Explain the reason for the differences between plate 1 and 2: ___

___

4. Explain how plate 4 made counting the transformed colonies easier compared to plate 2? ___

___

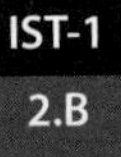

IST-1
2.B

ISBN: 978-1-98-856656-6

141 DNA Analysis

Key Question: What is the difference between DNA sequencing and DNA profiling and how are they used?

DNA can be analyzed in different ways depending on what information a researcher is seeking. **DNA sequencing** determines the sequence of nucleotides (As, Ts, Cs, and Gs) in a gene or section of DNA. Sequencing has many applications including in molecular biology, evolutionary biology, and medicine. **DNA profiling** looks at a specific DNA pattern (profile) and compares it to another. It can be used to identify individual people.

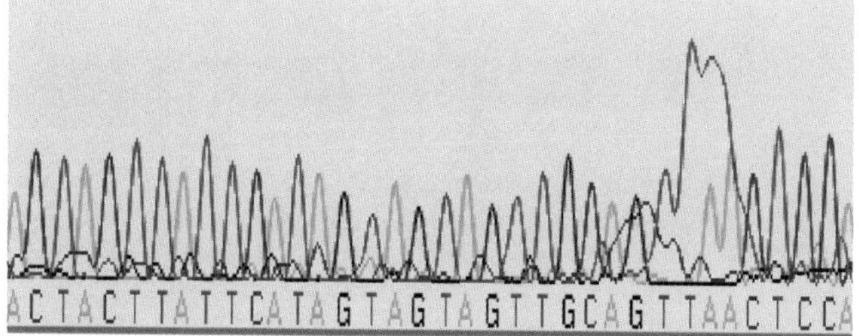

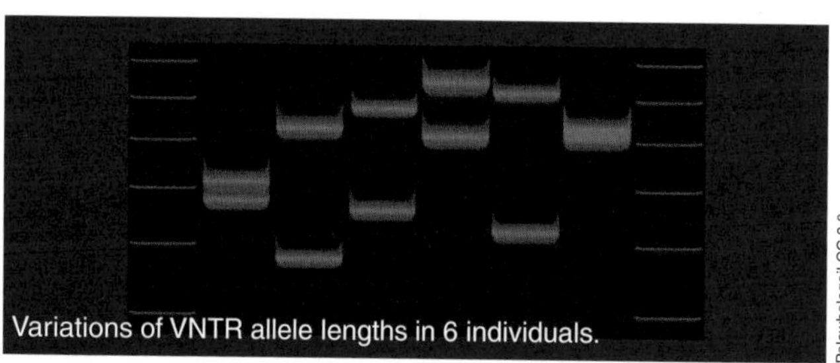
Variations of VNTR allele lengths in 6 individuals.

Palewhalegail CC 3.0

DNA sequencing

DNA sequencing can be used to sequence all of an organism's genetic material (its genome). Large genomes must be broken down into small pieces and amplified using PCR first. In chain termination methods (Sanger technology), the DNA fragments have fluorescent labels attached at the terminator end and the fragments are separated using gel electrophoresis. Each type of nucleotide base fluoresces a different color so when the gel is scanned the DNA sequence can be obtained (above). Current high throughput sequencing technologies have automated this basic process, running systems in parallel and producing thousands or millions of sequences at the same time.

Once the sequence is obtained, the information can be used to:

- Locate specific genes (e.g. associated with a disease) and target genes in gene therapy (correcting a defective gene).
- Determine the function of a gene.
- Provide information on the evolutionary history and/or relatedness between species.
- To improve genetic modification techniques.

DNA profiling

DNA profiling is also called DNA fingerprinting. Unlike sequencing, profiling does not attempt to determine DNA sequence. Instead the DNA profiles of individuals are compared to determine if a sample of DNA has come from a particular individual or not.

Within DNA there are regions containing short repeating DNA sequences. The sequences, called **short tandem repeats** (STRs), are only 2-6 base pairs long. STRs can repeat up to 100 times so there is STR variation between individuals. This variation can be used to identify a person's unique STR profile. Longer sequences of tandem repeats, called variable number tandem repeats (VNTRs), are also used in profiling (above).

Two common applications of DNA profiling are:

- Paternity testing (determining who the father of a child is).
- Forensic investigations. The DNA profile of a suspect is compared to DNA evidence collected at a crime scene to see if they were involved in the crime.

1. Explain the difference between DNA sequencing and DNA profiling: ______________________

2. There are about 3.2 billion base pairs in the human genome. 99.9% of the genome is identical between humans. Calculate the number of base pairs that are variable in humans:

____

3. (a) What are short tandem repeats? ______________________

(b) Explain how STRs cause variation between individuals: ______________________

ISBN: 978-1-98-856656-6

142 Applications of Profiling

Key Question: What are the forensic applications of DNA profiling?

The use of DNA as a tool for solving crimes such as homicide is well known, but it can also has several other applications. DNA evidence has been used to identify body parts, solve cases of industrial sabotage and contamination, for paternity testing, and even in identifying animal products illegally made from endangered species.

Using DNA to solve crimes

- Although it does not make a complete case on it own, DNA profiling (in conjunction with other evidence) is one of the most powerful tools in identifying offenders or unknown tissues.
- A lot of DNA is found at crime scenes and the information collected can be used to help identify the criminal. However, not all of the DNA collected will be from the criminal. Other DNA could belong to the victim, people who came to their aid (e.g. paramedics) or the police investigators (if they have not taken correct precautions).
- In the example (below) the criminal who broke into this home has left behind several samples of their DNA. Samples of material that may contain DNA are taken for analysis. At a crime scene, this may include blood and body fluids as well as samples of clothing or objects that the offender might have touched. Samples from the victim and the investigator are also taken to eliminate them as a possible source of contamination (below right). In this example the DNA of the people who live in the house and the investigator will also be collected so their profiles can be eliminated. A calibration or standard is run so the technician knows the profile has run correctly.

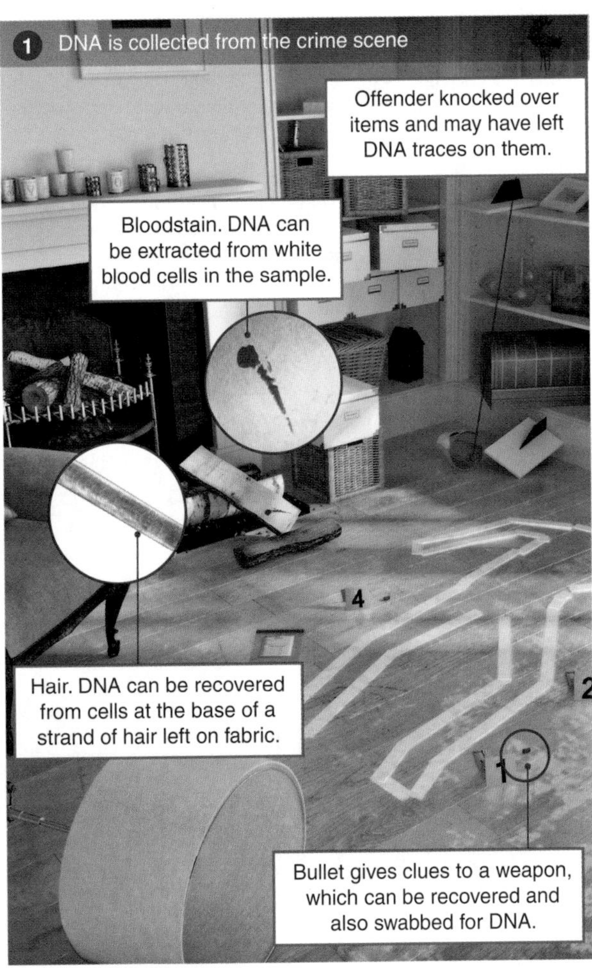

1 DNA is collected from the crime scene
Offender knocked over items and may have left DNA traces on them.
Bloodstain. DNA can be extracted from white blood cells in the sample.
Hair. DNA can be recovered from cells at the base of a strand of hair left on fabric.
Bullet gives clues to a weapon, which can be recovered and also swabbed for DNA.
4
2
1

2 DNA is isolated and profiles are made from all samples and compared to known DNA profiles such as that of the victim.

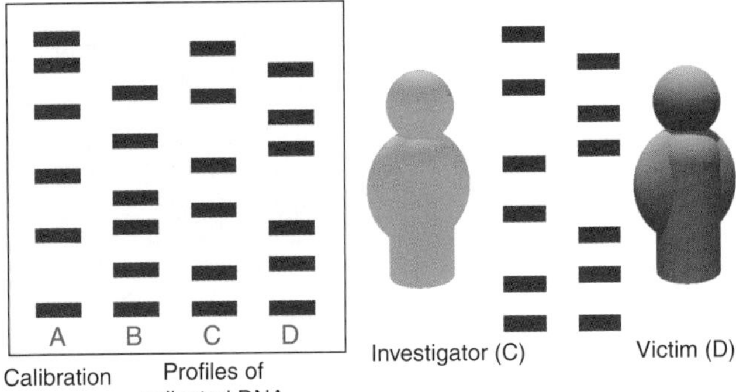

3 Unknown DNA samples are compared to DNA databases of convicted offenders and to the DNA of the alleged offender.

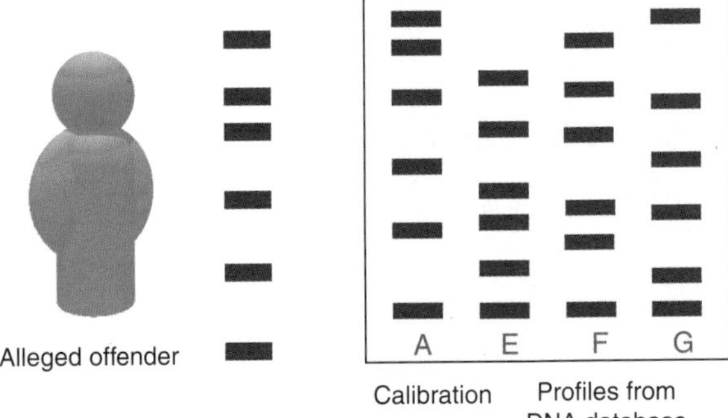

4 Although it does not make a complete case, DNA profiling, in conjunction with other evidence, is one of the most powerful tools in identifying offenders or unknown tissues.

1. Why are DNA profiles obtained for both the victim and investigator? ____________________

____

____

____

2. Use the evidence to decide if the alleged offender is innocent or guilty and explain your decision:

____

____

____

ISBN: 978-1-98-856656-6

Paternity testing

DNA profiling can be used to determine paternity (and maternity) by looking for matches in alleles between parents and children. It is used in cases such as child support or inheritance. DNA profiling can establish the certainty of paternity (and maternity) to a 99.99% probability of parentage.

Every STR allele is given the number of its repeats as its name, e.g. 8 or 9. In a paternity case, the mother may be 11, 12 and the father may be 8, 13 for a particular STR. The child will have a combination of these. The table below illustrates this:

DNA marker	Mother's alleles	Child's alleles	Father's alleles
CSF1PO	7, 8	8, 9	9, 12
D10S1248	14, 15	11, 14	10, 11
D12S391	16, 17	17, 17	17, 18
D13S317	10, 11	9, 10	8, 9

The frequency of the each allele occurring in the population is important when determining paternity (or maternity). For example, DNA marker CSF1PO allele 9 has a frequency of 0.0294 making the match between father and child very significant (whereas allele 12 has a frequency of 0.3446, making a match less significant). For each allele, a paternity index (PI) is calculated. These indicate the significance of the match. The PIs are combined to produce a probability of parentage. 10-13 different STRs are used to identify paternity. Mismatches of two STRs between the male and child is enough to exclude the male as the biological father.

Whale DNA: tracking illegal slaughter

Humpback whale

Under International Whaling Commission regulations, some species of whales can be captured for scientific research and their meat can be sold legally. Most whales, including humpback and blue whales, are fully protected and to capture or kill them is illegal.

Between 1999 and 2003, researchers used DNA profiling to investigate whale meat sold in markets in Japan and South Korea. They found 10% of the samples tested were from fully protected whales including western grey whales and humpbacks. They also found that many more whales were being killed than were being officially reported.

3. For the STR D10S1248 in the example above, what possible allele combinations could the child have?

____

4. A paternity test was carried out and the abbreviated results are shown below:

DNA marker	Mother's alleles	Child's alleles	Man's alleles
CSF1PO	7, 8	8, 9	9, 12
D10S1248	14, 15	11, 14	10, 11
D19S433	9, 10	10,15	14, 16
D13S317	10, 11	9, 10	8, 9
D2S441	7, 15	7, 9	14, 17

(a) Could the man be the biological father? ______________________________

(b) Explain your answer: ______________________________

____

____

5. (a) How could DNA profiling be used to refute official claims of the **type** of whales captured and sold in fish markets?

____

____

(b) How could DNA profiling be used to refute official claims of the **number** of whales captured and sold in fish markets?

____

____

____

ISBN: 978-1-98-856656-6

143 DNA Profiling Lab

STUDENT SUPPORT FOR INVESTIGATION 9: *Biotechnology: Restriction enzyme analysis of DNA*

- DNA profiling is a common forensic technique. Today profiling is done by using **PCR** to amplify short repeating segments of DNA, the length of which is unique to each person. The segments produced are then run on electrophoresis gels.
- An earlier technique for DNA profiling used restriction enzymes to cut the DNA into short pieces (called **restriction fragment length polymorphisms** or **RFLPs**) that are then again run on an electrophoresis gel.
- As you saw earlier, a restriction enzyme is an enzyme that cuts a double-stranded DNA molecule at a specific recognition site (a specific DNA sequence). There are many different types of restriction enzymes and each has a unique recognition site (below).

Recognition sites for selected restriction enzymes

Enzyme	Source	Recognition sites	Cuts between
***Eco*RI**	*Escherichia coli* RY13	G A A T T C	G and A
***Hae*III**	*Haemophilus aegyptius*	G G C C	G and C
***Hind*III**	*Haemophilus influenzae* Rd	A A G C T T	A and A
***Hpa*I**	*Haemophilus parainfluenzae*	G T T A A C	T and A
***Hpa*II**	*Haemophilus parainfluenzae*	C C G G	C and C
***Mbo*I**	*Moraxella bovis*	G A T C	Before G
***Taq*I**	*Thermus aquaticus*	T C G A	T and C

DNA fragments for gel electrophoresis are produced by **restriction digestion** of DNA using restriction enzymes. Restriction enzymes are produced by bacteria as a method of eliminating foreign DNA. About 3000 different restriction enzymes have been isolated. Around 600 are commonly used in laboratories.

Restriction enzymes are named according to the species they were first isolated from, followed by a number to distinguish different enzymes isolated from the same organism.

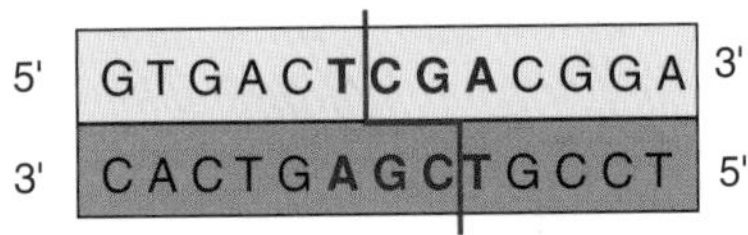

The *Taq*I restriction enzyme recognizes the site TCGA and cuts between the T and C.

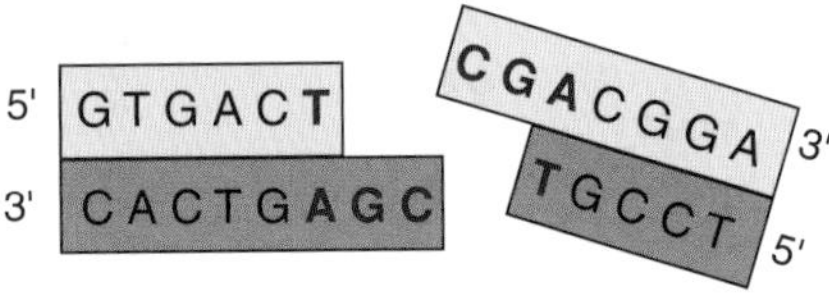

Two strands are produced with an overhang (stick ends) of two bp.

The recognition site for the restriction enzyme is normally **palindromic**, meaning it reads the same no matter what strand of DNA the restriction enzyme is reading.

1. (a) A scientist uses *Hpa*II to cut a length of DNA. State the recognition site for *Hpa*II: ______________________

   (b) Mark on the DNA sequence below (one strain is shown) where *Hpa*II would cut the following DNA sequence:

   GTTAGGCCCGGCTAGCTTGACCAGTCCCGGGTCACAGTCTCTGACCCGGCTTTAGACACACTCCGGTTACTACCG

Who-done-it?

Agent Smith of the Plant Crime Investigation Unit looked around the room. Rows of tables covered with flowers in vases and pots filled the competition display hall. All seemed as it should, expect for one particular display. A vase had been knocked over. A rose lay nearby, its petals scattered about.

Agent Smith followed the Curator over to the rose. The Curator pointed to it, "These are a very rare variety. Someone has stolen all but this one."

Agent Smith looked closer, light reflecting off his mirrored glasses. "They weren't too careful. There's blood on some of the thorns. Looks as if they pricked a finger on them. Any idea why they might have been stolen?"

The Curator shrugged. "Like I said, they are very rare. Possibly could have won the competition. The grower, Mr Anderson, hasn't won before, always comes second to Ms Trio. Very intense rivalry."

Agent Smith nodded. "I'll get my people on it. We can probably get a DNA profile from the blood on the rose. You find some suspects to match the profile against."

The Curator nodded knowingly. He'd dealt with this kind of thing before. "The usual suspects?"

Agent Smith nodded. "The usual."

Agent Smith obtained a DNA profile from the blood on the rose (far right). Three restriction enzymes were used on a specific part of the DNA.

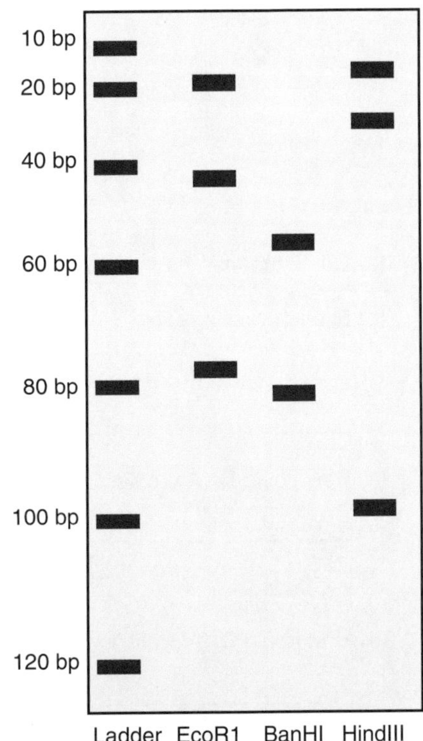

Profile obtained from the blood on the rose

ISBN: 978-1-98-856656-6

2. Agent Smith obtained DNA samples from three people, the Curator, Mr Anderson, and Ms Trio.

   The DNA sequence for the three samples is shown below (one strand is shown). Using the three restriction enzymes ECOR1, HaeIII, and HindIII mark on the DNA sequences where the DNA would be cut. Use a different color pen for each restriction enzyme.

The Curator

GTGACCTTCCGGAGGGCGAATTCCTAAAGCTTCGGCCTGTACTACCTGATGGACCTCTCTGATCAT ···➤
···➤ ATCGTCATGATGGCCACATAGACATAGAATTCCACAGATAGTGCAGGATAGTACAAGCTTTTGATAGTAG

Mr Anderson

GTGACCTTCCGGAGGGCGAATTCCTAAAGCTTCGCCCTGTACTACCTGATGGACCTCTTGATCAT ···➤
···➤ ATCGTCATGATGGCCACATAGACATAGAATTCCACAGATAGTACAGGATAGTACAAGCTTTTGATAGTAG

Ms Trio

GTGACCTTCCGGAGGGCGAATTCCTAAAGCTTCGGCCTGTACTACCTGATGGACCTCTTGATCAT ···➤
···➤ ATCGTCATGATGGCCACATAGACATAGAAATCCACAGATAGTGCAGGATAGTACAACCTTTGATAGTAG

3. Organize each sequence by counting the bases between each cut (the RFLP) and writing down the length of each RFLP in the spaces below.

The Curator:	Mr Anderson:	Ms Trio:
EcoRI: ____________	EcoRI: ____________	EcoRI: ____________
BanHI: ____________	BanHI: ____________	BanHI: ____________
HindIII: ____________	HindIII: ____________	HindIII: ____________

4. Use the lengths of the RFLPs to construct a DNA profile of each person on the electrophoresis gel below.

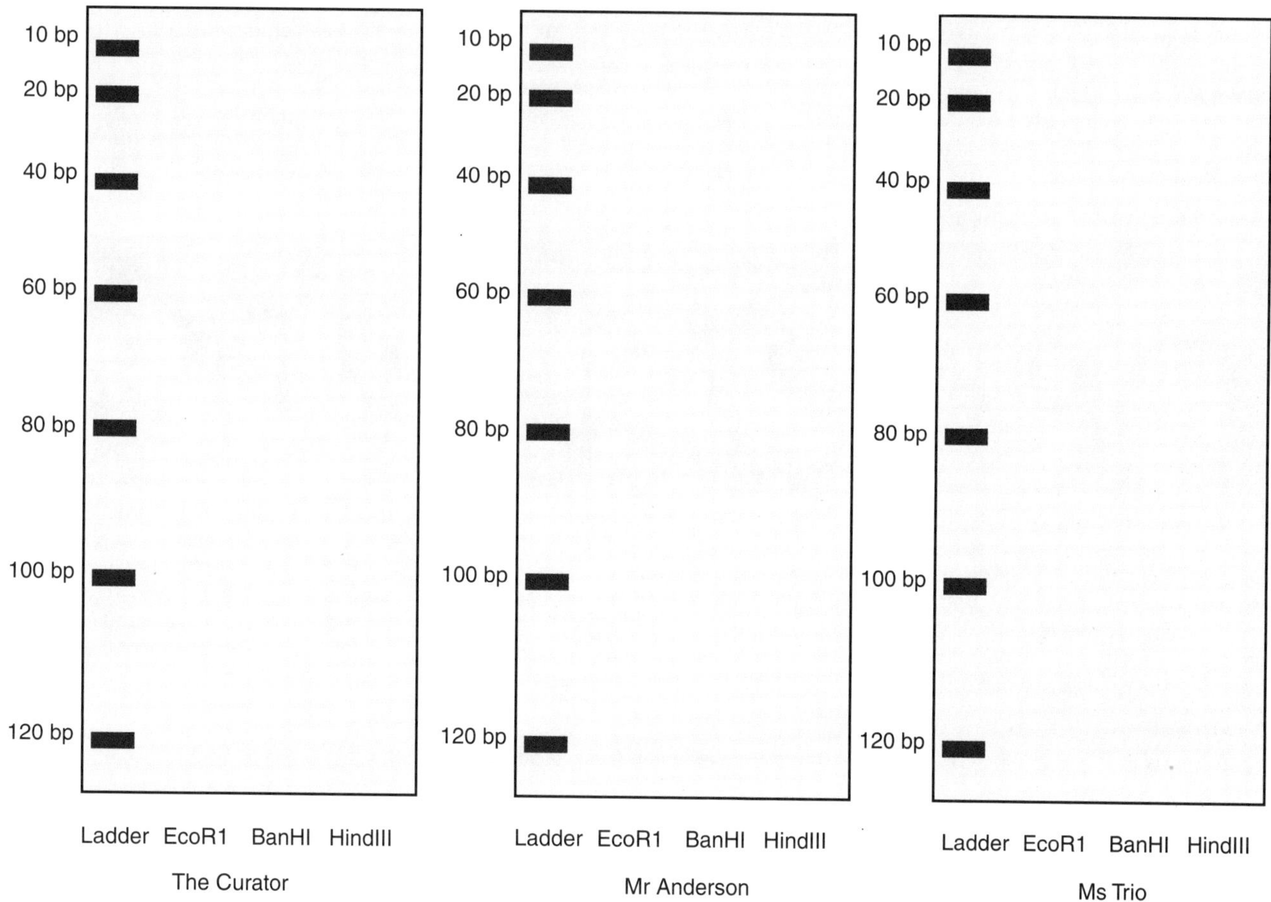

5. Compare the profiles you have made to the profile obtained by Agent Smith. Whose blood was on the rose?

____

ISBN: 978-1-98-856656-6

144 GMOs in Agriculture and Medicine

Key Question: What are some of the wider applications of genetic manipulation?

The technologies around genetic manipulation are not limited to modifying crops or livestock. As seen in previous activities, genetic manipulation can be used in a wide variety of applications. Current applications are highly varied and include food and enzyme technology, industry and medicine, environmental clean up, and many aspects of agriculture.

GMOs and agriculture

In the United States there is no specific legislation relating to genetically modified organisms or **GMOs**. Rather GMOs are regulated by the same health and safety regulations as other products. Specifically, these regulations are administered by the Department of Agriculture (plant and animal GMOs) and the Food and Drug Administration (GMOs in food).

What GM crops are grown in the United States?

Many GM crops are currently grown in the United States. They include **canola** (right), cotton, corn, alfalfa, potatoes, and soybeans.

Why GM crops?

There are many different reasons to genetically modify crops. Common reasons are to increase crop yield, decrease the cost of production, improve crop genetics, or enhance nutritional qualities.

IRRI CC2.0

Crop improvement: The nutrient content of crops can be enhanced to have higher protein or vitamin levels (e.g. golden rice has higher levels of β-carotene, which is needed to make vitamin A). Plants can also be engineered to use less water or to grow in conditions they could not normally tolerate (e.g. saline soils).

Scott Bauer, USDA ARS

Pest or herbicide resistance: Large amounts of money are spent on spraying chemicals to control plant pests. Plants can be engineered to express genes for insect toxins or herbicide resistance. Pest resistant crops do not require spraying and herbicide resistance allows the grower to control weeds without damaging the crops.

Extending shelf life: Food that spoils before it can be sold reduces profit. Shelf life in fresh produce (e.g. tomatoes) can be extended by switching off the genes for specific enzymes involved in the fruit ripening process (e.g. the enzymes involved in softening of the fruit wall or controlling the production of ethylene).

GMOs and pharmaceuticals

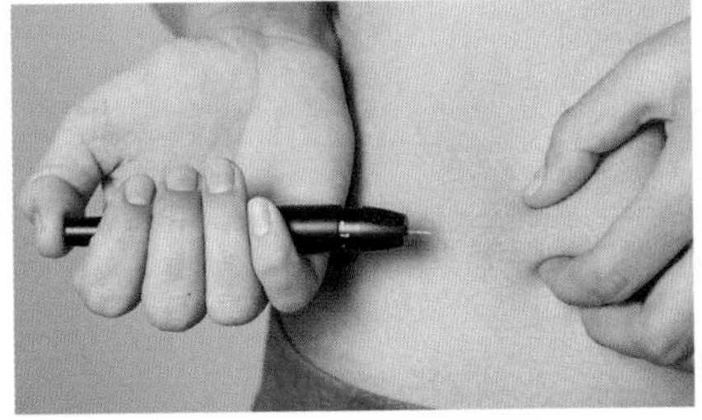

Vabampidis cc 0

Production of bioactive proteins: Transgenic bacteria are widely used to produce desirable commodities, such as hormones. Large quantities of a product can be produced commercially in large bioreactors. One example is injectable human insulin (above), which is now mainly produced in large quantities, at relatively low cost using recombinant bacteria or yeast. Transgenic sheep carrying the human gene for the protein α-1-antitrypsin, produce the protein in their milk. The antitrypsin is extracted from the sheep's milk and can be used to treat hereditary forms of emphysema.

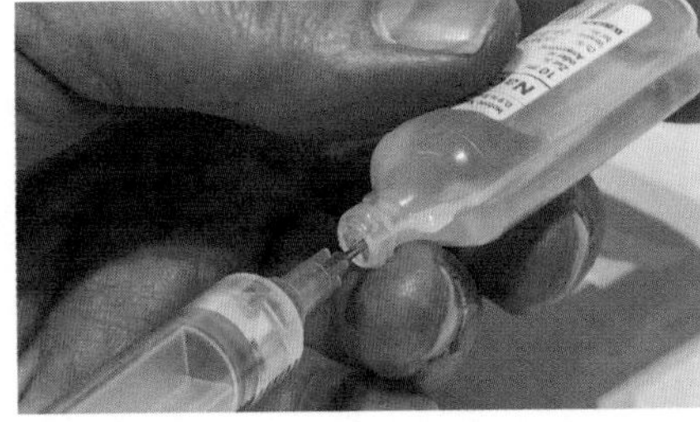

Vaccine development: Genes encoding antigenic components (e.g. viral proteins) are inserted into bacterial cells, which then express the genes. The gene product is purified to make a vaccine and generates an immune response without the risk of ever causing the disease.

1. Suggest one economic advantage of extending shelf life in fresh produce: ______________________

____

2. Explain the benefit of using GE bacteria to produce a human hormone such as insulin? ______________________

____

3. Explain why it is safer to produce a vaccine using gene technology, rather than the pathogen itself? ______________________

____

ISBN: 978-1-98-856656-6

Engineering herbicide resistance

Bt toxin

Bacillus thuringiensis is a soil living bacterium. It also occurs naturally in the gut of caterpillars and on leaf surfaces. The bacteria form spores that are associated with crystalline proteins called δ-endotoxins. These are lethal to lepidopteran (butterfly and moth) larvae but do not affect other insects such as beetles or bees (or any other animal). For this reason the Bt toxin has been used as a targeted insecticide since the 1960s.

In 1996 the seed company Monsanto released its first versions of Bt corn. This corn had been genetically modified to contain the gene that produces the Bt protein. The target insect pest for Bt corn is the larval stage of the European corn borer, which causes hundreds of millions of dollars worth of damage to crops annually.

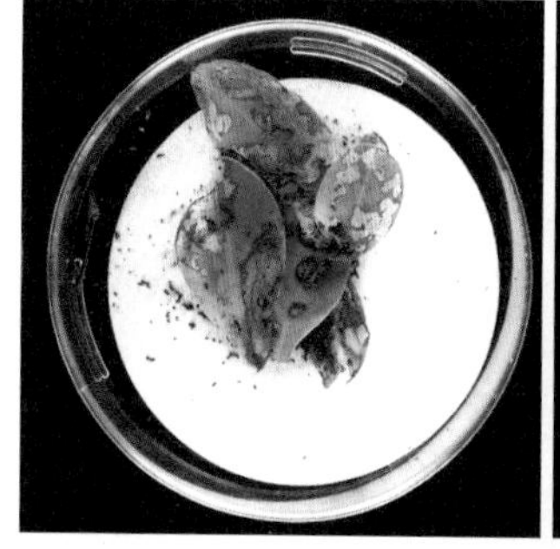

Both photos USDA

The effects of the Bt toxin on insect deterrence. The plant on the right has been treated with Bt toxin before being exposed to caterpillars. The plant on the left had not been treated with Bt toxin.

Producing a Bt plant

Genetic engineering has been used to produce **transgenic cotton**, corn, and potato varieties that produce the Bt toxin. The bacterium *Agrobacterium tumefaciens* is commonly used to transfer the Bt gene into plants, via a recombinant plasmid.

Agrobacterium tumefaciens

Bacillus thuringiensis

Bt gene

Bt gene inserted into *Ti* plasmid

Ti plasmid

Recombinant plasmid

Ti plasmid inserted back into *Agrobacterium*

Agrobacterium transfers plasmid into plant cell

Corn cell infected with *Agrobacterium*

Transformed plant cells are cultured into the lab and grown into new plants before being planted out.

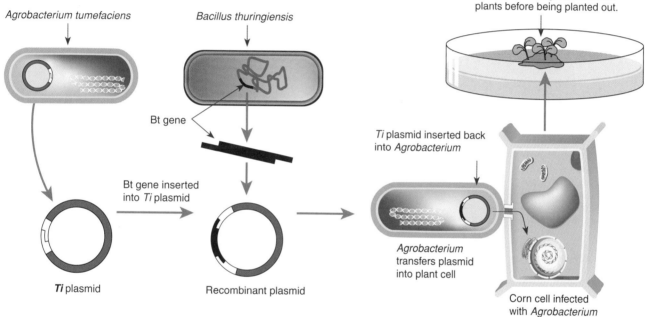

4. What is meant by a transgenic organism? ______________________________

____

5. Name the bacteria that produces Bt toxin: ______________________________

6. Why is Bt toxin a useful insecticide? ______________________________

____

7. What is the primary target of the Bt toxin in Bt corn? ______________________________

____

8. Explain how transgenic Bt corn is produced using *Agrobacterium tumefaciens*: ______________________________

____

____

____

____

ISBN: 978-1-98-856656-6

145 GM Techniques and Bioinformatics

Key Question: How are genetic engineering techniques applied to the analysis of species relatedness?

Increasingly advanced techniques in molecular biology are providing huge volumes of genomic data from many species. This information can be stored in databases where it can be easily retrieved, analyzed, and compared; a field of computing and biology called **bioinformatics**. Powerful computers and sophisticated software now allow DNA or protein sequences between species to be compared so that researchers can investigate and better understand evolutionary relationships.

Sequence comparisons using bioinformatics

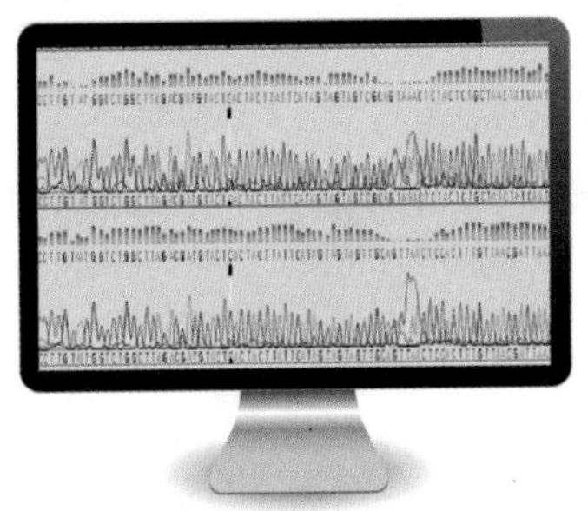

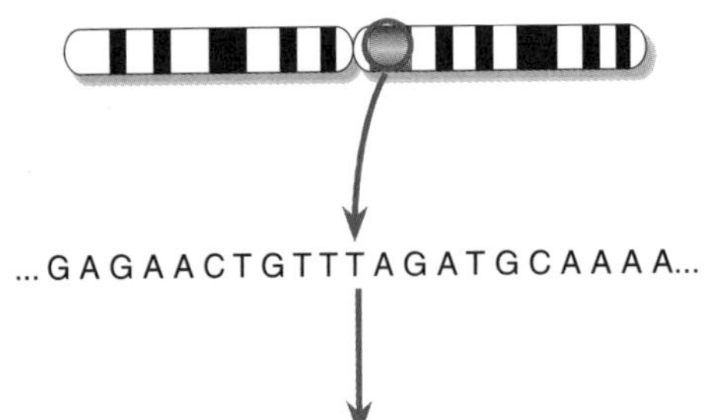

A gene of interest is selected for analysis.

High throughput 'Next-Gen' sequencing technologies allow the DNA sequence of the gene to be quickly determined.

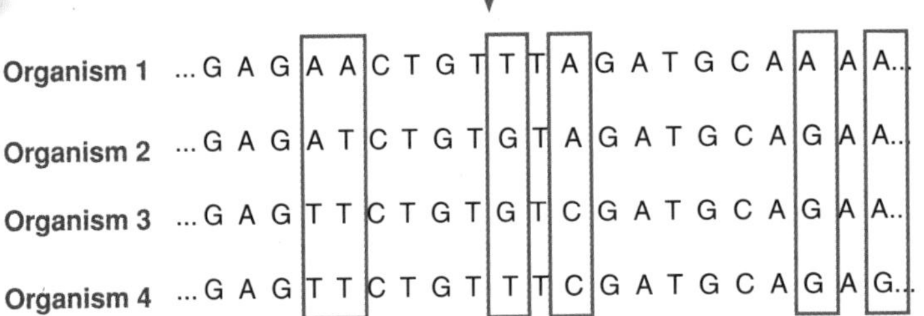

Powerful computer software can quickly compare the DNA sequences of many organisms. Commonalities and differences in the DNA sequence can help to determine the evolutionary relationships of organisms. The blue boxes indicate differences in the DNA sequences.

Once sequence comparisons have been made, the evolutionary relationships can be displayed as a phylogenetic tree. The example (right) shows the evolutionary relationships of the whales to some other land mammals.

Bioinformatics has played an important role in determining the origin of whales and their transition from a terrestrial (land) form to a fully aquatic form. This phylogenetic tree was determined by comparing retropositional events in whales and some of their closest relatives. Retroposons are repetitive DNA fragments that are inserted into chromosomes after they have been reverse transcribed from a mRNA molecule. Retroposons and their locations are predictable and stable, so they make reliable markers for determining species relationships. If two species have the same retroposons in the same location, they probably share a common ancestor.

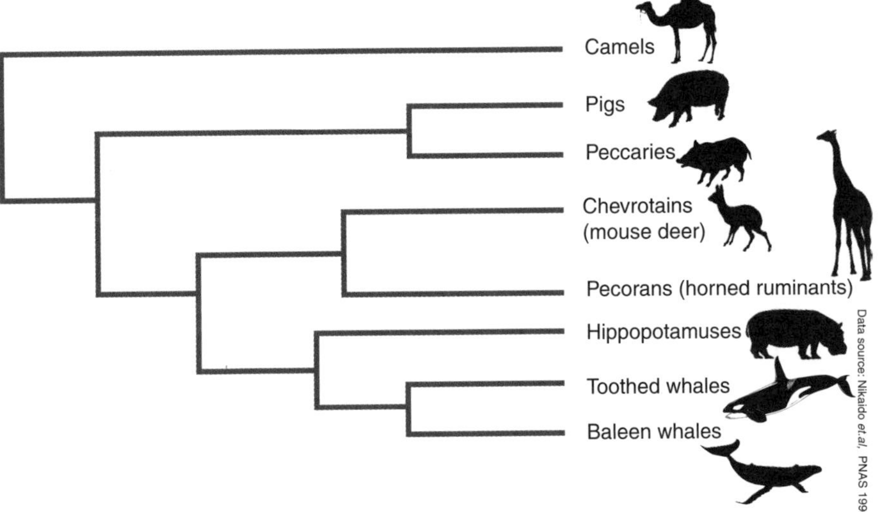

Data source: Nikaido *et al*, PNAS 1996

1. Explain how gene technology has helped scientists determine the evolutionary relationship of organisms: ______

2. The diagram above shows the relatedness of several mammals as determined by DNA sequencing of 10 genes:

   (a) Which land mammal are whales most related to? ______

   (b) Mark with an arrow on the diagram above where whales and the organism in (a) last shared a common ancestor.

   (c) Pigs were once considered to be the most closely related land ancestor to the whales. Use the phylogenetic tree above to describe the currently accepted relationship:

   ______

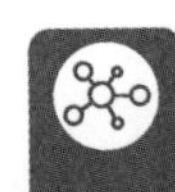

ISBN: 978-1-98-856656-6

146 Personal Progress Check

Answer the multiple choice questions that follow by circling the correct answer. Don't forget to read the question carefully!

1. Plasmids are:
   - (a) Small circular loops of DNA.
   - (b) Able to replicate independently of the chromosomes.
   - (c) Can be exchanged by bacteria during conjugation.
   - (d) All of the above.

2. Exons are regions of DNA that:
   - (a) Are left out during transcription of the DNA to RNA
   - (b) Are parts of the DNA that signal translation start and stop.
   - (c) Are the regions of the gene that code for proteins.
   - (d) Are found only in prokaryotic DNA.

3. Chargaff's rules state that:
   - (a) The % of A equals the % of T and the % C equals the % of G in both strands of DNA.
   - (b) The % of C equals the % of T and the % A equals the % of G in both strands of DNA.
   - (c) 50% of the DNA will A and T and 50% will be C and G.
   - (d) The % of A equal the % of C, but A always matches with T and C matches with G.

4. DNA nucleotides contain nitrogen atoms. Nitrogen atoms can be ^{15}N (heavy) or ^{14}N (light). DNA replication is semi-conservative. In an experiment, parental DNA was produced in an environment with nucleotides containing ^{15}N, producing heavy DNA (in both strands all nucleotides contain ^{15}N). All subsequent replications were carried out in an environment with ^{14}N nucleotides. What would the expected ratio of heavy DNA to light DNA be after 2 rounds of replication?
   - (a) 50% heavy DNA, 50% light DNA
   - (b) 75% heavy DNA, 25% light DNA
   - (c) 100% intermediate DNA
   - (d) 50% intermediate DNA, 50% light DNA

5. The role of the helicase enzyme is to:
   - (a) Relieve the tension of the DNA as it unwinds during replication.
   - (b) Unwind the DNA during replication.
   - (c) Rewind the DNA after replication.
   - (d) Copy the DNA during replication.

6. Cellular differentiation is a result of:
   - (a) Apoptosis
   - (b) Morphogenesis
   - (c) Cell division
   - (d) Differential gene expression

7. Which of the following single nucleotide mutations would affect the final protein the least?
   - (a) A substitution mutation
   - (b) A deletion mutation
   - (c) An insertion mutation
   - (d) None of the mutations will affect the protein

8. DNA polymerase:
   - (a) Adds nucleotides to the DNA in the 5' to 3' direction.
   - (b) Adds nucleotides to the DNA in the 3' to 5' direction.
   - (c) Adds amino acids to the growing polypeptide chain
   - (d) Joins fragments of DNA together.

9. DNA polymerase:
   - (a) Synthesizes DNA continuously on the lagging strand and discontinuously on the leading strand.
   - (b) Synthesizes DNA continuously on the leading strand and discontinuously on the lagging strand.
   - (c) Copies RNA from DNA to produce mRNA.
   - (d) Produces protein from mRNA.

10. Which is the correct sequence for gene expression?
    - (a) DNA → editing→ primary transcript → mRNA → translation
    - (b) DNA → editing→ primary transcript → Translation
    - (c) DNA → primary transcript → editing → mRNA → translation
    - (d) DNA → primary transcript → mRNA editing → translation

11.

First letter		Second letter: U	C	A	G	Third letter
	U	UUU Phe UUC Phe UUA Leu UUG Leu	UCU Ser UCC Ser UCA Ser UCG Ser	UAU Tyr UAC Tyr UAA STOP UAG STOP	UGU Cys UGC Cys UGA STOP UGG Trp	U C A G
	C	CUU Leu CUC Leu CUA Leu CUG Leu	CCU Pro CCC Pro CCA Pro CCG Pro	CAU His CAC His CAA Gln CAG Gln	CGU Arg CGC Arg CGA Arg CGG Arg	U C A G
	A	AUU Ile AUC Ile AUA Ile AUG Met	ACU Thr ACC Thr ACA Thr ACG Thr	AAU Asn AAC Asn AAA Lys AAG Lys	AGU Ser AGC Ser AGA Arg AGG Arg	U C A G
	G	GUU Val GUC Val GUA Val GUG Val	GCU Ala GCC Ala GCA Ala GCG Ala	GAU Asp GAC Asp GAA Glu GAG Glu	GGU Gly GGC Gly GGA Gly GGG Gly	U C A G

Using the amino acid table above the what are the amino acids produced by the following mRNA sequence?

AAA UCC GGA UUU

- (a) Lys Ser Gly Phe
- (b) Lys Gly Ser Phe
- (c) lie Asp Ser Ala
- (d) Val Leu Lys Phe

12. A genome is:
    - (a) The different version of genes on different chromosomes.
    - (b) All the genetic information in a haploid set of chromosomes.
    - (c) All the genetic information that defines a species.
    - (d) The genetic information that codes for a protein.

ISBN: 978-1-98-856656-6

13. What is the sequence of steps for splicing foreign DNA into a plasmid?

    I. Use ligase to seal plasmid DNA to non-plasmid DNA.
    II. Cut the plasmid DNA using restriction enzymes.
    III. Cut the foreign DNA using restriction enzymes and extract DNA.
    IV. Hydrogen-bond the plasmid DNA to non-plasmid DNA fragments.

    (a) I, IV, II, III
    (b) II, III, IV, I
    (c) III, I, II, IV
    (d) III, IV, I, II

14. What must happen before a eukaryotic gene can be inserted in a bacterial plasmid?

    (a) The exons must be removed from the gene.
    (b) The introns must be removed from the gene.
    (c) The DNA must be transcribed into mRNA.
    (d) The bacterial DNA must be cut with restriction enzymes.

15. Identify the steps for PCR (below) in the correct order:

    I. The primers hybridize to the target DNA.
    II. The mixture is heated to a high temperature to denature the double stranded target DNA.
    III. Fresh DNA polymerase is added.
    IV. DNA polymerase extends the primers to make a copy of the target DNA.

    (a) II, I, IV
    (b) I, III, II, IV
    (c) III, IV, I, II
    (d) III, IV, II

16. Which statement is correct?

    (a) All mutations have detrimental effects on the organism.
    (b) Whether or not a mutation is beneficial or detrimental can depend on the environment.
    (c) Silent mutations switch off the gene they affect.
    (d) Substitution mutations are always detrimental.

17. Genomic imprinting, DNA methylation, and histone acetylation are all examples of:

    (a) Genetic mutations.
    (b) Chromosomal rearrangements.
    (c) Karyotyping techniques.
    (d) Epigenetic phenomena.

18. The sequence of elements in a prokaryote operon can be described as:

    (a) Operator, promoter, structural genes.
    (b) Regulator gene, promoter, operator, structural genes.
    (c) Promoter, operator, structural genes.
    (d) Operator, promoter, regulator gene, structural genes.

19. In the *Lac* operon

    (a) The repressor is normally active, binds to the operator, and the genes are switched off.
    (b) The repressor is normally inactive, does no bind to the operator, and the genes are switched on.
    (c) The inducer activates repressor which binds to the operator and the genes are switched on.
    (d) The genes of switched off in the presence of lactose.

20. Which of the following statements about eukaryotic transcription is correct?

    (a) Transcription factors bind to the promoter and upstream enhancers. They act as a guide for DNA polymerase to start transcription.
    (b) Transcription factors bind to the promoter and upstream enhancers. They act as a guide for RNA polymerase to start transcription.
    (c) Enhancers bind to the promoter region to guide RNA polymerase to start region of the transcription region.
    (d) Activators bind to enhancers and act as a guide for transcription factors, which promote the transcription of genes by RNA polymerase.

21. The steps in the process of gel electrophoresis are:

    I. DNA samples are mixed with a "loading dye" to make the DNA sample visible.
    II. After the correct period of time the current is switch off and the gel is removed from the tray.
    III. DNA molecules are made visible by staining the gel with methylene blue or ethidium bromide.
    IV. The gel is covered, electrodes are attached to a power supply and turned on.
    V. The gel is placed in an electrophoresis chamber and the chamber is filled with buffer.

    (a) I, II, III, IV, V
    (b) V, II, III, I, IV
    (c) I, V, II, III, IV
    (d) V, I, IV, II, III

22. Which of the following can be used to join DNA fragments together to make recombinant DNA?

    (a) Restriction enzymes
    (b) Gene cloning
    (c) DNA ligase
    (d) Gel electrophoresis

23. Which of the following is used by viruses to produce DNA from RNA?

    (a) Restriction enzymes
    (b) Reverse transcriptase
    (c) DNA ligase
    (d) RNA polymerase

24. Which of the following cuts DNA molecules at specific locations?

    (a) Restriction enzymes
    (b) DNA polymerase
    (c) DNA ligase
    (d) Reverse transcriptase

ISBN: 978-1-98-856656-6

Free Response Question: *Interpreting and evaluating experimental results*

Studying the effect of diet on epigenetic changes in rats

One of the ways that environment can affect phenotype is by altering patterns of chromatin modification. These epigenetic modifications can be passed on to offspring and influence aspects of their phenotype including longevity and susceptibility to disease. Researchers were interested in the gene Hnf4a, which is associated with the ability to regulate glucose. They measured histone modifications at a regulatory region of the Hnf4a gene in two groups of rats. Their experimental design and results are shown below.

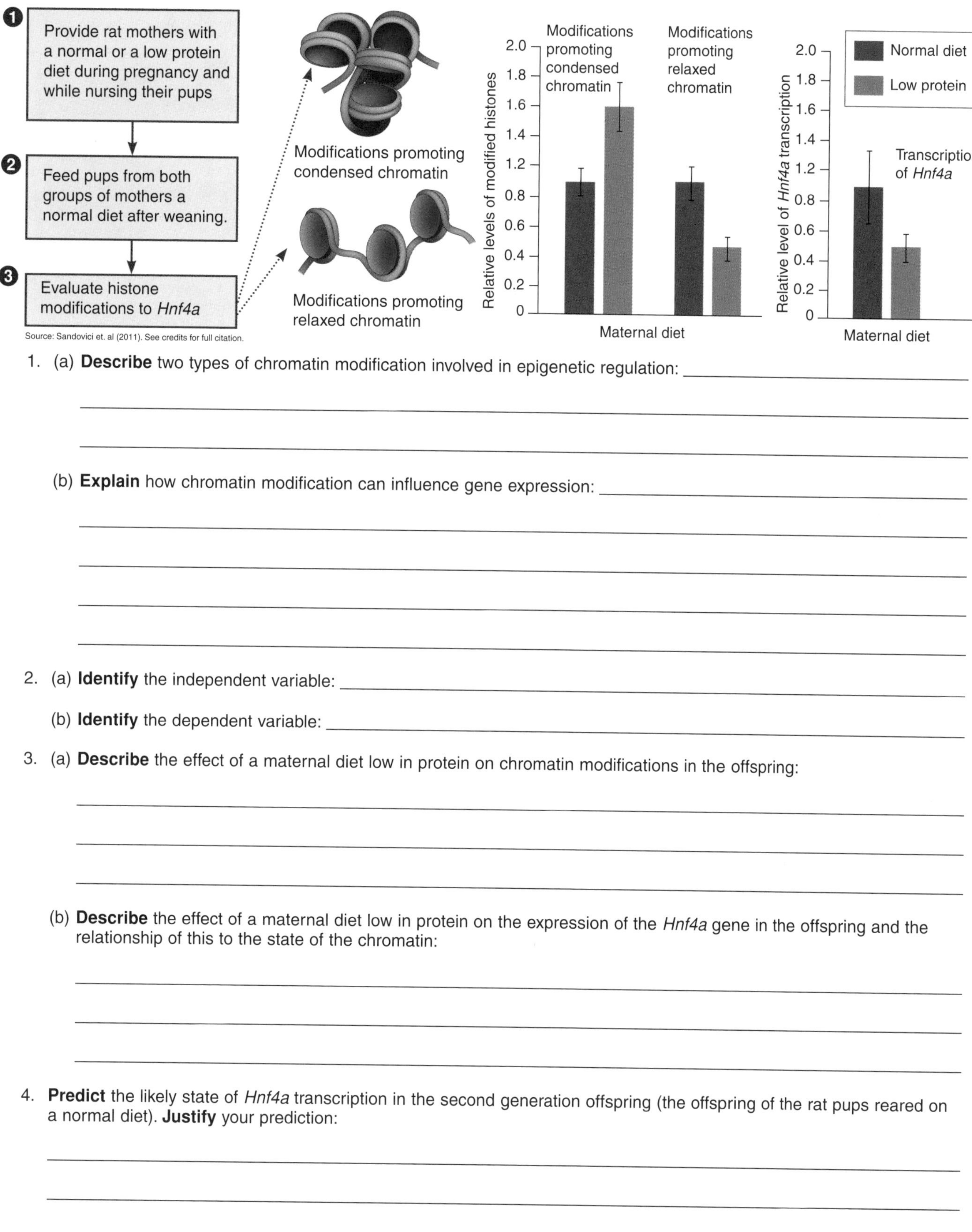

Source: Sandovici et. al (2011). See credits for full citation.

1. (a) **Describe** two types of chromatin modification involved in epigenetic regulation: ______

   (b) **Explain** how chromatin modification can influence gene expression: ______

2. (a) **Identify** the independent variable: ______

   (b) **Identify** the dependent variable: ______

3. (a) **Describe** the effect of a maternal diet low in protein on chromatin modifications in the offspring:

   ______

   (b) **Describe** the effect of a maternal diet low in protein on the expression of the *Hnf4a* gene in the offspring and the relationship of this to the state of the chromatin:

   ______

4. **Predict** the likely state of *Hnf4a* transcription in the second generation offspring (the offspring of the rat pups reared on a normal diet). **Justify** your prediction:

   ______

ISBN: 978-1-98-856656-6

Free Response Question 2: *Analyze model or visual representation*

Regulation of bioluminescence in *Aliivibrio fischeri*

As you saw in Unit 4, the bacterium *Aliivibrio fischeri* in the light organs of the Hawaiian bobtail squid luminesce in response to high levels of a signaling molecule called an autoinducer. The light-producing genes are organized in an operon that contains the genes for luminescence (*lux*CDABE). A schematic of the operon is shown right. Details are:

- The *luxI* gene codes for a synthase that catalyzes production of the autoinducer molecule. The autoinducer moves freely in and out of the cell.
- The *luxR* gene codes for LuxR, which can bind the autoinducer to form a complex that strongly activates transcription from the promoter.
- *luxO* and *luxP* are the operator and promoter.
- The LuxR-autoinducer complex also inhibits transcription of *luxR*.

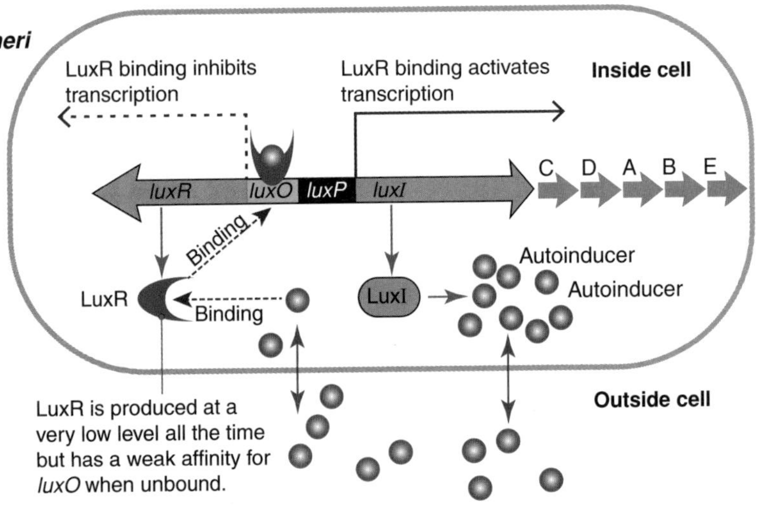

1. (a) **Describe** the basic structure of a prokaryotic operon and its regulation: ______

   (b) In a standard model of an operon, what gene does *luxR* represent? ______

2. (a) When transcription is activated by the LuxR-inducer complex, *luxI* is the first gene transcribed. **Explain** the effect of this to production of the inducer:

   (b) LuxR is an activator for transcription but also represses its own transcription. **Explain** the implications of this :

3. The signaling inducer molecule is an allosteric regulator of LuxR. Draw a labeled schematic (right) to illustrate what this means:

4. Use the model of the lux operon to **explain** why *Aliivibrio fischeri* only luminesces when the bacterial population is at high density:

ISBN: 978-1-98-856656-6

UNIT 7

Natural Selection

Learning Objectives

Developing understanding

CONTENT: In this unit, you will explore the evidence for and mechanisms of evolutionary change and learn about the consequences when species fail to adapt to the selection pressures imposed by their environment. The Hardy-Weinberg equilibrium is used as a mathematical model for describing and predicting allele frequencies in populations and you will use it to draw conclusions about genetic change in populations. This unit has strong connections with the final unit, in which you will explore aspects of population and community ecology.

SKILLS: This unit focuses on skills in using models and communicating what they mean. Data analysis, data interpretation, and argumentation are important skills in this and the final unit.

7.1 Introduction to natural selection ... activities 147 - 148

☐ 1. Describe the causes of natural selection and explain how it affects populations. Describe what is meant by fitness and explain how it is measured in populations.

7.2 Natural selection .... activities 149 - 153

☐ 2. Describe the importance of phenotypic variation in populations in terms of responses to selection pressures in a changing environment, and evolutionary change.

7.3 Artificial selection and the role of environment in convergence ...... activities 154 - 158

☐ 3. Explain how humans can affect variation and bring about phenotypic change in populations through artificial selection.

☐ 4. Use the example of convergent evolution to explain the relationship between changes in the environment and evolutionary change in a population.

7.4 Population genetics .... activities 159 - 163

☐ 5. Explain how random events affect the genetic make-up of populations, with reference to mutation, gene flow, and genetic drift in small populations (such as founder populations and those that have experienced bottlenecks).

☐ 6. Use an example to describe the role of random processes in the evolution of specific populations (e.g. brown anoles).

☐ 7. Recognize mutation as the source of all new alleles and so a source of new phenotypic variation in populations.

7.5 Hardy-Weinberg equilibrium ... activities 159, 164 - 165

☐ 8. Describe the conditions for genetic equilibrium in populations and recognize that they are rarely met, hence populations evolve. Use the Hardy-Weinberg equation to calculate allele frequencies for a population.

7.6 Evidence of evolution .... activities 166 - 177

☐ 9. Describe the types of data that provide evidence for evolution. Include reference to morphological, geological, and biochemical evidence from living and extinct organisms.

☐ 10. Describe the molecular and cellular features shared across all domains of life and explain how these provide powerful evidence for the common ancestry of all living things.

7.7 Common ancestry .... activities 177 - 178

☐ 11. Describe the structural and functional evidence on cellular and molecular levels that supports the common ancestry of all eukaryotes (including their origin).

7.8 Continuing evolution .... activities 179 - 183

☐ 12. Use examples to explain how evolution is an ongoing process in all living organisms. Examples include evidence of continuous change in the fossil record, genomic changes over time in extant populations such as the Galápagos finches, antibiotic resistance in bacteria, pesticide resistance in insects, and genomic change in viral pathogens.

7.9 Phylogeny .... activities 184 - 188

☐ 13. Describe the types of evidence that can be used to infer evolutionary history (phylogeny). Explain how phylogenetic trees and cladograms are constructed and why molecular data is increasingly important in the study of evolutionary relationships. Understand that phylogenetic trees and cladograms represent hypotheses for possible evolutionary relationships and are constantly being revised.

7.10 Speciation .... activities 189 - 197

☐ 14. Develop an understanding of the biological species concept, recognizing its strengths and deficiencies. Describe the conditions under which new species arise.

☐ 15. Describe the rate of speciation and evolution under different ecological conditions with reference to punctuated equilibrium and gradualism. Explain the role of environmental change/new habitats in rapid speciation rates and (consequently) divergent evolution.

☐ 16. Using examples, explain the processes and mechanisms that drive speciation, distinguishing between allopatric and sympatric speciation. Describe mechanisms by which species become, and stay, reproductively isolated.

7.11 Extinction .... activities 195,198 - 200

☐ 17. Describe the factors that lead to extinction of a population and how extinction risk is affected by environmental change. Recognize extinction as a natural process that has occurred throughout Earth's history and explain its consequences with reference to subsequent radiations.

☐ 18. Explain how diversity in a system is a function of the balance between speciation (origination) rates and extinction rates.

7.12 Variations in populations .... activities 201 - 202

☐ 19. Explain how the genetic diversity of a species or population affects its ability to withstand and adapt to new selection pressures imposed by environmental change.

7.13 Origins of Life on Earth............... activities 203 - 206

☐ 20. Describe the scientific evidence that supports models for the origin of life on Earth. Include reference to the geological evidence for the time of life's origins, models about the origin of life on Earth, and experimental evidence.

147 A Pictorial History of Evolutionary Thought

Key Question: What were the major milestones in the development of evolutionary theory?

Although Charles Darwin is largely credited with the development of the theory of evolution by natural selection, his ideas did not develop in isolation, but within the context of the work of others before him. The modern synthesis of evolution (below) has a long history with contributors from all fields of science. The diagram below summarizes just some of the important players in the story of evolutionary biology. This is not to say they were collaborators or always agreed. However, the work of many has contributed to a deeper understanding of evolutionary processes. This understanding continues to develop with the use of molecular techniques and work between scientists across many disciplines.

Find out more!
This timeline has been adapted from the University of California, Berkeley's excellent *Evolution 101* website. Go to the Resource Hub to find out more about the events and the people described.

1900 to present day

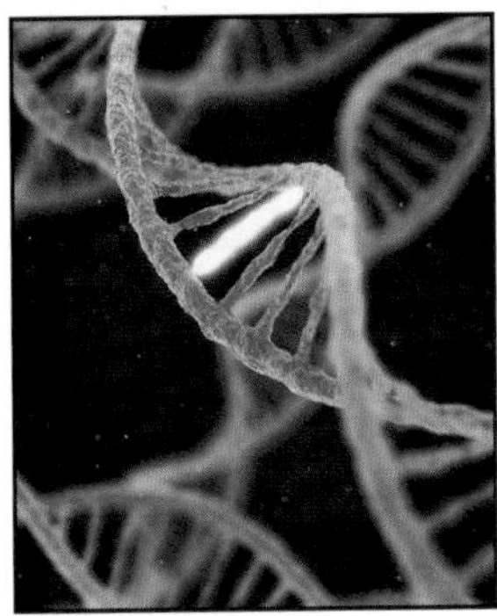

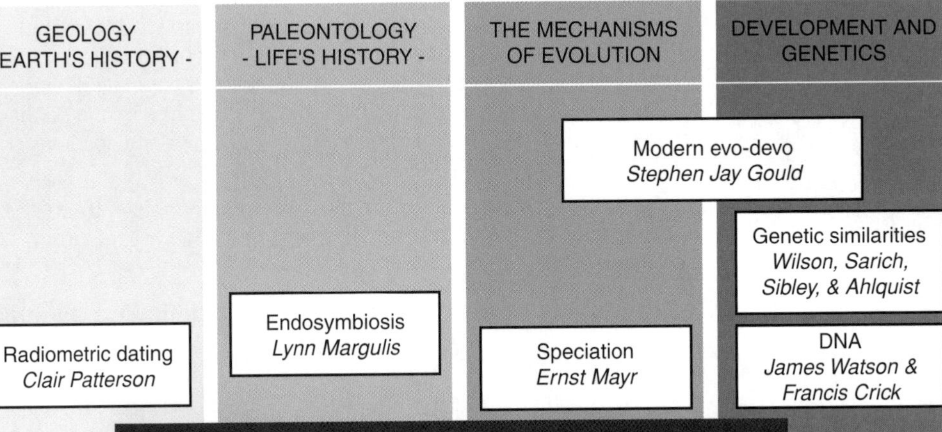

THE MODERN SYNTHESIS OF EVOLUTION
Brought together many disciplines and showed how mutation and natural selection could produce large-scale evolutionary change.
Theodosius Dobzhansky

1900

Human evolution *Huxley & Dubois*

The founding of population genetics *Fisher, Haldane, & Sewall Wright*

Chromosomes and mutation *Thomas Hunt Morgan*

Biogeography *Wallace & Wegener*

Early evo-devo *Ernst Haeckel*

Evolution by natural selection *Charles Darwin and Alfred Russel Wallace*

1800s

Genes are discrete *Gregor Mendel*

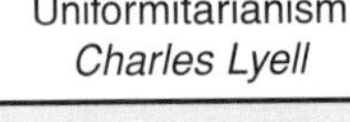

Chromosomal basis of heredity *August Weismann*

Biostratigraphy *William Smith*

Developmental studies *Karl Von Baer*

Evolution *Lamarck*

1800

Extinctions *Georges Cuvier*

Old Earth and ancient life *Comte de Buffon*

The ecology of human populations *Thomas Malthus*

Pre 1800

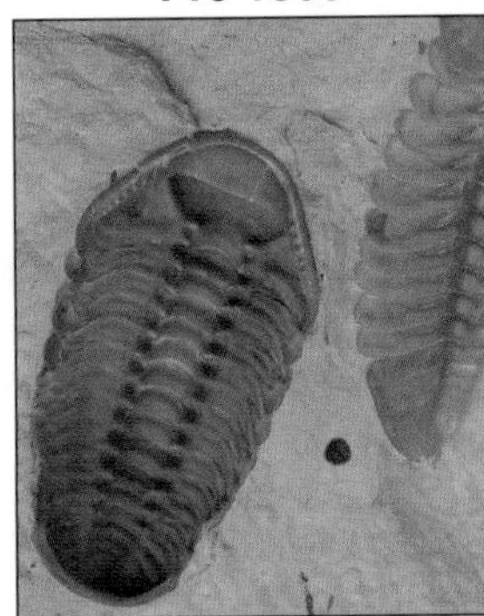

The order of nature *Carl Linnaeus*

1700

Fossils and the birth of paleontology

Observation and natural theology
Important because it addressed the question of how life works

Comparative anatomy *Andreas Vesalius*

ISBN: 978-1-98-856656-6

The development of the modern synthesis

Charles Darwin (1809-1882) and **Alfred Russel Wallace** (1823-1913) jointly and independently proposed the theory of evolution by natural selection. Both amassed large amounts of supporting evidence, Darwin from his voyages aboard the Beagle and in the Galápagos Islands and Wallace from his studies in the Amazon and the Malay archipelago. Wallace wrote to Darwin of his ideas, spurring Darwin to publish *The Origin of Species*.

Gregor Mendel (1822-1884) developed ideas of the genetic basis of inheritance. Mendel's ***particulate model of inheritance*** was recognized decades later as providing the means by which natural selection could occur.

From the Theodosius Dobzhansky Papers held by the APS. Used under Fair Use licence.

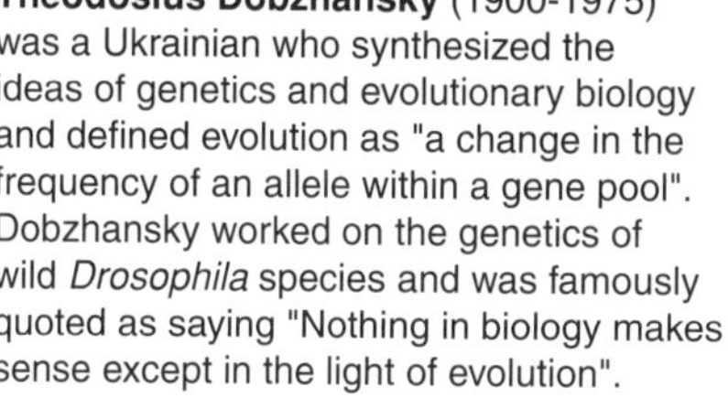

Theodosius Dobzhansky (1900-1975) was a Ukrainian who synthesized the ideas of genetics and evolutionary biology and defined evolution as "a change in the frequency of an allele within a gene pool". Dobzhansky worked on the genetics of wild *Drosophila* species and was famously quoted as saying "Nothing in biology makes sense except in the light of evolution".

PLoS, cc 2.5

Ernst Mayr (1904-2005) was a German evolutionary biologist who collaborated with Dobzhansky to formulate the modern evolutionary synthesis. He worked on and defined various mechanisms of speciation and proposed the existence of rapid speciation events, which became important for later ideas about punctuated equilibrium.

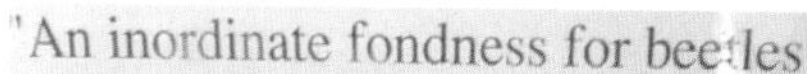

Display: Oxford University Museum of Natural History. z cc 3.0

Ronald Fisher, **JBS Haldane**, and **Sewall Wright** founded population genetics, building sophisticated mathematical models of genetic change in populations. Their models, together with the work of others like Mayr and Dobzhansky contributed to the development of the **modern synthesis.** Haldane was quoted as saying the Creator must have "an inordinate fondness for beetles".

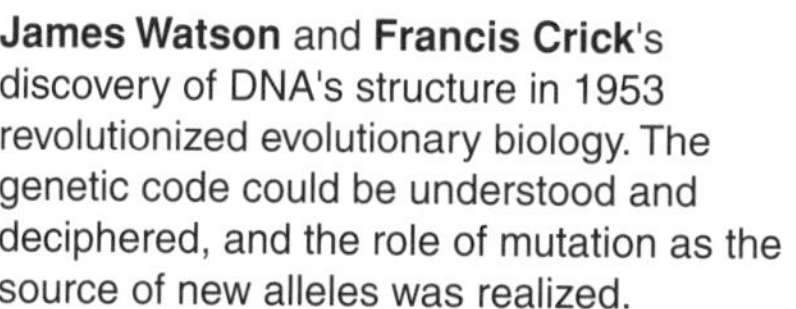

James Watson and **Francis Crick**'s discovery of DNA's structure in 1953 revolutionized evolutionary biology. The genetic code could be understood and deciphered, and the role of mutation as the source of new alleles was realized.

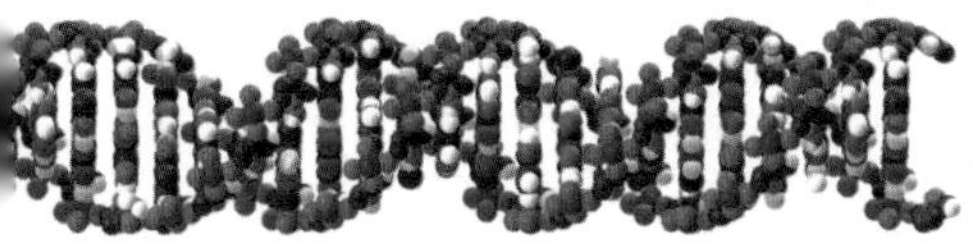

The modern synthesis today

After Haeckel's flawed work on embryology, the evolutionary study of embryos was largely abandoned for decades. However, in the 1970s, **Stephen Jay Gould**'s work on the genetic triggers for developmental change brought studies of embryological development back into the forefront. Today evo-devo provides strong evidence for how novel forms can rapidly arise.

Stephen Jay Gould (1941-2002)

Kathy Chapman online cc 3.0

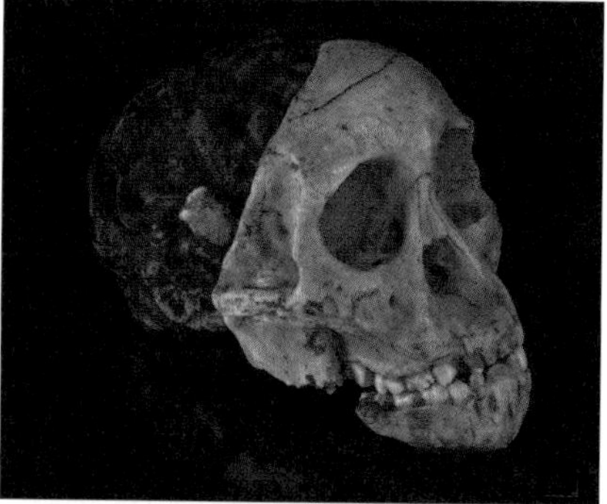

In recent decades, DNA and protein analyses have revolutionized our understanding of phylogeny. **Allan Wilson** was one of a small group of pioneers in this field, using molecular approaches to understand evolutionary change and reconstruct phylogenies, including those of human ancestors.

1. Using a separate sheet, research and then write a 150 word account of the development of evolutionary thought and the importance of contributors from many scientific disciplines in shaping what became the modern synthesis. You should choose specific examples to illustrate your points of discussion.

ISBN: 978-1-98-856656-6

148 Variation and Natural Selection

Key Question: What is the mechanism by which species evolve and become better adapted to their environment?

Evolution is simply the change in inherited characteristics in a population over generations. Darwin recognized this as the consequence of four interacting factors: (1) the capacity of populations to increase, (2) the phenotypic variation of individuals, (3) that there is competition for resources, and (4) proliferation of individuals with better survival and reproduction. Natural selection (the differential survival of favorable phenotypes) is a founding principle of science.

Natural selection is the varying survival and reproduction of individuals due to differences in phenotype. Organisms with more favorable phenotypes will survive in greater numbers to produce a greater number of viable offspring. The proportion of their alleles in subsequent generations will therefore increase. This is the basis of Darwin's theory of evolution by natural selection. Natural selection is one of the most important microevolutionary processes.

We can demonstrate the basic principles of evolution using the analogy of a 'population' of M&M's candy.

In a bag of M&M's, there are many colors, which represents the variation in a population. As you and a friend eat through the bag of candy, you both leave the blue ones, which you both dislike, and return them to bag.

The blue candy becomes more common...

Eventually, you are left with a bag of blue M&M's. Your selective preference for the other colors changed the make-up of the M&M's population. This is the basic principle of selection that drives evolution in natural populations.

Darwin's theory of evolution by natural selection

Darwin's theory of evolution by natural selection is outlined below. It is widely accepted by the scientific community today and is one of founding principles of modern science.

Overproduction

Populations produce too many young: many must die

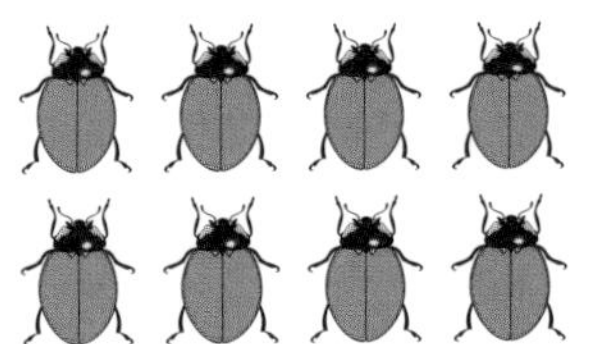

Populations generally produce more offspring than are needed to replace the parents. Natural populations normally maintain constant numbers. A certain number will die without reproducing.

Variation

Individuals show variation: some variations are more favorable than others

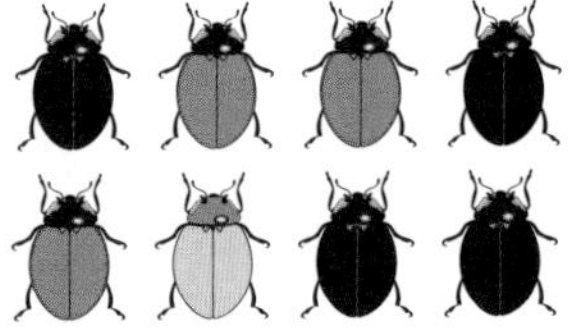

Individuals in a population have different phenotypes and therefore, genotypes. Some traits are better suited to the environment, and individuals with these have better survival and reproductive success.

Competition

Individuals compete for limited resources. Not all survive.

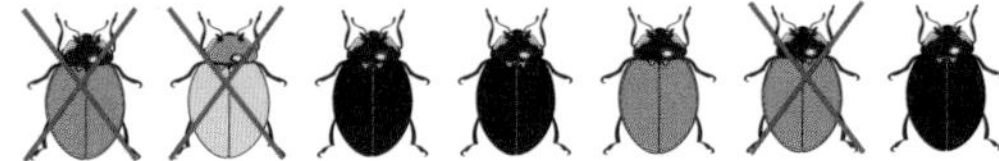

Natural selection favors the individuals best suited to the environment at the time. Those with favorable variations are more likely to survive and breed. Relatively more of those with less favorable variations will die.

Relative increase in favorable variants

Variations are inherited: the best suited variants leave more offspring

The variations (both favorable and unfavorable) are passed on to offspring. Each generation will contain proportionally more descendants of individuals with favorable characteristics.

1. Describe the four factors that interact to bring about evolution in populations: ______________________

____

____

____

ISBN: 978-1-98-856656-6

Variation, selection, and population change

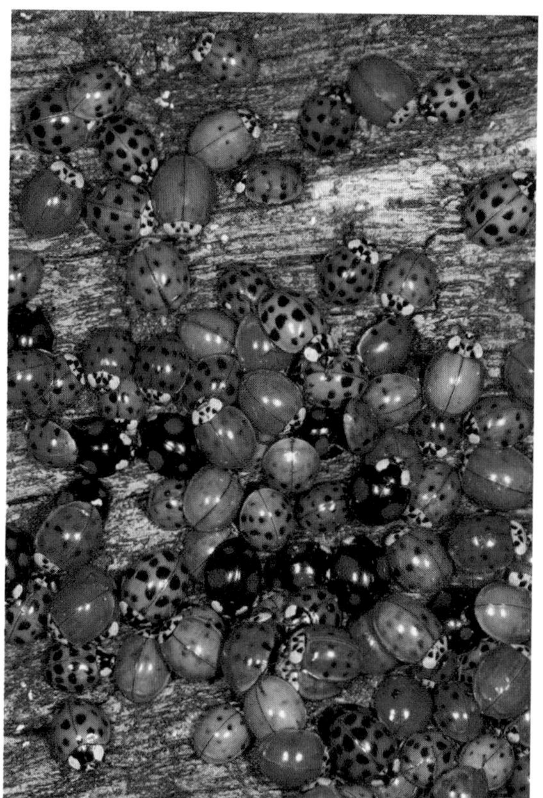

Natural populations, like the ladybug population above, show genotypic (and therefore phenotypic) variation. This is a result of **mutation** (which creates new alleles) and **sexual reproduction** (which produces new combinations of alleles). Some phenotypic variants are more suited to the environment of the time than others. These variants will leave more offspring, as described for the hypothetical population (right).

1. Variation through mutation and sexual reproduction:
In a population of brown beetles, mutations independently produce red coloration and 2 spot marking on the wings. The individuals in the population compete for limited resources.

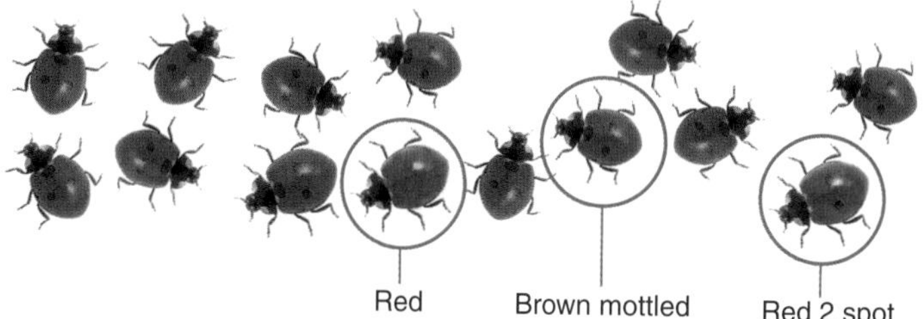

2. Selective predation:
Brown mottled beetles are eaten by birds but red ones are avoided.

3. Change in the genetics of the population:
Red beetles have better survival and fitness and become more numerous with each generation. Brown beetles have poor fitness and become rare.

2. What produces genetic variation in populations? ______________________________

3. What is meant by evolution? ______________________________

____

4. Explain how the genetic make-up of a population can change over time: ______________________________

____

____

____

____

____

____

5. Complete the table below by calculating the percentage of beetles in the example above right.

Beetle population	% Brown beetles	% Red beetles	% Red beetles with spots
1			
2			
3			

ISBN: 978-1-98-856656-6

149 Adaptation and Fitness

Key Question: What does fitness mean in an evolutionary context and what factors contribute to it?

In evolution, fitness is a mathematical measure of the genetic contribution and individual makes to the next generation. In the simplest terms it is a measure of reproductive success. The more offspring an individual (or genotype) contributes to the following generations, the greater its fitness. Fitness is linked to adaptation. The more well adapted an individual is to its environment, the more likely it is to reproduce successfully and therefore the greater its fitness will be.

Absolute fitness

- Absolute fitness is an absolute measure of the increase or decrease of a genotype or phenotype from generation to generation. Calculating fitness can depend on what is being measured: genotypes, individuals, population etc and the period over which it is measured (e.g. annual or lifetime).
- The absolute fitness of a genotype, (W), is calculated as the ratio between the number of individuals with that genotype after selection to those before selection. It is calculated for a single generation and may be calculated from numbers or from frequencies. A fitness value of >1 indicates that genotype is increasing. A value <1 indicates it is decreasing.
- In the example of a population of beetles (right), red beetles increase from 36% of the population to 56% of the population. This can be given as a ratio of 56/36 = 1.5.

Red beetles: 36%
Brown beetles: 64%

Red beetles: 56%. Absolute fitness 56/36 = 1.5.
Relative fitness = 1

Brown beetles: 44%. Absolute fitness 44/64 = 0.69
Relative fitness 0.69/1.5 = 0.46

Relative fitness

- Whereas absolute fitness determines changes in genotype **abundance**, relative fitness (w) determines changes in genotype **frequency**. The relative fitness of a genotype equals its absolute fitness divided by the absolute fitness of the fittest genotype (designated 1).
- For example, in the population of beetles, the absolute fitness of the red beetles is 1.5 and the absolute fitness of the brown beetles is 0.69. Relative fitness for the red beetles is then 1, whereas relative fitness for the brown beetles is 0.46. Even though in both cases the individuals of each genotype increased in number, the red beetles have a much greater fitness than the brown beetles. Over time we could expect that red beetles will come to dominate the population.
- When measuring changes in fitness over time, it is common to fix the fitness of the ancestral population at 1 and measure fitness relative to this. In this case, relative fitness can often exceed 1.

Fitness and adaptation

- An adaptation is any heritable characteristic (trait) that equips an organism for its niche, enhancing its exploitation of the environment and contributing to its fitness. Adaptations may be structural (morphological), physiological, or behavioral and are the result of evolution in particular environments.
- Traits that do not increase fitness will not be favored and will be lost. Genetic adaptation should not be confused with physiological adjustment (acclimatization), which refers to an organism's ability to adjust its physiology to changing conditions (e.g. a person's acclimatization to altitude). Acclimatization is a response to the need to maintain a stable internal state (homeostasis) although, of course, homeostatic mechanisms themselves are a product of evolution.

Drew Avery cc2.0

The **fennec fox** illustrates the adaptations for dessert survival: a small body size and lightweight fur, and long ears, legs, and nose.

The **arctic fox** illustrates adaptations for Arctic survival: a stocky, compact body shape with small ears, short legs and nose, and dense fur.

1. A small population of mice have brown coats or white coats. Out of a total of 500, 300 have brown coats. After a year the total population of mice remained at 500, but brown coated mice have reduced to 250.

   (a) What are the absolute fitness values of the brown and white coated mice? ______________________

   (b) What is the relative fitness of the brown coated mice relative to the white coated mice over the period of a year?

ISBN: 978-1-98-856656-6

Measuring fitness in a population

- Measuring fitness in a population is a matter of recording breeding and survival, often over many breeding seasons.
- Data on a population of Columbian ground squirrels was collected from 1992 to 2019 and followed the complete lifespan of numerous female squirrels. It was found that the date the squirrels emerged from hibernation affected their relative fitness with those emerging earlier having a higher fitness than those that emerged later.

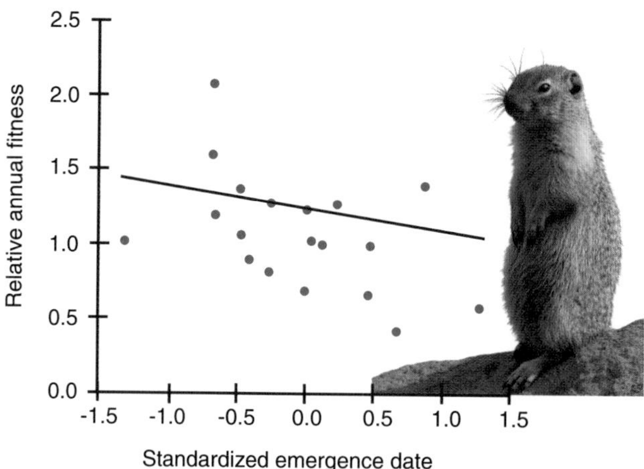

Fitness in *E. coli*

- The *E. coli* Long Term Evolution Experiment (**LTEE**) is an experiment in which samples of an *E. coli* population have been kept for over 50,000 generations. The *E. coli* are grown in a limited glucose solution, but no other selection is imposed on them. Every 500 generations, the fitness of each population was compared to the fitness of the ancestor (denoted as 1). The graph below shows the changes in the fitness of three separate populations over the first 10,000 generations.

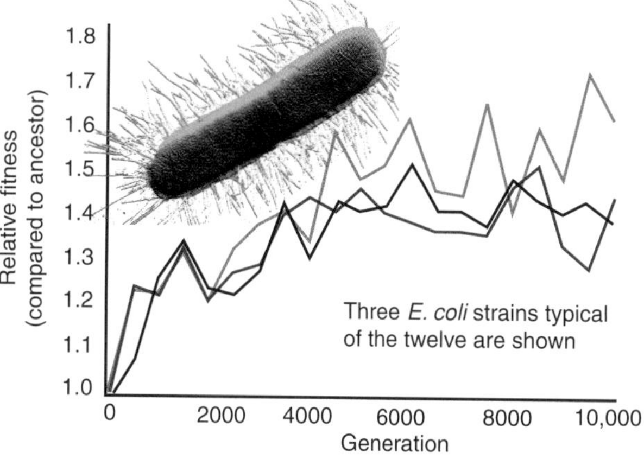

2. Describe the relationship between the length of extremities (such as limbs and ears) and climate: ____________________

3. Explain the adaptive advantage of a compact body with a relatively small surface area in a colder climate: ____________________

4. (a) Describe the relationship between emergence from hibernation and fitness in Columbian ground squirrels: ____________________

   (b) Suggest why a behavioral pattern of early emergence from hibernation increases fitness: ____________________

5. (a) Why did the fitness of the three *E. coli* populations increase over time? ____________________

   (b) Predict the result if the three populations from the 10,000th generation were mixed with the original population and placed in a high glucose environment? Justify your prediction based on your understanding of biological processes:

   ____

   (c) Why does the fitness of the three *E. coli* population flatten out over time? ____________________

ISBN: 978-1-98-856656-6

150 Environment and Evolution

Key Question: What factors can affect the rate and direction of evolution in a population?

Biotic and abiotic factors influence the direction and rate at which a population or species will evolve. Biotic factors are the living components of the environment and include interactions with other organisms and food resources. Abiotic factors are the physical components of the environment and include factors such as temperature and availability of water.

Biotic factors affect evolution

Biotic factors play an important role in evolution. All organisms must compete with others to gain the resources they need. Those that compete more successfully will have greater reproductive success. For example, in a predatory species, better adapted individuals will obtain more food and so can successfully raise more young.

Biotic factors create selection pressures that can result in species evolving together. For example, a predator exerts selection pressure on its prey and vice versa so predators and prey coevolve: the predators becoming better adapted to hunt and the prey better adapted to escape. This type of reciprocal evolution in common.

Other interactions also affect the direction of evolution in a species. Examples include symbioses such as plants attracting pollinators, or parasites living in or on a host. Changes in one of the symbionts (e.g. a redder flower) may ultimately affect the reproductive success of another symbiont and so influence its evolutionary path.

Abiotic factors affect evolution

Abiotic factors also play a part in the direction and rate of at which species evolve. Rapid changes in the environment can increase the rate of evolution by creating new selection pressures.

A gradual increase in the environment's temperature, such as is currently occurring, may favor phenotypes able to tolerate the greater heat or reduce heat uptake. These phenotypes will proliferate.

Desert plants such as cacti have evolved to tolerate the extreme heat and solar radiation in the desert. Many plants in tropical rainforest have evolved leaves that quickly drain water from their surfaces.

1. Explain how biotic factors might affect the evolution of a population: ______

2. Explain how abiotic factors might affect the evolution of a population: ______

3. Why is variation important in a population? ______

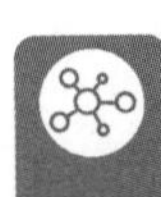

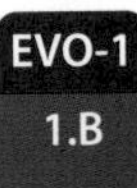

ISBN: 978-1-98-856656-6

151 Natural Selection Acts on Phenotype

Key Question: How does natural selection cause changes in phenotype and genotype over time?

Natural selection operates on the phenotypes of individuals, produced by their particular combinations of alleles. It results in the differential survival of some phenotypes over others. Individuals with phenotypes conferring greater fitness in the environment at the time will become relatively more numerous in the population. Over time, natural selection may lead to a permanent change in the genetic makeup of a population. Natural selection is always linked to phenotypic suitability in the prevailing environment so it is a dynamic process. It may favor existing phenotypes or shift the phenotypic median, (below).

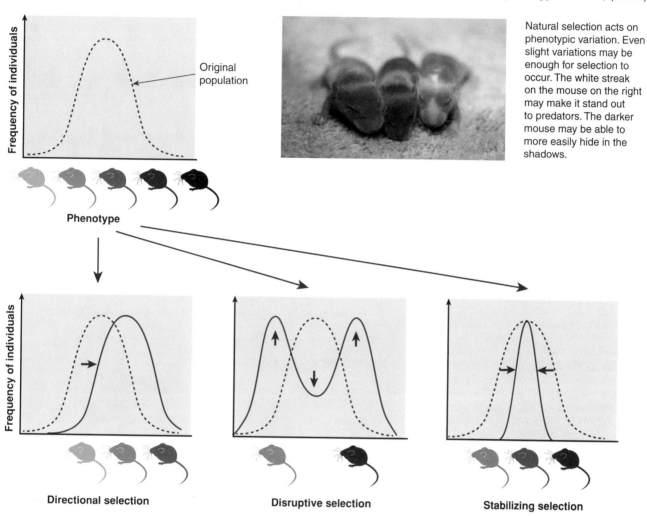

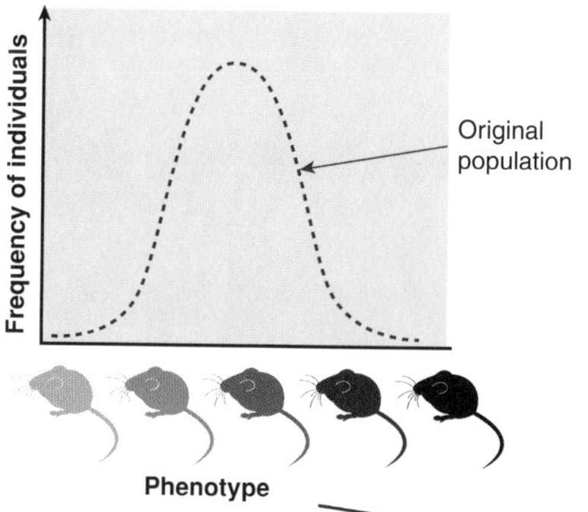

Frequency of individuals

Original population

Phenotype

Natural selection acts on phenotypic variation. Even slight variations may be enough for selection to occur. The white streak on the mouse on the right may make it stand out to predators. The darker mouse may be able to more easily hide in the shadows.

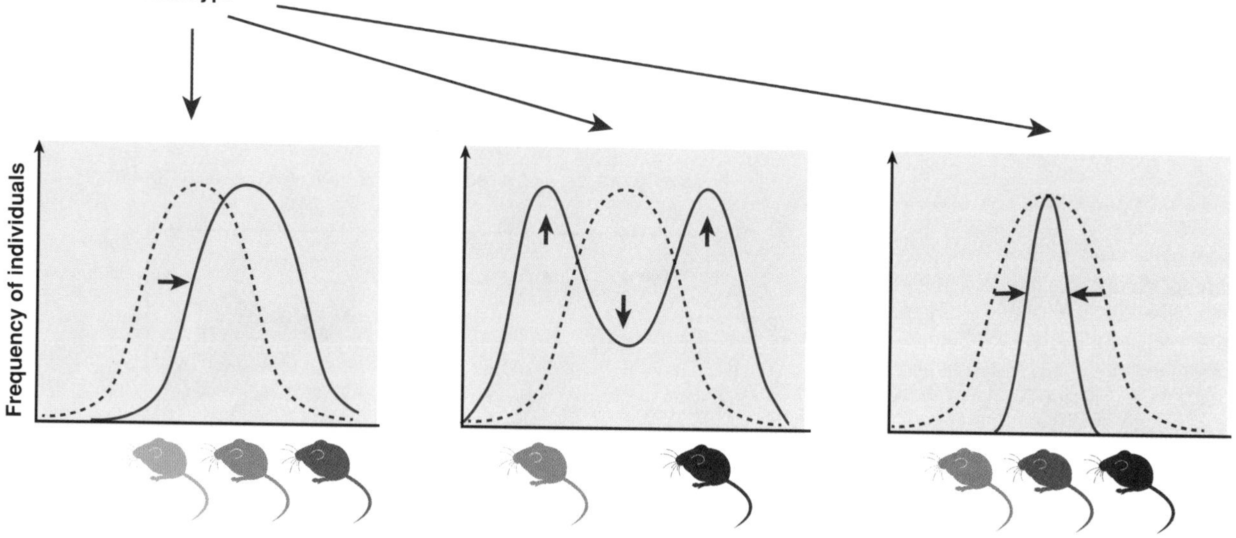

Frequency of individuals

Directional selection

An environmental pressure, e.g. predation, or higher temperatures, selects against one of the phenotypic extremes. The adaptive phenotype is shifted in one direction and one phenotype is favored over others.

Disruptive selection

Disruptive selection favors two phenotypic extremes at the expense of intermediate forms. Disruptive selection may occur when environments or resources are fluctuating or distinctly divergent.

Stabilizing selection

Extreme variations are selected against and the middle range (most common) phenotypes are retained in greater numbers. Stabilizing selection decreases variation for the phenotypic character involved.

1. Explain why fluctuating (as opposed to stable) environments favor disruptive (diversifying) selection: ______________

____

____

____

____

2. Predict the likely effect of rapid environmental change on a population with very low phenotypic variation: ______________

____

____

____

____

ISBN: 978-1-98-856656-6

152 Selection Pressure in Populations

Key Question: How can shifts in selection pressure result in a corresponding shift in phenotype?

Any factor that alters the reproductive success of a certain phenotype exerts a **selection pressure**. This pressure can shift the evolution of the population in the direction of the most well adapted phenotype. In **peppered moths** (*Biston betularia*) during the Industrial Revolution, selection favored the proliferation of dark (melanic) forms over the pale (non-melanic) forms. Intensive coal burning during this time caused trees to become dark with soot, which favored an increase in the relative fitness of the melanic forms. The phenotypic shift at this time is an example of **directional selection**.

The gene controlling color in the peppered moth, is located on a single locus. The allele for the melanic (dark) form (**M**) is dominant over the allele for the gray (light) form (**m**).

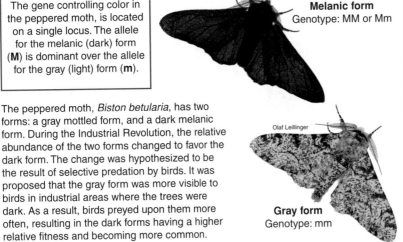

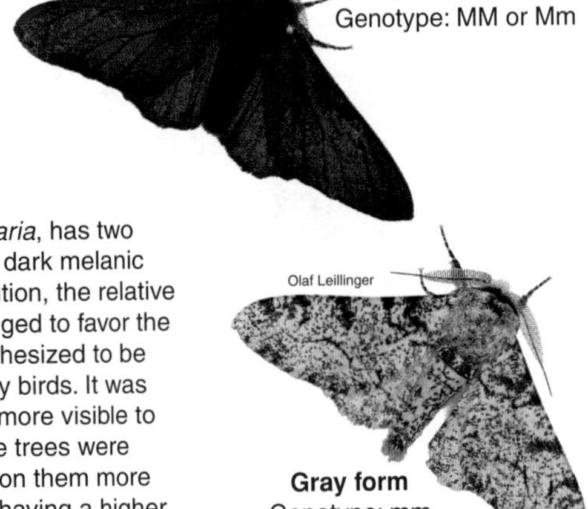

The peppered moth, *Biston betularia*, has two forms: a gray mottled form, and a dark melanic form. During the Industrial Revolution, the relative abundance of the two forms changed to favor the dark form. The change was hypothesized to be the result of selective predation by birds. It was proposed that the gray form was more visible to birds in industrial areas where the trees were dark. As a result, birds preyed upon them more often, resulting in the dark forms having a higher relative fitness and becoming more common.

Museum collections of the peppered moth over the last 150 years show a marked change in the frequency of the melanic form (above right). Moths collected in 1850, prior to the major onset of the Industrial Revolution in England, were mostly the gray form (above left). Fifty years later, the frequency of the darker melanic forms had increased.

In the 1940s and 1950s, coal burning was still at intense levels around the industrial centers of Manchester and Liverpool. During this time, the melanic form of the moth was still very dominant. In the rural areas further south and west of these industrial centers, the occurrence of the gray form increased dramatically. With the decline of coal burning factories and the introduction of the Clean Air Act in cities, air quality improved between 1960 and 1980. Sulfur dioxide and smoke levels dropped to a fraction of their previous levels. This coincided with a sharp fall in the relative numbers of melanic moths (right).

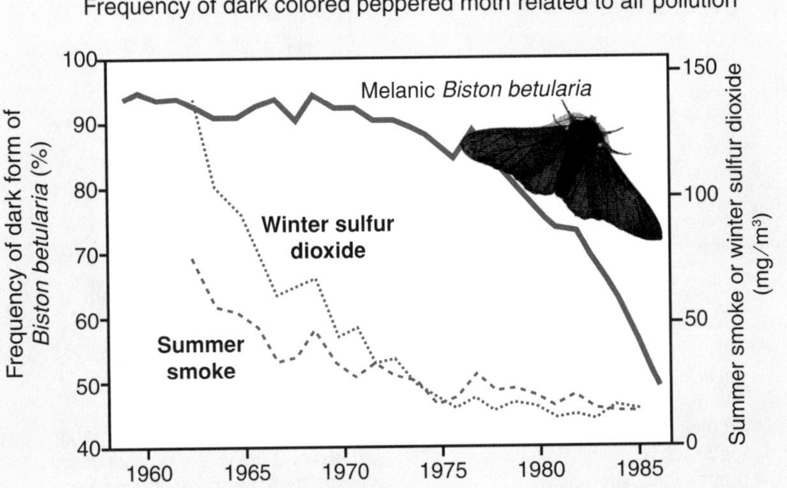

1. Describe how the selection pressure on the gray form has changed with change in environment over the last 150 years:

2. Describe the relationship between allele frequency and phenotype frequency:

3. The level of pollution dropped around Manchester and Liverpool between 1960 and 1985. How did the frequency of the darker melanic form change during this period?

ISBN: 978-1-98-856656-6

153 Phenotypic Variation and Fitness

Key Question: How does variation influence fitness?

Fitness depends how well an organism's adaptations suit an environment. For example, an insect may have an adaptation that helps it resist a certain pesticide, but unless the insect is exposed to the pesticide the adaptation is unlikely to become common. It may actually carry an energetic cost and so lower fitness. Some species, especially those with short generation times, have been able to evolve defenses against synthetic pesticides very rapidly. This may be because the genes for chemical defenses already exist in their genome and only require a favorable selective environment to proliferate. In humans, some genetic diseases that would ordinarily produce a phenotype of lower relative fitness can become relatively more common in certain selective environments.

The sickle cell allele (Hb^S)

- **Sickle cell disease** is caused by a mutation in a gene for the human blood protein hemoglobin. The mutant allele is known as $\mathbf{Hb^S}$ and produces a form of hemoglobin that differs from the normal form by just one amino acid in the β-chain. This small change causes a cascade of physiological problems in people with two copies of the allele. The red blood cells containing mutated hemoglobin alter their shape to become irregular and spiky: the so-called **sickle cells**. In people homozygous for the mutation, most of their red blood cells are sickled.
- Sickle cells work less efficiently and have a tendency to clump together and block circulation. In people with just one sickle cell allele (the heterozygote condition $\mathbf{Hb^SHb}$), there is a mixture of both red blood cell types and they have the sickle cell trait. They are generally unaffected by the disease except in low oxygen environments (e.g. climbing at altitude). People with two Hb^S genes ($\mathbf{Hb^SHb^S}$) suffer severe illness and even premature death. HbS is therefore considered a **lethal allele**.
- In tropical regions of the world the Hb^S allele is far more common (with a frequency of up to 20%) than would be expected given the allele's effect in reducing fitness (right).
- If we take the frequency of the $HbHb^s$ genotype as 20% (0.2) we can use Hardy-Weinberg equations* to determine genotype frequencies and apply the results to the equation for fitness: $W = 1 - s$ and $s = 1/(1 - q)$, where W is fitness and s is the selection coefficient.
- We then determine that the fitness of the homozygous dominant genotype relative to the heterozygote is about 0.88 in areas where malaria is prevalent. While the Hb^SHb^S genotype is lethal, the Hb^SHb genotype produces a resistance to the effects of malaria while producing few noticeable side effects. As a result the fitness of the heterozygote is greater than the homozygous condition HbHb. This explains why the Hb^S allele persists. This increase in fitness is called **heterozygous advantage.**

*The Hardy-Weinberg equation, $p^2 + 2pq + q^2 = 1$, is a simple equation that can be used to calculate probable genotype frequencies in a population and to track their changes. p^2 is the frequency of the dominant (HbHb) genotype, q^2 is the frequency of the recessive genotype (HbSHbS), and 2pq is the frequency of the heterozygote.

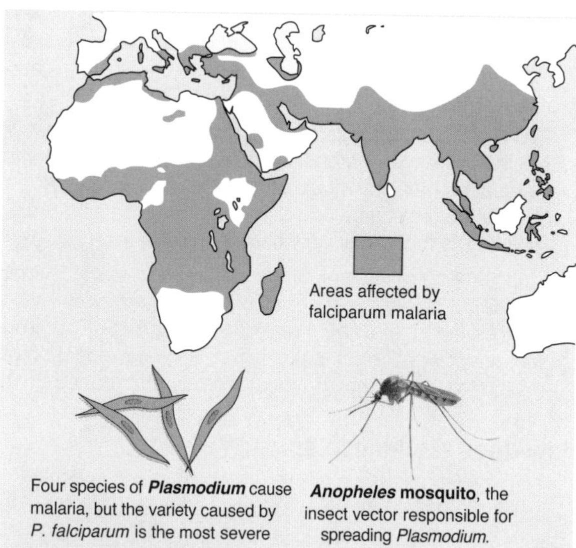
Areas affected by falciparum malaria
Four species of *Plasmodium* cause malaria, but the variety caused by *P. falciparum* is the most severe
Anopheles **mosquito**, the insect vector responsible for spreading *Plasmodium*.

Fig. 1: Incidence of falciparum malaria

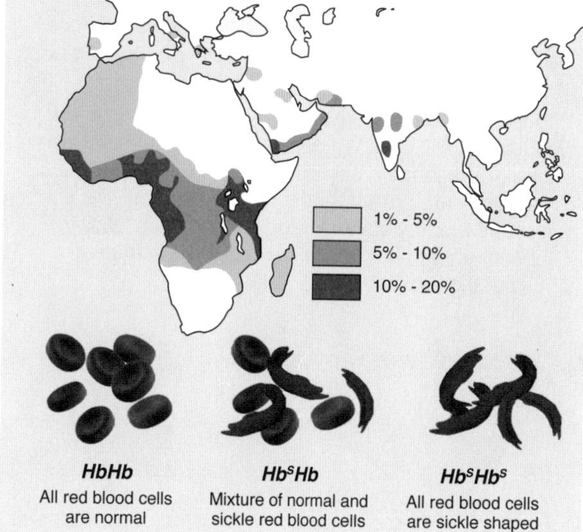
1% - 5%
5% - 10%
10% - 20%
HbHb
All red blood cells are normal
Hb^SHb
Mixture of normal and sickle red blood cells
Hb^SHb^S
All red blood cells are sickle shaped

Fig. 2: Frequency of the sickle cell allele

In areas affected by endemic malaria, there is generally a higher than usual frequency of the sickle cell allele.

1. What causes sickle cell disease? ______________________________

____

____

2. With respect to the sickle cell allele, explain how heterozygous advantage allows the retention of a generally deleterious mutation within a population:

____

____

____

____

ISBN: 978-1-98-856656-6

Insecticide resistance in insects

- Insecticides are pesticides used to control insect pests. They have been used for hundreds of years, but their use has increased since synthetic insecticides were first developed in the 1940s.
- Resistance can arise through behavioral, anatomical, biochemical, and physiological mechanisms, but the underlying process is a form of natural selection, in which the most resistant organisms have higher fitness.
- When insecticide resistance develops, the control agent will no longer control the target species. Examples of insecticide resistance include the Colorado potato beetle (right) and the *Anopheles* mosquito (top image).
- The Colorado potato beetle is a major potato pest that was originally found living on buffalo-bur in the Rocky mountains. The beetle has shown an extraordinary capability for insecticide resistance and since the 1940s it has become resistant to more than 50 different types of insecticides.
- Mosquitoes are vectors for the malaria parasite in humans. In 1955, a global malaria eradication program was established to eliminate the vectors using DDT. The program was effective at first, but resistance soon developed in many mosquito populations. It was eventually abandoned in 1969.

In some parts of West Africa, *Anopheles gambiae* is highly resistance to all classes of insecticides.

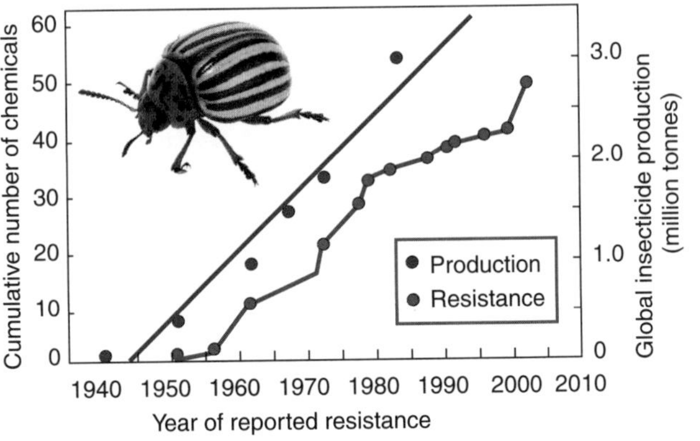

How does resistance spread?

- The application of an insecticide can act as a selective agent for chemical resistance in pest insects. Insects with a low natural resistance die from an insecticide application, but a few (those with a naturally higher resistance) will survive, particularly if the insecticide is not applied properly. These individuals will reproduce, giving rise to a new generation which will, on average, have a higher resistance to the insecticide.
- As the diagram right shows, a small proportion of the population will have the genetic makeup to survive the first application of a pesticide. The genes for pesticide resistance are passed to the next generation. The proportion of resistant individuals increases following subsequent applications of insecticide. Eventually, most of the population is resistant.

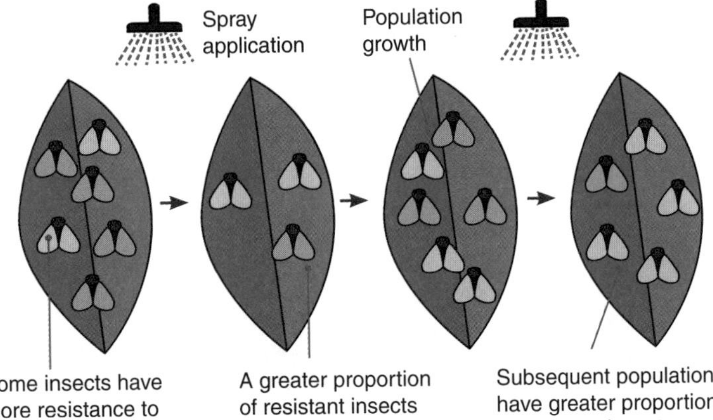

3. Give two reasons why widespread insecticide resistance can develop very rapidly in insect populations:

(a) ______________________________

(b) ______________________________

4. Explain how repeated insecticide applications act as a selective agent for evolutionary change in insect populations:

____

5. With reference to synthetic insecticides, discuss the implications of insecticide resistance to human populations:

____

ISBN: 978-1-98-856656-6

154 Artificial Selection

Key Question: What is artificial selection and how does it produce desirable qualities in animals?

Artificial selection (or selective breeding) is the process by which humans breed individuals with desirable traits together so that those traits appear in the offspring. Repeating this process over many generations leads to the traits becoming more common. Artificial selection reduces genetic diversity over time so that many alleles may become fixed (a frequency of 1 or 100%) and others may be lost. A reduction in genetic diversity in domestic species decreases the ability of breeders to influence future phenotypes, because the pool of genes to select from becomes smaller. For this reason, there is now an effort to maintain ancestral stocks and rare breeds to ensure genetic diversity for future breeding needs.

The origin of domestic animals

PIG

Wild ancestor: Boar (left)

Origin: Anatolia, 9000 years BP

Now: More than 12 distinct modern breeds, including the Berkshire (meat) and Tamworth (hardiness).

DOMESTIC FOWL

Wild ancestor: Red jungle fowl (right)

Origin: Indus Valley, 4000 BP

Now: More than 60 breeds including Rhode Island red (meat) and leghorn (egg production).

Each domesticated breed has been bred from the wild ancestor. The date indicates the earliest record of the domesticated form (years before present or BP). Different countries have different criteria for selection, based on their local environments and consumer preferences.

Bezoar ibex goat

Mouflon

Zebu: derived from Indian aurochs

USDA

GOAT

Wild ancestor: Bezoar goat

Origin: Iraq, 10,000 years BP

Now: approx. 35 breeds including Spanish (meat), Angora (fibre) and Nubian (dairy).

SHEEP

Wild ancestor: Asiatic mouflon

Origin: Iran, Iraq, Levant, 10,000 years BP

Now: More than 200 breeds including Merino (wool), Suffolk (meat), Friesian (milk), and dual purpose (Romney).

CATTLE

Wild ancestor: Auroch (extinct)

Origin: SW Asia, 10,000 years BP

Now: 800 modern breeds including the Aberdeen Angus (meat), Friesian and Jersey (milk), and zebu (draught).

1. (a) What is artificial selection? ____________________

(b) What are the advantages of artificial selection? ____________________

2. Explain the effect of artificial selection on the genetic diversity of a population: ____________________

ISBN: 978-1-98-856656-6

The origins of domestic dogs

- All breeds of dog are members of the same species, *Canis familiaris* and provide an excellent example of artificial selection. The dog was the first domesticated species and, over centuries, humans have selected for desirable traits, so extensively that there are now more than 400 breeds of dogs.
- Until very recently, the gray wolf was considered to the ancestor of the domestic dog. However, 2015 genetic studies provide strong evidence that domestic dogs and gray wolves are sister groups and shared a now extinct wolf-like common ancestor, which gave rise to the dog before the agricultural revolution 12,000 years ago. Based on genetic analysis, four major clusters of ancient dog breeds are recognized. Through artificial selection, all other breeds are thought to have descended from these clusters.

1: Older lineages
The oldest lineages, including Chinese breeds, basenji, huskies, and malamutes.

2: Mastiff-type
An older lineage that includes the mastiffs, bull terriers, boxers, and rottweilers.

3: Herding
Includes German shepherd, St Bernard, borzoi, collie, corgi, pug, and greyhound

4: Hunting
Most arose in Europe. Includes terriers, spaniels, poodles, and modern hounds.

Problems with artificial selection

- Selection for a desirable phenotype can result in undesirable traits being emphasized, often because genes for particular characteristics are linked and selection for one inadvertently selects for the other. For example, the German shepherd is a working dog, originally bred for its athleticism and ability to track targets.
- In German shepherds bred to meet the specific appearance criteria of show dogs, some traits have been exaggerated so much that it causes health issues. The body shape of the show German shepherd has been selected for a flowing trot and it has a pronounced slope in the back. This has resulted in leg, hip, and spinal problems. In addition, artificial selection has increased the incidence of some genetic diseases such as epilepsy and blood disorders.

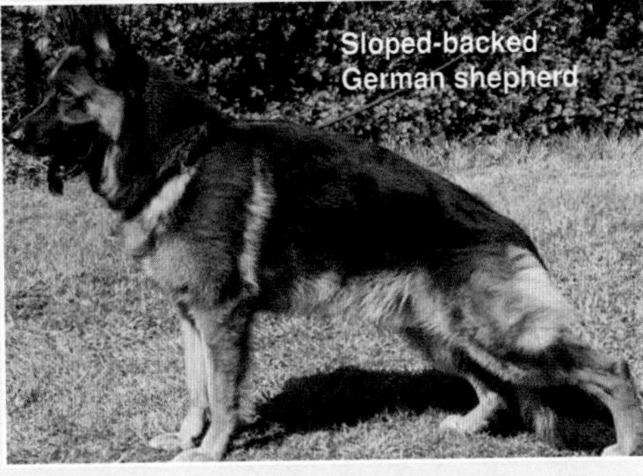

3. List physical and/or behavioral traits that would be desirable (selected for) in the following uses of a dog:

   (a) Hunting large game (e.g. boar and deer): ______________________

   (b) Stock control (sheep/cattle dog): ______________________

   (c) Family pet (house dog): ______________________

   (d) Guard dog: ______________________

4. As a group, discuss the ethical considerations of using artificial selection to "improve" dog breeds. What would it take to change breed standards to avoid health issues?

____

____

____

____

____

ISBN: 978-1-98-856656-6

155 Selection and Population Change

Key Question: How is selective breeding able to produce rapid change in the phenotypic characteristics of a population?

Humans may create the selection pressure for evolutionary change by choosing and breeding together individuals with particular traits. The example of milk yield in Holstein cows illustrates how humans have directly influenced the genetic makeup of Holstein cattle with respect to milk production and fertility. Since the 1960s, the University of Minnesota has maintained a Holstein cattle herd in which there has been no selection. They also maintain a herd that was selected for increased milk production between 1965 and 1985. They compared the genetic merit of milk yield in these groups to that of the USA Holstein average. Note that selective breeding is the term usually used in livestock improvement.

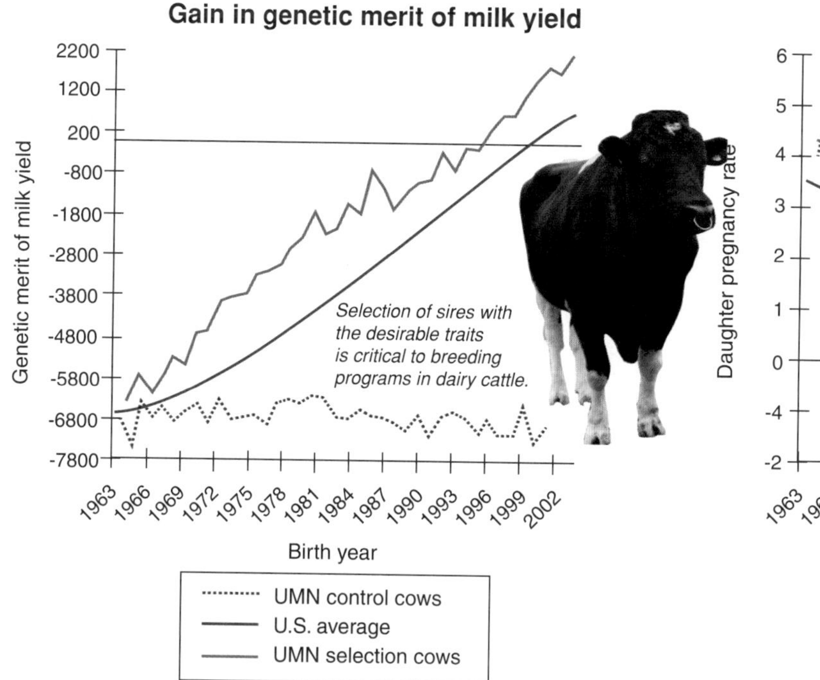

Milk production in the University of Minnesota (UMN) herd subjected to selective breeding increased in line with the U.S. average production. In real terms, milk production per cow per milking season increased by 3740 kg since 1964. The herd with no selection remained effectively constant for milk production.

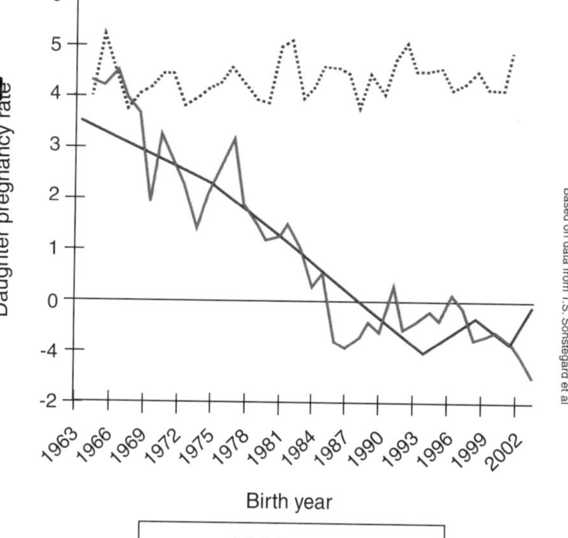

Along with increased milk production there has been a distinct decrease in fertility. The fertility of the University of Minnesota (UMN) herd that was not subjected to selection remained constant while the fertility of the herd selected for milk production decreased with the U.S. fertility average.

1. (a) Describe the relationship between milk yield and fertility on Holstein cows: ______

   (b) What does this suggest about where the genes for milk production and fertility are carried? ______

2. What limits might this place on maximum milk yield? ______

3. Why is sire selection important in selective breeding, even if the characters involved are expressed only in the female?

4. Natural selection is the mechanism by which organisms with favorable traits become proportionally more common in the population. How does artificial selection mimic natural selection? How does the example of the Holstein cattle show that reproductive success is a compromise between many competing traits?

ISBN: 978-1-98-856656-6

156 Artificial Selection in Crop Plants

Key Question: How has artificial selection produced the many crop plants available to us today?

For thousands of years, farmers have used the variation in wild and cultivated plants to develop crops. *Brassica oleracea* is a good example of the variety that can be produced by selectively growing plants with desirable traits. Not only are there six varieties of *Brassica oleracea*, but each of those has a number of sub-varieties as well. Although brassicas have been cultivated for several thousand years, cauliflower, broccoli, and brussels sprouts appeared only in the last 500 years.

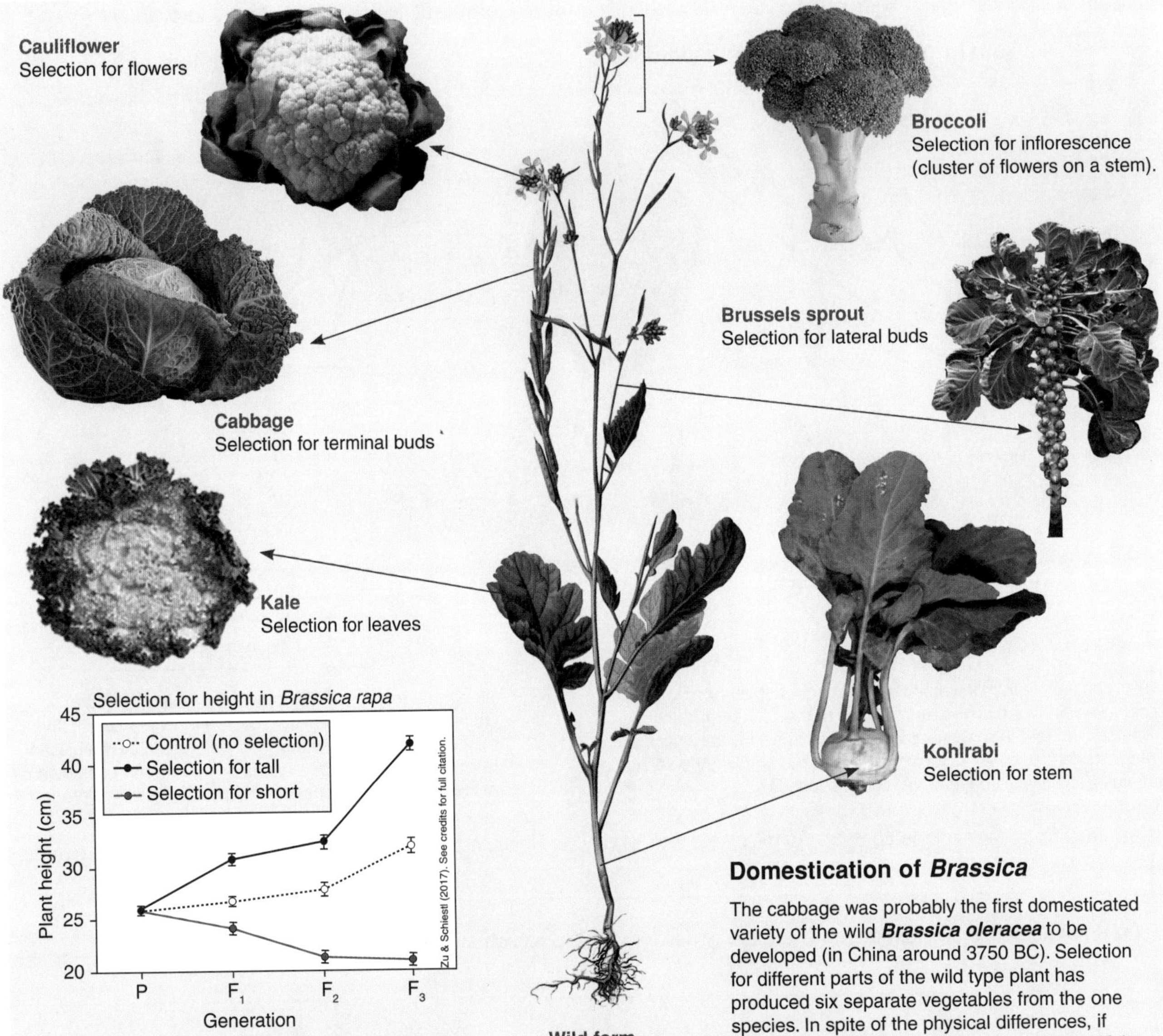

Cauliflower
Selection for flowers

Broccoli
Selection for inflorescence (cluster of flowers on a stem).

Cabbage
Selection for terminal buds

Brussels sprout
Selection for lateral buds

Kale
Selection for leaves

Kohlrabi
Selection for stem

Wild form
(*Brassica oleracea*)

Selection for height in *Brassica rapa*

Generation	Control (no selection)	Selection for tall	Selection for short
P	~26	~26	~26
F_1	~27	~31	~24
F_2	~28	~33	~21.5
F_3	~32.5	~42	~21.5

Plant height (cm); Generation. Zu & Schiestl (2017). See credits for full citation.

Species in the *Brassica* genus respond rapidly to selection as indicated by the plot above. This makes it easy to produce new varieties rapidly.

Domestication of *Brassica*

The cabbage was probably the first domesticated variety of the wild ***Brassica oleracea*** to be developed (in China around 3750 BC). Selection for different parts of the wild type plant has produced six separate vegetables from the one species. In spite of the physical differences, if allowed to flower, all six can cross-pollinate. Kale is closer to the wild type than the other varieties.

1. Describe the feature of these vegetables that suggests they are members of the same species: ____________

____

2. What features of *Brassica oleracea* would humans have selected to produce broccoli? ____________

____

____

3. Describe the data shown in the plot of height selection in *Brassica rapa* above: ____________

____

____

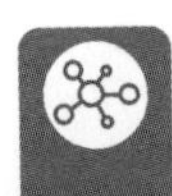

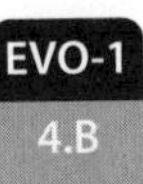

ISBN: 978-1-98-856656-6

The number of apple varieties available now is a fraction of the many hundreds grown a century ago. Apples are native to Kazakhstan and breeders are now looking back to this center of diversity to develop apples resistant to the bacterial disease that causes fire blight.

In 18th-century Ireland, potatoes were the main source of food for about 30% of the population, and farmers relied almost entirely on one very fertile and productive variety. That variety proved susceptible to the potato blight fungus which resulted in a widespread famine.

Hybrid corn varieties have been bred to minimize damage by insect pests such as corn rootworm (above). Hybrids are important because they recombine the genetic characteristics of parental lines and show increased heterozygosity and hybrid vigor.

4. (a) Describe a phenotypic characteristic that might be desirable in an apple tree: ______________________

(b) Outline how artificial selection could be used to establish this trait in the next generation: ______________________

5. (a) Explain why genetic diversity might decline during artificial selection for particular characteristics: ______________________

(b) With reference to an example, discuss why retaining genetic diversity in crop plants is important for food security:

6. Cultivated American cotton plants have a total of 52 chromosomes (2N = 52). In each cell there are 26 large chromosomes and 26 small chromosomes. Old World cotton plants have 26 chromosomes (2N = 26), all large. Wild American cotton plants have 26 chromosomes, all small. How might cultivated American cotton have originated from Old World cotton and wild American cotton?

7. Why is it important to maintain the biodiversity of wild plants and ancient farm breeds? ______________________

ISBN: 978-1-98-856656-6

157 Selection in Fast Plants

STUDENT SUPPORT FOR INVESTIGATION 1: *Artificial selection*

Artificial selection can be studied using Wisconsin Fast Plants®, plants bred to complete their life cycle in only five weeks. These plants show variation in quantifiable traits such hairiness (number of trichomes) and stem color. The students chose hairiness (number of trichomes) and selected plants by cross-pollinating the hairiest plants within a parental generation to produce a generation of offspring (F_1). The incidence of hairiness in the F_1 generation was studied to quantify the effect of artificial selection on phenotype.

Procedure

Students planted and grew Wisconsin Fast Plants® *Brassica rapa* seeds in the laboratory taking care to cultivate them in the soil, light, and moisture conditions required for optimal growth. At maturity (7-12 days) the students used a magnifier to count the number of trichomes (hairs) on the edge of the right hand side of the first true leaf of each plant. The class data for the parental generation are presented in Table 1. From the parental generation (F_0), students used small tags to identify and label the hairiest 10% of plants.

At day 14, when several flowers were present on each plant, the students cross pollinated the hairiest 10% of plants using pollination wands. This procedure was carried out for three consecutive days to ensure pollination was successful and fertilization had occurred.

Seeds were harvested from each plant between days 28-36, and placed in a paper bag for several days to dry. Once dry, the seeds were planted and grown under the same conditions as described above to produce the F_1 generation of plants. The number of hairs on each plant were counted at maturity using the same method described above. The results are presented in Table 1.

Students counted the number of hairs on the right hand side of the first true leaf

Cotyledon (seed leaf)

1. Record the frequency of trichomes for each of the categories listed below in table 2.

Table 2.
Frequency of trichomes in parental and first generation plants

Number of trichomes	Parental generation		F_1 generation	
	Working	Frequency	Working	Frequency
0-4	46+6+3+3+2			
5-9				
10-14				
15-19				
20-24				
25-29				
30-34				
35-39				
40-44				

Table 1. Trichome data for parental and F_1 generation fast plants

Number of trichomes	Parental generation		F_1 generation	
	Freq.	Total	Freq.	Total
0	46	0	8	0
1	6		3	
2	3		1	
3	3		0	
4	2		1	
5	6		1	
6	4		3	
7	2		4	
8	7		2	
9	2		3	
10	7		4	
11	3		4	
12	6		2	
13	0		5	
14	1		2	
15	2		6	
16	3		1	
17	1		7	
18	2		3	
19	1		5	
20	1		8	
21	3		1	
22	2		0	
23	0		3	
24	1		1	
25	0		1	
26	1		2	
27	0		0	
28	0		2	
29	1		2	
30	0		1	
31	0		2	
32	2		1	
33	1		0	
34	0		0	
35	0		1	
36	0		0	
37	0		0	
38	0		0	
39	0		0	
40	0		1	
41	0		0	
42	0		0	
43	0		0	
44	1		0	
Totals	120		91	

254

ISBN: 978-1-98-856656-6

2. (a) Select an appropriate graph type and plot trichome distribution in the parental and F_1 generation plants above.

(b) Describe the distribution of trichomes between the two sets: ______________________________

3. (a) Calculate the total number of trichomes in the totals columns of Table 1.

(b) Using the space right (or a spreadsheet) calculate the mean and standard deviation for the two data sets. Record them below:

Parental generation mean: ______________________________

Parental generation standard deviation: ______________________________

F_1 generation mean: ______________________________

F_1 generation standard deviation: ______________________________

(c) Are the two generations different? ______________________________

(d) How could you test if any difference was significant? ______________________________

(e) How could you further explore the heritability of trichome density under selection? ______________________________

ISBN: 978-1-98-856656-6

158 Convergence: The Influence of the Environment

Key Question: Why do species living in similar environments look the same even though they are not closely related?

Convergent evolution describes the process by which species from different evolutionary lineages come to resemble each other because they have similar habitats and ecological roles and natural selection has produced similar adaptations.

Convergence: same look, different origins

- We have seen how artificial selection applies selection pressure to bring about phenotypic change in a population. In natural environments, selection pressures to solve similar problems in particular environments can result in similar phenotypic characteristics in unrelated (or very distantly related) species.
- The evolution of succulence in unrelated plant groups (*Euphorbia* and cacti) is an example of convergence in plants. In the example (right), the selection pressures of the aquatic environment have produced a similar streamlined body shape in unrelated vertebrates. Icthyosaurs, penguins, and dolphins each evolved from terrestrial species that took up an aquatic lifestyle. Their body form has evolved similarities to that of the shark, which has always been aquatic. Note that flipper shape in mammals, birds, and reptiles is a result of convergence, but its origin from the pentadactyl limb is an example of common ancestry.

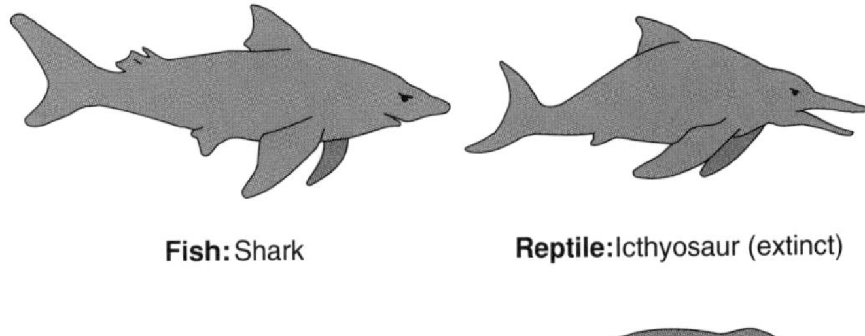

Fish: Shark

Reptile: Icthyosaur (extinct)

Mammal: Dolphin

Bird: Penguin

Analogous structures arise through convergence

- Analogous structures have the same function and often the same appearance, but different origins.
- The example (right) shows the structure of the **camera eye** in two unrelated taxa (mammals and cephalopod mollusks). The eyes appear similar, but have different embryonic origins and have evolved independently.
- The **wings** of birds and insects are also analogous. The wings have the same function, but the two taxa do not share a common ancestor. *Longisquama*, an extinct reptile, also had 'wings' that probably allowed gliding between trees. These 'wings' were highly modified long scales extending from its back and not a modification of the forearm (as in birds).

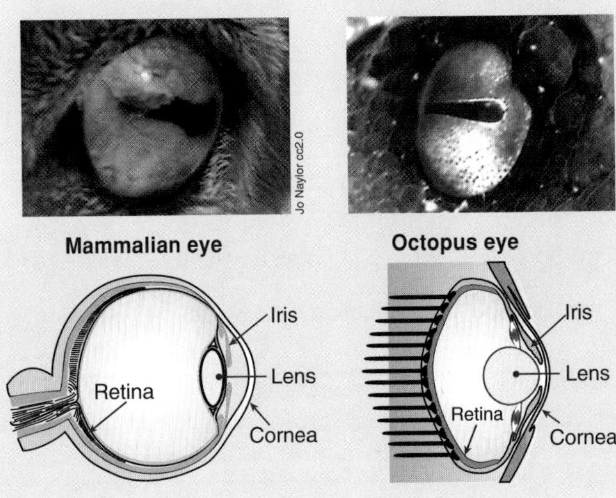

1. In the example above illustrating convergence in swimming form, describe two ways in which the body form has evolved in response to the particular selection pressures of the aquatic environment:

   (a) ____________________

   ____

   (b) ____________________

   ____

2. Describe two of the selection pressures that have influenced the body form of the swimming animals above:

   (a) ____________________

   (b) ____________________

3. When early taxonomists encountered new species in the Pacific region and the Americas, they were keen to assign them to existing taxonomic families based on their apparent similarity to European species. In recent times, many of the new species have been found to be quite unrelated to the European families they were assigned to. Explain why the traditional approach did not reveal the true evolutionary relationships of the new species:

   ____

   ____

   ____

ISBN: 978-1-98-856656-6

Convergence occurs in many taxa

- There are a wide range of species that have evolved similar solutions to similar ecological problems.

Rove beetles

- Rove beetles are a family of beetles comprising roughly 60,000 species. They generally have elongated bodies and short wing covers. At least 12 different groups of rove beetle have independently evolved to mimic ants.
- This convergence is ancient. Genetic and fossil analysis indicates that the ancestor of all ant mimicking rove beetles lived about 105 million years ago and the living species of ant mimics are not closely related. It is thought that this free living ancestor must have had traits that enabled the evolution of all the different ant mimicking taxa.

Taro Eldredge

Rove beetles: Isolated images show the usual appearance of a free living species (center) and four ant mimics.

Carrion flowers

- Many different groups of plants have evolved flowers that both look and smell similar to carrion (rotting meat). The purpose of this is to attract flies as pollinators.
- Examples include the titan arum, which produces the largest inflorescence in the plant world, *Rafflesia* (near right), which produces the world's largest single flower, and plants in the genus *Stapelia* (far right), cactus-like succulents native to South Africa.

Klaus Polak CC 3.0

Hypertrophic lips in cichlids

- Cichlids are a group of freshwater fish that are found in both Africa and Central and South America. They are particularly diverse in the African Rift Lakes.
- Many cichlids in different lakes and continents have evolved a characteristic called hypertrophic lips. There are large fleshy lips that protrude from the mouth. They are used to feed from rock surfaces, apparently sucking food from cracks and crevasses on the surface.

Amphilophus labiatus (South America) *Placidochromis phenochilus* (Africa)

4. Describe the selection pressures that would have been important in the convergence of the species pictured above:

   (a) Rove beetles: ____________________

   (b) Carrion flowers: ____________________

   (c) Cichlids: ____________________

5. Explain why unrelated organisms in separate but similar environments often tend to evolve similar characteristics:

____

ISBN: 978-1-98-856656-6

6. For each of the paired examples, briefly describe the adaptations of body shape, diet and locomotion that appear to be similar in both forms, and the likely selection pressures that are acting on these mammals to produce similar body forms:

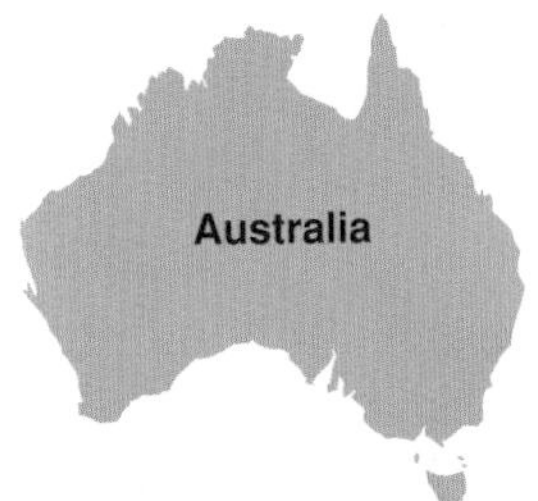

Convergence between marsupials and placentals

Marsupial and **placental** mammals diverged very early in mammalian evolution (about 120 mya), probably in what is now the Americas. Marsupials were widespread throughout the supercontinent of Gondwana as it began to break up through the Cretaceous, but became isolated on the southern continents, while the placentals diversified in the Americas and elsewhere, displacing the marsupials in most habitats around the world. Australia's isolation from other landmasses in the Eocene meant that the Australian marsupials escaped competition with placentals and diversified into many species, ecologically equivalent to the placental species in North America.

Wombat

(a) Adaptations: ______

Selection pressures: ______

Woodchuck (groundhog or marmot)

Sugar glider (flying phalanger)

(b) Adaptations: ______

Selection pressures: ______

Flying squirrel

Marsupial mouse (antechinus)

Patrick K59 cc 2.0

(c) Adaptations: ______

Selection pressures: ______

Deer mouse

Long eared bandicoot (bilby)

(d) Adaptations: ______

Selection pressures: ______

Jack rabbit

ISBN: 978-1-98-856656-6

159 Microevolutionary Processes in Gene Pools

Key Question: What are the factors that contribute to changes in the genetic makeup (frequency of different alleles) of a population?

A population can be regarded as a collection of all its alleles (the **gene pool**). Changes in the frequency of these alleles in the population over time is what we call **evolution**. These changes can be both random (happening by chance) and non-random. Four microevolutionary processes can contribute to genetic change in populations. **Mutation** creates new alleles. Migration creates **gene flow** as alleles enter or leave a population. **Natural selection** sorts variation and establishes adaptive phenotypes and is a major agent of evolution. **Genetic drift** alters alleles frequencies randomly and its effects are due to chance events. Increasingly, genetic drift is being recognized as an important agent of change, especially in small, isolated populations (e.g. island colonizers).

Genetic variation

Genetic variation refers to the number of different types of alleles in a population. Genetic variation produces **phenotypic variation** (e.g. color of ladybugs). It is this phenotypic variation that is the raw material for natural selection. This ladybug population has five different phenotypes (black, dark brown, tan, brick red, and pale).

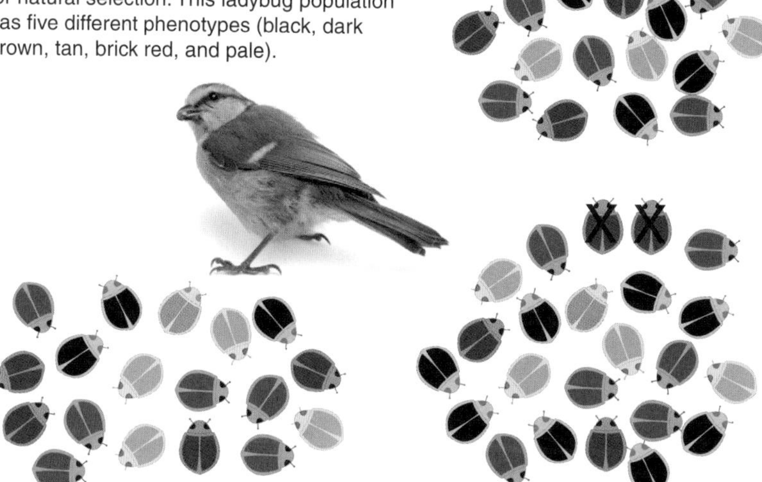

As we have seen in earlier activities, genetic variation arises through mutations and the recombination of alleles through sexual reproduction.

For example, a **mutation** produces a ladybug with a new spotted phenotype (below).

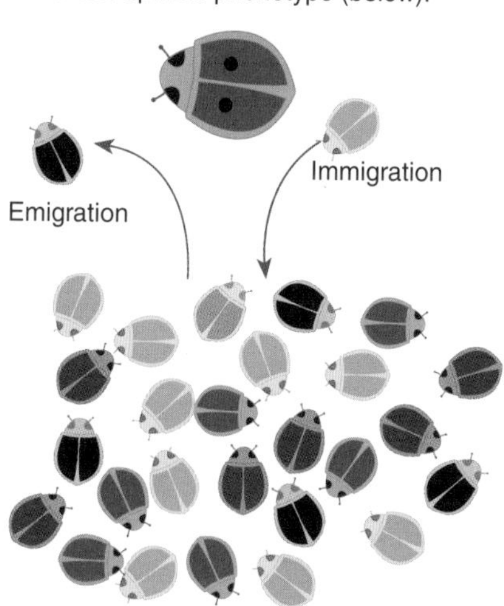

Natural selection

Natural selection acts on populations to maintain favorable phenotypes and eliminate unfavorable phenotypes. Over time, favorable phenotypes become more common in the population because those individuals reproduce more.

For example, black ladybugs are more easily seen by birds and are eaten more often than the other phenotypes. The lighter phenotypes become more common in the next generation.

Genetic drift

Genetic drift is the change in a population's allele frequency due to random events. Genetic drift has a more pronounced effect in small populations.

For example, falling rocks kill a number of ladybugs, but more of the dark brown ladybugs are crushed than any other phenotype. The proportion of dark brown ladybugs remaining in the population is drastically reduced, and their representation in the next generation is also reduced.

Migration (gene flow)

Migration is the movement of individuals into and out of a population. Through immigration or emigration, alleles can enter or leave the population. Gene flow tends to decrease the genetic differences between populations because alleles are being exchanged.

In the example above, several black ladybugs have left and some very pale lady birds have arrived changing the proportion of remaining phenotypes in the population.

1. Identify each of the following processes as random or non-random: *mutation, natural selection, genetic drift, gene flow*:

____

2. Explain clearly what is meant by the following terms:

(a) Gene flow: ____

____

____

(b) Genetic drift: ____

____

____

(c) Natural selection: ____

____

____

ISBN: 978-1-98-856656-6

3. One of the important theoretical concepts in population genetics is that of **genetic equilibrium**, which states that "***for a large, randomly mating population, allele frequencies do not change from generation to generation***". If allele frequencies in a population are to remain unchanged, all of the following criteria must be met: the population must be large, there must be no mutation or gene flow, mating must be random, and there must be no natural selection. Evolution is a consequence of few if any of these conditions ever being met in natural populations. For each of the five factors (a-e) below, explain how and why each would affect the allele frequency in a gene pool. Use the diagrams to help you.

(a) Population size: ______________________

____

____

____

____

(b) Mate selection: ______________________

____

____

____

____

(c) Gene flow: ______________________

____

____

____

____

____

(d) Mutation: ______________________

____

____

____

____

(e) Natural selection: ______________________

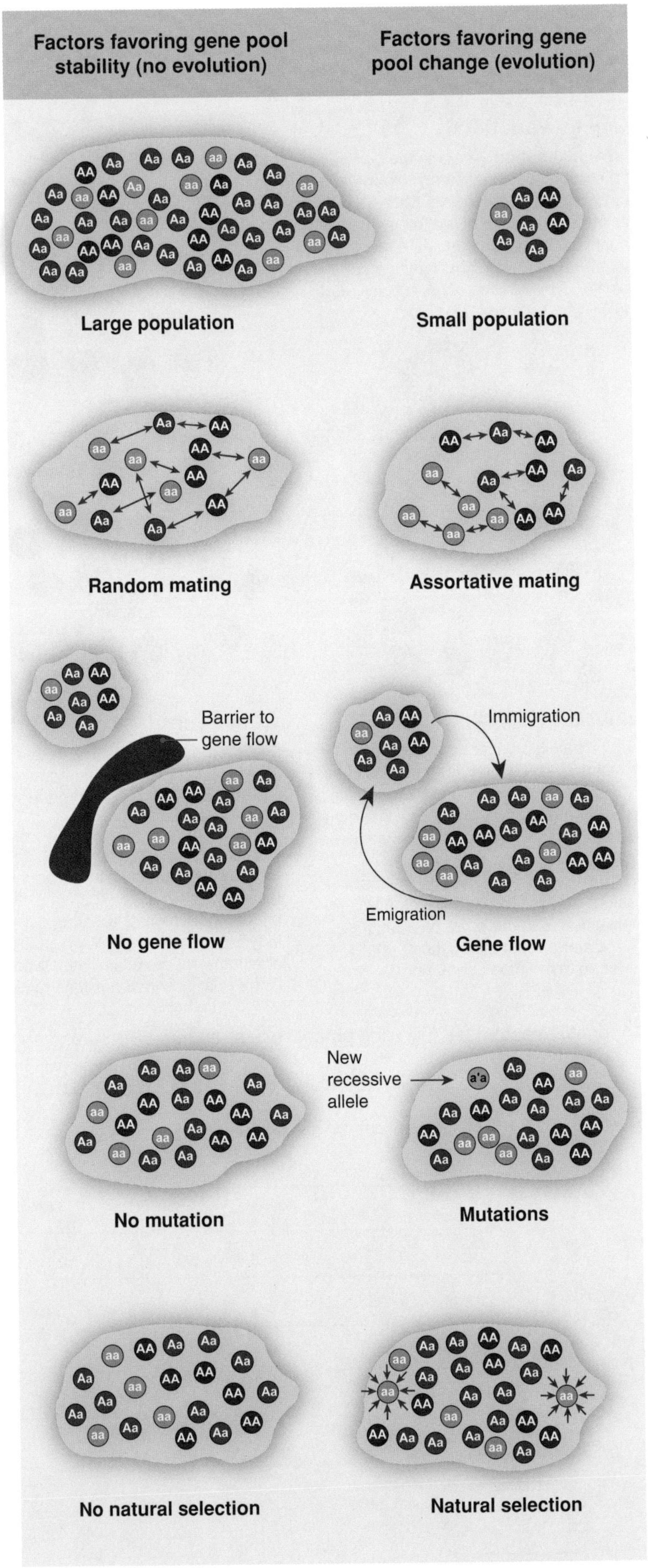

____

____

____

____

____

Factors favoring gene pool stability (no evolution)	Factors favoring gene pool change (evolution)
Large population	Small population
Random mating	Assortative mating
No gene flow	Gene flow
No mutation	Mutations
No natural selection	Natural selection

4. Identify a factor that tends to:

(a) Increase genetic variation in populations:

____

____

(b) Decrease genetic variation in populations:

____

____

ISBN: 978-1-98-856656-6

160 Changes in a Gene Pool

Key Question: How do natural selection and migration alter the allele frequencies in gene pools?

The diagram below shows an hypothetical population of beetles undergoing changes as it is subjected to two 'events'. The three phases represent a progression in time (i.e. the same gene pool, undergoing change). The beetles have two phenotypes (black and pale) determined by the amount of pigment deposited in the cuticle. The gene controlling this character is represented by two alleles **A** and **a**. Your task is to analyze the gene pool as it undergoes changes.

1. For each phase in the gene pool below fill in the following tables (the first has been done for you):

   (a) Count the number of A and a alleles separately. Enter the count into the top row of the table (left hand columns).
   (b) Count the number of each type of allele combination (AA, Aa and aa) in the gene pool. Enter the count into the top row of the table (right hand columns).
   (c) For each of the above, work out the frequencies as percentages (bottom row of table):

Allele frequency = No. counted alleles ÷ Total no. of alleles x 100

Phase 1: Initial gene pool

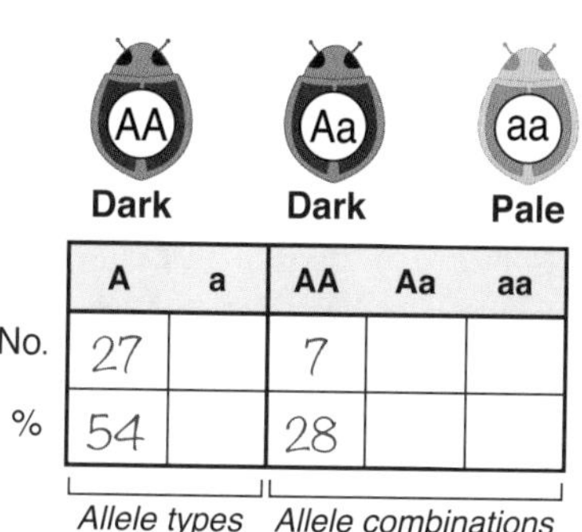

	A	a	AA	Aa	aa
No.	27		7		
%	54		28		

Allele types *Allele combinations*

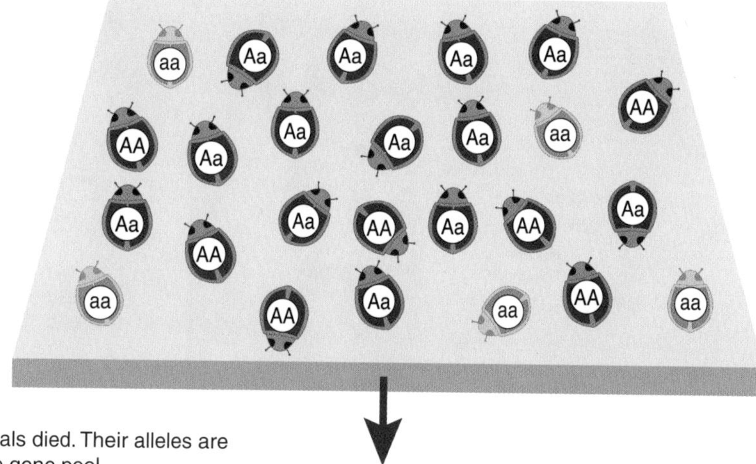

Two pale individuals died. Their alleles are removed from the gene pool.

Phase 2: Natural selection

In the same gene pool at a later time there was a change in the allele frequencies. This was due to the loss of certain allele combinations due to natural selection. Some of those with a genotype of aa were eliminated (poor fitness).
These individuals (surrounded by small white arrows) are not counted for allele frequencies; they are dead!

	A	a	AA	Aa	aa
No.					
%					

This individual is entering the population and will add its alleles to the gene pool.

This individual is leaving the population, removing its alleles from the gene pool.

Phase 3: Immigration and emigration

This particular kind of beetle exhibits wandering behavior. The allele frequencies change again due to the introduction and departure of individual beetles, each carrying certain allele combinations.
Individuals coming into the gene pool (AA) are counted for allele frequencies, but those leaving (aa) are not.

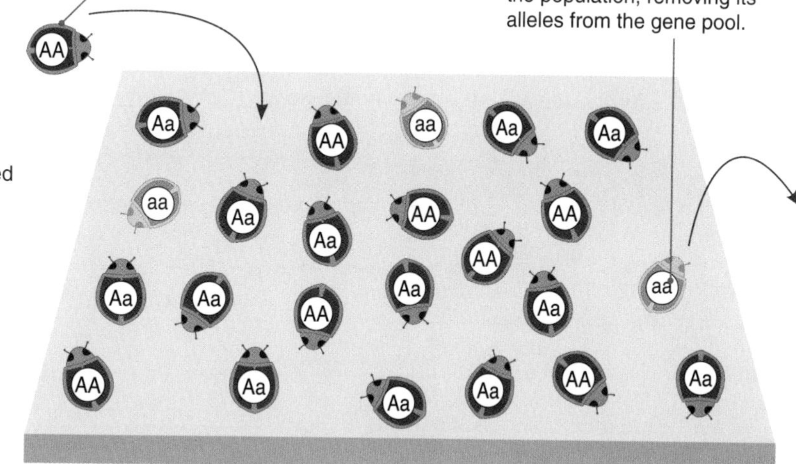

	A	a	AA	Aa	aa
No.					
%					

ISBN: 978-1-98-856656-6

161 Population Bottlenecks

Key Question: What are population bottlenecks, how do they occur, and how do they affect the genetic diversity of a species or population?

Populations may sometimes be reduced to low numbers by predation, disease, or periods of climatic change. These large scale reductions are called population (genetic) bottlenecks. The sudden population decline is not necessarily selective and it may affect all phenotypes equally. Large scale catastrophic events, such as fire or volcanic eruption, are examples of such non-selective events. Affected populations may later recover, having squeezed through a 'bottleneck' of low numbers. The diagram below illustrates how population numbers may be reduced as a result of a catastrophic event. Following such an event, the gene pool of the surviving remnant population may be markedly different to that of the original gene pool. Genetic drift may cause further changes to allele frequencies. The small population may return to previous levels but with a reduced genetic diversity.

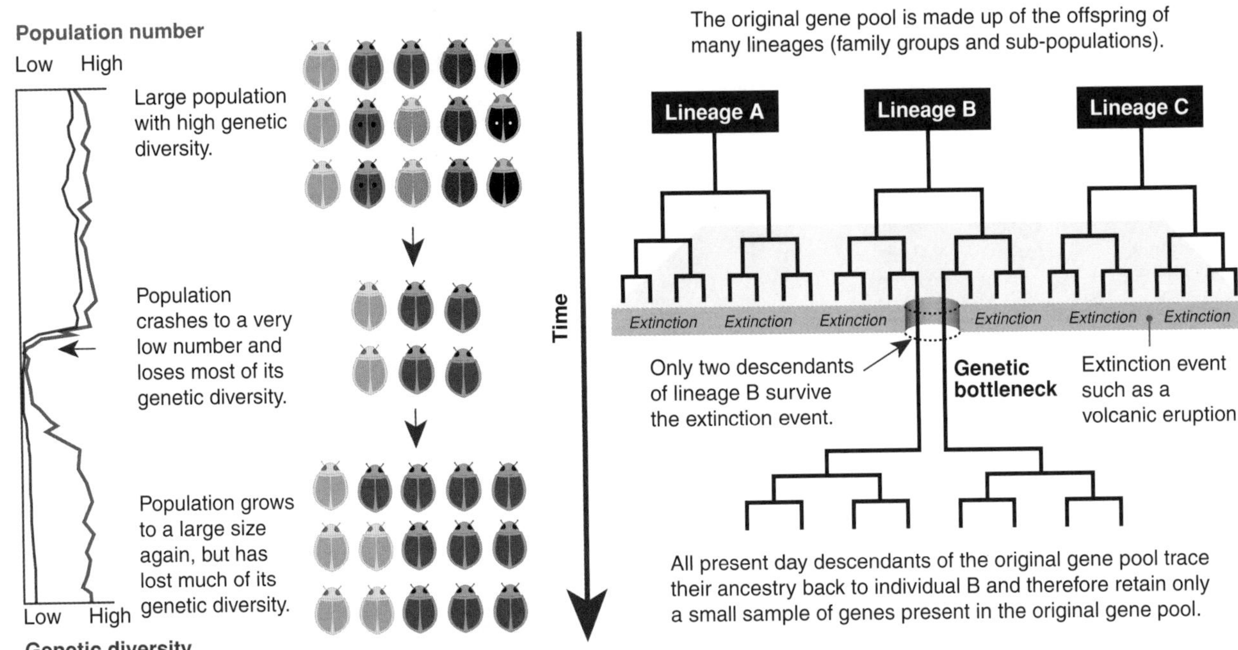

Population bottlenecks and low allelic diversity in Tasmanian devils

- Tasmanian devils are the largest surviving marsupial carnivore. They were once found throughout mainland Australia, but became locally extinct about 3000 years ago and are now restricted to Tasmania. Genetic evidence suggests that devils went through at least two historic population crashes, one about 30,000 years ago and another about 3000 years ago. Added to these historic declines are modern declines (1850 to 1950) as a result of trapping and disease. These population crashes are the likely cause of the very low diversity in the MHC I and II (immune) genes in devils.
- The MHC genes are important in immunity and the body's self recognition system. Low allelic diversity for MHC is implicated in the spread of devil facial tumor disease (DFTD), a contagious cancer that appeared in populations in the mid 1990s and has resulted in the loss of 80% of the devil population. The cancerous cells are transmitted when the devils fight. Ordinarily this foreign material would be recognized and destroyed by the immune system. In Tasmanian devils, the immune diversity is so low that tumors can spread without invoking an immune response.
- Recent evidence also shows that some populations have immunity to DFTD. This may originate in devils with MHC alleles distinctly different from susceptible animals.

1. Define the term population (genetic) bottleneck: ____________________

2. Explain how a population bottleneck can decrease genetic diversity in a population: ____________________

ISBN: 978-1-98-856656-6

Cheetahs have undergone a genetic bottleneck

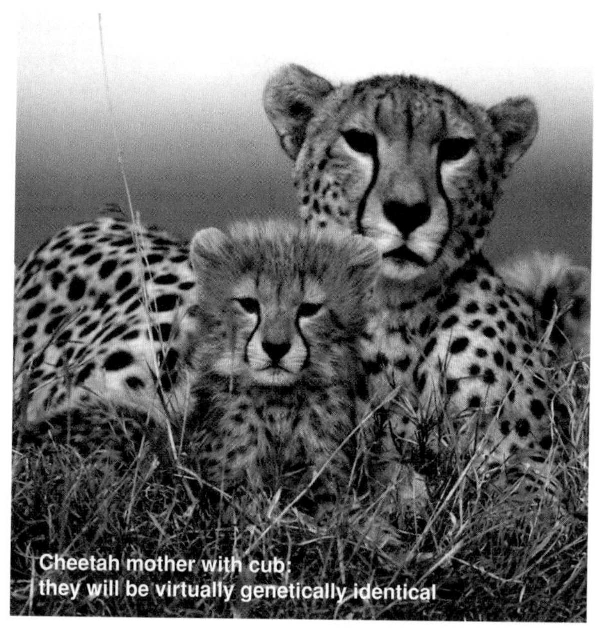

Cheetah mother with cub: they will be virtually genetically identical

- The global population of cheetahs currently stands at fewer than 8000. This is partially due to hunting and habitat loss, but also due to very low genetic diversity within the population.
- The low genetic variability in cheetahs is the result of past genetic bottlenecks, the first around 100,000 years ago and the second about 12,000 years ago. These bottlenecks were most likely associated with ice age migrations from North America into Africa and with a depletion of prey species at the end of the Pleistocene. The bottlenecks severely reduced genetic variability in the population and greatly increased the amount of inbreeding.
- Researchers measured genetic variation between seven individuals in two countries using a number of measures. They found cheetahs have very little genetic variation. In fact, their variation is so depleted, organs could be transplanted between individuals and not cause an immune response.
- A high level of inbreeding increases the incidence of harmful alleles and is associated with reproductive failures. Male cheetahs have a high occurrence of malformed sperm, which contributes to their poor reproductive success. In addition, the low allelic diversity means that the cheetahs are less able to respond to environmental changes or new pathogens, making extinction much more likely.

3. What events might cause a population bottleneck? ______________________________

____

4. (a) What has been the genetic consequence of bottleneck events in the Tasmanian devil population? ______________________________

____

____

____

(b) Explain how this has led to increased susceptibility to disease, specifically infectious cancer: ______________________________

____

____

____

5. Endangered species are often subjected to genetic bottlenecks. Explain how genetic bottlenecks affect the ability of a population of an endangered species to recover from its plight:

____

____

____

6. The New Zealand black robin experienced a severe population bottleneck in 1980 in which the entire species population dropped to just 5. Of that small group, only one female bred. The population is now just over 250, and all are related to the one breeding female. The graph shows the genetic diversity of the black robin compared to a related robin species. Use the graph to explain the effect of the population bottleneck on the black robin:

____

____

____

____

____

Total number of unique DNA fragments: 0, 10, 20, 30, 40, 50, 60, 70

Number of DNA fragments sampled: 0, 100, 200, 300, 400, 500, 600

South Island robin

Black robin

S.L. Ardern, D.M. Lambert 1997

ISBN: 978-1-98-856656-6

162 The Founder Effect

Key Question How can the founder effect result in differences in allele frequencies between parent and founder populations?

If a small number of individuals from a large population becomes isolated from their original parent population, their sample of alleles is unlikely to represent the allele proportions of the parent population. This phenomenon is called the **founder effect** and it can result in the colonizing (founder) population evolving in a different direction to the parent population. This is particularly the case if the founder population is subjected to different selection pressures in a new environment and if the population is missing alleles that are present in the parent population.

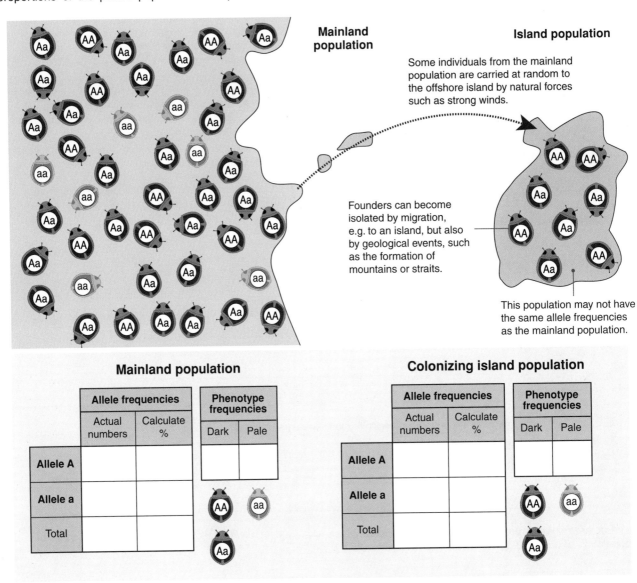

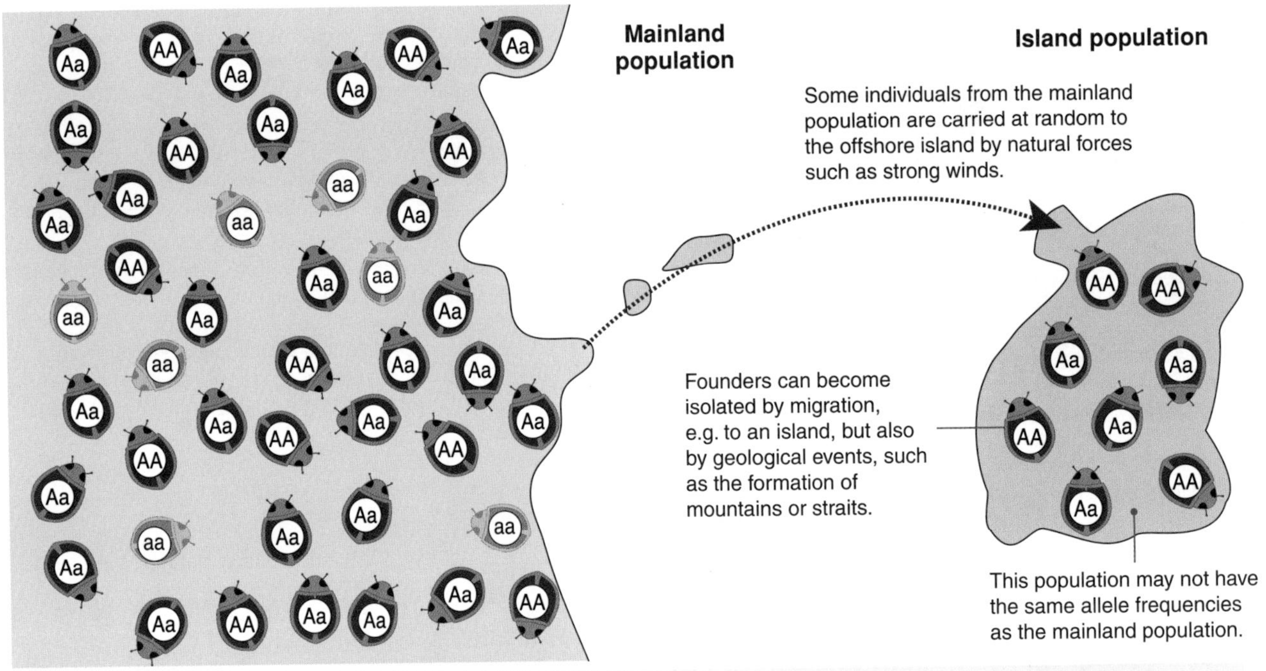

Mainland population

Island population

Some individuals from the mainland population are carried at random to the offshore island by natural forces such as strong winds.

Founders can become isolated by migration, e.g. to an island, but also by geological events, such as the formation of mountains or straits.

This population may not have the same allele frequencies as the mainland population.

Mainland population

	Allele frequencies	
	Actual numbers	Calculate %
Allele A		
Allele a		
Total		

Phenotype frequencies	
Dark	Pale

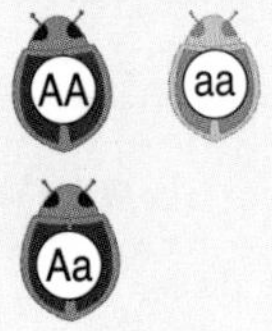

Colonizing island population

	Allele frequencies	
	Actual numbers	Calculate %
Allele A		
Allele a		
Total		

Phenotype frequencies	
Dark	Pale

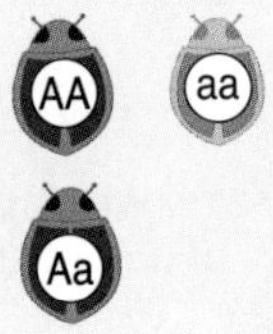

1. Compare the mainland population to the population which ended up on the island (use the spaces in the tables above):
   (a) Count the phenotype numbers for the two populations (i.e. the number of black and pale beetles).
   (b) Count the allele numbers for the two populations: the number of dominant alleles (A) and recessive alleles (a). Calculate these as a percentage of the total number of alleles for each population.

2. How are the allele frequencies of the two populations different? ______________________________

____

3. (a) Describe the likely changes when a founder population is isolated in a new environment: ______________________________

____

____

(b) Describe the factors that might influence the end result or the speed of the changes: ______________________________

____

____

ISBN: 978-1-98-856656-6

Founder effect in brown anole lizards

- In 2004 Hurricane Francis wiped out the brown anole lizard (*Anolis sagrei*) populations on several cays (small sandy islands) around the Bahamas. Scientists used this as a chance to study the founder effect. They took pairs of lizards from the mainland and placed them on different cays.
- The vegetation on the cays is much smaller and scrub-like with thin branches or twigs compared to the much larger trees of the mainland. On the mainland, scientists noted that the lizards use their long limbs to climb around the trees. They hypothesized that the populations isolated on the cays would eventually evolve shorter limbs to adapt to the scrub-like, less supportive vegetation. They measured the limb length over several years.
- It was found that limb length indeed became shorter over successive generations in all the populations. Importantly, populations founded by lizards with the longest legs still had the longest legs and populations founded by lizards with the shortest legs still had the shortest legs. The characteristics of the founder populations influenced the descendant populations.

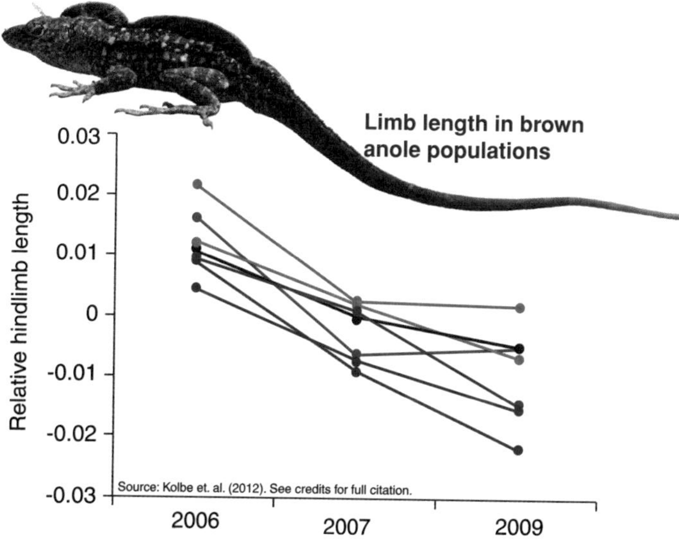

Founder effect in human populations

thinboyfatter CC 2.0

Brian Gratwicke CC 2.0

Due to the many episodes of human migration around the world there are many instances of the founder effect in human populations. In 1790, nine mutineers from the ship HMS Bounty along with six Tahitian men, eleven Tahitian women, and a baby girl settled on Pitcairn island. The population eventually grew to 193 by 1856.

In 1856 the entire population of Pitcairn Island resettled on Norfolk Island after it was decided Pitcairn was over populated. The effect of this can still be seen in genetic studies of the Norfolk Island population. In 1859, 16 people returned to Pitcairn Island and founded a new population, that eventually reached 250 people by 1936. The population is now around 56.

Tristan da Cunha sits 2,400 km from Africa and more than 3,500 km from South America. The current settlement of Tristan da Cunha was founded by the English in 1817. In 1961, a genetic study traced 14% of all genes in the population of 300 to one founding couple. Around 47% of the population are affected by asthma. From the 15 original settlers at least three had asthma.

4. (a) Why were conditions good for setting up an experiment on the founder effect on the cays around the Bahamas?

____

____

(b) Describe how the founder effect was demonstrated in the brown anole lizards: _______________

____

____

____

____

5. (a) The rate of asthma in the UK is about 8%. Calculate the rate of asthma in the original Tristan da Cunha settlers:

____

(b) Describe how this has affected the current population of Tristan da Cuhna: _______________

____

____

____

ISBN: 978-1-98-856656-6

163 Genetic Drift

Key Question: What is the effect of genetic drift on the allele frequencies of a population and how does population size affect its influence?

Genetic drift is the change in allele frequencies in a population due to random (chance) events. It may result in the loss (or fixation) of any allele, including beneficial ones. Genetic drift is effectively sampling error so its effects are greater when the population is small. In natural systems, small populations are generally the result of the founder effect or a genetic bottleneck. Both these mechanisms are well documented in natural populations. In these small populations, genetic drift is an important agent of genetic change.

How does genetic drift reduce variation in populations?

The change in allele frequencies within a population through genetic drift is often illustrated using the random sampling of marbles from a jar. The diagram below represents a population of 20 individuals. The different alleles are represented by blue and orange marbles. The starting population contains an equal number of blue and orange marbles. Random mating is represented by selecting 10 marbles at random. Twenty marbles representing the new allele proportions are placed into a new jar to represent the second generation, and the process is repeated for subsequent generations.

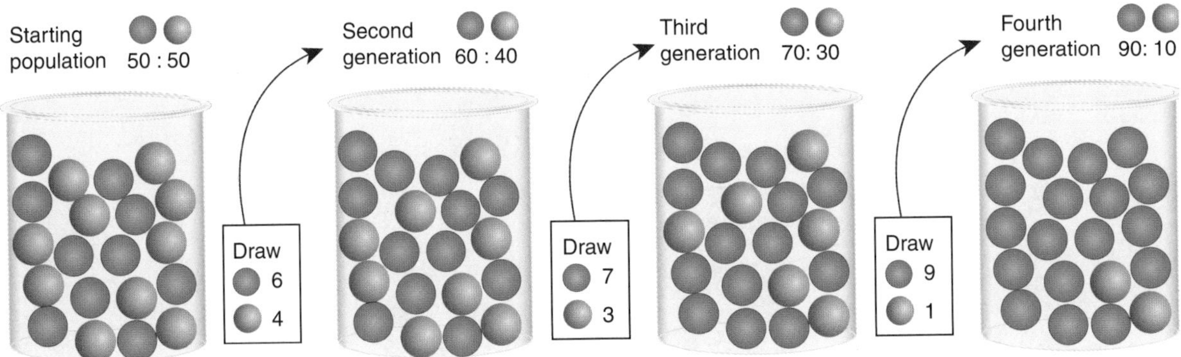

In the example above, the orange marbles are becoming less frequent within the population and the amount of genetic variation within the population is reducing. Unless the proportion of orange marbles increases, it will eventually be lost from the population altogether and the allele for the blue marble becomes fixed (the only variant). If environmental conditions change so that the blue allele becomes detrimental, the population may become extinct (the potentially adaptive orange allele has been lost).

In small populations, genetic drift can be a major agent of rapid change because the loss of any one individual represents a greater proportion of the total population.

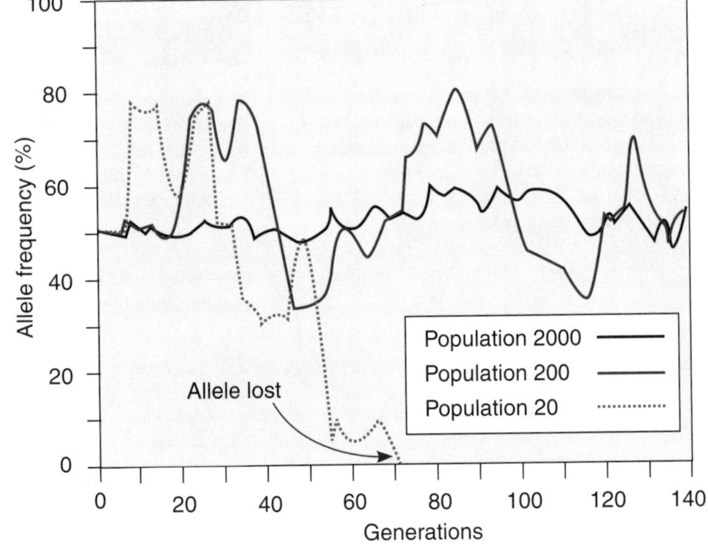

The graph on the right shows a simulation of the effect of genetic drift on populations of various sizes. Fluctuations are minimal for a large population (2000) but more pronounced in smaller populations (200 and 20), which may lose alleles.

1. Explain why the effects of genetic drift are more significant in small populations: ______________________

2. Use the diagram above to predict the shape of the line if a population of 200,000 was used in the simulation:

3. (a) Does genetic drift in a small population increase or decrease the number of heterozygotes? ______________________

(b) How could this affect a population's long term viability? ______________________

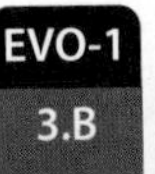

ISBN: 978-1-98-856656-6

164 Calculating Allele Frequencies in Populations

Key Question: How is the Hardy-Weinberg equation used to model the allele frequencies in a population?

Recall the principle of genetic equilibrium. The **Hardy-Weinberg equation** provides a simple mathematical model of genetic equilibrium in a gene pool, but its main application in population genetics is in calculating allele and genotype frequencies in populations, particularly as a means of studying changes and measuring their rate.

Punnett square

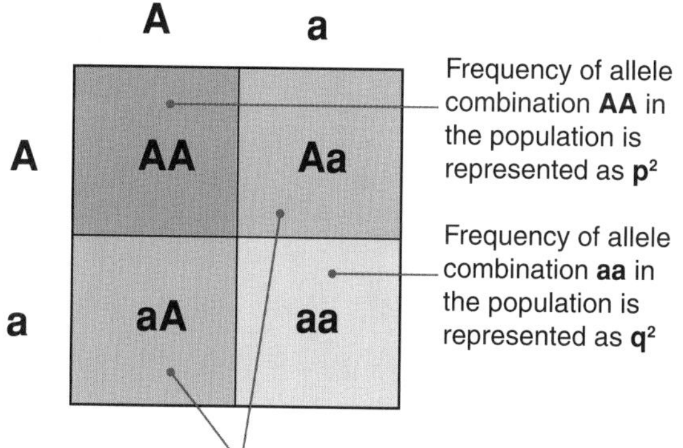

A
a
A
a
AA
Aa
aA
aa
Frequency of allele combination **AA** in the population is represented as **p²**
Frequency of allele combination **aa** in the population is represented as **q²**

Frequency of allele combination **Aa** in the population (add these together to get **2pq**)

$$(p + q)^2 = p^2 + 2pq + q^2 = 1$$

Frequency of allele types	Frequency of allele combinations
p = Frequency of allele A	p^2 = Frequency of AA (homozygous dominant)
q = Frequency of allele a	2pq = Frequency of Aa (heterozygous)
	q^2 = Frequency of aa (homozygous recessive)

The Hardy-Weinberg equation is applied to populations with a simple genetic situation: dominant and recessive alleles controlling a single trait. The frequency of all of the dominant (A) and recessive alleles (a) equals the total genetic complement, and adds up to 1 or 100% of the alleles present (i.e. p + q = 1).

How to solve Hardy-Weinberg problems

In most populations, the frequency of two alleles of interest is calculated from the proportion of homozygous recessives (q^2), as this is the only genotype identifiable directly from its phenotype. If only the dominant phenotype is known, q^2 may be calculated (1 – the frequency of the dominant phenotype). The following steps outline the procedure for solving a Hardy-Weinberg problem:

***Remember that all calculations must be carried out using proportions,* NOT PERCENTAGES!**

1. Examine the question to determine what piece of information you have been given about the population. In most cases, this is the percentage or frequency of the homozygous recessive phenotype q^2, or the dominant phenotype $p^2 + 2pq$ (see note above).
2. The first objective is to find out the value of p or q, If this is achieved, then every other value in the equation can be determined by simple calculation.
3. Take the square root of q^2 to find q.
4. Determine p by subtracting q from 1 (i.e. p = 1 – q).
5. Determine p^2 by multiplying p by itself (i.e. $p^2 = p \times p$).
6. Determine 2pq by multiplying p times q times 2.
7. Check that your calculations are correct by adding up the values for $p^2 + q^2 + 2pq$ (the sum should equal 1 or 100%).

Worked example

Among white-skinned people in the USA, approximately 70% of people can taste the chemical phenylthiocarbamide (PTC) (the dominant phenotype), while 30% are non-tasters (the recessive phenotype).

Determine the frequency of:	***Answers***
(a) Homozygous recessive phenotype(**q^2**).	30% - provided
(b) The dominant allele (**p**).	45.2%
(c) Homozygous tasters (**p^2**).	20.5%
(d) Heterozygous tasters (**2pq**).	49.5%

Data: The frequency of the dominant phenotype (70% tasters) and recessive phenotype (30% non-tasters) are provided.

Working:

Recessive phenotype: **q^2** = 30%
use 0.30 for calculation

therefore: **q** = 0.5477
square root of 0.30

therefore: **p** = 0.4523
1 – q = p
1 – 0.5477 = 0.4523

p + q = 1
p = 1 – q
q = 1 – p

Use p and q in the equation (top) to solve any unknown:

Homozygous dominant **p^2** = 0.2046
(p x p = 0.4523 x 0.4523)

Heterozygous: **2pq** = 0.4953

$p^2 + 2pq$ = dom. phen.

1. A population of hamsters has a gene consisting of 90% M alleles (black) and 10% m alleles (gray). Mating is random.
Data: Frequency of recessive allele (10% m) and dominant allele (90% M).

Determine the proportion of offspring that will be black and the proportion that will be gray (show your working):

99% black

1% gray

Recessive allele:	q	= 0.1
Dominant allele:	p	= 0.9
Recessive phenotype:	q^2	= 0.01
Homozygous dominant:	p^2	= 0.81
Heterozygous:	2pq	= 0.18

ISBN: 978-1-98-856656-6

2. You are working with pea plants and found 36 plants out of 400 were dwarf.
Data: Frequency of recessive phenotype (36 out of 400 = 9%)

(a) Calculate the frequency of the tall gene: 70% (280)

(b) Determine the number of heterozygous pea plants:
168 heterozygous
(400 × 0.42)

Recessive allele:	q	= 0.3
Dominant allele:	p	= 0.7
Recessive phenotype:	q^2	= .09
Homozygous dominant:	p^2	= 0.49
Heterozygous:	$2pq$	= 0.42

3. In humans, the ability to taste the chemical phenylthiocarbamide (PTC) is inherited as a simple dominant characteristic. Suppose you found out that 360 out of 1000 college students could not taste the chemical.
Data: Frequency of recessive phenotype (360 out of 1000).

(a) State the frequency of the gene for tasting PTC: 40%

(b) Determine the number of heterozygous students in this population:
480 heterozygous students

Recessive allele:	q	= 0.6
Dominant allele:	p	= 0.4
Recessive phenotype:	q^2	= 0.36
Homozygous dominant:	p^2	= 0.16
Heterozygous:	$2pq$	= 0.48

4. A type of deformity appears in 4% of a large herd of cattle. Assume the deformity was caused by a recessive gene.
Data: Frequency of recessive phenotype (4% deformity).

(a) Calculate the percentage of the herd that are carriers of the gene:
32%

(b) Determine the frequency of the dominant gene in this case:
80%

Recessive allele:	q	= 0.2
Dominant allele:	p	= 0.8
Recessive phenotype:	q^2	= .04
Homozygous dominant:	p^2	= 0.64
Heterozygous:	$2pq$	= 0.32

5. Assume you placed 50 pure bred black guinea pigs (dominant allele) with 50 albino guinea pigs (recessive allele) and allowed the population to attain genetic equilibrium (several generations have passed).
Data: Frequency of recessive allele (50%) and dominant allele (50%).

(genotype) Determine the proportion (%) of the population that becomes white:
50%

Recessive allele:	q	= 0.5
Dominant allele:	p	= 0.5
Recessive phenotype:	q^2	= 0.25
Homozygous dominant:	p^2	= 0.25
Heterozygous:	$2pq$	= 0.5

6. It is known that 64% of a large population exhibit the recessive trait of a characteristic controlled by two alleles (one is dominant over the other).
Data: Frequency of recessive phenotype (64%). Determine the following:

(a) The frequency of the recessive allele: 80%

(b) The percentage that are heterozygous for this trait: 32%

(c) The percentage that exhibit the dominant trait: 36%

(d) The percentage that are homozygous for the dominant trait: 4%

(e) The percentage that has one or more recessive alleles: 96%

Recessive allele:	q	= 0.8
Dominant allele:	p	= 0.2
Recessive phenotype:	q^2	= 0.64
Homozygous dominant:	p^2	= 0.04
Heterozygous:	$2pq$	= 0.32

7. Explain how the Hardy-Weinberg equations allow the calculation of allele frequencies in a population while needing to know only the frequency of the recessive phenotype. Use the example that the recessive phenotype cystic fibrosis occurs at a frequency of 1 in 2500 births.

$.0004 = q^2$ $\quad p = .98$ $\quad 2pq = 0.0392$
$.02 = q$ $\quad p^2 = 0.9604$

ISBN: 978-1-98-856656-6

165 Analysis of a Squirrel Gene Pool

STUDENT SUPPORT FOR INVESTIGATION 2: *Mathematical Modeling*

In Olney, Illinois, there is a unique population of albino (white) and gray squirrels. Between 1977 and 1990, students at Olney Central College carried out a study of this population. They recorded the frequency of gray and albino squirrels. The albinos displayed a mutant allele expressed as an albino phenotype only in the homozygous recessive condition. The data they collected are provided in the table below. Using the **Hardy-Weinberg equation**, it was possible to estimate the frequency of the normal 'wild' allele (G) providing gray fur coloring, and the frequency of the mutant albino allele (g) producing white squirrels when homozygous.

Thanks to **Dr. John Stencel**, Olney Central College, Olney, Illinois, US, for providing the data for this exercise.

Gray squirrel, usual color form

Albino form of gray squirrel

Population of gray and white squirrels in Olney, Illinois (1977-1990)

Year	Gray	White	Total	GG	Gg	gg	Freq. of g	Freq. of G
1977	602	182	784	26.85	49.93	23.21	48.18	51.82
1978	511	172	683	24.82	50.00	25.18	50.18	49.82
1979	482	134	616	28.47	49.77	21.75	46.64	53.36
1980	489	133	622	28.90	49.72	21.38	46.24	53.76
1981	536	163	699	26.74	49.94	23.32	48.29	51.71
1982	618	151	769	31.01	49.35	19.64	44.31	55.69
1983	419	141	560	24.82	50.00	25.18	50.18	49.82
1984	378	106	484	28.30	49.79	21.90	46.80	53.20
1985	448	125	573	28.40	49.78	21.82	46.71	53.29
1986	536	155	691	27.71	49.86	22.43	47.36	52.64
1987	*No data collected this year*							
1988	652	122	774	36.36	47.88	15.76	39.70	60.30
1989	552	146	698	29.45	49.64	20.92	45.74	54.26
1990	603	111	714	36.69	47.76	15.55	39.43	60.57

1. Graph population changes: Use the data in the first 3 columns of the table above to plot a line graph. This will show changes in the phenotypes: numbers of gray and white (albino) squirrels, as well as changes in the total population. Plot: gray, white, and total for each year:

(a) Determine by how much (as a %) the total population numbers have fluctuated over the sampling period:

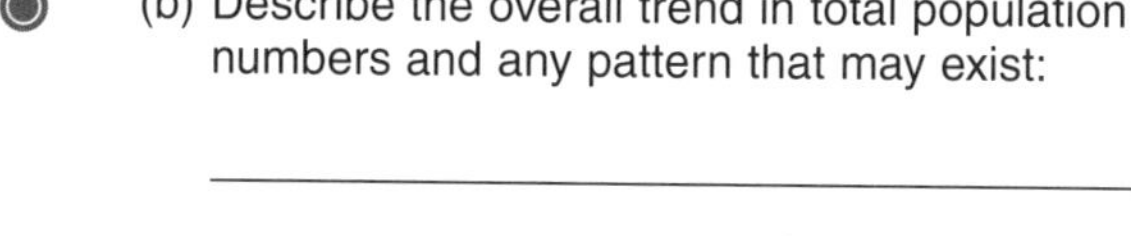

(b) Describe the overall trend in total population numbers and any pattern that may exist:

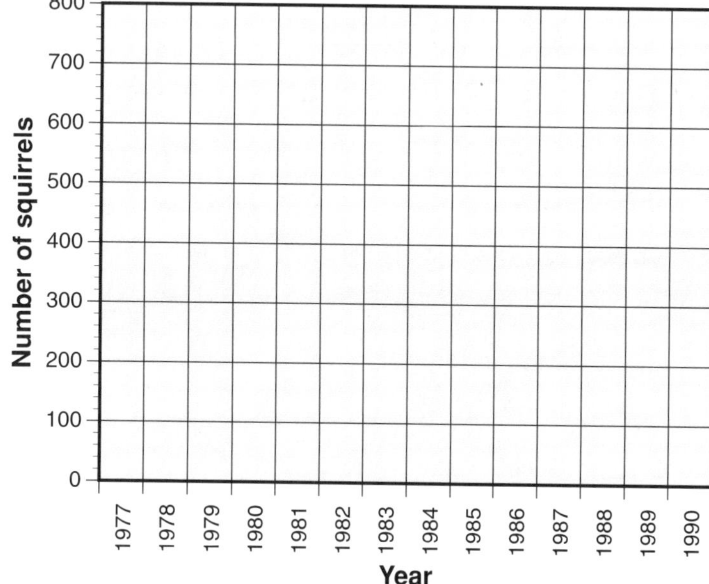

ISBN: 978-1-98-856656-6

253

164
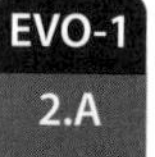
EVO-1 4.A

EVO-1 2.A

2. Graph genotype changes: Use the data in the genotype columns of the table on the previous page to plot a line graph. This will show changes in the allele combinations (**GG, Gg, gg**). Plot: **GG**, **Gg**, and **gg** for each year:

Describe the overall trend in the frequency of:

(a) Homozygous dominant (**GG**) genotype:

(b) Heterozygous (**Gg**) genotype:

(c) Homozygous recessive (**gg**) genotype:

3. Graph allele changes: Use the data in the last two columns of the table on the previous page to plot a line graph. This will show changes in the allele frequencies for each of the dominant (**G**) and recessive (**g**) alleles.
Plot: the frequency of **G** and the frequency of **g**:

(a) Describe the overall trend in the frequency of the dominant allele (**G**):

(b) Describe the overall trend in the frequency of the recessive allele (**g**):

4. (a) State which of the three graphs best indicates that a significant change may be taking place in the gene pool of this population of squirrels:

(b) Give a reason for your answer:

5. Describe a possible cause of the changes in allele frequencies over the sampling period:

6. Visit the simulation websites listed on the **Resource Hub** for this activity to model how gene pools change from one generation to the next when variables such as selection, mutation, and migration are manipulated.

ISBN: 978-1-98-856656-6

166 The Evidence for Evolution

Key Question: What evidence is there that life evolved from a single common ancestor that lived around 3.8 billion years ago?

Evolution is the heritable genetic change in a population over generations. The evidence that life evolved from a single common ancestor can be found in the fossil record and in the homology of body structures and DNA sequences, and is supported by laboratory experiments and field studies.

Example: humans and dogs: related by evidence

Fossil record

Fossils shows that few mammal groups existed 65 million years ago. After the extinction of the dinosaurs the fossil record very quickly becomes full of new mammalian groups. Transitional fossils can show the evolutionary changes as one group of organisms evolve into another. Very early mammalian ancestors show generalist features (e.g. tooth structure), that become progressively more specific as the mammalian common ancestor diverged to fill vacant niches.

Endogenous retroviruses (ERVs)

Retroviral DNA insertions are found in all organisms. The human genome is about 5% ERVs. They can be inherited. Closely related organisms carry more similar ERVs than more distantly related organisms.

Genetic code

With a very few exceptions, humans, dogs, and every other living thing all share the same genetic code. The same four bases are found in DNA and the triplet sequences in the DNA molecule code for the same amino acids in all organisms.

Vestigial structures

All mammals have tails. Adaptations to different lifestyles have changed the their appearance. In humans the tail is vestigial (as the coccyx) while in dogs the tail is still an important and large structure.

DNA homology

The more closely related organisms are the more similar their DNA. Humans share about 65% with chickens, 85% of their DNA with dogs, and 98% with chimpanzees.

Homologous structures

Humans and dogs share the same body plan. The skeletons have essentially the same arrangement of bones, e.g forelimb bones are arranged in the same way.

Human

Domestic dog

Last common mammal ancestor

Ancestral mammal

Experimentation

Artificial selection has produced all the breeds of dog present today, showing how selection operates in populations. Experiments with *Drosophila* flies and *E. coli* bacteria have documented evolution in real time.

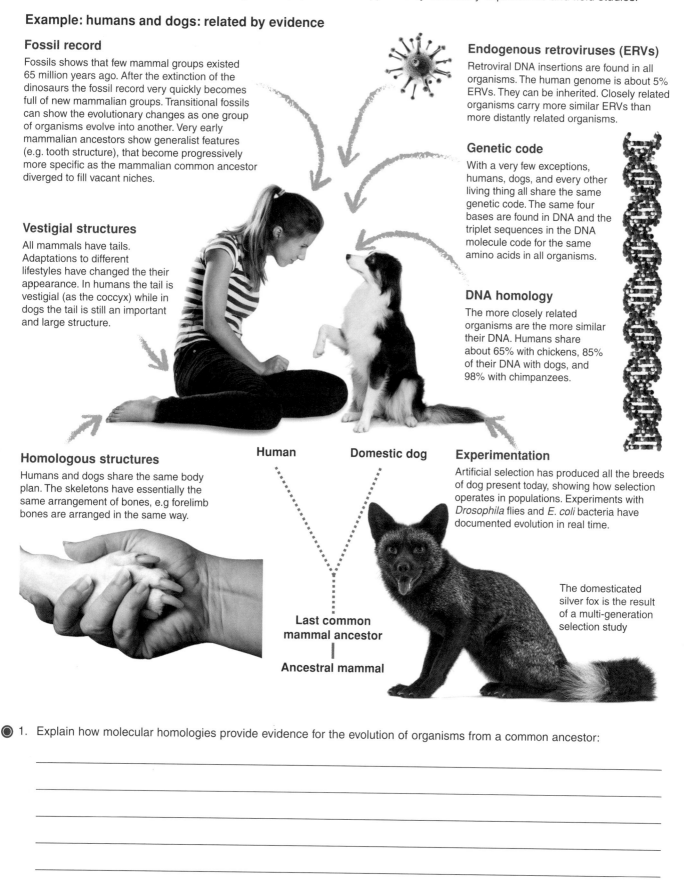

The domesticated silver fox is the result of a multi-generation selection study

1. Explain how molecular homologies provide evidence for the evolution of organisms from a common ancestor:

ISBN: 978-1-98-856656-6

177

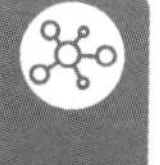

167 Fossils

Key Question: How are fossils formed and what can they tell us about the evolution of life on Earth?

A fossil may be the preserved remains of the organism itself, the impression of it in the sediment (a mould), or marks made by it during its lifetime (trace fossils). For fossilization to occur, rapid burial of the organism is required (usually in water-borne sediment). This is followed by chemical alteration, whereby minerals are added or removed. Fossilization requires the normal processes of decay to be permanently arrested. This can occur if the organism's remains are isolated from the air or water and decomposing microbes are prevented from breaking them down. Fossils provide a record of the appearance, evolution, and extinction of organisms, from species to whole taxonomic groups. Once this record is calibrated against a time scale (by using a broad range of dating techniques, including radiometric and relative dating), it is possible to build up a picture of the evolutionary changes that have taken place.

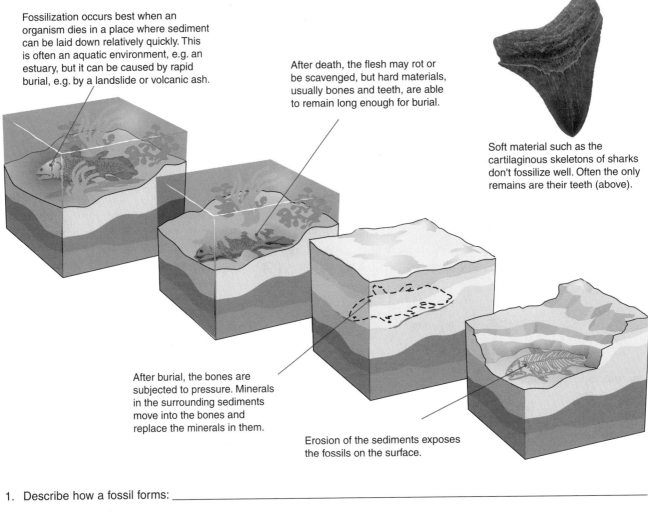

Fossilization occurs best when an organism dies in a place where sediment can be laid down relatively quickly. This is often an aquatic environment, e.g. an estuary, but it can be caused by rapid burial, e.g. by a landslide or volcanic ash.

After death, the flesh may rot or be scavenged, but hard materials, usually bones and teeth, are able to remain long enough for burial.

Soft material such as the cartilaginous skeletons of sharks don't fossilize well. Often the only remains are their teeth (above).

After burial, the bones are subjected to pressure. Minerals in the surrounding sediments move into the bones and replace the minerals in them.

Erosion of the sediments exposes the fossils on the surface.

1. Describe how a fossil forms:

2. Explain why the rapid burial of an organism is important in the formation of fossils:

3. Explain why the fossil record is biased towards marine organisms with hard parts:

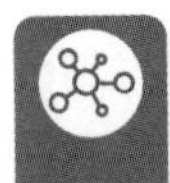

ISBN: 978-1-98-856656-6

Some fossils act as index fossils

- An **index fossil** is a fossil that is characteristic of a particular span of geologic time or environment. Index fossils help scientists with relative dating (placing rock layers in a relative order to each other), define boundaries in the geologic time scale, and correlate strata from different regions.
- Trilobites make excellent index fossils because they are easily recognizable, abundant in the fossil record, and different families are characteristic of different geographic distributions and different time periods.
- Trilobites (meaning three lobes) are a fossil group of extinct marine arthropods. They first appeared in the fossil record near the beginning of the Cambrian (520 mya) and disappeared in the mass extinction at the end of the Permian (250 mya).
- They were a very diverse group and underwent several radiations during the Cambrian, inhabiting a wide range of marine environments and exhibiting diverse life strategies. The wide diversity in their appearance reflects this.
- The trilobite fossil record provides evidence of several evolutionary trends in the different lineages. These included streamlined shape in swimming forms, broadening of the head in filter feeders, improvement in the ability to curl up into a defensive ball, decreased size, and the evolution of spines as defences (below).

Fossilized trilobite

Loss of surface detail could have helped with burrowing. A decrease in size allowed exploitation of new microhabitats.

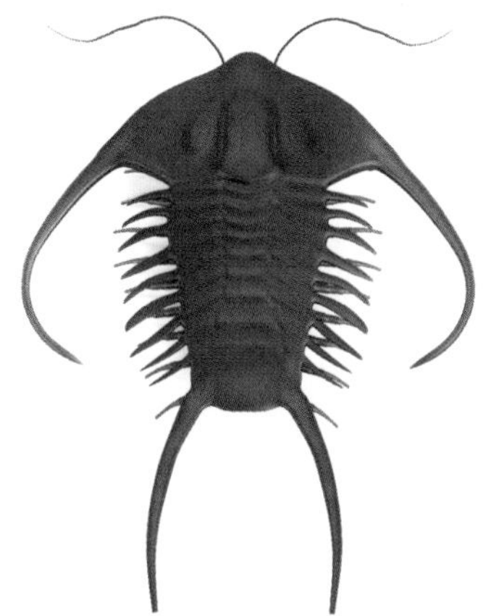
Spines provided defence from attack and stabilization on loose surfaces.

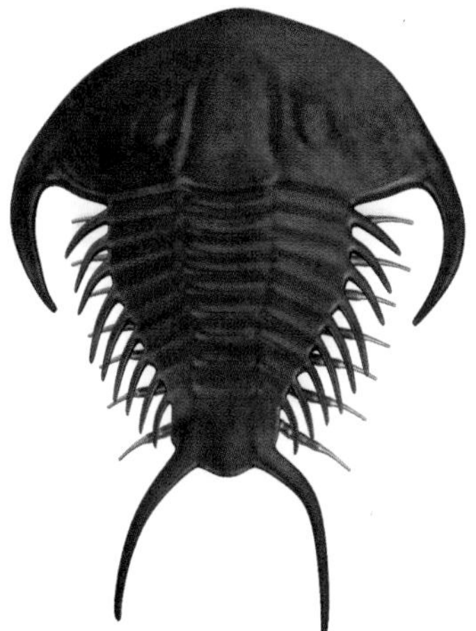
An enlargement of the head region was probably an adaptation to filter feeding.

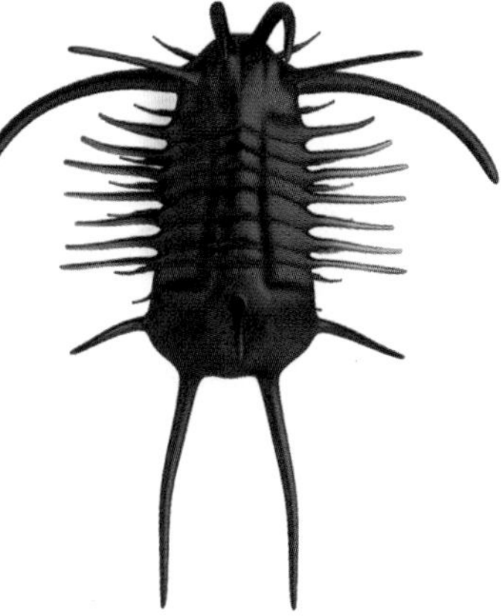
Elongated and streamlined bodies aided swimming in pelagic (open ocean) forms.

4. (a) Explain the importance of index fossils in determining relative time lines: ______

(b) Why do trilobites make good index fossils? ______

5. What fossil evidence do we have that trilobites were a diverse group adapted to many different niches? ______

ISBN: 978-1-98-856656-6

168 Methods of Dating Fossils

Key Question: What are the different methods for dating fossil remains and what are the differences between them?

Radiometric dating methods allow an **absolute date** to be assigned to fossils, most commonly by dating the rocks around the fossils. Multiple dating methods for samples provides cross-referencing, which gives confidence in a given date. Absolute, or **chronometric**, dating methods most often involve radiometric dating (e.g. **radiocarbon**, **potassium-argon**, **fission track**), which relies on the known rates of radioisotopic decay of elements to their stable isotopes. Non-radiometric methods can also be used to provide relative dates including the chemical analysis of bones, biostratigraphy, and even using tree rings.

Radiometric dating methods

Uranium-lead

Measures the decay of the two main isotopes of uranium (^{235}U and ^{238}U) into lead in igneous rocks. The ratio of these elements can be used to determine the time since the rocks formed.

Uranium series

Measures the decay of uranium-234 into thorium-230 in marine carbonates (e.g. corals). Uranium-234 is soluble and is incorporated into coral skeletons. As it decays, it produces thorium-230. The age of the coral is determined by the uranium to thorium ratio.

Fission track

When uranium decays, the subatomic particles emitted leave tracks through the mineral. The number of tracks increases over time and this can be used to calculate the time since the rock formed. Fission track dating is useful for dating pottery, glass, and volcanic minerals.

Potassium/argon (K-Ar)

Measures the decay of potassium-40 to argon-40 in volcanic rocks above or below fossil bearing strata. Argon is inert, so it only builds up in minerals by radioisotopic decay of potassium. The amount of argon is therefore related to the age of the rock.

Radiocarbon dating (carbon-14 or ^{14}C)

Measures the amount of the radioisotope carbon-14 (taken up by an organism when it was alive) within its fossilized remains. The older a sample is, the less ^{14}C there is to be detected.

Relative dating methods

Chemical analysis

Bones buried in the ground can absorb elements such as uranium and fluorine. The rate of absorption depends on factors in the immediate environment. Thus bones from the same site can be compared but bones from different sites cannot.

Stratigraphy

Layers of rock laid down oldest at the bottom to youngest at the top. Thus in areas where the layers are not severely deformed the order of deposition can be determined. Displaced deposits can be ordered using knowledge of the order of nearby deposits.

Biostratigraphy

The remains of organisms are incorporated as fossils as deposits are laid down. Older fossils are therefore found below younger ones. Some fossils are characteristic of various layers and times and can be used to date newly found rock layers.

Paleomagnetism

Magnetic minerals in rocks lock-in a record of the Earth's magnetic field when they form. The record of geomagnetic reversals preserved in rock sequences provides a time-scale that is used as a geochronological tool.

Obsidian hydration

Obsidian is a natural volcanic glass used by prehistoric humans to produce blades. The manufacture of these blades zeros the mineral hydration clock. Over time, the mineral becomes hydrated. If the hydration rate is known, an age can be obtained.

1. When the date of a sample has been determined, it is common practice to express it in the following manner: Example: **1.88 ± 0.02** million years old. Explain what the **± 0.02** means in this case:

2. Explain why it is best to test many small samples to find a date when dating a specimen using radiometric dating:

3. Suggest a possible source of error that could account for an incorrect dating measurement using radiocarbon dating:

4. Explain why relative dating methods can not give exact dates of when specimens formed or died:

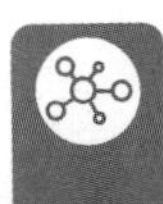

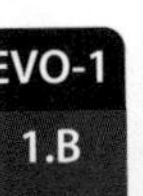

ISBN: 978-1-98-856656-6

169 Relative Dating and the Fossil Record

Key Question: How are fossils in a rock profile dated by relative dating?

Relative dating establishes the sequential (relative) order of past events in a rock profile, but it cannot provide an absolute date for an event. Each rock layer (**stratum**) is unique in terms of the type of rock (sedimentary or volcanic) and the type of fossils it contains. Rock layers (**strata**) are arranged in the order that they were deposited, with the oldest layers at the bottom (unless disturbed by geological events). This is called the **law of superposition**. Strata from widespread locations with the same fossils or characteristics can be correlated, even when their absolute date is unknown.

Profile with sedimentary rocks containing fossils

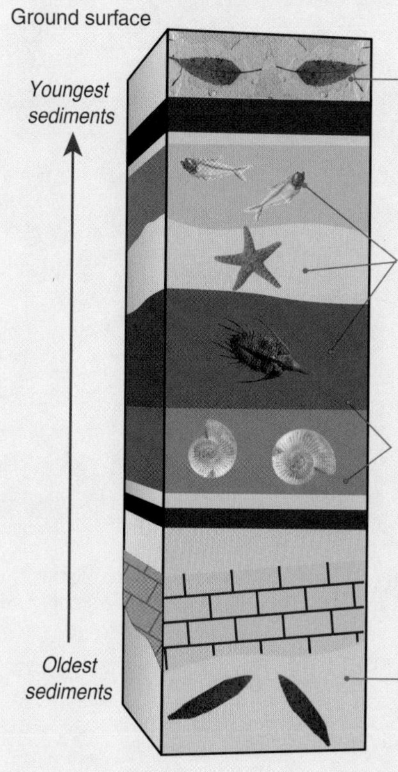

Recent fossils are found in more recent sediments
The more recent the layer of rock, the more resemblance there is between the fossils found in it and living forms.

Many extinct species
The number of extinct species is far greater than the number of species living today.

Fossil types differ in each stratum
Fossils in any given layer of sedimentary rock are generally quite different to fossils in other layers.

More primitive fossils are found in older sediments
Phyla are represented by more generalized forms in the older layers, and not by specialized forms (such as those alive today).

What is relative dating?

Relative dating is a way to determine the relative order of past events without necessarily determining absolute (chronometric) age. The same rocks and fossils can then be used to correlate stratigraphic records in different places. Material that can't be dated using absolute methods can therefore be correlated with the same material elsewhere for which an absolute date may be available.

New fossil types mark changes in environment

In the rocks marking the end of one geologic period, it is common to find many new fossils that become dominant in the next. Each geologic period had an environment very different from those before and after. Their boundaries coincided with drastic environmental changes and the appearance of new niches. New selection pressures resulted in new adaptive features as species responded to the changes. An absolute age can be assigned to fossils, usually by dating the rocks around them. Most often, this involves radiometric dating (e.g. radiocarbon, K-Ar).

The fossil record of proboscidea

African and Asian elephants have descended from a diverse group known as **proboscideans** (named for their long trunks). The first pig-sized, trunkless members of this group lived in Africa 40 million years ago. From Africa, their descendants invaded all continents except Antarctica and Australia. As the group evolved, they became larger, an effective evolutionary response to deter predators. Examples of extinct members of this group are illustrated below:

Columbian mammoth
Pleistocene, Costa Rica to northern US. Range overlap with woolly mammoths in the north.
~4 m at the shoulder

Deinotherium
Miocene-Pleistocene, Asia, Africa
~4 m at the shoulder

Gomphotherium
Miocene, Europe, Africa
~ 3 m at the shoulder

Platybelodon
One of several genera of shovel-tuskers. Middle Miocene, Northern Asia, Europe, Africa
~3 m at the shoulder

- **Modern day species can be traced:** The evolution of many present-day species can be very well reconstructed. For instance, the evolutionary history of the modern elephants is exceedingly well documented for the last 40 million years. The modern horse also has a well understood fossil record spanning the last 50 million years.
- **Fossil species are similar to but differ from today's species**: Most fossil animals and plants belong to the same major taxonomic groups as organisms living today. However, they do differ from the living species in many features.

1. Explain the importance of fossils in relative dating: ______________________

____

____

____

____

ISBN: 978-1-98-856656-6

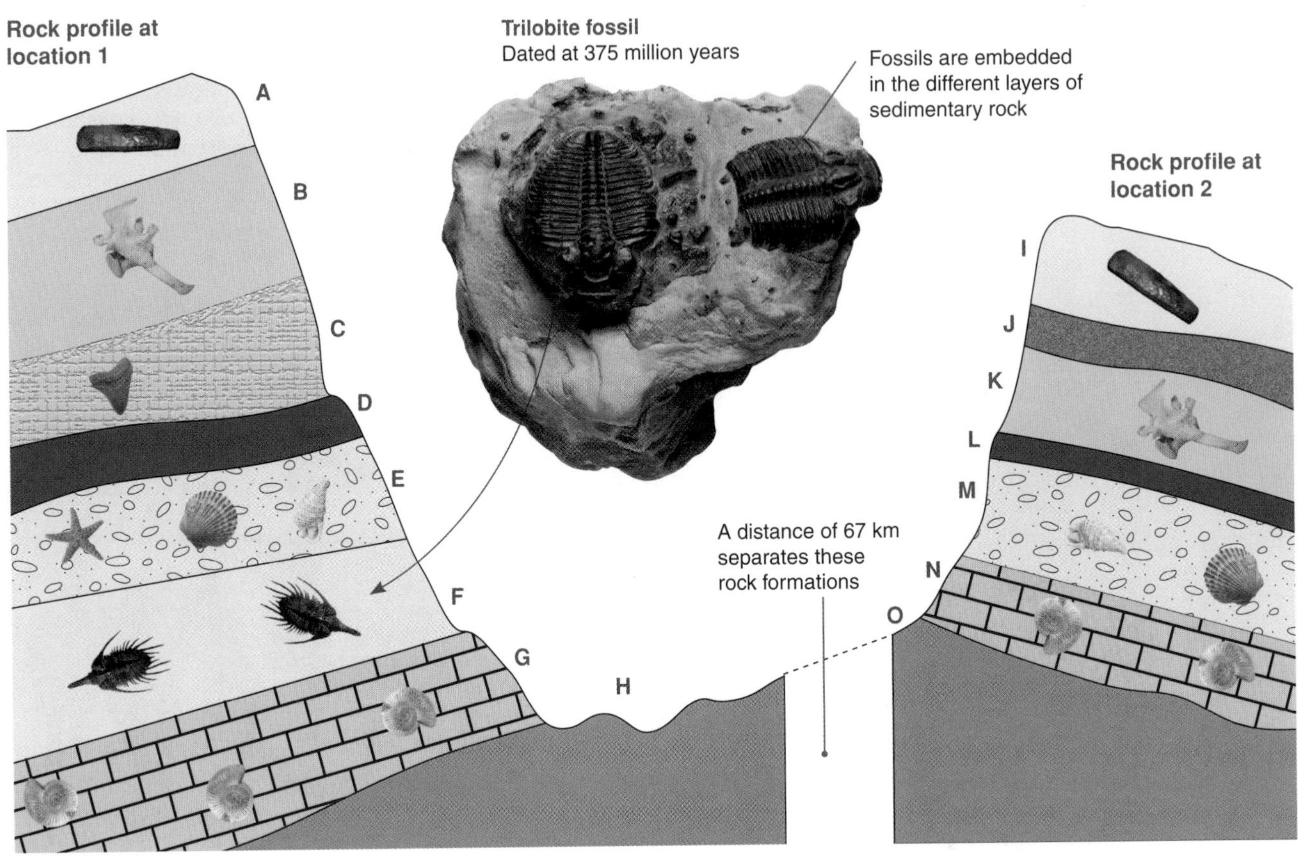

The questions below relate to the diagram above, showing a hypothetical rock profile from two locations separated by a distance of 67 km. There are some differences between the rock layers at the two locations. Apart from layers D and L which are volcanic ash deposits, all other layers comprise sedimentary rock.

2. Assuming there has been no geologic activity (e.g. tilting or folding), state in which rock layer (A-O) you would find:

   (a) The youngest rocks at location 1: ______________________

   (b) The oldest rocks at location 1: ______________________

   (c) The youngest rocks at location 2: ______________________

   (d) The oldest rocks at location 2: ______________________

3. (a) State which layer at location 1 is of the same age as layer M at location 2: ______________________

   (b) Explain the reason for your answer above: ______________________

4. The rocks in layer H and O are sedimentary rocks. Explain why there are no visible fossils in these layers:

   ____

5. (a) State which layers present at location 1 are missing at location 2: ______________________

   (b) State which layers present at location 2 are missing at location 1: ______________________

6. Using radiometric dating, the trilobite fossil was determined to be approximately 375 million years old. The volcanic rock layer (D) was dated at 270 million years old, while rock layer B was dated at 80 million years old. Give the approximate age range (i.e. greater than, less than, or between given dates) of the rock layers listed below:

   (a) Layer A: ______________________

   (b) Layer C: ______________________

   (c) Layer E: ______________________

   (d) Layer G: ______________________

   (e) Layer L: ______________________

   (f) Layer O: ______________________

7. Suggest why gaps in the fossil record can make it difficult to determine an evolutionary history: ______________________

ISBN: 978-1-98-856656-6

170 Chronometric Dating

Key Question: What radiometric techniques can be used for chronometric dating of fossil and other natural and human-made materials?

Many chronometric dating methods rely on the decay of radioactive isotopes (radioisotopes) to calculate the age of a specimen. A radioisotope may go through multiple decay events (a decay series) before reaching a stable non-radioactive isotope. The ratio of the original radioisotope to the stable isotope can be used to calculate the age of the specimen. In some cases the ratios of the different elements within the decay series can be used. Radioactivity can be used to date both once living (e.g. bone) or nonliving (e.g. volcanic rocks) materials. Isotopes are taken up by living organisms at relatively constant rates so that when they die the amount of radioisotope left in the body can be compared to that of living organisms to find a date of death.

Radioactive decay

The rate of decay of a radioisotope is measured by its half-life. **A half-life** is the time it takes for half the atoms in a sample of radioactive substance to decay into a new element, or the time in which there is a 50% chance any particular atom will have decayed. For example, uranium-238 has a half life of 4.5 billion years. Starting with a sample of 10 g of uranium-238, after 4.5 billion years there would be 5 g of uranium-238 and 5 g of various other elements (mostly lead) in the sample.

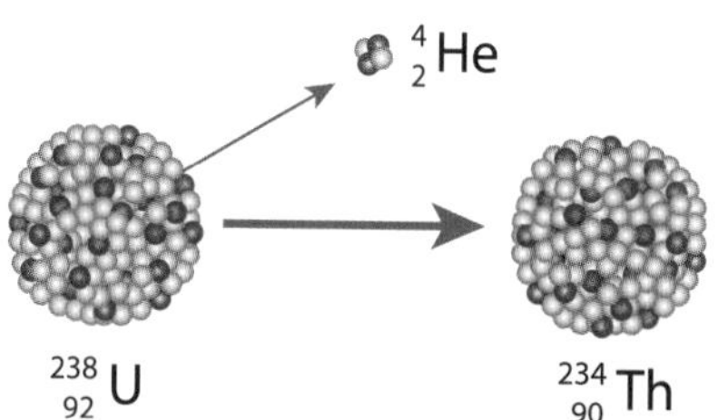

Uranium-238 has a half live of 4.5 billion years and decays to thorium-234. Thorium-234 has a half life of just 24.5 days.

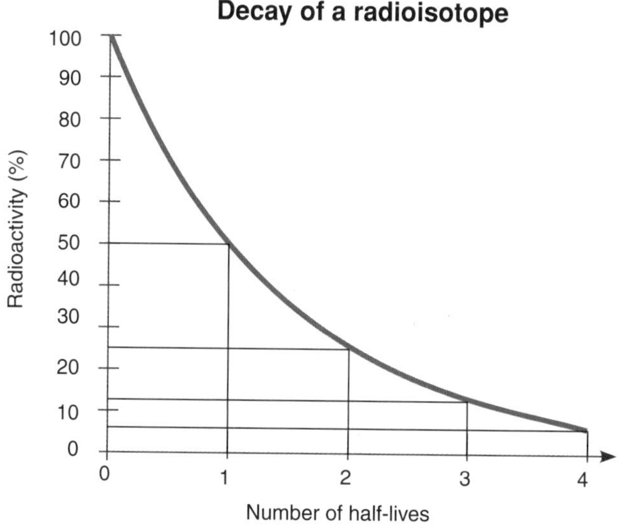

Isotope	Half-life
Uranium-238	4.5 billion years
Uranium-235	700 million years
Thorium-234	24.5 days
Thorium-230	76,000 years
Radium-226	1600 years
Lead-210	22 years
Potassium-40	1.25 billion years
Carbon-14	5730 years

Dating using radioactivity

The length of the half-life and the type of sample being dated are important when considering which dating method to use. Beyond a certain number of half-lives, the amount of radioisotope left may become so small that accurate dating becomes impossible.

Usable dating range in years *(Log scale)*: 1 billion, 100 million, 10 million, 1 million, 100,000, 10,000, 1000

Dating method	Datable materials
Fission track	Pottery, glass, and volcanic minerals
Radiocarbon	Wood, shells, peat, charcoal, bone, animal tissue, calcite, soil
Potassium/argon	Volcanic rocks and minerals
Uranium series	Marine carbonate, coral, mollusc shells
Uranium-lead	Rocks containing zircon minerals

Pottery amphora

Bone

Basalt

Mollusc shell

ISBN: 978-1-98-856656-6

Non-isotopic methods

Some methods for chronometric dating do not rely on measuring half-lives. Instead they use other properties of atoms in the sample, including electron spins and emission of light.

Electron spin resonance (ESR)

When minerals are exposed to radiation (e.g. cosmic rays or radioactive decay) their electrons may be knocked from one energy level to a higher energy level. As they return to the lower energy level they may become trapped between energy levels. Under ESR, these electrons can be detected and the number of electrons relates to the length of time since the sample formed. This method is useful for dating objects such as burnt flints, cave sediments, bone, teeth, and loess (wind-blown deposits).

Thermoluminescence

This method is useful for dating objects including ceramics, quartz, feldspar, and carbonates. It works by measuring the accumulated radiation dose (e.g. radioactivity or sunlight) of a crystalline sample. When the sample is heated, it emits light in proportion to the radiation dose. The larger the dose the older the object. Measurements of surrounding radiation can be used to identify the annual dose. The method is relatively cheap but requires the destruction of a significant amount of the sample.

1. Examine the diagram at the bottom of the previous page and describe the approximate dating range and datable materials for each of the methods listed below (Note the logarithmic time scale on the diagram):

   (a) Potassium-argon method: ______________________

   (b) Radiocarbon method: ______________________

   (c) Uranium series: ______________________

2. Radiocarbon dating compares the amount of carbon-14 in dead material to the amount in living material (adjusted to natural variations).

   (a) A piece of tree branch found in sediments of an ancient swamp is radiocarbon dated and found to have about 3% of the expected amount of ^{14}C in a living tree. Calculate the age of the tree:

   ____

   (b) Another tree branch from the same sediments is radiocarbon dated to 150,000 years. Is this date likely to be accurate? Explain your answer:

   ____

3. Use the following data to place the fossils A to E in the correct layers along with the age of the layers:
   Fossil C is never found with fossils A, B, D, and E. Fossil B is found in the same layers as fossil D. Fossil D is found below a layer of volcanic ash dated at 20 million years (MY) old. Fossil A is found above a layer of volcanic ash dated at 10 million years old. Fossil E is never found with any other fossils, but it resembles a fossil found elsewhere below a layer of rock dated at 27 million years old. Fossil B shows more derived skeletal features than fossil E.

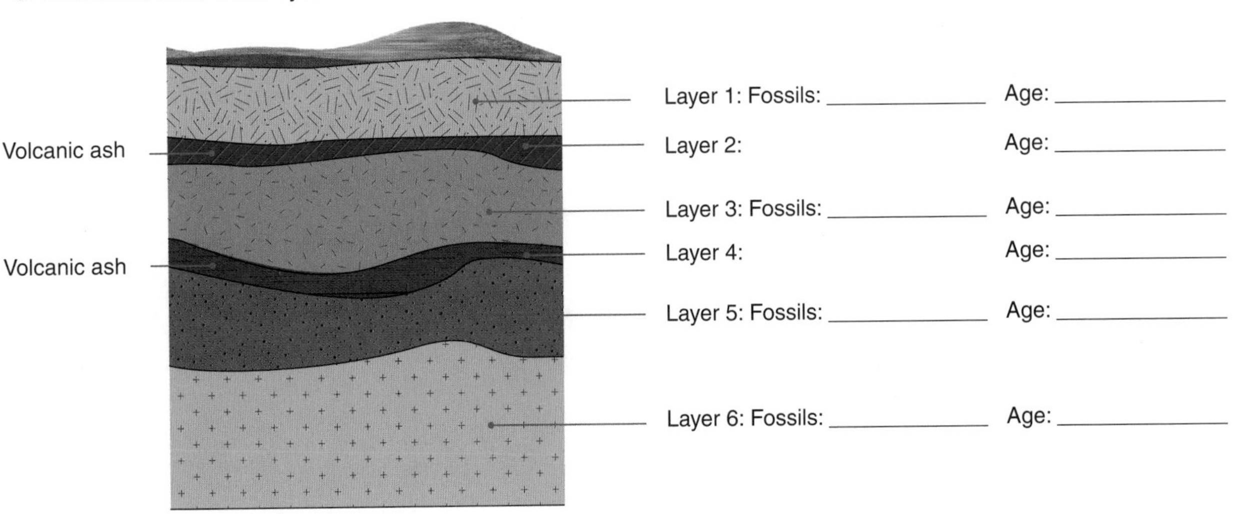

ISBN: 978-1-98-856656-6

171 Homologous Structures

Key Question: What are homologous structures and how do they provide evidence of evolution?

Homologous structures (homologies) are structural similarities present as a result of common ancestry. In air-breathing vertebrates, the bones of the forelimbs have the same components arranged in a comparable pattern. The early land vertebrates were amphibians with a **pentadactyl limb** structure (a limb with five fingers or toes). The pattern of bones in the forelimbs of all vertebrates that descended from these early amphibians indicates this common ancestry. They also illustrate the phenomenon known as **adaptive radiation**. The common structural components have been adapted to different purposes in different taxa as they evolved to occupy a diversity of different niches.

Generalized pentadactyl limb

The fore and hind limbs have the same arrangement of bones but they have different names. In many cases, the basic limb plan has been adapted (e.g. by loss or fusion of bones) to meet the requirements of different niches (e.g. during adaptive radiation of the mammals).

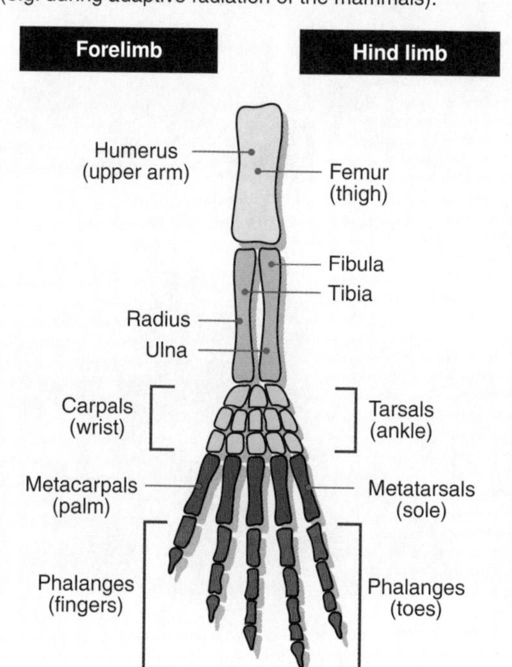

Specializations of pentadactyl limbs

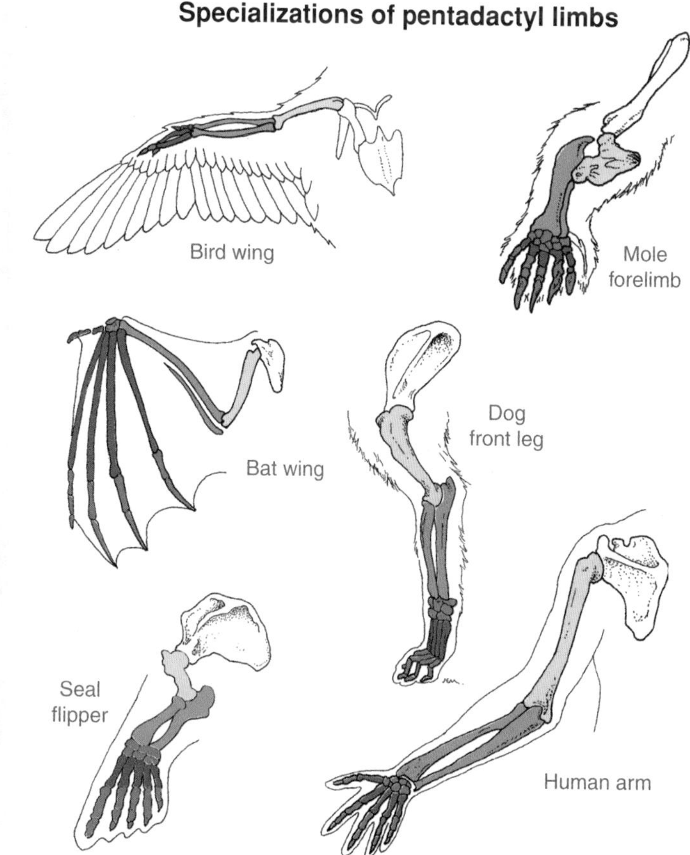

1. Briefly describe the purpose of the major anatomical change that has taken place in each of the limb examples above:

 (a) Bird wing: Highly modified for flight. Forelimb is shaped for aerodynamic lift and feather attachment.

 (b) Human arm: ________

 (c) Seal flipper: ________

 (d) Dog front leg: ________

 (e) Mole forelimb: ________

 (f) Bat wing: ________

2. Explain how homology in the pentadactyl limb provides evidence for adaptive radiation: ________

3. Homology in the innate behavior of animals (for example, sharing similar courtship or nesting rituals) is sometimes used to indicate the degree of relatedness between groups. How could behavior be used in this way?

ISBN: 978-1-98-856656-6

172 Vestigial Structures

Key Question: How does the persistence of vestigial structures provides evidence for common ancestry?

Vestigial structures are anatomical features that have been retained through a species' evolution but have lost most or all of their ancestral function (although they may retain some lesser function). Vestigial structures are often homologous to structures that retain their usual function in other species and so present evidence for biological evolution. For example, the human tail bone (coccyx) has lost its original function (balance and mobility) and is homologous to the fully functioning tail in many other primates. It retains a function in anchoring some pelvic muscles.

Vestigial structures

- Maintaining a structure (or behavior) that offers no benefit to fitness is costly. This means that there will be selection pressure for regression of characters with a function that is no longer required.
- Vestigial structures can therefore be used as evidence for relatedness by their presence. For example, the vestigial wing bones in birds such as emus and kiwi show they are related to flighted birds. Flightlessness is an evolved trait in response to environments where flight was not necessary for survival.
- In another example, along with other evidence, the vestigial limbs in pythons (far right), indicate they are related to reptiles that once walked with all four limbs.

Emus have vestigial wings hidden beneath their feathers. They still have a minor role in balance.

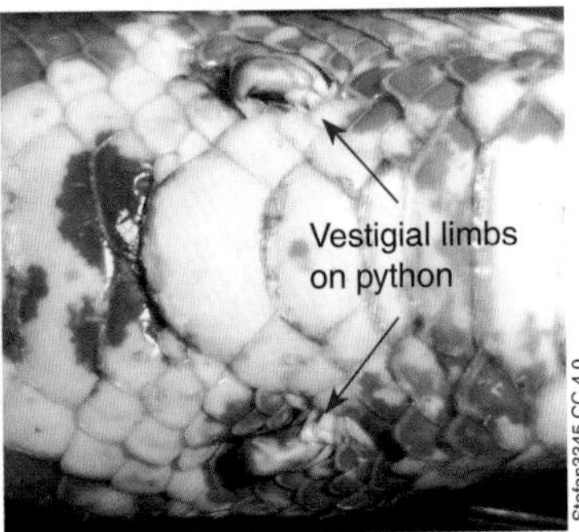

The vestigial limbs in pythons and boa constrictors are one indication of their relatedness to lizards.

Vestigial behaviors

- Vestigiality can also be seen in behaviors. Wild dogs turn around several times before lying down, to trample down vegetation and check for safety. Domestic dogs still exhibit this behavior even through it is no longer needed in human homes.
- The Galápagos flightless cormorant has small stubby wings too small for flying. Yet after coming out of the sea it still hold its wings out to dry the same as its flighted relatives. In flying cormorants, this behavior dries the wings in preparation for flight. But because flightless cormorants obviously don't fly, this behavior serves no purpose.

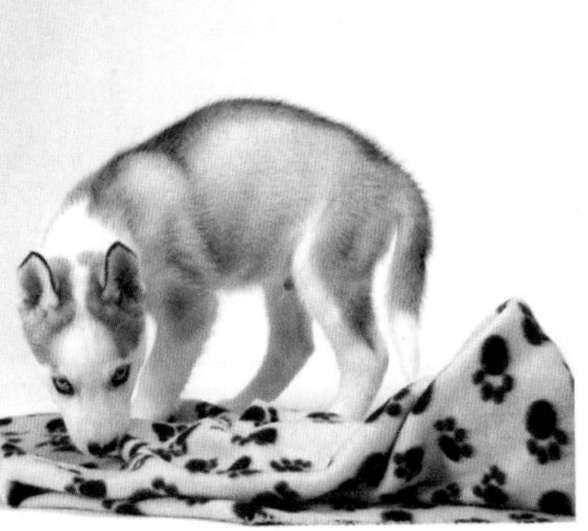

1. In terms of natural selection, explain how structures that were once functional could become vestigial:

2. Explain why some vestigial structures do not disappear altogether:

3. Explain how vestigial structures can show relationships between organisms:

4. Explain how vestigial behaviors can show relationships between organisms:

ISBN: 978-1-98-856656-6

173 Homologous Proteins

Key Question: How can the differences in proteins with similar roles in different species indicate common ancestry?

Proteins are the product of gene expression, so an analysis of the differences between the same protein in different taxa gives an indication of species relatedness. Traditionally, phylogenies were based largely on anatomical traits, and biologists attempted to determine the relationships between taxa based on similarity or by tracing the appearance of key characteristics. With the advent of new molecular techniques, homologies (similarities arising from shared ancestry) could be studied at the molecular level as well and the results compared to phylogenies established using other methods. Protein sequencing provides an excellent tool for establishing homologies. A protein has a specific number of amino acids arranged in a specific order. Any differences in the sequence reflect changes in the DNA sequence. Commonly studied proteins include blood proteins, such as hemoglobin, and the respiratory protein cytochrome c.

Hemoglobin homology

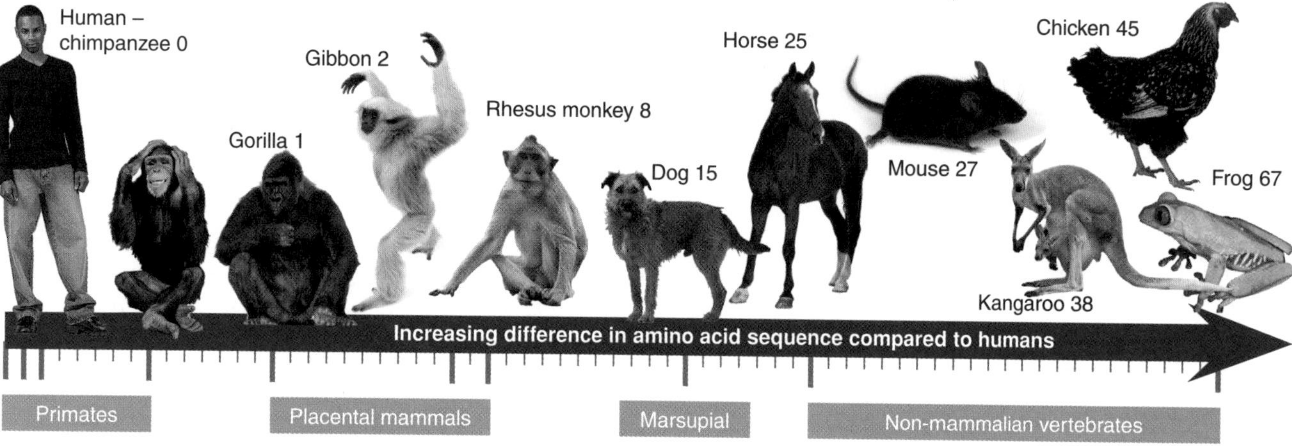

Hemoglobin is the oxygen-transporting blood protein found in most vertebrates. The beta chain hemoglobin sequences from different organisms can be compared to determine evolutionary relationships.

As genetic relatedness decreases, the number of amino acid differences between the hemoglobin beta chains of different vertebrates increases (above). For example, there are no amino acid differences between humans and chimpanzees, indicating they recently shared a common ancestor. Humans and frogs have 67 amino acid differences, indicating they had a common ancestor a very long time ago.

Highly conserved proteins

Some proteins are common in many different species. These proteins are called highly conserved proteins, meaning they change (mutate) very little over time. This is because they have critical roles in the organism (e.g. in cellular respiration) and mutations are likely to be lethal.

Evidence indicates that highly conserved proteins are homologous and have been derived from a common ancestor. Because they are highly conserved, changes in the amino acid sequence are likely to represent major divergences between groups during the course of evolution.

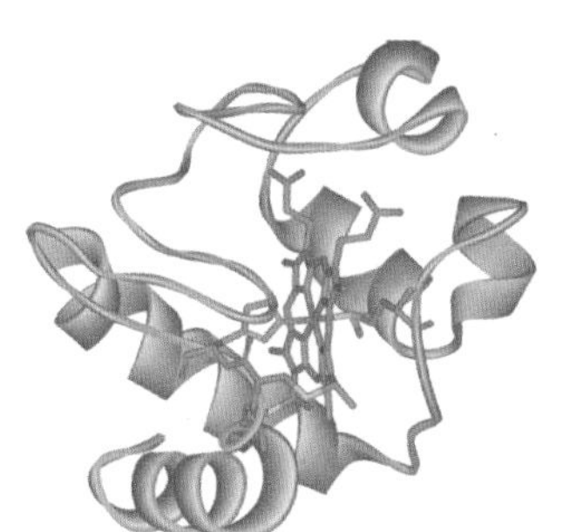

Cytochrome C (left) is a respiratory protein located in the electron transport chain in mitochondria.

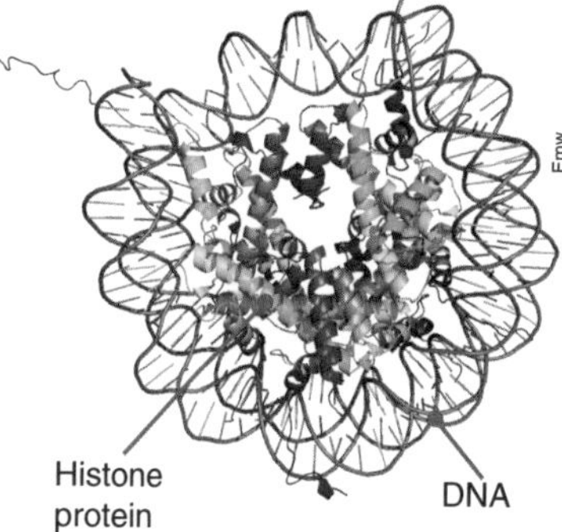

Histones (right) are a family of proteins that associate with DNA and organise it so that it can fit inside the cell nucleus.

1. (a) What is a highly conserved protein? ______________________________

(b) What type of proteins tend to be highly conserved? ______________________________

(c) Why are the proteins named in (b) highly conserved? ______________________________

(d) Why are highly conserved proteins good for constructing phylogenies? ______________________________

ISBN: 978-1-98-856656-6

Using immunology to determine phylogeny

The immune system of one species will recognise the blood proteins of another species as foreign and form antibodies against them. This property can be used to determine the extent of relatedness between species. Blood proteins, such as albumins, are used to prepare **antiserum** in rabbits, a distantly related species. The antiserum contains antibodies against the test blood proteins (e.g. human) and will react to those proteins in any blood sample they are mixed with. The extent of the reaction indicates how similar the proteins are; the greater the reaction, the more similar the proteins. This principle is illustrated (right) for antiserum produced to human blood and its reaction with the blood of other primates and a rat.

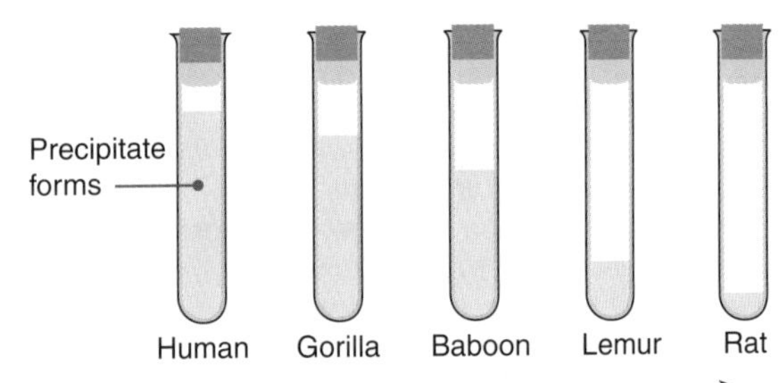

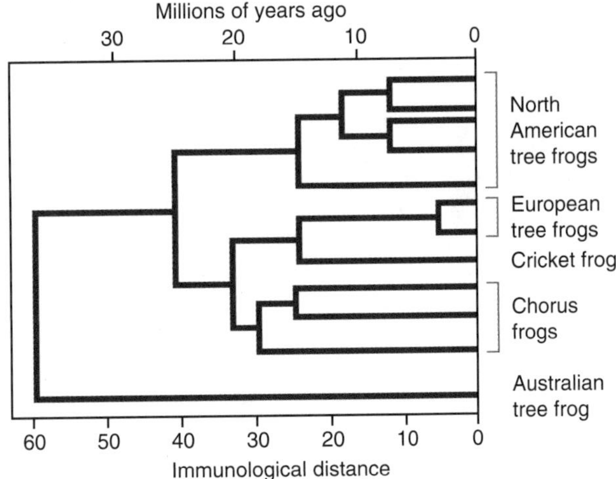

The relationships among tree frogs have been established by immunological studies based on blood proteins such as immunoglobulins and albumins. The **immunological distance** is a measure of the number of amino acid substitutions between two groups. This, in turn, has been calibrated to provide a time scale showing when the various related groups diverged.

2. (a) Compare the differences in the hemoglobin sequence of humans, rhesus monkeys, and horses. What do these tell you about the relative relatedness of these organisms?

(b) If the differences in the amino acid sequences in hemoglobin were not a result of evolutionary relatedness (i.e. the differences were unrelated to the time the species have been separated), what pattern of differences might be seen?

3. (a) Human antiserum extracted from the rabbit contains what kind of antibodies?

(b) If the antiserum was added to human albumin what percentage of reaction would you expect to see (e.g. 100% = full reaction 0% = no reaction).

(c) Now explain why human antiserum reacts more with gorilla albumin than with rat albumin:

(d) Explain how these reactions can be used to determine species relationships:

ISBN: 978-1-98-856656-6

174 What Can Highly Conserved Proteins Tell Us?

Key Question: What are highly conserved proteins and what can they tell us about evolutionary relationships?

Some proteins are common in many different species. These proteins are called highly conserved proteins, meaning they change (mutate) very little over time. This is because they have critical roles in the organism (e.g. in cellular respiration) and mutations are likely to be lethal. Evidence indicates that highly conserved proteins are homologous and have been derived from a common ancestor. Because they are highly conserved, changes in the amino acid sequence are likely to represent major divergences between groups during the course of evolution. Examples of highly conserved proteins are cytochrome c, a respiratory protein (below) and the Pax-6 protein (bottom).

Cytochrome *c* compared between species

		1	2	3	4	5	6	7	8	9	10	11	12	13	14	15	16	17	18	19	20	21	22
Human		Gly	Asp	Val	Glu	Lys	Gly	Lys	Lys	Ile	Phe	Ile	Met	Lys	Cys	Ser	Gln	Cys	His	Thr	Val	Glu	Lys
Pig												Val	Gln			Ala							
Chicken				Ile						Val		Val	Gln			Ala							
Dogfish										Val		Val	Gln			Ala							Asn
Drosophila	<<									Leu		Val	Gln	Arg		Ala							Ala
Wheat	<<		Asn	Pro	Asp	Ala		Ala				Lys	Thr	Arg		Ala						Asp	Ala
Yeast	<<		Ser	Ala	Lys			Ala	Thr	Leu		Lys	Thr	Arg		Glu	Leu						

Cytochrome C (right) is a respiratory protein located in the electron transport chain in mitochondria. Highly conserved proteins, such as cytochrome c, change very little over time and between species because they carry out important roles and if they changed too much they may no longer function properly.

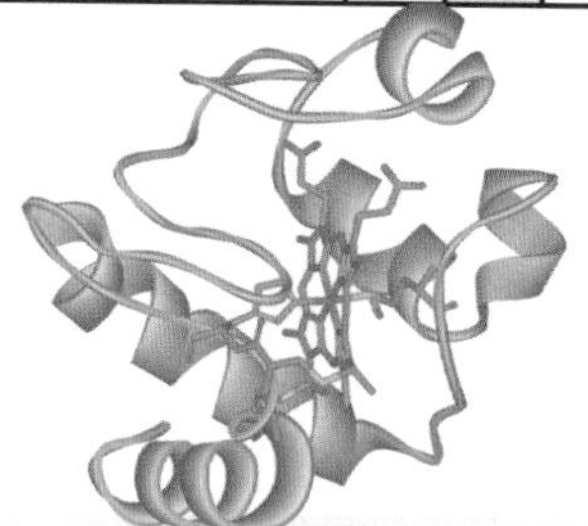

The table above shows the N-terminal 22 amino acid residues of human cytochrome c, with corresponding sequences from other organisms aligned beneath. Sequences are aligned to give the most position matches. A shaded square indicates no change. In every case, the cytochrome's heme group is attached to the Cys-14 and Cys-17. In *Drosophila*, wheat, and yeast, arrows indicate that several amino acids precede the sequence shown.

The Pax-6 protein provides evidence for evolution

- The Pax-6 gene belongs to a family of master genes that regulate the formation of a number of organs, including the eye, during embryonic development.
- The Pax-6 gene produces the Pax-6 protein, which acts as a transcription factor to control the expression of other genes.
- Scientists know the role of Pax-6 in eye development because they created a knockout model in mice where the Pax-6 gene is not expressed. The knockout model is eyeless or has very underdeveloped eyes.
- The Pax-6 gene is so highly conserved that the gene from one species can be inserted into another species, and still produce a normal eye.
- This suggests the Pax-6 proteins are homologous, and the gene has been inherited from a common ancestor.

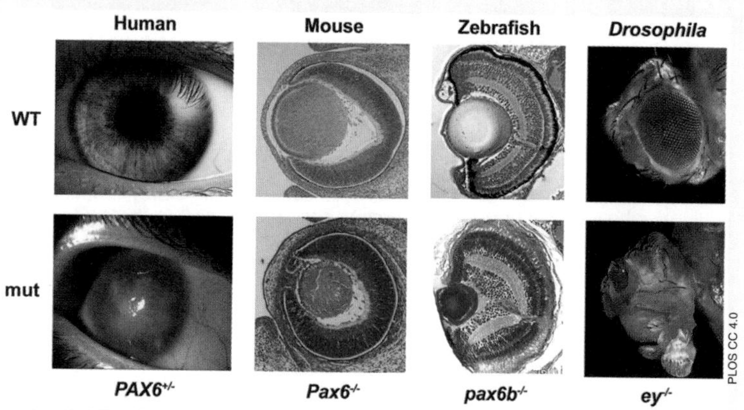

The images above show the effect of a non-functional Pax-6 gene. In all cases, a non-functional gene leads to non-functional eyes. In the case of the *Drosophila* the eye is missing. Experiments have shown that Pax-6 genes work across species. When a mouse Pax-6 gene was inserted into fly DNA and turned on in the fly's legs, the fly developed morphologically normal eyes on its legs!

1. Use the cytochrome c table above to answer the following:

   (a) Which two organisms in the table are most distantly related? Explain your answer: ____________

   ____

   ____

   (b) Which two organisms in the table are most closely related? Explain your answer: ____________

   ____

   ____

ISBN: 978-1-98-856656-6

Cytochrome *c* and phylogeny

Because conserved proteins are found across many species they can be used to create a phylogeny showing species relationships based on their mutations. The molecular clock hypothesis states that mutations occur at a relatively constant rate for any given gene. The genetic difference between any two species can indicate when two species last shared a common ancestor and can be used to construct a phylogenetic tree. The molecular clock for each species, and each protein, may run at different rates, so molecular clock data is calibrated with other evidence (e.g. morphological) to confirm phylogeny. Molecular clock calculations are carried out on DNA or amino acid sequences.

In this hypothetical example, the DNA sequence for a gene in two species (A and B) alive today differs by four bases. The mutation rate for the gene is approximately one base per 25 million years. Based on this rate, it can be determined that the common ancestor for these two species lived 50 million years ago.

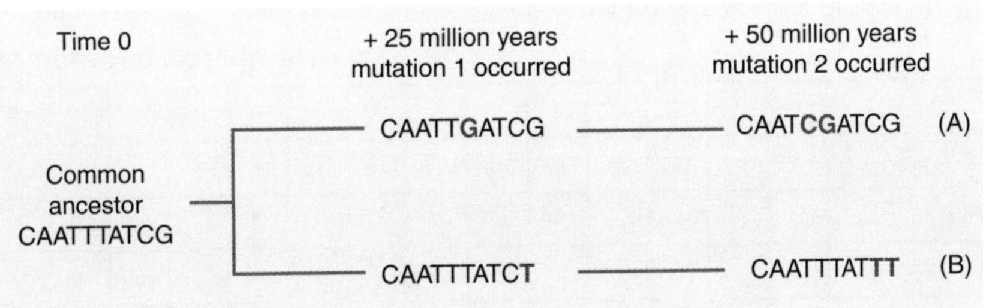

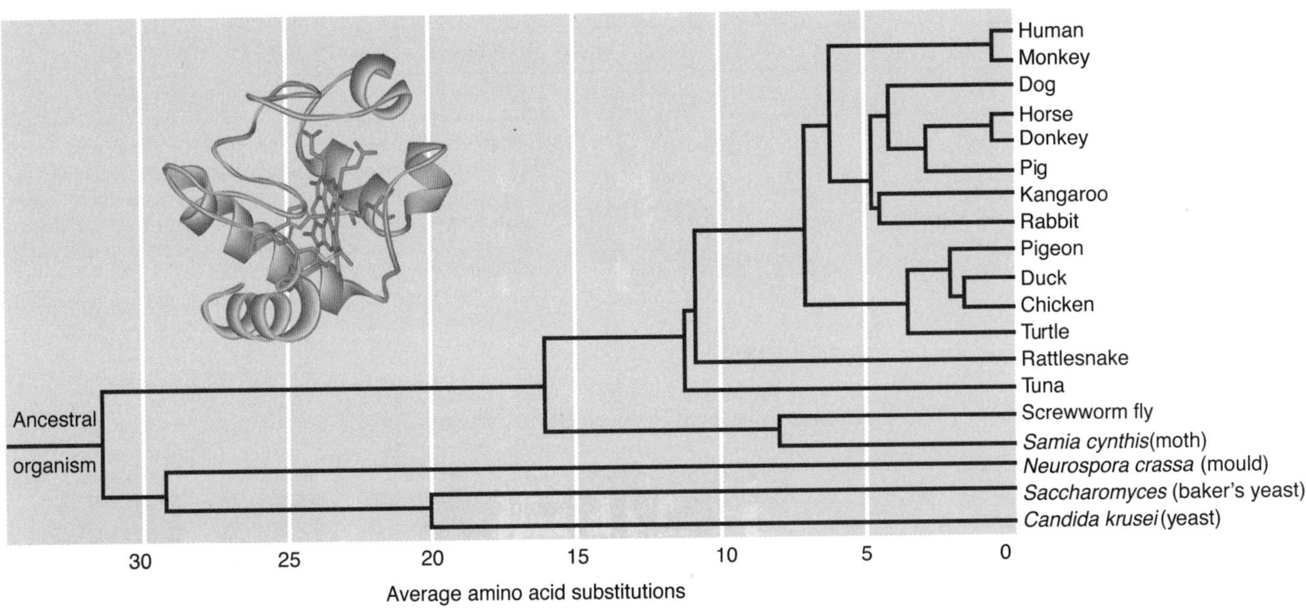

2. For cytochrome *c*, suggest why amino acids 14 and 17 are unchanged in all the organisms shown in the table: ________

3. (a) Describe the role of the Pax-6 gene: ________

   (b) What evidence is there that the Pax-6 protein is highly conserved? ________

4. (a) Describe a limitation of using molecular clocks to establish phylogeny: ________

   (b) Why are highly conserved proteins good for constructing phylogenies? ________

ISBN: 978-1-98-856656-6

175 Genomic Comparisons and Relatedness

Key Question: Relationships between species can be assessed by comparing the DNA directly.

Protein studies can show relatedness between species, but since those proteins are based on the DNA sequence, it makes sense to study the DNA directly. There are two main methods of doing this. An older technique is called DNA hybridization (below). The method provides information only about how much of the DNA is the same but cannot provide specific information about what the similarities or differences are. It has largely been superseded by direct DNA sequencing (opposite), which provides more accurate information about where the differences in the DNA occur.

1. Explain how DNA hybridization can give a measure of genetic relatedness between species:

2. Explain why the double strands of DNA break when they are heated:

3. What is responsible for the hybridization between the DNA strands?

4. The graph below shows the results of a DNA hybridization between humans and other primates.

Similarity of human DNA to that of other primates

Primate species	DNA similarity (%)
Human	100%
Chimpanzee	97.6%
Gibbon	94.7%
Rhesus monkey	91.1%
Vervet monkey	90.5%
Capuchin monkey	84.2%
Galago	58.0%

(a) Which primate is most closely related to humans?

(b) Which primate is most distantly related to humans?

5. Hybrid DNA from species A and B comes apart at a lower temperature that of species A and C. Which species is A most closely related to?

DNA hybridization technique

1. DNA from the two species to be compared is extracted, purified and cut into short fragments.
2. The mixture is heated so the DNA separates. The DNA from the two species is mixed together.
3. As it cools, bonds form between compatible nucleotides. Hybrid double-stranded DNA forms.
4. If species share low similarity, the hybrid DNA will have few bonds (and the strands will be weakly held together). The number of bonds (and therefore the strength of the hybrid DNA) increases with increasing similarity.
5. The similarity is measured by heating the hybrid DNA to force it to form single strands. The greater the similarity, the more heat that is required to break the hybrid DNA apart.

Human DNA

Chimpanzee DNA

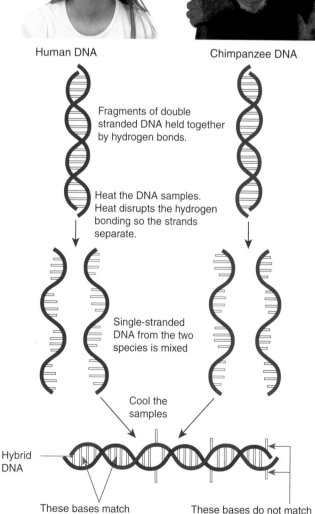

Fragments of double stranded DNA held together by hydrogen bonds.

Heat the DNA samples. Heat disrupts the hydrogen bonding so the strands separate.

Single-stranded DNA from the two species is mixed

Cool the samples

Hybrid DNA

These bases match

These bases do not match

ISBN: 978-1-98-856656-6

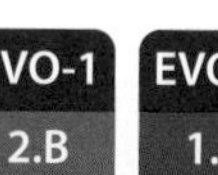

DNA sequencing

DNA sequencing provides the precise order of nucleotides in a DNA molecule. This information, which can now be analysed using sophisticated computing, allows researchers to compare sequences between species in much more detail than is possible with DNA hybridization. Not only can areas of difference be identified, but the variation between the nucleotides at a certain position can be determined. This information allows researchers to more accurately determine the relatedness between species, even between those with very minor differences.

Comparing DNA sequences

Improved DNA sequencing techniques and powerful computing software have allowed researchers to accurately and quickly sequence and compare entire genomes (all an organism's genetic material) within and between species.

Once DNA sequences have been determined, they are aligned and compared to see where the differences occur (right). DNA sequencing generates large volumes of data and the rise in computing power has been central to modern sequence analyses. The technological advances have been behind the new field of bioinformatics, which uses computer science, statistics, mathematics, and engineering to analyze and interpret biological data.

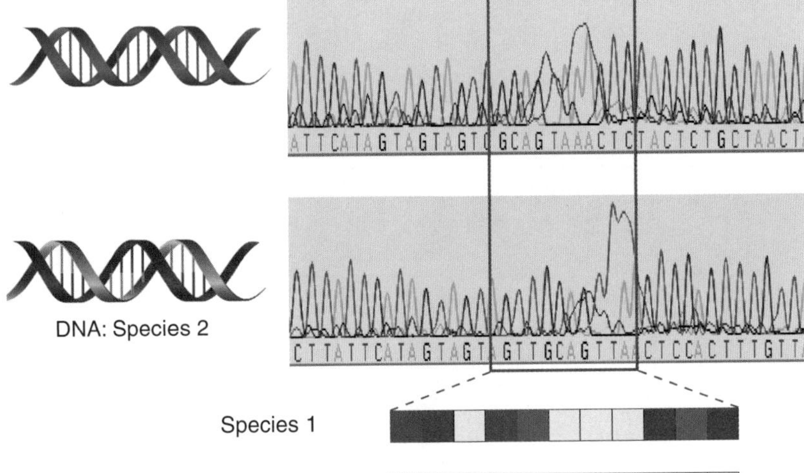

What type of sequences are compared?

Highly conserved sequences are often used for comparative genomic analysis because they are found in many organisms. The changes (mutations) of the sequences over time can be used to determine evolutionary relationships. As with other forms of molecular analysis, species with fewer nucleotide differences are more closely related than those with many.

Whole genome analysis has been important in classifying the primates. Historical views attributed special status to humans which often confused primate classification schemes. DNA evidence provides impartial quantitative evidence and modern classification schemes have been based on this data.

Based on DNA evidence, chimpanzees (center) are more closely related to humans than they are to gorillas (left) and there is no genetic basis for the taxon, "great apes".

6. (a) Compare the information obtained from DNA sequence comparisons relative to DNA hybridization:

____

____

____

(b) Explain why DNA sequence comparisons are therefore more useful in determining evolutionary relationships:

____

____

7. Three partial DNA sequences for three different species are presented below.

Species 1 ATGGCCCCCAACATTCGAAAATCGCACCCCCTGCTCAAAATTATCAAC

Species 2 ATGGCACCTAACATCCCCAACTCCCACCGTGTACTCAAAATCATCAAG

Species 3 ATGGCACCCAATATCCGCAAATCACACCCCCTGTTAAAAACAATCAAC

Based on the number of differences in the DNA sequences:

(a) Identify the two species that are most closely related: ______________________________

(b) Identify the two species that are the least closely related: ______________________________

ISBN: 978-1-98-856656-6

176 Gene Duplication and Evolution

Key Question: What do genomic comparisons reveal about the evolution and diversification of arthropod taxa?

Evolutionary developmental biology (or *evo-devo*) is a rapidly advancing area of evolutionary biology that examines how changes to developmental processes can result in the novel features we see appearing in evolutionary radiations.

Genomic comparisons among arthropod taxa have been important in revealing how the duplication and mutation of the genes regulating development have been involved in the evolution of novel structures and body plans. In particular, it explains how new characteristics in taxa can appear with apparent suddenness.

Evolution: you work with what you've got!

- Genomic studies have revealed the role of developmental genes in the evolution of novel forms and structures, and given valuable insight into the genetic mechanisms underlying evolutionary radiations.
- Arthropods, annelids, and vertebrates, all have highly modular bodies, i.e. the body is made up of repeating units. In arthropods, changes to individual segments through duplication and modification of genes has seen the evolution of a diverse range of body forms.
- For example, a gene involved in the development of appendages in arthropods can be duplicated and the duplicate gene modified. This produces modifications to some appendages, enabling a new set of functions without having to modify all other the appendages.

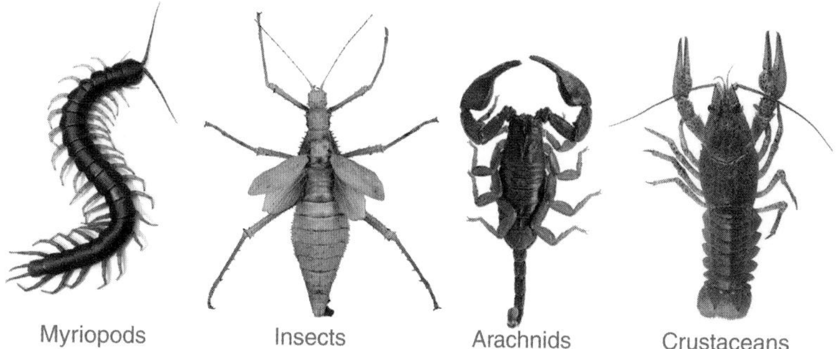

Evolution works with what is already present, and 'new' structures are just modifications of pre-existing structures. Segmental modifications produce a large amount of morphological variation in arthropods.

Developmental genes and arthropods

Antp

Scr *Antp*

Scr *Antp* *abd*

Scr *Antp* *Ubx* *abd-A*

- Head (mandible/maxillae)
- Head (other mouthparts)
- Thoracic legs
- Abdomen
- Wings
- Abdomen end

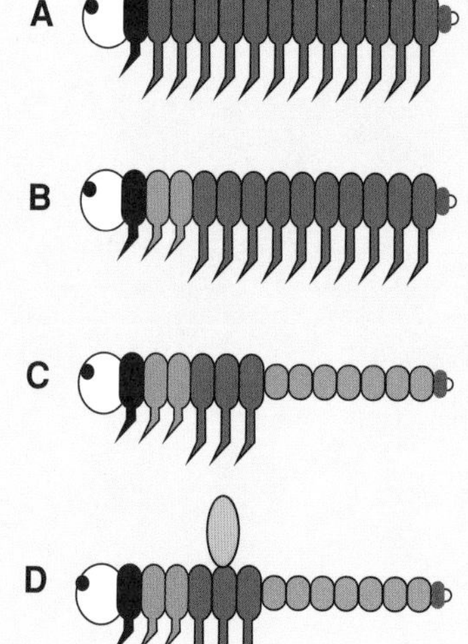

By looking at the DNA sequences in a series of genes we can piece together the order in which genes were duplicated and modified. The sequence above shows the order in which genes that are expressed in various parts of an arthropod appeared, starting with the original antennapedia (Antp) gene, which controls the development of appendages near the head.

We can identify which body segments the genes are expressed in and so work out the order in which body segments were modified. Above we start with a primitive arthropod (**A**). Three genes control development of the head, the middle segments, and the tail. Subsequent duplication and modification of genes produces an arthropod resembling a centipede (**B**), then a primitive wingless insect (**C**), and finally a modern winged insect (**D**).

1. Using the information above, explain how comparisons of developmental genes among different taxa can provide evidence for how different organisms are related and their evolutionary history:

ISBN: 978-1-98-856656-6

177 Descent and Common Ancestry

Key Question: How do we know there was a universal common ancestor?

Traditionally, the phylogeny (evolutionary history) of organisms was established using morphological comparisons. In recent decades, molecular techniques involving the analysis of DNA, RNA, and proteins have provided more information about how all life on Earth is related. These newer methods have enabled scientists to clarify the origin of the eukaryotes and to recognize two prokaryote domains. The universality of the genetic code and the similarities in the molecular machinery of all cells provide powerful evidence for a common ancestor to all life on Earth.

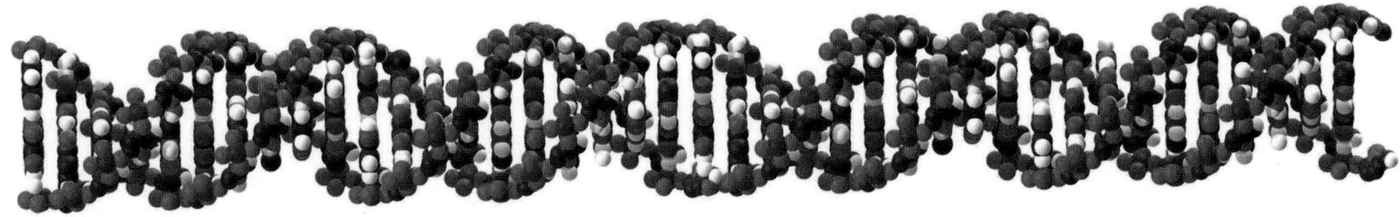

There is a universal genetic code (well almost)

DNA encodes the genetic instructions of all life. The form of these genetic instructions, called the **genetic code**, is effectively universal, i.e. the same combination of three DNA bases code for the same amino acid in almost all organisms. There are very few exceptions to this universality, restricted to mitochondrial DNA and the nuclear genome of a few protozoan species and the bacterium *Mycoplasma capricolum*. Notably, in these exceptions, a standard STOP codon encodes an amino acid. For example, UGA is normally a stop codon, but in the mitochondria of the fruit fly *Drosophila melanogaster*, it encodes the amino acid tryptophan.

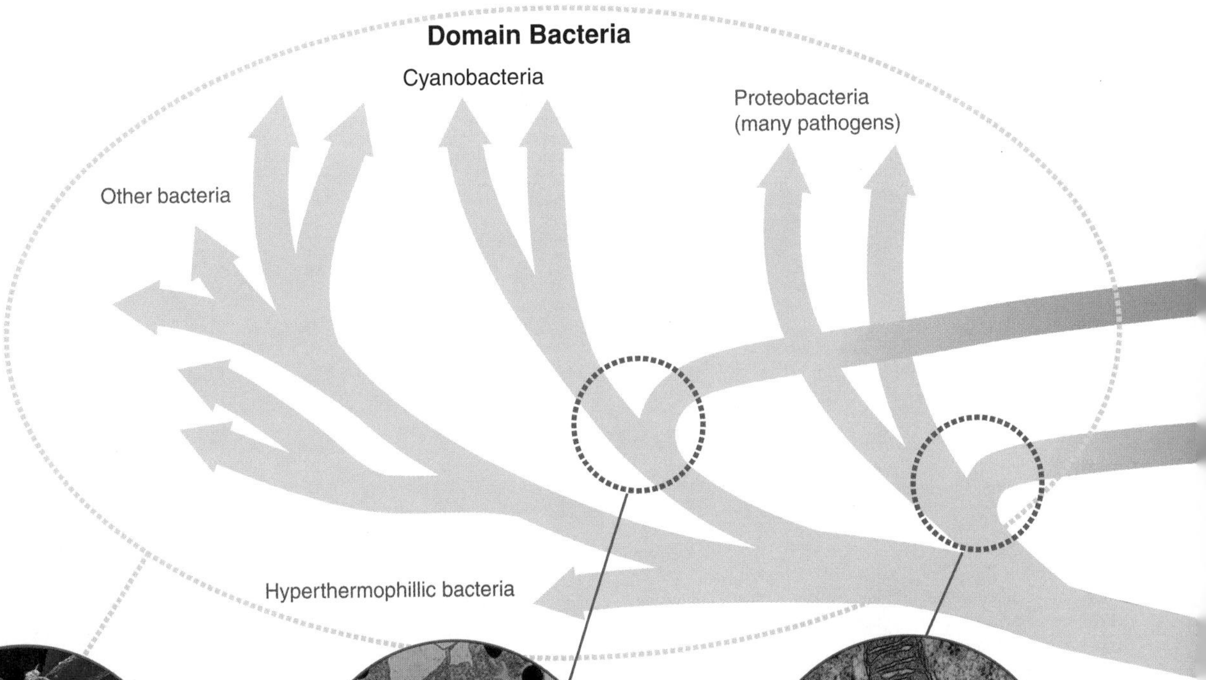

Domain Bacteria

Cyanobacteria

Proteobacteria (many pathogens)

Other bacteria

Hyperthermophillic bacteria

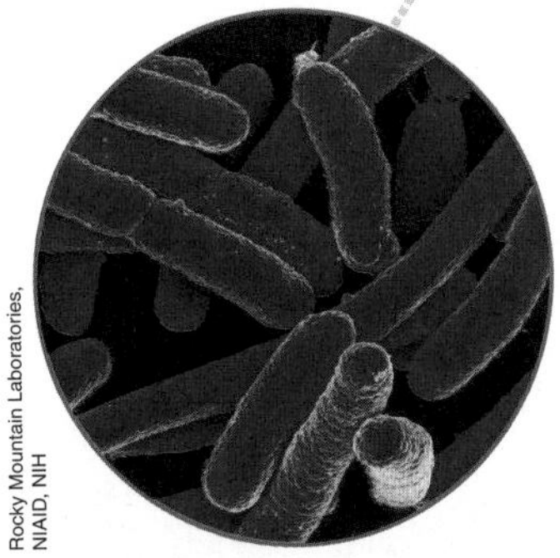

Rocky Mountain Laboratories, NIAID, NIH

EII

Bacteria lack a distinct nucleus and cell organelles. Features of the cell wall are unique to bacteria and are not found among archaea or eukaryotes. Typically found in less extreme environments than archaea.

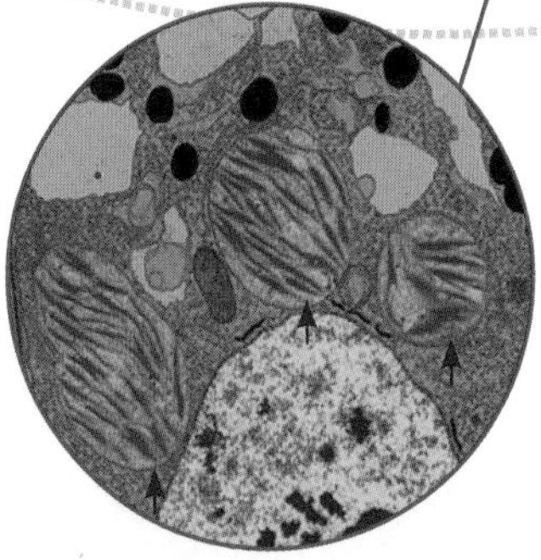

Chloroplasts have a bacterial origin

Cyanobacteria are considered to be the ancestors of chloroplasts. The evidence for this comes from similarities in the ribosomes and membrane organization , as well as from genomic studies. Chloroplasts were acquired independently of mitochondria, from a different bacterial lineage, but by a similar process.

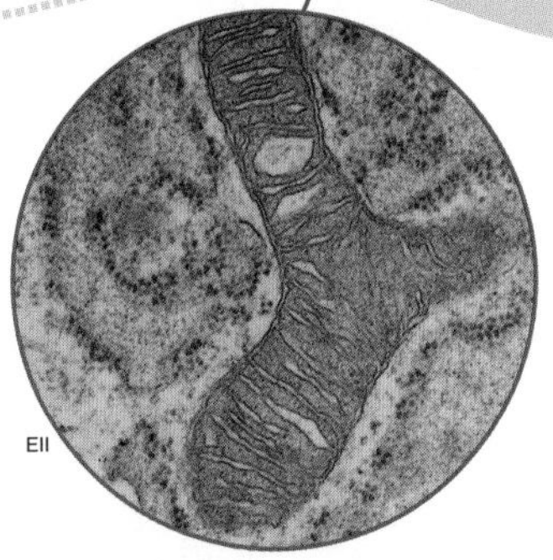

Mitochondria have a bacterial origin

Evidence from mitochondrial gene sequences, ribosomes, and protein synthesis indicate that mitochondria have a prokaryotic origin. Mitochondria were probably symbiotic inclusions in an early eukaryotic ancestor.

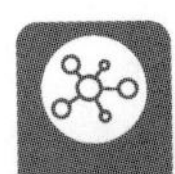

ISBN: 978-1-98-856656-6

1. Suggest why scientists believe that mitochondria were acquired before chloroplasts: ______________________

2. The few exceptions to the universality of the genetic code in some organisms (described opposite) do not imply multiple origins of life. Predict what you would expect to see in the DNA of these organisms if life has had multiple origins:

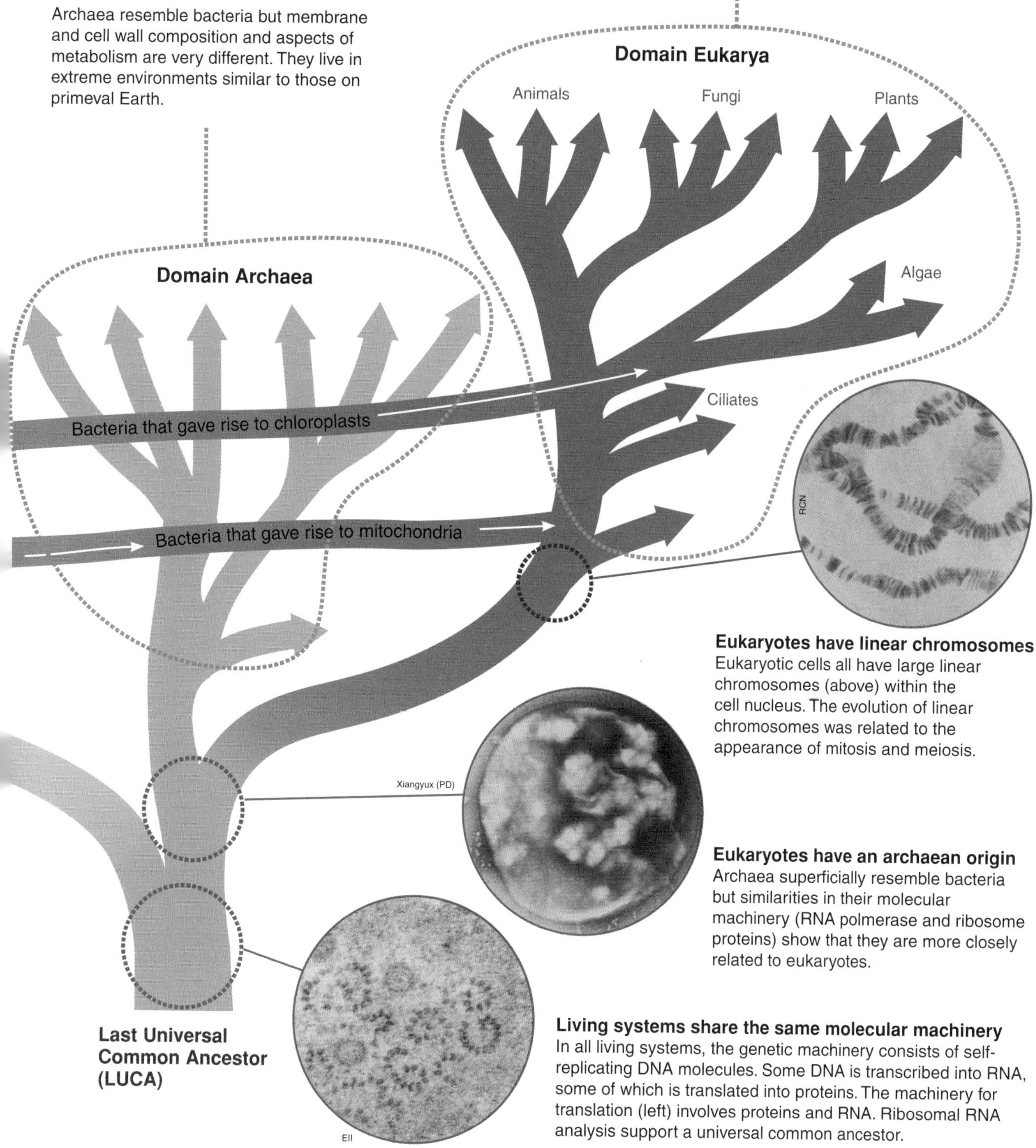

Eukarya (the eukaryotes) are characterized by complex cells with organelles and a membrane-bound nucleus. This domain contains four of the kingdoms recognized under a traditional scheme.

Archaea resemble bacteria but membrane and cell wall composition and aspects of metabolism are very different. They live in extreme environments similar to those on primeval Earth.

Domain Eukarya

Animals

Fungi

Plants

Algae

Ciliates

Domain Archaea

Bacteria that gave rise to chloroplasts

Bacteria that gave rise to mitochondria

RCN

Eukaryotes have linear chromosomes
Eukaryotic cells all have large linear chromosomes (above) within the cell nucleus. The evolution of linear chromosomes was related to the appearance of mitosis and meiosis.

Xiangyux (PD)

Eukaryotes have an archaean origin
Archaea superficially resemble bacteria but similarities in their molecular machinery (RNA polmerase and ribosome proteins) show that they are more closely related to eukaryotes.

Last Universal Common Ancestor (LUCA)

EII

Living systems share the same molecular machinery
In all living systems, the genetic machinery consists of self-replicating DNA molecules. Some DNA is transcribed into RNA, some of which is translated into proteins. The machinery for translation (left) involves proteins and RNA. Ribosomal RNA analysis support a universal common ancestor.

ISBN: 978-1-98-856656-6

178 The Origin of Eukaryotes

Key Question: How did eukaryotes evolve?

The first fossil evidence dates to 2.1 bya, but molecular evidence suggests that the eukaryotic lineage is much more ancient and closer to the origin of life. The original **endosymbiotic theory** (Margulis, 1970) proposed that eukaryotes arose as a result of an endosymbiosis between two prokaryotes, one of which was aerobic and gave rise to the mitochondrion. The hypothesis has since been modified to recognize that eukaryotes probably originated with the appearance of the nucleus and flagella, when a small prokaryote-like cell was engulfed by a larger one and formed an endosymbiotic relationship. Mitochondria and chloroplasts were then acquired later. Primitive eukaryotes probably acquired mitochondria by engulfing purple bacteria. Similarly, chloroplasts may have been acquired by engulfing primitive cyanobacteria. In both instances, the organelles produced became dependent on the nucleus of the host cell to direct some of their metabolic processes. Unlike mitochondria, chloroplasts were probably acquired independently by more than one organism, so their origin is polyphyletic.

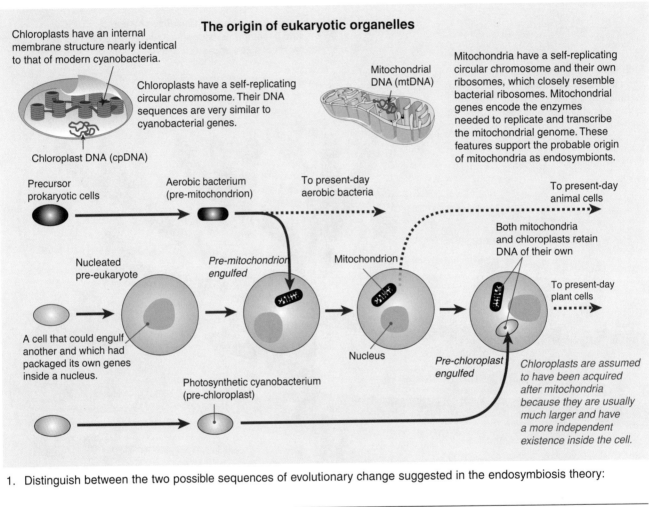

The origin of eukaryotic organelles

Chloroplasts have an internal membrane structure nearly identical to that of modern cyanobacteria.

Chloroplasts have a self-replicating circular chromosome. Their DNA sequences are very similar to cyanobacterial genes.

Chloroplast DNA (cpDNA)

Mitochondrial DNA (mtDNA)

Mitochondria have a self-replicating circular chromosome and their own ribosomes, which closely resemble bacterial ribosomes. Mitochondrial genes encode the enzymes needed to replicate and transcribe the mitochondrial genome. These features support the probable origin of mitochondria as endosymbionts.

Precursor prokaryotic cells

Aerobic bacterium (pre-mitochondrion)

To present-day aerobic bacteria

To present-day animal cells

Both mitochondria and chloroplasts retain DNA of their own

Nucleated pre-eukaryote

Pre-mitochondrion engulfed

Mitochondrion

To present-day plant cells

A cell that could engulf another and which had packaged its own genes inside a nucleus.

Nucleus

Pre-chloroplast engulfed

Photosynthetic cyanobacterium (pre-chloroplast)

Chloroplasts are assumed to have been acquired after mitochondria because they are usually much larger and have a more independent existence inside the cell.

1. Distinguish between the two possible sequences of evolutionary change suggested in the endosymbiosis theory:

2. How does the endosymbiotic theory account for the origins of the following eukaryotic organelles?

(a) Mitochondria:

(b) Chloroplasts:

3. Explain how the presence of mitochondria in all eukaryotes provides evidence for common ancestry:

ISBN: 978-1-98-856656-6

179 Continuing Evolution: Galapagos Finches

Key Question: Can direct measurements of a population show natural selection in action?

Natural selection acts on the phenotypes of a population. Individuals with phenotypes that produce more offspring have higher fitness, increasing the proportion of the genes corresponding to that phenotype in the next generation. Many population studies have shown natural selection can cause phenotypic changes in a population relatively quickly.

The finches on the Galápagos Islands (Darwin's finches) are famous in that they are commonly used as examples of how evolution produces new species. In this activity you will analyze data from the measurement of beaks depths of the **medium ground finch**, *Geospiza fortis* (below) on the island of Daphne Major near the center of the Galápagos Islands. The measurements were taken in 1976 before a major drought hit the island and in 1978 after the drought (survivors and survivors' offspring).

Beak depth (mm)	No. 1976 birds	No. 1978 survivors
7.30-7.79	1	0
7.80-8.29	12	1
8.30-8.79	30	3
8.80-9.29	47	3
9.30-9.79	45	6
9.80-10.29	40	9
10.30-10.79	25	10
10.80-11.29	3	1
11.30+	0	0

Beak depth of offspring (mm)	Number of birds
7.30-7.79	2
7.80-8.29	2
8.30-8.79	5
8.80-9.29	21
9.30-9.79	34
9.80-10.29	37
10.30-10.79	19
10-80-11.29	15
11.30+	2

1. Use the data above to draw two separate sets of histograms:

   (a) On the left hand grid draw side-by-side histograms for the number of 1976 birds per beak depth and the number of 1978 survivors per beak depth.

   (b) On the right hand grid draw a histogram of the beak depths of the offspring of the 1978 survivors.

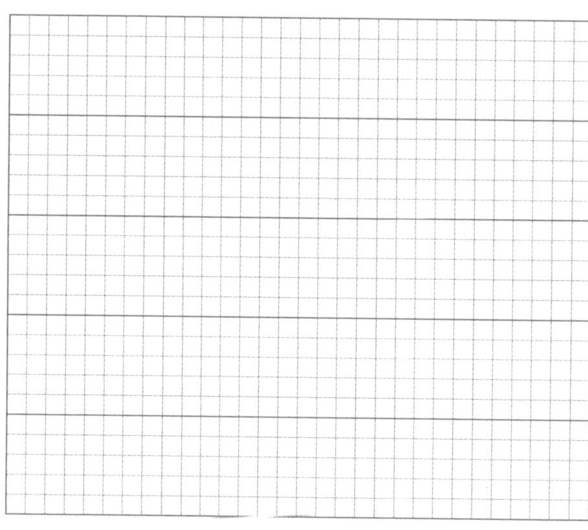

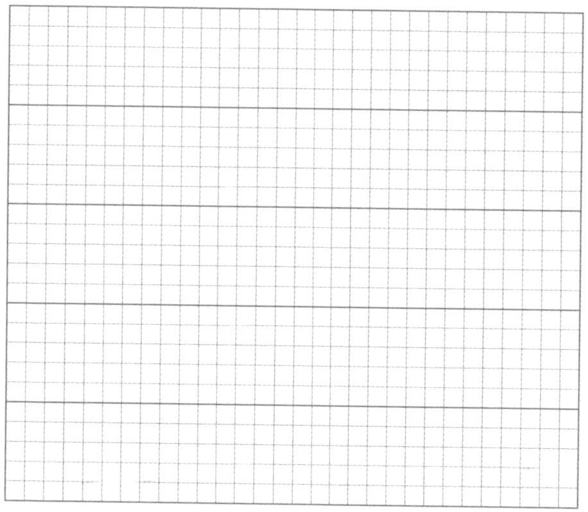

2. (a) Mark the approximate mean beak depth on the graphs of the 1976 beak depths and the 1978 offspring.

   (b) How much has the average moved from 1976 to 1978? ______________________________

   (c) Is beak depth heritable? What does this mean for the process of natural selection in the finches?

   ____

   ____

3. The 1976 drought resulted in plants dying back and not producing seed. Based on the graphs, what can you say about competition between the birds for the remaining seeds, i.e. in what order were the seeds probably used up?

   ____

   ____

   ____

ISBN: 978-1-98-856656-6

EVO-3
3.E

▸ A second study of a *Geospiza fortis* population during a prolonged drought on Santa Cruz Island in the Galápagos showed how **disruptive selection** can change the distribution of genotypes in a population. During the drought, large and small seeds were more abundant than the preferred intermediate seed size.

Beak sizes of *G. fortis* were measured over a three year period (2004-2006), at the start and end of each year. At the start of the year, individuals were captured, banded, and their beaks were measured.

The presence or absence of banded individuals was recorded at the end of the year when the birds were recaptured. Recaptured individuals had their beaks measured. The proportion of banded birds in the population at the end of the year gave a measure of fitness. Absent individuals were presumed dead (fitness = 0).

Fitness related to beak size showed a bimodal distribution (left) typical of disruptive selection.

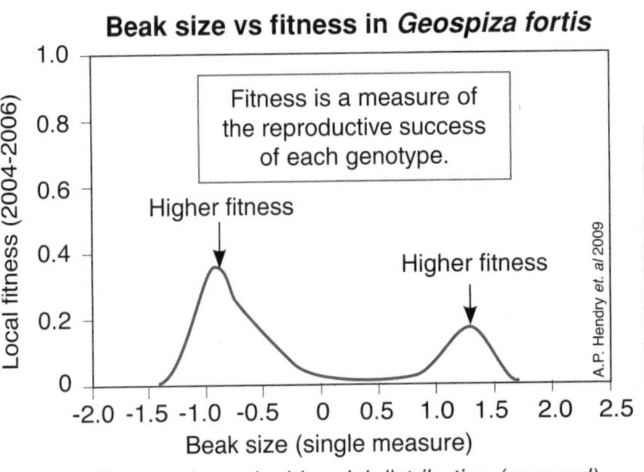

Fitness showed a bimodal distribution (arrowed) being highest for smaller and larger beak sizes.

Measurements of the beak length, width, and depth were combined into one **single measure**.

Beak size pairing in *Geospiza fortis*

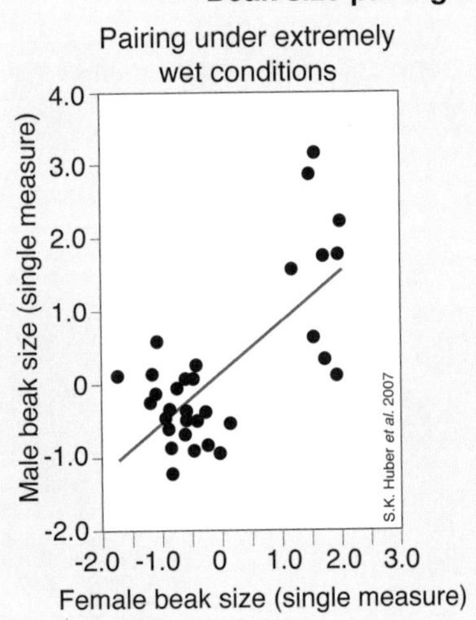

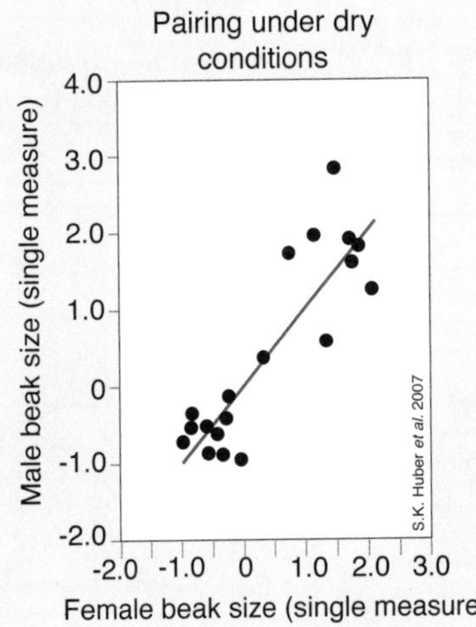

A 2007 analysis found that breeding pairs of birds had similar beak sizes. Male and females with small beaks tended to breed together, and males and females with large beaks tended to breed together. Mate selection maintained the bimodal distribution in the population during extremely wet conditions. If beak size wasn't a factor in mate selection, the beak size would even out.

4. (a) How did the drought affect seed size on Santa Cruz Island? ________________

   (b) How did the change in seed size during the drought create a selection pressure for changes in beak size?

5. How does beak size relate to fitness in *G. fortis*? ________________

6. Beak size in *G. fortis* was measured in wet and dry conditions, and showed non random mating. Suggest a next step in measuring beak size and mating preference:

ISBN: 978-1-98-856656-6

180 Master Genes and Evolutionary Change

Key Question: What is the effect of changes in gene expression on the evolution of a species?

Bone morphogenetic proteins (BMPs) regulate bone and cartilage growth in embryos. BMP4 is a signaling molecule in a signal transduction pathway for the expression of genes controlling development of the skull, face, and jaws.

The diverse shapes seen in the beaks of Darwin's finches and in the jaws of African cichlid fishes are the result of different levels of BMP4 expression. They show how different morphologies can arise by changing the expression of genes, and not necessarily the genes themselves. These processes are active in the continuing the evolution of organisms today.

Beak shape is regulated by BMP4 and CaM1 expression

Two regulatory proteins, BMP4 and calmodulin (CaM1), are involved in controlling the shape of beaks in birds. Calmodulins are a group of calcium binding proteins, they have important roles in regulating a number of different protein targets, so are involved in regulating a variety of cell functions. In beak development, BMP4 controls width and CaM1 influences length.

The two extremes of beak shape in Darwin's finches are shown right. A wide range of beak shapes occur between these two extremes as a result of the different levels of expression of BMP4 and CaM1. The images below show some of the beak variation observed in Darwin's finches.

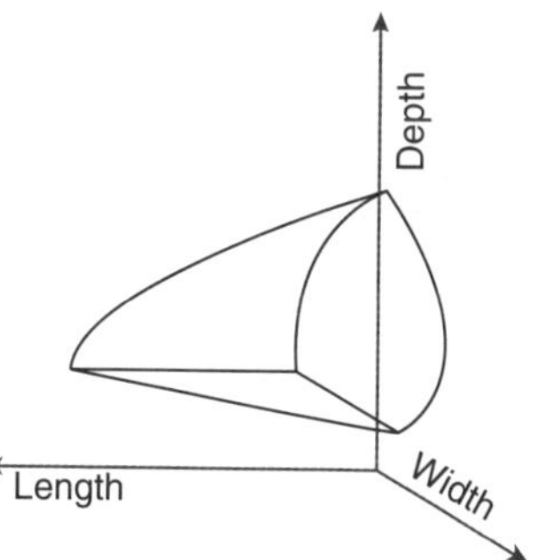

BMP4 (encoded by the BMP4 gene) controls beak width. Individuals expressing high levels of BMP4 early in development have deep, broad beaks, whereas individuals with low BMP4 expression developed narrower, shallower beaks.

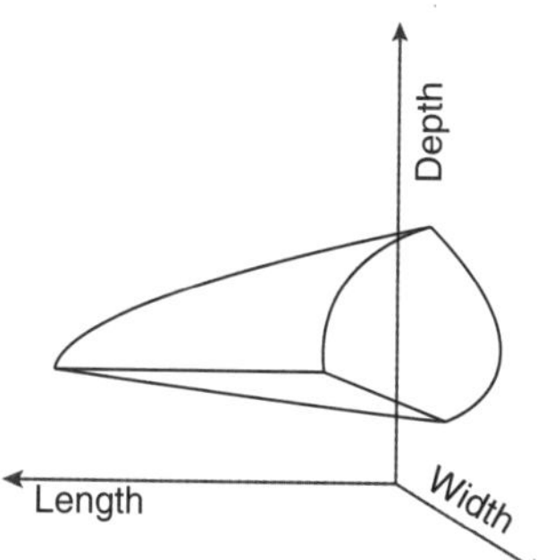

CaM1 (encoded by the CaM1 gene) controls the length of the beak. When CaM1 is strongly expressed the beak tends to be more long and pointed than in individuals where CaM1 expression is lower.

The finches of the Galápagos Islands have adapted to occupy a wide range of different ecological niches, each specializing on different food sources. The shape of their beaks reflects this. Although several species of ground finch eat seeds, the size and hardness of the seeds they preferentially eat depends on their beak morphology. For example, the large, deep beak of the large ground finch allows it to break much harder, larger seeds than the smaller beaks of the two other ground finches.

The sharp-beaked finch (*G. difficilis*) feeds on a mixed diet of seeds and insects.

Low BMP4 Low beak depth/width
Low CaM Short beak

Compiled from various sources including: LF DeLeon *et al*, J. Evol. Biol, 27 (2014) "*Darwin's finches and their diet niches: the sympatric coexistence of imperfect generalists*." and A Abzhanov *et al*. Nature 442 (2006) " *The calmodulin pathway and evolution of elongated beak morphology in Darwin's finches*."

Low BMP4 Low beak depth/width	Low/ moderate BMP4 Moderate beak depth/width	Moderate BMP4 Moderate beak depth/width	Early/high BMP4 High beak depth/width
High CaM Elongated beak	High CaM Elongated beak	Low CaM Short beak	Low CaM Short beak

Cactus finch *(G. scandens)* Probes cactus flowers and fruit.

Large cactus finch (*G. conirostris*) Feeds on seeds, insects, and cacti.

Medium ground finch (*G. fortis*) Crushes seeds up to 1.5cm.

Large ground finch (*G.magnirostris*) Crushes large, hard seeds up to 2 cm.

Finch photos all thanks to Prof. Jeff Podos unless otherwise stated

Cactus fruit

Cactus seeds

Roger Culos Muséum de Toulouse CC3.0

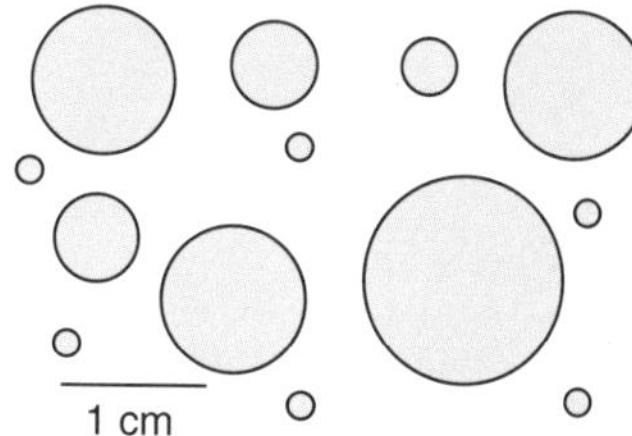

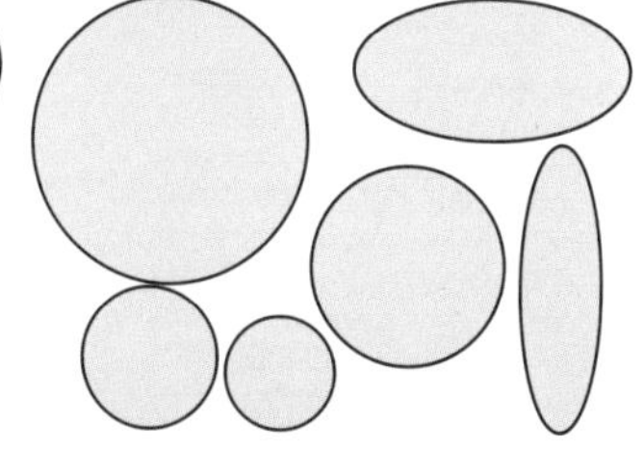

ISBN: 978-1-98-856656-6

179

166

EVO-3
1.B
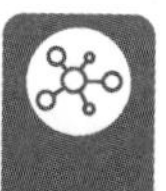

Variations in cichlid jaw shape

Labeotropheus fuelleborni

Metriaclima zebra

The cichlids are a large, diverse family of perch-like fishes. They are particularly diverse in the African Great Lakes where adaptive radiation has resulted in ~1500 species exploiting a range of feeding niches. The morphology of the jaws and teeth in cichlids is associated with the level of BMP4 expressed during embryonic development. High levels of BMP4 are detected in the jaws of developing *Labeotropheus fuelleborni*. As a result, this species develops a short, robust lower jaw, with small closely spaced teeth, ideal for stripping algae from rocky surfaces. At the same stage of development, lower levels of BMP4 are expressed in *Metriaclima zebra*. The resulting jaw is more elongated, with large well spaced teeth. The *M. zebra* jaw is suited to sucking up loose material. Further evidence for the importance of BMP4 in jaw development has come from the manipulation of BMP4 expression in zebrafish (*Danio rerio*). Over-expression of BMP4 resulted in deep jaws forming.

1. (a) Explain the role of BMP4 in beak development: __________

   (b) What role does CaM1 play in beak development? __________

2. The photos right show two species of Galápagos Island finches; the vegetarian finch (A) and the green warbler finch (B). Compare their beaks and suggest how the expression of BMP4 and CaM1 has likely differed between the two:

A

B

Finch photos courtesy of Prof. Jeff Podos

3. (a) What evidence is there that BMP4 plays a role in controlling the morphology of cichlid jaw development?

   (b) How is jaw shape is related to diet in the two cichlid species above?

4. Explain how the regulation of gene expression has produced diverse morphologies in related species and explain the significance of this to their adaptive radiation:

ISBN: 978-1-98-856656-6

181 Continuous Change in the Fossil Record

Key Question: Does the fossil record show change over time? The completeness of the fossil record for different taxa is highly variable. Soft bodies organisms typically have a poor fossil record whereas others with bones, shells or other hard body parts are more highly represented in the fossil record. Certain taxa, including trilobites and ammonites, have a comprehensive and well documented fossil record. The reasons for this include being particularly numerous and present in locations where fossilization was more likely. Examples of vertebrate taxa with rich fossil records include horses and whales. The fossils of both of these groups document their evolution from a smaller ancestor adapted to a lifestyle that was very different to that of their modern descendants. These fossils showing intermediate states between ancestral and modern form are called transitional fossils. They provide clear evidence for change over time.

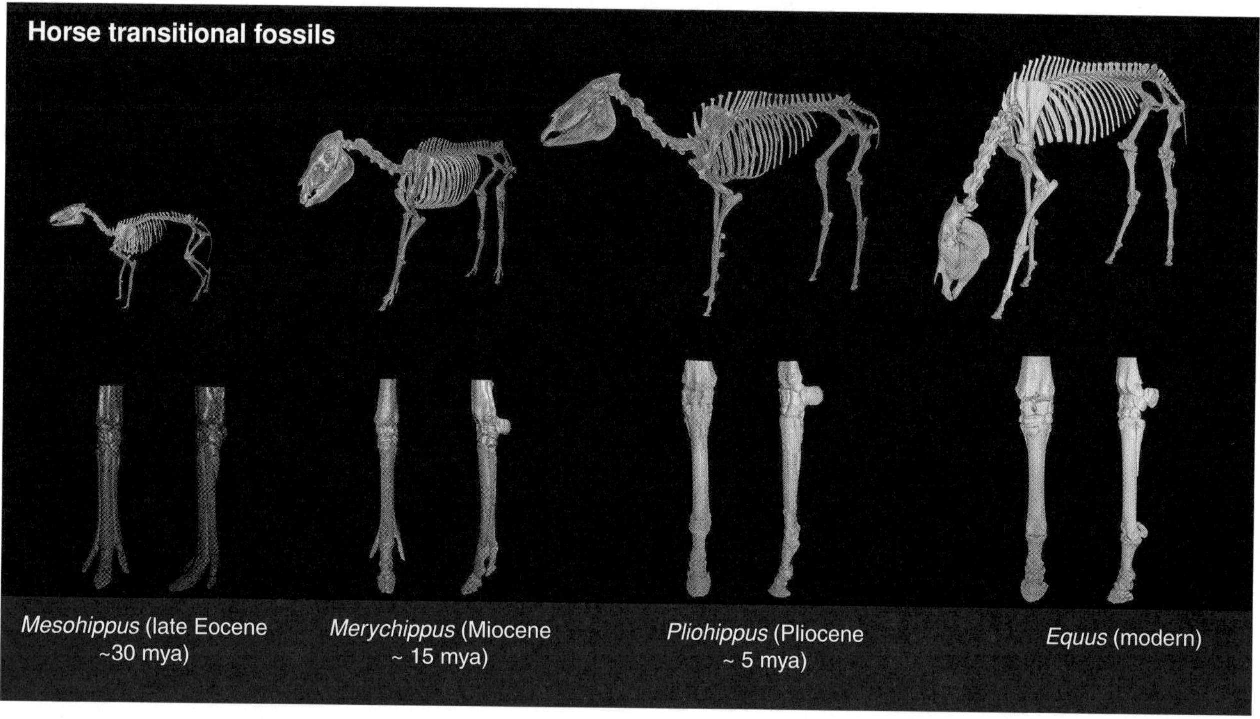

- The evolution of the horse from the ancestral *Hyracotherium* to modern *Equus* is well documented in the fossil record. The rich fossil record, which includes numerous **transitional fossils**, has enabled scientists to develop a robust model of horse phylogeny. It is a complex tree-like lineage with many divergences, and a diverse array of often coexisting species. The environmental transition from forest to grasslands drove many of the changes observed in the fossil record. These include reduction in toe number, increased size of cheek teeth, and increasing body size.
- Over time, equids became taller and faster, enabling them to detect and escape predators more easily. Their overall size increased and their limbs became more elongated. The reduction in the number of toes from four to one also enabled them to run faster and more efficiently (with less energy expenditure).

1. (a) What selection pressure(s) do you think might have acted on the horse's ancestors to produce the equids of today?

(b) Describe the general anatomical changes in horses over the last 30 million years:

2. Explain the importance of transitional fossils:

ISBN: 978-1-98-856656-6

166

145

EVO-3
1.B

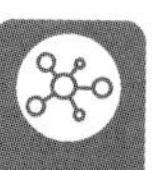

Evolution of whales

- The evolution of modern whales from an ancestral land mammal is well documented in the fossil record. The fossil record of whales includes many transitional forms, which has enabled scientists to develop an excellent model of whale evolution. The evolution of the whales shows a gradual accumulation of adaptive features that have equipped them for life in the open ocean.

Modern whales are categorized into two broad suborders based on the presence or absence of teeth.

- **Toothed whales**: These have full sets of teeth throughout their lives. Examples: sperm whale and orca.
- **Baleen whales**: Toothless whales, which have a comb-like structure (baleen) in the jaw. Baleen is composed of the protein keratin and is used to filter food from the water. Examples: blue whale, humpback whale.

Robert Pittman - NOAA
Orca

Humpback whale

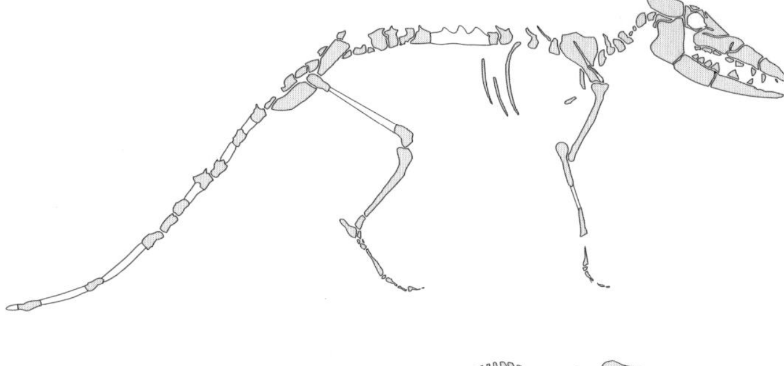

50 mya *Pakicetus*

Pakicetus was a transitional species between carnivorous land mammals and the earliest true whales. It was mainly land dwelling, but foraged for food in water. It had four, long limbs. Its eyes were near the top of the head and its nostrils were at the end of the snout. It had external ears, but they showed features of both terrestrial mammals and fully aquatic mammals.

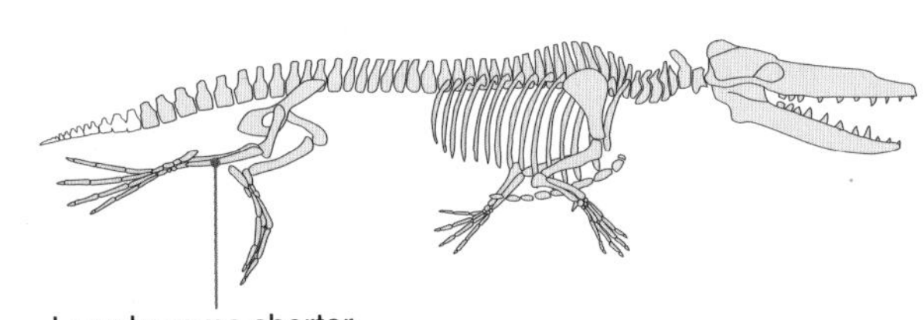
Legs became shorter

45 mya *Rhodocetus*

Rhodocetus was mainly aquatic (water living). It had adaptations for swimming, including shorter legs and a shorter tail. Its eyes had moved to the side of the skull, and the nostrils were located further up the skull. The ear showed specializations for hearing in water.

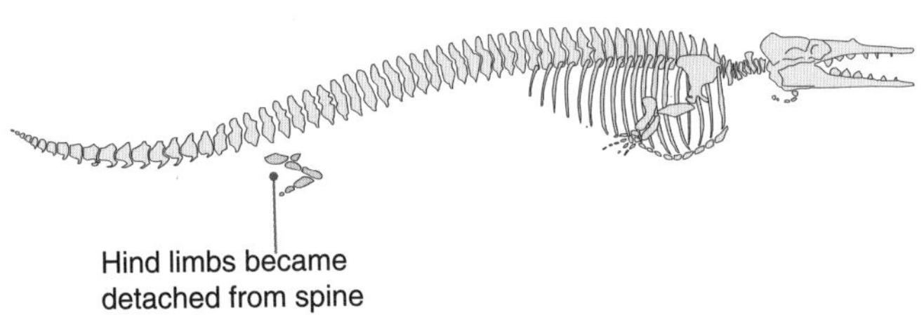
Hind limbs became detached from spine

40 mya *Dorudon*

Dorudon was fully aquatic. Its adaptations for swimming included a long, streamlined body, a broad powerful muscular tail, the development of flippers and webbing. It had very small hind limbs (not attached to the spine) which would no longer bear weight on land.

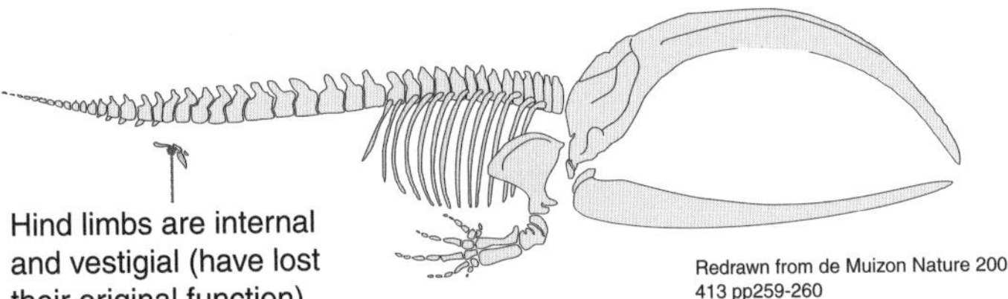
Hind limbs are internal and vestigial (have lost their original function).

Redrawn from de Muizon Nature 2001 413 pp259-260

***Balaena* (recent whale ancestor)**

The hind limbs became fully internal and vestigial. Studies of modern whales show that limb development begins, but is arrested at the limb bud stage. The nostrils became modified as blowholes. This recent ancestor to modern whales diverged into two groups (toothed and baleen) about 36 million years ago. Baleen whales have teeth in their early fetal stage, but lose them before birth.

3. Explain why the whale fossil record provides a good example of the evolutionary process: ____________________

____

____

____

4. Briefly describe the adaptations of whales for swimming that evolved over time: ____________________

____

____

ISBN: 978-1-98-856656-6

182 Modern Drivers in Evolution

Key Question: How are human actions, such as the use of antimicrobial drugs, driving the evolution of organisms today?

Resistance to antibiotics and other antimicrobial drugs is becoming increasingly common. Antimicrobial drugs create an environment that selects for resistance, which can arise and spread when chemical control agents do not remove all the targeted organisms. Those that survive as a result of their particular suite of heritable characteristics are able to pass on these genes and so resistance becomes more common in subsequent generations (i.e. natural selection). Resistance to antibiotics in bacteria and to antimalarial drugs in *Plasmodium* pose serious threats to current and future human health.

The evolution of antibiotic resistance in bacteria

Antibiotic resistance arises when genetic changes allow bacteria to tolerate levels of antibiotic that would normally inhibit growth. Resistance may arise spontaneously through mutation or by transfer of DNA between microbes (horizontal gene transfer). Genomic analyses from 30,000 year old permafrost sediments show that the genes for antibiotic resistance predate modern antibiotic use. In the current selective environment of widespread antibiotic use, these genes have proliferated and antibiotic resistance has spread. For example, methicillin resistant strains of *Staphylococcus aureus* (MRSA) have acquired genes for resistance to all penicillins. Such strains are called superbugs.

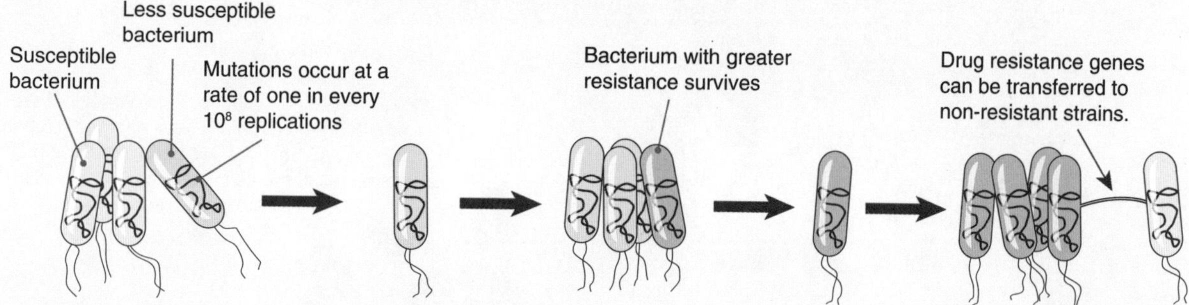

Any population, including bacterial populations, includes variants with unusual traits, in this case reduced sensitivity to an antibiotic. These variants arise as a result of mutations in the bacterial chromosome.

When a person takes an antibiotic, only the most susceptible bacteria will die. The more resistant cells remain alive and continue dividing. Note that the antibiotic does not create the resistance; it provides the environment in which selection for resistance can take place.

If the amount of antibiotic delivered is too low, or the course of antibiotics is not completed, a population of resistant bacteria develops. Within this population too, there will be variation in susceptibility. Some will survive higher antibiotic levels than others.

A highly resistant population has evolved. The resistant cells can exchange genetic material with other bacteria (via horizontal gene transmission), passing on the genes for resistance. The antibiotic initially used against this bacterial strain will now be ineffective.

Staphylococcus aureus is a common bacterium responsible for several minor skin infections in humans. Methicillin resistant *Staphylococcus aureus* (MRSA) is a strain that has evolved resistance to penicillin and related antibiotics. MRSA can be contracted in many environments, but is particularly troublesome in hospital-associated infections because patients with open wounds, invasive devices (e.g. catheters), or poor immunity are at greater risk for infection than the general public (far right).

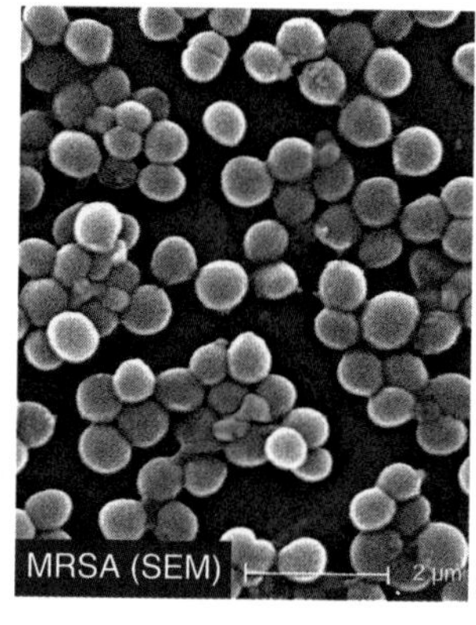

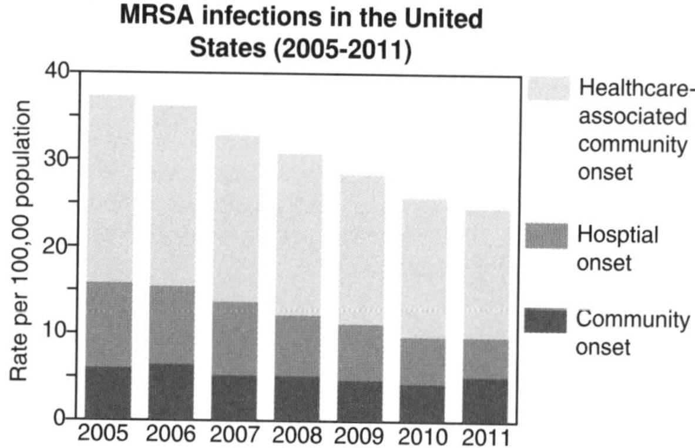

1. Genomic evidence indicates that the genes for antibiotic resistance are ancient:

(a) Explain how these genes could have arisen: ____________________

____

(b) Explain why these genes are proliferating now: ____________________

____

2. Explain how failing to complete a course of antibiotics can lead to antibiotic resistance, such as seen in MRSA:

____

____

ISBN: 978-1-98-856656-6

Chloroquine resistance

- Mutations in some strains of the protozoa that cause malaria allowed them to become more resistant to some antimalarial drugs. **Chloroquine** is an antimalarial drug discovered in 1934. It was first used clinically to prevent malaria in 1946. Chloroquine was widely used because it was cheap to produce, safe, and very effective.
- Chloroquine resistance in *Plasmodium falciparum* first appeared in the late 1950s, and the subsequent spread of resistance has significantly decreased chloroquine's effectiveness. However, chloroquine is still effective at preventing malaria in Central American countries (chloroquine resistance has not yet arisen there), with a 2014 study in Haiti showing no treatment failure. In 30 other countries, chloroquine failure rates ranged between 20 and 100%. In some regions, chloroquine used in combination with other anti-malarial drugs is still an effective treatment.

Global spread of chloroquine resistance

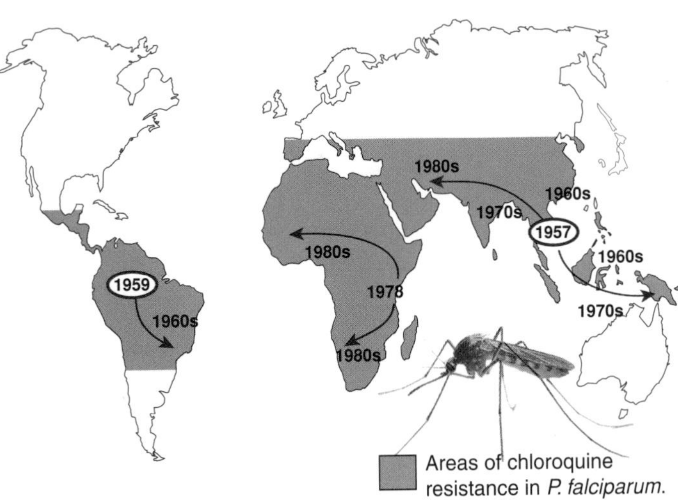

Malaria in humans is caused by various species of *Plasmodium*, a protozoan parasite transmitted by *Anopheles* mosquitoes. The inexpensive anti-malarial drug **chloroquine** was used successfully to treat malaria for many years, but its effectiveness has declined since resistance to the drug was first recorded in the 1950s.

Chloroquine resistance has spread steadily (above) and now two of the four *Plasmodium* species, *P. falciparum* and *P. vivax*, are chloroquine-resistant. *P. falciparum* alone accounts for 80% of all human malarial infections and 90% of the deaths, so this rise in resistance is of global concern.

New anti-malarial drugs have been developed, but are expensive and often have undesirable side effects. Resistance to even these newer drugs is already evident, especially in *P. falciparum*, although this species is currently still susceptible to artemisinin, a derivative of the medicinal herb *Artemisia annua*.

Studies have demonstrated a link between mutations in the chloroquine resistance transporter (PfCRT) gene and resistance to chloroquine in *P. falciparum*. PfCRT is a membrane protein involved in drug and metabolite transport.

T G T G T A A T G A A T A C A A T T

A point mutation coding for threonine instead of lysine at amino acid position 76 on the PfCRT gene produces resistance to chloroquine. Parasites with the mutation are better able to release the chloroquine from the vesicles in which it normally accumulates in the cell. Therefore, they accrue less chloroquine than susceptible parasites.

Chloroquine is a suppressive drug. It is only effective at killing the malarial parasite once the parasite has entered the blood-borne stage of its life cycle.

The use of chloroquine in many African countries was stopped during the 1990s because of resistance to the drug in *P. falciparum*. Recent studies in Malawi and Kenya have revealed a significant decrease in chloroquine resistance since the drug was withdrawn. There may be a significant fitness cost to the PfCRT mutants in the absence of anti-malarial drugs, leading to their decline in frequency once the selection pressure of the drugs is removed. This raises the possibility of re-introducing chloroquine as an anti-malarial treatment in the future.

3. Describe the benefits of using chloroquine to prevent malaria: ______________________

4. With reference to *Plasmodium falciparum*, explain how chloroquine resistance arises: ______________________

5. Describe two strategies to reduce the spread of chloroquine resistance while still treating malaria:

   (a) ______________________

   (b) ______________________

ISBN: 978-1-98-856656-6

183 The Emergence of New Diseases

Key Question: How do new pathogens arise and spread?

Evolution is not just a characteristic of cellular based life. Viruses have also been evolving since they emerged early in the evolution of life. Human pathogens, including viral pathogens, continually evolve, causing new disease outbreaks every few years. The rapid spread of an infectious disease through a nation is called an **epidemic**. When the disease spreads rapidly throughout the world, it becomes a **pandemic**. Examples of recent pandemic diseases include HIV/AIDS, influenza, Zika virus, and Covid-19.

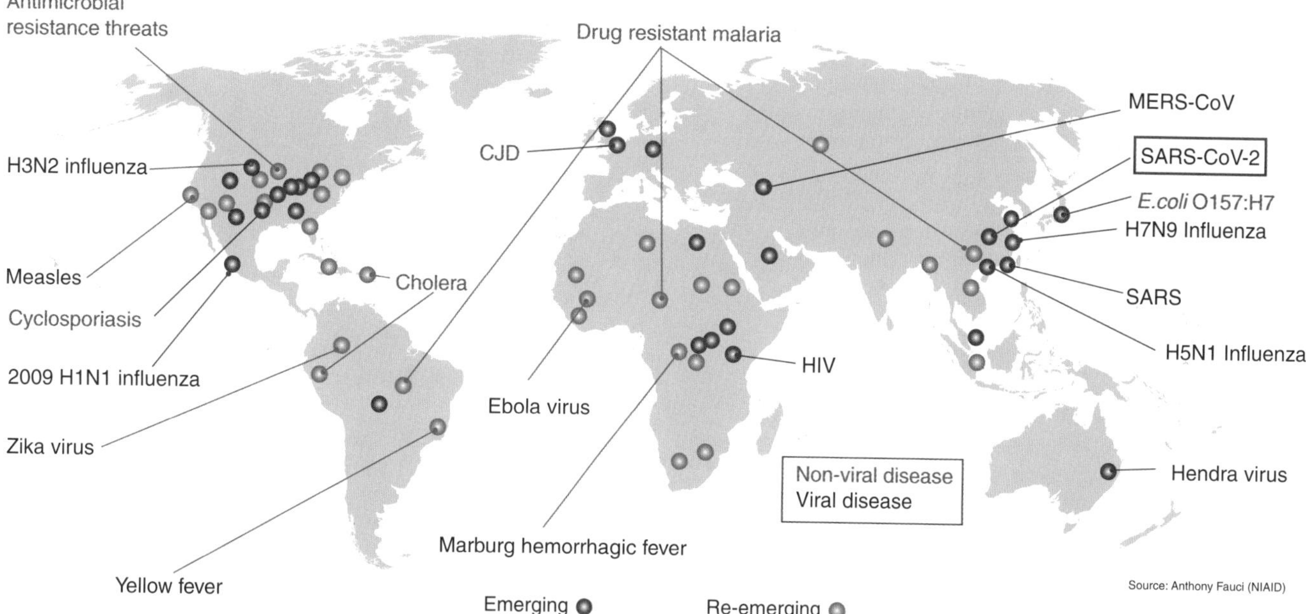

What are emerging and re-emerging diseases?

- Emerging infectious diseases are those that have never been encountered by humans (rare), have occurred previously but in small numbers and in isolated regions (e.g. Ebola), or have occurred throughout history but have only been recognized recently.
- Re-emerging infectious diseases are those that were once major health problems, then declined, but are now on the rise again. Examples include malaria and tuberculosis.
- The reasons for these emergences or re-emergences are varied and often particular to the disease. However some important factors include the movement of humans into previously uninhabited areas (e.g. by deforestation), greater movement of people from place to place and globally, or the failure of people to vaccinate or use antibiotics correctly (leading to antibiotic resistance).
- Although different countries have different abilities to identify new pathogens and diseases, the detection of new diseases over the last 40 years shows a uniform global pattern. No region appears to be more likely than any other to detect a new disease.

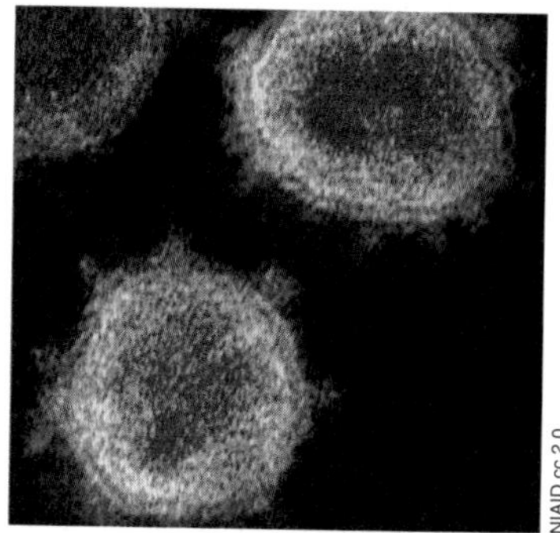

TEM of SARS-CoV-2, the cause of the Covid-19 pandemic, which emerged in China in 2019.

1. Explain the difference between emerging and re-emerging diseases: ______

2. (a) Describe factors involved in the emergence of new pathogens and diseases: ______

   (b) Describe factors involved in the re-emergence of once declining pathogens and diseases: ______

ISBN: 978-1-98-856656-6

The emergence of Covid-19

- Reports of viral pneumonia (a lung infection) in Wuhan, China were reported on the 31st December 2019. Early in January 2020, a new coronavirus, SARS-CoV-2, was identified as the cause of the infections.

What is Covid-19?

- Covid-19 is the disease caused by infection with the SARS-CoV-2 virus (right).
- The virus affects the respiratory system.
- 80% of infected people recover without hospital care.
- 20% of infected people develop severe breathing problems and may require high level hospital care. The elderly and people with underlying medical problems are most at risk of becoming very sick.
- The virus is spread through the environment in small droplets from the nose and mouth (e.g. when a person speaks, sneezes, or coughs). People become infected when they breathe these droplets in, or when they touch a surface contaminated with the virus.
- Vaccines have now been developed.

A representation of the SARS-CoV-2 virus

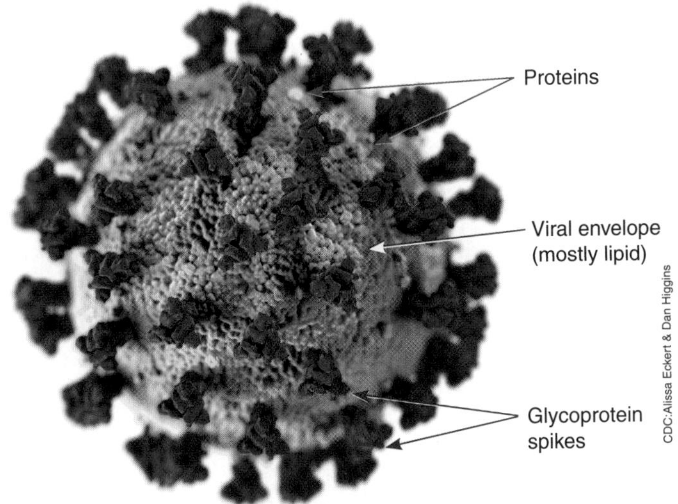

Changes in coronavirus

- Like *Influenzavirus*, SARS-CoV-2 stores its genetic material as strands of RNA. However, observation has shown that SARS-CoV-2 mutates about four times more slowly than *Influenzavirus*. Currently, it is believed that this is because SARS-CoV-2 has a better "proof-reading" system than *Influenzavirus*, so mutations are less common.
- Although various strains of SARS-CoV-2 have been identified, the virus does not appear to be drifting antigenically. Also its genome (as with all CoVs) is non-segmented, so it is not capable of antigenic shift through reassortment. This means that vaccines may last longer and work against a wider range of strains of SARS-CoV-2 than do vaccines for *Influenzavirus*.
- In the case of SARS-CoV-2, producing a vaccine is not necessarily more difficult than for other viruses. The main challenges were developing the vaccine in the shortest time possible, testing it, ensuring safety, and then distributing it.

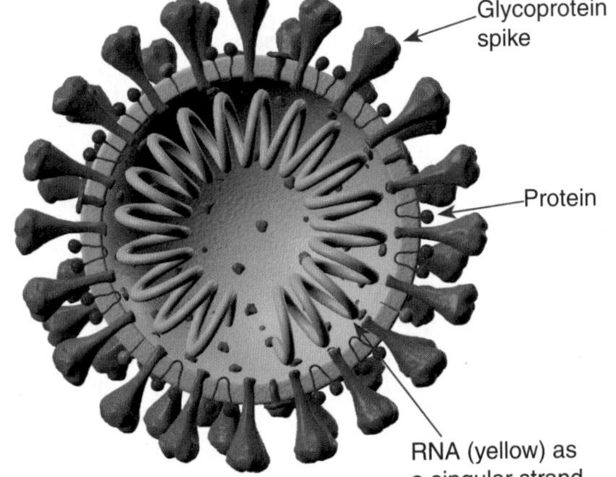

But where did SARS-CoV-2 come from?

- The exact pathway of SARS-CoV-2 evolution may not be known definitively for some time. Coronaviruses are common in bats and the best evidence to date suggests that the reservoir is bats. Genetic sequences obtained from viruses in bats show a 96.2% similarity with SARS-CoV-2.
- CoV sequences similar to SARS-CoV-2 have also been obtained from pangolins, but not from pangolins in China. At some stage, the proto-SARS-CoV-2 virus must have jumped from its animal host to humans where it likely then evolved into the current SARS-CoV-2 virus.

3. Explain why SARS-CoV-2 cannot undergo antigenic shift: ______________________

____

4. As a group, discuss the main challenges around **developing** a Covid-19 vaccine. Do some online searches of reliable sources and explain how were these were or are being overcome. Summarize your group's response as points below.

____

____

____

____

____

ISBN: 978-1-98-856656-6

184 What is a Phylogenetic Tree?

Key Question: What are phylogenetic trees?

Phylogenetics is the study of the evolutionary history and the relationships among individuals or groups of organisms. These relationships are often shown diagrammatically as a phylogenetic tree. A **phylogenetic tree** represents a likely hypothesis of the evolutionary relationships between biological groups or taxa (*sing.* taxon). A taxon may consist of individual species or be a larger group (e.g. an order).

Traditionally phylogenetic trees have been constructed based on similarities or differences in appearance, but in more recent times molecular comparisons have been used. Molecular phylogenetics can reveal differences not seen in morphological comparisons, and have resulted in the revision of some morphological phylogenies where organisms could not be separated on appearance. Phylogenetic trees are often constructed based on cladistics (below).

What do phylogenetic trees look like?

Phylogenetic trees represent possible evolutionary histories, and there are many different ways they can be drawn (right). Depending on how the tree is constructed, some represent evolutionary time through the length of the branches (lines). Phylogenetic trees based on cladistics (cladograms) do not represent evolutionary time.

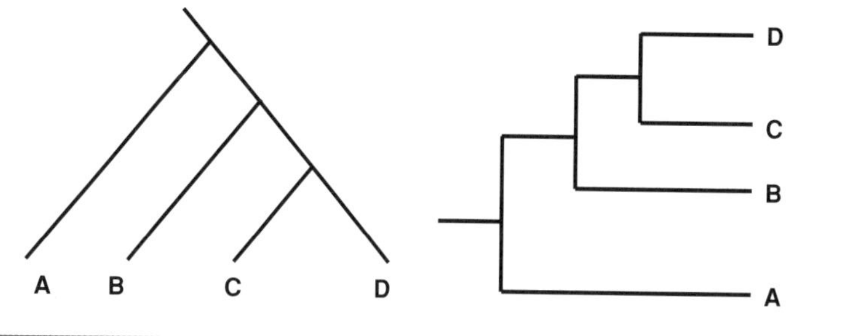

Determining phylogenetic relationships

- Increasingly, analyses to determine evolutionary relationships rely on cladistic analyses of character states. Cladistic analysis groups species according to their most recent common ancestor on the basis of **shared derived characteristics** or synapomorphies. All other characters are ignored.
- A phylogeny constructed using cladistics thus includes only monophyletic groups, i.e. the common ancestor and all of its descendants. It excludes both paraphyletic and polyphyletic groups (right). It is important to understand these terms when constructing cladograms and to also understand that the terms are relative to whereever you start in the phylogenetic tree (i.e. where the common ancestor is).
- The cladist restriction to using only synapomorphies creates an unambiguous branching tree. One problem with this approach is that a strictly cladistic classification could theoretically have an impractically large number of taxonomic levels and may be incompatible with a Linnaean system.

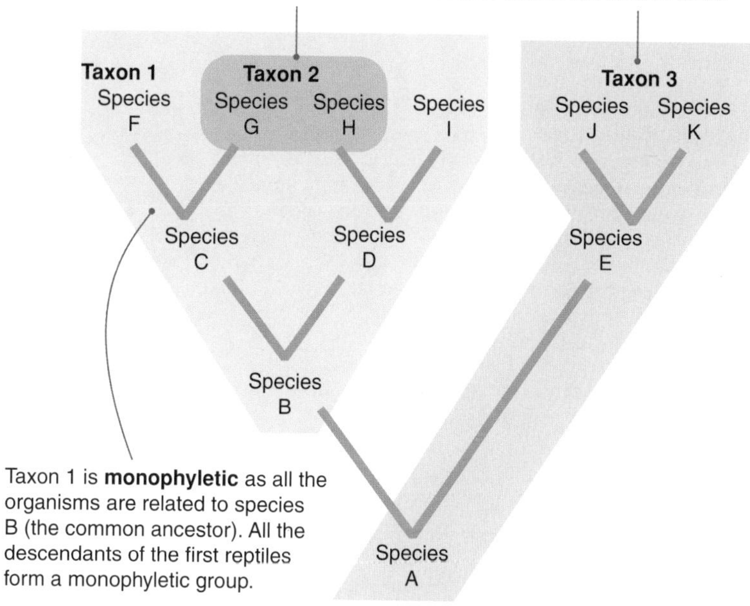

Taxon 2 is **polyphyletic** as it includes organisms with different ancestors. The group "warm-blooded (endothermic) animals" is polyphyletic as it includes birds and mammals.
Taxon 3 is **paraphyletic**. It includes species A without including all of A's descendants. The traditional grouping of reptiles is paraphyletic because it does not include birds.
Taxon 1
Species F
Taxon 2
Species G
Species H
Species I
Taxon 3
Species J
Species K
Species C
Species D
Species E
Species B
Species A
Taxon 1 is **monophyletic** as all the organisms are related to species B (the common ancestor). All the descendants of the first reptiles form a monophyletic group.

1. What does a phylogenetic tree show? ______________________________

2. Why might a phylogenetic tree based on molecular differences be preferred over phylogenies based on appearance?

3. Explain why it is useful to construct phylogenetic trees that are monophyletic: ______________________________

ISBN: 978-1-98-856656-6

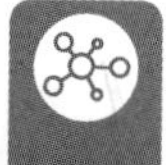

- Scientists can use the tools at their disposal, including anatomical and molecular evidence, to construct a branching diagram to illustrate how the species in a taxonomic group are related. These '**phylogenetic trees**' represent a hypothesis for the evolutionary history of the taxon and will be supported to greater or lesser extents by the evidence.
- Increasingly, DNA and protein analyses are indicating that many traditional phylogenies do not accurately portray evolutionary relationships. This is true at all levels of classification including class (e.g. reptiles and birds) and order e.g. primates. To illustrate this, the traditional classification of primates is compared with the revised classification based on cladistic analysis (a newer method of determining evolutionary relationships based on molecular evidence).

Two view of the phylogeny of primates

A classical taxonomic view

Hominidae

Pongidae

The 'great apes'

Humans

Chimpanzees

Gorillas

Orangutans

On the basis of overall anatomical similarity (e.g. bones and limb length, teeth, musculature), apes were grouped into a family (Pongidae) that is separate from humans and their immediate ancestors (Hominidae). The family Pongidae (the great apes) is not monophyletic (of one phylogeny with one common ancestor and all its descendants), because it stems from an ancestor that also gave rise to a species in another family (i.e. humans). This traditional classification scheme is now at odds with schemes derived after considering genetic evidence.

A view based on molecular evidence

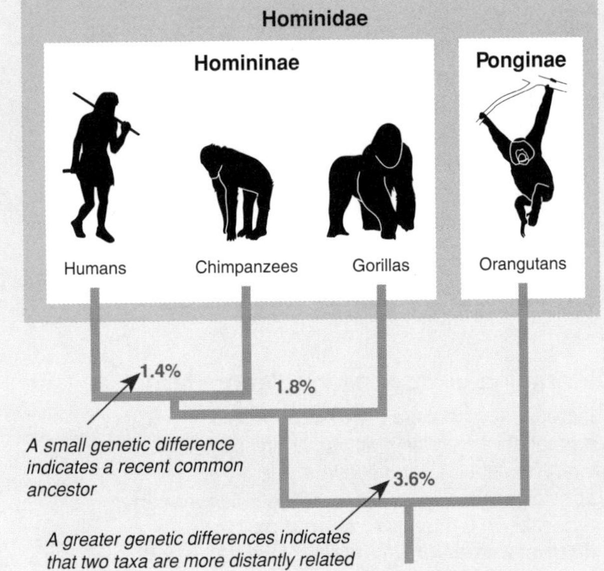
Hominidae
Homininae
Ponginae
Humans
Chimpanzees
Gorillas
Orangutans
1.4%
1.8%
3.6%
A small genetic difference indicates a recent common ancestor
A greater genetic differences indicates that two taxa are more distantly related

Based on the evidence of genetic differences (% values above), chimpanzees and gorillas are more closely related to humans than to orangutans, and chimpanzees are more closely related to humans than they are to gorillas. Under this scheme there is no true family of great apes. The family Hominidae includes two subfamilies: Ponginae and Homininae (humans, chimpanzees, and gorillas). This classification is monophyletic: the Hominidae includes all the species that arise from a common ancestor.

4. Interpret the phylogenies of primates above to explain how molecular evidence has contributed to revisions of the relatedness of the taxa pictured:

5. Suggest why classifications based on molecular evidence might provide a more likely phylogeny than one based on appearance alone:

6. What evidence has led to the reclassification of the primates?

ISBN: 978-1-98-856656-6

185 The Phylogeny of Animals

Key Question: What is the evolutionary history of animals?
The animals are a monophyletic group of multicellular eukaryotes that arose early in evolution from a group of protists called choanoflagellates. Their phylogeny is based on a number of characters including presence of tissues, body symmetry (radial or bilateral), the presence or absence of a body cavity, and the number of body layers (diploblastic (2) or triploblastic (3)). The animal phylogeny below is based on DNA sequence data of a number of genes from various phyla. The short vertical bars indicate when novel traits arose.

Choanoflagellates

Sponges

No body symmetry
Immobile
No tissues

Cnidaria

Ctenophora

TWO TISSUE LAYERS
RADIAL SYMMETRY

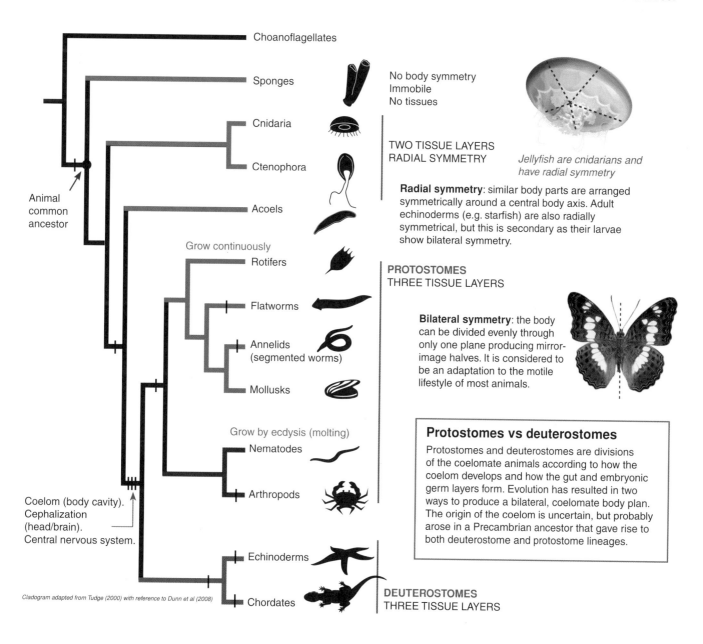

Jellyfish are cnidarians and have radial symmetry

Animal common ancestor

Acoels

Radial symmetry: similar body parts are arranged symmetrically around a central body axis. Adult echinoderms (e.g. starfish) are also radially symmetrical, but this is secondary as their larvae show bilateral symmetry.

Grow continuously

Rotifers

PROTOSTOMES
THREE TISSUE LAYERS

Flatworms

Annelids (segmented worms)

Mollusks

Bilateral symmetry: the body can be divided evenly through only one plane producing mirror-image halves. It is considered to be an adaptation to the motile lifestyle of most animals.

Grow by ecdysis (molting)

Nematodes

Arthropods

Coelom (body cavity).
Cephalization (head/brain).
Central nervous system.

Echinoderms

Chordates

DEUTEROSTOMES
THREE TISSUE LAYERS

Cladogram adapted from Tudge (2000) with reference to Dunn et al (2008)

Protostomes vs deuterostomes

Protostomes and deuterostomes are divisions of the coelomate animals according to how the coelom develops and how the gut and embryonic germ layers form. Evolution has resulted in two ways to produce a bilateral, coelomate body plan. The origin of the coelom is uncertain, but probably arose in a Precambrian ancestor that gave rise to both deuterostome and protostome lineages.

1. (a) In the phylogenetic tree above, short vertical bars indicate when certain traits originated. Identify when each of the following traits arose by assigning each bar its corresponding letter, as follows (one is completed for you). Note that segmentation arises independently three times in three lineages. Radial symmetry in adults (**R**). Secondary loss of coelom (**L**). Segmentation (**S**). Multicellularity (**M**). Bilateral symmetry (**B**). Protostomy (**P**). Deuterostomy (**D**).

   (b) Place a vertical bar where you think ecdysis (molting of the cuticle or exoskeleton) arose in animal evolution.

2. (a) The free-swimming larvae of cnidarians are bilaterally symmetric. Also, new research shows that a few primitive cnidarians show bilateral symmetry. Where would you place the origin of bilateral symmetry based on this information?

   (b) If the cnidarians were reclassified, on what basis would they remain distinct from other bilateral organisms?

ISBN: 978-1-98-856656-6

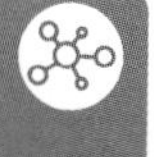

186 Constructing Phylogenies Using Cladistics

Key Question: What are cladograms and how are shared derived characters used to construct them?

A **cladogram** is a phylogenetic tree constructed using a taxonomic tool called cladistics. Cladistics groups organisms on the basis of their **shared derived characters** (features arising in an ancestor and shared by all its descendants) and ignores features that are not the result of shared ancestry. A clade, or branch on the tree, includes a common ancestor and all its descendants (i.e. it is monophyletic). Increasingly, cladistic methods rely on molecular data (e.g. DNA sequences) to determine phylogenies. Highly conserved DNA sequences are used because changes are likely to signal a significant evolutionary divergence. Cladograms may not always agree completely with phylogenies constructed using traditional methods but similarities in the trees indicate that the proposed relationships are likely to be correct.

Derived vs ancestral characters

When constructing cladograms, shared derived characters are used to separate the clades (branches on the tree). Using ancestral characters (those that arise in a species that is ancestral to more than one group) would result in distantly related organisms being grouped together and would not help to determine the evolutionary relationships within a clade. Whether or not a character is derived depends on the taxonomic level being considered. For example, a backbone is an ancestral character for mammals, but a derived character for vertebrates. Production of milk is a derived character shared by all mammals but no other taxa.

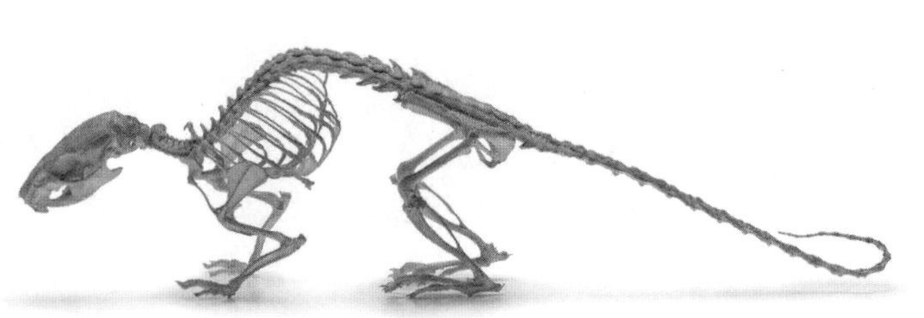

The backbone in a mammal, e.g. rat, is an ancestral character common to all vertebrate taxa. However, the production of milk from mammary glands is a derived character, shared by all mammals but no other taxa.

Constructing a simple cladogram

- A table listing the features for comparison allows us to identify where we should make branches in the cladogram. An **outgroup** (one which is known to have no or little relationship to the other taxa in the table) is used as a basis for comparison.
- The table (right) lists features shared by selected taxa. The outgroup (jawless fish) shares just one feature (vertebral column), so it gives a reference for comparison and the first branch of the cladogram. As the number of taxa in the table increases, the number of possible trees that could be drawn increases exponentially.
- Several different cladograms can be constructed from the same data. To determine the most likely relationships, the rule of **parsimony** is used. Parsimony assumes that the tree with the simplest explanation (the least number of evolutionary events) is most likely to show the correct (or most plausible) evolutionary relationship.
- A possible cladogram for the data in the table is shown on the right. Its construction assumed that six evolutionary events took place (labeled as blue bars on the cladogram). If other cladograms were constructed, but involved more evolutionary events, the one shown would be assumed to be correct because it is the most parsimonious.
- Parsimony can lead to some confusion. Some evolutionary events have occurred multiple times. An example is the evolution of the four chambered heart, which occurred separately in both birds and mammals. The use of fossil evidence and DNA analysis can help to solve problems like this.

Taxa

Comparative features	Jawless fish (outgroup)	Bony fish	Amphibians	Lizards	Birds	Mammals
Vertebral column	✔	✔	✔	✔	✔	✔
Jaws	✘	✔	✔	✔	✔	✔
Four supporting limbs	✘	✘	✔	✔	✔	✔
Amniotic egg	✘	✘	✘	✔	✔	✔
Diapsid skull	✘	✘	✘	✔	✔	✘
Feathers	✘	✘	✘	✘	✔	✘
Hair	✘	✘	✘	✘	✘	✔

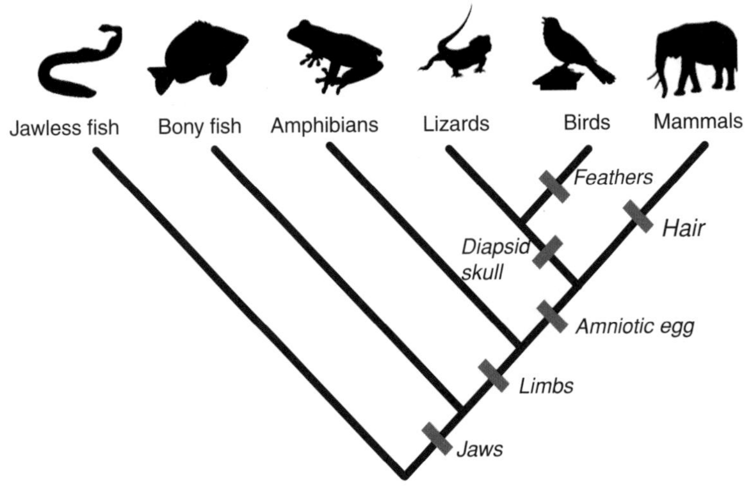

ISBN: 978-1-98-856656-6

1. (a) Distinguish between a shared derived characteristic and a shared ancestral characteristic: ____________________

(b) Why are ancestral characters not useful in constructing evolutionary histories? ____________________

2. What assumption is made when applying the rule of parsimony in constructing a cladogram? ____________________

3. Two possible phylogenetic trees constructed from the same character table are shown below. The numbers next to a blue bar represent an evolutionary event.

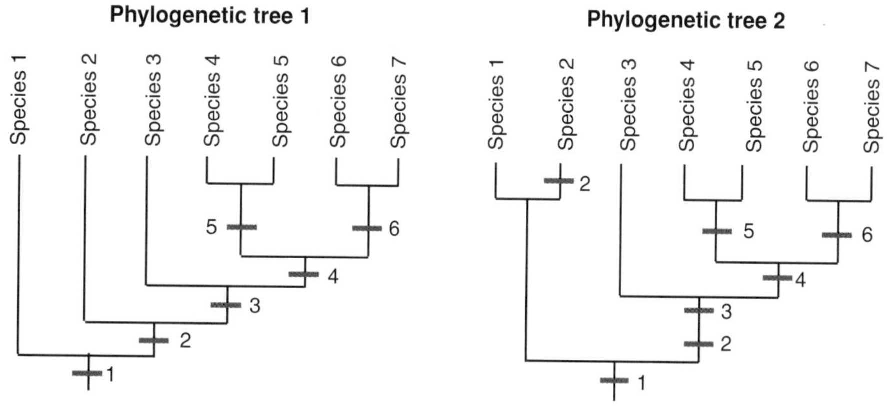

Phylogenetic tree 1

Species 1, Species 2, Species 3, Species 4, Species 5, Species 6, Species 7

Phylogenetic tree 2

Species 1, Species 2, Species 3, Species 4, Species 5, Species 6, Species 7

(a) Which tree is more likely to be correct? ____________________

(b) State your reason: ____________________

(c) Identify the event which has occurred twice in phylogenetic tree 2: ____________________

4. A phylogenetic tree is a hypothesis for an evolutionary history. How could you test it? ____________________

5. Use the shapes below to construct a cladogram that shows their phylogenetic relationships (hint: A is the outgroup).

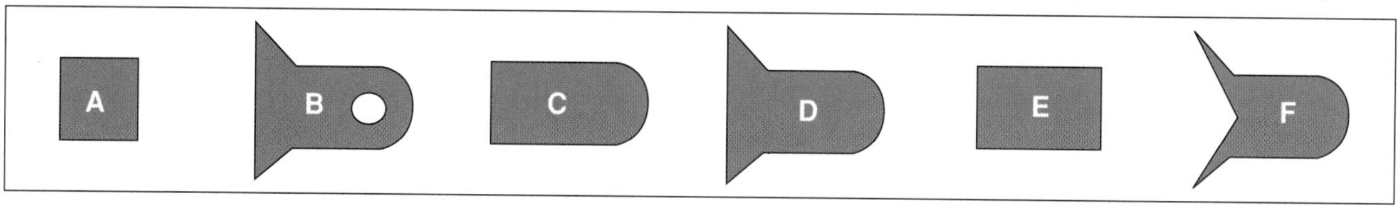

A B C D E F

ISBN: 978-1-98-856656-6

187 Why Are Birds Dinosaurs?

Key Question: What is the evidence from shared derived characters that puts birds and dinosaurs in the same taxon?

Defining groups of organisms and evaluating their ancestry using morphological features alone can be problematic because similarities in structure may not necessarily be the result of shared ancestry. This problem can be overcome by considering only **shared derived characters**, i.e. the characters of two of more taxa that are present in their most recent common ancestor but not in earlier ancestors. Tracing the evolution of derived character states can more accurately identify the evolutionary history of a taxon. The ancestry of birds illustrates this. Although birds are commonly regarded as a single taxon (and in modern terms they are) birds are simply the last in the lineage of the dinosaurs. Recent analysis of the protein structure of fossil collagen from *Tyrannosaur* fossils puts birds and dinosaurs in the same taxon.

Derived characters shared by birds and dinosaurs

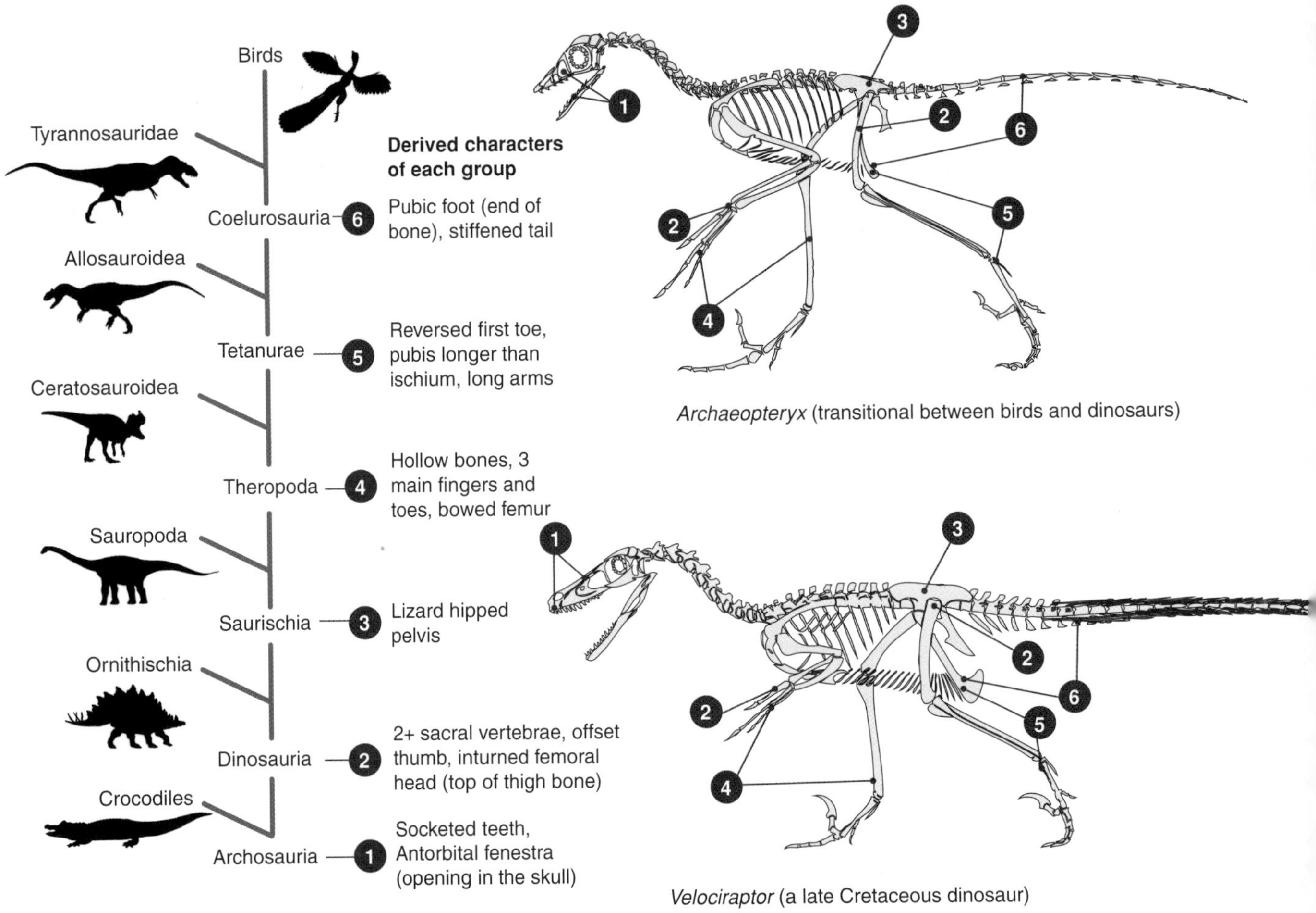

Birds
Tyrannosauridae
Coelurosauria
Allosauroidea
Tetanurae
Ceratosauroidea
Theropoda
Sauropoda
Saurischia
Ornithischia
Dinosauria
Crocodiles
Archosauria

Derived characters of each group

6. Pubic foot (end of bone), stiffened tail
5. Reversed first toe, pubis longer than ischium, long arms
4. Hollow bones, 3 main fingers and toes, bowed femur
3. Lizard hipped pelvis
2. 2+ sacral vertebrae, offset thumb, inturned femoral head (top of thigh bone)
1. Socketed teeth, Antorbital fenestra (opening in the skull)

Archaeopteryx (transitional between birds and dinosaurs)

Velociraptor (a late Cretaceous dinosaur)

1. Explain how grouping organisms based on shared derived characters can help explain their evolutionary history:

2. Interpret the ladder of derived character states to explain why birds are considered to be the last organisms in the lineage of dinosaurs:

ISBN: 978-1-98-856656-6

188 Constructing a Cladogram

Key Question: How is systematic organization of characters used to construct a cladogram?

	Character												
Taxon	**1**	**2**	**3**	**4**	**5**	**6**	**7**	**8**	**9**	**10**	**11**	**12**	**13**
Zebra-perch sea chub	0	0	0	0	0	0	0	0	0	0	0	0	0
Barred surfperch	1	0	0	0	0	0	0	0	0	1	1	0	0
Walleye surfperch	1	0	0	0	0	1	0	1	0	1	1	0	0
Black perch	1	1	1	0	0	0	0	0	0	0	0	1	0
Rainbow seaperch	1	1	1	0	0	0	0	0	0	0	0	1	0
Rubberlip surfperch	1	1	1	1	1	0	0	0	0	0	0	0	1
Pile surfperch	1	1	1	1	1	0	0	0	0	0	0	0	1
White seaperch	1	1	1	1	1	0	0	0	0	0	0	0	0
Shiner perch	1	1	1	1	1	1	0	0	0	0	0	0	0
Pink seaperch	1	1	1	1	1	1	1	1	0	0	0	0	0
Kelp perch	1	1	1	1	1	1	1	1	1	0	0	0	0
Reef perch	1	1	1	1	1	1	1	1	1	0	0	0	0

Steve Lonhart (SIMoN / MBNMS) PD NOAA

Surfperches are viviparous (live bearing) and the females give birth to well developed young. Some of the characters (below, left) relate to adaptations of the male for internal fertilization. Others relate to deterring or detecting predators. In the matrix, characters are assigned a 0 or 1 depending on whether they represent the ancestral (0) or derived (1) state. This coding is common in cladistics because it allows computer analysis of the data.

Selected characters for cladogram assembly

1. Viviparity (live bearing)	0 No	1 Yes
2. Males with flask organ	0 No	1 Yes
3. Orbit without bony front wall	0 Yes	1 No
4. Tail length	0 Short	1 Long
5. Body depth	0 Deep	1 Narrow
6. Body size	0 Large	1 Small
7. Length of dorsal fin base	0 Long	1 Short
8. Eye diameter	0 Moderate	1 Large
9 Males with anal crescent	0 No	1 Yes
10 Pectoral bone with process	0 No	1 Yes
11. Length of dorsal sheath	0 Long	1 Short
12. Body mostly darkish	0 No	1 Yes
13. Flanks with large black bars	0 No	1 Yes

Notes and working space

1. This activity provides the taxa and character matrix for 11 genera of marine fishes in the family of surfperches. The outgroup given is a representative of a sister family of rudderfishes (zebra-perch sea chub), which are not live-bearing. Your task is to create the most parsimonious cladogram from the matrix of character states provided. To help you, we have organized the matrix with genera having the smallest blocks of derived character states (1) at the top following the outgroup representative. Use a separate sheet of graph paper and work from left to right to assemble your cladogram. Identify the origin of derived character states with horizontal bars, as shown in Activity 186. CLUE: You should end up with 15 steps. Two derived character states arise twice independently. Staple your cladogram to this page.

2. (a) Why are the character states organized in a matrix? ______________________________

   (b) Why is it useful to designate the characters states as 0 (ancestral) or derived (1)? ______________________________

3. In the cladogram you have constructed for the surfperches, two characters have evolved twice independently:

   (a) Identify these two characters: ______________________________

   (b) What selection pressures do you think might have been important in the evolution of these two derived states?

____

ISBN: 978-1-98-856656-6

186

EVO-3
2.D

189 What is a Species?

Key Question How are species assigned and how can we distinguish distinct species with a similar appearance?

Humans have always tried to identify and classify the diversity of organisms but assigning species on the basis of appearance alone can be inaccurate because of phenomena such as convergence. A 'good' classification should accurately reflect phylogeny. Traditional classifications were based on similarities in morphology, but modern taxonomy relies heavily on molecular analysis to classify species on the basis of their evolutionary relationships. The **biological species concept** defines a species as group of organisms that can successfully interbreed and produce fertile offspring, *and* is reproductively isolated from other such groups. However, assigning an organism to a species is not trivial, as described below. How we identify species has important implications, because we cannot conserve what we cannot recognize.

Different species may look the same

Assigning species based on morphology alone can lead to mis-classification. Some organisms may be morphologically indistinguishable but DNA analysis or close examination of their biology may show them to be different species.

Example: The butterfly genus *Heliconius* comprises 39 species, many of which mimic each others' patterns and colors. *Heliconius* is a **species complex**, i.e. a group of closely related or sibling species with similar appearances and unclear boundaries between them. Their appearance varies with geographical location, but different species often adopt a similar pattern in the same location (left) making species determination based on appearance alone extremely difficult.

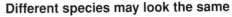

African bush elephant
Loxodonta africana
Yathin S Krishnappa CC3.0

African forest elephant
Loxodonta cyclotis
Thomas Breuer cc2.5

Molecular analysis can distinguish cryptic species

DNA variation occurs within species as well as between species, so scientists must determine what level of variation is acceptable within a species before a new species classification is made. If such boundaries were not set, every molecular variation observed would result in the classification of a new species.

Example: Molecular studies have been important in identifying **cryptic species**, i.e. two or more distinct species disguised under one species name. The African bush elephant and the African forest elephant were once considered subspecies, but recent genetic analysis has confirmed they are separate species, which diverged from each other 2-7 million years ago. Analysis of morphological differences, including skull anatomy, supports this.

A. muscaria muscaria

Amanita m. var. *formosa*

Amanita m. var. *guessowii*

Conservation and species assignment

The recognition of species complexes and cryptic species has important implications to our estimates of biodiversity, and affects decisions made in species conservation and in the management of economically important species (including pests and medically important organisms). DNA analyses indicate that cryptic species are more common than previously thought, providing a strong argument for "whole ecosystem" management of biodiversity.

Example: The fly agaric mushroom (*Amanita muscaria*, left) comprises several cryptic species. Genetic analyses in 2006 and 2008 showed at least four groups or clades that are genetically distinct enough to be considered separate species. The varieties identified left include the type specimen (far left) and two of the subspecies now considered to be separate species.

1. In what way have traditional methods of classification based on morphology been inadequate? ____________

____

____

____

2. Explain the implications of species complexes and cryptic species in conservation: ____________

____

____

____

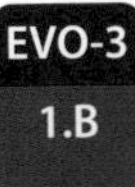
EVO-3 1.B

196

197

ISBN: 978-1-98-856656-6

190 Patterns of Evolution

Key Question: What evolutionary patterns can be observed when comparing species and their niches?

The diversification of one species into one or more separate species can follow one of four main patterns. **Divergent evolution** occurs when two species diverge from a common ancestor. Divergence is common in evolution and responsible for evolutionary radiations. When unrelated species evolve similar forms as a result of similar selection pressures it is called **convergent evolution** (convergence). A similar phenomenon in related lineages is called **parallel evolution** (parallelism). The fourth pattern, **coevolution**, involves reciprocal evolution in unrelated lineages.

Divergent evolution (cladogenesis). A lineage splits and evolves independently due to different selection pressures in different environments. Species may later occupy the same environment, e.g. black swan (*Cygnus atratus*) and mute swan (*Cygnus olor*).

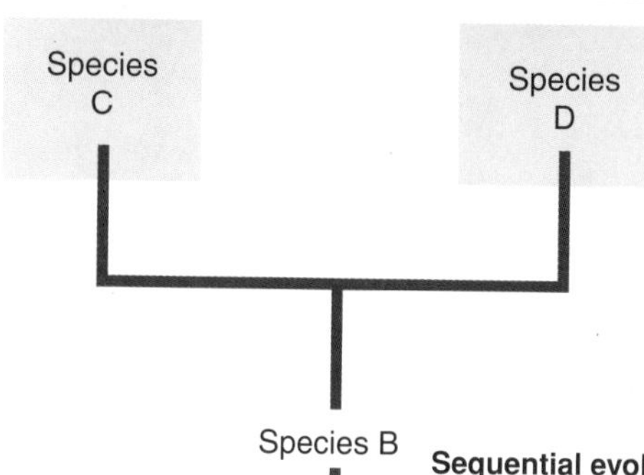

Sequential evolution (anagenesis)
A species accumulates enough genetic changes over time to form new species (remaining interbreeding).

Convergent evolution. Unrelated or distantly related species in similar environments and under similar selection pressures evolve similar features, e.g. streamlined swimming form in aquatic birds and mammals.

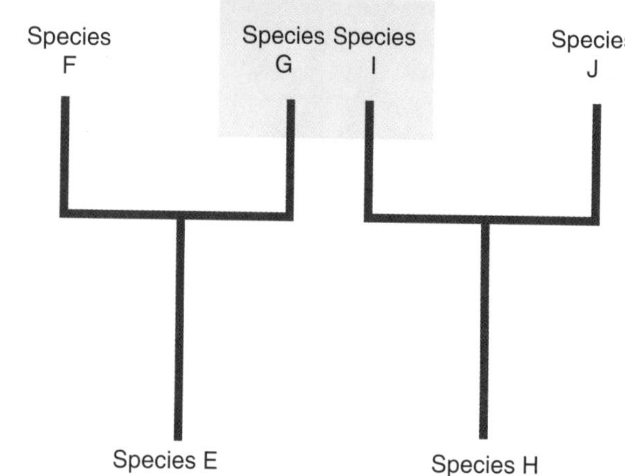

Parallel evolution. Closely related species living in separate but similar environments independently evolve similar features, e.g. the cichlid fishes of the East African Rift Valley lakes. Left: the frontosa (L. Tanganyika). Right: the Malawi blue dolphin (L. Malawi).

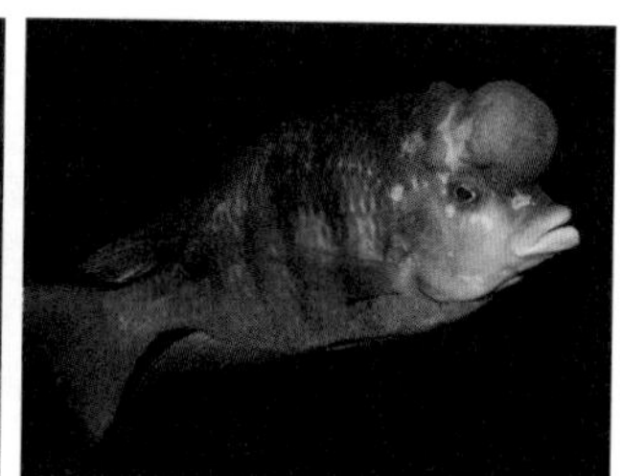

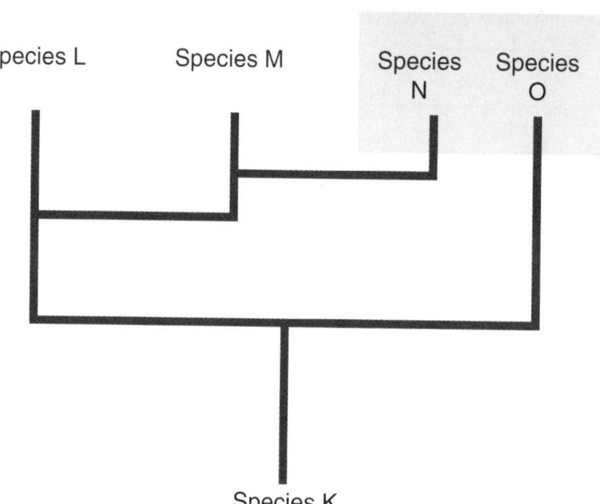

Coevolution. Reciprocal evolution in unrelated species as a result of selection pressures each imposes on the other. It results in complementary characteristics, e.g. flowering plants and their bird and insect pollinators.

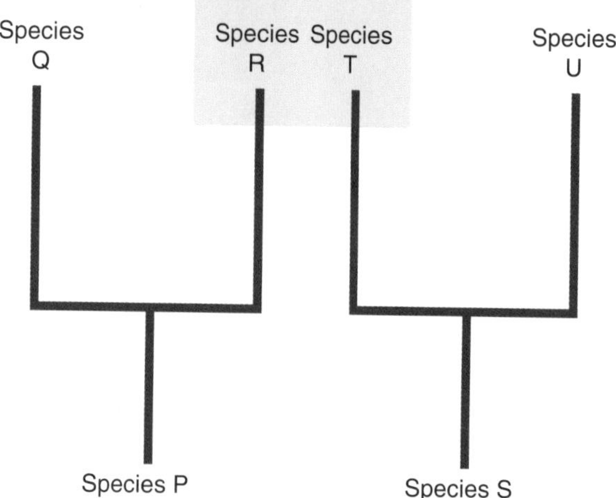

ISBN: 978-1-98-856656-6

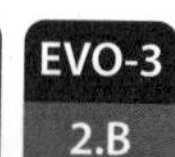

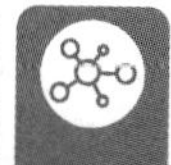

There are two basic models for the pace of evolutionary change: phyletic gradualism and punctuated equilibrium. It is most likely that both mechanisms operate at different times and in different situations. Interpretations of the fossil record vary depending on the time scales involved. During its formative millennia, a species may have accumulated changes gradually (e.g. over 50,000 years). If that species survives for 5 million years, the evolution of its characteristics would have been compressed into just 1% of its evolutionary history. In the fossil record, the species would appear quite suddenly.

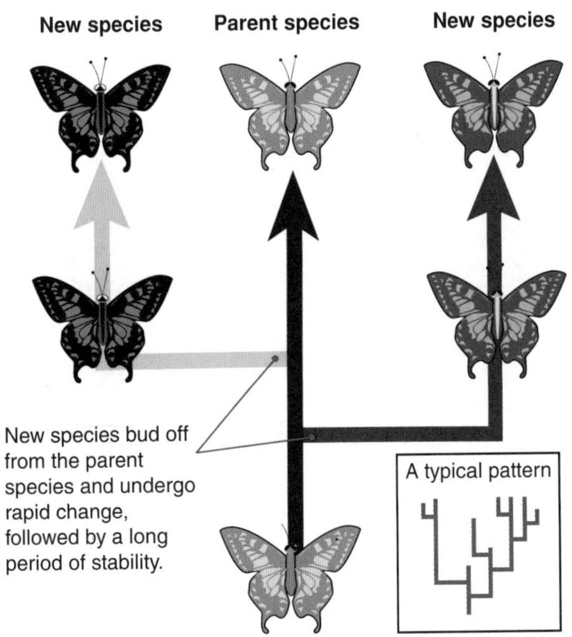

Punctuated equilibrium

According to the punctuated equilibrium theory, there is very little change for most of a species' existence and little time is spent in active evolutionary change. The stimulus for evolution occurs when some crucial aspect of the environment changes.

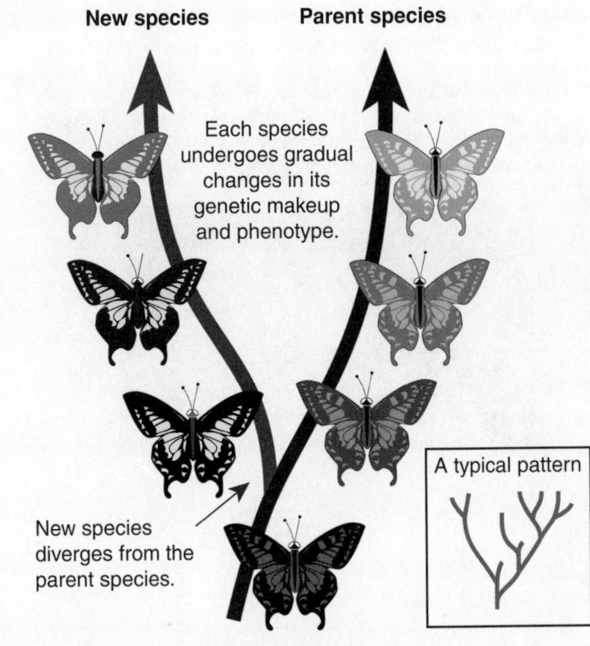

New species
Parent species
Each species undergoes gradual changes in its genetic makeup and phenotype.
New species diverges from the parent species.
A typical pattern

Phyletic gradualism

In a phyletic gradualism model, speciation is a uniform process and species diverge by slowly accumulating adaptations in response to new selection pressures. There is no clear line between an ancestral species and its descendant species.

1. Explain the likely causes of divergent evolution: ______________________________

____

____

2. What is the difference between divergence and sequential evolution? ______________________________

____

____

____

4. Explain how coevolution might occur: ______________________________

____

____

____

5. (a) Explain the characteristics of the two models for the pace of evolutionary change represented above:

____

____

____

(b) Explain how these contrasting patterns might appear differently in the fossil record: ______________________________

____

____

ISBN: 978-1-98-856656-6

191 Divergence is an Evolutionary Pattern

Key Question: How does divergent evolution occur?

Divergent evolution describes the divergence of two or more species from a common ancestor. It arises through the accumulation of genetic differences in diverging lines, usually following isolation, so that gene flow between them stops and new species arise. Divergence is a common evolutionary pattern. When it involves the diversification of a lineage into many different niches, it is called **adaptive radiation**.

An overview of divergent evolution

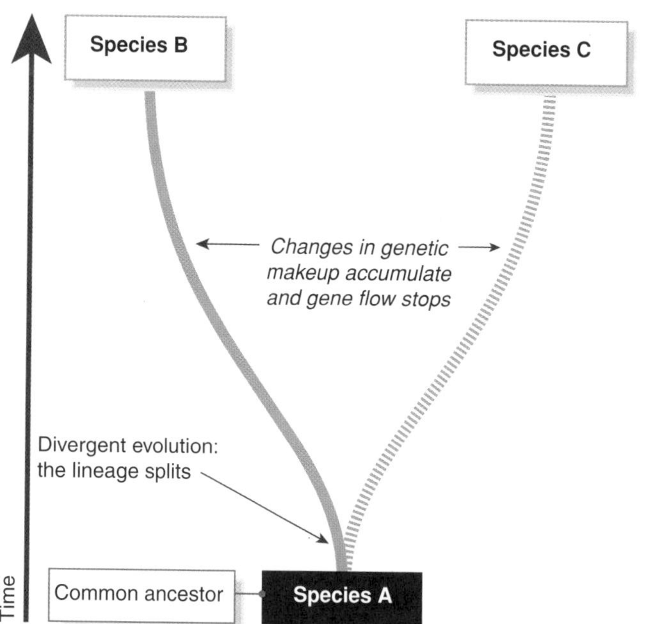

Adaptive radiation of trilobite orders

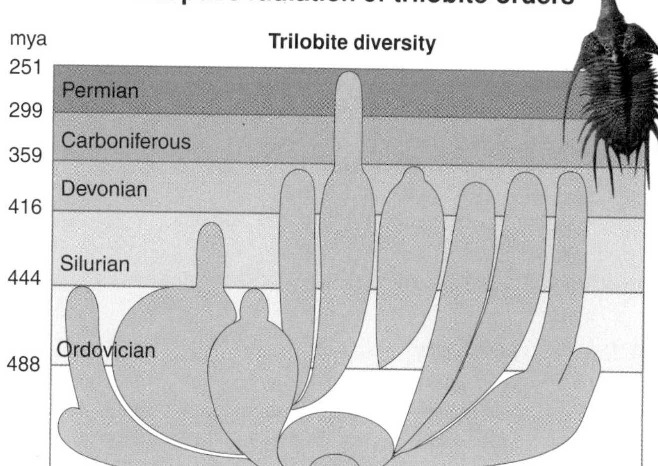

Trilobites are extinct marine arthropods. They were one of the earliest arthropod groups and were highly successful, diverging many times during their history to exploit a wide range of niches. They appeared in the fossil record near the beginning of the Cambrian and disappeared in the Permian mass extinction. Each blue shape represents an order. Its width indicates its diversity.

Dwergenpaartje CC 3.0

Paradoxides, late Cambrian

DanielCD CC 3.0

Dalmanites, Silurian

Ghedoghedo CC 3.0

Cheirurus, Ordivician

Daderot

Walliserops, middle Devonian

Because trilobites had a hard exoskeleton they fossilized well and have left an extensive fossil record. These fossils show that trilobites rapidly diversified early in their evolution. As many as 50,000 species of trilobite may have existed.

1. Distinguish between divergent evolution and adaptive radiation: ______________________

____

____

____

____

2. (a) How would you describe the evolution of the trilobites? ______________________

____

____

____

(b) When was the trilobite group most diverse? ______________________

ISBN: 978-1-98-856656-6

Divergent evolution: snapping shrimp

- The Isthmus of Panama separates the Pacific Ocean and Caribbean Sea in the region of Central America. The isthmus closed about 3 million years ago.
- On either side of the isthmus are numerous species of snapping shrimp. Every species on the Pacific side has a sister species on the Caribbean side.
- Genetic studies suggest that before the appearance of the isthmus there were already numerous species of snapping shrimps. After the isthmus formed, each species diverged, creating two new species, one on either side of the isthmus.

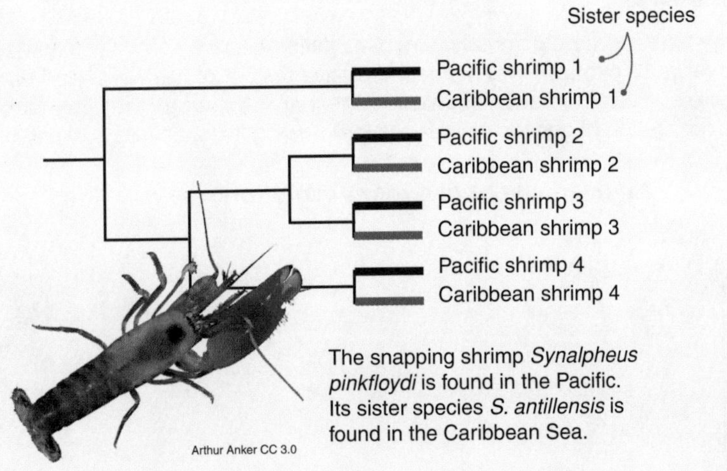

The snapping shrimp *Synalpheus pinkfloydi* is found in the Pacific. Its sister species *S. antillensis* is found in the Caribbean Sea.

Adaptive radiation

Adaptive radiation is a type of divergent evolution in which a single lineage diversifies rapidly to produce a large number of species occupying different niches. The example below right describes the radiation of the mammals, which took place after the extinction of the dinosaurs made new niches available. Note that the evolution of species may not necessarily involve branching.

- The earliest true mammals evolved about 195 million years ago, long before they underwent their major adaptive radiation some 65-50 million years ago. These ancestors to the modern forms were very small (12 cm long) and typically shrew-like. Many were nocturnal and fed on insects and other invertebrates. *Megazostrodon* is a typical example. This animal is known from fossil remains in South Africa and first appeared in the Early Jurassic period (about 195 million years ago).
- It was climatic change as well as the extinction of the dinosaurs (and their related forms) that suddenly left many niches vacant for exploitation by such adaptable 'generalists'. All modern mammal orders developed very quickly and early.

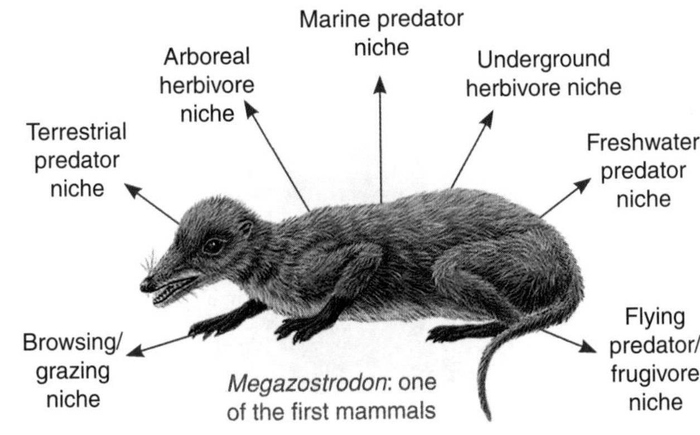

Megazostrodon: one of the first mammals

3. (a) Suggest why the trilobites diversified so quickly: __________

   (b) Considering the trilobites existed from 521 million years ago to 252 million years ago, approximately what percentage of their time in existence was spent in the evolution of new trilobite orders:

4. What evidence is there that the closing of the Isthmus of Panama was a factor in the divergence of snapping shrimps?

5. What factors were important in the adaptive radiation of the early mammals? __________

ISBN: 978-1-98-856656-6

192 Adaptive Radiation in Mammals

Key Question: What factors were important in the adaptive radiation of mammals?

Adaptive radiation is diversification among the descendants of a single ancestral group (one lineage) to occupy different niches. Most of the modern mammalian groups became established very early on. The diagram below shows the divergence of the mammals into the major orders that came to occupy the niches left vacant by the extinction of the dinosaurs. The vertical extent of each green shape shows the time span for which a particular order has existed. Those that reach the top of the chart have survived to the present day. The width of a shape shows how many species existed at any given time. The dotted lines indicate possible links between the orders for which there is no direct fossil evidence.

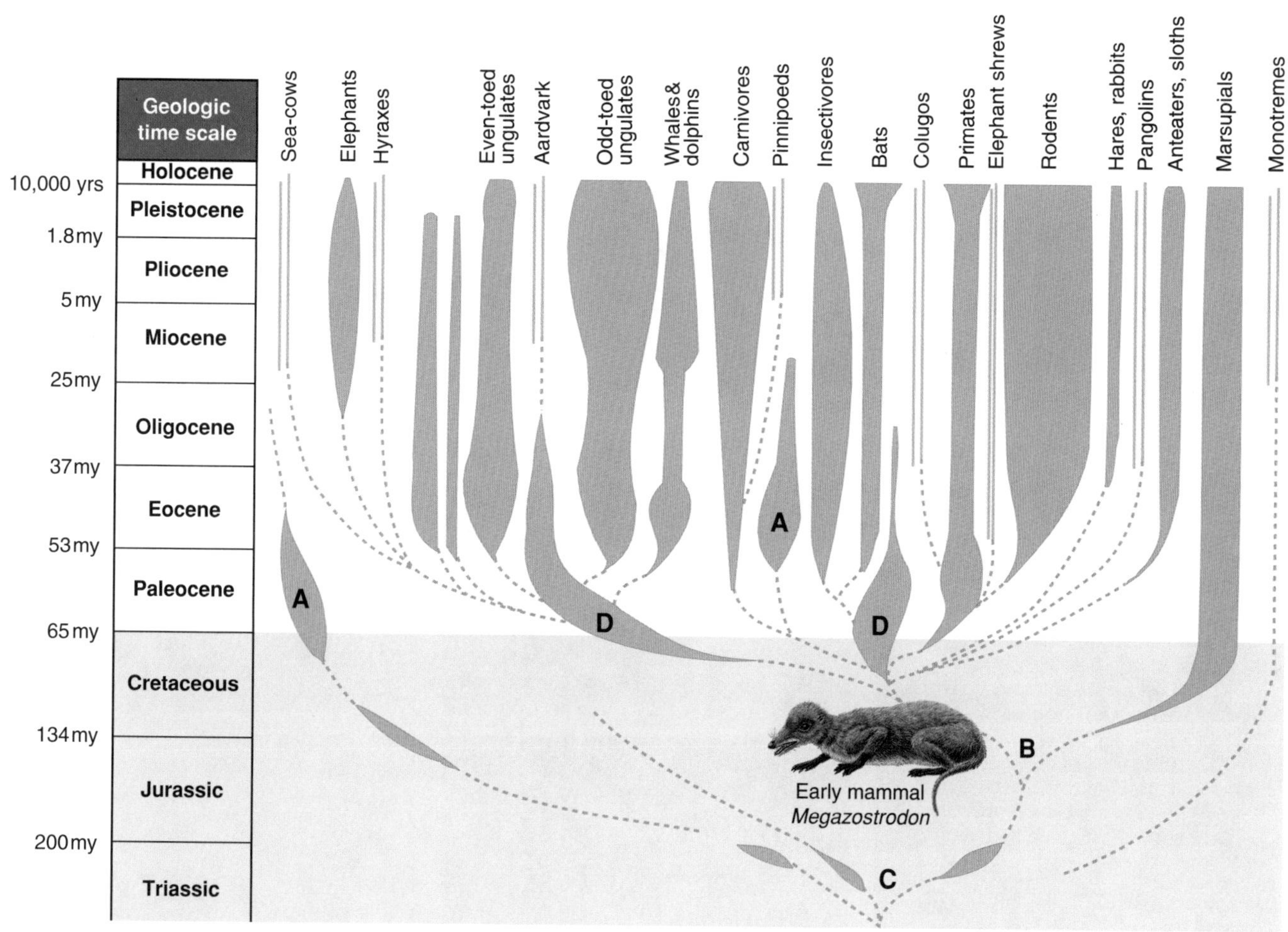

Geologic time scale
Holocene
Pleistocene
Pliocene
Miocene
Oligocene
Eocene
Paleocene
Cretaceous
Jurassic
Triassic
10,000 yrs
1.8my
5my
25my
37my
53my
65my
134my
200my
Sea-cows
Elephants
Hyraxes
Even-toed ungulates
Aardvark
Odd-toed ungulates
Whales & dolphins
Carnivores
Pinnipoeds
Insectivores
Bats
Colugos
Primates
Elephant shrews
Rodents
Hares, rabbits
Pangolins
Anteaters, sloths
Marsupials
Monotremes
A
A
D
D
B
C
Early mammal
Megazostrodon

1. In general terms, describe the adaptive radiation that occurred in mammals: ______________________

____

____

____

2. Name the term that you would use to describe the animal groups at point **C** (above): ______________________

3. Explain what occurred at point **B** (above): ______________________

____

4. Describe one thing that the animal orders labeled **D** (above) have in common: ______________________

____

5. Identify the two orders that appear to have been most successful in terms of the number of species produced:

____

6. Explain what has happened to the mammal orders labeled **A** in the diagram above: ______________________

____

7. Name the geological time period during which there was the most adaptive radiation: ______________________

ISBN: 978-1-98-856656-6

Vacant niches allow adaptive radiation

There have been at least two adaptive radiations during the evolution of placental mammals, occurring around the time of the extinction of the dinosaurs. Adaptive radiation occurs because of the appearance of new or vacant niches (ecological habitats and roles that can be exploited). The mammals shown below are representatives of one of these radiations and illustrate the features that evolved to exploit the vacant niches. The new mammals included large terrestrial and marine predators, nocturnal flying insect hunters, terrestrial invertebrate feeders, opportunistic generalists, and arboreal (tree based) frugivores (fruit eating).

8. Match the mammals shown at the top of the page with the niche/environment they have adapted to:

(a) Lion: ______________________

(b) Mouse: ______________________

(c) Sea lion: ______________________

(d) Hedgehog: ______________________

(e) Townsend bat: ______________________

(f) Gibbon: ______________________

9. The dinosaurs became extinct 65 million years ago. Predict the likely effect on mammalian evolution if dinosaurs had remained the dominant terrestrial animals.

____

____

____

____

ISBN: 978-1-98-856656-6

193 Allopatric Speciation

Key Question: How do geographical barriers lead to allopatric speciation?

Allopatric speciation refers to the genetic divergence of a species after a population becomes split and then isolated geographically. It is probably the most common mechanism by which new species arise and has certainly been important in regions where there have been cycles of geographical fragmentation, e.g. as a result of ice expansion and retreat (and accompanying sea level changes) during glacial and interglacial periods.

Stage 1: Moving into new environments

There are times when the range of a species expands for a variety of different reasons. A single population in a relatively homogeneous environment will move into new regions of their environment if there is intense competition for resources. Competition between members of the same species is the most intense because they are competing for identical resources in the same habitat. In the diagram on the right there is a 'parent population' of a single species with a common gene pool with regular 'gene flow'. Theoretically any individual can mate with any other individual of the opposite sex.

Stage 2: Geographical isolation

Parts of the population may become isolated by **physical barriers**, such as mountains, deserts, or stretches of water. These barriers may cut off those parts of the population that are at the extremes of the range and gene flow becomes rare or stops altogether. Climate change (e.g. ice ages and a consequent rise and fall in sea level) can leave 'islands' of habitat separated by large inhospitable zones that the species cannot traverse.

Example: In mountainous regions, alpine species can populate extensive areas of habitat during cool climatic periods. During warmer periods, they may become isolated because their habitat is reduced to 'islands' of high ground surrounded by inhospitable lowland habitat.

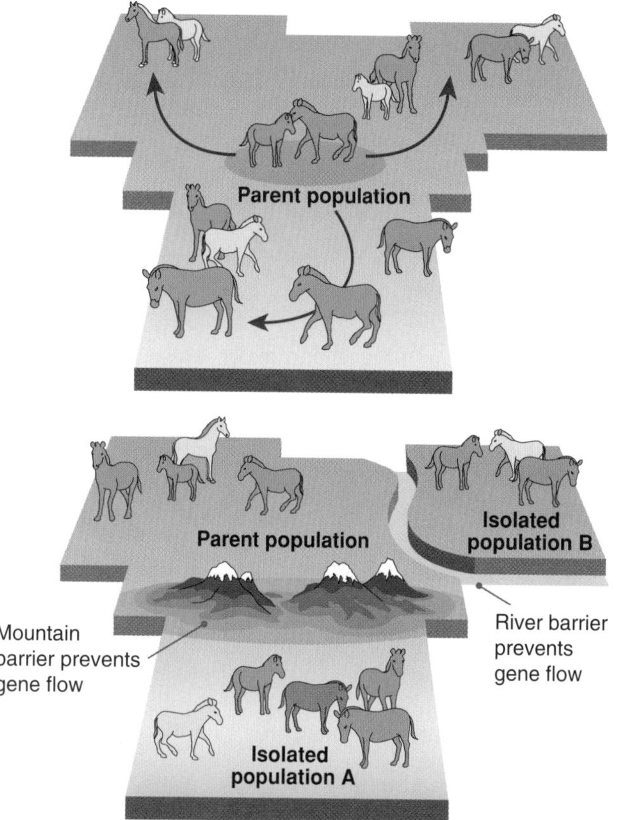

Stage 3: Different selection pressures

The isolated populations (A and B) may be subjected to quite different selection pressures. These will favor individuals with traits suited to each particular environment. For example, population A will be subjected to selection pressures found in drier conditions, favoring individuals with phenotypes (and genotypes) suited to dry conditions (e.g. better ability to conserve water). This would result in improved survival and reproductive performance. As allele frequencies for certain genes change, the population takes on the status of a subspecies. Reproductive isolation is not yet established but the subspecies are significantly different genetically from related populations.

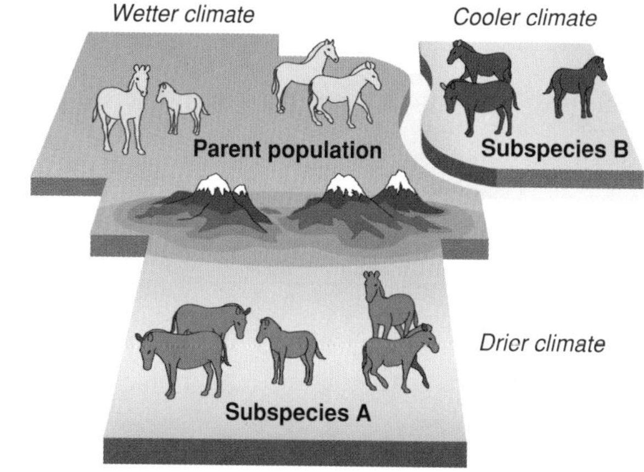

Stage 4: Reproductive isolation

The separated populations (isolated subspecies) undergo genetic changes to become reproductively isolated. Reproductive isolation can result through changes in morphology, behavior, or physiology and it prevents gene flow with other populations, even if they reunite at a later time (for example, if the geographical barrier is removed). In the diagram, gene flow does not occur but there is a zone of overlap between two species after species B has moves back into the range of the parent population. Closely-related species with an overlapping distribution like this are called **sympatric**. Those that remain geographically isolated are called **allopatric** species.

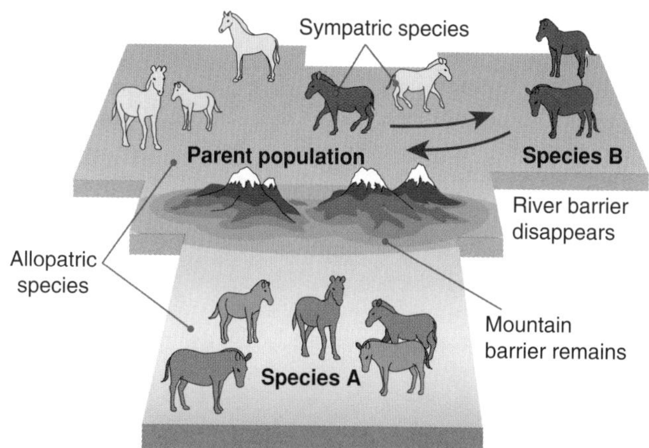

ISBN: 978-1-98-856656-6

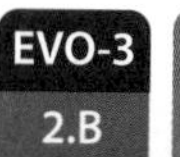

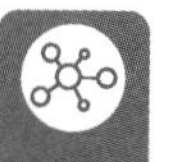

1. Why do some animals, given the opportunity, move into new environments?

2. Plants are unable to move. How might plants disperse to new environments?

3. Describe the amount of gene flow within a parent population prior to and during the expansion of a species' range:

4. Explain how cycles of climate change can cause large changes in sea level (up to 200 m):

5. (a) What kinds of physical barriers could isolate different parts of the same population?

(b) How might emigration achieve the same effect as geographical isolation?

6. (a) How might selection pressures differ for a population that becomes isolated from the parent population?

(b) Describe the general effect of the change in selection pressures on the allele frequencies of the isolated gene pool:

7. Use the diagram on the previous page to explain how allopatric populations become reproductively isolated:

8. Predict the consequence of removing barriers to gene flow in newly isolated populations:

ISBN: 978-1-98-856656-6

Allopatric speciation in Death Valley pupfish

During the last glacial period, the desert surrounding Death Valley in North America once had a relatively wet climate, with a large lake and numerous rivers. As the lake and rivers dried up, populations of pupfish in it were isolated in several small springs that still exist in the valley area. There are three species of pupfish in the area, each with several subspecies that have diverged in the last few thousand years since their separations.

There is still strong debate over the length of time these populations have been separated, with research suggesting the populations have been separated from anywhere between a few hundred years to up to 60,000 years.

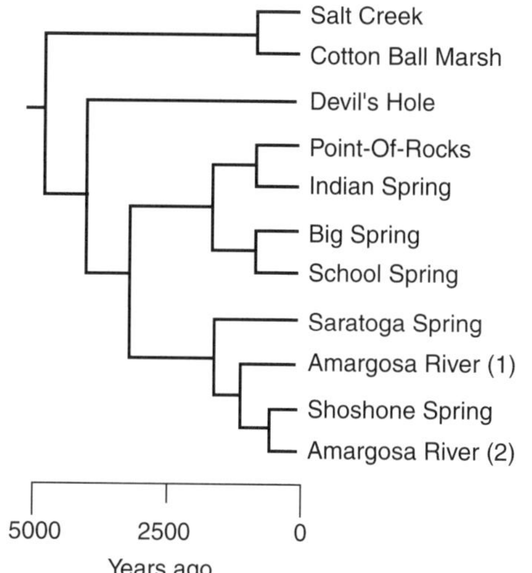

Map of Death Valley pupfish locations

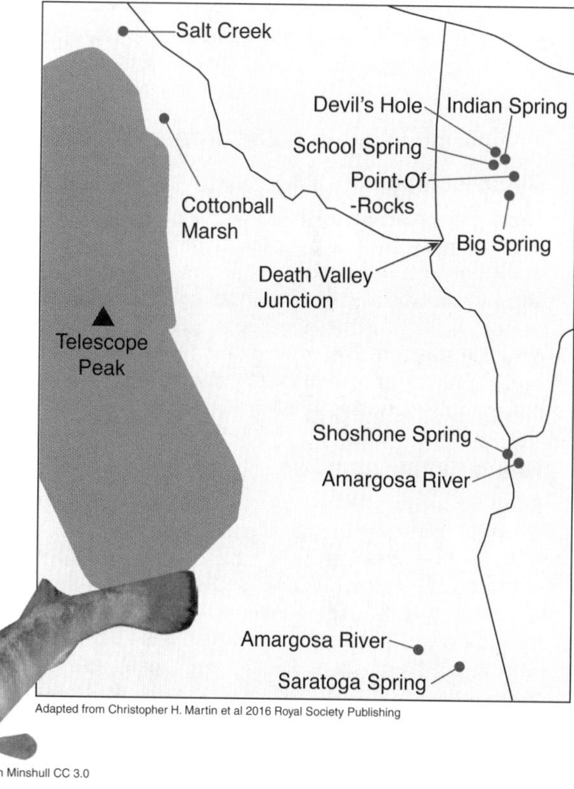

Adapted from Christopher H. Martin et al 2016 Royal Society Publishing

Jason Minshull CC 3.0

9. (a) What physical barriers separate the pupfish species? ___

(b) What environmental event caused these barriers to appear? ___

(c) Explain how this caused the split of the pupfish species: ___

10. How many subspecies of *Cyprinodon nevadensis* are there? ___

11. (a) Note the locations (above right) and phylogeny (above left) of *Cyprinodon* spp. Are they compatible? Explain:

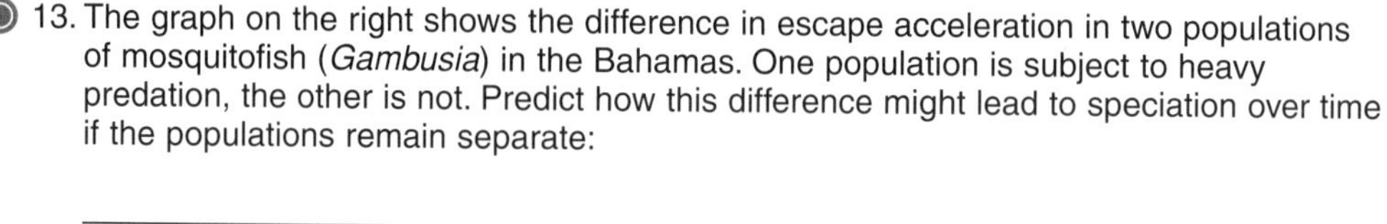

(b) Which species of pupfish appears anomalous in its location and phylogeny? ___

12. Approximately how many years ago did the Devil's Hole pupfish appear? ___

13. The graph on the right shows the difference in escape acceleration in two populations of mosquitofish (*Gambusia*) in the Bahamas. One population is subject to heavy predation, the other is not. Predict how this difference might lead to speciation over time if the populations remain separate:

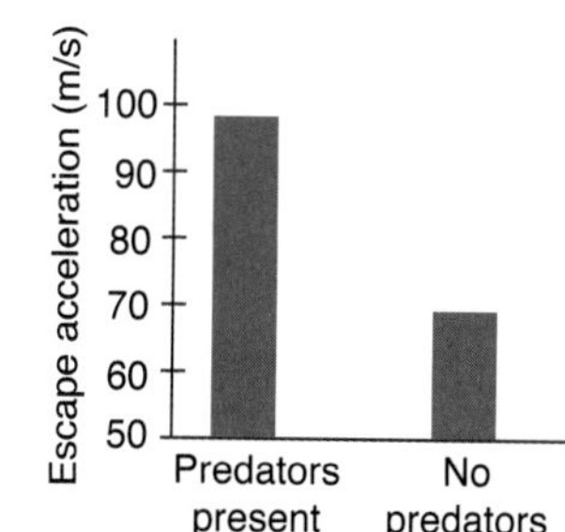

ISBN: 978-1-98-856656-6

194 Sympatric Speciation

Key Question: What mechanisms are involved in speciation when there is no geographical separation?

In sympatric (same place) speciation, a new species evolves from a single ancestral species while inhabiting the same geographic region. Sympatric speciation is rarer than allopatric speciation, although it is not uncommon in plants which form polyploids. There are two situations in which sympatric speciation is thought to occur. These are described below.

Speciation through niche differentiation

Niche isolation

There are many microhabitats within a heterogeneous environment (one that is not the same everywhere). Some individuals in a population may preferentially occupy to occupy one particular microhabitat, only rarely coming in contact with those that select other microhabitats. Some organisms become so dependent on the resources offered by their particular microhabitat that they never interact with others of their species in different microhabitats.

Reproductive isolation

Sub-populations, which have remained genetically isolated because of their microhabitat preferences, become reproductively isolated. They have become new species with subtle differences in behavior, structure, and physiology. Gene flow (via sexual reproduction) is limited to organisms that share similar microhabitat preferences (as shown right). **Example**: Some host-specific phytophagous insects (insects that feed on plants) lay eggs on plants identical to the species they themselves hatched on. Host plant preference leads to isolation despite the populations being sympatric.

An fly that lays its eggs on an unfamiliar plant species may give rise to a new population isolated from the original.

Original host plant species **New host plant species**

Original host plant species

New host plant species

Gene flow

No gene flow

Instant speciation by polyploidy

Polyploidy may result in the formation of a new species without isolation from the parent species. This event, occurring during meiosis, produces sudden reproductive isolation for the new group. Because the sex-determining mechanism is disturbed, animals are rarely able to achieve new species status this way (they are sterile). Many plants, on the other hand, are able to reproduce vegetatively, or self pollinate. This ability to reproduce on their own enables such polyploid plants to produce a breeding population.

Speciation by allopolyploidy

This type of polyploidy usually arises from the doubling of chromosomes in a hybrid between two different species. The doubling often makes the hybrid fertile. **Examples**: Modern wheat. Swedes are a polyploid species formed from a hybrid between a type of cabbage and a type of turnip.

Origin of polyploid event

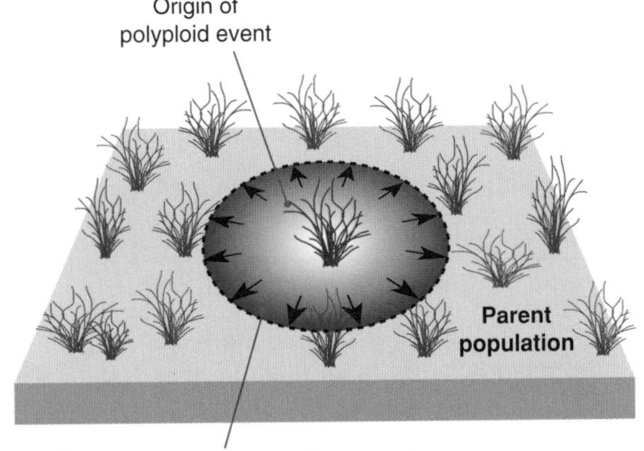

New polyploid plant species spreads out through the existing parent population

1. Use the diagram above to explain how niche differentiation can result in speciation: ______________________

____

____

____

____

____

2. What is the mechanism for instant speciation? Explain why it is more common in plants than in animals: ______________________

____

____

____

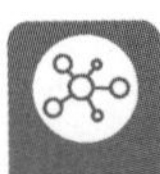
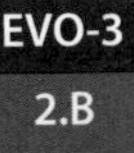

ISBN: 978-1-98-856656-6

Sympatric speciation in apple maggot flies

Apple maggot flies are native to North America. They infest the fruit of apple trees, laying eggs in the fruit, which develop into maggots that burrow into and eat the fruit. However, apple trees are not native to North America and were introduced less than 300 years ago.

Joseph Berger, Bugwood.org

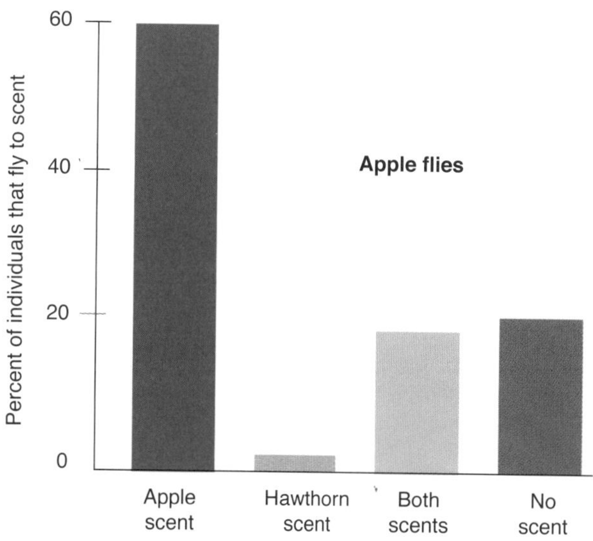

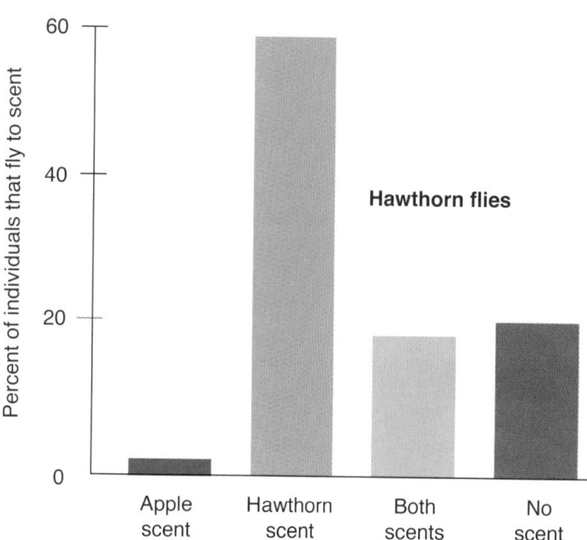

Research found that apple maggot flies also infest the fruit of native hawthorns. More importantly, flies that develop from maggots infesting hawthorns mated and laid eggs on hawthorns (hawthorn flies). Flies that develop from maggots that infested apples preferred to mate and lay eggs on apples (apple flies). Only 6% of matings took place between flies from different fruits.

Other experiments show the flies discriminate between scents on a genetic basis and have alleles associated with attraction to hawthorn or apple scent.

This separation of individuals by preference of apples or hawthorns has been a consequence of the introduction of apple trees. Although the flies are morphologically and genetically the same, their behavior has separated them into different populations on the pathway to speciation.

3. What plant did the apple maggot fly infest before apple trees were introduced to North America?

4. What kind of natural selection is occurring in the apple maggot fly?

5. (a) Explain the mechanisms that are causing this selection to occur:

(b) How might these mechanisms affect the future evolution of the apple maggot fly?

6. Apple fruits tend to drop earlier in the season that hawthorn fruits. How might this enhance the separation of apple flies and hawthorn flies?

ISBN: 978-1-98-856656-6

195 Habitat Fragmentation: Speciation and Extinction

Key Question: How does habitat fragmentation lead to the evolution of new species or the extinction of existing ones?

Habitat fragmentation occurs when a large area of habitat (e.g. a forest) becomes split up into separate smaller regions (e.g. patches of forest). This may occur naturally (e.g. by forest fire or lava flows) or it may occur because of human influences (e.g. logging large parts of the forest). Habitat fragmentation can lead to speciation, especially if a specific type of habitat is isolated or gene flow between populations in different habitat fragments ceases. If an isolated population is too small to breed effectively (or becomes inbred) and gene flow between fragmented areas ceases, then that population isolate may die out (a local extinction). If this occurs throughout the fragmented habitats then the species may also die out (extinction).

Habitat fragmentation and speciation

Hawai'i, the largest island of the Hawaiian islands (also known as Big Island) is also the youngest of the islands. The island is the tip of a volcano more than 10,000 m tall, which emerged from the ocean less than a million years ago. Hawai'i has since been colonized by many species, with some of these then giving rise to new species in the new island environment. The island is still very volcanically active and lava regularly flows from three active volcanic craters. These lava flows often intersect forests, producing forest fragments separated by black basalt lava. The fragmentation separates organisms and has been shown to produce quite different populations of organisms in each fragment. Two well studied examples are *Drosophilia* flies and *Tetragnatha* spiders.

Habitat fragmentation caused by a lava flow from Kilauea volcano.

USGS

- There are at least 12 species of *Tetragnatha* spiders on Hawai'i. Studies of three from forest fragmented by a 160 year old lava flow show genetic differences between isolated populations in two of the species. The third species showed little genetic difference between population isolates. This may be because it is a habitat generalist.
- Forest fragmentation is also important in Hawaiian *Drosophila*. There are 800 species of Drosophilidae in Hawaii, one of the highest concentrations anywhere in the world. *D. silvestris* males have a series of hairs on their forelegs, which they brush against females during courtship. Males in the northeastern part of the island have many more of these hairs than the males on the southwestern side of the island. While still the same species, the two populations are already displaying structural and behavioral isolation.

Habitat fragmentation and species loss

- Often habitat fragmentation causes a loss of biodiversity, especially in larger animals that require large areas of land to find food. Habitat fragmentation reduces population sizes and can reduce migration and therefore gene flow because individuals are unable to move easily between habitat fragments. Fragmentation also affects plants in a similar way. Because plants are immobile, genes are exchanged by the movement of pollen, either by the wind or by pollinators.
- A 2018 study examined bee pollination in tropical forest fragments surrounded by areas converted to pasture in north Queensland, Australia. The study found that the diversity and total number of bees pollinating tree flowers was lower in small forest fragments than larger ones (right).

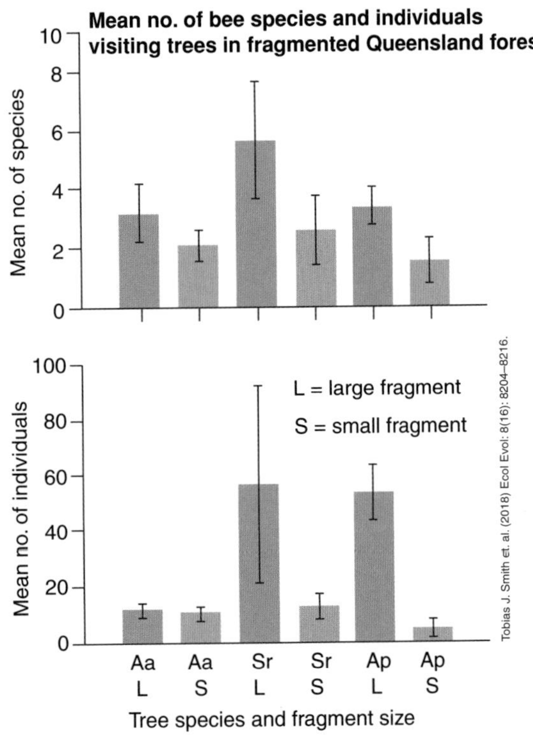

1. What is the difference between the mode of fragmentation in the Hawaiian and Queensland examples?

2. Suggest why was there little genetic difference between fragmented populations of the generalist *Tetragnatha* spider?

3. Explain why reduced numbers of pollinators would reduce gene flow between plants in small fragmented areas of forest:

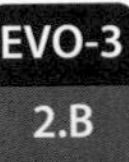
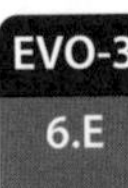
EVO-3 2.B

EVO-3 6.E
198

ISBN: 978-1-98-856656-6

196 Prezygotic Isolating Mechanisms

Key Question: What are the different types of reproductive isolating mechanism and how do they prevent interbreeding between different species?

Reproductive isolating mechanisms prevent successful interbreeding between species and are crucial to maintaining species' integrity. **Prezygotic isolating mechanisms** operate before fertilization can occur and prevent "gamete wastage". They are the most common type of isolating mechanism and may be associated with behavior, morphology, or reproductive timing. Single barriers to gene flow (such as geographical barriers) are usually insufficient to isolate a gene pool, so most species commonly have more than one type of barrier. Geographical barriers are not strictly a reproductive isolating mechanism, because they are not part of the species' biology, although they are usually a necessary precursor to reproductive isolation in sexually reproducing populations.

Geographical isolation

Geographical isolation describes the isolation of a species population (gene pool) by some kind of physical barrier, for example, mountain range, water body, isthmus, desert, or ice sheet. Geographical isolation is a frequent first step in the subsequent reproductive isolation of a species.

Example: Geological changes to the lake basins has been instrumental in the proliferation of cichlid fish species in the rift lakes of East Africa (far right). Similarly, many Galápagos Island species (e.g. iguanas, finches) are now quite distinct from the Central and South American mainland species from which they separated.

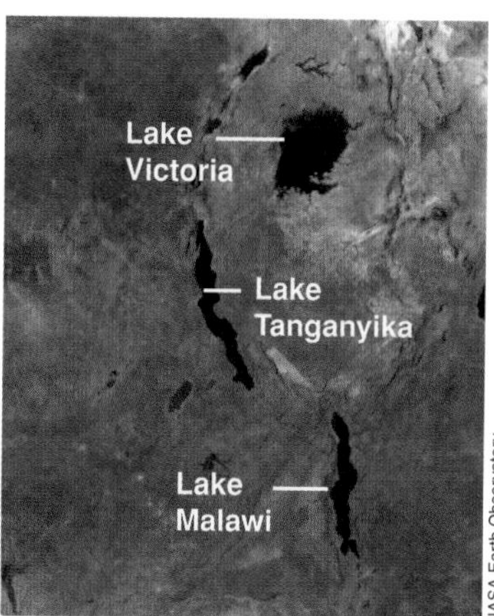

Ecological (habitat) isolation

Ecological isolation describes the existence of a prezygotic reproductive barrier between two species (or sub-species) as a result of them occupying or breeding in different habitats within the same general geographical area. Ecological isolation includes small scale differences (e.g. ground or tree dwelling) and broad differences (e.g. desert vs grasslands). Ecological isolation often follows geographical isolation, but in many cases the geographical barriers may remain in part.

Example: The red-browed and brown treecreepers (*Climacteris* spp.) are sympatric in south-eastern Australia and both species feed largely on ants. However the brown spends most of its time foraging on the ground or on fallen logs while the red-browed forages almost entirely in the trees.

Temporal isolation

Temporal isolation means isolated in time, and it prevents species interbreeding because they mate or they are active at different times. For example, individuals from different species do not mate because they are active during different times of the day (e.g. one species is active during the day and the other at night) or in different seasons.

Example: Closely related animal species may have different breeding seasons or periods of emergence to prevent interbreeding. The periodical cicadas (*Magicicada* genus) are an excellent example of this. Periodical cicadas are found in North America. There are several species and some have an overlapping distribution. Most of their life is spent underground as juveniles, emerging to complete their development and to mate. To prevent interbreeding, the various species spend either 13 or 17 years underground developing. Emergence of a single species is synchronized so the entire population emerges at the same time to breed.

ISBN: 978-1-98-856656-6

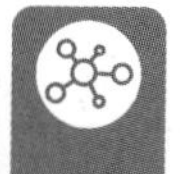

Gamete Isolation

The gametes (eggs and sperm) from different species are often incompatible, so even if the gametes meet, fertilization is unsuccessful. Gamete isolation is very important in aquatic environments where the gametes are released into the water and fertilization occurs externally (e.g. reproduction in frogs, fish, and corals). Where fertilization is internal, the sperm may not survive in the reproductive tract of another species. If the sperm does survive and reach the egg, chemical differences in the gametes prevent fertilization. Chemical recognition is also used by flowering plants to recognise pollen from the same species. Pollen from a different species is recognized as foreign and it does not germinate.

Example: Two species of sea urchin, the red sea urchin (*Strongylocentrotus franciscanus*) and the purple sea urchin (*Strongylocentrotus purpuratus*), share the same geographic range. Sea urchins release their gametes into the sea water, but the two species do not interbreed because their gametes are not compatible.

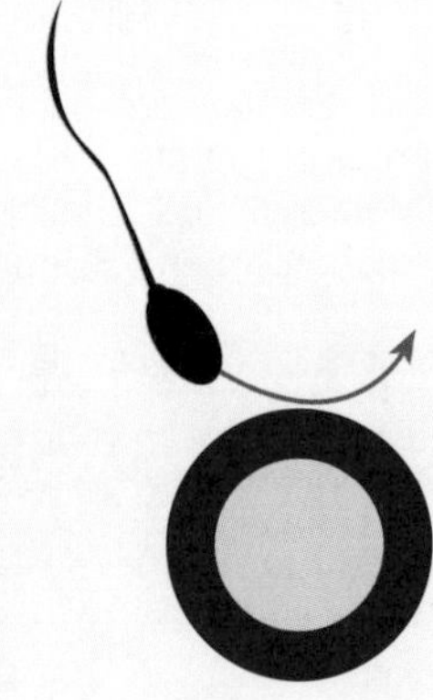

Purple sea urchin

Kirt L. Onthank cc3.0

Red sea urchin

Taollan82; Kirt L. Onthank cc3.0

Behavioral Isolation

In many species, courtship behaviors are a necessary prelude to successful mating. These behaviors may include dances, calls, displays, or the presentation of gifts. The displays are very specific and are unique to each species. This means that mates of the same species recognise and are attracted to the individual performing the behavior, but members of other species do not recognize or pay attention to the behaviors.

Birds exhibit a wide range of courtship displays. The use of song is widespread but ritualized movements, including nest building, are also common.
Examples: Galápagos frigatebirds have an elaborate display in which they inflate a bright red throat pouch to attract a mate. Frogs have species-specific calls.

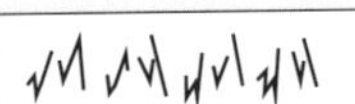

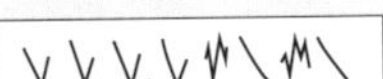

Male frigatebird display

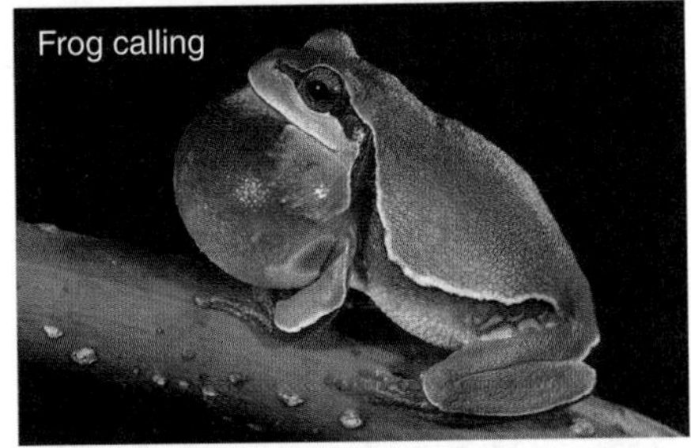

Frog calling

Mechanical (morphological) isolation

Structural differences (incompatibility) in the anatomy of reproductive organs prevents sperm transfer between individuals of different species. This is an important isolating mechanism preventing breeding between closely related species of arthropods.

Example: The sexual organs of empid flies have a lock-and-key mechanism. Without the right shaped genitalia, individuals cannot mate.

Many flowering plants have coevolved with their animal pollinators and have flower structures to allow only that insect access. Structural differences in the flowers and pollen of different plant species prevents cross breeding because pollen transfer is restricted to specific pollinators and the pollen itself must be species compatible.

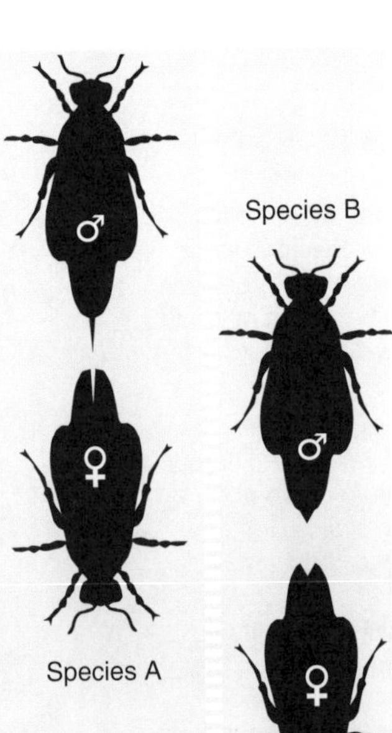

Empid flies mating

Orchid

ISBN: 978-1-98-856656-6

1. (a) What is a reproductive isolating mechanism? ____________________

____

(b) What role do isolating mechanisms have in maintaining the integrity of a species? ____________________

____

____

2. What is a prezygotic isolating mechanism? ____________________

____

____

3. (a) Explain why geographical isolation is not regarded as a reproductive isolating mechanism: ____________________

____

____

(b) Explain why, despite this, it often precedes, and is associated with, reproductive isolation: ____________________

____

____

____

4. Explain the difference between geographical and ecological isolation: ____________________

____

____

____

5. Identify the type(s) of reproductive isolation described in the following examples:

(a) Two species of butterfly (right) coexist in the same habitat but have different breeding seasons:

____

Breeding season for species A

Breeding season for species B

J F M A M J J A S O N D

(b) Male bowerbirds construct elaborate bowers (shelters) to attract a mate. One species, the MacGregor's bowerbird builds a tall structure and decorates it with charcoal. A second species, the satin bowerbird, decorates its bower with bright blue objects:

____

(c) Two species of New Zealand skinks, *Oligosoma smithi* and *O. suteri* are sympatric (same area) in north-eastern New Zealand. *O. smithi* is diurnal and gives birth to live young. *O. suteri* is nocturnal and lays eggs.

____

(d) The blackbird (*Turdus merula*) and the ring ouzel (*Turdus torquatus*) are two closely related species found in Europe. The blackbird is a woodland species and the ring ouzel tends to inhabit highlands:

____

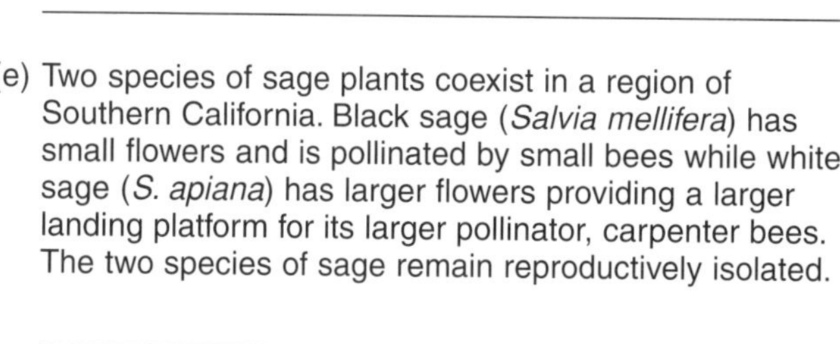

(e) Two species of sage plants coexist in a region of Southern California. Black sage (*Salvia mellifera*) has small flowers and is pollinated by small bees while white sage (*S. apiana*) has larger flowers providing a larger landing platform for its larger pollinator, carpenter bees. The two species of sage remain reproductively isolated.

____

Shan Shebs CC 3.0

ISBN: 978-1-98-856656-6

197 Postzygotic Isolating Mechanisms

Key Question: What mechanisms maintain reproductive isolation after fertilization in closely related species?

Postzyotic reproductive isolating mechanisms occur after fertilization (formation of the zygote) has occurred. Postzygotic isolating mechanisms are less common than prezygotic mechanisms, but are important in maintaining the integrity of closely related species. There are several different postzygotic mechanisms operating at different stages. The first prevents development of the zygote. Even if the zygote develops into a viable offspring there are further mechanisms to prevent long term viability. These include premature death or (more commonly) infertility.

Hybrid inviability

Mating between individuals of two species may produce a zygote (fertilized egg), but genetic incompatibility may stop development of the zygote. Fertilized eggs often fail to divide because of mis-matched chromosome numbers from each gamete. Very occasionally, the hybrid zygote will complete embryonic development but will not survive for long.

For example, although sheep and goats seem similar (right) and can be mated together, they belong to different genera. Any offspring of a sheep-goat pairing is generally stillborn.

Hybrid sterility

Even if two species mate and produce hybrid offspring that are vigorous, the species are still reproductively isolated if the hybrids are sterile (genes cannot flow from one species' gene pool to the other). Such cases are common among the horse family (such as the zebra and donkey shown on the right). One cause of this sterility is the failure of meiosis to produce normal gametes in the hybrid. This can occur if the chromosomes of the two parents are different in number or structure (see the "**zebronkey**" karyotype on the right).

The **mule**, a cross between a donkey stallion and a horse mare, is also an example of **hybrid vigor** (they are robust) as well as **hybrid sterility**. Female mules sometimes produce viable eggs but males are infertile.

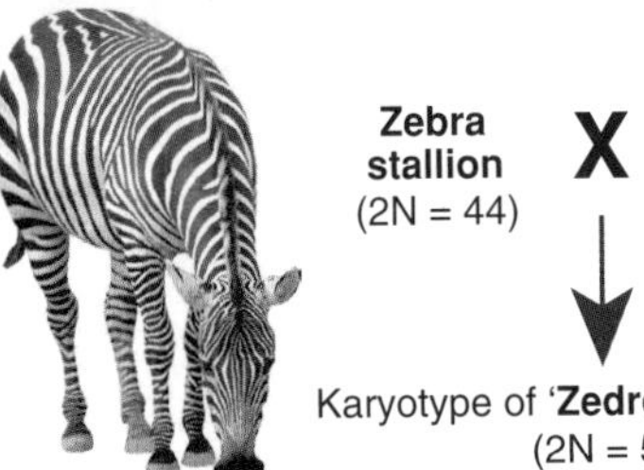

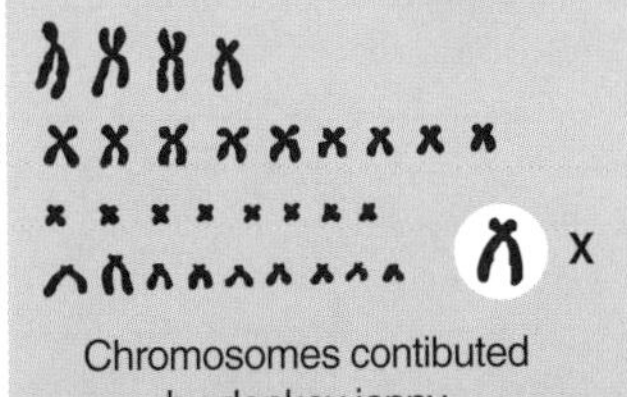

Hybrid breakdown

Hybrid breakdown is common feature of some plant hybrids. The first generation (F_1) may be fertile, but the second generation (F_2) are infertile or inviable. Examples include hybrids between species of cotton (near right), species within the genus *Populus*, and strains of the cultivated rice *Oryza* (far right).

1. Postzygotic isolating mechanisms are said to reinforce prezygotic ones. Explain why this is the case: ______

2. Briefly explain how each of the postzygotic isolating mechanisms below maintains reproductive isolation:

(a) Hybrid inviability: ______

(b) Hybrid sterility: ______

(c) Hybrid breakdown: ______

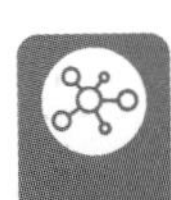

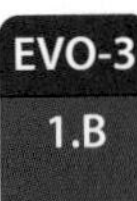

189 194

ISBN: 978-1-98-856656-6

198 Extinction

Key Question: How has the processes of extinction shaped the evolution and specification of life on Earth?

Extinction is a natural process and important in evolution because it provides opportunities, in the form of vacant niches, for the evolution of new species. The species alive today make up only a fraction of the total list of species that have lived on Earth throughout its history. The duration of a species is thought to range from as little as 1 million years for complex larger organisms to as long as 10-20 million years for simpler organisms. This constant extinction of species is called the **background extinction rate**. Superimposed on this rate are catastrophic events or **mass extinctions** that wipe out vast numbers of species, including entire families, in relatively brief periods of time in geologic terms. The diagram below shows how the number of species has varied over the history of life on Earth. The number of species is indicated on the graph by families: a taxonomic group comprising many genera and species. There have been five major extinction events and a likely sixth event, which began in the Late Pleistocene and continues today.

Major mass extinctions

Ordovician extinction (458-440 MYA)
Second largest extinction of marine life: >60% of marine invertebrates died. One of the coldest periods in Earth's history.

Permian extinction (252 MYA)
Nearly all life on Earth perished. More than 90% of marine species and many terrestrial species die out. Many families and genera lost.

Cretaceous extinction (66 MYA)
Marked by the extinction of flying reptiles and nearly all dinosaur species (their descendants the birds survive). Generally accepted as being caused by an asteroid that collided with Earth.

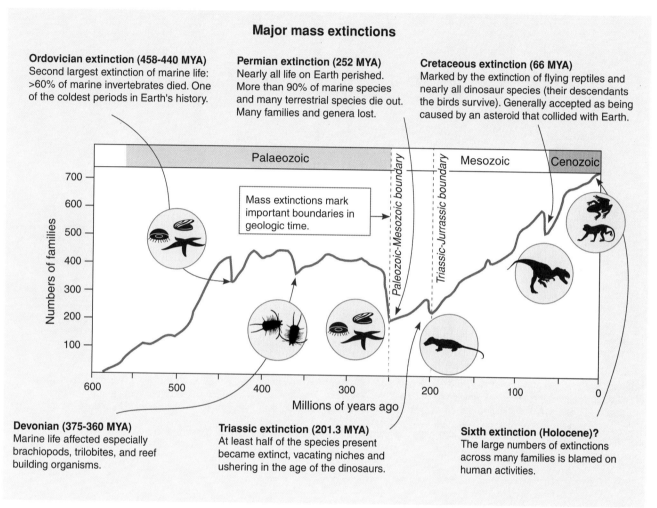

Palaeozoic
Mesozoic
Cenozoic
Mass extinctions mark important boundaries in geologic time.
Paleozoic-Mesozoic boundary
Triassic-Jurrassic boundary
Numbers of families
700
600
500
400
300
200
100
600
500
400
300
200
100
0
Millions of years ago

Devonian (375-360 MYA)
Marine life affected especially brachiopods, trilobites, and reef building organisms.

Triassic extinction (201.3 MYA)
At least half of the species present became extinct, vacating niches and ushering in the age of the dinosaurs.

Sixth extinction (Holocene)?
The large numbers of extinctions across many families is blamed on human activities.

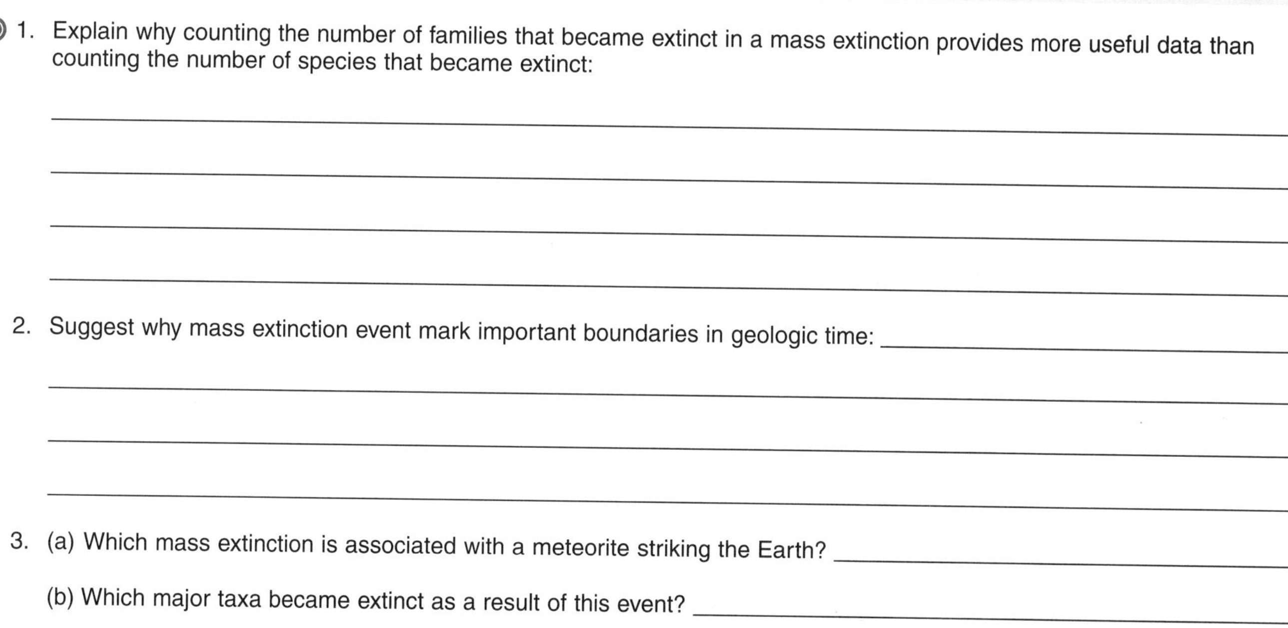

1. Explain why counting the number of families that became extinct in a mass extinction provides more useful data than counting the number of species that became extinct:

2. Suggest why mass extinction event mark important boundaries in geologic time:

3. (a) Which mass extinction is associated with a meteorite striking the Earth?

   (b) Which major taxa became extinct as a result of this event?

ISBN: 978-1-98-856656-6

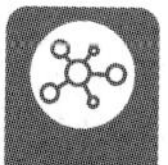

Extinction, speciation, and diversification

- As the figure on the previous page shows, the past 540 million years of life on Earth has been characterized by five major mass extinctions. These were events when there was a widespread and rapid decrease in the biodiversity on Earth. Overall though, biodiversity has increased over time. After each extinction events, biodiversity recovers as species diversify to occupy vacated (or completely new) niches, just as mammals diversified following the Cretaceous extinction of the dinosaurs.
- The level of species diversity at any point in time is the result of a balance between the rates at which new species form (the speciation or origination rate) and the rate at which species are lost (the extinction rate). Species richness declines when rates of extinction exceed rates of speciation. Whether or not species survive a mass extinction event is often a function of how widespread that species is and whether or not they were able to retreat to isolated areas or refugia.
- A study published in nature in 2000 analyzed the record of biodiversity for marine animals since the beginning of the Cambrian (~570 MYA). They looked at the relationship between the peaks in extinction of existing families and genera and the peaks in origination of new groups (rate of speciation). The results of their analysis are summarized below.

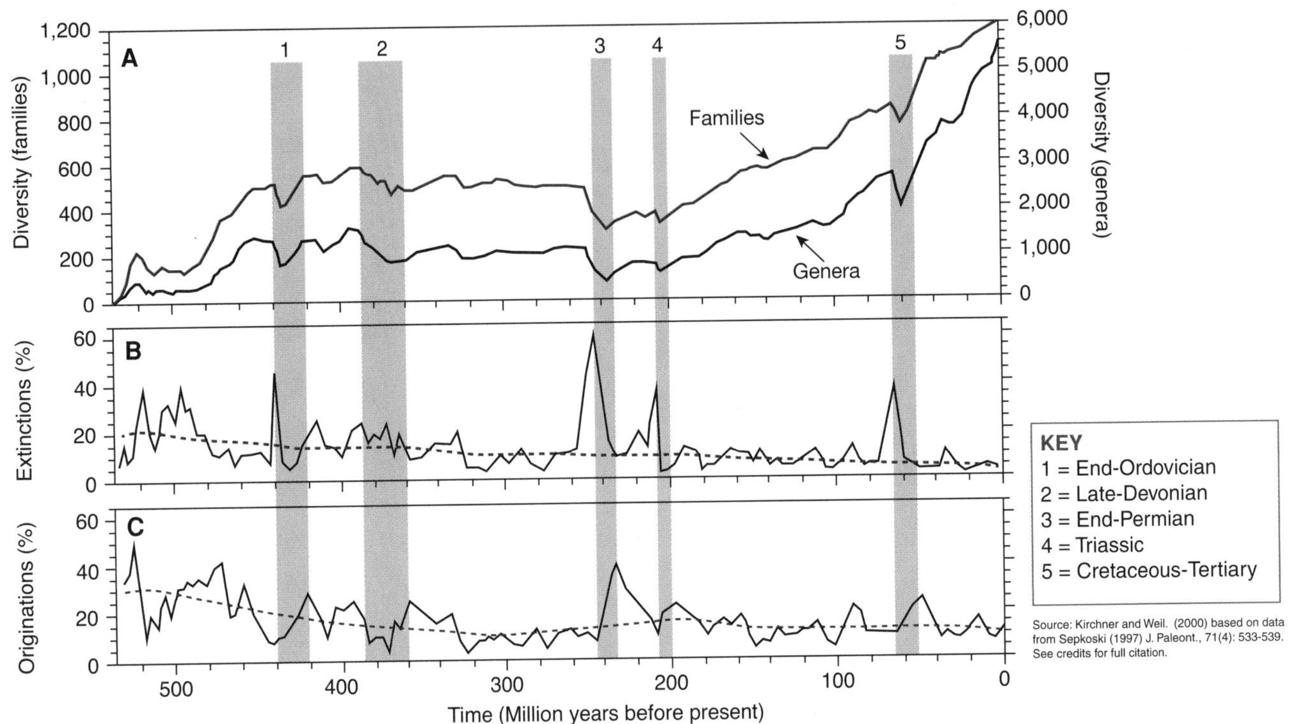

Above: Changes in marine animal diversity (A), percentage extinctions (B), and percentage originations (C) 540 MYA to present. The five major mass extinctions events are identified by numbers 1-5 (key right). The shaded bands show the recovery interval from the extinction rate peaks (center plot) to origination rate peaks (bottom plot). Dotted lines in (B) and (C) show computer-modeled long-term trends.

4. (a) Describe the patterns shown in the data presented above. Include reference to trends in overall diversity, patterns of originations, and time of recovery:

   (b) Suggest a reason for these patterns:

5. Given what the data show for the recovery period following a mass extinction, predict the consequences to Earth's biodiversity in light of a current Sixth Extinction:

ISBN: 978-1-98-856656-6

199 Causes of Mass Extinctions

Key Question: What events have caused the various mass extinctions seen on Earth?

There have been about 24 mass extinctions over the last 540 million years. Five of these were major and 19 were minor (based on the percentage of families that became extinct). Some extinction peaks coincided with known comet or asteroid impacts, implying that they may have been causal.

Environmental deterioration associated with climate change or a major cosmic, geologic, or biological event, is deemed the main cause of extinctions. The ability of the biosphere to recover from such crises is evident by the fact that life continues to exist today. The increasing number of extinctions in the current epoch provides evidence for the claim by many scientists that a sixth Holocene mass extinction is underway.

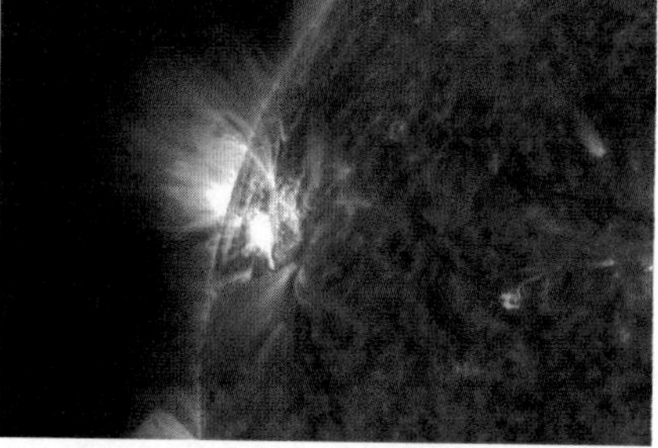

All images NASA

Possible causes of mass extinction	Effects on the extinction rate
Impacts by large asteroid/comet or 'showers': Shock waves, heat-waves, wildfires, impact 'winters' caused by global dust clouds, super-acid rain, toxic oceans, superwaves and superfloods from an oceanic impact.	Global extinction of much of the planet's biodiversity. Smaller comet showers could cause stepwise, regional extinctions.
Supernovae radiation: Direct exposure to X-rays and cosmic rays. Ozone depletion and subsequent exposure to excessive UV radiation from the sun.	Causes mutations and kills organisms. Selective mass extinctions, particularly of animals (but not plants) exposed to the atmosphere, as well as shallow-water aquatic forms.
Large solar flares: Exposure to large doses of X-rays, and UV radiation. Ozone depletion.	Mass extinctions.
Geomagnetic reversals: Increased flux of cosmic rays.	Mass extinctions.
Continental drift: Climatic changes, such as glaciations and droughts, occur when continents move towards or away from the poles.	Global cooling due to changes in the pattern of oceans currents caused by shifting land masses. Extinctions as species find themselves in inhospitable climates.
Intense volcanism: Cold conditions caused by volcanic dust reducing solar input. Volcanic gases causing acid rain and reduced alkalinity of oceans. Toxic trace elements.	Stepwise mass extinctions.
Sea level change: Loss of habitat.	Mass extinctions of susceptible species (e.g. marine reptiles, coral reefs, coastal species).
Arctic spill over: Release of cold fresh water or brackish water from an isolated Arctic Ocean. Ocean temperature falls by 10°C, resulting in atmospheric cooling and drought.	Mass extinctions in marine ecosystems. Change of vegetation with drastic effect on large reptiles.
Anoxia: Shortage of oxygen.	Mass extinctions in the oceans.
Spread of disease/predators: Direct effects due to changing geographic distribution.	Mass extinctions.

Source: *Environmental Change – The Evolving Ecosphere (1997)*, by R.J. Huggett

Examples of extinction events and their likely causes

Quaternary (15,000-10,000 ya)
Extinction of: Many large mammals and large flightless birds.

Probable cause: Warming of the global climate after the last ice age plus predation (hunting) by humans.

Late Cretaceous (66 mya)
Extinction of: Dinosaurs, plesiosaurs, icthyosaurs, mosasaurs, pterosaurs, ammonites and belemnites (squid-like animals), and many other groups.

Probable cause: Catastrophic asteroid impact near Yucatan peninsula.

Late Permian (250 mya)
Extinction of: 90% of marine species and 70% of land species. Coral reefs, trilobites, some amphibians, and mammal-like reptiles, were eliminated (the Great Dying).

Probable cause: An asteroid impact, followed by furious volcanic activity, a rapid heating of the atmosphere, and depletion of oxygen from the oceans.

Late Devonian (360 mya)
Extinction of: Many corals, bivalves, fish, sponges (21% of all marine families). Collapse of tropical reef communities.

Probable cause: Global cooling associated with (or causing?) widespread oxygen deficiency of shallow seas.

Source: *Evolution: A Biological and Paleontological Approach*, Skelton, P. (ed.), Addison-Wesley (1993)

1. Describe how a massive asteroid strike on the Earth might lead to a mass extinction: ______________________

____

____

____

____

ISBN: 978-1-98-856656-6

200

198

EVO-3
2.B

200 The Sixth Extinction

Key Question: Is there any evidence that the Earth is experiencing a sixth mass extinction event?

Human activity dominates Earth. Humans can be found almost everywhere on the globe, even at the South Pole. As humans have spread across the planet, from Africa into Europe and Asia, and across into the Americas and beyond, they have changed the environment around them to suit their needs. How these changes have occurred has varied according to the technology available and the general social environment and attitudes at the time. Human-associated change has had a profound impact on the globe's physical and biological systems. Only in the past century have we begun to fully evaluate the impact of human activity on the Earth. Humans have caused the deliberate or accidental extinction of numerous species and brought many more to the brink. So many species have been lost as a direct or indirect result of human activity that this period in history has been termed the **Sixth Extinction**. There is debate over when this extinction began, its extent, and the degree of human involvement. However, it is clear that many species are being lost and many that existed before humans appeared in their domains, no longer do.

Estimating extinction rates

Estimates of the rate of species loss can be made by using the **background extinction rate** as a reference. It is estimated that one species per million species per year becomes extinct. By totalling the number of extinctions known or suspected over a time period, we can compare the current rate of loss to the background extinction rate.

Birds provide one of the best examples. There are about 10,000 living or recently extinct species of birds. In the last 500 years an estimated 150 or more have become extinct. From the background extinction rate we would expect one species to become extinct every 100 years (10,000/1,000,000 = 0.01 extinctions per year = 1 extinction per 100 years). It then becomes apparent that 150/500 = 0.3 extinctions per year or 30 extinctions per century, 30 times greater than the background rate. The same can be calculated for most other groups of animals and plants.

Organism*	Total number of species (approx)*	Known extinction (since ~1500)*
Mammals	5487	87
Birds	9975	150
Reptiles	10,000	22
Amphibians	6700	39
Plants	300,000	114

*These numbers vastly underestimate the true numbers because so many species are undescribed.

The Carolina parakeet

The Carolina parakeet was the only parakeet (or parrot) native to the eastern United States. It was a very social bird, forming large flocks in upland forests and forest edges, from the Ohio Valley to the Gulf of Mexico. It was a spectacular bird, with bright green plumage, a yellow head, and orange face and bill. Its natural diet was wild fruit, seeds, and nuts, but when settlers began planting crops, it quickly exploited them and was treated as a pest (despite a useful role in destroying invasive weed species). Entire flocks were easily targeted and shot because the parakeets' behavioral strategy was to rally around distressed or injured birds. The last confirmed sighting of the parakeet in the wild was in 1904 and the last captive bird died in 1918.

The reasons for the Carolina parakeet's extinction are not fully known. Although large numbers were killed by hunting or habitat destruction, the last, apparently healthy, populations were left more or less alone. It appears disease may have been a major factor in the final extinction of the last populations, probably from introduced domestic fowl.

Carolina parakeet mounted specimen, Field Museum of Natural History, Chicago, Illinois, USA.

1. Define the **Sixth Extinction**: ______

2. Humans are frequently not directly responsible for the extinction of a species, yet recently extinct species have often become so after humans arrive in their habitat. Discuss the reasons for these extinctions:

______

198 199

ISBN: 978-1-98-856656-6

What is the Sixth Extinction?

There have been five previous major mass extinctions. The last, 66 mya, saw the end of the dinosaurs and most marine reptiles. The Sixth Extinction refers to the apparent human-induced loss of much of the Earth's biodiversity. Twenty years ago, Harvard biologist E.O. Wilson estimated that as many as 30,000 species a year were being lost – one every 20 minutes. The extinction dates for some examples are given right.

US Fish and Wildlife Service

Golden toad (Costa Rica) 1989 AD

Thylacine (Australia) 1930 AD

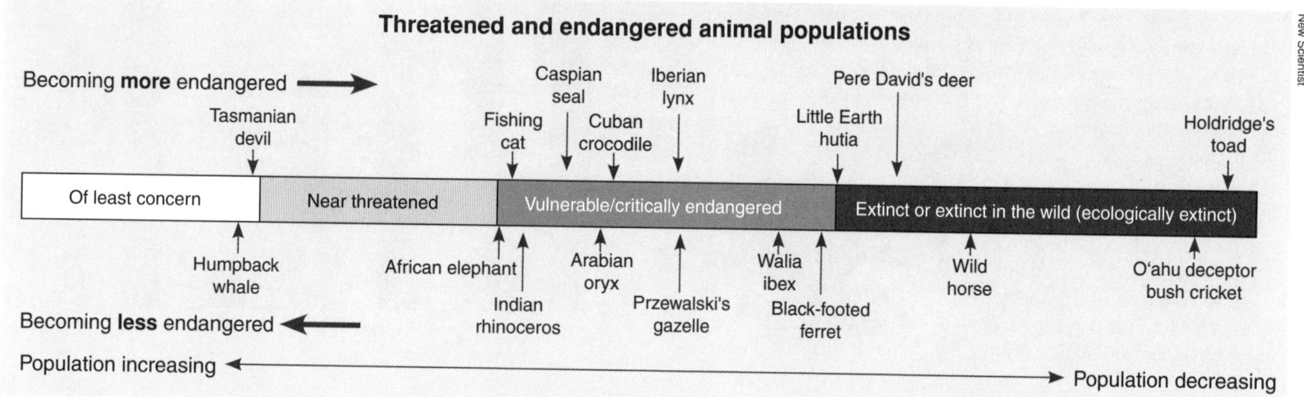

3. A scientist wanted to carry out a statistical test to see if there is a difference between the current extinction rate of animals and the background rate. State the null and alternative hypotheses for the statistical test:

4. Use the data in the table to calculate (1) the **rate of species extinction per century** for each of the groups and (2) how many times greater this is than the background extinction rate:

(a) Mammals:

(b) Reptiles:

(c) Amphibians:

(d) Plants:

5. Large appealing animals, e.g. pandas, are known as charismatic megafauna. Research shows these kinds of animals receive far more money and time for conservation efforts than less appealing organisms such as snakes, spiders and plants. Suggest why this might be the case and explain how this could affect the conservation of biodiversity:

6. Identify a species, other than one mentioned earlier, that has recently become extinct. Identify the date and possible reasons for its extinction:

ISBN: 978-1-98-856656-6

201 Diversity and Resilience

Key Question: How does genetic diversity affect a population's ability to resist and recover from disturbances?

Genetic diversity refers to the variety of alleles and genotypes present in a population. It is important to the survival and adaptability of a species because populations with low genetic diversity generally show poor resilience. This means that they are less able to respond to, or recover from, environmental changes and so are at greater risk of extinction. In contrast, species with greater genetic diversity are more likely to have the genetic resources to respond to environmental change through adaptation (in response to natural selection). This increases their chance of survival as a species.

Genetic diversity in prairie chickens

- Until 1992, the Illinois prairie chicken was destined for extinction. The population had fallen from millions before European arrival to 25,000 in 1933 and then to 50 in 1992.
- The dramatic decline in the population in such a short time resulted in a huge loss of genetic diversity, which led to inbreeding and in turn resulted in a decrease in fertility and an ever-decreasing number of eggs hatching successfully (right).
- In 1992, a translocation program began, bringing in 271 birds from Kansas and Nebraska. There was a rapid population response, as fertility and egg viability increased. The population is now recovering (1995, right).

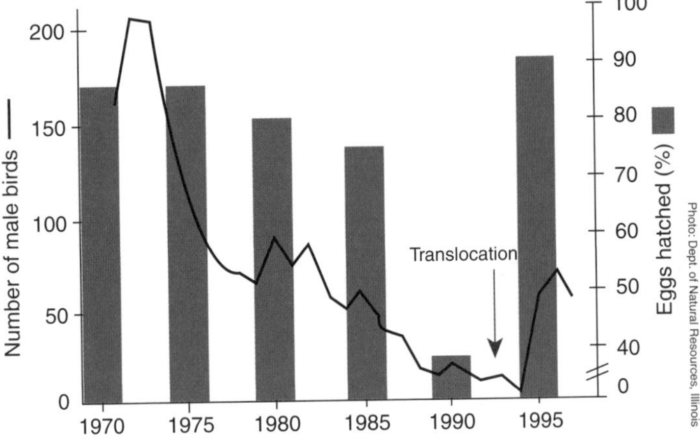

Photo: Dept. of Natural Resources, Illinois

Southern corn leaf blight

- A particularly devastating episode of corn blight occurred in crops of US corn (*Zea mays*) in 1970. At the time 85% of the US corn crop was the type T-cms (Texas cytoplasmic male sterile). At the same time, a new strain (race T) of the fungus *Bipolaris maydis* appeared, which produces a T-toxin. T-cms proved to be highly susceptible to the new fungus. Corn losses were 50-100% depending on the location. It is estimated that up to $1 billion dollars worth of crops were lost.
- There are various corn types, normal cytoplasm, T-cms, and cytoplasmic male sterile (C-cms). T-cms was developed because removing the pollen-producing bodies from the top of the plant was simpler, making cross breeding simpler.
- However, corn plants with T-cms cytoplasm have maternally inherited a gene encoding a protein on the inner mitochondrial membrane. T-toxin from race T-*B. maydis* acts on this protein, causing the leaf blight.

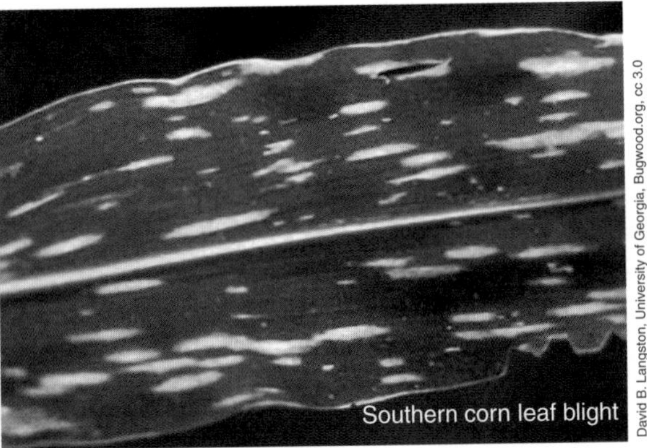

Southern corn leaf blight

David B. Langston, University of Georgia, Bugwood.org, cc 3.0

1. Explain the importance of genetic diversity to population resilience:

2. (a) What was the effect of low genetic diversity in the Illinois prairie chicken?

   (b) What was the result of introducing birds from Kansas and Nebraska?

3. What caused the susceptibility of corn to southern leaf blight in 1970?

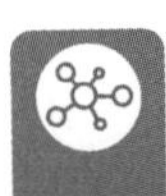

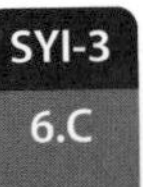

ISBN: 978-1-98-856656-6

Measuring genetic diversity

- There are many ways to measure genetic diversity and the information different methods produce does not always agree. Genetic diversity can be measured based on the DNA sequences, allele frequency, the heterozygote frequency, the number of different alleles for a gene, or even the variability of the genome.
- One of the simplest measures of genetic diversity involves calculating the proportions polymorphic loci across a genome or a species. Eukaryotic chromosomes contain many genes and, in any one population, each gene may have a number of alleles. The presence of more than one allele at a specific gene location (locus) is called **polymorphism**. When only one allele is present the locus is said to be monomorphic.
- The following equation can be used to calculate the proportion of polymorphic genes:

$$\text{Proportion of polymorphic gene loci} = \frac{\text{number of polymorphic gene loci}}{\text{total number of loci}}$$

Measuring genetic diversity in African lions

Allele variation at 26 enzyme loci in an African lion population was studied (below). Twenty loci showed no variation (they were monomorphic) and six loci showed variation (they were polymorphic).

	Allele		
Enzyme locus	**1**	**2**	**3**
ADA	0.56	0.33	0.11
DIAB	0.61	0.39	
ESI	0.88	0.12	
GPI	0.85	0.15	
GPT	0.89	0.11	
MPI	0.92	0.08	
20 Monomorphic loci	1.00		

Data: Newman et al. 1985

- Measuring genetic diversity can help identify at-risk populations and prioritize conservation efforts for rare breeds or animals in captive breeding programmes. Purebred animals ("pedigrees") may be tested for genetic diversity to assist when planning breeding programmes so that loss of genetic diversity and risks of inbreeding depression are minimized.
- Inbreeding depression describes the reduced survival and fertility of offspring of related individuals. Reducing this risk also increases the chance of a species being able to adapt to the selection pressures created by environmental change.

In 1987, the California condor population was reduced to just 14 breeding members and all remaining wild birds were captured for a captive breeding program. Even after this, the population (now over 500) retained a surprising amount of genetic diversity, which will help in its recovery and resilience.

In the 1840s the Irish potato famine was, in part, caused by the use of one particular type of potato (the "lumper"). This was susceptible to rot caused by *Phytophthora infestans*. Entire crops were lost and, as the potato was a staple food source at the time, it resulted in widespread starvation.

USFWS

The black-footed ferret was declared extinct in 1979 before a small population was rediscovered 1981. After captive breeding and reintroductions, the population is now about 1000, all related to just 7 individuals. Without management, the population may still decline due a lack of genetic diversity.

4. (a) For the lion data, identify the enzyme locus with the highest genetic diversity: ______________________

   (b) Calculate the genetic diversity for the 26 loci studied above: ______________________

5. Why is knowing the genetic diversity of a population important for captive breeding of endangered species?

____

____

____

6. Populations with low numbers and low genetic diversity sometimes enter what is known as an extinction vortex, where the population begins reducing very rapidly, sometimes even with active conservation. Explain why this might happen:

____

____

____

____

____

ISBN: 978-1-98-856656-6

202 Investigating Molecular Diversity

STUDENT SUPPORT FOR INVESTIGATION 3: *Comparing DNA sequences to understand evolutionary relationships with BLAST*

The advancement of DNA sequencing has produced enormous amounts of sequencing information. The collection, storage, and analysis of this information using computers is called **bioinformatics**. Bioinformatics allows DNA sequence comparisons between species, a field called comparative genomics. Comparative genomics has provided the information to support (or overturn) established phylogenies.

Using the sequence data

As genome sequencing has become faster and more genomes are sequenced there has been a corresponding growth in the use of bioinformatics. Online DNA databases allow the comparison of DNA being studied to known DNA sequences. This can allow quick identification of species, especially bacteria or viruses.

A gene of interest is selected for analysis.

...G A G A A C T G T T T A G A T G C A A A A...

Powerful computer software can quickly compare the DNA sequences of many organisms. Commonalities and differences in the DNA sequence can help to determine the organism and its evolutionary relationship to other organisms. The blue boxes indicate differences in the DNA sequences.

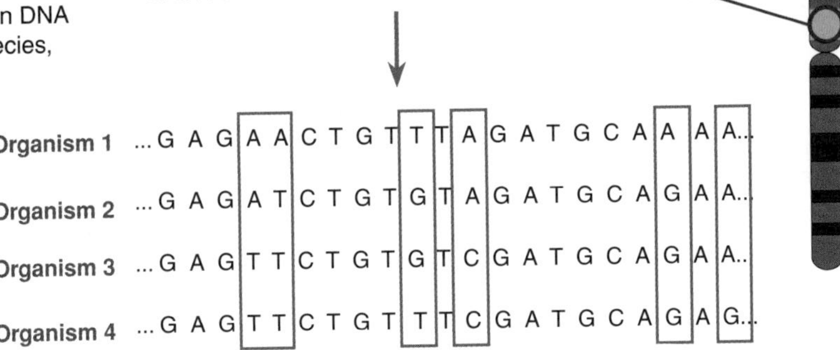

Online data bases

There are many easily accessible online data bases where DNA sequences can be studied. The example below uses NCBI data base at **www.ncbi.nlm.nih.gov**.

There is a search box at the top of the page with a drop down menu. Use the menu find and click **Gene** (**IMAGE 1**).

In the search box, type **SATB2**. This is a homeobox gene on the 2nd human chromosome. Homeobox genes control the early embryonic development of many body structures.

Click **search** and a new window will appear showing the results.

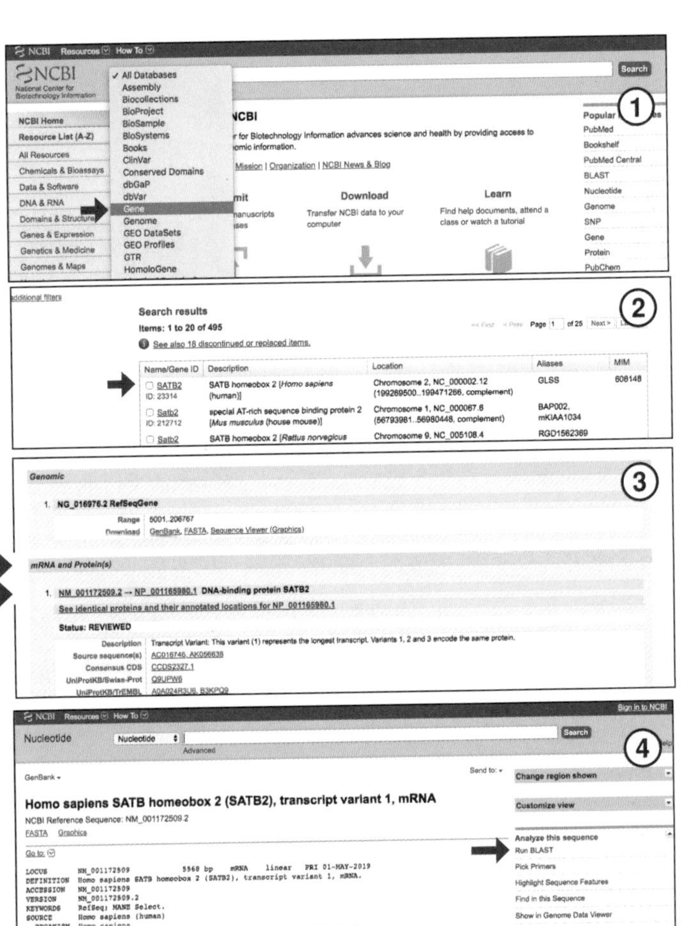

Click the first SATB2 on the list (ID 23314) (**IMAGE 2**). A new window appears showing known information on the SATB2 gene. Scrolling down the screen provides a huge amount of information about this gene.

Scroll down to the heading **NCBI Reference Sequences**. Under this is the smaller heading **mRNA and proteins** (**IMAGE 3**) listing all the mRNA transcripts of this gene.

Click the first on the list **(NM_001172509.2)**.

This brings up information on the transcript. Scroll to the bottom and the DNA sequence for the mRNA is shown.

Highlight and copy this sequence.

Scroll back to the top of the page. On the right is the heading **Analyze this sequence** (**IMAGE 4**). Under this, click the heading **Run BLAST**. This opens a search box where you can compare the SATB2 sequence from the previous website to other sequences.

Paste the SATB2 DNA sequence in your paste buffer into the box headed "**Enter accession number(s), gi(s), or FASTA sequence(s)**" or use the reference number shown in the box (**IMAGE 5**). Click on **BLAST** at the bottom of the page. The search may take a minute or so.

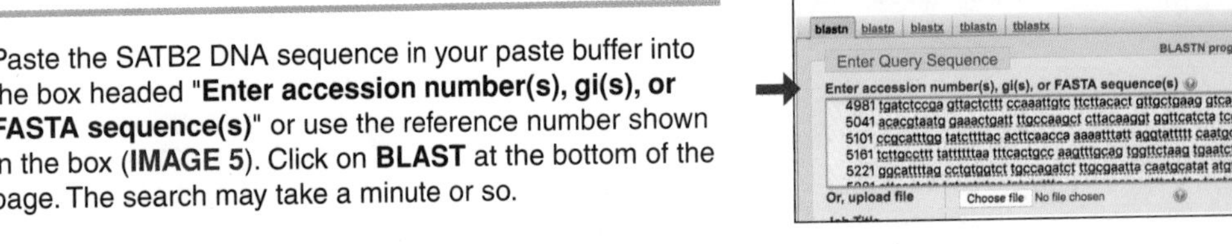

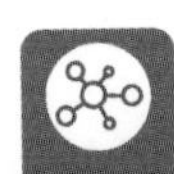

SYI-3
6.C

60

145

ISBN: 978-1-98-856656-6

A new screen will appear showing the BLAST results. Scroll down to see a list of all the species with similar SATB2 sequences. Clicking on a species shows a match of the DNA in the sequences. Once you are familiar with this process go back to the opening page **www.ncbi.nlm.nih.gov**. Find **HomoloGene** in the drop down menu beside the search box and click it. This is the homologous gene database. Type SATB2 in the search box and click **search**.

A new page comparing the SATB2 proteins in other species appears (**IMAGE 6**). Under the heading **Protein alignments** is a pair of drop down boxes. Here you can compare any two species' SATB2 proteins.

Compare humans and dogs (*Canis lupus familiaris*).

Click **BLAST** under the drop down boxes. After a minute all the amino acids coded for by the SATB2 gene will appear compared as a query (what you are comparing to) and a subject (what is being compared). Any differences are shown in the middle line of text.

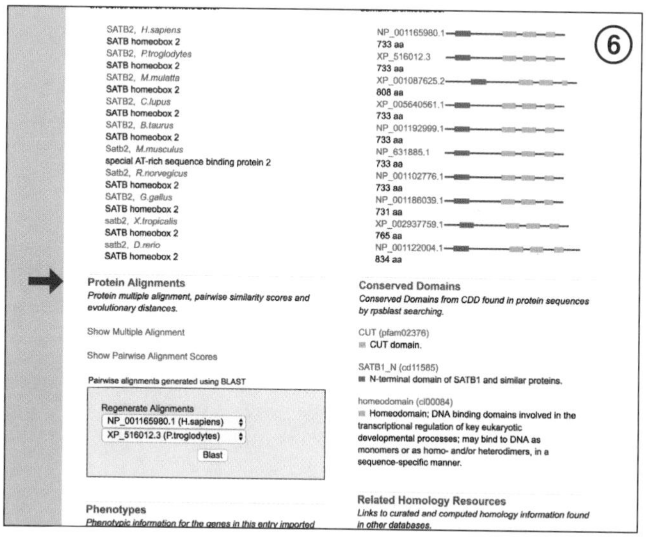

The steps above are a highly simplified step-through of the database. It is capable of many different searches and investigations and stores millions of DNA sequences. Even this simple process shows the power of technology when investigating species relationships.

1. Using the SATB2 gene and the NCBI gene database answer the following:

   (a) What is the % similarity of the DNA between a human and a chimpanzee for the SATB2 gene? ________________

   (b) What is the % similarity of the DNA between a human and a domestic dog for the SATB2 gene (variant X1)?

   ____

2. Computers scan the DNA sequences to find where the sequences most closely align. At what number DNA base pairs do the wolf and human DNA begin to align?

   ____

3. Using the Homologene search for the gene SATB2 answer the following:

   (a) What is the % similarity between the human and dog SATB2 amino acid sequence? ________________

   (b) At what number amino acids do the differences occur? __________________________

4. Go to the NCBI web page shown in image 5 above. The search box is useful in that the DNA sequence can be typed directly into the search box. How might this be useful in identifying the origin of a DNA sequence?

   ____

5. Type a short DNA sequence of your choosing in the search box (about 20 to 30 letters). Click Blast and see if there are any matches. The search may take some time. Have you "found" a unique DNA sequence or is it from a known species?

   ____

6. Use what you have learned in this activity to explain why bioinformatics is such a powerful tool:

   ____

ISBN: 978-1-98-856656-6

203 The Origin of Life on Earth

Key Question: How did life begin on Earth?

Through experiments and observations of extraterrestrial material (e.g. comets) scientists have determined how organic molecules most probably first arose on Earth. They believe that the conditions on primitive Earth provided the precursor molecules needed to produce small organic molecules. The organic molecules later served as building blocks for more complex molecules, including proteins and nucleic acids. The reactions required for these molecules to form may have occurred in a solution or on solid reactive surfaces (e.g. clay).

How did life on Earth arise?

- Most origin of life on Earth theories propose a sequence of events starting with the spontaneous formation of simple organic molecules, formation of more complex molecules, and finally the formation of self-sustaining biological molecules (right).
- In the 1920s Oparin and Haldane proposed that life on Earth arose through a process of gradual chemical evolution. They proposed that simple inorganic molecules reacted in the reducing (oxygen poor) atmosphere of early Earth to form simple organic molecules. These accumulated in the oceans to produce a primordial soup, eventually reacting and combining to form more complex molecules. The energy for the reaction would have been provided from lightning or the Sun.
- Miller and Urey tested Oparin and Haldane's theory by building a closed experimental system to see if organic molecules could be produced under the conditions thought to resemble early Earth. They were successful.
- Scientists now think the early atmosphere was not reducing, so Miller and Urey's (and Oparin and Haldane's) theories are not fully supported. However, several recent experiments have shown that organic building blocks can be produced under a wide range of conditions, lending weight to the theory that spontaneous formation of simple organic molecules led to more complex ones.

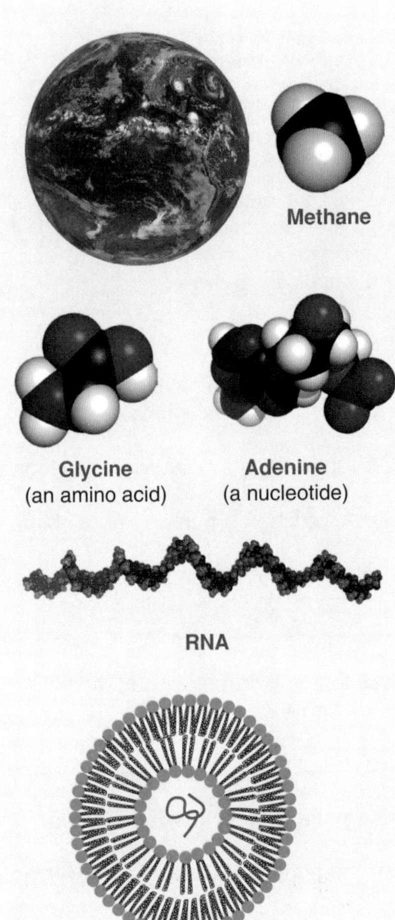

Formation of the Earth (4.6 billion years ago) and its acquisition of volatile organic chemicals by collision with comets and meteorites. The early atmosphere on Earth also provided the inorganic precursors needed to produce simple organic molecules.

The synthesis and accumulation of simple organic molecules occurred. Products included amino acids, purines, pyrimidines, sugars, and lipids.

Dehydration synthesis produced polymers of amino acids (proteins) and nucleic acids (RNA or DNA). RNA was probably the first self-replicating molecule on Earth. Evidence for this comes from the fact that RNA is able to act as a replication catalyst. It also carries genetic information which can be passed on to the next generation.

Larger lipids were synthesized, with the ability to self-assemble into double-layered membranes (liposomes). Liposomes could enclose organic self-replicating and catalytic molecules (e.g. RNA) to form a **protobiont**.

The protobiont is very simple, and often regarded as a very simple cell-like structure and an immediate precursor to the first living systems.

1. (a) Describe the proposed hypothesis for how life on Earth first evolved: ______________________________

____

____

____

____

____

(b) Describe the likely role of liposomes in the formation of protobionts: ______________________________

____

____

____

(c) Why are protobionts regarded as primitive cells? ______________________________

____

____

____

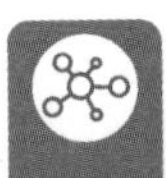

ISBN: 978-1-98-856656-6

When and where did life on Earth evolve?

- The Earth formed around 4.6 billion years ago (bya) but the conditions were too hostile to support life until around 3.9 bya. The oldest known fossil evidence for life are stromatolites (3.5 bya). Several hypotheses have been proposed for where life on Earth first originated.
- **The primordial soup model** proposes that the simple compounds (e.g amino acids and nucleotides) were synthesized and accumulated within various liquid environments (e.g. ponds, shallow pools, and oceanic vents). Once concentrated, these molecules could react together to form stable, more complex molecules essential for building living organisms.
- Another hypothesis is that the chemical reactions occurred on a **solid reactive surface** such as clay. Clay can act as a support structure and a catalyst for the formation of polymers. This was demonstrated in the 1990s when it was shown that RNA nucleotides linked together to form an RNA polymer when exposed to a clay surface. In addition, montmorillonite (a type of clay mineral) has been shown to cause lipid spheres to assemble together into cell membrane-like vesicles.
- **Undersea thermal vents** may also have been likely sites for the origin of life. This warm, nutrient rich environment provides the necessary gases, energy, and catalysts (metals) for life to evolve.
- Yet another hypothesis is that organic molecules or microorganisms arrived on Earth carried within extraterrestrial material (comets or meteorites). This is called **panspermia** (cosmic ancestry). Support for this comes from the fact that complex organic molecules have been detected in interstellar dust clouds and in meteorites that have landed on Earth. In addition, complex molecules have been formed in experiments using simulated space ice.

Leon Hupperichs CC2.0

Reactive clay surfaces, such as montmorillonite (above), have been shown to be capable of catalyzing the formation of RNA polymers.

Didier Descouens CC4.0

Stromatolites (such as the one above from a beach in Western Australia) provide records of the first life on Earth. They are created by mats of cyanobacteria. Fossilized stromatolites have been found in rocks dating back 3.5 billion years ago.

2. Explain why scientists think that RNA was the first self-replicating molecule on Earth: ______

3. There are several possible hypotheses regarding the origin of life on Earth.

   (a) Contrast the primordial soup and the solid reactive surface hypotheses: ______

   (b) What evidence is there to support the claim that the precursors for life on Earth may have originated in space?

4. How does stromatolite evidence add legitimacy to determining when life on Earth first arose? ______

ISBN: 978-1-98-856656-6

204 Prebiotic Experiments

Key Question: What happens to chemical formation when Earth's early atmospheric conditions are simulated?

In the 1950s, Stanley Miller and Harold Urey attempted to recreate the conditions of primitive Earth. They hoped to produce the biological molecules that preceded the development of the first living organisms. Researchers at the time believed that the Earth's early atmosphere was made up of methane, water vapor, ammonia, and hydrogen gas, so these were the components included in the experiments. Many variations on this experiment have produced similar results (below). It seems that the building blocks of life are relatively easy to create.

The Miller-Urey experiment

The experiment (right) was run for a week after which samples were taken from the collection trap for analysis. Up to 4% of the carbon (from the methane) had been converted to amino acids. In this and subsequent experiments, it has been possible to form all 20 amino acids commonly found in organisms, along with nucleic acids, several sugars, lipids, adenine, and even ATP (if phosphate is added to the flask). Researchers now believe that the early atmosphere may be similar to the vapors given off by modern volcanoes: carbon monoxide (CO), carbon dioxide (CO_2), and nitrogen (N_2). Note the absence of free atmospheric oxygen.

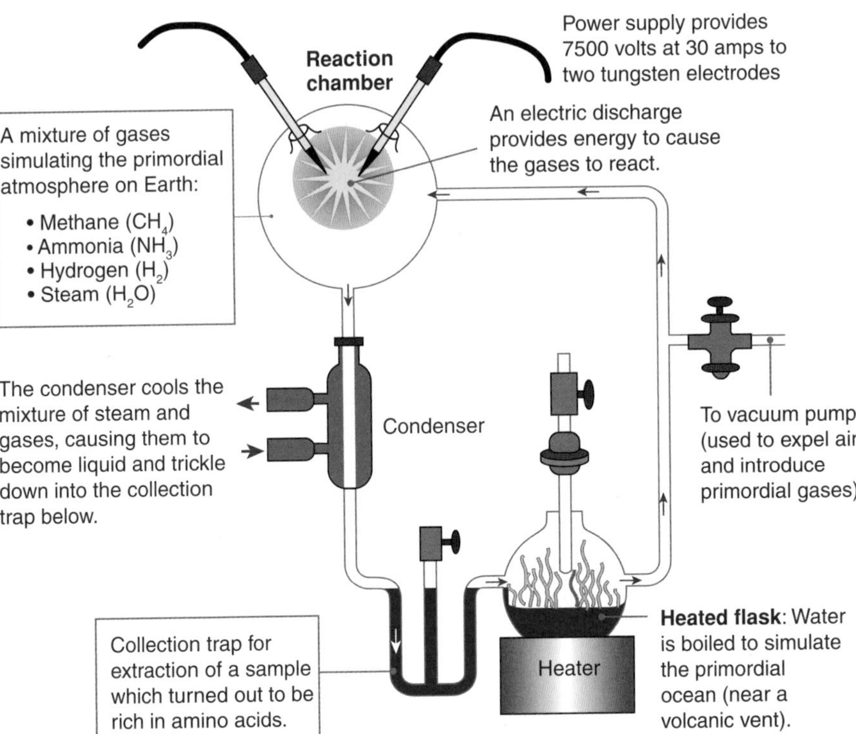

Reaction chamber
Power supply provides 7500 volts at 30 amps to two tungsten electrodes
An electric discharge provides energy to cause the gases to react.
A mixture of gases simulating the primordial atmosphere on Earth:
• Methane (CH_4)
• Ammonia (NH_3)
• Hydrogen (H_2)
• Steam (H_2O)
The condenser cools the mixture of steam and gases, causing them to become liquid and trickle down into the collection trap below.
Condenser
To vacuum pump (used to expel air and introduce primordial gases).
Collection trap for extraction of a sample which turned out to be rich in amino acids.
Heater
Heated flask: Water is boiled to simulate the primordial ocean (near a volcanic vent).

Iron pyrite (fool's gold) has been proposed as a possible stabilizing surface for the synthesis of organic compounds in the prebiotic world.

Some scientists envisage a global winter scenario for the formation of life. Organic compounds are more stable in colder temperatures and could combine in a lattice of ice. This "snowball Earth"' could thaw later.

Lightning is a natural phenomenon associated with volcanic activity. It may have supplied energy for the formation of new compounds (e.g. nitrogen oxides) which were incorporated into organic molecules.

The early Earth was subjected to volcanism everywhere. At volcanic sites such as deep sea hydrothermal vents and geysers (like the one above), gases delivered vital compounds to the surface, where reactions took place.

1. State a hypothesis for the Miller-Urey experiment: ______________________________

2. Discuss if the Miller-Urey experiment supported the theory that conditions on early Earth could have produced simple organic molecules:

____

3. Why is highly unlikely that life could ever begin again on present day Earth? ______________________________

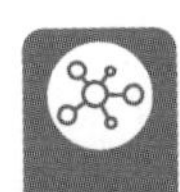

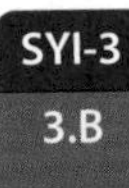

SYI-3
3.B

203

206

ISBN: 978-1-98-856656-6

205 An RNA World

Key Question: Did life begin with self replicating RNA?
Modern life requires complex proteins and other molecules for replication, but these did not exist in life's beginnings. The discovery of ribozymes in 1982 helped to solve the problem of how biological information was stored and replicated.

Ribozymes are enzymes formed from RNA, which itself can store biological information. The ribozymes can catalyze the replication of the original RNA molecule. This mechanism for self replication has led to the theory of an "**RNA world**".

1 Pre RNA world

The individual ribonucleotides of RNA are difficult to assemble without enzymes.

This has led to proposals of a pre-RNA world, where polymers similar to RNA formed and acted as the very first catalysts.

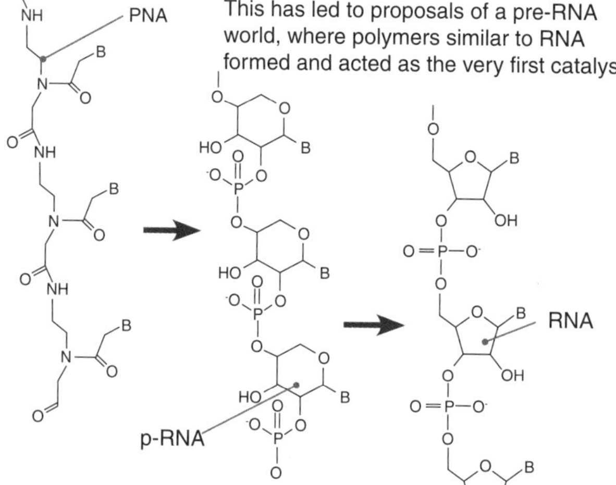

PNA
p-RNA
RNA

Evidence in laboratory experiments shows that PNA (a much simpler molecule than RNA) can act as a template for the formation of RNA.

2 RNA world

RNA is able to act as a vehicle for both information storage and catalysis. It therefore provides a way around the problem that genes require enzymes to form and enzymes require genes to form. The first stage of evolution may have proceeded by RNA molecules folding up to form ribozymes, which could then catalyze the replication of other similar RNAs.

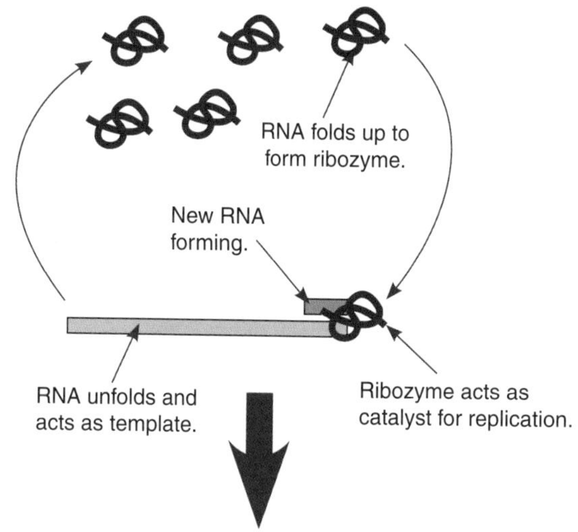

RNA folds up to form ribozyme.
New RNA forming.
RNA unfolds and acts as template.
Ribozyme acts as catalyst for replication.

3 Mutation and competition

From the establishment of self replicating RNA molecules there would have been competition, of a sort. Incorrect copies of the original RNA produced new varieties of RNA.

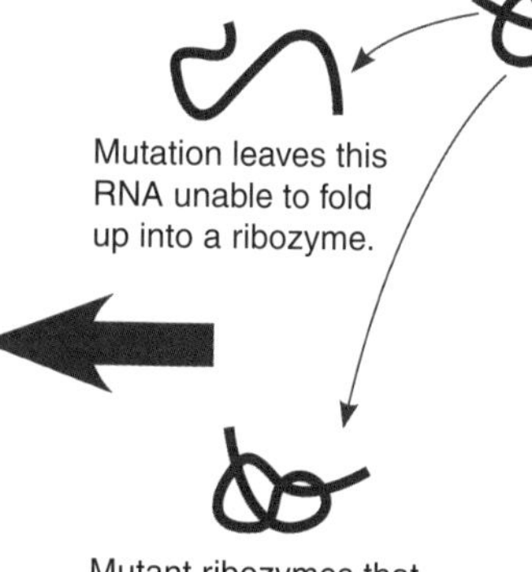

Original RNA

Mutation leaves this RNA unable to fold up into a ribozyme.

Some ribozymes may have added more ribonucleotide to the chain, allowing the RNA to grow in length.

Mutant ribozymes that allowed faster copying would have been able to gather resources faster than the original, becoming more prevalent.

Mutant ribozyme is able to translate RNA into proteins.

4 Proto-cells

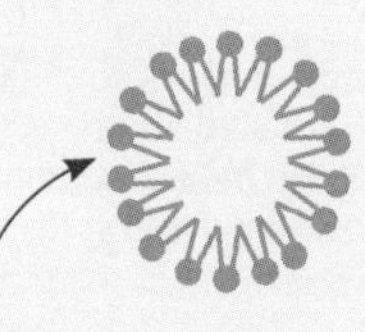

Large groups of micelles can interact to form vesicles large enough to contain other molecules.

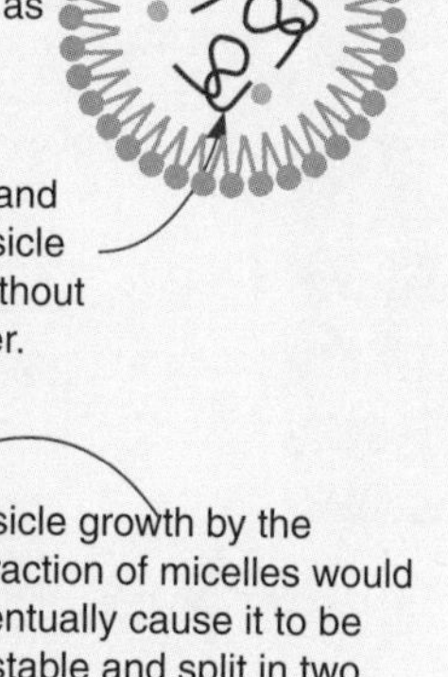

Certain types of organic molecule (such as fatty acids) spontaneously form micelles when placed in an aqueous solution.

Mutually cooperating RNAs and proteins trapped inside a vesicle would be able to replicate without moving away from each other.

Vesicle growth by the attraction of micelles would eventually cause it to be unstable and split in two. Each vesicle would take a random number of RNAs with it.

1. How did the discovery of ribozymes provide evidence for the RNA world hypothesis? ______

2. Explain how mutations in RNA templates led to the first form of evolution: ______

ISBN: 978-1-98-856656-6

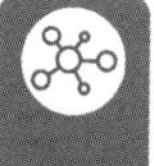

206 Landmarks in Earth's History

Key Question: How does the geological record show the progression of life on Earth?

Modern life forms arose from ancient ancestors that have long since become extinct. These ancient life forms themselves originally arose from primitive cells living some 3500 million years ago in conditions quite different from those on Earth today. The earliest fossil records of living things show only simple cell types. It is believed that the first cells arose as a result of evolution at the chemical level in a 'primordial soup' (a rich broth of chemicals in a warm pool of water, perhaps near a volcanic vent). Life appears very early in Earth's history, but did not evolve beyond the simple cell stage until much later (about 600 mya). This would suggest that the evolution of complex life forms required more difficult evolutionary hurdles to be overcome. One hypothesis is that fluctuating nutrient levels and rising oxygen following the end of the snowball glaciations may have been important in the evolution of multicellularity.

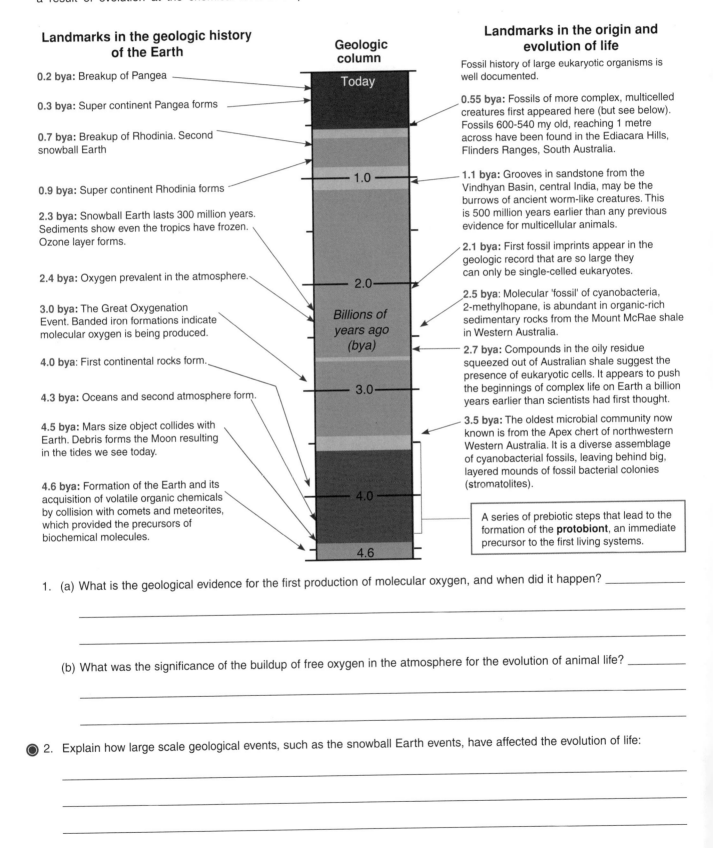

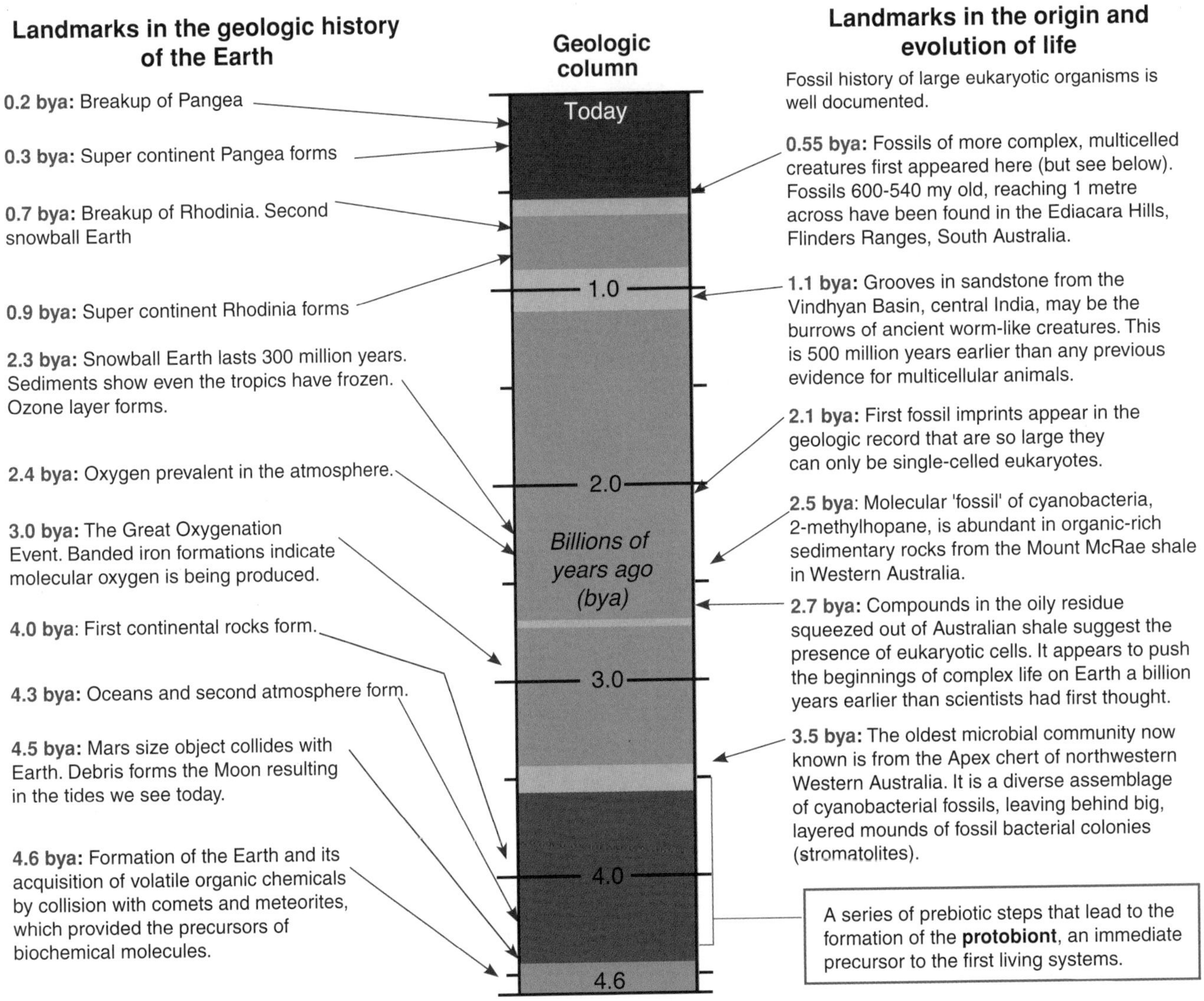

Landmarks in the geologic history of the Earth
0.2 bya: Breakup of Pangea
0.3 bya: Super continent Pangea forms
0.7 bya: Breakup of Rhodinia. Second snowball Earth
0.9 bya: Super continent Rhodinia forms
2.3 bya: Snowball Earth lasts 300 million years. Sediments show even the tropics have frozen. Ozone layer forms.
2.4 bya: Oxygen prevalent in the atmosphere.
3.0 bya: The Great Oxygenation Event. Banded iron formations indicate molecular oxygen is being produced.
4.0 bya: First continental rocks form.
4.3 bya: Oceans and second atmosphere form.
4.5 bya: Mars size object collides with Earth. Debris forms the Moon resulting in the tides we see today.
4.6 bya: Formation of the Earth and its acquisition of volatile organic chemicals by collision with comets and meteorites, which provided the precursors of biochemical molecules.
Geologic column
Today
1.0
2.0
Billions of years ago (bya)
3.0
4.0
4.6
Landmarks in the origin and evolution of life
Fossil history of large eukaryotic organisms is well documented.
0.55 bya: Fossils of more complex, multicelled creatures first appeared here (but see below). Fossils 600-540 my old, reaching 1 metre across have been found in the Ediacara Hills, Flinders Ranges, South Australia.
1.1 bya: Grooves in sandstone from the Vindhyan Basin, central India, may be the burrows of ancient worm-like creatures. This is 500 million years earlier than any previous evidence for multicellular animals.
2.1 bya: First fossil imprints appear in the geologic record that are so large they can only be single-celled eukaryotes.
2.5 bya: Molecular 'fossil' of cyanobacteria, 2-methylhopane, is abundant in organic-rich sedimentary rocks from the Mount McRae shale in Western Australia.
2.7 bya: Compounds in the oily residue squeezed out of Australian shale suggest the presence of eukaryotic cells. It appears to push the beginnings of complex life on Earth a billion years earlier than scientists had first thought.
3.5 bya: The oldest microbial community now known is from the Apex chert of northwestern Western Australia. It is a diverse assemblage of cyanobacterial fossils, leaving behind big, layered mounds of fossil bacterial colonies (stromatolites).
A series of prebiotic steps that lead to the formation of the protobiont, an immediate precursor to the first living systems.

1. (a) What is the geological evidence for the first production of molecular oxygen, and when did it happen? ______

(b) What was the significance of the buildup of free oxygen in the atmosphere for the evolution of animal life? ______

2. Explain how large scale geological events, such as the snowball Earth events, have affected the evolution of life:

______

ISBN: 978-1-98-856656-6

The clock of history

The visualization of Earth's history as a 24 hour clock enables almost unimaginable lengths of time to be compressed into a somewhat more meaningful, or at least imaginable, scale. Some of the key events in Earth's history are listed below:

Cenozoic Era
0.01 mya: Modern history begins.
0.2 mya: Modern humans evolve. Their activities, starting at the most recent ice age, are implicated in the extinction of the megafauna.
3 mya: Early humans arise from ape-like ancestors.
~65 mya: Major shifts in climate. Major adaptive radiations of angiosperms (flowering plants), insects, birds, and mammals. Start of Cenozoic Era.

Mesozoic Era
~65 mya: Apparent asteroid impact implicated in mass extinctions of many marine species and all dinosaurs. End of Mesozoic Era.
181 mya: Major radiations of dinosaurs and evolution of birds.
230 mya: Origin of mammals Gymnosperms become dominant land plants.

Paleozoic Era
240 mya: Mass extinction of nearly all species on land and in the sea.
340 mya: Reptiles evolve.
370 mya: Amphibians evolve.
435 mya: Major adaptive radiations of early fishes. Plants colonize the land.
550 mya: Cambrian explosion: Animals with hard parts appear. Simple marine communities indicated by early Cambrian fossil forms.

Precambrian Era (Hadean, Archean, and Proterozoic)
1100 mya: Multicellular life evolves.
3500 mya: First fossils of bacteria.
4300 mya: Oceans form.
4500 mya: Moon forms from planetary collision.
4600 mya: Origin of Earth.

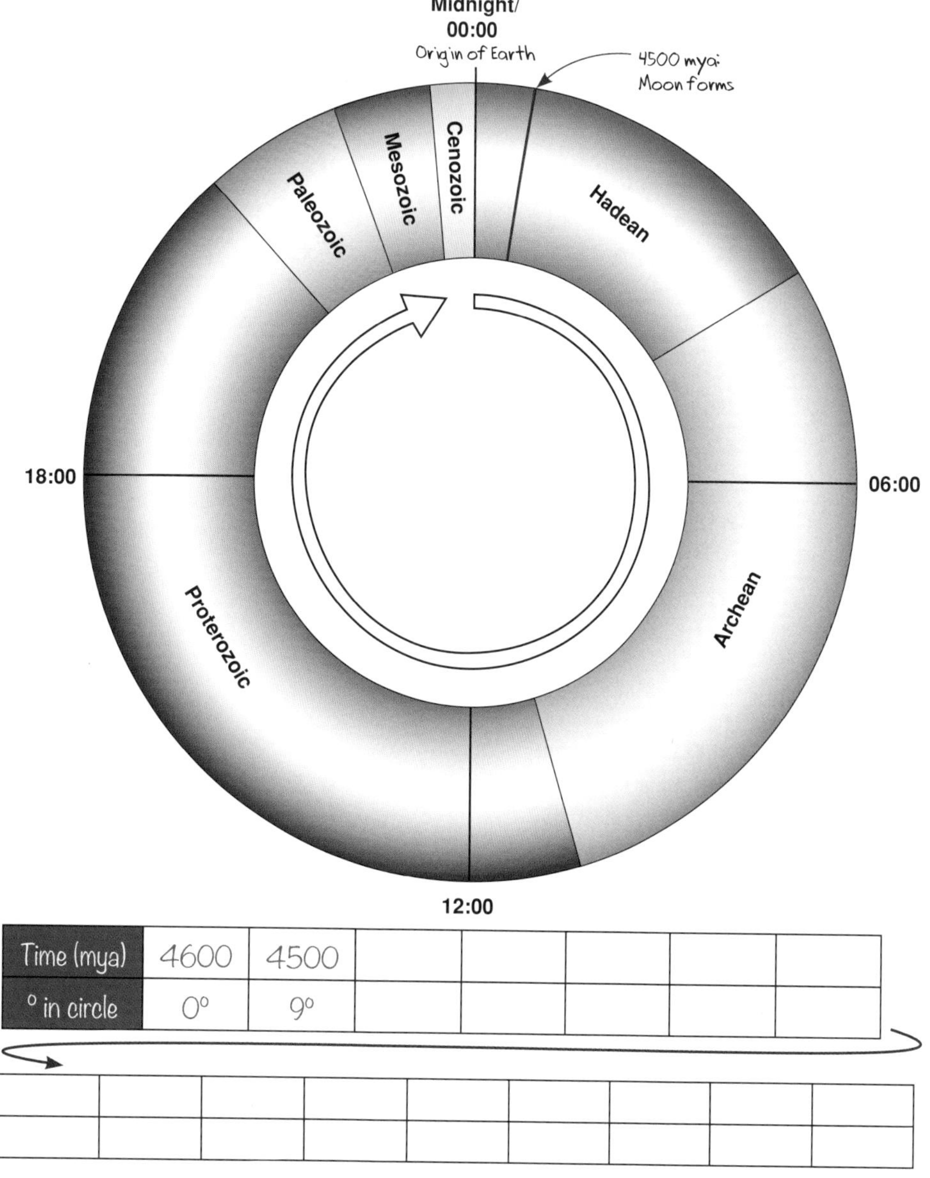

Time (mya)	4600	4500					
° in circle	0°	9°					

3. (a) Using the times given in the table above left, calculate the degrees each time represents and write it in the space provided. The first two are done for you. (Hint use the formula: 360 - (mya x 0.078)):

   (b) Using the degrees you have calculated, mark on the clock the events listed. The first two are done for you:

4. Explain how changes in selection pressures throughout Earth's history have influenced the evolution of life on Earth:

ISBN: 978-1-98-856656-6

207 Personal Progress Check

Answer the multiple choice questions that follow by circling the correct answer. Don't forget to read the question carefully!

1. The mean birth weight for babies born in the US is 3.5 kg but the range of typical birth weights is quite narrow. This is an example of:
   (a) Directional selection
   (b) Disruptive selection
   (c) Stabilizing selection
   (d) None of the above

2. Circle the graph below which shows directional selection:

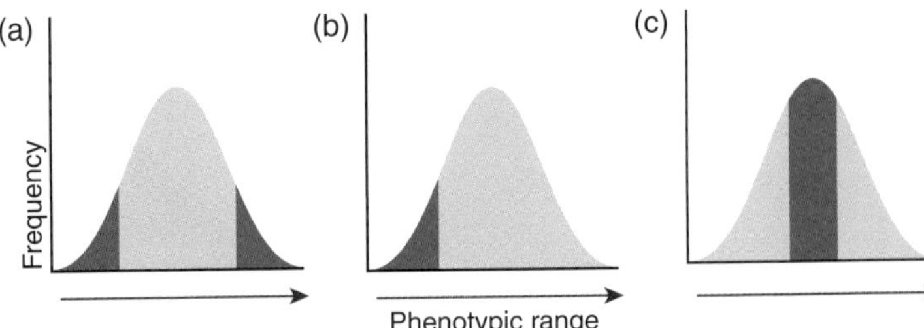

3. The diagrams (far right) show the forelimbs of a human, bird, and whale. These structures share many of the same bones. These type of structures are called:
   (a) Mutations
   (b) Homologous structures
   (c) Vestigial structures
   (d) Analogous structures

4. The structures pictured right arose through:
   (a) Mutation
   (b) Extinction
   (c) Convergent evolution
   (d) Adaptive radiation

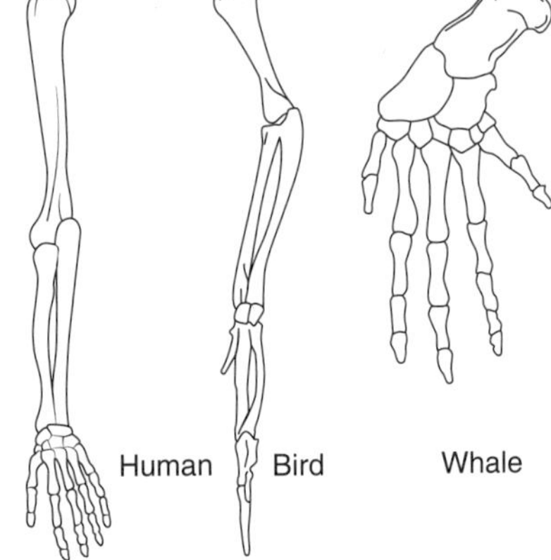

5. The statements (A)-(D) below describe scenarios in hypothetical populations:
   A A forest fire burns through an area containing black and gray squirrels. It kills 70% of the black squirrels and 30% of the gray squirrels.
   B Dark colored mice are able to avoid being eaten by owls more easily than light colored mice.
   C Deer from a population become isolated from another population because of a huge slip blocking a hilltop pass.
   D A plant nursery is infected with a fungal infection that affects the leaves of plants. Plants with thick leaf cuticles are more likely to survive.

   In which of the scenarios is genetic drift likely to have a significant effect on allele frequencies?
   (a) A
   (b) B and D
   (c) A and C
   (d) All of the above

6. A river changes its course, separating a population of snails into two. They can no longer interact and over time the two populations become separate species. Identify the type of speciation involved:
   (a) Sympatric speciation
   (b) Adaptive radiation
   (c) Allopatric speciation
   (d) Artificial selection

7. DDT was once extremely effective in reducing malaria by killing the *Anopheles* mosquito. Today DDT is largely reduced in its effectiveness and as higher percentage of mosquitoes survive. What might be a reason for this?
   (a) The concentration of DDT used is less than it was.
   (b) Many governments banned DDT so the reduced kill rate is related to it being used less.
   (c) Mosquitoes that weren't killed by DDT passed on their resistance to their offspring, so increasing the population's overall resistance.
   (d) DDT is no longer designed to target mosquitoes.

For questions 8 and 9:
In a population of beetles, 81% have spots on their forewings and 19% do not. Having spots is the dominant trait. Assume Hardy-Weinberg equilibrium.

8. What is percentage of the population is heterozygous?
   (a) 0.44
   (b) 0.56
   (c) 0.49
   (d) 0.32

9. What is percentage of the population is homozygous dominant?
   (a) 0.44
   (b) 0.56
   (c) 0.49
   (d) 0.32

10. Which statement is correct?
   (a) Allopatric speciation occurs when a population is separated by a geographical barrier.
   (b) Allopatric speciation occurs when a population is separated by temporal characteristics, such as flowering at different times.
   (c) Allopatric speciation occurs when the population is separated by behavioral barriers.
   (c) Allopatric speciation occurs when separated populations become no longer separated and interbreed to form a new hybrid species.

ISBN: 978-1-98-856656-6

11. The diagram below right represents part of a sedimentary rock profile from two states in the USA. Identify which statement is incorrect:
    (a) Species C is the youngest
    (b) Species B was not found in Virginia
    (c) Species A is the youngest
    (d) The order of fossils makes it possible to correlate rock layers of the same age

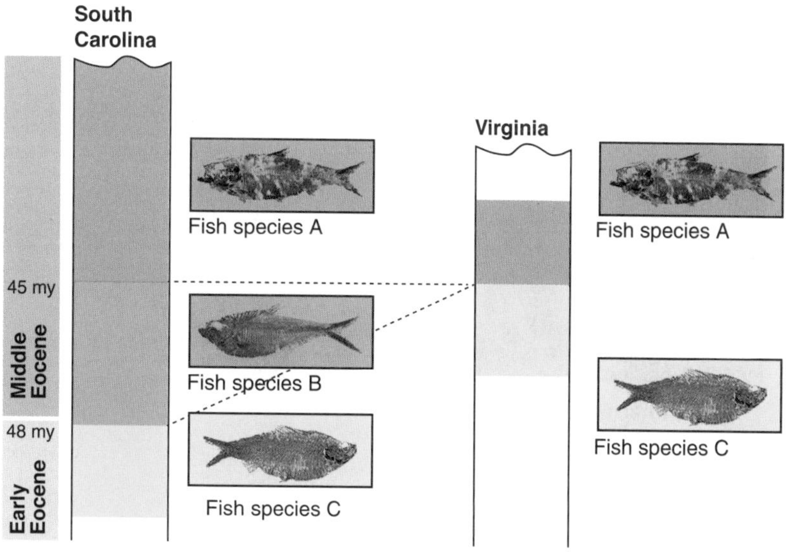

12. Again, with reference to the diagram right, what sort of dating is involved here?
    (a) Relative dating
    (b) Chronometric dating
    (c) Radiometric dating
    (d) None of the above

13. What age of rocks are missing from the profile in Virginia?
    (a) Early Eocene
    (b) Middle Eocene
    (c) Late Eocene
    (d) No layers are missing

South Carolina
Virginia
45 my
Middle Eocene
48 my
Early Eocene
Fish species A
Fish species B
Fish species C
Fish species A
Fish species C

14. In a population with two alleles, B and b, it was found that in the adult population the homozygous dominant genotype was the most common, the heterozygous condition persisted in a small percentage, and the homozygous recessive condition was absent (the condition being lethal in the young). This situation may have come about due to:
    (a) The homozygous dominant genotype being selected against
    (b) Heterozygous advantage
    (c) The homozygous recessive genotype being actively selected for
    (d) None of the above

15. Use the diagram below to answer the question:

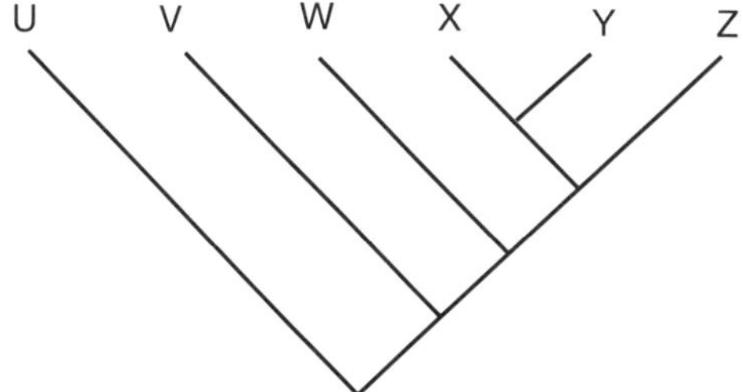

Which statement is correct:
    (a) U has the most advanced features
    (b) V is more closely related to W than to X
    (c) X shares its most recent ancestor with W
    (d) X is more advanced than Y

16. Carbon-14 has a half life of 5730 years. Its proportion is relatively constant in living organisms. A bone is found to have a quarter of the carbon-14 expected in living organisms. How old is the bone?
    (a) 5730 years old
    (b) 11,460 years old
    (c) 17,190 years old
    (d) 22,920 years old

17. The four important concepts of Darwin's theory of natural selection are:
    (a) Overproduction, overpopulation, variation, inheritance
    (b) Overproduction, variation, artificial selection, inheritance
    (c) Overproduction, natural selection, increased fitness, inheritance
    (d) Overproduction, variation, natural selection, inheritance

18. The image below shows a representative collection of pepper moth from 1850 to 1950. The image shows how the color of moths has changed over time. This is most probably the result of:

    (a) Stabilizing selection
    (b) Artificial selection
    (c) Directional selection
    (d) Disruptive selection

19. Which of the following are likely to have a greater effect on the allele frequencies in a small population than the allele frequencies of a large population:
    (a) Genetic drift
    (b) Natural selection
    (c) Gene flow
    (d) All of the above

ISBN: 978-1-98-856656-6

20. The two plants shown below are unrelated. The left hand image shows a cactus from North America, while the right hand image shows a Euphorbia from Africa. Both these plants live in deserts.

This pattern of evolution is:

(a) Divergent evolution
(b) Sequential evolution
(c) Parallel evolution
(d) Convergent evolution

21. Which of the following must exist in a population before natural selection can act upon that population?

(a) Heritable variation among individuals
(b) Variation among individuals caused by environmental factors
(c) Sexual reproduction
(d) An aging population

22. If two organisms are closely related in an evolutionary sense, then it would be expected that:

(a) They live in very different habitats
(b) They should share few homologous structures
(c) Conserved areas of DNA would be very similar
(d) They shared a very distant common ancestor

23. Which pieces of evidence most strongly supports the common origin of all life on Earth?

(a) All organisms require energy
(b) All organisms use essentially the same genetic code
(c) All organisms reproduce
(d) All organisms show genetic variation

24. The extinction event that caused the extinction of the dinosaurs:

(a) Caused the adaptive radiation of the mammals
(b) Allowed the expansion of birds
(c) Was most likely the result of a meteorite strike
(d) Also wiped out 80% of life on the planet

25. Breeders have improved milk quality from cattle by:

(a) Artificial selection
(b) Natural selection
(c) Stabilizing selection
(d) Random breeding

26. Which list of reproductive isolating mechanisms below identifies only prezygotic isolating mechanisms?

(a) Geographical, ecological, hybrid breakdown, gamete incompatibility
(b) Behavioral, ecological, temporal, gamete incompatibility
(c) Temporal, gamete incompatibility, hybrid inviability, hybrid breakdown
(d) Geographical, hybrid breakdown, mechanical, gamete incompatibility

27. *Archaeopteryx* is known from a fossil showing many avian and reptilian features. The fossil is an example of:

(a) A transitional fossil (from reptiles to birds)
(b) A transitional fossil (from birds to reptiles)
(c) The evolution of a new species
(d) A well crafted fake

28. Antibiotic resistance in bacteria occurs because:

(a) The bacteria need to resist the antibiotics and so evolve mechanisms that will help them do this.
(b) Variation in the bacterial population allows some of the bacteria to produce antibiotic resistant materials while others can not.
(c) Variation in the bacterial population allows some of the bacteria to survive an inadequate dose of antibiotics and pass these variations on to the next generation.
(d) Variation in bacteria allow some to avoid detection by host immune systems and then pass on these variations to the next generation.

29. Adaptive radiation

(a) Is a type of divergent radiation
(b) Occurs when a single species evolves to produce many species occupying many different niches
(c) Occurred in mammals about 66 million years ago
(d) All of the above

30. Which of the following would likely **not** increase the rate of speciation in a large population?

(a) High birth rates and death rates
(b) Fragmentation and low gene flow
(c) Specialized feeding behaviors and requirements
(d) Complex courtship and display behaviors

31. A population of beetles that have either light or dark wing covers were captured, counted and released into several environments. After several days they were recaptured and recounted. Based on the data, in which environment is the dark phenotype an advantage?

Area	Wing cover	Released	Recaptured
(a)	Dark	100	81
	Light	110	103
(b)	Dark	150	115
	Light	120	92
(c)	Dark	110	40
	Light	100	30

(d) The dark phenotype has no advantage

ISBN: 978-1-98-856656-6

Free Response Question: *Interpreting and evaluating experimental results with graphing*

- Parasites may adapt and radiate among host species in the same way that free-living species adapt when isolated on islands. Feather lice are host-specific parasites of birds that feed on the feathers, skin, and blood of birds, reducing fitness through energetic stress. Feather lice depend on feathers to move around and most dispersal is from parent to offspring in the nest.
- Birds reduce lice infestations by removing them during preening. Lice are thought to escape preening through camouflage because light-colored bird species have light-colored lice, and dark-colored species have dark-colored lice. Researchers carried out a multi-year experiment to investigate adaptive divergence in feather lice in response to host preening. The experiment tracked ~60 louse generations. At time 0, lice were transferred from wild caught gray feral rock pigeons to white, black, or gray rock pigeons that could either preen normally, or were stopped from preening with a harmless device on the beak. The luminosity (brightness) of the lice was quantified every 6 months through color-matching to color standards. The results were normalized to the control (gray) birds (as zero) to gain a relative luminosity. The results after 42 months are tabulated below.

	White pigeons		Gray (control) pigeons		Black pigeons	
	n	Relative luminosity mean ± 95% CI	n	Relative luminosity mean ± 95% CI	n	Relative luminosity mean ± 95% CI
Normal preening	71	23.39 ± 4.30	91	8.25 ± 1.5	75	4.47 ± 1.56
Impaired preening	193	9.26 ± 1.02	189	8.39 ± 1.18	184	9.17 ± 1.36

Adapted from data in Bush et al. (2019). See credits for full citation.

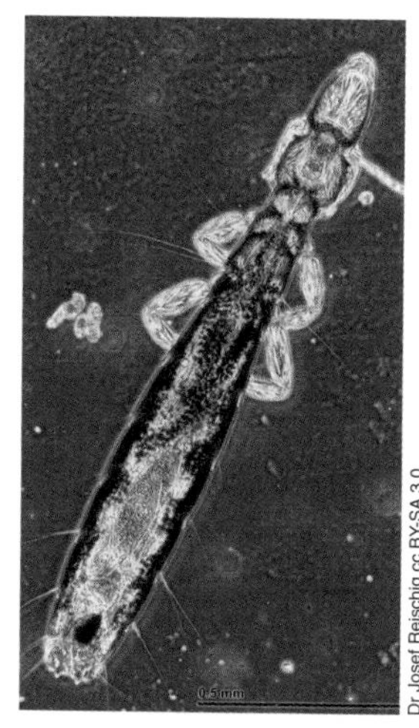

Feather louse (*Columba columbae*) used in this study.

1. (a) **Describe** what is meant by selection pressure: ____________________

   (b) **Explain** how selection pressure can result in phenotypic change over generations: ____________________

2. **Plot** an appropriate labeled graph of the data tabulated above.

3. **Describe** the results: ____________________

4. **Predict** the likely consequences to the luminosity of subsequent generations of feather lice if they were transferred from the white pigeons back to gray pigeons. **Justify** your prediction:

ISBN: 978-1-98-856656-6

Free Response Question: *Analyze data*

- This question reports on the results of 36 year long translocation experiment in the Italian wall lizard (*Podarcis sicula*), a small species native to south-eastern Europe.
- Researchers introduced five adult pairs of the lizards to the small islet of Pod Mrčaru (0.03 km^2) from a source population on the islet of Pod Kopište (0.09 km^2). Both islets are in the South Adriatic Sea. Pod Mrčaru was previously inhabited by a related lizard species, but repeated surveys showed it to be extinct on the islet.
- The researchers found through analysis of gut contents that the diet of the translocated population on Pod Mrčaru was 48-60% fibrous plant material compared to the Pod Kopište population which was dominated by invertebrates (only 4-9% plant material). The change in diet was accompanied by changes in the gut structure of the Pod Mrčaru population associated with digesting plant material.
- The researchers predicted that the change in diet would be associated with measurable phenotypic changes in the Pod Mrčaru population. They measured a range of characteristics in the two populations 36 years after the translocation. These measurements were associated with the size of the head and the strength of the bite. The results are plotted, right (±95% CI). Where error bars are not shown, they fall within the limit of the marker. Pod Kopište, n = 100. Pod Mrčaru, n = 158.

Divergence in populations of *P. sicula* 36 years after introducing 10 individuals to Pod Mrčaru. Filled symbol = Pod Mrčaru. Open symbol = Pod Kopište. * = $P < 0.05$

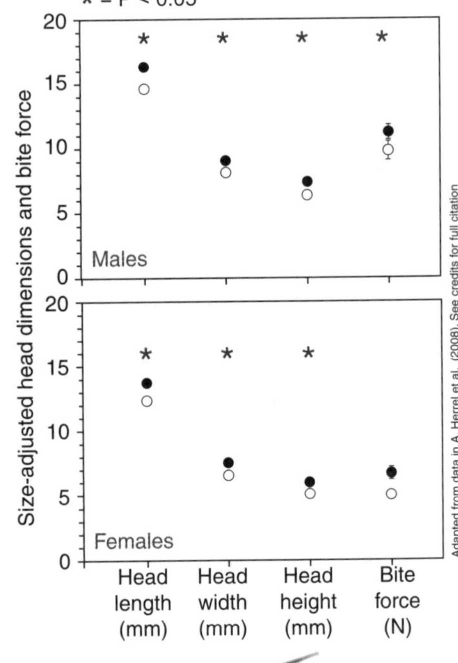

1. **Describe** the results of the translocation experiment:

2. **Explain** how the observed differences are related to the change in diet in the Pod Mrčaru population:

3. Use the data to **evaluate** the prediction of the researchers:

4. **Explain** how the experimental results relate to our understanding of the evolution of small founding populations:

ISBN: 978-1-98-856656-6

UNIT 8 Ecology

Learning Objectives

Developing understanding

CONTENT: This unit integrates the principles and concepts in all the other units to show how interactions, processes, and responses are related to available energy. When complex living systems interact, they will change based on those interactions. Population dynamics and community interactions both influence and are influenced by energy flows. Regardless of an ecosystem's characteristics, its health and resilience depend on biodiversity. Your understanding should now enable you to determine the outcome of disruptions within biological systems.

SKILLS: This unit focuses on understanding and evaluating experimental work. You should draw on the skills of earlier units demonstrate competency in data analysis and argumentation.

8.1 Responses to the environment ... activities 208 - 228

☐ 1. Explain how organisms respond to their environments through behavioral and physiological mechanisms. Examples include photoperiodism and phototropism in plants, and taxes and kineses in animals.

☐ 2. Use examples of responses to internal changes (e.g. hormones) and external cues (e.g. warning calls) to explain how an exchange of information between organisms can lead to a change in behavior.

☐ 3. Describe the mechanisms by which organisms communicate. Explain how the behavioral responses of organisms to communicated information contribute to fitness.

8.2 Energy flow through ecosystems.............................. activities 229 - 236

☐ 4. Describe how organisms use energy to maintain organization, grow, and reproduce. Examples include strategies for thermoregulation and reproduction in animals.

☐ 5. Describe the relationship between metabolic rate per unit body mass and animal size. Explain the consequences of a net loss or a net gain in energy in an organism.

☐ 6. Explain how changes in the availability of energy affect populations and communities, e.g. by affecting biomass at different trophic levels or the number of trophic levels.

☐ 7. Use examples and models to explain how the activities of autotrophs (including chemoautotrophs) and heterotrophs enable the flow of energy within an ecosystem.

8.3 Population ecology .... activities 237 - 238

☐ 8. Describe the factors that influence the growth dynamics of populations. Include reference to birth rates (natality), death rates (mortality), and migration.

☐ 9. Describe the characteristics of exponential population growth (also called density independent or geometric growth). When does it occur and why is it rarely sustained?

8.4 Effect of population density .... activity 239

☐ 10. Explain how the density of a population affects and is determined by resource availability. Explain the basis of logistic growth with reference to carrying capacity. How does the logistic growth model explain the population growth of most natural populations?

8.5 Community ecology .... activities 240 - 242

☐ 11. Use a diversity index to describe the structure of a community according to its composition and diversity.

☐ 12. Explain how interactions within and among populations influence community structure. Describe these relationships in terms of positive and negative effects and include reference to predator-prey interactions, trophic cascades, and resource (niche) partitioning.

☐ 13. Explain how species interactions, including predation, competition, and symbioses, can influence the dynamics of populations. Examples include predator-prey cycles, competitive displacement or exclusion, and niche specialization in species with symbiotic relationships.

☐ 14. Explain how community structure is related to energy availability. Use examples to show how cooperation between organisms, populations, and species can enhance the movement of, or access to, matter and energy.

8.6 Biodiversity .... activities 243 - 244

☐ 15. Describe the relationship between the diversity of an ecosystem and its resilience to environmental change.

☐ 16. Using examples, explain the role of keystone species in ecosystems. Explain how keystone species, producers, and essential biotic and abiotic factors contribute to maintaining the diversity of an ecosystem.

☐ 17. Explain how species diversity influences ecosystem organization. With respect to keystone species, explain how the addition or removal of a ecosystem component affects the ecosystem's short-term and long-term structure.

8.7 Disruptions to ecosystems .... activities 245 - 248

☐ 18. Explain how random or pre-existing variation in a population can interact with the environment to result in traits that benefit an organism in that environment.

☐ 19. Using examples, explain how invasive species affect ecosystem dynamics. Explain the rapid population growth of invasive species and the effect of this on energy flows and community structure.

☐ 20. Describe human activities that lead to changes in populations or in ecosystem structure. Describe examples to show how human activity accelerates change at both local and global levels. Examples include the introduction of new diseases and changes to habitats.

☐ 21. Explain how geological and meteorological activity can result in changes to ecosystem structure an/or dynamics. Examples include volcanic eruptions, ice ages, climate cycles (El Niño Southern Oscillation).

208 Responding to Changes in the Environment

Key Question: Why do organisms respond to environmental changes and what kinds of responses do they have?

The environment in which any organism lives is always changing. Organisms must respond appropriately to these changes in order to survive. A response by the organism is called its **behavior**, which may be simple, e.g. moving towards light, or complex, e.g. calling and displaying for a mate. A behavior that contributes to an organism's survival and reproductive success (fitness) is called an **adaptive behavior**. Behaviors (usually called responses in plants) are subject to natural selection. Those that increase fitness (have adaptive value) are retained in a population, whereas those that reduce fitness are eventually lost. Some behaviors are so important they are **innate**, i.e. genetically programmed, and do not require learning. For example, a maggot exposed to light will immediately seek shade because this behavior reduces the risk of being eaten or drying out. The behavior is not learned and every maggot responds the same way.

Orientation behaviors

Positioning in response to an environmental stimulus

Animals

- **Kineses**: Non-directional
- **Taxes**: Directional

Plants

- **Tropisms**: Directional
- **Nasties**: Non-directional

Honeybees orientate towards the light to escape confinement.

The position of the Sun is important in honeybee navigation.

Navigation

- Sun compass
- Magnetic compass
- Chemical cues
- Landmarks

The position of flowers (food sources) is communicated through body movements.

Timing behaviors

Predictable responses to environmental rhythms

- Annual, daily, lunar, tidal
- Involves a biological clock

Honeybees are day-active (diurnal)

Species interactions

- Communicating
- Competition
- Mutualism
- Exploitation
- Breeding behavior

1. (a) What is a behavior?

   (b) In what way is behavior adaptive?

2. Explain the difference between an orientation behavior and a timing behavior:

3. Suggest how a behavior might become innate:

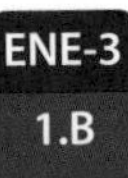

ISBN: 978-1-98-856656-6

209 Timing and Coordination in Plants

Key Question: How do plants coordinate their responses to changes in the environment?

In plants, responses to day length and temperature are mediated by plant growth regulators called **phytohormones** (or plant hormones). The ability to detect changes in day length allows plants to respond to annual cycles by making the appropriate structures at the appropriate time, e.g. flowers or frost tolerant buds. Plant hormones act as signal molecules to regulate plant growth and responses. Alone and together, plant hormones target specific parts of a plant and produce a specific effect. Many have roles in coordinating timing responses in plants including promoting and breaking bud dormancy, seed germination, and fruit ripening. In addition these rhythms are often linked to temperature.

Phytohormones, plant growth, and fruiting

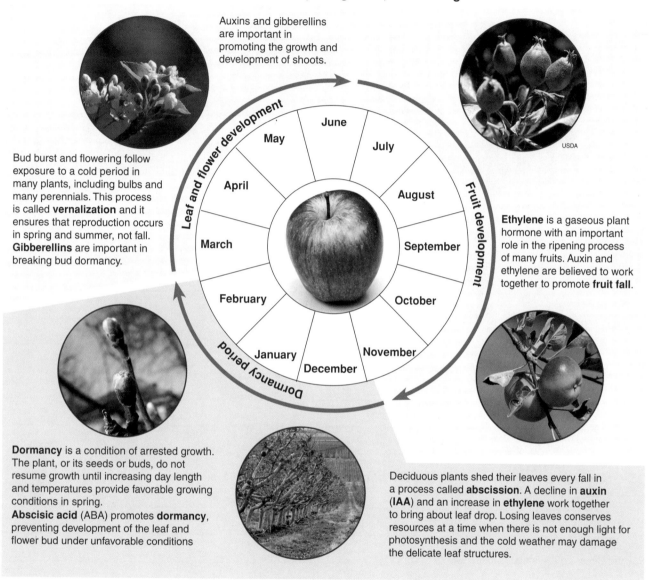

Auxins and gibberellins are important in promoting the growth and development of shoots.

Leaf and flower development

Fruit development

Dormancy period

June, July, August, September, October, November, December, January, February, March, April, May

USDA

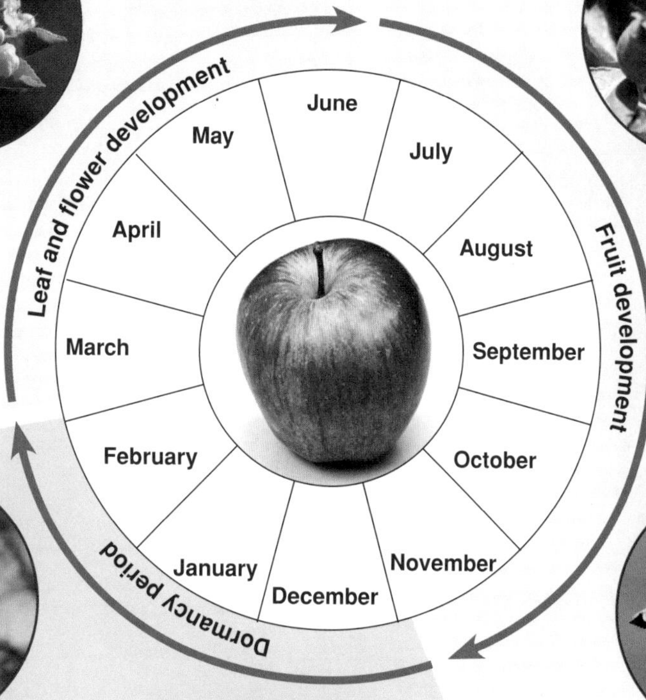

Bud burst and flowering follow exposure to a cold period in many plants, including bulbs and many perennials. This process is called **vernalization** and it ensures that reproduction occurs in spring and summer, not fall. **Gibberellins** are important in breaking bud dormancy.

Ethylene is a gaseous plant hormone with an important role in the ripening process of many fruits. Auxin and ethylene are believed to work together to promote **fruit fall**.

Dormancy is a condition of arrested growth. The plant, or its seeds or buds, do not resume growth until increasing day length and temperatures provide favorable growing conditions in spring.
Abscisic acid (ABA) promotes **dormancy**, preventing development of the leaf and flower bud under unfavorable conditions

Deciduous plants shed their leaves every fall in a process called **abscission**. A decline in **auxin** (**IAA**) and an increase in **ethylene** work together to bring about leaf drop. Losing leaves conserves resources at a time when there is not enough light for photosynthesis and the cold weather may damage the delicate leaf structures.

Daily rhythm in tulips

Many flowers, including tulips, show **sleep movements**. In most species, these are triggered by day length, but in tulips the environmental cue is temperature. This series of photographs shows the sleep movements of a single tulip flower over one 12 hour period during spring. Sleep movements may prevent flower damage, stop the entry of non-pollinating insects, or stop the pollen becoming wet with dew.

7.00 am

9.30 am

11.00 am

5.00 pm

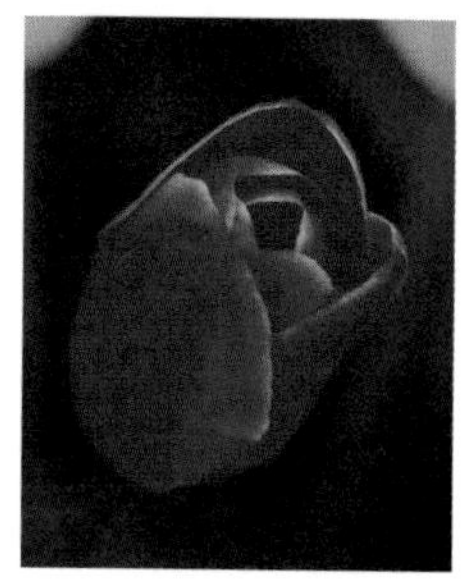
7.00 pm

All photos: RA

ISBN: 978-1-98-856656-6

The cycle of opening and closing of stomata

The opening and closing of stomata shows a daily cycle that is largely determined by the hours of light and dark.

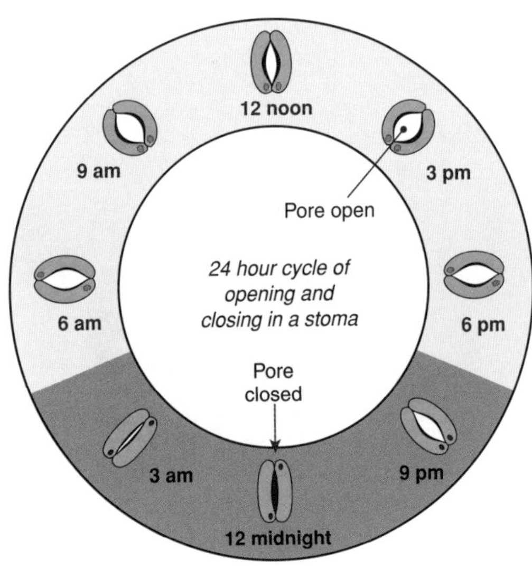

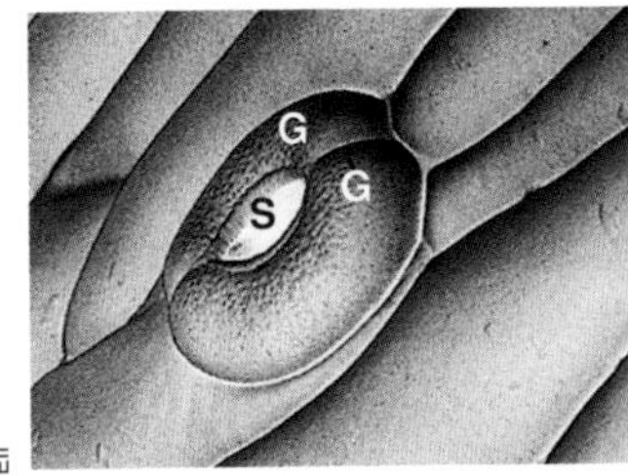

The image left shows a scanning electron micrograph (SEM) of a single stoma from the leaf epidermis of a dicot. Note the guard cells (G), which are swollen tight and open the pore (S) to allow gas exchange between the leaf tissue and the environment.

Factors influencing stomatal opening

Stomata	Guard cells	Daylight	CO_2	Soil water
Open	Turgid	Light	Low	High
Closed	Flaccid	Dark	High	Low

The opening and closing of stomata depends on environmental factors, the most important being light, CO_2 concentration in the leaf tissue, and water supply. Stomata tend to open during daylight in response to light, and close at night (left and above). Low CO_2 levels also promote stomatal opening. Conditions that induce water stress cause the stomata to close, regardless of light or CO_2 level.

1. (a) Explain the adaptive value of dormancy in plants: ______

   (b) What cues are likely to be involved in breaking dormancy? ______

2. Explain the adaptive value of leaf abscission: ______

3. Explain why the same hormones are involved in both leaf fall (abscission) and fruit fall in plants: ______

4. (a) Describe the sleep movements of tulips in response to temperature: ______

   (b) Explain the adaptive value of these movements: ______

   (c) What is the name of this type of response? ______

5. (a) When are stomata most likely to be open? ______

   (b) Explain why they are most likely to open at this time: ______

   (c) Explain why water stress would cause stomata to close: ______

ISBN: 978-1-98-856656-6

210 Tropisms and Growth Responses

Key Question: What is the general role of plant tropisms?

Tropisms are plant growth responses to external stimuli, in which the stimulus direction determines the direction of the growth response. Tropisms are identified according to the stimulus involved and direction (positive or negative). Stimuli are identified as photo- (light), gravi- (gravity), hydro- (water), chemo- (chemicals), and thigmo- (touch). Tropisms act to position the plant in the most favorable growth environment.

(a) ....

A positive growth response to a chemical stimulus. *Example: Pollen tubes grow towards a chemical, possibly calcium ions, released by the ovule of the flower.*

(b) ....

Stems, grow away from the direction of the Earth's gravitational pull. Coleoptiles (the sheath surrounding the young grass shoot) show the same response.

(c) ....

Growth response to water. Roots are influenced primarily by gravity but will also grow towards water.

(d) ....

Growth responses to light, particularly directional light. Coleoptiles, young stems, and some leaves show a positive response.

(e) ....

Roots respond positively to the Earth's gravitational pull, and curve downward after emerging through the seed coat.

(f) ....

Growth responses to touch or pressure. Tendrils (modified leaves) have a positive coiling response stimulated by touch.

Plant growth responses are adaptive in that they position the plant in a suitable growing environment, within the limits of the position in which it germinated. The responses to stimuli reinforce the appropriate growth behavior, e.g. shoots grow towards light and away from dark.

Root mass in a hydroponically grown plant

Tendril wrapping around twig

Germinating pollen

Thale cress bending to the light

Kristian Peters

1. Identify each of the plant tropisms described in (a)-(f) above. State whether the response is positive or negative.

2. Describe the adaptive value of the following tropisms:

   (a) Positive gravitropism in roots: ____________________

   (b) Positive phototropism in coleoptiles: ____________________

   (c) Positive thigmomorphogenesis in weak stemmed plants: ____________________

   (d) Positive chemotropism in pollen grains: ____________________

3. Explain the adaptive value of positive phototropism in a seedling: ____________________

____

____

____

ISBN: 978-1-98-856656-6

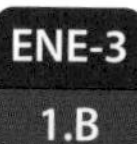

211 Plant Hormones as Signal Molecules

Key Question: What is the role of auxin in promoting apical growth in plants?

Auxins are plant hormones with a central role in a range of growth and developmental responses in plants. Auxins are responsible for apical dominance in shoots and are produced in the shoot tip. Indole-acetic acid (IAA) is the most potent native auxin in intact plants. The response of a plant tissue to IAA depends on the tissue itself, the hormone concentration, the timing of its release, and the presence of other hormones. Gradients in auxin concentration during growth prompt differential responses in specific tissues and contribute to directional growth.

- Light is an important growth requirement for all plants. Most plants show an adaptive response of growing towards the light. This growth response is called phototropism.
- The bending of the plants shown on the right is a phototropism in response to light shining from the left and is caused by the plant hormone **auxin**. Auxin causes the elongation of cells on the shaded side of the stem, causing it to bend (photo right).

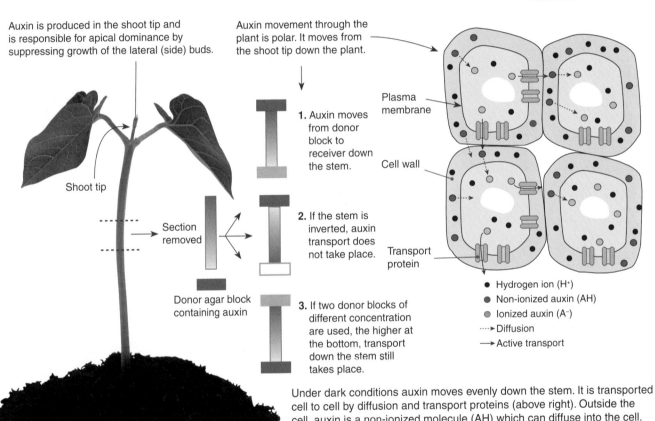

Auxin is produced in the shoot tip and is responsible for apical dominance by suppressing growth of the lateral (side) buds.

Shoot tip

Section removed

Donor agar block containing auxin

Auxin movement through the plant is polar. It moves from the shoot tip down the plant.

1. Auxin moves from donor block to receiver down the stem.
2. If the stem is inverted, auxin transport does not take place.
3. If two donor blocks of different concentration are used, the higher at the bottom, transport down the stem still takes place.

Plasma membrane

Cell wall

Transport protein

- Hydrogen ion (H^+)
- Non-ionized auxin (AH)
- Ionized auxin (A^-)
- Diffusion
- Active transport

Under dark conditions auxin moves evenly down the stem. It is transported cell to cell by diffusion and transport proteins (above right). Outside the cell, auxin is a non-ionized molecule (AH) which can diffuse into the cell. Inside the cell the pH of the cytoplasm causes auxin to ionize, becoming A^- and H^+. Transport proteins at the basal end of the cell then transport A^- out of the cell where it regains an H^+ ion and reforms AH. In this way auxin is transported in one direction through the plant.

When plant cells are illuminated by light from one direction, transport proteins in the plasma membrane on the shaded side of the cell are activated and auxin is transported to the shaded side of the plant.

1. What is the term given to the tropism being displayed in the photo (top right)? ______________________

2. Describe one piece of evidence that demonstrates the transport of auxin is polar: ______________________

____

____

____

3. Describe the effect of auxin on cell growth: ______________________

____

ISBN: 978-1-98-856656-6

Auxin and apical dominance

Auxin is produced in the shoot tip and diffuses down to inhibit the development of the lateral (side) buds. The effect of auxin on preventing lateral bud development can be demonstrated by removing the auxin source and examining the outcome (below).

- In many plants the growth of the shoot apex inhibits the growth of side (lateral) buds. As a result, plants tend to grow a single main stem upwards, which dominates over lateral branches. This response is called **apical dominance**.
- The hormone responsible for this response is **auxin**. It acts by stimulating cell elongation.

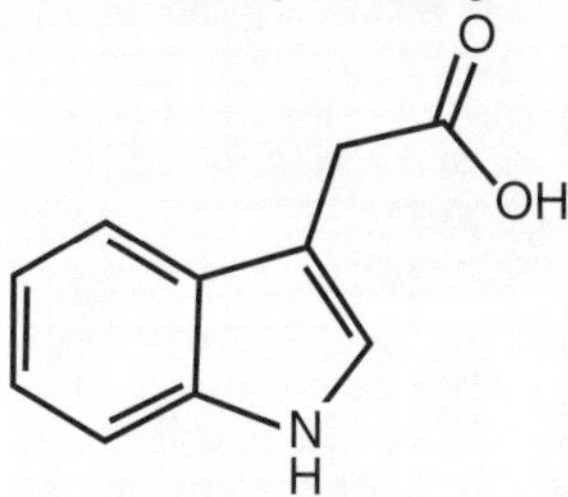

Indole-acetic acid (above) is the only known naturally occurring auxin. It is produced in the apical shoot and young leaves.

No treatment
Apical bud is left intact.

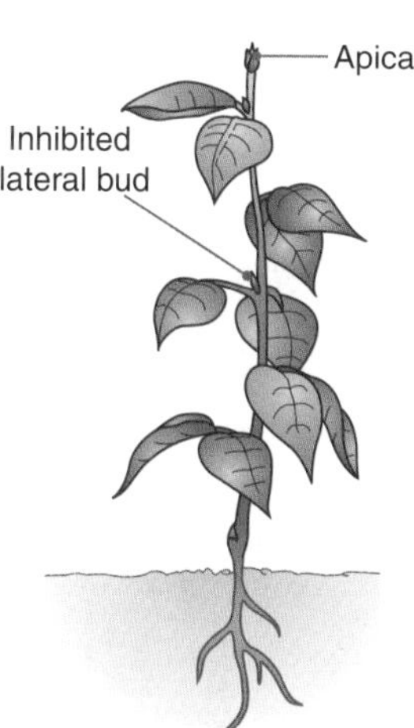

In an intact plant, the plant stem elongates and the lateral buds remain inactive. No side growth occurs.

Treatment one
Apical bud is removed. No auxin is applied.

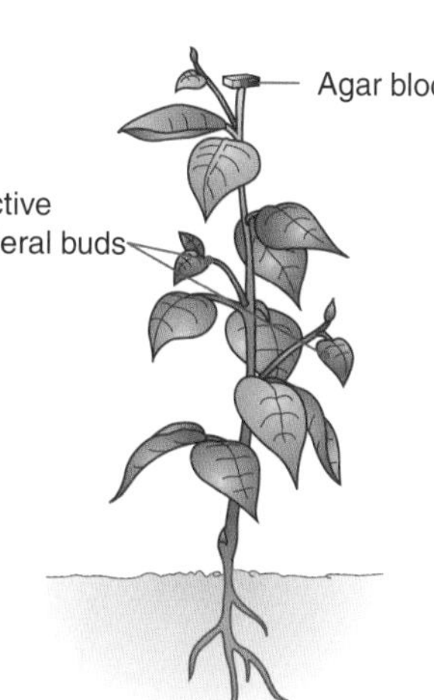

The apical bud is removed and an agar block without auxin is placed on the cut surface. The seedling begins to develop lateral buds.

Treatment two
Apical bud is removed. Auxin is applied.

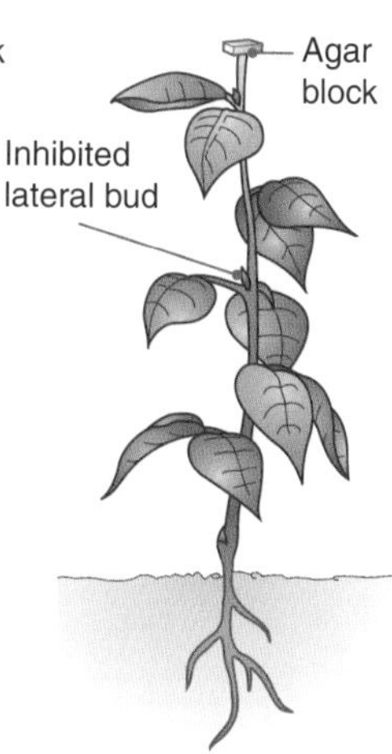

The apical bud is removed and an agar block containing auxin is placed on the cut surface. Lateral bud development is inhibited.

4. In the experiment described above, identify:

   (a) The independent variable: ____________________

   (b) The dependent variable: ____________________

   (c) The control: ____________________

5. Draw two conclusions fro the experiment described above: ____________________

6. Describe the role of auxins in apical dominance: ____________________

7. Study the photo (right) and then answer the following questions:

   (a) Which letter is the apical bud? ____ (b) Which letter is the lateral bud(s)? ____

   (c) Which buds are the largest? ____________________

   (d) Why would this be important? ____________________

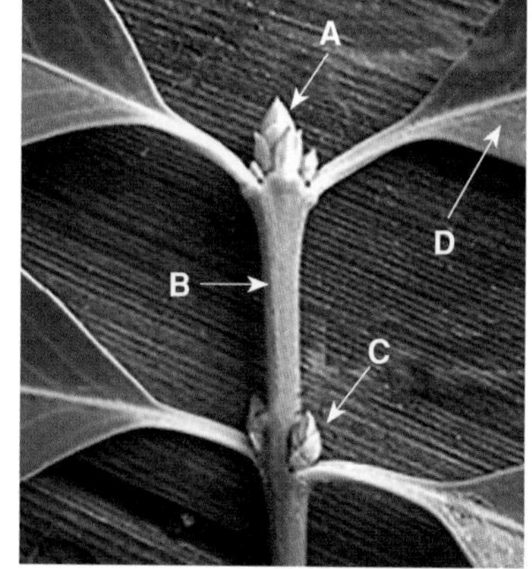

8. If you were a gardener, how would you make your plants bushier? ____________________

ISBN: 978-1-98-856656-6

212 Photoperiodism in Plants

Key Question: How is photoperiodism controlled in plants?

Photoperiodism is the response of a plant to the relative lengths of light and dark. Flowering is a photoperiodic activity that is dependent on the species' response to light. It is controlled through the action of a pigment called **phytochrome**. Phytochrome acts as a signal for some biological clocks in plants and exists in two forms, P*r* and P*fr*. It is important in initiating flowering in long-day and short-day plants, but is also involved in other light initiated responses, such as germination and shoot growth.

Phytochrome

Phytochrome is a blue-green pigment that acts as a photoreceptor for detection of night and day in plants and is universal in vascular plants. It has two forms: **P*r*** (inactive) and **P*fr*** (active).

P*r* is readily converted to P*fr* under natural light. P*fr* converts back to P*r* in the dark but more slowly. P*fr* predominates in daylight and the plant measures day length (or rather night length) by the amount of phytochrome in each form.

In **daylight** or **red light** (660 nm), P*r* converts rapidly, but reversibly, to P*fr*.

P*fr* is the physiologically active form of phytochrome. It promotes flowering in long-day plants and inhibits flowering in short-day plants.

Phytochrome interacts with genes collectively called "clock genes" that maintain the plant's biological clock.

In the **dark** or in **far red light** (730 nm) P*fr* reverts slowly, but spontaneously, back to the inactive form of phytochrome P*r*.

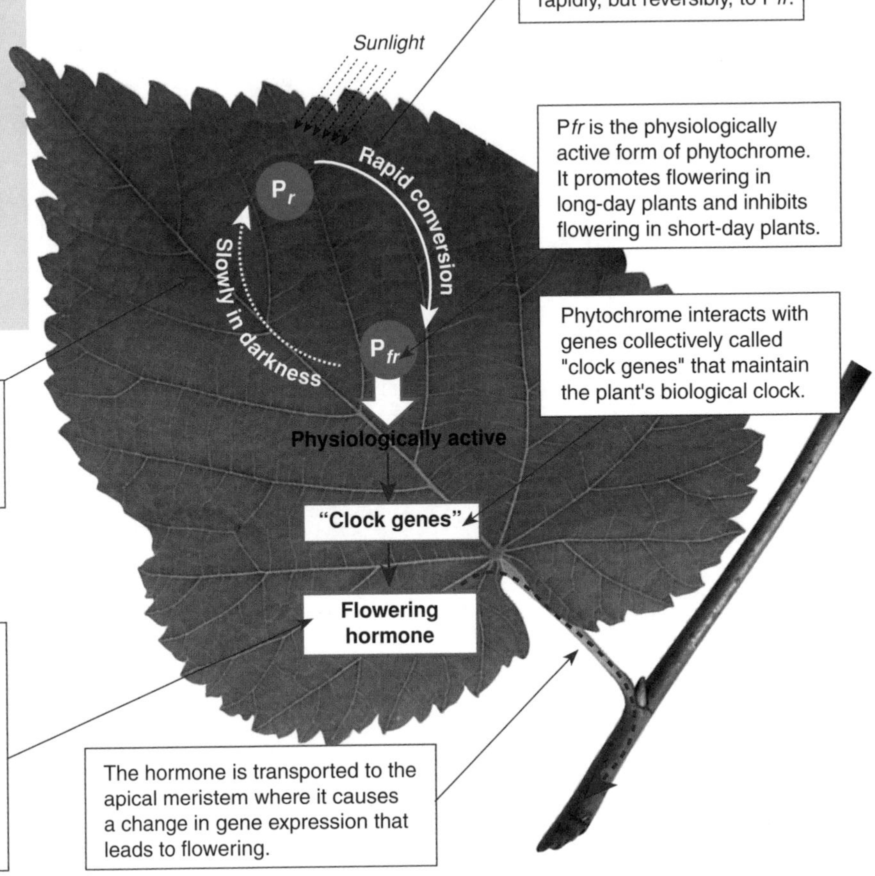

Sunlight

P_r

Rapid conversion

Slowly in darkness

P_{fr}

Physiologically active

"Clock genes"

Flowering hormone

There is still uncertainty over what the flowering hormone (commonly called **florigen**) is. Recent studies suggested it may be the protein product of the gene FLOWERING LOCUS T (FT) (in long day plants at least) which appears to influence gene expression that includes the gene LEAFY (LFY) in the apical meristem and causes flowering.

The hormone is transported to the apical meristem where it causes a change in gene expression that leads to flowering.

1. (a) Identify the two forms of phytochrome and the wavelengths of light they absorb: ______

   ______

   (b) Identify the biologically active form of phytochrome and describe how it behaves in long day plants and short day plants with respect to flowering:

   ______

   ______

2. (a) Use the diagram above to explain the role of phytochrome in a plant's ability to measure day length: ______

   ______

   ______

   ______

   ______

   (b) Explain how this helps to coordinate flower production in a plant species: ______

   ______

   ______

   ______

ISBN: 978-1-98-856656-6

Long day vs short day plants

1. Long-day plants (LDP) flower when the photoperiod is greater than a critical day length. Short-day plants (SDP) flower when the photoperiod is less than a critical day length.
2. Interruption of the long dark period inhibits flowering in SDP but promotes flowering in LDP.
3. Dark must be continuous in SDP but not in LDP.
4. Interruption of the light period inhibits flowering in LDP but not in SDP.
5. Alternating cycles of short light and short dark inhibit flowering in SDP.
6. Plants that do not use day length to initiate flowering are called day-neutral (e.g. cucumber, tomato).

Chrysanthemums

Manipulating flowering in plants

Controlling the light-dark regime has allowed flower growers and horticulturists to produce flowers out of season or to coincide flowering with specific dates. Plants kept in greenhouses can be subjected to artificial lighting or covered to control the amount of light they receive. To be totally effective at controlling flowering, temperature must also be controlled, as this is also an important flowering cue.

For the example of the *Chrysanthemum*, a short-day plant, flowering is can be controlled under the following conditions. The temperature is kept between 16°C and 25°C. The light-dark regime is controlled at 13 hours of light and 11 hours of dark for 4-5 weeks from planting to ensure vegetative growth. Then the regime changes to 10 hours light and 14 hours darkness to induce flowering.

Long-day plants

When subjected to the light regimes on the right, the 'long-day' plants below flowered as indicated:

Examples: *lettuce, clover, delphinium, gladiolus, beets, corn, coreopsis*

Photoperiodism in plants

An experiment was carried out to determine the environmental cue that triggers flowering in 'long-day' and 'short-day' plants. The diagram below shows 3 different light regimes to which a variety of long-day and short-day plants were exposed.

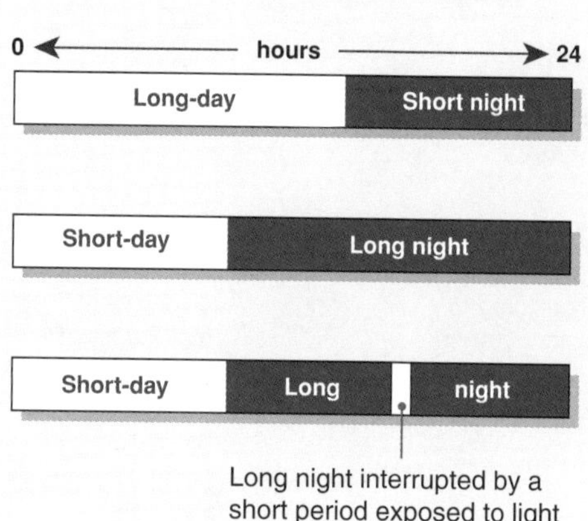

Short-day plants

When subjected to the light regimes on the left, the 'short-day' plants below flowered as indicated:

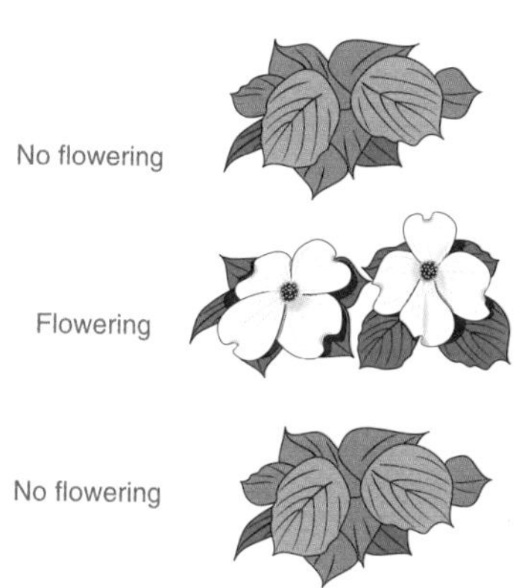

Examples: *potatoes, asters, dahlias, cosmos, chrysanthemums, pointsettias*

3. (a) What is the environmental cue that synchronizes flowering in plants? __________

   (b) What is a biological advantage of this synchronization to the plants? __________

4. Study the three light regimes above and the responses of short-day and long-day flowering plants to that light. From this observation, explain how the onset of flowering is controlled in:

   (a) Short-day plants: __________

   (b) Long-day plants: __________

5. Describe evidence to support the claim that short-day plants are best described as "long-night plants": __________

ISBN: 978-1-98-856656-6

213 Investigating Plant Transpiration

STUDENT SUPPORT FOR INVESTIGATION 11: *Transpiration*

Different kinds of plants have different shapes and sizes of leaves. Comparing the leaf area and stomatal density of different plants helps to explain differences in transpiration rate among them. The volume of water transpired can be measured using a potometer.

The potometer

A **potometer** is a simple instrument for investigating transpiration rate (water loss per unit time). The equipment is simple to use and easy to obtain. A basic potometer, such as the one shown right, can easily be moved around so that transpiration rate can be measured under different environmental (physical) conditions.

Physical factors that can affect transpiration rate include:

- Humidity or vapor pressure (high or low)
- Temperature (high or low)
- Air movement (high or low)
- Light level (high or low)
- Water supply

It is also possible to compare transpiration rates in plants with different adaptations, e.g. comparing transpiration rates in plants with rolled leaves vs rates in plants with broad leaves. If possible, experiments like these should be conducted simultaneously using replicate equipment. If conducted sequentially, care should be taken to keep the controlled variables the same for all plants used.

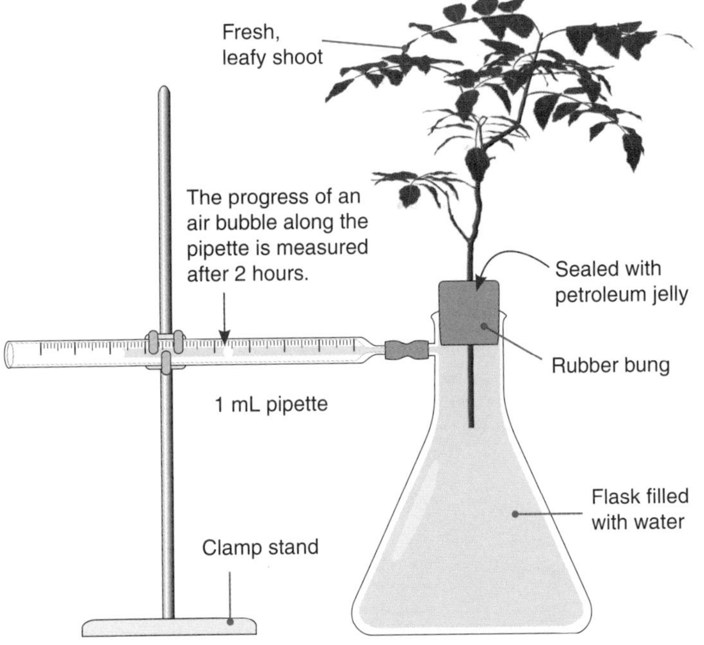

Measuring leaf area

Leaf area can be measured by tracing the leaves onto graph paper and counting the squares, or by tracing or photocopying the leaves onto a paper of a known mass per area, then cutting out the shapes and weighing them. For both methods, multiply by 2 for both leaf surfaces.

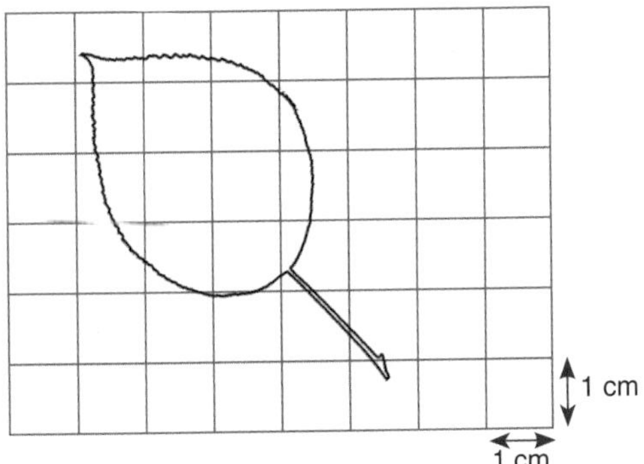

Calculating SA by mass:
Photocopying leaves onto paper with a known gsm (grams per square meter) allows you to calculate the surface area from the mass of paper they cover.

Calculating SA by leaf trace method:
Count entire squares covered by the leaf. Estimate the area of the partial squares by counting those that are at least half covered by the leaf and disregarding those that are less than half covered.

Determining the number of stomata per mm²

The number of stomata per mm² on the surface of a leaf can be determined by counting the stomata visible under a microscope. Painting clear nail polish over the surface of a leaf and leaving it to dry creates a layer with impressions of the leaf surface. This can be peeled off and viewed under the microscope to count stomata (below).

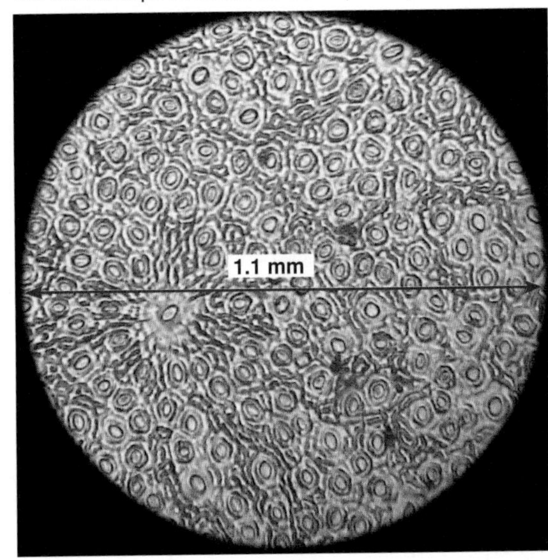

1. (a) Determine the area of the leaf traced onto the blue grid above: ____________________

   (b) Twenty leaves from plant A were taped to paper and photocopied on to 80 gsm paper. The shapes were cut out and weighed on a digital balance. The total weight of shapes was 3.21 grams. Calculate the surface area of the leaves.

   ____

2. Calculate the number of stomata per mm² in the microscope view of the leaf above: ____________________

____

ISBN: 978-1-98-856656-6

Investigation 1

The aim

To evaluate the relationship between transpiration rate and stomatal density by examining a variety of plant species.

Background

Plants lose water all the time by evaporation from the leaves and stem. This loss, mostly through pores in the leaf surfaces, is called **transpiration**. Despite the adaptations of plants to reduce water loss (e.g. waxy leaf cuticle), 99% of the water a plant absorbs from the soil is lost by evaporation. Different species of plant are adapted to different physical conditions. These conditions may affect the number of stomata per mm^2 of leaf and the transpiration rate of the plant.

The method

Six plant species from a range of habitats were chosen for use. The stems of several specimens of each species were cut while submerged and set up in a potometer similar to that described on the previous page but with a larger capacity. The temperature was measured at 21°C. The plants were left to transpire in still air at 70% relative humidity for 2 hours and the volume of water transpired was recorded. The surface area of the leaves was also determined as was the number of stomata per mm^2.

3. Write a hypothesis for the investigation: __________

Table 1: Water loss in various plant species over 2 hours

	Total leaf area (cm^2)	Total water lost (µL)	Transpiration rate (µL/cm/ h)	Number of stomata per mm^2 upper surface	Number of stomata per mm^2 lower surface	Total number of stomata per mm^2
Sunflower: *Helianthus annus*	2000	6081		71	172	
Busy Lizzie: *Impatiens sultani*	620	3017		29	143	
Geranium: *Pelargonium zonale*	3800	3721		19	52	
Garden bean: *Phaseolus vulgaris*	1340	4147		40	250	
Caster oil plant: *Ricinus communis*	860	3609		52	121	
Corn: *Zea mays*	4100	6402		60	101	

4. Complete the table by calculating the transpiration rate and total number of stomata per mm^2 for each plant in table 1:

5. (a) Which plant has the highest transpiration rate? __________

   (b) Which plant has the lowest transpiration rate? __________

6. (a) Which plant has the highest stomatal density? __________

   (b) Which plant has the lowest stomatal density? __________

7. (a) Is there a relationship between the number of stomata per mm^2 and the transpiration rate?

   (b) Explain your answer: __________

8. (a) Where are the majority of stomata located In a typical dicot leaf? __________

   (b) Suggest why this might be the case: __________

ISBN: 978-1-98-856656-6

Investigation 2

A second investigation focused on the effect of the environment on transpiration rate in one species of plant. Conditions investigated were ambient conditions (minimal air movement, 20°C, indirect lighting), wind, direct bright light, and high humidity. This time a potometer fitted with a very thin graduated pipette (0.01-0.5 mL) was used to measure water loss. The results are tabulated below.

Table 2. Potometer readings in μL water loss

Treatment \ Time (min)	0	3	6	9	12	15	18	21	24	27	30
Ambient	0	2	5	8	12	17	22	28	32	36	42
Wind	0	2.5	54	88	112	142	175	208	246	283	325
High humidity	0	2	4	6	8	11	14	18	19	21	24
Bright light	0	2.1	42	70	91	112	141	158	183	218	239

9. (a) Plot labeled graph (right) of the potometer data for time = 30 minutes from Table 2:

(b) Identify the independent variable:

(c) Identify the dependent variable:

10. (a) Identify the control:

(b) Explain the purpose of including a control in an experiment:

(c) Which factors increased water loss?

(d) How does each environmental factor influence water loss?

(e) Explain why the plant lost less water in humid conditions:

11. Imagine you plotted a labeled line graph of all the data in Table 2 to show how water changed over time for each treatment. How would you classify the variable of time?

ISBN: 978-1-98-856656-6

214 Kineses

Key Question: What is a kinesis and what is its purpose?

A **kinesis** (*pl.* kineses) is a non-directional response to a stimulus in which the rate of movement (**orthokinesis**) or the rate of turning (**klinokinesis**) is proportional to the stimulus intensity. In other words, the stronger the stimulus, the greater the rate of movement or turning. Kineses are typical of many invertebrates (including protozoa) and do not involve orientation directly to the stimulus.

Kinesis in woodlice

Woodlice are commonly found living in damp conditions under logs or bark. Many of the behavioral responses of woodlice are concerned with retaining moisture. Unlike most other terrestrial arthropods, they lack a waterproof cuticle, so water can diffuse through the exoskeleton, making them vulnerable to drying out. When exposed to low humidity, high temperatures, or high light levels, woodlice show a kinesis response to return them to their preferred, high humidity environment.

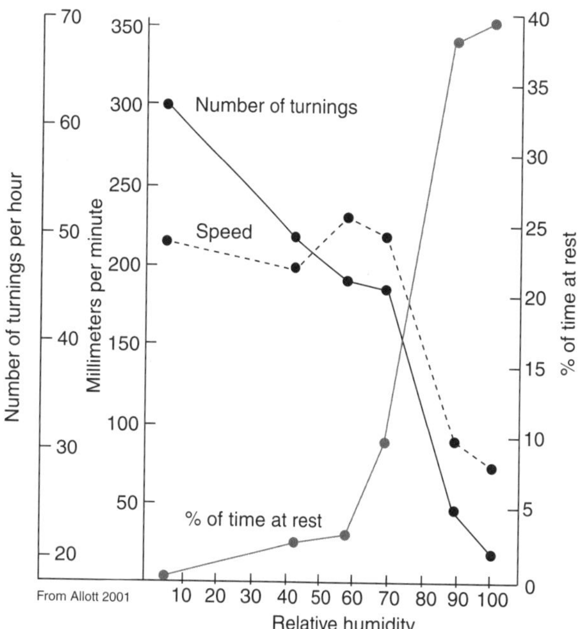

Investigating kinesis in woodlice (pillbugs)

Experiment 1

To investigate the effect of a light-dark regime on the orthokinetic behavior of woodlice.

Method

A petri dish was laid out with 1 cm x 1 cm squares. The investigation was carried out at room temperature (about 21°C). A woodlouse was placed in the petri dish under constant light. The number of squares the woodlouse passed over in five minutes was recorded. This was repeated four times. The woodlouse was then placed in constant dark and the number of squares it passed over in five minutes recorded. Again, this was repeated four times. The results are shown below.

Results

	Number of squares crossed	
Trial	**Light**	**Dark**
1	122	15
2	206	68
3	103	57
4	70	59
Mean		

Experiment 2

To investigate the effect of a light-dark regime on the klinokinetic behavior of woodlice.

Method

The woodlouse was again placed in the petri dish under constant light. The experiment was carried out at room temperature as in experiment 1. The number of turns the woodlouse performed in five minutes was recorded. This was repeated four times. The woodlouse was then placed in constant dark. Again the number of turns performed in five minutes was recorded. This was also carried out four times. The results are shown below.

Results

	Number of turns	
Trial	**Light**	**Dark**
1	80	10
2	165	20
3	110	122
4	90	55
Mean		

ISBN: 978-1-98-856656-6

Kinesis in body lice

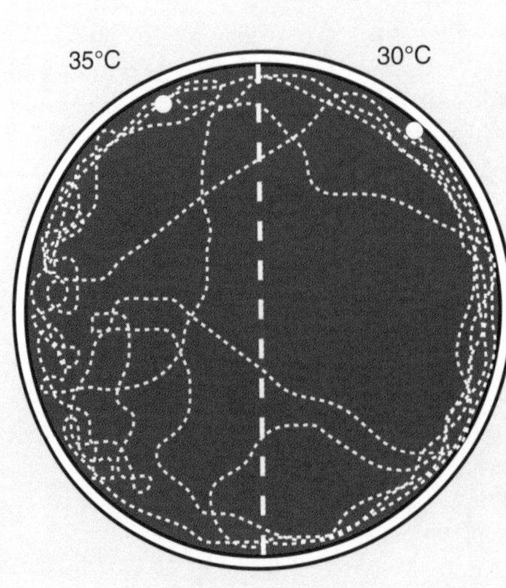

In a circular chamber, lice make relatively few turns at their preferred temperature of 30°C, but many random turns at 35°C. This response enables the lice to increase their chances of finding favorable conditions and remaining in them once found.

1. Use the graph on woodlice at the top of the previous page to answer the following questions:

   (a) At which relative humidities do the following occur:

   i. Largest number of turnings per hour: __________

   ii. Highest speed of movement: __________

   iii. Largest percentage of time at rest: __________

   (b) Explain the significance of these movements: __________

   (c) What is the preferred range of relative humidity for the woodlice? __________

2. (a) Complete the results tables on the previous page by calculating the mean for each of the experiments.

   (b) Which regime (light or dark) does the woodlice appear to prefer? __________

   (c) Explain your reasoning: __________

   (d) Explain how increasing the number of turns or the speed of movement increases a woodlice's likelihood of survival when in a unfavorable environment.

3. (a) Identify the preferred temperature of a body louse: __________

   (b) What is the name of this response? __________

   (c) Contrast the movements of the body louse when within and when outside its preferred temperature environment:

ISBN: 978-1-98-856656-6

215 Taxes

Key Question: What sort of behaviors are taxes, what do they involve, and what is their adaptive value?

Taxes (*sing.* taxis) involve orientation and movement in response to a directional stimulus or a gradient in stimulus intensity. Taxes often involve moving the head until the sensory input from both sides is equal. Many taxes involve a simultaneous response to more than one stimulus, e.g. fish orientate dorsal (back) side up in response to both light and gravity. As with plant tropisms, orientation responses are identified by the stimulus involved and whether the response is towards (positive) or away from (negative) the stimulus. Simple orientation responses are innate, whereas more complex orientation responses may involve learning (the behavior can be modified based on experience).

When confronted with a vertical surface, snails will reorientate themselves so that they climb vertically upwards. The adaptive advantage of this may be to help the snail find food or shelter, or to avoid overly wet surfaces.

A flying male moth, encountering an odor (pheromone) trail left by a female, will turn and fly upwind until it reaches the female. This behavior increases the chances of the male moth mating and passing on its genes to the next generation.

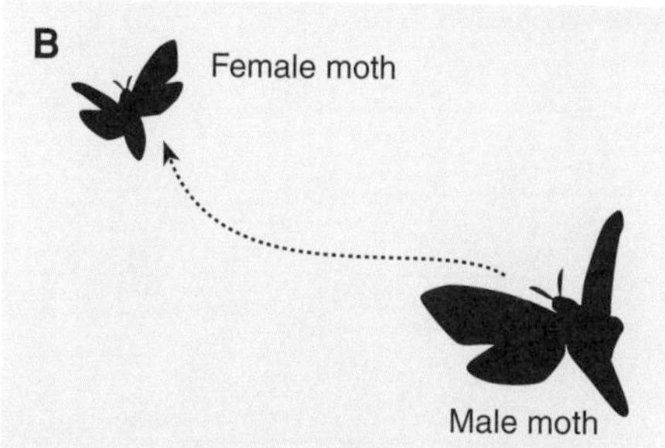

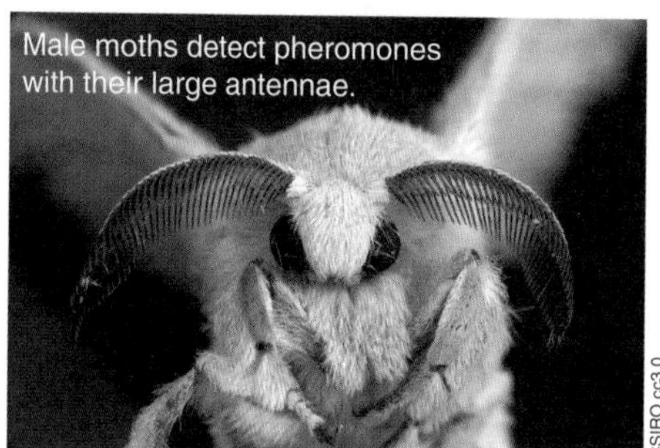

Male moths detect pheromones with their large antennae.

Spiny lobsters (crayfish) will back into tight crevices so that their body is touching the crevice sides. The antennae may be extended out. This behavior gives the lobsters greater protection from predators.

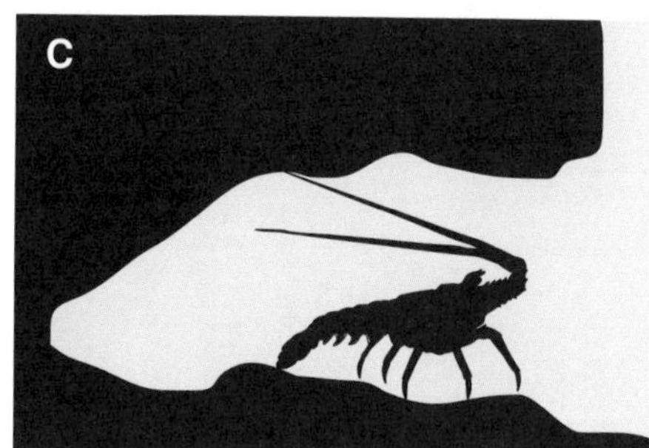

Spiny lobster in crevice

At close range, mosquitoes use the temperature gradient generated by the body heat of a host to locate exposed flesh. This allows the female to find the blood needed for the development of eggs.

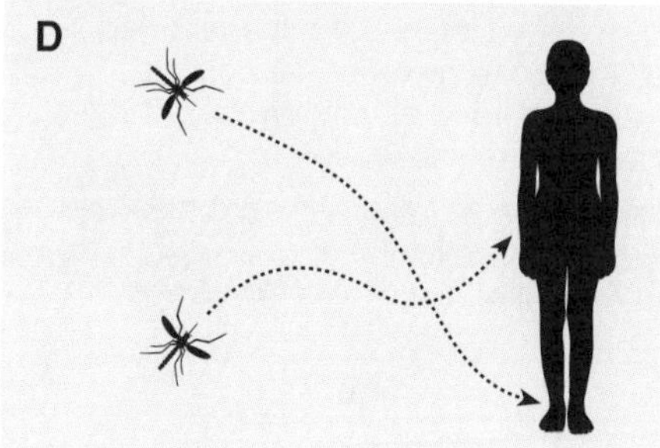

Blowfly maggots will turn and move rapidly away from a directional light source. Light usually indicates hot, dry areas and the maggots avoid predators and desiccation (drying out) by avoiding the light.

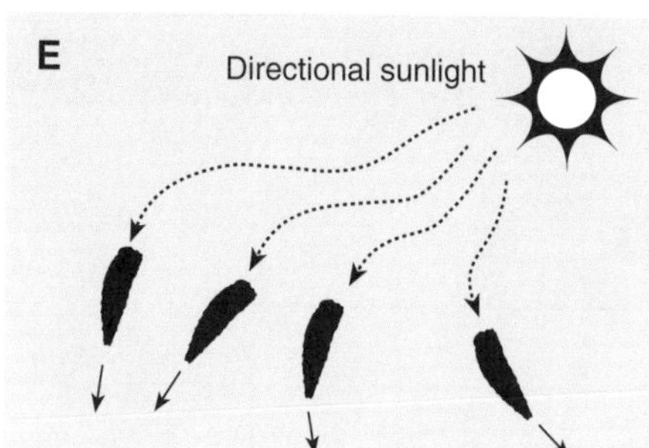

White fly larvae burrowing into soil.

ISBN: 978-1-98-856656-6

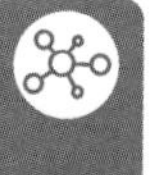

1. Distinguish between a taxis and a kinesis:

2. Describe the adaptive value of simple orientation behaviors such as taxes:

3. For each example (**A-E**) on the previous page, describe the orientation response and whether it is positive or negative:

(a) **A:**

(b) **B:**

(c) **C:**

(d) **D:**

(e) **E:**

4. The diagrams on the right show the movement of nematodes on plates where a salt (NH_4Cl) was added (**A**) and on a plate where no NH_4Cl was added (**B**).

(a) Describe the movements of the nematodes in plates A and B:

(b) Name the orientation behavior shown in plate A:

(c) Describe an advantage of this kind of behavior to nematodes:

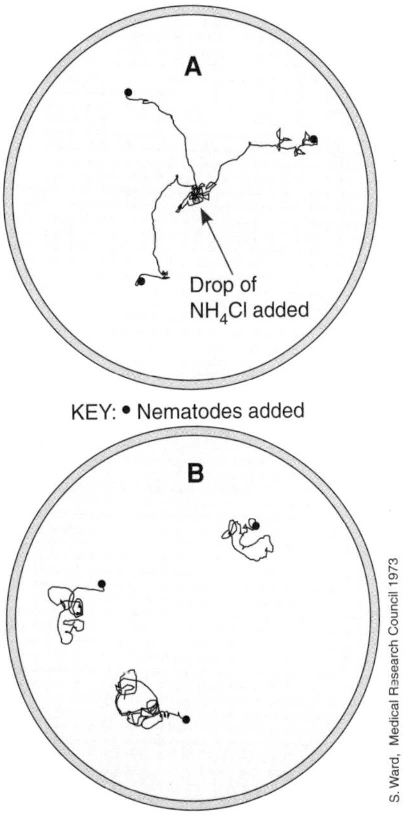

A

Drop of NH_4Cl added

KEY: • Nematodes added

B

S. Ward, Medical Research Council 1973

5. Some students carried out an investigation of the phototactic movements of maggots. They set up a lamp in a darkened room and placed a maggot on grid paper 10 cm from the lamp. They then recorded the distance the maggot had moved every 10 s. Movements towards the lamp were recorded as positive (+) while movements away from the lamp were recorded as negative (-). The investigation was repeated four times. The results are shown below:

Time (s)	Distance of maggot 1 from start point (cm)	Distance of maggot 2 from start point (cm)	Distance of maggot 3 from start point (cm)	Distance of maggot 4 from start point (cm)
10	-1.7	-3.7	-5.8	-3.0
20	-0.5	-0.0	+1.8	-1.5
30	+0.7	-0.8	-6.1	-0.2
40	+0.2	-1.4	+1.0	-1.0

Describe the movements of the maggots during the experiment. Include whether the maggots are positively or negatively phototactic and the rate of the movements.

ISBN: 978-1-98-856656-6

216 Choice Chamber Investigations

STUDENT SUPPORT FOR INVESTIGATION 12: *Fruit fly behavior*

Choice chambers are a simple way to investigate behavior in animals. A simple choice chamber consists of two distinct areas enclosing opposing environments, e.g. warm and cool, dry and humid, light and dark. Animals are placed in the middle of the chamber and given time to move to their preferred area before numbers in each chamber are counted.

Background

Students carried out two investigations on woodlice. The first was to determine woodlouse preference for light or dark. The second was to test preference for warm or cool environments.

Aim: investigation 1

To investigate if woodlice prefer a light or dark environment.

The method

A choice chamber was set up using two joined petri dishes, one painted black, the other left clear. The chamber was kept at room temperature (21°C). Ten woodlice were placed into the joining segment of the chamber and left for ten minutes to orientate themselves. The numbers of woodlice in each chamber were then recorded. The experiment was carried out a total of four times.

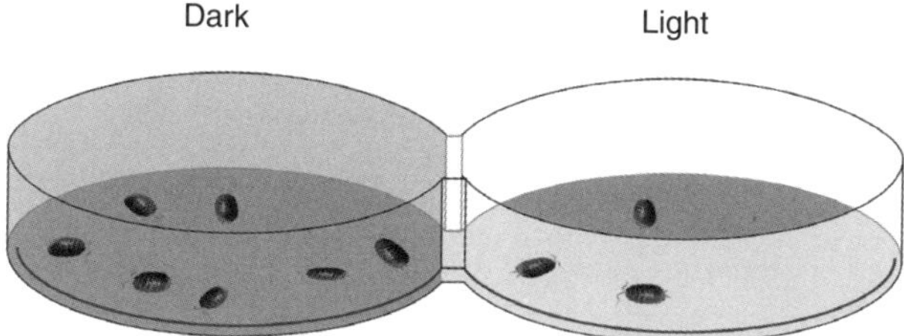

Results

Trial	Number of woodlice in chamber	
	Dark	Light
1	7	3
2	9	1
3	8	2
4	9	1

Aim: investigation 2

To investigate if woodlice prefer a warm or cool environment.

The method

A choice chamber was set up painted entirely black. One side was heated to 27°C by placing a heat pad underneath. The other side was kept cool at 14°C by placing a towel soaked in cool water around the chamber. Ten woodlice were placed into the joining segment of the chamber and left for ten minutes to orientate. The numbers of woodlice in each chamber were then recorded. The experiment was carried out a total of four times.

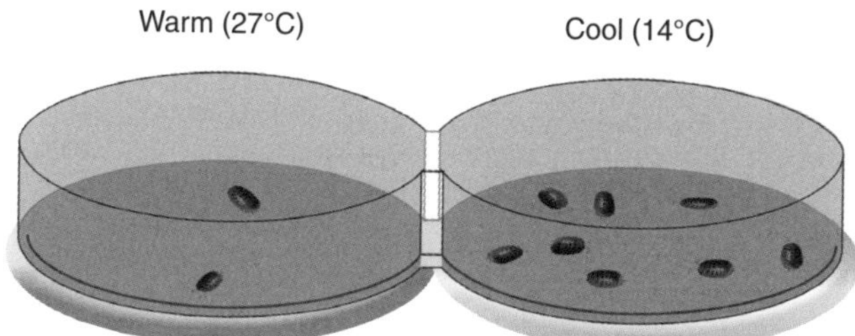

Results

Trial	Number of woodlice in chamber	
	Warm	Cool
1	2	8
2	3	7
3	2	8
4	1	9

1. (a) Write a hypothesis for investigation 1: ______________________

   (b) Write a hypothesis for investigation 2: ______________________

2. For each investigation, what would you expect if there was no difference in choice of environment by the woodlice?

   ____

3. How would you determine if the results for each investigation were significant? ______________________

4. Describe one way to improve investigation 1: ______________________

ISBN: 978-1-98-856656-6

Designing an investigation: fruit flies

Students wanted to investigate at which stage of ripeness bananas were the most attractive to fruit flies, *Drosophila melanogaster*.

They used a choice chamber made of two clear bottles end to end. Bananas of known age were used to determine the age of the banana that was most attractive. Bananas were purchased green and designated day 0. The age of the banana was determined from this date as they ripened.

Choice chamber made from soft drink bottles

5. Where will the bananas be placed in the choice chamber? ______________________________

6. What range of ages of bananas would be suitable to investigate? ______________________________

7. What number of bananas (separate investigations) should be carried out? ______________________________

8. Write a method that would allow you to determine the age of the banana that is most attractive to fruit flies:

9. The results for a trial between 0 and 10 day old bananas are shown below:

Time (minutes)	Position in chamber (number of fruit flies)		
	End with 10 day old banana	Middle	End with 0 day old banana
1	21	18	21
10	45	3	12

(a) Which banana appeared the most attractive to the fruit flies? ______________________________

(b) A student suggested that the sex of the flies might make a difference to their choice of banana ripeness. How could you test this?

ISBN: 978-1-98-856656-6

217 Stimuli and Behavior

Key Question: What are stimuli and why is it important that organisms respond to appropriately to them?

A **stimulus** is any physical or chemical change in the environment capable of provoking a response in an organism. Organisms respond to a variety of stimuli. The response depends on the stimulus and is adaptive (increases fitness). Stimuli may come from the physical environment, or from a member of the same or another species. In most cases, information of some kind is exchanged between the organisms at the same time. Potential mates may exchange information about their readiness to breed. Prey may exchange information with predators to avoid them (such as bright coloration indicating poisons). Plants also exchange information and respond to other organisms, usually through the production of toxins, which make leaves unpalatable, or signaling molecules, which warn nearby plants.

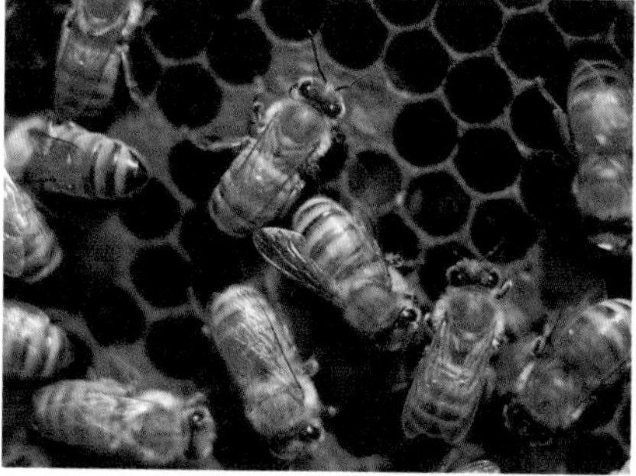

The warning coloration of wanderer butterflies communicates they are toxic

A **pheromone** is a chemical produced by an animal and released into the external environment where it affects the physiology or behavior of members of the same species. Pheromones produced by a honeybee queen and her daughters, the workers, maintain the social order of the colony. In mammals, pheromones are used to signal sexual receptivity and territory, or to synchronize group behavior.

Coloration is an important messenger. Bright colors may communicate anything from the health of an individual, to a warning of toxicity, to the ripeness of fruit on plants.

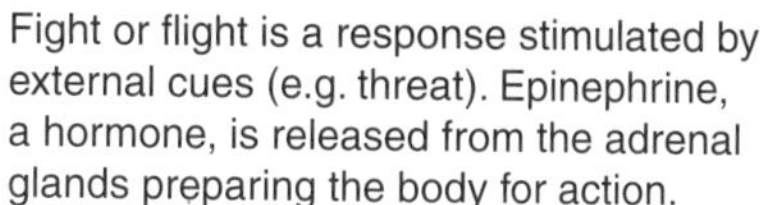
Fight or flight is a response stimulated by external cues (e.g. threat). Epinephrine, a hormone, is released from the adrenal glands preparing the body for action.

Plants attacked by herbivores may produce chemicals, including toxins, to defend themselves. These may make the leaves unpalatable or harm the herbivore.

Sagebrush releases the VOC methacrolein

Plants, including sagebrush (above) may produce and release volatile organic compounds (VOCs) when eaten. These may be detected by other plants, which can react by producing their own defenses.

1. (a) What is a pheromone? ______________________________

   (b) Using examples, explain the purpose of pheromones: ______________________________

2. Explain how coloration is used to communicate information: ______________________________

3. How are VOCs useful to plants? ______________________________

ISBN: 978-1-98-856656-6

The fight or flight response

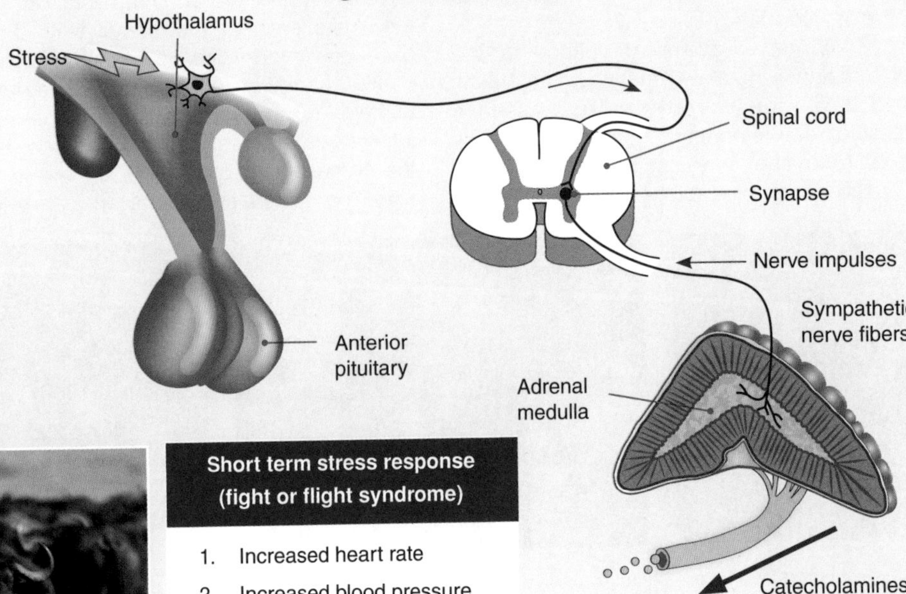

Short term stress response (fight or flight syndrome)

1. Increased heart rate
2. Increased blood pressure
3. Liver converts glycogen to glucose; blood glucose levels increase
4. Dilation of bronchioles
5. Blood flow to gut and kidney reduced . Blood flow to muscles and brain increased.
6. Increased metabolic rate

Internal changes or external cues can change the way an animal behaves in certain situations. A good example is the fight or flight response. When an animal is subjected to stress (e.g. being stalked by a predator) the way the animal reacts is controlled by complex hormonal and nervous interactions of the hypothalamus, and pituitary and adrenal glands.

The stress response is triggered through sympathetic stimulation of the central medulla region of the adrenal glands. This stimulation causes the release of catecholamines (epinephrine and norepinephrine). These physiological changes occur as part of the short term stress response so animals operate at peak efficiency when endangered, competing, or whenever a high level of performance is required.

A threat from another animal does not always cause an immediate fight or flight reaction. There may be a period of heightened awareness, during which each animal interprets behavioral signals and cues from the other before they decide to take action (fight or flight). The heightened awareness of one animal will be received by the rest of the group, potentially changing the behavior of the group as a whole (e.g. one individual's nervousness may unsettle the group to the point where a stampede occurs).

5. (a) What is the fight or flight response? ______________________________

____

____

(b) Describe some of the physiological changes that take place: ______________________________

____

____

____

(c) Explain how these changes prepare an animal to react to a threatening or potentially life threatening situation:

____

____

____

____

____

ISBN: 978-1-98-856656-6

218 Plant Responses to Threats

Key Question: What mechanisms do plants use to protect themselves against herbivores?

Plants have evolved a number of mechanisms to protect them from herbivory (being grazed or browsed by animals). The most well known of these mechanisms are physical (e.g. thick cuticles, protective thorns) or involve specific nastic responses (nasties) of plant parts. Increasingly, there is also experimental evidence of chemical communication among plants. When a plant is browsed, it is able to send chemical signals to nearby plants so that they can launch protective defenses of their own. These protective mechanisms improve the plant's chances of reproductive success.

Nastic responses to herbivory

- Nastic movements (**nasties**) are non-directional responses to stimuli, and include the folding of leaves in response to touch. This response is commonly observed in *Mimosa pudica*. *M. pudica* has long leaves composed of small leaflets. When a leaf is touched, it collapses and its leaflets fold together. Strong disturbances cause the entire leaf to droop from its base. This response takes only a few seconds and is caused by a rapid loss of turgor pressure from the cells at the bases of the leaves and leaflets.
- The message that the plant has been disturbed is passed quickly around the plant by electrical signals (changes in membrane potential) not by plant hormones (as occurs in tropisms). The response can be likened to the nerve impulses of animals, but it is much slower. After the disturbance is removed, turgor is restored to the cells, and the leaflets slowly return to their normal state.
- The adaptive value of leaf collapse nasties is most likely related to deterring browsers or reducing water loss during high winds.

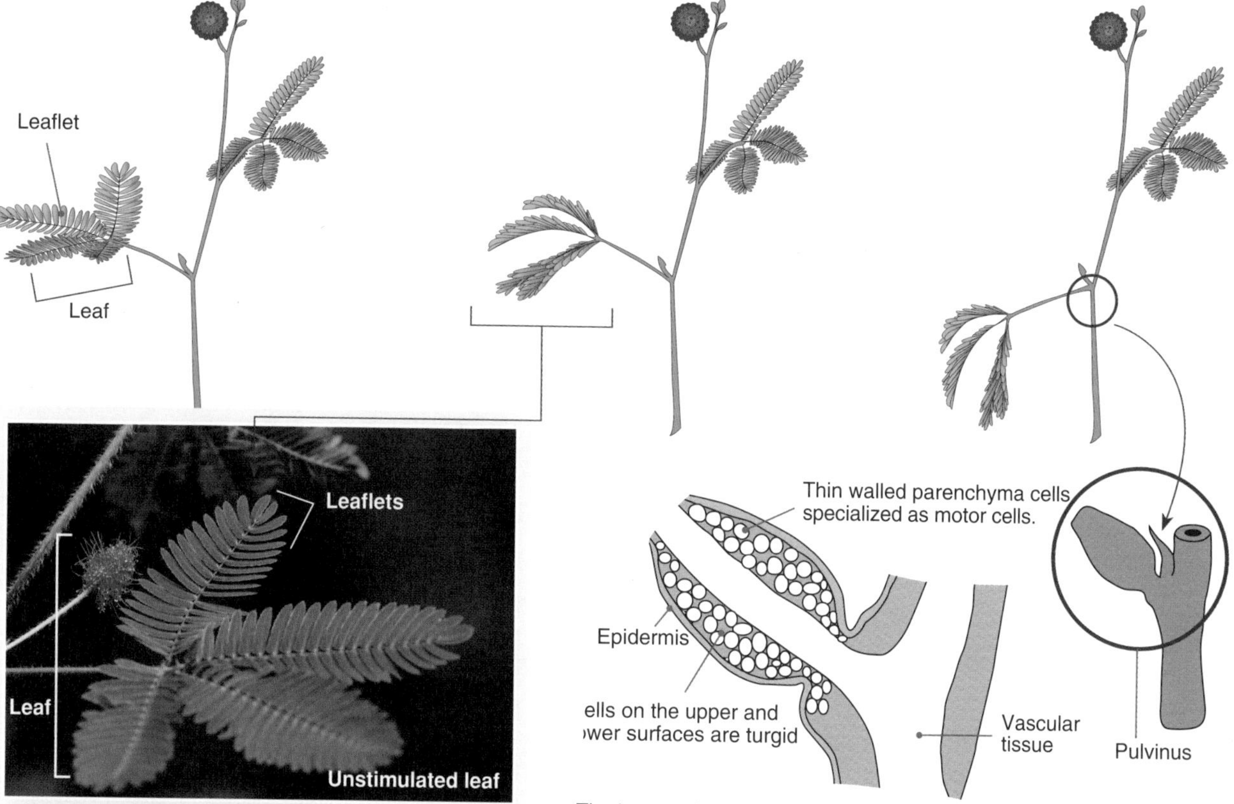

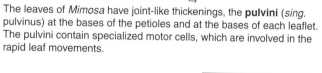

The leaves of *Mimosa* have joint-like thickenings, the **pulvini** (*sing.* pulvinus) at the bases of the petioles and at the bases of each leaflet. The pulvini contain specialized motor cells, which are involved in the rapid leaf movements.

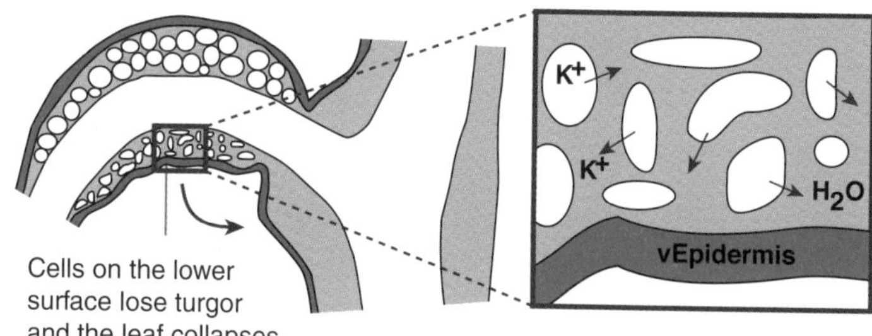

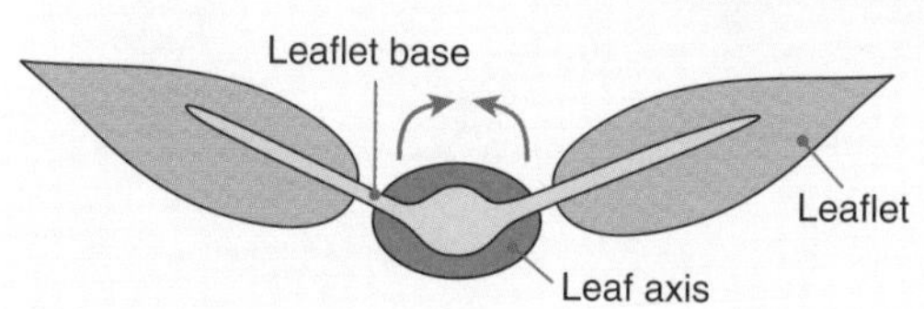

When disturbed, a change in membrane potential of the leaf cells is transmitted to the cells of the pulvinus. These cells respond by actively pumping potassium ions out of the cytoplasm (see inset above). Water follows osmotically and there is a sudden loss of turgor.

This mechanism also operates at the leaflet bases, except that the cells on the upper surface of the pulvinus lose turgor, and the individual leaflets fold up, rather than down (left).

ISBN: 978-1-98-856656-6

Plants transmit warning signals through the air

Arthropods (e.g. aphids, caterpillars, and beetles) are common browsers of plants. The plants respond to browsing damage by activating defense mechanisms. These include the production of unpalatable chemicals, protease inhibitors, or metabolites involved in defense pathways.

Browsing may also cause plants to release volatile organic compounds (VOCs). Often these chemicals attract carnivorous arthropods to the plant and these prey upon the browsers, limiting the browse damage.

The VOCs can travel through the air and act as chemical signals to nearby plants, warning them of potential danger from browsers (right). Neighboring plants receiving the signal activate the appropriate defense-related genes. These responses have been demonstrated experimentally among many plants, including between sagebrush and tobacco. Early activation of plant defenses can prevent or limit damage. These plants gain a competitive advantage over plants that have not received the warning. .

The composition of VOCs released from a plant under attack varies depending on the herbivore browsing on them. For example, the composition of VOC released in response to damage caused by chewing beetle is different to the composition released when cell feeders such as mites are feeding from the plant. The specific VOC message enables neighboring plants to better coordinate their defense response and increases their chances of successfully repelling an attack.

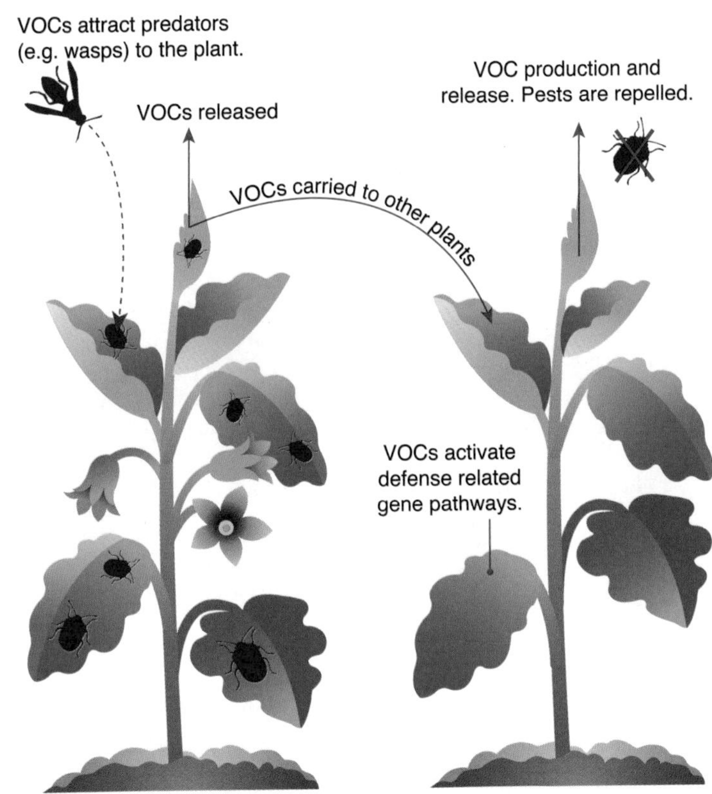
VOCs attract predators (e.g. wasps) to the plant.
VOCs released
VOCs carried to other plants
VOC production and release. Pests are repelled.
VOCs activate defense related gene pathways.
Plant infested with vegetable bugs
Non-infested plant

1. (a) Describe the basic mechanism behind the sudden leaf movements in *Mimosa*: ______

(b) Explain how the movements of the *Mimosa pudica* might help its survival: ______

2. (a) Name the compounds involved in plant-to-plant herbivory signaling: ______

(b) Explain how these compounds help protect a plant that is already under attack by browsers: ______

(c) Explain how plants communicate a browser attack to each other: ______

(d) Explain how this provides a competitive advantage to a plant not under attack: ______

ISBN: 978-1-98-856656-6

219 Communication

Key Question: How and why do organisms communicate?

Communication among organisms is a feature of biological systems. Animals communicate to avoid predators, coordinate foraging and hunting activities, maintain social behaviors, and attract mates. The messages are often highly ritualized (follow a fixed pattern) and therefore not easily misinterpreted. During conflict situations, ritualization often prevents interactions escalating to a point of injury. Messages can be passed between animals using a range of visual, chemical, auditory, or tactile signals. The type of signal used depends on the activity pattern and habitat of the animal, e.g. sound carries well in dense forest. Plants can also communicate information, using color and scent to signal to the animals they rely on for pollination and seed dispersal.

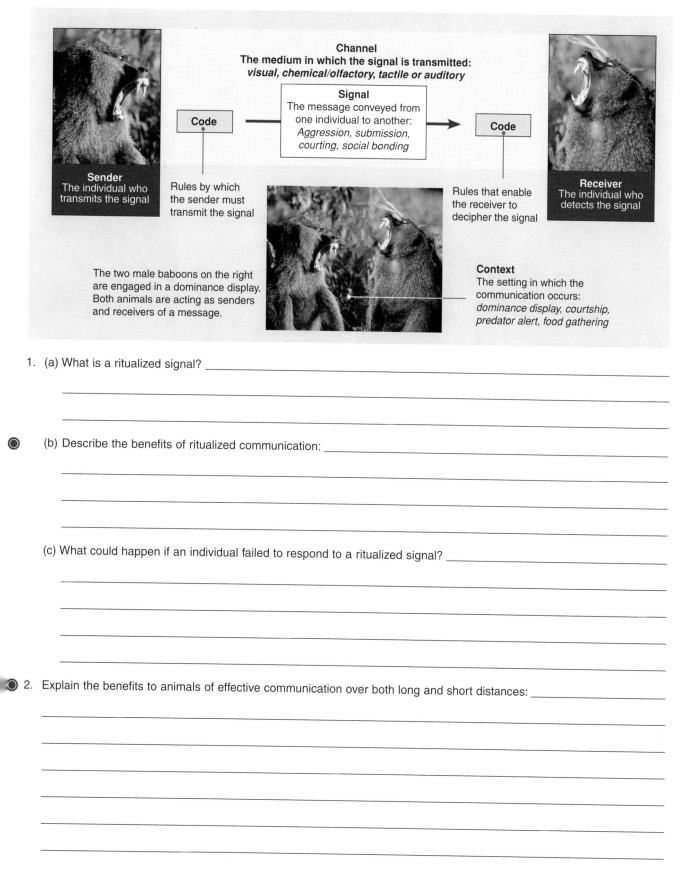

Channel
The medium in which the signal is transmitted:
visual, chemical/olfactory, tactile or auditory

The individual who detects the signal
Context
The setting in which the communication occurs:
dominance display, courtship, predator alert, food gathering

The two male baboons on the right are engaged in a dominance display. Both animals are acting as senders and receivers of a message.

1. (a) What is a ritualized signal? ______________________________

(b) Describe the benefits of ritualized communication: ______________________________

(c) What could happen if an individual failed to respond to a ritualized signal? ______________________________

2. Explain the benefits to animals of effective communication over both long and short distances: ______________________________

ISBN: 978-1-98-856656-6

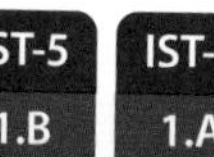

The individual who transmits the signal
Code
Rules by which the sender must transmit the signal

The message conveyed from one individual to another:
Aggression, submission, courting, social bonding
Code
Rules that enable the receiver to decipher the signal

217

208

IST-5

Animal to animal communication

Olfactory messages

Some animals produce scents that are carried by the wind. Scents may advertize for a mate or warn neighboring competitors to keep out of a territory. In some cases, mammals use their urine and feces to mark territorial boundaries. Sniffing genitals is common among mammals.

Tactile messages

Touch may be part of a cooperative or an aggressive interaction. Grooming behavior between members of a primate group communicates social bonding. Vibrations sent along a web by a male spider signal to a potential mate not to eat him.

Auditory messages

Sound may be used to communicate over great distances. Birds keep rivals away and advertize for mates with song. Fin whales send messages over thousands of kilometers of ocean. Mammals can use calls to attract mates, keep in touch with group members, or warn away competitors.

Pheromones

Communication in ants and other social insects occurs through pheromones. Foraging ants leave a chemical trail that other ants will follow and reinforce until the food source is depleted. Ants also release alarm substances, which will send other ants in the vicinity into an attack frenzy. These signals dissipate rapidly if not reinforced.

The feathery antennae of male moths are specialized to detect the pheromone released by females. Males can detect concentrations as low as 2 ppm. They use wind direction to orientate, flying upwind to find the female. The sex attractant property of pheromones is used in traps, which are widely used to trap insect pests in orchards.

Visual messages

Many animals convey information to other members of the species through body coverings and adornment, as well as through gestures and body language. Visual displays can show threat or submission, attract a mate, or exert control over a social group.

Bioluminescence

Many animals are bioluminescent (produce and emit light). The glow they produce can be used as a signal to others of their species, such as fireflies signaling to a mate. Some deep sea fish use bioluminescence to signal to other fish in the school.

Body position or facial expression

Social species with dominance hierarchies (e.g. wolves) use stereotyped expressions and body postures to avoid direct conflict with others in the group. The messages are well understood and rarely challenged, and are crucial to maintenance of the hierarchy.

Attraction

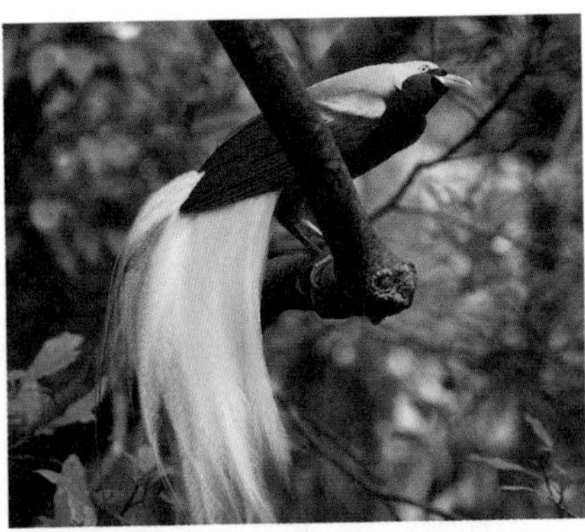

Many animals produce visual displays to attract a mate. The plumage of some birds can be very colorful and elaborate, such as in peacocks, birds-of-paradise (above), and lyrebirds. Display of the plumage is often accompanied by specific body postures.

ISBN: 978-1-98-856656-6

Plant to animal communication

David Kennard CC 3.0 www.davidkennardphotography.com

Flower color and color patterns are important mechanisms by which plants communicate with pollinating animals. Different types of animal see colors differently, so flower colors correspond to what the pollinator can perceive. Some pigments may be visible only in infrared or ultraviolet (UV) light.

Smell is also an important way in which plants communicate with animals. Plants produce scents that attract specific pollinators. For example, some plants produce scents like rotten meat to attract flies while other plants produce sweeter scents that attract bees and moths.

Plants often communicate the ripeness of fruit by changing their color. Green usually means an unripe fruit (and immature seeds). Other colors, such as red and orange, communicate that the fruit is ripe. Animals feeding on ripe fruit will then deposit its mature seeds away from the parent plant.

3. (a) Describe and explain the communication methods best suited to nocturnal animals in a forest habitat: __________

(b) Describe and explain the communication methods best suited to solitary animals with large home ranges: __________

4. Explain the role of dominant and submissive behaviors in animals with social hierarchies: __________

5. Explain how the response of a male moth to female pheromone is adaptive: __________

6. Explain the role of pheromones in orientation and communication in social insects: __________

7. Explain the need for plants to communicate with animals and describe some methods of communication:

ISBN: 978-1-98-856656-6

220 Courtship and Mating Behavior

Key Question: How do courtship behaviors ensure reproductive success?

Many behaviors in animals, including territorial behavior, are associated with reproduction, reflecting the importance of this event in an individual's life cycle. Most animals breed during a specific season and show no reproductive behavior outside this time. During the breeding season, reproductive signals must be given and interpreted correctly or the chance for successful reproduction may be missed. The short time period that most sexually reproducing animals have in which to breed creates strong selective pressure for behavior that improves the chances of reproductive success (therefore fitness). Breeding pairs often establish territories (defended areas) to ensure reliable access to resources during breeding, while ritualized courtship behaviors reduce conflict between the sexes so that mating is achieved without injury.

What is courtship?

- Courtship refers to the behavior of animals just before, during, and just after mating. Courtship is a way for both male and female to evaluate the health, strength, and potential fitness of a possible mate.
- A potential mate may initially be attracted by a call (e.g. male frog calling). The caller (usually male) may then perform a more intricate display once the responder (usually female) arrives. In other cases the male's call and display may be the same performance.
- Sometimes the male may attract a mate by offering a gift of food. This is relatively common in insects, such as empid flies (right and below). Sometimes the male himself is unwittingly the "gift of food", such as in praying mantises in which the male is invariably eaten during mating. This behavior is also common in spiders.

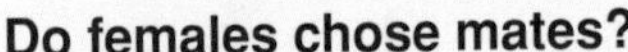

Do females chose mates?

- Mate choice (or intersexual selection) occurs where members of one biological sex choose mates of the other sex to mate with. Where there is mate choice, one sex competes with same-sex members and the other sex chooses. This competition often involves elaborate rituals, calls, and displays to the choosing sex.
- Females usually have more invested in offspring so their mate choice is important and they are often the choosy sex. Female preference for certain features, e.g. eyes on a peacock's tail, is thought to be behind the elaborate structures and displays that have evolved in many species (e.g. peafowl, right).

Courtship is a often crucial part of breeding behavior

Female empid flies are aggressive hunters, so males have to be careful about how they approach them. Ritualized courtship behavior by the male helps him to be accepted by the female as a mate. The male's gift of food for the female pacifies her during mating and is a crucial component of mating success.

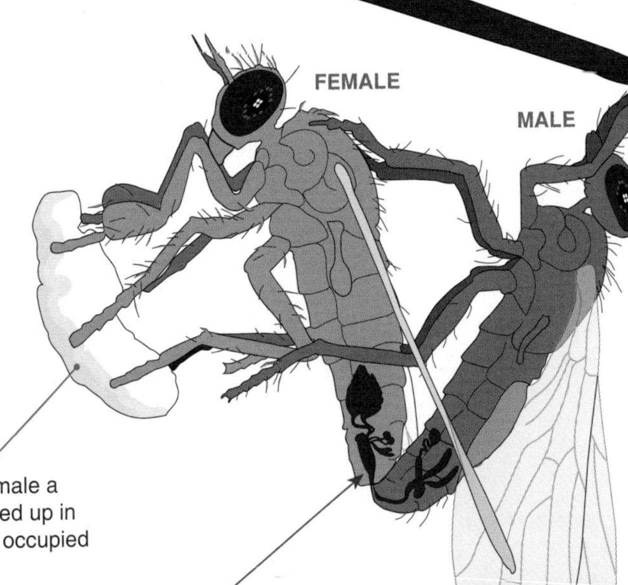

Male hangs on
The male empid fly grips on to a twig with its front legs during mating. It uses the other four legs to grip on to the female.

Courtship gift
The male gives the female a meal (an insect wrapped up in a cocoon) to keep her occupied while he mates.

Lock and key genitalia
The empid flies lock the tips of their abdomens together so that the male's sperm can enter the female. If the sperm were exposed to the air, they would dry out and die.

ISBN: 978-1-98-856656-6

In birds, song is an important mechanism for attracting a mate and proclaiming ownership of a territory. The song also acts as reproductive isolating mechanism, as differences between the songs of two species enables individuals to recognize their own species and mate only with them. Kakapo (a New Zealand ground parrot) is a lek species and males attempt to attract a mate to their lek (breeding territory) by producing a low frequency booming sound during the breeding season, which can be heard over many kilometers of forest. When a female arrives the male begins a display in which he spreads his wings and rocks side to side (above).

One of the functions of courtship behavior is to synchronize the behaviors of the male and female so that mating can occur, and to override attack or escape behavior. Although courtship rituals may be complex, they are very stereotyped and not easily misinterpreted. Males display, usually through exaggerated physical posturing, and the females then select their mates. Courtship displays are species specific and may include ritualized behavior such as dancing, feeding, and nest-building. Many birds may form life long bonds (e.g. albatross above) and renew these every year by displaying to each other when they arrive at breeding grounds.

1. (a) Why might courtship behavior be necessary prior to mating? ______________________

   (b) Explain why courtship behavior is often ritualized, with stereotyped displays: ______________________

2. Describe two aspects of mating behavior in empid flies that help to ensure successful mating:

   (a) ______________________

   (b) ______________________

3. (a) Explain why choosing the best mate is particularly important for females: ______________________

   (b) Explain how female choice could lead to elaboration of structures and displays in males: ______________________

   (c) In some species, the female is unable to choose a mate. Elephant seal males fight for the right to mate with a female and defend a harem. Females arriving at the beach often try to avoid the harem, but with males being up to four times heavier this is difficult. Explain how this system helps to ensure the offspring are likely to have the "best" genes:

   ____

ISBN: 978-1-98-856656-6

221 Territories and Breeding Behavior

Key Question: What is the benefit of establishing and defending a territory during the breeding season?

Territories (defended areas) are most often established in the breeding season, usually spring and summer. In fall and winter, migratory animals leave their territories and return to winter grounds. Other animals that do not migrate may still only defend a territory during the breeding season, when the benefits of territory defense are higher. Establishing a territory requires considerable energy and effort, but the benefit is the exclusive access to resources. During the breeding season, males in particular spend time defending a territory with the goal of attracting a female and reproducing. In many cases, where territories are established only for breeding purposes, the position of the territory is often the most important factor.

The **speckled wood butterfly** is found throughout northern Eurasia and Africa. During the breeding season, males have two breeding strategies. Dominant males defend a patch of sunlight in a wood, while others fly through the forest looking for unmated females. Studies have shown the males defending a territory have a greater chance of mating. This appears not to be because these males are more desirable *per se* but that they are more able to spot females flying through the sunlight than males with no sunlit patch.

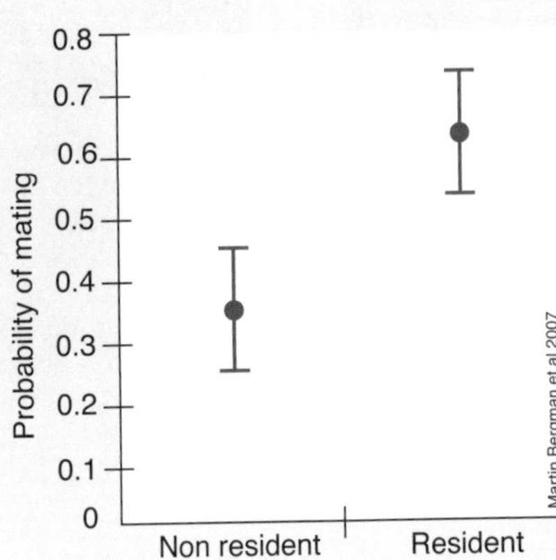

Lekking is a relatively common breeding behavior. Lekking areas (arenas) often contain numerous males. In most cases the more dominant males have leks in the center of the arena. The diagram right shows a schematic of a **greater sage-grouse** lek arena. The most dominant alpha male (A) is found in the middle where he displays strongly to females by drumming (photo right).

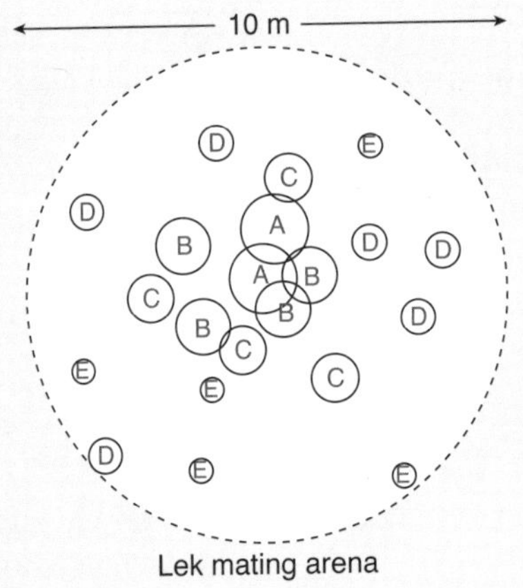

Topi are antelopes found on sub-Saharan grasslands. They establish leks during the mating season (March to May). Studies have shown that the closer the male is to the center of the lekking arena the larger the number of females that are mated with per day.

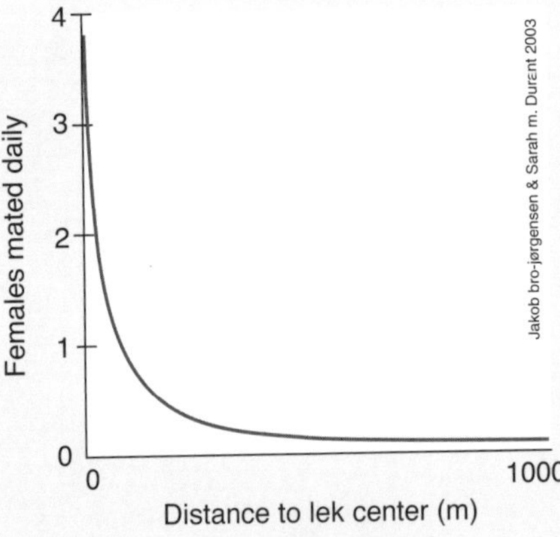

1. What is the purpose of establishing a territory during breeding season? ______________________

2. How do lek species indicate dominance in males? ______________________

3. Explain why establishing a lek system is efficient for both males and females: ______________________

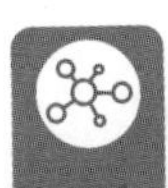

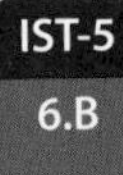

ISBN: 978-1-98-856656-6

Bird song

- Male birds defend territory and attract mates with song. The strength, quality, and type of song all factor into how well the bird is able to defend and maintain its territory. It may also be a factor in how much effort is put into defense against rivals. Studies of the New Zealand tui, a medium sized song bird, have shown that the owner of a territory will defend it more aggressively against rivals with particularly high quality songs.
- In song sparrows, birds with low quality or soft songs have their territory invaded more often and for longer than do birds with higher quality or louder songs (below left).
- In Cassin's finches, the type, length, and frequency of the song may change if a female present in a male's territory leaves. If she returns the male song usually returns to normal (below right).

Intrusion time and song type in song sparrows

Intrusions (seconds): 0, 500, 1000, 1500, 2000

Soft singing owner; Loud singing owner

Source: Searcy and Nowicki (2008). See credits for full citation.

Song length and female presence in Cassin's finch

Mean song length (seconds): 0, 100, 200, 300, 400, 500

Female status: Present Day 1; Absent Day 2; Absent Day 1; Present Day 2

Source: Sockman et al 2005. See credits for full citation. Image: Elaine R. Wilson CC 3.0

4. Use examples as evidence to support the claim that the position of a territory can be important for reproductive success:

5. (a) Explain how the quality of song affects how often a male's territory is invaded:

   (b) Explain why this might occur:

6. Suggest why a male bird would increase his song length if a female leaves his territory:

ISBN: 978-1-98-856656-6

222 Herds, Flocks, and Schools

Key Question: How do herding, flocking, and schooling behaviors contribute to fitness?

Some animals are solitary, interacting only to reproduce, but many live in groups, which may be non-social (as in fish schools) or highly organized social groupings, in which individuals within the groups interact to varying degrees. Schooling in fish, flocking in birds, and herding in grazing mammals are essentially all similar behaviors. These **group behaviors** provide survival advantages via protection from physical factors and predation. Each individual behaves in a way that helps its own survival regardless of the others within that group. Different groups have different levels of organization. Some will have a definite leader, although these are often small groups (e.g. elephants). Others may have several leaders (usually older, larger adults) that others in the herd or group tend to follow. Some groups have no leader but the individual behavior of each member contributes to the overall group behavior (e.g. fish schools and large bird flocks).

School of fish

A large flock of auklets (a small seabird)

D. Dibenski, cc0

Schooling in fish

Prey fish may school for defensive reasons. Schooling fish also benefit by better hydrodynamics within the school so less energy is expended in swimming. Schooling help avoid predators because:

- The movement of the school causes confusion.
- There is a reduced probability of individual capture.
- There are more prey than can be eaten (predator satiation).
- Predator detection is more efficient (the many eyes principle).

Herding in mammals

Herding is common in hoofed mammals, especially those on grasslands such as the African savanna.

A herd provides protection because while one animal is feeding, another will have its head up looking for predators. In this way, each individual benefits from a continual surveillance (again, this is the many eyes principle).

During an attack, individuals move closer to the center of the herd, as those on the outside are more frequently captured. The herd moves as one group, driven by individual needs.

Flocking in birds

Flocks follow similar rules to schools. In flight, each bird maintains a constant distance from others and keeps flying in the average direction of the group. Flocks can be very large, with thousands of birds flying together as a loosely organized unit, e.g. starlings flocking in the evening or queleas flocking over feeding or watering sites.

Most flocks are non-social, but there are exceptions. Flamingos form social groups with many hundreds of birds. The large colonies help the birds avoid predators, maximize food intake, and use suitable nesting sites more efficiently.

1. Describe some benefits of schooling to a:

   (a) Predatory fish species: ______________________________

   (b) Prey fish species: ______________________________

   ____

   ____

2. Explain how herding in grazing mammals provides a survival advantage: ______________________________

   ____

   ____

   ____

   ____

3. Many migratory birds navigate using an internal compass. These are not always fully accurate. Explain why a single bird migrating on its own has a greater likelihood of ending up in the wrong place than many birds migrating in flock:

   ____

   ____

   ____

   ____

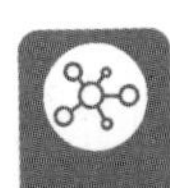
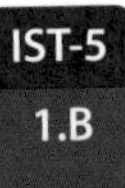

ISBN: 978-1-98-856656-6

223 The Adaptive Value of Cooperation

Key Questions: How does cooperation increase fitness?

Cooperative behavior involves two or more individuals working together to achieve a common goal (e.g. defense, food acquisition, or rearing young). Examples of cooperation include hunting as a team (e.g. hunts by wolves, lions, and chimpanzees), responding to the actions of others with the same goal (e.g. consensus decisions to migrate), or acting to benefit others (e.g. mobbing in small birds). Cooperation occurs most commonly between members of the same species and is adaptive in that it increases the probability of survival and successful reproduction for those that cooperate. **Altruism** is an extreme form of cooperative behavior in which one individual disadvantages itself for the benefit of another. Altruism is often seen in highly social animals. Most often the altruistic individual receives some non-material benefit (e.g. increased probability of breeding success).

Cooperation in the black-backed jackal

Black-backed jackal *(Canis mesomelas)*

Black-backed jackals live in the brushland of Africa. Monogamous pairs (single male and female parents) hunt cooperatively, share food and defend territories. Offspring from the previous year's litter frequently help rear their siblings by regurgitating food for the lactating mother and for the pups themselves. The pup survival results of 15 separate jackal groups are shown in the graph on the right.

Black-backed jackal adult, juvenile, and young pup

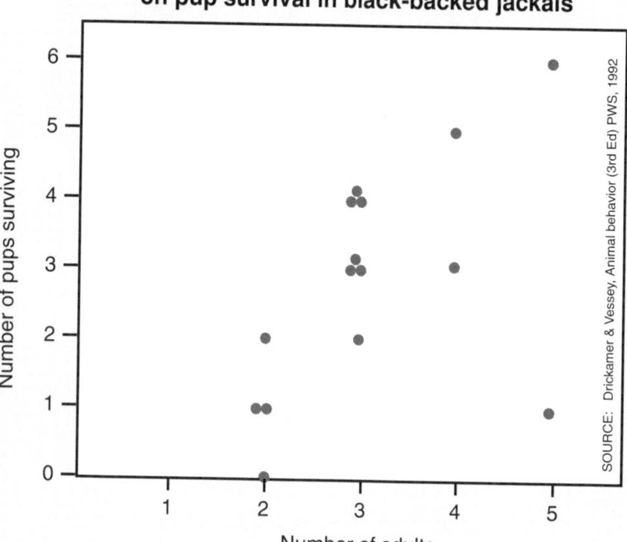

1. Use the data on black-backed jackals to explain how cooperative behavior benefits fitness:

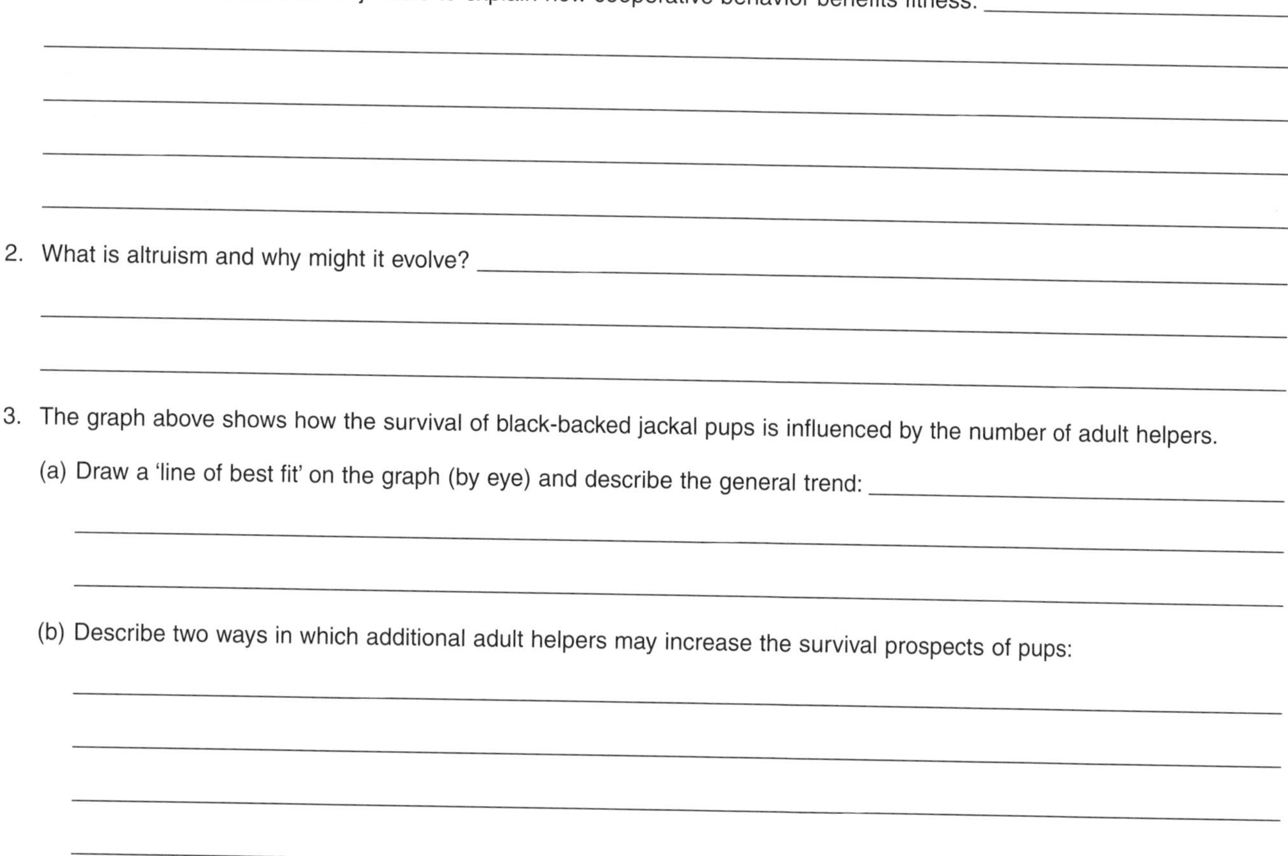

2. What is altruism and why might it evolve?

3. The graph above shows how the survival of black-backed jackal pups is influenced by the number of adult helpers.

   (a) Draw a 'line of best fit' on the graph (by eye) and describe the general trend:

   (b) Describe two ways in which additional adult helpers may increase the survival prospects of pups:

ISBN: 978-1-98-856656-6

- By working together (directly or indirectly), members of a group increase each other's chances of survival. However the level of help often depends on the level of relatedness.
- Living in a group can improve the survival of individual group members, e.g. by improving foraging success or decreasing the chances of predation. Animals such as meerkats, ground squirrels, and prairie dogs decrease the chances of predation to others by having sentries that produce alarms calls when a predator approaches. Many animals live as family groups that help with foraging and raising the young.

Crowned fairy wrens

Purple crowned fairy wrens are found in northern Australia. They are cooperative breeders and maintain territories along rivers year round. Groups consist of a breeding pair and up to six helpers (earlier offspring). The graphs right show the effect of the number of helpers (A and B) and group size (C and D) on various aspects on survival.

A: The number of fledglings per nest (current productivity).

B: The total feeding rate per nest.

C: Breeder survival probability (future productivity). D: The feeding rate per breeder.

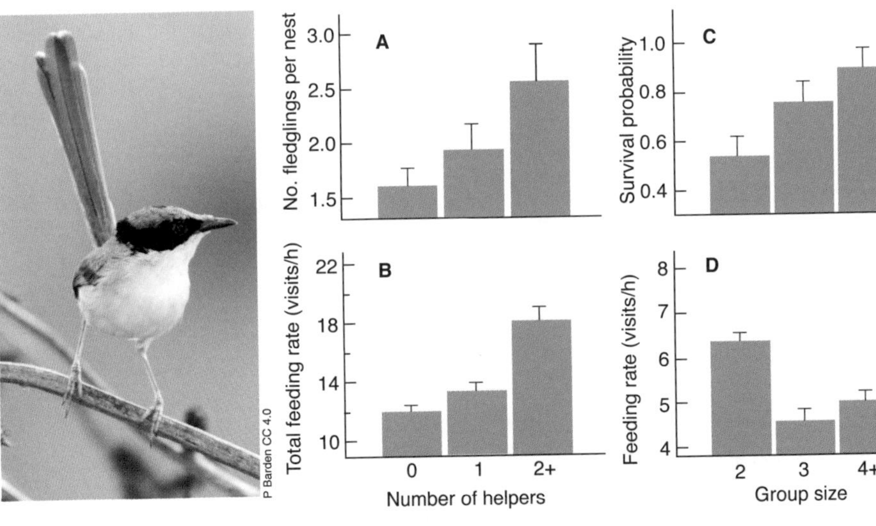

Sharing with friends

Cooperation does not have to be between family groups, or for direct actions such as feeding or defense. Sometimes cooperative activity occurs between unrelated individuals and involves sharing a resource with another in the knowledge that the act with be repaid at a later date. Common vampire bats feed on blood, usually of other mammals, by shaving off skin and lapping blood from the wound. Female bats live in colonies. Occasionally one bat may not feed successfully and will beg blood from a second bat, which the second bat may regurgitate. This sharing of blood between "friends" may be paid back at a later date. If the second bat refuses to share, the first bat often rebuffs any attempt by the second bat to beg a meal latter on. This is a "tit-for-tat" behavior.

Uwe Schmidt CC 4.0

4. (a) Describe the effect of number of helpers on the number of fledglings per nest in purple crowned fairy wrens:

(b) Describe the effect of number of helpers on the total feeding rate to the nest:

5. (a) Describe the effect of group size on the number of feeding visits breeders must make to the nest:

(b) Describe and explain the relationship between this and survival probability of breeders:

6. Explain how sharing a meal now helps survival in the future for vampire bats:

ISBN: 978-1-98-856656-6

224 Honeybee Communication

Key Question: How do honeybees communicate the distance and direction of food sources to other bees?

Honeybees navigate using a sun compass, so honeybees communicate the direction and distance to food relative to the current position of the sun. In the waggle dance, they adjust their dance to account for the changing direction of the sun.

The waggle dance

Bees communicate the direction and distance of the food source through the waggle dance (below). If food is located directly in line with the sun, the communicator (bee in the blue circle) demonstrates it by running directly up the comb. To direct bees to food located either side of the sun, the bee introduces the corresponding angle to the right or left of the upward direction into the dance. Bees adjust the angles of their dance to account the changing direction of the sun throughout the day. This means directions to the food source are still correct even though the sun has changed positions.

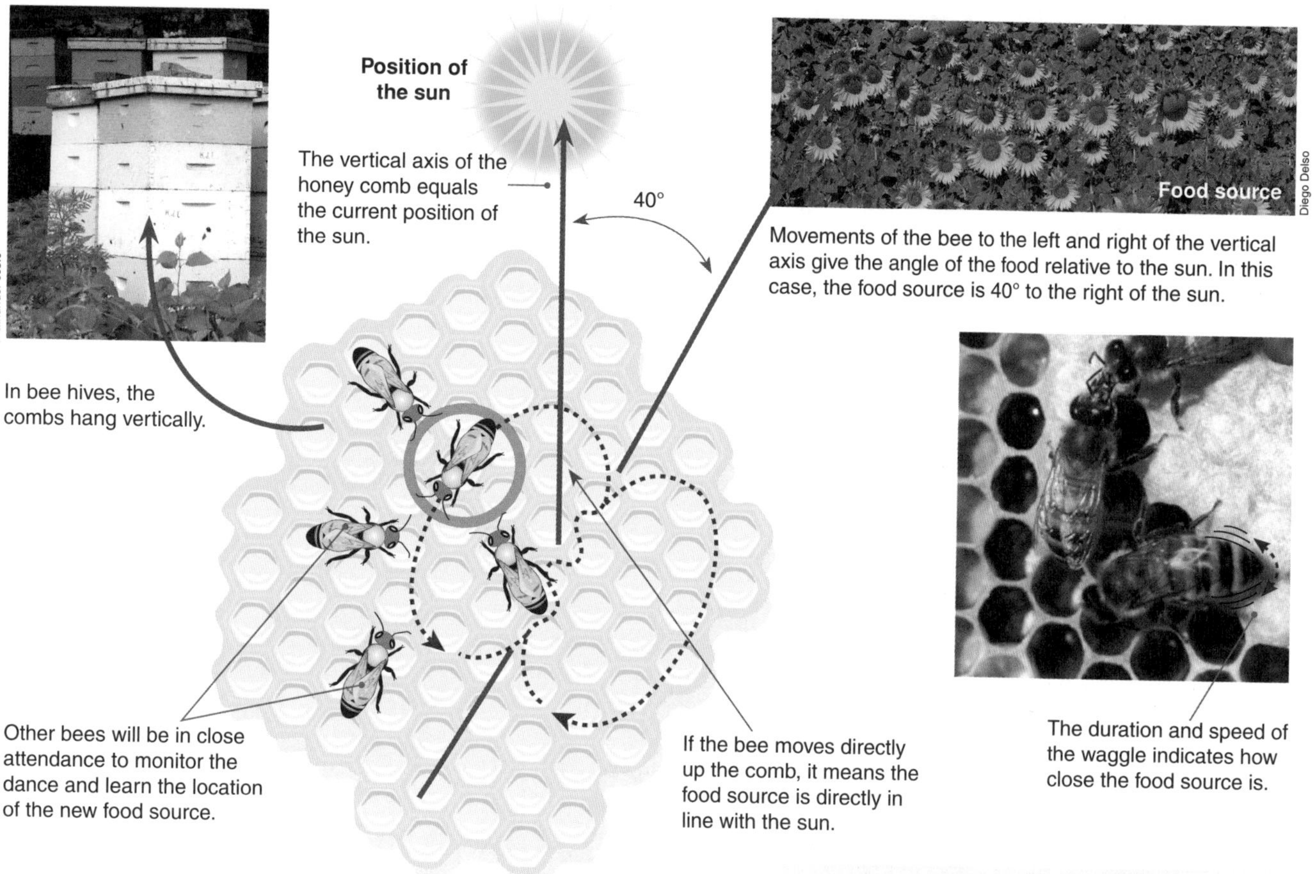

onathunder cc3.0

In bee hives, the combs hang vertically.

Position of the sun

The vertical axis of the honey comb equals the current position of the sun.

40°

Food source

Diego Delso

Movements of the bee to the left and right of the vertical axis give the angle of the food relative to the sun. In this case, the food source is 40° to the right of the sun.

Other bees will be in close attendance to monitor the dance and learn the location of the new food source.

If the bee moves directly up the comb, it means the food source is directly in line with the sun.

The duration and speed of the waggle indicates how close the food source is.

1. What environmental reference is used by honeybees to orientate for navigation?

2. How does a bee communicate the proximity of a food source in the waggle dance?

3. Explain the benefit of communicating flower location to other bees in the hive:

4. When is the round dance used?

The round dance

If the food source is very close (less than 50 m) the honeybee will perform a round dance. The honeybee's round dance stimulates other workers to leave the hive and search within 50 m for a food source (below).

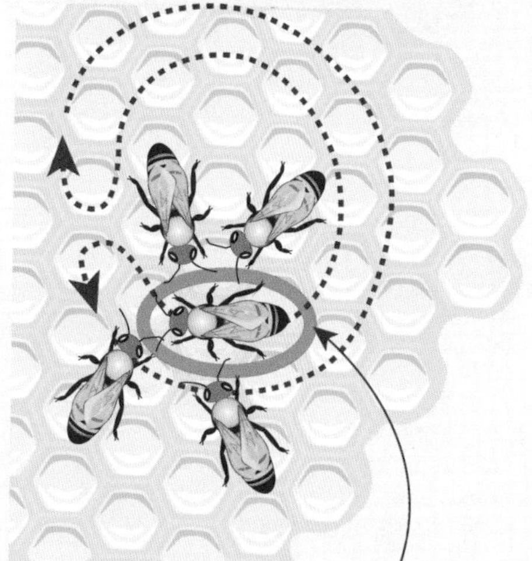

The bee communicating the presence of the food source (blue oval) follows a

ISBN: 978-1-98-856656-6

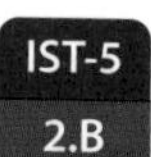

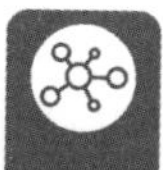

225 Cooperation and Foraging Success

Key Question: How does working together as a group increase the chance of an individual obtaining food?

Cooperating to gather food can be much more efficient than finding it alone because it increases the chances of finding food or capturing prey. Cooperative hunting will evolve in a species if there is a sustained benefit to the participants, the benefit for a single hunter is less than that of hunting in a group, and cooperation within the group is guaranteed.

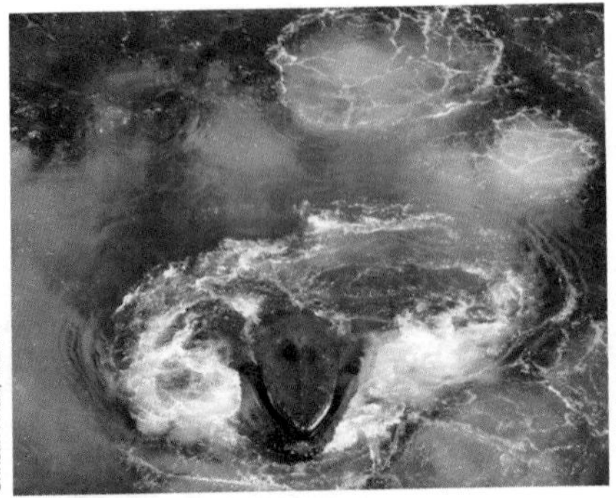

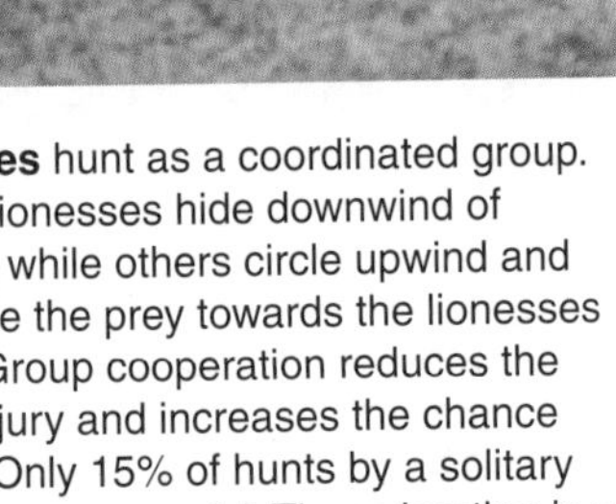

Lionesses hunt as a coordinated group. Several lionesses hide downwind of the prey, while others circle upwind and stampede the prey towards the lionesses in wait. Group cooperation reduces the risk of injury and increases the chance of a kill. Only 15% of hunts by a solitary lioness are successful. Those hunting in a group are successful 40% of the time.

Humpback whales (above) use a cooperative technique called bubble net feeding to catch small fish. The whales form a circle around a school of fish, and blow bubbles of air from their blowholes. The bubbles enclose the fish and prevent them escaping. The whales then simultaneously swim upwards and feed off the fish. Up to 60 individuals may be involved, so a high degree of learning and communication is required for this technique to be successful.

The mountain caracara in Peru (above) forages in groups of three or four, looking for prey hidden around rocks. Working together, the birds are able to overturn rocks far bigger than any individual could move. If a bird finds a rock that is worth turning over, it produces a high pitched call to attract the others. In most cases, only one bird (usually the initial caller) benefits from overturning the rock. However, the other birds may benefit when other rocks are overturned later (reciprocal altruism).

Cooperative foraging in ants

Army ants foraging

Cooperative foraging in ants often involves division of labor. Army ants (of which there are over 200 species) have several distinct worker castes. The smaller castes collect small prey, and larger porter ants collect larger prey. The largest workers defend the nest.

Different species of army ant have quite different raiding patterns (below right): The columns of *Eciton hamatum* go in many directions, whereas the swarm-raider *Eciton burchelli* forms a broad front. Both species cache food at various points along the way.

Through group cooperation, the tiny ants are able to subdue prey much larger than themselves, even managing to kill and devour animals such as lizards and small mammals. This would not be possible if they hunted as individuals.

Worker castes in army ants

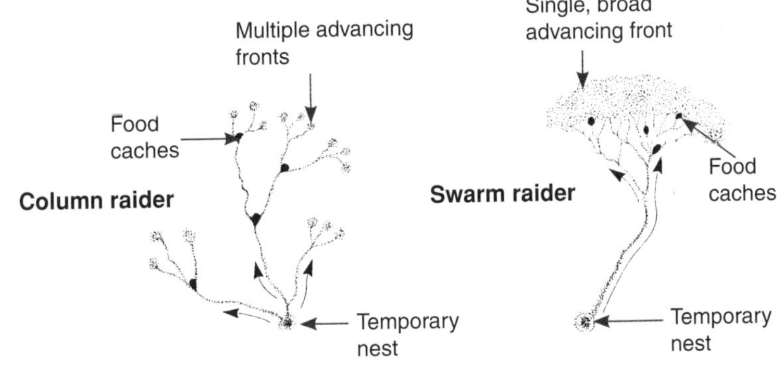

Honeypot ants

Honeypot ants of central Australia have a special group of workers called 'repletes'. These never leave the nest, but stay in underground galleries where they serve as vessels for storing a rich food supply.

Regular workers that have been foraging for honeydew and nectar return to the nest where they regurgitate food from their crops to feed the replete. The replete will continue to accept these offerings until its abdomen has swollen to the size of a pea (normally it is the size of a grain of rice). The repletes become so swollen that their movements are restricted to clinging to the gallery ceiling where many hundreds of them hang in a row.

When the dry season arrives and food supplies become scarce, workers return to the repletes, coaxing them to regurgitate droplets of honey.

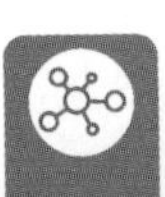

IST-5 4.B

ISBN: 978-1-98-856656-6

1. Describe the advantages of cooperative food gathering:

2. Describe the conditions that favor group cooperation in food gathering:

3. (a) Describe the advantages of reciprocal altruism in mountain caracara:

(b) Suggest why this a successful strategy, even when birds do not benefit all the time:

4. Explain how the division of roles within ants increases the foraging success of the colony as a whole:

5. How are honeypot ant repletes an extreme form of cooperation?

6. The graph on the right shows the hunting success of chimpanzee groups of various sizes. Explain how group size affects hunting success:

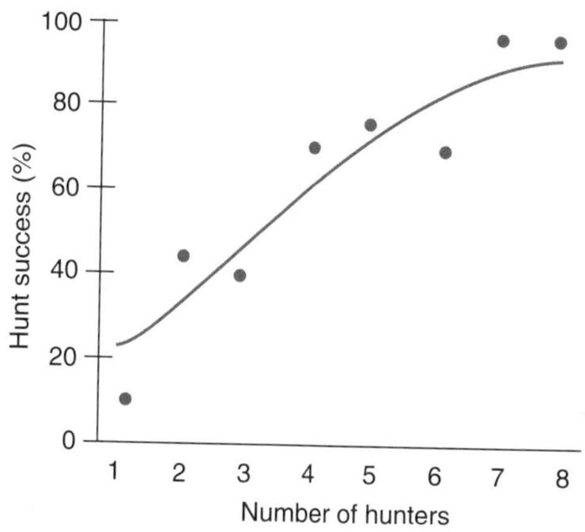

7. Increasing group size and hunting success are not always positively correlated. In many cases, groups above a certain number (which varies depending on the hunters and the situation) actually reduces the chances of a successful hunt. Explain why this might be the case:

ISBN: 978-1-98-856656-6

226 Cooperation and Improved Defense

Key Question: How does cooperative defense increase an individual's chance of survival?

Group defense is a key strategy for survival in social or herding mammals. Forming groups during an attack by a predator decreases the chances of being singled out, while also increasing the chances of a successful defense.

Group defense in musk oxen

In the Siberian steppes, which are extensive grasslands, musk oxen must find novel ways to protect themselves from predators. There is often no natural cover, so they must make their own barrier in the form of a defensive circle. When wolves (their most common predator) attack, they shield the young inside the circle. Lone animals have little chance of surviving an attack as wolves hunt in packs.

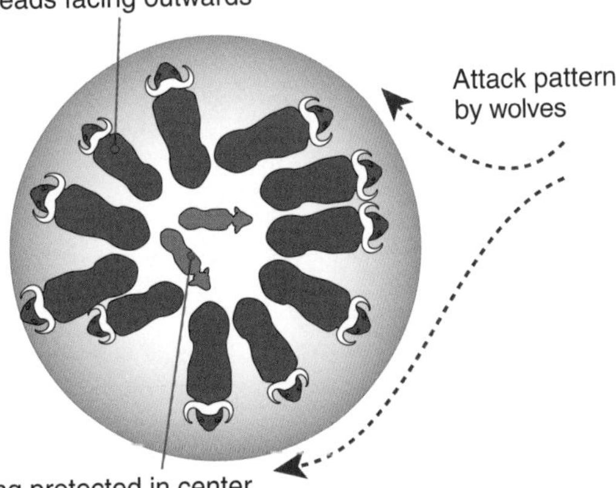

Red colobus monkey defense

Red colobus monkeys are a common target during chimpanzee hunts. They counter these attacks by fleeing (especially females with young), hiding, or mounting a group defense. The group defense is usually the job of the males and the more defenders there are, the greater the likelihood of the defense being successful.

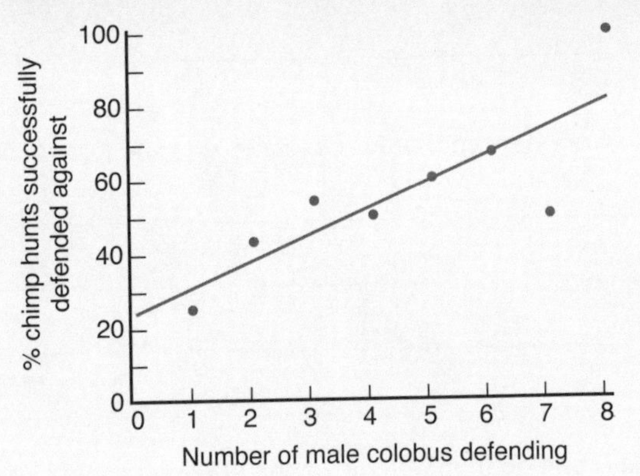

1. Describe two benefits of cooperative defense: ________________

2. How many colobus males are needed to effectively guarantee a successful defense against chimpanzees?

3. Sheep need to spend most of their day feeding on grass. They form mobs both naturally in the wild as well as on farms.

(a) Explain why sheep form mobs: ________________

(b) Explain how this might enhance an individual sheep's ability to feed: ________________

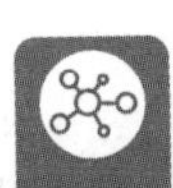

ISBN: 978-1-98-856656-6

227 Colony Behavior and Survival

Key Question: How does colony behavior contribute to survival and reproductive success in eusocial species?

A large variety of insects form colonies. A smaller set form social colonies. The most advanced and organized of these social colonies are the **eusocial colonies**. The most common and well known are the ants, wasps, honeybees, and termites. The colony provides numerous advantages to the group, including more efficient foraging, and improved attack and defense abilities. Eusocial colonies behave in way as to produce what is sometimes called a superorganism. In this case, the colony can not be thought of as many individuals working together but as one singular organism.

Eusocial insects

Eusocial animals are those in which a single female produces the offspring and non-reproductive individuals care for the young. They have the highest form of social organization. Individuals are divided into different castes with specific roles. In most cases, a queen produces all the young and members of the group are normally directly related to the queen. Non-reproductive members of the group may be involved in care of the young, foraging, or defense of the nest site. Examples include ants, honeybees, termites, and naked mole rats.

Termite queen

USDA

Swarming

One of the characteristics of many eusocial colonies is swarming behavior. Swarming may occur for many reasons, including reproduction and migration, but two important reasons are attack and defense. You will probably be aware of why you don't disturb a hornet nest. To do so often produces a mass defensive behavior in which large numbers of workers attack the provoking animal. In many cases, the insects (e.g. honeybees) produced alarm pheromones, which recruit other workers to the attack. These may be produced before or after a sting. In some species, such as Africanized honeybees, these pheromones can incite frenzied attacks.

Japanese honeybees

Japanese honeybees are often attacked by the aggressive Asian giant hornet (right), which also steals the bee colony's honey. When a hornet scout enters the honeybee hive, the honeybees mob it with more than 100 bees, forming a bee-ball (far right). The center of the ball can reach 50°C, literally baking the scout to death.

I, Kenpei cc 3.0

Takahashi cc. 2.1

Raiding parties

Many ant species, e.g. **slave-maker ants**, raid other ant nests (called slave-raiding), killing workers and capturing grubs (right). The grubs are carried back to the home nest where they grow and tend the slave-maker ants' own young (far right). Sometimes, however, the slaves rebel and can destroy the slave-maker nest.

In his book **Journey of Ants** Edward O. Wilson, the world's leading ant expert, noted that with ants *"their foreign policy can be summed up as follows: restless aggression, territorial conquest, and genocidal annihilation of neighboring colonies wherever possible. If ants had nuclear weapons, they would probably end the world in a week."*

James C Trager cc 3.0
Slave-maker ants raiding a nest

Queen and brood of a slave-maker ant attended by captured ant slaves
Adrian A. Smith

1. In eusocial animals, worker and soldier castes never breed but are normally all genetically related. Explain how their contribution to the group can help pass their own genes to the next generation (ensure the survival or their own genes):

2. Explain how swarming behavior in insects helps to defend a nest:

ISBN: 978-1-98-856656-6

228 Kin Selection

Key Question: What is kin selection and why does it occur? Individuals both within and between species may cooperate with each other for many reasons: for mutual defense and protection, to enhance food acquisition, or to rear young. To explain the evolution of cooperative behavior, it has been suggested that individuals benefit their own survival or the survival of their genes (offspring) by cooperating. **Kin selection** is a form of selection that favours altruistic (self-sacrificing) behavior towards relatives. In this type of behavior an individual will sacrifice its own opportunity to reproduce for the benefit of its close relatives, which carry a proportion of its own genes.

- Like any cooperative behavior, cooperative behavior towards relatives occurs when the benefit of cooperating outweighs the cost. Normally, cooperative behavior produces some direct benefit, e.g. obtaining food via cooperative hunting. This ultimately increases an individual's fitness by increasing the amount of energy (food) they have and can allocate to reproduction and raising offspring.
- Cooperative behavior that forgoes reproductive success does not mean losing genetic success. In genetic terms, a parent and its offspring are related by a half, siblings are related by a half, and an aunt or uncle is related to a nephew or niece by a quarter. Kin selection may evolve in systems where the resources available are sufficient to support only one breeding pair. Older siblings, aunts and uncles can pass on a reasonable fraction of their own genes by helping that pair to breed or raise offspring successfully, even if they are unable to breed themselves.
- Cooperation in this way becomes less as relatedness decreases because the genetic cost to the helper increases and eventually outweighs the genetic benefit.
- Kin selection and altruism can be explained by Hamilton's rule: $r \times B > C$ where r is the relatedness, B is the benefit to the recipient (how many more offspring are produced), and C is the cost to the altruist. If $r \times B$ is greater than C, then kin selection is likely to evolve.
- It is worth noting that unambiguous examples of kin selection are rare, as it can often be shown or speculated that helpers will gain genetic success at a later date.

Naked mole rat worker caring for newborn

Naked mole rats, from the arid regions of Kenya, are unique among mammals in having a social organization similar to that of social insects. Up to 300 of the rodents spend their lives underground in a **colony** with a **caste system**, which includes workers, soldiers, infertile females, and one breeding queen.

Honeybees: The ultimate in unselfish behavior?

Are honeybees altruistic?

Each female worker in the colony:

- Sacrifices her life to defend the colony against danger.
- Produces no eggs.
- Raises the young of the queen.

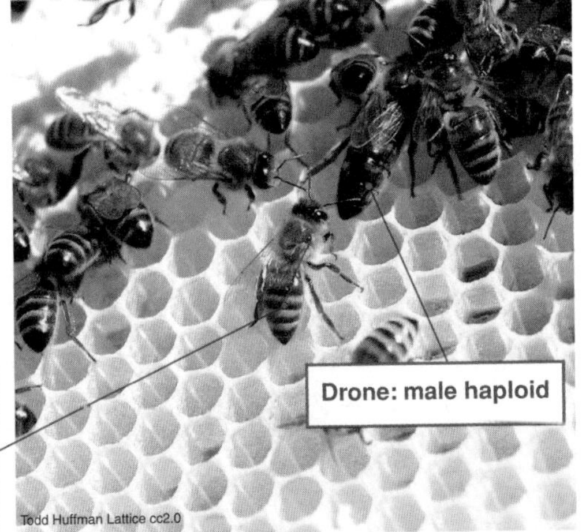
Workers: female diploid
The queen's daughters will share identical genes from the father and will share half the genes from the queen.
Drone: male haploid
Todd Huffman Lattice cc2.0

Kin selection explains the behavior

Kin selection is altruistic behavior towards relatives (i.e. animals help more often when more closely related).

- Honeybee males (drones) are haploid and females are diploid.
- Workers therefore all have the same male genes and half the queen's genes.
- Workers are more closely related to each other than they would be to their own daughters.
- Therefore care-giving behavior of sisters will increase faster than genes promoting investment in offspring.

1. (a) Explain how kin selection can account for the evolution of apparently altruistic behavior:

(b) Do you think such behavior is truly self sacrificing? Explain:

2. Explain how a worker honeybee is related to the queen and why these workers forgo their own reproductive success:

ISBN: 978-1-98-856656-6

229 How Organisms Allocate Energy

Key Question: How do organisms allocate their energy to maximize their survival and reproductive success?

The energy available to any organism is limited. This means that organisms must make compromises in terms of how they allocate available energy and their energy allocations may be prioritized differently at different times. For example, organisms may expend large amounts of energy in migration, but their overall energy gain at their destination enables them to allocate energy to breeding. Organisms make continual adjustments to these trade-offs to maximize fitness.

Energy gain and allocation

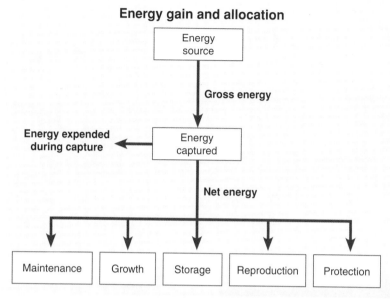

Energy source → **Gross energy** → Energy captured → **Energy expended during capture**

Energy captured → **Net energy** → Maintenance | Growth | Storage | Reproduction | Protection

The net energy gain from an energy source depends on the size of the energy source and the energy expended to obtain it. In the case of a predator, such as a cheetah, the energy expended in the chase must be less than the energy gained from the eating the prey. Enough energy must be left over to maintain the body, grow, or reproduce.

The energy a cheetah will expend during a hunt is very precisely regulated. If it doesn't make a kill in under a minute, it stops the chase.

A large amount of energy is expended during migration. The energy gained from abundant food sources at the destination is enough to allow the animal to breed, rear its young, and carry it through the return migration and winter.

Magne Flåten cc 3.0

Hibernation is a prolonged (usually seasonal) state of reduced activity and metabolic depression. It markedly reduces the animal's energy expenditure, allowing it to survive winter. Large amounts of energy must be stored (e.g. as fat) prior to hibernating.

Deciduous trees expend energy growing new leaves every spring. They produce all the energy needed to grow and reproduce before losing the leaves in fall. Losing leaves reduces frost or storm damage to the tree during winter months.

1. Why is it important for organisms to accurately assess energy gains against expenditure when selecting food sources:

2. In terms of energy allocation and expenditure, explain the following:

(a) Why many animals migrate every year despite the large energy cost:

(b) Why hibernation is a strategy for animals living in regions with extreme seasonal variations:

ISBN: 978-1-98-856656-6

Daily energy requirements for infants 0-12 months

Age (months)	Energy expenditure (E) (MJ/day)	Energy deposition (D) (MJ/day)	Total energy requirement (T = E + D) (MJ/day)	Percent D of T (D ÷ T) x100
0-1	2.5	1.63		
1-2	3.1	1.43		
2-3	3.6	1.14		
3-4	4.1	0.51		
4-5	4.5	0.43		
5-6	4.8	0.35		
6-7	5.0	0.15		
7-8	5.3	0.13		
8-9	5.5	0.12		
9-10	5.7	0.16		
10-11	5.9	0.15		
11-12	6.1	0.15		

Data: Combined data FAO

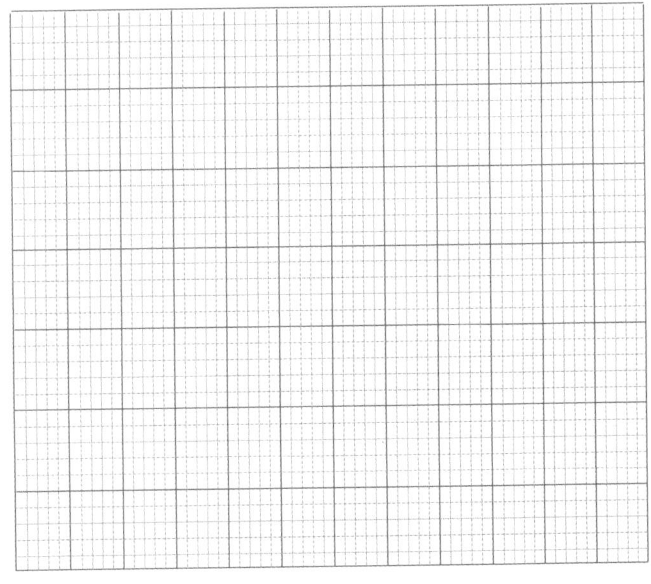

To grow, an organism must obtain more energy than it expends in activity and maintenance. As the body grows, new tissue also requires maintaining and so the daily energy needs of a growing organism increase. As growth slows, the daily energy requirement above that needed for maintenance is reduced. The table above lists daily total energy expenditure and energy deposition (used for growth) for infants from birth to 12 months.

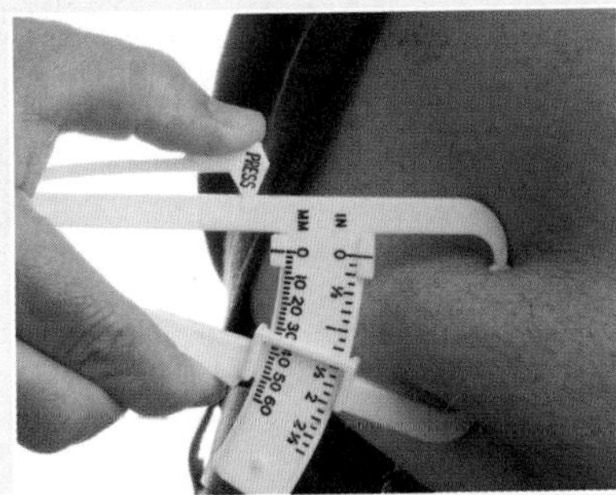

When people obtain more energy than they need for daily activities or growth, the extra energy is stored as fat. This is a growing problem many countries where high energy food is easily obtainable.

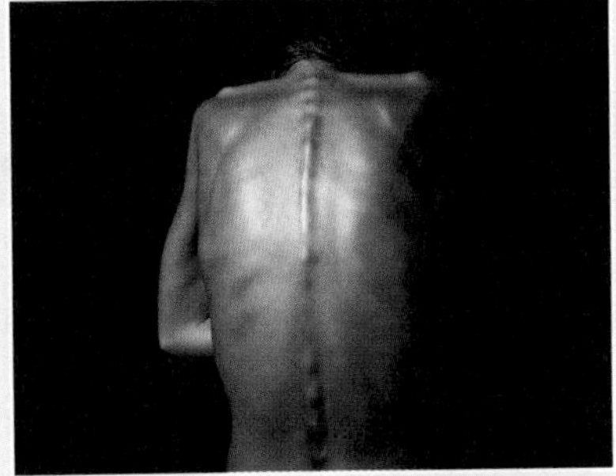

When the body does not get enough energy to carry out its daily activities, it starts to obtain energy by breaking down tissues in the body. This begins with fat tissue, then protein (normally muscle).

Balancing energy input and energy output is important for managing weight or being able to carry out high energy physical tasks like building muscle or playing sport. High energy tasks require greater energy input.

3. (a) Complete the calculations to fill in the missing columns in the table above.

(b) Plot the total energy expenditure, energy deposition, and energy requirement for infants aged 0 to 12 months.

(c) What happens to the total energy expenditure of infants as they grow? ______

______

(d) What happens to the amount of energy allocated to deposition as infants grow? ______

______

(e) How does the percentage of the total energy requirement allocated to energy deposition change as the infants grow?

______

4. How does the body deal with an excess energy intake in someone with a sedentary (inactive) lifestyle? ______

______

ISBN: 978-1-98-856656-6

230 Endothermy vs Ectothermy

Key Question: What is the difference between ectotherms and endotherms and how does each thermoregulate?

Animals are classified into two broad groups based on the source of their body heat. **Ectotherms** depend on the environment for their heat energy (e.g. heat from the sun) and their metabolic demands are relatively low, whereas **endotherms** generate their body heat from metabolism. All endotherms and many ectotherms **thermoregulate** (control body temperature) in order to maintain an optimum temperature for functioning. Ectotherms rely on behavioral mechanisms to do this. In endotherms, both behavioral and physiological responses are involved.

Most fish and all amphibians are ectothermic (they rely on environmental sources of heat energy). Unlike many reptiles, they do not thermoregulate, so their body temperature fluctuates with the environment (they are poikilothermic) and they are usually restricted to thermally stable environments.

Reptiles, such as snakes, lizards, and crocodiles, are also ectothermic but regulate body temperature using behavior. They bask and use body positioning to raise their body temperature for activity and seek shade when temperatures are too high. Some larger reptiles are able to maintain a relatively elevated body temperature for much of the time.

Birds and mammals are endotherms and achieve a high body temperature through metabolic activity and reduction of heat exchanges. They can function independently of the environmental temperature (within the species-specific tolerance range) and maintain high metabolic rates. Their body temperature remains stable (they are homeothermic) and their energy costs are high.

Daily temperature variations in ectotherms and endotherms

Ectotherm: Diurnal lizard
Body temperature is regulated by behavior so that it does not rise above 40°C. Basking increases heat uptake from the sun. Activity occurs when body temperature is high. Underground burrows are used for retreat.

Endotherm: Human
Body temperature fluctuates within narrow limits over a 24 hour period. Exercise and eating increase body temperature for a short time. Body temperature falls during rest and is partly controlled by an internal rhythm.

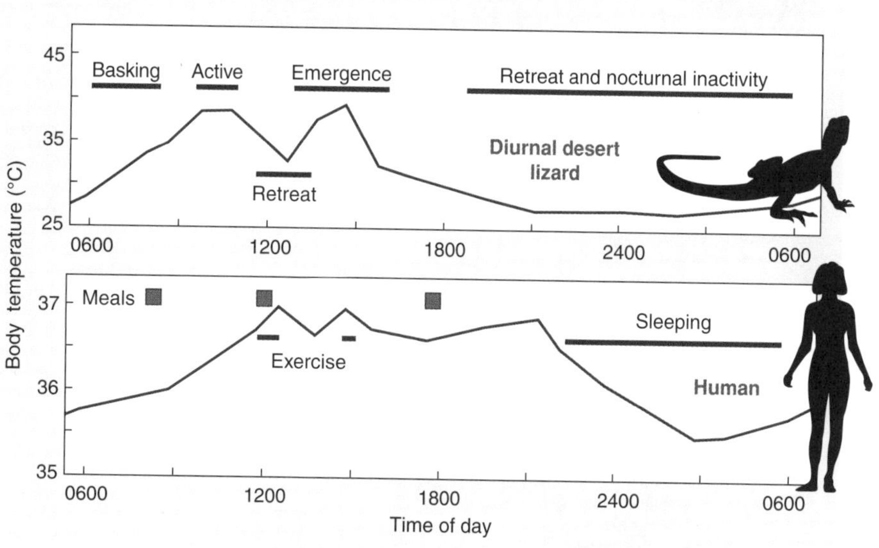

1. Distinguish between ectotherms and endotherms in terms of their sources of body heat: ______________________

2. Explain why ectotherms that do not thermoregulate are restricted to environments with relatively stable temperatures:

3. The diagrams above show daily temperature variations in an ectotherm and an endotherm.

(a) Which animal has the largest temperature variation? ______________________

(b) Explain why this is the case: ______________________

ISBN: 978-1-98-856656-6

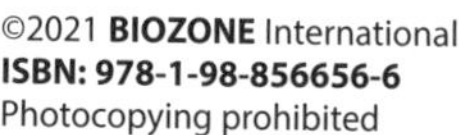

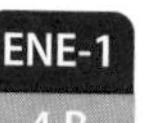

4. Again, with reference to the diagram of daily temperature fluctuations on the previous page:

(a) Describe the effect of eating and exercise on body temperature in humans: ______________________________

(b) What effect does sleeping have on human body temperature? ______________________________

(c) What do you think is happening to the metabolic rate during these times? ______________________________

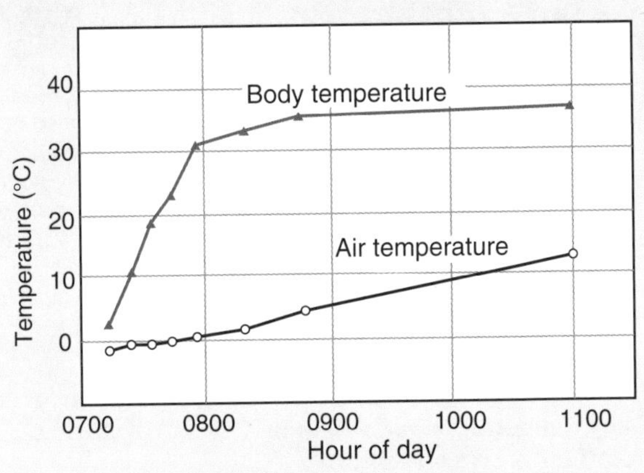

The Peruvian mountain lizard (*Liolaemus*) lives at altitudes of ~4000 m in Peru, where the air temperature is low, even in summer. It emerges in the morning when the air temperature is below freezing. By exposing itself to the sun, it rapidly heats up to a body temperature that enables it to be fully active. Once warm, the lizard maintains its preferred body temperature of around 35°C by changing posture and orientation to the sun and thereby controlling the amount of heat energy absorbed.

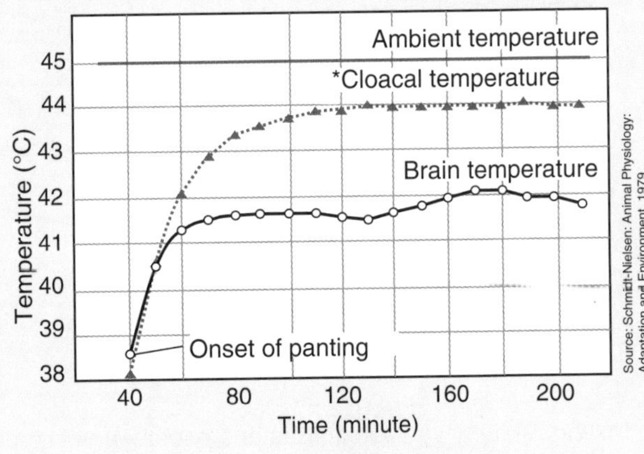

The chuckwalla (*Sauromalus*) is a widespread lizard species in the deserts of the southwestern United States and northern Mexico and is active in the temperature range 26-39°C (higher for basking). If moved from 15°C to 45°C, cloacal and brain temperatures increase rapidly. At ~41°C, these temperatures diverge and the brain stays at ~2°C below the cloacal temperature and 3°C below air temperature. The chuckwalla achieves this by panting. Its carotid arteries supplying the brain run close to the surface of the pharynx and heat is lost there by evaporative cooling. *Cloacal temperature measures deep body temperature through the cloaca. It is equivalent to rectal temperature in mammals.

5. (a) In the examples above, the increase in body temperature is very rapid. Why is this important for an ectotherm?

____

(b) What is the purpose of 'panting' in the chuckwalla? ______________________________

ISBN: 978-1-98-856656-6

6. Compare and contrast the thermoregulatory strategies of the Peruvian mountain lizard and the desert chuckwalla, relating any differences to the difference in their respective environments:

7. As illustrated in the examples opposite, ectotherms are capable of achieving and maintaining high, relatively constant body temperatures for relatively long periods in spite of environmental fluctuations. However, they also tolerate marked declines in body temperature to levels lower than are tolerated by most endotherms.

(a) Explain the advantage of allowing body temperature to fall when ambient temperature drops:

(b) Explain why ectothermy can be regarded as an adaptation to low or variable food supplies:

8. (a) In the generalized graph right, identify the optimum temperature range for an endotherm:

(b) Describe the energetic costs of thermoregulation (as measured by oxygen consumption) in an endotherm:

(c) Explain why this is the case:

Body temperature and oxygen consumption in an endotherm at different ambient temperatures

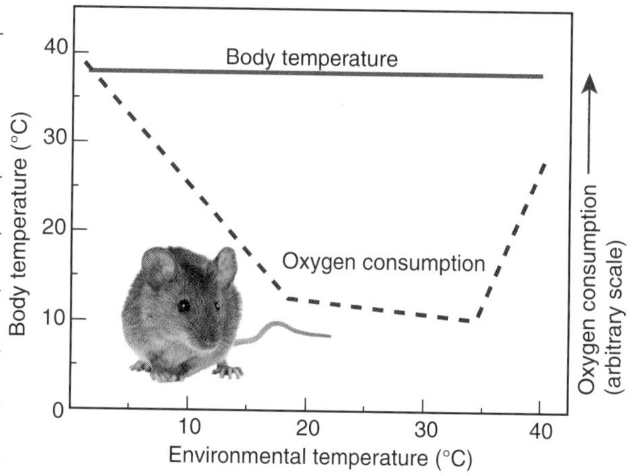

Some plants can also thermoregulate. Two of these are the sacred lotus and the eastern skunk cabbage (right). Both of these are able to maintain steady floral temperatures well above the air temperature even when the air temperature changes. High floral temperatures are maintained by uncoupling electron transport from ATP generation in the mitochondria, so energy is lost as heat. The skunk cabbage produces enough heat to melt the snow around it. The sacred lotus (*Nelumbo nucifera*) is able to maintain a floral temperature of around 30°C. This may help in dispersing scent and attracting pollinating insects to the warmth.

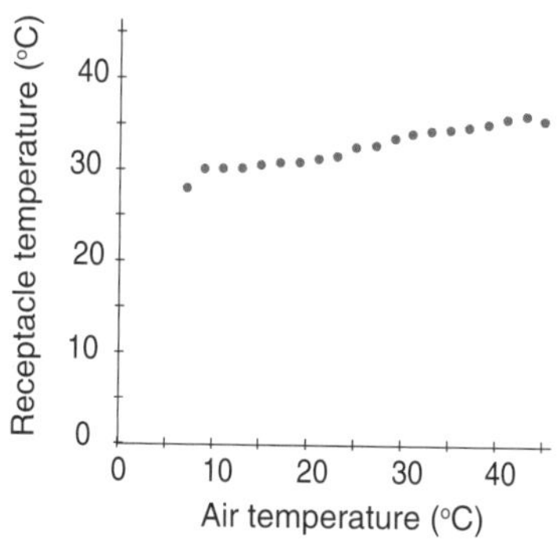

Eastern skunk cabbage

9. Give two reasons why regulating floral temperature could be an advantage to plants:

ISBN: 978-1-98-856656-6

231 Energy and Seasonal Breeding

Key Question: What strategies do animals use to ensure reproductive success?

Reproduction is an energetically expensive process, with energy expended in finding a mate, producing gametes, and raising young. The breeding cycles of organisms are normally timed so that young are produced when the food available (energy) is most abundant and conditions are favorable for survival of the young (spring and summer).

The reproductive cycle for animals that breed seasonally often begins in late fall, with a winter gestation, and birth of the young in spring. This maximizes the time for raising young before the next winter and coincides with the time of most food availability.

For Antarctic penguins, the environment dictates a slightly different strategy. Emperor penguins spend their summer feeding and begin their reproductive cycle at the beginning of the Antarctic winter. They move to breeding colonies where the chicks are raised through the winter, becoming independent by the start of the Antarctic summer. Raising chicks through the harsh Antarctic winter allows them to be independent by summer and so be better able to survive the following winter.

Emperor penguins must also have enough time after raising their chick to feed before their annual molt, during which they cannot enter the sea and so must again rely on their fat stores.

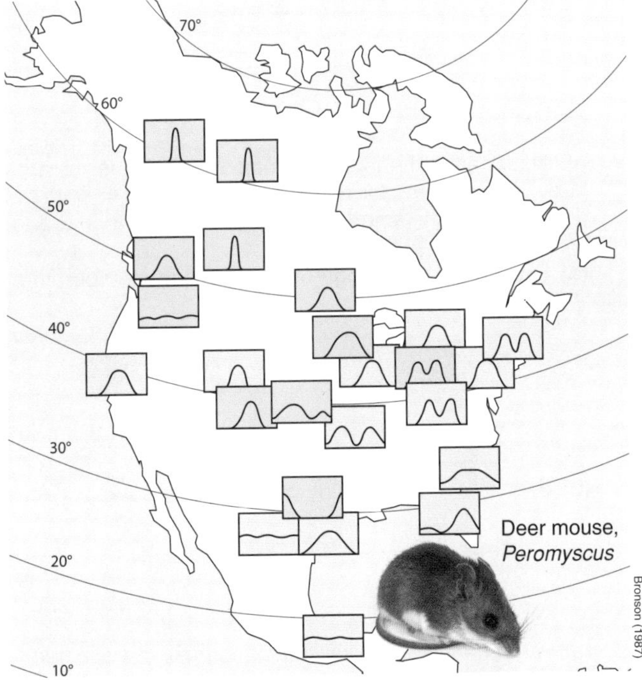

This diagram shows the relative proportions of female deer mice pregnant at any one time of the year (January on the left side of each graph, December on the right). At higher latitudes, females breed during summer months only, whereas at lower latitudes they breed throughout the year (the blue boxes show one single species).

- In many animals, male-male competition develops where the benefits (access to females or resources) outweigh the energy costs (fighting or territory defense). The amount of energy expended by males in attracting or monopolizing several females needs to be weighed against the assistance the females might need to raise the young and how far they range.
- It is energetically uneconomic for males to defend a large number of females if those females require male assistance to rear the young or travel a great distance to find food. Generally, the most energy expensive reproductive activities for males involve courtship and mating. In females, it is in pregnancy and rearing young.

1. Explain why many animals and plants have seasonal reproductive cycles:

2. Suggest why deer mice at 50°-60° latitude have a strict summer breeding period, unlike the deer mice at 20° latitude:

3. (a) In which part of the reproductive process do males tend to spend the most energy? Explain:

   (b) In which part of the reproductive process do females tend to spend the most energy?

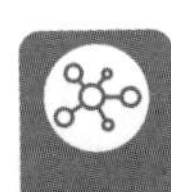
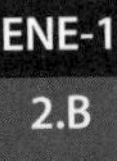
ENE-1 2.B

229

ISBN: 978-1-98-856656-6

232 Reproductive Allocation and Parental Care

Key Question: What are the costs and benefits of different reproductive strategies?

The **reproductive effort** is the amount of energy allocated to reproduction (production and care of young). Of the total reproductive effort, the amount remaining after production of the offspring can be allocated to parental care. At one extreme, most invertebrates expend their total reproductive effort in producing eggs and sperm and there is no parental care. At the other extreme, mammals invest heavily in a small number of offspring and the parental care cost is substantial. Between this is a continuum, with some animals adopting alternative strategies, such as brood parasitism. No strategy is necessarily 'better' than any other. They are different solutions to the problem of successful reproduction.

Many eggs or young produced

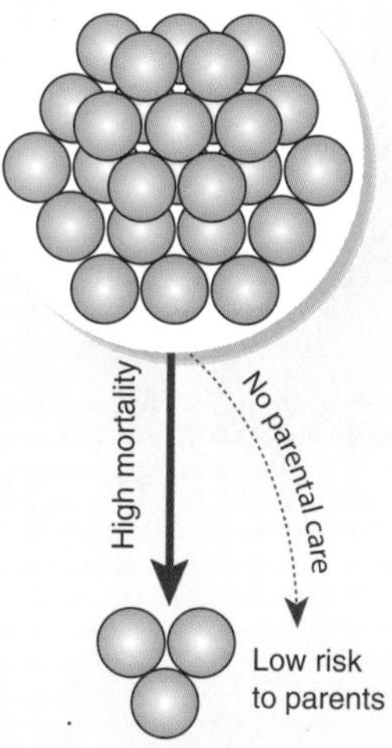

Low percentage of offspring survive to reproductive age

Little or no parental care

- Large number of offspring produced.
- Reproductive effort per offspring is low.
- Little or no parental care of offspring.
- Reproductive effort is put into producing the offspring, not parental care.
- Examples: most fish, amphibians, reptiles, and invertebrates.

Moderate number of eggs produced

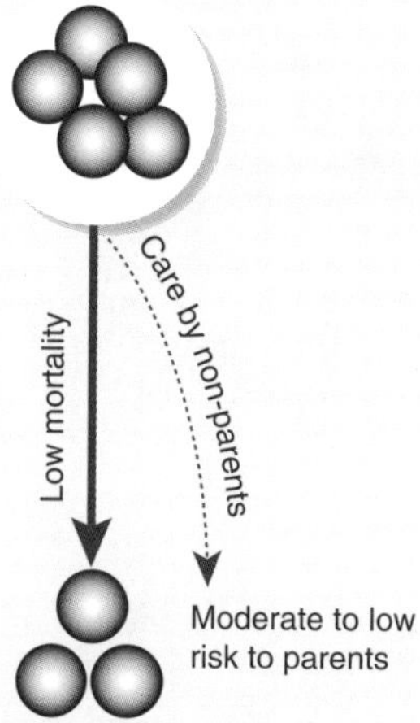

High percentage of offspring survive to reproductive age

Brood parasites

- Moderate number of offspring.
- Reproductive effort per offspring is moderate to low.
- Rely on others to raise offspring.
- Risk of egg loss is mitigated by distributing eggs amongst a number of hosts.
- Examples: some birds, insects, and fish.

Few eggs or young produced

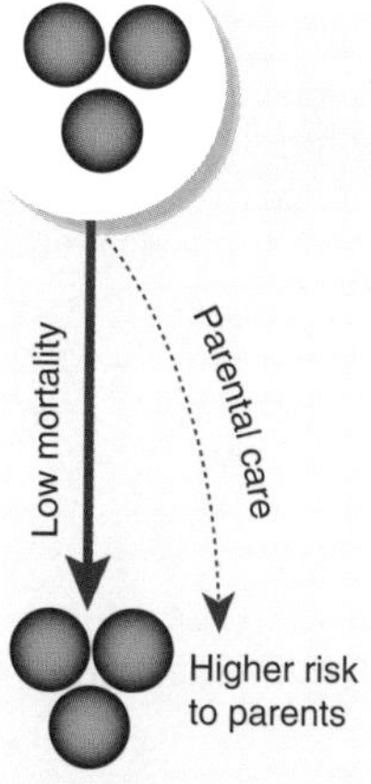

High percentage of offspring survive to reproductive age

Parental care

- Few offspring.
- Reproductive effort per offspring is high.
- Moderate to substantial care of offspring.
- Large reproductive effort put into raising offspring to a less vulnerable stage.
- Examples: most birds and mammals, some fish.

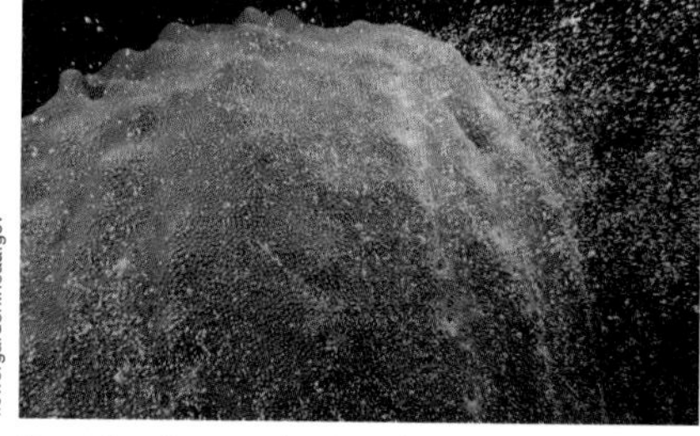

flowergarden.noaa.gov

Broadcast spawning involves no parental investment after the gametes are released.

Many invertebrates allocate all their reproductive effort to producing offspring and there is no parental care. Broadcast spawners such as clams and corals (above), release millions of gametes into the water. Very few of the planktonic larvae will survive. This is the most common reproductive strategy in the oceans and is typical of most marine invertebrates and many fish. Many amphibians are also broadcast spawners although there are many exceptions, including New Zealand's native frogs (*Leiopelma*) in which the males carry the offspring on their backs.

Dario Sanches cc 2.0

A shiny cowbird chick is fed by its host parent, a smaller rufous collared sparrow.

Brood parasitism is a strategy adopted by some birds, notably cuckoos and cowbirds. The brood parasite removes an egg from the nest of a host species and lays one of its own in its place. To reduce the risk of eggs being discovered and destroyed, the eggs are spread around a large number of hosts. Most avian brood parasites have short incubation times, so the egg hatches before those of the host and the imposter will eliminate all or most of the host's eggs/nestlings. The host then raises the parasite chick as if it were its own, even when the chick is larger and differs in appearance. The strategy is not without risk - only about half of the parasite's young survive.

Mammals have a high level of investment in offspring before and after birth.

Both mammals and birds are well known for their high levels of parental care and mammals also have a high level of prenatal investment. Other vertebrates, such as some amphibians, fish, and reptiles also provide care until the offspring are capable of fending for themselves. Bird parents are required to incubate their eggs in a nest and then feed the chicks until they are independent. Although most mammals give birth to well developed offspring, they are dependent on their mother for nourishment via suckling milk, as well as learning behaviors essential to their survival.

ISBN: 978-1-98-856656-6

The significance of reproductive investment

- Producing offspring demands enormous amount of energy and risk. In many vertebrate species, reproduction is almost entirely up to the female (males contributing only sperm) but in other species the male also provides support (e.g. by defending a territory or providing food for the female).
- Because the female is most heavily invested in the offspring, it is important that she has the best possible reproductive outcome each time she mates, and mate choice is critical. In general, females have a limited reproductive outcome and can only produce so many eggs or offspring in a lifetime. For example, a human female produces one egg a month for about 40 years, a maximum of ~480 eggs in a lifetime. Given that gestation and breast feeding (which suppresses ovulation) may take two years, only about 20 children can be raised in the average lifetime (the record is reportedly 69).
- Males, on the other hand, have less invested in offspring. They produce sperm continuously and put no direct energy into the offspring until at least birth or egg laying. Potentially, males could fertilize unlimited numbers of females and so produce far more young with little additional effort.
- These differences in reproductive investment have been important in the evolution of mating systems, e.g. monogamy, with animals adopting strategies that maximize reproductive success in their particular physical and social environment.

In ospreys, both parents are needed to successfully rear the chicks. Monogamy is a common mating system when biparental care is needed for offspring survival. Ospreys usually mate for life and raising the young requires a five month commitment.

A South American sea lion male keeps a harem of up to 18 females and their young, which he protects.

1. Describe the different ways in which animals can allocate their total reproductive effort:

2. Animals with parental care protect the investment they have already made in offspring. Explain how factors in the environment (e.g. food resources and risks to young) might influence how much care is provided by each parent:

3. (a) What might be the benefits of a brood parasitism strategy to the brood parasite?

   (b) What adaptations of the brood parasite help to maximize the success of its strategy?

4. The common cuckoo (*Cuculus canorus*) is a widespread brood parasite. It parasitizes a range of species including dunnocks, meadow pipits, and reed warblers but females specialize in parasitizing a single species, whose eggs it mimics. This characteristic is heritable, although males fertilize females of all lines, which maintains gene flow in the population.

   (a) Explain how a female cuckoo's strategy of parasitizing only a single species contributes to the success of their reproductive strategy:

   (b) What is the genetic effect of males showing no such preference for females?

Reed warbler feeds common cuckoo

Per Harald Olsen CC 3.0

ISBN: 978-1-98-856656-6

233 Metabolism and Body Size

Key Question: What is mass specific metabolic rate and why are mass-specific metabolic rates higher in smaller animals?

Metabolism is inefficient and produces heat. Animals that use this metabolic heat to maintain body temperature are called endotherms. Those that do not are called ectotherms. The baseline metabolic rate of an animal is measured as the basal metabolic rate (BMR) for an endotherm or as the standard metabolic rate (SMR) for an ectotherm. Clearly, larger animals have higher metabolic rates (total kJ used per day) because there is more metabolizing tissue, but when we look at the per-mass (per gram) metabolic rate, the situation is the opposite.

In both endotherms and ectotherms, smaller animals have higher mass-specific MRs than larger animals. This relationship holds true across many species and can be described mathematically. This is in part related to the higher surface area to volume ratios of small animals (they lose heat faster so must also generate it faster) but it is not the entire story as the relationship holds even for ectotherms.

For example, during a deep dive, the largest whales are able to stay submerged for almost two hours. However, small diving mammals, such as the water shrew, can only stay submerged for 30 s. Part of the reason for these variations is the obvious difference in the size of their lungs and their body's ability to store oxygen. The most important factor is the difference in the rate of oxygen consumption per unit mass (a measure of the mass-specific metabolic rate). The water shrew uses oxygen at a rate of 7.4 L/kg/h. The blue whale uses just 0.02 L/kg/ h.

Animal	Body mass (kg)	O_2 consumption (L/kg/h)
Shrew	0.005	7.40
Harvest mouse	0.009	2.50
Kangaroo mouse	0.015	1.80
Mouse	0.025	1.65
Ground squirrel	0.096	1.03
Rat	0.290	0.87
Cat	2.5	0.68
Dog	11.7	0.33
Sheep	42.7	0.22
Human	70	0.21
Horse	650	0.11
Elephant	3830	0.07

Data: Schmidt-Nielsen

Body mass vs oxygen consumption rate in mammals

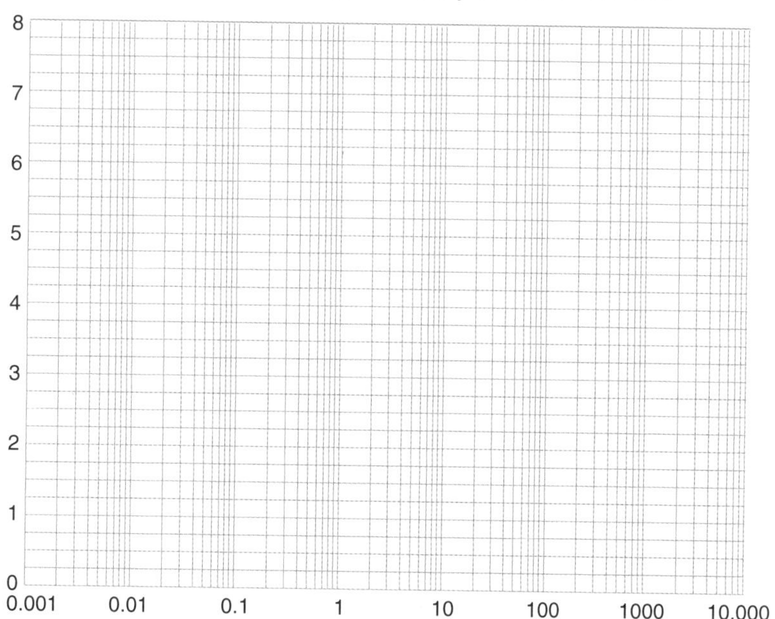

1. (a) Use the semi-log grid above to plot the rate of oxygen consumption for the animals listed in the table:

   (b) What is the shape of the graph? ______________________________

   (c) Explain why the data are plotted on a logarithmic scale for body mass: ______________________________

   (d) Using the graph, what is the expected oxygen consumption rate of a mammal with a body weight of exactly 1 kg?

ISBN: 978-1-98-856656-6

The relationship between specific metabolic rate and body mass for mammals is expressed as B ~ 70 $M^{-0.25}$. That is, the specific metabolic rate (B) of any mammal is proportional to its mass (M (kg)) to the power of -0.25. Thus a 2 kg cat has a specific metabolic rate 3.1 times less than a 0.02 kg mouse. However, there appear to be many exceptions so there is some debate over the validity of the function.

The relationship of specific metabolic rate and size also appears in organisms other than mammals. Birds follow a relationship very close to that of mammals. Invertebrates and unicellular organisms all follow similar patterns in that the bigger they are, the slower their mass-specific metabolic rate. Trees follow a relationship close to 1 (i.e. a tree half the size of another will have a specific metabolic rate twice as great).

Exactly why metabolic rates are slower in large animals is uncertain. Certainly the surface area to volume ratio of organisms appears to be involved (small animals radiate more heat per volume than large ones). However, this does not explain why ectotherms follow a similar relationship to mammals. It may be because smaller animals have more structural mass per volume, which has a higher cost to maintain.

2. Calculate the following:

   (a) How many times greater the specific metabolic rate of a shrew is than a horse: ____________________

   (b) How many times less the specific metabolic rate of a human is than a rat: ____________________

3. Explain why per mass oxygen consumption per hour is a good indicator of mass specific metabolic rate: ____________________

4. Explain why a small mammal (e.g. a shrew) needs to eat proportionally more than a large mammal (e.g. an elephant):

5. Explain how specific metabolic rate may affect the diving times of mammals: ____________________

6. The plot right shows the total surface area of lung tissue in various mammals against the rate of oxygen consumption:

   (a) Describe the relationship between a mammal's lung surface area and their oxygen consumption:

   (b) Is this what you would expect? Explain: ____________________

Lung alveolar surface area (m^2): 0.01, 0.1, 1.0, 10, 100, 1000

Oxygen consumption (L O_2/h): 0.001, 0.01, 0.1, 1, 10, 100

Whale, Slope = 1.0, Cow, Pig, Bear, Goat, Porpoise, Human, Manatee, Dog, Dugong, Raccoon, Rabbit, Armadillo, Cat, Woodchuck, Monkey, Rat, Guinea pig, Shrew, Bat, Mouse

ISBN: 978-1-98-856656-6

234 Energy in Ecosystems

Key Question: How is abundance or biomass related to the available energy in an ecosystem?

The Sun is the ultimate source of energy for most ecosystems on Earth. As energy moves through the biotic environment (life) on Earth, it is used to combine chemical elements into biologically useful forms (e.g. fats). These transformations result in some energy being stored as biomass and some being dissipated to the environment as heat, usually during cellular respiration. Energy is transferred between organisms by the exchange of matter (in feeding). Some of the energy stored in that matter is lost with each transfer, so each time matter is exchanged in one feeding event, less energy is available for the next. Each organism in an ecosystem is assigned to a **trophic level** based on its position in this chain of feeding relationships (**food chain**). The higher the trophic level, the less energy is available to support the total number of organisms at that level. Typically, only 10% of the energy available at one trophic level is transferred to the next. This loss is multiplied over the length of a food chain so that only abut 0.1% of the energy fixed in photosynthesis can flow all the way to a tertiary consumer. The reduction in energy availability at successive trophic levels limits the abundance of top level carnivores (**apex predators**) that an ecosystem can support and the number of links in a food chain.

Quantitative models of energy flow in ecosystems

- We can account for the transfer of energy from its input (as solar radiation) to its release as heat, because energy is conserved. An ecological study of a grazing food chain in a Michigan old field (a previously grazed, then abandoned, area) quantified energy transfers from vegetation to meadow voles (right) to weasels (see data below).
- Other feeding groups form supplementary food chains in ecosystems and the interaction of many food chains forms a complex model of interactions called a **food web**. By examining changes in one component of the system, it can be possible to predict the effects on other components. Detrital food webs are often connected to grazing food webs by consumers (generally primary consumers) that feature in both food webs.

Tabulated data of energy transfers in an old field community in Michigan

Data after Golley (1960). Figures in kJ/ha²/year

SUNLIGHT AND PRODUCERS	
Sun's energy utilized	1.97×10^7
Gross 1° production	2.44×10^5
Producer respiration	3.67×10^4
Net 1° production	2.07×10^5
Available to voles	6.61×10^4
To other consumers	6.46×10^4

VOLES (*Microtus*)	
Consumed by voles	1046.00
Vole respiration	711.00
Wasted/unused food	309.88
Vole (2°) production	21.63
Vole immigration	56.48
Population increase	1569

WEASELS (*Mustela*)	
To other consumers	50.21
Consumed by weasel	24.32
Weasel respiration	22.74
Wasted/unused food	1.08
Weasel production	0.54
Population increase	117

VISUAL MODEL

This model does not show the amount of incoming light plants do not utilize because it is not absorbed (it is reflected off surfaces or absorbed by other molecules).

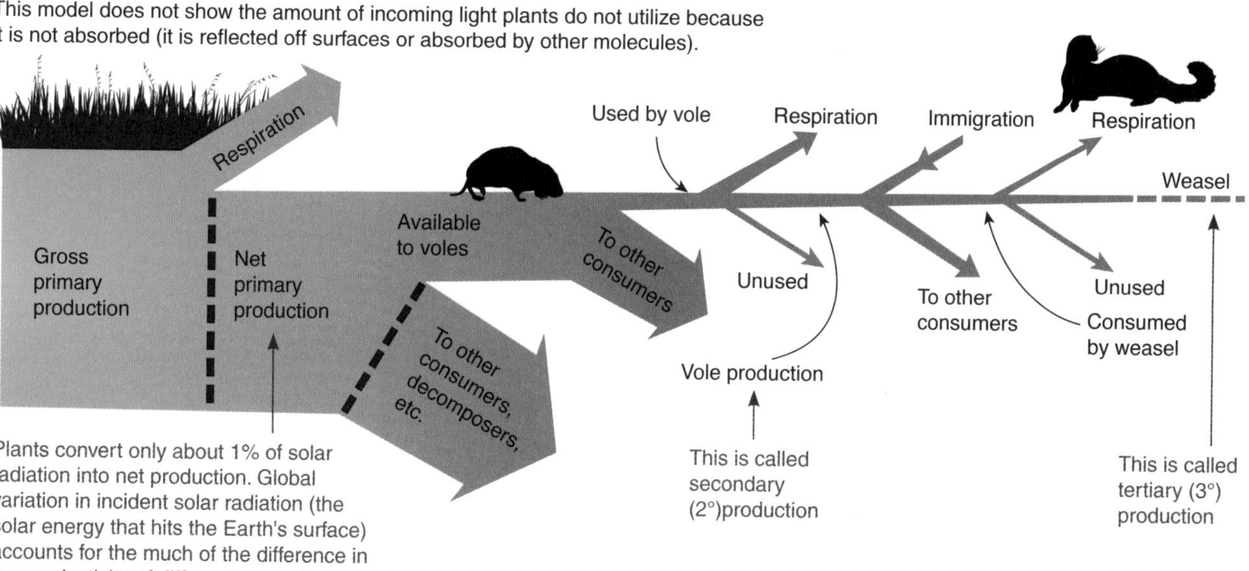
Respiration
Used by vole
Respiration
Immigration
Respiration
Weasel
Gross primary production
Net primary production
Available to voles
To other consumers
Unused
To other consumers
Unused
Consumed by weasel
To other consumers, decomposers, etc.
Vole production
Plants convert only about 1% of solar radiation into net production. Global variation in incident solar radiation (the solar energy that hits the Earth's surface) accounts for the much of the difference in the productivity of different ecosystems, assuming water is not limiting.
This is called secondary (2°)production
This is called tertiary (3°) production

ISBN: 978-1-98-856656-6

236

235
ENE-1 6.D
ENE-1 5.A
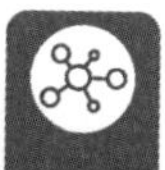

Ecological pyramids show energy and biomass relationships

- Ecological pyramids are graphical models of the quantitative differences between trophic levels in an ecosystem. The trophic structure can be represented using energy, biomass, or numbers of organisms at each trophic level. The first trophic level is placed at the bottom of the pyramid and subsequent trophic levels are stacked in their 'feeding sequence'. As with the model on the previous page, these energy transfers can be measured. Ecological pyramids therefore provide a convenient quantitative model for the relationship between different trophic levels in an ecosystem.
- Note how decomposers are not included in the models pictured. Sometimes decomposers are shown as a separate parallel level to first order consumers (see opposite), but often they are collapsed into the consumer levels.

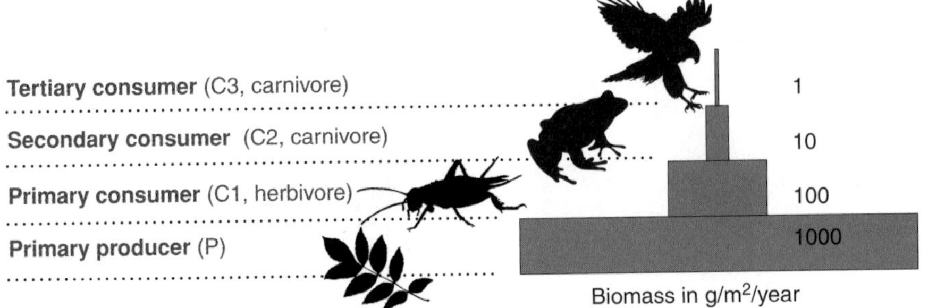

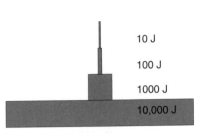

> The percentage of energy transferred from one trophic level to the next is the **trophic efficiency**. It varies between 5-20% and measures the efficiency of energy transfer. A figure of 10% trophic efficiency is often used.

Biomass in a forest community

Biomass pyramids measure the mass of biological material at each trophic level. Water content of organisms varies, so 'dry mass' is often used. Organism size is taken into account, allowing meaningful comparisons of different trophic levels.

Energy in a forest community

Pyramids of energy are often very similar to biomass pyramids. The energy content at each trophic level is generally comparable to the biomass (i.e. similar amounts of dry biomass tend to have about the same energy content).

1. For the energy flow diagram of the Michigan old field shown on the previous page, calculate (to the nearest whole value):

   (a) The % of the food available eaten by voles: ______________________

   (b) The % of voles available eaten by weasels: ______________________

   (c) The % of the energy assimilated voles lose through respiration: ______________________

   (d) The % of the energy assimilated weasels lose through respiration: ______________________

2. Do you think that weasels are the top predator in the grazing old field system described on the previous page? Explain:

3. What is the ultimate source of energy in most ecosystems? ______________________

4. Explain how the energy available at each trophic level is related to the biomass in the ecosystem:

5. Explain why a population of secondary consumers is smaller than the population of primary consumers they feed on:

ISBN: 978-1-98-856656-6

Why are some pyramids inverted?

- As you saw on the opposite page, pyramids of energy and biomass often look similar. In most pyramids of biomass, such as the pyramids for Wisconsin Lake and Enewetok, different trophic efficiencies are represented by the sizes of the stacked levels and the producer biomass is the largest. In the example of the English Channel, biomass of the lower trophic level is less than the biomass of the next higher trophic level. In the oceans, algal doubling rate is much higher than that of the zooplankton that eat them and, at any point in time, the total amount of biomass in the algae is small.
- If we examine a pyramid of energy where the decomposer contribution (D) is quantified, we can see how much energy flows through detrital-decomposer food chains. Pyramids of energy can never be inverted.

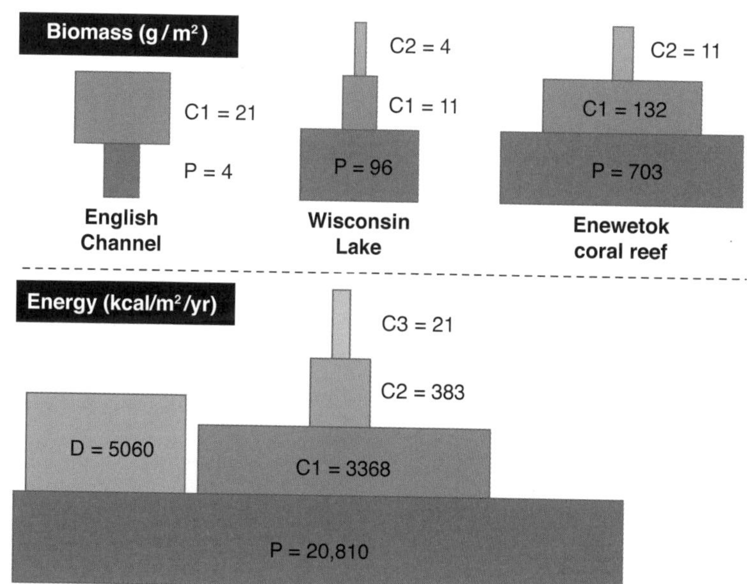

What about disturbances?

- Disruptions to ecosystems through loss of productivity can alter the abundance of organisms at higher levels and can even lead to a simplification of food chains and a loss of consumer species.
- In undisturbed communities, producer levels contain more biomass than higher trophic levels. Fires reduce producer biomass, which has an impact on the higher trophic levels from the bottom up. In contrast, an increase in predation, such as might occur with the introduction of predator from outside its natural range, affects lower levels from the top down.
- Communities already compromised by introduced predators will be more vulnerable to disturbances (such as fire) that reduce producer biomass, because primary consumers will feel the impact of both a reduction in producer biomass and predation.

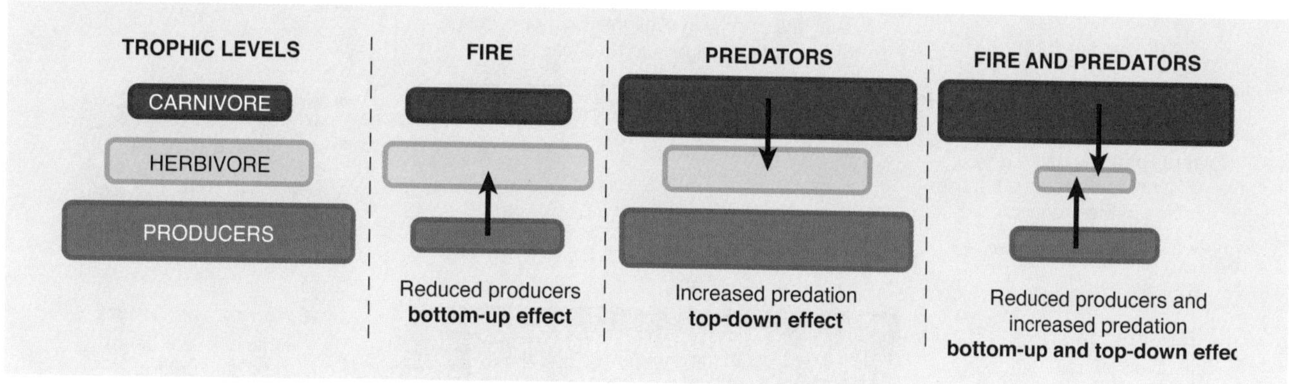

6. (a) Describe examples of events that could lead to a loss of producer biomass: ______

(b) Use the schematics above to predict the likely the effect of reduced producer biomass on other trophic levels: ______

7. In terms of energy availability, explain the effect of introduced carnivores on a system: ______

ISBN: 978-1-98-856656-6

235 The Flow of Energy In Ecosystems

Key Question: What is the difference between the way autotrophs and heterotrophs obtain their energy and the molecules they need to grow?

Living things obtain their energy for metabolism in two main ways. **Autotrophs** (producers) use the energy in sunlight or inorganic molecules to make their own food. **Heterotrophs** (consumers) rely on other organisms as a source of energy and carbon. All other organisms depend on producers, even if they do not consume them directly. The energy flow into and out of each trophic (feeding) level can be represented on a diagram using arrows of different sizes to represent relative amounts of energy lost from different trophic levels.

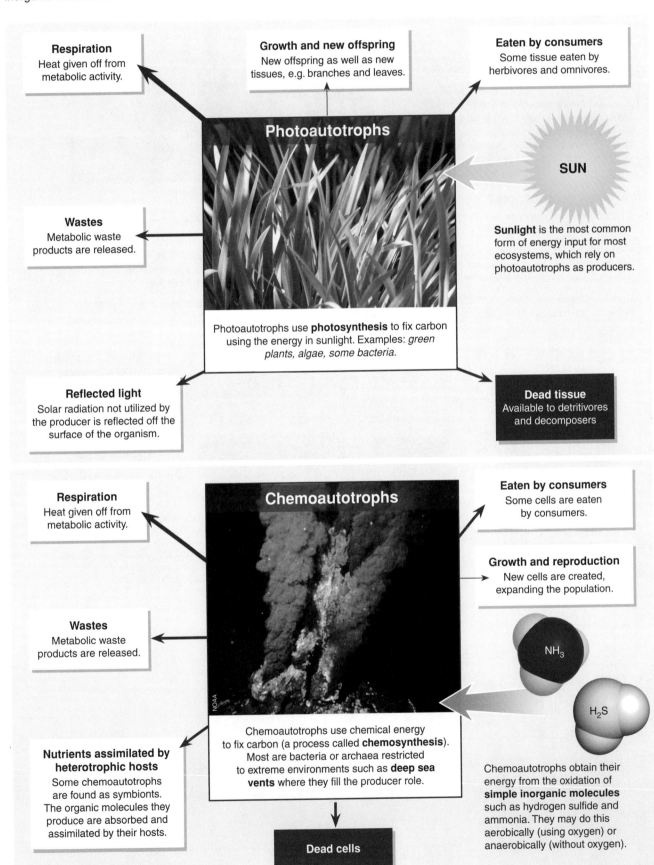

Respiration
Heat given off from metabolic activity.

Growth and new offspring
New offspring as well as new tissues, e.g. branches and leaves.

Eaten by consumers
Some tissue eaten by herbivores and omnivores.

Photoautotrophs

SUN

Sunlight is the most common form of energy input for most ecosystems, which rely on photoautotrophs as producers.

Wastes
Metabolic waste products are released.

Photoautotrophs use **photosynthesis** to fix carbon using the energy in sunlight. Examples: *green plants, algae, some bacteria*.

Reflected light
Solar radiation not utilized by the producer is reflected off the surface of the organism.

Dead tissue
Available to detritivores and decomposers

Respiration
Heat given off from metabolic activity.

Chemoautotrophs

Eaten by consumers
Some cells are eaten by consumers.

Growth and reproduction
New cells are created, expanding the population.

Wastes
Metabolic waste products are released.

NH_3

H_2S

NOAA

Chemoautotrophs use chemical energy to fix carbon (a process called **chemosynthesis**). Most are bacteria or archaea restricted to extreme environments such as **deep sea vents** where they fill the producer role.

Nutrients assimilated by heterotrophic hosts
Some chemoautotrophs are found as symbionts. The organic molecules they produce are absorbed and assimilated by their hosts.

Dead cells

Chemoautotrophs obtain their energy from the oxidation of **simple inorganic molecules** such as hydrogen sulfide and ammonia. They may do this aerobically (using oxygen) or anaerobically (without oxygen).

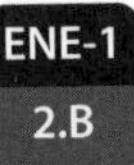

ISBN: 978-1-98-856656-6

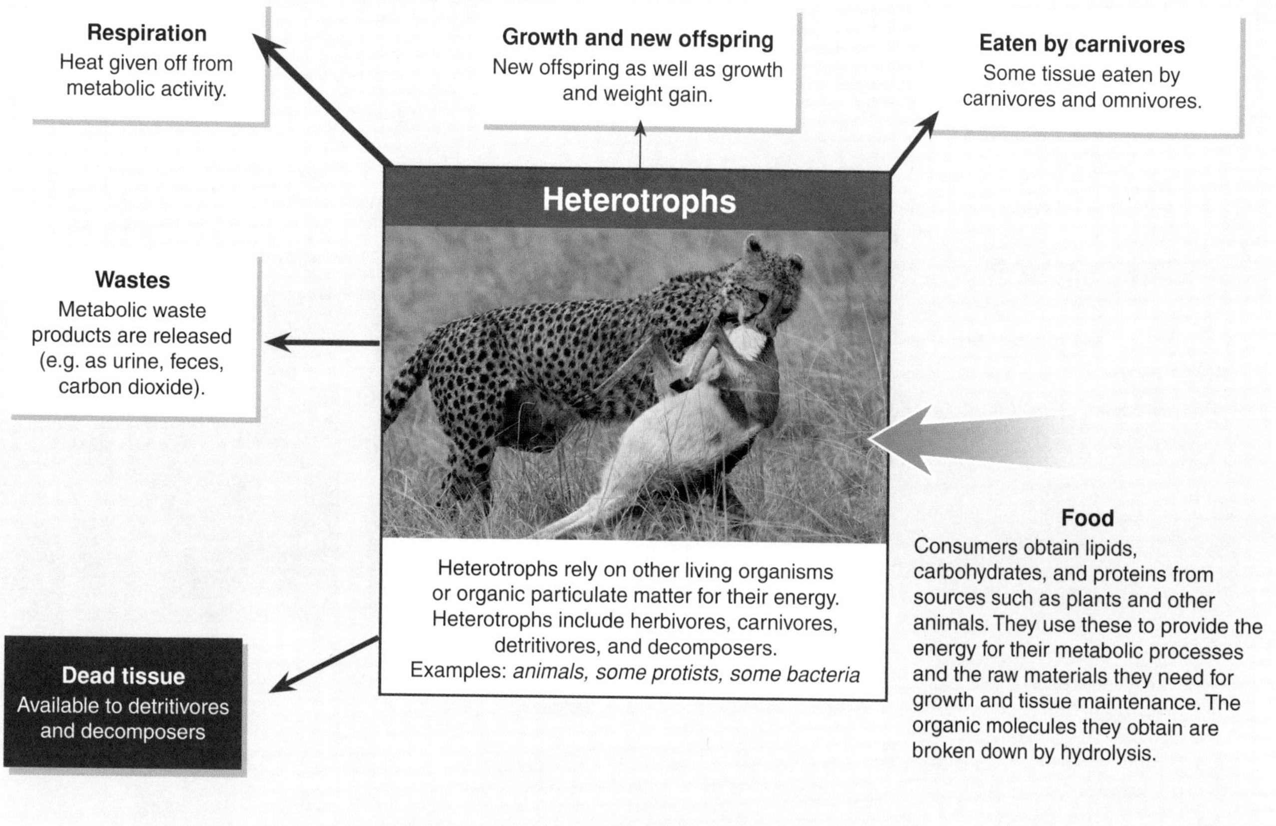

Respiration
Heat given off from metabolic activity.

Growth and new offspring
New offspring as well as growth and weight gain.

Eaten by carnivores
Some tissue eaten by carnivores and omnivores.

Heterotrophs

Wastes
Metabolic waste products are released (e.g. as urine, feces, carbon dioxide).

Heterotrophs rely on other living organisms or organic particulate matter for their energy. Heterotrophs include herbivores, carnivores, detritivores, and decomposers.
Examples: *animals, some protists, some bacteria*

Food
Consumers obtain lipids, carbohydrates, and proteins from sources such as plants and other animals. They use these to provide the energy for their metabolic processes and the raw materials they need for growth and tissue maintenance. The organic molecules they obtain are broken down by hydrolysis.

Dead tissue
Available to detritivores and decomposers

1. Study the diagrams on energy flow relating to **photoautotrophs**, **chemoautotrophs**, and **heterotrophs**. Explain how the activities of autotrophs and heterotrophs enable the flow of energy in an ecosystem:

2. Describe how energy may be lost from organisms in the form of:

   (a) Wastes:

   (b) Respiration:

3. Explain why so little energy is available for growth and reproduction, regardless of trophic group:

4. Explain the ecological importance of chemoautotrophic organisms in deep sea environments:

5. In what way is the chemoautotrophic system of the deep sea thermal vent linked to other ecological systems?

ISBN: 978-1-98-856656-6

236 Investigating Trophic Efficiencies

STUDENT SUPPORT FOR INVESTIGATION 10: *Energy dynamics*

The gross primary production of any ecosystem will be determined by the efficiency with which solar energy is captured by photosynthesis. The efficiency of subsequent energy transfers will determine the amount of energy available to consumers. These energy transfers can be quantified using measurements of dry mass. In this activity, you will calculate energy and biomass transfers in real and experimental systems. This analysis will help you to more easily plan and carry out your own investigation.

Production vs productivity: What's the difference?

Strictly speaking, the primary production of an ecosystem is distinct from its productivity, which is the amount of production per unit time (a rate). However because values for production (accumulated biomass) are usually given for a certain period of time in order to be meaningful, the two terms are often used interchangeably.

Corn field

Mature pasture

1. The energy budgets of two agricultural systems (4000 m^2 area) were measured over a growing season of 100 days. The results are tabulated right.

	Corn field	Mature pasture
	kJ x 10^6	kJ x 10^6
Incident solar radiation	8548	1971
Plant utilization		
Net primary production (NPP)	105.8	20.7
Respiration (R)	32.2	3.7
Gross primary production (GPP)	138.0	24.4

(a) For each system, calculate the percentage efficiency of energy utilization (how much incident solar radiation is captured by photosynthesis):

Corn: ______________________

Mature pasture: ______________________

(b) For each system, calculate the percentage losses to respiration:

Corn: ______________________

Mature pasture: ______________________

(c) For each system, calculate the percentage efficiency of NPP:

Corn: ______________________

Mature pasture: ______________________

(d) Which system has the greatest efficiency of energy transfer to biomass? ______________________

Estimating NPP in *Brassica rapa*

Background

Brassica rapa (right) is a fast growing brassica species, which can complete its life cycle in as little as 40 days if growth conditions are favorable. A class of students wished to estimate the gross and net primary productivity of a crop of these plants using wet and dry mass measurements made at three intervals over 21 days.

The method

- Seven groups of three students each grew 60 *B. rapa* plants in plant trays under controlled conditions. On day 7, each group made a random selection of 10 plants and removed them, with roots intact. The 10 plants were washed, blotted dry, and then weighed collectively (giving wet mass).
- The 10 plants were placed in a ceramic drying bowl and placed in a drying oven at 200°C for 24 hours, then weighed (giving dry mass).
- On day 14 and again on day 21, the procedure was repeated with a further 10 plants (randomly selected).
- The full results for group 1 are presented in Table 1 on the next page. You will complete the calculation columns.

ISBN: 978-1-98-856656-6

Table 1: Group 1's results for growth of 10 *B. rapa* plants over 21 days

Age in days	Wet mass of 10 plants (g)	Dry mass of 10 plants (g)	Percent biomass	Energy in 10 plants (kJ)	Energy per plant (kJ)	NPP (kJ/plant/d)
7	19.6	4.2				
14	38.4	9.3				
21	55.2	15.5				

2. Calculate percent biomass using the equation: % biomass = dry mass ÷ wet mass x 100. Enter the values in Table 1.

3. Each gram of dry biomass is equivalent to 18.2 kJ of energy. Calculate the amount of energy per 10 plants and per plant for plants at 7, 14, and 21 days. Enter the values in Table 1.

4. Calculate the Net Primary Productivity per plant, i.e. the amount of energy stored as biomass per day (kJ/plant/d). Enter the values in Table 1. We are using per plant in this exercise as we do not have a unit area of harvest.

5. The other 6 groups of students completed the same procedure and, at the end of the 21 days, the groups compared their results for NPP. The results are presented in Table 2, below.

   Transfer group 1's NPP results from Table 1 to complete the table of results and calculate the mean NPP for *B. rapa*.

Table 2: Class results for NPP of *B. rapa* over 21 days

Time in days (d)	Group NPP (kJ/plant/d)							
	1	2	3	4	5	6	7	Mean NPP
7		1.05	1.05	1.13	1.09	1.13	1.09	
14		1.17	1.21	1.25	1.21	1.25	1.17	
21		1.30	1.34	1.30	1.34	1.38	1.34	

6. On the grid (right), plot the class mean NPP vs time.

7. (a) What is happening to the NPP over time?

   (b) Explain why this is happening:

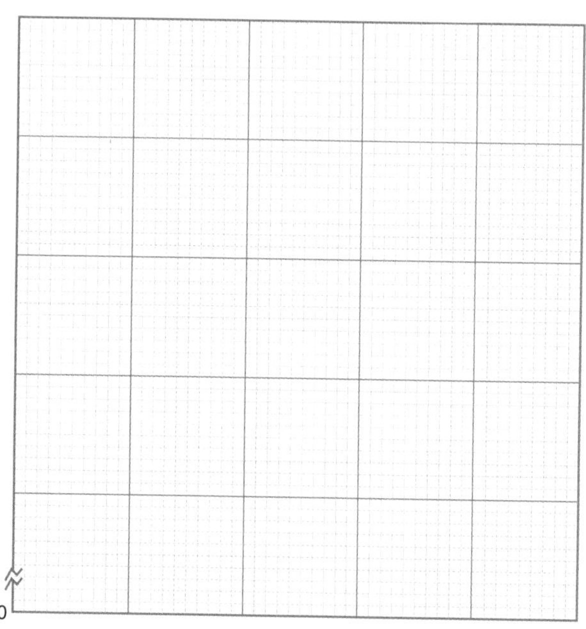

8. What would you need to know to determine the gross primary productivity of *B. rapa*?

9. Net production in consumers (N), can be expressed as **N = I – (W + R)**, where I = energy gain, W = wastes, and R = respiration. Red meat contains ~700 kJ per 100 g. If N = 20% of the energy gain, how much energy is lost as W and R?

ISBN: 978-1-98-856656-6

Calculating energy flow from producers to primary consumers

Secondary production is the generation of primary consumer (heterotrophic) biomass in a system. In this experiment, students determined the net secondary production and respiratory losses using 12 day old cabbage white larvae feeding on Brussels sprouts. Of the NPP from the Brussels sprouts that is consumed by the larvae, some will be used in cellular respiration, some will be available to secondary consumers (the **net secondary production**) and some will be lost as egested waste products (**frass**).

The method

- The wet mass of ten, 12 day old larvae, and approximately 30 g Brussels sprouts was accurately measured and recorded.
- The larvae and Brussel sprouts were placed into an aerated container. After three days the container was disassembled and the wet mass of the Brussels sprouts, larvae, and frass was individually measured and recorded.
- The Brussels sprouts, larvae and frass were placed in separate containers and placed in a drying oven and their dry mass was recorded.

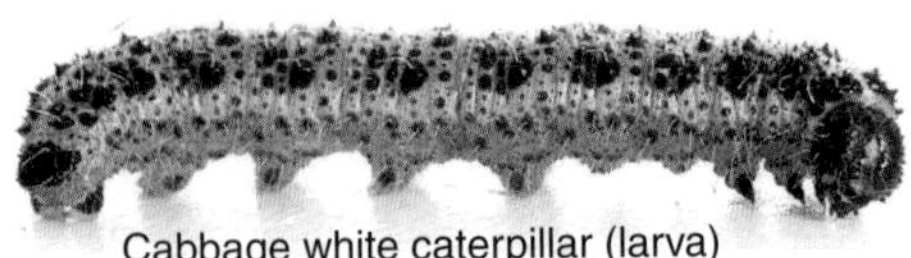

Cabbage white caterpillar (larva)

Note: We assume the % biomass of Brussels sprouts and caterpillars on day 1 is the same as the calculated value from day 3.

Table 3: Brussels sprouts

	Day 1	Day 3	
Wet mass of Brussels sprouts	30 g	11 g	g consumed =
Dry mass of Brussels sprouts	–	2.2 g	
Plant proportion biomass (dry/wet)			
Plant energy consumed (wet mass x proportion biomass x 18.2 kJ)			kJ consumed per 10 larvae =
Plant energy consumed ÷ no. of larvae			kJ consumed per larva (**E**) =

Table 4: Caterpillars (larvae)

	Day 1	Day 3	
Wet mass of 10 larvae	0.3 g	1.8 g	g gained =
Wet mass per larva			g gained per larva =
Dry mass of 10 larvae	–	0.27 g	
Larva proportion biomass (dry/wet)			
Energy production per larva (wet mass x proportion biomass x 23.0 kJ)			kJ gained per larva (**S**) =

Table 5: Frass

	Day 3
Dry mass frass from 10 larvae	0.5 g
Frass energy (waste) = frass dry mass x 19.87 kJ	
Energy from frass from 1 larva (**W**)	

10. Complete the calculations in tables 3-5 above.

11. (a) Write the net secondary production per larva value here: ______

(b) Write the equation to calculate the percentage efficiency of energy transfer from producers to consumers (use the notation provided) and calculate the value here:

______

(c) Is this value roughly what you would expect? Explain: ______

______

______

12. (a) Write the equation to calculate respiratory losses per larva (use the notation provided): ______

(b) Calculate the respiratory losses per larva here: ______

13. Why can't we measure the actual dry biomass of Brussels sprouts and larvae on day 1? ______

______

ISBN: 978-1-98-856656-6

237 The Dynamics of Populations

Key Question: What are the attributes of populations that are not shown by individuals and why are they important?

A population refers to all the organisms of a species in a particular area. Population ecologists are concerned about population attributes that can be measured or calculated to provide information about the population. Such attributes include aspects of population composition, distribution and abundance, and dynamics (below). One way to retrieve information about populations is to sample them. Sampling involves collecting data, directly or indirectly, about features of the population from samples (since populations are usually too large to examine in total).

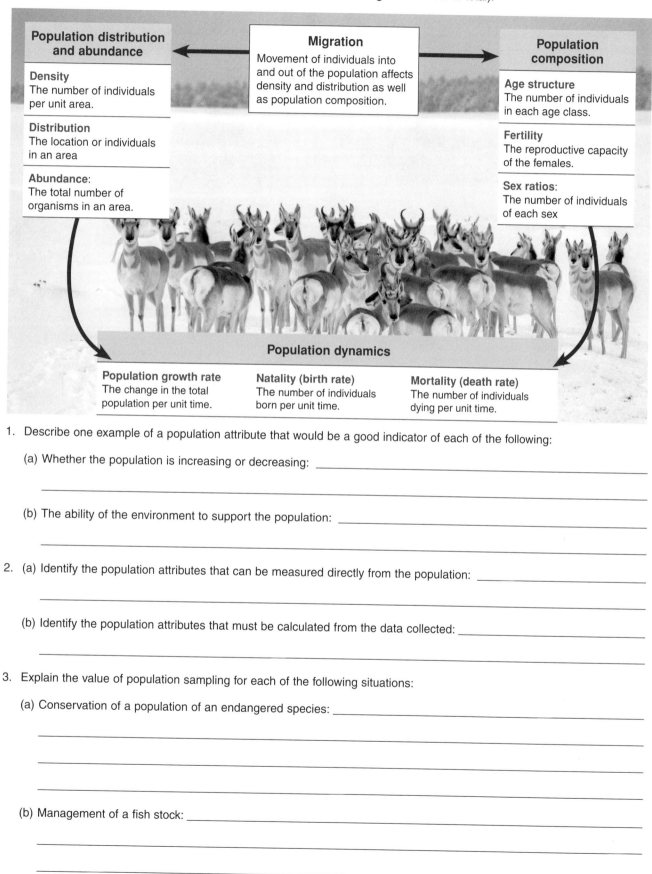

Population distribution and abundance
Density
The number of individuals per unit area.
Distribution
The location or individuals in an area
Abundance:
The total number of organisms in an area.
Migration
Movement of individuals into and out of the population affects density and distribution as well as population composition.
Population composition
Age structure
The number of individuals in each age class.
Fertility
The reproductive capacity of the females.
Sex ratios:
The number of individuals of each sex
Population dynamics
Population growth rate
The change in the total population per unit time.
Natality (birth rate)
The number of individuals born per unit time.
Mortality (death rate)
The number of individuals dying per unit time.

1. Describe one example of a population attribute that would be a good indicator of each of the following:

(a) Whether the population is increasing or decreasing: ______

(b) The ability of the environment to support the population: ______

2. (a) Identify the population attributes that can be measured directly from the population: ______

(b) Identify the population attributes that must be calculated from the data collected: ______

3. Explain the value of population sampling for each of the following situations:

(a) Conservation of a population of an endangered species: ______

(b) Management of a fish stock: ______

ISBN: 978-1-98-856656-6

Quantifying change in populations

- **Population dynamics** is the mathematical study of how and why populations change in size and structure over time.
- The number of individuals in a population (N) is calculated by knowing the gains and losses to the population. Births, deaths, immigrations (movements into the population) and emigrations (movements out of the population) are events that together determine the number of individuals in a population. Scientists usually measure the rate of these events, which are influenced by the resources available and the biotic potential, which varies among species.

Births, deaths, immigration (movements into the population) and emigration (movements out of the population) are events that determine the population size. Population growth depends on the number of individuals added to the population from births and immigration, minus the number lost through deaths and emigration. This is expressed as:

Population growth =
(Births + Immigration) – (Deaths + Emigration)
(B + I) – (D + E)

The difference between immigration and emigration gives net migration. Ecologists usually measure the **rate** of these events. These rates are influenced by **limiting factors** in the environment (such as availability of food, water, or habitat) and by the characteristics of the organisms themselves (their **biotic potential** or natural capacity to increase, *r*).

Rates in population studies are commonly expressed in one of two ways:

- **Numbers per unit time**, e.g. 20,150 live births per year. The birth rate is termed the natality, whereas the death rate is the mortality.
- **Per capita rate** (number per head of population), e.g. 122 live births per 1000 individuals per year (12.2%).

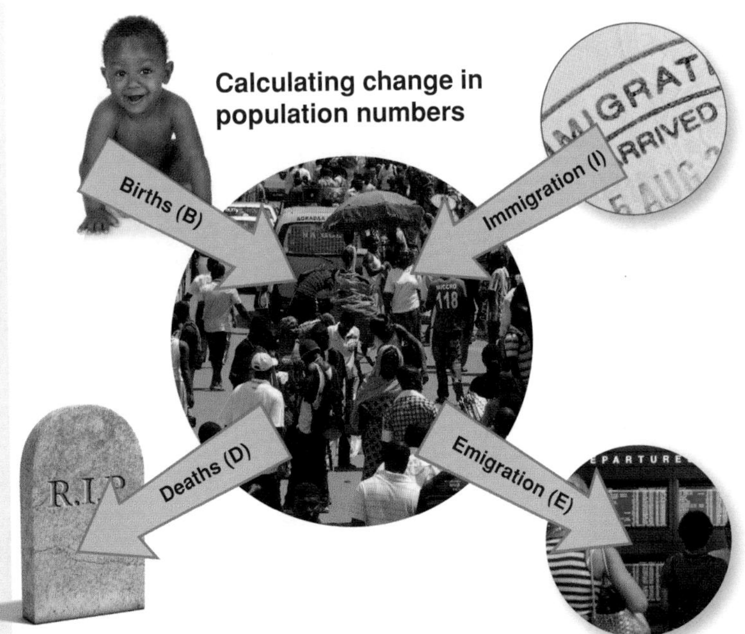

The human population is estimated to peak at around 9 billion by 2050 as a result of multiple factors, including falling birth rates. Humans have the technology and production efficiency to solve many resource problems and so might appear exempt from the direct influence of limiting factors. However, declining availability of water and land for food production are **limiting factors** likely to constrain population growth, at least regionally.

4. Define the following terms used to describe changes in population numbers:

 (a) Death rate (mortality): ______

 (b) Birth rate (natality): ______

 (c) Net migration rate: ______

5. Explain how the concept of limiting factors applies to population biology: ______

6. Using the terms, B, D, I, and E (above), construct equations to express the following:

 (a) A population in equilibrium: ______

 (b) A declining population: ______

 (c) An increasing population: ______

7. A population started with a total number of 100 individuals. Over the following year, population data were collected. Calculate birth rates, death rates, net migration rate, and rate of population change for the data below (as percentages):

 (a) Births = 14: Birth rate = ______

 (b) Net migration = +2: Net migration rate = ______

 (c) Deaths = 20: Death rate = ______

 (d) Rate of population change = ______

 (e) State whether the population is increasing or declining: ______

ISBN: 978-1-98-856656-6

238 Exponential Population Growth

Key Question: What does an exponential pattern of population growth look like and why does it occur?

Population growth is the change in a population's numbers over time (dN/dt or ΔN/Δt). **Exponential** (or geometric) **growth** occurs when resources are effectively unlimited and the population doubles with each generation. It typically occurs when a small population, with a high potential for increase (biotic potential), moves into an area with plentiful resources and few predators or competitors. Exponential growth plots as a J shaped curve on a linear scale.

Exponential growth

Recall the relationship between the factors determining population growth. If we want to compare populations of different sizes, it is useful to express population parameters such as rates of birth, death, and population growth on a **per capita** (per individual) basis.

The maximum per capita rate of population increase under ideal conditions (or **biotic potential**) is called r_{max}. We can calculate this using a simple equation (in words to the right, below):

r_{max} = B – D / N

r_{max} = Births – Deaths ÷ Population number

Exponential growth (right) is then expressed as:

dN/dt = r_{max}N

Population growth rate at time t = per capita rate of increase X population number

Exponential growth is **density independent** because per capita birth and death rates do not depend on the population size. It is a typical pattern of population growth when a few individuals enter a new area with unlimited resources, but it is rarely sustained.

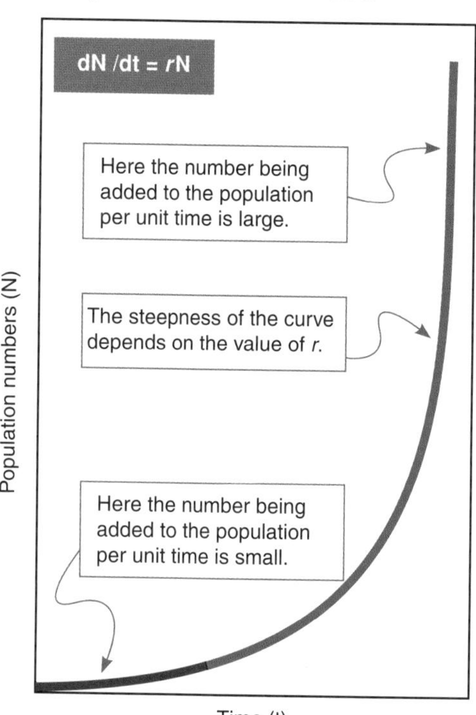
dN /dt = rN
Here the number being added to the population per unit time is large.
The steepness of the curve depends on the value of r.
Here the number being added to the population per unit time is small.
Population numbers (N)
Time (t)

Exponential curve: Note the lag (red) and exponential (blue) phases of the curve.

The biotic potential (recall this is the r_{max}) is constant for any one species. However, in natural populations, the per capita rate of increase (r) is usually lower than the r_{max} because resource limitation slows population growth. Organisms will show exponential growth if r is positive and constant so the equation is often given simply as **dN/dt = rN** (right).

More than a century ago, gray wolves were hunted almost to extinction in many parts of North America. In the 1980s, following their protection under law, packs began to repopulate parts of the US from Canada. The table below records the wolf population in Montana 1979-1995. Gray wolves were removed from the endangered species list in 2011 and hunting has since recommenced.

Gray wolf population in Montana

Year	Population	Year	Population
1979	5	1997	52
1981	5	1999	75
1983	9	2001	125
1985	20	2003	190
1987	15	2005	252
1989	16	2007	420
1991	38	2009	525
1993	52	2011	651
1995	60	2013	620
		2014	552

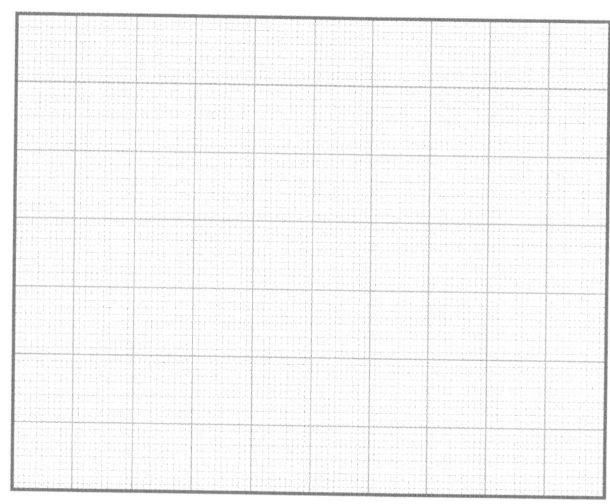

1. Produce a line graph of the gray wolf population on the grid above:

2. What would explain the lag in population growth before 1999? ______

3. Explain why wolves showed this pattern of population growth: ______

ISBN: 978-1-98-856656-6

239

237

SYI-1
4.A

239 The Effect of Population Density: Logistic Growth

Key Question: What happens to population growth when the population reaches the environment's carrying capacity?

Logistic growth begins exponentially, but slows as the population approaches carrying capacity. Populations do not generally continue to grow unchecked. Their numbers generally stabilize around a maximum that can be supported by the environment. This maximum number is called the **carrying capacity** (K). As the population number approaches K, the resources required for continued growth become limiting and there is increasing environmental resistance to further expansion. As a result, the rate of population growth slows. If the change in numbers is plotted over time, the curve is S shaped (sigmoidal), a pattern of called **logistic growth**. Logistic growth is typical of populations that live at or near carrying capacity and per capita birth and death rates are affected by population size (**density dependent**). Logistic growth is expressed as: **dN/dt = rN(K−N/K)**.

Logistic growth

- Under the logistic growth model, dN/dt = rN is multiplied by the proportion of K that is left unused.
- As the population increases (N approaches K), the proportion of K available decreases and individuals find it difficult to find or utilize space and resources.
- The rate of population increase slows as population size approaches carrying capacity.
- Often, there is a lag between depletion of resources and the population's response to that depletion. This can cause the population to overshoot K before declining again in response to lack of resources. In time, populations usually stabilize around K.

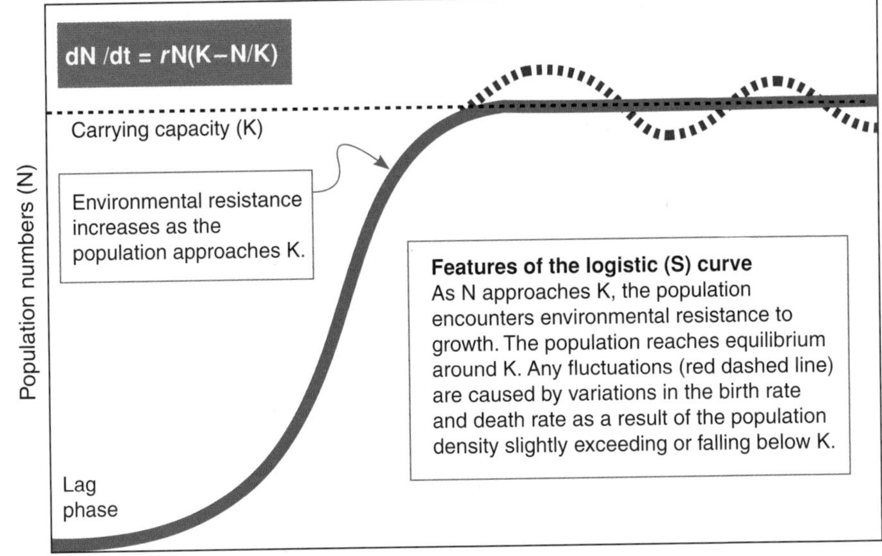

Population growth, West Virginia			
Year	Population	Year	Population
1800	78,592	1900	958,800
1810	105,469	1910	1,221,119
1820	136,808	1920	1,463,701
1830	176,924	1930	1,729,205
1840	224,537	1940	1,901,974
1850	308,313	1950	2,005,552
1860	376,688	1960	1,860,421
1870	442,014	1970	1,744,237
1880	618,457	1980	1,949,644
1890	762,794	1990	1,793,477

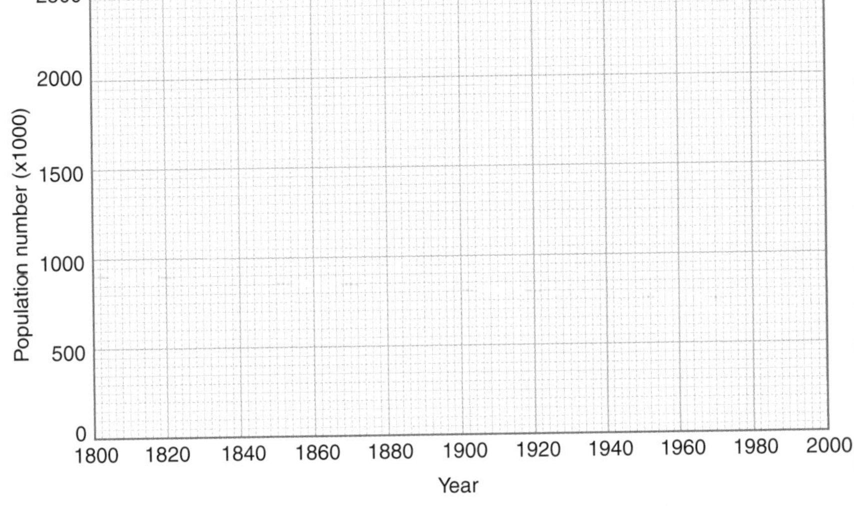

1. Census information provides a good test of the predictions of population growth models. The table of data above records census data for the human population of West Virginia 1800-1990.

   (a) Based on what you know so far, what sort of curve would you predict for a new settlement of humans? Explain:

   (b) Plot the data on the grid provided. The axes have been labeled to help you.

   (c) Did the plotted curve agree with your predictions?

2. Use the data to calculate r for the population of Virginia from 1800-1810 (if K = 1.9 million):

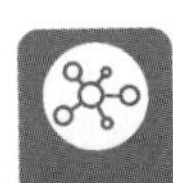

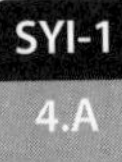

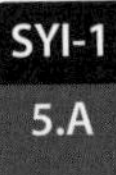

ISBN: 978-1-98-856656-6

Modeling logistic growth

Plotting a logistic growth curve on a spreadsheet can help in understanding logistic growth and the factors that affect population growth rate. In this exercise, you will create your own spreadsheet model of logistic growth for the population of Virginia as on the previous page, using r = 0.357 and K = 1,900,000. You can use Microsoft Excel or an equivalent spreadsheet program.

Plotting a logistic growth curve on a spreadsheet can help in understanding the effect of population size on the growth rate and how the logistic equation applies. For the population of Virginia the following formulae can be entered into the spreadsheet:

	A	B	C	D	E	F	G
1	r	t (year)	N	K	K-N/K	dN/dt	
2	0.356	1800	78592	1900000	=($D$2-C2)/$D$2	=$A$2*C2*E2	
3		=B2+10	=C2+F2				
4							
5							
6							
7							

Population at t_1 = population at t_0 + dN/dt (the amount of population change over ten years)

The cells can then be filled down. The first four steps have been filled here. Fill the cells down to about 1950 then plot t vs N.

	A	B	C	D	E	F
1	r	t (year)	N	K	K-N/K	dN/dt
2	0.357	1800	78592	1900000	0.958635789	26897
3		1810	105489		0.944479593	35569
4		1820	141057		0.925759265	46619
5		1830	187676		0.901222995	60382
6						

r and K selection

- Species with life histories characterized by short generation times, high biotic potential, and exponential population growth are called r-selected species (e.g. bacteria and many rodents).
- Species with life histories characterized by longer life spans and slower population growth are called K-selected species. They tend to live at or around the carrying capacity of their environments.

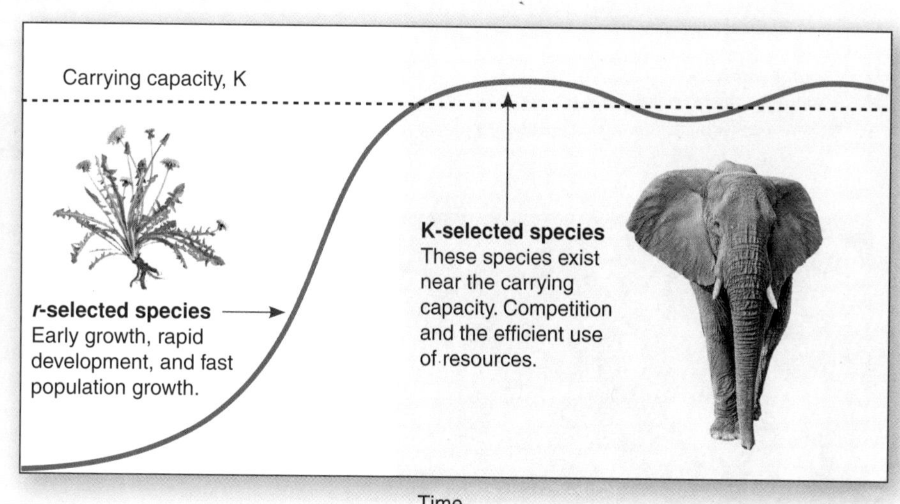

Carrying capacity, K
Population numbers (N)
r-selected species
Early growth, rapid development, and fast population growth.
K-selected species
These species exist near the carrying capacity. Competition and the efficient use of resources.
Time

3. Why don't populations continue to increase exponentially in an environment? ______________________

4. What is meant by **carrying capacity**? ______________________

5. Describe and explain the phases of the logistic growth curve: ______________________

6. (a) Describe how dN/dt changes over time in your spreadsheet: ______________________

   (b) Compare and contrast your spreadsheet graph to your plotted graph: ______________________

ISBN: 978-1-98-856656-6

240 Community Structure and Diversity

Key Question: How do diversity indices quantify the biodiversity in an area and measure ecosystem health?

The health of an ecosystem can be assessed by measuring both the number and relative abundances of organisms present. A change in species composition over time can therefore indicate changes in that ecosystem's status. Certain **indicator species** are also useful in this respect as they are associated with habitats of a particular status, e.g. unpolluted water. Scientists quantify biodiversity using a diversity index. Diversity indices take account of both the species evenness and species richness and can be used to assess environmental stress (or recovery).

Simpson's index of diversity

Simpson's Index of Diversity (below) produces values ranging between 0 and almost 1. There are other variants of this index, but the more limited range of values provided by this calculation makes it more easily interpreted. No single index offers the "best" measure of diversity; each is chosen on the basis of suitability to different situations.

Simpson's Index of Diversity (D) is easily calculated using the following simple formula. Communities with a wide range of species produce a higher score than communities dominated by larger numbers of only a few species.

$$D = 1 - (\Sigma(n/N)^2)$$

D = Diversity index
N = Total number of individuals (of all species) in the sample
n = Number of individuals of each species in the sample

Example of species diversity in a stream

The example below describes the results from a survey of stream invertebrates. It is not necessary to know the species to calculate a diversity index as long as the different species can be distinguished.

For the example below, Simpson's Index of Diversity using $D = 1 - (\Sigma(n/N)^2)$ is:

Species	n	n/N	$(n/N)^2$
A (backswimmer)	12	0.300	0.090
B (stonefly larva)	7	0.175	0.031
C (silver water beetle)	2	0.050	0.003
D (caddisfly larva)	6	0.150	0.023
E (water spider)	5	0.125	0.016
F (mayfly larva)	8	0.20	0.040
	$\Sigma n = 40$		$\Sigma(n/N)^2 = 0.201$

D = 1-0.201 = 0.799

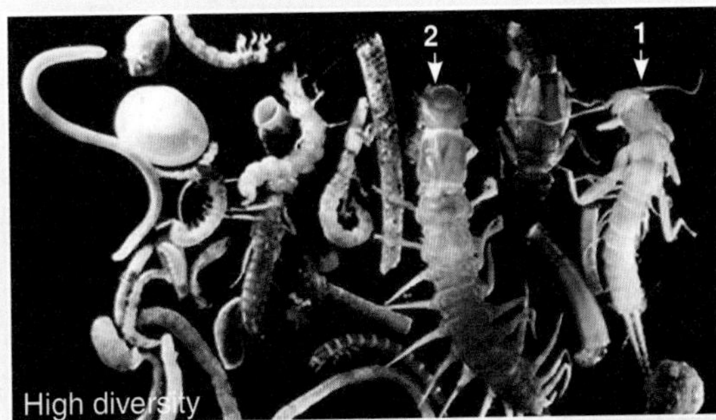

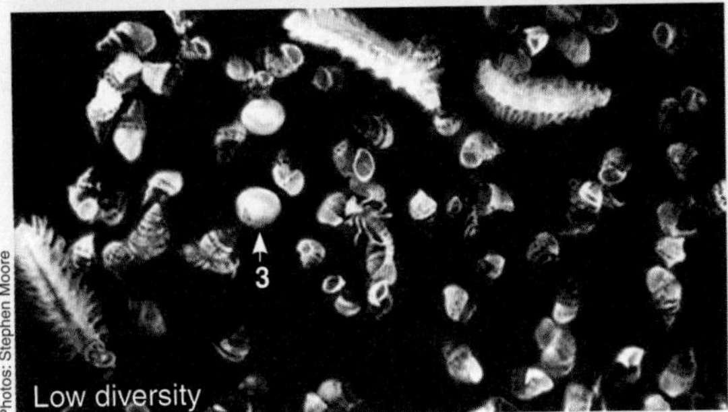

Photos: Stephen Moore

Using diversity indices and the role of indicator species

To be properly interpreted, indices are usually evaluated with reference to earlier measurement or a standard ecosystem measure. The photographs left show samples from two stream communities, a high diversity community with a large number of macroinvertebrate species (top) and a low diversity community (lower photograph) with fewer species in large numbers. These photographs also show indicator species. The top image shows a stonefly (1) and an alderfly larva (2). These species (together with mayfly larvae) are typical of clean, well oxygenated water. The lower image is dominated by snails (3), which are tolerant of a wide range of conditions, included degraded environments.

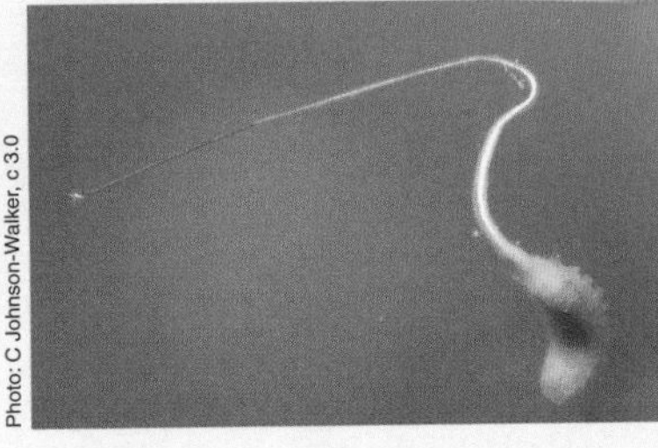

Photo: C Johnson-Walker, c 3.0

The aptly named rat-tail maggot is the larva of the drone fly. This species is an indicator of gross pollution. Its prominent feature is a long snorkel-like breathing siphon.

1. Why might it be useful to have baseline data (prior knowledge of a system) before interpreting a diversity index?

2. (a) How might you monitor the recovery of a stream ecosystem following an ecological restoration project?

(b) What role could indicator species play in the monitoring program?

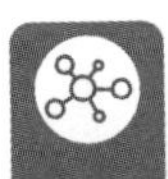

254

ISBN: 978-1-98-856656-6

Comparing diversity at two woodland sites

- Diversity indices are particularly useful when comparing the diversity of different areas or comparing the change in diversity over time. The investigation below gathered data using quadrats to survey of invertebrate diversity in two different types of forested land. The types and individuals of invertebrate species were recorded.

Observation

Walking through a conifer plantation, a student observed that there seemed to be only a few different invertebrate species in the forest leaf litter. They wondered if more invertebrate species would be found in a nearby oak woodland.

Hypothesis

The oak woodland has a more varied leaf litter composition than the conifer plantation, so will support a wider variety of invertebrate species.
The **null hypothesis** is that there is no difference between the diversity of invertebrate species in oak woodland and coniferous plantation litter.

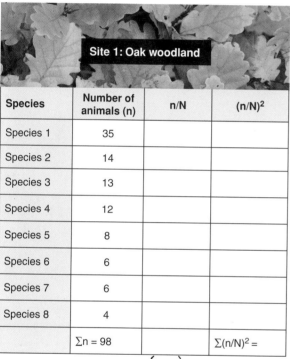

Site 1: Oak woodland

Species	Number of animals (n)	n/N	$(n/N)^2$
Species 1	35		
Species 2	14		
Species 3	13		
Species 4	12		
Species 5	8		
Species 6	6		
Species 7	6		
Species 8	4		
	$\Sigma n = 98$		$\Sigma(n/N)^2 =$

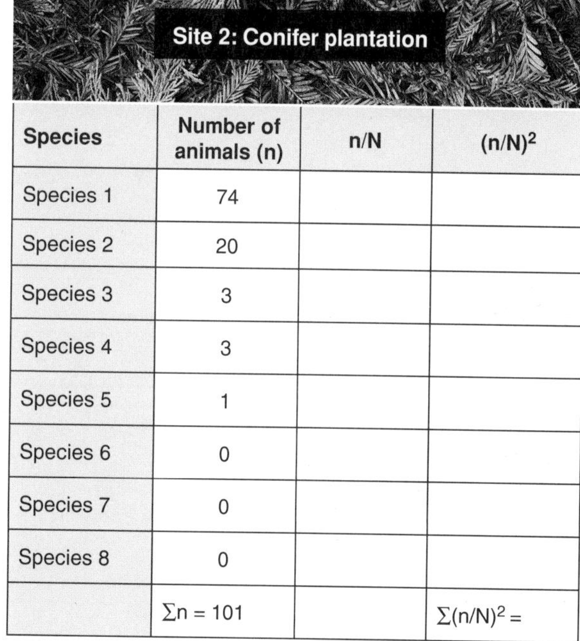

Site 2: Conifer plantation

Species	Number of animals (n)	n/N	$(n/N)^2$
Species 1	74		
Species 2	20		
Species 3	3		
Species 4	3		
Species 5	1		
Species 6	0		
Species 7	0		
Species 8	0		
	$\Sigma n = 101$		$\Sigma(n/N)^2 =$

Species 1 Mite

Species 2 Ant

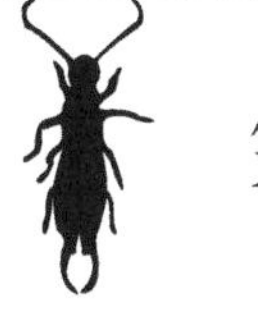
Species 3 Earwig

Species 4 Woodlice

Species 5 Centipede

Species 6 Longhorn beetle

Species 7 Small beetle

Species 8 Pseudoscorpion

3. (a) Complete the two tables above by calculating the values for n/N and $(n/N)^2$ for the student's two sampling sites:

   (b) Calculate the Simpson's Index of Diversity for site 1: ______

   (c) Calculate the Simpson's Index of Diversity for site 2: ______

   (d) Compare the diversity of the two sites and suggest any reasons for it: ______

ISBN: 978-1-98-856656-6

Survey differences in populations

Clover leaf

- Communities and populations can be affected by the interactions of the organisms in them. White clover (*Trifolium repens*) is a common pasture plant. It has white flowers and distinctive leaves with three (or occasionally four) leaflets. The leaves are held on petioles that can be 150 mm or more long if left undisturbed. In pasture that is regularly grazed petiole length can be shorter.
- Two paddocks containing white clover were grazed by cattle under different regimes during the peak growing season (late winter to early summer). Paddock A was grazed for one day every week whereas paddock B was grazed for one day every four weeks.
- At the end of the trial, quadrats were used to select random samples of clover and the lengths of the petioles were measured to evaluate the effect of grazing on morphology (in this case petiole length). The results are shown below.
- Using the data to calculate a 95% confidence interval will help establish if there is a significant difference in the effect of the grazing regimes. You can do this by hand or using a spreadsheet program.

4. Calculate the mean for:

   (a) Paddock A: ______________________

   (b) Paddock B: ______________________

5. Use the mean to complete the table on the left.

6. Use the equations below to calculate the standard deviation and standard error for the clover population in each paddock:

Standard deviation

$$s = \sqrt{\frac{\Sigma(x_i - \bar{x})^2}{n-1}}$$

Standard error

$$SE = \frac{s}{\sqrt{n}}$$

   (a) Standard deviation paddock A: ______________________

   (b) Standard error paddock A: ______________________

   (c) Standard deviation paddock B: ______________________

   (d) Standard error paddock B: ______________________

7. Calculate the 95% confidence interval using the equation 95% CI = SE × $t_{P(n-1)}$. Use the table right to identify the value of t at n - 1 d.f:

   (a) 95% CI for paddock A: ______________________

   (b) 95% CI for paddock B: ______________________

8. Express this as mean ± 95% CI

   (a) Paddock A: ______________________

   (b) Paddock B: ______________________

x (length in mm)		$x - \bar{x}$ (deviation from mean)		$(x - \bar{x})^2$ (deviation from mean)^2	
Paddock A	**Paddock B**	**Paddock A**	**Paddock B**	**Paddock A**	**Paddock B**
83	30	40.2	-77.5	1616.04	6006.25
70	87	27.2	-20.5	739.84	420.25
32	48				
61	92				
70	54				
45	33				
28	135				
34	60				
37	81				
20	139				
25	90				
30	78				
31	125				
35	174				
80	167				
22	184				
62	80				
35	125				
25	163				
44	197				
30	116				
			Sum of squares →	$\Sigma (x - \bar{x})^2$	$\Sigma (x - \bar{x})^2$

What could you do next?

- *A Student's t test*
- *Plot a labeled graph and attach it to this page*

Table of critical values of *t* at different levels of *P*.

Degrees of freedom	P 0.05
1	12.71
2	4.303
3	3.182
4	2.776
5	2.571
6	2.447
7	2.365
8	2.306
9	2.262
10	2.228
15	2.131
20	2.086

9. Is there evidence that the grazing produced a significant difference in the clover populations of paddocks A and B? Explain you reasoning:

10. What assumption is being made in this study? What would have increased its validity?

ISBN: 978-1-98-856656-6

241 Species Interactions and Community Structure

Key Question: How do the interactions within populations influence community structure?

Community structure is a result of the many complex interactions of the organisms in the community. These interactions can slowly change the community over time. Interactions include competition, predation, and symbioses.

Community changes over time: succession

- Newly established communities change over time in a process called **ecological succession**. It occurs as a result of the dynamic interactions between biotic and abiotic factors over time.
- Earlier communities modify the physical environment, making it more favorable for the species that will make up later communities. Over time, a succession may result in a stable, mature, or climax, community, although this is not always the case. Succession occurring where there is no pre-existing vegetation or soil is called **primary succession**.

The organisms at earlier stages of a succession modify the environment in such a way that it becomes more suitable for organisms at later stages. Existing communities are outcompeted and replaced by species more suited to the modified environment. This progression of species replacements generally leads to increase in diversity and complexity in late successional communities.

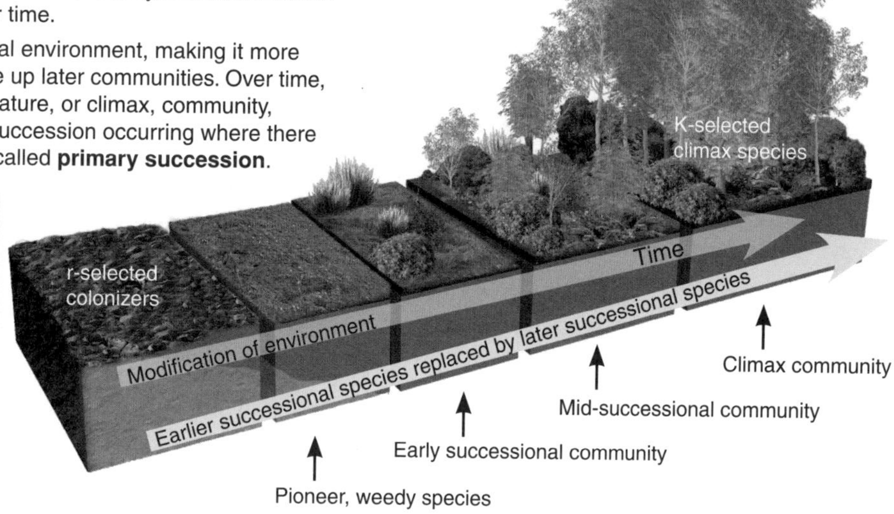

Primary succession occurs with the emergence of new volcanic islands, new coral atolls, or islands where the previous community has been destroyed by a volcanic eruption, such as occurred on Mount St Helens after it erupted in 1980. The sequence below shows the recolonization of Mount St Helens after the eruption.

Areas of Mount St. Helens were scoured bare by large flows of super-heated gas and volcanic ash in the eruption of 1980.

Organic acids secreted by **lichens** (above) chemically break down rock to produce **humus**, and eventually soil.

Nitrogen fixers enrich the soil over time, and other plant species can become established.

Community composition has been influenced by the species remaining after the eruption. Recovery has been more rapid in areas where vegetation was nearby.

1. Explain why succession naturally results from the interactions among species in an establishing community:

ISBN: 978-1-98-856656-6

235 234

Types of species interactions

- No organism exists in isolation. Each interacts with other organisms of its own and other species. Species interactions (those between different species) involve benefit to at least one party. If one party benefits at the expense of another, the relationship is an exploitation. If one species benefits and one is unaffected, the relationship is said to be commensal.
- Some species interactions involve a close association or **symbiosis** (living together) between the parties involved. Symbioses include parasitism and mutualism. Many species interactions involve coevolution, in which there is a reciprocal evolution of adaptations in both parties.
- Competition is an important influencer in community ecology. It can alter the distribution and abundance of both competing species (see case study opposite) and promotes niche partitioning as species specialize to avoid competition for resources.

Type of interaction between species				
Mutualism	Commensalism	Parasitism	Predation	Competition
A symbiosis in which both species benefit. If both species depend on the symbiosis for survival, the mutualism is obligate. Mutualism can involve more than two species. **Examples**: Flowering plants and their insect pollinators. The flowers are pollinated and the insect gains food. Ruminants and their rumen protozoa and bacteria. The microbes digest the cellulose in plant material and produce short-chain fatty acids, which the ruminant uses as an energy source.	A symbiosis in which one species benefits and the other is unaffected. It is likely that most commensal relationships involve some small benefit to the apparently neutral party. **Example**: The squat anemone shrimp (or sexy shrimp), lives among the tentacles of sea anemones, where it gains protection and scavenges scraps of food from the anemone. The anemone appears to be neither harmed, nor gain any benefit.	A symbiotic relationship in which the parasite lives in or on the host, taking all its nutrition from it. The host is harmed but not usually killed, at least not directly. Parasites may have multiple hosts and their transmission is often linked to food webs. **Example**: Parasitic tongue-replacing isopods cut the blood supply to the tongue of the host fish, causing it to fall off. The parasite attaches to what is left of the tongue, feeding on blood or mucus.	A predator kills the prey and eats it. Predators may prey on a range of species or they may prey exclusively on one species. Predation is a consumer-resource interaction and a type of exploitation. Herbivory is an equivalent exploitation between herbivores and plants. **Examples**: Praying mantis consuming insect prey. Canada lynx eating snowshoe hare. Starfish eating mussels and limpets.	Individuals of the same or different species compete for the same limited resources. Both parties are detrimentally affected. **Examples**: Neighboring plants of the same and different species compete for light and soil nutrients. Vultures compete for the remains of a carcass. Insectivorous birds compete for suitable food in a forest. Tree-nesting birds with similar requirements compete for nest sites.
			Luc Viatour www.Lucnix.be Marco vinci cc 3.0	
A ⇄ B Benefits Benefits				

2. In the spaces above, draw a simple model to show whether each species/individual in the interaction described is harmed or benefits. The first one has been completed for you.

3. Ticks are obligate blood feeders (meaning they must obtain blood to pass from one life stage to the next). Ticks attach to the outside of hosts where they suck blood and fluids and cause irritation.

   (a) Identify this type of interaction: ______

   (b) How would the tick population be affected if the host became rare? ______

   ______

4. Competition is common both within and between species. Predict which would be the most intense and explain why:

   ______

   ______

ISBN: 978-1-98-856656-6

Population changes over time: predator-prey cycles

- Predators hunt and eat other animals. As a result, their population growth can be closely linked that of their prey.
- In many herbivore-carnivore systems, prey populations fluctuate seasonally with changes in vegetation growth. Predators may respond to increases in prey by increasing their rate of reproduction. This type of numerical response shows a time lag, associated with the time it takes for the predator population to respond by producing more young. The most famous of these time-lagged predator-prey cycles is that recorded for the Canada lynx and its prey, the snowshoe hare (below).

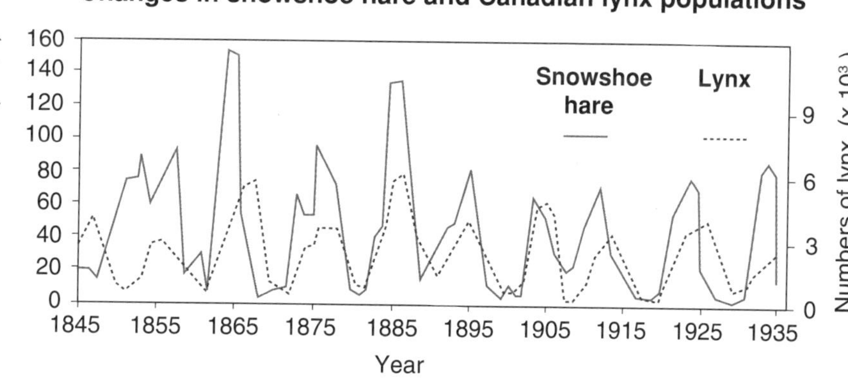

Trophic cascades and the role of top predators

Almost for as long as humans have been farming livestock or gathering animal resources, they have competed with the natural apex predator. Recall that apex predators occupy the top trophic level. They control prey density, regulate disease by taking old and sick individuals, and limit the numbers of smaller predators. Orca, saltwater crocodiles, and great skuas are all apex predators.

- In many regions of the world, the apex predators have been removed or severely reduced in numbers. This is often intentional, to protect people and livestock, or simply for trophy hunting. In other cases, habitat loss has made apex predators more vulnerable.
- The loss of key apex predators has resulted in many ecosystems being skewed towards herbivores. This in turn has resulted in over-grazing and ecosystem damage. The effects of apex predators on lower trophic levels are called **trophic cascades**.

Orca (killer whales) are the apex predator in the oceans. Orca hunt in packs and are capable of preying on any other marine species. Overfishing can alter normal trophic balances and cause orca to switch prey.

Gray wolves hunt in packs by running down their prey. Their reintroduction to Yellowstone Park in the USA resulted in large beneficial changes the park ecosystem, with a restoration of its former biodiversity.

Trophic cascades can be dramatic. When arctic foxes were introduced to the Aleutian Islands, they preyed on seabirds. This reduced sea to land nutrient transport and grassland plants were replaced with tundra species.

5. Explain why predator-prey cycles occur: ______________________

____

____

____

____

6. Suggest why a predator (such as the Canada lynx) that feeds on only one prey species is more vulnerable to population losses than a predator with multiple prey species and the capability for prey-switching.

____

____

____

ISBN: 978-1-98-856656-6

Competition can influence patterns of distribution

- Seashores provide a wide range of habitats and opportunities. Not surprisingly, this results in a high diversity and abundance of organisms competing for the benefits of living there.
- Competition in barnacle species was studied by J.H. Connell in Scotland. By removing one barnacle species and observing the effect on another, it was possible to determine how competition influenced distribution. Barnacles are sessile, filter-feeding crustaceans, common on rocky shores. The outcome of any competitive interaction depends not only on the biological characteristics and tolerances of the competing species, but also the habitat diversity, as more diverse habitats can provide more microhabitats in which species can avoid direct competition.

Competitive exclusion in natural populations of barnacles

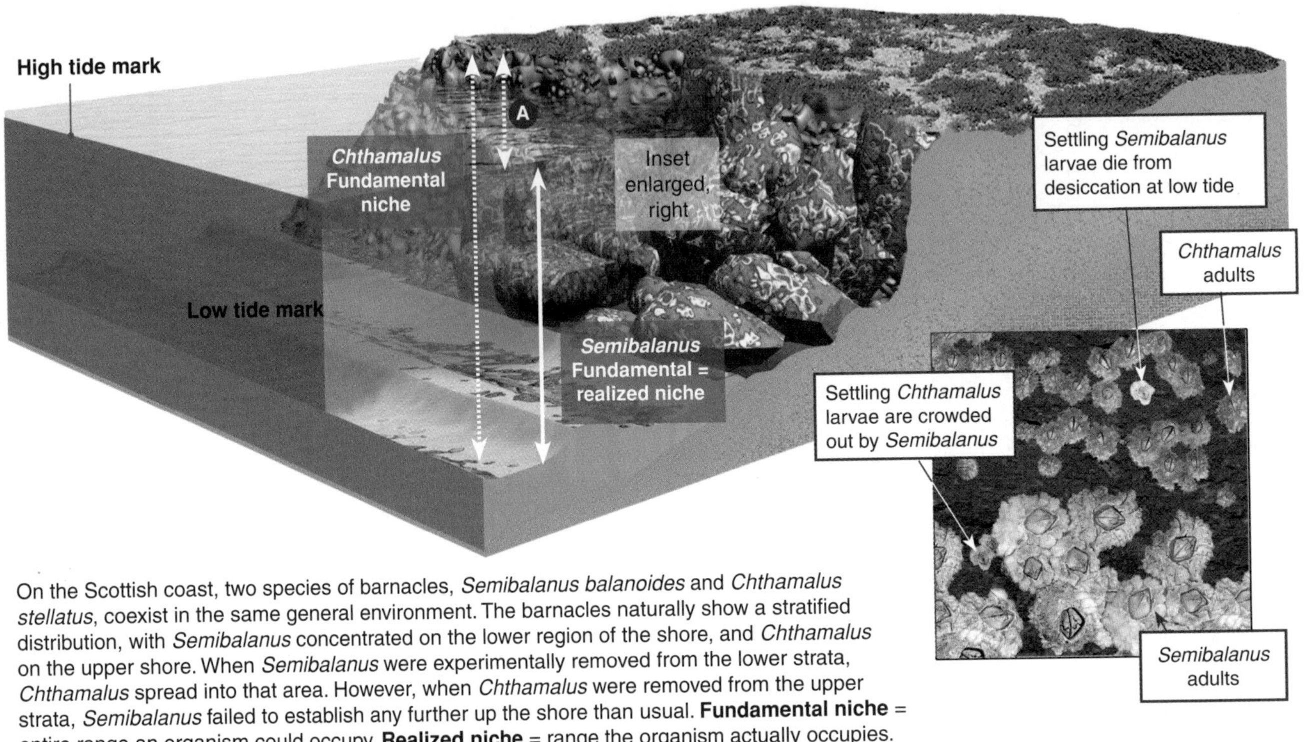

On the Scottish coast, two species of barnacles, *Semibalanus balanoides* and *Chthamalus stellatus*, coexist in the same general environment. The barnacles naturally show a stratified distribution, with *Semibalanus* concentrated on the lower region of the shore, and *Chthamalus* on the upper shore. When *Semibalanus* were experimentally removed from the lower strata, *Chthamalus* spread into that area. However, when *Chthamalus* were removed from the upper strata, *Semibalanus* failed to establish any further up the shore than usual. **Fundamental niche** = entire range an organism could occupy. **Realized niche** = range the organism actually occupies.

7. (a) In the example of the barnacles above, describe what is represented by the zone labeled with the arrow A:

(b) Outline the evidence for the barnacle distribution being the result of competitive exclusion:

8. (a) What keeps *Semibalanus* larvae from establishing at higher shore levels?

(b) What is the consequence of this to the realized niche compared to the fundamental niche of *Semibalanus*?

9. There are many studies underway about the effect global warming and rising sea levels might have on marine communities. Predict the effect a rise in sea level have on the *Chthamalus*/*Semibalanus* community:

ISBN: 978-1-98-856656-6

Competing species partition resources

Many field studies have indicated that different species partition the available resources to avoid direct competition. This evolutionary change in resource use, caused by competition over generations is called **niche differentiation**. It contributes to community diversity because a larger number of species can occupy the same general area of habitat.

In a study of three species of coexisting grassland sparrows in Pennsylvania, researchers found that although territory boundaries of all three species overlapped, they made use of the gradient in the vegetation to partition the grassland habitat and avoid competition. All species eat insects and seeds. Henslow's and grasshopper sparrows have a similar beak size but the savannah sparrow has a smaller beak and exploits slightly different food sizes than the grasshopper sparrow with which it has a 35% habitat overlap.

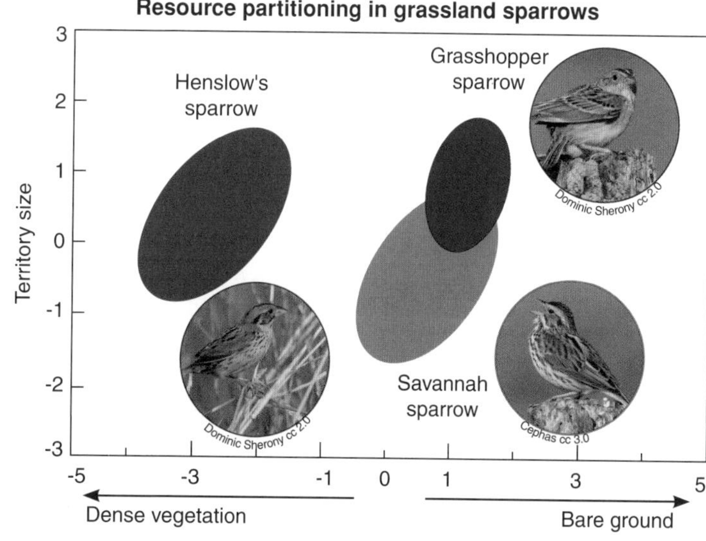

10. Study the diagram of resource partitioning in grassland sparrows. Describe two ways in which the species minimize the competition between them in their grassland ecosystem:

11. Use the examples and data presented earlier to explain how interactions within and among populations influence the structure of ecological communities:

ISBN: 978-1-98-856656-6

242 Community Structure and Energy Availability

Key Question: How does energy availability affect community structure?

The amount of energy in an ecosystem changes depending on location. Ecosystems in tropical regions (e.g. tropical rain-forest) have a large amount of available energy. Ecosystems in desert of polar regions do not have much energy available (although for different reasons). The availability of the energy affects the number of trophic levels possible in an ecosystem.

Boreal forests (taiga) are found at high latitudes in the northern hemisphere. The productivity of these forests changes seasonally, being very low in winter and high in summer. The number of trophic levels remains constant over the year, but the biomass and energy available at higher trophic levels is reduced in winter as many animals migrate to warmer climates.

The primary productivity of tropical rainforests is very high as a result of high incident light, non-limiting supplies of water, and favorable climate. Because the primary productivity is high, a large amount of energy is available to consumer levels and having five trophic levels is common.

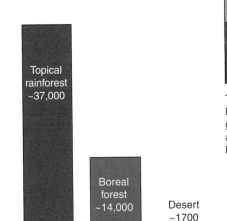

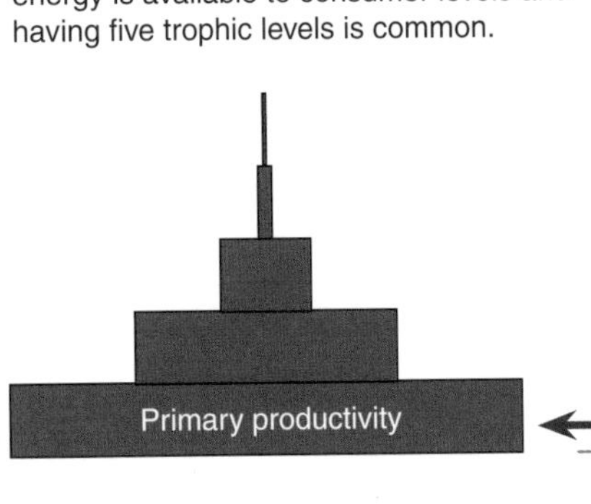

The primary productivity of deserts is very low because water is a limiting factor to plant growth. As a result, there is very little energy available to support a large consumer biomass and there are fewer trophic levels.

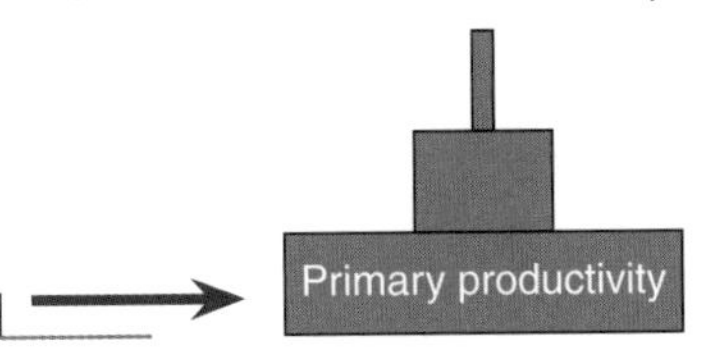

Topical rainforest ~37,000

Boreal forest ~14,000

Desert ~1700

Average net primary productivity (kJ/m^2/yr)

1. Explain why tropical rainforests support more consumer biomass and a greater number of trophic levels than deserts:

2. Would you expect tropical reefs to support more, fewer, or about the same number of trophic levels than a tropical rainforest? Explain your reasoning:

3. In terms of energy availability, explain why may large herbivores at high northern latitudes migrate south before winter:

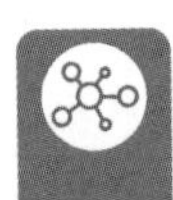

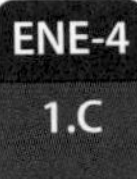

ISBN: 978-1-98-856656-6

Mutualistic relationships and access to energy

As you explored earlier, cooperation can include species-specific behaviors such as food sharing and group hunting. Cooperation between different species most often involves commensal or mutualistic relationships. These relationships provide one or both participants in the relationship with access to a resource that would otherwise be unavailable (usually food) and creates new pathways for energy flow in ecosystems.

Resource-resource relationships: One resource is traded for another (usually food or a nutrient)

Staghorn coral

Reef building corals rely on a mutualism with algae in their tissues. The algae supply the coral with energy (glucose and glycerol) and, in return, obtain a habitat and the compounds they need for photosynthesis and growth (CO_2 and nitrogen). This symbiosis is crucial to recycling nutrients within the reef.

Althepal cc 2.5

Worker termite

Termites eat wood and rely on a microbial community in their gut to break down the cellulose in wood and produce the fatty acids they use for energy. The obligate relationship provides food for both microbes and termites. Termites are responsible for recycling most of the dead wood in tropical ecosystems.

Lichens are a composite organism formed by an alga or cyanobacterium living among the filaments of a fungus. These symbioses are very successful, involving about 20% of all fungal species. Lichens are common pioneer species in ecosystems and make energy available to higher trophic levels that would otherwise be lost.

Service-resource relationships: A service is performed in exchange for a resource, e.g. food for protection

viamoi cc 2.0

Ant guards its aphids

Some ant species "farm" aphids by protecting the aphids from beetle predators. In return, the ants harvest and consume the honeydew that the aphids excrete. The relationship provides a reliable source of high-energy food for the ants, enabling them to meet their colony's needs.

Honeybee pollinating a purple crocus

Many flowering plant species have a mutualistic relationship with their bee pollinators. The bee obtains food (nectar) and the plant receives a service (pollination). The mutualism is normally, although not always facultative; neither species depends exclusively on the other for survival.

The High Fin Sperm Whale - cc 3.0

Many plants have symbiotic mycorrhizal relationships with fungi that live in or on their roots. The fungi help the plant extract nutrients from the soil. This means the plant is much more productive than would it might otherwise be, making more energy and matter available to the community as a whole.

4. Using examples, describe how symbiotic relationships increase resource availability for the species involved:

ISBN: 978-1-98-856656-6

243 Ecosystem Diversity and Resilience

Key Question: What factors contribute to ecosystem stability and how are diversity and ecosystem stability related?

Ecological theory suggests that all species in an ecosystem contribute in some way to ecosystem function. Therefore, species loss past a certain point is likely to have a detrimental effect on the functioning of the ecosystem and on its ability to resist change over time (its **stability**). More diverse systems generally show greater stability over time although they may not recover quickly from disturbance. Scientists estimate that human destruction of natural habitats is implicated in the extinction of up to 100,000 species every year. The loss of species, and repeated large scale disturbances in a relatively short time period compromise the stability of ecosystems and can permanently change their characteristics.

Ecosystem stability has various components, including **resistance** (the ability to resist disturbance) and **resilience** (ability to recover from external disturbances). Ecosystem stability is closely linked to the biodiversity of the system, although it is difficult to predict which factors will stress an ecosystem beyond its range of tolerance. It was once thought that the most stable ecosystems were those with the most species, because they had the greatest number of biotic interactions operating to buffer them against change. This assumption is supported by experimental evidence but there is uncertainty over what level of biodiversity provides long-term stability.

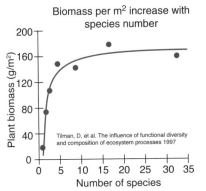

Biomass per m^2 increase with species number

Plant biomass (g/m^2): 0, 40, 80, 120, 160, 200

Number of species: 0, 5, 10, 15, 20, 25, 30, 35

Tilman, D, et al. The influence of functional diversity and composition of ecosystem processes 1997

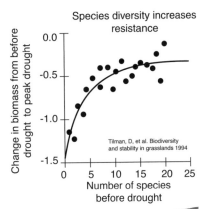

Species diversity increases resistance

Change in biomass from before drought to peak drought: 0.0, -0.5, -1.0, -1.5

Number of species before drought: 0, 5, 10, 15, 20, 25

Tilman, D, et al. Biodiversity and stability in grasslands 1994

- Resilience and resistance can be modeled by a rubber band and a piece of string.
- The rubber band is highly resilient. It can be stretched by an external force. Once the force is removed, the rubber band quickly returns to its original shape. However it is not very resistant, even a small external force can stretch the band out of shape.
- A rope is highly resistant, a large force does not change its shape. It is not resilient though as a large enough force will break the string so it can never return to its original shape.

A rope or string vs a rubber band: the rope has high resistance but very low resilience, whereas the opposite is true of the rubber band.

Monoculture

Brian Dell Public Domain

Natural grassland (savanna)

Lubasi cc 2.0

Amazon rainforest (aerial)

Deforestation

Single species crops (monocultures), such as the soy bean crop (above, left), represent low diversity systems that can be vulnerable to disease, pests, and disturbance. In contrast, natural grasslands (above, right) may appear homogeneous, but contain many species which vary in their predominance seasonally. Although they may be easily disturbed (e.g. by burning) they are very resilient and usually recover quickly.

Tropical rainforests (above, left) represent the highest diversity systems on Earth. Whilst these ecosystems are generally resistant to disturbance, once degraded, (above, right) they have little ability to recover. The biodiversity of ecosystems at low latitudes is generally higher than that at high latitudes, where climates are harsher, niches are broader, and systems may be dependent on a small number of key species.

1. (a) Define ecosystem resilience: ______

   (b) Define ecosystem resistance: ______

2. What is the effect of species number on plant biomass production? ______

3. What is the effect of latitude on biodiversity? ______

ISBN: 978-1-98-856656-6

Factors affecting ecosystem resilience

Ecosystem biodiversity

The greater the diversity of an ecosystem the greater the chance that all the roles (niches) in an ecosystem will be occupied, making it harder for invasive species to establish and easier for the ecosystem to recover after a disturbance.

Ecosystem health

Intact ecosystems are more likely to be resilient than ecosystems suffering from species loss or disease.

Disturbance frequency

Single disturbances to an ecosystem can be survived, but frequent disturbances make it more difficult for an ecosystem to recover. Some ecosystems depend on frequent natural disturbances for their maintenance, e.g. grasslands rely on natural fires to prevent shrubs and trees from establishing. The various grass species present have evolved to survive frequent fires.

- A study of coral and algae cover at two locations in Australia's Great Barrier Reef (right) showed how ecosystems recover after a disturbance. At Low Isles, frequent disturbances (e.g. from cyclones) made it difficult for corals to reestablish, while at Middle Reef, infrequent disturbances made it possible to coral to reestablish its dominant position in the ecosystem.

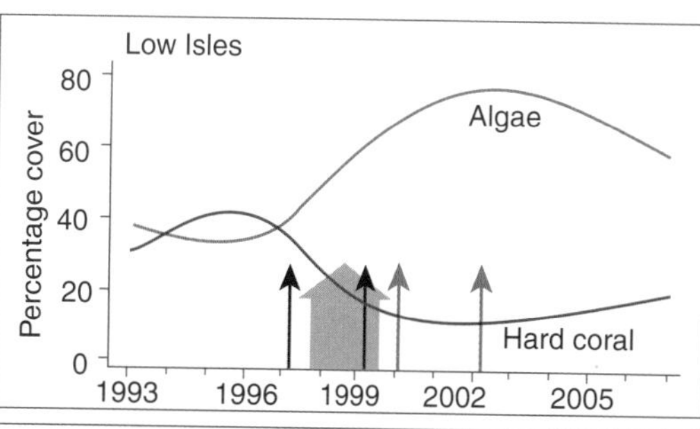

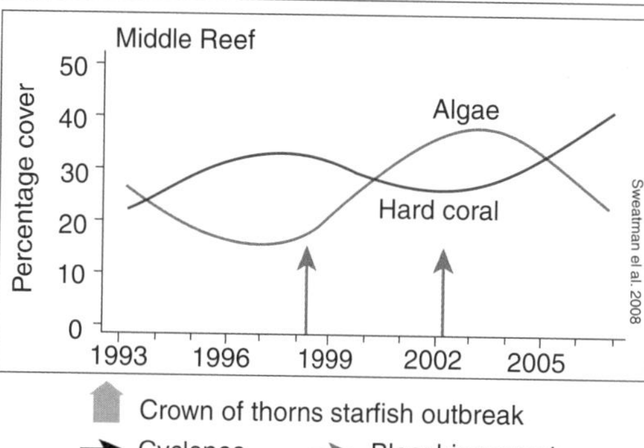

4. Explain the contrasting responses of the two coral populations shown in the graphs above: ______

5. Explain why monoculture crops require an input of energy (from the farmer) to maintain their structure: ______

6. A student used blocks to model ecosystem stability. They placed once set of blocks as in Figure 1 and another set as in Figure 2. Figure 1 they said modeled a low diversity ecosystem. Figure 2 they said modeled a high diversity ecosystem.

   Explain how well each model represents the system described, referring to stability, resilience, and resistance: ______

Figure 1

Figure 2

ISBN: 978-1-98-856656-6

244 The Role of Keystone Species

Key Question: What are keystone species and why do they have a disproportionate effect on ecosystem processes?

Every species has a functional role in an ecosystem (its niche), but some have a much bigger effect on ecosystem processes and stability than their abundance would suggest because their activities are crucial to the way the ecosystem as a whole functions. These species are called keystone species. They are often top (apex) predators, or have a critical role in seed dispersal or nutrient cycling. The loss of a keystone species can have a large and rapid impact on the structure and function of an ecosystem, changing the balance of relationships and leading to instability. This has important implications for the management of threatened ecosystems because many keystone species are endangered.

Why are keystone species important?

The term keystone species comes from the analogy of the keystone in a true arch. An archway is supported by a series of stones, the central one being the **keystone**. If the keystone is removed, the arch collapses.

The idea of the keystone species was first hypothesized in 1969 by Robert Paine. He determined through experimentation that the ochre starfish (*Pisaster*), a predator in rocky shore communities, had a role in maintaining community diversity. When the starfish were removed, their prey species increased, crowding out algae and reducing species richness in the area from 15 to 8.

Yellowstone wolves run down a bull elk

Trophic cascades following the return of gray wolves to Yellowstone

- Gray wolves are a top predators in North American ecosystems, yet federal extermination programs in the late 1800s-early 1900s reduced them to near extinction in the US, including in the Yellowstone National Park (YNP) where National Park status did not protect them.
- Once the wolves were gone, numbers of elk (their primary prey) increased and the deciduous vegetation became severely overgrazed. This had a number of consequences. Without wolves, coyotes also increased, and the numbers of pronghorn antelope (coyote prey) then declined. Beavers became largely absent.
- In 1974, the gray wolf was declared endangered under the Endangered Species Act (1973) and in 1995 its reintroduction to the park began. Since that time, wolf numbers in the park have grown, elk have declined and shifted into less favorable habitats, deciduous vegetation has recovered, beavers have returned, and the coyote population has stabilized at a lower level.

Figures, right, show some of the ecological changes recorded in YNP following the 1995/1996 reintroduction of gray wolves. Individual plots show numbers of wolves (A), elk (B), and beaver (C), together with vegetation changes. Aspen heights recorded in areas with downed logs, which regenerate somewhat faster than areas without downed logs. Dashed lines represent time periods with at least 1 year of missing data.

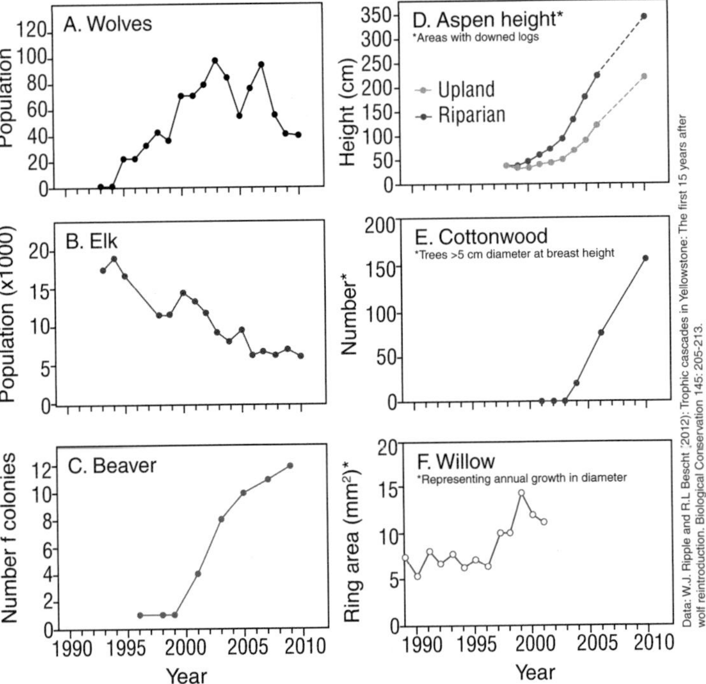

Data: W.J. Ripple and R.L Beschta (2012): Trophic cascades in Yellowstone: The first 15 years after wolf reintroduction. Biological Conservation 145: 205-213.

1. Use the figures (A-F) above to discuss the evidence for the role of gray wolves as a keystone species:

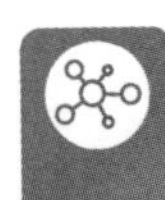
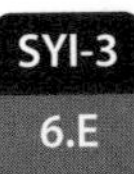

ISBN: 978-1-98-856656-6

Sea otters as keystone species

- Sometimes the significant keystone effects of a species are evident when a species declines rapidly to the point of near extinction. This is illustrated by the sea otter example described below.
- Sea otters live along the Northern Pacific coasts and had been hunted for hundreds of years for their fur. Extensive commercial hunting between 1741 and 1911 reduced the global population to fewer than 2000 animals.
- The drop in sea otter numbers had a significant effect on local marine environments. Sea otters feed on shellfish, particularly sea urchins, and keep their populations in check. Sea urchins eat kelp, on which many marine species depend for food and habitat. Without the sea otters, sea urchin numbers increased and the kelp forests were destroyed or severely reduced.
- Sea otters have been protected since 1911 and reintroduced throughout much of their original range. The most secure populations are now in Russia.

Sea otter feeding on a sea urchin

Matt knoth cc BY 2.0

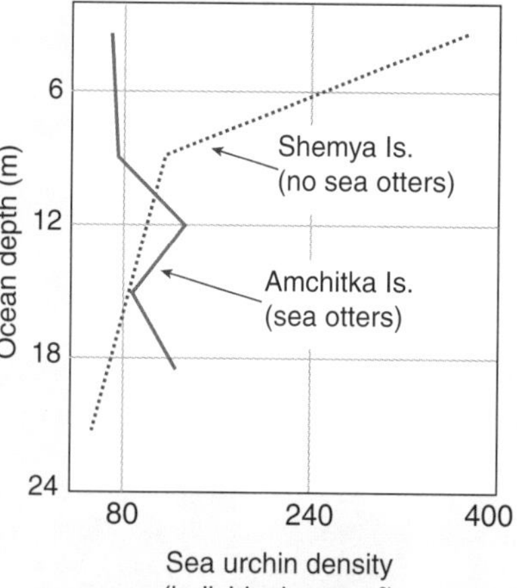

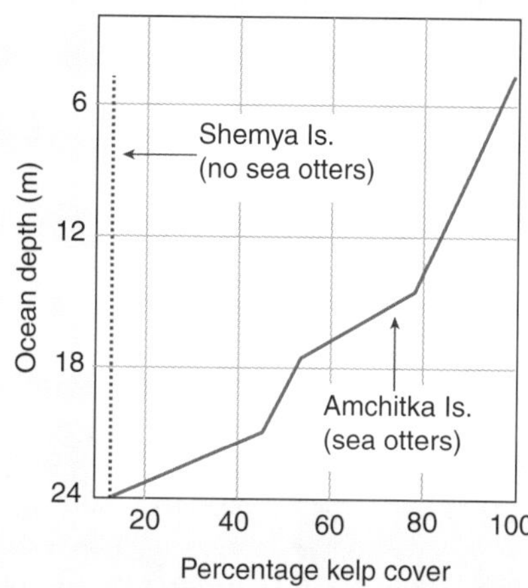

Sea otters are critical to the functioning of North Pacific coastal ecosystems. Their widespread decline, including many local extinctions, was associated with sea urchin increases and widespread disappearance of the kelp forests (above left). In the Aleutian Island group, most islands experienced local extinctions of sea otters. This provided the opportunity to record the ecology of coastal systems with and without sea otters (Palmisano and Estes 1976).

The effect can be seen on Shemya and Amchitka Islands. Where sea otters are absent, there are large numbers of sea urchins and almost no kelp. Sea otters began recolonizing Shemya in the 1990s and the kelp has since recovered.

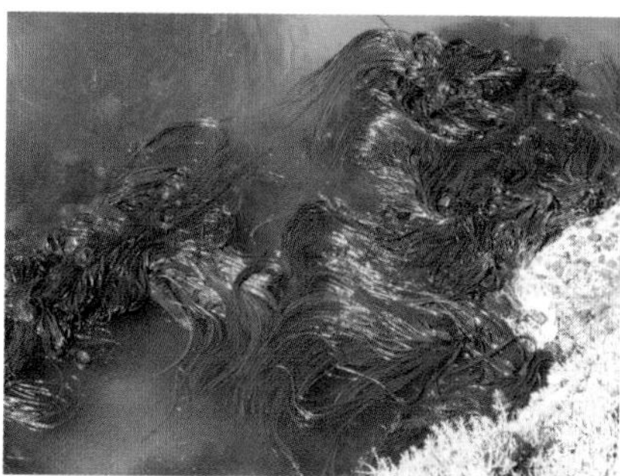

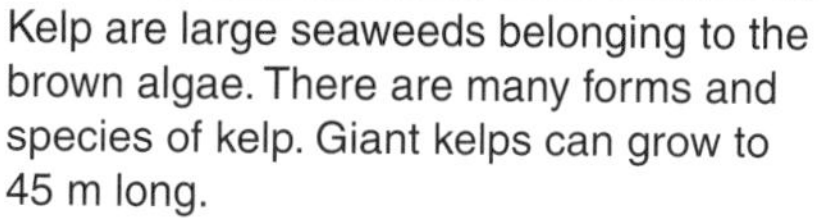
Kelp are large seaweeds belonging to the brown algae. There are many forms and species of kelp. Giant kelps can grow to 45 m long.

In much the same way that forests on land provide diverse habitats for terrestrial species, kelps provide habitat, food, and shelter for a variety of marine animals.

Urchin barren

NPS

Sea urchins kill kelp by eating the holdfast that secures the kelp to the seabed. Unchecked urchin populations can quickly turn a kelp forest into an **urchin barren**.

2. (a) What evidence is there that the sea otter is a keystone species in these Northern Pacific coastal ecosystems?

(b) Predict the effect on the Amchitka Island ecosystem if sea otters became locally extinct:

ISBN: 978-1-98-856656-6

245 Adaptation and Environmental Change

Key Question: How can mutations and preexisting variations help organisms adapt to their environments?

Recall that mutation is the source of all new alleles. Occasionally whole genes, chromosomes, or genomes are duplicated. Gene duplication (if it does not produce serious side effects) allows natural selection to act on and change a gene while also maintaining an unchanged gene to perform the original role. There are many examples of this recorded in the genomes of organisms. Genes for the enzymes in snake venom can be traced to duplicated genes involved in producing enzymes in other parts of the body, including the salivary glands. Mutations can give populations the ability to evolve new features and abilities, allowing them to exploit new opportunities or changes in the environment.

Gene duplication allows the evolution of new abilities

- Sometimes having two genes with the same role (functionality) can be an advantage and both genes retain their original function. For example, when there is a high demand for a particular protein.
- Unless two copies of the same gene provide an advantage, one of the duplicated genes may develop a new function while the other copy continues on with its original function.
- Gene duplication is an important mechanism for generating new genetic material that can be subject to natural selection. Duplicated genes can then follow different evolutionary paths.
- Gene duplication is widespread. The nematode, *Caenorhabditis elegans*, has 49% genes duplicated, the fruit fly, *Drosophila melanogaster*, 41%, and yeast, *Saccharomyces cerevisiae*, 30%.

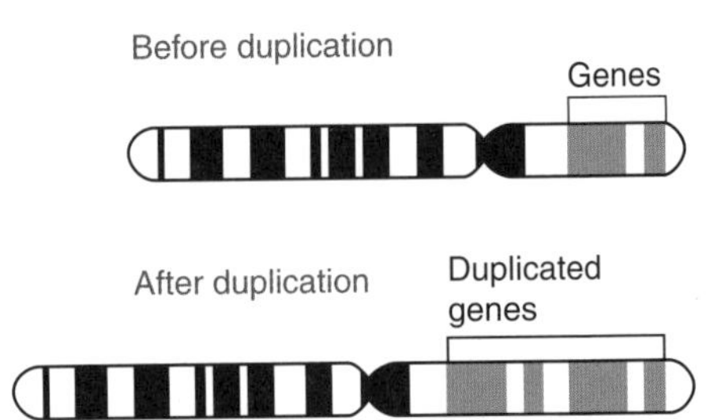

Gene duplication in Antarctic fish

Fish living in the near freezing waters of the Antarctic must have a way of ensuring their blood remains ice free. In many species, this is done by producing proteins with antifreeze properties. There are four major antifreeze proteins used by fish (called AFP types I - IV). The gene for the protein AFP III, found in Antarctic eelpout, is very similar to the gene that produces sialic acid synthase (SAS) (also found in humans).

Molecular studies have found that a slight modification to the SAS gene causes the production and secretion of AFP III protein. Importantly, the SAS gene product shows ice binding capability. It appears that duplication of the SAS gene produced a new gene that was selected for its ice binding capabilities and diverged to become the AFP III gene in Antarctic eelpout.

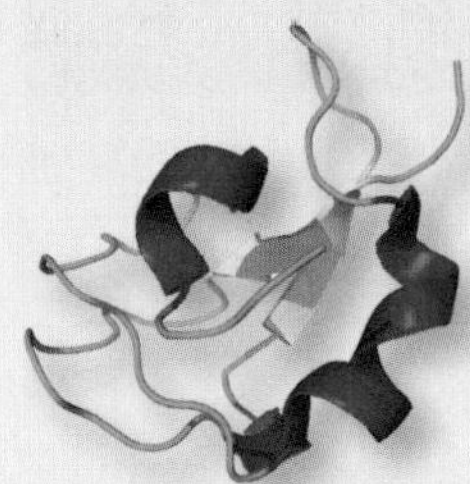

AFP III protein and SAS protein have similar structures and can be modified to have similar functions. This provides evidence for the likelihood of diversification of function after gene duplication.

Gene duplication in colobine monkeys

Gene duplication in colobine monkeys has enabled the production of enzymes that optimally perform similar functions in different bodily environments. Unlike most primates, the main food source of colobines is leaves. The leaves are fermented in the gut by bacteria. The monkeys, like ruminants, obtain their nitrogen through RNase-mediated digestion of RNA from these bacteria. In colobines, there are two forms of the RNase genes, **RNase1** and **RNase1B**, while other primates only have RNase1.

The optimal pH for the enzyme RNase1 and RNase1B are 7.4 and 6.3 respectively. In colobines, the pH of the digestive system is 6-7, but in other primates it is 7.4-8. RNase1B is six times more efficient at degrading RNA in the gut of colobines than RNase1. RNase1 is also expressed in cells outside the digestive system where it degrades ds RNA and may defend against viral infection. RNase1B is 300 times less efficient at this function.

Red colobus

1. Explain how gene duplication can result in the evolution of a new gene function: ______________________

2. Describe the evidence that the AFPIII protein in the Antarctic eel pout may have evolved through a duplication of the SAS gene:

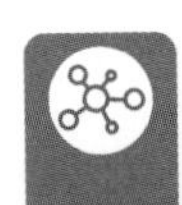
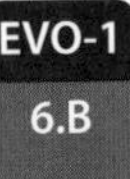

ISBN: 978-1-98-856656-6

Rapid adaptation in pasture grasses

- A well documented example of how environmental change can drive genetic change in populations is found in the grass browntop (*Agrostis capillaris*) growing on pasture and contaminated soil around a copper mine site. Tolerant plants were those able to grow on the contaminated mine soil whereas non-tolerant plants were less able to grow on the mine soil and had reduced fitness (survival and reproduction). Tolerant plants had reduced fitness when growing on uncontaminated soil.
- Flowering stages were used to calculate the number of days plants at each transect site were reproductively isolated (when they could not interbreed). Tolerant and not tolerant plants were genetically distinct, with a hybrid zone between. Similar results were obtained for sweet vernal growing on a zinc and lead mining site (also in Wales).

Drws-y-Coed mine (Wales) Browntop (*Agrostis capillaris*)

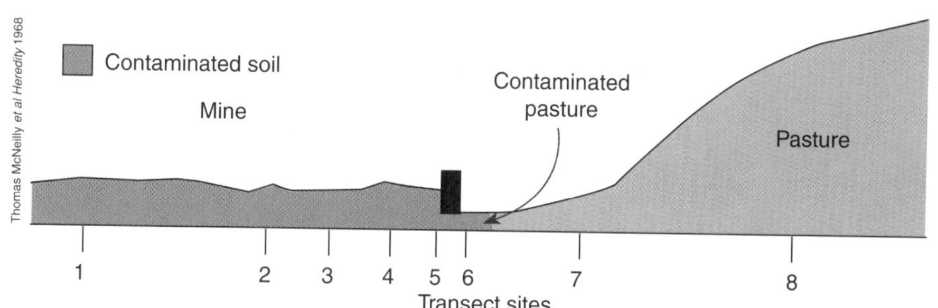

Dam below Drws-y-Coed copper mine

- About 25% of the tolerant plant population flowered earlier than non-tolerant plants, preventing interbreeding between the populations.
- These flowering differences were verified as genetic by removing plants to a controlled environment where the difference in flowering was still observed.

Flowering isolation in browntop

Isolation time (days)	Tolerant			Intermediate	Non-tolerant	
Year \ Site	2	3	4	5	6	7
1964	6.09	5.96	12.17	7.95	0	3.23
1965	3.73	4.86	8.49	7.85	0	2.79

3. Describe the evidence for the adaptation of browntop grass to soil contamination by copper: ______

4. Explain how tolerant and intolerant grasses have become genetically isolated: ______

5. How was the difference in flowering time between tolerant and non-tolerant plants confirmed to be genetically influenced rather than environmentally influenced?

6. The North American pika is a thermally sensitive, cold-adapted specialist species found in the mountains of western North America. In the southern extent of their range they are usually found above 2500 m. Pika are very sensitive to high temperatures and will die if exposed to temperatures above 25.5°C for even a few hours. Their strategies for avoiding thermal stress are largely behavioral and they seek out cool microclimates to avoid high temperatures. A survey in 2014-2015 found widespread evidence of a decrease in range, shifting to higher altitude, and local extinction. Explain why climate warming threatens pika populations and why biologists are worried for their future:

ISBN: 978-1-98-856656-6

246 Invasive Species and Community Change

Key Question: Why are invasive species such a problem and how can they be dealt with?

Introduced (or alien) species are those that have evolved at one place in the world and have been transported by humans, either intentionally or inadvertently, to another region. Some of these introductions are beneficial, e.g. introduced agricultural plants and animals. **Invasive species** are those alien species that have a detrimental effect on the ecosystems into which they have been imported. There are hundreds of these species with varying degrees of undesirability to humans and the environment they have invaded. Humans have deliberately introduced many of these species into new environments, whereas others have been accidentally imported with cargo shipments or in the ballast of ships. Some have been deliberately introduced to control another pest species and have themselves become a problem. Some of the most destructive of all alien species are fast growing plants, e.g. mile-a-minute weed (a perennial vine from Central and South America), velvet tree (a South American tree invading Hawaii and Tahiti), and *Caulerpa* seaweed, the aquarium strain now found in the Mediterranean. Below are two invasive species now causing real problems in the United States.

Kudzu

- Kudzu (*Pueraria lobata*) is a climbing vine native to south-east Asia. It spreads aggressively by vegetative reproduction and is a serious invasive pest in the southern US, where it has been spreading at a rate of 61,000 ha per annum. Kudzu was first introduced to the US in the 1800s as an ornamental plant for shade porches, and was subsequently widely distributed as a high-protein cattle fodder and as a cover plant to prevent soil erosion. It grew virtually unchecked in the climate of the Southeastern US and was finally listed as a weed in 1970, more than a decade after it was removed from a list of suggested cover plants. Today, kudzu is estimated to cover 3 million ha of land in the southeastern US.

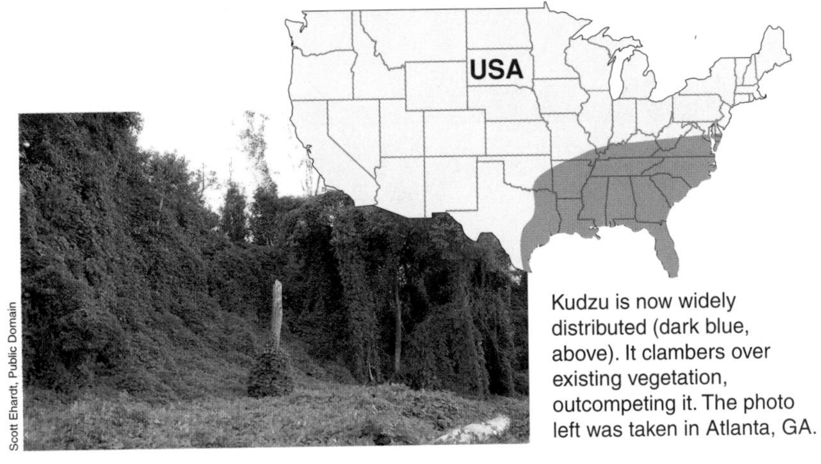

Kudzu is now widely distributed (dark blue, above). It clambers over existing vegetation, outcompeting it. The photo left was taken in Atlanta, GA.

Zebra mussels

- Zebra mussels (*Dreissena polymorpha*) are freshwater mussels native to the Black, Caspian, and Azov Seas. They have become a highly invasive species in many parts of the world. Zebra mussels reproduce prolifically, crowding out native species and severely affecting food chains where native mussels and clams are food for other species.
- Zebra mussels have also affected human activities. They often grow in the intake pipes of hydroelectric turbines and the bottom of boats and anchor chains, and must be regularly removed. Establishing prevention measures is costly. It is estimated zebra mussels have cost North American communities around $5 billion since their introduction.

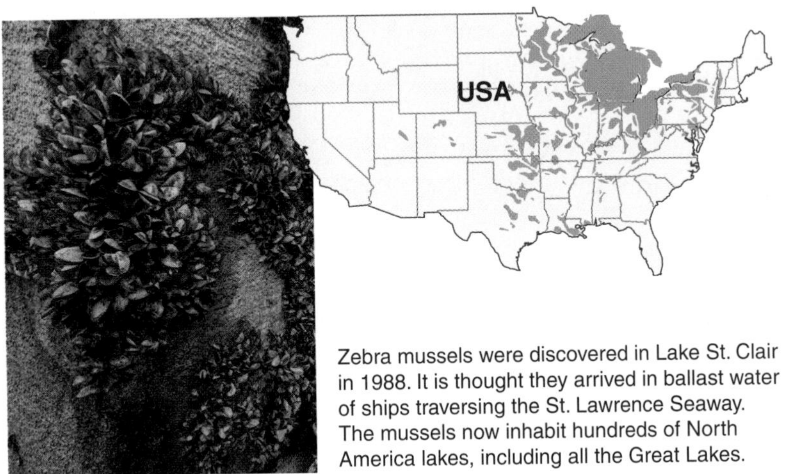

Zebra mussels were discovered in Lake St. Clair in 1988. It is thought they arrived in ballast water of ships traversing the St. Lawrence Seaway. The mussels now inhabit hundreds of North America lakes, including all the Great Lakes.

1. How do alien species arrive in a new environment? ____________________

2. Describe the factors involved in the spread of Kudzu through the USA: ____________________

3. Explain why zebra mussels are an economically-costly invasive species: ____________________

ISBN: 978-1-98-856656-6

What makes an invasive species?

- Many native species live in what can be called "balance with their ecosystem". Their population never gets too high because they normally have predators, parasites, or pathogens that reduce or keep the population in check, or they run out of food or space.
- Slow breeding species are unlikely to become invasive because of the time it takes for their population to increase, meaning they can be controlled by culling. Animals with specific habitats or diets are also unlikely to become invasive.
- Invasive species tend to be *r*-selected species and generalists. When in a new environment, they have few predators or pathogens and their population can increase rapidly. An example is the New Zealand mud snail (*Potamopyrgus antipodarum*).
- The NZ mud snail is a freshwater snail that lives in streams and lakes. It is endemic to New Zealand and is only about 12 mm long and 5 mm high.
- Despite being so small and from a country 2000 km away from the nearest larger landmass, the NZ mud snail has been accidently introduced to at least a dozen countries including in Europe and North America. Outside of New Zealand it is considered one of the worst invasive freshwater species.
- The snail is such a successful invader because it tolerates a wide range of environments. These include both fresh and brackish water, disturbed environments, temperatures from 0°C to 34°C, and long lengths of time out of water. It breeds both sexually and asexually and can produce up to 230 young per year. In Lake Zurich, Switzerland, it was reported to have reached population densities of 800,000 per m^2.
- Outside of New Zealand the snail has no predators, parasites, or pathogens. It survives passage through the gut of many fish and birds, and can float, allowing for rapid spread.

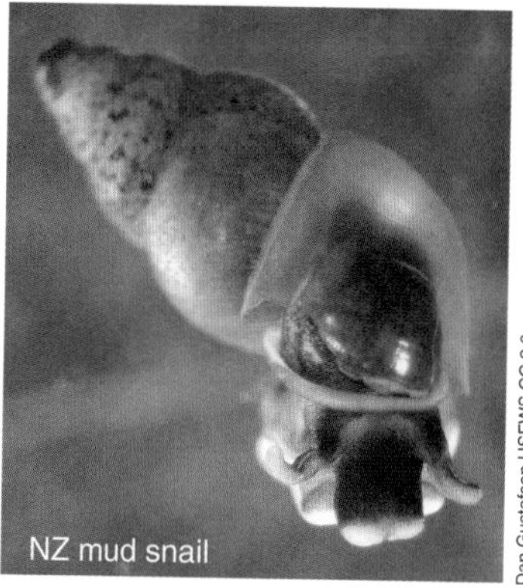
NZ mud snail

Dan Gustafson USFWS CC 2.0

NZ mud snail in the United States

- The NZ mud snail was first detected in the US in 1987 in Snake River in Idaho. It has since spread throughout the United States. It is thought the snail arrived in ship ballast or possibly via live game fish or contaminated wading gear.
- Densities have reached up to 500,000 per m^2 in some rivers. Native snail species have become endangered as they are out-competed. This affects species further up the food chain as their natural food source is reduced.

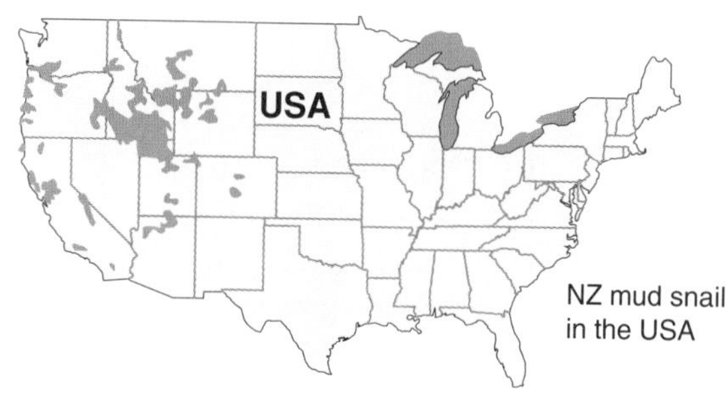

NZ mud snail in the USA

4. Describe the biological attributes of the NZ mud snail that make it such an invasive species:

5. Describe how it affects the ecosystem it invades:

6. Use the data provided above to support or reject the hypothesis that "*eradication of the New Zealand mud snail from freshwater waterways in the USA is possible.*" Justify your reasoning:

7. Use online searching to find out about an invasive species in your region. When did it arrive? What area does it cover? What are its effects on the environment? Are there any plans in place for its removal? Summarize your findings below:

ISBN: 978-1-98-856656-6

Invasive species affect community structure

- One of the major problems of invasive species is their effect on the food webs and trophic structure of the ecosystem they invade. Their impact depends on their trophic position in the ecosystem.
- New Zealand mud snails are scraper-grazers, eating epiphytic algae, periphyton, and biofilms on the lake bottom (see definitions right). They can outcompete other consumers of benthic (bottom-dwelling) algae, so they have a major bottom-up effect on the animals that feed at this level and the animals that feed on them.

Important definitions for understanding production in lakes

Planktonic algae: Algae floating in the open water.

Epiphytic algae: Algae growing on the surfaces of other algae and plants.

Periphyton: A mixture of algae, bacteria, and detritus that is attached to submerged surfaces.

Biofilms: Microbial communities attached to surfaces.

Food webs

- As you saw earlier, food webs show how food chains in an ecosystem are interconnected. The arrows show which organism eats which, and indicate the direction of the **flow of energy**. In the food web below, typical of the North American Great Lakes, mussels and bloodworms are eaten by freshwater drum and round goby.

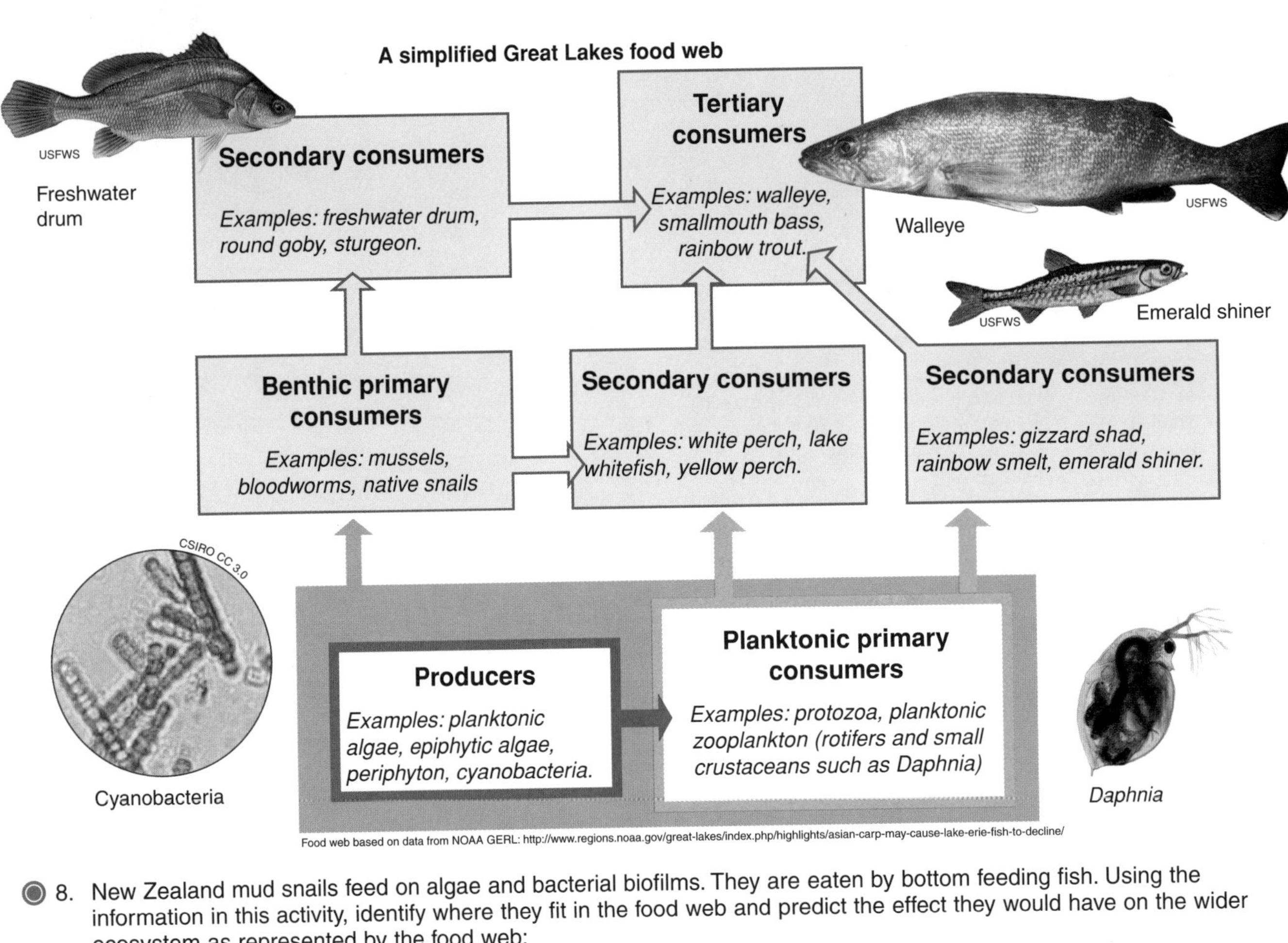

Food web based on data from NOAA GERL: http://www.regions.noaa.gov/great-lakes/index.php/highlights/asian-carp-may-cause-lake-erie-fish-to-decline/

8. New Zealand mud snails feed on algae and bacterial biofilms. They are eaten by bottom feeding fish. Using the information in this activity, identify where they fit in the food web and predict the effect they would have on the wider ecosystem as represented by the food web:

9. New Zealand mud snails have no natural predators or parasites in North America, nor do they have any real competitors. As a result they have unchecked growth. Describe the likely impact of this on community structure on the Great Lakes:

ISBN: 978-1-98-856656-6

247 Human Activity and Ecosystem Changes

Key Question: How have human activities affected local and global ecosystems?

There is no question that the world's ecosystems and biodiversity are under threat. The many factors that are causing this can be summarized as HIPPCO (**H**abitat destruction, **I**nvasive species, (human) **P**opulation growth, **P**ollution, **C**limate change, and **O**ver exploitation). Habitat destruction, and its consequent ecological changes, are a major component of HIPPCO. Vast areas of land and sea are exploited for their resources, often with little regard to the environmental impact of this exploitation. Invasive species, including new diseases, have also played an important role in changing ecosystems globally. Invasive species outcompete natives, and new diseases, especially those affecting plants, can drastically alter ecosystems. Global climate change has contributed to the spread of some diseases, including chytridiomycosis, which has caused the dramatic reduction in amphibian species around the world.

Habitat fragmentation and biodiversity

- Habitat fragmentation is the process by which large habitats become divided up into smaller ones, usually with areas of completely changed (and often uncrossable) land between them. This can happen naturally (e.g. lava flows dividing areas of forest) but more often it occurs as a result of human activities (e.g. building roads or removing large parts of forests).
- Habitat fragmentation can be a driver of evolution, creating greater biodiversity by separating species' populations. This has occurred many times on the islands of Hawaii for example. However this is usually a response of smaller organisms, such as insects.
- Usually habitat fragmentation causes a loss of biodiversity, especially in larger animals that are territorial or require large areas of land to find food. Habitat fragmentation reduces population sizes and can reduce gene flow because individuals are unable to move easily between habitat fragments. This can lead to inbreeding because access to mates is limited. Fragmentation also affects plants. Invasive plant species are more able to invade fragments due to more open edges, which often provide disturbed land where they can easily become established.
- The degree of fragmentation of a species' habitat is a significant predictor of the likelihood of a species going extinct. The IUCN (International Union for Conservation of Nature) lists species from least concern to critically endangered. When the species in these categories are matched against the degree of their habitat's fragmentation a clear pattern emerges (right).

Forest fragmentation, Brazil

NASA

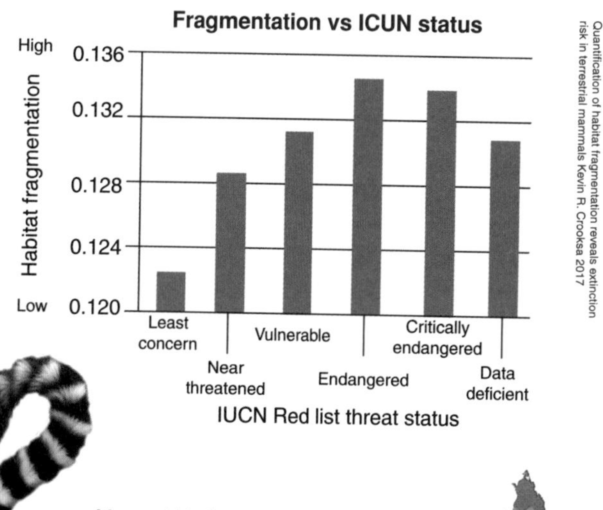

Quantification of habitat fragmentation reveals extinction risk in terrestrial mammals Kevin R. Crooksa 2017

Habitat fragmentation in Madagascar

- Madagascar has three main forest types, dry, humid, and spiny (diagram far right) and is known as a biodiversity "hotspot". Over 90% of its wildlife is endemic (found nowhere else).
- Madagascar's forests and wildlife are increasingly threatened by encroaching human activity. Many of its forests are being slowly destroyed by activities such as slash and burn farming. This has led to an increasing amount of forest fragmentation with large areas of forest becoming increasingly scarce.

Many of Madagascar's iconic lemur species are critically endangered

Dry

Humid

Spiny

Madagascar forest types

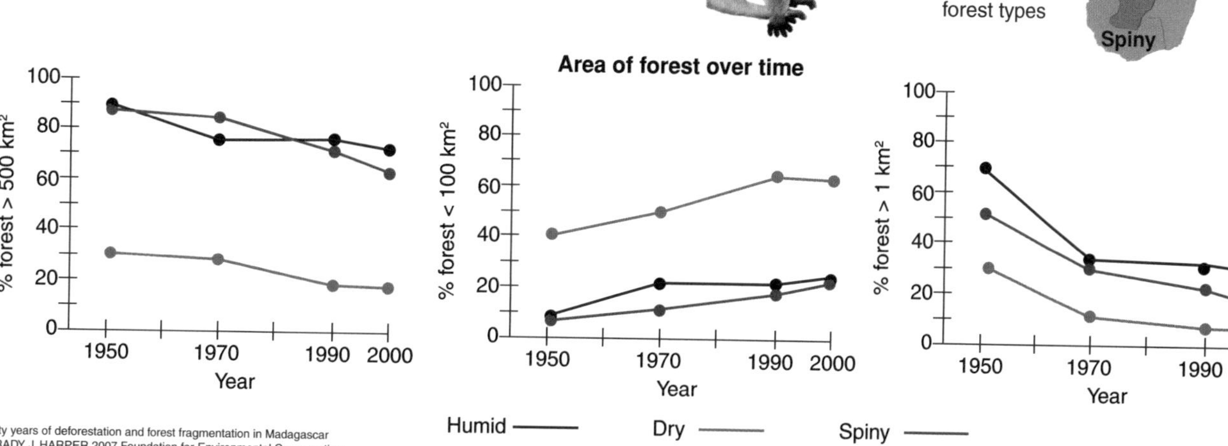

Fifty years of deforestation and forest fragmentation in Madagascar GRADY J. HARPER 2007 Foundation for Environmental Conservation

ISBN: 978-1-98-856656-6

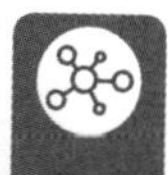

How humans affect the environment

Projections of current human population growth predict the human population will reach between 9 and 11 billion by 2050. This growth will create an increasing demand on natural resources, particularly water, arable land, and minerals. As the human population increases, cities expand, fragmenting or destroying the natural ecosystems surrounding them. Careful management of urban development and resource use will be needed to prevent loss of biodiversity.

Human exploitation of natural populations has driven some species to the brink of extinction, or significantly reduced their populations. Examples include overfishing of many fish populations such as North Sea cod. Most industry still depends on the combustion of fossil fuels and this contributes to climate change. Climate changes may affect species distributions, breeding cycles, and patterns of migration. Species unable to adapt are at risk of extinction

Eighty percent of Earth's documented species are found in tropical rainforests. These rainforests are being destroyed rapidly as land is cleared for agriculture or cattle ranching, to supply logs, for mining, or to build dams. Deforestation places a majority of the Earth's biodiversity at risk and threatens the stability of important ecosystems. More over rainforests have important roles in moderating climate and rainfall. Their loss could several affect global climate.

1. (a) What is habitat fragmentation? __________

   (b) Describe some of the causes of habitat fragmentation: __________

2. A study found a species habitat was moderately fragmented. What is its probable IUCN threat status?

3. Interpret the data on the previous page to describe how habitat fragmentation has affected forest size in Madagascar:

4. Why would loss of Madagascar's forests be particularly significant for global biodiversity? __________

5. The human population is growing at a rapid rate. As a result, the demand for resources in increasing. Discuss how human activities are affecting local and global ecosystems:

ISBN: 978-1-98-856656-6

The effect of a new disease in an environment: Dutch elm disease

- Dutch elm disease (DED) is caused by the fungus *Ophiostoma ulmi* and affects trees in the elm family (*Ulmus* and *Zelkova*) causing wilt. The disease is spread by the elm bark beetle. It originated in Asia and was accidently introduced to Europe, North America, and much later, New Zealand. Where the disease has been introduced it has quickly caused the loss of large numbers of elm trees by clogging their vascular tissue.

DED in North America

DED arrived in North America in 1928. Efforts to contain the disease were reduced during WWII and by 1989 North America has lost an estimated 75% of its elms.

DED in Minnesota

As in other U.S. states, elms were commonly used in Minnesota as shade trees in municipal areas, such as in parks and along streets. By 1950s, Minnesota had around 140 million elms in parks and lining streets and streams. DED did not reach Minnesota until about 1960, although it was known to be in many surrounding states. Measures that could have been taken to stop its introduction into Minnesota, such as restricting elm planting and controlling the import of logs, could have reduced the impact when the disease arrived. The city of Minneapolis was estimated to have an elm population of over 200,000 in 1970. Losses began slowly, but rapidly increased until an aggressive sanitation campaign began in 1977. However, by around 1990 the elm population had reduced to about 100,000.

This campaign, including trimming, stump removal, and replanting, cost Minneapolis around $60 million between 1978 and 1988.

Elm trees lost in Minneapolis

Year	Losses per year
1972	222
1973	225
1974	937
1975	1688
1976	7239
1977	31,475
1978	20,813
1979	6751
1980	4184
1981	5068
1982	3389
1983	2144
1984	4965
1985	4087
1986	2896
1987	2280

Elm afflicted by DED

DED in the United Kingdom

DED appeared in Europe in 1910 and a much deadlier strain appeared in 1967. In the UK, these strains have killed 60 million trees. France has lost nearly 90% of its elm trees.

Elm trees lost in the UK

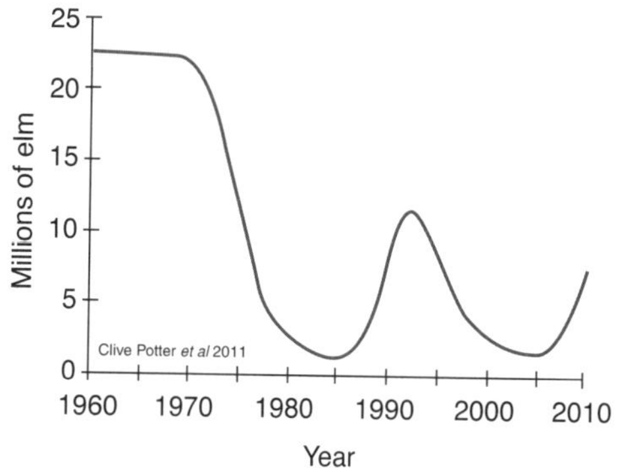

Tree numbers drop rapidly as management removes infected trees. New trees grow, but new infections, outbreaks, and repeated management reduces numbers.

Nests in elm trees for kestrel and stock dove

	Kestrel (*Falco tinnunculus*)	Stock dove (*Columba oenas*)
1970	15	20
1971	12	15
1972	11	11
1973	10	26
1974	11	5
1975	8	10
1976	8	8
1977	7	7

The number of nests of various British birds recorded in elm trees reduced significantly over the 1970s as elm trees succumbed to DED. Interestingly, the kestrel actually increased its population numbers five fold over this time.

6. (a) What causes Dutch elm disease? __________

   (b) How is it spread? __________

7. (a) In what year Dutch elm disease peak in Minnesota? __________

   (b) Why did cases begin to fall after this date? __________

8. Is there evidence for an indirect effect of Dutch elm disease on bird populations in the UK? Explain: __________

ISBN: 978-1-98-856656-6

248 Natural Events and Ecosystems

Key Question: What are the agents of natural ecosystem change and how do these changes vary in scale?

Ecosystems are dynamic systems, and natural disruptions are common. Environmental changes come from three sources: the biosphere, geological events (e.g volcanic eruptions, plate tectonics), and meteorological events (e.g. El Niño). All these can cause cycles, steady states, and directional changes (trends) in the environment. Many of these disruptions, e.g. seasonal changes and tidal movements, are periodic in occurrence and allow organisms to adapt to the predictable changes. Others, such as volcanic eruptions, are episodic and largely unpredictable. Ecosystem changes also occur over very different scales of time and space, from large scale geological and climate changes (below), to shorter term localized changes in weather. Extraordinary natural events, e.g. asteroid impacts, can result in the loss of ecosystems.

El Niño effect

- The El Niño-Southern Oscillation (ENSO) is a climate cycle that has a periodicity of three to seven years. El Niño years cause a reversal of the usual climate regime and are connected to such economically disastrous events as the collapse of fisheries stocks (e.g the Peruvian anchovy stock), severe flooding in the Mississippi Valley, drought-induced crop failures, and forest fires in Australia and Indonesia. It is also responsible for greening of the Chilean deserts.

- In **non-El Niño** conditions, a low pressure system over Australia draws the southeast trade winds across the eastern Pacific from a high pressure system over South America. This system produces rain in the area of Australasia and dry conditions on the coast of South America.

- In an **El Niño** event (right), the pressure systems over Australia and South America are weakened or reversed, beginning with a rise in air pressure over the Indian Ocean, Indonesia, and Australia. Warm waters block the nutrient upwelling along the west coast of the Americas. El Niño brings drought to Indonesia and northeastern South America, while heavy rain over Peru and Chile causes the deserts to bloom.

El Niño weather pattern

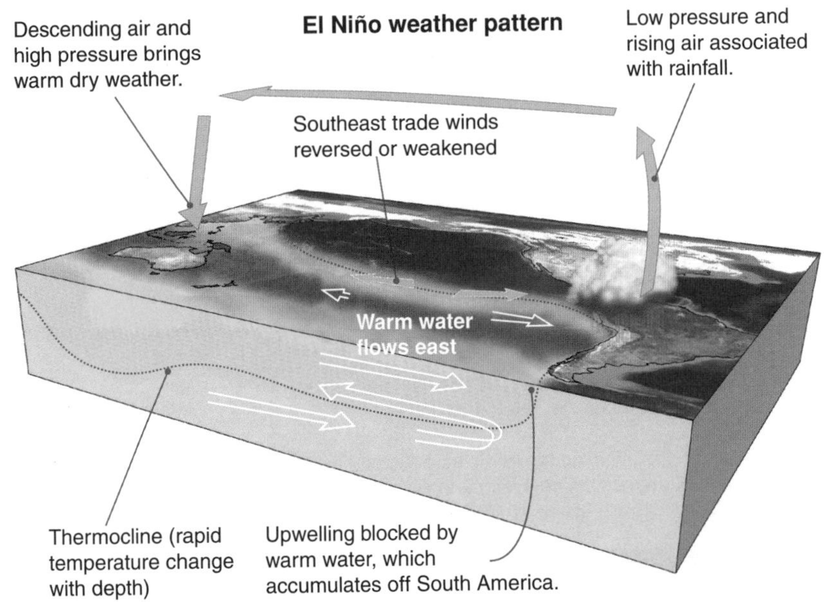
Descending air and high pressure brings warm dry weather.
Low pressure and rising air associated with rainfall.
Southeast trade winds reversed or weakened
Warm water flows east
Thermocline (rapid temperature change with depth)
Upwelling blocked by warm water, which accumulates off South America.

During non-El Niño years, cool nutrient-rich waters along the South American coast sustain huge populations of fish such as anchovy. During El Niño events, warm waters reduce nutrient supply, and fish populations either crash or move to feeding grounds elsewhere.

Javier Rubilar CC 2.0

El Niño events bring more rain to deserts in parts of South America and the Baja California. On the islands of the Gulf of California, plant cover increases from 0-4% during non-El Niño years to 54-89% during El Niño years. In Northern Chile plant cover increased over five times during El Niño.

Dan Harkless CC 4.0

El Niño events affect terrestrial animal communities too. On the islands of the Gulf of California, spider densities doubled in response to high levels of insect prey resulting from increases in plant abundance. The population later crashed as parasitoid wasps proliferated.

1. Describe the effects of El Niño on the ecosystems of:

(a) Chilean deserts: ______

(b) Islands of the Gulf of California: ______

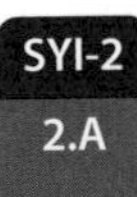
SYI-2
2.A

199

241

ISBN: 978-1-98-856656-6

Episodic events can disrupt ecosystems

- Periodically, the Earth experiences geological and meteorological events that can have long lasting effects. The size of the event often dictates how long the effects last for.

Eruptions

- Although there are 50-70 volcanic eruptions each year, most of these are small. Occasionally there are extremely large and long-lasting eruptions. These can affect the globe by blasting ash and aerosols into the atmosphere and producing tsunamis (when near the sea) that can travel vast distances.
- Modern examples of these effects include Mount Pinatubo, in the Philippines, which erupted in 1991. The Earth's climate was severely affected by Pinatubo's eruption. Over the course of the eruption, some 17 million tonnes of SO_2 and 10 km^3 of ash were released into the atmosphere. The ash caused an almost 10% reduction in sunlight reaching the Earth's surface over the following year, and global temperatures dropped by 0.5°C over the following 2-3 years. Similarly, the eruption of El Chichon in Mexico, 1982, lowered the global temperature by 0.5°C over two years, emitting about half the SO_2 volume of Pinatubo.
- In the 1800s, the eruptions of Tambora and Krakatau in Indonesia affected climate as far away as Europe and North America. Effects included early snow falls and cold wet weather. 1816, the year after the Tambora eruption, was called the year without summer.

The eruption column of Mount Pinatubo on June 12, 1991, three days before the final eruption phase.

Ice ages

- Some changes to the Earth happen on such vast time scales that they are not perceivable to humans. Changes may take place over thousands to million of years. Some changes occur in cycles (periodic), such as the advance and retreat of ice sheets, while others are continuous, such as continental drift.
- The Earth has gone through five ice ages, i.e. long periods of time when large ice sheets covered large parts of the globe. The latest ice age began about 2.7 million years ago and is still ongoing. Within an ice age, there are periods of warmer climate conditions called interglacials, such as the present. The cooler periods of time are called glacials. These tend to last longer than the interglacials.
- The current interglacial began about 12,000 years ago. Antarctic ice cores (right) confirm the cycle of glacials (blue) and interglacials (yellow) as ice sheets advanced and retreated. Ice cores reveal a lot of climate data, reaching depths of more than 3 km and extending back 800,000 years.

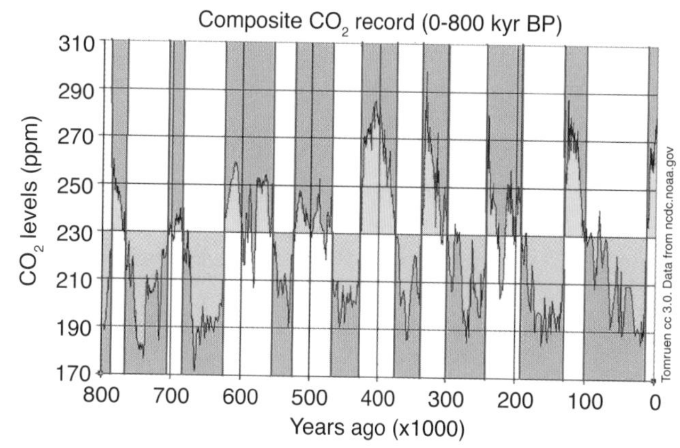

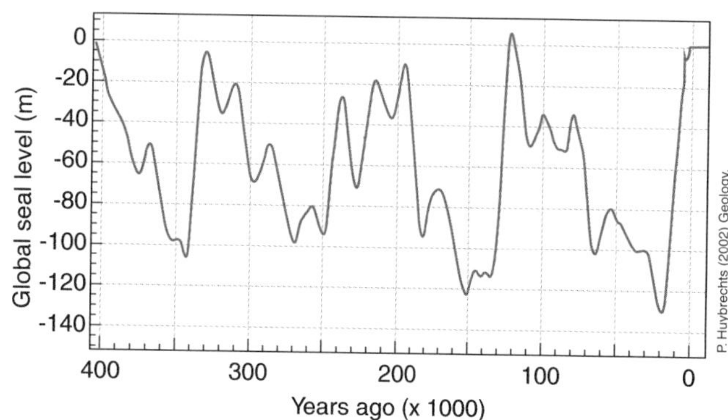

Asteroid impacts

- More rarely and unpredictably the Earth is hit by large asteroids. These asteroid impacts can totally change the Earth's ecosystems. It has been shown almost conclusively that the extinction of the dinosaurs was linked to global climate change (an impact winter) associated with the impact of a 10 km wide asteroid near the Yucatan Peninsula in Mexico.

2. Describe how volcanic eruptions can affect local ecosystems and the wider climate: ______

3. Using the data above, describe the climate and sea level changes during the latest (current) ice age: ______

ISBN: 978-1-98-856656-6

249 Personal Progress Check

Answer the multiple choice questions that follow by circling the correct answer. Don't forget to read the question carefully!

Questions 1-2 relate to the plot below.

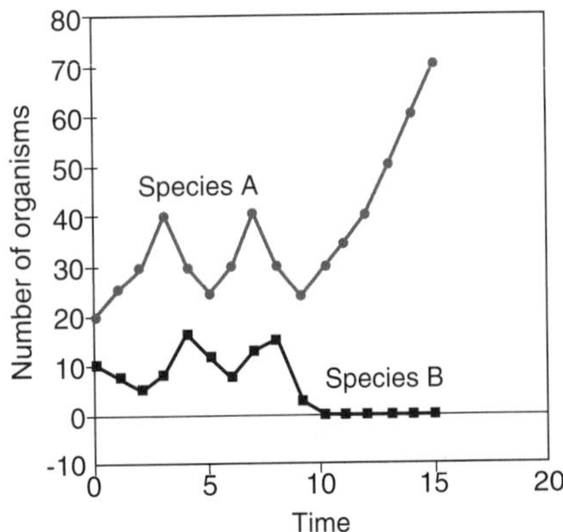

1. Species A and B are found in the same ecosystem. What could be inferred from the data presented:
   (a) Species B is the prey of species A
   (b) Species B is the predator of species A
   (c) Species A is a keystone species
   (d) Species A is a parasite of species B

2. Which of the following statements would explain why a species would show cyclic population changes:
   (a) A keystone species in the ecosystem is removed.
   (b) The vegetation on which it depends varies seasonally.
   (c) Climate shifts alter the prevalence of parasites that affect the species.
   (d) A predator of the species is preyed on by a species that is introduced to the ecosystem.

3. Pumas prey on a species of deer in a region. The deer feed on vegetation. What is the most likely outcome if the puma population declines markedly as a result of hunting by humans:
   (a) The deer population will cycle between high and low numbers until the predator returns.
   (b) The deer population will increase and strip the region of vegetation.
   (c) The deer population will decline and vegetation cover will increase.
   (d) The deer population will be stable.

4. Which of the following might be expected if a keystone species is eliminated from an ecosystem:
   (a) Interspecific competition increases.
   (b) There is one less niche available.
   (c) The ecosystem diversity declines.
   (d) There is no significant change.

5. When two species have a close relationship in which both obtain benefits, the relationship is called:
   (a) Symbiosis
   (b) Mutualism
   (c) Commensalism
   (d) Competition

6. The plot below shows the mean net productivity of various biomes. The productivity varies between them because:
   (a) Productivity increases from the poles to the equator.
   (b) The oceans have fewer photosynthetic organisms than terrestrial biomes.
   (c) Productivity is determined largely by available water, light, and nutrients.
   (d) Grasses have lower productivity than trees.

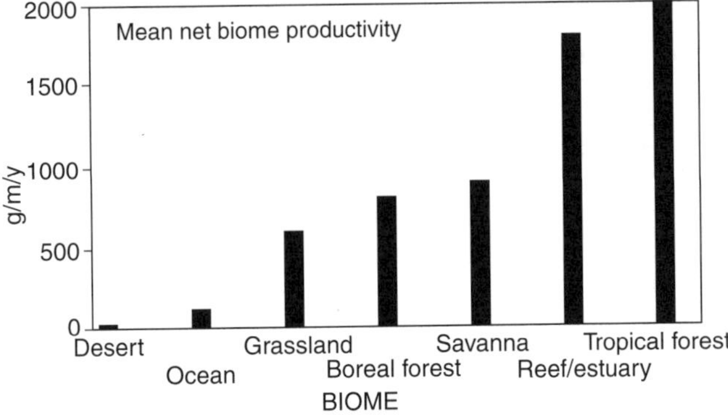

7. The photograph below depicts:
   (a) Intraspecific competition and predation
   (b) Cooperation
   (c) Intra- and interspecific competition and predation
   (d) Interspecific competition and predation

8. The cartoon sequence depicted below illustrates:
   (a) Primary succession
   (b) Secondary succession
   (c) Secondary succession and ecosystem resilience
   (d) Primary succession and ecosystem resistance

Rcole17 CC4.00

9. Maggots turn and move away from bright light towards a dark area. This is an example of:
   (a) Negative phototaxis
   (b) Klinokinesis
   (c) Orthokinesis
   (d) Positive phototaxis

ISBN: 978-1-98-856656-6

10. In which situation are you more likely to observe primary succession?
    (a) Tropical rainforest
    (b) Newly created volcanic island
    (c) Recently burned forest
    (d) A recently flooded field.

11. The plot right show the results of the experimental removal of the starfish *Pisaster* from a region of an ecosystem:

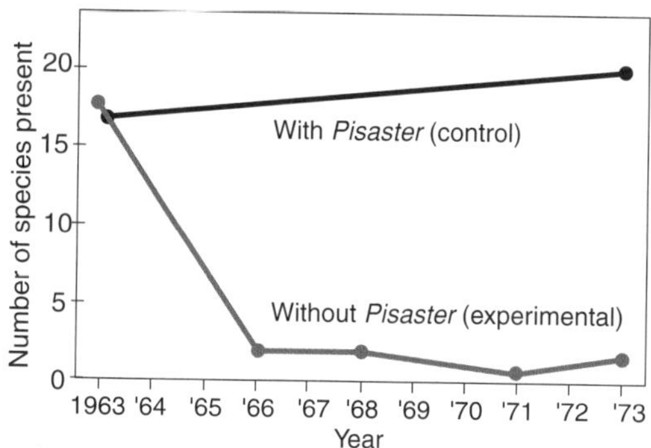

From information on the plot it could be said that:
    (a) *Pisaster* is an effective predator
    (b) Removing *Pisaster* only causes a short term effect
    (c) *Pisaster* has an important role in maintaining species diversity
    (d) Removing *Pisaster* in a benefit to the ecosystem

12. The diagram below depicts a food web for a meadow habitat.

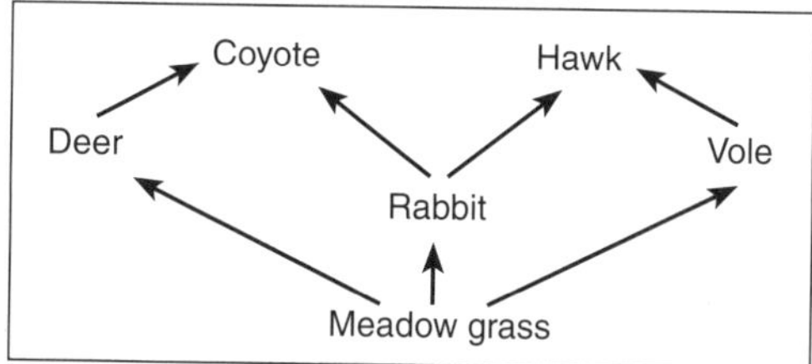

The effect of reducing deer and rabbits from this food web would:
    (a) Likely increase the hawk population because there would be more grass for voles
    (b) Likely reduce the coyote population but not affect the hawk population.
    (c) Likely reduce both the coyote and hawk population but increase the amount of grass available.
    (d) Cause no effect because there would still be deer and rabbits.

13. Which of the following is true about secondary consumers in an ecosystem?
    (a) They are greater in number than primary consumers
    (b) They are the prey of primary consumers
    (c) They are smaller and weaker than are primary consumers
    (d) They are fewer in number than primary consumers

14. The image below shows a:

    (a) Positive phototropism
    (b) Negative phototropism
    (c) Positive phototaxis
    (d) Negative phototaxis

15. The opening and closing of tulip flowers on a daily basis (open in the day closed at night) is:
    (a) A tropism
    (b) A photoperiodic response
    (c) A nastic response
    (d) A kinesis

16. The type of population growth labeled X in the graph below is:

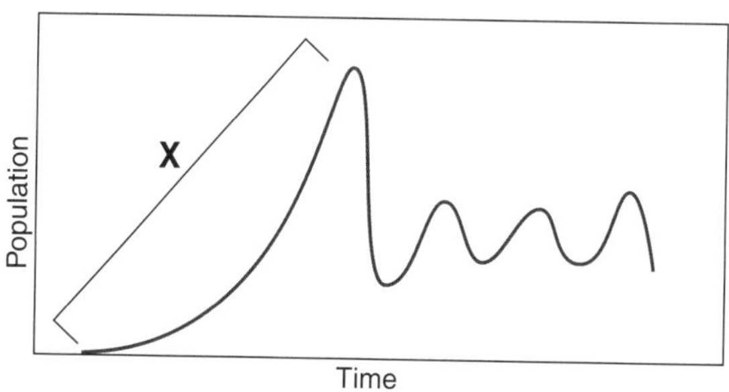

    (a) Exponential growth
    (b) Logistic growth
    (c) Stable
    (d) Density dependent

17. Most of the energy in the biotic ecosystem is found in:
    (a) The primary consumers
    (b) The primary producers
    (c) The secondary consumers
    (d) The primary carnivores

18. Which reason best explains why food chains never exceed more than five trophic levels?
    (a) Most consumers function at more than one trophic level.
    (b) Trophic levels above this number would not contain enough energy to sustain the consumers in them
    (c) Top carnivores are too few in number to prey effectively.
    (d) The ecosystem contains too much biomass

ISBN: 978-1-98-856656-6

Free Response Question: *Interpreting and evaluating experimental results with graphing*

- Disturbances to many coral reefs in the Caribbean is increasingly leading to a shift towards communities dominated by macroalgae, such as the brown alga *Dictyota*, rather than the stony corals (colonial tcnidarians) that build the physical structure of the Caribbean reef ecosystem. These corals depend on symbiotic zooxanthellae (algae) in their tissues, which photosynthesize and provide the coral with the organic compounds it needs to survive.
- Growing evidence that stony corals and macroalgae compete for space (right) led researchers to carry out an experimental study of coral-macroalgal interactions. The investigated the effect of shading and abrasion or young coral polyps (*Agaricia* spp.) by the alga *Dictyota* using experimental manipulations that involved placing cages over areas of coral and simulating crowding or shading of the polyps. Coral colony size in the two treatments was measured after 14 months and compared to cage controls (cages but no manipulation). Pre-treatment trials showed no difference in coral growth inside or outside of cages.
- To simulate crowding, *Dictyota* was added into the cages with the polyps. To simulate shading, *Dictyota* was draped over the cages to reduce the light reaching the polyps. The results are tabulated right.

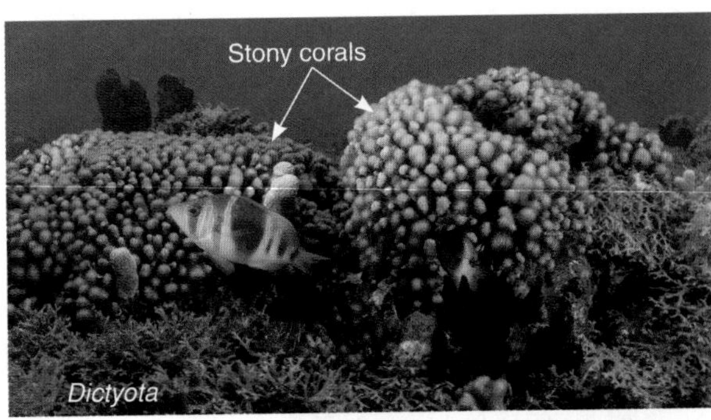

		Percentage increase in colony size	
	n	Mean	95% CI
Cage control	8	284	43
Dictyota added	8	61	19
Dictyota shading	8	71	52

Adapted from data in Box and Mumby (2007).See credits for full citation.

1. (a) **Describe** what is meant by interspecific competition in the context of this study: ______________________

   (b) **Explain** why stony corals would be affected by shading when in competition with macroalgae:

2. **Plot** an appropriate labeled graph of the data tabulated above.

3. **Describe** the results: ______________________

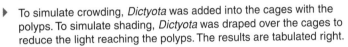

4. **Predict** the likely consequences to Caribbean coral reefs if disturbances that favor growth of macroalgae continue. **Justify** your prediction:

ISBN: 978-1-98-856656-6

Free Response Question: *Scientific investigation*

- Indole Acetic Acid (IAA) is a plant hormone belonging to the auxin group of hormones. Its effect on leaf fall (abscission) in deciduous plants can be investigated by observing how leaf fall is affected in the presence of IAA.

Aim

- To investigate the effect of IAA on leaf stalk abscission in *Coleus* plant sections.

Method

- *Coleus* stems were chosen for this experiment.
- The plant stems were cut 1 cm above and below where the leaf stalk (petiole) attached to the main stem. The stem sections were then cut in half vertically, so each half consisted of a leaf attached to the stem (diagram A). The leaves were cut off where the leaf blade and leaf stalk joined. A total of 10 samples (5 pairs) were prepared.
- One of each pair had waterproof lanolin applied to the cut end of the leaf stalk. Lanolin containing 1% of IAA was applied to the other stem section of each pair.
- The samples were placed cut surface down on wet filter paper and placed into a clear plastic box enclosed within a plastic bag so they did not dry out (diagram B). A light source was provided.
- The samples were examined daily for 4-8 days.

Diagram A

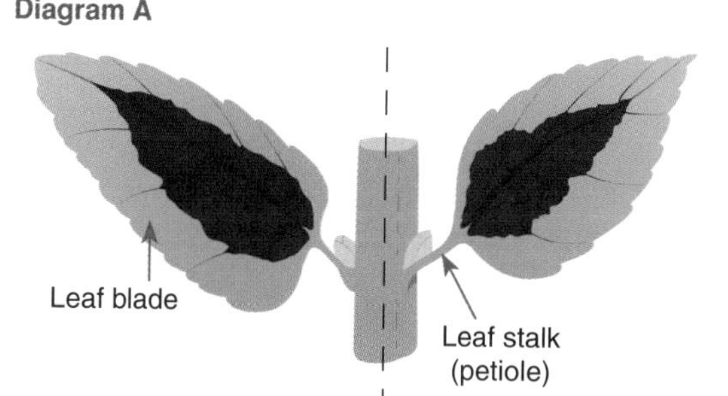

Coleus stems were cut in half vertically to produce two samples.

Diagram B

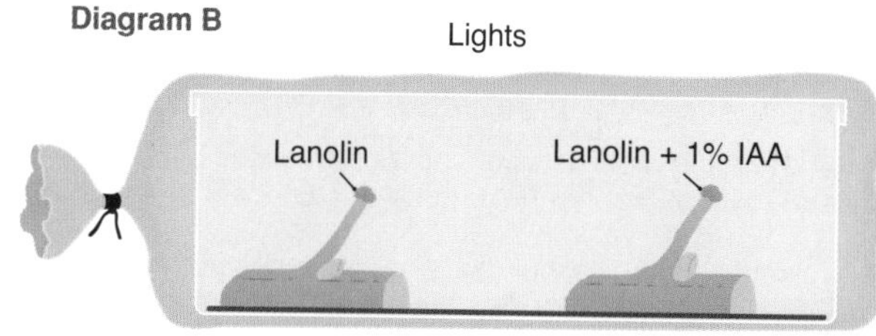

The leaves were removed from the leaf stalks. One of two treatments was applied to the cut surface of the leaf stalks before the samples were place in the experimental chamber.

Adapted from Science & Plants for Schools, www.saps.org.uk

1. **Describe** the biological basis for this investigation of plant growth regulation: ______

2. **Identify** the control for this experiment: ______

3. **Predict** the effect of IAA on leaf stalk abscission in this experiment: ______

4. **Justify** your prediction: ______

ISBN: 978-1-98-856656-6

SKILLS SUPPORT

Science Practices

Learning Objectives

Developing understanding

CONTENT: Science practices describe the things you should be able to do while you are covering the content of this AP® Biology course. They represent the practices that underlie the study of any science and are categorized into skills. See the table on page xii at the front of this book for a summary of skills and practices and a key to identifying them in the activities.

SKILLS: This supporting unit provides a background reference for the skills you will use throughout this course of study. You will develop competency in these skills as you complete the activities in this book. These skills form the basis of the tasks in the AP® Biology exam.

1 Concept explanation .... activity 250

Key: Use verbal and/or written skills

☐ V. In describing biological concepts or processes you will need to identify relevant features of a concept or process.

☐ W. To explain biological concepts or processes you will need to provide explanatory detail relating to the concept or process, rather than just describing its components.

☐ X. To explain biological concepts/processes in applied contexts you must relate your explanations to real world situations.

2 Analyze visual representations......... activity 251

Key: Create and use visual representations

☐ A. Describing the features of a biological concept, process, or model represented visually might involve describing the features of a diagram or a plot.

☐ B. Explaining relationships between characteristics of concepts/processes represented visually might involve comparing or predicting patterns or trends or explaining a visual model.

☐ C. Explaining how a visual representation relates to broader principles, concepts, processes, or theories might involve drawing a conclusion based on principles or concepts in the model or representation.

☐ D. Representing relationships within biological models might involve interacting with a mathematical formula or chemical equation, or creating a diagram or flowchart.

3 Questions and methods .... activity 252

Key: Pose, refine, and evaluate scientific questions

☐ A. Identifying/posing a testable question means asking, refining, and evaluating questions about natural phenomena and investigating answers, e.g. through experimentation.

☐ B. You should be able to state null and alternative hypotheses and predict the results of an experiment.

☐ C. Identifying experimental procedures includes identifying variables, and identifying and justifying controls.

☐ D. To make observations or collect data from laboratory setups you will need to collect first-hand data from observations.

☐ E. Proposing a new investigation may be based on evaluating the evidence from an experiment or the design/methods.

4 Representing and describing data ... activity 253

Key: Plotting and describing different types of data

☐ A. Constructing a graph/plot/chart involves correct choice of plot type (e.g. line or bar graph), orientation, labeling, units, scaling, plotting, and trend line (for line graphs).

☐ B. Describing data from a table or graph may involve identifying specific data points, describing trends or patterns in the data, or describing the relationships between variables.

5 Statistical tests and data analysis...... activity 254

Key: Use mathematics to solve problems and analyze data

☐ A. Performing mathematical calculations includes solving mathematical equations embedded in the curriculum, and calculating means, rates, ratios, and percentages.

☐ B. Using confidence intervals and/or error bars involves determining the significance of difference between means.

☐ C. Performing chi-square hypothesis-testing for appropriate data involves calculating the statistic, determining the *p*-value for the set of data, and drawing conclusions based on comparing the chi-square value to the *p*-value.

☐ D. Using data to evaluate a hypothesis or its prediction involves identifying when to reject or accept the null hypothesis (H_0) in favor of accepting or rejecting the alternative hypothesis (H_A). Given data, you should be able to make and justify predictions.

6 Argumentation .... activity 255

Key: Write & evaluate scientific descriptions & explanations

☐ A. Making a scientific claim may involve describing what is being shown in a graph or table, or drawing conclusions for your own or others' experimental results.

☐ B. Supporting a claim with evidence from biological principles, concepts, processes or data involves explaining how the claim is supported by the biological evidence provided.

☐ C. Providing reasoning to justify a claim by connecting evidence to theories involves explaining how the data relate to a biological theory, or explaining how reasoning supports the claim. For example, an analysis of the peppered moth experiments (original and follow-up).

☐ D. Explaining the relationship between experimental results and wider biological concepts, processes, or theories may involve explaining how the results of an investigation explain a biological principle, or connecting observational data to a broader theory. For example, connecting experimental evidence to endosymbiotic theory.

☐ E. Predicting the causes or effects of a change in, or disruption to, a biological system could be based on biological concepts or processes, visual representations (e.g. graphs) or data. For example, it might involve predicting the effect of removing a keystone species from an ecosystem, predicting the effect of increased temperature on photosynthetic rate, or interpreting a graph to predict the response of an organism to a change in the external environment.

250 Concept Explanation

Key Question: How can concepts, processes and models be presented in a written format?

Putting data or a diagram into words adds information that may not be obvious in the data. Explanations can be added to descriptions of data and so better explain the concept being shown. Sometimes data or diagrams can be complex or show multiple concepts. It is important to be able to describe and explain these and how they relate to each other.

Describing a concept *may include...*

- Describing characteristics and attributes using defining terms, e.g. describing a process as a positive or negative feedback loop.
- Classifying or grouping concepts or parts of concepts, e.g. identifying trophic levels.
- Describing components, e.g. describing the parts involved in carbon cycling.
- Describing how a process occurs, e.g. giving a simple description of an ecological process.
- Describing structure and function, e.g. describing the structure of energy pyramids and the function of each component.
- Describing trends and patterns, e.g. describing patterns in graphs or data tables.

Explaining a concept *may include...*

- Explaining each of the points in the description table on the left.
- Explaining these points in applied contexts. This might include:
  - Explaining the effect of domestication on biodiversity.
  - Explaining the relationship between photosynthesis and carbon cycling.
  - Explaining competition or cooperation between and within species.
  - Explaining how birth rates change as countries become more developed or industrialized.

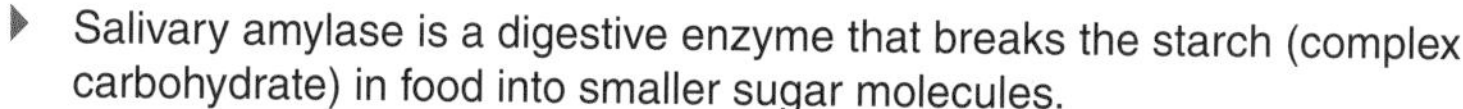

- Salivary amylase is a digestive enzyme that breaks the starch (complex carbohydrate) in food into smaller sugar molecules.
- The activity of amylase can be tracked using the iodine test. Iodine solution is a yellow/brown color and the test shows if starch is present. If the iodine indicator stays yellow/brown after the addition of a sample it means there is no starch present in the sample. If the sample turns blue/black it means that starch is present in the sample.
- The table below shows how long it took for salivary amylase to completely break down the starch over a range of temperatures.

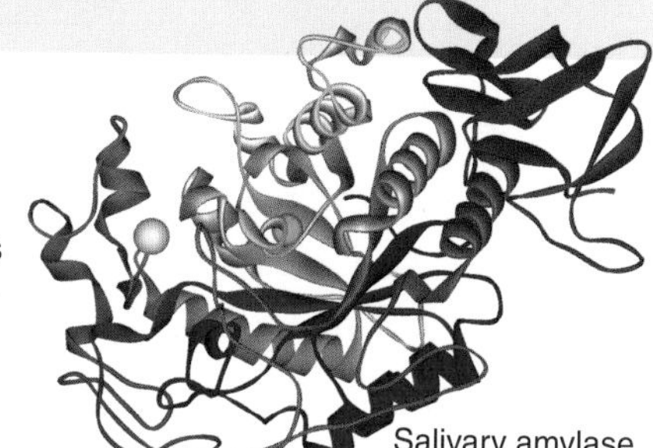

Salivary amylase

Time taken for salivary amylase to break starch down at various temperatures

Temperature (°C)	Time (minutes)														
	1	2	3	4	5	6	7	8	9	10	11	12	13	14	15
10	Y	Y	Y	Y	Y	Y	Y	Y	Y	Y	N	N	N	N	N
20	Y	Y	Y	Y	Y	Y	Y	N	N	N	N	N	N	N	N
30	Y	Y	Y	N	N	N	N	N	N	N	N	N	N	N	N
40	Y	N	N	N	N	N	N	N	N	N	N	N	N	N	N
50	Y	Y	Y	Y	Y	Y	Y	Y	N	N	N	N	N	N	N
60	Y	Y	Y	Y	Y	Y	Y	Y	Y	Y	Y	Y	Y	Y	Y

Y = starch is present, N = starch is absent.

Y N

Iodine solution turns blue/black if starch is present

1. Describe how temperature affects how quickly salivary amylase breaks down starch: ______

2. Explain the effect of temperature on the rate of this reaction: ______

ISBN: 978-1-98-856656-6

251 Visual Representations

Key Question: How are visual representations useful for explaining scientific concepts?

Diagrams and models are important ways of representing scientific concepts and ideas visually. They help to visualize trends and patterns in data and can be used to show the complexity of relationships within a system.

Describing visual representations *may include...*

- Describing the characteristics of the representation, e.g. describing the relationship between variables.
- Describing patterns or trends, e.g. describing a trend in a graph.

Explaining visual representations *may include...*

- Compare patterns or trends, e.g. comparing mitosis and meiosis.
- Explaining the concept being represented visually, e.g. explaining what the flow diagram is showing.
- Predicting patterns based on the representation/model.
- Drawing conclusions based on the information being represented visually.

1. Describe what each of the models, A - D, is showing:

A: ______________________________

____

____

B: ______________________________

____

____

C: ______________________________

____

____

D: ______________________________

____

____

2. Explain the pattern shown in the graph B (left):

____

____

____

____

____

____

____

____

____

____

____

____

____

____

Scientific information can be represented visually or modeled in many different ways. Representations vary widely, depending on what type of information is being conveyed. The ability to describe and explain visual representations helps you to communicate information about the biological principles, concepts, and processes they involve. Some examples of are shown below:

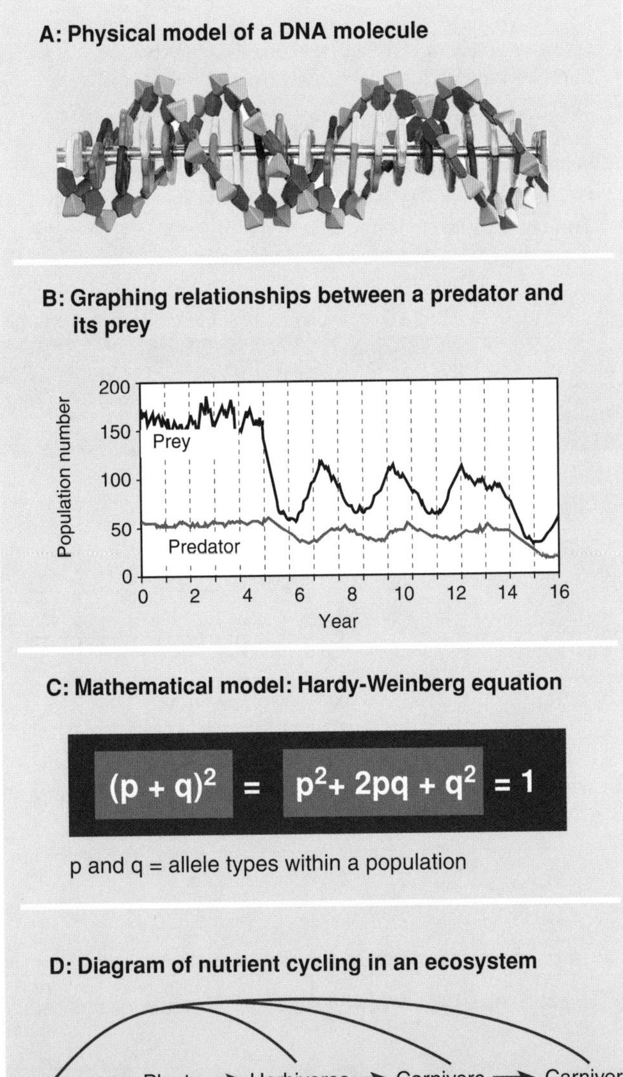

ISBN: 978-1-98-856656-6

252 Questions and Methods

Key Question: Once we have asked a scientific question, how do we then test it?

The process of science is dynamic but it follows a fairly standardized format that gives it rigor. A scientific question is asked and a hypothesis is generated. The researcher then designs an experimental procedure to collect the kind of data needed to answer their question. During the experiment, data is collected and recorded before undergoing analysis. Based on the findings, the hypothesis can be accepted or rejected. Often, results pose further questions, and experimental designs and protocols must be redesigned or reevaluated to address these new questions.

Describing aspects of scientific investigations *may include...*

- Identifying the purpose or aim of the investigation, or the hypothesis being tested.
- Identifying and describing the method, including the dependent and independent variables.
- Identifying the control (if present) and justifying any factors that need to controlled.
- Being able to draw data from the method and results, including photographs and diagrams (e.g. graphs).
- Identifying and describing how a method could be modified or refined to obtain more accurate data.

Carrying out a scientific investigation *may include...*

- Identifying the aim and writing a hypothesis.
- Deciding which variable will be changed (the independent variable) and which will be measured (the dependent variable) and how this will done.
- Writing the method of data collection so that it can be followed and repeated by someone else.
- Recording data in a systematic way.
- Drawing conclusions from the data.
- Writing a concluding discussion identifying what the results mean and any limitations in the investigation.

Start with observation, ask questions, make hypotheses and predictions

- Investigations normally start from observations, either from a previous investigation or from observing natural phenomena. An observation could be: there are more hurricanes occurring now than 10 years ago, there are fewer monarch butterflies around, measles is becoming more common, pepsin activity is slow near a neutral pH.
- These observations may or may not be true, but they allow us to ask questions: Has the incidence of hurricanes increased? Has the monarch butterfly population declined? Are measles infections increasing? Does pH affect pepsin activity? We can turn the questions into statements that can be tested to be true of not, that is, the statement (hypothesis) can be accepted or rejected.
- **For example**: Pepsin activity is highest at very low pH and decreases as pH increases towards neutral. The statement can be tested by measuring pepsin activity over a range of different pH values. If pepsin activity is highest at low pH and decreases as pH increases then the hypothesis can be accepted. If not, it can be rejected or revised.

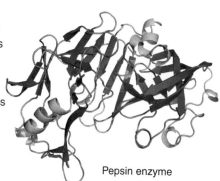

Pepsin enzyme

Identifying variables

- A **variable** is any characteristic or property able to take any one of a range of values. Investigations often look at the effect of changing one variable on another. It is important to identify all variables in an investigation: independent, dependent, and controlled, although there may be nuisance factors of which you are unaware. In a fair test, only one variable is changed by the investigator.

Dependent variable

- Measured during the investigation.
- Recorded on the **y axis** of the graph.

Independent variable

- Set by the experimenter.
- Recorded on the graph's **x axis**.
- Ideally (for a fair test) it should include at least four different values.

Dependent variable

Independent variable

Controlled variables

- Factors that are kept the same or controlled by the experimenter.
- List these in the method, as appropriate to your own investigation.

TIME IS TRICKY!

- Time is often plotted on the X axis because the response to treatments is often followed over a period of time, **but it is rarely the independent variable**.
- Time is a **covariate** (it is not part of the experimental manipulation).

1. What are the independent and dependent variables for the example in red text above:

(a) Dependent: ______________________________

(b) Independent: ______________________________

ISBN: 978-1-98-856656-6

Experimental controls

- A **control** refers to a standard or reference treatment or group in an experiment.
- It is the same as the experimental (test) group, except that it lacks the one variable being manipulated by the experimenter.
- Controls are used to demonstrate that the response in the test group is due a specific variable (e.g. temperature).
- The control undergoes the same preparation, experimental conditions, observations, measurements, and analysis as the test group. This helps to ensure that responses observed in the treatment groups can be reliably interpreted.
- Data-gathering investigations sometimes have the control built into the investigation. For example, when testing water quality, researchers would sample both upstream and downstream of a pollution source. The upstream sample acts as the control (reference).

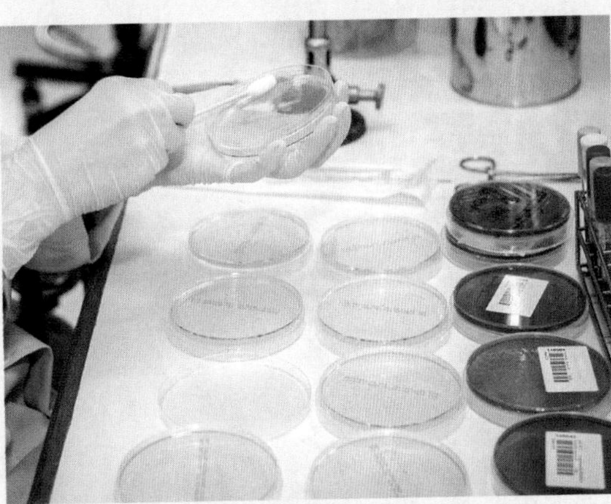

- The experiment above tests the effect of a certain nutrient on microbial growth. All the agar plates are prepared in the same way, but the control plate does not have the test nutrient applied.
- Each plate is inoculated from the same stock solution, incubated under the same conditions, and examined at the same set periods. The control plate sets the baseline; any growth above that seen on the control plate is attributed to the nutrient.

Gathering data and evaluating evidence

- Investigations should be carried out multiple times in order to make sure the data collected is reliable.
- Multiple trials and measurements for the same variable allow descriptive statistics (e.g. the mean and standard deviation) to be calculated.
- The more trials and data gathered, the more confident you can be of the final results, providing there is no **systematic bias** in your methodology.
- You should be able to justify all the decisions you make in your experimental methodology and identify any assumptions inherent in your design. Assumptions are things you assume to be true but do not test. They should be based on sound scientific principles.
- These considerations apply when evaluating the design and methods of the work of others.

Accuracy, precision, reliability, and validity

- How do we describe the confidence we have in the primary data we collect? If the data are complete and accurate (i.e. **reliable**), we can be more confident that the conclusions we draw based on the data are valid.
- In its broadest sense, **validity** is a measure of how well your investigation measures what it sets out to measure. Validity is increased by controlling more variables, improving measurement technique, reducing sampling bias, increasing sample size, and replication (repeating the entire experiment at the same time). A sound understanding of validity will help you to evaluate your own and others' work.
- **Accuracy** refers to how close a measured or derived value is to its true value. **Precision** refers to how close repeated measurements are to each other, i.e. **repeatability**. A balance with a fault in it could give very precise (repeatable) but inaccurate (untrue) results. This is an example of a systematic error.
- **Systematic errors** are consistent, repeatable errors associated with faulty equipment or a flawed design. They differ from **random errors** caused by unknown or unpredictable changes in the experimental conditions.

2. (a) A researcher is trying to determine the temperature at which an enzyme becomes denatured. Their temperature probe is incorrectly calibrated. Explain how this might affect the accuracy and precision of the data collected:

(b) Explain how this might affect the validity of any conclusions made:

ISBN: 978-1-98-856656-6

Investigation: Effect of light on rate of photosynthesis

Background

The aquarium plant, *Cabomba aquatica*, will produce a stream of oxygen bubbles when illuminated. The oxygen bubbles are a waste product of the process of photosynthesis (overall equation below right), which produces glucose ($C_6H_{12}O_6$) for the plant. The rate of oxygen production provides an approximation of photosynthetic rate.

The method

- 6 x 1.0 g of *Cabomba* stems were placed into each of 6 test-tubes filled with 10 mL room temperature solution of 0.2 mol/L sodium hydrogen carbonate (to supply CO_2).
- Test tubes were placed at distances (20, 25, 30, 35, 40 cm) from a 60W light source (light intensity reduces with distance at a predictable rate). One test tube was not exposed to the light source.
- Before recording, the *Cabomba* stems were left to acclimatize to the new light level for 5 minutes. The bubbles emerging from the stem were counted for a period of three minutes at each distance.

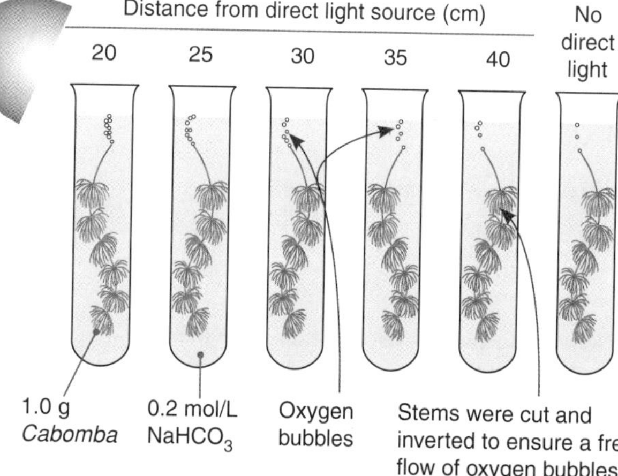

$$6CO_2 + 12H_2O \xrightarrow{\text{Light}} C_6H_{12}O_6 + 6O_2 + 6H_2O$$

3. Write a suitable aim for this experiment: ______________________

4. Write a possible hypothesis for this experiment: ______________________

5. (a) What is the independent variable in this experiment? ______________________

   (b) What is the range of values for the independent variable? ______________________

   (c) Name the unit for the independent variable: ______________________

   (d) How could you better quantify the independent variable? ______________________

6. (a) What is the dependent variable in this experiment? ______________________

   (b) Name the unit for the dependent variable: ______________________

   (c) What equipment might have made it easier to record the response of the dependent variable accurately? Predict when it would have been most needed:

   ____

   (d) What is the sample size for each treatment? ______________________

   (e) What could you change in the design of the experiment to guard against unexpected or erroneous results?

   ____

7. Which tube is the control for this experiment? ______________________

8. Identify two assumptions being made about this system:

   (a) ______________________

   (b) ______________________

9. Identify one variable that might have been controlled in this experiment, and how it could have been monitored:

   ____

10. How might you test the gas being produced is oxygen: ______________________

ISBN: 978-1-98-856656-6

253 Representing and Describing Data

Key Question: How can we display and describe data?
Once data has been collected it, needs to be displayed and analyzed. Representing your findings in tables or graphs is an excellent way to concisely display your data. Graphs provide a visual way to summarize trends in data or show relationships between variables. It is important to know how to properly construct graphs, and to select the correct graph for your data.

Interpreting data may include:

- Describing patterns or trends (e.g. does a variable rise or fall over time).
- Describing how the dependent variable changes in response to changes in the independent variable.
- Explaining why the dependent variable changes in response to changes in the independent variable.
- Making predictions based on trends in the data and justifying the prediction.
- Justifying the predictions of others based on the data presented.

Types of data

Quantitative (interval or ratio)
Characteristics for which measurements or counts can be made, e.g. height, weight, number.
Summary measures: mean, median, standard deviation

- **Discontinuous (discrete)**
  e.g. Number of children in a family (3, 0, 4)
- **Continuous**
  e.g. Height of children in a family (1.5 m, 0.8 m)

Qualitative (nominal)
Non-numerical and descriptive, e.g. sex, color, viability (dead/alive), presence or absence of a specific feature.
Summary measures: frequencies and proportions

e.g. Sex of children in a family (male, female)

Ranked (ordinal)
Data are ranked in order, although the intervals between the orders may not be equal, e.g. abundance (abundant, common, rare).
Summary measures: frequencies and proportions

e.g. Birth order in a family (1, 2, 3)

Discontinuous or discrete data:
The unit of measurement cannot be split up (e.g. you cannot have half a child).

Continuous data:
The unit of measurement can be a part number (e.g. 5.25 kg).

Presenting data in tables

- Tables provide a way to systematically record and condense a large amount of information. They provide an accurate record of numerical data and allow you to organize your data in a way that allows you to identify relationships and trends. This can help to decide the best way to graph the data if graphing is required.
- Table titles and row and column headings must be clear and accurate so the reader knows exactly what the table is about. Calculations such as rates and summary statistics (such as mean or standard deviation) may be included on a table.
- Summary statistics make it easier to identify trends and compare different treatments. Rates are useful in making multiple data sets comparable, e.g. if recordings were made over different time periods.

Table 1: Incidence of red and white clover in different areas.

Clover plant type	Frost free area		Frost prone area		Totals
	Number	%	Number	%	
Red	124	78	26	18	150
White	35	22	115	82	150
Total	159	100	141	100	300

1. For each of the photographic examples A-C below use the flow chart top to classify the data.

A: Flower color

B: Eggs per nest

C: Tree trunk diameter

A: ____________________

B: ____________________

C: ____________________

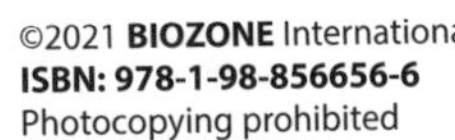

ISBN: 978-1-98-856656-6

Tally charts and tables

- If collating some types of data from a logbook, such as data for organisms measured in the field, it can be useful to create a **tally chart**, grouping the measurements into classes and recording the number in each class. This is a useful way to organize the data and get an early idea of any trends or patterns.
- **Tables** provide a way to systematically record and condense a large amount of information. They provide an accurate record of numerical data and allow you to organize and summarize your data.
- Table titles and row and column headings must be clear and accurate. In a **fair test**, where only one variable is manipulated, the independent variable is recorded in the left column, with control values at the top and rows for each treatment. Calculations such as rates and summary statistics (such as mean or standard deviation) may be included on a table.
- Summary statistics make it easier to identify trends and compare different treatments. Rates are useful in making multiple data sets comparable, e.g. if recordings were made over different time periods.

Table 2: Tally chart of size classes of crawfish from stream site A

Size class (cm)	Tally	Number
0-4.9	III	3
5.0-9.9	卌	5
10.0-14.9	卌 IIII	9
15.0-19.9	卌 II	7
20.0-24.9	II	2

Table 3: Mass (g) of radish plant roots under six different fertiliser concentrations (data given to 1dp).

Fertilizer concn (g/L)	Mass of radish root (g) †						
	Sample (*n*)					Total mass	Mean mass
	1	2	3	4	5		
0	80.1	83.2	82.0	79.1	84.1	408.5	81.7
0.06	109.2	110.3	108.2	107.9	110.7	546.3	109.3
0.12	117.9	118.9	118.3	119.1	117.2	591.4	118.3
0.18	128.3	127.3	127.7	126.8	DNG*	510.1	127.5
0.24	23.6	140.3	139.6	137.9	141.1	558.9**	139.7
0.30	122.3	121.1	122.6	121.3	123.1	610.4	122.1

*DNG = Did not germinate
** Calculation excludes sample #1

† Based on data from M S Jilani, et al Journal Agricultural Research

2. Using evidence from Table 3 above, explain the value in having a sample size (n) of more than 1 at each treatment:

3. A page from a student logbook is presented right. Using the data presented, create a tally chart size classes of 10 mm:

Size class (mm)	Tally	Total

Length of smelt from the Red River

Cloudy, 16°C 2-July-2021

81	71	42	61
47	47	78	41
57	57	47	61
31	63	46	41
63	71	67	53
66	43	33	43
36	54	68	49
54	48	36	37
29	28	56	34
26	68	56	51
51	62	38	38
27	25	62	25
52	51	64	52
11	18	58	6
74	66	57	58

All fish netted and returned after measuring (n = 60)

Stephen Moore

ISBN: 978-1-98-856656-6

Presenting data in graphs

- Graphs are a good way to show trends, patterns, and relationships visually without taking up too much space. Complex data sets tend to be presented as a graph rather than as a table, although the raw data can sometimes be tabulated as an appendix.
- Presenting graphs properly requires attention to a few basic details, including correct orientation and labeling of the axes, accurate plotting of points, and a descriptive, accurate title.
- Before representing data graphically, it is important to identify the kind of data you have. Common graphs include scatter plots and line graphs (for continuous data), and bar charts (for categorical data). For continuous data with calculated means, points can be connected. On scatter plots, a line of best fit is often drawn.

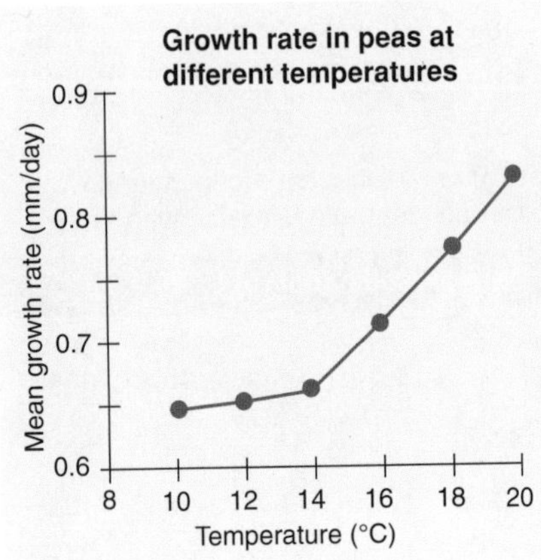

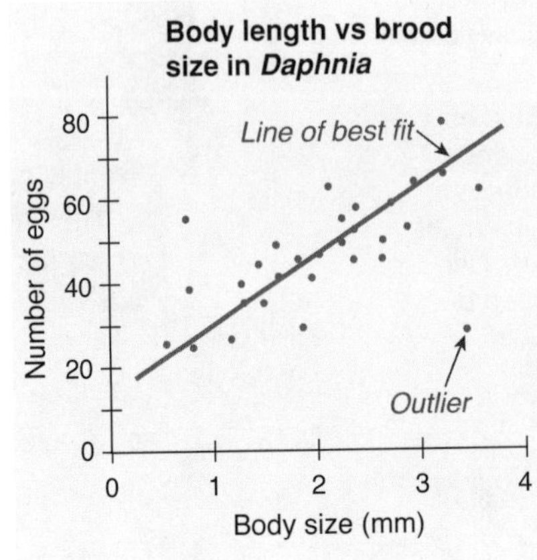

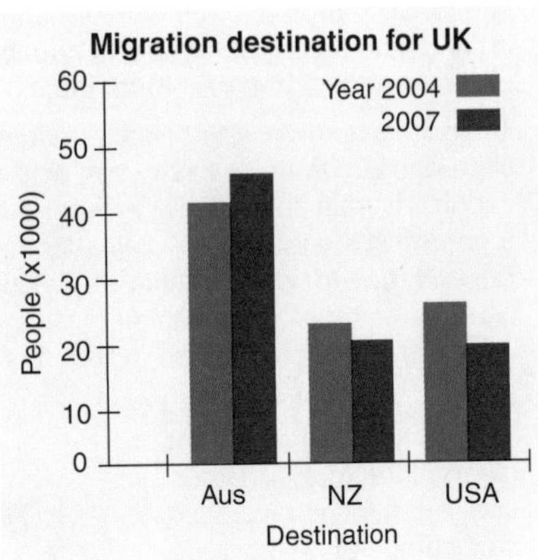

Guidelines for line graphs

- Line graphs are used when one variable (the independent variable) affects another, the dependent variable.
- The data must be continuous for both variables. The independent variable is the experimental treatment. The dependent variable is the response.
- The relationship between two variables can be represented as a continuum and the plotted data points are connected directly (point to point).

Guidelines for scatter graphs

- A scatter graph is a common way to display continuous data where there is a relationship between **two interdependent variables**.
- There is no manipulated variable, but the variables are often correlated (vary together in a predictable way).
- The points on the graph are not connected, but a line of best fit is often drawn through the points to show the relationship between the variables

Guidelines for bar/column graphs

- Bar and column graphs are appropriate for data that are non-numerical and discrete (categorical) for one variable. There are no dependent or independent variables.
- Data is discontinuous so bars do not touch (continuous data can be shown on a **histogram** where bars do touch).
- Multiple sets of data can be displayed side by side for comparison (e.g. males and females in the same age group).

4. Explain the choice of graph types for the three data sets above: ______________________________

____

____

____

____

5. The ability of mammals to remain submerged for long periods of time depends on the ability to maintain the oxygen supply to the tissues. This depends on oxygen stores. The graph right compares the amount of oxygen in different regions of the body during a dive in various seal and sea lion (SL) species and a human (not on scuba).

   (a) Describe where seals store oxygen in their body:

   ____

   ____

   ____

   (b) How does this compare to a human? ______________________________

   ____

   ____

   ____

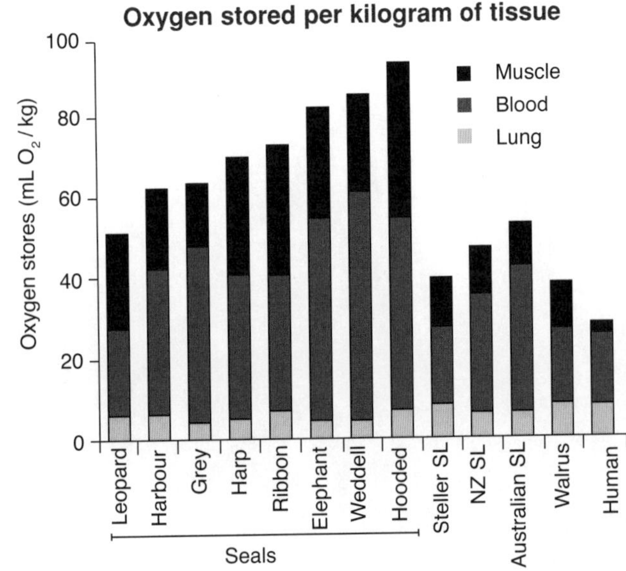

ISBN: 978-1-98-856656-6

254 Statistical Tests and Data Analysis

Key Question: How are descriptive statistics and statistical tests used to describe and analyze data?

Describing quantitative data using descriptive statistics

- Descriptive statistics, such as mean and standard deviation, are used to summarize a set of data values and its features. These values can be calculated for an entire population, e.g. mean condition score of great grey owls in Idaho, or from a sample, e.g. mean condition score of great grey owls in Salmon–Challis National Forest. When we talk about descriptive statistics, we are usually talking about a sample of the entire population. In experimental studies, the mean is often used to "average out" the different values obtained for samples undergoing the same treatment (e.g. the mean of 5 samples of enzyme reaction rate at pH 7).
- When we describe a set of data, it is usual to give a measure of **central tendency**. This is a single value (a mean, a median, or a modal value) identifying the central position within that set of data. The type of statistic calculated depends on the type of data (quantitative, qualitative) and its distribution (normal, skewed, bimodal).
- The sample mean ($\bar{x}$) is calculated by summing all the data values (x) and dividing them by the total number of data points (n). **Outliers** (very extreme values) are usually excluded from calculations of the mean. For very skewed data sets, it is better to use the median (the middle value) as a measure of central tendency. Qualitative data are described using mode (the most common value or values).

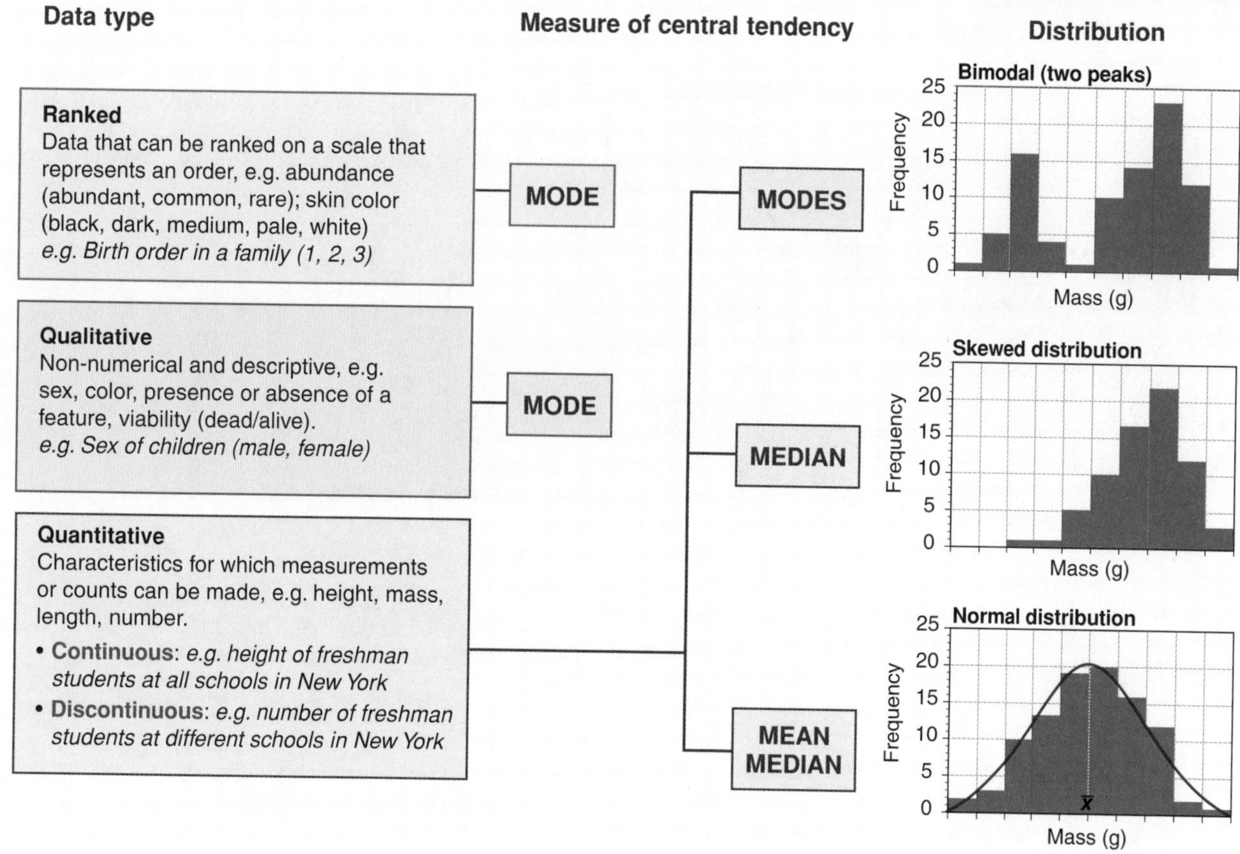
Data type
Measure of central tendency
Distribution
Ranked
Data that can be ranked on a scale that represents an order, e.g. abundance (abundant, common, rare); skin color (black, dark, medium, pale, white)
e.g. Birth order in a family (1, 2, 3)
MODE
Qualitative
Non-numerical and descriptive, e.g. sex, color, presence or absence of a feature, viability (dead/alive).
e.g. Sex of children (male, female)
MODE
Quantitative
Characteristics for which measurements or counts can be made, e.g. height, mass, length, number.
• Continuous: e.g. height of freshman students at all schools in New York
• Discontinuous: e.g. number of freshman students at different schools in New York
MODES
MEDIAN
MEAN MEDIAN
Bimodal (two peaks)
Skewed distribution
Normal distribution
Frequency
Mass (g)
0
5
10
15
20
25
x̄

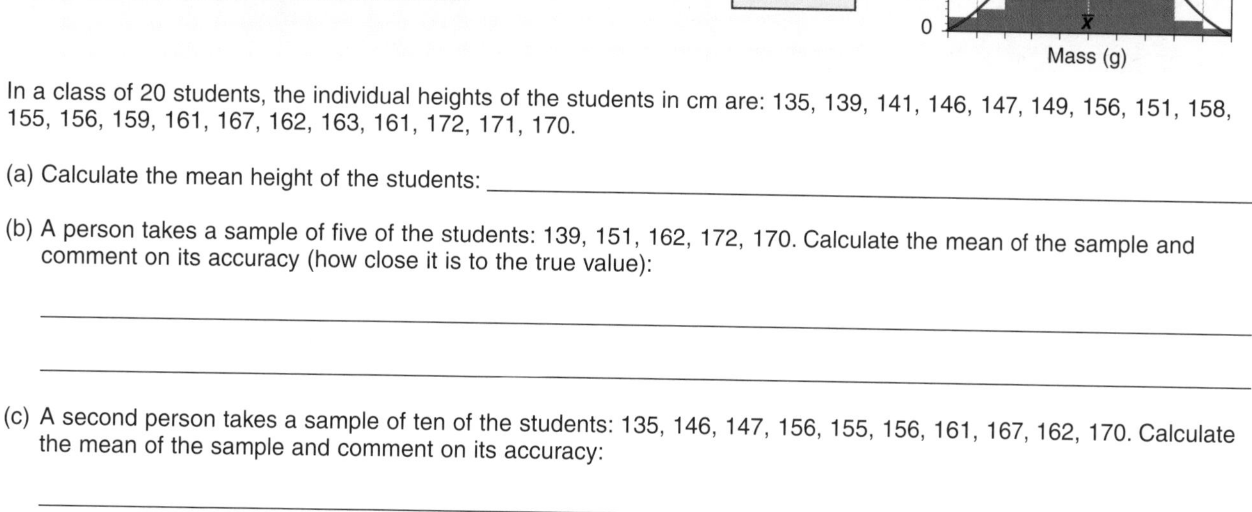

1. In a class of 20 students, the individual heights of the students in cm are: 135, 139, 141, 146, 147, 149, 156, 151, 158, 155, 156, 159, 161, 167, 162, 163, 161, 172, 171, 170.

(a) Calculate the mean height of the students: ______________________

(b) A person takes a sample of five of the students: 139, 151, 162, 172, 170. Calculate the mean of the sample and comment on its accuracy (how close it is to the true value):

____

____

(c) A second person takes a sample of ten of the students: 135, 146, 147, 156, 155, 156, 161, 167, 162, 170. Calculate the mean of the sample and comment on its accuracy:

____

____

ISBN: 978-1-98-856656-6

Expressing confidence in your data

- When we take measurements (e.g. fish length) from samples of a larger population, we are using the samples as indicators of what the whole population looks like. Therefore, when we calculate a sample mean for a variable, it is useful to know how close that value is to the true population mean for that same variable (i.e. its accuracy). If you are confident that your data set fairly represents the entire population, you are justified in making inferences about the population from your sample.
- You can start by calculating a simple measure of dispersion called standard deviation. Standard deviation is a measure of the amount of variation in a set of values. Are the individual data values all close to the mean, or are the data values highly variable? Standard deviation provides a way to evaluate the distribution of your data, which can help you decide the step in your analysis.

Standard deviation

- Sample standard deviation (s) is presented as $\bar{x} \pm s$.
- In normally distributed data, 68% of all data values will lie within one standard deviation ($1s$) of the mean. 95% of all values will lie within two standard deviations ($2s$) of the mean (see the distribution plotted right).
- The lower the standard deviation, the more closely the data values cluster around the mean.
- The formula for calculating standard deviation is shown in the green box (below).

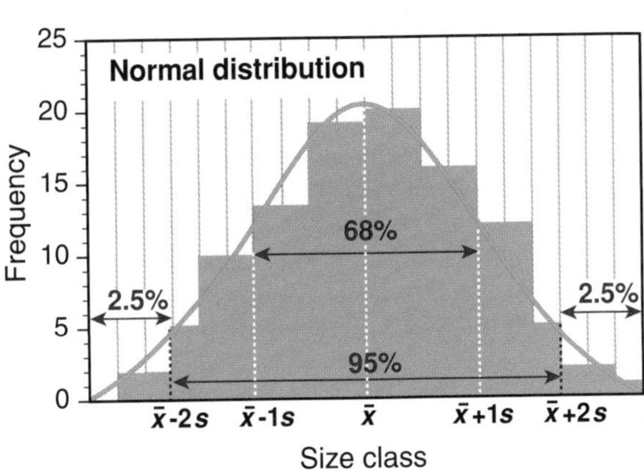

Calculating standard deviation

$$s = \sqrt{\frac{\sum(x - \bar{x})^2}{n-1}}$$

$\sum(x - \bar{x})^2$ = sum of squared deviations from the mean

n = sample size.

$n-1$ provides a unbiased s for small sample sizes (large samples can use n).

Both of the histograms below show a normal distribution of data with the values spread symmetrically about the mean. However, their standard deviations are different. In histogram A, the data values are widely spread around the mean. In histogram B, most of the data values are close to the mean. Sample B has a smaller standard deviation than sample A.

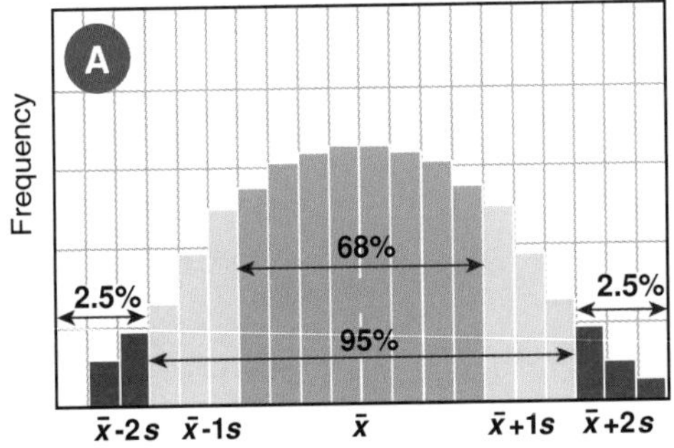

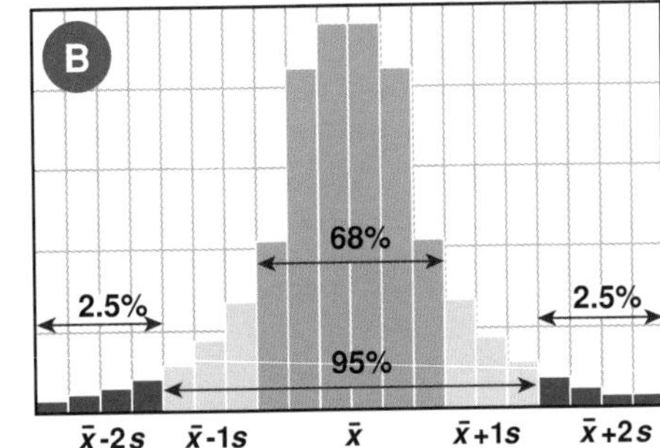

2. Two sample data sets of rat body length have the same mean. The first data set has a much larger standard deviation than the second data set. What does this tell you about the spread of data around the mean in each case? Which data set is likely to provide the most reliable estimate of body length in the rat population being sampled and why?

3. The data on the right shows the heights for 29 male swimmers.

   (a) Calculate the mean for the data:

   (b) Use manual calculation, a calculator, or a spreadsheet to calculate the standard deviation (s) for the data:

   (c) State the mean ± 1s:

   (d) What percentage of values are within 1s of the mean?

   (e) What does this tell you about the spread of the data?

Raw data: Height (cm)

178	177	188	176	186	175
180	181	178	178	176	175
180	185	185	175	189	174
178	186	176	185	177	176
176	188	180	186	177	

ISBN: 978-1-98-856656-6

95% confidence intervals

- So how can you tell if your sample is giving a fair representation of the entire population? We can do this using the **95% confidence interval**. This statistic allows you to make a claim about the **reliability** your sample data. The mean ± the 95% confidence interval (95% CI) gives the **95% confidence limits** (95% CL). This tells us that, on average, 95 times out of 100, the true population mean will lie within the confidence limits. Having a large sample size greatly increases the reliability of your data.
- You can plot the 95% CL on to graphs to determine if observed differences between sets of sample data (e.g. between field plots or treatments) are statistically significant. If the 95% CL do not overlap it is likely that the differences between the sample sets is significant. The 95% CI is very easy to calculate (below). You can also use the spreadsheet on **BIOZONE's Resource Hub**.

Step 1 is to calculate the standard error of the mean (SE). It is simple to calculate and is usually a small value.

$$SE = \frac{s}{\sqrt{n}}$$

Step 2 is to calculate the 95% confidence interval (95% CI). It is calculated by multiplying SE by the value of t at P = 0.05 for the appropriate degrees of freedom (df) for your sample.

$$95\%\ CI = SE \times t_{(P=0.05)}$$

An experiment was carried out to see how different types of feed affected the growth of newly weaned rats. Rats were placed into four different groups and each group was fed a different type of feed. There were 10 rats in each group. They were weighed after a further 28 days of growth. The results are shown right.

Individual	Mass (g) of rats after 28 days on four feeds			
	Feed type			
	Feed 1	Feed 2	Feed 3	Feed 4
1	28.0	28.5	25.6	48.6
2	36.0	31.2	28.6	51.2
3	36.2	30.9	27.1	55.3
4	28.5	35.0	33.0	42.7
5	27.9	27.2	40.0	40.5
6	32.6	26.9	25.9	49.8
7	35.0	34.0	32.9	47.9
8	27.2	29.0	33.1	50.8
9	26.9	34.8	33.6	39.9
10	35.0	23.9	35.0	47.0
Sum (∑)				
Mean ($\bar{x}$)				
Std dev. (s)				
Std error (SE)				
95% CI				

4. Complete the table by calculating the sum (∑), mean ($\bar{x}$), standard deviation (s), standard error (SE), and 95% confidence interval (95% CI) for each group. You can do this using a calculator or a spreadsheet. The t value at P=0.05 for 9 df = 2.262

5. (a) Plot a column graph of the mean mass of the rats in each group. Add the 95% CL bars ($\bar{x}$ ± 95% CI) to your graph. To do this, add the 95% CI value to the mean to get the upper value and subtract it to get the lower value. Feed 1 is completed for you.

(b) Is there any significant difference between the groups? Explain your answer:

Mass of rats after 28 days on 4 different feeds (mean ± 95% CL)

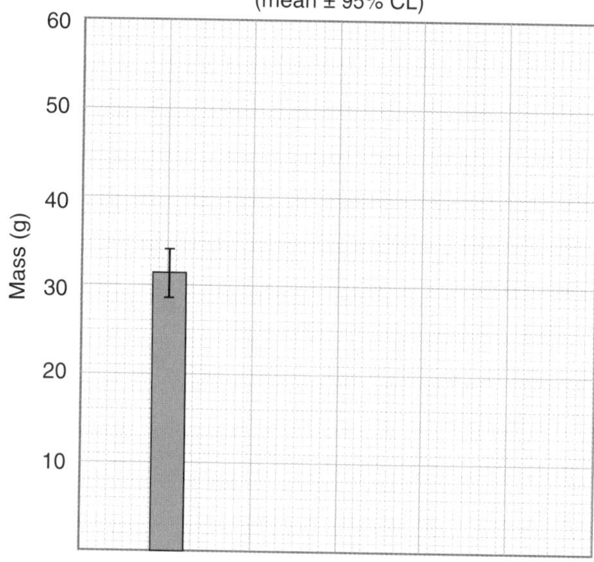

ISBN: 978-1-98-856656-6

Statistical tests

- Data analysis provides information on the biological significance of your investigation. How your data is analyzed depends on the type of data you have collected. Plotting your data, even at the very early stages of your investigation, can help you to decide what statistical analysis to carry out. Sometimes, a statistical test is not needed to determine the significance of your findings. Plotting your data with 95% confidence intervals will very often provide you with the information you need to make a conclusion.
- The panels below briefly describe the criteria for some of the simplest and most common statistical analyses you will come across. If your data do not meet the criteria, e.g. a t test is not appropriate when you are comparing more than two groups and a linear regression is not appropriate if your data plot as a curve. There are other tests for these types of data.

Tests for difference

Data type: Frequencies (counts only) in categories.

Purpose: Compare the observed results versus the calculated expected results.

Data plot as a column chart.

Criteria:
- Performed on raw counts
- Requires large sample size

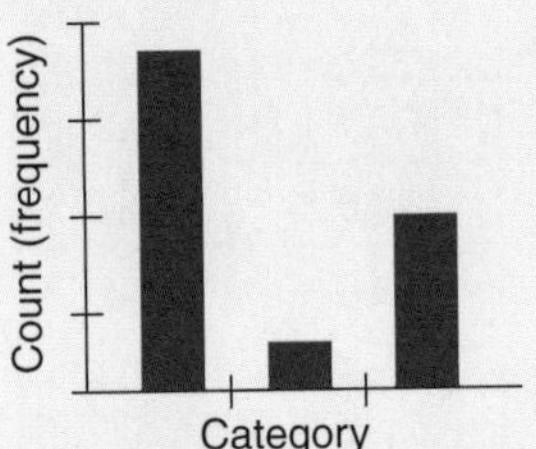

USE: **Chi squared for goodness of fit** (χ^2)

Examples:
Compare observed and expected outcomes of genetic crosses.

Compare observed and expected behaviors (choice chamber experiments).

Data type: Measurements or counts in two categories.

Purpose: Compare the means of two groups.

Data plot as a column chart.

Criteria:
- Distribution of the data must be normal
- Compares only two groups

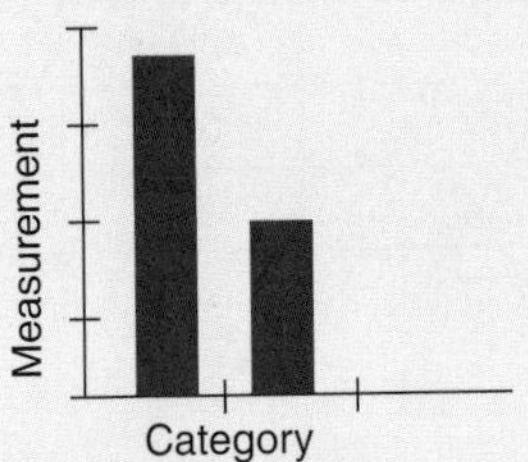

USE: **Unpaired t-test (student's t test)**

Examples:
Compare means of plants grown in clay plots vs plastic pots.

Compare the mean density of invertebrates in two areas of stream (e.g. forested vs not forested).

Tests for a trend or relationship

Data type: Continuous for both variables.

Purpose: Determining the relationship between two variables. Often predictive.

Data plot as a **linear scatter**. The X variable is independent by virtue of the regression equation. A line of best fit can be drawn through the points.

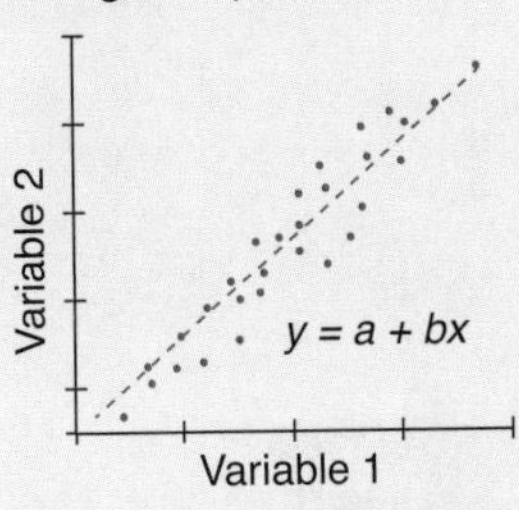

USE: **Linear regression**

The coefficient of determination (r^2) tells you how much of the variation in y is predictable from the independent variable.

Examples:
Fish-length and weight.

Petal length and width.

Data type: Continuous for both variables.

Purpose: Test how strongly two variables are associated.

Data plot as a **linear scatter**. There is no independent variable.

No line should be drawn through the data.

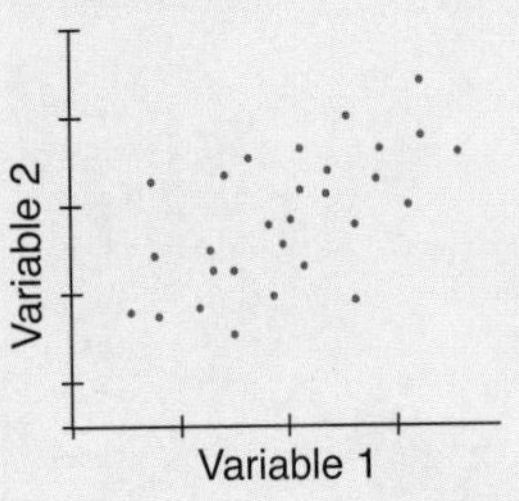

USE: **Pearson r correlation**

The correlation coefficient (r) tells you about the strength of the association between the two variables.

Examples:
Arm length vs leg length.

Blood pressure and waist circumference.

6. Identify an appropriate statistical analysis for the following scenarios and briefly explain your choice:

(a) Comparing the observed numbers of four phenotypes in a genetic cross with those expected by Mendelian ratios:

(b) Analyzing linear body weight and heart disease data:

(c) Using measurements of tree height and trunk diameter to assist in evaluating forest structure:

(d) You measured growth rates in two group of rats on different diets:

7. Suggest why statistical tests and predictive models, such as a regression, are useful in practical applications such as in population analysis and medicine:

ISBN: 978-1-98-856656-6

255 Argumentation

Key Question: What is the role of scientific argumentation and what does it involve?

An important part of your studies in biology is developing skills in argumentation. This means using evidence-based reasoning to support a claim or explanation that you make (or some else makes) with respect to your own or others' investigations. During your studies in AP Biology, you will be required to use argumentation to make claims (statements), support them with evidence, and justify your reasoning. You will also need to be able to explain the relationship between experimental results and larger biological concepts, processes, or theories. As with all science, you can then make predictions based on evidence and logical reasoning. Part of this process, is learning to evaluate source material critically. It is important to note that argumentation is not the same as arguing! It is about evidence-based reasoning.

Opinion, anecdote, and scientific evidence

As well as collecting primary data from your own investigations, much of your study of biology will involve collating and interpreting the results of others (secondary data) or evaluating the claims they have made based on their findings.

The validity of scientific claims depends on the evidence used to support the claim. The schematic below shows a hierarchy of evidence as might apply to developing a new pharmaceutical drug. Although this applies to a particular case, the concepts are applicable across all science.

ANECDOTAL EVIDENCE	SCIENTIFIC EVIDENCE
Uncontrolled, therefore very susceptible to bias	Controlled for subject and experimenter bias
Very small sample size	Large sample sizes
Only exceptional cases reported	Everything is reported
Vague outcomes	Defined outcomes
Claim from memory	Claim from data

WEAK → STRONG

OPINIONS ANECDOTES	LAB STUDIES (cellular and animal studies)	OBSERVATIONAL STUDIES IN HUMANS	RANDOMIZED CONTROLLED CLINICAL TRIALS	SYSTEMATIC REVIEW
Anecdotal evidence and expert opinion provide weak evidence, although expert opinion is often used in law and matters of public policy.	Research on model animals and on cell cultures is useful but the results may not necessarily apply to humans.	Studies involving case studies or cohort analysis often show correlation, but cause and effect is more difficult to determine.	Subjects are randomly assigned to test groups and tests are run blind or double blind. Such trials help remove bias.	Statistical analysis of a large number of randomized controlled trials. Important in issues of medical, public health, and environmental policy.

Not all information should be treated equally

- Many topics in science are emotive. Peoples' viewpoints are not necessarily based on reliable evidence, but on their personal belief system, their experiences, and the opinions of those around them.
- While the internet has made accessing information very easy, the quality of the information people consume varies greatly, and not all information should be given equal weighting. For example, someone's opinion shared on their blog does not have the scientific validity of a peer-reviewed journal article.
- As a student of science, you must think critically about the material you are consuming. Can you confirm the validity of the source? Does it make sense? Is it unbiased? These questions will help you identify biased or flawed information and help you make an informed decision to guide your own decisions.

NIH cc0

As more studies, trials, and reviews are carried out, a larger body of evidence is obtained. This allows researchers to predict effects with greater confidence and also allows them to see how data collected from earlier stages relates to the final outcomes.

1. Suggest why opinion and anecdote are weak forms of evidence for constructing an evidence-based argument

ISBN: 978-1-98-856656-6

Constructing an evidence-based argument

Once you have planned your investigation, collected and analyzed your data, and justified your methodology, you will be ready to make an evidence-based argument. To do this, you need to determine the degree to which the evidence (the data you have collected or collated) supports the aim of your investigation (the question you asked). The evidence might raise further questions, or support an alternative explanation (hypothesis). This doesn't mean your investigation was a failure. Sometimes unexpected findings are the most exciting!

You can use the graphic organizer below to help in constructing a scientific argument. A scientific argument makes a claim based on evidence (data, statistical analysis, anecdotal evidence, expert opinion), and justified by logical reasoning. Bear in mind, the more you rely on opinion and anecdote, the weaker your argument will be. Any evidence-based argument should address the reliability of the data and the limitations of the study. Acknowledging strengths as well as weaknesses is important to planning future research.

If you have been careful about the design of your experiment and collection of data, you can then draw and justify conclusions that are consistent with the evidence.

1 Evidence *What data or observations address your question?*

2 Science concepts *What science concepts might help to answer the question?*

? *What is your scientific aim or question?*

3 Scientific reasoning *How do the science concepts connect to the evidence and to the question you're trying to answer?*

4 Claim *What claim can you make based on the evidence and reasoning?*

? + 1 + 2 + 3 + 4

Your evidence-based argument

Combine all the elements into a coherent scientific argument.

Draw conclusions, justify them, and describe their limitations. Discuss how your findings fit or don't fit with current knowledge.

Having a complete logbook can help with this stage, allowing you to reflect on your research.

2. Explain why evidenced-based argumentation would be more credible than argumentation based on opinion:

3. The table (below) outlines some common problems students encounter when presenting a scientific argument. For each of the examples below, describe how the problem could result in a weak or flawed argument

(a) Scientific misconceptions:

(b) Discounting evidence that does not support your claim:

Some problematic patterns in scientific argumentation...	
Value judgments (normative reasoning)	Making an argument based on social norms
Fallacious reasoning	Not distinguishing between opinion and scientific evidence
	Fusion of scientific facts and personal beliefs
	Scientific misconceptions
Claims unsupported by data	Can be the result of extrapolation
Disregarding evidence contrary to the claim	Lack of critical thinking and dishonesty
Check during your work that you don't fall into these traps!	

ISBN: 978-1-98-856656-6

A-1 Appendix 1: Summary of Mathematical Formulas

Mathematics is used to analyze, interpret, and compare data. It is important that you are familiar with mathematical notation (the language of mathematics) and can confidently apply some basic mathematical principles and calculations to your data. Data collected in the field or laboratory is called raw data. It often needs to be transformed to reveal trends or patterns. This page summarizes some of the transformations and statistical formulae you might use to summarize and test your data. Some of the required mathematical formulas are covered in the book as indicated.

Using mathematical routines may include:

- Determining the best method to solve a mathematical problem, e.g. explaining the best way to compare water intake in different plants.
- Applying appropriate mathematical routines or relationships to solve a problem, with working shown, e.g. calculating population growth over time.
- Calculating a numeric answer to a problem, using the appropriate units, e.g. calculating the rate of water loss from a plant over 24 hours.

Units of measure

Name	Unit	Symbol
Mass	gram*	*g*
Length	meter	*m*
Time	second	*s*
Temperature	Celsius	°C
	Kelvin	K
Volume	Liter	*L*

*Gram (g) is the unit of mass, but kilogram (kg) is the SI unit.

Prefixes

Units of measure can be prefixed with a multiplier:

milli: 10^{-3} centi: 10^{-2} deci: 10^{-1}

hecto: 10^{2} kilo: 10^{3} mega: 10^{4}

Ratios

- Ratios give the relative amount of two or more quantities, and provide an easy way to identify patterns.
- Ratios do not require units.
- Ratios are expressed as **a : b**.
- Ratios are calculated by dividing all the values by the smallest number.

Pea pod shape	Number	Ratio
Inflated	882	2.95
Constricted	299	1

Pea seed shape and color	Number	Ratio
Round, yellow	495	9
Wrinkled yellow	152	2.8
Round green	158	2.9
Wrinkled green	55	1

Percentages

- To calculate percentage, simply calculate the fraction of the total x 100. For example 2/5 = 0.4 x 100 = 40%
- Percentages will show what fraction (out of 100) falls into any particular category, e.g. for pie graphs.
- Percentages can be used to express concentrations and to allow meaningful comparison between samples with different starting points, e.g. different numbers or masses.

Volume of food coloring (cm^3)	Volume of water (cm^3)	Concentration of coloring (%)
10	0	100
8	2	80
6	4	60
4	6	40
2	8	20
0	10	0

Percentage change

Percentage change shows how much a value has changed (e.g. between time t and time t + 1). Calculating percentage change is easy. Determine the difference between the old and new values, divide by the old value, and multiply by 100.

$$\%\text{ change} = \frac{\text{new value} - \text{old value}}{\text{old value}} \times 100$$

- A positive value = percentage increase.
- A negative value = percentage decrease.
- Percentage change is useful in studies of natural populations and when analyzing mass changes in experiments.

Example: There were 116 mice in a local population, but after a successful breeding season, the number was 160. What was the percentage change?

Working:
160 – 116 ÷ 160 = 0.275
0.275 x 100 = 27.5% increase.

Rates

Rates are expressed as a measure per unit of time and show how a variable changes over time. Rates are used to provide meaningful comparisons of data that may have been recorded over different time periods.

Often rates are expressed as a mean rate over the duration of the measurement period, but it can be useful to calculate the rate at various times to understand how rate changes over time. The table below shows the reaction rates for gas production during a chemical reaction. A worked example for the rate at 4 minutes is provided below the table.

Time (minute)	Cumulative gas produced (cm^3)	Rate of reaction (cm^3 / min)
0	0	0
2	34	17
4	42	4*
6	48	3
8	50	1
10	50	0

* Gas produced between 2 – 4 min: 42 cm^3 – 34 cm^3 = 8 cm^3
Rate of reaction between 2 – 4 min:8 ÷ 2 min = 4 cm^3 /min

Basic statistical formulae

	Symbol	Formula
Mean	$\bar{x}$	$\bar{x} = \sum x \div n$
Sample standard deviation	s	$s = \sqrt{\dfrac{\sum(x-\bar{x})^2}{n-1}}$
Standard error	SE	$SE = \dfrac{s}{\sqrt{n}}$
95% confidence interval	*95% CI*	$95\%\ CI = SE \times t_{(P=0.05)}$

Worked example from a data set of fern sori

64, 69, 71, 67, 60, 70, 69, 64, 64, 63, 59, 63, 62, 70, 70, 64, 68, 70, 66, 63, 66, 63, 61, 62, 70

Mean:
$\bar{x} = \sum x \div n$: $\sum x$ = 1638. n = 25.
1638 ÷ 25 = 65.52 = **66**

Sample standard deviation:
$(x - \bar{x})^2$ (for each data point) (the first two workings are shown):
$(64 - 65.52)^2 = 2.3104$, $(69 - 65.52)^2 = 12.1104$ ...

$\sum(x - \bar{x})^2$ = 2.3104 + 12.1104 + 30.0304 + 2.1904 + 30.4704 + 20.0704 + 12.1104 + 2.3104 + 2.3104 + 6.3504 + 42.5104 + 6.3504 + 12.3904 + 20.0704 + 20.0704 + 2.3104 + 6.1504 + 20.0704 + 0.2304 + 6.3504 + 0.2304 + 6.3504 + 20.4304 + 12.3904 + 20.0704 = 316.24 = **316**.

n – 1 = 25 – 1 = 24. 316 ÷ 24 = 13.18. √13.18 = 3.63 = **4**.

Standard error:
SE = 3.63 ÷ √ 25 = 0.73 = **1**

95% Confidence interval:
0.73 x t (from t tables) = 0.73 x 2.064 = 1.50 = **2**.

Formulas for statistical tests

	Symbol	Formula
Chi squared for goodness of fit	χ^2	$\chi^2 = \sum \dfrac{(O-E)^2}{E}$ O = observed results E = expected results
Unpaired *t*-test (Student's *t*-test)	t	$t = \dfrac{(\bar{x}_A - \bar{x}_B)}{\sqrt{\dfrac{s^2_A}{n_A} + \dfrac{s^2_B}{n_B}}}$ $\bar{x}$ = the mean for each data set s^2 = the variance for each data set n = number of samples in each data set
Linear regression	r^2	$y = a + bx$ y = dependent variable a = the y intercept b = the slope of the line x = independent variable
Pearson *r* correlation	r	$r = \dfrac{\sum xy - n\bar{x}\bar{y}}{ns_x s_y}$ $\bar{x}$ = mean of all the x variables $\bar{y}$ = mean of all the y variables s_x = standard deviation of x s_y = standard deviation of y n = number of pairs of readings

Probability tables are provided on the **Resource Hub**:

Probability

SEE PAGE 156

If A and B are mutually exclusive, then use the **sum rule**:
P(A or B) = *P*(A) + *P*(B)

If A and B are independent, then use the **product rule**:
P(A and B) = *P*(A) x *P*(B)

Hardy-Weinberg equations

SEE PAGE 291

$p^2 + 2pq + q^2 = 1$
$P + q = 1$
p = frequency of allele 1 in the population
q = frequency of allele 2 in the population

Population growth

SEE PAGES 427-428

Exponential growth: $dN/dt = r_{max}N$
Logistic growth: $dN/dt = r_{max}N(K - N/K)$
were r_{max} is maximum per capita growth rate
N = population size
K = carrying capacity

Solute potential

SEE PAGE 58

$\psi_s = -iCRT$

A-2 Appendix 2: Glossary

A

abscission
Breaking off; usually referring to the loss of leaves or fruit in plants.

absolute dating
A method for determining the age of an object based on the proportion of a radioactive isotope within it and the half-life of that isotope (*cf. relative dating*).

absolute fitness
An absolute measure of the increase or decrease of a phenotype or genotype from generation to generation (*cf. relative fitness*).

accuracy
How close measurements are to the true value.

acetyl coenzyme A, acetyl coA
A coenzyme that adds acetyl groups in biochemical reactions.

activation energy
The minimum amount of energy needed to initiate a chemical reaction.

active site
Region of an enzyme where the substrate binds and undergoes a chemical reaction.

active transport
The movement of molecules or ions across a cell membrane against a concentration gradient, requiring an expenditure of energy.

adaptation (*verb*)
The genetic process by which populations become more suited to their environments.

adaptive behavior
Behavior that increases fitness.

adaptive radiation
Diversification from an ancestral species into many species occupying many different niches.

adaptive value
The extent to which a trait positively influences the fitness of an individual.

adhesion
The tendency of certain dissimilar molecules to cling to one another forces (*cf. cohesion*).

alcoholic fermentation
A biological process carried out by yeasts, in which simple sugars (e.g. glucose) are converted to ethanol and carbon dioxide.

allele
Any of the alternative versions of a gene that may produce distinguishable phenotypes.

allopatric speciation
Speciation that occurs when biological populations become geographically isolated.

amino acid
Any organic compound containing both an amino group and a carboxylic acid group.

anabolic reaction
A chemical reaction that constructs large, complex molecules from simpler molecules.

anaerobic metabolism
Biological processes that produce usable energy for an organism without oxygen.

anaphase
A stage in cell division when chromosomes are pulled toward opposite ends of the cell.

aneuploidy
A deviation from the normal number of chromosomes.

anticodon
A sequence of three adjacent nucleotides in tRNA that binds to a corresponding codon in mRNA during protein synthesis (*cf. codon*).

antigenic drift
A mechanism for genetic variation in viruses, involving the accumulation of mutations (*cf. antigenic shift*).

antigenic shift
The process by which the genomes of two or more different viruses or strains recombine to form a new subtype.

apoptosis
A controlled process of programmed cell death in multicellular organisms.

argumentation
An attempt to validate or refute a claim using logical reasoning.

artificial selection
Intervention by humans in animal or plant reproduction in order to preserve selected genetic traits.

aseptic technique
The practice of maintaining sterility.

ATP
An organic compound that serves as an energy source for metabolic processes.

ATP synthase
A protein that catalyzes the formation of ATP from ADP and inorganic phosphate.

autoinducer
Signaling molecules in bacteria produced in response to changes in cell density.

autosomal dominant trait
A trait or disorder that may be passed from one generation to the next, where only one allele is required to pass on the trait.

autosomal recessive trait
A trait or disorder that may be passed from one generation to the next, where two copies of an abnormal gene must be present in order for the trait to be expressed.

autotroph
An organism that produces its own food using materials from inorganic sources.

auxin
Any of several plant hormones that regulate the growth and development of plants.

B

behavior
An organism's external reactions to its environment.

biodiversity
The amount of biological variation present in a region (genetic, species, and habitat diversity).

bioinformatics
The use of computer science, mathematics, and information theory to organize and analyze complex biological data.

C

Calvin cycle
The light-independent phase of photosynthesis during which chemical reactions convert carbon dioxide into sugars.

cancer
The malignant growth of cells due to uncontrolled cell division.

carbohydrate
Any of a class of molecules that contain carbon, hydrogen and oxygen, with a general formula $C_n(H_2O)_n$.

carrying capacity (K)
The maximum number of organisms that can be sustained by a specific environment.

catabolic reaction
The breakdown of large, complex molecules into smaller, simpler molecules.

catalyst
A substance that modifies and increases the rate of a chemical reaction without being consumed in the process.

cell cycle
The cycle of stages that occur in a cell as it grows and divides to produce new daughter cells.

cell division
Any process by which a parent cell divides into two or more daughter cells.

cell wall
The rigid outermost cell layer found in plants and certain algae, bacteria, and fungi but absent from animal cells.

cellular differentiation
The process by which a cell changes from one cell type to another, usually to a more specialized type of cell.

cellular respiration
The series of metabolic reactions that oxidize organic molecules to produce ATP.

chlorophyll
A green photosynthetic pigment found primarily in the chloroplasts of algae and plants, essential to photosynthesis.

chloroplast
An organelle within the cells of plants and green algae that contains chlorophyll and is the site of photosynthesis.

chromatid
One half of a replicated chromosome, held to its other half at the centromere.

chromatin
A complex of DNA and proteins, making up the chromosomes.

chromosome
A cellular structure consisting of one DNA molecule and associated protein molecules.

chronometric dating
See **absolute dating**.

cladistics
A biological classification system in which organisms are categorized in groups ("clades") based on hypotheses of most recent common ancestry.

cladogram
A *phylogenetic tree* constructed using cladistic techniques.

codominance
A phenomenon in which two alleles are expressed equally within an organism.

codon
A sequence of three adjacent nucleotides in a DNA or mRNA sequence that is part of the genetic code (*cf. anticodon*).

coenzyme
A non-protein compound that binds to an enzyme to initiate or aid in its function.

coevolution
Evolution that occurs among interdependent species as a result of specific interactions.

cohesion
The tendency of certain like-molecules to cling together due to attractive forces (*cf. adhesion*).

commensalism
A relationship between two organisms in which one benefits, and one is unaffected.

communication *(behavior)*
The transmission of understood information among individuals.

competition
Interaction within or between species in which individuals attempt to access the same limited resource.

competitive inhibition
A form of enzyme inhibition in which an inactive molecule reversibly binds to the active site, preventing the actual substrate from binding (*cf. non-competitive inhibition*).

condensation reaction
A chemical reaction in which two molecules are joined covalently with the removal of an -OH ion from one and a -H ion from the other to form water (*cf. hydrolysis*).

consumer
An organism that feeds on producers, other consumers, or non-living organic material.

continuous data
Quantitative data representing a scale of measurement that can consist of numbers other than whole numbers.

continuous variation
Variation in phenotypic traits in which in which there is a complete spread of forms (phenotypes) across a range.

convergent evolution
The independent evolution of similar traits or features in unrelated species.

cooperative behavior
An evolutionary response to reduce the competition between individuals of the same species.

cotransport
Transport of substances across a membrane in which the energy required to move one substance against its concentration gradient is provided by the movement of another down its concentration gradient.

covalent bond
A type of chemical bond in which two atoms share one or more pairs or electrons (*cf. hydrogen bond, ionic bond*).

CRISPR-Cas9
A prokraryotic gene sequence used as a tool in the editing of genomes.

cristae
One of the inward projections or folds of the inner membrane of a mitochondrion.

crossing over
The reciprocal exchange of genetic material between non-sister chromatids during prophase 1 of meiosis.

cyclic photophosphorylation
ATP is generated using light energy during photosynthesis but the electrons from photosystem I flow back to the electron carriers in the membrane (cyclic flow). Photosystem II is inactive and no NADPH is generated.

cyclin
One of several regulatory proteins whose concentrations fluctuate cyclically throughout the cell cycle. Involved in cell cycle regulation via cyclin-dependent kinases.

cyclin dependent kinase (CDK)
A family of enzymes involved in regulation of the cell cycle.

cytokinesis
The part of the cell division process when the cytoplasm of a single eukaryotic cell divides to produce two daughter cells.

cytosis
A mechanism involving movement of the plasma membrane, which enables the transport of large quantities of molecules into and out of cells.

D

data analysis
The systematic application of statistical and logical techniques to describe and evaluate data and derive meaningful conclusions.

dehydration synthesis
See **condensation reaction**.

denaturation
The alteration of a protein shape resulting in a loss of function.

diffusion
The net movement of molecules from a region of high concentration to one of lower concentration.

dihybrid cross
A cross between two organisms that differ in two observed traits.

diploid
Having paired sets of chromosomes, one from each parent, in a cell or cell nucleus.

dipole
A molecule that has both negative and positive charges.

directional selection
A mode of natural selection in which one phenotypic extreme is favored over others, causing the allele frequency of a population to shift towards that phenotype (*cf. disruptive selection, stabilizing selection).*

disaccharide
A carbohydrate consisting of two monosaccharides linked together.

discontinuous data
A quantitative data set representing a scale of measurement that can consist only of whole numbers (*cf. continuous data*).

discreet data
See **discontinuous data**.

disruptive selection
A natural selection mechanism in which opposing extremes for a trait are favored, creating phenotypic divergence (*cf. directional selection, stabilizing selection).*

divergent evolution
The accumulation of differences between closely related populations within a species, leading to the formation of new species.

DNA profiling
The process of determining an individual's DNA characteristics (fingerprint).

DNA replication
The duplication of a DNA molecule, producing two identical copies from one original DNA molecule.

DNA sequencing
The process of determining the nucleic acid sequence in DNA.

dominant allele
An allele that is expressed (as a trait) even if the individual only has one copy of the allele.

dominant trait
See **dominant allele**.

dormancy
A period in an organism's life cycle when growth, development, and (in animals) physical activity are temporarily stopped.

E

ecological pyramid
A graphical representation of the relationship between different organisms in an ecosystem, and their trophic levels.

ecosystem
All the organisms in a given area as well as the abiotic factors with which they interact.

ectothermy
The regulation of body temperature by the external environment (*cf. endothermy*).

electron transport chain
A series of protein complexes that transfer electrons from donors to acceptors across a membrane via redox reactions.

endocytosis
A process of cellular ingestion by which the plasma membrane folds inward to bring substances into the cell (*cf. exocytosis*).

endoplasmic reticulum
A membranous network found in eukaryotic cells, composed of ribosome-studded (rough) and ribosome-free (smooth) regions.

endosymbiotic theory
The theory describing the evolution of organelles in eukaryotic cells, whereby different types of free-living prokaryotes became incorporated inside larger prokaryotic cells and eventually gave rise to organelles (mitochondria and chloroplasts).

endothermy
A form of thermoregulation in which heat is generated by metabolism (*cf. ectothermy*).

enzyme
Globular proteins that act as biological catalysts for specific reactions.

enzyme inhibition
A reaction between a molecule and an enzyme that blocks the action of the enzyme, either temporarily or permanently.

epigenetics
Heritable phenotypic changes that do not involve changes to the DNA sequence.

ester bond
A covalent bond formed by condensation between a carboxyl and a hydroxyl group.

evolution
The change in the heritable characteristics of populations over successive generations.

exocytosis
Secretion of intracellular molecules, contained within membrane-bound vesicles, to the outside of the cell by fusion of vesicles with the plasma membrane (*cf. endocytosis*).

exon
A protein coding region of a gene.

exponential growth
A pattern of population growth where the growth rate is proportional to the size of the population itself. (*cf. logistic growth*).

extinction
The dying out or extermination of a species.

extracellular
Located or occurring outside a cell or cells.

F

facilitated diffusion
The passive movement of molecules along the concentration gradient.

FAD/FADH$_2$
A redox coenzyme that can accept or donate electrons. H_2 is the oxidized version.

feedback inhibition
A cellular control mechanism in which enzyme activity is inhibited by the end product.

fermentation
An anaerobic metabolic process by which a carbohydrate, such as starch or a sugar, is converted into an alcohol or an acid.

fertilization
The union of haploid gametes to produce a diploid zygote, initiating the development of a new organism.

fight or flight response
A response to an acute threat to survival that is marked by physical changes, including nervous and endocrine changes.

first gap phase (G_1)
The first gap, or growth phase, of the cell cycle, consisting of the portion of interphase before DNA synthesis.

fitness
A mathematical measure of the genetic contribution to the next generation.

fossil record
The history of life as documented by fossils.

founder effect
The loss of genetic variation that occurs when a new population is established by a very small number of individuals.

G

gamete
A mature sexual reproductive cell, as a sperm or egg, that unites with another cell to form a new organism.

gametic mutation
A mutation that occurs in a gamete, germ cell, or gametocyte (*cf. somatic mutation*).

gel electrophoresis
The separation and analysis of protein molecules of varying sizes by moving them through a block of gel using an electric field.

gene
A unit of hereditary information consisting of a specific nucleotide sequence in DNA.

gene cloning
The production of exact copies of a particular gene or DNA sequence using genetic engineering techniques.

gene duplication
A duplication of a section of DNA within a chromosome. An important mechanism in molecular evolution.

gene expression
The transcription and translation of a gene.

genetic cross
The purposeful mating of two individuals resulting in the combination of genetic material in the offspring.

genetic drift
The random changes in allele frequency in a population over generations.

genetic engineering
The process of making changes to an organism's genes, e.g. to give it new traits.

genetic equilibrium
Allele frequencies in a population that are static, or unchanging, over time.

genetic variation
The differences in the genetic makeup of individuals in a population.

GMO (genetically modified organism)
Any organism whose genetic material has been altered using genetic engineering.

genome
The genetic material of an organism, and all the heritable traits encoded in its DNA.

genotype
The genetic makeup of an organism.

glucose
A simple sugar that functions as the main source of metabolic energy in living things.

glycolysis
The metabolic pathway that converts glucose into pyruvate.

glycosidic bond
A covalent bond that joins a carbohydrate (sugar) molecule to another group, which may or may not be another carbohydrate.

Golgi apparatus
An organelle found in eukaryotic cells that packages and transports molecules from the endoplasmic reticulum to their destination.

granum (*pl., grana*)
Stack of thylakoids found in the stroma of chloroplasts, where the light-dependent reactions of photosynthesis take place.

H

haploid
Having a single set of each chromosome in a cell or cell nucleus, e.g. as in gametes.

Hardy-Weinberg equation
An equation used to predict genetic outcomes in a non-evolving population over time, $p^2 + 2pq + q^2 = 1$.

heterotroph
See **consumer**.

heterozygous
Having two different alleles for any hereditary characteristic.

heterozygous advantage
The higher fitness of heterozygotes for a condition relative to either homozygote.

histone
A small basic protein found in the nucleus of eukaryotic cells that organizes DNA strands to form chromatin.

homologous chromosomes
A pair of chromosomes, one inherited from each parent, with the same genes in the same order along their chromosomal arms.

homology
Similarity between two different species of organisms due to shared ancestry.

homozygous
Having two identical alleles for any hereditary characteristic.

hormone
Chemical messengers secreted directly into the blood, where they circulate to exert specific effects on target tissues and organs.

***Hox* gene**
A group of related genes that specify regions of the body plan of an embryo along the head-tail axis of animals.

hydrogen bond
A weak dipole-dipole bond in which a hydrogen atom in one molecule is attracted to an electronegative atom in the same or a different molecule.

hydrolysis
A reaction in which a molecule is split into smaller molecules by reacting with water.

hydrophilic
Interacting readily with, or attracted to, water (*cf. hydrophobic*).

hydrophobic
Not readily interacting with water; a molecule or substance that does not dissolve in or mix with water (*cf. hydrophilic*).

IJ

incomplete dominance
A gene interaction in which both alleles of a gene at a locus are partially expressed, resulting in an intermediate phenotype.

independent assortment
With reference to inheritance, describing how alleles for separate traits are passed to the gametes independently of one another.

index fossil
A fossil (usually) with a narrow time range and wide spatial distribution, used to define periods of geologic time.

indole-acetic acid (IAA)
See **auxin**.

induced fit model
A model for the interactions between an enzyme and substrate involving conformational change in the enzyme.

insulin
A hormone secreted by pancreatic β cells that lowers blood glucose levels by promoting cellular uptake of glucose and synthesis and storage of glycogen in the liver.

interphase
The period in the cell cycle when the cell is not dividing, accounting for about 90% of the cell cycle. During interphase, metabolic activity is high and cell size may increase.

intracellular
Occurring or situated within a cell or cells.

intron
A segment of DNA that does not code for a protein and is removed before translation.

ion pump
Membrane proteins that is capable of transporting ions against a concentration gradient using the energy from ATP.

ionic bond
A chemical bond between two ions with opposite charges, formed when an electron is transferred from one atom to another.

K

K selection
A form of selection that occurs in an environment at or near carrying capacity, favoring species with long gestation that produce few offspring (*cf. r selection*).

karyogram
A photograph of the chromosomes of a cell, arranged in homologous pairs and in a numbered sequence.

karyotype (*noun*)
The observed characteristics of the chromosomes of an individual or species.

keystone species
A species that occupies an essential role in an ecosystem and on which most or all of the other species in an ecosystem depend, directly or indirectly.

Krebs cycle
A cycle of aerobic catalyzed reactions in respiration occurring within mitochondria. Generates ATP and reducing power.

kinesis (*pl., kineses*) *(biology)*
The non-directional movement of an animal in response to a stimulus. *Orthokinesis* involves the rate of movement, whereas *klinokinesis* involves the rate of turning.

L

lactic acid fermentation
A metabolic process by which glucose is converted into cellular energy and lactate.

latent heat of fusion
The energy required to change the state of a substance from a solid to a liquid.

latent heat of vaporization
The energy required to change the state of a substance from a liquid to a gas.

ligand
An ion, molecule, or molecular group that binds to another chemical entity to form a larger complex. A signal molecule.

light dependent phase
The phase of photosynthesis during which light energy is converted into chemical energy through chemical reactions.

light independent phase
See **Calvin cycle**.

limiting factor
A resource or environmental condition that limits the growth, distribution or size of a population within an ecosystem.

link reaction
The stage in respiration that converts pyruvate into acetyl CoA, linking glycolysis to the Krebs cycle.

linked genes
Genes located on the same chromosome. Functionally refers to genes located close enough together on a chromosome that they tend to be inherited together.

lipid
Any organic substance that does not dissolve in water, but dissolves well in nonpolar organic solvents. Lipids include fatty acids, fats, oils, waxes and steroids.

local regulation
A method by which cells signal to and interact with other cells in the vicinity.

locus (*pl., loci*)
A specific place along the length of a chromosome where a given gene is located.

logistic growth
A pattern of population growth in which growth rate declines as the population nears carrying capacity (*cf. exponential growth*).

M

M phase
The period in the cell cycle during which cell division takes place.

mass extinction
The extinction of a large number of species within a relatively short period of global time.

maternal chromosome
The chromosomes in the nucleus received from the female gamete during fertilization.

matrix *(of mitochondria)*
The space within the inner membrane of a mitochondrion.

meiosis
The process of double nuclear division in sexually reproducing organisms, which results in cells with half the original number of chromosomes (haploid).

Mendelian inheritance
Patterns of inheritance that are characteristic of organisms that reproduce sexually, such as independent assortment and segregation of chromosomes.

metabolic pathway
A linked series of chemical reactions occurring within a cell.

metabolism
The chemical processes occurring within a living cell/organism that sustain life.

metaphase
The third stage of mitosis, in which the spindle is complete and the chromosomes are all aligned at the equator of the cell.

microRNA (miRNA)
A short non-coding segment of RNA that regulates the function of messenger RNA.

mitochondrion (*pl., mitochondria*)
An organelle in eukaryotic cells that serves as the site of cellular respiration.

mitosis
The phase of the cell cycle resulting in nuclear division.

molecular cloning
See **gene cloning**.

monohybrid cross
A cross between two organisms that differ in one observed trait.

monomer
A simple molecule that can covalently bind to other similar molecules to form a polymer.

monophyletic
A taxon that includes an ancestor and all its descendants.

monosaccharide
A molecule that has the chemical formula $(CH_2O)n$ and cannot be hydrolyzed to form any smaller carbohydrates. Also called a simple sugar.

morphogen
A chemical substance that governs the movement and development of cells during embryonic development.

multiple alleles
The existence of more than two alleles for a gene in the population.

multiple genes
When many genes contribute to a single phenotype.

mutation
A change in the nucleotide sequence of an organism's DNA (or RNA).

mutualism
Biological interaction between (usually two) species that benefits both parties.

N

NAD/NADH
Electron carriers in cellular respiration (oxidized/reduced forms).

NADP/NADPH
Electron carriers in photosynthesis (oxidized/reduced forms).

nastic response/nasty
Non-directional response to stimuli in plants.

natural selection
The differential survival and reproduction of favorable phenotypes.

negative feedback
In physiology, a primary mechanism of homeostasis where a change in a variable triggers a response that counteracts the initial change.

niche differentiation
An evolved response in which species partition resources in an environment in order to minimize competition between them.

non-competitive inhibition
Enzyme inhibition where the inhibitor binds to the enzyme at a region other than the active site (*cf. competitive inhibition).*

non-cyclic photophosphorylation
The generation of ATP using light energy during photosynthesis. The electrons lost in this process are replaced by the splitting of water.

nondisjunction
The failure of homologous chromosomes or sister chromatids to separate properly during cell division.

non-Mendelian inheritance
Any inheritance pattern in which traits do not segregate in accordance with Mendel's laws.

nuclear membrane
The double-layered membrane enclosing the nucleus of a cell (aka *nuclear envelope*).

nucleic acid
A polymer consisting of many nucleotide monomers. Serves as a blueprint for proteins and therefore for all cellular activities. The two types are DNA and RNA.

nucleolus (*pl., nucleoli*)
A specialized spherical structure in the nucleus, consisting of chromosomal regions containing ribosomal RNA (rRNA); the site of rRNA synthesis and ribosomal assembly.

nucleotide (*pl., nucleotides*)
An organic molecule that is the building block of DNA and RNA. Consist of a sugar molecule (ribose in RNA or deoxyribose in DNA) attached to a phosphate group and a nitrogen-containing base.

nucleus
The organelle of a eukaryotic cell that contains the genetic material in the form of chromosomes, made up of chromatin.

O

operator
A segment of DNA that is the binding site for proteins that initiate transcription.

operon
A cluster of functionally-related genes in prokaryotes controlled by a shared operator.

optimum *(enzyme)*
The conditions under which a particular enzyme is most active.

organelle
A subcellular structure with one or more specific jobs to perform in the cell.

osmolarity
The concentration of a solution expressed as the total number of solute particles per liter; number of moles of solute per liter.

osmosis
The diffusion of free water across a selectively permeable membrane.

outgroup
A more distantly related group of organisms that serves as a reference group when determining the evolutionary relationships.

oxidative phosphorylation
The process in which ATP is formed as a result of the step-wise transfer of electrons to a final acceptor, oxygen.

P

paraphyletic
A group that includes an ancestral species but not all of its descendants.

parasitism
Interaction in which one organism, the parasite, benefits at the expense of the other, the host.

parsimony
A principle that argues that the simplest of competing explanations is the most likely to be correct. Also known as Occam's razor.

passive transport
Diffusion of a substance across a biological membrane with no expenditure of energy.

paternal chromosome
The chromosomes in the nucleus received from the male gamete during fertilization.

pedigree
A diagram of a family tree, with conventional symbols, showing the occurrence of heritable characters in parents and offspring over multiple generations.

peptide bond
A covalent bond between two amino acids; the primary linkage in all protein structures.

phagocytosis
The engulfing and ingestion of foreign bodies such as bacteria by phagocytes.

phenotype
The observable traits of an organism, determined by its genetic makeup, environment and epigenetic factors.

pheromone
A chemical released by an organism, to the outside, which triggers a behavioral response in members of the same species.

phospholipid
A polar lipid composed of glycerol joined to two fatty acids and a phosphate group. Phospholipids form bilayers that function as biological membranes.

photolysis
Chemical decomposition induced by light or other radiant energy.

photoperiodism
The functional or behavioral response of organisms to changes in the duration in cycles of light and darkness.

photosynthesis
A process used by green plants, algae, and some bacteria to convert light energy into chemical energy (carbohydrate).

photosystem
Membrane-bound pigment complexes that capture light in photosynthesis.

phyletic gradualism
Evolutionary model proposing that species arise through the gradual and continuous transformation of populations (*cf. punctuated equilibrium*).

phylogenetic tree
A branching diagram showing evolutionary relationships among organisms. Can be based on cladistic analysis, in which case it is called a cladogram.

phylogeny
The evolutionary history of a taxon.

phytohormone
A plant growth regulator; plant hormone.

pinocytosis
A form of endocytosis in which the cell takes in fluids by infolding of its membrane.

plant hormone
Chemical compounds produced within plants that control growth and development.

plasma membrane
The membrane at the boundary of every cell that acts as a selective barrier, regulating the cell's chemical composition.

plasmid
A circular extra-chromosomal segment of DNA capable of self replication.

plasmodesma (*pl., plasmodesmata*)
A thin membrane-lined channel in the cell walls of plant cells and some algal cells, enabling transport and communication between adjacent cells.

polar
A molecule that carries a partial positive charge on one side and a partial negative charge on the other.

polygenes
See **multiple genes**.

polymers
Very large molecules (macromolecules) composed of many repeating subunits.

polymerase chain reaction (PCR)
An *in-vitro* technique for rapid synthesis of a given DNA sequence.

polypeptide
A chain of amino acids linked together by peptide bonds.

polyphyletic
A group of organisms that includes organisms with different ancestors, e.g. warm-blooded animals.

polyploidy
A condition in which the cells of an organism have more than two complete sets of chromosomes.

polysaccharide
A carbohydrate chain consisting of many monosaccharides joined by glycosidic bonds, e.g. starch and cellulose.

population bottleneck
An evolutionary event in which the size of a population is sharply reduced, leading to a loss of genetic diversity.

population density
A measurement of population per unit area or unit volume.

population growth
Change in the size of a population over time.

positive feedback
In physiology, a control mechanism in which a change in a variable triggers a response that reinforces or amplifies the change.

precision
How close repeated measurements are to each other, i.e. repeatability.

predation
Biological interaction in which one organism, the predator, kills and eats another, its prey.

pressure potential
A component of the potential energy of water caused by physical pressures on a solution. Can be positive or negative (*cf. solute potential*).

primary active transport
The movement of molecules across a membrane against a concentration gradient, using energy from ATP (*cf. secondary active transport*).

primary structure
The linear sequence of amino acids in a polypeptide chain.

primary transcript
The initial single-stranded ribonucleic acid product synthesized by DNA transcription.

probability
The chance or likelihood that a certain event will occur or that a prediction will be correct.

producer
See **autotroph**.

programmed cell death
See **apoptosis**.

prometaphase
A stage in mitosis or meiosis during which the nuclear membrane breaks down and microtubules attach to kinetochores.

prophase
The first stage of mitosis, in which the chromatin condenses into discrete chromosomes, the miotic spindle begins to form, and the nucleolus disappears.

protein
A biologically functional molecule consisting of one or more polypeptides folded into a specific three-dimensional structure.

punctuated equilibrium
Evolutionary model proposing that evolution occurs primarily through short bursts of speciation, followed by lengthy periods of stasis. (*cf. phyletic gradualism*).

Punnett square
A diagram used in the study of inheritance to show the predicted genotypic results of random fertilization in genetic crosses between individuals of known genotype.

pyruvate
A versatile biological molecule that is the end product of glycolysis.

Q

quaternary structure
The structure formed by the association of two or more polypeptides.

quorum sensing
A type of cell signaling in unicellular organisms in which cells sense population density by detecting signaling molecules secreted by other cells. Cell activity often changes dramatically when the population reaches a threshold size, or quorum.

R

R group
Part of an amino acid's core structure that varies from a single hydrogen atom to large structures containing carbon rings. Variation in the R group is responsible for variation in amino acid structure and function.

***r* selection**
A form of selection in non-limiting environments favoring short life spans and high reproductive rates (*cf. K selection*).

radiometric dating
See **absolute dating**.

receptor
A protein molecule inside a target cell or on its surface that receives a chemical signal and brings about a response.

recessive allele
An allele that is only expressed if the individual has two copies of the allele.

recessive trait
See **recessive allele**.

recombination
The process by which genes are exchanged between different chromosomes to produce new combinations of alleles.

regulatory gene
A gene that produces a repressor substance to control the expression of other gene(s).

relative dating
A method for determining the age of a fossil by comparing its placement with that of fossils in other strata (*cf. absolute dating).*

relative fitness
A measure of fitness that describes the changes in genotype frequency relative to other genotypes (*cf. absolute fitness).*

reproductive effort
The proportion of its resources that an organism expends on reproduction.

reproductive isolating mechanism
An ecological, physiological, anatomical or behavioral barrier that prevents interbreeding between different species.

resilience *(of ecosystems)*
The property of ecosystems or populations to recover from disturbances.

resistance *(of ecosystems)*
The property of ecosystems or populations to remain largely unchanged when subjected to a disturbance.

resting phase (G_0)
A cellular state outside of the replicative cell cycle, during which the cell enters a resting state and is not dividing.

rough endoplasmic reticulum (rER)
The portion of the endoplasmic reticulum with ribosomes attached.

RuBisCo
A plant enzyme involved in fixing atmospheric CO_2 during photosynthesis.

S

S phase
The synthesis phase of the cell cycle, during which chromosomes are replicated.

saturated fatty acid
A fatty acid whose carbon chain cannot contain any more hydrogen atoms.

second gap phase (G_2)
The second gap, or growth phase, of the cell cycle, during which there is rapid cell growth and the cell prepares for mitosis.

secondary active transport
Active transport across a membrane in which movement of one ion down its concentration gradient is coupled to the movement of a molecule against its concentration gradient (*cf. primary active transport*).

secondary structure
The folding of a polypeptide chain into an alpha helix, beta sheet, or random coil.

selection pressure
Any factor that reduces or increases fitness in a portion of a population.

sex linkage
An association between genes in sex chromosomes that makes some characteristics appear more frequently in one sex.

sexual reproduction
A type of reproduction in which offspring are created by combining genetic information from two individuals of different sexes.

shared derived character
Characters arising in an ancestor and shared by all of its descendants.

signal transduction
The process by which a stimulus outside a cell is converted to an intracellular signal required for a cellular response.

signaling molecule
See **ligand**

smooth endoplasmic reticulum (sER)
The portion of the endoplasmic reticulum that lacks ribosomes.

solute potential
A component of the potential energy of water caused by a difference in solute concentrations at two locations. Can be zero or negative (*cf. pressure potential*).

somatic mutation
A mutation in DNA that occurs after conception, and which can occur in any of the body's cells except the gametes (*cf. gametic mutation*).

speciation
The formation of new biological species through the process of evolution.

species *(biological)*
A group of organisms that can successfully interbreed and produce fertile offspring, and is reproductively isolated from other such groups.

specific heat capacity
The amount of heat that must be added (or removed) from a unit mass of a substance to change its temperature by one Kelvin.

stabilizing selection
A mode of natural selection that favors retention of the median phenotype (*cf. directional selection, disruptive selection).*

stimulus
In neural or hormonal circuits, a fluctuation in a variable that triggers a response.

stroma
The fluid filling up the inner space of chloroplasts, which surrounds the thylakoids and grana.

stroma lamellae
Hollow tube-like structures within chloroplasts that connect thylakoids in different grana.

structural gene
A gene that encodes the amino acid sequence of a protein.

substrate level phosphorylation
The synthesis of ATP by the transfer of a phosphate from a substrate directly to ADP.

symbiosis
A very close ecological relationship which may be beneficial to both parties (e.g. mutualism) or only to one (parasitism).

sympatric speciation
The evolution of a new species from an ancestral species while both continue to inhabit the same geographic region.

synapomorphy
A shared derived character state. Cladistic analysis of evolutionary relationships is based only on synapomorphies.

systematic bias, systematic error
Consistent, repeatable error associated with faulty equipment or a flawed design.

T

taxis (*pl., taxes*)
A directional response to a stimulus.

telophase
The final stage of mitosis in which daughter nuclei are forming.

territory
Any area defended by an animal for such purposes as mating, nesting, or feeding.

tertiary structure
The three-dimensional structure of a protein, created by the folding of the helices or sheets.

thermoregulation
The maintenance of internal body temperature within a tolerable range.

thylakoid discs
Membrane-bound sacs containing chlorophyll; the site of the light-dependent reactions of photosynthesis.

trait
One of two or more detectable variants in a genetic character.

transcription
The process of copying a segment of DNA into a strand of mRNA.

transcription factor
A protein that binds to specific DNA sequences, controlling the transcription of genetic information from DNA to mRNA.

transformation *(genetics)*
Genetic alteration of a cell resulting from the direct uptake and incorporation of foreign DNA from its surroundings through the cell membrane.

translation
The process of decoding a strand of mRNA to produce a sequence of amino acids.

transmembrane receptor
A protein embedded in the plasma membrane of a cell that acts in cell signaling by binding to extracellular molecules and initiating a response the other side. Specialized integral membrane proteins that allow communication between the cell and the extracellular space.

transpiration
The evaporative loss of water from a plant.

triose phosphate
A 3-C molecule produced in photosynthesis.

trophic cascades
The multiple effects of top predators on lower trophic levels.

trophic efficiency
A description of how effectively energy is transferred from one trophic level to the next.

trophic level
A level or position in a food chain, food web or ecological pyramid. An organism's trophic level is determined by its feeding behavior.

tropism *(plants)*
Directional growth in response an external stimulus, such as light or gravity.

turgor
Distention or rigidity of plant cells, resulting from fluid pressure against the rigid cell wall.

U

unsaturated fatty acid
A fatty acid whose carbon chain contains at least one double bond.

V

validity
How well and investigation measures what it sets out to measure.

variable
A measurable property that changes over time or can take on different values.

vestigial structure
An organ or structure retained during evolution but which has been reduced in size and/or function and is no longer (evidently) useful.

visual representation
A graph, diagram or schematic created to present information or data.

W

water potential
The potential energy of water in a certain environment compared with the potential energy of pure water at room temperature and atmospheric pressure.

XYZ

X-linkage
Sex linkage involving the X chromosome.

Credits

ACKNOWLEDGEMENTS

The writing team would like to thank the following people and organizations for their contributions to this edition:

• Andrea Braakhuis (Waikato Institute of Technology, Wintec) for the photo of the athletes on the stationary bikes • Waikato Hospital for the images of the karyograms • Prof. Jeff Podos for the photos of the finches • Stephen Moore for freshwater invertebrate photos.

SPECIAL REFERENCES

Source paper for FRQ (milk processing) (page 25):
Qian, F., Sun, J., Cao, D., Tuo, Y., Jiang, S., & Mu, G. (2017). Experimental and modelling study of the denaturation of milk protein by heat treatment. Korean journal for food science of animal resources, 37(1), 44–51.

Source paper for FRQ (osmosis in RBCs) (page 69):
L.K. Goodhead and F.M. MacMillan. (2017). Measuring osmosis and hemolysis of red blood cells. Adv Physiol Educ 41: 298 –305.

Source paper for FRQ (pulse and chase experiment) (page 70):
J.D. Jamieson and G.E. Palade (1967). Intracellular transport of secretory proteins in the pancreatic exocrine cell: II Transport to condensing vacuoles and zymogen granules. J Cell Biol 34(2): 597-615.

Source paper for FRQ (mitosis in bean root tips) (page 142):
C. C. Moh & J. J. Alán (1964). The effect of low temperature on mitosis in the root tips of beans, Caryologia, 17:2, 409-415,

Source paper for FRQ (effect of stathmin on cancer) (page 143):
Miceli, C., Tejada, A., Castaneda, A. *et al.* Cell cycle inhibition therapy that targets stathmin in *in vitro* and *in vivo* models of breast cancer. Cancer Gene Therapy 20, 298–307 (2013). https://doi.org/10.1038/cgt.2013.21

Source paper for trichome length in *Acacia* (page 179)
A.V. Milewski, Truman P. Young, and Derek Madden (1990). Thorns as induced defenses: experimental evidence. School for Field Studies, 16 Broadway, Beverly, MA, 01915, USA.

Data for FRQ (effect of reindeer browsing) (page 191) **based on**:
M. Den Herder, R. Virtanen, & H. Roininen (2004). Effects of reindeer browsing on tundra willow and its associated insect herbivores. Journal of Applied Ecology 41: 870–879

Background information for FRQ (temperature dependent sex determination in tongue sole) (page 192):
Jiang, L., & Li, H. (2017). Single locus maintains large variation of sex reversal in half-smooth tongue sole (*Cynoglossus semilaevis*). G3 (Bethesda, Md.), 7(2), 583–589.

Bicheng Yang (2014). Two papers unraveled the mystery of sex determination and benthic adaptation of the flatfish. https://www.eurekalert.org/pub_releases/2014-02/bs-tpu020114.php

Source paper for apoptosis in *C. elegans* (page 217):
Lettre, G. and Hengartner MO (2006) Developmental apoptosis in *C. elegans*: a complex CEDnario. Nat Rev Mol Cell Biol 7: 97–108.

Source paper for microRNA function in zebra fish (page 226):
Schier, A.F and Giraldex, A.J (2006). MicroRNA function and mechanism: Insights from zebra fish. Cold Spring Harbor Symposia on Quantitative Biology, 2006

Source paper for whale evolution (page 256):
Nikaido, M., Rooney, A. P. , and Okada, N (1999). Phylogenetic relationships among cetartiodactyls based on insertions of short and long interpersed elements: Hippopotamuses are the closest extant relatives of whales. PNAS August 31, 1999 96 (18) 10261-10266

Source paper for diet and epigenetic changes in rats (page 259)
Sandovici I., Smith N.H., Nitert M.D., Ackers-Johnson M., Uribe-Lewis S., Ito Y., Jones R.H., Marquez V.E., Cairns W., Tadayyon M., O'Neill L.P., Murrell A., Ling C., Constância M., Ozanne S.E. (2011). Maternal diet and aging alter the epigenetic control of a promoter-enhancer interaction at the Hnf4a gene in rat pancreatic islets. Proc Natl Acad Sci USA. 108(13):5449-54.

Source paper for plot of artificial selection in *B. rapa* (page 276)
Zu, P. and Schiestl, F.P. (2017). The effects of becoming taller: direct and pleiotropic effects of artificial selection on plant height in *Brassica rapa*. Plant J, 89: 1009-1019. https://doi.org/10.1111/tpj.13440

Source paper for founder effect in anole lizards (page 289)
Kolbe J.J., Leal M., Schoener T.W., Spiller D.A., Losos J.B. (2012).Founder effects persist despite adaptive differentiation: a field experiment with lizards. Science 335(6072):1086-9.

Source for rates of species origination and extinction (page 350)
James W. Kirchner and Anne Weil (2000). Delayed biological recovery from extinctions throughout the fossil record. Nature 404: 177-180.

Source paper for selection in feather lice (page 367)
Bush, S.E., Villa, S.M., Altuna, J.C., Johnson, K.P., Shapiro, M.D. and Clayton, D.H. (2019), Host defense triggers rapid adaptive radiation in experimentally evolving parasites. Evolution Letters, 3: 120-128.

Source paper for rapid evolution in wall lizards (page 368)
Anthony Herrel, Katleen Huyghe, Bieke Vanhooydonck, Thierry Backeljau, Karin Breugelmans, Irena Grbac, Raoul Van Damme, Duncan J. Irschick (2008). Rapid large-scale evolutionary divergence in morphology and performance associated with exploitation of a different dietary resource. Proceedings of the National Academy of Sciences: 105(12) 4792-4795.

Source papers for songbird data (page 397)
Searcy, W.A., Nowicki, S. (2008). Bird song and the problem of honest communication. American Scientist, 96(2).

Sockman, K. W., Sewall, K. B., Ball, G. F., & Hahn, T. P. (2005). Economy of mate attraction in the Cassin's finch. Biology letters, 1(1), 34–37.

Source paper for coral-macroalga competition (page 397)
Box, S. and Mumby, P. (2007). Effect of macroalgal competition on growth and survival of juvenile Caribbean corals. Marine Ecology Progress Series. 342. 139-149.

PHOTO CREDITS

We also acknowledge the photographers who have made images available through Wikimedia Commons under Creative Commons Licences 0, 1.0, 2.0, 2.5, 3.0, or 4.0:

• Christian Schmelzer • Rufino Uribe • J. Miquel, D. Vilavella, Z.widerski, V. V. Shimalov and J. Torres • STM Erwinrossen • BAN127 • Dr Graham Beards • tooony • Eduard Solà • Vossman • A2-33 • Capkuckokos • Ericlin1337 • Professor Dr. habil. Uwe Kils • Böhler et al. (2018) • HG6996 • Piotr Kuczynski • Alison Roberts • Margaret McFall-Ngai • Ragesoss • Jpbarrass • Matthias Zepper • dsworth Center- New York State Department of Health • Emmanuelm • Paulo Henrique Orlandi Mourao • Craig. Mcclenagha • Emw • Zephyris • KTBN • Walter Siegmund • Noor et al PLOS0 • Jeevan Jose • Megan McCarty • NYWTS • Dr Graham Beards • Shirely Owens MSU • Fdardel • emNL • Ltshears • Toony • PhiLiP • Cybercobra • Boghog • GT • Palewhalegail • IRRI • Scott Bauer, USDA ARS • PLos • GDallimore • Kathy Chapman • Drew Avery • Olaf Leillinger • Jo Naylor • Klaus Polak • Patrick K59 • thinboyfatter • Brian Gratwicke •Stefan3345 • Sharp Photography • Rocky Mountain Laboratories, NIAID, NIH • Xiangyux • H. Zell • Robert Pittman - NOAA • CDC:Alissa Eckert & Dan Higgins • Steve Lonhart (SIMoN / MBNMS) PD NOAA • Meyer A, PLoS Biology • Thomas Breuer • Yathin S Krishnappa • Tony Wills • Ron Pastorino • The High Fin Sperm Whale • Hectonichus • Dwergenpaartje • DanielCD • Ghedoghedo • Daderot • Arthur Anker • • Evancez • Jason Minshull • Joseph Berger, Bugwood.org • Aviceda • Bruce Marlin • Bruce Marlin • Kirt L. Onthank • Taollan82; Kirt L. Onthank • Shan Shebs • AKA • James St. John • David B. Langston, University of Georgia, Bugwood.org,• Leon Hupperichs • Didier Descouens • Dr Josef Reischig • Taro Eldredge • EMW • Kristian Peters • Yug • CSIRO • Sini Merikallio • Opzwartbeek • artfarmer • David Kennard • Onno Zweers • Charlesjsharp • Snake3yes • D. Dibenski • P Barden • Uwe Schmidt • onathunder • Diego Delso • Christin Khan, NOAA • maciejbledowski • Alex Wild • Greg Hume at en.wikipedia • Olivier Lejade • I, Kenpei • Takahashi • James C Trager • Adrian A. Smith • Todd Huffman Lattice • Magne Flåten • Magne Flåten • Bronson (1987) • flowergarden.noaa.gov • Dario Sanches • Nestor Galina • Per Harald Olsen • C Johnson-Walker • Hardyplants • Ryan Batten • Walter Siegmund • Luc Viatour www.Lucnix.be • Marco vinci • Robert Pitman • dominic sherony • Cephas • Althepal • viamoi • The High Fin Sperm Whale • Lubasi •Brian Dell • NPS • matt knoth • John M • Scott Ehardt • Dan Gustafson USFWS • Piet Spaans • Javier Rubilar • Dan Harkless • Rcole17 • Tangopaso • Stephen Moore • NY State Dept of Health • John Hayman • Robert Scarth • Vabampidis • Azul • Dept. of Natural Resources, Illinois

Contributors identified by coded credits are:

• BCC: Berkshire Community College Image Library • BF: Brian Finerran • CDC: Centers for Disease Control and Prevention, Atlanta, USA • EII: Educational Interactive Imaging • FH: Felix Hicks • JDG: John Green (University of Waikato) • KP: Kent Pryor • TG: Tracey Greenwood • NASA: National Aeronautics and Space Administration • NCI: National Cancer Institute • NIAD: National Institute of Allergy and Infectious Diseases • NIH: National Institute of Health • NOAA: National Oceanic and Atmospheric Administration • PDB: Protein Data Base • RA: Richard Allan • RCN: Ralph Cocklin • USDA: United States Department of Agriculture • USFWS: US Fish and Wildlife Service • USGS: United States Geological Survey • WMU: Waikato Microscope Unit (University of Waikato)

Royalty free images, purchased by BIOZONE International Ltd, are used throughout this workbook and have been obtained from the following sources:
• Adobe Stock • Black Diamond Images • iStock images • Corel Corporation from their Professional Photos CD-ROM collection; ©Digital Vision; PhotoDisc®, Inc. USA, www.photodisc.com • 3D images created using Bryce, Poser, and Pymol

Index

95% confidence intervals 432, 469

A
Absorption spectrum 88
Abiotic factors, role in evolution 268
Abscission in plants 371
Absolute fitness 266
Accuracy 462
Acetylation of histones 215
Action spectrum 88
Activation energy 74
Active site 12, 72
Active transport 60-63
Adaptation 266-267, 444-445
Adaptive radiation 335-338
Adenosine triphosphate, structure 82
Adhesion 2
Aerobic respiration 93
Age structure, populations 425
Agriculture, GMOs in 254-255
Agrobacterium 196, 255
Albinism 235
Alcoholic fermentation 93, 103
Allele frequencies 291-292
Alleles, definition 194
Allelic diversity, Tasmanian devils 286
Allopatric speciation 339-341
Allosteric enzyme regulation 78
Alpha helix 11
Altruism 399, 406
Amino acids 9-10
Anabolic reactions 74
Anaerobic metabolism 93, 103
Anaerobic respiration 93
Anagenesis 333
Analogous structures 280
Anaphase 130, 145
Anecdote 471
Aneuploidy 233
Animal cells 31-32
Animal phyla, phylogenetic tree 327
Anoxygenic photosynthesis 86
Antennapedia 225
Antibiotic resistance, acquiring 236
Antibiotic resistance, evolution of 321
Anticodon 209
Antigen-presenting cell 113
Antigenic drift 237
Antigenic shift 237-238
Antihistamine, action of 123
Antisense strand 207
Apex predators 417, 435, 442
Apical dominance 375
Apoptosis 137-138, 217
Aquaporins 49
Argumentation 471-472
Army ants, cooperation in 402
Arrow of time 83
Arsenic, effect on enzymes 79
Artificial selection 273-277
Aseptic technique 246-247
Asteroid impact, effect of 350, 453
Asymmetry of DNA 7
ATP 6, 60, 82, 85
ATP synthase 73, 98-99
ATP yield, aerobic respiration 95-96
Autocrine signaling, defined 112
Autoinducers, in quorum sensing 121
Auxins, role of 371, 374-375
ATP generation, uncoupling 99

B
Background extinction rate 349, 352
Bacterial cell walls 52
Bacterial conjugation 195
Bacterial structure 28
Bacterial transformation 239, 244, 248
Bar charts 466
Bases in nucleic acids 6
Beak size, finches 315-317
Behavior, types of 370
Beneficial mutations 227, 235
Beta oxidation of lipids 20
Beta pleated sheet 11
Binary fission, energy for 82
Bioinformatics 256
Biological species concept 332
Bioluminescence, control of 121
Biomass pyramids 418-419
Biotic factors, role in evolution 268
Biotic potential 427
Birds, derived characters 330
BLAST 356-357
Blood cell differentiation 120
Blood glucose, regulation 125
Blood group alleles 167
BMP4, role in evolution 317-318
Body mass and O_2 consumption 415
Bottleneck effect 286-287
Brassica, artificial selection in 276
BRCA1 137
Breeding, energy costs 412
Brood parasites, advantages 413
Bt toxin 255

C
Calvin cycle 87, 91
Cancer 137, 181
Caps, mRNA processing 208
Carbohydrates 4, 15-19
Carbon dioxide, limiting factor 91
Carbon, bonding in 5
Carolina parakeet, extinction of 352
Carotenoids 88
Carrier proteins 53
Carrion flowers, convergence in 281
Carrying capacity 428-429
Catabolic reactions 74
Catalyst 72, 74
Cattle, artificial selection in 275
CdK 136
Cell cycle, eukaryotic 128, 130
- regulation of 135-137
Cell differentiation, control 120
Cell division 127-138
Cell plate, plant cell cytokinesis 131
Cell signaling 111-121
- role in differentiation 214
- transcription factors 218
Cell size, limitations to 41
Cell sizes 39
Cell walls 33, 52
Cell-to-cell communication 112-113
Cells, biochemical nature of 4
Cells, types of 28-34
Cellular compartments, origin of 66
Cellular differentiation 214
Cellular respiration 84, 93-97, 100
Cellulose 17, 19
Central dogma 204
Centrioles 31
Centromere 130, 145-146
CFTR, mutation 230
Channel proteins 12, 53
Checkpoints in mitosis 128, 135
Cheetah, genetic bottleneck 287
Chemiosmosis 89, 97-99
Chemoautotrophs, in ecosystems 420
Chi squared test 134, 163, 174, 470
Chitin 17
Chlorophylls 88-89
Chloroplast DNA, inheritance of 180
Chloroplasts 33, 38, 87
- bacterial origin of 312, 314
Chloroquine resistance 322
Choice chamber experiments 385-386
Chromatin 197
Chromosomal theory 186-187
Chromosome mapping 172
Chromosomes, changes to 233-234
Chromosomes 195, 197
Chronic myelogenous leukemia 139
Chronometric dating 298, 301
Cichlid fishes, convergence in 281
Cichlid fishes, evolution in 318
Clades, animals 327
Cladistics 325
Cladograms, constructing 328-331
Cleavage furrow 131
Climax community 433
Clock of history 363
Coat color, mutations in 229
Coding strand 207
Codominance 166-167
Coevolution 333
Cohesion 2-3
Collagen 14
Commensalism 434
Common ancestry, evidence 312-313
Communication 390-393, 401
Communities, changes in 433
Compartmentalization in cells 64-65
Competition 434, 436-437
Competitive inhibition 78
Concentration gradients 41
Concept explanation, skill 459
Condensation, in lipids 20
Condensation, in sugars 16
Condensation, nucleic acids 7
Condensation, nucleotides 6
Condensation, polypeptides 10
Conjugation, bacterial 195
- and antibiotic resistance 236
Conservation and diversity 355
Conserved proteins 305, 307
Consumers 417, 420
- in the Great Lakes 448
Continuous data 464
Continuous variation 184
- and multiple genes 178
Controls, experimental 462
Convergent evolution 280-282, 333
Cooperative behavior 399-406
Corn blight, cause of 354
Correlation 470
Cotransport 61
Courtship behavior 394-397
Covariate 461
Covid-19 323-324
CRISPR-Cas9 239
Cristae 37, 94, 97
Crops, artificial selection in 276-277
Crossing over 145-146
Cryptic species 332
Cyanobacteria 28, 362
Cyclic AMP, second messenger 120
Cyclic phosphorylation 89
Cyclin dependent kinases 136
Cystic fibrosis, mutation 230
Cytochrome c homology 307-308
Cytokines, signal molecules 120
Cytokinesis 128, 130-131
Cytoplasm 31, 33
Cytosis in cells 62-63

D
Darwin, Charles 262-264
Data, distribution of 467
Data, types of 464
Deep sea vents, origin of life 359
Deep sea vents, production in 420
Defense, cooperative 404
Deforestation 449-450
Degeneracy of genetic code 205-206
Dehydration synthesis 7, 10
Deletion mutation 231
Denaturation 12, 75
Density
- effect on population growth 428
- of water 2-3
- population 425
Deoxynucleosides, role of 203
Dependent variable 461
Development
- control of 217, 224-225
- role of miRNA 226
Developmental genes 311
Diffusion 41, 53
Dihybrid inheritance 154, 159
Dinosaurs and bird evolution 330
Directional selection 269-270, 315
Disaccharides 16
Discontinuous variation 184
Discontinuous data 464
Disease
- and antigenic shift 238
- emerging 323-324
- effects on ecosystems 451
Disorders, human 187-188
Disruptive selection 269-270, 316
Disruptive selection, in finches 316
Distribution of data 467
Distribution, population 425
Disturbance, effect on diversity 441
Disulfide bond, in proteins 10-12
Divergent evolution 333-338
Diversity
- and ecosystem stability 440-441
- indices, calculating 430-431
- and community structure 430-432
- changes over time 350
DNA 6-7
DNA homology 295, 309-310
DNA ligase, in DNA replication 203
DNA model 198
DNA polymerase 201, 203
DNA profiling 249-253
DNA replication 201, 203
DNA sequencing 249, 256
DNA, information storage 151
Dogs, artificial selection in 274
Domains of life 312-313
Domestic animals, selection 273-275
Dormancy in plants 371
Down syndrome 188, 233
Drosophila, genes in 170-171, 225
Drug resistance, evolution of 321-322
Drugs, effects on enzymes 79
Dutch elm disease 451

E
E. coli LTEE 267
Earth's history, landmarks in 362-363
Ecological pyramids 418-419
Ecological 433
Ecosystem change 452-453, 449-450
Ecosystem disturbance 419
Ecosystem diversity 440-441
Ecosystem resilience 440-441
Ecosystem resistance 440
Ecosystem stability 440-441
Ectothermy 409-410
Edward syndrome 233
El Niño 452
Elastin 14
Electrochemical gradients 61
Electromagnetic spectrum 88
Electron transport chain 93-97
Electron-spin resonance 302
Electrophoresis, DNA analysis of 241
Elements in organisms 5
Elongation phase, translation 210
Emerging diseases 323-324
End products 73-74
Endergonic reactions 74
Endocrine signaling 112, 115
Endocytosis 63
Endoplasmic reticulum 31, 33
Endosymbiotic theory 66, 314
Endothermy 409

Energy allocation 407-408
Energy and community structure 438
Energy flow diagram 417
Energy pyramids 418-419
Energy resources, and mutualism 439
Energy transformations 85
Energy yielding pathways 93
Energy, in lipids 20
Enhancer sequences 222-223
Entropy 83
Environment
- effect on mitosis 134
- effects on phenotype 181-183
- role in evolution 268
Enzyme activity 75-77, 80
Enzymes 12, 72-80
Epigenetics 184, 215-216
Epinephrine 118, 120
Ester bond 20
Estrogen 115, 118
Ethylene in plants 371
Euchromatin 215
Euglena 28
Eukaryotes 28, 39
- cell cycle 128
- chromosomes 197
- gene expression 204, 207-211
- gene regulation 221
- gene structure 213
- origin 313-314
Eusocial insects 401, 405-406
Evolution 280-283, 295-324, 333-343
Evolutionary thought, history of 262
Exchanges in organisms 46-47
Exergonic reactions 74
Exocytosis 62
Exons 197, 221
Experimental control 462
Experimental methods 461
Exploitation, species interactions 434
Exponential growth 427
Extinction 344, 349-353
Extracellular enzymes 72
Extracellular receptor, defined 112
Eye development, cavefish 224

F
Facilitated diffusion 53
Fast plants, selection in 278
Fatty acids, types of 21
Feedback inhibition 78, 84
Feedback, in physiology 124-126
Fermentation 93, 103
Fetal hemoglobin 105
Fever, positive feedback in 126
Fibrous proteins 14
Fight or flight response 388
First messenger 118
Fission track dating 298
Fitness, and sickle cell 271
Fitness, measuring 266-267
Fluid mosaic model 48
Food chains 417
Food webs 417
Foraging, cooperative 402
Forensics 240, 250
Fossil record 295, 319-320
- dating methods 298-300
Fossilization 296
Fossils, formation 296
Fossils, index 297
Founder effect 288-289
Frameshift mutation 231
Fruit fly genetics 186
Fundamental niche 436
Fungal cells walls 52

G
G-coupled receptor 49, 118
Galápagos finches 315-317
Gametes, production of 127
Gametic mutation 228
Gap phase, cell cycle 128, 135
Gas exchanges in humans 47
Gel electrophoresis 241
Gene 197
Gene duplication 311, 444
Gene expression 204, 207-211
- epigenetic regulation of 215
- evidence for control 224
Gene flow 283
Gene induction 219
Gene markers 244
Gene pool analysis 293
Gene pools, changes in 285, 293
Gene regulation 219-223
Gene repression 220, 223
Gene structure 213
Gene, definition 194
Genetic bottlenecks 286
Genetic code 205
- evidence for evolution 295
- universality of 151, 312
Genetic crosses 154-155
Genetic diversity 354-355
Genetic drift 283, 290
Genetic engineering, tools in 239
Genetic equilibrium, principle of 284
Genetic variation, in gene pools 283
Genome, definition 194
Genome, prokaryotic 194-195
Genotype, defined 152
Geographical isolation 339, 345
Geometric growth 427
gfp, marker 244
Gibberellins, role of 218, 371
Globular proteins 13
Glucose transport 61, 115
GLUT-1 glucose transporter 49
Glycerate 3-phosphate 91
Glycogen 17
Glycolysis 93-97
Glycosidic bond 16, 19
GMOs, applications of 254-255
GMOs, producing 240
Golgi apparatus 31, 33, 62
Graphing 466
Great Lakes food web 448
Group behavior 398, 402, 404-405
Growth rate, populations 425-429
Gut structure in humans 47

H
Habitat fragmentation
- effect on biodiversity 449
- role in speciation 344
Haemoglobin 11, 13
Hardy-Weinberg equation 291
Harmful mutations 227, 230, 235
Hawaiian bobtail squid 121
Hb-O_2 dissociation curve 105
Heat capacity, water 2-3
HeLa cells 138-139
Helicase 201, 203
Hematopoiesis, control of 120
Hemoglobin homology 305
Hemoglobin, variation in 104
Herbicide resistance 255
Herbivory, response of plants to 182
Heterochromatin 215
Heterotrophs 421
Heterozygous advantage 271
Hibernation, energy conservation 407
Histogram 466
Histone modification 215
Histone proteins 197
HIV, life cycle 212
Homologous proteins 305
Homologous structures 295, 303
Hormones 115
Horses, evolution in 319
Hox genes 225
Human disorders 187-188
Human impact 449-450
Huntington disease 187
Hybrid sterility 348
Hydrogen atom 5
Hydrogen bonding in water 2-3
Hydrolysis 7, 10, 16, 20
Hydrophilic signal molecules 118
Hydrophobic signal molecules 118
Hypertonic 54
Hypotheses 461
Hypotonic 54

I
Ice ages, ecosystem change 453
Immunoglobulins 13
Immunological distance 306
Incomplete dominance 163, 168
Independent assortment, law of 153
Index fossils 297
Indicator species 430
Independent variable 461
Induced fit model 73
Industrial melanism 270
Influenzavirus, evolution in 237
Inheritance
- chromosomal basis of 186-187
- laws of 153
- pedigree analysis 157-158
Inhibition, signal transduction 122
Inhibitors, enzyme 78-79
Initiation phase, translation 210
Inorganic ions, in cells 4
Insect colonies, behavior in 405
Insecticide resistance 272
Insertion mutation 231
Instant speciation, by polyploidy 342
Insulin 13, 115, 117
Intermolecular bonds, in water 2
Interphase 128, 130
Interspecific competition 436-437
Intracellular enzymes 72
Intracellular receptor, defined 112
Introns 197, 221
Invasive species, effects of 446-447
Ion pumps 61
Ionization constant 59
Ionizing radiation, mutagen 232
Irreversible inhibition 79
Isomers, sugars 15
Isotonic 54

JK
K selection 429
Karyogram, analysis of 139
Keratin 14
Keystone species 442-443
Kin selection 406
Kineses 370, 381-382
Klinokinesis 381
Krebs cycle 93-97
Kudzu, invasive species 446

L
Lac operon 219
Lactate shuttle 103
Lactic acid fermentation 93, 103
Lactose intolerance, pedigree 158
Lactose tolerance 235
Lagging strand 203
Latent heat of fusion 2-3
Latent heat of vaporization 2-3
Law of superposition 299
Laws of inheritance 153
Leading strand, 203
Leaf disc experiment 92
Lectin, effect on mitosis 134
Leks 396
Lethal allele 163, 169, 271
Life, origin of 358-359
Lifestyle, and mutation risk 232
Ligation in genetic engineering 239
Light dependent phase 87, 89
Light independent phase 87, 91
Light microscopy 29
Limiting factors
- in photosynthesis 91
- in population growth 426
Line graphs 466
Linear chromosomes, in evolution 313
Linear regression 470
Link reaction 93-97
Linked genes 163, 170-174
Lipid bilayer 22, 48
Lipids 4, 20-21
Lipolysis 20
Liposomes, in life's origins 358
Local regulators 112, 114
Logistic growth 428-429
Long-day plants 377
Lysosomes 31

M
M phase 128-129
M-phase promoting factor 136
Macroevolution 333
Madagascar, habitat loss 449
Magnification, defined 30
Malaria and drug resistance 322
Mammalian evolution 282, 336-338
Map units, defined 172
Mass extinction 349-351
Mass-specific metabolic rate 415-416
Master genes, role in evolution 317
Maternal age effect 188
Maternal chromosome 130, 145
Mating behavior 394-397
Matrix, of mitochondrion 37 94, 97
Meiosis vs mitosis 150
Meiosis, in life cycle 127
Meiosis, modeling 148
Meiosis, stages in 145
Membrane permeability 50
Mendel, Gregor 263
Mendelian genetics 152-153
Meristems, mitosis in 129
Messenger RNA 8
Metabolic pathways, conserved 151
Metabolic pathways, efficiency 83
Metabolic rate 415
Metabolism, and body size 415
Metaphase 130, 145
Metaphase checkpoint 135
Metastasis 135
Methylation, in epigenetics 215
microRNA, in gene regulation 226
Microevolution 283-284
Middle lamella 33
Migration 283, 407, 425
Miller-Urey experiment 358, 360
Mimosa, nastic responses 389
miRNA and development 226
Mitochondria 31, 33, 37, 94, 97
- bacterial origin of 312, 314
- compartments in 46
Mitochondrial DNA, inheritance 180
Mitosis 127-138
- energy for 82
Mitosis vs meiosis 150
Mitotic index 129, 132
Model, DNA 198
Modeling logistic growth 429
Modeling meiosis 148
Modeling, mitosis 132
Modern synthesis 262-263
Molecular diversity, investigating 356
Monohybrid cross explained 154
Monosaccharides 15
Morphogens 217
Mortality 425-426
mRNA 204
mRNA -amino acid table 205
mRNA processing 208
Mt St Helens, succession 433
Multicellular organisms
- exchanges in 43, 47
Multiple alleles 163, 167
Multiple genes 63, 178
Mutagens 232
Mutation 227-235
- source of variation 265
- conferring drug resistance 322
Mutualism 434, 439
Myoglobin 105

N
Nastic behaviors 370-371, 389
Natality 425-426
Natural ecosystem change 452-453
Natural selection 269-270
- in gene pools 283
Navigation behavior 370
Negative feedback 124-125
Neurotransmitter, local regulator 114
Niche differentiation 437
Nitrogen atom 5
Non-competitive inhibition 78
Non-cyclic phosphorylation 89
Non-disjunction in meiosis 188
Non-isotopic dating methods 302
Non-Mendelian inheritance 163
Non-nuclear inheritance 163, 180
Nuclear division 128, 135
Nuclear membrane 31, 33

Nucleic acids 4, 6-8
Nucleolus 31, 33
Nucleosome 197
Nucleotide derivatives 6
Nucleotides 6
Nucleus 31, 33

O
Okazaki fragments 203
Oldfield mice, mutations in 229
Olfactory messages 392
One gene-one protein hypothesis 195
Operator, prokaryote operon 219-220
Operon 219-220
Optimum, enzyme activity 77
Organelles 31, 33, 36-38, 42, 64-65
Organochlorines, action of 123
Orientation behavior 370
Origin of life on Earth 358-359
Orthokinesis 381
Osmolarity, defined 54
Osmosis 54-59
Oxidative phosphorylation 96-98
Oxygen atom 5
Oxygen consumption 100-101, 415
Oxygenic photosynthesis 86

P
p53 gene 137
Parallel evolution 333
Parasitism 434
Parental care, energetic costs 413
Particulate inheritance, law of 153
Passive transport 53
Paternal chromosome 130, 145
Paternity testing 251
Pax-6 gene 307
PCR 242
Pedigree analysis 157-158
Penicillin, action of 79
Pentadactyl limb 303
Peppered moth, selection in 270
Pepsin 75, 77
Peptide bond 9-10
Per capita growth rates 426
Peroxidase, action of 80
Pesticides, and cell signaling 123
pH, effect on enzyme activity 75, 77
pH, effect on plant phenotype 183
Phagocytosis 63, 82
Pharmaceuticals, engineering 254
Phenotype, defined 152
Phenotype, influences on 184-185
Phenotypic plasticity 184-185
Pheromones 392
Phosphodiester bond 7
Phospholipids 22, 48
Phosphorus in organisms 5
Phosphorylation cascade 117, 120
Photoautotrophs, in ecosystems 420
Photolysis of water 89
Photoperiodism, plants 376-377
Photosynthesis 85-92
- in ecosystems 420
Photosystems 89
Phototropism 374
Phyletic gradualism 334
Phylogenetic trees, 325, 328-331
Phylogenetics 240
Phylogeny, protein homology 307-308
Phytochrome, role of 376
Pigments, and light absorption 88
Pinocytosis 63
Pioneer species 433
Plant cell walls 52
Plant cells 33-34
Plant responses to herbivory 390
Plants, exchanges in 46
Plants, timing and coordination 371
Plasma membrane, structure 22, 48
Plasmid 195-196
Plasmodesmata 33, 113
Plasmolysis, plant cell 57
Pleiotropy, defined 163
Poisons 79, 232
Polarity, of water 2-3
Poly-A tails 208, 221
Polygenes 178
Polymerase chain reaction 242
Polymorphism, genetic 355
Polypeptide 10-11
Polyphenism 185
Polyploidy 234, 342
Polysaccharides 17-19
Population bottlenecks 286-287
Population growth 426-429
Populations 425
Positive feedback 126
Post-transcriptional modification 208
Postzygotic isolating mechanism 348
Potassium-argon dating 298
Prebiotic experiments 360
Precision 462
Predation 434-435, 442
Predator-prey cycles 435
Predictions 461
Pressure potential, defined 56
Prezygotic isolating mechanism 345
Primary active transport 60
Primary production 417, 438
Primary structure, protein 10-11
Primary succession 433
Primary transcript 204, 207, 221
Primates, phylogenetic trees 326
Probability 156
Producers 417, 422
Producers, in the Great Lakes 448
Product rule, probability 156
Prokaryote gene expression 211
Prokaryotes, ATP generation in 99
Prokaryotic cells 28, 39
Prokaryotic chromosomes 195
Prokaryotic gene structure 213
Prokayotes gene regulation 219-220
Prometaphase 130, 145
Promoter, in gene regulation 219-222
Prophase 130, 145
Protein homologies 305
Protein kinases in mitosis 136
Proteins 4, 11-14
Proto-oncogenes 137
Protobiont 358, 362
Proton pump 61, 83
Proton-sucrose cotransporter 83
Punctuated equilibrium 334
Purines 6
Pyrimidines 6

Q
Q10 76
Qualitative data 464, 467
Qualitative traits 184
Quantitative data 464, 467
Quantitative models, energy flow 417
Quantitative traits 184
Quaternary structure, protein 11
Quorum sensing, bacteria 121

R
R group 9-10
r selection 429
Radioactive decay curve 301
Radiocarbon dating 298, 301
Ranked data 464, 467
Reaction rate 76
Realized niche 436
Receptor-mediated endocytosis 63
Receptors 112
Recombinant offspring 159, 170, 172
Recombination
- in dihybrid inheritance 159
- of alleles in meiosis 145-146
Redundancy, genetic code 205-206
Regression 470
Regulatory genes 213, 219-220
- role in development 224-225
Relative dating, methods 298-300
Relative fitness 266-267
Renaturation 75
Replica plating 244-245
Replication, DNA 201, 203
Repressor, in operon 219-220
Reproductive investment 413-414
Reproductive isolation 339, 345-348
Reproductive strategies 413
Resistance, ecosystems 440
Resistance, to insecticide 272
Resistance to antibiotics 236, 321
Resolution 30
Resource exploitation 450
Resource partitioning 437
Respiration 85
Respiratory pigments 104
Respirometer 100-101
Resting phase, in cell cycle 128, 135
Restriction enzymes 239, 244
Retroviruses 212, 295
Reverse transcriptase 212
Reversible inhibition 78, 84
Ribosomal RNA 8
Ribosomes 151, 204, 209-211
Ribozymes 361
r_{max} 427
RNA 6-8
RNA polymerase 207, 219-223
RNA world 361
Round dance 401
RuBisCo 13, 73, 87, 91

S
S phase 128, 135
SARS-CoV-2 323-324
Saturated fatty acids 21
Scanning electron microscopy 29
Scatter graphs 466
Scientific evidence, defined 471
Scientific investigations 461-462
Seasonal breeding 412
Second gap phase 128, 135
Second messenger 118, 120
Secondary active transport 60
Secondary production 417
Secondary structure, protein 11
Secretion in cells 62
Segregation, law of 153
Selection in fast plants 278
Selection pressure 269-270, 280
- role in speciation 339
Selective breeding 273-277
Sequence data 356-357
Sequential evolution 333
Sex determination 177, 183
Sex linked genes 163, 175-176
Sex ratio, populations 425
Sexual reproduction 265
Shared conserved processes 151
Shared derived characteristics 325
Short tandem repeats 249
Short-day plants 377
Sickle cell disease 187
Sickle cell trait 271
Signal cascades 120
Signal transduction 116-122
Signaling in cells 111-121
Silent mutation 227
Simpson's index of diversity 430-431
Sixth Extinction 352-353
Sleep movements, tulips 371
Sodium-potassium pump 61
Solute potential, 56, 58
Solvent, water 2-3
Somatic mutation 228
Song, role in breeding behavior 397
Speciation 339-344, 350
Species interaction, behavior in 370
Species interactions 434-437
Species, recognizing 332
Spindle in cell division 130, 145-146
Squirrel gene pool, analysis 293
Stability, ecosystem 440-441
Stabilizing selection 269
Staining, cells 28
Standard deviation of the mean 468
Starch 17, 19
Statistical test 470
Stimuli, and behavior 370, 387-388
Stomata 46, 372, 378
Streak plating 246-247
Stress response, and behavior 388
Stroma of chloroplast 38, 91
Stromatolites 359
STRs, in DNA profiling 249
Structural genes 213, 219-220
Student's t test, criteria for 470
Sub-unit proteins 11-13
Substitution mutation 231
Substrates 72-74
Succession, ecological 433
Sugars 15-16
Sum rule, probability 156
Surface area of cells, calculating 40
Surface area-volume ratios 42-47
Symbiosis 434
Sympatric speciation 342-343
Synapse 114
Systematic bias 462

T
Tables, use of 464-465
Tally charts 465
Taxes 370, 383
Telophase 130, 145
Temperature, enzyme activity 76-77
Template strand 207
Termination phase, translation 210
Terminator region 221
Territories, role of 396
Tertiary structure, protein 11-12
Test cross 154-155
Thermoluminescence 302
Thermoregulation 82, 124, 409-411
Thylakoid membranes 38, 87-89
Time, as a covariate 461
Timeline of evolutionary thought 262
Timing behaviors 370-372
Tissues, and SA:V 43
Tonicity, defined 54
Topoisomerase, DNA replication 203
Transcellular transport 114
Transcription 204, 207, 211
Transcription factors 118, 214
- in development 217-218
- in gene regulation 222-223
Transduction, bacterial 236
Transfer RNA 8
Transformation 236, 239, 244, 248
Transition state, enzyme 74
Transitional fossils 319-320
Translation 204, 209-211
Transmembrane receptor 112
Transmission electron microscopy 29
Transpiration, investigating 378
Transposons 236
Triacylglycerols 20
Trilobites, evolution of 297, 334
Trisomy 21 188
tRNA 209-210
Trophic cascades 435, 442
Trophic efficiency 418, 422
Trophic structure 438
Tropisms 370, 373-374
Trp operon 220
Tumor-suppressor genes 137
Turgor, plant cell 57
Turner syndrome 233
Twin studies, epigenetics 216

UVW
Unicellular organisms, exchanges 46
Universal solvent 2-3
Unsaturated fatty acids 21
Uranium-lead dating 298
UTRs in genes 213, 221
Vaccine development 254
Vacuoles 31, 33
Validity of data 462
Variables, identifying 461
Variation, and natural selection 264
Variation, causes of 184
Vernalization 371
Vestigial structures 295, 303
Viral diseases, emerging 323-324
Viruses, role in mutation 232
VOCs in plants 390
Volcanic eruptions, effects of 453
Volume of cells, calculating 40
Waggle dance 401
Wallace, Alfred Russel 262-263
Water potential 56, 59
Water, 2-4
Watson and Crick 263
Whales, evolution in 320

XYZ
X-linked traits, pedigree 176
Zygote 127